CONSTITUTIONAL LAW

LEADING CASES

2010 Edition

By

Jesse H. Choper

Earl Warren Professor of Public Law,
University of California, Berkeley

Richard H. Fallon, Jr.

Ralph S. Tyler, Jr. Professor of Constitutional Law,
Harvard University

Yale Kamisar

Distinguished Professor of Law, University of San Diego
Clarence Darrow Distinguished University Professor Emeritus of Law,
University of Michigan

Steven H. Shiffrin

Charles Frank Reavis, Sr., Professor of Law,
Cornell University

AMERICAN CASEBOOK SERIES®

WEST®

A Thomson Reuters business

Mat #40922138

© West, a Thomson business, 2007, 2008
© 2009 Thomson Reuters
© 2010 Thomson Reuters

 610 Opperman Drive
 St. Paul, MN 55123
 1–800–313–9378

Printed in the United States of America

ISBN: 978–0–314–26173–1

Preface

It may seem ironic that the authors of a 1600–page constitutional law casebook would turn out a compact casebook of less than 900 pages. But in recent years we have heard many of our colleagues express the need for such a book for a basic course in constitutional law—and we decided to do something about it. By judicious editing of the most important decisions of the Supreme Court and careful summarizing of less significant cases, we have sought to produce a book containing "the essentials" for a single course on the subject.

Leading Cases in Constitutional Law is published every year and includes all the significant opinions handed down during the just-concluded Supreme Court Term.

The organization of the compact book is very similar to our much larger one, which we shall continue to revise and supplement annually, and which will be available as a "resource" book for those who use this volume.

Case and statute citations, as well as footnotes of the Court, have been omitted without so specifying; other omissions are indicated by asterisks or by brackets. Numbered footnotes are from the original material; lettered footnotes are ours.

JESSE H. CHOPER
RICHARD H. FALLON, JR.
YALE KAMISAR
STEVEN H. SHIFFRIN

July 2010

Table of Contents

Table of Cases

The principal cases are in bold type. Cases cited or discussed in the text are in roman type. References are to pages.

CONSTITUTIONAL LAW

LEADING CASES

2010 Edition

Chapter 1

NATURE AND SCOPE OF
JUDICIAL REVIEW

SECTION 1. ORIGINS, EARLY CHALLENGES,
AND CONTINUING CONTROVERSY

"Whoever hath an absolute authority to interpret any written or spoken laws, it is he who is truly the lawgiver, to all intents and purposes, and not the person who first spoke or wrote them."

— Bishop Hoadly's Sermon, preached before the King, 1717.

MARBURY v. MADISON

5 U.S. (1 Cranch) 137, 2 L.Ed. 60 (1803).

[Thomas Jefferson, an Anti–Federalist (or Republican), who defeated John Adams, a Federalist, in the presidential election of 1800, was to take office on March 4, 1801. On January 20, 1801, Adams, the defeated incumbent, nominated John Marshall, Adams' Secretary of State, as fourth Chief Justice of the United States. Marshall assumed office on February 4 but continued to serve as Secretary of State until the end of the Adams administration. During February, the Federalist Congress passed (1) the Circuit Court Act, which, inter alia, doubled the number of federal judges and (2) the Organic Act which authorized appointment of 42 justices-of-the-peace in the District of Columbia. Senate confirmation of Adams' "midnight" appointees, virtually all Federalists, was completed on March 3. Their commissions were signed by Adams and sealed by Acting Secretary of State Marshall, but due to time pressures, several for the justices-of-the-peace (including that of William Marbury) remained undelivered when Jefferson assumed the presidency the next day. Jefferson ordered his new Secretary of State, James Madison, to withhold delivery.

[Late in 1801, Marbury and several others sought a writ of mandamus in the Supreme Court to compel Madison to deliver the commissions. The Court ordered Madison "to show cause why a mandamus should not issue" and the case was set for argument in the 1802 Term.

[While the case was pending, the new Republican Congress—incensed at Adams' efforts to entrench a Federalist judiciary and at the "Federalist" Court's order against a Republican cabinet officer—moved to repeal the Circuit Court Act. Federalist congressmen argued that repeal would be unconstitutional as violative of Art. III's assurance of judicial tenure "during good behavior" and of the Constitution's plan for separation of powers assuring the independence of the

1

Judiciary. It "was in this debate that for the first time since the initiation of the new Government under the Constitution there occurred a serious challenge of the power of the Judiciary to pass upon the constitutionality of Acts of Congress. Hitherto, [it had been the Republicans] who had sustained this power as a desirable curb on Congressional aggression and encroachment on the rights of the States, and they had been loud in their complaints at the failure of the Court to hold the Alien and Sedition laws unconstitutional. Now, however, in 1802, in order to counteract the Federalist argument that the Repeal Bill was unconstitutional and would be so held by the Court, [Republicans] advanced the proposition that the Court did not possess the power."a

[The Repeal Law passed early in 1802. To forestall its constitutional challenge in the Supreme Court until the political power of the new administration had been strengthened, Congress also eliminated the 1802 Supreme Court Term. Thus, the Court did not meet between December, 1801 and February, 1803.]

[On] 24th February, the following opinion of the court was delivered by CHIEF JUSTICE MARSHALL: * * *

No cause has been shown, and the present motion is for a mandamus. The peculiar delicacy of this case, the novelty of some of its circumstances, and the real difficulty attending the points which occur in it require a complete exposition of the principles on which the opinion to be given by the court is founded. * * *

1st. Has the applicant a right to the commission he demands? * * *

Mr. Marbury, [since] his commission was signed by the President and sealed by the Secretary of State, was appointed; and as the law creating the office gave the officer a right to hold for five years, independent of the executive, the appointment was not revocable, but vested in the officer legal rights, which are protected by the laws of his country.

To withhold his commission, therefore, is an act deemed by the court not warranted by law, but violative of a vested legal right. * * *

2dly. If he has a right, and that right has been violated, do the laws of his country afford him a remedy?

The very essence of civil liberty certainly consists in the right of every individual to claim the protection of the laws, whenever he receives an injury. One of the first duties of government is to afford that protection. * * *

The government of the United States has been emphatically termed a government of laws, and not of men. It will certainly cease to deserve this high appellation, if the laws furnish no remedy for the violation of a vested legal right. * * *

[W]here the heads of departments are the political or confidential agents of the executive, merely to execute the will of the president, or rather to act in cases in which the executive possesses a constitutional or legal discretion, nothing can be more perfectly clear than that their acts are only politically examinable. But where a specific duty is assigned by law, and individual rights depend upon the performance of that duty, it seems equally clear that the individual who considers himself injured, has a right to resort to the laws of his country for a remedy. * * *

It remains to be inquired whether,

3dly. He is entitled to the remedy for which he applies? This depends on,

1st. The nature of the writ applied for; and,

a. Charles Warren, *The Supreme Court in*   United States History *215 (1922).*

2dly. The power of this court.

1st. The nature of the writ. * * *

This writ, if awarded, would be directed to an officer of government, and its mandate to him would be, to use the words of Blackstone, "to do a particular thing therein specified, which appertains to his office and duty, and which the court has previously determined, or at least supposes, to be consonant to right and justice." Or, in the words of Lord Mansfield, the applicant, in this case, has a right to execute an office of public concern, and is kept out of possession of that right.

These circumstances certainly concur in this case.

Still, to render the mandamus a proper remedy, the officer to whom it is to be directed, must be one to whom, on legal principles, such writ may be directed; and the person applying for it must be without any other specific and legal remedy.

1st. With respect to the officer to whom it would be directed. The intimate political relation subsisting between the President of the United States and the heads of departments, necessarily renders any legal investigation of the acts of one of those high officers peculiarly irksome, as well as delicate; and excites some hesitation with respect to the propriety of entering into such investigation. Impressions are often received without much reflection or examination, and it is not wonderful that in such a case as this the assertion, by an individual, of his legal claims in a court of justice, to which claims it is the duty of that court to attend, should at first view be considered by some, as an attempt to intrude into the cabinet, and to intermeddle with the prerogatives of the executive.

It is scarcely necessary for the court to disclaim all pretensions to such a jurisdiction. An extravagance, so absurd and excessive, could not have been entertained for a moment. The province of the court is, solely, to decide on the rights of individuals, not to inquire how the executive, or executive officers, perform duties in which they have a discretion. Questions in their nature political, or which are, by the constitution and laws, submitted to the executive, can never be made in this court.

But [what] is there in the exalted station of the officer, which shall bar a citizen from asserting, in a court of justice, his legal rights, or shall forbid a court to listen to the claim, or to issue a mandamus, directing the performance of a duty, not depending on executive discretion, but on particular acts of congress, and the general principles of law? * * *

This, then, is a plain case for a mandamus, either to deliver the commission, or a copy of it from the record; and it only remains to be inquired,

Whether it can issue from this court.

The act to establish the judicial courts of the United States authorizes the supreme court "to issue writs of mandamus, in cases warranted by the principles and usages of law, to any courts appointed, or persons holding office, under the authority of the United States."**b**

b. § 13 of the Judiciary Act of 1789 provided: "That the Supreme Court shall have exclusive jurisdiction of all controversies of a civil nature, where a state is a party, except between a state and its citizens; and except also between a state and citizens of other states, or aliens, in which latter case it shall have original but not exclusive jurisdiction. And shall have exclusively all such jurisdiction of suits or proceedings against ambassadors or other public ministers, or their domestics, or domestic servants, as a court of law can have or exercise consistently with the law of nations; and original, but not exclusive jurisdiction of all suits brought by ambassadors or other public ministers, or in which a consul, or vice consul, shall be a party. And the trial of issues of fact in the Supreme Court in all actions at law against citizens of the United States shall be by jury. The Supreme Court shall also have appellate jurisdiction from the circuit courts and courts

The secretary of state, being a person holding an office under the authority of the United States, is precisely within the letter of the description; and if this court is not authorized to issue a writ of mandamus to such an officer, it must be because the law is unconstitutional, and therefore absolutely incapable of conferring the authority, and assigning the duties which its words purport to confer and assign. * * *

In the distribution of [the judicial power of the United States] it is declared that "the supreme court shall have original jurisdiction in all cases affecting ambassadors, other public ministers and consuls, and those in which a state shall be a party. In all other cases, the supreme court shall have appellate jurisdiction."

It has been insisted, at the bar, that as the original grant of jurisdiction, to the supreme and inferior courts, is general, and the clause, assigning original jurisdiction to the supreme court, contains no negative or restrictive words, the power remains to the legislature, to assign original jurisdiction to that court in other cases than those specified in the article which has been recited; provided those cases belong to the judicial power of the United States.

If it had been intended to leave it in the discretion of the legislature to apportion the judicial power between the supreme and inferior courts according to the will of that body, it would certainly have been useless to have proceeded further than to have defined the judicial power, and the tribunals in which it should be vested. The subsequent part of the section is mere surplusage, is entirely without meaning, if such is to be the construction. If congress remains at liberty to give this court appellate jurisdiction, where the constitution has declared their jurisdiction shall be original; and original jurisdiction where the constitution has declared it shall be appellate; the distribution of jurisdiction, made in the constitution, is form without substance.

Affirmative words are often, in their operation, negative of other objects than those affirmed; and in this case, a negative or exclusive sense must be given to them, or they have no operation at all.

It cannot be presumed that any clause in the constitution is intended to be without effect; and, therefore, such a construction is inadmissible, unless the words require it. * * *

The authority, therefore, given to the Supreme Court, by the Act establishing the judicial courts of the United States, to issue writs of mandamus to public officers, appears not to be warranted by the Constitution; and it becomes necessary to inquire whether a jurisdiction so conferred can be exercised.

The question whether an Act repugnant to the Constitution can become the law of the land, is a question deeply interesting to the United States; but, happily, not of an intricacy proportioned to its interest. It seems only necessary to recognize certain principles, supposed to have been long and well established, to decide it.

That the people have an original right to establish, for their future government, such principles as, in their opinion, shall most conduce to their own happiness, is the basis on which the whole American fabric has been erected. The exercise of this original right is a very great exertion; nor can it nor ought it to be frequently repeated. The principles, therefore, so established, are deemed funda-

of the several states, in the cases hereinafter specially provided for; and shall have power to issue writs of prohibition to the district courts, when proceeding as courts of admiralty and maritime jurisdiction, and writs of mandamus, in cases warranted by the principles and usages of law, to any courts appointed, or persons holding office under the authority of the United States."

mental. And as the authority from which they proceed is supreme, and can seldom act, they are designed to be permanent.

This original and supreme will organizes the government, and assigns to different departments their respective powers. It may either stop here, or establish certain limits not to be transcended by those departments.

The government of the United States is of the latter description. The powers of the legislature are defined and limited; and that those limits may not be mistaken, or forgotten, the constitution is written. To what purpose are powers limited, and to what purpose is that limitation committed to writing, if these limits may, at any time, be passed by those intended to be restrained? The distinction between a government with limited and unlimited powers is abolished, if those limits do not confine the persons on whom they are imposed, and if acts prohibited and acts allowed, are of equal obligation. It is a proposition too plain to be contested, that the constitution controls any legislative act repugnant to it; or, that the legislature may alter the constitution by an ordinary act.

Between these alternatives there is no middle ground. The constitution is either a superior paramount law, unchangeable by ordinary means, or it is on a level with ordinary legislative acts, and, like other acts, is alterable when the legislature shall please to alter it.

If the former part of the alternative be true, then a legislative act contrary to the constitution is not law: if the latter part be true, then written constitutions are absurd attempts, on the part of the people, to limit a power in its own nature illimitable.

Certainly all those who have framed written constitutions contemplate them as forming the fundamental and paramount law of the nation, and consequently, the theory of every such government must be, that an act of the legislature, repugnant to the constitution, is void.

This theory is essentially attached to a written constitution, and is, consequently, to be considered, by this court, as one of the fundamental principles of our society. It is not therefore to be lost sight of in the further consideration of this subject.

If an act of the legislature, repugnant to the Constitution, is void, does it, notwithstanding its invalidity, bind the courts, and oblige them to give it effect? Or, in other words, though it be not law, does it constitute a rule as operative as if it was a law? This would be to overthrow in fact what was established in theory; and would seem, at first view, an absurdity too gross to be insisted on. It shall, however, receive a more attentive consideration.

It is emphatically the province and duty of the judicial department to say what the law is. Those who apply the rule to particular cases, must of necessity expound and interpret that rule. If two laws conflict with each other, the courts must decide on the operation of each.

So if a law be in opposition to the constitution; if both the law and the constitution apply to a particular case, so that the court must either decide that case conformably to the law, disregarding the constitution; or conformably to the constitution, disregarding the law; the court must determine which of these conflicting rules governs the case. This is of the very essence of judicial duty.

If, then, the courts are to regard the constitution, and the constitution is superior to any ordinary act of the legislature, the constitution, and not such ordinary act, must govern the case to which they both apply.

Those then who controvert the principle that the constitution is to be considered in court, as a paramount law, are reduced to the necessity of maintaining that courts must close their eyes on the constitution, and see only the law.

This doctrine would subvert the very foundation of all written constitutions. It would declare that an Act which, according to the principles and theory of our government, is entirely void, is yet, in practice, completely obligatory. It would declare that if the legislature shall do what is expressly forbidden, such Act, notwithstanding the express prohibition, is in reality effectual. It would be giving to the legislature a practical and real omnipotence, with the same breath which professes to restrict their powers within narrow limits. It is prescribing limits, and declaring that those limits may be passed at pleasure.

That it thus reduces to nothing what we have deemed the greatest improvement on political institutions, a written constitution, would of itself be sufficient, in America, where written constitutions have been viewed with so much reverence, for rejecting the construction. But the peculiar expressions of the Constitution of the United States furnish additional arguments in favor of its rejection.

The judicial power of the United States is extended to all cases arising under the Constitution.

Could it be the intention of those who gave this power, to say that in using it the Constitution should not be looked into? That a case arising under the Constitution should be decided without examining the instrument under which it arises?

This is too extravagant to be maintained.

In some cases, then, the Constitution must be looked into by the judges. And if they can open it at all, what part of it are they forbidden to read or to obey?

There are many other parts of the Constitution which serve to illustrate this subject.

It is declared that "no tax or duty shall be laid on articles exported from any State." Suppose a duty on the export of cotton, of tobacco, or of flour; and a suit instituted to recover it. Ought judgment to be rendered in such a case? Ought the judges to close their eyes on the Constitution, and only see the law?

The Constitution declares "that no bill of attainder or ex post facto law shall be passed."

If, however, such a bill should be passed, and a person should be prosecuted under it, must the court condemn to death those victims whom the Constitution endeavors to preserve?

"No person," says the Constitution, "shall be convicted of treason unless on the testimony of two witnesses to the same overt act, or on confession in open court."

Here the language of the Constitution is addressed especially to the courts. It prescribes, directly for them, a rule of evidence not to be departed from. If the legislature should change that rule, and declare one witness, or a confession out of court, sufficient for conviction, must the constitutional principle yield to the legislative act?

From these, and many other selections which might be made, it is apparent, that the framers of the constitution contemplated that instrument as a rule for the government of courts, as well as of the legislature.

Why otherwise does it direct the judges to take an oath to support it? This oath certainly applies in an especial manner, to their conduct in their official character. How immoral to impose it on them, if they were to be used as the instruments, and the knowing instruments, for violating what they swear to support!

The oath of office, too, imposed by the legislature, is completely demonstrative of the legislative opinion on this subject. It is in these words: "I do solemnly swear that I will administer justice without respect to persons, and do equal right to the poor and to the rich; and that I will faithfully and impartially discharge all the duties incumbent on me as ___, according to the best of my abilities and understanding agreeably to the constitution and laws of the United States."

Why does a judge swear to discharge his duties agreeably to the constitution of the United States, if that constitution forms no rule for his government? If it is closed upon him, and cannot be inspected by him?

If such be the real state of things, this is worse than solemn mockery. To prescribe, or to take this oath, becomes equally a crime.

It is also not entirely unworthy of observation, that in declaring what shall be the supreme law of the land, the constitution itself is first mentioned; and not the laws of the United States generally, but those only which shall be made in pursuance of the constitution, have that rank.

Thus, the particular phraseology of the Constitution of the United States confirms and strengthens the principle, supposed to be essential to all written constitutions, that a law repugnant to the constitution is void; and that courts, as well as other departments, are bound by that instrument.

The rule must be discharged.c

———

"We are under a Constitution, but the Constitution is what the judges say it is."

— Charles Evans Hughes, Speech, 1907.

COMMENTARY ON MARBURY

Further Historical Context

RANDY E. BARNETT, *Restoring the Lost Constitution* 144 (2004): "While historical evidence strongly supports the conclusion that the original meaning of 'judicial power'a included the power to nullify [unconstitutional legislation], there is little if any evidence to support a claim that the original meaning of 'judicial power' also included a power to command other branches. Nor was such a power exercised by the Supreme Court in *Marbury*. This famous case grew out of legislation enacted by a lame-duck Congress dominated by Federalists to create numerous judicial positions that could be filled with Federalists by outgoing President Adams before the newly elected Republican Thomas Jefferson could assume the presidency. In a bizarre twist by today's lights, all these 'midnight commissions' had been sealed by John Marshall himself—who was not only chief justice, but also the outgoing secretary of state—and delivered by his brother

---

c. Six days later, the Circuit Court Act Repeal Law was held to be constitutional. *Stuart v. Laird,* 5 U.S. (1 Cranch) 299, 2 L.Ed. 115 (1803). After *Marbury,* the Court did not hold an act of Congress unconstitutional until *Dred Scott v. Sandford,* 60 U.S. (19 How.) 393, 15 L.Ed. 691 (1857).

a. This is a reference to Art. III, § 2, cl.1, providing that "[t]he judicial power of the United States shall extend to all cases * * * arising under this Constitution [and] the Laws of the United States * * *."

James. In the haste to seal and deliver the commissions, Marbury's was left behind. At the instructions of incoming President Jefferson, James Madison, the incoming secretary of state, refused to deliver it.''

"Marbury then brought suit in the Supreme Court to issue a writ of mandamus to compel the secretary of state 'either to deliver the commission, or a copy of it from the record.' The Court rejected this request because the Judiciary Act that authorized the Court to grant writs of mandamus on government officials exceeded the powers of Congress and was unconstitutional. By avoiding the issue of whether a judicial command of this kind to the executive branch would exceed the judicial power, Marshall needed only to justify in his opinion the judicial power to nullify the Judiciary Act as beyond the powers of Congress to enact. Although this conclusion could have been well-supported by evidence of the original meaning of the 'judicial power,' Marshall's opinion in *Marbury* is entirely an exercise in constitutional construction.''

———

CHARLES WARREN, 1 *The Supreme Court in United States History,* 232, 242–43 (1922): "Contemporary writings make it very clear that the republicans attacked the [*Marbury*] decision, not so much because it sustained the power of the court to determine the validity of congressional legislation, as because it enounced the doctrine that the court might issue mandamus to a cabinet official who was acting by direction of the president. In other words, Jefferson's antagonism to Marshall and the court at that time was due more to his resentment at the alleged invasion of his executive prerogative than to any so-called 'judicial usurpation' of the field of congressional authority. [It] seems plain [that Marshall might] have construed the language of the section of the judiciary act [to escape the necessity] to pass upon its constitutionality. Marshall naturally felt that in view of the recent attacks on judicial power it was important to have the great principle firmly established, and undoubtedly he welcomed the opportunity of fixing the precedent in a case in which his action would necessitate a decision in favor of his political opponents.''

———

MORRIS COHEN, *The Faith of a Liberal* 178–80 (1946) (written in 1938): "The section of [the] act of 1789 which Marshall declared unconstitutional had been drawn up by Ellsworth, his predecessor as chief justice, and by others who a short time before had been the very members of the constitutional convention that had drafted its judicial provisions. It was signed by George Washington who had presided over the deliberations of that convention. Fourteen years later, John Marshall by implication accused his predecessor on the bench, the members of congress such as James Madison, the father of the constitution, and President Washington, of either not understanding the constitution (which some of them had drawn up), or else wilfully disregarding it. [To] a secular historian, it is obvious that John Marshall was motivated by the fear of impeachment if he granted the mandamus or dared to declare the republican judiciary repeal act of 1802 unconstitutional. Having thus refused aid to his fellow federalists ousted from offices created for them by a 'lame duck' congress, he resorted to a line of sophistical dicta to get even with his political enemy, as indeed he did also in the *Aaron Burr* case. In his letter to his colleague Chase, Marshall offered to abandon judicial supremacy in the interpretation of the constitution in return for security against impeachment."b

The Three Faces of Marbury

RICHARD H. FALLON, Jr., *Marbury and the Constitutional Mind: A Bicentennial Essay on the Wages of Doctrinal Tension*, 91 Calif.L.Rev. 1, 12 (2003): "John Marshall's canonical opinion includes at least three facets or faces. It could plausibly be claimed that any of these reflects an essential element of Marshall's reasoning and expresses the foundational insights that subsequent judicial practice must follow in order to be true to *Marbury*. * * *

"1. *The Private–Rights Face*. Judicial review gives federal judges, who are not directly accountable to the electorate, a power that is potentially threatening to more representative branches of the government and to political democracy. *Marbury*'s private-rights face responds directly to this threat and attempts to disarm it. This face represents *Marbury* as a species of traditional private litigation. It casts the Justices of the Supreme Court as ordinary judges humbly doing their best to apply the law to disputes between individuals. In *Marbury*, the Justices claimed no general authority to resolve constitutional issues that might arise in American politics. Rather, Marshall's reasoning grounds the Court's exercise of judicial review in its need to decide the case before it, which involved Marbury's claimed right to judicial relief under the law of the United States. * * *

"2. *The Special–Functions Face*. In justifying the Court's exercise of judicial review, *Marbury* asserted that 'it is emphatically the province and duty of the judicial department to say what the law is.' The force of this proposition can be seen as conditioned by the case's facts, involving a concrete and traditional claim of individual right, but acceptance of this limit is not strictly necessary. The grounds for a broader view lie in *Marbury*'s expressly functional argument: If other branches of government, especially Congress, could exceed constitutional bounds without being subject to judicial check, then the restraining function of a written constitution would be obliterated. [According] to what has been called a 'special functions' or 'public rights' model, the courts should provide safeguards against constitutional violations by other branches, even in cases that do not involve the kinds of private rights and material injuries that typically underlie suits at common law. * * *

"3. *The Political or Prudential Face*. *Marbury*'s third face becomes visible when one looks beneath the Court's rhetoric and considers the decision in its political context. This is a political face of judicial prudence tinctured with guile. Its central prescription is that the Court must sometimes recede from the conflict with the political branches or with aroused public opinion in order to maintain its prestige and thus its power. [To] sustain and legitimatize its place in a constitutional democracy, the Court must define for itself a democratically acceptable role. The sources of the Court's vulnerability are several. First, the Court's orders are not self-executing. Thomas Jefferson and James Madison seemed poised to ignore the Supreme Court's writ of mandamus if one had issued in *Marbury*. [Second,] Article III vests Congress with express power to control and limit the appellate jurisdiction of the Supreme Court. [Third,] the political branches possess constitutional authority not only to determine the membership of the Supreme Court through appointment and confirmation processes, but also to adjust its size. In

b. In 1804, the House impeached Justice Chase due, inter alia, to what the Republicans believed to be Chase's partisan Federalist activities and statements both on and off the Bench. After a lengthy trial in the Senate, the constitutional majority to convict was not obtained. It was generally assumed that, if the effort had been successful, Marshall and other Federalist judges would suffer the same fate.

conjunction, these powers make 'Court packing' at least a potential response to judicial decisions that aroused political majorities adjudge intolerable. In *Marbury* the Court reached the only prudent conclusion: It could not, indeed must not, issue a quixotic order to Madison to deliver Marbury's commission. But never before or since has the Court, in prudent retreat, displayed more guile to emerge in glory from the spectre of defeat."

The Court as "Final" Arbiter

THOMAS JEFFERSON, writing in 1804, 8 *The Writings of Thomas Jefferson* 310 (1897): "The judges, believing the [sedition law] constitutional, had a right to pass a sentence of fine and imprisonment; because that power was placed in their hands by the constitution. But the executive, believing the law to be unconstitutional, was bound to remit the execution of it; because that power has been confided to him by the constitution. The instrument meant that its co-ordinate branches should be checks on each other. But the opinion which gives to the judges the right to decide what laws are constitutional, and what not, not only for themselves in their own sphere of action, but for the legislative and executive also in their spheres, would make the judiciary a despotic branch."

––––––––

ANDREW JACKSON, veto message in 1832 on Act to Recharter Bank of United States (the constitutionality of which had earlier been upheld by the Court), 2 Richardson, *Messages and Papers of the Presidents* 576, 581–82 (1900): "It is as much the duty of the house of representatives, of the senate, and of the president to decide upon the constitutionality of any bill or resolution which may be presented to them for passage or approval as it is of the supreme judges when it may be brought before them for judicial decision. The opinion of the judges has no more authority over congress than the opinion of congress has over the judges, and on that point the president is independent of both. The authority of the supreme court must not, therefore, be permitted to control the congress or the executive when acting in their legislative capacities, but to have only such influence as the force of their reasoning may deserve."

––––––––

ABRAHAM LINCOLN, inaugural address in 1861, 2 Richardson, supra, at ___, 9–10: "[The] candid citizen must confess that if the policy of the government upon vital questions affecting the whole people is to be irrevocably fixed by decisions of the Supreme Court, the instant they are made in ordinary litigation between parties in personal actions the people will have ceased to be their own rulers, having to that extent practically resigned their government into the hands of that eminent tribunal. Nor is there in this view any assault upon the court or the judges. It is a duty from which they may not shrink to decide cases properly brought before them, and it is no fault of theirs if others seek to turn their decisions to political purposes."

––––––––

COOPER v. AARON, 358 U.S. 1 (1958) (also in Ch. 9, Sec.2, IV) arose several years after the landmark reading in *Brown v. Board of Education* (1954) that segregation of public school children on the basis of race violated fourteenth amendment equal protection. A plan approved by the lower federal courts to desegregate Little Rock public schools was blocked by the Governor of Arkansas and other state officials. In the face of a federal court injunction, the Governor backed off, and National Guard soldiers, called out to keep the public schools desegregated, were withdrawn. For a short time, black students were able to attend previously all-white public schools under the protection of federally-commanded troops. However, in early 1958, citing deep tension and concern about violence, the school board sought, and a federal court granted, a long postponement of the desegregation plan. The Court of Appeals reversed, and the Supreme Court affirmed—in an opinion delivered not by any one justice, as is ordinarily the case, but signed by all nine. Arkansas contended that since it was not a party to the litigation that culminated in the *Brown* ruling, it was not "bound" by that decision. This claim stirred the Supreme Court to make a broad and forceful statement about its supremacy in constitutional matters—as Laurence H. Tribe, *American Constitutional Law* 255 (3d ed. 2000) (hereafter Tribe, 3d ed.) described it, "a statement uniquely punctuated by the Justices' individual signatures of the opinion":

"Article VI of the Constitution makes the Constitution the 'supreme law of the land.' In 1803, Chief Justice Marshall, speaking for a unanimous Court, referring to the Constitution as 'the fundamental and paramount law of the nation,' declared [in] *Marbury* [the] basic principle that the federal judiciary is supreme in the exposition of the law of the Constitution, and that principle has ever since been respected by this Court and the Country as a permanent and indispensable feature of our constitutional system. It follows that the interpretation of the Fourteenth Amendment enunciated by this Court in the *Brown* case is the supreme law of the land. [Every] state legislator and executive and judicial officer is solemnly committed by oath taken pursuant to art. VI, cl. 3 'to support this Constitution.' * * * No state legislature or executive or judicial officer can war against the Constitution without violating his undertaking to support it. Chief Justice Marshall spoke for a unanimous court in saying that: 'If the legislatures of the several states may, at will, annul the judgments of the courts of the United States, and destroy the rights acquired under those judgments, the constitution itself becomes a solemn mockery * * *.' *United States v. Peters,* 5 Cranch 115. A Governor who asserts a power to nullify a federal court order is similarly restrained."

Judicial Review and Democracy: The Countermajoritarian Difficulty

ALEXANDER BICKEL, *The Least Dangerous Branch* 16–20 (1962): "The root difficulty is that judicial review is a counter-majoritarian force in our system. [W]hen the Supreme Court declares unconstitutional a legislative act or the action of an elected executive, it thwarts the will of representatives of the actual people of the here and now; it exercises control, not in behalf of the prevailing majority, but against it. That [is] the reason the charge can be made that judicial review is undemocratic.

"[It] does not follow from the complex nature of a democratic system that, because admirals and generals and the members, say, of the Federal Reserve Board or of this or that administrative agency are not electorally responsible, judges who exercise the power of judicial review need not be responsible either, and in neither case is there a serious conflict with democratic theory. For admirals and generals and the like are most often responsible to officials who are themselves elected and through whom the line runs directly to a majority. What is more significant, the policies they make are or should be interstitial or technical only and are reversible by legislative majorities * * *—a fact of great consequence."

JESSE CHOPER, *The Supreme Court and the Political Branches: Democratic Theory and Practice,* 122 U.Pa.L.Rev. 810, 830–32 (1974): "In the main, the effect of judicial review in ruling legislation unconstitutional is to nullify the finished product of the lawmaking process. It is the very rare supreme court decision on constitutionality that affirmatively mandates the undertaking of government action. To make the point in another way, when the Supreme Court finds legislative acts unconstitutional it holds invalid only those enactments that have survived the many hurdles fixed between incipient proposals and standing law.

"The significance of this [is] that most of the antimajoritarian elements that have been found in the American legislative process [are] negative ones. They work to *prevent* the translation of popular wishes into governing rules rather than to *produce* laws that are contrary to majority sentiment.

"[Although] exceptions exist, '[a] distinguishing feature of our system, perhaps impelled by heritage of sectional division and heterogeneity, is that our governmental structure, institutional habits, and political parties with their internal factional divisions, have combined to produce a system in which major programs and major new directions cannot be undertaken unless supported by a fairly broad popular consensus. This normally has been far broader than 51 percent and often bipartisan as well.' [Consequently,] when the Supreme Court, itself without conventional political responsibility, says 'thou shalt not' to acts of Congress, it usually cuts sharply against the grain of majority rule. The relatively few laws that finally overcome the congressional obstacle course generally illustrate the national political branches operating at their majoritarian best while the process of judicial review depicts that element of the Court's work and that exertion of federal authority with the most brittle democratic roots.[59]"

A "Double Standard" of Judicial Review?

For a discussion of the view that the courts should utilize a "double standard" of review, upholding economic legislation so long as it is supported by any rational basis but subjecting laws restricting political processes likely to bring about repeal of undesirable legislation or laws aimed at racial or religious minorities to a more exacting judicial scrutiny, see fn. 4 of the *Carolene Products* case, p. 173 infra.

MARTIN v. HUNTER'S LESSEE
14 U.S. (1 Wheat.) 304, 4 L.Ed. 97 (1816).

[Lord Fairfax, a Virginia citizen, willed his Virginia land known as the Northern Neck of Virginia to his nephew, Martin, a British subject resident in England. In 1789, Virginia, acting pursuant to state laws confiscating lands owned by British subjects, granted land in the Northern Neck to Hunter. The latter brought an action of ejectment against Martin. The Virginia district court ruled

---

59. Although no detailed examination of the legislative systems in the states and their political subdivisions has been ventured here, the same conclusion appears to have substantially similar merit in respect to the Court's overturning the laws they produce.

for Martin, whose claim was fortified by the anti-confiscation clauses of the treaties of 1783 and 1794 with Great Britain. But the Virginia Court of Appeals reversed, holding that (1) the state's title to the Northern Neck had been perfected before any treaty and (2) in any event, a 1796 Act of Compromise between the Fairfax claimants and the state claimants, formally adopted by the Virginia legislature, had settled the matter against Martin.

[Acting for the purchasers of the Fairfax estate, John Marshall, then a member of the Virginia legislature, had negotiated the compromise. Since he and his brother had organized a syndicate which purchased 160,000 acres of Northern Neck from Martin in 1793, Marshall had a great interest in the case's outcome.

[In *Fairfax's Devisee v. Hunter's Lessee,* 11 U.S. (7 Cranch) 603, 3 L.Ed. 453 (1813), the Supreme Court (Marshall, C.J., not participating) reversed the Virginia Court of Appeals, ruling that Virginia had not perfected title to Northern Neck prior to the grant to Hunter and that therefore the Treaty of 1794 confirmed the title remaining in Martin. Neither Story, J.'s majority opinion nor Johnson, J.'s dissent mentioned the Act of Compromise.

[The cause was remanded to the Virginia Court of Appeals with instructions to enter judgment for appellant, but that court refused to obey the Supreme Court's mandate. All four judges then sitting maintained that in so far as it extended the appellate jurisdiction of the Supreme Court to "this court," § 25 of the Judiciary Act was unconstitutional. Judge Roane—Marshall's arch political enemy—and Judge Fleming (the two judges sitting when the court had decided the case against Martin on the merits) contended further that even if the Judiciary Act were valid the case had not properly been before the Supreme Court since the Virginia decision turned not upon a treaty, but "upon another and ordinary ground of jurisdiction—the act of compromise."

[The case again came to the Supreme Court, Marshall again not sitting.]

STORY, J., delivered the opinion of the court. * * *

The third article of the constitution is that which must principally attract our attention. [A]ppellate jurisdiction is given by the constitution to the supreme court, in all cases [within "the judicial power of the United States"] where it has not original jurisdiction; subject, however, to such exceptions and regulations as congress may prescribe. [W]hat is there to restrain its exercise over state tribunals, in the enumerated cases? [If] the judicial power extends to the case, it will be in vain to search in the letter of the constitution for any qualification as to the tribunal where it depends. It [is] plain, that the framers of the constitution did contemplate that cases within the judicial cognisance of the United States, not only might, but would, arise in the state courts, in the exercise of their ordinary jurisdiction [pointing to the supremacy clause]. Suppose, an indictment for a crime, in a state court, and the defendant should allege in his defence, that the crime was created by an ex post facto act of the state, must not the state court [have] a right to pronounce on the validity and sufficiency of the defence? [It] was foreseen, that in the exercise of their ordinary jurisdiction, state courts would incidentally take cognisance of cases arising under the constitution, the laws and treaties of the United States. Yet, to all these cases, the judicial power, by the very terms of the constitution, is to extend. It cannot extend, by original jurisdiction, if that was already rightfully and exclusively attached in the state courts, which (as has been already shown) may occur; it must, therefore, extend by appellate jurisdiction, or not at all. It would seem to follow, that the appellate power of the United States must, in such cases, extend to state tribunals. * * *

It has been argued, that such an appellate jurisdiction over state courts is inconsistent with the genius of our governments, and the spirit of the constitution. That the latter was never designed to act upon state sovereignties, but only upon the people, and that if the power exists it will materially impair the sovereignty of the states, and the independence of their courts. [But the Constitution] is crowded with provisions which restrain or annul the sovereignty of the states, in some of the highest branches of their prerogatives. The tenth section of the first article contains a long list of disabilities and prohibitions imposed upon the states. [The] language of the constitution is also imperative upon the states, as to the performance of many duties. It is imperative upon the state legislatures, to make laws prescribing the time, places and manner of holding elections for senators and representatives, and for electors of president and vice-president. And in these, as well as some other cases, congress have a right to revise, amend or supersede the laws which may be passed by state legislatures. When, therefore, the states are stripped of some of the highest attributes of sovereignty, and the same are given to the United States; when the legislatures of the states are, in some respects, under the control of congress, and in every case are, under the constitution, bound by the paramount authority of the United States; it is certainly difficult to support the argument, that the appellate power over the decisions of state courts is contrary to the genius of our institutions. The courts of the United States can, without question, revise the proceedings of the executive and legislative authorities of the states, and if they are found to be contrary to the constitution, may declare them to be of no legal validity. Surely, the exercise of the same right over judicial tribunals is not a higher or more dangerous act of sovereign power.

Nor can such a right be deemed to impair the independence of state judges. It is assuming the very ground in controversy, to assert that they possess an absolute independence of the United States. In respect to the powers granted to the United States, they are not independent; they are expressly bound to obedience, by the letter of the constitution * * *.

The argument urged from the possibility of the abuse of the revising power, is equally unsatisfactory. [From] the very nature of things, the absolute right of decision, in the last resort, must rest somewhere—wherever it may be vested, it is susceptible of abuse. [A]dmitting that the judges of the state courts are, and always will be, of as much learning, integrity and wisdom, as those of the courts of the United States (which we very cheerfully admit), it does not aid the argument. It is manifest, that the constitution has proceeded upon a theory of its own, and given or withheld powers according to the judgment of the American people, by whom it was adopted. We can only construe its powers, and cannot inquire into the policy or principles which induced the grant of them. The constitution has presumed (whether rightly or wrongly, we do not inquire), that state attachments, state prejudices, state jealousies, and state interests, might sometimes obstruct, or control, or be supposed to obstruct or control, the regular administration of justice. * * *

This is not all. A motive of another kind, perfectly compatible with the most sincere respect for state tribunals, might induce the grant of appellate power over their decisions. * * * Judges of equal learning and integrity, in different states, might differently interpret the statute, or a treaty of the United States, or even the constitution itself: if there were no revising authority to control these jarring and discordant judgments, and harmonize them into uniformity, the laws, the treaties and the constitution of the United States would be different, in different states, and might, perhaps, never have precisely the same construction, obligation or efficiency, in any two states. The public mischiefs that would attend such a state of things would be truly deplorable * * *.

On the whole, the court are of opinion, that the appellate power of the United States does extend to cases pending in the state courts; and that the 25th section of the judiciary act, which authorizes the exercise of this jurisdiction in the specified cases, by a writ of error, is supported by the letter and spirit of the constitution. [It] is an historical fact, that this exposition of the constitution, extending its appellate power to state courts, was, previous to its adoption, uniformly and publicly avowed by its friends, and admitted by its enemies, as the basis of their respective reasonings, both in and out of the state conventions. It is an historical fact, that at the time when the judiciary act was submitted to the deliberations of the first congress, composed, as it was not only of men of great learning and ability, but of men who acted a principal part in framing, supporting or opposing that constitution, the same exposition was explicitly declared and admitted by the friends and by the opponents of that system. It is an historical fact, that the supreme court of the United States have, from time to time, sustained this appellate jurisdiction, in a great variety of cases, brought from the tribunals of many of the most important states in the Union,[a] and that no state tribunal has ever breathed a judicial doubt on the subject or declined to obey the mandate of the supreme court, until the present occasion. * * *

[The Court next rejected the contention that the case was not properly before it because the Virginia decision turned on the Act of Compromise.]

We have not thought it incumbent on us to give any opinion upon the question, whether this court have authority to issue a writ of mandamus to the court of appeals, to enforce the former judgments, as we did not think it necessarily involved in the decision of this cause.

It is the opinion of the whole court, that the judgment of the court of appeals of Virginia, rendered on the mandate in this cause, be reversed, and the judgment of the district court [be] affirmed.

JOHNSON, J. It will be observed, in this case, that the court disavows all intention to decide on the right to issue compulsory process to the state courts; thus leaving us, in my opinion, where the constitution and laws place us— supreme over persons and cases, so far as our judicial powers extend, but not asserting any compulsory control over the state tribunals. In this view, I acquiesce in their opinion, but not altogether in the reasoning or opinion of my brother who delivered it. * * *

———

COHENS v. VIRGINIA, 19 U.S. (6 Wheat.) 264 (1821)—which sustained the Court's appellate jurisdiction under § 25 of the Judiciary Act to review state criminal proceedings, and is generally viewed as reaffirming and "supplementing" *Martin*—has stronger historical links with *McCulloch v. Maryland* (Ch. 2, Sec. 1 infra).

Appellants were found guilty in a Virginia court of selling lottery tickets in violation of state law. Their defense was that the lottery was organized by the City of Washington, under a congressional statute authorizing the lottery. On appeal to the Supreme Court, they were met with the contentions that the Court had no

a. See, e.g., *Clerke v. Harwood,* 3 U.S. (3 Dall.) 342 (1797) (state law in conflict with treaty). The first Supreme Court decision holding a state law unconstitutional was *Fletcher v. Peck,* 10 U.S. (6 Cranch) 87 (1810) but the case arose in a lower federal court.

jurisdiction to review a state criminal case and, in any event, Congress had no power to permit the sale of lottery tickets in a state which prohibited such sale. On the jurisdictional point, Virginia argued that (1) if when the state is a party the Supreme Court has original jurisdiction, this grant excludes appellate jurisdiction; (2) federal courts cannot take original jurisdiction over criminal cases, since that rightfully belongs to the courts of the state whose laws have been violated; (3) consequently, the Supreme Court has no jurisdiction at all. As in *Marbury*, MARSHALL, C.J., used the occasion to express a broad view of the Court's powers, but decided the case on a narrow ground in favor of the Jeffersonians—the federal statute authorizing a lottery had no effect outside the City of Washington.

SECTION 2.   POLITICAL QUESTIONS

Notwithstanding the assertion in *Marbury v. Madison* that it is "the province and duty of the judicial department to say what the law is," the Court has long recognized that at least a few constitutional issues present "political questions" that are inappropriate for judicial resolution and thus "nonjusticiable."

In PACIFIC STATES TEL. & T. CO. v. OREGON, 223 U.S. 118 (1912), four years after Oregon amended its constitution to allow the people to enact laws through an initiative process, petitioner challenged a tax enacted by an initiative on the ground that the process violated Art. IV, § 4, which provides that "[t]he United States shall guarantee to every State in this Union a Republican Form of Government." In essence, the company argued that the initiative process is democratic, not republican. The Court, per WHITE, J., held that the case presented a political question, quoting from *Luther v. Borden,* 48 U.S. (7 How.) 1 (1849), an action arising out of the Dorr Rebellion in Rhode Island, in which the question of whether the defendant's arrest of the plaintiff was a trespass turned on which of two groups was the lawful government of the state: "[Under Art. IV, § 4], it rests with Congress to decide what government is the established one in a State. For, as the United States guarantee to each State a republican government, Congress must necessarily decide what government is established in the State before it can determine whether it is republican or not. And when the senators and representatives of a State are admitted into the councils of the Union, the authority of the government under which they are appointed, as well as its republican character, is recognized by the proper constitutional authority. And its decision is binding on every other department of the government, and could not be questioned in a judicial tribunal. It is true that the contest in this case did not last long enough to bring the matter to this issue; and as no senators or representatives were elected under the authority of the government of which Mr. Dorr was the head, Congress was not called upon to decide the controversy. Yet the right to decide is placed there, and not in the courts."

Turning from *Luther,* the Court noted that the telephone company's argument proceeds "upon the theory that the adoption of the initiative and referendum destroyed all government republican in form in Oregon. This being so, the contention, if held to be sound, would necessarily affect the validity, not only of the particular statute which is before us, but of every other statute passed in Oregon since the adoption of the initiative and referendum. And indeed the propositions go further than this, since in their essence they assert that there is no governmental function, legislative or judicial, in Oregon, because it cannot be assumed, if the proposition be well founded, that there is at one and the same time one and the same government which is republican in form and not of that character. * * *

"Do the provisions of § 4, Art. IV, bring about these strange, far-reaching and injurious results? [D]o they authorize the judiciary to substitute its judgment as to a matter purely political for the judgment of Congress on a subject committed to it and thus overthrow the Constitution upon the ground that thereby the guarantee to the States of a government republican in form may be secured, a conception which after all rests upon the assumption that the States are to be guaranteed a government republican in form by destroying the very existence of a government republican in form in the Nation?

"[The] defendant company does not contend here that it could not have been required to pay a license tax. It does not assert that it was denied an opportunity to be heard as to the amount for which it was taxed, or that there was anything inhering in the tax or involved intrinsically in the law which violated any of its constitutional rights. If such questions had been raised they would have been justiciable, and therefore would have required the calling into operation of judicial power. Instead, however, of doing any of these things, the attack on the statute here made is of a wholly different character. Its essentially political nature is at once made manifest by understanding that the assault which the contention here advanced makes is not on the tax as a tax, but on the State as a State. It is addressed to the framework and political character of the government by which the statute levying the tax was passed. It is the government, the political entity, which (reducing the case to its essence) is called to the bar of this court, not for the purpose of testing judicially some exercise of power assailed, on the ground that its exertion has injuriously affected the rights of an individual because of repugnancy to some constitutional limitation, but to demand of the State that it establish its right to exist as a State, republican in form."

———

BAKER v. CARR, 369 U.S. 186 (1962), per Brennan, J., held that a suit challenging Tennessee's legislative apportionment scheme, under which some districts had vastly larger populations than others, presented a justiciable question under the Equal Protection Clause: "Judicial standards under the Equal Protection Clause are well developed. [This] case does, in one sense, involve the allocation of political power within a State, and the appellants might conceivably have added a claim under the Guarantee Clause. [Although such a claim] could not have succeeded it does not follow that appellants may not be heard on the equal protection claim which in fact they tender."

In the course of holding the equal protection challenge before the Court to be justiciable, Brennan, J., noted the existence of entire subject areas in which all challenges to congressional or executive authority had sometimes been said to raise non-justiciable political questions, including foreign relations, questions involving dates of duration of hostilities, the formal validity of legislative enactments, the status of the Indian tribes, and questions about whether a republican form of government exists in the states. But the categories were misleading: "Much of the confusion results from the capacity of the 'political question' label to obscure the need for case-by-case inquiry."

A survey of the cases yielded a list of governing criteria: "Prominent on the surface of any case held to involve a political question is found a textually demonstrable constitutional commitment of the issue to a coordinate political department; or a lack of judicially discoverable and manageable standards for resolving it; or the impossibility of deciding without an initial policy determination of a kind clearly for nonjudicial discretion; or the impossibility of a court's undertaking independent resolution without expressing lack of the respect due coordinate branches of government; or an unusual need for unquestioning adherence to a political decision already made; or the potentiality of embarrassment from multifarious pronouncements by various departments on one question."

CLARK, J., concurred: "The majority of the voters have been caught up in a legislative straight jacket. [The existing apportionment scheme] has riveted the present seats in the assembly to their respective constituencies, and by the votes of their incumbents a reapportionment of any kind is prevented."

FRANKFURTER, J., joined by Harlan, J., dissented: "The present case [is], in effect, a Guarantee Clause claim masquerading under a different label. But it cannot make the case more fit for judicial action that appellants invoke the Fourteenth Amendment rather than Art. IV, § 4, where, in fact, the gist of their complaint is the same."

———

In GILLIGAN v. MORGAN, 413 U.S. 1 (1973), students at Kent State University sought relief against government officials to prevent the repetition of events that had included the shooting of a number of students by National Guard members on that campus in May 1970. The court of appeals instructed the federal district court to evaluate the "pattern of training, weaponry and orders in the Ohio National Guard" so as to determine whether it made "inevitable the use of fatal force in suppressing civilian disorders." The Court, per BURGER, C.J., reversed, relying heavily on Art. I, § 8, cl. 16—which grants to Congress "the responsibility for organizing, arming and disciplining the Militia (now the National Guard), with certain responsibilities being reserved to the respective States"— and on federal legislation enacted pursuant thereto: "[T]he nature of the questions to be resolved on remand are subjects committed expressly to the political branches of government. [It] would be difficult to think of a clearer example of the type of governmental action that was intended by the Constitution to be left to the political branches [or] of an area of governmental activity in which the courts have less competence. The complex, subtle, and professional decisions as to the composition, training, equipping, and control of a military force are essentially professional military judgments, subject *always* to civilian control of the Legislative and Executive Branches [which] are periodically subject to electoral accountability."

BLACKMUN, J., joined by Powell, J., concurred: "This case relates to prospective relief in the form of judicial surveillance of highly subjective and technical matters involving military training and command. As such, it presents an '[inappropriate] subject matter for judicial consideration,' for respondents are asking the District Court, in fashioning that prospective relief, 'to enter upon policy determinations for which judicially manageable standards are lacking.' *Baker.* [On] the understanding that this is what the Court's opinion holds, I join that opinion."

Cf. *Scheuer v. Rhodes*, 416 U.S. 232 (1974) (holding that *Gilligan* did not bar a damages action by estates of students killed at Kent State).

NIXON v. UNITED STATES

506 U.S. 224, 113 S.Ct. 732, 122 L.Ed.2d 1 (1993).

CHIEF JUSTICE REHNQUIST delivered the opinion of the Court.

Petitioner Walter L. Nixon, Jr., [a] former Chief Judge of the United States District Court for the Southern District of Mississippi, was convicted by a jury of two counts of making false statements before a federal grand jury and sentenced to prison. The grand jury investigation stemmed from reports that Nixon had accepted a gratuity from a Mississippi businessman in exchange for asking a local district attorney to halt the prosecution of the businessman's son. Because Nixon refused to resign from his office as a United States District Judge, he continued to collect his judicial salary while serving out his prison sentence.

On May 10, 1989, the House of Representatives adopted three articles of impeachment for high crimes and misdemeanors. The first two articles charged Nixon with giving false testimony before the grand jury and the third article charged him with bringing disrepute on the Federal Judiciary.

After the House presented the articles to the Senate, the Senate voted to invoke its own Impeachment Rule XI, under which the presiding officer appoints a committee of Senators to "receive evidence and take testimony." The Senate committee held four days of hearings, during which 10 witnesses, including Nixon, testified. Pursuant to Rule XI, the committee presented the full Senate with a complete transcript of the proceeding and a report stating the uncontested facts and summarizing the evidence on the contested facts. Nixon and the House impeachment managers submitted extensive final briefs to the full Senate and delivered arguments from the Senate floor during the three hours set aside for oral argument in front of that body. Nixon himself gave a personal appeal, and several Senators posed questions directly to both parties. The Senate voted by more than the constitutionally required two-thirds majority to convict Nixon on the first two articles. The presiding officer then entered judgment removing Nixon from his office as United States District Judge.

Nixon thereafter commenced the present suit, arguing that Senate Rule XI violates the constitutional grant of authority to the Senate to "try" all impeachments because it prohibits the whole Senate from taking part in the evidentiary hearings. [The] District Court held that his claim was nonjusticiable and the Court of Appeals for the District of Columbia Circuit agreed.

A controversy is nonjusticiable—i.e., involves a political question—where there is "a textually demonstrable constitutional commitment of the issue to a coordinate political department; or a lack of judicially discoverable and manageable standards for resolving it." *Baker v. Carr,* 369 U.S. 186, 217 (1962). But [the] lack of judicially manageable standards may strengthen the conclusion that there is a textually demonstrable commitment to a coordinate branch.

In this case, we must examine Art. I, § 3, cl. 6, to determine the scope of authority conferred upon the Senate by the Framers regarding impeachment. It provides: "The Senate shall have the sole Power to try all Impeachments. When sitting for that Purpose, they shall be on Oath or Affirmation. When the President of the United States is tried, the Chief Justice shall preside: And no Person shall be convicted without the Concurrence of two thirds of the Members present." * * *

Petitioner argues that the word "try" in the first sentence imposes by implication an additional requirement on the Senate in that the proceedings must be in the nature of a judicial trial. From there petitioner goes on to argue that this limitation precludes the Senate from delegating to a select committee the task of hearing the testimony of witnesses * * *.

There are several difficulties with this position which lead us ultimately to reject it. The word "try," both in 1787 and later, has considerably broader meanings than those to which petitioner would limit it. [Thus], we cannot say that the Framers used the word "try" as an implied limitation on the method by which the Senate might proceed in trying impeachments. * * *

The conclusion that the use of the word "try" in the first sentence of the Impeachment Trial Clause lacks sufficient precision to afford any judicially manageable standard of review of the Senate's actions is fortified by the existence of the three very specific requirements that the Constitution does impose on the Senate when trying impeachments: the members must be under oath, a two-thirds vote is required to convict, and the Chief Justice presides when the President is tried. These limitations are quite precise, and their nature suggests that the Framers did not intend to impose additional limitations on the form of the Senate proceedings by the use of the word "try" in the first sentence.

Petitioner devotes only two pages in his brief to negating the significance of the word "sole" in the first sentence of Clause 6. [We] think that the word "sole" is of considerable significance. Indeed, the word "sole" appears only one other time in the Constitution—with respect to the House of Representatives' "*sole* Power of Impeachment." Art. I, § 2, cl. 5 (emphasis added). The common sense meaning of the word "sole" is that the Senate alone shall have authority to determine whether an individual should be acquitted or convicted. The dictionary definition bears this out. "Sole" is defined as "having no companion," "solitary," "being the only one," and "functioning . . . independently and without assistance or interference." If the courts may review the actions of the Senate in order to determine whether that body "tried" an impeached official, it is difficult to see how the Senate would be "functioning . . . independently and without assistance or interference."

Nixon [argues] that even if significance be attributed to the word "sole" in the first sentence of the clause, the authority granted is to the Senate, and this means that "the Senate—not the courts, not a lay jury, not a Senate Committee—shall try impeachments." Brief for Petitioner 42. It would be possible to read the first sentence of the Clause this way, but it is not a natural reading. Petitioner's interpretation would bring into judicial purview not merely the sort of claim made by petitioner, but other similar claims based on the conclusion that the word "Senate" has imposed by implication limitations on procedures which the Senate might adopt. Such limitations would be inconsistent with the construction of the Clause as a whole, which, as we have noted, sets out three express limitations in separate sentences.

The history and contemporary understanding of the impeachment provisions support our reading of the constitutional language. The parties do not offer evidence of a single word in the history of the Constitutional Convention or in contemporary commentary that even alludes to the possibility of judicial review in the context of the impeachment powers. This silence is quite meaningful in light of the several explicit references to the availability of judicial review as a check on the Legislature's power with respect to bills of attainder, ex post facto laws, and statutes. See *The Federalist* No. 78.

The Framers labored over the question of where the impeachment power should lie. Significantly, in at least two considered scenarios the power was placed with the Federal Judiciary. [See] *The Federalist* No. 65. The Supreme Court was not the proper body because the Framers "doubted whether [it] would possess the degree of credit and authority" to carry out its judgment if it conflicted with the accusation brought by the Legislature—the people's representative. In addition, the Framers believed the Court was too small in number: "The awful discretion, which a court of impeachments must necessarily have, to doom to honor or to infamy the most confidential and the most distinguished characters of the community, forbids the commitment of the trust to a small number of persons." Id.

There are two additional reasons why the Judiciary, and the Supreme Court in particular, were not chosen to have any role in impeachments. First, the Framers recognized that most likely there would be two sets of proceedings for individuals who commit impeachable offenses—the impeachment trial and a separate criminal trial. In fact, the Constitution explicitly provides for two separate proceedings. See Art. I, § 3, cl. 7. The Framers deliberately separated the two forums to avoid raising the specter of bias and to ensure independent judgments. [Certainly] judicial review of the Senate's "trial" would introduce the same risk of bias as would participation in the trial itself.

Second, judicial review would be inconsistent with the Framers' insistence that our system be one of checks and balances. In our constitutional system, impeachment was designed to be the *only* check on the Judicial Branch by the Legislature. * * * Judicial involvement in impeachment proceedings, even if only for purposes of judicial review, is counterintuitive because it would eviscerate the "important constitutional check" placed on the Judiciary by the Framers. * * *

Nevertheless, Nixon argues [that] if the Senate is given unreviewable authority to interpret the Impeachment Trial Clause, there is a grave risk that the Senate will usurp judicial power. The Framers anticipated this objection and created two constitutional safeguards to keep the Senate in check. The first safeguard is that the whole of the impeachment power is divided between the two legislative bodies [which] "avoids the inconvenience of making the same persons both accusers and judges; and guards against the danger of persecution from the prevalency of a factious spirit in either of those branches." The second safeguard is the two-thirds supermajority vote requirement. * * *

In addition to the textual commitment argument, we are persuaded that the lack of finality and the difficulty of fashioning relief counsel against justiciability. See *Baker*. We agree with the Court of Appeals that opening the door of judicial review to the procedures used by the Senate in trying impeachments would "expose the political life of the country to months, or perhaps years, of chaos." This lack of finality would manifest itself most dramatically if the President were impeached. The legitimacy of any successor, and hence his effectiveness, would be impaired severely, not merely while the judicial process was running its course, but during any retrial that a differently constituted Senate might conduct if its first judgment of conviction were invalidated. Equally uncertain is the question of what relief a court may give other than simply setting aside the judgment of conviction. Could it order the reinstatement of a convicted federal judge, or order Congress to create an additional judgeship if the seat had been filled in the interim?

Petitioner finally contends that a holding of nonjusticiability cannot be reconciled with our opinion in *Powell v. McCormack*, 395 U.S. 486 (1969). The relevant issue in *Powell* was whether courts could review the House of Representatives' conclusion that Powell was "unqualified" to sit as a Member because he had been accused of misappropriating public funds and abusing the process of the New York courts. We stated that the question of justiciability turned on whether the Constitution committed authority to the House to judge its members' qualifications, and if so, the extent of that commitment. Article I, § 5 provides that "Each House shall be the Judge of the Elections, Returns and Qualifications of its own Members." In turn, Art. I, § 2 specifies three requirements for membership in the House: The candidate must be at least 25 years of age, a citizen of the United States for no less than seven years, and an inhabitant of the State he is chosen to represent. We held that, in light of the three requirements specified in the Constitution, the word "qualifications"—of which the House was to be the

Judge—was of a precise, limited nature. [The] claim by the House that its power to "be the Judge of the Elections, Returns and Qualifications of its own Members" was a textual commitment of unreviewable authority was defeated by the existence of this separate provision specifying the only qualifications which might be imposed for House membership. The decision as to whether a member satisfied these qualifications was placed with the House, but the decision as to what these qualifications consisted of was not.

In the case before us, there is no separate provision of the Constitution which could be defeated by allowing the Senate final authority to determine the meaning of the word "try" in the Impeachment Trial Clause. We agree with Nixon that courts possess power to review either legislative or executive action that transgresses identifiable textual limits. [But] we conclude, after exercising that delicate responsibility, that the word "try" in the Impeachment Clause does not provide an identifiable textual limit on the authority which is committed to the Senate.

Affirmed.

JUSTICE STEVENS, concurring.

[Respect] for a coordinate Branch of the Government forecloses any assumption that improbable hypotheticals like those mentioned by Justice White and Justice Souter will ever occur. * * *

JUSTICE WHITE, with whom JUSTICE BLACKMUN joins, concurring in the judgment.

[The] Court is of the view that the Constitution forbids us even to consider [petitioner's constitutional] contention. I find no such prohibition and would therefore reach the merits of the claim. I concur in the judgment because the Senate fulfilled its constitutional obligation to "try" petitioner.

I. It should be said at the outset that, as a practical matter, it will likely make little difference whether the Court's or my view controls this case. This is so because the Senate has very wide discretion in specifying impeachment trial procedures and because it is extremely unlikely that the Senate would abuse its discretion and insist on a procedure that could not be deemed a trial by reasonable judges. Even taking a wholly practical approach, I would prefer not to announce an unreviewable discretion in the Senate to ignore completely the constitutional direction to "try" impeachment cases. When asked at oral argument whether that direction would be satisfied if, after a House vote to impeach, the Senate, without any procedure whatsoever, unanimously found the accused guilty of being "a bad guy," counsel for the United States answered that the Government's theory "leads me to answer that question yes." Especially in light of this advice from the Solicitor General, I would not issue an invitation to the Senate to find an excuse, in the name of other pressing business, to be dismissive of its critical role in the impeachment process.

Practicalities aside, however, since the meaning of a constitutional provision is at issue, my disagreement with the Court should be stated.

II. [T]he issue in the political question doctrine is not whether the Constitutional text commits exclusive responsibility for a particular governmental function to one of the political branches. There are numerous instances of this sort of textual commitment, e.g., Art. I, § 8, and it is not thought that disputes implicating these provisions are nonjusticiable. Rather, the issue is whether the Constitution has given one of the political branches final responsibility for interpreting the scope and nature of such a power.

[T]here are few, if any, explicit and unequivocal instances in the Constitution of this sort of textual commitment. [In] drawing the inference that the Constitution has committed final interpretive authority to one of the political branches, courts are sometimes aided by textual evidence that the judiciary was not meant to exercise judicial review—a coordinate inquiry expressed in *Baker's* "lack of judicially discoverable and manageable standards" criterion. See, e.g., *Coleman v. Miller,* 307 U.S. 433, 452–454 (1939), where the Court refused to determine the life span of a proposed constitutional amendment given Art. V's placement of the amendment process with Congress and the lack of any judicial standard for resolving the question.

A. [That] the word "sole" is found only in the House and Senate Impeachment Clauses demonstrates that its purpose is to emphasize the distinct role of each in the impeachment process. As the majority notes, the Framers, following English practice, were very much concerned to separate the prosecutorial from the adjudicative aspects of impeachment. Giving each House "sole" power with respect to its role in impeachments effected this division of labor. While the majority is thus right to interpret the term "sole" to indicate that the Senate ought to " 'function independently and without assistance or interference,' " it wrongly identifies the judiciary, rather than the House, as the source of potential interference with which the Framers were concerned when they employed the term "sole."

Even if the Impeachment Trial Clause is read without regard to its companion clause, the Court's willingness to abandon its obligation to review the constitutionality of legislative acts merely on the strength of the word "sole" is perplexing. Consider, by comparison, the treatment of Art. I, § 1, which grants "All legislative powers" to the House and Senate. As used in that context "all" is nearly synonymous with "sole"—both connote entire and exclusive authority. Yet the Court has never thought it would unduly interfere with the operation of the Legislative Branch to entertain difficult and important questions as to the extent of the legislative power. * * *

The historical evidence reveals above all else that the Framers were deeply concerned about placing in any branch the "awful discretion, which a court of impeachments must necessarily have." *The Federalist* No. 65. Viewed against this history, the discord between the majority's position and the basic principles of checks and balances underlying the Constitution's separation of powers is clear. In essence, the majority suggests that the Framers conferred upon Congress a potential tool of legislative dominance yet at the same time rendered Congress' exercise of that power one of the very few areas of legislative authority immune from any judicial review. [In] a truly balanced system, impeachments tried by the Senate would serve as a means of controlling the largely unaccountable judiciary, even as judicial review would ensure that the Senate adhered to a minimal set of procedural standards in conducting impeachment trials.

B. [The] majority finds this case different from *Powell* only on the grounds that, whereas the qualifications of Art. I, § 2 are readily susceptible to judicial interpretation, the term "try" does not provide an "identifiable textual limit on the authority which is committed to the Senate." [Yet, the] term "try" is hardly so elusive as the majority would have it. Were the Senate, for example, to adopt the practice of automatically entering a judgment of conviction whenever articles of impeachment were delivered from the House, it is quite clear that the Senate will have failed to "try" impeachments. Indeed in this respect, "try" presents no greater, and perhaps fewer, interpretive difficulties than some other constitutional standards that have been found amenable to familiar techniques of judicial construction, including, for example, "Commerce . . . among the several States," Art. I, § 8, cl. 3, and "due process of law." Amdt. 5.3

III. [T]extual and historical evidence reveals that the Impeachment Trial Clause was not meant to bind the hands of the Senate beyond establishing a set of minimal procedures. Without identifying the exact contours of these procedures, it is sufficient to say that the Senate's use of a factfinding committee under Rule XI is entirely compatible with the Constitution's command that the Senate "try all impeachments." * * *

JUSTICE SOUTER, concurring in the judgment.

[As] we cautioned in *Baker,* "the 'political question' label" tends "to obscure the need for case-by-case inquiry." The need for such close examination is nevertheless clear from our precedents, which demonstrate that the functional nature of the political question doctrine requires analysis of "the precise facts and posture of the particular case," and precludes "resolution by any semantic cataloguing."

[Whatever] considerations feature most prominently in a particular case, the political question doctrine is "essentially a function of the separation of powers," ibid., existing to restrain courts "from inappropriate interference in the business of the other branches of [the Federal] Government," and deriving in large part from prudential concerns about the respect we owe the political departments. Not all interference is inappropriate or disrespectful, however, and application of the doctrine ultimately turns, as Learned Hand put it, on "how importunately the occasion demands an answer." Learned Hand, *The Bill of Rights* 15 (1958).

This occasion does not demand an answer. The Impeachment Trial Clause [contemplates] that the Senate may determine, within broad boundaries, such subsidiary issues as the procedures for receipt and consideration of evidence necessary to satisfy its duty to "try" impeachments. Other significant considerations confirm a conclusion that this case presents a nonjusticiable political question: the "unusual need for unquestioning adherence to a political decision already made," as well as "the potentiality of embarrassment from multifarious pronouncements by various departments on one question." * * *

One can, nevertheless, envision different and unusual circumstances that might justify a more searching review of impeachment proceedings. If the Senate were to act in a manner seriously threatening the integrity of its results, convicting, say, upon a coin-toss, or upon a summary determination that an officer of the United States was simply "a bad guy," judicial interference might well be appropriate. In such circumstances, the Senate's action might be so far beyond the scope of its constitutional authority, and the consequent impact on the Republic so great, as to merit a judicial response despite the prudential concerns that would

---

3. The majority's in terrorem argument against justiciability—that judicial review of impeachments might cause national disruption and that the courts would be unable to fashion effective relief—merits only brief attention. In the typical instance, court review of impeachments would no more render the political system dysfunctional than has this litigation. Moreover, the same capacity for disruption was noted and rejected as a basis for not hearing *Powell.* The relief granted for unconstitutional impeachment trials would presumably be similar to the relief granted to other unfairly tried public employee-litigants. Finally, as applied to the special case of the President, the majority's argument merely points out that, were the Senate to convict the President without any kind of a trial, a constitutional crisis might well result. It hardly follows that the Court ought to refrain from upholding the Constitution in all impeachment cases. Nor does it follow that, in cases of Presidential impeachment, the Justices ought to abandon their Constitutional responsibilities because the Senate has precipitated a crisis.

ordinarily counsel silence. "The political question doctrine, a tool for maintenance of governmental order, will not be so applied as to promote only disorder." *Baker.*

———

In VIETH v. JUBELIRER, 541 U.S. 267 (2004), SCALIA, J., concluded for a four-Justice plurality that no judicially manageable standards exist to determine when partisan political gerrymanders of voting districts violate the Constitution. The plurality opinion appeared to accept that partisan gerrymanders would violate the Constitution if they went "too far" in deliberately advantaging the candidates of one party and disadvantaging those of another, but maintained that the courts lack sufficiently clear standards, rooted in the Constitution, for determining when partisan scheming exceeds constitutional bounds.

KENNEDY, J., concurred in the judgment dismissing the plaintiffs' complaint. He agreed with the plurality that no constitutionally adequate and judicially manageable standard for identifying forbidden partisan gerrymanders "has emerged in this case," but he declined to pronounce partisan gerrymandering claims categorically non-justiciable, based on the possibility that an administrable standard might emerge in the future. In separate dissenting opinions, Stevens, J., Souter, J. (joined by Ginsburg, J.), and Breyer, J., all disagreed about the absence of judicially manageable standards and indeed identified the (diverse) standards that they would apply.

SECTION 3.   DISCRETIONARY REVIEW

The Supreme Court's original jurisdiction, which typically comprises at most a handful of cases each year (mainly concerning "controversies between two or more states"), is presently governed by 28 U.S.C.A. § 1251. The most important current provisions respecting the Court's appellate jurisdiction are 28 U.S.C.A. §§ 1254 (federal courts of appeals) and 1257 (state courts), both of which provide for review of lower court decisions only by "writ of certiorari"—a discretionary writ that permits the Court to decide for itself which cases most deserve its attention.[1]

In recent years, more than 7,000 cases have been filed annually in the Supreme Court. The Court decided only 80 cases with written opinions in the 2004–05 Term, down from an average of 172 cases each year for the five Terms spanning 1984–88 and an average of 113 for the five Terms spanning 1990–97. By long tradition, it takes the votes of four Justices to put a case on the Court's plenary docket.

UNITED STATES SUPREME COURT RULES

Rule 10. Considerations Governing Review on Writ of Certiorari

1. A review on writ of certiorari is not a matter of right, but of judicial discretion. A petition for a writ of certiorari will be granted only when there are special and important reasons therefor. The following, while neither controlling nor fully measuring the Court's discretion, indicate the character of reasons that will be considered: (a) When a United States court of appeals has rendered a decision in conflict with the decision of another United States court of appeals on the same matter; or has decided a federal question in a way in conflict with a state

---

1. Until 1988, Sections 1254 and 1257 both provided for appeal as of right in some cases, although they gave the Court discretion with respect to others.

court of last resort; or has so far departed from the accepted and usual course of judicial proceedings, or sanctioned such a departure by a lower court, as to call for an exercise of this Court's power of supervision. (b) When a state court of last resort has decided a federal question in a way that conflicts with the decision of another state court of last resort or of a United States court of appeals. (c) When a state court or a United States court of appeals has decided an important question of federal law which has not been, but should be, settled by this Court, or has decided a federal question in a way that conflicts with applicable decisions of this Court. * * *

MARYLAND v. BALTIMORE RADIO SHOW, INC.

338 U.S. 912, 70 S.Ct. 252, 94 L.Ed. 562 (1950).

Opinion of JUSTICE FRANKFURTER respecting the denial of the petition for writ of certiorari. * * *

A variety of considerations underlie denials of the writ, and as to the same petition different reasons may lead different Justices to the same result. This is especially true of petitions for review on writ of certiorari to a State court. Narrowly technical reasons may lead to denials. A decision may satisfy all these technical requirements and yet may commend itself for review to fewer than four members of the Court. Pertinent considerations of judicial policy here come into play. A case may raise an important question but the record may be cloudy. It may be desirable to have different aspects of an issue further illumined by the lower courts. Wise adjudication has its own time for ripening.

Since there are these conflicting and, to the uninformed, even confusing reasons for denying petitions for certiorari, it has been suggested from time to time that the Court indicate its reasons for denial. Practical considerations preclude. [The] time that would be required is prohibitive, apart from the fact as already indicated that different reasons not infrequently move different members of the Court * * *. It becomes relevant here to note that failure to record a dissent from a denial of a petition for writ of certiorari in nowise implies that only the member of the Court who notes his dissent thought the petition should be granted. * * *

Chapter 2

NATIONAL LEGISLATIVE POWER

SECTION 1. SOURCES AND NATURE

INTRODUCTION

By 1787, the minimal power of the national government under the Articles of Confederation—including its inability to directly raise armies, collect taxes, regulate foreign commerce (in particular to establish tariffs to protect new domestic industries), enforce domestic laws, and require the states to conform to the Peace Treaty with Great Britain[a]—produced what many considered to be a political crisis. Among the major defects in the Articles that led to the Constitutional Convention was the lack of authority to eliminate trade barriers erected by the individual states that treated other states like foreign nations and threatened to result in interstate commercial warfare.

With these concerns in mind, the framers set out to construct a new central government that would have sufficient authority to address national problems, but whose powers would be limited to those designated in the Constitution. The framers recognized the conflict between generalized grants of federal power (which might threaten the liberty of the people) and in overly specific listing of powers (which might leave the new government as ineffective as its predecessor). At one point, the Convention tentatively approved Virginia's proposal that the national legislature should have power "to legislate in all cases for the general interests of the Union, and also in those to which the States are separately incompetent." But the Committee on Detail's final report chose instead to enumerate a series of powers—mainly in Art. I, § 8—and to add at the end the power to "make all laws that shall be necessary and proper for carrying into execution the foregoing powers, and all other powers vested, by this Constitution."

Although the Necessary and Proper Clause was adopted by the Convention with little discussion, it was hardly understood uniformly. In 1791, before signing a bill chartering a national bank, President Washington sought opinions on its constitutionality. Secretary of the Treasury Alexander Hamilton argued that the Necessary and Proper Clause had to be interpreted broadly. Although Hamilton

---

a. See *The Federalist* No. 15 (Alexander Hamilton). The Federalist was a series of essays published in New York newspapers in late 1787 and early 1788 to defend the proposed Constitution against attacks aimed at defeating its ratification in New York. The essays were republished in book form as "The Federalist" in the Spring of 1788. The principal authors, anonymous at time of publication, were Alexander Hamilton, James Madison, and John Jay.

acknowledged limits on the federal legislative power, he took the Necessary and Proper Clause to mean that Congress had implied powers. Laws "necessary" to carry out Congress' powers meant laws "needful, requisite, incidental, useful" to such powers. Limiting Congress' authority to strict necessity would unreasonably curtail the government's ability to act.

Secretary of State Thomas Jefferson strictly read the Necessary and Proper Clause: a national bank was in no sense *essential* to carry out the duties of the federal government. If the clause were read so broadly as to make the bank "necessary," then Congress would effectively be authorized to enact any legislation that would be "convenient" in carrying out its goals, thus rendering the Convention's careful enumeration irrelevant.

Background of McCulloch v. Maryland. The first Bank of the United States engaged in a private banking business, but also acted as a depository for United States funds wherever it established branches. The preamble of the Act incorporating the Bank stated that its establishment "will be very conducive to the successful conducting of the national finances; will tend to give facility to the obtaining of loans, for the use of the government, in sudden emergencies; and will be productive of considerable advantages to trade and industry in general." The second Bank was incorporated over strenuous political opposition, and made itself extremely unpopular, particularly in the West and South, when it over-expanded credits and later drastically curtailed them, contributing to the failure of many state-incorporated banks. As a result, a number of states sought to exclude the Bank, either by state constitutional prohibitions against operating within the state any bank not chartered by the state, or by imposing heavy discriminatory taxes on such banks. The tax in *McCulloch* was one of the milder taxes.

McCULLOCH v. MARYLAND

17 U.S. (4 Wheat.) 316, 4 L.Ed. 579 (1819).

CHIEF JUSTICE MARSHALL delivered the opinion of the Court.

[Maryland taxed any bank operating in the state without state authority 2% of the face value of all banknotes issued unless it paid a $15,000 tax. The Maryland Court of Appeals upheld judgment for the statutory penalty against the cashier of the Baltimore branch of the Bank of United States for issuing bank notes without payment of the tax. The Supreme Court reversed only three days after completion of nine days of oral argument.]

The first question [is], has Congress power to incorporate a bank? * * *

This government is acknowledged by all to be one of enumerated powers.a [Among] the enumerated powers, we do not find that of establishing a bank or

---

a. The Court rejected Maryland's argument that the Constitution was "the Act of sovereign and independent states," who "delegated" the "powers of the federal government," which must be exercised in subordination to the states: "The convention which framed the Constitution was, indeed, elected by the state legislatures. But the instrument, when it came from their hands, was a mere proposal [to] the then existing Congress of the United States, with a request that it might 'be submitted to a convention of delegates, chosen in each state, by the people thereof, under the recommendation of its legislature, for their assent and ratification.' This mode of proceeding was adopted; and by the convention, by Congress, and by the state legislatures, the instrument was submitted to the people. They acted upon it, in the only manner in which they can act safely, effectively, and wisely, on such a subject, by assembling in convention [in] their several states * * *.

"From these conventions the Constitution derives its whole authority. The government proceeds directly from the people; is 'ordained and established' in the name of the people. [The] assent of the states, in their sovereign capacity, is implied in calling a convention, and thus submitting that instrument to the people.

creating a corporation. But there is no phrase in the instrument which, like the Articles of Confederation [Article II: "Each state retains [every] power [not] expressly delegated."] excludes incidental or implied powers; and which requires that everything granted shall be expressly and minutely described. Even the tenth amendment, which was framed for the purpose of quieting the excessive jealousies which had been excited, omits the word "expressly," and declares only that the powers "not delegated to the United States, nor prohibited to the states, are reserved to the states or to the people"; thus leaving the question, whether the particular power which may become the subject of contest has been delegated to the one government, or prohibited to the other, to depend on a fair construction of the whole instrument. The men who drew and adopted this amendment had experienced the embarrassments resulting from the insertion of this word in the Articles of Confederation, and probably omitted it to avoid those embarrassments. A constitution, to contain an accurate detail of all the subdivisions of which its great powers will admit, and of all the means by which they may be carried into execution, would partake of the prolixity of a legal code, and could scarcely be embraced by the human mind. It would probably never be understood by the public. Its nature, therefore, requires, that only its great outlines should be marked, its important objects designated, and the minor ingredients which composed those objects be deduced from the nature of the objects themselves. [In] considering this question, then, we must never forget, that it is *a constitution* we are expounding.

Although, among the enumerated powers of government, we do not find the word "bank," or "incorporation," we find the great powers to lay and collect taxes; to borrow money; to regulate commerce; to declare and conduct a war; and to raise and support armies and navies. The sword and the purse, all the external relations, and no inconsiderable portion of the industry of the nation, are intrusted to its government. It can never be pretended that these vast powers draw after them others of inferior importance, merely because they are inferior. [But] it may, with great reason be contended that a government, intrusted with such ample powers, on the due execution of which the happiness and prosperity of the nation so vitally depends, must also be intrusted with ample means for their execution. The power being given, it is the interest of the nation to facilitate its execution. It can never be their interest, and cannot be presumed to have been their intention, to clog and embarrass its execution by withholding the most appropriate means. [The] exigencies of the nation may require, that the treasure raised in the North should be transported to the South, that raised in the East conveyed to the West, or that this order should be reversed. Is that construction of the Constitution to be preferred which would render these operations difficult, hazardous, and expensive? Can we adopt that construction (unless the words imperiously require it) which would impute to the framers of that instrument, when granting these powers for the public good, the intention of impeding their exercise by withholding a choice of means? * * *

But the Constitution of the United States has not left the right of Congress to employ the necessary means, for the execution of the powers conferred on the government, to general reasoning. To its enumeration of powers is added that of [the Necessary and Proper Clause].

But the people were at perfect liberty to accept or reject it; and their act was final. [The] Constitution, when thus adopted, was of complete obligation, and bound the state sovereignties. * * *

"The government of the Union, then (whatever may be the influence of this fact on the case), is emphatically and truly a government of the people. In form and in substance it emanates from them, its powers are granted by them, and are to be exercised directly on them, and for their benefit."

The counsel for the state of Maryland have urged [that] this clause, though in terms a grant of power, is not so in effect; but is really restrictive of the general right, which might otherwise be implied, of selecting means for executing the enumerated powers. * * *

Is it true, that this is the sense in which the word "necessary" is always used? [If] reference be had to its use, in the common affairs of the world, or in approved authors, we find that it frequently imports no more than that one thing is convenient, or useful, or essential to another. To employ the means necessary to an end, is generally understood as employing any means calculated to produce the end, and not as being confined to those single means, without which the end would be entirely unattainable. [A] thing may be necessary, very necessary, absolutely or indispensably necessary. To no mind would the same idea be conveyed, by these several phrases. This comment on the word is well illustrated [by] the tenth section of the first article of the Constitution. It is, we think, impossible to compare the sentence which prohibits a state from laying "imposts, or duties on imports or exports, except what may be *absolutely* necessary for executing its inspection laws," with that which authorizes Congress "to make all laws which shall be necessary and proper for carrying into execution" the powers of the general government, without feeling a conviction that the convention understood itself to change materially the meaning of the word "necessary" by prefixing the word "absolutely." This word, then like others, is used in various senses; and in its construction, the subject, the context, the intention of the person using them, are all to be taken into view.

Let this be done in the case under consideration. The subject is the execution of those great powers on which the welfare of a nation essentially depends. It must have been the intention of those who gave these powers, to insure, as far as human prudence could insure, their beneficial execution. [This] provision is made in a constitution intended to endure for ages to come, and, consequently, to be adapted to the various crises of human affairs. To have prescribed the means by which government should, in all future time, execute its powers, would have been to change, entirely, the character of the instrument, and give it the properties of a legal code. It would have been an unwise attempt to provide, by immutable rules, for exigencies which, if foreseen at all must have been seen dimly, and which can be best provided for as they occur. To have declared that the best means shall not be used, but those alone without which the power given would be nugatory, would have been to deprive the legislature of the capacity to avail itself of experience, to exercise its reason, and to accommodate its legislation to circumstances. If we apply this principle of construction to any of the powers of the government, we shall find it so pernicious in its operation that we shall be compelled to discard [it.]

But the argument which most conclusively demonstrates the error of the construction contended for by the counsel for the state of Maryland, is founded on the intention of the convention, as manifested in the whole clause: * * *

1st. The clause is placed among the powers of Congress, not among the limitations on those powers.

2nd. Its terms purport to enlarge, not to diminish the powers vested in the government. It purports to be an additional power, not a restriction on those already granted. [If] no other motive for its insertion can be suggested, a sufficient one is found in the desire to remove all doubts respecting the right to legislate on that vast mass of incidental powers which must be involved in the Constitution, if that instrument be not a splendid bauble.

We admit, as all must admit, that the powers of the government are limited, and that its limits are not to be transcended. But we think the sound construction of the Constitution must allow to the national legislature that discretion, with respect to the means by which the powers it confers are to be carried into [execution]. Let the end be legitimate, let it be within the scope of the Constitution, and all means which are appropriate, which are plainly adapted to that end, which are not prohibited, but consist with the letter and spirit of the Constitution, are constitutional. * * *

If a corporation may be employed indiscriminately with other means to carry into execution the powers of the government, no particular reason can be assigned for excluding the use of a bank, if required for its fiscal operations. [That] it is a convenient, a useful, and essential instrument in the prosecution of its fiscal operations, is not now a subject of controversy. * * *

But were its necessity less apparent, none can deny its being an appropriate measure; and if it is, the degree of its necessity, as has been very justly observed, is to be discussed in another place. [S]hould Congress, under the pretext of executing its powers, pass laws for the accomplishment of objects not entrusted to the government; it would become the painful duty of this tribunal, should a case requiring such a decision come before it, to say that such an act was not the law of the land. But where the law is not prohibited, and is really calculated to effect any of the objects entrusted to the government, to undertake here to inquire into the degree of its necessity, would be to pass the line which circumscribes the judicial department, and to tread on legislative ground. * * *

[The Court invalidated Maryland's tax on the United States Bank, invoking the Supremacy Clause (Art. VI, cl. 2). This ruling and its progeny are considered in Sec. 5 infra.]

The most recent extensive consideration of McCulloch, UNITED STATES v. COMSTOCK, 130 S.Ct. ___ (2010), per BREYER, J., basing its "conclusion on five considerations, taken together," upheld a "federal civil-commitment statute [that] authorizes the Department of Justice to detain a mentally ill, sexually dangerous federal prisoner beyond the date the prisoner would otherwise be released. 18 U.S.C. § 4248. [The government] must first 'make all reasonable efforts to cause' the State where that person was tried, or the State where he is domiciled, to 'assume responsibility for his custody, care and treatment.'

[1] "[We have] made clear that, in determining whether the Necessary and Proper Clause grants Congress the legislative authority to enact a particular federal statute, we look to see whether the statute constitutes a means that is rationally related to the implementation of a constitutionally enumerated power. *Sabri v. United States,* [Sec. 3, II infra]; *Gonzales v. Raich,* [Sec. 2, IV infra]. Congress routinely exercises its authority to enact criminal laws in furtherance of, for example, its enumerated powers to regulate interstate and foreign commerce, to enforce civil rights, to spend funds for the general welfare, to establish federal courts, to establish post offices, to regulate bankruptcy, to regulate naturalization, and so forth. [2. Here,] Congress has long been involved in the delivery of mental health care to federal prisoners, and has long provided for their civil commitment [including] insane criminals [who are sexually dangerous] upon the expiration of their terms of confinement, where it would be dangerous to turn them loose upon society and where no state will assume responsibility for their custody.

[3] "[Section] 4248 is 'reasonably adapted,' *United States v. Darby*, [Sec. 2, II, B infra], to Congress' power to act as a responsible federal custodian (a power that rests, in turn, upon federal criminal statutes that legitimately seek to implement constitutionally enumerated authority,) [and] Congress could have reasonably concluded [that] § 4248 satisfies 'review for means-end rationality', i.e., that it satisfies the Constitution's insistence that a federal statute represent a rational means for implementing a constitutional grant of legislative authority.

[4] "[T]he statute properly accounts for state interests. The powers 'delegated to the United States by the Constitution' include those specifically enumerated powers listed in Article I along with the implementation authority granted by the Necessary and Proper Clause. Virtually by definition, these powers are not powers that the Constitution 'reserved to the States.' [Nor] does this statute invade state sovereignty or otherwise improperly limit the scope of 'powers that remain with the States.' To the contrary, it requires *accommodation* of state interests. [5. The argument] that Congress' authority can be no more than one step removed from a specifically enumerated power [is] irreconcilable with our precedents. [A]s Chief Justice Marshall recognized in *McCulloch*, 'the power to "to establish post offices and post roads" ... is executed by the single act of *making* the establishment. [F]rom this has been inferred the power and duty of *carrying* the mail along the post road, from one post office to another. And, from this *implied* power, has *again* been inferred the right to *punish* those who steal letters from the post office, or rob the mail.' "

Kennedy, J., concurred in the judgment because § 4248 "is a discrete and narrow exercise of authority over a small class of persons already subject to the federal power," but: "When the inquiry is whether a federal law has sufficient links to an enumerated power to be within the scope of federal authority, the analysis depends not on the number of links in the congressional-power chain but on the strength of the chain. * * *

"The terms 'rationally related' and 'rational basis' must be employed with care, particularly if either is to be used as a stand-alone test. The phrase 'rational basis' [as used in connection with the Due Process Clause is] one of the most deferential formulations of the standard for reviewing legislation in all the Court's precedents, [and] should not be extended uncritically to the issue before us. [The] Court's discussion of the Tenth Amendment invites the inference that restrictions flowing from the federal system are of no import when defining the limits of the National Government's power, as it proceeds by first asking whether the power is within the National Government's reach, and if so it discards federalism concerns entirely. [But it] is of fundamental importance to consider whether essential attributes of state sovereignty are compromised by the assertion of federal power under the Necessary and Proper Clause; if so, that is a factor suggesting that the power is not one properly within the reach of federal power."

Alito, J., also concurred only in the judgment: "The Necessary and Proper Clause does not give Congress carte blanche. Although the term 'necessary' does not mean 'absolutely necessary' or indispensable, the term requires an 'appropriate' link between a power conferred by the Constitution and the law enacted by Congress. And it is an obligation of this Court to enforce compliance with that limitation.

"The law in question here satisfies that requirement. This is not a case in which it is merely possible for a court to think of a rational basis on which Congress might have perceived an attenuated link between the powers underlying the federal criminal statutes and the challenged civil commitment provision. Here, there is a substantial link to Congress' constitutional powers."

THOMAS, J., joined by SCALIA, J., dissented: Under *McCulloch*, "unless the end itself is 'legitimate,' the fit between means and end is irrelevant. In other words, no matter how 'necessary' or 'proper' an Act of Congress may be to its objective, Congress lacks authority to legislate if the objective is anything other than 'carrying into Execution' one or more of the Federal Government's enumerated powers. [But the] Government identifies no specific enumerated power or powers as a constitutional predicate for § 4248, and none are readily discernable. [Section] 4248 closely resembles the involuntary civil-commitment laws that States have enacted under their parens patriae and general police powers. Indeed, it is clear, on the face of the Act and in the Government's arguments urging its constitutionality, that § 4248 is aimed at protecting society from acts of sexual violence, not [to] execute *any* enumerated power. Section 4248 is therefore unconstitutional.

"[The] Necessary and Proper Clause does not provide Congress with authority to enact any law simply because it furthers *other laws* Congress has enacted in the exercise of its incidental [authority]. Federal laws that criminalize conduct that interferes with enumerated powers, establish prisons for those who engage in that conduct, and set rules for the care and treatment of prisoners awaiting trial or serving a criminal sentence satisfy this test because each helps to 'carr[y] into Execution' the enumerated powers that justify a criminal defendant's arrest or conviction. [Civil] detention under § 4248, on the other hand, lacks any such connection to an enumerated power.a * * *

"First, the statute's definition of a 'sexually dangerous person' contains no element relating to the subject's crime. [The] Government concedes that nearly 20% of individuals against whom § 4248 proceedings have been brought fit this description.

"Second, § 4248 permits the term of federal civil commitment to continue beyond the date on which a convicted prisoner's sentence expires or the date on which the statute of limitations on an untried defendant's crime has run. The statute therefore authorizes federal custody over a person at a time when the Government would lack jurisdiction to detain him for violating a criminal law that executes an enumerated power. [It] authorizes federal detention of a person even *after* the Government loses the authority to prosecute him for a federal crime.

"Third, the definition of a 'sexually dangerous person' relevant to § 4248 does not require the court to find that the person is likely to violate a law executing an enumerated power in the future.

"[Finally, the] Court and both concurrences suggest that Congress must have had the power to enact § 4248 because a long period of federal incarceration might 'seve[r]' a sexually dangerous prisoner's 'claim to legal residence' in any particular State, thus leaving the prisoner without any 'home State to take charge' of him upon release. I disagree with the premise of that argument. As an initial matter, States plainly have the constitutional authority to 'take charge' of a federal prisoner released within their jurisdiction. In addition, the assumption that a State knowingly would fail to exercise that authority is, in my view, implausible. [E]ven in the event a State made such a decision, the Constitution assigns the responsibility for that decision, and its consequences, to the state government alone."

As for § 4248's "accommodation of state interests," once it is determined that Congress has the authority to provide for the civil detention of sexually dangerous persons, Congress 'is acting within the powers granted it under the Constitution,'

---

a. Scalia, J., did not join the analysis of this paragraph.

and 'may impose its will on the States.' Section 4248's right of first refusal is thus not a matter of constitutional necessity, but an act of legislative grace.

"Nevertheless, 29 States appear as amici and argue that § 4248 is constitutional. * * * Congress' power, however, is fixed by the Constitution; it does not expand merely to suit the States' policy preferences, or to allow State officials to avoid difficult choices regarding the allocation of state funds. [T]he duty to protect citizens from violent crime, including acts of sexual violence, belongs solely to the States. [The] Constitution gives States no more power to decline this responsibility than it gives them to infringe upon those liberties in the first instance."

SECTION 2.   THE NATIONAL COMMERCE POWER

I.   DEVELOPMENT OF BASIC CONCEPTS

GIBBONS v. OGDEN

22 U.S. (9 Wheat.) 1, 6 L.Ed. 23 (1824).

CHIEF JUSTICE MARSHALL delivered the opinion of the Court.

[A New York statute granted Livingston and Fulton the exclusive right to navigate steamboats in state waters; they assigned to Ogden the right to navigate between New York City and New Jersey. Ogden secured an injunction in the state courts against Gibbons, who was navigating two steamboats licensed under an act of Congress between New York and New Jersey.]

The appellant contends that this decree is erroneous, because the laws which purport to give the exclusive privilege it sustains, are repugnant [to] that clause in the constitution which authorizes Congress to [regulate] "commerce with foreign nations, and among the several states, and with the Indian tribes."

The subject to be regulated is commerce [and to] ascertain the extent of the power, it becomes necessary to settle the meaning of the word. The counsel for the appellee would limit it to traffic, to buying and selling, or the interchange of commodities, and do not admit that it comprehends navigation. This would restrict a general term, applicable to many objects, to one of its significations. Commerce, undoubtedly, is traffic, but it is something more,—it is intercourse. It describes the commercial intercourse between nations, and parts of nations in all its branches, and is regulated by prescribing rules for carrying on that intercourse. [All] America understands, and has uniformly understood the word "commerce" to comprehend navigation. It was so understood, and must have been so understood, when the Constitution was framed. The power over commerce, including navigation, was one of the primary objects for which the people of America adopted their government, and must have been contemplated in forming [it].

To what commerce does this power extend? The Constitution informs us, to commerce "with foreign nations, and among the several states, and with the Indian tribes." It has, we believe, been universally admitted that these words comprehend every species of commercial intercourse between the United States and foreign nations. No sort of trade can be carried on between this country and any other to which this power does not extend. * * *

The subject to which the power is next applied is to commerce "among the several States." The word "among" means intermingled [with.] Commerce among the states cannot stop at the external boundary-line of each state, but may be introduced into the interior. * * * Comprehensive as the word "among" is, it may very properly be restricted to that commerce which concerns more states than one. [The] enumeration of the particular classes of commerce to which the power was to be extended [presupposes] something not enumerated; and that something, if we regard the language or the subject of the sentence, must be the exclusively internal commerce of a state. The genius and character of the whole government seem to be, that its action is to be applied to all the external concerns of the nation, and to those internal concerns which affect the states generally; but not to those which are completely within a particular state, which do not affect other states, and with which it is not necessary to interfere for the purpose of executing some of the general powers of the government. The completely internal commerce of a state, then, may be considered as reserved for the state itself.

But, in regulating commerce[,] the power of Congress does not stop at the jurisdictional lines of the several states. [They] either join each other, in which case they are separated by a mathematical line, or they are remote from each other, in which case other states lie between them. What is commerce "among" them; and how is it to be conducted? Can a trading expedition between two adjoining states commence and terminate outside of each? And if the trading intercourse be between two states remote from each other, must it not commence in one, terminate in the other, and probably pass through a third? Commerce among the states must, of necessity, be commerce with the states. [The] power of Congress, then, whatever it may be, must be exercised within the territorial jurisdiction of the several states. * * *

We are now arrived at the inquiry, What is this power? It is the power to regulate; that is, to prescribe the rule by which commerce is to be governed. This power, like all others vested in Congress, is complete in itself, may be exercised to its utmost extent, and acknowledges no limitations other than are prescribed in the Constitution. These are expressed in plain terms, and do not affect the questions which arise in this case. [A]s has always been understood, the sovereignty of Congress, though limited to specified objects, is plenary as to those objects. [The] wisdom and the discretion of Congress, their identity with the people, and the influence which their constituents possess at elections, are, in this, as in many other instances, as that, for example, of declaring war, the sole restraints on which they have relied, to secure them from its abuse. They are the restraints on which the people must often rely solely, in all representative governments. * * *a

[Ch. 4, Sec. 1 considers Marshall, C.J.'s discussion of Gibbons' claim that Congress' power to regulate commerce was exclusive. The Court left that issue unresolved when it ruled that Ogden's claim of a steamboat monopoly under New York's law must yield to the federal law under which Gibbons held a license.]

Note

The Court's Commerce Clause concepts were first developed largely in cases challenging state regulatory laws and taxes as regulations of "commerce," which were claimed to be exclusively within the power of Congress. Congress had left most business regulation to the states,b and had made little use of its power to regulate commerce until the Interstate Commerce Act in 1887 and the Sherman Act in 1890. *Paul v. Virginia*, 75 U.S. (8 Wall.) 168 (1869), upheld state regulation of interstate insurance business on the ground that "issuing a policy of insurance is not a transaction of commerce" and insurance contracts "are not articles of commerce." *Kidd v. Pearson*, 128 U.S. 1 (1888), upheld Iowa's ban on manufac-

a. Johnson, J., concurred on the ground that the power of Congress to regulate commerce was exclusive.

b. Ch. 4 concerns the Court's protecting interstate commerce from harmful state regulation and taxes without thwarting state efforts to protect legitimate interests.

ture of liquor as applied to an Iowa distillery that sold its entire output in other states. It rejected the contention that manufacture for exclusively out-of-state sales was interstate commerce subject only to congressional regulation. The Court continued to adhere to this ruling in *United States v. E.C. Knight Co.*, 156 U.S. 1 (1895) (Sherman Act could not be applied to monopoly of sugar refiners: "commerce succeeds to manufacture, and is not part of it"). But *The Daniel Ball*, 77 U.S. (10 Wall.) 557 (1871) sustained, a federal safety regulation as applied to a small ship navigating in shallow water on a river exclusively within Michigan: "So far as she was employed in transporting goods destined for other States, or goods brought from without the limits of Michigan and destined to places within that State, she was engaged in commerce between the States. [She] was employed as an instrumentality of that commerce."

FOUNDATIONS FOR EXTENDING THE REACH OF CONGRESSIONAL POWER

Significant problems concerning Congress' commerce power have related to its use over (1) national economic problems by regulating local aspects that may be neither "commerce" nor "among the several states," such as crops produced and consumed on a farm; (2) disfavored local activities, such as gambling and distribution of harmful or improperly labeled foods and drugs; and (3) other socially undesirable conduct, such as discrimination based on race.

The next two cases develop two different methods of using the Commerce Clause to deal with such problems, followed by the evolution of these two "approaches."

THE LOTTERY CASE (CHAMPION v. AMES)

188 U.S. 321, 23 S.Ct. 321, 47 L.Ed. 492 (1903).

JUSTICE HARLAN delivered the opinion of the Court.

[The Federal Lottery Act, prohibiting interstate carriage of lottery tickets, was applied to shipping a box of tickets from Texas to California.] These tickets were the subject of traffic; they could have been sold; and the holder was assured that the company would pay to him the amount of the prize drawn. [L]ottery tickets [therefore] are subjects of commerce, and the regulation of the carriage of such tickets from state to state, at least by independent carriers, is a regulation of commerce among the several states.

[Are] we prepared to say that a provision which is, in effect, a *prohibition* of the carriage of such articles from state to state is not a fit or appropriate mode for the *regulation* of that particular kind of commerce? If lottery traffic, *carried on through interstate commerce,* is a matter of which Congress may take cognizance and over which its power may be exerted, can it be possible that it must tolerate the traffic, and simply regulate the manner in which it may be carried on? Or may not Congress, for the protection of the people of all the states, and under the power to regulate interstate commerce, devise such means, within the scope of the Constitution, and not prohibited by it, as will drive that traffic out of commerce among the states? * * *

If a state, when considering legislation for the suppression of lotteries within its own limits, may properly take into view the evils, that inhere in the raising of money, in that mode, why may not Congress, invested with the power to regulate commerce among the several states, provide that such commerce shall not be polluted by the carrying of lottery tickets from one state to another? [I]t must not be forgotten that the power of Congress to regulate commerce among the states is plenary, is complete in itself, and is subject to no limitations except such as may be found in the Constitution. [What] clause can be cited which, in any degree, countenances the suggestion that one may, of right, carry or cause to be carried from one state to another that which will harm the public morals? * * *

Congress [does] not assume to interfere with traffic or commerce in lottery tickets carried on exclusively within the limits of any state, but has in view only commerce of that kind among the several states [and] has only legislated in respect of a matter which concerns the people of the United States. * * * Congress, for the purpose of guarding the people of the United States against the "widespread pestilence of lotteries" and to protect the commerce which concerns all the states, may [supplement] the action of those states—perhaps all of them— which, for the protection of the public morals, prohibit the drawing of lotteries, as well as the sale or circulation of lottery tickets, within their respective limits. It said, in effect, that it would not permit the declared policy of the states, which sought to protect their people against the mischiefs of the lottery business, to be overthrown or disregarded by the agency of interstate commerce. We should hesitate long before adjudging that an evil of such appalling character, carried on through interstate commerce, cannot be met and crushed by the only power competent to that end. * * *

It is said, however, that if, in order to suppress lotteries carried on through interstate commerce, Congress may exclude lottery tickets from such commerce, that principle leads necessarily to the conclusion that Congress may arbitrarily exclude from commerce among the states any article, commodity, or thing, of whatever kind or nature, or however useful or valuable, which it may choose, no matter with what motive. [It] will be time enough to consider the constitutionality of such legislation when we must do so. [T]he possible abuse of a power is not an argument against its existence. * * *

CHIEF JUSTICE FULLER, with whom concur JUSTICE BREWER, JUSTICE SHIRAS, and JUSTICE PECKHAM, dissenting.

[D]oubtless an act prohibiting the carriage of lottery matter would be necessary and proper to the execution of a power to suppress lotteries; but that power belongs to the states and not to Congress. To hold that Congress has general police power would be to hold that it may accomplish objects not intrusted to the general government, and to defeat the operation of the 10th Amendment.c * * * The power to prohibit the transportation of diseased animals and infected goods over railroads or on steamboats is an entirely different thing, for they would be in themselves injurious to the transaction of interstate commerce, [and] are essentially commercial in their nature. And the exclusion of diseased persons rests on different ground, for nobody would pretend that persons could be kept off the trains because they were going from one state to another to engage in the lottery business. However enticing that business may be, we do not understand these pieces of paper themselves can communicate bad principles by contact. * * *

HOUSTON, EAST & WEST TEXAS RY. v. UNITED STATES (SHREVEPORT CASE)

234 U.S. 342, 34 S.Ct. 833, 58 L.Ed. 1341 (1914).

JUSTICE HUGHES delivered the opinion of the Court.

[The Interstate Commerce Commission fixed interstate railroad rates westward from Shreveport, La., to Texas markets. The ICC also ordered the affected

---

c. The dissent later quoted the sentence in *McCulloch* about Congress, "under the pretext of executing its powers, pass[ing] laws for the accomplishment of objects not entrusted to the government."

railroads to raise their rates for intrastate shipments to the same Texas markets. These rates were prescribed by the Texas Railroad Commission and discriminated against interstate commerce.a

[Where the power of Congress to regulate commerce] exists, it dominates. Interstate trade was not left to be destroyed or impeded by the rivalries of local government. The purpose was to make impossible the recurrence of the evils which had overwhelmed the Confederation, and to provide the necessary basis of national unity by insuring "uniformity of regulation against conflicting and discriminating state legislation." By virtue of the comprehensive terms of the grant, the authority of Congress is at all times adequate to meet the varying exigencies that arise. [Its] authority, extending to these interstate carriers as instruments of interstate commerce, necessarily embraces the right to control their operations in all matters having such a close and substantial relation to interstate traffic that the control is essential or appropriate to the security of that traffic, to the efficiency of the interstate service, and to the maintenance of conditions under which interstate commerce may be conducted upon fair terms and without molestation or hindrance.

[While *Baltimore & O.R. Co. v. ICC*, 221 U.S. 612 (1911),b and *Southern R. Co. v. United States*, 222 U.S. 20 (1911)c] relate to measures adopted in the interest of the safety of persons and property, they illustrate the principle that Congress [may] prevent the common instrumentalities of interstate and intrastate commercial intercourse from being used in their intrastate operations to the injury of interstate commerce. This is not to say that Congress possesses the authority to regulate the internal commerce of a state, as such, but that it does possess the power to foster and protect interstate commerce, and to take all measures necessary or appropriate to that end, although intrastate transactions of interstate carriers may thereby be controlled.

This principle is applicable here. We find no reason to doubt that Congress is entitled to keep the highways of interstate communication open to interstate traffic upon fair and equal terms. That an unjust discrimination in the rates of a common carrier, by which one person or locality is unduly favored as against another under substantially similar conditions of traffic, constitutes an evil, is undeniable; and where this evil consists in the action of an interstate carrier in unreasonably discriminating against interstate traffic over its line, the authority of Congress to prevent it is equally clear. It is immaterial, so far as the protecting power of Congress is concerned, that the discrimination arises from intrastate rates as compared with interstate rates. [In] removing the injurious discriminations against interstate traffic arising from the relation of intrastate to interstate rates, Congress is not bound to reduce the latter below what it may deem to be a proper standard, fair to the carrier and to the public. Otherwise, it could prevent the injury to interstate commerce only by the sacrifice of its judgment as to interstate rates. Congress is entitled to maintain its own standard as to these rates, and to forbid any discriminatory action by interstate carriers which will

a. For example "a rate of 60 cents carried first-class traffic [160 miles] from Dallas, while the same rate [carried] the same class of traffic only 55 miles into Texas from Shreveport. [The] rate on wagons from Dallas to Marshall, Texas, 147.7 miles, was 36.8 cents, and from Shreveport to Marshall, 42 miles, 56 [cents]."

b. *Baltimore & O.R.* upheld federal regulation of hours of service of employees working on interstate railroads, even though the effect

was to control their hours on intrastate service as well, because of the impracticality of limiting their work to one or the other.

c. *Southern R.* upheld the federal safety appliance act's application to vehicles used by an interstate railroad only in intrastate traffic, as well as those used interstate, in order to assure the safety of interstate traffic moving over the same railroad as the intrastate.

obstruct the freedom of movement of interstate traffic over their lines in accordance with the terms it establishes. * * *

JUSTICE LURTON and JUSTICE PITNEY dissent.

II. REGULATION OF NATIONAL ECONOMIC PROBLEMS

A. LIMITATIONS ON COMMERCE POWER THROUGH 1936

HAMMER v. DAGENHART

247 U.S. 251, 38 S.Ct. 529, 62 L.Ed. 1101 (1918).

JUSTICE DAY delivered the opinion of the Court.

[Ruling that Congress exceeded its commerce power by prohibiting interstate transportation of products from factories that used child labor, the Court distinguished the *Lottery* line of cases:] In each of these instances the use of interstate transportation was necessary to the accomplishment of harmful results. In other words, although the power over interstate transportation was to regulate, that could only be accomplished by prohibiting the use of the facilities of interstate commerce to effect the evil intended.

This element is wanting in the present case. [The] act in its effect does not regulate transportation among the states, but aims to standardize the ages at which children may be employed in mining and manufacturing within the states. The goods shipped are of themselves harmless. [B]efore transportation begins, the labor of their production is over, and the mere fact that they were intended for interstate commerce transportation does not make their production subject to federal control. [O]therwise, all manufacture intended for interstate shipment would be brought under federal control to the practical exclusion of the authority of the states, a result certainly not contemplated by the framers of the Constitution * * *.

It is further contended that the authority of Congress may be exerted to control interstate commerce in the shipment of child-made goods because of the effect of the circulation of such goods in other states where the evil of this class of labor has been recognized by local legislation, [but there] is no power vested in Congress to require the states to exercise their police power so as to prevent possible unfair competition. Many causes may cooperate to give one state, by reason of local laws or conditions, an economic advantage over others. The commerce clause was not intended to give to Congress a general authority to equalize such conditions. In some of the states laws have been passed fixing minimum wages for women, in others the local law regulates the hours of labor of women in various employments. Business done in such states may be at an economic disadvantage when compared with states which have no such regulations; surely, this fact does not give Congress the power to deny transportation in interstate commerce to those who carry on business where the hours of labor and the rate of compensation for women have not been fixed by a standard in use in other states and approved by Congress. [To] sustain this statute [would] sanction an invasion by the federal power of the control of a matter purely local in its character * * *.

JUSTICE HOLMES, [joined by McKenna, Brandeis, and Clarke, JJ.,] dissenting.

* * * Regulation means the prohibition of something, and when interstate commerce is the matter to be regulated I cannot doubt that the regulation may prohibit any part of such commerce that Congress sees fit to forbid. * * *

The question then is narrowed to whether the exercise of its otherwise constitutional power by Congress can be pronounced unconstitutional because of its possible reaction upon the conduct of the States in a matter upon which [they] are free from direct control. I [should] have thought that the most conspicuous decisions of this Court had made it clear that the power to regulate commerce and other constitutional powers could not be cut down or qualified by the fact that it might interfere with the carrying out of the domestic policy of any [State.]

The Act does not meddle with anything belonging to the States. They may regulate their internal affairs and their domestic commerce as they like. But when they seek to send their products across the State line they are no longer within their rights. If there were no Constitution and no Congress their power to cross the line would depend upon their neighbors. Under the Constitution such commerce belongs not to the States but to Congress to regulate. It may carry out its views of public policy whatever indirect effect they may have upon the activities of the States. Instead of being encountered by a prohibitive tariff at her boundaries the State encounters the public policy of the United States which it is for Congress to express. [The] national welfare as understood by Congress may require a different attitude within its sphere from that of some self-seeking State. * * *

CONSTITUTIONAL STRUGGLE: THE NEW DEAL VS. THE GREAT DEPRESSION

The great depression of the 1930s gave rise to unprecedented unemployment, drastic cutbacks in production, 60% declines in farm and labor income, widespread business and bank failures, devastating home and farm mortgage foreclosures, all reacting on each other in an extraordinary downward spiral. Congress used the Commerce Clause to respond. SCHECHTER POULTRY CORP. v. UNITED STATES, 295 U.S. 495 (1935), per HUGHES, C.J., struck down a Code, adopted under the National Industrial Recovery Act, to regulate trade practices, wages, hours, and collective bargaining in the New York poultry wholesale slaughtering market where 96% of the poultry came from other states. Schechter bought poultry only on the local market and, after slaughtering, sold it only to local retailers. The Court ruled that the regulation fell outside the commerce power because the regulated conduct had no "direct" effect upon interstate commerce, but said little to clarify this, possibly because the major basis for invalidity was that the Act unconstitutionally delegated legislative power to the Act's Administrator, see Ch. 3, Sec. 2, I.

One year later, CARTER v. CARTER COAL CO., 298 U.S. 238 (1936), per SUTHERLAND, J., expanded on *Schechter's* "direct effect" test ruling that the Commerce Clause did not give Congress power to require Bituminous Coal Code members to observe the hours and wages agreed upon between producers of two-thirds of the bituminous coal volume and one-half of the employed bituminous mine workers: "[T]he effect of the labor provisions of the [act] primarily falls upon production and not upon commerce; [p]roduction is a purely local activity. It follows that none of these essential antecedents of production constitutes a transaction in or forms any part of interstate commerce. [T]he local character of mining, of manufacturing, and of crop growing is a fact, and remains a fact, whatever may be done with the products. * * *

"That the production of every commodity intended for interstate sale and transportation has some effect upon interstate commerce may [be] freely granted; and we are brought to the final and decisive inquiry, whether here that effect is direct [or] indirect. The distinction is not formal, but substantial in the highest degree, as we pointed out in *Schechter*. 'If the commerce clause were construed

[to] reach all enterprises and transactions which could be said to have an indirect effect upon interstate commerce, the federal authority would embrace practically all the activities of the people, and the authority of the state over its domestic concerns would exist only by sufferance of the federal government.' * * *

"Whether the effect of a given activity or condition is direct or indirect is not always easy to determine. The word 'direct' implies that the activity or condition invoked or blamed shall operate proximately—not mediately, remotely, or collaterally—to produce the effect. It connotes the absence of an efficient intervening agency or condition. [The] distinction between a direct and an indirect effect turns, not upon the magnitude of either the cause or the effect, but entirely upon the manner in which the effect has been brought about. [It] is quite true that rules of law are sometimes qualified by considerations of degree, as the government argues. But the matter of degree has no bearing upon the question here, since that question is not—What is the *extent* of the local activity or condition, or the *extent* of the effect produced upon interstate commerce? but—What is the *relation* between the activity or condition and the effect?

"[The] only perceptible difference between [*Schechter*] and this is that in the *Schechter Case* the federal power was asserted with respect to commodities which had come to rest after their interstate transportation; while here, the case deals with commodities at rest before interstate commerce has begun. That difference is without significance. The federal regulatory power ceases when interstate commercial intercourse ends; and, correlatively, the power does not attach until interstate commercial intercourse begins."a

B.   EXPANSION OF COMMERCE POWER AFTER 1936

By the 1936 Presidential election the Court had invalidated six federal laws designed to advance President Franklin D. Roosevelt's New Deal program for economic recovery, four of major importance: the National Industrial Recovery Act and the Bituminous Coal Act, both supra, the Agricultural Adjustment Act, *United States v. Butler*, Sec. 3, II infra, the Railway Pension Act, the Farm Mortgage Act and the Municipal Bankruptcy Act. Only one New Deal measure had been sustained, the Gold Clause legislation. *Norman v. Baltimore & O.R. Co.*, 294 U.S. 240 (1935) (5–4). More vital laws of the New Deal program still awaited the Court's scrutiny. These included the National Labor Relations Act, the Social Security Act (both old age pensions and unemployment compensation), and the Public Utility Holding Company Act. In addition, new legislation was needed to replace the minimum labor standards lost in *Schechter* and *Carter Coal* and the control over agricultural surpluses lost in *Butler*.

After his overwhelming victory in the 1936 elections, President Roosevelt sought congressional approval of what became known popularly as the "Court Packing" plan, which would have authorized appointment of as many as six new justices, one to sit in addition to each justice over seventy years of age. The first major Commerce Clause decision after *Carter*, several months before Congress rejected the Court–Packing plan,b NLRB v. JONES & LAUGHLIN STEEL CORP., 301 U.S. 1 (1937), per HUGHES, C.J., upheld application of the National

a. Hughes, C.J., concurred in the result, stating only: "Congress may not use this protective authority [over commerce] as a pretext [to] regulate activities and relations within the states which affect interstate commerce only indirectly." Cardozo, J., joined by Brandeis and Stone, JJ., found the labor provisions not ripe for decision, but would uphold those fixing intrastate coal prices.

b. Two weeks earlier, *West Coast Hotel Co. v. Parrish*, Ch. 5, Sec. 3, held that a state minimum wage law did not violate the Fourteenth Amendment Due Process Clause, overruling several earlier decisions.

Labor Relations Act to the nation's fourth largest steel producer, with facilities throughout the country, most of whose production was shipped and sold in interstate commerce. The NLRB found that J & L had engaged in unfair labor practices by discharging employees at one of its plants: "[Respondent's] argument rests upon the proposition that manufacturing in itself is not commerce. [Although] activities may be intrastate in character when separately considered, if they have such a close and substantial relation to interstate commerce that their control is essential or appropriate to protect that commerce from burdens and obstructions, Congress cannot be denied the power to exercise that control. Undoubtedly the scope of this power must be considered in the light of our dual system of government and may not be extended so as to embrace effects upon interstate commerce so indirect and remote that to embrace them, in view of our complex society, would effectually obliterate the distinction between what is national and what is local and create a completely centralized government. The question is necessarily one of degree.

"[In] *Schechter,* we found that the effect there was so remote as to be beyond the federal power. To find 'immediacy or directness' there was to find it 'almost everywhere,' a result inconsistent with the maintenance of our federal system. In *Carter Coal,* the Court was of the opinion that the provisions of the statute relating to production were invalid upon several grounds,—that there was improper delegation of legislative power, and that the requirements not only went beyond any sustainable measure of protection of interstate commerce but were also inconsistent with due process. These cases are not controlling here.

"[T]he stoppage of [J & L's] operations by industrial strife would have a most serious effect upon interstate commerce. In view of respondent's far-flung activities, it is idle to say that the effect would be indirect or remote. It is obvious that it would be immediate and might be catastrophic. We are asked to shut our eyes to the plainest facts of our national life and to deal with the question of direct and indirect effects in an intellectual vacuum. Because there may be but indirect and remote effects upon interstate commerce in connection with a host of local enterprises throughout the country, it does not follow that other industrial activities do not have such a close and intimate relation to interstate commerce as to make the presence of industrial strife a matter of the most urgent national concern." McReynolds J., joined by Van Devanter, Sutherland and Butler, JJ., dissented.

UNITED STATES v. DARBY

312 U.S. 100, 61 S.Ct. 451, 85 L.Ed. 609 (1941).

Justice Stone delivered the opinion of the Court. * * *

The Fair Labor Standards [Act's] purpose [is] to exclude from interstate commerce goods produced for the commerce and to prevent their production for interstate commerce, under conditions detrimental to the maintenance of the minimum standards of living necessary for health and general well-being; and to prevent the use of interstate commerce as the means of competition in the distribution of goods so produced, and as the means of spreading and perpetuating such substandard labor conditions among the workers of the several [states].

The indictment charges that appellee is engaged, in the state of Georgia, in the business of acquiring raw materials, which he manufactures into finished lumber with the intent when manufactured, to ship it in interstate [commerce].

The prohibition of shipment of the proscribed goods in interstate commerce. Section 15(a)(1) prohibits, and the indictment charges, the shipment in interstate commerce, of goods produced for interstate commerce by employees whose wages and hours of employment do not conform to the requirements of the Act. * * *

While manufacture is not of itself interstate commerce the shipment of manufactured goods interstate is such commerce and the prohibition of such shipment by Congress is indubitably a regulation of the commerce. The power to regulate [extends] not only to those regulations which aid, foster and protect the commerce, but embraces those which prohibit it. It is conceded that the power of Congress to prohibit transportation in interstate commerce includes noxious articles, stolen articles, [and] articles such as intoxicating liquor or convict made goods, traffic in which is forbidden or restricted by the laws of the state of destination.

But it is said that the present prohibition falls within the scope of none of these categories; that while the prohibition is nominally a regulation of the commerce its motive or purpose is regulation of wages and hours of persons engaged in manufacture, the control of which has been reserved to the states and upon which Georgia and some of the states of destination have placed no restriction. [But] Congress, following its own conception of public policy concerning the restrictions which may appropriately be imposed on interstate commerce, is free to exclude from the commerce articles whose use in the states for which they are destined it may conceive to be injurious to the public health, morals or welfare even though the state has not sought to regulate their use. * * *

The motive and purpose of the present regulation are plainly to make effective the Congressional conception of public policy that interstate commerce should not be made the instrument of competition in the distribution of goods produced under substandard labor conditions. [The] motive and purpose of a regulation of interstate commerce are matters for the legislative judgment upon the exercise of which the Constitution places no restriction and over, which the courts are given no control [citing cases on Congress' taxing power, Sec. 3, I infra]. Whatever their motive and purpose, regulations of commerce which do not infringe some constitutional prohibition are within the plenary power conferred on Congress by the Commerce Clause. Subject only to that limitation, presently to be considered [fn. a infra], we conclude that the prohibition of the shipment interstate of goods produced under the forbidden substandard labor conditions is within the constitutional authority of Congress.

[T]hese principles of constitutional interpretation have been so long and repeatedly recognized by this Court as applicable to the Commerce Clause, that there would be little occasion for repeating them now were it not for the decision of this Court twenty-two years ago in *Dagenhart* [by] a bare majority of the Court over the powerful and now classic dissent of Mr. Justice Holmes [*Dagenhart*] has not been followed. The distinction on which the decision was rested that Congressional power to prohibit interstate commerce is limited to articles which in themselves have some harmful or deleterious property—a distinction which was novel when made and unsupported by any provision of the Constitution—has long since been abandoned. The thesis of the opinion that the motive of the prohibition or its effect to control in some measure the use or production within the states of the article thus excluded from the commerce can operate to deprive the regulation of its constitutional authority has long since ceased to have force. [It] should be and now is overruled.

Validity of the wage and hour requirements. Section 15(a)(2) and §§ 6 and 7 require employers to conform to the wage and hour provisions with respect to all employees engaged in the production of goods for interstate commerce. As appellee's employees are not alleged to be "engaged in interstate commerce" the validity of the prohibition turns on the question whether [their employment] in the production of goods for interstate commerce is so related to the commerce and so affects it as to be within the reach of the power of Congress to regulate it.

[The]   purpose of the Act was [to] stop the initial step toward transportation, production with the purpose [of] transporting it. [T]he power of Congress to regulate interstate commerce extends to the regulation [of] activities intrastate which have a substantial effect on the commerce or the exercise of the Congressional power over it. In such legislation Congress has sometimes left it to the courts to determine whether the intrastate activities have the prohibited effect on the commerce, as in the Sherman Act. It has sometimes left it to an administrative board or agency to determine[,] as in the case [of] the National Labor Relations Act. [S]ometimes Congress itself has said that a particular activity affects the commerce, as it did in the present Act, the Safety Appliance Act and the Railway Labor Act. In passing on the validity of legislation of the class last mentioned the only function of courts is to determine whether the particular activity regulated or prohibited is within the reach of the federal power.

Congress, having by the present Act adopted the policy of excluding from interstate commerce all goods produced for the commerce which do not conform to the specified labor standards, it may choose the means reasonably adapted to the attainment of the permitted end, even though they involve control of intrastate activities. Such legislation has often been sustained with respect to powers, other than the commerce power granted to the national government, when the means chosen, although not themselves within the granted power, were nevertheless deemed appropriate aids to the accomplishment of some purpose within an admitted power of the national government. [A] familiar like exercise of power is the regulation of intrastate transactions which are so commingled with or related to interstate commerce that all must be regulated if the interstate commerce is to be effectively controlled. *Shreveport*; *Wisconsin Railroad Comm.* [Similarly], Congress may require inspection and preventive treatment of all cattle in a disease infected area in order to prevent shipment in interstate commerce of some of the cattle without the treatment. [And] we have recently held that Congress in the exercise of its power to require inspection and grading of tobacco shipped in interstate commerce may compel such inspection and grading [at] local auction rooms from which a substantial part but not all of the tobacco sold is shipped in interstate commerce. *Currin v. Wallace,* 306 U.S. 1 (1939). * * *

We think also that § 15(a)(2), now under consideration, is sustainable independently of § 15(a)(1), which prohibits shipment or transportation of the proscribed goods. As we have said the evils aimed at by the Act are the spread of substandard labor conditions through the use of the facilities of interstate commerce for competition by the goods so produced with those produced under the prescribed or better labor conditions; and the consequent dislocation of the commerce itself caused by the impairment or destruction of local businesses by competition made effective through interstate commerce. The Act is thus directed at the suppression of a method or kind of competition [which] it has in effect condemned as "unfair", as the Clayton Act, has condemned other "unfair methods of competition" made effective through interstate commerce. * * *

The means adopted by § 15(a)(2) for the protection of interstate commerce by the suppression of the production of the condemned goods [is] so related to the commerce and so affects it as to be within the reach of the commerce power. Congress, to attain its objective in the suppression of nationwide competition in interstate commerce by goods produced under substandard labor conditions, has made no distinction as to the volume or amount of shipments in the commerce or of production for commerce by any particular shipper or producer. * * *

So far as *Carter* is inconsistent with this conclusion, its doctrine is limited in principle by the decisions under the Sherman Act and the National Labor Relations Act, which we have cited and which we follow.

Our conclusion is unaffected by the Tenth Amendment [which] states but a truism that all is retained which has not been surrendered. There is nothing in the history of its adoption to suggest that it was more than declaratory of the relationship between the national and state governments as it had been established by the Constitution before the amendment or that its purpose was other than to allay fears that the new national government might seek to exercise powers not granted, and that the states might not be able to exercise fully their reserved powers.**b**

Reversed.

Notes

1. *After interstate commerce ends.* (a) UNITED STATES v. SULLIVAN, 332 U.S. 689 (1948), per BLACK, J. upheld the conviction of a retail druggist under the federal Food, Drug and Cosmetic Act for selling two pill boxes, in which he had placed 12 tablets, and failing to affix the required warning label that was printed on the large bottle of pills bought from an in-state wholesaler, who had secured them through interstate commerce: "[The Act] was designed [to] safeguard the consumer by applying the Act to articles from the moment of their introduction into interstate commerce all the way to the moment of their delivery to the ultimate consumer. [We affirm] the constitutional power of Congress under the commerce clause to regulate the branding of articles that have completed an interstate shipment and are being held for future sales in purely local or intrastate commerce." Rutledge, J., concurred. Frankfurter, J., joined by Reed and Jackson, JJ., dissented. All were concerned only with statutory construction.

(b) SCARBOROUGH v. UNITED STATES, 431 U.S. 563 (1977), per MARSHALL, J., interpreted a federal statute as making it a crime for a convicted felon to possess a firearm as long as there existed "the minimal nexus that the firearm have been, at some time, in interstate commerce, [with] little concern for when the nexus with commerce occurred"—even before the accused was convicted. Although the Court did not resolve any constitutional issue, it indicated that "Congress [asserted] its full Commerce Clause power so as to cover all activity substantially affecting interstate commerce."

2. *Local activities affecting commerce.* (a) WICKARD v. FILBURN, 317 U.S. 111 (1942), per JACKSON, J., upheld a penalty imposed under the Agricultural Adjustment Act of 1938 on Filburn for raising 239 bushels of wheat in excess of his marketing allotment. Filburn's practice was to plant a small acreage of wheat, to sell some, feed some to livestock, and use some for home-consumed flour and for seed: "[The commerce clause] question would merit little consideration since

b. The Court also held that the minimum wage and maximum hours provisions did not violate the Due Process Clause of the Fifth Amendment, citing *West Coast Hotel Co. v. Parrish*, Ch. 5, Sec. 3.

The unanimity in *Darby* can be attributed to the departure of the four justices who dissented in *Jones & Laughlin*, Butler, J., by death in 1938, and the other three by retirement: Van Devanter, J., in 1937, Sutherland, J., in 1938 and McReynolds, J., in 1940, just two days before the announcement of *Darby*. Of the five who joined the majority opinion in *Carter Coal*, only Roberts, J., remained, and his views appeared to have undergone much change since 1936.

our decision in [*Darby*], except for the fact that this Act extends federal regulation to production not intended in any part for commerce but wholly for consumption on the farm. [But once] an economic measure of the reach of the power granted to Congress in the Commerce Clause is accepted, questions of federal power cannot be decided simply by finding the activity in question to be 'production' nor can consideration of its economic effects be foreclosed by calling them 'indirect.' [E]ven if appellee's activity be local and though it may not be regarded as commerce, it may still, whatever its nature, be reached by Congress if it exerts a substantial economic effect on interstate commerce * * *.

"The wheat industry has been a problem industry for some years. [The] effect of consumption of home-grown wheat on interstate commerce * * * constitutes the most variable factor in the disappearance of the wheat crop. [The] effect of the statute before us is to restrict the amount which may be produced for market and the extent as well to which one may forestall resort to the market by producing to meet his own needs. That appellee's own contribution to the demand for wheat may be trivial by itself is not enough to remove him from the scope of federal regulation where, as here, his contribution, taken together with that of many others similarly situated, is far from trivial. [*NLRB v. Fainblatt*, 306 U.S. 601 (1939); *Darby*].

"It is well established by decisions of this Court that the power to regulate commerce includes the power to regulate the prices at which commodities in that commerce are dealt in and practices affecting such prices. One of the primary purposes of the Act in question was to increase the market price of wheat and to that end to limit the volume thereof that could affect the market. It can hardly be denied that a factor of such volume and variability as home-consumed wheat would have a substantial influence on price and market conditions. This may arise because being in marketable condition such wheat overhangs the market and if induced by rising prices tends to flow into the market and check price increases. But if we assume that it is never marketed, it supplies a need of the man who grew it which would otherwise be reflected by purchases in the open market. Home-grown wheat in this sense competes with wheat in commerce. The stimulation of commerce is a use of the regulatory function quite as definitely as prohibitions or restrictions thereon. This record leaves us in no doubt that Congress may properly have considered that wheat consumed on the farm where grown if wholly outside the scheme of regulation would have a substantial effect in defeating and obstructing its purpose to stimulate trade therein at increased prices."

(b) MARYLAND v. WIRTZ, 392 U.S. 183 (1968), per Harlan, J., upheld expanded congressional coverage of the Fair Labor Standards Act (1) from employees "engaged in commerce or in the production of goods for commerce" to *all* employees of any "*enterprise*" so engaged and (2) to include hospitals, nursing homes, and educational institutions—elementary, secondary or higher education—whether private or public.c The "enterprise" extension was justified on two grounds: (1) the competitive position of an interstate enterprise is affected by *all* its labor costs, not simply the costs of employees producing goods for commerce; and (2) a labor dispute caused by substandard labor conditions "among any group of employees, whether or not they are personally engaged in commerce or production, may lead to strife disrupting an entire enterprise." Extension of coverage to schools and hospitals was sustained under the commerce power on the ground that these institutions are major users of goods imported from other

---

c. For application of the Act to state gov-   ernment activities, see Sec. 5 infra.

states, and work stoppages involving their employees would interrupt this flow of goods across state lines.

(c) PEREZ v. UNITED STATES, 402 U.S. 146 (1971), per Douglas, J., upheld the federal Consumer Credit Protection Act's ban on "extortionate credit transactions, though purely intrastate, [because they] may in the judgment of Congress affect interstate commerce. [R]eports and hearings [supplied] Congress with the knowledge that the loan shark racket provides organized crime with its second most lucrative source of revenue, exacts millions from the pockets of people, coerces its victims into the commission of crimes against property, and causes the takeover by racketeers of legitimate businesses.

"We have mentioned in detail the economic, financial, and social setting of the problem as revealed to Congress [not] to infer that Congress need make particularized findings in order to legislate [but because of petitioner's claim] that all that is involved in loan sharking is a traditionally local activity. It appears, instead, that loan sharking in its national setting is one way organized interstate crime holds its guns to the heads of the poor and the rich alike and syphons funds from numerous localities to finance its national operations."

The Court rejected the contention that the extortionate activities of Perez were not shown to have any effect on commerce: "Where the *class of activities* is regulated and that *class* is within the reach of federal power, the courts have no power 'to excise, as trivial, individual instances' of the class. *Wirtz.*" Stewart, J., dissented.

III. PROTECTION OF OTHER INTERESTS THROUGH THE COMMERCE CLAUSE

HEART OF ATLANTA MOTEL, INC. v. UNITED STATES

379 U.S. 241, 85 S.Ct. 348, 13 L.Ed.2d 258 (1964).

Justice Clark delivered the opinion of the Court. * * *

Appellant owns and operates the Heart of Atlanta Motel which has 216 rooms, [readily] accessible to interstate [and] state highways. [A]pproximately 75% of its registered guests are from out of State. Prior to [1964] the motel had followed a practice of refusing to rent rooms to Negroes. [The] sole question posed is, therefore, the constitutionality of the Civil Rights Act of 1964a as applied to these facts. * * *

The Senate Commerce Committee made it quite clear that the fundamental object of Title II was to vindicate [pursuant to the Equal Protection Clause of the Fourteenth Amendment] "the deprivation of personal dignity that surely accompanies denials of equal access to public establishments." At the same time, however, it noted that such an objective has been and could be readily achieved "by congressional action based on the commerce power of the Constitution." Our study of the legislative record [has] brought us to the conclusion that Congress

a. Sec. 201(a) provided: "All persons shall be entitled to the full and equal enjoyment of the goods, services, facilities, [and] accommodations of any place of public accommodation * * * without discrimination or segregation on the ground of race, color, religion, or national origin." Sec. 201(b) defined of several types of establishments as "a place of public accommodation [if] its operations affect [interstate or foreign commerce], or if discrimination or segregation by it is supported by State action." Sec. 201(c) provided that "any inn, hotel, motel or other establishment which provides lodging to transient guests" is a place of public accommodation whose "operations * * * affect commerce," except when a live-in owner rents five or less rooms.

possessed ample power [under the Commerce Clause], and we have therefore not considered the other grounds relied upon. * * *

While the Act [carried] no congressional findings the [legislative record is] replete with evidence of the burdens that discrimination by race or color places upon interstate commerce. This testimony included the fact that our people have become increasingly mobile with millions of all races traveling from State to State; that Negroes in particular have been the subject of discrimination in transient accommodations, having to travel great distances to secure the same; that often they have been unable to obtain accommodations and have had to call upon friends to put them up overnight; and that these conditions had become so acute as to require the listing of available lodging for Negroes in a special guidebook which was itself "dramatic testimony of the difficulties" Negroes encounter in travel. These exclusionary practices were found to be nationwide [and] there is "no question that this discrimination in the North still exists to a large degree" and in the West and Midwest as well. This testimony indicated a qualitative as well as quantitative effect on interstate travel by Negroes. The former was the obvious impairment of the Negro traveler's pleasure and convenience. [As] for the latter, there was evidence that this uncertainty stemming from racial discrimination had the effect of discouraging travel on the part of a substantial portion of the Negro community. [T]he voluminous testimony presents overwhelming evidence that discrimination by hotels and motels impedes interstate travel.

[The] same interest in protecting interstate commerce which led Congress to deal with segregation in interstate carriers and the white slave traffic has prompted it to extend the exercise of its power to gambling, to criminal enterprises, to deceptive practices in the sale of products, to fraudulent security transactions, to misbranding of drugs, [to] discrimination against shippers, to the protection of small business from injurious price cutting, [and] to racial discrimination by owners and managers of terminal restaurants.

That Congress was legislating against moral wrongs in many of these areas rendered its enactments no less valid. In framing Title II of this Act Congress was also dealing with what it considered a moral problem. But that fact does not detract from the overwhelming evidence of the disruptive effect that racial discrimination has had on commercial intercourse. [G]iven this basis for the exercise of its power, Congress was not restricted by the fact that the particular obstruction to interstate commerce with which it was dealing was also deemed a moral and social wrong.

[T]he power of Congress to promote interstate commerce also includes the power to [regulate] local activities in both the States of origin and destination, which might have a substantial and harmful effect upon that commerce. One need only examine the evidence which we have discussed above to see that Congress may—as it has—prohibit racial discrimination by motels serving travelers, however "local" their operations may appear. * * *

[The concurring opinions of Douglas and Goldberg, JJ., appear after *Katzenbach v. McClung,* infra.]

KATZENBACH v. McCLUNG, 379 U.S. 294 (1964), per CLARK, J., upheld application of Sec. 201 to Ollie's Barbecue, a Birmingham restaurant eleven blocks from an interstate highway. It catered to a family and white collar trade with a take-out service for African Americans, whom it had refused to serve since opening in 1927: "There is no claim that interstate travelers frequented the restaurant. The sole question, therefore, narrows down to whether Title II, as applied to a restaurant receiving about $70,000 worth of food which has moved in commerce [out of a total of $150,000], is a valid exercise of the power of Congress.b The [legislative] record is replete with testimony of the burdens placed on interstate commerce by racial discrimination in restaurants. A comparison of per capita spending by Negroes in restaurants, theaters, and like establishments indicated less spending, after discounting income differences, in areas where discrimination is widely practiced. This condition, which was especially aggravated in the South, was attributed in the testimony of the Under Secretary of Commerce to racial segregation. This diminutive spending [has,] regardless of the absence of direct evidence, a close connection to interstate commerce. The fewer customers a restaurant enjoys the less food it sells and consequently the less it buys. [In] addition, the Attorney General testified that this type of discrimination imposed 'an artificial restriction on the market' and interfered with the flow of merchandise. [In] addition, there were many references to discriminatory situations causing wide unrest and having a depressant effect on general business conditions in the respective communities.

"Moreover there was an impressive array of testimony that discrimination in restaurants had a direct and highly restrictive effect upon interstate travel by Negroes. This resulted, it was said, because discrimination practices prevent Negroes from buying prepared food served on the premises while on a trip, except in isolated and unkempt restaurants and under most unsatisfactory and often unpleasant conditions. This obviously discourages travel and obstructs interstate commerce for one can hardly travel without eating. Likewise, it was said, that discrimination deterred professional, as well as skilled, people from moving into areas where such practices occurred and thereby caused industry to be reluctant to establish there. * * *

"It goes without saying that, viewed in isolation, the volume of food purchased by Ollie's Barbecue from sources supplied from out of state was insignificant when compared with the total foodstuffs moving in commerce. But, as [said] in *Wickard:* 'That appellee's own contribution to the demand for wheat may be trivial by itself is not enough to remove him from the scope of federal regulation where, as here, his contribution, taken together with that of many others similarly situated, is far from trivial.'

"[Appellees] object to the omission of a provision for a case-by-case determination—judicial or administrative—that racial discrimination in a particular restaurant affects commerce. [But here, as *in Darby*], Congress has determined for itself that refusals of service to Negroes have imposed burdens both upon the interstate flow of food and upon the movement of products generally. Of course, the mere fact that Congress has said when particular activity shall be deemed to affect commerce does not preclude further examination by this Court. But where we find that the legislators, in light of the facts and testimony before them, have a rational basis for finding a chosen regulatory scheme necessary to the protection of commerce, our investigation is at an end. * * *

"The absence of direct evidence connecting discriminatory restaurant service with the flow of interstate food, a factor on which the appellees place much reliance, is not, given the evidence as to the effect of such practices on other aspects of commerce, a crucial matter."

b. Sec. 201(b)(2) classified as a public accommodation, "any restaurant [or] other facility principally engaged in selling food for consumption on the premises." Sec. 201(c)(2) stated that the operations of such an establishment "affect commerce [if] it serves or offers to serve interstate travelers or a substantial portion of the food it serves [has] moved in commerce."

DOUGLAS, J., concurred: "Though I join the Court's opinion, I am somewhat reluctant [to] rest solely on the Commerce Clause. My reluctance is not due to any conviction that Congress lacks power to regulate commerce in the interests of human rights. It is rather my belief that the right of people to be free of state action that discriminates against them because of race * * *, 'occupies a more protected position in our constitutional system than does the movement of cattle, fruit, steel and coal across state lines.' [Hence] I would prefer to rest on the assertion of legislative power contained in § 5 of the Fourteenth Amendment."c

---

HODEL v. VIRGINIA SURFACE MINING AND RECLAMATION ASS'N, 452 U.S. 264 (1981), per MARSHALL, J., unanimously upheld the Surface Mining Control and Reclamation Act of 1977: "In light of the evidence available to Congressa and the detailed consideration that the legislation received, we cannot say that Congress did not have a rational basis for concluding that surface coal mining has substantial effects on interstate commerce."b REHNQUIST, J., concurred in the judgment, emphasizing that "there *are* constitutional limits on the power of Congress to regulate pursuant to the Commerce Clause. [I]t has long been established that the commerce power does not reach activity which merely 'affects' interstate commerce. There must instead be [a] *substantial effect* on that commerce. [Moreover,] simply because Congress may conclude that a particular activity substantially affects interstate commerce does not necessarily make it so. Congress' findings must be supported by a 'rational basis' and are reviewable by the courts."

IV. NEW LIMITATIONS AT THE END OF THE 20TH CENTURY

UNITED STATES v. MORRISON

529 U.S. 598, 120 S.Ct. 1740, 146 L.Ed.2d 658 (2000).

CHIEF JUSTICE REHNQUIST delivered the opinion of the Court.

[Petitioner Brzonkala, alleging that respondent, a fellow student at Virginia Polytechnic Institute, had assaulted and repeatedly raped her, sued him under 42 U.S.C. § 13981 (part of the Violence Against Women Act of 1984) which provides a federal civil remedy for the victims of gender-motivated violence. The United States intervened to defend § 13981's constitutionality.]

As we discussed at length in *United States v. Lopez*, 514 U.S. 549 (1995), our interpretation of the Commerce Clause has changed as our Nation has developed. [I]n the years since *Jones & Laughlin*, Congress has had considerably greater

---

c. Goldberg, J., also joined the opinion of the Court but in a separate opinion stated his view that the Fourteenth Amendment also authorized enactment of the Civil Rights Act, stressing that its "primary purpose" was "vindication of human dignity."

a. The opinion recited these findings of Congress: "[M]any surface mining operations result in disturbances of surface areas that burden and adversely affect commerce and the public welfare by destroying or diminishing the utility of land for commercial, industrial, residential, recreational, agricultural, and forestry purposes, by causing erosion and landslides, by contributing to floods, by polluting the water, by destroying fish and wildlife habitats, by impairing natural beauty, by damaging the property of citizens, by creating hazards dangerous to life and property by degrading the quality of life in local communities, and by counteracting governmental programs and efforts to conserve soil, water, and other natural resources."

b. The opinion expressly rejected the claim that "land as such" is not subject to regulation under the Commerce Clause.

latitude in regulating conduct and transactions under the Commerce Clause than our previous case law permitted.

Lopez emphasized, however, [that] Congress' regulatory authority is not without effective bounds. [In] *Jones & Laughlin,* the Court warned that the scope of the interstate commerce power "must be considered in the light of our dual system of government and may not be extended so as to embrace effects upon interstate commerce so indirect and remote that to embrace them, in view of our complex society, would effectually obliterate the distinction between what is national and what is local and create a completely centralized government."

As we observed in *Lopez,* modern Commerce Clause jurisprudence has "identified three broad categories of activity that Congress may regulate under its commerce power." "First, Congress may regulate the use of the channels of interstate commerce" (citing *Heart of Atlanta; Darby*). "Second, Congress is empowered to regulate and protect the instrumentalities of interstate commerce, or persons or things in interstate commerce, even though the threat may come only from intrastate activities" (citing *Shreveport*). "Finally, Congress' commerce authority includes the power to regulate those activities having a substantial relation to interstate commerce, i.e., those activities that substantially affect interstate commerce" (citing *Jones & Laughlin*).

Petitioners [seek] to sustain § 13981 as a regulation of activity that substantially affects interstate commerce. Given § 13981's focus on gender-motivated violence wherever it occurs (rather than violence directed at the instrumentalities of interstate commerce, interstate markets, or things or persons in interstate commerce), we agree that this is the proper inquiry.

[In] *Lopez,* we held that the Gun–Free School Zones Act of 1990, 18 U.S.C. § 922(q)(1)(A), which made it a federal crime to knowingly possess a firearm in a school zone, exceeded Congress' authority under the Commerce Clause. Several significant considerations contributed to our decision.

First, we observed that § 922(q) was "a criminal statute that by its terms has nothing to do with 'commerce' or any sort of economic enterprise, however broadly one might define those terms." [A] fair reading of *Lopez* shows that the noneconomic, criminal nature of the conduct at issue was central to our decision in that case. See, e.g., ("Even *Wickard,* which is perhaps the most far reaching example of Commerce Clause authority over intrastate activity, involved economic activity in a way that the possession of a gun in a school zone does not"), ("Admittedly, a determination whether an intrastate activity is commercial or noncommercial may in some cases result in legal uncertainty. But, so long as Congress' authority is limited to those powers enumerated in the Constitution, and so long as those enumerated powers are interpreted as having judicially enforceable outer limits, congressional legislation under the Commerce Clause always will engender 'legal uncertainty' "), ("The possession of a gun in a local school zone is in no sense an economic activity that might, through repetition elsewhere, substantially affect any sort of interstate commerce"); see also id. (Kennedy, J., concurring) (stating that *Lopez* did not alter our "practical conception of commercial regulation" and that Congress may "regulate in the commercial sphere on the assumption that we have a single market and a unified purpose to build a stable national economy"), ("Were the Federal Government to take over the regulation of entire areas of traditional state concern, areas having nothing to do with the regulation of commercial activities, the boundaries between the spheres of federal and state authority would blur"), ("[In] a sense any conduct in this interdependent world of ours has an ultimate commercial origin or consequence, but we have not yet said the commerce power may reach so far"). * * *

The second consideration that we found important [was] that the statute contained "no express jurisdictional element which might limit its reach to a discrete set of firearm possessions that additionally have an explicit connection with or effect on interstate commerce." Such a jurisdictional element may establish that the enactment is in pursuance of Congress' regulation of interstate commerce.a

Third, we noted that neither § 922(q) "nor its legislative history contains express congressional findings regarding the effects upon interstate commerce of gun possession in a school zone." While "Congress normally is not required to make formal findings as to the substantial burdens that an activity has on interstate commerce," (citing *McClung*, *Perez*), the existence of such findings may "enable us to evaluate the legislative judgment that the activity in question substantially affects interstate commerce, even though no such substantial effect [is] visible to the naked eye."

Finally, our decision in *Lopez* rested in part on the fact that the link between gun possession and a substantial effect on interstate commerce was attenuated. The United States argued that the possession of guns may lead to violent crime, and that violent crime "can be expected to affect the functioning of the national economy in two ways. First, the costs of violent crime are substantial, and, through the mechanism of insurance, those costs are spread throughout the population. Second, violent crime reduces the willingness of individuals to travel to areas within the country that are perceived to be unsafe." The Government also argued [that] guns at schools poses a threat to the educational process, which in turn threatens to produce a less efficient and productive workforce, which will negatively affect national productivity and thus interstate commerce.

We rejected these "costs of crime" and "national productivity" arguments because they would permit Congress to "regulate not only all violent crime, but all activities that might lead to violent crime, regardless of how tenuously they relate to interstate commerce." We noted that, under this but-for reasoning: "Congress could regulate any activity that it found was related to the economic productivity of individual citizens: family law (including marriage, divorce, and child custody), for example. Under these theories, [it] is difficult to perceive any limitation on federal power, even in areas such as criminal law enforcement or education where States historically have been sovereign. Thus, if we were to accept the Government's arguments, we are hard pressed to posit any activity by an individual that Congress is without power to regulate."

With these principles underlying our Commerce Clause jurisprudence as reference points, the proper resolution of the present cases is clear. Gender-motivated crimes of violence are not, in any sense of the phrase, economic activity. While we need not adopt a categorical rule against aggregating the effects of any noneconomic activity in order to decide these cases, thus far in our Nation's history our cases have upheld Commerce Clause regulation of intrastate activity only where that activity is economic in nature.

Like the Gun–Free School Zones Act at issue in *Lopez*, § 13981 contains no jurisdictional element establishing that the federal cause of action is in pursuance of Congress' power to regulate interstate commerce. Although *Lopez* makes clear that such a jurisdictional element would lend support to the argument that

a. After *Lopez*, Congress amended the Gun–Free School Zones Act to add that the prosecution must demonstrate that the gun "has moved in or otherwise affects interstate or foreign commerce."

§ 13981 is sufficiently tied to interstate commerce, Congress elected to cast § 13981's remedy over a wider, and more purely intrastate, body of violent crime.5

In contrast with the lack of congressional findings that we faced in *Lopez*, § 13981 *is* supported by numerous findings regarding the serious impact that gender-motivated violence has on victims and their families. But [as] we stated in *Lopez*, "Simply because Congress may conclude that a particular activity substantially affects interstate commerce does not necessarily make it so." (quoting *Hodel* (Rehnquist, J., concurring in judgment)). Rather, " 'whether particular operations affect interstate commerce sufficiently to come under the constitutional power of Congress to regulate them is ultimately a judicial rather than a legislative question, and can be settled finally only by this Court.' "(quoting *Heart of Atlanta* (Black, J., concurring)).

In these cases, Congress [found] that gender-motivated violence affects interstate commerce "by deterring potential victims from traveling interstate, from engaging in employment in interstate business, and from transacting with business, and in places involved in interstate commerce; [by] diminishing national productivity, increasing medical and other costs, and decreasing the supply of and the demand for interstate products." Given these findings and petitioners' arguments, the concern that we expressed in *Lopez* that Congress might use the Commerce Clause to completely obliterate the Constitution's distinction between national and local authority seems well founded. The reasoning that petitioners advance seeks to follow the but-for causal chain from the initial occurrence of violent crime (the suppression of which has always been the prime object of the States' police power) to every attenuated effect upon interstate commerce. If accepted, petitioners' reasoning would allow Congress to regulate any crime as long as the nationwide, aggregated impact of that crime has substantial effects on employment, production, transit, or consumption. Indeed, if Congress may regulate gender-motivated violence, it would be able to regulate murder or any other type of violence since gender-motivated violence, as a subset of all violent crime, is certain to have lesser economic impacts than the larger class of which it is a part.7

[The] regulation and punishment of intrastate violence that is not directed at the instrumentalities, channels, or goods involved in interstate commerce has always been the province of the States. See, e.g., *Cohens v. Virginia,* (Marshall, C. J.) (stating that Congress "has no general right to punish murder committed within any of the States," and that it is "clear [that] congress cannot punish felonies generally"). Indeed, we can think of no better example of the police

---

5. Title 42 U.S.C. § 13981 is not the sole provision of the Violence Against Women Act of 1994 to provide a federal remedy for gender-motivated crime. Section 40221(a) of the Act creates a federal criminal remedy to punish "interstate crimes of abuse including crimes committed against spouses or intimate partners during interstate travel and crimes committed by spouses or intimate partners who cross State lines to continue the abuse." [The] Courts of Appeals have uniformly upheld this criminal sanction as an appropriate exercise of Congress' Commerce Clause authority, reasoning that the provision properly falls within the first of *Lopez's* categories as it regulates the use of channels of interstate commerce—i.e., the use of the interstate transportation routes through which persons and goods move.

7. Justice Souter's dissent theory [is] remarkable because it undermines this central

principle of our constitutional system. As we have repeatedly noted, the Framers crafted the federal system of government so that the people's rights would be secured by the division of power. [No] doubt the political branches have a role in interpreting and applying the Constitution, but ever since *Marbury* this Court has remained the ultimate expositor of the constitutional text. Contrary to Justice Souter's suggestion, [that] from *Gibbons* on, public opinion has been the only restraint on the congressional exercise of the commerce power is true only insofar as it contends that political accountability is and has been the only limit on Congress' exercise of the commerce power within that power's outer bounds. As the language surrounding that relied upon by Justice Souter makes clear, *Gibbons* did not remove from this Court the authority to define that boundary.

power, which the Founders denied the National Government and reposed in the States, than the suppression of violent crime and vindication of its victims. * * *

[The issue of Congress' power to enact § 13981 under § 5 of the Fourteenth Amendment is discussed in Ch. 11, Sec. 2.]

JUSTICE THOMAS, concurring.

The majority opinion correctly applies our decision in *Lopez,* and I join it in full. I write separately only to express my view that the very notion of a "substantial effects" test under the Commerce Clause is inconsistent with the original understanding of Congress' powers and with this Court's early Commerce Clause cases. [Thomas, J.'s concurring opinion in *Lopez* contended:

["At the time the original Constitution was ratified, 'commerce' consisted of selling, buying, and bartering, as well as transporting for these purposes [in] contradistinction to productive activities such as manufacturing and agriculture. Alexander Hamilton, for example, repeatedly treated commerce, agriculture, and manufacturing as three separate endeavors. * * *

["The Constitution not only uses the word 'commerce' in a narrower sense than our case law might suggest, it also does not support the proposition that Congress has authority over all activities that 'substantially affect' interstate commerce. [After] all, if Congress may regulate all matters that substantially affect commerce, there is no need for the Constitution to specify that Congress may enact bankruptcy laws, cl. 4, or coin money and fix the standard of weights and measures, cl. 5, or punish counterfeiters of United States coin and securities, cl. 6. [As] the Framers surely understood, these other branches of trade substantially affect interstate commerce. [An] interpretation of cl. 3 that makes the rest of § 8 superfluous simply cannot be correct."]

By continuing to apply this rootless and malleable standard, however circumscribed, the Court has encouraged the Federal Government to persist in its view that the Commerce Clause has virtually no limits. Until this Court replaces its existing Commerce Clause jurisprudence with a standard more consistent with the original understanding, we will continue to see Congress appropriating state police powers under the guise of regulating commerce.

JUSTICE SOUTER, with whom JUSTICE STEVENS, JUSTICE GINSBURG, and JUSTICE BREYER join, dissenting. * * *

One obvious difference from *Lopez* is the mountain of data assembled by Congress, here showing the effects of violence against women on interstate commerce. Passage of the Act in 1994 was preceded by four years of hearings [and] includes reports on gender bias from task forces in 21 [States]. Congress received evidence for the following findings:

"Three out of four American women will be victims of violent crimes sometime during their life. [A]s many as 50 percent of homeless women and children are fleeing domestic violence. [B]attering 'is the single largest cause of injury to women in the United States.' An estimated 4 million American women are battered each year by their husbands or partners. * * * Between 2,000 and 4,000 women die every year from [domestic] abuse. [A]rrest rates may be as low as 1 for every 100 domestic assaults. [E]stimates suggest that we spend $5 to $10 billion a year on health care, criminal justice, and other social costs of domestic violence."

The evidence as to rape was similarly extensive, supporting these conclusions:

"[The incidence of] rape rose four times as fast as the total national crime rate over the past 10 years. According to one study, close to half a million girls now in high school will be raped before they graduate. [T]hree-quarters of women never go to the movies alone after dark because of the fear of rape and nearly 50 percent do not use public transit alone after dark for the same reason. [Forty-one] percent of judges surveyed believed that juries give sexual assault victims less credibility than other crime victims. Less than 1 percent of all [rape] victims have collected damages. '[A]n individual who commits rape has only about 4 chances in 100 of being arrested, prosecuted, and found guilty of any offense.' Almost one-quarter of convicted rapists never go to prison and another quarter received sentences in local jails where the average sentence is 11 months. [A]lmost 50 percent of rape victims lose their jobs or are forced to quit because of the crime's severity." * * *

Congress thereby explicitly stated the predicate [quoted in the second to last paragraph of Court's opinion] for the exercise of its Commerce Clause power. [T]he sufficiency of the evidence before Congress to provide a rational basis for the finding cannot seriously be questioned. * * *

The Act would have passed muster at any time between *Wickard* in 1942 and *Lopez* in 1995. [I]t is clear that some congressional conclusions about obviously substantial, cumulative effects on commerce are being assigned lesser values than the once-stable doctrine would assign them. These devaluations are accomplished not by any express repudiation of the substantial effects test or its application through the aggregation of individual conduct, but by supplanting rational basis scrutiny with a new criterion of review.

* * * From the fact that Art. I, § 8, cl. 3 grants an authority limited to regulating commerce, [it] does not at all follow that an activity affecting commerce nonetheless falls outside the commerce power, depending on the specific character of the activity, or the authority of a State to regulate it along with Congress. My disagreement with the majority is not, however, confined to logic. [F]or significant periods of our history, the Court has defined the commerce power as plenary, unsusceptible to categorical exclusions. [T]oday's attempt to distinguish between primary activities affecting commerce in terms of the relatively commercial or noncommercial character of the primary conduct proscribed comes with the pedigree of near-tragedy that I outlined in *Lopez*. In the half century following the modern activation of the commerce power with passage of the Interstate Commerce Act in 1887, this Court from time to time created categorical enclaves beyond congressional reach by declaring such activities as "mining," "production," "manufacturing," and union membership to be outside the definition of "commerce" and by limiting application of the effects test to "direct" rather than "indirect" commercial consequences.

Since adherence to these formalistically contrived confines of commerce power in large measure provoked the judicial crisis of 1937, one might reasonably have doubted that Members of this Court would ever again toy with a return to the days before *Jones & Laughlin*, which brought the earlier and nearly disastrous experiment to an end. And yet [today's] enquiry into commercial purpose, first intimated by the *Lopez* concurrence (opinion of Kennedy, J.), is cousin to the intent-based analysis employed in *Hammer*, but rejected for Commerce Clause purposes in *Heart of Atlanta* and *Darby*.

Why is the majority tempted to reject the lesson so painfully learned in 1937? An answer emerges from contrasting *Wickard* with one of the predecessor cases it superseded. It was obvious in *Wickard* that growing wheat for consumption right on the farm was not "commerce" in the common vocabulary.[13] [Just] a few years

---

13. [I]f substantial effects on commerce are proper subjects of concern under the Com- merce Clause, what difference should it make whether the causes of those effects are them-

before *Wickard*, however, it had certainly been no less obvious that "mining" practices could substantially affect commerce, even though *Carter Coal* had held mining regulation beyond the national commerce power. When we try to fathom the difference between the two cases, it is clear that they did not go in different directions because the *Carter Coal* Court could not understand a causal connection that the *Wickard* Court could grasp; the difference, rather, turned on the fact that the Court in *Carter Coal* had a reason for trying to maintain its categorical, formalistic distinction. [It] was still trying to create a laissez-faire world out of the 20th-century economy, and formalistic commercial distinctions were thought to be useful instruments in achieving that object. * * *

The Court finds it relevant that the statute addresses conduct traditionally subject to state prohibition under domestic criminal law, a fact said to have some heightened significance when the violent conduct in question is not itself aimed directly at interstate commerce or its instrumentalities. Again, history seems to be recycling, for the theory of traditional state concern as grounding a limiting principle has [been repudiated in *Garcia v. San Antonio Met. Trans. Auth.* (1985) [Sec. 5 infra], which held that the concept of "traditional governmental function" [was] incoherent* * *.14

The objection to reviving traditional state spheres of action as a consideration in commerce analysis [is] compounded by a further defect[:] the majority's rejection of the Founders' considered judgment that politics, not judicial review, should mediate between state and national interests as the strength and legislative jurisdiction of the National Government inevitably increased through the expected growth of the national economy. [quoting Madison (in *Federalist* No. 46), James Wilson, and Marshall, C.J., in *Gibbons*]. * * *

The *Garcia* Court's rejection of "judicially created limitations" in favor of the intended reliance on national politics was all the more powerful owing to the Court's explicit recognition that in the centuries since the framing the relative powers of the two sovereign systems have markedly changed. Nationwide economic integration is the norm, the national political power has been augmented by its vast revenues, and the power of the States has been drawn down by the Seventeenth Amendment, eliminating selection of senators by state legislature in favor of direct election. * * *19

Amendments that alter the balance of power between the National and State Governments, like the Fourteenth, or that change the way the States are represented within the Federal Government, like the Seventeenth, are not rips in the

---

selves commercial? The Court's answer is that it makes a difference to federalism, and the legitimacy of the Court's new judicially derived federalism is the crux of our disagreement.

14. The Constitution of 1787 did, in fact, forbid some exercises of the commerce power. Article I, § 9, cl. 6, barred Congress from giving preference to the ports of one State over those of another. More strikingly, the Framers protected the slave trade from federal interference, see Art. I, § 9, cl. 1. [These] reservations demonstrate the plenary nature of the federal power; the exceptions prove the rule. [T]o suppose that enumerated powers must have limits is sensible; to maintain that there exist judicially identifiable areas of state regulation immune to the plenary congressional commerce

power even though falling within the limits defined by the substantial effects test is to deny our constitutional history.

19. The majority tries to deflect the objection that it blocks an intended political process by explaining that the Framers intended politics to set the federal balance only within the sphere of permissible commerce legislation, whereas we are looking to politics to define that sphere (in derogation even of *Marbury*). * * * Neither Madison nor Wilson nor Marshall, nor the *Jones & Laughlin, Darby, Wickard,* or *Garcia* Courts, suggested that politics defines the commerce power. Nor do we, even though we recognize that the conditions of the contemporary world result in a vastly greater sphere of influence for politics than the Framers would have envisioned. * * *

fabric of the Framers' Constitution, inviting judicial repairs. The Seventeenth Amendment may indeed have lessened the enthusiasm of the Senate to represent the States as discrete sovereignties, but the Amendment did not convert the judiciary into an alternate shield against the commerce power.

The Court [finds] no significance whatever in the state support for the Act based upon the States' acknowledged failure to deal adequately with gender-based violence in state courts, and the belief of their own law enforcement agencies that national action is essential. The National Association of Attorneys General supported the Act unanimously, and [as] the 1993 Senate Report put it, "The Violence Against Women Act is intended to respond both to the underlying attitude that this violence is somehow less serious than other crime and to the resulting failure of our criminal justice system to address such violence. Its goals are both symbolic and practical." [It] is, then, not the least irony of these cases that the States will be forced to enjoy the new federalism whether they want it or not. * * *

JUSTICE BREYER, with whom JUSTICE STEVENS joins, and with whom JUSTICE SOUTER and JUSTICE GINSBURG join as to Part I–A, dissenting.

No one denies the importance of the Constitution's federalist principles. [The] question is how the judiciary can [best] impose some meaningful limit, but not too great a limit, upon the scope of the legislative authority that the Commerce Clause delegates to Congress.

A. Consider the problems. The "economic/noneconomic" distinction is not easy to apply. Does the local street corner mugger engage in "economic" activity or "noneconomic" activity when he mugs for money? Would evidence that desire for economic domination underlies many brutal crimes against women save the present statute?

The line becomes yet harder to draw given the need for exceptions. The Court itself would permit Congress to aggregate, hence regulate, "noneconomic" activity taking place at economic establishments. See *Heart of Atlanta*. And it would permit Congress to regulate where that regulation is "an essential part of a larger regulation of economic activity, in which the regulatory scheme could be undercut unless the intrastate activity were regulated." *Lopez*.[b] Given the former exception, can Congress simply rewrite the present law and limit its application to restaurants, hotels, perhaps universities, and other places of public accommodation? Given the latter exception, can Congress save the present law by including it, or much of it, in a broader "Safe Transport" or "Workplace Safety" act?

More important, why should we give critical constitutional importance to the economic, or noneconomic, nature of an interstate-commerce-affecting cause? If chemical emanations through indirect environmental change cause identical, severe commercial harm outside a State, why should it matter whether local factories or home fireplaces release them? * * *

Most important, the Court's complex rules seem unlikely to help secure the very object that they seek, namely, the protection of "areas of traditional state regulation" from federal intrusion. The Court's rules, even if broadly interpreted, are underinclusive. The local pickpocket is no less a traditional subject of state regulation than is the local gender-motivated assault. Regardless, the Court reaffirms, as it should, Congress' well-established and frequently exercised power

---

b. In *Lopez*, Breyer, J., joined by Stevens, Souter and Ginsburg, JJ., dissenting, noted that "although the majority today attempts to categorize *Perez*, *McClung*, and *Wickard*, as involving intrastate 'economic activity,' the Courts that decided each of those cases did *not* focus upon the economic nature of the activity regulated. Rather, they focused upon whether that activity *affected* interstate or foreign commerce."

to enact laws that satisfy a commerce-related jurisdictional prerequisite—for example, that some item relevant to the federally regulated activity has at some time crossed a state line. *Heart of Atlanta*; see also *Scarborough*.

And in a world where most everyday products or their component parts cross interstate boundaries, Congress will frequently find it possible to redraft a statute using language that ties the regulation to the interstate movement of some relevant object, thereby regulating local criminal activity or, for that matter, family affairs. See, e.g., Child Support Recovery Act of 1992. [How] much would be gained, for example, were Congress to reenact the present law in the form of "An Act Forbidding Violence Against Women Perpetrated at Public Accommodations or by Those Who Have Moved in, or through the Use of Items that Have Moved in, Interstate Commerce"? Complex Commerce Clause rules creating fine distinctions that achieve only random results do little to further the important federalist interests that called them into being. That is why modern (pre-*Lopez*) case law rejected them.

* * * We live in a Nation knit together by two centuries of scientific, technological, commercial, and environmental change. Those changes, taken together, mean that virtually every kind of activity, no matter how local, genuinely can affect commerce, or its conditions, outside the State—at least when considered in the aggregate. And that fact makes it close to impossible for courts to develop meaningful subject-matter categories that would exclude some kinds of local activities from ordinary Commerce Clause "aggregation" rules without, at the same time, depriving Congress of the power to regulate activities that have a genuine and important effect upon interstate commerce.

Since judges cannot change the [world,] Congress, not the courts, must remain primarily responsible for striking the appropriate state/federal balance. Congress is institutionally motivated to do so. Its Members represent state and local district interests. They consider the views of state and local officials when they legislate, and they have even developed formal procedures to ensure that such consideration takes place. See, e.g., Unfunded Mandates Reform Act of 1995. Moreover, Congress often can better reflect state concerns for autonomy in the details of sophisticated statutory schemes than can the judiciary, which cannot easily gather the relevant facts and which must apply more general legal rules and categories.

B. I would also note [that] attorneys general in the overwhelming majority of States (38) supported congressional legislation, telling Congress that "our experience as Attorneys General strengthens our belief that the problem of violence against women is a national one, requiring federal attention, federal leadership, and federal funds."

Moreover, [Congress] focused the federal law upon documented deficiencies in state legal systems. And it tailored the law to prevent its use in certain areas of traditional state concern, such as divorce, alimony, or child custody. Consequently, the law before us seems to represent an instance, not of state/federal conflict, but of state/federal efforts to cooperate in order to help solve a mutually acknowledged national problem. * * *

I continue to agree with Justice Souter that the Court's traditional "rational basis" approach is sufficient. But I recognize that the law in this area is unstable and that time and experience may demonstrate both the unworkability of the majority's rules and the superiority of Congress' own procedural approach—in which case the law may evolve towards a rule that, in certain difficult Commerce

Clause cases, takes account of the thoroughness with which Congress has considered the federalism issue.c * * *

Notes

1. ***"Substantial effects" of local activities.*** GONZALES v. RAICH, 545 U.S. 1 (2005), per STEVENS, J., upheld Congress' power to apply the Controlled Substances Act—which was part of "a comprehensive regime to combat the international and interstate traffic in illicit drugs"—to "prohibit the local cultivation and use of marijuana" even when state law authorized its use for medical purposes: "[*Wickard*] establishes that Congress can regulate purely intrastate activity that is not itself 'commercial,' in that it is not produced for sale, if it concludes that failure to regulate that class of activity would undercut the regulation of the interstate market in that commodity. [Here] too, Congress had a rational basis for concluding that leaving home-consumed marijuana outside federal control would similarly affect price and market conditions [given] the likelihood that the high demand in the interstate market will draw such marijuana into that market [and given] the enforcement difficulties that attend distinguishing between marijuana cultivated locally and marijuana grown elsewhere, and concerns about diversion into illicit channels [which] would leave a gaping hole in the CSA. [W]e have never required ['that legislation must contain detailed findings proving that each activity regulated within a comprehensive statute is essential to the statutory scheme'], absent a special concern such as the protection of free speech.

"[I]n both *Lopez* and *Morrison,* the parties asserted that a particular statute or provision fell outside Congress' commerce power in its entirety. This distinction is pivotal for we have often reiterated that '[w]here the class of activities is regulated and that class is within the reach of federal power,' the courts have no power 'to excise, as trivial, individual instances' of the class.' *Perez.* [Unlike] *Lopez* and *Morrison,* the activities regulated by the CSA are quintessentially economic [—] production, distribution, and consumption of commodities for which there is an established, and lucrative, interstate market.

"[If] the personal cultivation, possession, and use of marijuana for medicinal purposes is beyond the 'outer limits' of Congress' Commerce Clause authority,' (O'Connor, J., dissenting), it must also be true that such personal use of marijuana (or any other homegrown drug) for recreational purposes is also beyond those 'outer limits,' whether or not a State elects to authorize or even regulate such use. Justice Thomas' separate dissent suffers from the same sweeping implications. [One] need not have a degree in economics to understand why a nationwide exemption for the vast quantity of marijuana (or other drugs) locally cultivated for personal use (which presumably would include use by friends, neighbors, and family members) may have a substantial impact on the interstate market for this extraordinarily popular substance. The congressional judgment that an exemption for such a significant segment of the total market would undermine the orderly enforcement of the entire regulatory scheme is entitled to a strong presumption of validity.

"[L]imiting the activity to marijuana possession and cultivation 'in accordance with state law' cannot serve to place respondents' activities beyond congressional reach. The Supremacy Clause unambiguously provides that if there is any

---

c. The question of whether the national political process or judicial review is more de- sirable and effective in "safeguarding" federalism is considered further in Sec. 5, IV infra.

conflict between federal and state law, federal law shall prevail. * * *38 [The] notion that California law has surgically excised a discrete activity that is hermetically sealed off from the larger interstate marijuana market is a dubious proposition,a and, more importantly, one that Congress could have rationally rejected."

SCALIA, J., concurred in the judgment to describe a "more nuanced doctrinal foundation" and to respond to O'Connor, J.'s dissent: Although *Lopez* and *Morrison* "rejected the argument that Congress may regulate *noneconomic* activity based solely on the effect that it may have on interstate commerce through a remote chain of inferences," under the Necessary and Proper Clause, Congress has "regulatory authority over intrastate activities that are not themselves part of interstate commerce [even when they] do not themselves substantially affect interstate commerce [if they are] 'an essential part of a larger regulation of economic activity, in which the regulatory scheme could be undercut unless the intrastate activity were regulated.' [*Lopez*.] Unlike the power to regulate activities that have a substantial effect on interstate commerce, the power to enact laws enabling effective regulation of interstate commerce can only be exercised in conjunction with congressional regulation of an interstate market. [Therefore, that] simple possession [of drugs] is a noneconomic activity is immaterial to whether it can be prohibited as a necessary part of a larger regulation. [T]hat the CSA regulates an area typically left to state regulation [is] not enough to render federal regulation an inappropriate means."

O'CONNOR, J., joined by Rehnquist, C.J., and Thomas, J., dissented: "This case exemplifies the role of States as laboratories. The States' core police powers have always included authority to define criminal law and to protect the health, safety, and welfare of their citizens. [Today's] decision suggests that the federal regulation of local activity is immune to Commerce Clause challenge because Congress chose to act with an ambitious, all-encompassing statute, rather than piecemeal. [If so], then *Lopez* stands for nothing more than a drafting guide: Congress should have described the relevant crime as 'transfer or possession of a firearm anywhere in the nation'—thus including commercial and noncommercial activity, and clearly encompassing some activity with assuredly substantial effect on interstate commerce. [This is] a signal to Congress to enact legislation that is more extensive and more intrusive into the domain of state power. * * *

"A number of objective markers are available to confine the scope of constitutional review here. Both federal and state legislation [recognize] that medical and nonmedical (i.e., recreational) uses of drugs are realistically distinct and can be [regulated] differently. [To] ascertain whether Congress' encroachment is constitutionally justified in this case, then, I would focus here on the personal cultivation, possession, and use of marijuana for medicinal purposes.

---

38. California's decision (made 34 years after the CSA was enacted) to impose "stric[t] controls" on the "cultivation and possession of marijuana for medical purposes," (Thomas, J., dissenting), cannot retroactively divest Congress of its authority under the Commerce Clause.

[Thomas, J.'s dissent responded: "The majority apparently believes that even if States prevented any medical marijuana from entering the illicit drug market, and thus even if there were no need for the CSA to govern medical marijuana users, we should uphold the CSA under the *Commerce* Clause and the *Nec-*

essary and Proper Clause. [T]o invoke the Supremacy Clause, as the majority does, is to beg the question. The CSA displaces California's Compassionate Use Act if the CSA is constitutional as applied to respondents' conduct, but that is the very question at issue."]

a. The Court refers here to O'Connor, J's argument "that California's Compassionate Use Act and similar state legislation may well isolate activities relating to medicinal marijuana from the illicit market," through controls such as the requirement of a "recommendation by a physician" and "an identification card system for qualified patients."

"[It] will not do to say that Congress may regulate noncommercial activity simply because it may have an effect on the demand for commercial goods, or because the noncommercial endeavor can, in some sense, substitute for commercial activity. Most commercial goods or services have some sort of privately producible analogue. Home care substitutes for daycare. Charades games substitute for movie tickets. Backyard or windowsill gardening substitutes for going to the supermarket. To draw the line wherever private activity affects the demand for market goods is to draw no line at all, and to declare everything economic. [As for *Wickard*, in] contrast to the CSA's limitless assertion of power, Congress provided an exemption within the AAA for small producers.

"[S]omething more than mere assertion is required when Congress purports to have power over local activity whose connection to an interstate market is not self-evident. Otherwise, the Necessary and Proper Clause will always be a back door for unconstitutional federal regulation. [And] here, in part because common sense suggests that medical marijuana users may be limited in number, [the] effect of those activities on interstate drug traffic is not self-evidently substantial.

"[T]his case is readily distinguishable from *Wickard* [because] the parties had 'stipulated a summary of the economics of the wheat industry' [which showed] that consumption of homegrown wheat was the most variable factor in the size of the national wheat crop, and that on-site consumption could have the effect of varying the amount of wheat sent to market by as much as 20 percent. [The] Court recognizes that 'the record in the *Wickard* case itself established the causal connection between the production for local use and the national market' and argues that 'we have before us findings by Congress *to the same effect*.' The Court refers to a series of declarations in the introduction to the CSA saying that (1) local distribution and possession of controlled substances causes 'swelling' in interstate traffic; (2) local production and distribution cannot be distinguished from interstate production and distribution; (3) federal control over intrastate incidents 'is essential to effective control' over interstate drug trafficking. These bare declarations cannot be compared to the record before the Court in *Wickard*. [If] as the Court claims, today's decision does not break with precedent, how can it be that voluminous findings, documenting extensive hearings about the specific topic of violence against women, did not pass constitutional muster in *Morrison*, while the CSA's abstract, unsubstantiated, generalized findings about controlled substances do?"

THOMAS, J., dissented: "The Government contends that banning ['a distinct and separable subclass (local growers and users of state-authorized, medical marijuana)'] is 'necessary and proper for carrying into Execution' its regulation of interstate drug trafficking. However, in order to be 'necessary,' the intrastate ban must be more than 'a reasonable means [of] effectuat[ing] the regulation of interstate commerce.' [See] (majority opinion) (employing rational-basis review). It must be 'plainly adapted' to regulating interstate marijuana trafficking—in other words, there must be an 'obvious, simple, and direct relation' between the intrastate ban and the regulation of interstate commerce. *Sabri v. United States,* [Sec. 3, II infra] (Thomas, J., concurring in judgment). * * *

"In *Lopez,* I argued that allowing Congress to regulate intrastate, noncommercial activity under the Commerce Clause would confer on Congress a general 'police power' over the Nation. This is no less the case if Congress ties its power to the Necessary and Proper Clause rather than the Commerce Clause. [The] means selected by Congress to regulate interstate commerce cannot be 'prohibited' by, or inconsistent with the 'letter and spirit' of, the Constitution. *McCulloch.* * * *

"[E]ven assuming Congress has 'obvious' and 'plain' reasons why regulating intrastate cultivation and possession is necessary to regulating the interstate drug trade, none of those reasons applies to medical marijuana. [E]ven assuming that States' controls[b] allow some seepage of medical marijuana into the illicit drug market, [i]t is difficult to see how [this] makes regulating intrastate medical marijuana obviously essential to controlling the interstate drug market. [I]t is implausible that this Court could set aside entire portions of the United States Code as outside Congress' power in *Lopez* and *Morrison,* but it cannot engage in the more restrained practice of invalidating particular applications of the CSA that are beyond Congress' power. This Court has regularly entertained as-applied challenges under constitutional provisions, including the Commerce Clause, see *McClung*; *Heart of Atlanta*; *Wickard*. * * *

"The majority's rewriting of the Commerce Clause seems to be rooted in the belief that, unless the Commerce Clause covers the entire web of human activity, Congress will be left powerless to regulate the national economy effectively. The interconnectedness of economic activity is not a modern phenomenon unfamiliar to the Framers. *Lopez* (Thomas, J., concurring). Moreover, the Framers understood what the majority does not appear to fully appreciate: There is a danger to concentrating too much, as well as too little, power in the Federal Government. This Court [has] casually allowed the Federal Government to strip States of their ability to regulate *intra* state commerce—not to mention a host of local activities, like mere drug possession, that are not commercial."

2. ***"Instrumentalities of interstate commerce."*** PIERCE COUNTY v. GUILLEN, 537 U.S. 129 (2003), per THOMAS, J., upheld Congress' power to grant a privilege from pretrial discovery in state and federal courts, for information (e.g., data regarding "potential accident sites, hazardous roadway conditions"), "compiled or collected" in connection with a federal program funding highway improvement: the law was "aimed at improving safety in the channels of commerce and increasing protection for the instrumentalities of interstate commerce." See also *Reno v. Condon*, Sec. 5, IV infra.

SECTION 3. THE NATIONAL TAXING AND SPENDING POWERS

Art. I, § 8, cl. 1, grants Congress power "to lay and collect taxes, duties, imposts and excises, to pay the debts and provide for the common defense and general welfare of the United States." Its language includes both power to tax and to spend. This section is concerned primarily with use of these two related powers to achieve regulatory ends.

The Court has long recognized that Congress may use its taxing power as both a "necessary and proper" way to enforce its regulatory powers, and as a way to raise revenue which may produce "incidental" regulatory effects. The issues raised by the latter use of the taxing power, and analogous use of the spending power, declined in importance as the expanded view of Congress' regulatory powers after 1936 left few occasions for Congress to resort to taxing or spending for regulatory purposes. But the limitations imposed on the commerce power by *Lopez* and *Morrison* (as well as on Congress' ability to enforce the Civil War Amendments, see Ch. 11, Sec. 2) have given the national taxing and spending powers a potentially renewed importance.

b. See fn. a to the Court's opinion.

I. REGULATION THROUGH TAXING

Between 1922 and 1935, the Court thwarted the efforts of Congress to bypass the Court's narrow interpretation of the commerce clause by imposing burdensome taxes for deviation from a specified course of conduct beyond the congressional power to regulate.a Because Congress has had little occasion to resort to the taxing power for regulatory purposes after *Darby* and *Wickard* approved a greatly expanded commerce power, the Court has not found it necessary to review critically the distinction it drew in the Child Labor Tax Case (1922) between (a) taxes it condemned as a "penalty" for departure from a detailed and specified course of conduct and (b) those typical excise taxes it sustained on sales or businesses set at a burdensome amount designed to discourage the taxed activity.b

II. REGULATION THROUGH SPENDING

UNITED STATES v. BUTLER, 297 U.S. 1 (1936), per ROBERTS, J., held invalid the Agricultural Adjustment Act of 1933. To raise farm prices by reducing supply, the Act authorized the government to contract with farmers to reduce their acreage for particular commodities in exchange for benefit payments derived from a tax on processors of that commodity: "The government concedes that the phrase 'to provide for the general welfare' [in cl.1] qualifies the power 'to lay and collect taxes,' [but] sharp differences of opinion have persisted as to the true interpretation of the phrase. Madison asserted [that], as the United States is a government of limited and enumerated powers, the grant of power to tax and spend for the general national welfare must be confined to the enumerated legislative fields committed to the Congress. * * * Hamilton, on the other hand, maintained the clause confers a power separate and distinct from those later enumerated, [and] Congress consequently has a substantive power to tax and to appropriate, limited only by the requirement that it shall be exercised to provide for the general welfare of the United States."

Although the Court adopted Hamilton's view, it ruled that "the act invades the reserved rights of the states. It is a statutory plan to regulate and control agricultural production, a matter beyond the powers delegated to the federal government. [May] the taxing power [be] employed to raise the money necessary to purchase a compliance which the Congress is powerless to command? [The] regulation is not in fact voluntary. [If] the cotton grower elects not to accept the benefits, he will receive less for his crops; those who receive payments will be able to undersell him. The result may well be financial ruin. [This] is coercion by economic pressure."

STONE, J., joined by Brandeis and Cardozo, JJ., dissented: "As the present depressed state of agriculture is nation wide in its extent and effects, there is no basis for saying that the expenditure of public money in aid of farmers is not within the specifically granted power of Congress to levy taxes to 'provide for [the] general welfare.' [The] suggestion of coercion finds no support in the record or in

---

a. *Bailey v. Drexel Furniture Co.* (Child Labor Tax Case), 259 U.S. 20 (1922) (struck down 10% net profit tax on manufacturers who employed children deviating from standards like those in *Dagenhart*); *Hill v. Wallace*, 259 U.S. 44 (1922) (struck down tax on futures contracts in grain unless made through a board of trade meeting federal requirements); *United States v. Constantine*, 296 U.S. 287 (1935) (struck down tax on liquor manufacturers and dealers operating in violation of state law 10 to 40 times greater than tax on those operating lawfully). Since 1935, no federal tax with a regulatory effect has been invalidated.

b. *McCray v. United States*, 195 U.S. 27 (1904); *United States v. Doremus*, 249 U.S. 86 (1919).

any data showing the actual operation of the act. [The] power of Congress to spend is inseparable from persuasion to action over which Congress has no legislative control. Congress may not command that the science of agriculture be taught in state universities. But if it would aid the teaching of that science by grants to state institutions, it is appropriate, if not necessary, that the grant be on the condition [that] it be used for the intended purpose."

———

STEWARD MACHINE CO. v. DAVIS, 301 U.S. 548 (1937), per CARDOZO, J., upheld the Social Security Act program for unemployment compensation. Although proceeds of a federal tax on employers went into the general federal treasury, these employers received 90% credit on this tax for payments to a state unemployment compensation fund under a state law that met federal requirements: "To draw the line intelligently between duress and inducement, there is need to remind ourselves of facts as to the problem of unemployment. [During] the years 1929 to 1936, when the country was passing through a cyclical depression, [the] states were unable to give the requisite relief. Many held back through alarm lest in laying such a toll upon their industries, they would place themselves in a position of economic disadvantage as compared with neighbors or competitors. [It] is too late today for the argument to be heard with tolerance that in a crisis so extreme the use of the moneys of the nation to relieve the unemployed and their dependents is a use for any purpose narrower than the promotion of the general welfare. Cf. *Butler*; *Helvering v. Davis* [infra], decided herewith. * * *

"The Social Security Act is an attempt to find a method by which all these public agencies may work together to a common end. [Who] is coerced[?] Not the taxpayer. He pays in fulfillment of the mandate of the local legislature. Not the state. Even now she does not offer a suggestion that in passing the unemployment law she was affected by duress. For all that appears, she is satisfied with her choice, and would be sorely disappointed if it were now to be annulled. [E]very rebate from a tax when conditioned upon conduct is in some measure a temptation. But to hold that motive or temptation is equivalent to coercion is to plunge the law in endless difficulties. [It] is one thing to impose a tax [where] the conduct to be stimulated or discouraged is unrelated to the fiscal need subserved by the tax in its formal operation, or to any other end legitimately national. [It is another] to say that a tax will be abated upon the doing of an act that will satisfy the fiscal need. [In] such circumstances, if in no others, inducement or persuasion does not go beyond the bounds of power."a

Note

Definition of "general welfare." (a) HELVERING v. DAVIS, 301 U.S. 619 (1937), per CARDOZO, J., upheld the Social Security Act's old age pension program, supported exclusively by federal taxes: "The line must still be drawn between one welfare and another, between the particular and the general. [The] discretion [belongs] to congress, unless the choice is clearly wrong, a display of arbitrary power, not an exercise of judgment. [Nor] is the concept of the general welfare static. Needs that were narrow or parochial a century ago may be interwoven in our day with the well-being of the nation. * * *

a. McReynolds and Butler, JJ., dissented in separate opinions. Sutherland, J., joined by Van Devanter, J., agreed that the act did not coerce the states, but contended that the administrative provisions of the act unconstitutionally encroached on state powers (an issue considered in Sec. 5 infra).

"The problem is plainly national in area and dimensions. Moreover, laws of the separate states cannot deal with it effectively. Congress, at least, had a basis for that belief. States and local governments are often lacking in the resources that are necessary to finance an adequate program of security for the aged. [Apart] from the failure of resources, states and local governments are at times reluctant to increase so heavily the burden of taxation to be borne by their residents for fear of placing themselves in a position of economic disadvantage as compared with neighbors or competitors. [A] system of old age pensions has special dangers of its own, if put in force in one state and rejected in another. The existence of such a system is a bait to the needy and dependent elsewhere, encouraging them to migrate and seek a haven of repose. Only a power that is national can serve the interests of all." Butler and McReynolds, JJ., dissented.

(b) UNITED STATES v. GERLACH LIVE STOCK CO., 339 U.S. 725 (1950), upheld federal spending for large scale federal land reclamation projects: "Congress has substantive power to tax and appropriate for the general welfare, limited only by the requirement that it shall be exercised for the common benefit as distinguished from some mere local purpose."

SOUTH DAKOTA v. DOLE

483 U.S. 203, 107 S.Ct. 2793, 97 L.Ed.2d 171 (1987).

CHIEF JUSTICE REHNQUIST delivered the opinion of the Court.

Petitioner South Dakota permits persons 19 years of age or older to purchase beer containing up to 3.2% alcohol. In 1984 Congress enacted 23 U.S.C. § 158 [withholding 5%] of federal highway funds otherwise allocable from States "in which the purchase or public possession [of] any alcoholic beverage by a person who is less than twenty-one years of age is lawful." * * *

The spending power is of course not unlimited, *Pennhurst State School and Hospital v. Halderman*, 451 U.S. 1, 17, and n. 13 (1981). [The] first of these limitations is derived from the language of the Constitution itself: the exercise of the spending power must be in pursuit of "the general welfare." In considering whether a particular expenditure is intended to serve general public purposes, courts should defer substantially to the judgment of Congress. *Helvering*.[2] Second, we have required that if Congress desires to condition the States' receipt of federal funds, it "must do so unambiguously, [enabling] the States to [be] cognizant of the consequences of their participation." *Pennhurst*. Third, our cases have suggested (without significant elaboration) that conditions on federal grants might be illegitimate if they are unrelated "to the federal interest in particular national projects or programs." *Massachusetts v. United States*, 435 U.S. 444, 461 (1978) (plurality opinion). Finally, we have noted that other constitutional provisions may provide an independent bar to the conditional grant of federal funds.

South Dakota does not seriously claim that § 158 is inconsistent with any of the first three restrictions mentioned [above.] Indeed, the condition imposed by Congress is directly related to one of the main purposes for which highway funds are expended—safe interstate travel. [A] Presidential commission appointed to study alcohol-related accidents and fatalities on the Nation's highways concluded that the lack of uniformity in the States' drinking ages created "an incentive to drink and drive" because "young persons commut[e] to border States where the drinking age is lower." * * *

2. The level of deference to the congressional decision is such that the Court has more recently questioned whether "general welfare" is a judicially enforceable restriction at all. See *Buckley v. Valeo*, 424 U.S. 1, 90–91 (1976) (per curiam).

The remaining question about the validity of § 158—and the basic point of disagreement between the parties—is whether the Twenty-first Amendment constitutes an "independent constitutional bar." [Petitioner] asserts that "Congress may not use the spending power to regulate that which it is prohibited from regulating directly under the Twenty-first Amendment." But our cases [have] established that the constitutional limitations on Congress when exercising its spending power are less exacting than those on its authority to regulate directly.

[In] *Oklahoma v. Civil Service Comm'n*, 330 U.S. 127 (1947), the Court considered the validity of the Hatch Act insofar as it was applied to political activities of state officials whose employment was financed in whole or in part with federal funds. The State contended that an order under this provision to withhold certain federal funds unless a state official was removed invaded its sovereignty in violation of the Tenth Amendment. [See Sec. 5 infra.] Though finding that "the United States is not concerned with, and has no power to regulate, local political activities as such of state officials," the Court nevertheless held that the Federal Government "does have power to fix the terms upon which its money allotments to states shall be disbursed." The Court found no violation of the State's sovereignty because the State could, and did, adopt "the 'simple expedient' of not yielding to what she urges is federal coercion. The offer of benefits to a state by the United States dependent upon cooperation by the state with federal plans, assumedly for the general welfare, is not unusual."

[T]he language in our earlier opinions stands for the unexceptionable proposition that the [spending] power may not be used to induce the States to engage in activities that would themselves be unconstitutional. Thus, [a] grant of federal funds conditioned on invidiously discriminatory state action or the infliction of cruel and unusual punishment would be an illegitimate exercise of the Congress' broad spending power. But no such claim can be or is made here. Were South Dakota to succumb to the blandishments offered by Congress and raise its drinking age to 21, [it] would not violate the constitutional rights of anyone.

Our decisions have recognized that in some circumstances the financial inducement offered by Congress might be so coercive as to pass the point at which "pressure turns into compulsion." *Steward*. Here, however, Congress has directed only that a State desiring to establish a minimum drinking age lower than 21 lose a relatively small percentage of certain federal highway funds. [A] conditional grant of federal money of this sort is [not] unconstitutional simply by reason of its success in achieving the congressional objective.a * * *

Here Congress has offered relatively mild encouragement to the States to enact higher minimum drinking ages than they would otherwise choose. But the enactment of such laws remains the prerogative of the States not merely in theory but in fact. Even if Congress might lack the power to impose a national minimum drinking age directly, we conclude that encouragement to state action found in § 158 is a valid use of the spending power. * * *

JUSTICE O'CONNOR, dissenting.

[T]he Court's application of the requirement that the condition imposed be reasonably related to the purpose for which the funds are expended is cursory and unconvincing. [When] Congress appropriates money to build a highway, it is entitled to insist that the highway be a safe one. But it is not entitled to insist as a

---

a. *Pennhurst*, per Rehnquist, J., observed that "legislation enacted pursuant to the spending power is much in the nature of a contract: in return for federal funds, the States agree to comply with federally imposed conditions. The legitimacy of Congress' power to legislate under the spending power thus rests on whether the State voluntarily and knowingly accepts the terms of the 'contract.' "

condition of the use of highway funds that the State impose or change regulations in other areas of the State's social and economic life because of an attenuated or tangential relationship to highway use or safety. Indeed, if the rule were otherwise, the Congress could effectively regulate almost any area of a State's social, political, or economic life on the theory that use of the interstate transportation system is somehow enhanced. If, for example, the United States were to condition highway moneys upon moving the state capital, I suppose it might argue that interstate transportation is facilitated by locating local governments in places easily accessible to interstate highways—or, conversely, that highways might become overburdened if they had to carry traffic to and from the state capital. In my mind, such a relationship is hardly more attenuated than the one which the Court finds supports § 158.

There is a clear place at which the Court can draw the line between permissible and impermissible conditions on federal grants. [It] turns on whether the requirement specifies in some way how the money should be spent, so that Congress' intent in making the grant will be effectuated. [A] requirement that is not such a specification is not a condition, but a regulation, which is valid only if it falls within one of Congress' delegated regulatory powers. [The] error in *Butler* was not the Court's conclusion that the Act was essentially regulatory, but rather its crabbed view of the extent of Congress' regulatory power under the Commerce Clause. The Agricultural Adjustment Act was regulatory but it was regulation that today would likely be considered within Congress' commerce power.

[If] the spending power is to be limited only by Congress' notion of the general welfare, the reality, given the vast financial resources of the Federal Government, is that the Spending Clause gives "power to the Congress to tear down the barriers, to invade the states' jurisdiction, and to become a parliament of the whole people, subject to no restrictions save such as are self-imposed." This, of course, as *Butler* held, was not the Framers' plan and it is not the meaning of the Spending Clause. Our later cases are consistent with the notion that, under the spending power, the Congress may only condition grants in ways that can fairly be said to be related to the expenditure of federal funds [discussing *Oklahoma v. CSC*. But] a condition that a State will raise its drinking age to 21 [has] nothing to do with how the funds Congress has appropriated are expended. Rather [it] is a regulation determining who shall be able to drink liquor. As such it is not justified by the spending power.

Of the other possible sources of congressional authority for regulating the sale of liquor only the commerce power comes to mind. But in my view, the regulation of the age of the purchasers of liquor, just as the regulation of the price at which liquor may be sold, falls squarely within the scope of those powers reserved to the States by the Twenty-first Amendment.b * * *

SABRI v. UNITED STATES, 541 U.S. 600 (2004), per SOUTER, J., held that Congress had power to make it a crime to bribe state or local officials whose government agency received federal funds in excess of $10,000 in any year: "Congress has authority under the Spending Clause to appropriate federal monies to promote the general welfare, and it has corresponding authority under the Necessary and Proper Clause to see to it that taxpayer dollars appropriated under that power are in fact spent for the general welfare, and not frittered away in graft or on projects undermined when funds are siphoned off or corrupt public

b. Brennan, J., agreed with this point in a brief, separate dissent.

officers are derelict about demanding value for dollars. See generally *McCulloch* (establishing review for means-ends rationality under the Necessary and Proper Clause).''

Although concurring in the judgment on the basis of pre-*Lopez* and *Morrison* precedents, THOMAS, J. observed that "the Court appears to hold that the Necessary and Proper Clause authorizes the exercise of any power that is no more than a 'rational means' to effectuate one of Congress' enumerated powers. This conclusion derives from the Court's characterization [of] *M'Culloch*, as having established a 'means-ends rationality' test, a characterization that I am not certain is correct. [The Court] does not explain how there could be any federal interest in 'prosecut [ing] a bribe paid to a city's meat inspector in connection with a substantial transaction just because the city's parks department had received a federal grant of $10,000.' It would be difficult to describe the chain of inferences and assumptions in which the Court would have to indulge to connect such a bribe to a federal interest in any federal funds or programs as being 'plainly adapted' to their protection.''

SECTION 4. TREATIES AS A SOURCE OF LEGISLATIVE POWER

The preceding materials on the commerce, taxing, and spending powers should provide adequate background for consideration of issues relating to the many other congressional powers. This section, however, involves a significant, atypical congressional power.

––––––––

MISSOURI v. HOLLAND, 252 U.S. 416 (1920), per HOLMES, J., upheld a federal statute implementing a treaty with Canada that obligated both countries to seek legislation[a] protecting birds that traversed both countries, and were valued for food and as destroyers of insects harmful to vegetation: "[It] is not enough to refer to the Tenth Amendment [because] by Article 2, Section 2, the power to make treaties is delegated expressly, and by Article 6 treaties [are] declared the supreme law of the land.[b] If the treaty is valid there can be no dispute about the validity of the statute [as] a necessary and proper means to execute the powers of the Government. * * *

"It is said [that] there are [constitutional limits] to the treaty-making power, and that one such limit is that what an act of Congress could not do unaided, in derogation of the powers reserved to the States, a treaty cannot do. [Acts] of Congress are the supreme law of the land only when made in pursuance of the Constitution, while treaties are declared to be so when made under the authority of the United States. It is open to question whether the authority of the United States means more than the formal acts prescribed to make the convention. We do not mean to imply that there are no qualifications to the treaty-making power; but they must be ascertained in a different way. It is obvious that there may be matters of the sharpest exigency for the national well being that an act of Congress could not deal with but that a treaty followed by such an act could, and

a. Thus, the treaty was not, by its terms, "self-executing," but rather required congressional implementation.

b. "[A] treaty is placed on the same footing [with] an act of legislation. [When] the two relate to the same subject, the courts will always endeavor to construe them so as to give effect to both, [but] if the two are inconsistent, the one last in date will control the other." *Whitney v. Robertson*, 124 U.S. 190 (1888).

it is not lightly to be assumed that, in matters requiring national action, 'a power which must belong to and somewhere reside in every civilized government' is not to be found. [W]hen we are dealing with words [in] the Constitution of the United States, we must realize that they have called into life a being the development of which could not have been foreseen completely by the most gifted of its begetters. It was enough for them to realize or to hope that they had created an organism; it has taken a century and has cost their successors much sweat and blood to prove that they created a nation. The case before us must be considered in the light of our whole experience and not merely in that of what was said a hundred years ago. The treaty in question does not contravene any prohibitory words to be found in the Constitution. The only question is whether it is forbidden by some invisible radiation from the general terms of the Tenth Amendment. We must consider what this country has become in deciding what that amendment has reserved. * * *

"Here a national interest of very nearly the first magnitude is involved. It can be protected only by national action in concert with that of another power. The subject matter is only transitorily within the State and has no permanent habitat therein. But for the treaty and the statute there soon might be no birds for any powers to deal with. We see nothing in the Constitution that compels the Government to sit by while a food supply is cut off and the protectors of our forests and our crops are destroyed. It is not sufficient to rely upon the States. The reliance is vain, and were it otherwise, the question is whether the United States is forbidden to act. We are of opinion that the treaty and statute must be upheld." Van Devanter and Pitney, JJ., dissented without opinion.

SECTION 5.   APPLYING NATIONAL POWERS TO STATE GOVERNMENTS: INTERGOVERNMENTAL IMMUNITIES

I. ORIGINS OF IMMUNITIES

Intergovernmental immunity as a constitutional limit on state and federal power started with McCULLOCH v. MARYLAND, Sec. 1 supra, which held invalid Maryland's taxes on the Bank of United States: "[The] great principle [that sustains the bank's] claim to be exempted from the power of the state to tax its operations [is] that the Constitution and the laws made in pursuance thereof are supreme. [From] this, [other] propositions are deduced as corollaries[:] 1st. That a power to create implies a power to preserve. 2d. That a power to destroy, if wielded by a different hand, is hostile to, and incompatible with, these powers to create and to preserve. 3d. That where this repugnancy exists, that authority which is supreme must control. [That] the power of taxing [the bank] by the states may be exercised so as to destroy it, is too obvious to be denied."

Invoking *McCulloch*, many cases afforded state officials a fairly broad immunity from federal taxes. But beginning in 1938, this line of cases was abandoned. On the other hand, the Court has invalidated no federal tax since 1938 on a state, its activities, agencies or property—except for discrimination against state employees. But both cases to reach the Court have not questioned a state's right to immunity in appropriate situations, although in neither did a majority agree on a statement of the controlling considerations. See *New York v. United States*, 326 U.S. 572 (1946); *Massachusetts v. United States*, 435 U.S. 444 (1978). Finally, since *McCulloch* the Court has never questioned absolute federal immunity from state taxation without the consent of Congress. But such immunity has been restricted to state taxes imposed on the United States itself, or an agency or instrumentality so closely connected to the Government that the two cannot realistically be viewed as separate entities, at least insofar as the activity being taxed is concerned.

II. STATE IMMUNITY FROM FEDERAL REGULATION

MARYLAND v. WIRTZ (1968), Sec. 2, III, B supra, per HARLAN, J., upheld application of the Fair Labor Standards Act to state schools and hospitals, stressing that "Congress has 'interfered with' these state functions only to the extent of providing that when the state employs people in performing such functions it is subject to the same restrictions as a wide range of other employers whose activities affect commerce, including privately operated schools and hospitals." in exercising a "delegated power" the federal government "may override countervailing state interests whether these be described as 'governmental' or 'proprietary' in character." See also *United States v. California*, 297 U.S. 175 (1936), unanimously upholding application of the federal Safety Appliance Act to a state-owned railroad, which served San Francisco wharves and industrial plants. Douglas, J., joined by Stewart, J., dissented.

———

NATIONAL LEAGUE OF CITIES v. USERY, 426 U.S. 833 (1976), per REHNQUIST, J., overruled *Wirtz* on this issue: "The Court has never doubted that there are limits upon the power of Congress to override state sovereignty, even when exercising its otherwise plenary powers to tax or to regulate commerce." Federal regulation of the wages, hours, and overtime compensation for those whom states employ "to carry out their governmental functions" would increase costs and "substantially restructure" ways by which "state and local governments [discharge] their dual function of administering the public law and furnishing public services." It is not within Congress' commerce power "to directly displace the States' freedom to structure integral operations in areas of traditional governmental functions." Blackmun, J., joined it "with the understanding" that it "adopts a balancing approach, and does not outlaw federal power where [it] would be essential." Brennan, J., joined by White, Marshall and Stevens, JJ., dissented.

———

During the next seven years, the *National League of Cities* principle was unsuccessfully urged upon the Court five times. The first two decisions were unanimous.[a] In the next two, Blackmun, J., joined the *National League of Cities* dissenters to rule 5 to 4 that the principle was not applicable.[b] The fifth follows:

GARCIA v. SAN ANTONIO METROPOLITAN
TRANSIT AUTHORITY
469 U.S. 528, 105 S.Ct. 1005, 83 L.Ed.2d 1016 (1985).

JUSTICE BLACKMUN delivered the opinion of the Court.

[The Court upheld application of the Fair Labor Standards Act wage and hour provisions to a municipally-owned and operated mass transit system.]

a. *Hodel v. Virginia Surface Mining* (1981), note 4 after *Heart of Atlanta* (upholding federal regulation of surface mining, displacing state regulation except when a state adopts the federal regulation, and drawing a "sharp distinction between congressional regulation of private persons and federal regulation 'directed to States as States'"); *United Transp. Union v. Long Island R. R.,* 455 U.S. 678 (1982) (Long Island R.R. ruled not a "traditional government function").

b. *Federal Energy Regulatory Com'n v. Mississippi* (1982), fn. c. in *Printz* infra; *Equal Employment Opportunity Com'n v. Wyoming,* 460 U.S. 226 (1983) (upholding federal ban on mandatory age retirement for state game wardens as not involving a "serious federal intrusion").

The prerequisites for governmental immunity under *National League of Cities* were summarized by this Court in *Hodel*[:] First, it is said that the federal statute at issue must regulate "the 'States as States.' " Second, the statute must "address matters that are indisputably 'attribute[s] of state sovereignty.' " Third, state compliance with the federal obligation must "directly impair [the States'] ability 'to structure integral operations in areas of traditional governmental functions.' " "Finally, the relation of state and federal interests must not be such that 'the nature of the federal [interest] justifies state submission.' "

The controversy in the present cases has focused on the [third] requirement. [It] normally might be fair to venture the assumption that case-by-case development would lead to a workable standard for determining whether a particular governmental function should be immune from federal regulation under the Commerce Clause. * * *

The distinction [between governmental and proprietary functions that] the Court discarded as unworkable in the field of tax immunity has proved no more fruitful in the field of regulatory immunity under the Commerce Clause. Neither do any of the alternative standards that might be employed to distinguish between protected and unprotected governmental functions appear manageable. We rejected the possibility of making immunity turn on a purely historical standard of "tradition" in *Long Island* [because] it prevents a court from accommodating changes in the historical functions of States [that] have resulted in a number of once-private functions like education being assumed by the States and their subdivisions. At the same time, [r]eliance on history as an organizing principle results in linedrawing of the most arbitrary sort; the genesis of state governmental functions stretches over a historical continuum from before the Revolution to the present, and courts would have to decide by fiat precisely how longstanding a pattern of state involvement had to be for federal regulatory authority to be defeated.

A nonhistorical standard for selecting immune governmental functions is likely to be just as unworkable. [I]dentifying "uniquely" governmental functions, for example, has been rejected by the Court in the field of government tort liability in part because the notion of a "uniquely" governmental function is unmanageable. * * *

We believe, however, that there is a more fundamental problem at work here [—] neither the governmental/proprietary distinction nor any other that purports to separate out important governmental functions can be faithful to the role of federalism in a democratic society. The essence of our federal system is that within the realm of authority left open to them under the Constitution, the States must be equally free to engage in any activity that their citizens choose for the common weal, no matter how unorthodox or unnecessary anyone else—including the judiciary—deems state involvement to be. Any rule of state immunity that looks to the "traditional," "integral," or "necessary" nature of governmental functions inevitably invites an unelected federal judiciary to make decisions about which state policies it favors and which ones it dislikes. [If] there are to be limits on the Federal Government's power to interfere with state functions—as undoubtedly there are—we must look elsewhere to find them. We accordingly return to the underlying issue that confronted this Court in *National League of Cities*. [The] central theme of *National League of Cities* was [that] the Constitution precludes

"the National Government [from] devour[ing] the essentials of state sovereignty."
* * *

We doubt that courts ultimately can identify principled constitutional limitations on the scope of Congress' Commerce Clause powers over the States merely by relying on a priori definitions of state sovereignty. In part, this is because of the elusiveness of objective criteria for "fundamental" elements of state sovereignty, a problem we have witnessed in the search for "traditional governmental functions." There is, however, a more fundamental reason: [the] States unquestionably do "retai[n] a significant measure of sovereign authority." They do so, however, only to the extent that the Constitution has not divested them of their original powers and transferred those powers to the Federal Government. [The] fact that the States remain sovereign as to all powers not vested in Congress or denied them by the Constitution offers no guidance about where the frontier between state and federal power lies. In short, we have no license to employ freestanding conceptions of state sovereignty when measuring congressional authority under the Commerce Clause.

When we look for the States' "residuary and inviolable sovereignty," *The Federalist* No. 39 (J. Madison), in the shape of the constitutional scheme rather than in predetermined notions of sovereign power, a different measure of state sovereignty emerges. Apart from the limitation on federal authority inherent in the delegated nature of Congress' Article I powers, the principal means chosen by the Framers to ensure the role of the States in the federal system lies in the structure of the Federal Government itself. It is no novelty to observe that the composition of the Federal Government was designed in large part to protect the States from overreaching by Congress.[11] [The] States were vested with indirect influence over the House of Representatives and the Presidency by their control of electoral qualifications and their role in presidential elections. They were given more direct influence in the Senate, where each State received equal representation and each Senator was to be selected by the legislature of his State. The significance attached to the [former] is underscored by the prohibition of any constitutional amendment divesting a State of equal representation without the State's consent. Art. V.

The extent to which the structure of the Federal Government itself was relied on to insulate the interests of the States is evident in the views of the Framers. James Madison explained that the Federal Government "will partake sufficiently of the spirit [of the States], to be disinclined to invade the rights of the individual States, or the prerogatives of their governments." *The Federalist* No. 46. [State] sovereign interests, then, are more properly protected by procedural safeguards inherent in the structure of the federal system than by judicially created limitations on federal power.

The effectiveness of the federal political process in preserving the States' interests is apparent even today in the course of federal legislation. [T]he States have been able to direct a substantial proportion of federal revenues into their own treasuries in the form of general and program-specific grants in aid. [At] the same time [they] have been able to exempt themselves from a wide variety of obligations imposed by Congress under the Commerce Clause. For example, the Federal Power Act, the National Labor Relations Act, the Labor–Management Reporting and Disclosure Act, the Occupational Safety and Health Act, the

---

11. See, e.g., Jesse H. Choper, *Judicial Review and the National Political Process* 175–184 (1980); Herbert Wechsler, *The Political Safeguards of Federalism: The Role of the States in the Composition and Selection of the* *National Government,* 54 Colum.L.Rev. 543 (1954); D. Bruce La Pierre, *The Political Safeguards of Federalism, Redux: Intergovernmental Immunity and the States as Agents of the Nation,* 60 Wash.U.L.Q. 779 (1982).

Employee Retirement Insurance Security Act, and the Sherman Act all contain express or implied exemptions for States and their subdivisions. The fact that some federal statutes such as the FLSA extend general obligations to the States cannot obscure the extent to which the political position of the States in the federal system has served to minimize the burdens that the States bear under the Commerce Clause.

[A]gainst this background, we are convinced that the fundamental limitation that the constitutional scheme imposes on the Commerce Clause to protect the "States as States" is one of process rather than one of result. Any substantive restraint on the exercise of Commerce Clause powers must find its justification in the procedural nature of this basic limitation, and it must be tailored to compensate for possible failings in the national political process rather than to dictate a "sacred province of state autonomy." [W]e perceive nothing in the overtime and minimum-wage requirements of the FLSA, as applied to SAMTA, that is destructive of state [sovereignty]. SAMTA faces nothing more than the same minimum-wage and overtime obligations that hundreds of thousands of other employers, public as well as private, have to meet.**b** [The] political process ensures that laws that unduly burden the States will not be promulgated. In the factual setting of these cases the internal safeguards of the political process have performed as intended. * * * *National League of Cities* is overruled. * * *

JUSTICE POWELL, with whom THE CHIEF JUSTICE, JUSTICE REHNQUIST, and JUSTICE O'CONNOR join, dissenting.

[T]oday's decision effectively reduces the Tenth Amendment to meaningless rhetoric when Congress acts pursuant to the Commerce Clause. * * *

Much of the Court's opinion is devoted to arguing that it is difficult to define a priori "traditional governmental functions." *National League of Cities* neither engaged in, nor required, such a task [but rather] adopted a familiar type of balancing test for determining whether Commerce Clause enactments transgress constitutional limitations imposed by the federal nature of our system of government. [In] reading *National League of Cities* to embrace a balancing approach, Justice Blackmun quite correctly cited the part of the opinion that reaffirmed *Fry v. United States* [which] explicitly weighed the seriousness of the problem addressed by the federal legislation at issue in that case, against the effects of compliance on State sovereignty.**a** Our subsequent decisions also adopted this [approach].**5** * * *

Today's opinion does not explain how the States' role in the electoral process guarantees that particular exercises of the Commerce Clause power will not infringe on residual State sovereignty. Members of Congress are elected from the various States, but once in office they are members of the federal government.

---

b. The Court noted that when FLSA changes subjected state mass-transit systems to higher costs the federal government simultaneously provided "substantial countervailing financial assistance."

a. *Fry*, 421 U.S. 542 (1975) upheld Congress' commerce power to combat inflation by limiting wage increases for state and local government employees, along with all others, citing *Wirtz:* "It seems inescapable that the effectiveness of federal action would have been drastically impaired if wage increases to this sizeable group of employees (14% of the Nation's work force) were left outside [these] emergency federal wage controls." Rehnquist, J., dissented, urging the overruling of *Wirtz.*

Douglas, J., would have dismissed the writ as improvidently granted.

5. In undertaking such balancing, we have considered [the] strength of the federal interest in the challenged legislation and the impact of exempting the States from its reach. Central to our inquiry into the federal interest is how closely the challenged action implicates the central concerns of the Commerce Clause, viz., the promotion of a national economy and free trade among the states. [On] the other hand, we have also assessed the injury done to the States if forced to comply with federal Commerce Clause enactments.

Although the States participate in the Electoral College, this is hardly a reason to view the President as a representative of the States' interest against federal encroachment. We noted recently "the hydraulic pressure inherent within each of the separate Branches to exceed the outer limits of its [power]." *INS v. Chadha,* [Ch. 3, Sec. 2, II]. The Court offers no reason to think that this pressure will not operate when Congress seeks to invoke its powers under the Commerce Clause, notwithstanding the electoral role of the States.[9]

[The] States' success at obtaining federal funds for various projects and exemptions from the obligations of some federal statutes [is] not relevant to the question whether the political *processes* are the proper means of enforcing constitutional limitations. The fact that Congress generally does not transgress constitutional limits on its power to reach State activities does not make judicial review any less necessary to rectify the cases in which it does do so.[b] [Far] from being "unsound in principle," judicial enforcement of the Tenth Amendment is essential to maintaining the federal system so carefully designed by the Framers and adopted in the Constitution. [Indeed,] the Court's view of federalism appears to relegate the States to precisely the trivial role that opponents of the Constitution feared they would occupy.

[Under] the balancing test [the] state interest [in this case] is compelling. The financial impact on States and localities of displacing their control over wages, hours, overtime regulations, pensions, and labor relations with their employees could have serious, as well as unanticipated, effects on state and local planning, budgeting, and the levying of taxes. [I]ntracity mass transit system [is] a classic example of the type of service traditionally provided by local government. It [is] indistinguishable in principle from the traditional services of providing and maintaining streets, public lighting, traffic control, water, and sewerage systems. Services of this kind are precisely those "with which citizens are more 'familiarly and minutely conversant.'" The *Federalist,* No. 46. State and local officials [know] that their constituents and the press respond to the adequacy, fair distribution, and cost of these services. It is this kind of state and local control and accountability that the Framers understood would insure the vitality and preservation of the federal system that the Constitution explicitly requires. * * *c

9. * * * Professor Wechsler, whose seminal article in 1954 proposed the view adopted by the Court today, [wrote]: "National action [has] always been regarded as exceptional in our polity, an intrusion to be justified by some necessity, the special rather than the ordinary case." Not only is the premise of this view clearly at odds with the proliferation of national legislation over the past 30 years, but "a variety of structural and political changes in this century have combined to make Congress particularly *insensitive* to state and local values." Advisory Comm'n on Intergovernmental Relations, *Regulatory Federalism: Policy, Process, Impact and Reform* 50 (1984). The adoption of the Seventeenth Amendment (providing for direct election of senators), the weakening of political parties on the local level, and the rise of national media, among other things, have made Congress increasingly less representative of State and local interests, and more likely to be responsive to the demands of various national constituencies. Id. [See] also Lewis B. Kaden, *Politics, Money, and State Sovereignty: The Judicial Role,* 79 Colum.L.Rev. 847 (1979). * * *

b. Consider Kennedy, J., joined by O'Connor, J., concurring in *Lopez,* Sec. 2, IV supra: "[T]he federal balance is too essential a part of our constitutional structure and plays too vital a role in securing freedom for us to admit [the Court's] inability to intervene when one or the other level of Government has tipped the scales too far. [T]he substantial element of political judgment in Commerce Clause matters leaves our institutional capacity to intervene more in doubt than when we decide cases, for instance, under the Bill of Rights even though clear and bright lines are often absent in the latter class of disputes. But our cases do not teach that we have no role at all in determining the meaning of the Commerce Clause."

c. O'Connor, J., joined by Rehnquist, C.J., and Powell, J., added a dissent that called for "weighing state autonomy as a factor in the balance when interpreting the means by which Congress can exercise its authority on the State as States."

While joining the Powell and O'Connor dissents, Rehnquist, J., withheld full acceptance of their "balancing" approaches and conclud-

Notes

1. *"Failings in national political process."* SOUTH CAROLINA v. BAKER, 485 U.S. 505 (1988), per Brennan, J., again recognized the possibility of a process-based attack on federal regulation of state government operations, but ruled that the "national political process did not operate in a defective manner" when Congress banned certain types of state bonds by relying on anecdotal, not "concrete" evidence that such bonds were being used to conceal taxable income.

2. *Alternative approach.* GREGORY v. ASHCROFT, 501 U.S. 452 (1991), per O'Connor, J., advanced many of the considerations in the *Garcia* dissent in refusing to apply the federal Age Discrimination in Employment Act to a state judge required by state law to retire at 70, by importing a "plain statement" rule from Eleventh Amendment cases: "If Congress intends to alter the 'usual constitutional balance between the States and the Federal Government' it must make its intention to do so unmistakably clear in the language of the statute." Of the five justices in the *Garcia* majority, the four remaining on the Court dissented from this reasoning because it "directly contravenes our decision in *Garcia.*"

PRINTZ v. UNITED STATES

521 U.S. 898, 117 S.Ct. 2365, 138 L.Ed.2d 914 (1997).

Justice Scalia delivered the opinion of the Court.

[T]he Brady Handgun Violence Prevention Act purports to direct state law enforcement officers to participate, albeit only temporarily, in the administration of a federally enacted regulatory scheme. Regulated firearms dealers are required to forward Brady Forms not to a federal officer or employee, but to the CLEOs ["chief law enforcement officers"], whose obligation [is] to make "reasonable efforts" within five days to determine whether the sales reflected in the forms are lawful. While the CLEOs are subjected to no federal requirement that they prevent the sales determined to be unlawful (it is perhaps assumed that their state-law duties will require prevention or apprehension), they are empowered to grant, in effect, waivers of the federally prescribed 5–day waiting period for handgun purchases by notifying the gun dealers that they have no reason to believe the transactions would be illegal.

The petitioners here object to being pressed into federal service * * *. Because there is no constitutional text speaking to this precise question, the answer to the CLEOs' challenge must be sought in historical understanding and practice, in the structure of the Constitution, and in the jurisprudence of this Court.

[The Court concluded that the relevant historical practice "tends to negate" Congress' power to impose federal responsibilities on state officers without the States' consent. "[E]nactments of the early Congresses [contain] no evidence of an assumption that the Federal Government may command the States' executive power in the absence of a particularized constitutional authorization," such as the Extradition Clause of Art IV, Sec. 2. The "early laws establish, at most, that the Constitution was originally understood to permit imposition of an obligation on

ed: "[U]nder any one of these approaches the judgment in this case should be affirmed, and I do not think it incumbent on those of us in dissent to spell out further the fine points of a principle that will, I am confident, in time again command the support of a majority of this Court." O'Connor, J., added her "belief that this Court will in time again assume its constitutional responsibility."

state judges to enforce federal prescriptions, insofar as those prescriptions related to matters appropriate for the judicial power." Finally, there is "an absence of executive-commandeering statutes [in] our later history as well."]a

* * * We turn next to consideration of the structure of the Constitution, to see if we can discern among its "essential postulate[s]" a principle that controls the present cases. * * * We have set forth the historical record in more detail elsewhere, see *New York v. United States,* [505 U.S. 144 (1992), per O'Connor, J. (discussed below)], and need not repeat it here. It suffices to repeat the conclusion: "The Framers explicitly chose a Constitution that confers upon Congress the power to regulate individuals, not States." [This] separation of the two spheres is one of the Constitution's structural protections of liberty. [The] power of the Federal Government would be augmented immeasurably if it were able to impress into its service—and at no cost to itself—the police officers of the 50 States.

[F]ederal control of state officers would [also] have an effect upon [the] separation and equilibration of powers between the three branches of the Federal Government itself. The Constitution [says] the President "shall take Care that the Laws be faithfully executed," personally and through officers whom he appoints. [The] Brady Act effectively transfers this responsibility to thousands of CLEOs in the 50 States, who are left to implement the program without meaningful Presidential control (if indeed meaningful Presidential control is possible without the power to appoint and remove).b [T]he power of the President would be subject to reduction, if Congress could act as effectively without the President as with him, by simply requiring state officers to execute its laws.12 * * *

Finally, and most conclusively in the present litigation, we turn to the prior jurisprudence of this Court. Federal commandeering of state governments is such a novel phenomenon that this Court's first experience with it did not occur until the 1970's, when [several] opinions of ours have made clear that the Federal Government may not compel the States to implement, by legislation or executive action, federal regulatory programs. [*Hodel*, note 4 after *Katzenbach v. McClung*] concluded that the Surface Mining Control and Reclamation Act of 1977 did not present the problem they raised because it merely made compliance with federal standards a precondition to continued state regulation in an otherwise pre-empted field. In *FERC* [*v. Mississippi*, 456 U.S. 742 (1982),] we construed the most troubling provisions of the Public Utility Regulatory Policies Act of 1978 to contain only the "command" that state agencies "consider" federal standards, and again only as a precondition to continued state regulation of an otherwise pre-empted field.c * * *

a. The dissents disputed each point, as well as the meaning of *The Federalist* Nos. 27 and 44: "[T]he majority's opinion consists almost entirely of arguments against the substantial evidence weighing in opposition to its [view.] Absent even a modicum of textual foundation for its judicially crafted constitutional rule, there should be a presumption that if the Framers had actually intended such a rule, at least one of them would have mentioned it."

b. The subject is considered in Ch. 3, Sec. 2, III.

12. There is not, as the dissent believes, "tension" between the proposition that impressing state police officers into federal service will massively augment federal power, and the proposition that it will also sap the power of the Federal Presidency. It is quite possible to have a more powerful Federal Government that is, by reason of the destruction of its Executive unity, a less efficient one. The dissent is correct that control by the unitary Federal Executive is also sacrificed when States voluntarily administer federal programs, but the condition of voluntary state participation significantly reduces the ability of Congress to use this device as a means of reducing the power of the Presidency.

c. *FERC*, per Blackmun, J., emphasized that since "Congress could have preempted the field of utility regulation, at least insofar as private rather than state activity is concerned, [the Act] should not be invalid simply because, out of deference to state authority, Congress adopted a less intrusive scheme and allowed the States to continue regulating in the area on the condition that they *consider* the sug-

When we were at last confronted squarely with a federal statute that unambiguously required the States to enact or administer a federal regulatory program, our decision should have come as no surprise. At issue in *New York* [were] the so-called "take title" provisions of the Low–Level Radioactive Waste Policy Amendments Act of 1985, which required States either to enact legislation providing for the disposal of radioactive waste generated within their borders, or to take title to, and possession of, the waste—effectively requiring the States either to legislate pursuant to Congress's directions, or to implement an administrative solution. We concluded that Congress could constitutionally require the states to do neither. * * *

The Government contends that *New York* is distinguishable on the following ground: unlike the "take title" provisions invalidated there, [the] Brady Act does not require state legislative or executive officials to make policy. [But executive] action that has utterly no policymaking component is rare, particularly at an executive level as high as a jurisdiction's chief law-enforcement officer. Is it really true that there is no policymaking involved in deciding, for example, what "reasonable efforts" shall be expended to conduct a background check? It may well satisfy the Act for a CLEO to direct that (a) no background checks will be conducted that divert personnel time from pending felony investigations, and (b) no background check will be permitted to consume more than one-half hour of an officer's time. [Is] this decision whether to devote maximum "reasonable efforts" or minimum "reasonable efforts" not preeminently a matter of policy?d It is quite impossible, in short, to draw the Government's proposed line at "no policymaking," and we would have to fall back upon a line of "not too much policymaking." [Even assuming,] that the Brady Act leaves no "policymaking" discretion with the States, we fail to see how that improves rather than worsens the intrusion upon state sovereignty. Preservation of the States as independent and autonomous political entities is arguably less undermined by requiring them to make policy in certain fields than [by] "reduc[ing] [them] to puppets of a ventriloquist Congress." * * *

The Government purports to find support for its proffered distinction of *New York* [in] *Testa v. Katt,* 330 U.S. 386 (1947), [which] stands for the proposition that state courts cannot refuse to apply federal law—a conclusion mandated by the terms of the Supremacy Clause. [T]hat says nothing about whether state executive officers must administer federal law. * * *

The Government also maintains that requiring state officers to perform discrete, ministerial tasks specified by Congress does not violate the principle of *New York* because it does not diminish the accountability of state or federal officials.e [But by] forcing state governments to absorb the financial burden of

gested federal standards. [Thus, the provisions] do not threaten the States' 'separate and independent existence,' and do not impair the ability of the States 'to function effectively in a federal system.' To the contrary, they offer the States a vehicle for remaining active in an area of overriding concern."

d. Dissenting in *FERC*, O'Connor, J., joined by Burger, C.J. and Rehnquist, J., argued that: "the power to make decisions and set [policy] embraces more than the ultimate authority to enact laws; it also includes the power to decide which proposals are most worthy of consideration, the order in which they should be taken up, and the precise form in which they should be debated. [The Act] in-

trudes upon all of these functions. It chooses twelve proposals, forcing their consideration even if the state agency deems other ideas more worthy of immediate attention. [By] taxing the limited resources of these commissions, and decreasing their ability to address local regulatory ills, [the Act] directly impairs the power of state utility commissions to discharge their traditional functions efficiently and effectively."

e. *New York* reasoned that "where the Federal Government compels States to regulate, the accountability of both state and federal officials is diminished. If the citizens of New York, for example, do not consider that making provision for the disposal of radioactive waste

implementing a federal regulatory program, Members of Congress can take credit for "solving" problems without having to ask their constituents to pay for the solutions with higher federal taxes. And even when the States are not forced to absorb the [costs,] they are still put in the position of taking the blame for its burdensomeness and for its defects. Under the present law, for example, it will be the CLEO and not some federal official who stands between the gun purchaser and immediate possession of his gun. And it will likely be the CLEO, not some federal official, who will be blamed for any error (even one in the designated federal database) that causes a purchaser to be mistakenly rejected.

[The] Brady Act, the dissent asserts, is different [from] *New York* because the former is addressed to individuals—namely CLEOs—while the latter were directed to the State itself. [But while] the Brady Act is directed to "individuals," it is directed to them in their official capacities as state officers; it controls their actions, not as private citizens, but as the agents of the State. * * *

Finally, the Government puts forward a cluster of arguments [under] the heading: "The Brady Act serves very important purposes, is most efficiently administered by CLEOs during the interim period, and places a minimal and only temporary burden upon state officers." [Assuming] the mentioned factors were true, they might be relevant if we were evaluating whether the incidental application to the States of a federal law of general applicability excessively interfered with the functioning of state governments. See, e.g., *Fry; National League of Cities.* But where, as here, it is the whole object of the law to direct the functioning of the state executive, and hence to compromise the structural framework of dual sovereignty, such a "balancing" analysis is inappropriate.17 * * *

JUSTICE O'CONNOR, concurring.

[T]he Court appropriately refrains from deciding [whether] purely ministerial reporting requirements imposed by Congress on state and local authorities pursuant to its Commerce Clause powers are similarly invalid. See, e.g., 42 U.S.C. § 5779(a) (requiring state and local law enforcement agencies to report cases of missing children to the Department of Justice).a The provisions [here,] however, which directly compel state officials to administer a federal regulatory program, utterly fail to adhere to the design and structure of our constitutional scheme.b

is in their best interest, they may elect state officials who share their view. That view can always be preempted under the Supremacy Clause if is contrary to the national view, but in such a case it is the Federal Government that makes the decision in full view of the public, and it will be federal officials that suffer the consequences if the decision turns out to be detrimental or unpopular. But where the Federal Government directs the States to regulate, it may be state officials who will bear the brunt of public disapproval, while the federal officials who devised the regulatory program may remain insulated from the electoral ramifications of their decision."

17. The dissent observes that "Congress could require private persons, such as hospital executives or school administrators, to provide arms merchants with relevant information about a prospective purchaser's fitness to own a weapon," and that "the burden on police officers [imposed by the Brady Act] would be permissible if a similar burden were also im-

posed on private parties with access to relevant data." That is undoubtedly true, but [t]he Brady Act does not merely require CLEOs to report information in their private possession. It requires them to provide information that belongs to the State and is available to them only in their official capacity; and to conduct investigations in their official capacity, by examining databases and records that only state officials have access to. In other words, the suggestion that extension of this statute to private citizens would eliminate the constitutional problem posits the impossible.

a. The Court commented that "federal statutes [which] require only the provision of information to the Federal Government, do not involve the precise issue before us [here]."

b. The concurring opinion of Thomas, J., who joined the Court's opinion—and added that if "the Second Amendment is read to confer a *personal* right to 'keep and bear arms,' a colorable argument exists that the Federal Government's regulatory scheme, at

JUSTICE STEVENS, with whom JUSTICE SOUTER, JUSTICE GINSBURG, and JUSTICE BREYER join, dissenting. * * *

These cases do not implicate the more difficult questions associated with congressional coercion of state legislatures addressed in *New York*. Nor need we consider the wisdom of relying on local officials rather than federal agents to carry out aspects of a federal program, or even the question whether such officials may be required to perform a federal function on a permanent basis.

[S]ince the ultimate issue is one of power, we must consider its implications in times of national emergency. Matters such as the enlistment of air raid wardens, the administration of a military draft, the mass inoculation of children to forestall an epidemic, or perhaps the threat of an international terrorist, may require a national response before federal personnel can be made available to respond. If the Constitution empowers Congress and the President to make an appropriate response, is there anything in the Tenth Amendment, "in historical understanding and practice, in the structure of the Constitution, [or] in the jurisprudence of this Court," that forbids the enlistment of state officers to make that response effective? More narrowly, what basis is there in any of those sources for concluding that it is the Members of this Court, rather than the elected representatives of the people, who should determine whether the Constitution contains the unwritten rule that the Court announces today? * * *

Unlike the First Amendment, which prohibits the enactment of a category of laws that would otherwise be authorized by Article I, the Tenth Amendment [does] not purport to limit the scope or the effectiveness of the exercise of powers that are delegated to Congress.c Thus, the Amendment provides no support for a rule that immunizes local officials from obligations that might be imposed on ordinary citizens.2 * * *

Recent developments demonstrate that the political safeguards protecting Our Federalism are effective. The majority expresses special concern that were its rule not adopted the Federal Government would be able to avail itself of the services of state government officials "at no cost to itself." But this [problem] of imposing so-called "unfunded mandates" on the States has been identified and meaningfully addressed by Congress in recent legislation.18 * * *

least as it pertains to the purely intrastate sale or possession of firearms, runs afoul of that Amendment's protections"—is omitted.

c. *New York*, however, explained that "the Tenth Amendment confirms that the power of the Federal Government is subject to limits that may, in a given instance, reserve power to the States. [It] thus directs us to determine [whether] an incident of state sovereignty is protected by a limitation on an Article I power."

2. Recognizing the force of the argument, the Court suggests that this reasoning is in error because—even if it is responsive to the submission that the Tenth Amendment roots the principle set forth by the majority today—it does not answer the possibility that the Court's holding can be rooted in a "principle of state sovereignty" mentioned nowhere in the constitutional text. As a ground for invalidating important federal legislation, this argument is remarkably weak. The majority's further claim that, while the Brady Act may be legislation "necessary" to Congress' execution

of its undisputed Commerce Clause authority to regulate firearms sales, it is nevertheless not "proper" because it violates state sovereignty, is wholly circular. [Our] ruling in *New York* that the Commerce Clause does not provide Congress the authority to require States to enact legislation—a power that affects States far closer to the core of their sovereign authority—does nothing to support the majority's unwarranted extension of that reasoning today.

18. The majority also makes the more general claim that requiring state officials to carry out federal policy causes states to "tak[e] the blame" for failed programs. The Court cites no empirical authority to support the proposition. [Unlike] state legislators, local government executive officials routinely take action in response to a variety of sources of authority: local ordinance, state law, and federal law. It doubtless may therefore require some sophistication to discern under which authority an executive official is acting. [But] the majority's rule neither creates nor alters this basic truth. The problem is of little real consequence in any

Perversely, the majority's rule seems more likely to damage [the] safeguards against tyranny provided by the existence of vital state governments. By limiting the ability of the Federal Government to enlist state officials in the implementation of its programs, the Court creates incentives for the National Government to aggrandize itself. In the name of State's rights, the majority would have the Federal Government create vast national bureaucracies to implement its policies.d

Finally, the majority provides an incomplete explanation of our decision in *Testa* [which] unanimously held that state courts of appropriate jurisdiction must occupy themselves adjudicating claims brought by private litigants under the federal Emergency Price Control Act of 1942, regardless of how otherwise crowded their dockets might be with state-law matters. That is a much greater imposition on state sovereignty than the Court's characterization of the [case]. Even if the Court were correct in its suggestion that it was the reference to judges in the Supremacy Clause, rather than the central message of the entire Clause, that dictated the result in *Testa*, the Court's implied expressio unius argument that the Framers therefore did not intend to permit the enlistment of other state officials is implausible. Throughout our history judges, state as well as federal, have merited as much respect as executive agents. The notion that the Framers would have had no reluctance to "press state judges into federal service" against their will but would have regarded the imposition of a similar—indeed, far lesser— burden on town constables as an intolerable affront to principles of state sovereignty can only be considered perverse. * * *

JUSTICE BREYER, with whom JUSTICE STEVENS joins, dissenting.

[At] least some other countries [have] found that local control is better maintained through application of a principle that is the direct opposite of the principle the majority derives from the silence of our Constitution. The federal systems of Switzerland, Germany, and the European Union, for example, all provide that constituent states, not federal bureaucracies, will themselves implement many of the laws, rules, regulations, or decrees enacted by the central "federal" body. [Of] course, we are interpreting our own Constitution, [but] their experience may nonetheless cast an empirical light on the consequences of different solutions to a common legal problem. * * *

[T]he fact that there is not more precedent—that direct federal assignment of duties to state officers is not common—likely reflects, not a widely shared belief that any such assignment is incompatible with basic principles of federalism, but rather a widely shared practice of assigning such duties in other ways. See, e.g., *Dole* (spending power); *New York* (general statutory duty); *FERC* (pre-emption). Thus, there is neither need nor reason to find in the Constitution an absolute principle, the inflexibility of which poses a surprising and technical obstacle to the

event, because to the extent that a particular action proves politically unpopular, we may be confident that elected officials charged with implementing it will be quite clear to their constituents where the source of the misfortune lies. These cases demonstrate the point. Sheriffs Printz and Mack have made public statements, including their decisions to serve as plaintiffs in these actions, denouncing the Brady Act.

d. White, J., joined by Blackmun and Stevens, JJ., dissenting in *New York,* made a similar argument: "The ultimate irony of the decision today is that in its formalistically rigid obeisance to 'federalism,' the Court gives Congress fewer incentives to defer to the wishes of state officials in achieving local solutions to local problems. This legislation was a classic example of Congress acting as arbiter among the States in their attempts to accept responsibility for managing a problem of grave import. The States urged the National Legislature not to impose [a] solution to the country's low-level radioactive waste management problems. [By] invalidating the measure designed to ensure compliance for recalcitrant States, such as New York, the Court upsets the delicate compromise achieved among the States."

enactment of a law that Congress believed necessary to solve an important national problem.* * *e

———

RENO v. CONDON, 528 U.S. 141 (2000), per REHNQUIST, C.J., unanimously sustained Congress' power under the Commerce Clause to pass the Driver's Privacy Protection Act, which bars state motor vehicle departments from disclosing (or selling) personal information (such as name, address, telephone number, vehicle description, Social Security number, medical information, and photograph) required for a driver's license or car registration: "[T]he vehicle information which the States have historically sold is used by insurers, manufacturers, direct marketers, and others engaged in interstate commerce [and] is also used in the stream of interstate commerce by various public and private entities for matters related to interstate motoring. Because drivers' information is, in this context, an article of commerce, its sale or release into the interstate stream of business is sufficient to support congressional regulation. * * *

"We agree [that] the DPPA's provisions will require time and effort on the part of state employees ['to learn and apply its complex provisions'], but reject the State's argument that the DPPA violates the principles laid down in either *New York* or *Printz*. [Such] 'commandeering' [is] an inevitable consequence of regulating ['States acting purely as commercial sellers.'] That a State wishing to engage in certain activity must take administrative and sometimes legislative action to comply with federal standards regulating that activity is a commonplace that presents no constitutional defect.

"Like the statute at issue in [*South Carolina v. Baker*, note 1 after *Garcia*, which prohibited States from issuing unregistered bonds"], the DPPA does not require the States in their sovereign capacity to regulate their own citizens. The DPPA regulates the States as the owners of databases. It does not require the South Carolina Legislature to enact any laws or regulations, and it does not require state officials to assist in the enforcement of federal statutes regulating private individuals. We accordingly conclude that the DPPA is consistent with the constitutional principles enunciated in *New York* and *Printz*."

Nor does the DPPA "regulate the States exclusively. [It] regulates the universe of entities that participate as suppliers to the market for motor vehicle information—the States as initial suppliers of the information in interstate commerce and private resellers or redisclosers of that information in commerce."

e. Souter, J., who reaffirmed his view that *New York* "was rightly decided," filed a separate dissent, noting (1) that "in deciding these cases, which I have found closer than I had anticipated, it is *The Federalist* that finally determines my position," and (2) that "I do not read any of *The Federalist* material as requiring the conclusion that Congress could require administrative support without an obligation to pay fair value for it."

Chapter 3

DISTRIBUTION OF FEDERAL POWERS: SEPARATION OF POWERS

This chapter addresses the distribution of powers *within* the federal government. Its principal concern is how the Constitution's text and structure, and the separation-of-powers and checks-and-balances concepts they embody, define the powers of the branches of government, especially of Congress and the Executive. A related issue is the extent that a power expressly granted to one branch must be exercised to avoid interference with the powers of another branch. These matters are considered in this chapter's four sections: (1) presidential action affecting "congressional powers"; (2) congressional action affecting "presidential powers"; (3) executive privilege and immunity; and (4) impeachment of the president.

SECTION 1. PRESIDENTIAL ACTION AFFECTING "CONGRESSIONAL" POWERS

I. INTERNAL MATTERS: DOMESTIC LAWMAKING

YOUNGSTOWN SHEET & TUBE CO. v. SAWYER [THE STEEL SEIZURE CASE]

343 U.S. 579, 72 S.Ct. 863, 96 L.Ed. 1153 (1952).

JUSTICE BLACK delivered the opinion of the Court. * * *

We are asked to decide whether [President Truman] was acting within his constitutional power when he issued an order directing the Secretary of Commerce [Sawyer] to take possession of and operate most of the Nation's steel mills. The mill owners argue that the President's order amounts to lawmaking, a legislative function which the Constitution has expressly confided to the Congress and not to the President. The Government's position is that the order was made on findings of the President and that his action was necessary to avert a national catastrophe which would inevitably result from a stoppage of steel production [during the Korean War].

[When efforts to settle a labor dispute—including reference to the Federal Wage Stabilization Board—failed, the union called a nationwide strike to begin April 9, 1952. Finding that the strike would jeopardize national defense, a few hours before the strike deadline the President issued Executive Order 10340, directing the Secretary of Commerce to take possession of most of the country's steel mills and keep them operating. The President sent a message to Congress reporting his actions on the next day. On May 3, the Court granted direct review of a U.S. District Court order that enjoined the Secretary's possession of the steel mills, and set argument for May 12. On June 2, the Court upheld the injunction, ruling the seizure unconstitutional.]

The President's power, if any, to issue the order must stem either from an act of Congress or from the Constitution itself.

[T]he use of the seizure [to] prevent work stoppage was not only unauthorized by any congressional enactment; prior to this controversy, Congress had refused to adopt that method of settling labor disputes. When the [Labor Management Relations Act of 1947] was under [consideration], Congress rejected an amendment which would have authorized such governmental seizures in cases of emergency. [Instead], the plan sought to bring about settlements by use of the customary devices of mediation, conciliation, investigation by boards of inquiry, and public reports. In some instances temporary injunctions were authorized to provide cooling-off periods. All this failing, unions were left free to strike after a secret vote by employees * * *.1

It is clear that if the President had authority to issue the order he did, it must be found in some provision of the Constitution. [The] contention is that presidential power should be implied from the aggregate of his powers under the Constitution. Particular reliance is placed on provisions in Article II which say that "The executive Power shall be vested in a President"; that "he shall take Care that the Laws be faithfully executed"; and that he "shall be Commander in Chief of the Army and Navy of the United States."

* * * We cannot with faithfulness to our constitutional system hold that the Commander in Chief of the Armed Forces has the ultimate power as such to take possession of private property in order to keep labor disputes from stopping production. This is a job for the Nation's lawmakers, not for its military authorities.

Nor can the seizure order be sustained because of the several constitutional provisions that grant executive power to the President. In the framework of our Constitution, the President's power to see that the laws are faithfully executed refutes the idea that he is to be a lawmaker. The Constitution limits his functions in the lawmaking process to the recommending of laws he thinks wise and the vetoing of laws he thinks bad. And the Constitution is neither silent nor equivocal about who shall make laws which the President is to execute. The first section of the first article says that "All legislative Powers herein granted shall be vested in a Congress of the United States." * * *

The President's order does not direct that a congressional policy be executed in a manner prescribed by Congress—it directs that a presidential policy be executed in a manner prescribed by the President. The preamble of the order itself, like that of many statutes, sets out reasons why the President believes certain policies should be adopted, proclaims these policies as rules of conduct to be followed, and again, like a statute, authorizes a government official to promulgate additional rules and regulations consistent with the policy proclaimed and needed to carry that policy into execution. The power of Congress to adopt such

---

1. Sections 206–210 of the Act provided that "[w]henever in the opinion of the President [a] threatened or actual strike [will], if permitted to occur or to continue, imperil the national health or safety," on the President's initiative, the strike could be enjoined while a board of inquiry studied the dispute, but that the strike could continue after 80 days if the employees reject the employer's last offer of settlement. The President was then obligated under the Act to report on the emergency to Congress.

public policies as those proclaimed by the order is beyond question. It can authorize the taking of private property for public use. It can make laws regulating the relationships between employers and employees, prescribing rules designed to settle labor disputes, and fixing wages and working conditions in certain fields of our economy. The Constitution did not subject this lawmaking power of Congress to presidential or military supervision or control.

It is said that other Presidents without congressional authority have taken possession of private business enterprises in order to settle labor disputes. But even if this be true, Congress has not thereby lost its exclusive constitutional authority to make [laws].

Affirmed.

JUSTICE FRANKFURTER, concurring in the judgment and opinion of the Court.

Although the considerations relevant to the legal enforcement of the principle of separation of powers seem to me more complicated and flexible than may appear from what Mr. Justice Black has written, I join his opinion because I thoroughly agree with the application of the principle to this case. * * *

[We] must [put] to one side consideration of what powers the President would have had if there had been no legislation whatever bearing on the authority asserted by the seizure, or if the seizure had been only for a short, explicitly temporary period, to be terminated automatically unless Congressional approval were given. These and other questions, like or unlike, are not now here. * * *

[It] cannot be contended that the President would have had power to issue this order had Congress explicitly negated such authority in formal legislation. [And Congress's decision reflected in the Labor Management Relations Act of 1947 should be given the same effect, since] Congress has expressed its will to withhold this power from the President as though it had said so in so many words. [It has] said to the President, "You may not seize. Please report to us and ask for seizure power if you think it is needed in a specific [situation]."

[The] content of the three authorities of government is not to be derived from an abstract analysis. The areas are partly interacting, not wholly disjointed. The Constitution is a framework for government. Therefore the way the framework has consistently operated fairly establishes that it has operated according to its true nature. Deeply embedded traditional ways of conducting government cannot supplant the Constitution or legislation, but they give meaning to the words of a text. [But the] list of executive assertions of the power of seizure in circumstances comparable to the present reduces to three in the six-month period from June to December of 1941. [T]hese three isolated instances do not add up [to] the kind of executive construction of the Constitution [necessary to justify the action here]. Nor do they come to us sanctioned by the long-continued acquiescence of Congress* * *.

JUSTICE JACKSON, concurring in the judgment and opinion of the Court.

The actual art of governing under our Constitution does not and cannot conform to judicial definitions of the power of any of its branches based on isolated clauses or even single Articles torn from context. While the Constitution diffuses power the better to secure liberty, it also contemplates that practice will integrate the dispersed powers into a workable government. It enjoins upon its branches separateness but interdependence, autonomy but reciprocity. Presidential powers are not fixed but fluctuate, depending upon their disjunction or conjunction with those of Congress. We may well begin by a somewhat over-simplified grouping of practical situations in which a President may doubt, or others may challenge, his powers * * *.

1.   When the President acts pursuant to an express or implied authorization of Congress, his authority is at its maximum, for it includes all that he possesses in his own right plus all that Congress can delegate. * * *

2.   When the President acts in absence of either a congressional grant or denial of authority, he can only rely upon his own independent powers, but there is a zone of twilight in which he and Congress may have concurrent authority, or in which its distribution is uncertain. Therefore, congressional inertia, indifference or quiescence may sometimes, at least as a practical matter, enable, if not invite, measures on independent presidential responsibility. In this area, any actual test of power is likely to depend on the imperatives of events and contemporary imponderables rather than on abstract theories of law.

3.   When the President takes measures incompatible with the expressed or implied will of Congress, his power is at its lowest ebb, for then he can rely only upon his own constitutional powers minus any constitutional powers of Congress over the matter. Courts can sustain exclusive Presidential control in such a case only by disabling the Congress from acting upon the subject. Presidential claim to a power at once so conclusive and preclusive must be scrutinized with caution, for what is at stake is the equilibrium established by our constitutional system.

Into which of these classifications does this executive seizure of the steel industry fit? It is eliminated from the first by admission, for it is conceded that no congressional authorization exists for this seizure. [It] seems clearly eliminated from [the "second category"] because Congress has not left seizure of private property an open field but has covered it by three statutory policies inconsistent with this seizure [e.g., fn. a supra, none of which] were invoked. In choosing a different and inconsistent way of his own, the President cannot claim that it is necessitated or invited by failure of Congress to legislate upon the occasions, grounds and methods for seizure of industrial properties.

This leaves the current seizure to be justified only by the severe tests under the third grouping, [where] we can sustain the President only by holding that seizure of such strike-bound industries is within his domain and beyond control by Congress. * * * I cannot accept the view that [Art. II, § 1, cl. 1, vesting "the executive power" in the President] is a grant in bulk of all conceivable executive power but regard it as an allocation to the presidential office of the generic powers thereafter stated.

The [Commander in Chief] appellation is sometimes advanced as support for any presidential action, internal or external, involving use of force, the idea being that it vests power to do anything, anywhere, that can be done with an army or navy. [But the] Constitution expressly places in Congress power "to raise and *support* Armies" and "to *provide* and *maintain* a Navy." (Emphasis supplied.) * * * Congress alone controls the raising of revenues and their appropriation and may determine in what manner and by what means they shall be spent for military and naval procurement. I suppose no one would doubt that Congress can take over war supply as a Government enterprise. * * *

The third clause in which the Solicitor General finds seizure powers is that "he shall take Care that the Laws be faithfully executed." That authority must be matched against [the Due Process Clause of the Fifth Amendment]. One [clause] gives a governmental authority that reaches so far as there is law, the other gives a private right that authority shall go no farther. * * *

The Solicitor General lastly grounds support of the seizure upon nebulous, inherent powers never expressly granted but said to have accrued to the office from the customs and claims of preceding administrations. The plea is for a resulting power to deal with a crisis or an emergency according to the necessities of the case, the unarticulated assumption being that necessity knows no law. Loose and irresponsible use of adjectives colors all non-legal and much legal discussion of presidential powers. "Inherent" powers, "implied" powers, "incidental" powers, "plenary" powers, "war" powers and "emergency" powers are used, often interchangeably and without fixed or ascertainable meanings. * * *

In view of the ease, expedition and safety with which Congress can grant and has granted large emergency powers, certainly ample to embrace this crisis, I am quite unimpressed with the argument that we should affirm possession of them without statute. Such power either has no beginning or it has no end. If it exists, it need submit to no legal restraint. I am not alarmed that it would plunge us straightway into dictatorship, but it is at least a step in that wrong direction.

[The] Executive, except for recommendation and veto, has no legislative power. The executive action we have here originates in the individual will of the President and represents an exercise of authority without law. [With] all its defects, delays, and inconveniences, men have discovered no technique for long preserving free government except that the Executive be under the law, and that the law be made by parliamentary deliberations.[2]

CHIEF JUSTICE VINSON, with whom JUSTICE REED and JUSTICE MINTON join, dissenting.

[The dissent emphasized the country's international commitments for economic and military aid to preserve the free world and congressional action directing the President to strengthen the armed forces. It called attention to the legislation directly related to supporting the Korean War. It quoted affidavits showing the enormous demand for steel in vital defense programs and attesting that a work stoppage would imperil the national defense.] Accordingly, if the President has any power under the Constitution to meet a critical situation in the absence of express statutory authorization, there is no basis whatever for criticizing the exercise of such power in this case.

[Our] Presidents have on many occasions exhibited the leadership contemplated by the Framers when they made the President Commander in Chief, and imposed upon him the trust to "take Care that the Laws be faithfully executed." With or without explicit statutory authorization, Presidents have [dealt] with national emergencies by acting promptly [to] enforce legislative programs, at least to save those programs until Congress could act. Congress and the courts have responded to such executive initiative with consistent approval. [Historic episodes from George Washington to Franklin D. Roosevelt were summarized in 17 pages. A brief excerpt follows:]

Some six months before Pearl Harbor, a dispute at a single aviation [plant] interrupted a segment of the production of military aircraft. [President] Roosevelt ordered the seizure of the plant "pursuant to the powers vested in [him] by the Constitution and laws of the United States, as President [and] Commander in Chief of the Army and Navy of the United States." The Attorney General

---

2. Burton, J., also concurred in Black, J.'s opinion but also wrote a separate concurrence, similar in thrust to those of Frankfurter and Jackson, JJ., stressing that "the President's [order] invaded the jurisdiction of Congress," which "reserved to itself" the remedy of seizure. Douglas, J., concurred in Black, J.'s opinion, noting that "the branch of government that has the power to pay compensation for a seizure [Congress] is the only one able to au-

thorize a seizure [under] the condemnation provision in the Fifth Amendment." Clark, J., concurred in the judgment because "Congress had prescribed methods to be followed by the President in meeting the emergency at hand, [but] in the absence of such action by Congress, the President's independent power to act depends upon the gravity of the situation confronting the nation."

(Jackson) vigorously proclaimed that the President had the moral duty to keep this Nation's defense effort a "going concern." [A]lso prior to Pearl Harbor, the President ordered the seizure of a ship-building company and an aircraft parts plant. Following the declaration of war, [five] additional industrial concerns were seized to avert interruption of needed production. During the same period, the President directed seizure of the Nation's coal mines to remove an obstruction to the effective prosecution of the war.

[This] is but a cursory summary of executive leadership. But it amply demonstrates that Presidents have taken prompt action to enforce the laws and protect the country whether or not Congress happened to provide in advance for the particular method of execution. [T]he fact that Congress and the courts have consistently recognized and given their support to such executive action indicates that such a power of seizure has been accepted throughout our history.

Flexibility as to mode of execution [of the laws] to meet critical situations is a matter of practical necessity. [The] broad executive power granted by Article II [cannot], it is said, be invoked to avert disaster. Instead, the President must confine himself to sending a message to Congress recommending action. Under this messenger-boy concept of the Office, the President cannot even act to preserve legislative programs from destruction so that Congress will have something left to act upon.

[T]here [is no] question of unlimited executive power in this case. The President himself closed the door to any such claim when he sent his Message to Congress stating his purpose to abide by any action of Congress, whether approving or disapproving his seizure action [or] regulating the manner in which the mills were to be administered and returned to the owners. [J]udicial, legislative and executive precedents throughout our history demonstrate that in this case the President acted in full conformity with his duties under the Constitution.

Notes

Executive "lawmaking." (a) ***Delegation***. As discussed more fully in Sec. 2 infra, executive branch agencies, typically pursuant to authority delegated by Congress, routinely engage in rulemaking, and the President himself has developed and implemented tariff schedules.a Is the exercise of delegated rulemaking authority legislative action that is forbidden to executive officials?

(b) ***Executive orders***. Presidents have long asserted a power to issue"Executive Orders" relating to organization of the executive branch, use of federal property, and the terms on which the federal government will enter contracts. The most prominent include President Lincoln's Emancipation Proclamation and President Truman's racial integration of the armed forces. See also *United States v. Midwest Oil Co.*, 236 U.S. 459 (1915), upholding presidential authority to protect oil resources on public lands, pending proposed legislation, by suspending statutory rights to file oil claims. Presidents have issued executive orders forbidding race discrimination by private firms receiving federal contracts, and later mandating "affirmative action" by federal contractors.

DAMES & MOORE v. REGAN, 453 U.S. 654 (1981), per REHNQUIST, J., unanimously upheld presidential executive orders to implement an executive

---

a. See, e.g., *J.W. Hampton, Jr., & Co. v. United States*, 276 U.S. 394 (1928); *Field v.* *Clark*, 143 U.S. 649 (1892); *The Aurora*, 11 U.S. (7 Cranch) 382 (1813).

agreement between Iran and the United States securing release of American hostages held in Iran for 15 months in 1979–81. The executive agreement called for termination of "all litigation between the government of each party and the nationals of the other" and for settlement of pending claims through binding arbitration before a tribunal established under the agreement. The executive orders (1) suspended all claims in American courts that were within the jurisdiction of the claims tribunal, (2) nullified all prejudgment attachments against Iran's assets in actions against Iran in American, except for one billion dollars to cover awards against Iran by the claims tribunal.

Dames & Moore's prejudgment attachment of Iranian bank assets, to secure its large claim for services rendered to Iran, was vacated pursuant to the executive orders. The Court rejected Dames & Moore's challenge: "Because the President's action in nullifying the attachments and ordering the transfer of the assets was taken pursuant to specific congressional authorization [under the International Emergency Economic Powers Act (IEEPA)]a it is 'supported by the strongest of presumptions and the widest latitude of judicial interpretation, and the burden of persuasion would rest heavily upon any who might attack it.' [*Youngstown*] (Jackson, J., concurring). [We] cannot say that petitioner has sustained that heavy burden. A contrary ruling would mean that the Federal Government as a whole lacked the power exercised by the President, and that we are not prepared to say."

By contrast, "neither the IEEPA nor the Hostage Act constitutes specific authorization of the President's action suspending claims. [But this is] not to say that these statutory provisions are entirely irrelevant to the question of the validity of the President's [action.] Congress cannot anticipate and legislate with regard to every possible action the President may find it necessary to take. [E]nactment of legislation closely related to the question of the President's authority in a particular case which evinces legislative intent to accord the President broad discretion may be considered to 'invite' 'measures on independent presidential responsibility.' *Youngstown* (Jackson, J., concurring). At least this is so where there is no contrary indication of legislative intent and when, as here, there is a history of congressional acquiescence in conduct of the sort engaged in by the President. * * *

"Crucial to our decision today is the conclusion that Congress has implicitly approved the practice of claim settlement by executive agreement. This is best demonstrated by Congress' enactment of the International Claims Settlement Act of 1949. The Act had two purposes: (1) to allocate to United States nationals funds received in the course of an executive claims settlement with Yugoslavia, and (2) to provide a procedure whereby funds resulting from future settlements could be distributed. To achieve these ends Congress created the International Claims Commission, now the Foreign Claims Settlement Commission, and gave it jurisdiction to make final and binding decisions with respect to claims by United States nationals against settlement funds. By creating a procedure to implement future settlement agreements, Congress placed its stamp of approval on such agreements. Indeed, the legislative history of the Act observed that the United States was seeking settlements with countries other than Yugoslavia and [stated] that the bill contemplates settlements of a similar nature in the future.

"[As] Justice Frankfurter pointed out in *Youngstown*, 'a systematic, unbroken executive practice, long pursued to the knowledge of the Congress and never

---

a. Section 1702(a)(1)(B) of IEEPA empowered the President to "compel," "nullify," or "prohibit" any "transfer" with respect to, or transactions involving, any property subject to the jurisdiction of the United States in which any foreign country has any interest.

before questioned [may] be treated as a gloss on "Executive Power" vested in the President by § 1 of Art. II.' * * *

"Our conclusion is buttressed by the fact that the means chosen by the President to settle the claims of American nationals provided an alternative forum, the Claims Tribunal, which is capable of providing meaningful relief. [Just] as importantly, [we are] clearly not confronted with a situation in which Congress has in some way resisted the exercise of Presidential authority.

" * * * We do not decide that the President possesses plenary power to settle claims, even as against foreign governmental entities. [But] where, as here, the settlement of claims has been determined to be a necessary incident to the resolution of a major foreign policy dispute between our country and another, and where, as here, we can conclude that Congress acquiesced in the President's action, we are not prepared to say that the President lacks the power to settle such claims."

MEDELLIN v. TEXAS, 552 U.S. 491 (2008), per ROBERTS, C.J., (6–3) invalidated President G.W. Bush's "Memorandum" that state courts must adhere to the International Court of Justice's decision that the Vienna Convention on Consular Relations required (1) that law enforcement authorities inform arrested foreign nationals of their right to notify their consulate of their detention, and if this was not done, (2) that the United States provide reconsideration of convictions without regard to state procedural default rules:a While the treaty "constitutes an *international* law obligation on the part of the United States," it is "not domestic law unless Congress has either enacted implementing statutes or the treaty itself conveys an intention that it be 'self-executing' and is ratified on these terms. * * * Because none of [the] treaty sources creates binding federal law in the absence of implementing legislation, and because it is uncontested that no such legislation exists, we conclude that the [ICJ's decision] is not automatically binding domestic law."

As for the President's independent constitutional power under Art.II, "given the absence of congressional legislation, [the] non-self-executing treaties at issue here did not 'express[ly] or implied[ly]' vest the President with the unilateral authority to make them self-executing. Accordingly, the President's Memorandum does not fall within the first category of the *Youngstown* framework. * * * When the President asserts the power to 'enforce' a non-self-executing treaty by unilaterally creating domestic law, he acts in conflict with the implicit understanding of the ratifying Senate [and] is therefore within Justice Jackson's third category, not the first or even the second."b

As for *Dames & Moore*, "the claims-settlement cases involve a narrow set of circumstances: the making of executive agreements to settle civil claims between American citizens and foreign governments or foreign nationals. They are based on the view that 'a systematic, unbroken, executive practice, long pursued to the

a. Petitioner, a Mexican national, was convicted of gang rape and murder and sentenced to death. Although he had been given the *Miranda* warnings prior to his confession, he was not informed of his Vienna Convention right. The Texas courts refused to consider this claim because he had not raised it in timely fashion.

b. Therefore, even if there were "congressional acquiescence" in respect to the Presi-

dent's action—"which does not exist here"—it would be of no consequence: "Under the *Youngstown* tripartite framework, congressional acquiescence is pertinent when the President's action falls within the second category—that is, when he 'acts in absence of either a congressional grant or denial of authority.' "

knowledge of the Congress and never before questioned,' can 'raise a presumption that the [action] had been [taken] in pursuance of its consent.' *Dames & Moore.* [The] President's Memorandum is not supported by a 'particularly longstanding practice' of congressional acquiescence, but rather is what the United States itself has described as 'unprecedented action.' Indeed, the Government has not identified a single instance in which the President has attempted (or Congress has acquiesced in) a Presidential directive issued to state courts, much less one that reaches deep into the heart of the State's police powers and compels state courts to reopen final criminal judgments and set aside neutrally applicable state laws. [The] Executive's narrow and strictly limited authority to settle international claims disputes pursuant to an executive agreement cannot stretch so far as to support the current Presidential Memorandum.''c

BREYER, J., joined by Souter and Ginsburg, JJ. dissented, concluding that "a strong line of precedent, likely reflecting the views of the Founders, indicates that the treaty provisions [and the ICJ judgment] address themselves to the Judicial Branch and consequently are self-executing." STEVENS, J., concurred in the Court's judgment, although agreeing largely with Breyer, J., because "the text and history of the Supremacy Clause, as well as this Court's treaty-related cases, do not support a presumption against self-execution. I also endorse the proposition that the [treaty] is itself self-executing and judicially enforceable." But its unclear language leaves the manner of compliance "to the political, not the judicial department."

II. EXTERNAL MATTERS: FOREIGN AFFAIRS AND WAR

UNITED STATES v. CURTISS–WRIGHT EXPORT CORP.

299 U.S. 304, 57 S.Ct. 216, 81 L.Ed. 255 (1936).

JUSTICE SUTHERLAND delivered the opinion of the Court.

[A joint resolution of Congress authorized the President to prohibit the sale of arms to Bolivia and Paraguay, which were engaged in armed conflict, if the President found that such prohibition would "contribute to the reestablishment of peace between those countries." The President proclaimed an embargo, and Curtiss–Wright was indicted for violating its terms. The lower court found the joint resolution an unconstitutional delegation of legislative power.]

The powers of the federal government in respect of foreign or external affairs and those in respect of domestic or internal affairs [are] different, both in respect of their origin and their nature. The broad statement that the federal government can exercise no powers except those specifically enumerated in the Constitution, and such implied powers as are necessary and proper to carry into effect the enumerated powers, is categorically true only in respect of our internal affairs.

As a result of the separation from Great Britain by the colonies acting as a unit, the powers of external sovereignty passed from the Crown not to the colonies severally, but to the colonies in their collective and corporate capacity as the United States of America. [The] powers to declare and wage war, to conclude peace, to make treaties, to maintain diplomatic relations with other sovereignties, if they had never been mentioned in the Constitution, would have vested in the federal government as necessary concomitants of nationality.

---

c. For further discussion of similar issues arising in connection with executive agree-   ments, see fn. d (last ¶), Sec. II infra.

[Another difference is that] participation in the exercise of power [over external affairs] is significantly limited. In this vast external realm, with its important, complicated, delicate and manifold problems, the President alone has the power to speak or listen as a representative of the nation. He *makes* treaties with the advice and consent of the Senate; but he alone negotiates [and] the Senate cannot intrude. [As] Marshall said [in] the House of Representatives, "The President is the sole organ of the nation in its external relations, and its sole representative with foreign nations."

It is important [that] we are here dealing not alone with an authority vested in the President by an exertion of legislative power, but with such an authority plus the very delicate, plenary and exclusive power of the President as the sole organ of the federal government in the field of international relations. [If] embarrassment—perhaps serious embarrassment—is to be avoided and success for our aims achieved, congressional legislation [must] often accord to the President a degree of discretion and freedom from statutory restriction which would not be admissible were domestic affairs alone involved. Moreover, he, not Congress, has the better opportunity of knowing the conditions which prevail in foreign countries, and especially is this true in time of war. He has his confidential sources of information. * * * Secrecy in respect of information gathered by them may be highly necessary. [In] the light of the foregoing observations, it is evident that this court should not be in haste to apply a general rule which will have the effect of condemning legislation like that under review as constituting an unlawful delegation of legislative power. * * *

Reversed.a

Notes

1. *Constitutional sources of power to wage war.* The phrase "war powers" does not appear in the Constitution. Art. I, § 8 authorizes Congress to "lay and collect Taxes, [to] provide for the common Defence" (cl. 1); to "declare War (cl. 11);" to "grant Letters of Marque and Reprisal (cl. 11);" to "raise and support Armies" (cl. 12); to "provide and maintain a Navy" (cl. 13); to "make Rules for the Government and Regulation of the land and naval Forces" (cl. 14); to "provide for calling forth the Militia to execute the Laws of the Union, suppress Insurrections and repel Invasions" (cl. 15); to "provide for organizing, arming, and disciplining, the Militia" (cl. 16); and (in § 9, cl. 2) to suspend the "privilege of the Writ of Habeas Corpus [in] Cases of Rebellion or Invasion." As for the President, Art. II, § 1, cl. 1 grants him the "executive Power," § 2, cl. 1 declares that he "shall be Commander in Chief of the Army and Navy of the United States, and of the Militia of the several States, when called into the actual Service of the United States," and § 3 charges the President to "take Care that the Laws be faithfully executed." Especially because relatively few Supreme Court opinions address foreign affairs or war powers, much modern debate involving a host of controversial issues has concerned the original understanding and historical practice.

2. *Executive agreements.* Executive agreements with foreign nations originally played a minor role as compared to treaties, but since World War II, they have overwhelmed the process. Between 1939–1989, the nation entered into 11,698 non-treaty agreements but only 702 treaties. These agreements often have been authorized or approved by congressional action or entered into pursuant to treaties. But from early days Presidents have entered into significant internation-

a. McReynolds, J., dissented without opin-   ion. Stone, J., did not participate.

al executive agreements strictly on their own authority. *United States v. Belmont*, 301 U.S. 324 (1937), *United States v. Pink*, 315 U.S. 203 (1942), and *Dames & Moore* upheld the President's authority to enter into such executive agreements without Senate or congressional approval.**b**

III. INDIVIDUAL RIGHTS AND THE WAR ON TERRORISM

HAMDI v. RUMSFELD, 542 U.S. 507 (2004): Hamdi is an American citizen who by 2001 resided in Afghanistan. In the immediate aftermath of the al Qaeda terrorist attacks of September 11, 2001, Congress authorized the President to "use all necessary and appropriate force" against "nations, organizations, or persons" that he determines "planned, authorized, committed, or aided" in the attacks. Authorization for Use of Military Force (AUMF). A short time later, the President ordered the Armed Forces to Afghanistan to subdue al Qaeda and oust the ruling Taliban regime. Hamdi was seized late in 2001 by the Northern Alliance, a military group opposed to the Taliban, and, according to a declaration by a Defense Department official, was turned over to the U.S. military as a Taliban fighter captured on the battlefield. He was initially taken to the American base at Guantanamo Bay, Cuba, but when it was learned that he was an American citizen, he was transferred to a naval brig in the United States.

Hamdi's father filed a habeas petition, alleging, inter alia, that the Government was holding his son in violation of the Due Process Clause. He also claimed that his son's detention was prohibited by the Non–Detention Act, 18 U.S.C. § 4001(a), which forbids any imprisonment or detention of an American citizen "except pursuant to an Act of Congress." Hamdi's father contended that less than two months before the September 11 attacks his son went to Afghanistan to do "relief work" and could not have received any military training.

There was no opinion of the Court. The principal opinion was written by O'CONNOR, J., joined by Rehnquist, C.J., and Kennedy and Breyer, JJ. She found that the initial detention of Hamdi was "explicitly authorized" by the AUMF, and thus the Non–Detention act was satisfied because Hamdi's detention was "pursuant to an Act of Congress": "We conclude that detention of individuals falling into the limited category we are considering [those 'who fought against the United States in Afghanistan as part of the Taliban'], for the duration of the particular conflict in which they were captured, is so fundamental and accepted an incident to war as to be an exercise of the 'necessary and appropriate force' Congress has authorized the President to use." But O'Connor, J., rejected the government's argument that Hamdi could be held indefinitely as an "enemy combatant," without formal charges or proceedings. Under the Due Process Clause, "the process due in any given instance is determined by weighing 'the private interest that will be affected by the official action' against the Government's asserted interest, 'including the function involved' and the burdens the Government would face in providing greater process. [A]s critical as the Government's interest may

b. *Belmont* and *Pink* involved the Soviet Union's assignment to the United States of amounts owed to it by American nationals so that outstanding claims of other American nationals could be paid. The Court ruled that the executive agreement became the "supreme Law of the Land," overriding New York's court-made policy not to recognize government appropriation of property. *Pink* explained: "The powers of the President in the conduct of foreign relations included the power, without consent of the Senate, to determine the public policy of the United States with respect to the Russian nationalization [decrees]. Power to remove such obstacles to full recognition as [claims settlement] certainly is a modest implied power of the President who is the 'sole organ of the federal government in the field of international relations.' *Curtiss-Wright*. Effectiveness in handling the delicate problems of foreign relations requires no [less]."

be in detaining those who actually pose an immediate threat to the national security of the United States during ongoing international conflict, history and common sense teach us that [i]t is during our most challenging and uncertain moments that our Nation's commitment to due process is most severely tested; and it is in those times that we must preserve our commitment at home to the principles for which we fight abroad.

"[We hold] that a citizen-detainee seeking to challenge his classification as an enemy combatant must receive notice of the factual basis for his classification, and a fair opportunity to rebut the Government's factual assertions before a neutral decisionmaker. [These] essential constitutional promises may not be eroded." Nonetheless, the plurality ruled that due process does not forbid some tailoring of the proceedings to alleviate burdens they may impose on Executive authority during an ongoing military conflict. This may include accepting some use of hearsay, permitting government rebuttable presumptions, and "there remains the possibility that the standards we have articulated could be met by an appropriately authorized and properly constituted military tribunal."

SOUTER, J., joined by Ginsburg, J., disagreed with the plurality that if Hamdi's designation as an enemy combatant were correct, his detention, at least for some period, was authorized by the AUMF. Thus, not only was detention of a citizen like Hamdi unauthorized by the AUMF, but it was forbidden by the Non–Detention Act of 1971 whose purpose was to avoid "a repetition of the World War II internment of citizens of Japanese ancestry; Congress meant to preclude another episode like the one described in *Korematsu v. United States* [Ch. 9, Sec. 2, II]." Therefore, Hamdi was entitled to immediate release. However, in order to "give practical effect" to the conclusions of eight Justices rejecting the government's position, Souter, J., "join[ed] with the plurality in ordering remand on terms closest to those I would impose. Although I think litigation of Hamdi's status as an enemy combatant is unnecessary, the terms of the plurality's remand will allow Hamdi to offer evidence that he is not an enemy combatant, and he should at the least have the benefit of that opportunity."

SCALIA, J., joined by Stevens, J., dissented: Absent suspension of the writ of habeas corpus by Congress, which no one claimed was done, an American citizen accused of waging war against his country could not be imprisoned indefinitely regardless of "the Executive's assertion of military exigency"; he had to be prosecuted for treason or some other crime.

THOMAS, J., dissenting, maintained that the Executive Branch had acted "with explicit congressional approval" and that Hamdi's detention "comports with the Due Process Clause" and "falls squarely within the Federal Government's war powers," and we lack the expertise and capacity to second-guess that decision. * * * I do not think that the Federal Government's war powers can be balanced away by this Court. * * * "Of all the cares or concerns of government, the direction of war most peculiarly demands those qualities which distinguish the exercise of power by a single hand." The Federalist No. 74, (A.Hamilton).

HAMDAN v. RUMSFELD, 548 U.S. 557 (2006): In November 2001, while the United States was engaged in active combat with the Taliban, the President issued the November 13 Order, which gave the Secretary of Defense the authority to appoint military commissions. Shortly after American forces invaded Afghanistan, militia forces captured Hamdan, a Yemini national, and turned him over to the Americans. Hamdan was then transported to Guantanamo. In July 2003, the

President announced his determination that Hamdan was subject to the November 13 Order and thus triable by military commission. A year later, he was charged with having conspired with al Quaeda to commit offenses "triable by military commission," including "attacking civilians" and "terrorism."

A 5–3 majority, per STEVENS, J., emphasized that the military commission at issue was not authorized by any congressional act: "Together, the Uniform Code of Military Justice (UCMJ), the Authorization for Use of Military Force (AUMF) and the Detainee Treatment Act of 2005 (DTA) at most acknowledge a general Presidential authority to convene military commissions where justified under the 'Constitution and Laws,' including the law of war."

Moreover, concluded the Court, "the UCMJ conditions the President's use of military commissions on compliance with the rest of the UCMJ itself and with the 'rules and precepts of the law of nations, including the four Geneva conventions signed in 1949.' [But] the procedure that the Government has decreed will govern Hamdan's trial by commission violate these laws. [At] a minimum, [a] military commission 'can be regularly constituted by' the standards of our military justice system only if some practical need explains deviation from court-martial practice [and] no such need has been demonstrated here."

The Court underscored the fact "that Hamdan does not challenge, and we do not address, the Government's power to detain him for the duration of active hostilities in order to prevent [great] harm. But in undertaking to try Hamdan and subject him to criminal punishment, the Executive is bound to comply with the Rule of Law that prevails in this jurisdiction."

BREYER, J., joined by Kennedy, Souter and Ginsburg, JJ., all of whom joined the Court's opinion, concurred: "Nothing prevents the President from returning to Congress to seek the authority he believes necessary. Where, as here, no emergency prevents consultation with Congress, judicial insistence upon that consultation does not weaken our Nation's ability to deal with danger. To the contrary, that insistence strengthens the Nation's ability to determine—through democratic means—how best to do so."

BOUMEDIENE v. BUSH

553 U.S. 723, 128 S.Ct. 2229, 171 L.Ed.2d 41 (2008).

JUSTICE KENNEDY delivered the opinion of the Court.

[In prosecuting the War on Terrorism, the United States has apprehended a number of foreign nationals that it has subsequently designated as "enemy combatants" and detained at the United States Naval Station at Guantanamo Bay, Cuba. In *Rasul v. Bush*, 542 U.S. 466 (2004), the Court held that the then existing statutory scheme vested the United States district court in Washington, D.C., with statutory habeas corpus jurisdiction to review the lawfulness of the Guantanamo detainees' incarceration as enemy combatants. In response to *Rasul* and *Hamdan v. Rumsfeld*, Congress enacted the Military Commissions Act of 2006 (MCA), which purported to strip all United States courts of habeas corpus jurisdiction over the Guantanamo detainees. As a substitute for habeas corpus–the traditional mechanism by which courts have ruled on the lawfulness of executive detentions of persons not convicted of crimes by civilian courts–Congress provided a limited form of review by the D.C. Circuit over decisions of Combatant Status Review Tribunals (CSRTs) that had been set up by the Department of Defense under the Detainee Treatment Act of 2005 (DTA). The D.C. Circuit could exercise review only after the CSRTs had found detention to be warranted on the ground that the detainees were enemy combatants, with review limited to whether the

CSRTs had acted in accordance with applicable law and procedures specified by the Secretary of Defense.

[Petitioners argue that the MCA's withdrawal of habeas corpus jurisdiction violate the Suspension Clause, Art. I, § 9, cl. 2, which provides that "The Privilege of the Writ of Habeas Corpus shall not be suspended, unless when in Cases of Rebellion or Invasion, the public Safety may require it," and thereby implicitly guarantees that the writ must be available unless Congress validly suspends it. In response, the Government did not argue that Congress had invoked its Art. I, § 9, cl. 2 power to suspend the writ on grounds of "Rebellion or Invasion," but contended instead that the Suspension Clause did not guarantee the availability of the writ to noncitizens held outside the United States and thus conferred no right on petitioners. Even if the Clause did apply, the Government argued, withdrawal of habeas jurisdiction did not violate it, because the DTA provided enough judicial review to qualify as a constitutionally adequate substitute for habeas corpus.

[The Suspension Clause ensures] that, except during periods of formal suspension, the Judiciary will have a time-tested device, the writ, to maintain the delicate balance of governance that is itself the surest safeguard of liberty. [The] Court has been careful not to foreclose the possibility that the protections of the Suspension Clause have expanded along with post–1789 developments that define the present scope of the writ. See *INS* v. *St. Cyr*, 533 U. S. 289, 300–301 (2001). But the analysis may begin with precedents as of 1789, for the Court has said that "at the absolute minimum" the Clause protects the writ as it existed when the Constitution was drafted and ratified. Id.

[In] none of the cases cited [by the parties] do we find that a common-law court would or would not have granted, or refused to hear for lack of jurisdiction, a petition for a writ of habeas corpus brought by a prisoner deemed an enemy combatant, under a standard like the one the Department of Defense has used in these cases, and when held in a territory, like Guantanamo, over which the Government has total military and civil control.

We know that at common law a petitioner's status as an alien was not a categorical bar to habeas corpus relief. [T]he Government says the Suspension Clause affords petitioners no rights because the United States does not claim sovereignty over the place of detention. [Admittedly,] Guantanamo Bay is not formally part of the United States. And under the terms of the lease between the United States and Cuba, Cuba retains ultimate sovereignty over the territory while the United States exercises complete jurisdiction and control. [But] the history of common-law habeas corpus provides scant support for [the proposition that de jure sovereignty is the touchstone of habeas corpus jurisdiction, and] that position would be inconsistent with our precedents and contrary to fundamental separation-of-powers principles.

[Fundamental] questions regarding the Constitution's geographic scope first arose at the dawn of the 20th century when the Nation [acquired] Puerto Rico, Guam, and the Philippines [at] the conclusion of the Spanish–American War. [In] a series of opinions later known as the *Insular Cases*, the [Court] held that the Constitution has independent force in these territories. [Yet the Court was wary of applying the Anglo–American legal tradition (for example, the use of grand and petit juries) to territories that followed the civil law system, especially when, as with the Philippines, the United States intended to grant independence to the territory.] These considerations resulted in the doctrine of territorial incorporation, under which the Constitution applies in full in incorporated Territories surely destined for statehood but only in part [and mostly in cases involving fundamental rights] in unincorporated Territories.

[Practical] considerations weighed heavily as well in *Johnson* v. *Eisentrager*, 339 U. S. 763 (1950), where the Court addressed whether habeas corpus jurisdiction extended to enemy aliens who had been convicted of violating the laws of war. The prisoners were detained at Landsberg Prison in Germany during the Allied Powers' postwar occupation. The Court stressed the difficulties of ordering the Government to produce the prisoners in a habeas corpus proceeding. It "would require allocation of shipping space, guarding personnel, billeting and rations" and would damage the prestige of military commanders at a sensitive time.

[True,] the Court in *Eisentrager* denied access to the writ, and it noted the prisoners "at no relevant time were within any territory over which the United States is sovereign, and [that] the scenes of their offense, their capture, their trial and their punishment were all beyond the territorial jurisdiction of any court of the United States." 339 U. S., at 778. The Government seizes upon this language as proof positive that the *Eisentrager* Court adopted a formalistic, sovereignty-based test for determining the reach of the Suspension Clause. We reject this reading.

[Because] the United States lacked both de jure sovereignty and plenary control over Landsberg Prison, it is far from clear that the *Eisentrager* Court used the term sovereignty only in the narrow technical sense. [Moreover, the Government's reading] of *Eisentrager* overlooks [a] common thread uniting the *Insular Cases* and *Eisentrager*, [namely] the idea that questions of extraterritoriality turn on objective factors and practical concerns, not formalism.

The Government's formal sovereignty-based test raises troubling separation-of-powers concerns as well. [If the Constitution had no effect at Guantanamo Bay, at least as to noncitizens, because the United States disclaimed formal sovereignty, then the political branches would be able to govern without legal constraint by surrendering formal sovereignty over any unincorporated territory to a third party, while at the same time entering into a lease that grants total control over the territory back to the United States.] Our basic charter cannot be contracted away like this.

Based on [language] from *Eisentrager*, and the reasoning in our other extraterritoriality opinions, we conclude that at least three factors are relevant in determining the reach of the Suspension Clause: (1) the citizenship and status of the detainee and the adequacy of the process through which that status determination was made; (2) the nature of the sites where apprehension and then detention took place; and (3) the practical obstacles inherent in resolving the prisoners entitlement to the writ.

Applying this framework, we note [that the detainees here, unlike those in *Eisentrager*, deny they are enemy combatants. Moreover, whereas the *Eisentrager* petitioners were represented by counsel and could introduce evidence on their own behalf and could cross-examine the prosecution's witnesses,] the procedural protections afforded to the detainees in the CSRT hearings are far more limited, and [fall] well short of the procedures and adversarial mechanisms that would eliminate the need for habeas corpus review. Although the detainee is assigned a "Personal Representative" to assist him during CSRT proceedings, [that] person is not the detainee's lawyer or even his "advocate." The Government's evidence is accorded a presumption of validity.

[With respect to the sites of the petitioners' apprehension and detention], Guantanamo Bay [is] no transient possession. In every practical sense Guantanamo is not abroad; it is within the constant jurisdiction of the United States.

As to the third factor, we recognize, as the Court did in *Eisentrager*, that there are costs to holding the Suspension Clause applicable in a case of military detention abroad, [but] we do not find them dispositive. [The] Government presents no credible arguments that the military mission at Guantanamo would be compromised if habeas corpus courts had jurisdiction to hear the detainees' claims.

[It] is true that before today the Court has never held that noncitizens detained by our Government in territory over which another country maintains de jure sovereignty have any rights under our Constitution. But the cases before us lack any precise historical parallel.

[Because we] hold that Art. I, § 9, cl. 2, of the Constitution has full effect at Guantanamo Bay [and that this] Court may not impose a de facto suspension by abstaining from these controversies, the question becomes whether [Congress] has provided adequate substitute procedures for habeas corpus. [We] do not endeavor to offer a comprehensive summary of the requisites for an adequate substitute for habeas corpus. We do consider it uncontroversial, however, that the privilege of habeas corpus entitles the prisoner to a meaningful opportunity to demonstrate that he is being held pursuant to "the erroneous application or interpretation" of relevant law.

[To] determine the necessary scope of habeas corpus review, therefore, we must assess the CSRT process. [The] Government [argues that the CSRT scheme under which determinations of enemy combatants status are initially made by military tribunals] was designed to conform to the procedures suggested by the plurality in *Hamdi v. Rumsfeld* as providing the requisites of due process to a citizen detained within the United States as an enemy combatant. But even] if we were to assume that the CSRTs satisfy due process standards, [habeas] corpus is a collateral process that exists, in Justice Holmes' words, to "cu[t] through all forms and g[o] to the very tissue of the structure. It comes in from the outside, not in subordination to the proceedings, and although every form may have been preserved opens the inquiry whether they have been more than an empty shell." *Frank* v. *Mangum*, 237 U. S. 309, 346 (1915) (dissenting opinion). Even when the procedures authorizing detention are structurally sound, the Suspension Clause remains applicable and the writ relevant.

[We can assume that the DTA may be read to authorize the Court of Appeals to order the release of an applicant, even though the statute does not explicitly so provide. And the DTA might be read to permit judicial review of] most, if not all, of the legal claims [the petitioners] seek to advance, including their most basic claim: that the President has no authority under the AUMF to detain them indefinitely.

[More] difficult [is] whether the DTA permits the Court of Appeals to make requisite findings of fact. [But assuming] the DTA can be construed to allow the Court of Appeals to review or correct the CSRT's factual determinations, as opposed to merely certifying that the tribunal applied the correct standard of proof, we see no way to construe the statute to allow what is also constitutionally required in this context: an opportunity for the detainee to present relevant exculpatory evidence that was not made part of the record in the earlier proceedings. [N]ewly discovered evidence [may] be critical to the detainee's argument that he is not an enemy combatant and there is no cause to detain him.

[We] do not imply DTA review would be a constitutionally sufficient replacement for habeas corpus but for these limitations on the detainee's ability to present exculpatory evidence. For even if it were possible [to] read into the statute each of the necessary procedures we have identified, [the] cumulative effect of [holding] that the detainees at Guantanamo may, under the DTA, challenge the President's legal authority to detain them, contest the CSRT's findings of fact, supplement the record on review with exculpatory evidence, and request an order of release would come close to reinstating the § 2241 habeas corpus process Congress sought to deny them. The language of the statute, read in light of Congress' reasons for enacting it, cannot bear this interpretation.

[T]he question remains whether there are prudential barriers to habeas corpus review under these circumstances. [It likely would be an impractical and unprecedented extension of judicial power to make habeas corpus available at the moment a foreign citizen is detained abroad by the Executive. Proper] deference can be accorded to reasonable procedures for screening and initial detention under lawful and proper conditions of confinement and treatment for a reasonable period of time. [The] cases before us, however, do not involve detainees who have been held for a short period of time while awaiting their CSRT determinations. [And] there has been no showing that the Executive faces such onerous burdens that it cannot respond to habeas corpus actions. To require these detainees to complete DTA review before proceeding with their habeas corpus actions would be to require additional months, if not years, of delay.

[The] only law we identify as unconstitutional is [the provision of the MCA barring habeas review.] Accordingly, both the DTA and the CSRT process remain intact. [Moreover, except] in cases of undue delay, federal courts should refrain from entertaining an enemy combatant's habeas corpus petition at least until after the Department, acting via the CSRT, has had a chance to review his status.

[We] make no attempt to anticipate all of the evidentiary and access-to-counsel issues that will arise during the course of the detainees habeas corpus proceedings. We recognize, however, that the Government has a legitimate interest in protecting sources and methods of intelligence gathering; and we expect that the District Court will use its discretion to accommodate this interest to the greatest extent possible. These and the other remaining questions are within the expertise and competence of the District Court to address in the first instance.

[In considering the procedural and substantive standards used to detain and to prevent terrorist acts, the Executive, which, unlike the judiciary, has access to intelligence, should be accorded substantial deference. But security depends not only on the actions of intelligence and military officials, but also on] fidelity to freedom's first principles. Chief among these are freedom from arbitrary and unlawful restraint and the personal liberty that is secured by adherence to the separation of powers. [The] laws and Constitution are designed to survive, and remain in force, in extraordinary times. Liberty and security can be reconciled; and in our system they are reconciled within the framework of the law. The Framers decided that habeas corpus, a right of first importance, must be a part of that framework. * * *

CHIEF JUSTICE ROBERTS, with whom JUSTICE SCALIA, JUSTICE THOMAS, and JUSTICE ALITO join, dissenting.

[The] critical threshold question in these cases, prior to any inquiry about the writ's scope, is whether the system the political branches designed protects whatever rights the detainees may possess. [If] the CSRT procedures meet the minimal due process requirements outlined in *Hamdi*, and if an Article III court is available to ensure that these procedures are followed in future cases, there is no need to reach the Suspension Clause question. [And the existing system] is adequate to vindicate whatever due process rights petitioners may have. * * *

Because the central purpose of habeas corpus is to test the legality of executive detention, the writ requires most fundamentally an Article III court able to hear the petitioner's claims and, when necessary, order release. [Beyond] that, the process a given prisoner is entitled to receive depends on the circumstances and the rights of the prisoner. After much hemming and hawing, the majority appears to concede that the DTA provides an Article III court competent to order release. The only issue in dispute is the process the Guantanamo prisoners are entitled to use to test the legality of their detention. *Hamdi* concluded that American citizens detained as enemy combatants are entitled to only limited process, and that much of that process could be supplied by a military tribunal, with review to follow in an Article III court. That is precisely the system we have here. It is adequate to vindicate whatever due process rights petitioners may have. * * *

[The] scope of federal habeas review is traditionally more limited in some contexts than in others, depending on the status of the detainee and the rights he may assert. [And] the DTA [provides] more opportunity and more process, in fact, than that afforded prisoners of war or any other alleged enemy combatants in history.

Despite these guarantees, the Court finds the DTA system an inadequate habeas substitute, for one central reason: Detainees are unable to introduce at the appeal stage exculpatory evidence discovered after the conclusion of their CSRT proceedings. The Court hints darkly that the DTA may suffer from other infirmities, [but] it does not bother to name them. [The flaw in its reasoning is that if new evidence materializes *after* the CSRT's determination but before review in the Court of Appeals, the DTA permits the D.C. Circuit to remand to for a new CSRT determination.] The Court objects to the detainees' limited access to witnesses and classified material, but proposes no alternatives of its own. Indeed, it simply ignores the many difficult questions its holding presents. What, for example, will become of the CSRT process? The majority says federal courts should *generally* refrain from entertaining detainee challenges until after the petitioner's CSRT proceeding has finished. [But] to what deference, if any, is that CSRT determination entitled?

There are other problems. Take witness availability. What makes the majority think witnesses will become magically available when the review procedure is labeled "habeas"? Will the location of most of these witnesses change?—will they suddenly become easily susceptible to service of process? * * * Speaking of witnesses, will detainees be able to call active-duty military officers as witnesses? If not, why not?

The majority has no answers for these difficulties. What it does say leaves open the distinct possibility that its "habeas" remedy will, when all is said and done, end up looking a great deal like the DTA review it rejects. * * *

So who has won? Not the detainees. The Court's analysis leaves them with only the prospect of further litigation to determine the content of their new habeas right, followed by further litigation to resolve their particular cases, followed by further litigation before the D. C. Circuit—where they could have started had they invoked the DTA procedure. Not Congress, whose attempt to "determine—through democratic means—how best" to balance the security of the American people with the detainees liberty interests has been unceremoniously brushed aside. Not the Great Writ, whose majesty is hardly enhanced by its extension to a jurisdictionally quirky outpost, with no tangible benefit to anyone.

Not the rule of law, unless by that is meant the rule of lawyers, who will now arguably have a greater role than military and intelligence officials in shaping policy for alien enemy combatants. And certainly not the American people, who today lose a bit more control over the conduct of this Nation's foreign policy to unelected, politically unaccountable judges. * * *

JUSTICE SCALIA, with whom THE CHIEF JUSTICE, JUSTICE THOMAS, and JUSTICE ALITO join, dissenting.

[The] writ of habeas corpus does not, and never has, run in favor of aliens abroad; the Suspension Clause thus has no application, and the Court's intervention in this military matter is entirely ultra vires.

[The terrorist threat is grave, and the Court's opinion] will make the war harder on us. It will almost certainly cause more Americans to be killed. [At least 30 of the prisoners previously released from Guantanamo Bay have returned to the battlefield, and some have committed atrocities. And these] were detainees whom *the military* had concluded were not enemy combatants. Their return to the kill illustrates the incredible difficulty of assessing who is and who is not an enemy combatant in a foreign theater of operations where the environment does not lend itself to rigorous evidence collection. Astoundingly, the Court today raises the bar, requiring military officials to appear before civilian courts and defend their decisions under procedural and evidentiary rules that go beyond what Congress has specified.

[But] even when the military has evidence that it can bring forward, it is often foolhardy to release that evidence to the attorneys representing our enemies. [During] the 1995 prosecution of Omar Abdel Rahman, federal prosecutors gave the names of 200 unindicted co-conspirators to the "Blind Sheik's" defense lawyers; that information was in the hands of Osama Bin Laden within two weeks. In another case, trial testimony revealed to the enemy that the United States had been monitoring their cellular network, whereupon they promptly stopped using it, enabling more of them to evade capture and continue their atrocities.

[What] competence does the Court have to second-guess the judgment of Congress and the President on [the questions in issue with respect to the necessity and wisdom of the scheme that Congress created]? None whatever.

[The] Court admits that it cannot determine whether the writ historically extended to aliens held abroad, and it concedes (necessarily) that Guantanamo Bay lies outside the sovereign territory of the United States. Together, these two concessions establish that it is (in the Court's view) perfectly ambiguous whether the common-law writ would have provided a remedy for these petitioners. If that is so, the Court has no basis to strike down the Military Commissions Act, and must leave undisturbed the considered judgment of the coequal branches.

[The Court relies on *Eisentrager*, from which it purports to derive a "functional" test for the extraterritorial reach of the writ, but its claim of support is falsified by the plain language of Justice Jackson's Court opinion]: "We are cited to no instance where a court, in this or any other country where the writ is known, has issued it on behalf of an alien enemy who, at no relevant time and in no stage of his captivity, has been within its territorial jurisdiction. Nothing in the text of the Constitution extends such a right, nor does anything in our statutes." [*Eisentrager*] mentioned practical concerns [only] to support *its holding* that the Constitution does not empower courts to issue writs of habeas corpus to aliens abroad *in any circumstances*. [And the *Insular Cases* are similarly inapposite because they all concerned sovereign territories of the United States.]

What drives today's decision is neither the meaning of the Suspension Clause, nor the principles of our precedents, but rather an inflated notion of judicial supremacy. The Court says that if the extraterritorial applicability of the Suspension Clause turned on formal notions of sovereignty, "it would be possible for the political branches to govern without legal constraint" in areas beyond the sovereign territory of the United States. That cannot be, the Court says, because it is the duty of this Court to say what the law is. It would be difficult to imagine a more question-begging analysis. [Our] power "to say what the law is" is circumscribed by the limits of our statutorily and constitutionally conferred jurisdiction. [And] that is precisely the question in these cases: whether the Constitution confers habeas jurisdiction on federal courts to decide petitioners' claims. It is both irrational and arrogant to say that the answer must be yes, because otherwise we would not be supreme.

[Putting] aside the conclusive precedent of *Eisentrager*, it is clear that the original understanding of the Suspension Clause was that habeas corpus was not available to aliens abroad. [The] Court finds it significant that there is no recorded case *denying* jurisdiction to such prisoners. [But] a case standing for the remarkable proposition that the writ could issue to a foreign land would surely have been reported, whereas a case denying such a writ for lack of jurisdiction would likely not. At a minimum, the absence of a reported case either way leaves unrefuted the voluminous commentary stating that habeas was confined to the dominions of the Crown. * * *

Today [the Court] breaks a chain of precedent as old as the common law that prohibits judicial inquiry into detentions of aliens abroad absent a statutory authorization. And, most tragically, it sets our military commanders the impossible task of proving to a civilian court, under whatever standards the Court devises in the future, that evidence supports the confinement of each and every prisoner.

The Nation will live to regret what the Court has done today. * * *

SECTION 2. CONGRESSIONAL ACTION AFFECTING "PRESIDENTIAL" POWERS

I. DELEGATION OF RULEMAKING POWER

YAKUS v. UNITED STATES, 321 U.S. 414 (1944): The World War II emergency price control act authorized the president-appointed administrator to issue regulations establishing maximum prices and rents to carry out the act's purposes "to stabilize prices and to prevent speculative, unwarranted, and abnormal increases in prices and rents; [and] protect persons with relatively fixed and limited incomes [from] undue impairment of their standard of living * * *." When in the administrator's judgment prices "have risen or threaten to rise in a manner inconsistent with the purposes of this act," the administrator was to establish maximum prices and rents that "in his judgment [would] be generally fair and equitable [and] effectuate the purposes of this act." So far as practicable, the administrator was to "give due consideration to the prices prevailing between October 1 and October 15, 1941" and to "make adjustments for such relevant factors as he may determine and deem to be of general applicability." The Court, per STONE, C.J., upheld this delegation: "The Act [is] an exercise by Congress of its legislative power. In it Congress has stated the legislative objective, has prescribed the method of achieving that objective—maximum price fixing—, and has laid down standards to guide the administrative determination of both the occasions for the exercise of the price-fixing power, and the particular prices to be established.

"The Act is unlike the National Industrial Recovery Act [in] *Schechter Poultry Corp.*, [Ch. 2, Sec. 2, III, A], which proclaimed in the broadest terms its purpose 'to rehabilitate industry and to conserve natural resources.' It prescribed no method of attaining that end save by the establishment of codes of fair competition, the nature of whose permissible provisions was left undefined. It provided no standards to which those codes were to conform.

"[The] Constitution as a continuously operative charter of government does not demand the impossible or the impracticable. It does not require that Congress find for itself every fact upon which it desires to base legislative action or that it make for itself detailed determinations which it has declared to be prerequisite to the application of the legislative policy to particular facts and circumstances impossible for Congress itself properly to investigate. The essentials of the legislative function are the determination of the legislative policy and its formulation and promulgation as a defined and binding rule of conduct. [These] essentials are preserved when Congress has specified the basic conditions of fact upon whose existence or occurrence, ascertained from relevant data by a designated administrative agency, it directs that its statutory command shall be effective. It is no objection that the determination of facts and the inferences to be drawn from them in the light of the statutory standards and declaration of policy call for the exercise of judgment, and for the formulation of subsidiary administrative policy within the prescribed statutory framework." Only Roberts, J., dissented on the delegation issue.a

––––––––

WHITMAN v. AMERICAN TRUCKING ASSN'S, INC., 531 U.S. 457 (2001), per SCALIA, J. held that the Clean Air Act's delegation to the EPA to set air quality standards—"the attainment and maintenance of which [are] requisite to protect the public health" with "an adequate margin of safety"—stated an "intelligible principle." THOMAS, J., agreed, but was "not convinced that the intelligible principle doctrine serves to prevent all cessions of legislative power. [On] a future [day], I would be willing to address the question whether our delegation jurisprudence has strayed too far from our Founders' understanding of separation of powers."

––––––––

The broad scope of Congress' power to delegate in the modern administrative state is further emphasized by CHEVRON U.S.A. INC. v. NATURAL RESOURCES DEFENSE COUNCIL, INC., 467 U.S. 837 (1984), as elaborated in UNITED STATES v. MEAD, 533 U.S. 218 (2001), which concern a federal agency's interpretation of a statutory authorization when "Congress has not directly addressed the precise question at issue." The Court held that "if Congress has explicitly left a gap for the agency to fill," the agency's interpretations of its governing statute are valid "unless they are procedurally arbitrary, capricious, or manifestly contrary to the statute"; if the delegation is "implicit rather than

––––––––

a. In only two cases, both involving New Deal legislation, has the Court invalidated congressional delegation of legislative power to a federal officer or agency. *Schechter*, supra; *Panama Refining Co. v. Ryan*, 293 U.S. 388 (1935). See also *Carter v. Carter Coal Co.*, Ch. 2, Sec. 2, III, A, invalidating a congressional delegation to a private industry association with a potentially adverse interest to the objects of the regulation.

explicit," the agency's interpretation is valid if "reasonable." If the authorization is neither explicit nor implicit, "considerable weight should be accorded to an executive department's construction of a statutory scheme it is entrusted to administer," with the outcome ultimately based on multiple factors. In addition to this judicial "deference" to the agency's interpretations, "an agency to which Congress has delegated policymaking responsibilities may, within the limits of that delegation, properly rely upon the incumbent administration's views of wise policy to inform its judgments. While agencies are not directly accountable to the people, the Chief Executive is, and it is entirely appropriate for this political branch of the Government to make such policy choices—resolving the competing interests which Congress itself either inadvertently did not resolve, or intentionally left to be resolved by the agency charged with the administration of the statute in light of everyday realities."

II. LEGISLATIVE AND LINE ITEM VETOES

INS v. CHADHA

462 U.S. 919, 103 S.Ct. 2764, 77 L.Ed.2d 317 (1983).

CHIEF JUSTICE BURGER delivered the opinion of the Court.

[The Immigration and Nationality Act authorized the Attorney General to suspend deportation of a deportable alien if he met specified conditions and would suffer "extreme hardship" if deported. It required a report to Congress on each suspension. Sec. 244(c)(2) provided that if, within a specified period thereafter, either house of Congress "passes a resolution stating [that] it does not favor the suspension [the] Attorney General shall thereupon deport such alien." The Attorney General suspended the deportation of Chadha. Accepting a House Committee's conclusion that Chadha did not satisfy the hardship requirements, the House of Representatives passed a resolution that the "deportation should not be suspended." It was not submitted to the Senate, nor "presented to the President" under Art. I, § 7.]

Although not "hermetically" sealed from one another, the powers delegated to the three Branches are functionally identifiable. [Whether] actions taken by either House are, in law and fact, an exercise of legislative power depends not on their form but upon "whether they contain matter which is properly to be regarded as legislative in its character and effect."

[In] purporting to exercise power defined in Art. I, § 8, cl. 4, to "establish an uniform Rule of Naturalization," the House took action that had the purpose and effect of altering the legal rights, duties, and relations of persons, including the Attorney General, Executive Branch officials and Chadha, all outside the legislative branch. [The] one-House veto operated in [this case] to overrule the Attorney General and mandate Chadha's deportation; absent the House action, Chadha would remain in the United States. Congress has *acted* and its action has altered Chadha's status.

The legislative character of the one-House veto in [this case] is confirmed by the character of the congressional action it supplants. Neither the House of Representatives nor the Senate contends that, absent the veto provision in § 244(c)(2), either of them, or both of them acting together, could effectively require the Attorney General to deport an alien once the Attorney General, in the exercise of legislatively delegated authority,[16] had determined the alien should

---

16. Congress protests that affirming the Court of Appeals in [favor of Chadha] will   sanction "lawmaking by the Attorney General." * * * Executive action under legislatively

remain in the United States. Without the challenged provision in § 244(c)(2), this could have been achieved, if at all, only by legislation requiring deportation. * * *

The nature of the decision implemented by the one-House veto in [this case] further manifests its legislative character. After long experience with the clumsy, time-consuming private bill procedure, Congress made a deliberate choice to delegate to [the] Attorney General, the authority to allow deportable aliens to remain in this country in certain specified circumstances. [Disagreement] with the Attorney General's decision on Chadha's deportation—that is, Congress' decision to deport Chadha—no less than Congress' original choice to delegate to the Attorney General the authority to make that decision, involves determinations of policy that Congress can implement in only one way; bicameral passage followed by presentment to the President. Congress must abide by its delegation of authority until that delegation is legislatively altered or revoked.19

Finally, we see that when the Framers intended to authorize either House of Congress to act alone and outside of its prescribed bicameral legislative role, they narrowly and precisely defined the procedure for such action. There are [only] four provisions in the Constitution, explicit and unambiguous, by which one House may act alone with the unreviewable force of law, not subject to the President's veto: [the House of Representatives' power to initiate impeachments, and the Senate's powers to try impeachments, to approve presidential appointments, and to ratify treaties.]

The bicameral requirement, the Presentment Clauses, the President's veto, and Congress' power to override a veto were intended to erect enduring checks on each Branch and to protect the people from the improvident exercise of power by mandating certain prescribed steps. To preserve those checks, and maintain the separation of powers, the carefully defined limits on the power of each Branch must not be eroded. [In] purely practical terms, it is obviously easier for action to be taken by one House without submission to the President; but it is crystal clear from the records of the Convention, contemporaneous writings and debates, that the Framers ranked other values higher than efficiency. * * *

The choices we discern as having been made in the Constitutional Convention [were] consciously made by men who had lived under a form of government that permitted arbitrary governmental acts to go unchecked. There is no support in the

delegated authority that might resemble "legislative" action in some respects is not subject to the approval of both Houses of Congress and the President for the reason that the Constitution does not so require. That kind of Executive action is always subject to check by the terms of the legislation that authorized it; and if that authority is exceeded it is open to judicial review as well as the power of Congress to modify or revoke the authority entirely. A one-House veto is clearly legislative in both character and effect and is not so checked; the need for the check provided by Art. I, §§ 1, 7, is therefore clear. Congress' authority to delegate portions of its power to administrative agencies provides no support for the argument that Congress can constitutionally control administration of the laws by way of a Congressional veto.

19. This does not mean that Congress is required to capitulate to "the accretion of policy control by forces outside its chambers." [Beyond] the obvious fact that Congress ultimately controls administrative agencies in the legislation that creates them, other means of control, such as durational limits on authorizations and formal reporting requirements, lie well within Congress' constitutional power. See also n.9, supra.

[Fn. 9 stated: "Without the one-House veto, § 244 resembles the 'report and wait' provision approved by the Court in *Sibbach v. Wilson & Co.*, 312 U.S. 1 (1941). [The statute in] *Sibbach* did *not* provide that Congress could unilaterally veto the Federal Rules. Rather, it gave Congress the opportunity to review the Rules before they became effective and to pass legislation barring their effectiveness if the Rules were found objectionable. This technique was used by Congress when it acted in 1973 to stay, and ultimately to revise, the proposed Rules of Evidence."]

Constitution or decisions of this Court for the proposition that the cumbersomeness and delays often encountered in complying with explicit constitutional standards may be avoided, either by the Congress or by the President. * * *

JUSTICE POWELL concurring in the judgment.

[In] my view, the case [may] be decided on a narrower ground. When Congress finds that a particular person does not satisfy the statutory criteria for permanent residence in this country it has assumed a judicial function in violation of the principle of separation of powers. [The Framers'] concern that a legislature should not be able unilaterally to impose a substantial deprivation on one person was expressed not only in [the] general allocation of power, but also in more specific provisions, such as the Bill of Attainder Clause, Art. I, § 9, cl. 3 [,both of which] reflect the Framers' concern that trial by a legislature lacks the safeguards necessary to prevent the abuse of power. * * *

JUSTICE WHITE dissenting. * * *

The prominence of the legislative veto mechanism in our contemporary political system [has] become a central means by which Congress secures the accountability of executive and independent agencies. Without the legislative veto, Congress is faced with a Hobson's choice: either to refrain from delegating the necessary authority, leaving itself with a hopeless task of writing laws with the requisite specificity to cover endless special circumstances across the entire policy landscape, or in the alternative, to abdicate its lawmaking function to the Executive Branch and independent agencies. To choose the former leaves major national problems unresolved; to opt for the latter risks unaccountable policymaking by those not elected to fill that role. Accordingly, over the past five decades, the legislative veto has been placed in nearly 200 statutes. The device is known in every field of governmental concern: reorganization, budgets, foreign affairs, war powers, and regulation of trade, safety, energy, the environment, and the economy. [T]he increasing reliance of Congress upon the legislative veto suggests that the alternatives to which Congress must now turn are not entirely satisfactory.10

The history of the legislative veto also makes clear that it has not been a sword with which Congress has struck out to aggrandize itself at the expense of the other branches—the concerns of Madison and Hamilton. Rather, the veto has been a means of defense, a reservation of ultimate authority necessary if Congress is to fulfill its designated role under Art. I as the Nation's lawmaker. While the President has often objected to particular legislative vetoes, generally those left in the hands of congressional Committees, the Executive has more often agreed to legislative review as the price for a broad delegation of authority. * * *

I do not dispute the Court's truismatic exposition of [the prerequisites for lawmaking set forth in Art. I of the Constitution.] [But the] power to exercise a legislative veto is not the power to write new law without bicameral approval or Presidential consideration. The veto must be authorized by statute and may only negative what an Executive department or independent agency has proposed. On its face, the legislative veto no more allows one House of Congress to make law than does the Presidential veto confer such power upon the President. * * *

If Congress may delegate lawmaking power to independent and Executive agencies, it is most difficult to understand Art. I as prohibiting Congress from also reserving a check on legislative power for itself. Absent the veto, the agencies

---

10. While Congress could write certain statutes with greater specificity, it is unlikely that this is a realistic or even desirable substitute for the legislative veto. [Political volatility] and [t]he controversial nature of many issues would prevent Congress from reaching agreement on many major problems if specificity were required in their enactments.

receiving delegations of legislative or quasi-legislative power may issue regulations having the force of law without bicameral approval and without the President's signature. It is thus not apparent why the reservation of a veto over the exercise of that legislative power must be subject to a more exacting test. In both cases, it is enough that the initial statutory authorizations comply with the Art. I requirements. * * *

The central concern of the presentation and bicameralism requirements of Art. I is that when a departure from the legal status quo is undertaken, it is done with the approval of the President and both Houses of Congress—or, in the event of a Presidential veto, a two-thirds majority in both Houses. This interest is fully satisfied by the operation of § 244(c)(2). The President's approval is found in the Attorney General's action in recommending to Congress that the deportation order for a given alien be suspended. The House and the Senate indicate their approval of the Executive's action by not passing a resolution of disapproval within the statutory period. Thus, a change in the legal status quo—the deportability of the alien—is consummated only with the approval of each of the three relevant actors. The disagreement of any one of the three maintains the alien's pre-existing status* * *.

———

Two weeks after *Chadha,* PROCESS GAS CONSUMERS GROUP v. CONSUMER ENERGY COUNCIL OF AMERICA, 463 U.S. 1216 (1983), summarily affirmed decisions invalidating a one-house legislative veto of regulatory rulemaking by the Federal Energy Regulatory Commission and a two-house veto of such rulemaking by the Federal Trade Commission. Rehnquist, J., would have noted probable jurisdiction and set the cases for oral argument. Powell, J., took no part. WHITE, J., dissented: "Where the veto is placed as a check upon the actions of the independent regulatory agencies, the Art. I analysis relied upon in *Chadha* has a particularly hollow ring. [These] regulations have the force of law without the President's concurrence; nor can he veto. [To] invalidate the [legislative veto,] which allows Congress to maintain some control over the lawmaking process, merely guarantees that the independent agencies, once created, for all practical purposes are a fourth branch of the Government not subject to the direct control of either Congress or the Executive Branch."

———

CLINTON v. NEW YORK, 524 U.S. 417 (1998), per STEVENS, J., invalidated the Line Item Veto Act which gave the President the power to "cancel" certain expenditures and tax benefits that have been enacted by Congress and signed into law: "The Act requires the President [to] determine, with respect to each cancellation, that it will '(i) reduce the Federal budget deficit; (ii) not impair any essential Government functions; and (iii) not harm the national interest.' Moreover, he must transmit a special message to Congress notifying it of each cancellation within five calendar days. [If] a 'disapproval bill' pertaining to a special message is enacted into law, the cancellations set forth in that message become 'null and void.'

"[There] are important differences between the President's 'return' of a bill pursuant to Article I, § 7, and the exercise of the President's cancellation authority pursuant to the Line Item Veto Act. The constitutional return takes place before the bill becomes law; the statutory cancellation occurs after the bill becomes law. The constitutional return is of the entire bill; the statutory cancellation is of only a part. [The] procedures governing the enactment of statutes set forth [in] Article I were the product of the great debates and compromises that produced the Constitution itself. [What] has emerged in these cases from the President's exercise of his statutory cancellation powers, however, are truncated versions of two bills that passed both Houses of Congress. They are not the product of the 'finely wrought' procedure that the Framers designed.

"[In *Field v. Clark*, 143 U.S. 649 (1892)], the Court upheld the constitutionality of the Tariff Act of 1890. That statute contained a 'free list' of almost 300 specific articles that were exempted from import duties[, but] directed the President to suspend [the] exemption for sugar, molasses, coffee, tea, and hides 'whenever, and so often' as he [determined] that any country producing and exporting those products imposed duties on the agricultural products of the United States that he deemed to be 'reciprocally unequal and unreasonable.'

"[But there are] three critical differences between the power to suspend the exemption from import duties and the power to cancel portions of a duly enacted statute. First, the exercise of the suspension power was contingent upon a condition that did not exist when the Tariff Act was passed: the imposition of 'reciprocally unequal and unreasonable' import duties by other countries. In contrast, the exercise of the cancellation power [was] based on the same conditions that Congress evaluated when it passed those statutes. Second, under the Tariff Act, when the President determined that the contingency had arisen, he had a duty to suspend; in contrast, [the Line Item Veto Act] did not qualify his discretion to cancel or not to cancel. Finally, whenever the President suspended an exemption under the Tariff Act, he was executing the policy that Congress had embodied in the statute. In contrast, whenever the President cancels an item of new direct spending or a limited tax benefit he is rejecting the policy judgment made by Congress and relying on his own policy judgment."

KENNEDY, J., concurred: "Liberty is always at stake when one or more of the branches seek to transgress the separation of powers. Separation of powers was designed to implement a fundamental insight: concentration of power in the hands of a single branch is a threat to liberty."

SCALIA, J. joined by O'Connor and Breyer, JJ., dissented: Art. 1, § 7 "no more categorically prohibits the Executive reduction of congressional dispositions in the course of implementing statutes that authorize such reduction, than it categorically prohibits the Executive augmentation of congressional dispositions in the course of implementing statutes that authorize such augmentation—generally known as substantive rulemaking. [T]here is not a dime's worth of difference between Congress's authorizing the President to cancel a spending item, and Congress's authorizing money to be spent on a particular item at the President's discretion. And the latter has been done since the Founding of the Nation."

III. APPOINTMENT AND REMOVAL OF OFFICERS

Art. II, Sec. 2, cl.2 states the President's power to "appoint * * * Officers of the United States," but nowhere does the Constitution address the power to remove officers, an issue disputed in the First Congress concerning President Washington's authority to unilaterally remove the Secretary of the Department of Foreign Affairs. In a sweeping opinion that went well beyond the issues raised, MYERS v. UNITED STATES, 272 U.S. 52 (1926), ruled that the President's executive power included the power to remove executive officers of the United States, even when their appointment was subject to the advice and consent of the

Senate.a TAFT, C.J., reasoned that, as the President's "selection of administrative officers is essential to the execution of the laws by him, so must be his power of removing those for whom he can not continue to be responsible." This point soon became increasingly important as to which branch of government would have "control" over the greatly enlarged administrative state.

———

HUMPHREY'S EXECUTOR v. UNITED STATES, 295 U.S. 602 (1935), per SUTHERLAND, J., held that Congress could limit the grounds for removal of a Commissioner of the Federal Trade Commission: "[*Myers*] cannot be accepted as controlling our decision here. A postmaster is an executive officer restricted to the performance of executive functions. He is charged with no duty at all related to either the legislative or judicial power. [*Myers*] finds support in the theory that such an officer is merely one of the units in the executive department [and] the decision goes far enough to include all purely executive officers. It goes no farther * * *.

"[The] authority of Congress, in creating quasi-legislative or quasi-judicial agencies, to require them to act in discharge of their duties independently of executive control, cannot well be doubted; and that authority includes, as an appropriate incident, power to fix the period during which they shall continue in office, and to forbid their removal except for cause in the meantime. For it is quite evident that one who holds his office only during the pleasure of another, cannot be depended upon to maintain an attitude of independence against the latter's will.

"The fundamental necessity of maintaining each of the three general departments of government entirely free from the control or coercive influence, direct or indirect, of either of the others, has often been stressed and is hardly open to serious question. [The] power of removal here claimed for the President falls within this principle, since its coercive influence threatens the independence of a commission, which is not only wholly disconnected from the executive department, but [which] was created by Congress [as] an agency of the legislative and judicial departments."

———

BUCKLEY v. VALEO, 424 U.S. 1 (1976), per curiam, invalidated the Federal Election Campaign Act's provision for the Federal Election Commission because it assigned appointment of two commissioners to the President pro tem of the Senate and two to the Speaker of the House of Representatives, leaving two for Presidential appointment: "[A]ny appointee exercising significant authority pursuant to the laws of the United States is an Officer of the United States,' and must, therefore, be appointed in the manner prescribed by [the Appointments Clause]. While the second part of the Clause authorizes Congress to vest the appointment of the officers described in that part in 'the Courts of Law, or in the Heads of Departments,' neither the Speaker of the House nor the President pro tempore of the Senate comes within this language.

"[The] position that because Congress has been given explicit and plenary authority to regulate a field of activity, it must therefore have the power to

a. *Myers* held unconstitutional a statute establishing a four year term for first class postmasters, subject to removal for cause "by the President [with] the advice and consent of the Senate."

appoint those who are to administer the regulatory statute is both novel and contrary to the language of the Appointments Clause [which] controls the appointment of the members of a typical administrative agency even though its functions, as this Court recognized in *Humphrey's Executor*, may be 'predominantly quasi-judicial and quasi-legislative' rather than executive. The Court in that case carefully emphasized that although the members of such agencies were to be independent of the Executive in their day-to-day operations, the Executive was not excluded from selecting them. * * *

"All aspects of the Act are brought within the Commission's broad administrative powers: rulemaking, advisory opinions, and determinations of eligibility for funds and even for federal elective office itself. These functions [are] of kinds usually performed by independent regulatory agencies or by some department in the Executive Branch under the direction of an Act of Congress. [Yet] each of these functions also represents the performance of a significant governmental duty exercised pursuant to a public law. While the President may not insist that such functions be delegated to an appointee of his removable at will, *Humphrey's Executor*, none of them operates merely in aid of congressional authority to legislate or is sufficiently removed from the administration and enforcement of public law to allow it to be performed by the present Commission."

———

BOWSHER v. SYNAR, 478 U.S. 714 (1986): The Balanced Budget and Emergency Deficit Act of 1985 set maximum yearly permissible deficits with the goal of reducing the federal deficit to zero by 1991. If needed to keep the deficit within the maximum, the Act required across-the-board cuts, half in defense programs and half elsewhere. Sec. 251 set out the procedure: (1) For each year the directors of the Office of Management and Budget and of the Congressional Budget Office were to estimate the deficit and calculate, program by program, the cuts required to meet the goal, and to report their estimates and calculations to the Comptroller General. (2) After reviewing the directors' figures, the Comptroller was to report to the President on the estimates and required budget reductions. (3) The President was then to issue an order placing in effect reductions specified by the Comptroller, unless within a specified period congress met the deficit goal in other ways. The Court, per BURGER, C.J., held this procedure unconstitutional: "Congress cannot reserve for itself the power of removal of an officer charged with the execution of the laws except by impeachment.

"[Although] the Comptroller General is nominated by the President from a list of three individuals recommended by the Speaker of the House of Representatives and the President pro tempore of the Senate, and confirmed by the Senate,[a] he is removable only at the initiative of Congress [not] only by impeachment but also by joint resolution of Congress 'at any [time'].[7] [In] constitutional terms, the removal powers over the Comptroller General's office dictate that he will be subservient to Congress.

"[The] Comptroller General heads the General Accounting Office, 'an instrumentality of the United States Government independent of the executive departments,' which was created by Congress [in] 1921 [because] it believed that it 'needed an officer, responsible to it alone, to check upon the application of public

a. The Comptroller General was limited to a single 15–year term.

7. Although the President could veto such a joint resolution, the veto could be overridden by a two-thirds vote of both Houses of Congress. Thus, the Comptroller General could be removed in the face of Presidential opposition. [We] therefore read the removal provision as authorizing removal by Congress alone.

funds in accordance with appropriations.' Harvey C. Mansfield, *The Comptroller General* 65 (1939).

"It is clear that Congress has consistently viewed the Comptroller General as an officer of the Legislative Branch. [Over] the years, the Comptrollers General have also viewed themselves as part of the Legislative Branch. [The] remaining question is whether the Comptroller General has been assigned [executive powers under the Act].

"[Under] § 251, the Comptroller General must exercise judgment concerning facts that affect the application of the Act. He must also interpret the provisions of the Act to determine precisely what budgetary calculations are required. Decisions of that kind are typically made by officers charged with executing a statute."

In deciding the remedy, the Court invalidated the procedure that gave "executive" authority to the Comptroller General, and called for resort to the Act's "fallback" provisions[b] that were to take effect "[i]n the event [any] of the reporting procedures described in section 251 are invalidated."[c]

WHITE, J., dissented: "Determining the level of spending by the Federal Government is [a] peculiarly legislative function, and one expressly committed to Congress by Art. I, § 9. [Delegating] the execution of this legislation—that is, the power to apply the Act's criteria and make the required calculations—to an officer independent of the President's will does not deprive the President of any power that he would otherwise have or that is essential to the performance of the duties of his office. Rather, the result of such a delegation, from the standpoint of the President, is no different from the result of more traditional forms of appropriation: under either system, the level of funds available to the Executive Branch to carry out its duties is not within the President's discretionary control.

" * * * Congress may remove the Comptroller only through a joint resolution, which by definition must be passed by both Houses and signed by the President. [In] other words, a removal of the Comptroller under the statute *satisfies the requirements of bicameralism and presentment laid down in Chadha.* '[Those] who have studied the office agree that the procedural and substantive limits on the power of Congress and the President to remove the Comptroller make dislodging him against his will practically impossible.'[d]

MORRISON v. OLSON

487 U.S. 654, 108 S.Ct. 2597, 101 L.Ed.2d 569 (1988).

CHIEF JUSTICE REHNQUIST delivered the opinion of the Court.

b. Under the fallback provision, Congress makes the ultimate budget decision by joint resolution, which is subject to Presidential veto unless overridden by two-thirds votes in both houses of Congress.

c. Stevens, J., joined by Marshall, J., concurred in the judgment but dissented from "labeling the function assigned to the Comptroller General as 'executive powers.' I am convinced that the Comptroller General must be characterized as an agent of Congress because of his longstanding statutory responsibilities; that the powers assigned to him under the [Act] require him to make policy that will bind the Nation; and that, when Congress, or a component or an agent of Congress, seeks to

make policy that will bind the Nation, it must follow the procedures mandated by Article I of the Constitution—through passage by both Houses and presentment to the President."

d. Blackmun, J., separately dissenting, agreed with White, J., that it was "unrealistic" to claim that the removal power makes the Comptroller General "subservient to Congress." But to the extent removal power was found incompatible with the constitutional separation of powers, he would "cure" it by refusing to allow congressional removal "—if it ever is attempted—and not by striking down the central provisions of the Deficit Control Act."

[The Ethics in Government Act of 1978 called for appointment of an "independent counsel" to investigate, and, if appropriate, to prosecute certain high-ranking government officials[a] for violating any federal criminal law.[b] Upon receipt of information that the Attorney General considers "sufficient grounds," the Attorney General conducts a preliminary investigation and then reports to a special division of the Court of Appeals for the District of Columbia Circuit whether there are "reasonable grounds to believe that further investigation or prosecution is warranted." If so, the Attorney General must request the Special Division to appoint, and provide it with sufficient information to enable it to appoint, "an appropriate independent counsel and define that independent counsel's prosecutorial jurisdiction."[c] The act grants the independent counsel the "full power and independent authority" of the Department of Justice to investigate and prosecute. The department must suspend all its investigations and proceedings regarding any matter referred to independent counsel.[d] The Special Division appointed Morrison to investigate a charge of perjury before the House Judiciary Committee by Olson, an Assistant Attorney General. The first issue] is whether the provision of the Act restricting the Attorney General's power to remove the independent counsel to only those instances in which he can show "good cause," taken by itself, impermissibly interferes with the President's exercise of his constitutionally appointed functions. * * *

Unlike both *Bowsher* and *Myers,* this case does not involve an attempt by Congress itself to gain a role in the removal of executive officials other than its established powers of impeachment and conviction. The Act instead puts the removal power squarely in the hands of the Executive Branch. [There] is no requirement of congressional approval of the Attorney General's removal decision, though the decision is subject to judicial review. * * *

We undoubtedly did rely on the terms "quasi-legislative" and "quasi-judicial" to distinguish the officials involved in *Humphrey's Executor* and *Wiener* from those in *Myers,* but our present considered view is that the determination of whether the Constitution allows Congress to impose a "good cause"-type restriction on the President's power to remove an official cannot be made to turn on whether or not that official is classified as "purely executive." The analysis contained in our removal cases is designed not to define rigid categories of those officials who may or may not be removed at will by the President, but to ensure that Congress does not interfere with the President's exercise of the "executive power" [under] Article II. *Myers* was undoubtedly correct in its holding, and in its broader suggestion that there are some "purely executive" officials who must be removable by the President at will if he is to be able to accomplish his constitu-

---

a. These include the President, Vice-President, cabinet officers, high ranking officers in the Executive Office of the President and the Justice Department, and the like.

b. Except Class B or C misdemeanors.

c. The Act created the Special Division of three Circuit Court Judges appointed by the Chief Justice of the United States for two-year terms. The Court upheld the Special Division's authority to appoint the independent counsel and specify her jurisdiction. It invoked the Appointments Clause reference to courts of law appointing "inferior officers," the congruity of "a court having the power to appoint prosecutorial officers" with a "court's normal functions," and the Act's ban on Special Division

judges' participation in other matters relating to the independent counsel.

d. After having been allowed to lapse during the G.H.W. Bush Administration, the statute involved in *Morrison* was re-enacted, with amendments, in the Independent Counsel Reauthorization Act of 1994. Among its more significant changes, the new statute applied to members of Congress. Its most famous use was in the Whitewater/Lewinsky investigation under Kenneth W. Starr, lasting more than six years, costing in excess of $55 million and leading to the impeachment of President Clinton. This new law expired in 1999 and was not reauthorized.

tional role.29 [At] the other end of the spectrum from *Myers,* the characterization of the agencies in *Humphrey's Executor* and *Wiener* as "quasi-legislative" or "quasi-judicial" in large part reflected our judgment that it was not essential to the President's proper execution of his Article II powers that these agencies be headed up by individuals who were removable at will.30 [There] is no real dispute that the functions performed by the independent counsel are "executive" in the sense that they are law enforcement functions that typically have been undertaken by officials within the Executive Branch. As we noted above, however, the independent counsel is an inferior officer under the Appointments Clause, with limited jurisdiction and tenure and lacking policymaking or significant administrative authority. Although the counsel exercises no small amount of discretion and judgment in deciding how to carry out his or her duties under the Act, we simply do not see how the President's need to control the exercise of that discretion is so central to the functioning of the Executive Branch as to require as a matter of constitutional law that the counsel be terminable at will by the President. [Here,] as with the provision of the Act conferring the appointment authority of the independent counsel on the special court, the congressional determination to limit the removal power of the Attorney General was essential, in the view of Congress, to establish the necessary independence of the office. We do not think that this limitation as it presently stands sufficiently deprives the President of control over the independent counsel to interfere impermissibly with his constitutional obligation to ensure the faithful execution of the laws. * * *

JUSTICE SCALIA, dissenting.

[It] effects a revolution in our constitutional jurisprudence for the Court, once it has determined that (1) purely executive functions are at issue here, and (2) those functions have been given to a person whose actions are not fully within the supervision and control of the President, nonetheless to proceed further to sit in judgment of whether "the President's need to control the exercise of [the independent counsel's] discretion is *so central* to the functioning of the Executive Branch" as to require complete control (emphasis added), whether the conferral of his powers upon someone else "*sufficiently* deprives the President of control over the independent counsel [and] whether 'the Act give[s] the Executive Branch *sufficient* control over the independent counsel to ensure that the President is able to perform his constitutionally assigned duties' (emphasis added). It is not for us to determine [how] much of the purely executive powers of government must be within the full control of the President. The Constitution prescribes that they *all* are."

[Before] this statute was passed, the President, in taking action disagreeable to the Congress, or an executive officer giving advice to the President or testifying before Congress concerning one of those many matters on which the two branches are from time to time at odds, could be assured that his acts and motives would be

29. The dissent says that the language of Article II vesting the executive power of the United States in the President requires that every officer of the United States exercising any part of that power must serve at the pleasure of the President and be removable by him at will. This rigid demarcation—a demarcation incapable of being altered by law in the slightest degree, and applicable to tens of thousands of holders of offices neither known nor foreseen by the Framers—depends upon an extrapolation from general constitutional language which we think is more than the text will bear. * * *

30. The terms also may be used to describe the circumstances in which Congress might be more inclined to find that a degree of independence from the Executive, such as that afforded by a "good cause" removal standard, is necessary to the proper functioning of the agency or official. It is not difficult to imagine situations in which Congress might desire that an official performing "quasi-judicial" functions, for example, would be free of executive or political control.

adjudged—insofar as the decision whether to conduct a criminal investigation and to prosecute is concerned—in the Executive Branch, that is, in a forum attuned to the interests and the policies of the Presidency. That was one of the natural advantages the Constitution gave to the Presidency, just as it gave Members of Congress (and their staffs) the advantage of not being prosecutable for anything said or done in their legislative capacities. [It] deeply wounds the President, by substantially reducing the President's ability to protect himself and his staff. That is the whole object of the law, of course, and I cannot imagine why the Court believes it does not succeed.

[Worse] than what [the Court] has done, however, is the manner in which it has done it. A government of laws means a government of rules. Today's decision on the basic issue of fragmentation of executive power is ungoverned by rule, and hence ungoverned by law. It extends into the very heart of our most significant constitutional function the "totality of the circumstances" mode of analysis that this Court has in recent years become fond of. Taking all things into account, we conclude that the power taken away from the President here is not really *too* much. The next time executive power is assigned to someone other than the President we may conclude, taking all things into account, that it *is* too much. That opinion, like this one, will not be confined by any rule. We will describe [the] effects of the provision in question, and will authoritatively announce: "The President's need to control the exercise of the [subject officer's] discretion *is* so central to the functioning of the Executive Branch as to require complete control." This is not analysis; it is ad hoc judgment. And it fails to explain why it is not true that—as the text of the Constitution seems to require, as the Founders seemed to expect, and as our past cases have uniformly assumed—all purely executive power must be under the control of the President. * * *e

---

MISTRETTA v. UNITED STATES, 488 U.S. 361 (1989), per BLACKMUN, J., upheld the Sentence Reform Act of 1984, which created the U.S. Sentencing Commission charged with devising guidelines for federal sentencing that would establish, within the limits of existing law, ranges of determinate sentences for categories of offenses and defendants according to specified factors, "among others." The Commission was established as an independent commission in the Judicial Branch, consisting of seven voting members appointed by the President, of whom three must be federal judges:

"[Jackson, J.'s *Youngstown* opinion] summarized the pragmatic, flexible view of differentiated governmental power to which we are heir. [As] a general [principle], 'executive or administrative duties of a nonjudicial nature may not be imposed on [Art. III judges].' *Morrison*. Nonetheless, we have recognized significant exceptions to this general rule [as in] *Sibbach* [fn. 19 in *Chadha*, in which] we upheld a challenge to certain rules promulgated under the Rules Enabling Act of 1934, which conferred upon the Judiciary the power to promulgate federal rules of civil procedure." Thus, the constitutionality of conferring rulemaking authority on federal judges lay within the "twilight area" recognized by Jackson, J. In light of the judiciary's traditional role in sentencing, there was nothing "incongruous" about the judicial role on the Commission and no "vesting within the Judiciary [of] responsibilities that more appropriately belong to another Branch." Whatever "constitutional problems might arise if the powers of the Commission were vested in a court, the Commission is not a court, does not exercise judicial power, and is

---

e.   Kennedy, J., took no part.

not controlled by or accountable to members of the Judicial Branch. The Commission [is] an independent agency in every relevant sense." Moreover, "placement of the Sentencing Commission in the Judicial Branch has not increased the Branch's authority. Prior to the passage of the Act, the Judicial Branch, as an aggregate, decided precisely the questions assigned to the Commission: what sentence is appropriate to what criminal conduct under what circumstances." The Court also ruled that this "extrajudicial assignment" did not undermine the integrity or independence of the Judicial Branch, nor "threaten, either in fact or in appearance, [its] impartiality."a

---

METROPOLITAN WASHINGTON AIRPORTS AUTH. v. CITIZENS FOR THE ABATEMENT OF AIRPORT NOISE, INC., 501 U.S. 252 (1991), per STEVENS, J., invalidated a compact between the District of Columbia and Virginia, approved by Congress, leasing Reagan and Dulles airports from the federal government. The compact conditioned the lease on the vesting of veto power over the management of the airports in a Review Board comprised of nine members of Congress, selected from designated congressional committees but serving in their "individual" capacities. If the powers of the Review Board were "executive," congressional involvement in their exercise was impermissible under *Bowsher*. If the functions of the Review Board were instead classified as legislative, the arrangement ran afoul of principles laid down in *Chadha*: This statute is "a blueprint for extensive expansion of the legislative power beyond its constitutionally defined role. [Congress] could [use] similar expedients to enable its Members or its agents to retain control, outside the ordinary legislative process, of the activities of state grant recipients charged with executing virtually every aspect of national policy." White, J., joined by Rehnquist, C.J., and Marshall, J., dissented.

EDMOND v. UNITED STATES, 520 U.S. 651 (1997), upheld the authority of the Secretary of Transportation to appoint civilian members of the Coast Guard Court of Criminal Appeals, which hears appeals from courts martial. The Court, per SCALIA, J., reasoned that these judges were "inferior" officers, subject to appointment by heads of departments, because they were supervised by the Judge Advocate General, who could remove them without cause, and by the Court of Appeals for the Armed Forces, which has appellate jurisdiction over Coast Guard Court of Criminal Appeals judgments: "[T]he term 'inferior officer' connotes a relationship with some higher ranking officer or officers below the President: Whether one is an inferior officer depends upon whether he has a superior." Souter, J., concurred in the result.

---

a. Only Scalia, J., dissented. He would uphold "delegation of legislative authority" under "congressionally prescribed standards" only "in conjunction with the lawful exercise of executive or judicial power. [The] whole theory of *lawful* congressional 'delegation' is [that] a certain degree of discretion, and thus of lawmaking, *inheres* in most executive or judicial action, and it is up to Congress, by the relative specificity or generality of its statutory com- mands, to determine—up to a point—how small or how large that degree shall be. [But] the lawmaking function of the Sentencing Commission is completely divorced from any responsibility for execution of the law or adjudication of private rights under the law. [The] only governmental power the Commission possesses is the power to make law; and it is not the Congress."

FREE ENTERPRISE FUND v. PUBLIC COMPANY ACCOUNTING OVER-SIGHT BOARD, 130 S.Ct. ___ (2010): Respondent (Board) was created by the Sarbanes–Oxley Act of 2002 as part of a set of reforms in response to a "series of celebrated accounting debacles." It has "expansive powers" to govern the accounting industry, including promulgating rules whose violations may be punished by the Board issuing "severe sanctions in its disciplinary proceedings" or by up to 20 years imprisonment or $25 million in fines. It has five members who are "Officers of the United States" appointed by the SEC, which has oversight of the Board but cannot remove Board members except "for good cause shown," defined as "willful violations of the Act, Board rules, or the securities laws; willful abuse of authority; or unreasonable failure to enforce compliance—as determined in a formal Commission order, rendered on the record and after notice and an opportunity for a hearing." SEC Commissioners "cannot themselves be removed by the President except [for] inefficiency, neglect of duty, or malfeasance in office." The Court, per ROBERTS, C.J., held this to "contravene the Constitution's separation of powers" because it was "contrary to Article II's vesting of the executive power in the President.

"[W]e have previously upheld limited restrictions on the President's removal power [discussing *Humphrey's Executor* and *Morrison*]. In those cases, however, only one level of protected tenure separated the President from an officer exercising executive power. [The] Act before us [not] only protects Board members from removal except for good cause, but withdraws from the President any decision on whether that good cause exists. That decision is vested instead in other tenured officers—the Commissioners—none of whom is subject to the President's direct control. [The] President therefore cannot hold the Commission fully accountable for the Board's conduct to the same extent that he may hold the Commission accountable for everything else that it does. The Commissioners are not responsible for the Board's actions. They are only responsible for their own determination of whether the Act's rigorous good-cause standard is met. And even if the President disagrees with their determination, he is powerless to intervene—unless that determination is so unreasonable as to constitute 'inefficiency, neglect of duty, or malfeasance in office.'

"This novel structure does not merely add to the Board's independence, but transforms it. Neither the President, nor anyone directly responsible to him, nor even an officer whose conduct he may review only for good cause, has full control over the Board. The President is stripped of the power our precedents have preserved, and his ability to execute the laws—by holding his subordinates accountable for their conduct—is impaired. * * *4

"[T]he 'fact that a given law or procedure is efficient, convenient, and useful in facilitating functions of government, standing alone, will not save it if it is contrary to the Constitution,' for '[c]onvenience and efficiency are not the primary objectives—or the hallmarks—of democratic government.' *Bowsher* (quoting *Chadha*). [Moreover, neither] respondents nor the dissent explains why the Board's task, unlike so many others, requires *more* than one layer of insulation from the President—or, for that matter, why only two."

---

4. [Without] a second layer of protection, the Commission has no excuse for retaining an officer who is not faithfully executing the law. With the second layer in place, the Commission can shield its decision from Presidential review by finding that good cause is absent—a finding that, given the Commission's own protected tenure, the President cannot easily overturn. The dissent describes this conflict merely as one of four possible "scenarios," but it is the central issue in this case: The second layer matters precisely when the President finds it necessary to have a subordinate officer removed, and a statute prevents him from doing so.

Concerning the dissent's lengthy review leading to its conclusion that it could "see no way to avoid sweeping hundreds, perhaps thousands of high level government officials within the scope of the Court's holding, putting their job security and their administrative actions and decisions constitutionally at risk," the Court responded: "The parties have identified only a handful of isolated positions [in the government] in which inferior officers might be protected by two levels of good-cause tenure. [But none, such as "civil service tenure-protected employees in independent agencies or administrative law judges,"] are similarly situated to the Board."a

BREYER, J., joined by STEVENS, GINSBURG and SOTOMAYOR, JJ., dissented: "[T]oday vast numbers of statutes governing vast numbers of subjects, concerned with vast numbers of different problems, provide for, or foresee, their execution or administration through the work of administrators organized within many different kinds of administrative structures, exercising different kinds of administrative authority, to achieve their legislatively mandated objectives. [The] functional approach required by our precedents recognizes this administrative complexity and, more importantly, recognizes the various ways presidential power operates within this context—and the various ways in which a removal provision might affect that power. [Compared] to Congress and the President, the Judiciary possesses an inferior understanding of the realities of administration, and the manner in which power, including and most especially political power, operates in context."

The dissent then described at length, including "four scenarios that might arise," why "the 'for cause' restriction before us will not restrict presidential power significantly," emphasizing that "the Commission's control over the Board's investigatory and legal functions is virtually absolutely," and asking, "What is left? The Commission's inability to remove a Board member whose perfectly *reasonable* actions cause the Commission to overrule him with great frequency? What is the practical likelihood of that occurring, or, if it does, of the President's serious concern about such a matter? [And] if the President's control over the Commission is sufficient, and the Commission's control over the Board is virtually absolute, then, as a practical matter, the President's control over the Board should prove sufficient as well.

"At the same time, Congress and the President had good reason for enacting the challenged 'for cause' provision. First and foremost, the Board adjudicates cases. This Court has long recognized the appropriateness of using 'for cause' provisions to protect the personal independence of those who even only sometimes engage in adjudicatory functions. [Moreover, the] Accounting Board members supervise, and are themselves, technical professional experts [and] the justification for insulating the 'technical experts' on the Board from fear of losing their jobs due to political influence is particularly strong. [And] historically, this regulatory subject matter—financial regulation—has been thought to exhibit a particular need for independence."

Finally, despite the fact that "it is certainly not obvious that the SEC Commissioners enjoy 'for cause' protection, [the Court has] *created* a constitutional defect in a statute and then relied on that defect to strike a statute down as unconstitutional."

a. The Court also held that the Board members have been validly appointed: The Commission constitutes a 'Departmen[t]' for purposes of the Appointments Clause, and under *Edmond* the Board members are inferior officers whose appointment Congress may permissibly vest in a 'Hea[d] of Departmen[t].' The dissent did not disagree with this point.

SECTION 3. EXECUTIVE PRIVILEGE AND IMMUNITY

UNITED STATES v. NIXON, 418 U.S. 683 (1974), grew out of the burglary of Democratic national headquarters in the Watergate hotel, during the 1972 presidential campaign, by employees of the president's re-election committee. After investigations by the press and a Senate committee revealed involvement by high officials in the Nixon administration, the President authorized appointment of a special prosecutor,[a] who subpoenaed presidential tapes and documents based on an indictment that named Nixon an unindicted "co-conspirator," and charged seven of his staff and political associates with obstructing justice and other Watergate-related offenses. The Court, per BURGER, C.J., rejected Nixon's claim of executive privilege: "The President's counsel [reads] the Constitution as providing an absolute privilege of confidentiality for all presidential communications. Many decisions of this Court, however, have unequivocally reaffirmed the holding of *Marbury v. Madison* that '[i]t is emphatically the province and duty of the judicial department to say what the law is.' [Notwithstanding] the deference each branch must accord the others, the 'judicial power of the United States' [can] no more be shared with the Executive Branch than the Chief Executive, for example, can share with the judiciary the veto power.

"[T]he President's counsel urges [the] valid need for protection of communications between high government officials and those who advise and assist them in the performance of their manifold duties; the importance of this confidentiality is too plain to require further discussion. Human experience teaches that those who expect public dissemination of their remarks may well temper candor with a concern for appearances and for their own interests to the detriment of the decisionmaking process. Whatever the nature of the privilege of confidentiality of presidential communications in the exercise of Art. II powers, the privilege can be said to derive from the supremacy of each branch within its own assigned area of constitutional duties. Certain powers and privileges flow from the nature of enumerated powers; the protection of the confidentiality of presidential communications has similar constitutional underpinnings. * * *

"However, neither the doctrine of separation of powers, nor the need for confidentiality of high level communications, without more, can sustain an absolute, unqualified presidential privilege of immunity from judicial process under all circumstances. [When] the privilege depends solely on the broad, undifferentiated claim of public interest in the confidentiality of such conversations, a confrontation with other values arises. Absent a claim of need to protect military, diplomatic, or sensitive national security secrets, we find it difficult to accept the argument that even the very important interest in confidentiality of presidential communications is significantly diminished by production of such material for in camera inspection with all the protection that a district court will be obliged to provide.

"The impediment that an absolute, unqualified privilege would place in the way of the primary constitutional duty of the Judicial Branch to do justice in criminal prosecutions would plainly conflict with the function of the courts under Art. III. In designing the structure of our Government and dividing and allocating the sovereign power among three coequal branches, the Framers [sought] to provide a comprehensive system, but the separate powers were not intended to operate with absolute independence.

"[The need for confidentiality justifies] a presumptive privilege for presidential communications." [But] this presumptive privilege must be considered in light

---

a. Footnote 8 of the opinion provides details concerning the Special Prosecutor's independence.

of our historic commitment to the rule of law. [To] ensure that justice is done, it is imperative to the function of courts that compulsory process be available for the production of evidence needed either by the prosecution or by the defense. * * *

"In this case the President [does] not place his claim of privilege on the ground [of] military or diplomatic secrets [where courts] have traditionally shown the utmost deference to presidential [responsibilities]. No case of the Court [has] extended this high degree of deference to a President's generalized interest in confidentiality. * * *

"The right to the production of all evidence at a criminal trial similarly has constitutional dimensions. The Sixth Amendment explicitly confers upon every defendant in a criminal trial the right 'to be confronted with the witnesses against him' and 'to have compulsory process for obtaining witnesses in his favor.' Moreover, the Fifth Amendment also guarantees that no person shall be deprived of liberty without due process of law. It is the manifest duty of the courts to vindicate those guarantees and to accomplish that it is essential that all relevant and admissible evidence be produced.

"In this case we must weigh the importance of the general privilege of confidentiality of presidential communications in performance of [the President's] responsibilities against the inroads of such a privilege on the fair administration of criminal justice.19 The interest in preserving confidentiality is weighty indeed and entitled to great respect. However, we cannot conclude that advisers will be moved to temper the candor of their remarks by the infrequent occasions of disclosure because of the possibility that such conversations will be called for in the context of a criminal prosecution.

"On the other hand, [the] constitutional need for production of relevant evidence in a criminal proceeding is specific and central to the fair adjudication of a particular criminal case in the administration of justice. Without access to specific facts a criminal prosecution may be totally frustrated. [The] generalized assertion of privilege must yield to the demonstrated, specific need for evidence in a pending criminal trial."b Rehnquist, J., did not participate.

———

NIXON v. ADMINISTRATOR OF GENERAL SERVICES, 433 U.S. 425 (1977), per BRENNAN, J., rejected a claim of executive privilege in upholding the "facial validity" of the Presidential Recordings and Materials Preservation Act. The Act, passed after President Nixon's resignation and pardon by President Ford, required the Administrator to take "possession and control" of Nixon's presidential materials, to screen them and return those that were private and not of "general historical interest," and to promulgate regulations to protect the remaining materials from loss and to govern eventual access to them:

"[A]dequate justifications are shown for this limited intrusion into executive confidentiality comparable to those held to justify the in camera inspection [in *Nixon I.*] Congress acted to establish regular procedures [to] preserve the materials for legitimate historical and governmental purposes. [Other] substantial public

---

19. We are not here concerned with the balance between the President's generalized interest in confidentiality and the need for relevant evidence in civil litigation, nor with that between the confidentiality interest and congressional demands for information, nor with the President's interest in preserving state secrets.

b. The Court stressed the obligation of the District Court to examine the tapes and documents in camera and to excise and keep confidential all material not admissible and relevant.

interests [were] the desire to restore public confidence in our political processes by preserving the materials as a source for facilitating a full airing of the events leading to appellant's resignation, and Congress' need to understand how those political processes had in fact operated in order to gauge the necessity for remedial legislation. [And], of course, the Congress repeatedly referred to the importance of the materials to the Judiciary in the event that they shed light upon issues in civil or criminal litigation, a social interest that cannot be doubted."

BURGER, C.J., dissented, noting that all prior Presidents were allowed "to provide unilaterally for disposition of [their] workpapers. [No] one has suggested that Congress will find its own 'core' functioning impaired by lack of the impounded papers, as we expressly found the judicial function would be impaired by lack of the material subpoenaed in *Nixon I.*" Rehnquist, J., dissenting, "fully subscribe[d] to most of what is said respecting the separation of powers" in Burger, C.J.'s dissent.

———

After his departure from office, President Nixon was sued by Fitzgerald, who claimed that Nixon and White House aides caused him to be fired from his federal job (for "whistle-blowing") in violation of his statutory and constitutional rights. NIXON v. FITZGERALD, 457 U.S. 731 (1982), per POWELL, J., affirmed summary dismissal of the action against Nixon: A President is entitled to *absolute immunity* from "damages liability predicated on his official acts."[27] This immunity is "a functionally mandated incident of the President's unique office, rooted in the constitutional tradition of the separation of powers and supported by our history. * * *

"Because of the singular importance of the President's duties, diversion of his energies by concern with private lawsuits would raise unique risks to the effective functioning of government. As is the case with prosecutors and judges—for whom absolute immunity now is established—a President must concern himself with matters likely to 'arouse the most intense feelings.' Yet [it] is in precisely such cases that there exists the greatest public interest in providing an official 'the maximum ability to deal fearlessly and impartially with' the duties of his office. This concern is compelling where the officeholder must make the most sensitive and far-reaching decisions entrusted to any official under our constitutional system.

"[O]ur decisions have held that an official's absolute immunity should extend only to acts in performance of particular functions of his office. [See *Butz v. Economou,* 438 U.S. 478 (1978). But in] view of the special nature of the President's constitutional office and functions, we think it appropriate to recognize absolute Presidential immunity from damages liability for acts within the 'outer perimeter' of his official responsibility. * * *

"A rule of absolute immunity for the President will not leave the Nation without sufficient protection against misconduct on the part of the chief executive. There remains the constitutional remedy of impeachment. In addition, there are formal and informal checks on Presidential action that do not apply with equal force to other executive officials. The President is subjected to constant scrutiny by the press. Vigilant oversight by Congress also may serve to deter Presidential

27. [Our] holding today need only be that the President is absolutely immune from civil damages liability for his official acts in the absence of explicit affirmative action by Congress. We decide only this constitutional issue, which is necessary to disposition of the case before us.

abuses of office, as well as to make credible the threat of impeachment. Other incentives to avoid misconduct may include a desire to earn re-election, the need to maintain prestige as an element of Presidential influence, and a President's traditional concern for his historical stature."

WHITE, J., joined by Brennan, Marshall and Blackmun, JJ., dissented: "Attaching absolute immunity to the office of the President, rather than to particular activities that the President might perform, places the President above the law. [The] scope of immunity is determined by function, not office. The wholesale claim that the President is entitled to absolute immunity in all of his actions stands on no firmer ground than did the claim that all presidential communications are entitled to an absolute privilege *[Nixon I]*. Therefore, whatever may be true of the necessity of such a broad immunity in certain areas of executive responsibility,[30] the only question that must be answered here is whether the dismissal of employees falls within a constitutionally assigned executive function, the performance of which would be substantially impaired by the possibility of a private action for damages. I believe it does not." Blackmun, J., joined by Brennan and Marshall, JJ., also dissented.

Notes

1. **Constitutional foundation.** Art. I, § 6, cl. 1, expressly confers a limited immunity on members of Congress by providing that "for any Speech or Debate in either House, they shall not be questioned in any other Place."[a]

2. **Types of immunity.** There are generally two types of immunity from suits for damages: (i) absolute immunity, protecting an official even for egregious or intentional constitutional violations, and (ii) "qualified" or "good faith" immunity, permitting liability only for violations of "clearly established" rights of which a reasonable person would have known. See *Harlow v. Fitzgerald*, 457 U.S. 800 (1982). Qualified immunity is the norm; absolute immunity is the exception. *Harlow* made clear that high presidential aides are not entitled to absolute presidential immunity. *Butz* had held that "members of the Cabinet ordinarily enjoy only qualified immunity from suit," and it would be "untenable" to hold that all White House aides enjoy absolute immunity when cabinet members do not.[b]

CLINTON v. JONES, 520 U.S. 681 (1997): An Arkansas state employee, filed a federal civil suit against President Clinton, seeking damages for " 'abhorrent' sexual advances that she vehemently rejected," allegedly made while he was governor of Arkansas. The Court, per STEVENS, J., rejected Clinton's effort to have the suit dismissed without prejudice, and the statute of limitations tolled, until expiration of his term: "Petitioner's strongest argument [relies] on separation of powers. [He] contends that this particular case—as well as the potential additional

30. I will not speculate on the presidential functions which may require absolute immunity, but a clear example would be instances in which the President participates in prosecutorial decisions.

a. Decisions have limited the immunity to suits for damages predicated on the performance of expressly *legislative* functions. See, e.g., *Hutchinson v. Proxmire*, 443 U.S. 111 (1979).

b. Burger, C.J., dissenting, was "at a loss" to reconcile the Court's decision with the derivative extension of absolute congressional immunity under the Speech and Debate Clause to congressional aides in *Gravel v. United States*, 408 U.S. 606 (1972).

litigation that [it] may spawn—may impose an unacceptable burden on the President's time and energy, and thereby impair the effective performance of his office. [But this] predictive judgment finds little support in either history or the relatively narrow compass of the issues raised in this particular case. [In] the more than 200 year history of the Republic, only three sitting Presidents have been subjected to suits for their private actions. [It therefore] seems unlikely that a deluge of such litigation will ever engulf the Presidency. As for the case at hand, if properly managed by the District Court, it appears to us highly unlikely to occupy any substantial amount of petitioner's time.

"[Of] greater significance, petitioner errs by presuming that interactions between the Judicial Branch and the Executive, even quite burdensome interactions, necessarily rise to the level of constitutionally forbidden impairment of the Executive's ability to perform its constitutionally mandated functions. [We] have long held that when the President takes official action, the Court has the authority to determine whether he has acted within the law. [E.g., *Youngstown*. If] the Judiciary may severely burden the Executive Branch by reviewing the legality of the President's official conduct, and if it may direct appropriate process to the President himself [e.g., *Nixon*], it must follow that the federal courts have power to determine the legality of his unofficial conduct [including that occurring before he became President.]"

The Court went on to consider whether "a stay of either trial or discovery might be justified [in the discretion of the District Court] by considerations that do not require the recognition of any constitutional immunity. The District Court has broad discretion to stay proceedings as an incident to its power to control its own docket [and] potential burdens on the President [are] appropriate matters for the District Court to evaluate in its management of the case. The high respect that is owed to the Office of the Chief Executive [is] a matter that should inform the conduct of the entire proceeding, including the timing and scope of discovery." Nonetheless, "the proponent of a stay bears the burden of establishing its need." And so far there was "nothing in the record to enable a judge to assess the potential harm that may ensue from scheduling the trial promptly after discovery is concluded."

BREYER, J., concurred in the judgment only, agreeing "that the Constitution does not automatically grant the President an immunity from civil lawsuits based upon his private conduct." But "once the President sets forth and explains a conflict between judicial proceeding and public duties, [the] Constitution permits a judge to schedule a trial in an ordinary civil damages action [only] within the constraints of a constitutional principle [that] forbids a federal judge in such a case to interfere with the President's discharge of his public duties." Breyer, J., was less "sanguine" than the majority that permitting suits against sitting Presidents would not lead to a proliferation of such actions. He therefore thought that "ordinary case-management principles are unlikely to prove sufficient" and would make clear that the Constitution does "not grant a single judge more than a very limited power to second guess a President's reasonable determination (announced in open court) of his scheduling needs."

———

CHENEY v. U.S. DIST. CT., 542 U.S. 367 (2004), involved a discovery order against Vice President Cheney seeking information about the members and activities of a task force established to develop a national energy policy for the President. After noting that "the need for information for use in civil cases, while far from negligible, does not share the urgency or significance of the criminal subpoena requests in *[Nixon]* where a court's ability to fulfill its constitutional responsibility to resolve cases and controversies within its jurisdiction hinges on the availability of certain indispensable information," the Court, per KENNEDY, J., remanded to the D.C. Circuit because that court had "labored under the mistaken assumption that the assertion of executive privilege is a necessary precondition to the Government's separation-of-powers objections. [T]here is sound precedent in the District of Columbia itself for district courts to explore other avenues, short of forcing the Executive to invoke privilege, when they are asked to enforce against the Executive Branch unnecessarily broad subpoenas." Scalia, Souter, Thomas, and Ginsburg, JJ., dissented on procedural issues.

Chapter 4

STATE POWER TO REGULATE

INTRODUCTION

As discussed in Ch. 2, the Commerce Clause is principally a grant of legislative power to Congress. When the Constitution gave Congress the power to regulate commerce, it did not expressly negate state power.1 From the beginning, however, it has been assumed that the grant of authority to Congress necessarily implies a withdrawal of at least some regulatory power from the states. This chapter explores the impact of national legislative authority on state power to regulate. The focus is on the "dormant Commerce Clause"—the term commonly used to refer to the Commerce Clause in cases in which Congress possesses regulatory power but has not exercised it—though similar problems arise under other grants of federal authority.

When Congress enacts valid legislation under the Commerce Clause (and thus asserts its power, rather than leaving it "dormant"), there is no doubt that Congress can preclude, displace, or "preempt" state law. CROSBY v. NATIONAL FOREIGN TRADE COUNCIL, 530 U.S. 363, 372–73 (2000), summarized the relevant principles as follows: "A fundamental principle of the Constitution is that Congress has the power to preempt state law. Art. VI, cl. 2; *Gibbons v. Ogden* [which appears immediately below]. Even without an express provision for preemption, we have found that state law must yield to a congressional Act in at least two circumstances. When Congress intends federal law to 'occupy the field,' [all] state law in that area is preempted. And even if Congress has not occupied the field, state law is naturally preempted to the extent of any conflict with a federal statute. We will find preemption where it is impossible for a private party to comply with both state and federal law, and where 'under the circumstances of [a] particular case, [the challenged state law] stands as an obstacle to the accomplishment and execution of the full purposes and objectives of Congress.' " The basic concept of preemption is taken for granted, rather than studied, in the materials that follow.2 Once the principle is accepted, preemption questions essentially involve the interpretation of federal statutes, not the Constitution, and are better addressed in a course on statutory interpretation.

Accepting that valid federal legislation will "preempt" any incompatible state law, this chapter considers issues that arise in contexts where Congress' power is "dormant"—where Congress has the power to legislate, but has not done so.

---

1. Except for the special, express limits on tonnage duties and duties on imports and exports. Art. I, § 10.

2. For a more extensive introduction, see Tribe 3d ed., at 1172–1220.

SECTION 1.   STATE REGULATION WHEN CONGRESS' POWER IS "DORMANT": A HISTORICAL AND DOCTRINAL INTRODUCTION

I.   EARLY VIEWS OF THE IMPLICATIONS OF FEDERAL AUTHORITY FOR STATE POWER

In GIBBONS v. OGDEN (1824), Ch. 2, Sec. 2, MARSHALL, C.J., discussed but did not decide whether the grant of commerce power to Congress impliedly excluded all state regulation of interstate and foreign commerce: "In support of [the argument for concurrent power] it is said, that [the states] possessed it as an inseparable attribute of sovereignty, before the formation of the constitution, and still retain it, except so far as they have surrendered it by that instrument; that this principle results from the nature of the government, and is secured by the tenth amendment; that an affirmative grant of power is not exclusive, unless in its own nature it be such that the continued exercise of it by the former possessor is inconsistent with the grant, and that this is not of that description.

"The appellant [contends, however], that full power to regulate a particular subject, implies the whole power, and leaves no residuum; that a grant of the whole is incompatible with the existence of a right in another to any part of it.

"[The] grant of the power to lay and collect taxes is, like the power to regulate commerce, made in general terms, [but it] is capable of residing in, and being exercised by, different authorities at the same time. [When], then, each government exercises the power of taxation, neither is exercising the power of the other. But, when a State proceeds to regulate commerce with foreign nations, or among the several States, it is exercising the very power that is granted to Congress, and is doing the very thing which Congress is authorized to do. There is no analogy, then, between the power of taxation and the power of regulating commerce.

"[The] inspection laws are said to be regulations of commerce, and are certainly recognized in the constitution, as being passed in the exercise of a power remaining with the States. That inspection laws may have a remote and considerable influence on commerce, will not be denied; but that a power to regulate commerce is the source from which the right to pass them is derived, cannot be admitted. The object of inspection laws, is to improve the quality of articles produced by the labor of a [country]. They act upon the subject before it becomes an article of foreign commerce, or of commerce among the States, and prepare it for that purpose. They form a portion of that immense mass of legislation, which embraces every thing within the territory of a State, not surrendered to the general government: all which can be most advantageously exercised by the States themselves. Inspection laws, quarantine laws, health laws of every description, as well as laws for regulating the internal commerce of a State, and those which respect turnpike roads, ferries, & c., are component parts of this mass.

"No direct general power over these objects is granted to Congress, and, consequently, they remain subject to State legislation. [It] is obvious that the government of the Union, in the exercise of its express powers, that, for example, of regulating commerce with foreign nations and among the States, may use means that may also be employed by a State, in the exercise of its acknowledged powers; that, for example, of regulating commerce within the State. [If] a State, in passing laws on subjects acknowledged to be within its control, and with a view to those subjects, shall adopt a measure of the same character with one which

Congress may adopt, it does not derive its authority from the particular power which has been granted, but from some other, which remains with the State, and may be executed by the same means. All experience shows, that the same measures, or measures scarcely distinguishable from each other, may flow from distinct powers; but this does not prove that the powers themselves are [identical. The] acknowledged power of a State to regulate its police, its domestic trade, and to govern its own citizens, may enable it to legislate on this subject to a considerable [extent].

"It has been contended by the counsel for the appellant, that, as the word to 'regulate' implies in its nature, full power over the thing to be regulated, it excludes, necessarily, the action of all others that would perform the same operation on the same thing. That regulation is designed for the entire result, applying to those parts which remain as they were, as well as to those which are altered. It produces a uniform whole, which is as much disturbed and deranged by changing what the regulating power designs to leave untouched, as that on which it has operated. There is great force in this argument, and the Court is not satisfied that it has been refuted."

———

An early judicial response to question of exclusive vs. concurrent power involved an appeal to the states' "police" power—a power not to regulate "commerce" but to protect their citizens in ways that might sometimes affect commerce. WILLSON v. BLACK–BIRD CREEK MARSH CO., 27 U.S. (2 Pet.) 245 (1829), per MARSHALL, C.J., upheld a Delaware statute authorizing a dam that obstructed a small navigable stream, impeding the passage of a boat licensed by the federal navigation laws: "The act of assembly by which the plaintiffs were authorized to construct their dam, shows plainly that this is one of those many creeks, passing through a deep level marsh adjoining the Delaware [River], up which the tide flows for some distance. The value of the property on its banks must be enhanced by excluding the water from the marsh, and the health of the inhabitants probably improved. Measures calculated to produce these objects, provided they do not come into collision with the powers of the general government, are undoubtedly within those [police powers] which are reserved to the states. But the measure authorized by this act stops a navigable creek, and must be supposed to abridge the rights of those who have been accustomed to use it.

"[If] Congress had passed any act which bore upon the case; any act in execution of the power to regulate commerce, the object of which was to control state legislation over those small navigable creeks into which the tide flows, and which abound throughout the lower country of the middle and southern states; we should feel not much difficulty in saying that a state law coming in conflict with such act would be void. But Congress has passed no such act. The repugnancy of the law of Delaware to the constitution is placed entirely on its repugnancy to the power to regulate commerce with foreign nations and among the several states; a power which has not been so exercised as to affect the question.

"We do not think that the act empowering the [company] to place a dam across the creek, can, under all the circumstances of the case, be considered as repugnant to the power to regulate commerce in its dormant state, or as being in conflict with any law passed on the subject."

COOLEY v. BOARD OF WARDENS

53 U.S. (12 How.) 299, 13 L.Ed. 996 (1852).

JUSTICE CURTIS delivered the opinion of the Court.

[The Court upheld Pennsylvania's 1803 law that required ships using the Philadelphia port to hire a local pilot,[a] considered in the light of a 1789 Act of Congress providing that harbors and ports of the United States shall "continue to be regulated in conformity with the existing laws of the States [or] with such laws as the States [may] hereafter enact."]

If the Constitution excluded the States from making any law regulating commerce, certainly Congress cannot regrant, or in any manner reconvey to the States that power. And yet this act of 1789 gives its sanction only to laws enacted by the [States]. Entertaining these views we are brought [to the] question, whether the grant of the commercial power to Congress, did *per se* deprive the States of all power to regulate [pilots].

[When] it is said that the nature of the power requires that it should be exercised exclusively by Congress, it must be intended to refer to the subjects of that power, and to say they are of such a nature as to require exclusive legislation by Congress. Now the power to regulate commerce, embraces a vast field, containing not only many, but exceedingly various subjects, quite unlike in their nature; some imperatively demanding a single uniform rule, operating equally on the commerce of the United States in every port; and some, like the subject now in question, as imperatively demanding that diversity, which alone can meet the local necessities of navigation.

Either absolutely to affirm, or deny that the nature of this power requires exclusive legislation by Congress, is to lose sight of the nature of the subjects of this power, and to assert concerning all of them, what is really applicable but to a part. Whatever subjects of this power are in their nature national, or admit only of one uniform system, or plan of regulation, may justly be said to be of such a nature as to require exclusive legislation by Congress. That this cannot be affirmed of laws for the regulation of pilots and pilotage is plain. The act of 1789 contains a clear and authoritative declaration by the first Congress, that the nature of this subject is such, that until Congress should find it necessary to exert its power, it should be left to the legislation of the States; that it is local and not national; that it is likely to be the best provided for, not by one system, or plan of regulations, but by as many as the legislative discretion of the several States should deem applicable to the local peculiarities of the ports within their limits.

[The] practice of the States, and of the national government, has been in conformity with this declaration, from the origin of the national government to this time; and the nature of the subject, when examined, is such as to leave no doubt of the superior fitness and propriety, not to say the absolute necessity, of different systems of regulation, drawn from local knowledge and experience, and conformed to local wants. How then can we say, that by the mere grant of power to regulate commerce, the States are deprived of all the power to legislate on this subject, because from the nature of the power the legislation of Congress must be exclusive? * * *[b]

---

a. Ships not doing so were required to pay a fee for "the use of the society for the relief of distressed and decayed pilots" and their families.

b. Daniel, J., concurred on other grounds. McLean and Wayne, JJ., dissented.

An early application of the *Cooley* formula struck down a state statute that required only peddlers of out-of-state merchandise to secure a license and pay a tax. WELTON v. MISSOURI, 91 U.S. (1 Otto) 275 (1876), per FIELD, J.: "[T]rans-portation and exchange of commodities is of national importance, and admits and requires uniformity of regulation. The very object of investing this power in the General Government was to insure this uniformity against discriminating State legislation. [If state power to exact such a license tax were admitted,] all the evils of discriminating State legislation, favorable to the interests of one State and injurious to the interests of other states and countries, which existed previous to the adoption of the Constitution, might follow, and the experience of the last fifteen years shows would follow, from the action of some of the States. [It] is sufficient to hold now that the commercial power continues until the commodity has ceased to be the subject of discriminating legislation by reason of its foreign character. That power protects it, even after it has entered the State, from any burdens imposed by reason of its foreign origin."

II. CONGRESSIONAL AUTHORIZATION OF STATE REGULATION

Cooley assumed that "Congress cannot regrant" regulatory power to the states once the power of regulation has been given to Congress under the Commerce Clause. But *Cooley* was not the Court's last word.

PRUDENTIAL INS. CO. v. BENJAMIN, 328 U.S. 408 (1946), per RUTLEDGE, J., upheld Congress' power to authorize state taxes that discriminate against interstate commerce and thereby insulate such taxes from challenge under the dormant Commerce Clause:a "Prudential chiefly relies [on] the cases which from *Welton* until now have outlawed state taxes found to discriminate against inter-state commerce. [Those cases] presented no question of the validity of such a tax where Congress had taken affirmative action consenting to it or purporting to give it validity.

"[In] all the variations of Commerce Clause theory it has never been the law that what the states may do in the regulation of commerce, Congress being silent, is the full measure of its power. Much less has this boundary been thought to confine what Congress and the states acting together may [accomplish].

"[The] cases most important for the decision in this cause [are] the ones involving situations where the silence of Congress or the dormancy of its power has been taken judicially, [as] forbidding state action, only to have Congress later disclaim the prohibition or undertake to nullify it. Not yet has this Court held such a disclaimer invalid or that state action supported by it could not stand. On the contrary, in each instance it has given effect to the congressional judgment contradicting its own previous one.

"[The McCarran Act] was a determination by Congress that state taxes, which in its silence might be held invalid as discriminatory, do not place on interstate insurance business a burden which it is unable generally to bear or should not bear in the competition with local business. Such taxes were not uncommon among the states, and the statute clearly included South Carolina's tax now in issue.

a. *Prudential* upheld a South Carolina stat-ute that imposed a tax on gross insurance premiums from South Carolina business but exempted South Carolina insurance companies. The Court ruled that Congress had authorized such taxes by the McCarran Act, which made insurance companies subject to state taxes and regulations after *South–Eastern Underwriters,* Ch. 2, Sec. 2, I, had given rise to doubts about state power over interstate insurance business.

"That judgment was one of policy and reflected long and clear experience. For, notwithstanding the long incidence of the tax and its payment by Prudential without question prior to the *South–Eastern* decision, the record of Prudential's continuous success in South Carolina over decades refutes any idea that payment of the tax handicapped it in any way tending to exclude it from competition with local business or with domestic insurance companies.

"[This] broad authority [over commerce] Congress may exercise alone [or] in conjunction with coordinated action by the states, in which case limitations imposed for the preservation of their powers become inoperative and only those designed to forbid action altogether by any power or combination of powers in our governmental system remain effective. Here both Congress and South Carolina have acted, and in complete coordination, to sustain the tax. It is therefore reinforced by the exercise of all the power of government residing in our scheme. [Congress and the states] were not forbidden to cooperate or by doing so to achieve legislative consequences, particularly in the great fields of regulating commerce and taxation, which, to some extent at least, neither could accomplish in isolated exertion."

Although Congress can waive impediments to state discrimination under the Commerce Clause, Congress cannot waive individual rights to be free from discrimination under the Privileges and Immunities Clause of Art. IV, see Sec. 4 of this chapter, or the Equal Protection Clause of the Fourteenth Amendment, see Ch. 9. The leading equal protection case, METROPOLITAN LIFE INS. CO. v. WARD, 470 U.S. 869 (1985), per POWELL, J., struck down a discriminatory state tax on out-of-state insurance companies under the Equal Protection Clause, notwithstanding the statute's immunity from attack on dormant Commerce Clause grounds under the McCarran Act and *Prudential Ins. Co.*

III. THE QUEST FOR AN ADEQUATE STANDARD

Although the Court, since *Cooley*, has regularly reviewed state legislation for possible conflict with the negative implications of the Commerce Clause, uncertainty and controversy have persisted concerning the standard against which legislation should be tested. Through the nineteenth and into the twentieth century, the *Cooley* distinction between subjects that did and did not require national uniformity was consistently applied to invalidate purposefully discriminatory regulations that favored local interests, but other applications were less certain. After the turn of the century, the Court frequently distinguished between "direct" burdens on commerce, which were impermissible, and "indirect" burdens that could be sustained.[a] But observers complained that these labels were conclusory and, what is more, that it had become "difficult, if not impossible," to tell "whether these expressions merely constituted different methods of stating the *Cooley* doctrine, or whether the Court was applying different tests."[b]

In *Di Santo v. Pennsylvania*, 273 U.S. 34, 44 (1927), Stone, J., dissenting, mounted a forceful attack on the direct-indirect "formula." In its place, he suggested a balancing test, under which the validity of a state regulation would depend upon whether "a consideration of all the facts and circumstances, such as the nature of the regulation, its function, the character of the business involved and the actual effect on the flow of commerce, leads to the conclusion that the

a. The Court also "used many other expressions—such as whether the state law was a 'burden,' or a 'substantial' or 'undue' burden, on commerce, [and] whether the regulation was or was not imposed 'on' interstate commerce itself." Robert L. Stern, *The Problems of Yesteryear—Commerce and Due Process,* 4 Vand.L.Rev. 446, 451–52 (1951).

b. Id.

regulation concerns interests peculiarly local and does not infringe the national interest in maintaining the freedom of commerce across state lines.''c

Although Stone, J., wrote in dissent in *DiSanto*, the Court adopted a balancing approach in *Southern Pacific Co. v. Arizona* (1945), Sec. 2, V infra, involving a challenge to a state law prohibiting railroad trains of more than 14 passenger or 70 freight cars. In an opinion by now-Chief Justice Stone, the Court framed the judicial inquiry as turning on "the nature and extent of the burden which the state regulation of interstate trains, adopted as a safety measure, imposes on interstate commerce, and whether the relative weights of the state and national interests" justify the prohibition.

Subsequent decisions have refined the Court's state approach by adopting a sharply two-tiered framework. Under it, the Court engages in relatively even-handed balancing in cases involving state regulations that only "incidentally" (rather than facially or purposefully) restrict the flow of interstate commerce—for example, by regulating containers in which an item of commerce can be marketed, regardless of where it was produced. The most frequently invoked formulation of the balancing formula was first articulated in PIKE v. BRUCE CHURCH, INC., 397 U.S. 137, 142 (1970): "Where [a state statute] regulates evenhandedly to effectuate a legitimate local public interest, and its effects on interstate commerce are only incidental, it will be upheld unless the burden imposed on such commerce is clearly excessive in relation to the putative local benefits. If a legitimate local purpose is found, then the question [whether the regulation should be invalidated] becomes one of degree. And the extent of the burden that will be tolerated [will] depend on the nature of the local interest involved, and on whether it could be promoted as well with a lesser impact on interstate activities."

By contrast, state regulations that purposely or facially discriminate against interstate commerce—such as restrictions on the sale of goods imported from other states—are invalid unless supported by an extraordinary justification. WYOMING v. OKLAHOMA, 502 U.S. 437, 454–55 (1992), formulated this aspect of the doctrine as follows: "[The] 'negative' aspect of the Commerce Clause prohibits economic protectionism—that is, regulatory measures designed to benefit in-state economic interests by burdening out-of-state competitors. When a state statute clearly discriminates against interstate commerce, it will be struck down unless the discrimination is demonstrably justified by a valid factor unrelated to economic protectionism. Indeed, when the state statute amounts to simple economic protectionism, a 'virtually per se rule of invalidity' has applied."

As you study Sec. 2 infra, consider whether the Court's two-tiered analytical framework, including the balancing test articulated in *Pike,* (i) is constitutionally defensible and (ii) actually describes the Court's processes of decision.

SECTION 2. CASES AND DOCTRINE

I. REGULATIONS THAT BURDEN OUT–OF–STATE SUPPLIERS SEEKING IN–STATE MARKETS: BASIC THEMES AND DISTINCTIONS

BALDWIN v. G.A.F. SEELIG, INC.

294 U.S. 511, 55 S.Ct. 497, 79 L.Ed. 1032 (1935).

JUSTICE CARDOZO delivered the opinion of the Court.

---

c. Holmes and Brandeis, JJ., joined Stone, J.'s opinion.

[New York regulated minimum milk prices for sales by producers to dealers, and prohibited the sale in New York of milk bought outside the state at lower prices. The Court held the prohibition invalid.]

New York has no power to project its legislation into Vermont by regulating the price to be paid in that state for milk acquired there. [It] is equally without power to prohibit the introduction within her territory of milk of wholesome quality acquired in Vermont, whether at high prices or [low]. Accepting those postulates, New York asserts her power to outlaw milk so introduced by prohibiting its sale thereafter if the price that has been paid for it to the farmers of Vermont is less than would be owing in like circumstances to farmers in New York. The importer in that view may keep his milk or drink it, but sell it he may not.

Such a power, if exerted, will set a barrier to traffic between one state and another as effective as if customs duties, equal to the price differential, had been laid upon the thing transported.

[Nice] distinctions [between] direct and indirect burdens [are] irrelevant when the avowed purpose of the obstruction, as well as its necessary tendency, is to suppress or mitigate the consequences of competition between the states. [If] New York, in order to promote the economic welfare of her farmers, may guard them against competition with the cheaper prices of Vermont, the door has been opened to rivalries and reprisals that were meant to be averted by subjecting commerce between the states to the power of the nation.

The argument is pressed upon us, however, that the end to be served by the Milk Control Act is something more than the economic welfare of the farmers. [The] end to be served is the maintenance of a regular and adequate supply of pure and wholesome milk; the supply being put in jeopardy when the farmers of the state are unable to earn a living income. [On] that assumption we are asked to say that intervention will be upheld as a valid exercise by the state of its internal police power, though there is an incidental obstruction to commerce between one state and another. [Let] such an exception be admitted, and all that a state will have to do in times of stress and strain is to say that its farmers and merchants and workmen must be protected against competition from without, lest they go upon the poor relief lists or perish altogether. To give entrance to that excuse would be to invite a speedy end of our national solidarity. The Constitution was framed under the dominion of a political philosophy less parochial in range. It was framed upon the theory that the peoples of the several states must sink or swim together, and that in the long run prosperity and salvation are in union and not division.

[Another argument] seeks to establish [that] farmers who are underpaid will be tempted to save the expense of sanitary precautions. [But] the evils springing from uncared for cattle must be remedied by measures of repression more direct and certain than the creation of a parity of prices between New York and other states. Appropriate certificates may be exacted from farmers in Vermont and elsewhere (*Mintz v. Baldwin*, 289 U.S. 346; *Reid v. Colorado*, 187 U.S. 137); milk may be excluded if necessary safeguards have been omitted; but commerce between the states is burdened unduly when one state regulates by indirection the prices to be paid to producers in another, in the faith that augmentation of prices will lift up the level of economic welfare, and that this will stimulate the observance of sanitary requirements in the preparation of the [product.] Whatever relation there may be between earnings and sanitation is too remote and indirect to justify obstructions to the normal flow of commerce in its movement between states.

[The Court applied its ruling both to New York sales in the 40 gallon cans used to import the milk from Vermont and those in retail bottles after transfer from the cans]: The test of the "original package," which came into our law with *Brown v. Maryland*, 25 U.S. (12 Wheat.) 419 (1827), is not inflexible and final for the transactions of interstate commerce. [It] is not an ultimate principle. It is an illustration of a principle. [It] marks a convenient boundary, and one sufficiently precise save in exceptional conditions. What is ultimate is the principle that one state in its dealings with another may not place itself in a position of economic isolation. Formulas and catch-words are subordinate to this over-mastering requirement. Neither the power to tax nor the police power may be used by the state of destination with the aim and effect of establishing an economic barrier against competition with the products of another state or the labor of its residents. Restrictions so contrived are an unreasonable clog upon the mobility of commerce. They set up what is equivalent to a rampart of customs duties designed to neutralize advantages belonging to the place of origin. They are thus hostile in conception as well as burdensome in result. The form of the packages in such circumstances is immaterial, whether they are original or broken. The importer must be free from imposts framed for the very purpose of suppressing competition from without and leading inescapably to the suppression so intended. * * *

DEAN MILK CO. v. MADISON

340 U.S. 349, 71 S.Ct. 295, 95 L.Ed. 329 (1951).

JUSTICE CLARK delivered the opinion of the Court.

[A Madison, Wis., ordinance prohibited sale of milk not processed at approved pasteurization plants within five miles of Madison's central square. Madison officials inspected such plants monthly. Dean Milk, based in Illinois, bought milk from Wisconsin and Illinois farms, which it pasteurized at its two Illinois plants 65 and 85 miles from Madison. Chicago public health authorities licensed and inspected these plants under the Chicago ordinance, which required U.S. Public Health Service rating standards. Both ordinances were patterned after the Public Health Service Model Ordinance, though the Court noted that "Madison contends and we assume that in some particulars its ordinance is more rigorous than Chicago's."]

[W]e agree with appellant that the ordinance imposes an undue burden on interstate commerce. [T]his regulation, like the provision invalidated in *Baldwin,* in practical effect excludes from distribution in Madison wholesale milk produced and pasteurized in Illinois. [In] thus erecting an economic barrier protecting a major local industry against competition from without the State, Madison plainly discriminates against interstate commerce.[4] This it cannot do, even in the exercise of its unquestioned power to protect the health and safety of its people, if reasonable nondiscriminatory alternatives, adequate to conserve legitimate local interests, are available. Cf. *Baldwin*. A different view, that the ordinance is valid simply because it professes to be a health measure, would mean that the Commerce Clause of itself imposes no limitations on state action other than those laid down by the Due Process Clause, save for the rare instance where a state artlessly discloses an avowed purpose to discriminate against interstate goods. Our issue then is whether the discrimination inherent in the Madison ordinance can be justified in view of the character of the local interests and the available methods of protecting them.

---

4. It is immaterial that Wisconsin milk from outside the Madison area is subjected to the same proscription as that moving in interstate commerce.

It appears that reasonable and adequate alternatives are available. If Madison prefers to rely upon its own officials for inspection of distant milk sources, such inspection is readily open to it without hardship for it could charge the actual and reasonable cost of such inspection to the importing producers and processors. Moreover, appellee Health Commissioner of Madison testified that as a proponent of the local milk ordinance he had submitted the provisions here in controversy and an alternative proposal based on § 11 of the Model Milk Ordinance recommended by the United States Public Health Service. The model provision imposes no geographical limitation on location of milk sources and processing plants but excludes from the municipality milk not produced and pasteurized conformably to standards as high as those enforced by the receiving city, [subject to verification of ratings through the P.H.S.] The Commissioner testified that Madison consumers "would be safeguarded adequately" under either proposal and that he had expressed no preference.

[To] permit Madison to adopt a regulation not essential for the protection of local health interests and placing a discriminatory burden on interstate commerce would invite a multiplication of preferential trade areas destructive of the very purpose of the Commerce Clause. Under the circumstances here presented, the regulation must yield to the principle that "one state in its dealings with another may not place itself in a position of economic isolation." [*Baldwin*].

JUSTICE BLACK, with whom JUSTICE DOUGLAS, and JUSTICE MINTON concur, dissenting. * * *

Characterization of § 7.21 as a "discriminatory burden" on interstate commerce is merely a statement of the Court's result, which I think incorrect. [B]oth state courts below found that § 7.21 represents a good-faith attempt to safeguard public health by making adequate sanitation inspection possible. [The] fact that § 7.21, like all health regulations, imposes some burden on trade, does not mean that it "discriminates" against interstate commerce.

[W]hile the "reasonable alternative" concept has been invoked to protect First Amendment rights, [it] has not heretofore been considered an appropriate weapon for striking down local health laws. [In] my view, to use this ground now elevates the right to traffic in commerce for profit above the power of the people to guard the purity of their daily diet of [milk].

From what this record shows, and from what it fails to show, I do not think that either of the alternatives suggested by the Court would assure the people of Madison as pure a supply of milk as they receive under their own ordinance. On this record I would uphold the Madison law. At the very least, however, I would not invalidate it without giving the parties a chance to present evidence and get findings on the ultimate issues the Court thinks crucial—namely, the relative merits of the Madison ordinance and the alternatives suggested by the Court today.

———

BREARD v. ALEXANDRIA, 341 U.S. 622 (1951), per REED, J., upheld, over a Commerce Clause claim, an ordinance forbidding door-to-door soliciting of orders for the sale of merchandise, as applied to Breard and his crew of sales persons seeking subscriptions to out-of-state magazines.[5] The Court viewed the ordinance as protecting an important social interest in residential privacy: "Unwanted knocks on the door by day or night are a nuisance, or worse, to peace and quiet.

---

5. The Court also denied a freedom of the press claim.

[As] the exigencies of trade are not ordinarily expected to have a higher rating constitutionally than the tranquillity of the fireside, responsible municipal officers have sought a way to curb the annoyances while preserving complete freedom for desirable visitors to the homes." No less restrictive alternative was available. "The idea of barring classified salesmen from homes by means of notices posted by individual householders was rejected early as less practical than an ordinance regulating solicitors."

Although acknowledging that "the local retail merchant [has] not been unmindful of the effective competition furnished by house-to-house selling" and recognizing "the importance to publishers of our many periodicals" of house-to-house solicitation, the Court found it constitutionally adequate that the "usual methods of seeking business are left open by the ordinance." "That such methods do not produce as much business as house-to-house canvassing is, constitutionally, [immaterial.] Taxation that threatens interstate commerce with prohibition or discrimination is bad, but regulation that leaves out-of-state sellers on the same basis as local sellers cannot be invalid for that reason."

The Court was "not willing even to appraise the suggestion, unsupported in the record, that [widespread use of comparable ordinances] springs predominantly from the selfish influence of local merchants. [When] there is a reasonable basis for legislation to protect the social, as distinguished from the economic, welfare of a community, it is not for this Court because of the Commerce Clause to deny the exercise locally of the sovereign power of Louisiana."

VINSON, C.J., joined by DOUGLAS, J., dissented: "I think it plain that a 'blanket prohibition' upon appellant's solicitation discriminates against and unduly burdens interstate commerce in favoring local retail merchants. 'Whether or not it was so intended, those are its necessary effects.' The fact that this ordinance exempts solicitation by the essentially local purveyors of farm products shows that local economic interests are relieved of the burdensome effects of the ordinance."

————

HUNT v. WASHINGTON STATE APPLE ADVERTISING COMM'N, 432 U.S. 333 (1977), per BURGER, C.J., ruled unanimously that North Carolina violated the Commerce Clause when it barred from the state closed apple containers bearing any grade marks except those of U.S.D.A. or a "not graded" mark. The regulation was challenged on behalf of Washington apple growers, who routinely packed their apples in containers bearing Washington grades that were viewed in the trade as equivalent or superior to the USDA grades, due to 60 years of state inspection, grading, and advertising of Washington apples.

In reaching that conclusion, the Chief Justice held that a finding that a state regulation disproportionately disadvantages interstate commerce shifts the burden onto the state to justify its regulation. Though noting "some indications" of an "economic protection motive," the Court did not question the "declared purpose of protecting consumers from deception and fraud in the market place," where apples from seven states with divergent grading standards competed with North Carolina apples. But the mere fact that "state legislation furthers matters of legitimate local concern, even in the health and consumer protection areas, does not end the inquiry. [Rather], when such state legislation comes into conflict with the Commerce Clause's overriding requirement of a national 'common market', we are confronted with the task of effecting an accommodation of the competing national and local interests. *Pike.*

"[T]he challenged statute has the practical effect of not only burdening interstate sales of Washington apples, but also discriminating against them. This discrimination takes various forms. [The statute raised] the costs of doing business in the North Carolina market for Washington apple growers and dealers, while leaving those of their North Carolina counterparts unaffected.1 [The] statute [stripped] away from the Washington apple industry the competitive and economic advantages it has earned for itself through its expensive inspection and grading system. [By] prohibiting Washington growers and dealers from marketing apples under their State's grades, the statute has a leveling effect which insidiously operates to the advantage of local apple producers."

The Court further reasoned that "[w]hen discrimination against commerce of the type we have found is demonstrated, the burden falls on the state to justify it in terms of the local benefit flowing from the statute and the unavailability of nondiscriminatory alternatives adequate to preserve the local interests at stake. *Dean Milk*; *Baldwin*." The state did not meet this burden. By permitting no grades at all the statute "can hardly be thought to eliminate the problems of deception and confusion created by the multiplicity of different state grades." And a nondiscriminatory alternative was available by permitting state grades to be used on the same containers as USDA grades.

────────

BENDIX AUTOLITE CORP. v. MIDWESCO ENTERPRISES, INC., 486 U.S. 888 (1988), is noteworthy largely because of the argument presented in an influential dissenting opinion by Scalia, J. The Court, per KENNEDY, J., applied *Pike* balancing to invalidate an Ohio statute that tolled the statute of limitations when foreign corporations did not appoint an agent to accept process for the exercise of general judicial jurisdiction: "Where the burden of a state regulation falls on interstate commerce, restricting its flow in a manner not applicable to local business or trade, there may be either a discrimination that renders the regulation invalid without more, or cause to weigh and assess the State's putative interests against the interstate burden to determine if the burden imposed is a reasonable one. [We] find that the burden imposed on interstate commerce by the tolling statute exceeds any local interest that the state might advance.

"[The] Ohio statutory scheme [forces] a foreign corporation to choose between exposure to the general jurisdiction of Ohio courts or forfeiture of the limitations defense, remaining subject to suit in Ohio in perpetuity. Requiring a foreign corporation to appoint an agent for service in all cases and to defend itself with reference to all transactions, including those in which it did not have the minimum contacts necessary for supporting personal jurisdiction, is a significant [burden].

"The ability to execute service of process on foreign corporations and entities is an important factor to consider in assessing the local interest. [However,] Ohio cannot justify its statute as a means of protecting its residents from corporations who become liable for acts done within the State but later withdraw from the jurisdiction, for it is conceded by all parties that the Ohio long-arm statute would have permitted service on Midwesco throughout the period of limitations."

---

1. For the North Carolina market, Washington growers had to obliterate Washington grades imprinted on their standard containers, repack all shipments to North Carolina, or pack and store specially marked containers of apples for the estimated North Carolina market.

SCALIA, J., concurred in the judgment: "I cannot confidently assess whether the Court's evaluation and balancing of interests in this case is right or wrong. [He pointed out uncertainties regarding both the burden on a foreign corporation and the benefits to local interests.]

"Having [roughly] evaluated the interests on both sides, [the] Court then proceeds to judge which is more important. This process is ordinarily called 'balancing,' *Pike,* but the scale analogy is not really appropriate, since the interests on both sides are incommensurate. It is more like judging whether a particular line is longer than a particular rock is heavy. All I am really persuaded of by the Court's opinion is that the burdens the Court labels 'significant' are more determinative of its decision than the benefits it labels 'important.' Were it not for the brief implication that there is here a discrimination unjustified by *any* state interest, I suggest an opinion could as persuasively have been written coming out the opposite way. We sometimes make similar 'balancing' judgments in determining how far the needs of the State can intrude upon the liberties of the individual, but that is of the essence of the courts' function as the nonpolitical branch. Weighing the governmental interests of a State against the needs of interstate commerce is, by contrast, a task squarely within the responsibility of Congress, and 'ill suited to the judicial function.' *CTS Corp. v. Dynamics Corp.,* 481 U.S. 69 (1987) (Scalia, J., concurring in part and concurring in the judgment).

"I would therefore abandon the 'balancing' approach to these negative Commerce Clause cases, first explicitly adopted [in] *Pike,* and leave essentially legislative judgments to the Congress. Issues already decided I would leave untouched, but would adopt for the future an analysis more appropriate to our role and our abilities. [In] my view, a state statute is invalid under the Commerce Clause if, and only if, it accords discriminatory treatment to interstate commerce in a respect not required to achieve a lawful state purpose. When such a validating purpose exists, it is for Congress and not us to determine it is not significant enough to justify the burden on [commerce].

"Because the present statute discriminates against interstate commerce by applying a disadvantageous rule against nonresidents for no valid state purpose that requires such a rule, I concur in the judgment that the Ohio statute violates the Commerce Clause."1

SUBSIDIES AND LINKAGES

NEW ENERGY CO. OF IND. v. LIMBACH, 486 U.S. 269 (1988), per SCALIA, J., invalidated an Ohio statute that provided a tax credit to users of a gasoline substitute, ethanol, that was produced in Ohio or in a state that gave a reciprocal tax credit for Ohio-produced ethanol. The Court ruled unanimously that Ohio discriminated in violation of the Commerce Clause when it denied the tax credit for ethanol produced in Indiana, which granted a direct subsidy to Indiana ethanol producers, but furnished no reciprocal tax credit: "The Ohio provision at issue here explicitly deprives certain products of generally available beneficial tax treatment because they are made in certain other states, and thus on its face appears to violate the cardinal requirement of nondiscrimination.

---

1. See also *Tyler Pipe Industries, Inc. v. Washington State Dep't of Revenue,* 483 U.S. 232, 265 (1987) (Scalia, J., concurring in part and dissenting in part). Scalia, J., has since made clear that, despite his "recorded [view] that the Commerce Clause contains no 'negative' component," he will enforce contrary doctrine "[o]n stare decisis grounds [in] two cir- cumstances: (1) against a state law that facially discriminates against interstate commerce, and (2) against a state law that is indistinguishable from a type of law previously held unconstitutional by this Court." *Itel Containers International Corp. v. Huddleston,* 507 U.S. 60, 79 (1993) (Scalia, J., concurring in part and concurring in the judgment).

"[It] has not escaped our notice that the appellant here, which is eligible to receive a cash subsidy under Indiana's program for in-state ethanol producers, is the potential beneficiary of a scheme no less discriminatory than the one that it attacks, and no less effective in conferring a commercial advantage over out-of-state competitors. To believe the Indiana scheme is valid, however, is not to believe that the Ohio scheme must be valid as well. The Commerce Clause does not prohibit all state action designed to give its residents an advantage in the marketplace, but only action of that description *in connection with the State's regulation of interstate commerce.* Direct subsidization of domestic industry does not ordinarily run afoul of that prohibition; discriminatory taxation of out-of-state manufacturers does."

WEST LYNN CREAMERY, INC. v. HEALY

512 U.S. 186, 114 S.Ct. 2205, 129 L.Ed.2d 157 (1994).

JUSTICE STEVENS delivered the opinion of the Court.

[Massachusetts taxed all sales of milk by wholesalers to Massachusetts retailers, regardless of whether the milk was produced in or out of state. The proceeds of the tax went to a fund used to make subsidy payments to Massachusetts milk producers.]

The paradigmatic example of a law discriminating against interstate commerce is the protective tariff or customs duty, which taxes goods imported from other states, but does not tax similar products produced in state. A tariff is an attractive measure because it simultaneously raises revenue and benefits local producers by burdening their out-of-state competitors. Nevertheless, it violates the principle of the unitary national market by handicapping out-of-state competitors, thus artificially encouraging in-state production even when the same goods could be produced at lower cost in other states.

[In] fact, tariffs against the products of other states are so patently unconstitutional that our cases reveal not a single attempt by any state to enact one. Instead, the cases are filled with state laws that aspire to reap some of the benefits of tariffs by other means.

[Massachusetts' combination of a facially nondiscriminatory tax with a subsidy to in-state farmers] is clearly unconstitutional. Its avowed purpose and its undisputed effect are to enable higher cost Massachusetts dairy farmers to compete with lower cost dairy farmers in other States. [The net result is to make] milk produced out of State more expensive. Although the tax also applies to milk produced in Massachusetts, its effect on Massachusetts producers is entirely (indeed more than) offset by the subsidy provided exclusively to Massachusetts dairy farmers. Like an ordinary tariff, the tax is thus effectively imposed only on out-of-state products.

[Respondent] argues that the payments to Massachusetts dairy farmers from the Dairy Equalization Fund are valid, because subsidies are constitutional exercises of state power, and that the order premium which provides money for the Fund is valid, because it is a nondiscriminatory tax. [Even] granting respondent's assertion that both components of the pricing order would be constitutional standing alone,[15] the pricing order nevertheless must fall. [R]espondent errs in assuming that the constitutionality of the pricing order follows logically from the constitutionality of its component parts. By conjoining a tax and a subsidy,

---

15. We have never squarely confronted the constitutionality of subsidies, and we need not do so now. We have, however, noted that "[d]i-rect subsidization of domestic industry does not ordinarily run afoul" of the negative Commerce Clause. *New Energy.*

Massachusetts has created a program more dangerous to interstate commerce than either part alone. Nondiscriminatory measures, like the evenhanded tax at issue here, are generally upheld, in spite of any adverse effects on interstate commerce, in part because "[t]he existence of major in-state interests adversely affected [is] a powerful safeguard against legislative abuse." However, when a nondiscriminatory tax is coupled with a subsidy to one of the groups hurt by the tax, a state's political processes can no longer be relied upon to prevent legislative abuse, because one of the in-state interests which would otherwise lobby against the tax has been mollified by the subsidy. So, in this case, one would ordinarily have expected at least three groups to lobby against the order premium, which, as a tax, raises the price (and hence lowers demand) for milk: dairy farmers, milk dealers, and consumers. But because the tax was coupled with a subsidy, one of the most powerful of these groups, Massachusetts dairy farmers, instead of exerting their influence against the tax, were in fact its primary supporters.

[Respondent] also argues that "the operation of the [scheme] disproves any claim of protectionism," because "*only* in-state consumers feel the effect of any retail price increase [and] [t]he dealers themselves [have] a substantial in-state presence." This argument, if accepted, would undermine almost every discriminatory tax case. State taxes are ordinarily paid by in-state businesses and consumers, yet if they discriminate against out-of-state products, they are unconstitutional. [The] cost of a tariff is also borne primarily by local consumers, yet a tariff is the paradigmatic Commerce Clause violation.

SCALIA, J., joined by THOMAS, J., concurred in the judgment.

[The] Court notes that, in funding this subsidy, Massachusetts has taxed milk produced in other States, and thus "not only assists local farmers, but burdens interstate commerce." But the same could be said of almost all subsidies funded from general state revenues, which almost invariably include monies from use taxes on out-of-state products. And even where the funding does not come in any part from taxes on out-of-state goods, "merely assist[ing]" in-state businesses unquestionably neutralizes advantages possessed by out-of-state enterprises. Such subsidies, particularly where they are in the form of cash or (what comes to the same thing) tax forgiveness, are often admitted to have as their purpose—indeed, *are nationally advertised as having as their purpose*—making it more profitable to conduct business in-state than elsewhere, i.e., distorting normal market incentives.

[There] are at least four possible devices that would enable a State to produce the economic effect that Massachusetts has produced here: (1) a discriminatory tax upon the industry, imposing a higher liability on out-of-state members than on their in-state competitors; (2) a tax upon the industry that is nondiscriminatory in its assessment, but that has an "exemption" or "credit" for in-state members; (3) a nondiscriminatory tax upon the industry, the revenues from which are placed into a segregated fund, which fund is disbursed as "rebates" or "subsidies" to in-state members of the industry (the situation at issue in this case); and (4) with or without nondiscriminatory taxation of the industry, a subsidy for the in-state members of the industry, funded from the State's general revenues. It is long settled that the first of these methodologies is unconstitutional under the negative Commerce Clause. The second of them, "exemption" from or "credit" against a "neutral" tax, is no different in principle from the first, and has likewise been held invalid. The fourth methodology, application of a state subsidy from general revenues, is so far removed from what we have hitherto held to be unconstitutional, that prohibiting it must be regarded as an extension of our negative–Commerce–Clause jurisprudence and therefore, to me, unacceptable. See *Limbach*.

[The] issue before us in the present case is whether the third of these methodologies must fall. Although the question is close, I conclude it would not be a principled point at which to disembark from the negative–Commerce–Clause train. The only difference between methodology (2) (discriminatory "exemption" from nondiscriminatory tax) and methodology (3) (discriminatory refund of non-discriminatory tax) is that the money is taken and returned rather than simply left with the favored in-state taxpayer in the first place. The difference between (3) and (4), on the other hand, is the difference between assisting in-state industry through discriminatory taxation, and assisting in-state industry by other means.

I would therefore allow a State to subsidize its domestic industry so long as it does so from nondiscriminatory taxes that go into the State's general revenue fund. Perhaps, as some commentators contend, that line comports with an important economic reality: a State is less likely to maintain a subsidy when its citizens perceive that the money (in the general fund) is available for any number of competing, non-protectionist purposes. That is not, however, the basis for my position, for as the Chief Justice explains, "[a]nalysis of interest group partic-ipation in the political process may serve many useful purposes, but serving as a basis for interpreting the dormant Commerce Clause is not one of them. [I] draw the line where I do because it is a clear, rational line.

REHNQUIST, C.J., joined by Blackmun, J., dissenting: [The] wisdom of a messianic insistence on a grim sink-or-swim policy of laissez-faire economics would be debatable had Congress chosen to enact it; but Congress has done nothing of the kind. It is the Court which has imposed the policy under the dormant Commerce Clause, a policy which bodes ill for the values of federalism which have long animated our constitutional jurisprudence.

II. REGULATION TO PROTECT THE ENVIRONMENT AND PRESERVE NATURAL RESOURCES FOR IN–STATE USE

PHILADELPHIA v. NEW JERSEY

437 U.S. 617, 98 S.Ct. 2531, 57 L.Ed.2d 475 (1978).

JUSTICE STEWART delivered the opinion of the Court.

[Operators of New Jersey landfills, and out-of-state cities that had agreements with them for waste disposal, challenged under the Commerce Clause Ch. 363, N.J.Laws, 1973, which provided: "No person shall bring into this State any solid or liquid waste which originated or was collected outside [the] State." The New Jersey Supreme Court upheld the statute, ruling that it advanced vital health and environmental objectives with no economic discrimination against interstate com-merce and that its substantial benefits outweighed its "slight" burden on inter-state commerce. The Supreme Court reversed.]

[The] New Jersey Supreme Court questioned whether the interstate move-ment of [wastes] is "commerce" at all within the meaning of the Commerce Clause. [All] objects of interstate trade merit Commerce Clause protection; none is excluded by definition at the outset. [Just] as Congress has power to regulate the interstate movement of these wastes, States are not free from constitutional scrutiny when they restrict that movement.

[The] opinions of the Court through the years have reflected an alertness to the evils of "economic isolation" and protectionism, while at the same time recognizing that incidental burdens on interstate commerce may be unavoidable when a State legislates to safeguard the health and safety of its people. Thus, where simple economic protectionism is effected by state legislation, a virtually per se rule of invalidity has been erected. See, e.g., *Hood; Baldwin.* [But] where other legislative objectives are credibly advanced and there is no patent discrimination against interstate trade, the Court has adopted a much more flexible approach, the general contours of which were outlined in [*Pike*]. [The] crucial inquiry, therefore, must be directed to determining whether Ch. 363 is basically a protectionist measure, or whether it can fairly be viewed as a law directed to legitimate local concerns, with effects upon interstate commerce that are only incidental.

The purpose of Ch. 363 is set out in the [statute]: "The Legislature finds and determines that [the] volume of solid and liquid waste continues to rapidly increase, that the treatment and disposal of these wastes continues to pose an even greater threat to the quality of the environment of New Jersey, that the available and appropriate landfill sites within the State are being diminished, that the environment continues to be threatened by the treatment and disposal of waste which originated or was collected outside the State." [The] state court additionally found that New Jersey's existing landfill sites will be exhausted within a few years; that to go on using these sites or to develop new ones will take a heavy environmental [toll;] that new techniques to divert waste from landfills to other methods of disposal and resource recovery processes are under development, but that these changes will require time; and finally, that "the extension of the lifespan of existing landfills, resulting from the exclusion of out-of-state waste, may be of crucial importance in preventing further virgin wetlands or other undeveloped lands from being devoted to landfill purposes."

[The] dispute about ultimate legislative purpose need not be resolved, because [the] evil of protectionism can reside in legislative means as well as legislative ends. Thus, it does not matter whether the ultimate aim of ch. 363 is to reduce the waste disposal costs of New Jersey residents or to save remaining open lands from pollution, for we assume New Jersey has every right to protect its residents' pocketbooks as well as their environment. And it may be assumed as well that New Jersey may pursue those ends by slowing the flow of *all* waste into the State's remaining landfills, even though interstate commerce may incidentally be affected. But whatever New Jersey's ultimate purpose, it may not be accomplished by discriminating against articles of commerce coming from outside the State unless there is some reason, apart from their origin, to treat them differently. Both on its face and in its plain effect, ch. 363 violates this principle of nondiscrimination.

[Also] relevant here are the Court's decisions holding that a State may not accord its own inhabitants a preferred right of access over consumers in other States to natural resources located within its borders. [E.g.,] *West v. Kansas Natural Gas Co.*, 221 U.S. 229 (1911). [On] its face, [the New Jersey law] imposes on out-of-state commercial interests the full burden of conserving the State's remaining landfill space. It is true that in our previous cases the scarce natural resource was itself the article of commerce, whereas here the scarce resource and the article of commerce are distinct. But that difference is without consequence. In both instances, the State has overtly moved to slow or freeze the flow of commerce for protectionist reasons. It does not matter that the State has shut the article of commerce inside the State in one case and outside the State in the other. What is crucial is the attempt by one State to isolate itself from a problem common to many by erecting a barrier against the movement of interstate trade.

[It] is true that certain quarantine laws have not been considered forbidden protectionist measures, even though they were directed against out-of-state commerce. But those quarantine laws banned the importation of articles such as diseased livestock that required destruction as soon as possible because their very movement risked contagion and other evils. Those laws thus did not discriminate against interstate commerce as such, but simply prevented traffic in noxious articles, whatever their origin.

The New Jersey statute is not such a quarantine law. There has been no claim here that the very movement of waste into or through New Jersey endangers health, or that waste must be disposed of as soon and as close to its point of generation as possible. The harms caused by waste are said to arise after its disposal in landfill sites, and at that point, as New Jersey concedes, there is no basis to distinguish out-of-state waste from domestic waste. If one is inherently harmful, so is the other. Yet New Jersey has banned the former while leaving its landfill sites open to the latter. The New Jersey law blocks the importation of waste in an obvious effort to saddle those outside the State with the entire burden of slowing the flow of refuse into New Jersey's remaining landfill sites. That legislative effort is clearly impermissible under the Commerce Clause of the Constitution.

Today, cities in Pennsylvania and New York find it expedient or necessary to send their waste into New Jersey for disposal, and New Jersey claims the right to close its borders to such traffic. Tomorrow, cities in New Jersey may find it expedient or necessary to send their waste into Pennsylvania or New York for disposal, and those States might then claim the right to close their borders. The Commerce Clause will protect New Jersey in the future, just as it protects her neighbors now, from efforts by one State to isolate itself in the stream of interstate commerce from a problem shared by all.

Justice Rehnquist, with whom Chief Justice Burger joins, dissenting.

[New] Jersey should be free under our past precedents to prohibit the importation of solid waste because of the health and safety problems that such waste poses to its citizens. The fact that New Jersey continues to, and indeed must continue to, dispose of its own solid waste does not mean that New Jersey may not prohibit the importation of even more solid waste into the State.

[I] do not see why a State may ban the importation of items whose movement risks contagion, but cannot ban the importation of items which, although they may be transported into the State without undue hazard, will then simply pile up in an ever increasing danger to the public's health and safety. The Commerce Clause was not drawn with a view to having the validity of state laws turn on such pointless distinctions.

[T]hat New Jersey has left its landfill sites open for domestic waste does not, of course, mean that solid waste is not innately harmful. Nor does it mean that New Jersey prohibits importation of solid waste for reasons other than the health and safety of its population. New Jersey must out of sheer necessity treat and dispose of its solid waste in some fashion, just as it must treat New Jersey cattle suffering from hoof-and-mouth disease. It does not follow that New Jersey must, under the Commerce Clause, accept solid waste or diseased cattle from outside its borders and thereby exacerbate its problems. * * *

With *Philadelphia* compare MAINE v. TAYLOR, 477 U.S. 131 (1986), per Blackmun, J., upholding a Maine law that prohibited importation into Maine of live baitfish that competed with Maine's native baitfish industry. The Court relied on two district court findings: (1) "Maine 'clearly has a legitimate and substantial purpose in prohibiting the importation of live bait fish' because 'substantive uncertainties' surrounded the effects that baitfish parasites would have on the State's unique population of wild fish, and the [unpredictable] consequences of introducing non-native species." (2) "[L]ess discriminatory means of protecting against these threats were currently unavailable" despite the "abstract possibility" of developing acceptable testing procedures in the future. The Court added:

"[A] State must make reasonable efforts to avoid restraining the free flow of commerce across its borders, but it is not required to develop new and unproven means of protection at an uncertain cost. Appellee, of course, is free to work on his own or in conjunction with other bait dealers to develop scientifically acceptable sampling and inspection procedures for golden shiners; if and when such procedures are developed, Maine no longer may be able to justify its import ban. The State need not join in those efforts, however, and it need not pretend they already have succeeded.

"[The] evidence in this case amply supports the District Court's findings that Maine's ban on the importation of live baitfish serves legitimate local purposes that could not adequately be served by available nondiscriminatory alternatives. This is not a case of arbitrary discrimination against interstate commerce; the record suggests that Maine has legitimate reasons, 'apart from their origin, to treat [out-of-state baitfish] differently,' *Philadelphia.*"

Stevens, J., dissented, contending that "uncertainty" and "[a]mbiguity about dangers and alternatives should actually defeat, rather than sustain, the discriminatory measure." His summary: "There is something fishy about this case."

––––––

Whereas *Philadelphia v. New Jersey* found a waste management regulation to be facially discriminatory, MINNESOTA v. CLOVER LEAF CREAMERY CO., 449 U.S. 456 (1981), considered a statute held to be even-handed on its face. The Court, per BRENNAN, J., upheld a state law that banned nonreturnable milk containers made of plastic but permitted other nonreturnable milk containers, largely cartons made of pulpwood, though the plastic originated out of state and the pulpwood in state. The legislature had found that use of nonreturnable milk containers "presents a solid waste management problem for the state, promotes energy waste, and depletes natural resources" in violation of a legislative policy to encourage "the reduction of the amount and type of material entering the solid waste stream":

"[Minnesota's statute] does not effect 'simple protectionism,' but 'regulates even-handedly' by prohibiting all milk retailers from selling their products in plastic, nonreturnable milk containers, without regard to whether the milk, the containers, or the sellers are from outside the State. [Since] the statute does not discriminate between interstate and intrastate commerce, the controlling question is whether the incidental burden imposed on interstate commerce [is] 'clearly excessive in relation to the putative local benefits.' *Pike.* We conclude that it is not.' [Within] Minnesota, business will presumably shift from manufacturers of plastic nonreturnable containers to producers of paperboard cartons, refillable bottles, and plastic pouches, but there is no reason to suspect that the gainers will be Minnesota firms, or the losers out-of-state firms. Indeed, two of the three dairies, the sole milk retailer, and the sole milk container producer challenging the statute in this litigation are Minnesota firms.17

"Pulpwood producers are the only Minnesota industry likely to benefit significantly from the Act at the expense of out-of-state firms. Respondents point out that plastic resin, the raw material used for making plastic nonreturnable milk jugs, is produced entirely by non-Minnesota firms, while pulpwood, used for making paperboard, is a major Minnesota product. Nevertheless, it is clear that respondents exaggerate the degree of burden on out-of-state interests, both because plastics will continue to be used in the production of plastic pouches, plastic returnable bottles, and paperboard itself, and because out-of-state pulpwood producers will presumably absorb some of the business generated by the Act.

"Even granting that the out-of-state plastics industry is burdened relatively more heavily than the Minnesota pulpwood industry, we find that this burden is not 'clearly excessive' in light of the substantial state interest in promoting conservation of energy and other natural resources and easing solid waste disposal problems. [We] find these local benefits ample to support Minnesota's decision under the Commerce Clause. Moreover, we find that no approach with 'a lesser impact on interstate activities,' *Pike,* is [available].

"In *Exxon* [*Corp. v. Maryland,* 437 U.S. 117 (1978), we] stressed that the Commerce Clause 'protects the interstate market, not particular interstate firms, from prohibitive or burdensome regulations.' A nondiscriminatory regulation serving substantial state purposes is not invalid simply because it causes some business to shift from a predominantly out-of-state industry to a predominantly in-state industry. Only if the burden on interstate commerce clearly outweighs the State's legitimate purposes does such a regulation violate the Commerce Clause."a

PRESERVING NATURAL RESOURCES FOR IN–STATE USE

SPORHASE v. NEBRASKA, 458 U.S. 941 (1982), per STEVENS, J., held invalid a Nebraska law requiring denial of a permit to withdraw and transport water for use in an adjoining state unless that state "grants reciprocal rights" to withdraw and transport its water for use in Nebraska. Rejecting an earlier precedentb that itself had relied primarily on *Geer,* supra, the court ruled that ground water is an "article of commerce," requiring Commerce Clause analysis of state laws restricting its transfer to other states: "[because] Colorado forbids the exportation of its ground water, the reciprocity provision operates as an explicit barrier to commerce between the two states. The state therefore bears the initial burden of demonstrating a close fit between the reciprocity requirement and its asserted local purpose. [The] reciprocity requirement does not survive the 'strictest scrutiny' reserved for facially discriminatory legislation."

III. REGULATION OF TRANSPORTATION

SOUTHERN PACIFIC CO. v. ARIZONA, 325 U.S. 761 (1945), per STONE, C.J., reversed an Arizona Supreme Court decision that upheld an Arizona law limiting the length of trains in Arizona to 70 freight cars: "[E]ver since *Gibbons,* the states have not been deemed to have authority to impede substantially the free flow of commerce from state to state, or to regulate those phases of the national commerce which, because of the need of national uniformity, demand that their

17. The existence of major in-state interests adversely affected by the Act is a powerful safeguard against legislative abuse.

a. Powell and Stevens, JJ., dissenting separately, would have referred the Commerce Clause issue back to the Minnesota Supreme Court.

b. *Hudson County Water Co. v. McCarter,* 209 U.S. 349 (1908).

regulation, if any, be prescribed by a single authority.[3] [T]he matters for ultimate determination here are the nature and extent of the burden which the state regulation of interstate trains, adopted as a safety measure, imposes on interstate commerce, and whether the relative weights of the state and national interests involved are such as to make inapplicable the rule, generally observed, that the free flow of interstate commerce and its freedom from local restraints in matters requiring uniformity of regulation are interests safeguarded by the Commerce Clause from state [interference].

"The findings show that the operation [of trains of] more than seventy freight cars is standard practice over the main lines of the railroads of the United States, and that, if the length of trains is to be regulated at all, national uniformity [is] practically indispensable to the operation of an efficient and economical national railway system. [Compliance with the Arizona law increases the costs of operation by $1,000,000 annually for the two railroads in Arizona, and impedes efficient operation by delays in breaking up and remaking long trains.]

"[In] considering the effect of the statute as a safety measure, [the] decisive question is whether in the circumstances the total effect of the law as a safety measure in reducing accidents and casualties is so slight or problematical as not to outweigh the national interest in keeping interstate commerce free from interferences which seriously impede [it]. [The Court noted that increased crossing accidents from more but shorter trains more than offset the increased risk of accidents from greater 'slack' in longer trains.]

"[The state's] regulation of train lengths, admittedly obstructive to interstate train operation, and having a seriously adverse effect on transportation efficiency and economy, passes beyond what is plainly essential for safety. [E]xamination of all the relevant factors makes it plain that the state interest is outweighed by the interest of the nation in an adequate economical and efficient railway transportation service, which must prevail."

BLACK, J., dissenting, argued that in collecting evidence concerning the efficacy of safety legislation, and in weighing safety against other interests, the trial court "acted, and this Court today is acting, as a 'super-legislature.' [The] balancing of [such] probabilities" as the Court relied on "is not in my judgment a matter for judicial determination, but one which calls for legislative consideration."

KASSEL v. CONSOLIDATED FREIGHTWAYS CORP.

450 U.S. 662, 101 S.Ct. 1309, 67 L.Ed.2d 580 (1981).

JUSTICE POWELL announced the judgment of the Court and delivered an opinion in which JUSTICE WHITE, JUSTICE BLACKMUN, and JUSTICE STEVENS joined.

The question is whether an Iowa statute that prohibits the use of certain large trucks within the State unconstitutionally burdens interstate commerce.

I. Appellee Consolidated Freightways Corporation of Delaware (Consolidated) is one of the largest common carriers in the country. [Among] other routes, Consolidated carries commodities through Iowa on Interstate 80, the principal east-west route linking New York, Chicago, and the west coast, and on Interstate 35, a major north-south route.

Consolidated mainly uses two kinds of trucks. One consists of a three-axle tractor pulling a 40–foot two-axle trailer. This unit, commonly called a single, or

3. In applying this rule the Court has often recognized that to the extent that the burden of state regulation falls on interests outside the state, it is unlikely to be alleviated by the operation of those political restraints normally exerted when interests within the state are affected. * * *

"semi," is 55 feet in length overall. Such trucks have long been used on the Nation's highways. Consolidated also uses a two-axle tractor pulling a single-axle trailer which, in turn, pulls a single-axle dolly and a second single-axle trailer. This combination, known as a double, or twin, is 65 feet long overall. Many trucking companies, including Consolidated, increasingly prefer to use doubles to ship certain kinds of commodities. Doubles have larger capacities, and the trailers can be detached and routed separately if necessary. Consolidated would like to use 65–foot doubles on many of its trips through Iowa.

[Unlike] all other States in the West and Midwest, Iowa generally prohibits the use of 65–foot doubles within its borders. Instead, most truck combinations are restricted to 55 feet in length. Doubles, mobile homes, trucks carrying vehicles such as tractors and other farm equipment, and singles hauling livestock, are permitted to be as long as 60 feet. [T]he District Court found that the "evidence clearly establishes that the twin is as safe as the semi. * * * Twins are more maneuverable, are less sensitive to wind, and create less splash and spray. However, they are more likely than semis to jackknife or upset. They can be backed only for a short distance. The negative characteristics are not such that they render the twin less safe than semis overall. Semis are more stable but are more likely to 'rear end' another vehicle."

In light of these findings, the District Court applied the standard we enunciated in *Raymond Motor Transportation, Inc. v. Rice*, 434 U.S. 429 (1978), and concluded that the state law impermissibly burdened interstate commerce: "[The] total effect of the law as a safety measure in reducing accidents and casualties is so slight and problematical that it does not outweigh the national interest in keeping interstate commerce free from interferences that seriously impede it." The Court of Appeals for the Eighth Circuit affirmed. * * *

II. [R]egulations that touch upon safety—especially highway safety—are those that "the Court has been most reluctant to invalidate." [Indeed], "if safety justifications are not illusory, the Court will not second-guess legislative judgment about their importance in comparison with related burdens on interstate commerce."

[But] the incantation of a purpose to promote the public health or safety does not insulate a state law from Commerce Clause attack. Regulations designed for that salutary purpose nevertheless may further the purpose so marginally, and interfere with commerce so substantially, as to be invalid under the Commerce Clause. * * *

III.   The State failed to present any persuasive evidence that 65–foot doubles are less safe than 55–foot singles. Moreover, Iowa's law is now out of step with the laws of all other Midwestern and Western States. Iowa thus substantially burdens the interstate flow of goods by truck. [Trucking] companies that wish to continue to use 65–foot doubles must route them around Iowa or detach the trailers of the doubles and ship them through separately. Alternatively, trucking companies must use the smaller 55–foot singles or 60–foot doubles permitted under Iowa law. Each of these options engenders inefficiency and added expense. The record shows that Iowa's law added about $12.6 million each year to the costs of trucking companies. Consolidated alone incurred about $2 million per year in increased costs.

In addition to increasing the costs of the trucking companies (and, indirectly, of the service to consumers), Iowa's law may aggravate, rather than ameliorate, the problem of highway accidents. Fifty-five foot singles carry less freight than 65–foot doubles. Either more small trucks must be used to carry the same quantity of goods through Iowa, or the same number of larger trucks must drive longer distances to bypass Iowa. In either case, as the District Court noted, the restriction requires more highway miles to be driven to transport the same quantity of goods. Other things being equal, accidents are proportional to distance traveled. Thus, if 65–foot doubles are as safe as 55–foot singles, Iowa's law tends to *increase* the number of accidents, and to shift the incidence of them from Iowa to other States.

IV. [The] Court normally does accord "special deference" to state highway safety regulations. [Less] deference to the legislative judgment is due, however, where the local regulation bears disproportionately on out-of-state residents and businesses. Such a disproportionate burden is apparent here. Iowa's scheme, although generally banning large doubles from the State, nevertheless has several exemptions that secure to Iowans many of the benefits of large trucks while shunting to neighboring States many of the costs associated with their use.

At the time of trial there were two particularly significant exemptions. First, singles hauling livestock or farm vehicles were permitted to be as long as 60 feet. [Second,] cities abutting other States were permitted to enact local ordinances adopting the larger length limitation of the neighboring State. This exemption offered the benefits of longer trucks to individuals and businesses in important border cities without burdening Iowa's highways with interstate through traffic.

The origin of the "border cities exemption" also suggests that Iowa's statute may not have been designed to ban dangerous trucks, but rather to discourage interstate truck traffic. In 1974, the legislature passed a bill that would have permitted 65–foot doubles in the State. Governor Ray vetoed the bill. He said: "I find sympathy with those who are doing business in our state and whose enterprises could gain from increased cargo carrying ability by trucks. However, with this bill, the Legislature has pursued a course that would benefit only a few Iowa-based companies while providing a great advantage for out-of-state trucking firms and competitors at the expense of our Iowa citizens." After the veto, the "border cities exemption" was immediately enacted and signed by the Governor.

[In] the District Court and Court of Appeals, the State explicitly attempted to justify the law by its claimed interest in keeping trucks out of Iowa. The Court of Appeals correctly concluded that a State cannot constitutionally promote its own parochial interests by requiring safe vehicles to detour around [it].

V. Because Iowa has imposed [a] burden [on interstate commerce] without any significant countervailing safety interest, its statute violates the Commerce Clause.

JUSTICE BRENNAN, with whom JUSTICE MARSHALL joins, concurring in the judgment.

For me, analysis of Commerce Clause challenges to state regulations must take into account three principles: (1) The courts are not empowered to second-guess the empirical judgments of lawmakers concerning the utility of legislation. (2) The burdens imposed on commerce must be balanced against the local benefits actually sought to be achieved by the State lawmakers, and not against those suggested after the fact by counsel. (3) Protectionist legislation is unconstitutional under the Commerce Clause, even if the burdens and benefits are related to safety rather than economics.

Both the opinion of my Brother Powell and the opinion of my Brother Rehnquist are predicated upon the supposition that the constitutionality of a state regulation is determined by the factual record created by the State's lawyers in trial court. But that supposition cannot be correct, for it would make the constitutionality of state laws and regulations depend on the vagaries of litigation rather than on the judgments made by the State's lawmakers.

[A]lthough Iowa's lawyers in this litigation have defended the truck-length regulation on the basis of the safety advantages of 55–foot singles and 60–foot doubles over 65–foot doubles, Iowa's actual rationale for maintaining the regulation had nothing to do with these purported differences. Rather, Iowa sought to discourage interstate truck traffic on Iowa's highways. Thus, the safety advantages and disadvantages of the types and lengths of trucks involved in this case are irrelevant to the decision.

[Though] my Brother Powell recognizes that the State's actual purpose in maintaining the truck-length regulation was "to limit the use of its highways by deflecting some through traffic," he fails to recognize that this purpose, being *protectionist* in nature, is *impermissible* under the Commerce Clause.

[Iowa] may not shunt off its fair share of the burden of maintaining interstate truck routes, nor may it create increased hazards on the highways of neighboring States in order to decrease the hazards on Iowa highways. Such an attempt has all the hallmarks of the "simple * * * protectionism" this Court has condemned in the economic area. *Philadelphia v. New Jersey.*

JUSTICE REHNQUIST, with whom CHIEF JUSTICE BURGER and JUSTICE STEWART join, dissenting.

A determination that a state law is a rational safety measure does not end the Commerce Clause inquiry. A "sensitive consideration" of the safety purpose in relation to the burden on commerce is required. *Raymond.* When engaging in such a consideration the Court does not directly compare safety benefits to commerce costs and strike down the legislation if the latter can be said in some vague sense to "outweigh" the former. Such an approach would make an empty gesture of the strong presumption of validity accorded state safety measures, particularly those governing highways. It would also arrogate to this Court functions of forming public policy, functions which, in the absence of congressional action, were left by the Framers of the Constitution to state legislatures. [For a court to make such policy judgments would be especially inappropriate] when, as here, the question involves the difficult comparison of financial losses and "the loss of lives and limbs of workers and people using the highways."

The purpose of the "sensitive consideration" referred to above is rather to determine if the asserted safety justification, although rational, is merely a pretext for discrimination against interstate commerce. We will conclude that it is if the safety benefits from the regulation are demonstrably trivial while the burden on commerce is great.

[There] can be no doubt that the challenged statute is a valid highway safety regulation and thus entitled to the strongest presumption of validity against Commerce Clause challenges. As noted, all 50 States regulate the length of trucks which may use their highways. [There] can also be no question that the particular limit chosen by Iowa—60 feet—is rationally related to Iowa's safety objective. Most truck limits are between 55 and 65 feet, and Iowa's choice is thus well within the widely accepted range.

[The] District Court approached the case as if the question were whether Consolidated's 65–foot trucks were as safe as others permitted on Iowa highways, and the Court of Appeals as if its task were to determine if the District Court's factual findings in this regard were "clearly erroneous." The question, however, is whether the Iowa Legislature has acted rationally in regulating vehicle lengths and whether the safety benefits from this regulation are more than slight or problematical.

[The] answering of the relevant question is not appreciably advanced by comparing trucks slightly over the length limit with those at the length limit. It is emphatically not our task to balance any incremental safety benefits from prohibiting 65–foot doubles as opposed to 60–foot doubles against the burden on interstate commerce. Lines drawn for safety purposes will rarely pass muster if the question is whether a slight increment can be permitted without sacrificing safety. [The] particular line chosen by Iowa—60 feet—is relevant only to the question whether the limit is a rational one. Once a court determines that it is, it considers the overall safety benefits *from the regulation* against burdens on interstate commerce, and not any marginal benefits from the scheme the State established as opposed to that the plaintiffs desire.

[The] difficulties with the contrary approach are patent. While it may be clear that there are substantial safety benefits from a 55–foot truck as compared to a 105–foot truck, these benefits may not be discernible in 5–foot jumps. Appellee's approach would permit what could not be accomplished in one lawsuit to be done in 10 separate suits, each challenging an additional five feet.

IV. DISCRIMINATORY TAXATION OF GOVERNMENT BONDS

DEP'T OF REVENUE v. DAVIS, 553 U.S. 328 (2008), per SOUTER, J., upheld a Kentucky income tax statute that exempted interest on bonds issued by Kentucky and its political subdivisions, but not on bonds issued by other states or their local governments: "Municipal bonds currently finance roughly two-thirds of capital expenditures by state and local governments [and] by the [year 2000], over '$1.5 trillion in municipal bonds were outstanding.' Differential tax schemes like Kentucky's have a long pedigree, too. [Today], 41 states have laws like the one before us.

"It follows a fortiori from *United Haulers Ass'n, Inc. v. Oneida–Herkimer Solid Waste Management Auth.*, 550 U.S. 330 (2007), [also discussed p. 151, *infra*, which upheld an ordinance requiring trash haulers to deliver their solid waste to a publicly owned processing plant, rather than to private competitors] that Kentucky must prevail. In *United Haulers*, we explained that a government function is not susceptible to standard dormant Commerce Clause scrutiny owing to its likely motivation by legitimate objectives distinct from the simple economic protectionism the Clause abhors. [In] fact, this emphasis on the public character of the enterprise supported by the tax preference is just a step in addressing a fundamental element of dormant Commerce Clause jurisprudence, the principle that 'any notion of discrimination assumes a comparison of substantially similar entities.' [Viewed] through this lens, the Kentucky tax scheme parallels the ordinance upheld in *United Haulers:* it 'benefit[s] a clearly public [issuer, that is, Kentucky and its municipalities], while treating all private [issuers] exactly the same.' There is no forbidden discrimination because Kentucky, as a public entity, does not have to treat itself as being 'substantially similar' to the other bond issuers in the market."

Having found no forbidden discrimination, Souter, J., also concluded that the balancing test of *Pike v. Bruce Church, Inc.*, did not apply because "the current record and scholarly material convince us that the Judicial Branch is not institutionally suited to draw reliable conclusions of the kind that would be necessary." For example, the Court was not well situated to predict whether national capital markets would accommodate the bonds issued by smaller municipalities in the absence of tax benefits for in-state purchasers or whether "capital [would] to some degree simply dry up, eliminating a class of municipal improvements. [What] is most significant about these cost-benefit questions is not even the difficulty of answering them or the inevitable uncertainty of the predictions that might be made in trying to come up with answers, but the unsuitability of the judicial process and judicial forums for making whatever predictions and reaching whatever answers are possible at all."

Stevens, J., filed a concurring opinion. So did Roberts, C.J., and Scalia, J., both of whom declined to join parts of the majority opinion. Thomas, J., concurred in the judgment only, on the ground that the Court's dormant commerce clause jurisprudence lacked constitutional foundations and should be abandoned altogether.

KENNEDY, J., joined by Alito, J., dissented: "The Court holds the Kentucky law is valid because bond issuance fulfills a public function [but] the premise is wrong. The law in question operates on those who hold the bonds and trade them, not those who issue them." Moreover, even if the case were about bond issuance rather than taxation, "the discrimination against interstate commerce would be too plain and prejudicial to be sustained."

"[A] state has no authority to use its taxing power to erect local barriers to out-of-state goods or commodities. Nothing in our cases even begins to suggest this rule is inapplicable simply because the State uses a discriminatory tax to favor its own enterprise."

Kennedy, J., thought that the Court's reliance on *United Haulers* was misplaced, for the ordinance upheld there "applied equally to interstate and instate commerce. [Nondiscrimination], not just state involvement, was central to the rationale."

SECTION 3. THE STATE AS A MARKET PARTICIPANT

REEVES, INC. v. STAKE

447 U.S. 429, 100 S.Ct. 2271, 65 L.Ed.2d 244 (1980).

JUSTICE BLACKMUN delivered the opinion of the Court.

[Responding to a 1919 cement shortage, South Dakota built and operated a cement plant, which sold to both in-state and out-of-state buyers. The latter bought 40% of the plant's production in the mid–70's. When booming construction caused a cement shortage in 1978, the state "reaffirmed its policy of supplying all South Dakota customers" before offering cement to buyers from out of state. Reeves, an out-of-state buyer for 20 years, challenged South Dakota's preferential sales policy as a violation of the Commerce Clause.]

The issue in this case is whether, consistent with the Commerce Clause, the State of South Dakota, in a time of shortage, may confine the sale of cement that it produces solely to its residents. [The court of appeals upheld the law]. It concluded that the state had "simply acted in a proprietary capacity," as permitted by *Hughes v. Alexandria Scrap Corp.*, 426 U.S. 794 (1976).

Alexandria Scrap concerned a Maryland program designed to remove abandoned automobiles from the State's roadways and junkyards. To encourage recycling, a "bounty" was offered for every Maryland-title junk car converted into scrap. [The law] imposed more exacting documentation requirements on out-of-state than in-state processors. [*Alexandria Scrap*] did not involve "the kind of action with which the Commerce Clause is concerned." Unlike prior cases voiding state laws inhibiting interstate trade, "Maryland has not sought to prohibit the flow of [junk cars], or to regulate the conditions under which it may occur. Instead, it has entered into the market itself to bid up their price as a purchaser, in effect, of a potential article of interstate commerce," and has restricted "its trade to its own citizens or businesses within the State."

Having characterized Maryland as a market participant, rather than as a market regulator, the Court found no reason to "believe the Commerce Clause was intended to require independent justification for [the State's] action." The Court couched its holding in unmistakably broad terms. "Nothing in the purposes animating the Commerce Clause prohibits a State, in the absence of congressional action, from participating in the market and exercising the right to favor its own citizens over others."

The basic distinction drawn in *Alexandria Scrap* between States as market participants and States as market regulators makes good sense and sound law. As that case explains, the Commerce Clause responds principally to state taxes and regulatory measures impeding free private trade in the national marketplace. [There] is no indication of a constitutional plan to limit the ability of the States themselves to operate freely in the free market. See Laurence H. Tribe, *American Constitutional Law* 336 (1978) ("the Commerce Clause was directed, as an historical matter, only at regulatory and taxing actions taken by states in their sovereign capacity"). The precedents comport with this distinction.9

Restraint in this area also counseled by considerations of state sovereignty, the role of each State "as guardian and trustee for its people," and "the long recognized right of trader or manufacturer, engaged in an entirely private business, freely to exercise his own independent discretion as to parties with whom he will deal." *United States v. Colgate & Co.*, 250 U.S. 300, 307 (1919). Moreover, state proprietary activities may be, and often are, burdened with the same restrictions imposed on private market participants. Evenhandedness suggests that, when acting as proprietors, States should similarly share existing freedoms from federal constraints, including the inherent limits of the Commerce Clause. Finally, as this case illustrates, the competing considerations in cases involving state proprietary action often will be subtle, complex, politically charged, and difficult to assess under traditional Commerce Clause analysis. Given these factors, *Alexandria Scrap* wisely recognizes that, as a rule, the adjustment of interests in this context is a task better suited for Congress than this Court.

[We] find the label "protectionism" of little help in this context. The State's refusal to sell to buyers other than South Dakotans is "protectionist" only in the sense that it limits benefits generated by a state program to those who fund the state treasury and whom the State was created to serve. Petitioner's argument apparently also would characterize as "protectionist" rules restricting to state residents the enjoyment of state educational institutions, energy generated by a state-run plant, police and fire protection, and agricultural improvement and business development programs. Such policies, while perhaps "protectionist" in a loose sense, reflect the essential and patently unobjectionable purpose of state government—to serve the citizens of the State.

9. *Alexandria Scrap* does not stand alone. In *American Yearbook Co. v. Askew*, 339 F.Supp. 719 (M.D.Fla.1972), a three-judge District Court upheld a Florida statute requiring the State to obtain needed printing services from in-state shops. It reasoned that "state proprietary functions" are exempt from Commerce Clause scrutiny. This Court affirmed summarily. 409 U.S. 904 (1972). Numerous courts have rebuffed Commerce Clause challenges directed at similar preferences that exist in "a substantial majority of the states." Note, 58 Iowa L.Rev. 576 (1973). [The opinion cites state court decisions from eight states.]

[Cement] is not a natural resource, like coal, timber, wild game, or minerals. Cf. *Philadelphia v. New Jersey* (landfill sites). It is the end-product of a complex process whereby a costly physical plant and human labor act on raw materials. South Dakota has not sought to limit access to the State's limestone or other materials used to make cement. Nor has it restricted the ability of private firms or sister States to set up plants within its borders.

JUSTICE POWELL, with whom JUSTICE BRENNAN, JUSTICE WHITE, and JUSTICE STEVENS join, dissenting.

The application of the Commerce Clause to this case should turn on the nature of the governmental activity involved. [In] procuring goods and services for the operation of government, a State may act without regard to the private marketplace and remove itself from the reach of the Commerce Clause. See *American Yearbook Co.* [footnote 9 of the majority opinion, supra]. But when a State itself becomes a participant in the private market for other purposes, the Constitution forbids actions that would impede the flow of interstate commerce. These categories recognize no more than the "constitutional line between the State as Government and the State as trader." *New York v. United States,* [Ch. 2, Sec. 5, II supra].

The Court holds that South Dakota, like a private business, should not be governed by the Commerce Clause when it enters the private market. But precisely because South Dakota is a State, it cannot be presumed to behave like an enterprise "engaged in an entirely private business." A State frequently will respond to market conditions on the basis of political rather than economic concerns. To use the Court's terms, a State may attempt to act as a "market regulator" rather than a "market participant." In that situation, it is a pretense to equate the State with a private economic actor. State action burdening interstate trade is no less state action because it is accomplished by a public agency authorized to participate in the private market.

[Unlike] the market subsidies at issue in *Alexandria Scrap,* the marketing policy of the South Dakota Cement Commission has cut off interstate trade.3 The State can raise such a bar when it enters the market to supply its own needs. In order to ensure an adequate supply of cement for public uses, the State can withhold from interstate commerce the cement needed for public projects.

The State, however, has no parallel justification for favoring private, in-state customers over out-of-state customers.4 In response to political concerns that likely would be inconsequential to a private cement producer, South Dakota has shut off its cement sales to customers beyond its borders. That discrimination constitutes a direct barrier to trade "of the type forbidden by the Commerce Clause, and involved in previous cases." *Alexandria Scrap.* The effect on interstate trade is the same as if the state legislature had imposed the policy on private

3. One distinction between a private and a governmental function is whether the activity is supported with general tax funds, as was the case for the reprocessing program in *Alexandria Scrap,* or whether it is financed by the revenues it generates. In this case, South Dakota's cement plant has supported itself for many years. There is thus no need to consider the question whether a state-subsidized business could confine its sales to local residents.

4. The consequences of South Dakota's "residents-first" policy were devastating to petitioner Reeves, Inc., a Wyoming firm. For 20 years, Reeves had purchased about 95% of its cement from the South Dakota plant. When the State imposed its preference for South Dakota residents in 1978, Reeves had to reduce its production by over 75%. As a result, its South Dakota competitors were in a vastly superior position to compete for work in the region.

cement producers. The Commerce Clause prohibits this severe restraint on commerce.

———

UNITED HAULERS ASS'N, INC. v. ONEIDA–HERKIMER SOLID WASTE MANAGEMENT AUTH., 550 U.S. 330 (2007), upheld two county ordinances requiring trash haulers to deliver all solid waste generated within their borders to publicly owned waste processing facilities that charged a fee for their services. The majority reasoned that a preference for publicly owned facilities performing a traditional governmental function was unlikely to be motivated by economic protectionism. ALITO, J., joined by Stevens and Kennedy, JJ., dissented: "Respondents are doing exactly what the market-participant doctrine says they cannot: While acting as market participants by operating a fee-for-service business enterprise in an area in which there is an established interstate market, respondents are also regulating that market in a discriminatory manner and claiming that their special governmental status somehow insulates them from a dormant Commerce Clause challenge."

———

SOUTH–CENTRAL TIMBER DEVELOPMENT, INC. v. WUNNICKE, 467 U.S. 82 (1984), held that the market participant concept did not free Alaska from Commerce Clause invalidation of the state's contractual requirement that purchasers of state-owned standing timber must generally saw it into "cants" less than nine inches wide before shipping it out of state. WHITE, J.'s plurality opinion, joined by Brennan, Blackmun, and Stevens, JJ., stressed that the requirement reached beyond the market transaction in which the state participated: "[The] market-participant doctrine permits a state to influence 'a discrete, identifiable class of economic activity in which [it] is a major participant.' Contrary to the state's contention, the doctrine is not carte blanche to impose any conditions that the state has the economic power to dictate, and does not validate any requirement merely because the state imposes it upon someone with whom it is in contractual privity.

"The limit of the market-participant doctrine must be that it allows a State to impose burdens on commerce within the market in which it is a participant, but allows it to go no further. The State may not impose conditions, whether by statute, regulation, or contract, that have a substantial regulatory effect outside of that particular market. Unless the 'market' is relatively narrowly defined, the doctrine has the potential of swallowing up the rule that States may not impose substantial burdens on interstate commerce even if they act with the permissible state purpose of fostering local industry.

"At the heart of the dispute in this case is a disagreement about the definition of the market. Alaska contends that it is participating in the processed timber market, although it acknowledges that it participates in no way in the actual processing. South–Central argues, on the other hand, that although the State may be a participant in the timber market, it is using its leverage in that market to exert a regulatory effect in the processing market, in which it is not a participant. We agree with the latter position.

"[We] reject the contention that a State's action as a market regulator may be upheld against Commerce Clause challenge on the ground that the State could achieve the same end as a market participant. We therefore find it unimportant for present purposes that the State could support its processing industry by selling only to Alaska processors, by vertical integration, or by direct subsidy."

Having found the Commerce Clause applicable, the opinion concluded that Alaska's log processing requirement fell within the *Pike* and *Philadelphia* "rule of virtual per se invalidity" because of its "protectionist nature."a

Rehnquist, J., joined by O'Connor, J., dissented: "Alaska is merely paying the buyer of the timber indirectly, by means of a reduced price, to hire Alaska residents to process the timber. Under existing precedent, the State could accomplish that same result in any number of ways. [T]he State could choose to sell its timber only to those companies that maintain active primary-processing plants in Alaska. *Reeves.* Or the State could directly subsidize the primary-processing industry within the State. *Alexandria Scrap.* The State could even pay to have the logs processed and then enter the market only to sell processed logs. It seems to me unduly formalistic to conclude that the one path chosen by the State as best suited to promote its concerns is the path forbidden it by the Commerce Clause."

With *South Central Timber*, compare *White v. Massachusetts Council of Constr. Employers*, 460 U.S. 204 (1983), which rejected a Commerce Clause challenge to a mandate from the Mayor of Boston that had instituted employment preferences for Boston residents on city-funded construction projects. Is *White* persuasively distinguishable from *South-Central Timber*? Should it matter that the state, in *South-Central Timber*, entered the market to sell a natural resource that it had not created, whereas the city in *White* had raised money from taxpayers to create public benefits?

SECTION 4. INTERSTATE PRIVILEGES AND IMMUNITIES CLAUSE

Art. IV, § 2, cl. 1 provides that "The Citizens of each State shall be entitled to all Privileges and Immunities of Citizens in the several States." In most cases, the relationship between the dormant Commerce Clause and the Privileges and Immunities Clause is "mutually reinforcing." *Hicklin v. Orbeck*, 437 U.S. 518, 531 (1978). As a result, many of the claims brought under the dormant Commerce Clause could equally well be brought under the Privileges and Immunities Clause and vice versa. Nonetheless, the overlap between the dormant commerce and Privileges and Immunities Clauses is not complete. One clear and important difference is that corporations cannot sue under the Privileges and Immunities Clause because they are not "citizens." *Paul v. Virginia*, 75 U.S. (8 Wall.) 168 (1868). Claims on behalf of corporations must thus be brought under the dormant Commerce Clause if they are to be brought at all. Other differences are more subtle. As you read the following materials on the Privileges and Immunities Clause, you should keep the following questions in mind. First, what exactly are the "Privileges and Immunities of Citizens" that Art. IV, § 2, cl. 1 protects? Second, is the applicable test for the permissibility of state infringements on the "Privileges and Immunities of Citizens" more or less stringent than the test for

---

a. Powell, J., joined by Burger, C.J., would have remanded the foregoing issues for consideration by the court of appeals. But they joined Part II of White, J.'s opinion, which ruled that longstanding federal policy forbidding shipment from Alaska of unprocessed timber from federal lands did not negate the implied invalidity under the Commerce Clause of a similar state policy for timber from state lands: for "a state regulation to be removed from the reach of the dormant Commerce Clause, congressional intent must be unmistakably clear."

state violations of the Commerce Clause? Third, and perhaps most important, to what extent, if any, does the Privileges and Immunities Clause undermine the significance of "the market participant exception" to dormant Commerce Clause doctrine?

UNITED BUILDING & CONSTRUCTION TRADES COUNCIL v. MAYOR OF CAMDEN

465 U.S. 208, 104 S.Ct. 1020, 79 L.Ed.2d 249 (1984).

JUSTICE REHNQUIST delivered the opinion of the Court.

A municipal ordinance of the city of Camden, New Jersey, requires that at least 40% of the employees of contractors and subcontractors working on city construction projects be Camden residents. Appellant, the United Building and Construction Trades Council of Camden County and Vicinity (Council), challenges that ordinance as a violation of the Privileges and Immunities Clause, Art. IV, § 2, cl. 1, of the United States Constitution[1] [and] as unconstitutional under the Commerce Clause.

Citing *Reeves* and *Alexandria Scrap*, the [New Jersey Supreme Court] held that the resident quota was not subject to challenge under the Commerce Clause because the State was acting as a market participant rather than as a market regulator. [Since] the Council filed its appeal, [this Court] decided *White*, which held that an executive order of the Mayor of Boston, requiring that at least 50% of all jobs on construction projects funded in whole or in part by city funds be filled with bona fide city residents, was immune from scrutiny under the Commerce Clause because Boston was acting as a market participant rather than as a market regulator. In light of the decision in *White*, appellant has abandoned its Commerce Clause challenge. [The] only question left [is] whether the [ordinance] violates the Privileges and Immunities Clause.

[The City argues] that the Clause only applies to laws passed by a *State*. [But the] fact that the ordinance [is] municipal [does] not somehow place it outside the scope of the Privileges and Immunities Clause. [What] would be unconstitutional if done directly by the State can no more readily be accomplished by a city deriving its authority from the State. [Nor can we accept] that the Privileges and Immunities Clause does not apply to an ordinance that discriminates solely on the basis of *municipal* residency. The Clause is phrased in terms of *state* citizenship and was designed "to place the citizens of each State upon the same footing with citizens of other States, as far as the advantages resulting from citizenship in those States are concerned." [But we] have never read the Clause so literally as to apply it only to distinctions based on state citizenship. [A] person who is not residing in a given State is ipso facto not residing in a city within that State. Thus, whether the exercise of a privilege is conditioned on state residency or on municipal residency he will just as surely be excluded.

[It] is true that New Jersey citizens not residing in Camden will be affected by the ordinance as well as out-of-state citizens. And it is true that the disadvantaged New Jersey residents have no claim under the Privileges and Immunities Clause. *Slaughter-House Cases.* But New Jersey residents at least have a chance to remedy at the polls any discrimination against them. Out-of-state citizens have no similar opportunity.

---

1. "The Citizens of each State shall be enti-   zens in the several States."
tled to all Privileges and Immunities of Citi-

[Application] of the Privileges and Immunities Clause to a particular instance of discrimination against out-of-state residents entails a two-step inquiry. As an initial matter, the Court must decide whether the ordinance burdens one of those privileges and immunities protected by the Clause. *Baldwin v. Montana Fish and Game Comm'n.*, 436 U.S. 371 (1978).a Not all forms of discrimination against citizens of other States are constitutionally suspect: "Some distinctions between residents and nonresidents merely reflect the fact that this is a Nation composed of individual States, and are permitted; other distinctions are prohibited because they hinder the formation, the purpose, or the development of a single Union of those States. Only with respect to those 'privileges' and 'immunities' bearing upon the vitality of the Nation as a single entity must the State treat all citizens, resident and nonresident, equally." Ibid.

As a threshold matter, then, we must determine whether an out-of-state resident's interest in employment on public works contracts in another State is sufficiently "fundamental" to the promotion of interstate harmony so as to "fall within the purview of the Privileges and Immunities Clause." Id.

Certainly, the pursuit of a common calling [or job] is one of the most fundamental of those privileges protected by the Clause. Many, if not most, of our cases expounding the Privileges and Immunities Clause have dealt with this basic and essential activity. See, e.g., *Hicklin v. Orbeck*, 437 U.S. 518 (1978); *Toomer v. Witsell*, 334 U.S. 385 (1948). Public employment, however, is qualitatively different from employment in the private sector; it is a subspecies of the broader opportunity to pursue a common calling. We have held that there is no fundamental right to government employment for purposes of the Equal Protection Clause. And in *White*, we held that for purposes of the Commerce Clause everyone employed on a city public works project is, "in a substantial if informal sense, 'working for the city.' "

It can certainly be argued that for purposes of the Privileges and Immunities Clause everyone affected by the Camden ordinance is also "working for the city" and, therefore, has no grounds for complaint when the city favors its own residents. But we decline to transfer mechanically into this context an analysis fashioned to fit the Commerce Clause. Our decision in *White* turned on a distinction between the city acting as a market participant and the city acting as a market regulator. [But] the distinction between market participant and market regulator relied upon in *White* to dispose of the Commerce Clause challenge is not dispositive in this context. The two Clauses have different aims and set different standards for state conduct.

The Commerce Clause acts as an implied restraint upon state regulatory powers. Such powers must give way before the superior authority of Congress to

---

a. *Baldwin* upheld Montana's non-resident license fee of $225 for hunting elk, compared with $30 for residents, on the ground that hunting for sport was not a protected "fundamental" right under the Privileges and Immunities Clause. In holding that the Privileges and Immunities Clause protects only fundamental rights, the Court relied heavily on the opinion of Justice Bushrod Washington in *Corfield v. Coryell*, 6 F.Cas. 546, 552 (No. 3,230) (C.C.E.D.Pa.1823): "The inquiry is, what are the privileges and immunities of citizens in the several states? We feel no hesitation in confining these expressions to those privileges and immunities which are, in their nature, fundamental; which belong, of right, to the citizens of all free governments; and which have, at all times, been enjoyed by the citizens of the several states, [from] the time of their becoming free, independent, and sovereign. What these fundamental principles are, it would perhaps be more tedious than difficult to enumerate. They may, however, be all comprehended under the following general heads: Protection by the government; the enjoyment of life and liberty, with the right to acquire and possess property of every kind, and to pursue and obtain happiness and safety; subject nevertheless to such restraints as the government may justly prescribe for the general good of the whole."

legislate on (or leave unregulated) matters involving interstate commerce. When the State acts solely as a market participant, no conflict between state regulation and federal regulatory authority can arise. *White; Reeves; Alexandria Scrap.* The Privileges and Immunities Clause, on the other hand, imposes a direct restraint on state action in the interests of interstate harmony.

[In] *Hicklin,* we struck down as a violation of the Privileges and Immunities Clause an "Alaska Hire" statute containing a resident-hiring preference for all employment related to the development of the State's oil and gas resources. Alaska argued in that case that "because the oil and gas that are the subject of Alaska Hire are *owned* by the State, this ownership, of itself, is sufficient justification for the Act's discrimination against nonresidents, and takes the Act totally without the scope of the Privileges and Immunities Clause." We concluded, however, that the State's interest in controlling those things it claims to own is not absolute. "Rather than placing a statute completely beyond the Clause, the State's ownership of the property with which the statute is concerned is a factor— although often the crucial factor—to be considered in evaluating whether the statute's discrimination against noncitizens violates the Clause." Much the same analysis, we think, is appropriate to a city's efforts to bias private employment decisions in favor of its residents on construction projects funded with public moneys. The fact that Camden is expending its own funds or funds it administers in accordance with the terms of a grant is certainly a factor—perhaps the crucial factor—to be considered in evaluating whether the statute's discrimination violates the Privileges and Immunities Clause. But it does not remove the Camden ordinance completely from the purview of the Clause.

[Every] inquiry under the Privileges and Immunities Clause "must [be] conducted with due regard for the principle that the States should have considerable leeway in analyzing local evils and in prescribing appropriate cures." This caution is particularly appropriate when a government body is merely setting conditions on the expenditure of funds it controls. The Alaska Hire statute at issue in *Hicklin* swept within its strictures not only contractors and subcontractors dealing directly with the State's oil and gas; it also covered suppliers who provided goods and services to those contractors and subcontractors. We invalidated the Act as "an attempt to force virtually all businesses that benefit in some way from the economic ripple effect of Alaska's decision to develop its oil and gas resources to bias their employment practices in favor of the State's residents." No similar "ripple effect" appears to infect the Camden ordinance. It is limited in scope to employees working directly on city public works projects.

Nonetheless, we find it impossible to evaluate Camden's justification on the record as it now stands. No trial has ever been held in the case. No findings of fact have been made. [We], therefore, [remand for] proceedings not inconsistent with this opinion.

Justice Blackmun, dissenting.

[The] Framers had every reason to believe that interstate discrimination based on municipal residence would be dealt with by the States themselves. [Nor] is this mechanism for relief merely a theoretical one; in the past decade several States, including California and Georgia, have repealed or forbidden protectionist ordinances like the one at issue here. [Because] I believe that the [Privileges and Immunities Clause] does not apply to discrimination based on municipal residence, I dissent.

The Court, per O'CONNOR, J., stated a standard for testing discriminations against out-of-staters under the Privileges and Immunities Clause in LUNDING v. NEW YORK TAX APPEALS TRIBUNAL, 522 U.S. 287 (1998), which invalidated a New York statute that effectively denied non-resident taxpayers a state income tax deduction for alimony payments that was available to resident taxpayers." [W]hen confronted with a challenge under the Privileges and Immunities Clause to a law distinguishing between residents and nonresidents, a State may defend its position by demonstrating that (i) there is a substantial reason for the difference in treatment; and (ii) the discrimination practiced against nonresidents bears a substantial relationship to the State's objective." Ginsburg, J., joined by Rehnquist, C.J., and Kennedy, J., dissented.

Compare the much quoted formulation in *Toomer*, which invalidated a discriminatory state tax on non-residents' access to migratory shrimp, said: "Like many other constitutional provisions, the Privileges and Immunities Clause is not an absolute. It does bar discrimination against citizens of other States where there is no substantial reason for the discrimination beyond the mere fact that they are citizens of other States. But it does not preclude disparity of treatment in the many situations where there are perfectly valid independent reasons for it. Thus the inquiry in each case must be concerned with whether such reasons do exist and whether the degree of discrimination bears a close relation to [them. The] purpose [is] to outlaw classifications based on the fact of non-citizenship unless there is something to indicate that non-citizens constitute a peculiar source of the evil at which the statute is aimed."

Chapter 5

SUBSTANTIVE PROTECTION OF
ECONOMIC INTERESTS

INTRODUCTION

Most of the remaining chapters are concerned with constitutional limitations on government power, independent of limitations arising out of the distribution of powers within the federal system. Some of the limitations are identical, or nearly so, whether applied to the state or federal governments, but are based on different sources. The major limitations on the federal government are found in the Bill of Rights and in Art. I, § 9, while those on state government are based largely on the Thirteenth, Fourteenth, and Fifteenth Amendments and on Art. I, § 10. But the Fourteenth Amendment has now been held to impose on the states most of the limitations the Bill of Rights imposes on the federal government.

These materials do not deal with all the federal constitutional limitations but only those of major significance and difficulty. State constitutions include additional limitations on state government, some similar to federal limitations though occasionally interpreted differently, and some quite dissimilar in terms and purposes. Study of the federal limitations should provide adequate background for handling many of the state-imposed limitations.

SECTION 1.   ORIGINS OF SUBSTANTIVE
DUE PROCESS

One important concern of this and later chapters is the extent to which the Due Process Clauses of the Fifth and Fourteenth Amendments may be invoked to impose limits on the *substance* of governmental regulations and other activities, as well as to govern the *procedures* by which government affects "life, liberty and property." That these clauses embody *any* limits on the substance of legislation requires some initial explanation, since their terms refer only to "process."

I.   EARLY EXPRESSIONS OF THE NOTION
THAT GOVERNMENTAL AUTHORITY
HAS IMPLIED LIMITS

The most notable early expression in this country of the view that there are implied or inherent limits on governmental power is CHASE, J.'s opinion in CALDER v. BULL, 3 U.S. (3 Dall.) 386 (1798). Although the Supreme Court rejected the claim of potential heirs that a Connecticut statute amounted to an *ex post facto* law (because the *ex post facto* clause only applied to criminal laws), Chase, J., made plain his willingness in an appropriate case to strike down legislation without regard to explicit constitutional limitations:

"I cannot subscribe to the omnipotence of a State Legislature, or that it is absolute and without control; although its authority should not be expressly restrained by the Constitution, or fundamental law of the State. The people of the United States erected their constitutions, or forms of government, to establish justice, to promote the general welfare, to secure the blessings of liberty, and to protect their persons and property from violence. The purposes for which men enter into society will determine the nature and terms of the social compact; and as they are the foundation of the legislative power, they will decide what are the proper objects of it. The nature and ends of legislative power will limit the exercise of it. This fundamental principle flows from the very nature of our free Republican governments, that no man should be compelled to do what the laws do not require; nor to refrain from acts which the laws permit. There are acts which the Federal, or State, Legislature cannot do, without exceeding their authority. There are certain vital principles in our free Republican governments, which will determine and overrule an apparent and flagrant abuse of legislative power; as to authorize manifest injustice by positive law; to take away that security for personal liberty, or private property, for the protection whereof the government was established. An ACT of the legislature (for I cannot call it a law), contrary to the great first principles of the social compact, cannot be considered a rightful exercise of legislative authority. The obligation of a law in governments established on express compact, and on republican principles, must be determined by the nature of the power on which it is founded. A few instances will suffice to explain what I mean. A law that punished a citizen for an innocent action or, in other words, for an act, which, when done, was in violation of no existing law; a law that destroys, or impairs, the lawful private contracts of citizens; a law that makes a man a Judge in his own cause; or a law that takes property from A and gives it to B: It is against all reason and justice, for a people to intrust a Legislature with SUCH powers; and therefore, it cannot be presumed that they have done it. The genius, the nature, and the spirit, of our State Governments, amount to a prohibition of such acts of legislation; and the general principles of law and reason forbid them. [To] maintain that our Federal, or State Legislature possesses such powers, if they had not been expressly restrained, would, in my opinion, be a political heresy, altogether inadmissible in our free republican governments."

IREDELL, J., disagreed: "[If] a government, composed of Legislative, Executive and Judicial departments, were established, by a constitution which imposed no limits on the legislative power, the consequence would inevitably be, that whatever the legislative power chose to enact, would be lawfully enacted, and the judicial power could never interpose to pronounce it void. It is true, that some speculative jurists have held, that a legislative act against natural justice must, in itself, be void; but I cannot think that, under such a government any Court of Justice would possess a power to declare it so. [I]t has been the policy of all the American states, which have, individually, framed their state constitutions, since the revolution, and of the people of the United States, when they framed the Federal Constitution, to define with precision the objects of the legislative power, and to restrain its exercise within marked and settled boundaries. If any act of Congress, or of the Legislature of a state, violates those constitutional provisions, it is unquestionably void. [If], on the other hand, the Legislature of the Union, or the Legislature of any member of the Union, shall pass a law, within the general scope of their constitutional power, the Court cannot pronounce it to be void, merely because it is, in their judgment, contrary to the principles of natural justice. The ideas of natural justice are regulated by no fixed standard: the ablest and the purest men have differed upon the subject; and all that the Court could properly say, in such an event, would be that the Legislature (possessed of an equal right of opinion) had passed an act which, in the opinion of the judges, was inconsistent with the abstract principles of natural justice.''

———

Concurring in the judgment in WASHINGTON v. GLUCKSBERG (1997) (Ch. 6, Sec.2), which rejected the argument that there is a constitutional right to physician-assisted suicide, SOUTER, J., noted that the physicians who asserted this right ''also invoke two centuries of American constitutional practice in recognizing unenumerated substantive limits on governmental action.'' ''Although this practice has neither rested on any single textual basis nor expressed a consistent theory, [the] persistence of substantive due process in our cases points to the legitimacy of the modern justification for such judicial review * * *.

''Before the ratification of the Fourteenth Amendment, substantive constitutional review resting on a theory of unenumerated rights occurred largely in the state courts applying state constitutions that commonly contained either due process clauses like that of the Fifth Amendment (and later the Fourteenth) on the textual antecedents of such clauses, repeating Magna Carta's guarantee of 'the law of the land.' On the basis of such clauses, or of general principles untethered to specific constitutional language, state courts evaluated the constitutionality of a wide range of statutes. [The] middle of the 19th century brought the famous *Wynehamer* case, invalidating a statute purporting to render possession of liquor immediately illegal except when kept for narrow, specified purposes, the state court finding the statute inconsistent with the State's due process clause. WYNE-HAMER v. PEOPLE, 13 N.Y. 378, 486 (1856). The statute was deemed an excessive threat to the 'fundamental rights of the citizen' to property (opinion of Comstock, J.).

''Even in this early period, however, this Court anticipated the developments that would presage both the Civil War and the ratification of the Fourteenth Amendment, by making it clear on several occasions that it too had no doubt of the judiciary's power to strike down legislation that conflicted with important but unenumerated principles of American government. [In] FLETCHER v. PECK, 6 Cranch 87 (1810), [the Court] struck down an Act of the Georgia Legislature that purported to rescind a sale of public land ab initio and reclaim title for the State, and so deprive subsequent, good-faith purchasers of property conveyed by the original grantees. The Court rested the invalidation on alternative sources of authority: the specific prohibitions against bill of attainder, *ex post facto* laws, laws impairing contracts in Article 1, § 10, of the Constitution; and 'general principles which are common to our free institutions,' by which Chief Justice Marshall meant that a simple deprivation of property by the State could not be an authentically 'legislative' Act.

''*Fletcher* was not, though, the most telling early example of such review. For its most salient instance in the Court before the adoption of the Fourteenth Amendment was, of course, the case that the Amendment would in due course overturn, DRED SCOTT v. SANDFORD, 19 How. 393 (1857). Unlike *Fletcher*, *Dred Scott* was textually based on a Due Process Clause (in the Fifth Amendment, applicable to the National Government), and it was in reliance on that Clauses's protection of property that the Court invalidated the Missouri Compromise. This substantive protection of an owner's property in a slave taken to the territories was traced to the absence of any enumerated power to affect that property granted to the Congress by Article 1 of the Constitution, the implication being that the Government had no legitimate interest that could support the earlier congressional compromise. The ensuing judgment of history needs no recounting here."

II. THE SEARCH FOR A CONSTITUTIONAL BASIS

Before the adoption of the Fourteenth Amendment in 1868, the federal constitution provided little basis for challenging state regulation of economic interests. In BARRON v. MAYOR AND CITY COUNCIL OF BALTIMORE, 32 U.S. (7 Pet.) 243 (1833), in the course of rejecting appellant's argument that by ruining the use of his wharf the city had violated his Fifth Amendment guarantee that private property shall not be "taken for public use, without just compensation," the Court, per MARSHALL, C.J., held that the Bill of Rights applied only to the federal government: "[The] great revolution which established the constitution of the United States was not effected without immense opposition. Serious fears were extensively entertained that [the new national powers] might be exercised in a manner dangerous to liberty. In almost every convention by which the constitution was adopted, amendments to guard against the abuse of power were recommended. These amendments demanded security against the apprehended encroachments of the general government. [They] contain no expression indicating an intention to apply them to the state governments. This court cannot so apply them."

Moreover, the Court narrowed the scope of the constitutional provision (Act 1, § 10) prohibiting the states from passing any laws "impairing the obligation of contracts."[1] Indeed, *Charles River Bridge* seemed designed to discourage resort to the federal constitution to escape regulation of economic interests: "It is well settled by the decisions of this court, that a state law may be retrospective in its character, and may divest vested rights; and yet not violate the constitution of the United States, unless it also impairs the obligation of a contract."

With federal constitutional grounds not available to protect against most encroachments on economic interests, state judges resorted to the "due process" and "law of the land" clauses of state constitutions. These provisions originally referred to proceeding in accordance with the law and accepted legal procedure. The "law of the land" clause of the early State constitutions was usually a nearly literal translation of the famous chapter 29 of the Magna Carta of 1225, the Magna Carta of history. The phrase "due process of law" comes from chapter 3 of the statute of 28 Edward III (1355) which [reads]: "No man of what state or condition he be, shall be put out of his lands or tenements, nor taken, nor imprisoned, nor disinherited, nor put to death, without he be brought to answer by due process of law."

The state courts began to evolve out of these clauses a substantive limitation on legislative power, aimed first at special legislation designed to affect the rights of specific individuals, and then applied to general legislation interfering with vested rights. Most State constitutions contained from the outset a paraphrase of

1. *Proprietors of Charles River Bridge v. Proprietors of Warren Bridge,* 36 U.S. (11 Pet.) 420 (1837) (state grant of right to operate toll bridge did not imply obligation not to authorize competing bridge); *West River Bridge Co. v. Dix,* 47 U.S. (6 How.) 507 (1848) (state grant of exclusive right to operate toll bridge does not bar state from acquiring it by eminent domain); *Stone v. Mississippi,* 101 U.S. 814 (1880) (vital public interest permits state to ban lottery business 3 years after it granted 25 year charter).

chapter 29 of Magna Carta, which declared that no person should be deprived of his "estate" "except by the law of the land or a judgment of his peers"; and following the usage of the Fifth Amendment of the United States Constitution, more and more State constitutions came after 1791 to contain a clause which declared that "no person shall be deprived of life, liberty or property without due process of law." By the outbreak of the Civil War a more or less complete transference of the doctrine of vested rights and most of its Kentian corollaries had been effected in the vast majority of the State jurisdictions.

III. FOURTEENTH AMENDMENT

The Thirteenth Amendment forbidding involuntary servitude was ratified in 1865, but freeing the slaves did not produce the fruits of freedom, due to the "Black Codes" and other repressive measures. The plight of the blacks and their need at the time was reflected in the Civil Rights Act of 1866, which recognized "all persons born in United States" as United States citizens, and gave to "such citizens, of every race or color, without regard to any previous condition of slavery [the] same right, in every State and Territory in the United States, to make and enforce contracts, to sue, be parties, and give evidence, to inherit, purchase, lease, sell, hold, and convey real and personal property, and to full and equal benefit of all laws and proceedings for the security of person and property, as is enjoyed by white citizens."

Even while that 1866 Civil Rights Act was awaiting enactment, action was under way designed, in part at least, to remove existing doubts as to the power of Congress to enact such legislation. One week after the Senate passed the Civil Rights Act, the Congressional Joint Committee on Reconstruction submitted to both houses of Congress its early version of a Fourteenth Amendment authorizing Congress to enact laws to protect equal rights. After Congress passed the Civil Rights Act in April over a presidential veto based in part on the view that Congress lacked power to enact the law, the Joint Commission on Reconstruction hammered out a revised proposal that added privileges and immunities, due process, and equal protection provisions as limitations on the states, and authorized Congress to enact legislation to "enforce this article." After further modifications, Congress approved the Fourteenth Amendment in June, 1866 and sent it to the states for ratification.

———

SLAUGHTER–HOUSE CASES, 83 U.S. (16 Wall.) 36 (1873), per MILLER, J., upheld a Louisiana law granting a monopoly to operate slaughterhouses in the New Orleans area, regarding this an "appropriate, stringent, and effectual" means to "remove from the more densely population of the city, the noxious slaughterhouses and large and offensive collections of animals." Excluded butchers claimed that the law violated their right "to exercise their trade" and invoked the 13th and 14th Amendments: "The challengers claim that the law created an 'involuntary servitude' in violation of the 13th Amendment, and that it violated the 14th Amendment by abridging the 'privileges and immunities' of citizens of the United States, denying them 'of their property without due process of law.' [We are] thus called upon for the first time to [construe these Amendments].

"[The Civil War] being over, those who had succeeded in re-establishing the authority of the Federal government were not content to permit [the] great act of emancipation to rest on the actual results of the contest or the proclamation of the Executive, both of which might have been questioned in after times, and they determined to place this main and most valuable result in the Constitution of the restored Union as one of its fundamental articles. Hence the [13th Amendment]. To withdraw the mind from the contemplation of this grand yet simple declaration of the personal freedom of all the human race within the jurisdiction of this government [and] with a microscopic search endeavor to find in it a reference to servitudes, which may have been attached to property in certain localities, requires an effort, to say the least of it. That a personal servitude was meant is proved by the use of the word 'involuntary,' which can only apply to human beings.

"[The] process of restoring to their proper relations with the Federal government and with the other States those which had sided with the [rebellion] developed the fact that, notwithstanding the formal recognition by those States of the abolition of slavery, the condition of the slave race would, without further protection of the Federal government, be almost as bad as it was before. Among the first acts of legislation adopted by several of the States [were] laws which imposed upon the colored race onerous disabilities and burdens, and curtailed their rights [to] such an extent that their freedom was of little value. [These] circumstances [forced upon those] who had conducted the Federal government in safety through [the war], and who supposed that by [the 13th Amendment] they had secured the result of their labors, the conviction that something more was necessary in the way of constitutional protection to the unfortunate race who had suffered so much. They accordingly [proposed the 14th Amendment]. A few years experience satisfied [those] who had been the authors of the other two amendments that [these] were inadequate for the protection of life, liberty, and property, without which freedom to the slave was no boon. [It] was urged that a race of men distinctively marked as was the negro, living in the midst of another and dominant race, could never be fully secured in their person [and] property without the right of suffrage. Hence [the 15th Amendment].

"[In] the light of this recapitulation of events, almost too recent to be called history, [and] on the most casual examination of the language of these amendments, no one can fail to be impressed with the one pervading purpose found in them all, [and] without which none of them would have been even suggested; we mean the freedom of the slave race [and] the protection of the newly-made freeman and citizen from the oppressions of those who had formerly exercised unlimited dominion over him. It is true that only the 15th amendment, in terms, mentions the negro, [but] it is just as true that each of the other articles was addressed to the grievances of that race, and designed to remedy them as the fifteenth. We do not say that no one else but the negro can share in this protection. [But] what we do say [is] that in any fair and just construction of any section or phrase of these amendments, it is necessary to look to the purpose which [was] the pervading spirit of them all, the evil [they] were designed [to remedy].

"The first section of the [14th Amendment], to which our attention is more specially invited, opens with a definition of citizenship—not only citizenship of the United States, but citizenship of the states. * * * 'All persons born or naturalized in the United States, and subject to the jurisdiction thereof, are citizens of the United States and of the state wherein they reside.' [The section] overturns the *Dred Scott* decision by making *all persons* born within the United States * * * citizens of the United States. [The] next observation is more important in view of the arguments of counsel in the present case. [T]he distinction between citizenship of the United States and citizenship of a State is clearly recognized and established. Not only may a man be a citizen of the United States without being a citizen of a State, but an important element is necessary to convert the former into the latter. He must reside within the state to make him a citizen of it, but it is only necessary that he should be born or naturalized in the United States to be a citizen of the Union. * * *

"We think [the distinction between citizenship of the United states and citizenship of a State] of great weight in this argument, because the next paragraph of this same section, which is the one mainly relied on by plaintiffs in error, speaks only of privileges and immunities of citizens of the United States, and does not speak of those of citizens of the several states. The argument, however, in favor of the plaintiffs, rests wholly on the assumption that the citizenship is the same and the privileges and immunities guaranteed by the clause are the same. The language is, 'No state shall make or enforce any law which shall abridge the privileges or immunities of citizens of the United States.' It is a little remarkable, if this clause was intended as a protection to the citizen of a state against the legislative power of his own state, that the word citizen of the state should be left out when it is so carefully used, and used in contradistinction to citizens of the United States, in the very sentence which precedes it. It is too clear for argument that the change in phraseology was adopted understandingly and with a purpose.

"Of the privileges and immunities of the citizen of the United States, and, of the privileges and immunities of the citizen of the state, and what they respectively are, we will presently consider; but we wish to state here that it is only the former which are placed by this clause under the protection of the federal Constitution, and that the latter, whatever they may be, are not intended to have any additional protection by this paragraph of the amendment.

"[Art. IV, § 2 states:] 'The citizens of each State shall be entitled to all the privileges and immunities of citizens of the several States.' [It] did not create those rights, which it called privileges and immunities of citizens of the States. It threw around them in that clause no security for the citizen of the State in which they claimed or exercised. Nor did it profess to control the power of the State governments over the rights of its own citizens. Its sole purpose was to declare to the several States, that whatever those rights, as you grant or establish them to your own citizens, or as you limit or qualify, [the] same, neither more nor less, shall be the measure of the rights of citizens of other States within your jurisdiction.

"[Up] to the adoption of the recent amendments, no claim or pretense was set up that those rights depended on the Federal government for their existence or protection, beyond the very few express limitations which the Federal Constitution imposed upon the States—such, for instance, as the prohibition against ex post-facto laws, bills of attainder, and laws impairing the obligation of contracts. But with the exception of these and a few other restrictions, the entire domain of the privileges and immunities of citizens of the states [lay] within the constitutional and legislative power of the states, and without that of the Federal government. Was it the purpose of the fourteenth amendment, by the simple declaration that no state should make or enforce any law which shall abridge the privileges and immunities of *citizens of the United States,* to transfer the security and protection of all the civil rights [from] the States to the Federal government? And where it is declared that Congress shall have the power to enforce that article, was it intended to bring within the power of Congress the entire domain of civil rights heretofore belonging exclusively to the States?

"[Such] a construction [would] constitute this court a perpetual censor upon all legislation of the states, on the civil rights of their own citizens, with authority to nullify such as it did not approve as consistent with those rights, as they existed at the time of the adoption of this amendment. [Such a construction] radically changes the whole theory of the relations of the State and Federal governments to each other and of both these governments to the people. [We] are convinced that no such results were intended by the Congress which proposed these amendments, nor by the legislatures of the States which ratified them.

"The argument has not been much pressed in these cases that the defendant's charter deprives the plaintiffs of their property without due process of law, or that it denies to them the equal protection of the law. The first of these paragraphs has been in the Constitution since the adoption of the Fifth Amendment, as a restraint upon the federal power. It is also to be found in some form of expression in the constitutions of nearly all the states, as a restraint upon the power of the States. [U]nder no construction of that provision that we have ever seen, or any that we deem admissible, can the restraint imposed [by] Louisiana upon the exercise of their trade by the butchers of New Orleans be held to be a deprivation of property within the meaning of that provision.

"[In] the light of the history of these amendments, and the pervading purpose of them, which we have already discussed, [it] is not difficult to give a meaning to [the equal protection] clause. [Laws discriminating against 'the newly emancipated negroes'] was the evil to be remedied by this clause, and by it such laws are forbidden. [We] doubt very much whether any action of a state not directed by way of discrimination against the negroes as a class, or on account of their race, will ever be held to come within the purview of this provision. It is so clearly a provision for that race and that emergency, that a strong case would be necessary for its application to any other. Unquestionably [the recent was] added largely to the number of those who believe in the necessity of a strong National government. But, however pervading this sentiment, and however it may have contributed to the adoption of the amendments we have been considering, we do not see in those amendments any purpose to destroy the main features of the general system."

FIELD, J., joined by Chase, J., and Swayne and Bradley, JJ., dissented: "[The] question presented [is] whether the recent [amendments] protect the citizens of the United States against the deprivation of their common rights by State legislation. In my judgment, the fourteenth amendment does afford such [protection]. The amendment does not attempt to confer any new privileges or immunities upon citizens, or to enumerate or define those already existing. It assumes that there are such privileges and immunities which belong of right to citizens as such, and ordains that they shall not be abridged by State legislation. If this inhibition [only] refers, as held by the [majority], [to] such privileges and immunities as were before its adoption specially designated in the Constitution or necessarily implied as belonging to citizens of the United States, it was a vain and idle enactment, which accomplished nothing, and most unnecessarily excited Congress and the people on its passage. With privileges and immunities thus designated or implied no State could ever have interfered by its laws, and no new constitutional provision was required to inhibit such interference. [But] if the amendment refers to the natural and inalienable rights which belong to all citizens, the inhibition has a profound significance and consequence. * * *

"The terms, privileges and immunities, are not new in the amendment; they were in the Constitution before the amendment was adopted. They are found in [Art. IV, § 2.] In *Corfield v. Coryell*, 6 F. 546 (C.C.E.D. Pa. 1823), Cas. Mr. Justice Washington said he had 'no hesitation in confining these expressions to those privileges and immunities which were, in their nature, fundamental; which belong of right to the citizens of all free governments.' [This] appears to me to be a sound construction of the clause in question. Clearly among [these rights] must be placed the right to pursue a lawful employment in a lawful manner, without other restraint than such as equally affects all persons. In the discussions in Congress upon the passage of the Civil Rights Act repeated reference was made to this language of Mr. Justice Washington. It was cited by Senator Trumbull with the observation that it enumerated the very rights belonging to a citizen of the United States set forth in the first section of the act.

"[The] privileges and immunities designated in [Art. IV, § 2] are, then, according to the decision cited, those which of right belong to the citizens of all free governments. [What] the clause in question did for the protection of the citizens of one State against hostile and discriminating legislation of other States, the fourteenth amendment does for the protection of every citizen of the United States against hostile and discriminating legislation against him in favor of others, whether they reside in the same or in different [States].

"This equality of right, with exemption from all disparaging and partial enactments, in the lawful pursuits of life, throughout the whole country, is the distinguishing privilege of citizens of the United States. To them, everywhere, all pursuits, all professions, all avocations are open without other restrictions than such as are imposed equally upon all others of the same age, sex, and condition. The State may prescribe such regulations for every pursuit and calling of life as will promote the public health, secure the good order and advance the general prosperity of society, but when once prescribed, the pursuit or calling must be free to be followed by every citizen who is within the conditions designated, and will conform to the regulations. This is the fundamental idea upon which our institutions rest, and unless adhered to in the legislation of the country our government will be a republic only in name. The fourteenth amendment, in my judgment, makes it essential to the validity of the legislation of every State that this equality of right should be respected."

BRADLEY, J., also dissented: "[In] my judgment, it was the intention of the people of this country in adopting [the 14th] amendment to provide National security against violation by the States of the fundamental rights of the citizen. [A] law which prohibits a large class of citizens from adopting a lawful employment, or from following a lawful employment previously adopted, does deprive them of liberty as well as property, without due process of law. [Such] a law also deprives those citizens of the equal protection of the laws. [It] is futile to argue that none but persons of the African race are intended to be benefitted by this amendment. They may have been the primary cause of the amendment, but its language is general, embracing all citizens, and I think it was purposely so expressed. The mischief to be remedied was not merely slavery and its incidents and consequences; but that spirit of insubordination and disloyalty to the National government which had troubled the country for so many years in some of the States, and that intolerance of free speech and free discussion which often rendered life and property insecure, and led to much unequal legislation.

"[But] great fears are expressed that this construction of the amendment will lead to enactments by Congress interfering with the internal affairs of the States. [In] my judgment no such practical inconveniences would arise. Very little, if any, legislation on the part of Congress would be required to carry the amendment into effect. Like the prohibition against passing a law impairing the obligation of a contract, it would execute itself. [Even] if the business of the National courts should be increased, Congress could easily supply the remedy by increasing their number and efficiency. The great question is: What is the true construction of the amendment? [The] argument from inconvenience ought not to have a very controlling influence in questions of this sort. The National will and National interest are of far greater importance."

SECTION 2.   THE *LOCHNER* ERA

I.   THE ROAD TO *LOCHNER*

In *Munn v. Illinois*, 94 U.S. (4 Otto) 113 (1876), although the Court, per Waite, C.J., upheld a state law regulating the rates of grain elevators, pointing out that private property may be regulated when it is "affected with a public interest," the Court made a comment that was to be relied upon years later to justify judicial control of state regulation: "Undoubtedly, in mere private contracts, relating to matters in which the public has no interest, what is reasonable must be ascertained judicially." *Mugler v. Kansas*, 123 U.S. 623 (1887), upheld a state law prohibiting intoxicating beverages, but the Court, per Harlan, J., made clear that not every statute said to be enacted for the promotion of "the public morals, the public health, or the public safety" would be sustained. If a law supposedly enacted pursuant to the police powers of the state "has no real or substantial relation to these objects, or is a palpable invasion of rights secured by the fundamental law, it is the duty of the courts to so adjudge."

ALLGEYER v. LOUISIANA, 165 U.S. 578 (1897), was the first reasoned Supreme Court decision actually to hold that the substance of economic legislation violated Fourteenth Amendment Due Process. A unanimous Court, per PECKHAM, J., struck down a Louisiana law prohibiting any act in the state to effect a contract for marine insurance on state property with a company not licensed to do business in the state. The statute exceeded the police power of the state and deprived the defendants of their Fourteenth Amendment liberty to contract for insurance. The "liberty" mentioned in that amendment, the Court told us, means not only one's right to be free of physical restraint of his person, but "embrace[s] the right of the citizen to be free in the enjoyment of all his faculties, to be free to use them in all lawful ways; to live and work where he will; [to] pursue any livelihood or avocation; and for that purpose to enter into all contracts which may be proper, necessary, and essential to his carrying out to a successful conclusion the purpose above mentioned."

LOCHNER v. NEW YORK
198 U.S. 45, 25 S.Ct. 539, 49 L.Ed. 937 (1905).

JUSTICE PECKHAM delivered the opinion of the Court.

[The Court held invalid a New York statute forbidding employment in a bakery for more than 60 hours a week or 10 hours a day.]

The statute necessarily interferes with the right of contract between the employer and employees. [The] general right to make a contract in relation to his business is part of the liberty of the individual protected by the 14th Amendment. [*Allgeyer.*] The right to purchase or to sell labor is part of the liberty protected by this amendment, unless there are circumstances which exclude the right. [This court has] upheld the exercise of the police powers of the States in many cases, [among them] *Holden v. Hardy*, 169 U.S. 366 (1898), [where it] was held that the kind of employment, mining, smelting, etc., and the character of the employees in such kinds of labor, were such as to make it reasonable and proper for the State to interfere to prevent the employees from being constrained by the rules laid down by the proprietors in regard to labor. [There] is nothing in *Holden v. Hardy* which covers the case now before us.

It must, of course, be conceded that there is a limit to the valid exercise of the police power by the state. [Otherwise] the 14th Amendment would have no efficacy and the legislatures of the states would have unbounded power. [In] every case that comes before this court, therefore, where legislation of this character is concerned, and where the protection of the Federal Constitution is sought, the question necessarily arises: Is this a fair, reasonable, and appropriate exercise of the police power of the state, or is it an unreasonable, unnecessary, and arbitrary interference with the right of the individual to his personal liberty, or to enter into those contracts in relation to labor which may seem to him appropriate or necessary for the support of himself and his family? Of course the liberty of contract relating to labor includes both parties to it. The one has as much right to purchase as the other to sell labor. This is not a question of substituting the judgment of the court for that of the legislature. If the act be within the power of the State it is valid, although the judgment of the court might be totally opposed to the enactment of such a law. But the question would still remain: Is it within the police power of the State? and that question must be answered by the court.

The question whether this act is valid as a labor law, pure and simple, may be dismissed in a few words. There is no reasonable ground for interfering with the liberty of person or the right of free contract, by determining the hours of labor, in the occupation of a baker. There is no contention that bakers as a class are not equal in intelligence and capacity to men in other trades or manual occupations, or that they are not able to assert their rights and care for themselves without the protecting arm of the State. [They] are in no sense wards of the State. Viewed in the light of a purely labor law, with no reference whatever to the question of health, we think that a law like the one before us involves neither the safety, the morals, nor the welfare, of the public, and that the interest of the public is not in the slightest degree affected by such an act. The law must be upheld, if at all, as a law pertaining to the health of the individual engaged in the occupation of a baker. It does not affect any other portion of the public than those who are engaged in that occupation. Clean and wholesome bread does not depend upon whether the baker works but ten hours per day or only sixty hours a week. [There] is, in our judgment, no reasonable foundation for holding this to be necessary or appropriate as a health law to safeguard the public health, or the health of the individuals who are following the trade of a baker. * * *

We think that there can be no fair doubt that the trade of a baker, in and of itself, is not an unhealthy one to that degree which would authorize the legislature to interfere with the right to labor, and with the right of free contract on the part of the individual, either as employer or employee. [Some] occupations are more healthy than others, but we think there are none which might not come under the power of the legislature to supervise and control the hours of working therein, if the mere fact that the occupation is not absolutely and perfectly healthy is to confer that right upon the legislative department of the government. [It] is unfortunately true that labor, even in any department, may possibly carry with it the seeds of unhealthiness. But are we all, on that account, at the mercy of legislative majorities? A printer, a tinsmith, a locksmith, a carpenter, a cabinet maker, a dry goods clerk, a bank's, a lawyer's, or a physician's clerk, or a clerk in almost any kind of business, would all come under the power of the legislature, on this assumption. No trade, no occupation, no mode of earning one's living, could escape this all-pervading power, and the acts of the legislature in limiting the hours of labor in all employments would be valid, although such limitation might seriously cripple the ability of the laborer to support himself and his family.

[It] is also urged [that] it is to the interest of the State that its population should be strong and robust, and therefore any legislation which may be said to tend to make people healthy must be valid as health laws, enacted under the police power. If this be a valid argument and a justification for this kind of legislation, it follows that the protection of the Federal Constitution from undue interference with liberty of person and freedom of contract is visionary, wherever the law is sought to be justified as a valid exercise of the police power. Scarcely any law but might find shelter under such assumptions. [Not] only the hours of employees, but the hours of employers, could be regulated, and doctors, lawyers, scientists, all professional men, as well as athletes and artisans, could be forbidden to fatigue their brains and bodies by prolonged hours of exercise, lest the fighting strength of the state be impaired. We mention these extreme cases because the contention is extreme. We do not believe in the soundness of the views which uphold this law. [The] act is not, within any fair meaning of the term, a health law, but is an illegal interference with the rights of individuals, both employers and employees, to make contracts regarding labor upon such terms as they may think best, or which they may agree upon with the other parties to such contracts. Statutes of the nature of that under review, limiting the hours in which grown and intelligent men may labor to earn their living, are mere meddlesome interferences with the rights of the individual, and they are not saved from condemnation by the claim that they are passed in the exercise of the police power and upon the subject of the health of the individual whose rights are interfered with, unless there be some fair ground, reasonable in and of itself, to say that there is material danger to the public health, or to the health of the employees, if the hours of labor are not curtailed. * * *

This interference on the part of the legislatures of the several states with the ordinary trades and occupations of the people seems to be on the increase. [It] is impossible for us to shut our eyes to the fact that many of the laws of this character, while passed under what is claimed to be the police power for the purpose of protecting the public health or welfare, are, in reality, passed from other motives. We are justified in saying so when, from the character of the law and the subject upon which it legislates, it is apparent that the public health or welfare bears but the most remote relation to the [law].

Justice Harlan (with whom Justice White and Justice Day concurred) dissenting:

I take it to be firmly established that what is called the liberty of contract may, within certain limits, be subjected to regulations designed and calculated to promote the general welfare or to guard the public health, the public morals or the public safety. [It] is plain that this statute was enacted in order to protect the physical well-being of those who work in bakery and confectionery establishments. [The] statute must be taken as expressing the belief of the people of New York that, as a general rule, and in the case of the average man, labor in excess of sixty hours during a week in such establishments may endanger the health of those who thus labor. Whether or not this be wise legislation it is not the province of the court to inquire. Under our systems of government the courts are not concerned with the wisdom or policy of legislation. So that in determining the question of power to interfere with liberty or contract, the court may inquire whether the means devised by the State are germane to an end which may be lawfully accomplished and have a real or substantial relation to the protection of health, as involved in the daily work of the persons, male and female, engaged in bakery and confectionery establishments. But when this inquiry is entered upon I find it impossible, in view of common experience, to say that there is here no real or substantial relation between the means employed by the State and the end sought to be accomplished by its legislation. Nor can I say that the statute has no appropriate or direct connection with that protection to health which each State owes to her citizens or that it is not promotive of the health of the employees in question or that the regulation prescribed by the State is utterly unreasonable and extravagant or wholly arbitrary. Still less can I say that the statute is, beyond question, a plain, palpable invasion of rights secured by the fundamental law.

[The opinion quoted from writers on health problems of workers, pointing out that long hours, night hours, and difficult working conditions, such as excessive heat and exposure to flour dust, were injurious to the health of bakers, who "seldom live over their fiftieth year."] We judicially know that the question of the number of hours during which a workman should continuously labor has been, for a long period, and is yet, a subject of serious consideration among civilized peoples, and by those having special knowledge of the laws of health. We also judicially know that the number of hours that should constitute a day's labor in particular occupations involving the physical strength and safety of workmen has been the subject of enactments by Congress and by nearly all of the states. Many, if not most, of those enactments fix eight hours as the proper basis of a day's labor.

I do not stop to consider whether any particular view of this economic question presents the sounder theory. [It] is enough for the determination of this case [that] the question is one about which there is room for debate and for an honest difference of opinion. There are many reasons of a weighty, substantial character, based upon the experience of mankind, in support of the theory that, all things considered, more than ten hours' steady work each day, from week to week, in a bakery or confectionery establishment, may endanger the health and shorten the lives of the workmen, thereby diminishing their physical and mental capacity to serve the State and to provide for those dependent upon them.

If such reasons exist that ought to be the end of this case, for the state is not amenable to the judiciary, in respect of its legislative enactments, unless such enactments are plainly, palpably, beyond all question, inconsistent with the Constitution of the United States. * * *

JUSTICE HOLMES dissenting: * * *

This case is decided upon an economic theory which a large part of the country does not entertain. If it were a question whether I agree with that theory, I should desire to study it further and long before making up my mind. But I do not conceive that to be my duty, because I strongly believe that my agreement or disagreement has nothing to do with the right of a majority to embody their opinions in law. It is settled by various decisions of this court that state constitutions and state laws may regulate life in many ways which we as legislators might think as injudicious, or if you like as tyrannical, as this, and which, equally with this, interfere with the liberty to contract. Sunday laws and usury laws are ancient examples. A more modern one is the prohibition of lotteries. The liberty of the citizen to do as he likes so long as he does not interfere with the liberty of others to do the same, which has been a shibboleth for some well-known writers, is interfered with by school laws, by the Post Office, by every state or municipal institution which takes his money for purposes thought desirable, whether he likes it or not. The 14th Amendment does not enact Mr. Herbert Spencer's *Social Statics*. [A] Constitution is not intended to embody a particular economic theory, whether of paternalism and the organic relation of the citizen to the state or of laissez faire. It is made for people of fundamentally differing views, and the accident of our finding certain opinions natural and familiar, or novel, and even shocking, ought not to conclude our judgment upon the question whether statutes embodying them conflict with the Constitution of the United States.

General propositions do not decide concrete cases. [But] I think that the proposition just stated, if it is accepted, will carry us far toward the end. [I] think that the word "liberty," in the 14th Amendment, is perverted when it is held to prevent the natural outcome of a dominant opinion, unless it can be said that a rational and fair man necessarily would admit that the statute proposed would infringe fundamental principles as they have been understood by the traditions of our people and our law. It does not need research to show that no such sweeping condemnation can be passed upon the statute before us. * * *

II. THREE DECADES OF CONTROL OVER LEGISLATIVE POLICY

From *Lochner* in 1905 to *Nebbia* in 1934, infra, the Court frequently substituted its judgment for that of Congress and state legislatures on the wisdom of economic regulation said to interfere with contract and property interests. The Court relied mainly upon the Due Process Clauses of the Fifth and Fourteenth Amendments, with occasional resort to the Equal Protection Clause. Between 1899 and 1937, after excluding the civil rights cases, 159 Supreme Court decisions held state statutes unconstitutional under the Due Process and Equal Protection Clauses and 25 more statutes were struck down under the Due Process Clause coupled with some other provision of the Constitution.

The Court most freely substituted its judgment for that of the legislature in labor legislation, regulation of prices, and limitations on entry into business. It was most tolerant in the regulation of trade and business practices. A few examples will suffice to show the extent to which the Court interfered with legislative policymaking in economic regulation. With regularity Holmes, J., dissented from this use of the Due Process Clause, joined later by Brandeis and Stone, JJ., and Hughes, C.J.

1. ***Control over hours of labor.*** We have already seen how the Court barred control over the hours of labor, even in an industry where long hours threatened health. *Lochner* (1905). But in 1908 the Court sustained regulation of work hours for women in MULLER v. OREGON, 208 U.S. 412 (1908), basing the decision on special considerations relating to women. The Court, per BREWER, J., thought it plain that "women's physical structure" put her at a disadvantage in the struggle for subsistence and that since "healthy mothers are essential to vigorous offspring, the physical well-being of woman becomes an object of public interest." In 1917 the Court overruled *Lochner* (but not its philosophy) in sustaining a regulation of work hours for men in manufacturing establishments. *Bunting v. Oregon,* 243 U.S. 426. In *Muller*, the majority was influenced by the so-called "Brandeis brief," which furnished the Court with overwhelming documentation justifying regulation of hours of labor for women.

2. ***Control over anti-union discrimination.*** At an early date the Court struck down labor legislation forbidding discrimination by employers for union activity and prohibiting employers from requiring employees to sign "yellow dog" contracts, i.e., agreements not to remain or become union members. ADAIR v. UNITED STATES, 208 U.S. 161 (1908) (5th Amendment); COPPAGE v. KANSAS, 236 U.S. 1 (1915) (14th Amendment). *Adair* maintained that an employer and his employees "have equality of right, and any legislation that disturbs that equality is an arbitrary interference with the liberty of contract." PITNEY, J.'s majority opinion in *Coppage* has been called perhaps the clearest and fullest statement of the era's dominant philosophy. The Court was not impressed by the argument that "employees, as a rule, are not financially able to be as independent in making contracts for the sale of their labor as are employers in making contracts of purchase thereof." It is "from the nature of things impossible,"

responded the Court, "to uphold freedom of contract and the right of private property without at the same time recognizing as legitimate those inequalities of fortune that are the necessary result of the exercise of those rights." HOLMES, J., dissented.

These restrictive decisions were distinguished away in *Texas & N.O.R.R. v. Brotherhood of Ry. & S.S. Clerks,* 281 U.S. 548 (1930) and *NLRB v. Jones & Laughlin Steel Corp.* (1937). They were finally expressly overruled in *Phelps Dodge Corp. v. NLRB,* 313 U.S. 177 (1941) and *Lincoln Fed. Labor Union v. Northwestern Iron & Met. Co.* (1949), Sec. 3 infra.

3. ***Regulation of wages.*** Six years after it had upheld regulation of *hours* of labor in *Bunting,* the Court, per SUTHERLAND, J., ruled that a federal statute prescribing minimum *wages* for women in the District of Columbia violated due process. ADKINS v. CHILDREN'S HOSPITAL, 261 U.S. 525 (1923). The Court viewed the statute as "simply and exclusively a price-fixing law, confined to adult women, [who] are legally as capable of contracting for themselves as men." The Court noted that the 19th Amendment had recently been adopted, thus reducing the civil inferiority of women almost to the "vanishing point." Therefore, "liberty of contract" could not be subjected to greater infringement in the case of women than of men.

HOLMES, J., dissenting, expressed his inability to "understand the principle on which the power to fix a minimum for the wages of women can be denied by those who admit the power to fix a maximum for their hours of work." As he saw it, the bargain is "equally affected whichever half you regulate."

4. ***Regulation of prices.*** The Court also held that regulation of prices for commodities and services violated due process except for a limited class labeled "business affected with a public interest." *Nebbia v. New York* (1934) severely limited these rulings and they were expressly overruled in *Olsen v. Nebraska ex rel. Western Ref. & Bond Ass'n,* 313 U.S. 236 (1941).

SECTION 3.   THE ABANDONMENT OF *LOCHNER*

NEBBIA v. NEW YORK

291 U.S. 502, 54 S.Ct. 505, 78 L.Ed. 940 (1934).

JUSTICE ROBERTS delivered the opinion of the Court.

[In 1933, after a year's legislative study of the state's dairy industry, New York enacted a law which established a Milk Control Board with power to fix maximum and minimum retail prices. The Board fixed nine cents as the price to be charged by a store. Nebbia, the proprietor of a grocery store, was convicted of selling milk below the minimum price set.]

[Under] our form of government the use of property and the making of contracts are normally matters of private and not of public concern. The general rule is that both shall be free of governmental interference. But neither property rights nor contract rights are absolute; for government cannot exist if the citizen may at will use his property to the detriment of his fellows, or exercise his freedom of contract to work them harm. Equally fundamental with the private right is that of the public to regulate it in the common interest. [T]he guaranty of due process [demands] only that the law shall not be unreasonable, arbitrary, or capricious, and that the means selected shall have a real and substantial relation to the object sought to be attained.

[The opinion then summarized many different kinds of business and property regulations and controls previously sustained against due process attacks.]

The legislative investigation of 1932 was persuasive of the fact [that] unrestricted competition aggravated existing evils and the normal law of supply and demand was insufficient to correct maladjustments detrimental to the community. The inquiry disclosed destructive and demoralizing competitive conditions and unfair trade practices which resulted in retail price cutting and reduced the income of the farmer below the cost of production. [The Legislature] believed conditions could be improved by preventing destructive price-cutting by stores which, due to the flood of surplus milk, were able to buy at much lower prices than the larger distributors and to sell without incurring the delivery costs of the latter. [In] the light of the facts the [Milk Control Board's] order appears not to be unreasonable or arbitrary, or without relation to the purpose to prevent ruthless competition from destroying the wholesale price structure on which the farmer depends for his livelihood, and the community for an assured supply of milk. But we are told that because the law essays to control prices it denies due process. Notwithstanding the admitted power to correct existing economic ills by appropriate regulation of business, [the] appellant urges that direct fixation of prices is a type of regulation absolutely forbidden. [The] argument runs that the public control of rates or prices is per se unreasonable and unconstitutional, save as applied to businesses affected with a public interest; that a business so affected is [one] such as is commonly called a public utility; or a business in its nature a monopoly. [But] if, as must be conceded, the industry is subject to regulation in the public interest, what constitutional principle bars the state from correcting existing maladjustments by legislation touching prices? We think there is no such principle. The due process clause makes no mention of sales or of prices any more than it speaks of business or contracts or buildings or other incidents of property. The thought seems nevertheless to have persisted that there is something peculiarly sacrosanct about the price one may charge for what he makes or sells, and that, however able to regulate other elements of manufacture or trade, with incidental effect upon price, the state is incapable of directly controlling the price itself. This view was negatived many years ago. *Munn v. Illinois.*

[It] is clear that there is no closed class or category of businesses affected with a public interest, and the function of courts in the application of the Fifth and Fourteenth Amendments is to determine in each case whether circumstances vindicate the challenged regulation as a reasonable exertion of governmental authority or condemn it as arbitrary or discriminatory. The phrase "affected with a public interest" can, in the nature of things, mean no more than that an industry, for adequate reason, is subject to control for the public good. [There] can be no doubt that upon proper occasion and by appropriate measures the state may regulate a business in any of its aspects, including the prices to be charged for the products or commodities it sells.

So far as the requirement of due process is concerned, [a] state is free to adopt whatever economic policy may reasonably be deemed to promote public welfare, and to enforce that policy by legislation adapted to its purpose. The courts are without authority either to declare such policy, or, when it is declared by the legislature, to override it. If the laws passed are seen to have a reasonable relation to a proper legislative purpose, and are neither arbitrary nor discriminatory, the requirements of due process are satisfied. [With] the wisdom of the policy adopted, with the adequacy or practicability of the law enacted to forward it, the courts are both incompetent and unauthorized to deal. * * *

JUSTICE MCREYNOLDS, joined by JUSTICE VAN DEVANTER, JUSTICE SUTHERLAND, and JUSTICE BUTLER, dissenting:

[P]lainly, I think, this Court must have regard to the wisdom of the enactment. At least, we must inquire concerning its purpose and decide whether the means proposed have reasonable relation to something within legislative power—whether the end is legitimate, and the means appropriate. [Here,] we find direct interference with guaranteed rights defended upon the ground that the purpose was to promote the public welfare by increasing milk prices at the farm. [Not] only does the statute interfere arbitrarily with the rights of the little grocer to conduct his business according to standards long accepted—complete destruction may follow; but it takes away the liberty of 12,000,000 consumers to buy a necessity of life in an open market. [Grave] concern for embarrassed farmers is everywhere; but this should neither obscure the rights of others nor obstruct judicial appraisement of measures proposed for relief. The ultimate welfare of the producer, like that of every other class, requires dominance of the Constitution.

————

In WEST COAST HOTEL CO. v. PARRISH, 300 U.S. 379 (1937), a 5–4 majority, per HUGHES, C.J., overruled *Adkins v. Children's Hospital* and sustained a state minimum wage law for women. "[The] Legislature of the state was clearly entitled to consider [the] fact that [women] are in the class receiving the least pay, that their bargaining power is relatively weak, and that they are the ready victims of those who would take advantage of their necessitous circumstances. [We] may take judicial notice of the unparalleled demands for relief which arose during the recent period of depression. [The] community is not bound to provide, what is in effect a subsidy for unconscionable employers. [Even] if the wisdom of the policy be regarded as debatable and its effects uncertain, still the Legislature is entitled to its judgment."

As for the contention that the law violated "freedom of contract": "The Constitution does not speak of freedom of contract. It speaks of liberty [and in] prohibiting that deprivation the Constitution does not recognize an absolute and uncontrollable liberty. [Liberty] under the Constitution [is] necessarily subject to the restraints of due process, and regulation which is reasonable in relation to its subject and is adopted in the interests of the community is due process."

"THE MOST CELEBRATED FOOTNOTE IN CONSTITUTIONAL LAW": FOOTNOTE 4 OF THE *CAROLENE PRODUCTS* CASE

UNITED STATES v. CAROLENE PRODUCTS CO., 304 U.S. 144 (1938), upheld the constitutionality of a federal statute that prohibited the shipment in interstate commerce of "filled milk," a product compounded with fat or oil so as to resemble milk or cream. Appellee argued that the legislation violated both the commerce and due process clauses. The government countered that appellee's product was an impure, adulterated substance that posed a danger to the public. Writing for the Court, STONE, J., took the position that economic regulatory legislation, such as the statute at issue, was entitled to a presumption of constitutionality and should be upheld if supported by any rational basis. "Where the existence of a rational basis for legislation whose constitutionality is attacked depends upon facts beyond the sphere of judicial notice," continued Stone, "such facts may properly be made the subject of judicial inquiry, and the constitutionality of a statute predicated upon the existence of a particular state of facts may be challenged by showing to the court that those facts have ceased to exist. [B]y their very nature such inquiries, where the legislative judgment is drawn in question, must be restricted to the issue whether any state of facts either known or which could reasonably be assumed affords support for it." Under this approach, the challenged legislation easily passed constitutional muster. In the course of writing his opinion, Stone, J., dropped a footnote (fn. 4) that has been called "the most celebrated footnote in constitutional law" and "the great and modern charter for ordering the relations between judges and other agencies of government." That footnote (case citations omitted) reads as follows:

"There may be narrower scope for operation of the presumption of constitutionality when legislation appears on its face to be within a specific prohibition of the Constitution, such as those of the first ten Amendments, which are deemed equally specific when held to be embraced within the Fourteenth.

"It is unnecessary to consider now whether legislation which restricts those political processes which can obviously be expected to bring about repeal of undesirable legislation, is to be subjected to more exacting judicial scrutiny under the general prohibitions of the Fourteenth than are most other types of legislation [referring to cases dealing with restrictions on voting rights and freedom of expression and political association].

"Nor need we enquire whether similar considerations enter into the review of statutes directed at particular religious or national or racial minorities[:] whether prejudice against discrete and insular minorities may be a special condition, which tends seriously to curtail the operation of those political processes ordinarily to be relied upon to protect minorities, and which may call for a correspondingly more searching judicial inquiry."

THE 1940S, 50S AND 60S: A FAR CRY FROM *LOCHNER*

West Coast Hotel was followed quickly by a number of cases upholding New Deal legislation. See, e.g., *NLRB v. Jones & Laughlin Steel Corp.*, 301 U.S. 1 (1937) (the National Labor Relations Act); *United States v. Darby*, 312 U.S. 100 (1941) (the Fair Labor Standards Act); *Wickard v. Filburn*, 317 U.S. 111 (1942) (the Agricultural Adjustment Act). A great deal of challenged state economic legislation was also sustained. Some representative cases follow:

In LINCOLN FED. LABOR UNION v. NORTHWESTERN IRON & METAL CO., 335 U.S. 525 (1949), a unanimous Court, per BLACK, J., sustained a state "right-to-work" law that barred a preference for union membership in employment decisions. The Court noted that at least since *Nebbia*, it had "steadily rejected the due process philosophy enunciated in the [*Lochner-Coppage*] line of cases and returned closer to the earlier constitutional principle that states may legislate 'against what are found to be injurious practices in their internal commercial and business affairs, so long as they do not run afoul of some specific federal constitutional prohibition [or] some valid federal law.'"

WILLIAMSON v. LEE OPTICAL OF OKLAHOMA, 348 U.S. 483 (1955), where a unanimous Court, per DOUGLAS, J., upheld an Oklahoma law regulating opticians and optometrists, well demonstrates the great distance the Court had moved away from *Lochner* by the 1950s.

One provision forbid opticians from fitting or duplicating lenses without a prescription from an ophthalmologist or optometrist. "In practical effect, it means that no optician can fit old glasses into new frames or supply a lens, whether it be a new lens or one to duplicate a lost or broken lens, without a prescription." The Court rejected the argument that since an optician, by mechanical devices or ordinary skills, could take a fragment of a broken lens and reduce it to prescriptive terms, the particular means chosen by the legislature were "neither reasonably necessary nor reasonably related to the end sought to be achieved": "The legislature might have concluded that the frequency of occasions when a prescription is necessary was sufficient to justify this regulation of the fitting of eyeglasses. [Or] the legislature may have concluded that eye examinations were so critical [that] every change in frames and every duplication of a lens should be accompanied by a prescription from a medical expert. To be sure, the present law does not require a new examination of the eyes every time the frames are changed or the lenses duplicated. [But] the law need not be in every respect logically consistent with its aims to be constitutional. [The] day is gone when this Court uses the Due Process Clause [to] strike down state laws, regulatory of business and industrial conditions, because they may be unwise, improvident, or out of harmony with a particular school of thought."

FERGUSON v. SKRUPA, 372 U.S. 726 (1963), saw the Court, per BLACK, J., without a dissent, rejected a due process challenge to a state law barring all but lawyers from the business of debt adjusting. And it did so in the strongest terms: "Under the system of government created by our Constitution, it is up to the legislatures, not the courts, to decide on the wisdom and utility of legislation. [The] doctrine that prevailed in *Lochner, Coppage, Adkins*, and like cases [has] long since been discarded. We have returned to the original constitutional proposition that courts do not substitute their social and economic beliefs for the judgment of legislative bodies, who are elected to pass laws. [Whether] the legislature takes for its textbook Adam Smith, Herbert Spencer, Lord Keynes or some other is no concern of ours." Harlan, J., concurred on the ground that "[this] measure bears a rational relation to a constitutionally permissible objective."

A Note on Substantive Due Process and Punitive Damage Constraints

Do recent Supreme Court cases placing some limits on punitive damage awards constitute a reentry of substantive due process into an economic area?

Although opinions in earlier cases had indicated that there were some constitutional limits on punitive damage awards, BMW OF NORTH AMERICA, INC. v. GORE, 517 U.S. 559 (1996), marked the first time the Court invalidated a state-court punitive assessment as "grossly excessive," considering such factors as the degree of reprehensibility of the defendant's conduct and the disparity between the harm suffered by the plaintiff and his punitive damage award, and thus a violation of due process. The defendant had been assessed $2 million in punitive damages for having knowingly failed to tell an automobile buyer that, at a cost of $600, it had repainted portions of his new $40,000 car, thereby lowering its potential resale value by about 10%. A 5–4 majority, per STEVENS, J., recognized that the Court had "consistently rejected the notion that the constitutional line is marked by a simple mathematical formula, even one that compares actual *and potential* damages to the punitive award," but added: "When the ratio [between punitive damages and actual harm] is a breathtaking 500 to 1, the award must surely 'raise a suspicious judicial eyebrow.'"

SCALIA, J., joined by Thomas, J., dissented: "I do not regard the Fourteenth Amendment's Due Process Clause as a secret repository of substantive guarantees against 'unfairness'—neither the unfairness of an excessive civil compensatory award, nor the unfairness of an 'unreasonable' punitive award. What the Fourteenth Amendment's procedural guarantee assures is an opportunity to contest the reasonableness of a damages judgment in state court; but there is no federal guarantee a damages award actually *be* reasonable."

In a separate dissent, GINSBURG, J., joined by the Chief Justice, maintained that "[the] Court is not well equipped for this mission. Tellingly, [it] repeats that it brings to the task no 'mathematical formula,' no 'categorical approach.' [It] has only a vague concept of substantive due process, a 'raised eyebrow' test, as its ultimate guide."

———

STATE FARM MUT. AUTO INS. CO. v. CAMPBELL, 538 U.S. 408 (2003), struck down another punitive damages award. The case involved a $145 million punitive damages award where full compensatory damages were only $1 million. A 6–3 majority, per Kennedy, J., observed: "[Due process] prohibits the imposition of grossly excessive or arbitrary punishments on a tortfeasor. * * * We decline again to impose a bright-line ratio which a punitive damages award cannot exceed. Our jurisprudence and the principles it has now established demonstrate, however, that, in practice, few awards exceeding a single-digit ratio between punitive and compensatory damages, to a significant degree, will satisfy due process." Justice Scalia, Thomas and Ginsburg each filed separate dissents.

———

PHILIP MORRIS v. WILLIAMS, 549 U.S. 346 (2007), addressed a new punitive damages issue: After Jesse Williams, a heavy smoker, died of lung cancer, his widow brought a state lawsuit against a cigarette manufacturer for negligence and deceit. The jury decided in the widow's favor and awarded her $821,000 in compensatory damages and $79.5 million in punitive damages. In light of the plaintiff's argument that the jury should "think about how many other Jesse Williams" there had been in Oregon in the last 40 years and how many other people "cigarettes are going to kill," defendant asked the trial court to instruct the jury "not to punish the defendant for the impact of its alleged misconduct on other persons, who may bring lawsuits of their own in which other juries can resolve their claims." The judge rejected the request and instead told the jury that "punitive damages are awarded against a defendant to punish misconduct and to deter misconduct." A 5–4 majority, per Breyer, J., vacated the Oregon Supreme Court's judgment, holding that a punitive damages award based upon a jury's "desire to *punish* the defendant for harming persons who are not before the court [would] amount to a taking of 'property' from the defendant without due process":

"[A] defendant threatened with punishment for injuring a nonparty victim has no opportunity to defend against the charge, by showing, for example, [that] the other victim was not entitled to damages because he or she knew that smoking was dangerous or did not rely upon the defendants statements to the contrary. [Moreover,] to permit punishment for injuring a nonparty victim would add a near standardless dimension to the punitive damages equation. How many such victims are there? Under what circumstances did injury occur? [Given] the risks of unfairness we have mentioned, [the] Due Process Clause requires States to provide assurance that juries are not asking the wrong question, i.e., seeking, not simply, to determine reprehensibility, but also to punish for harm caused strangers.

"[At] the same time, we recognize that conduct that risks harm to many is likely more reprehensible than conduct that risks harm to only a few. And a jury consequently may take this fact into account in determining reprehensibility. [How] can we know whether a jury, in taking account of harm caused others under the rubric of reprehensibility, also seeks to *punish* the defendant for having caused injury to others? Our answer is that state courts cannot authorize procedures that create an unreasonable and unnecessary risk of any such confusion occurring. In particular, we believe that where the risk of that misunderstanding is a significant one—because, for instance, of the sort of evidence that was introduced at trial or the kinds of argument that plaintiff made to the jury—a court, upon request, must protect against that risk.''a

STEVENS, J., dissented, "see[ing] no reason why an interest in punishing a wrongdoer 'for harming persons who are not before the court' should not be taken into consideration when assessing the appropriate sanction for reprehensible conduct. [In] the case before us, evidence attesting to the possible harm the defendant's extensive deceitful conduct caused other Oregonians was properly presented to the jury. No evidence was offered to establish an appropriate measure of damages to compensate such third parties for their injuries, and no one argued that the punitive damages award would serve any such purpose. To award compensatory damages to remedy such third-party harm might well constitute a taking of property from the defendant without due process. But a punitive damages award, instead of serving a compensatory purpose, serves the entirely different purposes of retribution and deterrence that underlie every criminal sanction."

GINSBURG, J., joined by Scalia and Thomas, JJ., wrote a separate dissent: "[The Court] conveys that, when punitive damages are at issue, a jury is properly instructed to consider the extent of harm suffered by others as a measure of reprehensibility, but not to mete out punishment for injuries in fact sustained by nonparties. The Oregon courts did not rule otherwise. [The] right question regarding reprehensibility, the Court acknowledges, would train on 'the harm that Philip Morris was prepared to inflict on the smoking public at large.' [The] Court identifies no evidence introduced and no charge delivered inconsistent with that inquiry.''b

SECTION 4. OTHER LIMITS ON ECONOMIC LEGISLATION: THE PROHIBITION AGAINST "TAKING" "PRIVATE PROPERTY" WITHOUT JUST COMPENSATION

The Fifth Amendment limits the federal government's power of eminent domain: "nor shall private property be taken for a public use without just compensation." This specific provision of the Bill of Rights was one of the first to be deemed binding on the states via fourteenth amendment due process. See *Chicago, B. & Q. R. Co. v. Chicago*, 166 U.S. 226 (1897); *Missouri Pac. Ry. Co. v. Nebraska*, 164 U.S. 403 (1896).

Among the questions considered by this section are: What limits, if any, are there on the purposes for which private property may be taken *even with compensation*? When should a government action be regarded as a "taking," requiring just compensation and when should it be viewed merely as a "regulation" under the police power (in which case no compensation is required)? What constitutes "property" for purposes of the takings clause?

a. The Court noted that because the application of its standard on remand might lead to the need for a new trial or a change in the level of the punitive damages award, it would not consider the argument that the roughly 100–to–1 ratio the $79.5 million award bore to the compensatory damage amount rendered the punitive award "grossly excessive."

b. Thomas, J., also wrote a separate dissent to "reiterate my view that 'the Constitution does not constrain the size of punitive damage awards.' ''

What Constitutes a Taking for a "Public Purpose"?

As illustrated by *Kelo v. New London* (set forth infra), the Court's role in determining whether a taking is for a "public purpose" is extremely limited. A use is considered "public" if it furthers moral, economic, political, or even aesthetic objectives. A use may be deemed "public" so long as there is public advantage or benefit—even though the property may not be *used by* the general public.

What Government Action Should Be Regarded as a "Taking," Requiring Just Compensation?

In *Pennsylvania Coal Co. v. Mahon*, 260 U.S. 393 (1922), the Court, per Holmes, J., observed that "the general rule at least is, that while property may be regulated to a certain extent, if regulation goes too far it will be recognized as a taking." Such a rule may strike many as quite hazy and unmanageable. But is the "general rule" represented by the modern cases any more helpful?

The question presented in PENN CENTRAL TRANSP. CO. v. NEW YORK CITY, 438 U.S. 104 (1978) was whether a preservation commission's denial of approval for Penn Central to construct a 55–story office building on the roof of its property–Grand Central Terminal, which had been designated as a "landmark"—constituted a "taking." In holding that it did not, the Court, per Brennan, J., emphasized that the denial of approval to build the structure "does not interfere in any way" with the present and past uses of the Terminal. "More importantly, on this record, we must regard the [restriction] as permitting Penn Central not only to profit from the Terminal but also to obtain a 'reasonable return' on its investment."

The *Penn Central* Court recognized that "what constitutes a 'taking' has proved to be a problem of considerable difficulty. [T]his Court, quite simply, has been unable to develop any 'set formula' for determining when 'justice and fairness' require that economic injuries caused by public action be compensated by the government, rather than remain disproportionately concentrated on a few persons."

"A 'taking' may more readily be found," noted the Court, "when the interference with property can be characterized as a physical invasion by government [than] when interference arises from some public program adjusting the benefits and burdens of economic life to promote the common good." A good illustration is *Loretto v. Teleprompter Manhattan CATV Corp.*, 458 U.S. 419 (1982), which held that a state law requiring landlords to allow television cable companies to install cable facilities in their apartment buildings amounted to a "taking," despite the fact that the facilities occupied at most only 1 ½ cubic feet of the landlord's property.

Another situation in which the Court has considered categorical treatment appropriate is where the regulation denies all economically beneficial or productive use of land. A good illustration is *Lucas v. South Carolina Coastal Council*, 505 U.S. 1003 (1992), where the enactment of an anti-erosion law prevented the owner from erecting any permanent habitable structure on his land. The Court, per Scalia, J., observed:

"[R]egulations that leave the owner without economically beneficial or productive options for its use—typically, as here, by requiring land to be left substantially in its natural state—carry with them a heightened risk that private property is being pressed into some form of public service under the guise of mitigating serious public harm. [When] the owner of real property has been called upon to sacrifice *all* economically beneficial uses in the name of the common good, that is, to leave the property economically idle, he has suffered a taking."

In STOP THE BEACH RENOURISHMENT v. FLORIDA DEPT. OF ENVI-RONMENTAL PROTECTION, 130 S.Ct. ___ (2010), although all eight justices (Stevens, J., not participating) agreed that a Florida Supreme Court ruling did not constitute a "judicial taking," four (SCALIA, J., joined by Roberts, C.J., and Thomas and Alito, JJ.) would have used the case to establish the possibility that a *judicial decision* could violate the Takings Clause: "The Clause bars *the State* from taking private property without paying for it, no matter which branch is the instrument of the taking. [If] a legislature *or a court* declares that what was once an established right of private property no longer exists, it has taken that property, no less than if the State had physically appropriated it or destroyed its value by regulation." Kennedy, J., joined by Sotomayor, J., and Breyer, J., joined by GINSBURG, J., declined (a) to decide whether the judiciary can ever effect a taking or (b) to establish what the standard for doing so should be.

Can (Does) a Temporary Moratorium on a New Economic Development Constitute a "Taking"?

Consider *Tahoe-Sierra Preservation Council, Inc. v. Tahoe Regional Planning Agency*, 535 U.S. 302 (2002). A regional planning compact imposed two moratoria, totaling 32 months, on land development in the Lake Tahoe Basin while formulating a comprehensive land-use plan for the area. A 6–3 majority, per Stevens, J., held that *Lucas* did not apply and that *Penn Central*'s ad hoc balancing approach was the appropriate framework for analyzing whether a "taking" occurred:

"[The] categorical rule that we applied in *Lucas* states that compensation is required when a regulation deprives an owner of '*all* economically beneficial uses' of his land. Under that rule, a statute that 'wholly eliminated the value' of Lucas' fee simple clearly qualified as a taking. But our holding was limited to the extraordinary circumstance when *no* productive or economically beneficial use of land is permitted. * * *

"[The] duration of the restriction is one of the important factors that a court must consider in the appraisal of a regulatory takings claim, but with respect to that factor as with respect to [others], the 'temptation to adopt what amount to per se rules in either direction must be resisted.' *Palazzolo v. Rhode Island*, 533 U.S. 606 (2001) (O'Connor, J., concurring). [The] interest in 'fairness and justice' will be best served by relying on the familiar *Penn Central* approach when deciding cases like this, rather than by attempting to craft a new categorical rule."

May One Claim that a Restriction Imposed on Her Property Before She Acquired It Constitutes A "Taking"?

As *Palazzolo v. Rhode Island*, 533 U.S. 606 (2001), makes plain, the right to claim a "taking" is *not* limited to persons who held title to the property at the time the challenged regulation was imposed. To accept a contrary rule, observed the *Palazzolo* Court, per Kennedy, J., would mean that "the post-enactment transfer of title would absolve the State of its obligation to defend any action restricting land use, no matter how extreme or unreasonable. A State would be allowed, in effect, to put an expiration date on the Takings Clause. This ought not to be the rule. Future generations, too, have a right to challenge unreasonable limitations on the use and value of land."

What Constitutes "Property" for Purposes of the Takings Clause?

The Takings Clause applies where a *specific* interest in physical or intellectual property is involved. But no opinion of the Court has held that the Takings Clause applies when a *general obligation* to pay money to the government or to a third party is at issue.

In *Eastern Enterprises v. Apfel*, 524 U.S. 498 (1998), the Court struck down a federal statute that imposed a monetary assessment on the prior owner of a coal mine that would have been used to fund benefits for now-retired miners who had once worked for the coal mine. However, there was no opinion of the Court. Speaking for four Justices, O'Connor, J., concluded that as the statute affected Eastern Enterprises, it violated the Takings Clause. Concurring in the judgment, but rejecting the plurality's Takings Clause analysis, Kennedy, J., concluded that the statute "must be invalidated as contrary to essential due process principles" because it went "far outside the bounds of retroactivity permissible under our law." It is noteworthy that (a) the O'Connor plurality seemed to avoid reliance upon the Due Process Clause at least in part out of fear of resurrecting *Lochner*, but (b) Justice Kennedy pointed out that if the plurality had adopted what he called its "novel" concept of a "taking" in order to avoid making a "normative judgment" about the statute it would have had to make the normative judgment anyway. Indeed, maintained Kennedy, the malleability of the Court's takings doctrine "open[s] the door to normative considerations about the wisdom of government decisions." Moreover, dissenting Justice Stevens, joined by Souter, Ginsburg and Breyer, JJ., concluded that whether the statute "is analyzed under the Takings Clause *or* the Due Process Clause" (emphasis added), the company "has not carried its burden of overcoming the presumption of constitutionality accorded to an act of Congress."

When the smoke had cleared, a four-Justice plurality had maintained that a general obligation could be the subject of a taking, but *five* Justices (in concurring and dissenting opinions) had disagreed.

KELO v. NEW LONDON

545 U.S. 469, 125 S.Ct. 2655, 162 L.Ed.2d 439 (2005).

JUSTICE STEVENS delivered the opinion of the Court.

[Decades of economic decline prompted state and local officials to target New London, Conn. (hereinafter City), and especially its Fort Trumbell area, for economic revitalization. The New London Development Corp. (NLDC), a private entity designed to help the City in planning economic development, was revitalized. Shortly thereafter, the pharmaceutical company Pfizer announced that it would build a $300 million facility on a site immediately adjacent to Fort Trumbell. Local planners hoped that the new facility would serve as a catalyst to the area's rejuvenation.

[The city council approved the NLDC plan and authorized the entity to purchase property or to acquire it by exercising eminent domain in the City's name. When petitioners in the case, nine persons who owned 15 properties in Fort Trumbell, refused to sell, the City initiated condemnation proceedings. There is no allegation that any of their properties was blighted or otherwise in poor condition. Rather, they were condemned only because they happened to be in the development area.

[Petitioner brought this action in state court, maintaining that the City's taking of their properties would violate the "public use" restriction in the taking clause. The state supreme court disagreed.]

[The] disposition of this [case] turns on the question whether the City's development plan serves a "public purpose." Without exception, our cases have defined that concept broadly, reflecting our longstanding policy of deference to legislative judgments in this field. [For] more than a century, our public use jurisprudence has wisely eschewed rigid formulas and intrusive scrutiny in favor of affording legislatures broad latitude in determining what public needs justify the use of the takings power.

Those who govern the City were not confronted with the need to remove blight in the Fort Trumbull area, but their determination that the area was sufficiently distressed to justify a program of economic rejuvenation is entitled to our deference. The City has carefully formulated an economic development plan that it believes will provide appreciable benefits to the community, including—but by no means limited to—new jobs and increased tax revenue. [Because] that plan unquestionably serves a public purpose, the takings challenged here satisfy the public use requirement of the Fifth Amendment.

[Petitioners] contend that using eminent domain for economic development impermissibly blurs the boundary between public and private takings. Again, our cases foreclose this objection. Quite simply, the government's pursuit of a public purpose will often benefit individual private parties.

[It] is further argued that without a bright-line rule nothing would stop a city from transferring citizen A's property to citizen B for the sole reason that citizen B will put the property to a more productive use and thus pay more taxes. Such a one-to-one transfer of property, executed outside the confines of an integrated development plan, is not presented in this case. While such an unusual exercise of government power would certainly raise a suspicion that a private purpose was afoot, the hypothetical cases posited by petitioners can be confronted if and when they arise. They do not warrant the crafting of an artificial restriction on the concept of public use.

* * * We emphasize that nothing in our opinion precludes any State from placing further restrictions on its exercise of the takings power. Indeed, many States already impose "public use" requirements that are stricter than the federal baseline. [This] Court's authority, however, extends only to determining whether the City's proposed condemnations are for a "public use" within the meaning of the Fifth Amendment to the Federal Constitution. Because over a century of our case law interpreting that provision dictates an affirmative answer to that question, we may not grant petitioners the relief that they seek. * * *

JUSTICE KENNEDY, concurring, [joined the opinion of the Court but made some additional observations:]

[A] court confronted with a plausible accusation of impermissible favoritism to private parties should treat the objection as a serious one and review the record to see if it has merit, though with the presumption that the government's actions were reasonable and intended to serve a public purpose. Here, the trial court [did so] and concluded [that] benefitting Pfizer was not "the primary motivation or effect of this development plan." [This] case, then, survives the meaningful rational basis review that in my view is required under the Public Use Clause. [While] there may be categories of cases in which the transfers are so suspicious, or the procedures employed so prone to abuse, or the purported benefits are so trivial or implausible, that courts should presume an impermissible private purpose, no such circumstances are present in this case. * * *

JUSTICE O'CONNOR, with whom THE CHIEF JUSTICE, JUSTICE SCALIA, and JUSTICE THOMAS join, dissenting.

[To] reason, as the Court does, that the incidental public benefits resulting from the subsequent ordinary use of private property render economic development takings "for public use" is to wash out any distinction between private and public use of property—and thereby effectively to delete the words "for public use" from the Takings Clause of the Fifth Amendment.

[Where] is the line between "public" and "private" property use? [Were] the political branches the sole arbiters of the public-private distinction, the Public Use Clause would amount to little more than hortatory fluff. An external, judicial check on how the public use requirement is interpreted, however limited, is necessary if this constraint on government power is to retain any meaning.

[This case] presents an issue of first impression: Are economic development takings constitutional? I would hold that they are not.

[The Court] protests that it does not sanction the bare transfer from A to B for B's benefit. It suggests two limitations on what can be taken after today's decision. First, it maintains a role for courts in ferreting out takings whose sole purpose is to bestow a benefit on the private transferee—without detailing how courts are to conduct that complicated inquiry. [The] trouble with economic development takings is that private benefit and incidental public benefit are, by definition, merged and mutually reinforcing. In this case, for example, any boon for Pfizer or the plan's developer is difficult to disaggregate from the promised public gains in taxes and jobs.

Even if there were a practical way to isolate the motives behind a given taking, the gesture toward a purpose test is theoretically flawed. If it is true that incidental public benefits from new private use are enough to ensure the "public purpose" in a taking, why should it matter, as far as the Fifth Amendment is concerned, what inspired the taking in the first place?

[A]   second proposed limitation is implicit in the Court's opinion. The logic of today's decision is that eminent domain may only be used to upgrade—not downgrade—property. At best this makes the Public Use Clause redundant with the Due Process Clause, which already prohibits irrational government action. [In] any event, this constraint has no realistic import. For who among us can say she already makes the most productive or attractive possible use of her property? The specter of condemnation hangs over all property. Nothing is to prevent the State from replacing any Motel 6 with a Ritz–Carlton, any home with a shopping mall, or any farm with a factory. * * *

Any property may now be taken for the benefit of another private party, but the fallout from this decision will not be random. The beneficiaries are likely to be those citizens with disproportionate influence and power in the political process, including large corporations and development firms. As for the victims, the government now has license to transfer property from those with fewer resources to those with more. The Founders cannot have intended this perverse result. * * *

JUSTICE THOMAS, dissenting. * * *

[There]   is no justification [for] affording almost insurmountable deference to legislative conclusions that a use serves a "public use." To begin with, a court owes no deference to a legislature's judgment concerning the quintessentially legal question of whether the government owns, or the public has a legal right to use, the taken property. Even under the "public purpose" interpretation, moreover, it is most implausible that the Framers intended to defer to legislatures as to what satisfies the Public Use Clause, uniquely among all the express provisions of the Bill of Rights. We would not defer to a legislature's determination of the various circumstances that establish, for example, when a search of a home would be reasonable, or when a convicted double-murderer may be shackled during a sentencing proceeding without on-the-record findings, or when state law creates a property interest protected by the Due Process Clause.

Still worse, it is backwards to adopt a searching standard of constitutional review for nontraditional property interests, such as welfare benefits, while deferring to the legislature's determination as to what constitutes a public use when it exercises the power of eminent domain, and thereby invades individuals' traditional rights in real property. [Though] citizens are safe from the government in their homes, the homes themselves are not. Once one accepts, as the Court at least nominally does, that the Public Use Clause is a limit on the eminent domain power of the Federal Government and the States, there is no justification for the almost complete deference it grants to legislatures as to what satisfies it.

* * * I would revisit our Public Use Clause cases and consider returning to the original meaning of the Public Use Clause: that the government may take property only if it actually uses or gives the public a legal right to use the property.

* * * Allowing the government to take property solely for public purposes is bad enough, but extending the concept of public purpose to encompass any economically beneficial goal guarantees that these losses will fall disproportionately on poor communities. Those communities are not only systematically less likely to put their lands to the highest and best social use, but are also the least politically powerful. If ever there were justification for intrusive judicial review of constitutional provisions that protect "discrete and insular minorities," surely that principle would apply with great force to the powerless groups and individuals the Public Use Clause protects. * * *

A Note on the Prohibition Against "Impairing the Obligation of Contracts"

Art. 1, § 10, prohibits the state from enacting any "Law impairing the Obligation of Contracts." In *Home Building & Loan Ass'n v. Blaisdell* (1934) (below), Hughes, C.J., recalled the reasons that led to the adoption of this clause: "The widespread distress following the revolutionary period, and the plight of debtors, had called forth in the States an ignoble array of legislative schemes for the defeat of creditors and the invasion of contractual obligations. Legislative interferences had been so numerous and extreme that the confidence essential to prosperous trade had been undermined and the utter destruction of credit was threatened. It was necessary to interpose the restraining power of a central authority in order to secure the foundations even of 'private faith.' "

As pointed out in John E. Nowak & Ronald D. Rotunda, *Constitutional Law* 474 (7th ed. 2004): "Under the leadership of Chief Justice Marshall, [the Contract Clause] received an expansive reading. During the Marshall years, the Court used the provision to invalidate statutes that retrospectively impaired almost any contractual obligation of private parties. The Court never used the clause to void laws that prospectively modified contractual obligations. Nevertheless, until the late nineteenth century the contract clause was the principal provision the Court used to void legislation that infringed on private property rights."

Then the Contract Clause lost its importance. For one thing, "the states rarely would enact a statutory grant that [failed] to give [them] the necessary flexibility to pass legislation that [could] modify the previously issued public grant." Moreover, "the Court began to rely on the doctrine of substantive due process to void legislation that would infringe on property or business interests. More often than not, any state legislation that impaired the obligation of contract would not only violate the contract clause but would also violate the Court's notions of economic substantive due process," [a doctrine that] gave the Court more discretion and flexibility than the contract clause in passing on the constitutionality of state legislation. Hence, if the Court had a choice, it would use substantive due process analysis rather than contract clause analysis to void state legislation." Nowak & Rotunda, supra, at 183.

In HOME BUILDING & LOAN ASS'N v. BLAISDELL, 290 U.S. 398 (1934)—decided the same year the *Nebbia* case struck the economic due process doctrine a heavy blow—the Court upheld what might be called a "debtor relief law" despite its retrospective impact. As *Nebbia* and *Blaisdell* indicated, the Court's growing reluctance to invoke the contract clause would parallel its abandonment of substantive due process analysis to strike down economic legislation.

Blaisdell arose as follows: During the Great Depression, Minnesota enacted a Mortgage Moratorium Law—a law that was to remain in effect "only during the continuance of the emergency and in no event beyond May 1, 1935"—which gave the state courts the authority to extend the redemption period after real estate foreclosure sales provided the mortgagor paid a reasonable part of the rental value of the property. Thus mortgagees could not obtain possession of the real estate and convey title in fee as they would have been able to do if a mortgage moratorium law had not been adopted. A 5–4 majority, per Hughes, C.J., held that the challenged law "does not impair the integrity of the mortgage indebtedness. The obligation for interest remains. [Aside] from the extension of time, the other conditions of redemption are unaltered. [While] the mortgagee-purchaser is debarred from actual possession, he has, so far as rental value is concerned, the equivalent of possession during the extended period. [Not] only is the constitutional provision qualified by the measure of control which the State retains over remedial processes, but the State also continues to possess authority to safeguard the vital interests of its people. [Not] only are existing laws read into contracts in order to fix obligations as between the parties, but the reservation of existing attributes of sovereign power is also read into contracts as a postulate of the legal order. [The Constitution would not] permit the State to adopt as its policy the repudiation of debts or the destruction of contracts or the denial of means to enforce them. But it does not follow that conditions may not arise in which a temporary restraint of enforcement may be consistent with the spirit and purpose of the constitutional provision and thus found to be within the range of the reserved power of the State to protect the vital interests of the community."

In upholding the law, the Court found five factors significant: there was an emergency need "to protect the vital interests of the community"; the law was not designed to favor a special group "but for the protection of a basic interest of society"; the relief was appropriately tailored to the emergency; the conditions imposed were reasonable; and the legislation was "temporary in operation" and "limited to the exigency which called it forth."

UNITED STATES TRUST CO. v. NEW JERSEY, 431 U.S. 1 (1977) was the first case in thirty years to revive the Contract Clause. To assure bondholders of the Port Authority of New York and New Jersey that the Authority would not in the future take over mass transit deficit operations beyond its financial reserves in 1962, the two states entered into a covenant limiting the numbers of such operations the Authority would absorb. In 1974, however, in order to subsidize more mass transportation, both states repealed the legislation implementing the covenant. A 4–3 majority, per Blackmun, J., agreed with the bondholders that the retroactive repeal of the covenant, which reduced the financial security of their bonds, violated the Contract Clause.

The following year saw the major modern expansion of the Contract Clause: ALLIED STRUCTURAL STEEL v. SPANNAUS, 438 U.S. 234 (1978). Allied Steel adopted a pension plan that vested pension rights only when an employee had worked to age 65, or 15 years to age 60 or 20 years to age 55. However, Minnesota then enacted a law requiring employers of 100 workers or more who had established employee pension plans and who then went out of business in the state to pay full pensions to all its Minnesota employees who had worked ten years or more. A 6–3 majority, per Stewart, J., held that the law could not survive challenge under the contract clause: The law had "change[d] the company's obligations in an area where the element of reliance was vital—the funding of a pension [plan]" and "impose[d] a completely unexpected liability in potentially disabling amounts." Moreover, the law did not "deal with a situation remotely approaching the broad and desperate emergency economic conditions of the early 1930s—conditions of which the Court in *Blaisdell* took official notice."

BRENNAN, J., wrote forceful dissenting opinions in both the *U.S. Trust* and *Allied Steel* cases. Noting that *U.S. Trust* was "the first case in some 40 years in which the Court has seen fit to invalidate purely economic and social legislation on the strength of the Contract Clause," Brennan, J., voiced fear that the case might signal "a return to substantive constitutional review of States' policies and a new resolve to protect property owners whose interest or circumstances may happen to appeal to Members of the Court." Dissenting in *Allied Steel*, Brennan, J., maintained that the majority's "conversion of the Contract Clause into a limitation on the power of states to enact laws that impose duties additional to obligations assumed under private contracts must inevitably produce results difficult to square with any rational conception of a constitutional order." The "necessary consequences" of the majority's approach "is to best judges with broad subjective discretion to protect property interests that happen to appeal to them."

Although the Court appeared to have revitalized the Contract Clause, it retreated sharply in two 1983 cases: *Energy Reserves Group v. Kansas Power & Light Co.*, 459 U.S. 400 (unanimously upholding a Kansas law that imposed price controls on intrastate gas and prohibited natural gas producers from raising the purchase price despite provisions in contracts with consumers for raising the purchase price in the event of changes in the law); *Exxon Corp. v. Eagerton*, 462 U.S. 176 (unanimously upholding an Alabama law prohibiting oil producers from passing increases in a severance tax on to consumers despite pre-existing contracts requiring consumers to reimburse producers for such taxes).

Chapter 6

PROTECTION OF INDIVIDUAL RIGHTS: DUE PROCESS, THE BILL OF RIGHTS, AND NONTEXTUAL CONSTITUTIONAL RIGHTS

SECTION 1.   NATURE AND SCOPE OF FOURTEENTH AMENDMENT DUE PROCESS; APPLICABILITY OF THE BILL OF RIGHTS TO THE STATES

I.   THE "ORDERED LIBERTY—FUNDAMENTAL FAIRNESS," "TOTAL INCORPORATION" AND "SELECTIVE INCORPORATION" THEORIES

Twining v. New Jersey, 211 U.S. 78 (1908); *Palko v. Connecticut,* 302 U.S. 319 (1937); and *Adamson v. California,* 332 U.S. 46 (1947), rejected the "total incorporation" view of the history of the Fourteenth Amendment, the view—which has never commanded a majority—that the Fourteenth Amendment made all of the provisions of the Bill of Rights fully applicable to the states.[a] But *Twining* recognized that "it is possible that some of the personal rights safeguarded by the first eight Amendments against National action may also be safeguarded against state action, because a denial of them would be a denial of due process" or because "the specific pledge of particular amendments have been found to be implicit in the concept of ordered liberty and thus through the Fourteenth Amendment, become valid as against the states" (*Palko*). And the Court early found among the procedural requirements of Fourteenth Amendment due process certain rules paralleling provisions of the first eight amendments. For example, *Powell v. Alabama,* 287 U.S. 45 (1932), held that defendants in a capital case were denied due process when a state refused them the aid of counsel. "The logically critical thing, however," pointed out Harlan, J., years later, "was not that the

---

a. *Palko,* which held that the Fourteenth Amendment did not encompass at least certain aspects of the double jeopardy prohibition of the Fifth Amendment, was overruled in *Benton v. Maryland* (1969), discussed below. The *Twining-Adamson* view that the Fifth Amendment privilege against self-incrimination is not incorporated in the fourteenth was rejected in *Malloy v. Hogan* (1964), discussed below. *Grif-* *fin v. California,* 380 U.S. 609 (1965), subsequently applied *Malloy* to overrule the specific holdings of *Twining* and *Adamson,* which had permitted comment on a defendant's failure to take the stand at his criminal trial. These later decisions, however, were still consistent with the rejection of the "total incorporation" interpretation.

rights had been found in the Bill of Rights, but that they were deemed * * * fundamental."**b**

Under the "ordered liberty"-"fundamental fairness" test, which procedural safeguards included in the Bill of Rights were applicable to the states and which were not? Consider CARDOZO, J., speaking for the *Palko* Court: "[On reflection and analysis there] emerges the perception of a rationalizing principle which gives to discrete instances a proper order and coherence. The right to trial by jury and the immunity from prosecution except as the result of an indictment [are] not of the very essence of a scheme of ordered liberty. To abolish them is not to violate a 'principle of justice so rooted in the traditions and conscience of our people as to be ranked as fundamental.' [What] is true of jury trials and indictments is true also, as the cases show, of the immunity from compulsory self-incrimination. This too might be lost, and justice still be [done.]**c**

"We reach a different plane of social and moral values when we pass [to those provisions of the Bill of Rights] brought within the Fourteenth Amendment by a process of absorption. These in their origin were effective against the federal government alone. If the Fourteenth Amendment has absorbed them, the process of absorption has had its course in the belief that neither liberty nor justice would exist if they were sacrificed. This is true, for illustration, of freedom of thought and speech. Of that freedom one may say that it is the matrix, the indispensable condition, of nearly every other form of freedom. * * * Fundamental too in the concept of due process, and so in that of liberty, is the thought that condemnation shall be rendered only after trial. The hearing, moreover, must be a real one, not a sham or pretense [discussing *Powell* which] did not turn upon the fact that the benefit of counsel would have been guaranteed to the defendants by [the] Sixth Amendment if they had been prosecuted in a federal court [but on] the fact that in the particular situation laid before us [the aid of counsel] was essential to the substance of a hearing."

The "total incorporation" position received its strongest support in the *Adamson* dissents. In the principal dissent, BLACK, J., joined by Douglas, J., observed: "I cannot consider the Bill of Rights to be an outworn 18th Century 'strait jacket' as the *Twining* opinion did. Its provisions may be thought outdated abstractions by some. And it is true that they were designed to meet ancient evils. But they are the same kind of human evils that have emerged from century to century wherever excessive power is sought by the few at the expense of the many. In my judgment the people of no nation can lose their liberty so long as a Bill of Rights like ours survives and its basic purposes are conscientiously interpreted, enforced and respected so as to afford continuous protection against old, as well as new, devices and practices which might thwart those purposes. I fear to see the consequences of the Court's practice of substituting its own concepts of decency and fundamental justice for the language of the Bill of Rights as its point of departure in interpreting and enforcing that Bill of Rights. If the choice must be between the selective process of the *Palko* decision applying some of the Bill of Rights to the States, or the *Twining* rule applying none of them, I would choose the *Palko* selective process. But rather than accept either of these choices, I would follow what I believe was the original purpose of the Fourteenth Amendment—to extend to all the people of the nation the complete protection of the Bill of Rights.

b. *Duncan v. Louisiana* (dissent joined by Stewart, J.), discussed below.

c. As pointed out in fn. a supra, the Fifth Amendment privilege against self-incrimination was subsequently held to be fully applica-ble to the states via the Fourteenth Amendment. So was the Sixth Amendment right to jury trial in criminal cases. *Duncan v. Louisiana* (1968), discussed below.

"[T]o pass upon the constitutionality of statutes by looking to the particular standards enumerated in the Bill of Rights and other parts of the Constitution is one thing; to invalidate statutes because of application of 'natural law' deemed to be above and undefined by the Constitution is another. 'In the one instance, courts proceeding within clearly marked constitutional boundaries seek to execute policies written into the Constitution; in the other they roam at will in the limitless area of their own beliefs as to reasonableness and actually select policies, a responsibility which the Constitution entrusts to the legislative representatives of the people.' "d

Responding, FRANKFURTER, J.'s concurrence in *Adamson* stressed the "independent potency" of the Fourteenth Amendment Due Process Clause, maintaining that it "neither comprehends the specific provisions by which the founders deemed it appropriate to restrict the federal government nor is confined to them": "Between the incorporation of the Fourteenth Amendment into the Constitution and the beginning of the present membership of the Court—a period of 70 years— the scope of that Amendment was passed upon by 43 judges. Of all these judges only one, who may respectfully be called an eccentric exception, ever indicated the belief that the Fourteenth Amendment was a shorthand summary of the first eight Amendments theretofore limiting only the Federal Government, and that due process incorporated those eight Amendments as restrictions upon the powers of the States. [To] suggest that it is inconsistent with a truly free society to begin prosecutions without an indictment, to try petty civil cases without the paraphernalia of a common law jury, to take into consideration that one who has full opportunity to make a defense remains silent is, in de Tocqueville's phrase, to confound the familiar with the necessary.

"[Those] reading the English language with the meaning which it ordinarily conveys, those conversant with the political and legal history of the concept of due process, those sensitive to the relations of the States to the central government as well as the relation of some of the provisions of the Bill of Rights to the process of justice, would hardly recognize the Fourteenth Amendment as a cover for the various explicit provisions of the first eight Amendments. Some of these are enduring reflections of experience with human nature, while some express the restricted views of Eighteenth–Century England regarding the best methods for the ascertainment of facts. The notion that the Fourteenth Amendment was a covert way of imposing upon the States all the rules which it seemed important to Eighteenth Century statesmen to write into the Federal Amendments, was rejected by judges who were themselves witnesses of the process by which the Fourteenth Amendment became part of the Constitution. * * *

"Indeed, the suggestion that the Fourteenth Amendment incorporates the first eight Amendments as such is not unambiguously urged. [There] is suggested merely a selective incorporation of the first eight Amendments into the Fourteenth Amendment. Some are in and some are out, but we are left in the dark as to which are in and which are out. [If] the basis of selection is merely that those provisions of the first eight Amendments are incorporated which commend themselves to individual justices as indispensable to the dignity and happiness of a free man, we are thrown back to a merely subjective test. [In] the history of thought

d. Dissenting separately in *Adamson,* Murphy, J., joined by Rutledge, J., "agree[d] that the specific guarantees of the Bill of Rights should be carried over intact into [the Fourteenth Amendment but was] not prepared to say that the latter is entirely and necessarily limited by the Bill of Rights. Occasions may arise where a proceeding falls so far short of conforming to fundamental standards of procedure as to warrant constitutional condemnation in terms of a lack of due process despite the absence of a specific provision of the Bill of Rights."

'natural law' has a much longer and much better founded meaning and justification than such subjective selection of the first eight Amendments for incorporation into the Fourteenth. If all that is meant is that due process contains within itself certain minimal standards which are 'of the very essence of a scheme of ordered liberty,' *Palko,* putting upon this Court the duty of applying these standards from time to time, then we have merely arrived at the insight which our predecessors long ago expressed.

"[A] construction which gives to due process no independent function but turns it into a summary of the specific provisions of the Bill of Rights [would] deprive the States of opportunity for reforms in legal process designed for extending the area of freedom. It would assume that no other abuses would reveal themselves in the course of time than those which had become manifest in 1791. Such a view not only disregards the historic meaning of 'due process.' It leads inevitably to a warped construction of specific provisions of the Bill of Rights to bring within their scope conduct clearly condemned by due process but not easily fitting into the pigeonholes of the specific provisions.

" * * * Judicial review of [the Due Process Clause] of the Fourteenth Amendment inescapably imposes upon this Court an exercise of judgment upon the whole course of the proceedings in order to ascertain whether they offend those canons of decency and fairness which express the notions of justice of English-speaking peoples even toward those charged with the most heinous offenses. These standards of justice are not authoritatively formulated anywhere as though they were prescriptions in a pharmacopoeia. But neither does the application of the Due Process Clause imply that judges are wholly at large. The judicial judgment in applying the Due Process Clause must move within the limits of accepted notions of justice and is not to be based upon the idiosyncracies of a merely personal judgment."

———

Although the Court continued to apply the *"Palko* selective process" approach to the Bill of Rights, DUNCAN v. LOUISIANA, 391 U.S. 145 (1968) (holding the Sixth Amendment right to jury trial applicable to the states via the Fourteenth Amendment), no longer employed the Cardozo–Frankfurter terminology (e.g., whether a particular guarantee was "implicit in the concept of ordered liberty" or required by "the 'immutable principles of justice' as conceived by a civilized society") but instead inquired whether the procedural safeguard included in the Bill of Rights was "fundamental to the *American scheme of justice"* (emphasis added) or "fundamental *in the context of the criminal processes maintained by the American states"* (emphasis added). As WHITE, J., noted for the *Duncan* majority (fn. 14), the different phraseology is significant:

"Earlier the Court can be seen as having asked, when inquiring into whether some particular procedural safeguard was required of a State, if a civilized system could be imagined that would not accord the particular protection [quoting from *Palko*]. The recent cases, on the other hand, have proceeded upon the valid assumption that state criminal processes are not imaginary and theoretical schemes but actual systems bearing virtually every characteristic of the common-law system that has been developing contemporaneously in England and this country. The question thus is whether given this kind of system a particular procedure is fundamental—whether, that is, a procedure is necessary to an Anglo–American regime of ordered liberty. It is this sort of inquiry that can justify the conclusions that state courts must exclude evidence seized in violation of the Fourth Amendment, *Mapp v. Ohio* [Part III infra] [and] that state prosecutors may not comment on a defendant's failure to testify, *Griffin v. California* [fn. a supra]. [Of] each of these determinations that a constitutional provision originally written to bind the Federal Government should bind the States as well it might be said that the limitation in question is not necessarily fundamental to fairness in every criminal system that might be imagined but is fundamental in the context of the criminal processes maintained by the American States.

"When the inquiry is approached in this way the question whether the States can impose criminal punishment without granting a jury trial appears quite different from the way it appeared in the older cases opining that States might abolish jury trial. A criminal process which was fair and equitable but used no juries is easy to imagine. It would make use of alternative guarantees and protections which would serve the purposes that the jury serves in the English and American systems. Yet no American State has undertaken to construct such a system. Instead, every American State, including Louisiana, uses the jury extensively, and imposes very serious punishments only after a trial at which the defendant has a right to a jury's verdict. In every State, including Louisiana, the structure and style of the criminal process—the supporting framework and the subsidiary procedures—are of the sort that naturally complement jury trial, and have developed in connection with and in reliance upon jury trial."**e**

Because the *Duncan* Court believed that "trial by jury in criminal cases is fundamental to the American scheme of justice," it held that it was guaranteed by the Fourteenth Amendment: "The guarantees of jury trial in the Federal and State Constitutions reflect a profound judgment about the way in which law should be enforced and justice administered. A right to jury trial is granted to criminal defendants in order to prevent oppression by the Government. Those who wrote our constitutions knew from history and experience that it was necessary to protect against unfounded criminal charges brought to eliminate enemies and against judges too responsive to the voice of higher authority. * * * Providing an accused with the right to be tried by a jury of his peers gave him an inestimable safeguard against the corrupt or overzealous prosecutor and against the compliant, biased, or eccentric judge. * * * Fear of unchecked power, so typical of our State and Federal Governments in other respects, found expression in the criminal law in this insistence upon community participation in the determination of guilt or innocence. The deep commitment of the Nation to the right of jury trial in serious criminal cases as a defense against arbitrary law enforcement qualifies for protection under the Due Process Clause of the Fourteenth Amendment, and must therefore be respected by the States."

Harlan, J., joined by Stewart, J., dissented: "Even if I could agree that the question before us is whether Sixth Amendment jury trial is totally ['incorporated into' the Fourteenth Amendment] or totally 'out' [see Sec. II infra], I can find in the Court's opinion no real reasons for concluding that it should be 'in'. The basis for distinguishing among clauses in the Bill of Rights cannot be that [only] some are old and much praised, or that only some have played an important role in the

e. See also Powell, J., concurring in the companion 1972 "jury unanimity" cases of *Johnson v. Louisiana* and *Apodaca v. Oregon,* discussed below: "I agree with Mr. Justice White's analysis in *Duncan* that the departure from earlier decisions was, in large measure, a product of a change in focus in the Court's approach to due process. No longer are questions regarding the constitutionality of particular criminal procedures resolved by focusing alone on the element in question and ascer- taining whether a system of criminal justice might be imagined in which a fair trial could be afforded in the absence of that particular element. Rather, the focus is, as it should be, on the fundamentality of that element viewed in the context of the basic Anglo–American jurisprudential system common to the States. That approach to due process readily accounts both for the conclusion that jury trial *is* funda- mental and that unanimity *is not.*"

development of federal law. These things are true of all. The Court says that some clauses are more 'fundamental' than others, but [uses] this word in a sense that would have astonished Mr. Justice Cardozo and which, in addition, is of no help. The word does not mean 'analytically critical to procedural fairness' for no real analysis of the role of the jury in making procedures fair is even attempted. Instead, the word turns out to mean 'old,' 'much praised,' and 'found in the Bill of Rights.' The definition of 'fundamental' thus turns out to be circular.

"[Jury trial] is of course not without virtues [but its] principal original virtue—[the limitations it] imposes on a tyrannous judiciary—has largely disappeared. [The] jury system [is] a cumbersome process, not only imposing great cost in time and money on both the State and the jurors themselves, but also contributing to delay in the machinery of justice. [That] trial by jury is not the only fair way of adjudicating criminal guilt is well attested by the fact that it is not the prevailing way, either in England or in this country.

"[In] sum, there is a wide range of views on the desirability of trial by jury, and on the ways to make it most effective when it is used; there is also considerable variation from State to State in local conditions such as the size of the criminal caseload, the ease or difficulty of summoning jurors, and other trial conditions bearing on fairness. We have before us, therefore, an almost perfect example of a situation in which [the states should serve as laboratories.] [Instead,] the Court has chosen to impose upon every State one means of trying criminal cases; it is a good means, but it is not the only fair means, and it is not demonstrably better than the alternatives States might devise."f

---

Although the Court has remained unwilling to accept the total incorporationists' reading of the Fourteenth Amendment, in the 1960s it "selectively" "incorporated" or "absorbed" more and more of the specifics of the Bill of Rights into the Fourteenth Amendment. As White, J., observed in *Duncan*:

"In resolving conflicting claims concerning the meaning of this spacious [Fourteenth Amendment] language, the Court has looked increasingly to the Bill of Rights for guidance; many of the rights guaranteed by the first eight Amendments to the Constitution have been held to be protected against state action by the Due Process Clause of the Fourteenth Amendment.g That clause now protects [the] Fourth Amendment rights to be free from unreasonable searches and seizures and to have excluded from criminal trials any evidence illegally seized; the right guaranteed by the Fifth Amendment to be free of compelled self-incrimination; and the Sixth Amendment rights to counsel, to a speedy and public trial [*Klopfer v. North Carolina*, 386 U.S. 213 (1967); *In re Oliver*, 333 U.S. 257 (1948)], to confrontation of opposing witnesses [*Pointer v. Texas*, 380 U.S. 400

f. For a recent discussion of the history of the "incorporation" of the various provisions of the Bill of Rights, see Alito, J.'s plurality opinion in *McDonald v. Chicago*, p. 305 infra. Consider, too, the strongly-worded exchange between Scalia, J., concurring, and Stevens, J., dissenting, in that case.

g. See also Black, J., joined by Douglas, J., concurring in *Duncan*: "[I] believe as strongly as ever that the Fourteenth Amendment was intended to make the Bill of Rights applicable to the States. I have been willing to support the selective incorporation doctrine, however, as an alternative, although perhaps less historically supportable than complete incorporation [because it] keeps judges from roaming at will in their own notions of what policies outside the Bill of Rights are desirable and what are not. And, most importantly for me, the selective incorporation process has the virtue of having already worked to make most of the Bill of Rights' protections applicable to the States."

(1965)] and to compulsory process for obtaining witnesses [*Washington v. Texas,* 388 U.S. 14 (1967)].''**h**

II. SHOULD THE "SELECTED" PROVISION APPLY TO THE STATES "JOT–FOR–JOT"? "BAG AND BAGGAGE"?

In the 1960s, the Court seemed to be "incorporating" not only the basic notion or general concept of the "selected" provision of the Bill of Rights, but applying the provision to the states *to the same extent* it applied to the federal government. Thus, BRENNAN, J., observed for a majority in *Malloy v. Hogan,* 378 U.S. 1 (1964): "We have held that the guarantees of the First Amendment, the prohibition of unreasonable searches and seizures of the Fourth Amendment, and the right to counsel guaranteed by the Sixth Amendment, are all to be enforced against the States under the Fourteenth Amendment *according to the same standards that protect those personal rights against federal encroachment.* [The] Court thus has rejected the notion that the Fourteenth Amendment applies to the States only a 'watered-down, subjective version of the individual guarantees of the Bill of Rights.' " (Emphasis added.) And WHITE, J., put it for a majority in *Duncan:* "Because we believe that trial by jury in criminal cases is fundamental to the American scheme of justice, we hold that the Fourteenth Amendment guarantees a right of jury trial in all criminal cases which—*were they to be tried in a federal court*—would come within the Sixth Amendment's guarantee." (Emphasis added.)**i**

HARLAN, J., was the most persistent and powerful critic of the *Malloy–Duncan* approach to Fourteenth Amendment Due Process. "The consequence," he protested in his *Malloy* dissent, "is inevitably disregard of all relevant differences which may exist between state and federal criminal law and its enforcement. The ultimate result is compelled uniformity, which is inconsistent with the purpose of our federal system and which is achieved either by encroachment on the State's sovereign powers or by dilution in federal law enforcement of the specific protections found in the Bill of Rights." See also Harlan, J.'s concurring opinion in *Pointer v. Texas,* 380 U.S. 400 (1965) (holding that an accused's Sixth Amendment right to confront the witnesses against him applies in its entirety to the states via the Fourteenth Amendment) and his dissenting opinions in *Duncan* and *Benton v. Maryland* (fn. a supra).

––––––––

In the 1970s matters were brought to a head by the "right to jury trial" cases: *Baldwin v. New York,* 399 U.S. 66 (1970) (no offense can be deemed "petty," thus dispensing with the Fourteenth and Sixth Amendment rights to jury trial, where more than six months incarceration is authorized); *Williams v. Florida,* 399 U.S. 78 (1970) ("that jury at common law was composed of precisely 12 is an historical accident, unnecessary to effect the purposes of the jury system"; thus 6–person jury in criminal cases does not violate Sixth Amendment, as applied to the states via Fourteenth);**a** and the 1972 *Apodaca* and *Johnson* cases, discussed below, dealing with whether unanimous jury verdicts are required in criminal cases.

h. In the area of criminal procedure, the Court has come very close to incorporating all of the relevant Bill of Rights guarantees. But still on the books, is a lonely exception. *Hurtado v. California,* 110 U.S. 516 (1884), refusing to apply to the states the Fifth Amendment requirement that prosecution be initiated by grand jury indictment.

i. See also Justice Marshall's opinion for the Court in *Benton v. Maryland,* 395 U.S. 784 (1969) (the validity of the state conviction "must be judged not by the watered-down standard enumerated in *Palko,* but *under this Court's interpretations of the Fifth Amendment double jeopardy provision*"). (Emphasis added.)

a. But *Ballew v. Georgia,* 435 U.S. 223 (1978), subsequently held that a state trial in a

Dissenting in *Baldwin* and concurring in *Williams,* HARLAN, J., maintained: "[*Williams*] evinces [a] recognition that the 'incorporationist' view of the Due Process Clause of the Fourteenth Amendment, which underlay *Duncan* and is now carried forward into *Baldwin,* must be tempered to allow the States more elbow room in ordering their own criminal systems. With that much I agree. But to accomplish this by diluting constitutional protections within the federal system itself is something to which I cannot possibly subscribe. Tempering the rigor of *Duncan* should be done forthrightly, by facing up to the fact that at least in this area the 'incorporation' doctrine does not fit well with our federal structure, and by the same token that *Duncan* was wrongly decided.

"[Rather] than bind the States by the hitherto undeviating and unquestioned federal practice of 12–member juries, the Court holds, based on a poll of state practice, that a six-man jury satisfies the guarantee of a trial by jury in a federal criminal system and consequently carries over to the States. This is a constitutional renvoi. With all respect, I consider that before today it would have been unthinkable to suggest that the Sixth Amendment's right to a trial by jury is satisfied by a jury of six, or less, as is left open by the Court's opinion in *Williams,* or by less than a unanimous verdict, a question also reserved in today's decision.[b]

"[These decisions] demonstrate that the difference between a 'due process' approach, that considers each particular case on its own bottom to see whether the right alleged is one 'implicit in the concept of ordered liberty,' and 'selective incorporation' is not an abstract one whereby different verbal formulae achieve the same results. The internal logic of the selective incorporation doctrine cannot be respected if the Court is both committed to interpreting faithfully the meaning of the federal Bill of Rights and recognizing the governmental diversity that exists in this country. The 'backlash' in *Williams* exposes the malaise, for there the Court dilutes a federal guarantee in order to reconcile the logic of 'incorporation,' the 'jot-for-jot and case-for-case' application of the federal right to the States, with the reality of federalism. Can one doubt that had Congress tried to undermine the common law right to trial by jury before *Duncan* came on the books the history today recited would have barred such action? Can we expect repeated performances when this Court is called upon to give definition and meaning to other federal guarantees that have been 'incorporated'?

"[I]t is time [for] for this Court to face up to the reality implicit in today's holdings and reconsider the 'incorporation' doctrine before its leveling tendencies further retard development in the field of criminal procedure by stifling flexibility in the States and by discarding the possibility of federal leadership by example."

In the companion cases of *Apodaca v. Oregon,* 406 U.S. 404 (1972) and *Johnson v. Louisiana,* 406 U.S. 356 (1972), upholding the constitutionality of less-than-unanimous jury verdicts in state criminal cases, eight justices adhered to the *Duncan* position that each element of the Sixth Amendment right to jury trial applies to the states to the same extent it applies to the federal government, but split 4–4 over whether the federal guarantee *did require* jury unanimity in criminal cases. State convictions by less than unanimous votes were sustained only because the ninth member of the Court, newly appointed POWELL, J., read the

non-petty criminal case to a jury of only five persons did deprive a defendant of the right to trial by jury guaranteed by the Sixth and Fourteenth Amendments.

b. Cf. Frankfurter, J., for the Court in *Rochin v. California* (1952) (discussed in Part III infra): "Words being symbols do not speak without a gloss. [T]he gloss may be the deposit of history, whereby a term gains technical content. Thus the requirements of the Sixth and Seventh Amendments for trial by jury in the federal courts have a rigid meaning. No changes or chances can alter the content of the verbal symbol of 'jury'—a body of twelve men who must reach a unanimous conclusion if the verdict is to go against the defendant."

Sixth Amendment as requiring jury unanimity, but—taking a Harlan-type approach—concluded that *this feature* of the federal right is not "so fundamental to the essentials of jury trial" as to require unanimity in state criminal cases as a matter of Fourteenth Amendment Due Process:[c]

"[I]n holding that the Fourteenth Amendment has incorporated 'jot-for-jot and case-for-case' every element of the Sixth Amendment, the Court derogates principles of federalism that are basic to our system. In the name of uniform application of high standards of due process, the Court has embarked upon a course of constitutional interpretation that deprives the States of freedom to experiment with adjudicatory processes different from the federal model. At the same time, the Court's understandable unwillingness to impose requirements that it finds unnecessarily rigid (e.g., *Williams*), has culminated in the dilution of federal rights that were, until these decisions, never seriously questioned. The doubly undesirable consequence of this reasoning process, labeled by Mr. Justice Harlan as 'constitutional schizophrenia,' may well be detrimental both to the state and federal criminal justice systems."[d]

BRENNAN, J., joined by Marshall, J., dissented: "Readers of today's opinions may be understandably puzzled why convictions by 11–1 and 10–2 jury votes are affirmed [when] a majority of the Court agrees that the Sixth Amendment requires a unanimous verdict in federal criminal jury trials, and a majority also agrees that the right to jury trial guaranteed by the Sixth Amendment is to be enforced against the States according to the same standards that protect that right against federal encroachment. The reason is that while my Brother Powell agrees that a unanimous verdict is required in federal criminal trials, he does not agree that the Sixth Amendment right to a jury trial is to be applied in the same way to State and Federal Governments. In that circumstance, it is arguable that the affirmance of the convictions [is] not inconsistent with a view that today's decision is a holding that only a unanimous verdict will afford the accused in a state criminal prosecution the jury trial guaranteed him by the Sixth Amendment. In any event, the affirmance must not obscure that the majority of the Court remains of the view that, as in the case of every specific of the Bill of Rights that extends to the States, the Sixth Amendment's jury trial guarantee, however it is to be construed, has identical application against both State and Federal Governments."[e]

III. BODILY EXTRACTIONS: ANOTHER LOOK AT THE "DUE PROCESS" AND "SELECTIVE INCORPORATION" APPROACHES

As noted earlier, Harlan, J., maintained that "the difference between a 'due process' approach [and] 'selective incorporation' is not an abstract one whereby

c. But *Burch v. Louisiana,* 441 U.S. 130 (1979), subsequently held, without a dissent on this issue, that conviction by a nonunanimous *six-person* jury in a state criminal trial for a nonpetty offense did violate the sixth and Fourteenth Amendment rights to trial by jury.

d. See also Powell, J., joined by Burger, C.J., and Rehnquist, J., dissenting in *Crist v. Bretz,* 437 U.S. 28 (1978) (holding that federal rule as to when jeopardy "attaches" in jury trials applies to state cases). Consider, too, Burger, C.J.'s separate opinion in *Crist v. Bretz* and Rehnquist, J.'s separate opinion in *Buckley v. Valeo,* p. 579 infra, maintaining that "not all

of the strictures which the First Amendment imposes upon Congress are carried over against the States by the Fourteenth Amendment, [but] only the 'general principle' of free speech."

e. In a separate dissent, Stewart, J., joined by Brennan and Marshall, JJ., protested that "unless *Duncan* is to be overruled," "the only relevant question here is whether the Sixth Amendment's guarantee of trial by jury embraces a guarantee that the verdict of the jury must be unanimous. The answer to that question is clearly 'yes,' as my Brother Powell has cogently demonstrated."

different formulae achieve the same results." But he made this observation in the context of the applicability to the states of the Sixth Amendment right to trial by jury, which had, or was thought to have, a relatively rigid meaning. Most language in the Bill of Rights, however, is rather vague and general, at least when specific problems arise under a particular phrase.

In considering whether, and under what conditions, the police may direct the "pumping" of a person's stomach to uncover incriminating evidence, or the taking of a blood sample from him, without his consent, do the "specific guarantees" in the Bill of Rights against "unreasonable searches and seizures" and against compelling a person to be "a witness against himself" free the Court from the demands of appraising and judging involved in answering these questions by interpreting the "due process" clause?

ROCHIN v. CALIFORNIA, 342 U.S. 165 (1952): Having "some information" that Rochin was selling narcotics, three deputy sheriffs "forced upon the door of [his] room and found him sitting partly dressed on the side of the bed, upon which his wife was lying. On a 'night stand' beside the bed the deputies spied two capsules. When asked 'whose stuff is this?' Rochin seized the capsules and put them in his mouth. A struggle ensued, in the course of which the three officers 'jumped upon him' and [unsuccessfully] attempted to extract the capsules. [Rochin] was handcuffed and taken to a hospital. At the direction of one of the officers a doctor forced an emetic solution through a tube into Rochin's stomach against his will. This 'stomach pumping' produced vomiting. In the vomited matter were found two capsules which proved to contain morphine. [Rochin was convicted of possessing morphine] and sentenced to sixty days' imprisonment. The chief evidence against him was the two capsules."

The Court, per FRANKFURTER, J., concluded that the officers' conduct violated Fourteenth Amendment due process: "This is conduct that shocks the conscience. Illegally breaking into the privacy of the petitioner, the struggle to open his mouth and remove what was there, the forcible extraction of his stomach's contents—this course of proceeding by agents of government to obtain evidence is bound to offend even hardened sensibilities. They are methods too close to the rack and the screw to permit of constitutional differentiation. * * * Due process of law, as a historic and generative principle, precludes defining, and thereby confining, [civilized] standards of conduct more precisely than to say that convictions cannot be brought about by methods that offend 'a sense of justice.' It would be a stultification of the responsibility which the course of constitutional history has cast upon this Court to hold that in order to convict a man the police cannot extract by force what is in his mind but can extract what is in his stomach. [E]ven though statements contained in them may be independently established as true[,] [c]oerced confessions offend the community's sense of fair play and decency. So here, to sanction the brutal conduct which naturally enough was condemned by the court whose judgment is before us, would be to afford brutality the cloak of law. Nothing would be more calculated to discredit law and thereby to brutalize the temper of a society."

BLACK, J., concurring, maintained that the Fifth Amendment's protection against compelled self-incrimination applied to the states and that "a person is compelled to be a witness against himself not only when he is compelled to testify, but also when as here, incriminating evidence is forcibly taken from him by a contrivance of modern science." In his view, "faithful adherence to the specific guarantees in the Bill of Rights insures a more permanent protection of individual liberty than that which can be afforded by the nebulous [Fourteenth Amendment due process] standards stated by the majority."

DOUGLAS, J., concurring, also criticized the majority's approach. He contended that the privilege against self-incrimination applied to the states as well as the federal government and barred the prosecution's use of capsules seized from a suspect's stomach. "[This] is an unequivocal, definite and workable rule of evidence for state and federal courts. But we cannot in fairness free the state courts from the [restraints of the Fifth Amendment privilege] and yet excoriate them for flouting the 'decencies of civilized conduct' when they admit the evidence. This is to make the rule turn not on the Constitution but on the idiosyncracies of the judges who sit here."

————

Irvine v. California, 347 U.S. 128 (1954) limited *Rochin* to situations involving police violence or brutality.a BREITHAUPT v. ABRAM, 352 U.S. 432 (1957), illustrated that under the *Rochin* test state police had considerable leeway even when the body of the accused was "invaded." In *Breithaupt*, the police took a blood sample from an unconscious person who had been involved in a fatal automobile collision. A majority, per CLARK, J., affirmed a manslaughter conviction based on the blood sample (which showed intoxication), stressing that the sample was "taken under the protective eye of a physician" and that "the blood test procedure has become routine in our everyday life." The "interests of society in the scientific determination of intoxication, one of the great causes of the mortal hazards of the road," outweighed "so slight an intrusion" of a person's body.

WARREN, C.J., joined by Black and Douglas, JJ., dissenting, deemed *Rochin* controlling and argued that police efforts to curb the narcotics traffic, involved in *Rochin,* "is surely a state interest of at least as great magnitude as the interest in highway law enforcement. [Only] personal reaction to the stomach pump and the blood test can distinguish the [two cases]."

DOUGLAS, J., joined by Black, J., dissented, maintaining that "if the decencies of a civilized state are the test, it is repulsive to me for the police to insert needles into an unconscious person in order to get the evidence necessary to convict him, whether they find the person unconscious, give him a pill which puts him to sleep, or use force to subdue him."

Nine years later, even though in the meantime the Court had held in *Mapp v. Ohio,* fn. a supra, that the federal exclusionary rule in search and seizure cases was binding on the states and in *Malloy v. Hogan,* that the Fifth Amendment's protection against compelled self-incrimination was likewise applicable to the states, the Court upheld the taking by a physician, at police direction, of a blood sample from an injured person, over his objection. SCHMERBER v. CALIFORNIA, 384 U.S. 757 (1966). In affirming the conviction for operating a vehicle while under the influence of intoxicating liquor, a 5–4 majority, per BRENNAN, J., ruled: (1) that the extraction of blood from petitioner under the aforementioned circumstances "did not offend 'that' sense of justice' 'of which we spoke in *Rochin,*' thus

---

a. In *Irvine* the police made repeated illegal entries into petitioner's home, first to install a secret microphone and then to move it to the bedroom, in order to listen to the conversations of the occupants—for over a month. Jackson, J., who announced the judgment of the Court and wrote the principal opinion, recognized that "few police measures have come to our attention that more flagrantly, deliberately, and persistently violated the fundamental principle declared by the Fourth Amendment as a restriction on the Federal Government," but adhered to the holding in *Wolf v. Colorado*, 338 U.S. 25 (1949), that the exclusionary rule in federal search and seizure cases is not binding on the states. (*Wolf* was overruled in *Mapp v. Ohio*, 367 U.S. 643 (1961)). Nor did Jackson, J., deem *Rochin* applicable: "However obnoxious are the facts in the case before us, they do not involve coercion, violence or brutality to the person [as did *Rochin*], but rather a trespass to property, plus eavesdropping."

reaffirming *Breithaupt;* (2) that the privilege against self-incrimination, now binding on the states, 'protects an accused only from being compelled to testify against himself, or otherwise provide the State with evidence of a testimonial or communicative nature and that the withdrawal of blood and use of the analysis in question did not involve compulsion to these ends'; and (3) that the protection against unreasonable search and seizure, now binding on the states, was satisfied because (a) 'there was plainly probable cause' to arrest and charge petitioner and to suggest 'the required relevance and likely success of a test of petitioner's blood for alcohol';" (b) the officer "'might reasonably have believed that he was confronted with an emergency, in which the delay necessary to obtain a warrant, under the circumstances, threatened 'the destruction of evidence' "; and (c) "the test chosen to measure petitioner's blood-alcohol level was [reasonable and] performed in a reasonable manner."

BLACK, J., joined by Douglas, J., dissenting, expressed amazement at the majority's "conclusion that compelling a person to give his blood to help the State to convict him is not equivalent to compelling him to be a witness against himself." "It is a strange hierarchy of values that allows the State to extract a human being's blood to convict him of a crime because of the blood's content but proscribes compelled production of his lifeless papers."a

The "shocks-the-conscience" test and substantive due process claims. SACRAMENTO v. LEWIS, 523 U.S. 833 (1998), held, per SOUTER, J., that a police officer did not violate substantive due process by causing death through "reckless indifference" to, or "reckless disregard" for, a person's life in a high-speed automobile chase of a speeding motorcyclist. (The chase resulted in the death of the motorcyclist's passenger when the police car skidded into the passenger after the cycle had tipped over). In such circumstances, concluded the Court, "only a purpose to cause harm unrelated to the legitimate object of arrest will satisfy the element of arbitrary conduct shocking to the conscience, necessary for a due process violation [and for police liability under 42 U.S.C. § 1983]." Since the time of its early explanations of due process, observed the Court, "we have understood the core of the concept to be protection against arbitrary action. [Since *Rochin*] we have spoken of the cognizable level of executive abuse of power as that which shocks the conscience. [In] the intervening years we have repeatedly adhered to *Rochin*'s benchmark.' * * * Regardless whether [the officer's] behavior offended the reasonableness [of] tort law or the balance struck in law enforcement's own codes of sound practice, it does not shock the conscience."b

A Note on the Retroactive Effect of a Holding of Unconstitutionality

In recent decades, the Court has considered the retroactive effect of a holding that a law or practice is unconstitutional primarily in the context of criminal procedure decisions. A key case in the development of this body of law is *Shea v.*

a. Warren, C.J., and Douglas, J., dissented in separate opinions, each adhering to his dissenting views in *Breithaupt.* In a third dissent, Fortas, J., maintained that "petitioner's privilege against self-incrimination applies" and, moreover, "under the Due Process Clause, the State, in its role as prosecutor, has no right to extract blood from [anyone] over his protest."

b. Kennedy, J., joined by O'Connor, J. joined the opinion of the Court, but also wrote separately. They "share[d] Justice Scalia's concerns about using the phrase 'shocks the con-

science' in a manner suggesting that it is a self-defining test." The phrase, they observed, "has the unfortunate connotation of a standard laden with subjective assessments. In that respect, it must be viewed with considerable skepticism."

Concurring in the judgment, Scalia, J., joined by Thomas, J., would not have decided the case by applying the "shocks-the-conscience" test but "on the ground that respondents offer no textual or historical support for their alleged due process right."

Louisiana, 470 U.S. 51 (1985). While Shea's appeal from a conviction based on his confession was pending, the Court ruled that when the government uses a confession obtained by police-instigated interrogation, without a lawyer present, after the suspect has asked for a lawyer, the suspect's rights are violated. (*Edwards v. Arizona*, 451 U.S. 477 (1981).) This was exactly what happened in the *Shea* case. A 5–4 majority, per Blackmun, J., held that Shea was entitled to the benefit of the new ruling. The *Shea* majority was heavily influenced by Justice Harlan, who, dissenting in an earlier case, *Desist v. United States*, 394 U.S. 244 (1969), had maintained that all new rules of constitutional law "must, at a minimum, be applied to all those cases which are still subject to direct review by the Court at the time the 'new' decision is handed down."

In defending the distinction between a case pending on direct review and a case on collateral attack, BLACKMUN, J., observed that the distinction "properly rests on considerations of finality in the judicial process. The one litigant already has taken his case through the primary system. The other has not. For the latter, [someone in Shea's situation], the curtain of finality has not been drawn. Somewhere, the closing must come."

WHITE, J., joined by Burger, C.J., and Rehnquist and O'Connor, JJ., dissenting, maintained that "the attempt to distinguish between direct and collateral challenges for purposes of retroactivity is misguided": "Under the majority's rule, otherwise identically situated defendants may be subject to different constitutional rules, depending on just how long ago now-unconstitutional conduct occurred and how quickly cases proceed through the criminal justice system. The disparity is no different in kind from that which occurs when the benefit of a new constitutional rule is retroactively afforded to the defendant in whose case it is announced but to no others; the Court's new approach equalizes nothing except the numbers of defendants within the disparately treated classes."

There were two parts to Harlan, J.'s approach to retroactivity. He believed that new rulings should always be applied retroactively to cases on *direct* review (a position adopted in *Shea*), but he was also of the view that generally new rulings should not be applied retroactively to cases on *collateral* review. In *Teague v. Lane*, 489 U.S. 288 (1989), seven members of the Court adopted this position as well. In a plurality opinion that subsequently was adopted by the Court (see, e.g., *Sawyer v. Smith*, 497 U.S. 227 (1990)), O'CONNOR, J., joined by Rehnquist, C.J., and Scalia and Kennedy, JJ., maintained that generally on collateral review a court should evaluate a conviction by reference to "the law prevailing at the time [the] conviction became final," i.e., at the time when the opportunity for direct review was exhausted. In describing the "new rule" concept, the O'Connor plurality stated that "a case announces a new rule if the result was not *dictated* by precedent existing at the time the defendant's conviction became final." Later cases made clear that a result was not so dictated simply because it followed from the general rationale of that precedent.[a]

---

a. However, *Teague* did recognize two exceptions to the general approach. A habeas corpus court could overturn a final conviction based on a new rule if, but only if, (1) the rule "places 'certain kinds of primary, private individual conduct beyond the power of the criminal lawmaking authority to proscribe' " or (2) the rule mandates "new procedures without which the likelihood of an accurate conviction is seriously diminished."

SECTION 2. THE RIGHT OF "PRIVACY" (OR "AUTONOMY" OR "PERSONHOOD")

Introductory Note

"Whether as substantive due process or as Privacy, 'fundamentality' needs elaboration, especially with respect to the weight particular rights are to enjoy in the balance against public good. Justices Stone and Cardozo suggested that the freedoms of speech, press and religion required extraordinary judicial protection against invasions even for the public good, because of their place at the foundations of democracy and because of the unreliability of the political process in regard to them. If other rights—those to be described as within the Rights of Privacy—are also to be specially guarded against the democratic political process, similar or other justifications must be found—if there are any. Perhaps unusual respect for autonomy and idiosyncrasy as regards some 'personal' matters is intuitively felt by all of us, including Justices; that such deference is 'self-evident' is not self-evident."

— Louis Henkin, *Privacy and Autonomy,* 74 Colum.L.Rev. 1410, 1428–29 (1974).

————

As noted in Ira Lupu, *Untangling the Strands of the Fourteenth Amendment,* 77 Mich.L.Rev. 981, 1029–30 (1979), "unlike the all-inclusive theory of the *Lochner* era that held all liberties equally inviolable, and unlike the procedural due process theory that assesses the weight of any protected interest in a refined way for purposes of 'balancing' [Sec. 5 infra], [what might be called] modern substantive due process theory has a distinct all-or-nothing quality to it. Most liberties lacking textual support are of the garden variety—like liberty of contract—and thus their deprivation is constitutional if rationally necessary to the achievement of a public good. [See, e.g., *Williamson v. Lee Optical Co.,* Ch. 5, Sec. 3]. Several select liberties, on the other hand, have attained the status of 'fundamental' or 'preferred,' with the consequence that the Constitution permits a state to abridge them only if it can demonstrate an extraordinary justification." A notable example is *Roe v. Wade,* infra, where the Court held that the "right of privacy" encompassed "a woman's decision whether or not to terminate her pregnancy" and thus certain restrictions on abortion could be justified "only by a 'compelling state interest.'" See also *Shapiro v. Thompson,* Ch. 9, Sec. 5, II, which can be viewed as a "right to travel" case, which, in the course of invalidating a one-year durational residence requirement for welfare, rejected the argument that "a mere showing of a rational relationship between the waiting period and [administrative governmental] objectives will suffice [for] in moving from state to state [appellees] were exercising a constitutional right, and any classification which serves to penalize the exercise of that right, unless shown to be necessary to promote a *compelling* governmental interest, is unconstitutional." As Lupu observes, supra, "[b]ecause the review standard for ordinary liberties is so deferential, and the standard for preferred liberties so rigid, outcomes are ordained by the designation of 'preferred' [or 'fundamental'] or not."

Regulations dealing with "fundamental rights" call for "strict scrutiny" review just as government classifications based upon what have come to be known as "suspect" criteria trigger "strict" equal protection review. Not infrequently, as in *Skinner v. Oklahoma,* 316 U.S. 535 (1942),a an "equal protection" case in form

---

a. *Skinner,* per Douglas, J., held violative of equal protection Oklahoma's Habitual Criminal Sterilization Act, which authorized the sterilization of persons previously convicted and imprisoned two or more times of crimes "amounting to felonies involving moral turpitude" and thereafter convicted of such a felony and sentenced to prison. (Petitioner, previously convicted of "chicken-stealing" and robbery, had again been convicted of robbery.) Express-

which never mentioned any "right of privacy," can be viewed as either an "equal protection" or a "fundamental rights" (or "substantive due process") case.

GRISWOLD v. CONNECTICUT

381 U.S. 479, 85 S.Ct. 1678, 14 L.Ed.2d 510 (1965).

Justice Douglas delivered the opinion of the Court.

Appellant Griswold is Executive Director of the Planned Parenthood League of Connecticut. Appellant Buxton [is] Medical Director for the League at its Center in New Haven—a center open [when] appellants were arrested. They gave information, instruction, and medical advice to *married persons* as to the means of preventing conception. [Fees] were usually charged, although some couples were serviced free.

[The constitutionality of two Connecticut statutes is involved.] [One] provides: "Any person who uses any drug, medicinal article or instrument for the purpose of preventing conception shall be fined not less than fifty dollars or imprisoned not less than sixty days nor more than one year or be both fined and imprisoned." [The other] provides: "Any person who assists, abets, counsels, causes, hires or commands another to commit any offense may be prosecuted and punished as if he were the principal offender." The appellants were found guilty as accessories and fined $100 [each].

Coming to the merits,a we are met with a wide range of questions that implicate the Due Process Clause * * *. Overtones of some arguments suggest that *Lochner* should be our guide. But we decline that invitation * * *. We do not sit as a super-legislature to determine the wisdom, need, and propriety of laws that touch economic problems, business affairs, or social conditions. This law, however, operates directly on an intimate relation of husband and wife and their physician's role in one aspect of that relation.

The association of people is not mentioned in the Constitution nor in the Bill of Rights. The right to educate a child in a school of the parents' choice—whether public or private or parochial—is also not mentioned. Nor is the right to study any

---

ly exempted were such felonies as embezzlement. Thus one convicted three times of larceny could be subjected to sterilization, but the embezzler could not—although "the nature of the two crimes is intrinsically the same" and they are otherwise punishable in the same manner. The Oklahoma law "runs afoul of the equal protection clause" because—

"We are dealing here with legislation which involves one of the basic civil rights of man. Marriage and procreation are fundamental to the very existence and survival of the race. [In] evil or reckless hands [the power to sterilize] can cause races or types which are criminal to the dominant group to wither and disappear. There is no redemption for the individual whom the law touches. [He] is forever deprived of a basic liberty. We mention these matters [in] emphasis of our view that strict scrutiny of the classification which a State makes in a sterilization law is essential, lest unwittingly, or otherwise, invidious discriminations are made against groups or types of individuals in violation of the constitutional guaranty of just and equal laws."

Stone, C.J., concurring in the result, thought that "the real question [is] not one of equal protection, but whether the wholesale condemnation of a class to such as invasion of personal liberty, without opportunity to any individual to show that his is not the type of case which would justify resort to it, satisfies the demands of due process. [A] law which condemns, without hearing, all the individuals of a class to so harsh a measure as the present because some or even many merit condemnation, is lacking in the first principles of due process."

Skinner distinguished *Buck v. Bell*, 274 U.S. 200 (1927), upholding a sterilization law applicable only to mental defectives in state institutions: "[It] was pointed out [in that case] that 'so far as the operations enable those who otherwise must be kept confined to be returned to the world, and thus open the asylum to others, the equality aimed at will be more nearly reached.' Here there is no such saving feature."

a. The Court held that appellants had standing to assert the constitutional rights of the married persons they advised.

particular subject or any foreign language. Yet the First Amendment has been construed to include certain of those rights. [See] *Pierce v. Society of Sisters,* 268 U.S. 510 (1925) [and] *Meyer v. Nebraska,* 262 U.S. 390 (1923). [T]he State may not, consistently with the spirit of the First Amendment, contract the spectrum of available knowledge. The right of freedom of speech and press includes not only the right to utter or to print, but the right to distribute, the right to receive, the right to read and freedom of inquiry, freedom of thought, and freedom to teach— indeed the freedom of the entire university community. Without those peripheral rights the specific rights would be less secure. And so we reaffirm the principle [of] *Pierce* [and] *Meyer.*

In *NAACP v. Alabama* [Ch. 7, Sec. 9], we protected the "freedom to associate and privacy in one's associations," noting that freedom of association was a peripheral First Amendment right. [In] other words, the First Amendment has a penumbra where privacy is protected from governmental intrusion. In like context, we have protected forms of "association" that are not political in the customary sense but pertain to the social, legal, and economic benefit of the members. *NAACP v. Button,* 371 U.S. 415 (1963). [W]hile [association] is not expressly included in the First Amendment its existence is necessary in making the express guarantees fully meaningful.

The foregoing cases suggest that specific guarantees in the Bill of Rights have penumbras, formed by emanations from those guarantees that help give them life and substance. Various guarantees create zones of privacy. The right of association contained in the penumbra of the First Amendment is one, as we have seen. The Third Amendment in its prohibition against the quartering of soldiers "in any house" [is] another facet of that privacy. The Fourth Amendment [is another]. The Fifth Amendment in its Self–Incrimination Clause enables the citizen to create a zone of privacy which government may not force him to surrender to his detriment. The Ninth Amendment provides: "The enumeration in the Constitution, of certain rights, shall not be construed to deny or disparage others retained by the people." * * *

We have had many controversies over these penumbral rights of "privacy and repose." [*Skinner* and other cases] bear witness that the right of privacy which presses for recognition here is a legitimate one.

The present case, then, concerns a relationship lying within the zone of privacy created by several fundamental constitutional guarantees. And it concerns a law which, in forbidding the *use* of contraceptives rather than regulating their manufacture or sale, seeks to achieve its goals by means having a maximum destructive impact upon that relationship. Such a law cannot stand in light of the familiar principle [that] a "governmental purpose to control or prevent activities constitutionally subject to state regulation may not be achieved by means which sweep unnecessarily broadly and thereby invade the area of protected freedoms." *NAACP v. Alabama.* Would we allow the police to search the sacred precincts of marital bedrooms for telltale signs of the use of contraceptives? The very idea is repulsive to the notions of privacy surrounding the marriage relationship.

We deal with a right of privacy older than the Bill of Rights * * *. Marriage is a coming together for better or for worse, hopefully enduring, and intimate to the degree of being sacred. It is an association that promotes a way of life, not causes; a harmony in living, not political faiths; a bilateral loyalty, not commercial or social projects. Yet it is an association for as noble a purpose as any involved in our prior decisions.

Reversed.

JUSTICE GOLDBERG, whom THE CHIEF JUSTICE and JUSTICE BRENNAN join, concurring.

I [join the Court's opinion]. Although I have not accepted the view that "due process" as used in the Fourteenth Amendment includes all of the first eight Amendments, I do agree that the concept of liberty protects those personal rights that are fundamental, and is not confined to the specific terms of the Bill of Rights. My conclusion [that liberty] embraces the right of marital privacy though that right is not mentioned explicitly in the Constitution is supported both by numerous decisions [and] by the language and history of the Ninth Amendment [which] reveal that the Framers of the Constitution believed that there are additional fundamental rights, protected from governmental infringement. [The] Ninth Amendment [was] proffered to quiet expressed fears that a bill of specifically enumerated rights could not be sufficiently broad to cover all essential rights and that the specific mention of certain rights would be interpreted as a denial that others were protected.

[While] this Court has had little occasion to interpret the Ninth Amendment, "[i]t cannot be presumed that any clause in the constitution is intended to be without effect." [To] hold that a right so basic and fundamental and so deep-rooted in our society as the right of privacy in marriage may be infringed because that right is not guaranteed in so many words by the first eight amendments to the Constitution is to ignore the Ninth Amendment and to give it no effect whatsoever. [The] Ninth Amendment shows a belief of the Constitution's authors that fundamental rights exist that are not expressly enumerated in the first eight amendments and an intent that the list of rights included there not be deemed exhaustive.

[Surely] the Government, absent a showing of a compelling subordinating state interest, could not decree that all husbands and wives must be sterilized after two children have been born to them. Yet by [the dissenters'] reasoning such an invasion of marital privacy would not be subject to constitutional challenge because, while it might be "silly," no provision of the Constitution specifically prevents the Government from curtailing the marital right to bear children and raise a family. [I]f upon a showing of a slender basis of rationality, a law outlawing voluntary birth control by married persons is valid, then, by the same reasoning, a law requiring compulsory birth control also would seem to be valid. In my view, however, both types of law would unjustifiably intrude upon rights of marital privacy which are constitutionally protected.

In a long series of cases this Court has held that where fundamental personal liberties are involved, they may not be abridged by the States simply on a showing that a regulatory statute has some rational relationship to the effectuation of a proper state purpose. [The] State, at most, argues that there is some rational relation between this statute and what is admittedly a legitimate subject of state concern—the discouraging of extra-marital relations. It says that preventing the use of birth-control devices by married persons helps prevent the indulgence by some in such extra-marital relations. The rationality of this justification is dubious, particularly in light of the admitted widespread availability to all persons [in] Connecticut, unmarried as well as married, of birth-control devices for the prevention of disease, as distinguished from the prevention of conception. But in any event, it is clear that the state interest in safeguarding marital fidelity can be served by a more discriminately tailored statute, which does not, like the present one, sweep unnecessarily broadly, reaching far beyond the evil sought to be dealt with and intruding upon the privacy of all married couples. * * *

JUSTICE HARLAN, concurring in the judgment.

I [cannot] join the Court's opinion [as] it seems to me to evince an approach [that] the Due Process Clause of the Fourteenth Amendment does not touch this Connecticut statute unless the enactment is found to violate some right assured by the letter or penumbra of the Bill of Rights. [W]hat I find implicit in the Court's opinion is that the "incorporation" doctrine may be used to *restrict* the reach of Fourteenth Amendment Due Process. For me this is just as unacceptable constitutional doctrine as is the use of the "incorporation" approach to *impose* upon the States all the requirements of the Bill of Rights. * * *

[T]he proper constitutional inquiry in this case is whether this Connecticut statute infringes the Due Process Clause of the Fourteenth Amendment because the enactment violates basic values "implicit in the concept of ordered liberty." For reasons stated at length in my dissenting opinion in *Poe v. Ullman* [discussed below], I believe that it does. While the relevant inquiry may be aided by resort to one or more of the provisions of the Bill of Rights, it is not dependent on them or any of their radiations. The Due Process Clause of the Fourteenth Amendment stands, in my opinion, on its own bottom.

[While] I could not more heartily agree that judicial "self restraint" is an indispensable ingredient of sound constitutional adjudication, I do submit that the formula suggested [by the dissenters] for achieving it is more hollow than real. "Specific" provisions of the Constitution, no less than "due process," lend themselves as readily to "personal" interpretations by judges whose constitutional outlook is simply to keep the Constitution in supposed "tune with the times".

[Judicial self-restraint will] be achieved in this area, as in other[s], only by continual insistence upon respect for the teachings of history, solid recognition of the basic values that underlie our society, and wise appreciation of the great roles that the doctrines of federalism and separation of powers have played in establishing and preserving American freedoms. Adherence to these principles will not, of course, obviate all constitutional differences of opinion among judges, nor should it. Their continued recognition will, however, go farther toward keeping most judges from roaming at large in the constitutional field than will the interpolation into the Constitution of an artificial and largely illusory restriction on the content of the Due Process Clause.

[Dissenting in POE v. ULLMAN, 367 U.S. 497 (1961), which failed to reach the merits of the constitutional challenge to the Connecticut anti-birth control statute, Harlan, J., had maintained that the statute, "as construed to apply to these appellants, violates the Fourteenth Amendment" because "a statute making it a criminal offense for *married couples* to use contraceptives is an intolerable and unjustifiable invasion of privacy in the conduct of the most intimate concerns of an individual's personal life." Harlan, J., "would not suggest that adultery, homosexuality, fornication and incest are immune from criminal enquiry, however privately practiced," but "the intimacy of husband and wife is necessarily an essential and accepted feature of the institution of marriage, an institution which the State not only must allow, but which always and every age it has fostered and protected. It is one thing when the State exerts its power either to forbid extra-marital sexuality altogether, or to say who may marry, but it is quite another when, having acknowledged a marriage and the intimacies inherent in it, it undertakes to regulate by means of the criminal law the details of that intimacy."

[Although the state had argued the constitutional permissibility of the moral judgment underlying the challenged statute, Harlan, J., could not find anything that "even remotely suggests a justification for the obnoxiously intrusive means it has chosen to effectuate that policy." He deemed "the utter novelty" of the statute "conclusive." "Although the Federal Government and many States have at one time or another [prohibited or regulated] the distribution of contraceptives, none [has] made the *use* of contraceptives a crime. Indeed, a diligent search has revealed that no nation, including several which quite evidently share Connecticut's moral policy, had seen fit to effectuate that policy by the means presented here."

[Because the constitutional challenges to the Connecticut statute "draw their basis from no explicit language of the Constitution, and have yet to find expression in any decision of this Court," Harlan, J., deemed it "desirable at the outset to state the framework of Constitutional principles in which I think the issue must be judged":

["[Were] due process merely a procedural safeguard it would fail to reach those situations where the deprivation of life, liberty or property was accomplished by legislation which by operating in the future could, given even the fairest possible procedure in application to individuals, nevertheless destroy the enjoyment of all three. [I]t is not the particular enumeration of rights in the first eight Amendments which spells out the reach of Fourteenth Amendment due process, but rather [those concepts embracing] rights 'which [are] *fundamental;* which belong [to] the citizens of all free governments.'

["[T]hrough the course of this Court's decisions [due process] has represented the balance which our Nation, built upon postulates of respect for the liberty of the individual, has struck between that liberty and the demands of organized society. [The] balance of which I speak is the balance struck by this country, having regard to what history teaches are the traditions from which it developed as well as the traditions from which it broke. That tradition is a living thing. A decision of this Court which radically departs from it could not long survive, while a decision which builds on what has survived is likely to be sound. No formula could serve as a substitute, in this area, for judgment and restraint.

["[The] full scope of the liberty guaranteed by the Due Process Clause cannot be found in or limited by the precise terms of the specific guarantees elsewhere provided in the Constitution. This 'liberty' is not a series of isolated points pricked out in terms of [the] freedom of speech, press, and religion; [the] freedom from unreasonable searches and seizures; and so on. It is a rational continuum which, broadly speaking, includes a freedom from all substantial arbitrary impositions and purposeless restraints [and] which also recognizes, what a reasonable and sensitive judgment must, that certain interests require particularly careful scrutiny of the state needs asserted to justify their abridgment. Cf. *Skinner.*"]b

Justice White, concurring in the judgment.

In my view this Connecticut law as applied to married couples deprives them of "liberty" without [due process] guaranteed by the Fourteenth Amendment against arbitrary or capricious [denials]. Surely the right [to] be free of regulation of the intimacies of the marriage relationship, "come[s] to this Court with a momentum for respect lacking when appeal is made to liberties which derive merely from shifting economic arrangements." *Kovacs v. Cooper,* 336 U.S. 77 (1949) (opinion of Frankfurter, J.).

The Connecticut anti-contraceptive statute deals rather substantially with this relationship. [And] the clear effect of these statutes, as enforced, is to deny disadvantaged citizens of Connecticut, those without either adequate knowledge or resources to obtain private counseling, access to medical assistance and up-to-date information in respect to proper methods of birth control. In my view, a

b. See also the extracts from this dissent in Planned Parenthood v. Casey, *infra.*

statute with these effects bears a substantial burden of justification when attacked under the Fourteenth Amendment.

An examination of the justification offered, however, cannot be avoided by saying that the Connecticut anti-use statute invades a protected area of privacy and association or that it demeans the marriage relationship. The nature of the right invaded is pertinent, to be sure, for statutes regulating sensitive areas of liberty do, under the cases of this Court, require "strict scrutiny," *Skinner,* and "must be viewed in the light of less drastic means for achieving the same basic purpose." But such statutes, if reasonably necessary for the effectuation of a legitimate and substantial state interest, and not arbitrary or capricious in application, are not invalid under the Due Process Clause. [There] is no serious contention that Connecticut thinks the use of artificial or external methods of contraception immoral or unwise in itself, or that the anti-use statute is founded upon any policy of promoting population expansion. Rather, the statute is said to serve the State's policy against all forms of promiscuous or illicit sexual relationships, be they premarital or extramarital, concededly a permissible and legitimate legislative goal.

[But] I wholly fail to see how the ban on the use of contraceptives by married couples in any way reinforces the State's ban on illicit sexual relationships. [Perhaps] the theory is that the flat ban on use prevents married people from possessing contraceptives and without the ready availability of such devices for use in the marital relationship, there will be no or less temptation to use them in extramarital ones. This reasoning rests on the premise that married people will comply with the ban in regard to their marital relationship, notwithstanding total nonenforcement in this context and apparent nonenforcibility, but will not comply with criminal statutes prohibiting extramarital affairs and the anti-use statute in respect to illicit sexual relationships, a premise whose validity has not been demonstrated and whose intrinsic validity is not very evident. At most the broad ban is of marginal utility to the declared objective. A statute limiting its prohibition on use to persons engaging in the prohibited relationship would serve the end posited by Connecticut in the same way, and with the same effectiveness, or ineffectiveness, as the broad anti-use statute under attack in this case. I find nothing in this record justifying the sweeping scope of this [statute].

Justice Black, with whom Justice Stewart joins, dissenting.

[There are] guarantees in certain specific constitutional provisions which are designed in part to protect privacy at certain times and places with respect to certain activities. [But] I think it belittles [the Fourth] Amendment to talk about it as though it protects nothing but "privacy." [The] average man would very likely not have his feelings soothed any more by having his property seized openly than by having it seized privately and by stealth. [And] a person can be just as much, if not more, irritated, annoyed and injured by an unceremonious public arrest by a policeman as he is by a seizure in the privacy of his office or home.

One of the most effective ways of diluting or expanding a constitutionally guaranteed right is to substitute for the crucial word or words of a constitutional guarantee another word or words, more or less flexible and more or less restricted in meaning. This fact is well illustrated by the use of the term "right of privacy" as a comprehensive substitute for the Fourth Amendment's guarantee against "unreasonable searches and seizures." * * *1 I like my privacy as well as the next

---

1. The phrase "right to privacy" appears first to have gained currency from an article written by Messrs. Warren and (later Mr. Justice) Brandeis in 1890 which urged that States should give some form of tort relief to persons whose private affairs were exploited by others. *The Right to Privacy,* 4 Harv.L.Rev. 193. * * * Observing that "the right of privacy presses

one, but I am nevertheless compelled to admit that government has a right to invade it unless prohibited by some specific constitutional provision.

[This] brings me to the arguments made by [the concurring justices]. I discuss the due process and Ninth Amendment arguments together because on analysis they turn out to be the same thing—merely using different words to claim for this Court and the federal judiciary power to invalidate any legislative act [that] it considers to be arbitrary, capricious, unreasonable, or oppressive, or this Court's belief that a particular state law under scrutiny has no "rational or justifying" purpose, or is offensive to a "sense of fairness and justice." If these formulas based on "natural justice" [are] to prevail, they require judges to determine what is or is not constitutional on the basis of their own appraisal of what laws are unwise or unnecessary. [I] do not believe that we are granted power by the Due Process Clause or any [other] provisions to measure constitutionality by our belief that legislation is arbitrary, capricious or unreasonable, or accomplishes no justifiable purpose, or is offensive to our own notions of "civilized standards of conduct." Such an appraisal of the wisdom of legislation is an attribute of the power to make laws, [a] power which was specifically denied to federal courts by the [Framers].

Of the cases on which my [Brothers] rely so heavily, undoubtedly the reasoning of two of them supports their result here—[*Meyer* and *Pierce*]. *Meyer* [relying on *Lochner,*] held unconstitutional, as an "arbitrary" and unreasonable interference with the right of a teacher to carry on his occupation and of parents to hire him, a state law forbidding the teaching of modern foreign languages to young children in the schools.7 [*Pierce,* per McReynolds, J.] said that a state law requiring that all children attend public schools interfered unconstitutionally with the property rights of private school corporations because it was an "arbitrary, unreasonable, and unlawful interference" which threatened "destruction of their business and property." Without expressing an opinion as to whether either of those cases reached a correct result in light of our later decisions applying the First Amendment to the States through the Fourteenth, I merely point out that the reasoning stated in *Meyer* and *Pierce* was the same natural law due process philosophy which many later opinions repudiated, and which I cannot accept.
* * *

My Brother Goldberg has adopted the recent discovery12 that the Ninth Amendment as well as the Due Process Clause can be used by this Court as authority to strike down all state legislation which this Court thinks violates "fundamental principles of liberty and justice," or is contrary to the "traditions and collective conscience of our people." [One] would certainly have to look far beyond the language of the Ninth Amendment to find that the Framers vested in this Court any such awesome veto powers over lawmaking. [The Ninth] Amendment was passed [to] limit the Federal Government to the powers granted expressly or by necessary implication. [This] fact is perhaps responsible for the peculiar phenomenon that for a period of a century and a half no serious

for recognition here," today this Court, which I did not understand to have power to sit as a court of common law, now appears to be exalting a phrase which Warren and Brandeis use in discussing grounds for tort relief, to the level of a constitutional [rule].

7. In *Meyer,* in the very same sentence quoted in part by my Brethren in which he asserted that the Due Process Clause gave an abstract and inviolable right "to marry, establish a home and bring up children," Justice

McReynolds asserted also that the Due Process Clause prevented States from interfering with "the right of the individual to contract."

12. See Patterson, *The Forgotten Ninth Amendment* (1955) [who] urges that the Ninth Amendment be used to protect unspecified "natural and inalienable rights." The Introduction by Roscoe Pound states that "there is a marked revival of natural law ideas throughout the world. Interest in the Ninth Amendment is a symptom of that revival." * * *

suggestion was ever made that [that] Amendment, enacted to protect state powers against federal invasion, could be used as a weapon of federal power to prevent state legislatures from passing laws they consider appropriate to govern local affairs. * * *

I realize that many good and able men have eloquently spoken and written [of] the duty of this Court to keep the Constitution in tune with the times [but I] reject that philosophy. The Constitution makers knew the need for change and provided for it. [The] Due Process Clause with an "arbitrary and capricious" or "shocking to the conscience" formula was liberally used by this Court to strike down economic legislation in the early decades of this century, threatening, many people thought, the tranquility and stability of the Nation. See, e.g., *Lochner.* That formula, based on subjective considerations of "natural justice," is no less dangerous when used to enforce this Court's views about personal rights than those about economic rights. [So] far as I am concerned, Connecticut's law as applied here is not forbidden by any provision of the Federal Constitution as that Constitution was written, and I would therefore affirm.

JUSTICE STEWART, whom JUSTICE BLACK joins, dissenting.

[T]his is an uncommonly silly law. As a practical matter, the law is obviously unenforceable, except in the oblique context of the present case. As a philosophical matter, I believe the use of contraceptives in the relationship of marriage should be left to personal and private [choice]. As a matter of social policy, I think professional counsel about methods of birth control should be available to all, so that each individual's choice can be meaningfully made. But we are not [asked] whether we think this law is unwise, or even asinine. We are asked to hold that it violates the United States Constitution. And that I cannot do.

In the course of its opinion the Court refers to no less than six Amendments [but] does not say which of these Amendments, if any, it thinks is infringed by this Connecticut law. [As] to the First, Third, Fourth, and Fifth Amendments, I can find nothing in any of them to invalidate this Connecticut law, even assuming that all those amendments are fully applicable against the States. [The] Ninth Amendment, like its companion the Tenth [was] simply to make clear that the adoption of the Bill of Rights did not alter the plan that the *Federal* Government was to be a government of express and limited powers, and that all rights and powers not delegated to it were retained by the people and the individual States. Until today no member of this Court has ever suggested that the Ninth Amendment meant anything [else].

What provision of the Constitution, then, does make this state law invalid? The Court says it is the right of privacy "created by several fundamental constitutional guarantees." [I] can find no such general right of privacy in the Bill of Rights, in any other part of the Constitution, or in any case ever before decided by this Court. * * *

———

Griswold invalidated a ban on the *use* of contraceptives by *married* couples. EISENSTADT v. BAIRD, 405 U.S. 438 (1972), overturned a conviction for violating a Massachusetts law making it a felony to *distribute* contraceptive materials, *except* in the case of registered physicians and pharmacists furnishing the materials to *married* persons. Baird had given a woman a package of vaginal foam at the end of his lecture on contraception. He was not charged with distributing to an unmarried person. No proof was offered as to the recipient's marital status. The crime charged was that Baird had no license, and thus no authority, to distribute to anyone. The Court, per BRENNAN, J., concluded that, since the statute is riddled with exceptions making contraceptives freely available and since, if protection of health were the rationale, the statute would be both discriminatory and overbroad, "the goals of deterring premarital sex and regulating the distribution of potentially harmful articles cannot reasonably be regarded as legislative aims." "[V]iewed as a prohibition on contraception per se" the statute "violates the rights of single persons under the Equal Protection Clause." For, "whatever the rights of the individual to access to contraceptives may be, the rights must be the same for the unmarried and the married alike":

"If under *Griswold* the distribution of contraceptives to married persons cannot be prohibited, a ban on distribution to unmarried persons would be equally impermissible. It is true that in *Griswold* the right of privacy in question inhered in the marital relationship. Yet the marital couple is not an independent entity with a mind and heart of its own, but an association of two individuals each with a separate intellectual and emotional make-up. If the right of privacy means anything, it is the right of the *individual,* married or single, to be free from unwarranted governmental intrusion into matters so fundamentally affecting a person as the decision whether to bear or beget a child. On the other hand, if *Griswold* is no bar to a prohibition on the distribution of contraceptives, the State could not, consistently with [equal protection,] outlaw distribution to unmarried but not to married persons. In each case the evil, as perceived by the State, would be identical, and the underinclusion would be invidious."

WHITE, J., joined by Blackmun, J., concurred, emphasizing that "the State did [not] convict Baird for distributing to an unmarried person [but because] Baird had no license and therefore no authority to distribute to anyone." "Given *Griswold,* and absent proof of the possible hazards of using vaginal foam, we could not sustain [Baird's] conviction had it been for selling or giving away foam to a married person. Just as in *Griswold,* where the right of married persons to use contraceptives was 'diluted or adversely affected' by permitting a conviction for giving advice as to its exercise, so here to sanction a medical restriction upon distribution of a contraceptive not proved hazardous to health would impair the exercise of the constitutional right. That Baird could not be convicted for distributing [foam] to a married person disposes of this case. Assuming arguendo that the result would be otherwise had the recipient been unmarried, nothing has been placed in the record to indicate her marital status."a

Burger, C.J., dissented, "see[ing] nothing in the Fourteenth Amendment or any other part of the Constitution that even vaguely suggests that these medicinal forms of contraceptives must be available in the open market. [By] relying on *Griswold* in the present context, the Court has passed beyond the penumbras of the specific guarantees into the uncircumscribed area of personal predilections."

———

CAREY v. POPULATION SERVICES INTERN., 431 U.S. 678 (1977), to invalidate a New York law which allowed only pharmacists to sell non-medical contraceptive devices to persons over 16 and prohibited the sale of such items to those under 16. (The Court relied in part on the 1973 *Abortion Cases,* infra.) In striking down the restriction on sales to adults, BRENNAN, J., spoke for six justices;

a. Douglas, J., who joined the Court's opinion, also concurred on free speech grounds.   Powell and Rehnquist, JJ., did not participate.

in invalidating the ban on sales to those under 16, he spoke for a four-justice plurality.

As for the restriction on distribution to adults, "where a decision as fundamental as that whether to bear or beget a child is involved, regulations imposing a burden on it may be justified only by compelling interests, and must be narrowly drawn to express only those interests"—and the Court found none of the state interests advanced (e.g., protecting health, facilitating enforcement of other laws) to be "compelling."a The state argued that *Griswold* dealt only with the *use* of contraceptives, not their manufacture or sale, but read "in light of its progeny, the teaching of *Griswold* is that the Constitution protects individual decisions in matters of childbearing from unjustified intrusion by the State."

As for the ban on sales to those under 16, Brennan, J., joined by Stewart, Marshall, and Blackmun, JJ., applied a test "apparently less rigorous than the 'compelling state interest' test applied to restrictions on the privacy rights of adults"—restrictions inhibiting privacy rights of minors are valid "only if they serve 'any significant state interest [that] is not present in the case of an adult.' *Planned Parenthood v. Danforth,* infra]." The plurality then rejected what it called "the argument [that] minors' sexual activity may be deterred by increasing the hazards attendant on it," pointing out that that argument had already been rejected by the Court in related areas.b

POWELL, J., concurred in the judgment, observing that by restricting not only the kinds of retail outlets that may distribute contraceptives, "but even prohibit[ing] distribution by mail to adults"—"thus requiring individuals to buy contraceptives over the counter"—the New York provision "heavily burdens constitutionally protected freedom." He saw "no justification for subjecting restrictions on the sexual activity of the young to heightened judicial review"—"a standard that for all practical purposes approaches the 'compelling interest' standard"—but concurred in the invalidation of the "distribution to minors" restriction on narrow grounds.c

---

ORAL ARGUMENTS IN THE ABORTION CASES*

* * *

THE COURT: [I]s it critical to your case that the fetus not be a person under the due process clause? [W]ould you lose your case if the fetus was a person?

a. The Court recognized, however, that "other restrictions may well be reasonably related to the objective of quality control," and thus "express[ed] no opinion on, for example, restrictions on the distribution of contraceptives through vending machines."

b. Nor was the restriction on the privacy rights of minors "saved" by another provision authorizing physicians to supply minors with contraceptives. As with limitations on distribution to adults, "less than total restrictions on access to contraceptives that significantly burden the right to decide whether to bear children must also pass constitutional muster. [This provision] delegates the State's authority to disapprove of minors' sexual behavior to physicians, who may exercise it arbitrarily * * *."

c. White and Stevens, JJ., concurred only in the judgment with respect to the restriction on minors. Rehnquist, J., dissented, observing that if those responsible for the Bill of Rights and Civil War Amendments could have lived to know what their efforts had wrought "it is not difficult to imagine their reaction." Burger, C.J., dissented without opinion.

* These extracts are taken from 75 *Landmark Briefs and Arguments of the Supreme Court of the United States: Constitutional Law* 807–33 (Philip Kurland & Gerhard Casper eds.).

SARAH WEDDINGTON [on behalf of appellant Roe]: Then you would have a balancing of interests.

THE COURT: Well you say you have [that] anyway, don't you? * * *

THE COURT: [If] it were established that an unborn fetus is a person, [protected by] the Fourteenth Amendment, you would have almost an impossible case here, would you not?

WEDDINGTON: I would have a very difficult case. * * *

THE COURT: Could Texas constitutionally, in your view, declare [by] statute [that] the fetus is a person, for all constitutional purposes, after the third month of gestation?

WEDDINGTON: I do not believe that the State legislature can determine the meaning of the Federal Constitution. It is up to this Court to make that determination. * * *

ROBERT FLOWERS [on behalf of appellee]: [I]t is the position of the State of Texas that, upon conception, we have a human being; a person, within the concept of the Constitution of the United States, and that of Texas, also.

THE COURT: Now how should that question be decided? Is it a legal question? A constitutional question? A medical question? A philosophical question? Or, a religious question? Or what is it?

FLOWERS: [W]e feel that it could be best decided by a legislature, in view of the fact that they can bring before it the medical testimony * * *.

THE COURT: So then it's basically a medical question?

FLOWERS: From a constitutional standpoint, no, sir. * * *

THE COURT: Of course, if you're right about [the fetus being a person within the meaning of the Constitution], you can sit down, you've won your case. * * * Except insofar as, maybe, the Texas abortion law presently goes too far in allowing abortions.

FLOWERS: Yes, sir. That's exactly right. * * *

THE COURT: Do you think [you have] lost your case, then, if the fetus or the embryo is not a person? Is that it?

FLOWERS: Yes sir, I would say so. * * *

THE COURT: Well, if you're right that an unborn fetus is a person, then you can't leave it to the legislature to play fast and loose dealing with that person. [I]f you're correct, in your basic submission that an unborn fetus is a person, then abortion laws such as that which New York has are grossly unconstitutional, isn't it?

FLOWERS: That's right, yes.

THE COURT: Allowing the killing of people.

FLOWERS: Yes, sir. * * *

[Rebuttal argument of Weddington]

THE COURT: [I] gather your argument is that a state may not protect the life of the fetus or prevent an abortion [at] any time during pregnancy? Right up until the moment of birth? * * *

WEDDINGTON: [T]here is no indication [that] the Constitution would give any protection prior to birth. That is not before the Court. * * *

THE COURT: Well, I don't know whether it is or isn't. * * *

ROE v. WADE

410 U.S. 113, 93 S.Ct. 705, 35 L.Ed.2d 147 (1973).

JUSTICE BLACKMUN delivered the opinion of the Court.

This Texas federal appeal and its Georgia companion, *Doe v. Bolton,* [infra,] present constitutional challenges to state criminal abortion legislation. The Texas statutes [are] typical of those that have been in effect in many States for approximately a century. The Georgia statutes, in contrast, have a modern cast and are a legislative product that, to an extent at least, obviously reflects the influences of recent attitudinal change, of advancing medical knowledge and techniques, and of new [thinking]. The Texas statutes [make procuring an abortion a crime except] "by medical advice for the purpose of saving the life of the mother."

[Jane] Roe alleged that she was unmarried and pregnant [and] that she was unable to get a "legal" abortion in Texas because her life did not appear to be threatened by the continuation of her pregnancy. [The district court held the Texas abortion statutes unconstitutional, but denied the injunctive relief requested. Roe appealed.]

[R]estrictive criminal abortion laws [like Texas'] in effect in a majority of States [today] derive from statutory changes effected, for the most part, in the latter half of the 19th century. [The Court then reviewed, in some detail, "ancient attitudes," "the Hippocratic Oath" which forbids abortion, "the common law," "the English statutory law," and "the American law." Subsequently, it described the positions of the American Medical Association, the American Public Health Association, and the American Bar Association. Thus,] at common law, at the time of the adoption of our Constitution, and throughout the major portion of the 19th century, [a] woman enjoyed a substantially broader right to terminate a pregnancy than she does in most States today. * * *

Three reasons have been advanced to explain historically the enactment of criminal abortion laws in the 19th century and to justify their [continuance].

It has been argued occasionally that these laws were the product of a Victorian social concern to discourage illicit sexual conduct. Texas, however, does not advance this justification [and] it appears that no court or commentator has taken the argument seriously.

[A] second reason is [that when] most criminal abortion laws were first enacted, the procedure was a hazardous one for the woman. [But] medical data indicat[es] that abortion in early pregnancy, that is, prior to the end of first trimester, although not without its risk, is now relatively safe.

[The] third reason is the State's interest—some phrase it in terms of duty—in protecting prenatal life. Some of the argument for this justification rests on the theory that a new human life is present from the moment of conception. [Only] when the life of the pregnant mother herself is at stake, balanced against the life she carries within her, should the interest of the embryo or fetus not prevail. [In] assessing the State's interest, recognition may be given to the less rigid claim that as long as at least *potential* life is involved, the State may assert interests beyond the protection of the pregnant woman alone. [It] is with these interests, and the weight to be attached to them, that this case is concerned.

The Constitution does not explicitly mention any right of privacy. [But] the Court has recognized that a right of personal privacy, or a guarantee of certain areas or zones of privacy, does exist under the Constitution. In varying contexts the Court or individual Justices have indeed found at least the roots of that right in the First Amendment, *Stanley v. Georgia* [p. 367 infra]; in the Fourth and Fifth Amendments; in the penumbras of the Bill of Rights, *Griswold;* in the Ninth Amendment, id. (Goldberg, J., concurring); or in the concept of liberty guaranteed by the first section of the Fourteenth Amendment, see *Meyer.* These decisions make it clear that only personal rights that can be deemed "fundamental" or "implicit in the concept of ordered liberty," are included in this guarantee of personal privacy. They also make it clear that the right has some extension to activities relating to marriage, *Loving;* procreation, *Skinner;* contraception, *Eisenstadt;* family relationships, *Prince v. Massachusetts* [discussed at p. 649 infra]; and child rearing and education, *Pierce.*

This right of privacy, whether it be founded in the Fourteenth Amendment's concept of personal liberty [as] we feel it is, [or] in the [Ninth Amendment], is broad enough to encompass a woman's decision whether or not to terminate her pregnancy. The detriment that the State would impose upon the pregnant woman by denying this choice altogether is apparent. Specific and direct harm medically diagnosable even in early pregnancy may be [involved]. Psychological harm may be imminent. Mental and physical health may be taxed by child care. There is also the distress, for all concerned, associated with the unwanted child, and there is the problem of bringing a child into a family already unable, psychologically and otherwise, to care for it. In other cases, as in this one, the additional difficulties and continuing stigma of unwed motherhood may be involved. All these are factors the woman and her responsible physician necessarily will consider in consultation.

On the basis of elements such as these, appellants and some amici argue that the woman's right is absolute and that she is entitled to terminate her pregnancy at whatever time, in whatever way, and for whatever reason she alone chooses. With this we do not agree. [The] Court's decisions recognizing a right of privacy also acknowledge that some state regulation in areas protected by that right is appropriate. [A] state may properly assert important interests in safeguarding health, in maintaining medical standards, and in protecting potential life. At some point in pregnancy, these respective interests become sufficiently compelling to sustain regulation of the factors that govern the abortion decision.

[Where] certain "fundamental rights" are involved, the Court has held that regulation limiting these rights may be justified only by a "compelling state interest," and that legislative enactments must be narrowly drawn to express only the legitimate state interests at stake.

[Appellee argues] that the fetus is a "person" within the language and meaning of the Fourteenth Amendment. [If so,] appellant's case, of course, collapses, for the fetus' right to life is then guaranteed specifically by the Amendment.

[The] Constitution does not define "person" in so many words. [The Court then listed each provision in which the word appears.] But in nearly all these instances, the use of the word is such that it has application only postnatally. None indicates, with any assurance, that it has any possible pre-natal application. All this, together with our observation that throughout the major portion of the 19th century prevailing legal abortion practices were far freer [than] today, persuades us that the word "person," as used in the Fourteenth Amendment, does not include the unborn. [Thus,] we pass on to other considerations.

The pregnant woman cannot be isolated in her privacy. She carries an embryo and, later, a fetus. [The] situation therefore is inherently different from marital intimacy, or bedroom possession of obscene material, or marriage, or procreation, or education, with which *Eisenstadt, Griswold, Stanley, Loving, Skinner, Pierce,* and *Meyer* [were] concerned.

[Texas] urges that, apart from the Fourteenth Amendment, life begins at conception and is present throughout pregnancy, and that, therefore, the State has a compelling interest in protecting that life from and after conception. We need not resolve the difficult question of when life begins. When those trained [in] medicine, philosophy, and theology are unable to arrive at any consensus, the judiciary, at this point in the development of man's knowledge, is not in a position to speculate as to the answer.

[W]e do not agree that, by adopting one theory of life, Texas may override the rights of the pregnant woman that are at stake. We repeat, however, that the State does have an important and legitimate interest in preserving and protecting the health of the pregnant woman [and] that it has still *another* important and legitimate interest in protecting the potentiality of human life. These interests are separate and distinct. Each grows in substantiality as the woman approaches term and, at a point during pregnancy, each becomes "compelling."

With respect to [the] interest in the health of the mother, the "compelling" point, in the light of present medical knowledge, is at approximately the end of the first trimester. This is so because of the now established medical fact that until the end of the first trimester mortality in abortion is less than mortality in normal childbirth. It follows that, from and after this point, a State may regulate the abortion procedure to the extent that the regulation reasonably relates to the preservation and protection of maternal health. Examples of permissible state regulation in this area are requirements as to the qualifications of the person who is to perform the abortion; [as] to the facility in which the procedure is to be performed, [and] the like. This means, on the other hand, that, for the period of pregnancy prior to this "compelling" point, the attending physician, in consultation with his patient, is free to determine, without regulation by the State, that in his medical judgment the patient's pregnancy should be terminated. If that decision is reached, the judgment may be effectuated by an abortion free of interference by the State.

With respect to [the] interest in potential life, the "compelling" point is at viability [which "is usually placed at about seven months (28 weeks) but may occur earlier, even at 24 weeks."] This is so because the fetus then presumably has the capability of meaningful life outside the mother's womb.a State regulation

---

a. Earlier in its opinion, the Court described the point "at which the fetus becomes 'viable' " as the point that the fetus is "potentially able to live outside the mother's womb, albeit with artificial aid." *Planned Parenthood v. Danforth*, 428 U.S. 52 (1976), per Blackmun, J., upheld a Missouri abortion statute defining "viability" as "that stage of fetal development when the life of the unborn child may be continued indefinitely outside the womb by natural or artificial life-supportive systems." In rejecting contentions that the Missouri statute unduly expanded the *Roe* Court's definition of "viability," failed to contain any reference to a gestational time period, and failed to incorporate and reflect the three stages of pregnancy, the Court observed: "[W]e recognized in *Roe* that viability was a matter of medical judgment, skill, and technical ability, and we preserved the flexibility of the term. [The Missouri statute] does the same. [I]t is not the

proper function of the legislature or the courts to place viability, which essentially is a medical concept, at a specific point in the gestation period. The time when viability is achieved may vary with each pregnancy, and the determination of whether a particular fetus is viable is, and must be, a matter for the judgment of the responsible attending physician. [The statutory definition] merely reflects this fact."

Consider, too, *Colautti v. Franklin*, 439 U.S. 379 (1979), per Blackmun, J., [reaffirming] that the determination of "viability" is "a matter for medical judgment" and that viability is reached "when, in the judgment of the attending physician on the particular facts of the case before him, there is a reasonable likelihood of the fetus' sustained survival outside the womb, with or without artificial support. Because this point may differ with each pregnancy, neither the legislature nor the courts may proclaim

protective of fetal life after viability thus has both logical and biological justifications. If the State is interested in protecting fetal life after viability, it may go as far as to proscribe abortion during that period except when it is necessary to preserve the life or health of the mother.

Measured against these standards, [the Texas statute] sweeps too broadly [and] therefore, cannot survive the constitutional attack made upon it here.

[In] *Doe* [infra], procedural requirements contained in one of the modern abortion statutes are considered. That opinion and this one [are] to be read together.67

This holding, we feel, is consistent with the relative weights of the respective interests involved, with the lessons and examples of medical and legal history, with the lenity of the common law, and with the demands of the profound problems of the present day. The decision leaves the State free to place increasing restrictions on abortion as the period of pregnancy lengthens, so long as those restrictions are tailored to the recognized state interests. The decision vindicates the right of the physician to administer medical treatment according to his professional judgment up to the points where important state interests provide compelling justifications for intervention. Up to those points, the abortion decision in all its aspects is inherently, and primarily, a medical decision, and basic responsibility for it must rest with the physician. If an individual practitioner abuses the privilege of exercising proper medical judgment, the usual remedies, judicial and intra-professional, are available. * * *

JUSTICE STEWART, concurring.

In 1963, this Court, in *Ferguson v. Skrupa* [Ch. 5, Sec. 3], purported to sound the death knell for the doctrine of substantive due process, [but] [b]arely two years later, in *Griswold,* the Court held a Connecticut birth control law unconstitutional. [T]he *Griswold* decision can be rationally understood only as a holding that the Connecticut statute substantively invaded the "liberty" that is protected by the Due Process Clause of the Fourteenth Amendment. As so understood, *Griswold* stands as one in a long line of pre-*Skrupa* cases decided under the doctrine of substantive due process, and I now accept it as such.

[The] Constitution nowhere mentions a specific right of personal choice in matters of marriage and family life, but the "liberty" protected by the Due Process Clause of the Fourteenth Amendment covers more than those freedoms explicitly named in the Bill of Rights. [As] recently as last Term, in *Eisenstadt,* we recognized "the right of the *individual,* married or single, to be free from unwarranted governmental intrusion into matters so fundamentally affecting a person as the decision whether to bear or beget a child." That right necessarily includes the right of a woman to decide whether or not to terminate her pregnancy. [It] is evident that the Texas abortion statute infringes that right directly. [The] question then becomes whether the state interests advanced to justify this abridgment can survive the "particularly careful scrutiny" that the Fourteenth Amendment here requires.

The asserted state interests are protection of the health and safety of the pregnant woman, and protection of the potential future human life within her. These are legitimate objectives, amply sufficient to permit a State to regulate

one of the elements entering into the ascertainment of viability—be it weeks of gestation or fetal weight or any other single factor—as the determinant of when the State has a compelling interest in the life or health of the fetus."

67. Neither in this opinion nor in *Doe* do we discuss the father's rights, if any exist in the constitutional context, in the abortion decision. No paternal right has been asserted in either of the [cases].

abortions as it does other surgical procedures, and perhaps sufficient to permit a State to regulate abortions more stringently or even to prohibit them in the late stages of pregnancy. But such legislation is not before us, and I think the Court today has thoroughly demonstrated that these state interests cannot constitutionally support the broad abridgment of personal liberty worked by the existing Texas law. * * *

JUSTICE DOUGLAS, concurring [in *Doe* as well as in *Roe*].

While I join the opinion of the Court, I add a few words.

[The] Ninth Amendment obviously does not create federally enforceable rights. [But] a catalogue of [the rights "retained by the people"] includes customary, traditional, and time-honored rights, amenities, privileges, and immunities that come within the sweep of "the Blessings of Liberty" mentioned in the preamble to the Constitution. Many of them in my view come within the meaning of the term "liberty" as used in the Fourteenth Amendment.

First is the autonomous control over the development and expression of one's intellect, interests, tastes, and personality. These are rights protected by the First Amendment and in my view they are absolute * * *.

Second is freedom of choice in the basic decisions of one's life respecting marriage, divorce, procreation, contraception, and the education and upbringing of children. These rights, unlike those protected by the First Amendment, are subject to some control by the police power. [They] are "fundamental" and we have held that in order to support legislative action the statute must be narrowly and precisely drawn and that a "compelling state interest" must be shown in support of the limitation. * * *4

[Third] is the freedom to care for one's health and person, freedom from bodily restraint or compulsion, freedom to walk, stroll, or loaf. These rights, though fundamental, are likewise subject to regulation on a showing of "compelling state interest." * * * Elaborate argument is hardly necessary to demonstrate that childbirth may deprive a woman of her preferred life style and force upon her a radically different and undesired future.

[Such reasoning] is, however, only the beginning of the problem. [V]oluntary abortion at any time and place regardless of medical standards would impinge on a rightful concern of society. The woman's health is part of that concern; as is the life of the fetus after quickening. These concerns justify the State in treating the procedure as a medical one.

[T]he Georgia statute outlaws virtually all such operations—even in the earliest stages of pregnancy. In light of modern medical evidence [it] cannot be seriously urged that so comprehensive a ban is aimed at protecting the woman's health. Rather, [this ban] can rest only on a public goal of preserving both embryonic and fetal life.

The present statute has struck the balance between the woman and the State's interests wholly in favor of the latter. [We] held in *Griswold* that the States may not preclude spouses from attempting to avoid the joinder of sperm

---

4. My Brother Stewart, writing in the present cases, says that our decision in *Griswold* reintroduced substantive due process that had been rejected in [*Skrupa*]. There is nothing specific in the Bill of Rights that covers [the marital relation]. Nor is there anything in the Bill of Rights that in terms protects the right of association or the privacy in one's association. [Other] peripheral rights are the right to educate one's children as one chooses, and the right to study the German language. These decisions with all respect, have nothing to do with substantive due process. One may think they are not peripheral rights to other rights that are expressed in the Bill of Rights. But that is not enough to bring into play the protection of substantive due process. * * *

and egg. [I]t is difficult to perceive any overriding public necessity which might attach precisely at the moment of conception.

[The] protection of the fetus when it has acquired life is a legitimate concern of the State. Georgia's law makes no rational, discernible decision on that score. For under the Act the developmental stage of the fetus is irrelevant when pregnancy is the result of rape or when the fetus will very likely be born with a permanent defect or when a continuation of the pregnancy will endanger the life of the mother or permanently injure her health. When life is present is a question we do not try to resolve. While basically a question for medical experts, [it is], of course, caught up in matters of religion and morality. * * *

JUSTICE WHITE, with whom JUSTICE REHNQUIST joins, dissenting [in *Doe* as well as in *Roe*].

At the heart of the controversy in these cases are those recurring pregnancies that pose no danger whatsoever to the life or health of the mother but are nevertheless unwanted for any one or more of a variety of reasons—convenience, family planning, economics, dislike of children, the embarrassment of illegitimacy, etc. The common claim before us is that for any one of such reasons, or for no reason at all, and without asserting or claiming any threat to life or health, any woman is entitled to an abortion at her request if she is able to find a medical advisor willing to [perform it].

The Court for the most part sustains this position [and] simply fashions and announces a new constitutional right [and], with scarcely any reason or authority for its action, invests that right with sufficient substance to override most existing state abortion statutes. The upshot is that the people and the legislatures of the 50 States are constitutionally disentitled to weigh the relative importance of the continued existence and development of the fetus on the one hand against a spectrum of possible impacts on the mother on the other hand. As an exercise of raw judicial power, the Court perhaps has authority [but] in my view its judgment is an improvident and extravagant exercise of the power of judicial review * * *.

JUSTICE REHNQUIST, dissenting. * * *

I have difficulty in concluding [that] the right of "privacy" is involved in this case. [Texas] bars the performance of a medical abortion by a licensed physician on a plaintiff such as Roe. A transaction resulting in an operation such as this is not "private" in the ordinary usage of that word. Nor is the "privacy" which the Court finds here even a distant relative of the freedom from searches and seizures protected by the Fourth Amendment.

[If] the Court means by the term "privacy" no more than that the claim of a person to be free from unwanted state regulation of consensual transactions may be a form of "liberty" * * * I agree [with] Mr. Justice Stewart [that that "liberty"] embraces more than the rights found in the Bill of Rights. But that liberty is not guaranteed absolutely against deprivation, but only against deprivation without due process of law. The test traditionally applied in the area of social and economic legislation is whether or not a law such as that challenged has a rational relation to a valid state objective. [If] the Texas statute were to prohibit an abortion even where the mother's life is in jeopardy, I have little doubt that such a statute would lack a rational relation to a valid state [objective]. But the Court's sweeping invalidation of any restrictions on abortion during the first trimester is impossible to justify under that [standard]. As in *Lochner* and similar cases applying substantive due process standards to economic and social welfare legislation, the adoption of the compelling state interest standard will inevitably require this Court to examine the legislative policies and pass on the wisdom of these policies in the very process of deciding whether a particular state interest put forward may or may not be "compelling." The decision here to break the term of pregnancy into three distinct terms and to outline the permissible restrictions the State may impose in each one, for example, partakes more of judicial legislation than it does of a determination of the intent of the drafters of the Fourteenth Amendment.

The fact that a majority of the States, reflecting after all the majority sentiment in those States, have had restrictions on abortions for at least a century seems to me as strong an indication there is that the asserted right to an abortion is not "so rooted in the traditions and conscience of our people as to be ranked as fundamental." Even today, when society's views on abortion are changing, the very existence of the debate is evidence that the "right" to an abortion is not so universally accepted as the appellants would have us believe.

[By] the time of the adoption of the Fourteenth Amendment in 1868 there were at least 36 laws enacted by state or territorial legislatures limiting abortion. [The] only conclusion possible from this history is that the drafters did not intend to have the Fourteenth Amendment withdraw from the States the power to legislate with respect to this matter. * * *

———

DOE v. BOLTON, 410 U.S. 179 (1973), the companion case to *Roe v. Wade,* sustained, against the contention that it had been rendered unconstitutionally vague by a three-judge district court's interpretation, a Georgia provision that permitted a physician to perform an abortion when "based upon his best clinical judgment that an abortion is necessary." (The district court had struck down the statutorily specified reasons: because continued pregnancy would endanger a pregnant woman's life or injure her health; the fetus would likely be born with a serious defect; or the pregnancy resulted from rape.) "The net result of the district court's decision," observed the court, "is that the abortion determination, so far as the physician is concerned, is made in the exercise of his professional, that is, his 'best clinical,' judgment in the light of all the attendant circumstances. He is not now restricted to the three situations originally specified. Instead, [the] medical judgment may be exercised in light of all factors—physical, emotional, psychological, familial, and the woman's age—relevant to the well-being of the patient. All these factors may relate to health. This allows the attending physician the room he needs to make his best medical judgment. And it is room that operates for the benefit, not the disadvantage, of the pregnant woman."

However, despite the fact that the Georgia statute was patterned after the American Law Institute's Model Penal Code (1962), which had served as the model for recent legislation in about one-fourth of the states, the Court, per BLACKMUN, J., invalidated substantial portions of the statute. Struck down were requirements (1) that the abortion be performed in a hospital accredited by the Joint Commission on Accreditation of Hospitals (JCAH); (2) that the procedure be approved by a hospital staff abortion committee; and (3) that the performing physician's judgment be confirmed by independent examinations of the patient by two other physicians.

As for (1): There is no restriction of the performance of nonabortion surgery in a hospital not accredited by the JCAH. This requirement is also invalid "because it fails to exclude the first trimester of pregnancy, see *Roe.* [As] for (2), [we] see no constitutionally justifiable pertinence [for] the advance approval by the abortion committee. We are not cited to any other surgical procedure made subject to committee approval as a matter of state criminal law. The woman's right to receive medical care in accordance with the licensed physician's best judgment and the physician's right to administer it are substantially limited by this statutorily imposed overview." As for (3), the two-doctor concurrence, "the statute's emphasis [is] on the attending physician's 'best clinical judgment that an abortion is necessary.' That should be sufficient. [No] other voluntary medical or surgical procedure for which Georgia requires confirmation by two other physicians has been cited to us."

ROE v. WADE AND THE DEBATE IT STIRRED OVER "NONINTERPRETIVIST" OR "NONORIGINALIST" CONSTITUTIONAL DECISIONMAKING

1. **What happened on the day Roe was decided?** "The subject of abortion," observes Robert Bork, *The Tempting of America* 111–16 (1990), "had been fiercely debated in state legislatures for many years. [Whatever] the proper resolution of the moral debate, [few] imagined that the Constitution resolved it. [The] discovery this late in our history that the question was not one for democratic decision but one of constitutional law was so implausible that it certainly deserved a fifty-one page explanation. Unfortunately, in the entire opinion there is not one line of explanation, not one sentence that qualifies as legal argument. [It] is unlikely that [the Court] ever will [provide the explanation lacking in 1973] because the right to abort, whatever one thinks of it, is not to be found in the Constitution. * * *

Compare Laurence Tribe, *Abortion: The Clash of Absolutes* 99 (1990): "Judge Bork says that 'the right to abort, whatever one thinks of it, is not to be found in the Constitution.' In a sense this is obviously right. Indeed, not one of the words 'abortion,' 'pregnancy,' 'reproduction,' 'sex,' 'privacy,' 'bodily integrity,' and 'procreation' appears anywhere in [the] Constitution. But neither do such phrases as 'freedom of thought,' 'rights of parenthood,' 'liberty of association,' 'family self-determination,' and 'freedom of marital choice.' Yet nearly everyone supposes that at least some of these dimensions of personal autonomy and independence are aspects of the 'liberty' which the Fourteenth Amendment says no state may deny to any person 'without due process of law.'

2. **Are the Abortion Cases "bad constitutional law" or "not constitutional law"?** Consider John H. Ely, *The Wages of Crying Wolf: A Comment on Roe v. Wade,* 82 Yale L.J. 920, 935–37, 939, 943, 947–49 (1973): "What is frightening about *Roe* is that this super-protected right is not inferable from the language of the Constitution, the framers' thinking respecting the specific problem in issue, any general value derivable from the provisions they included, or the nation's governmental structure. Nor is it explainable in terms of the unusual political impotence of the group judicially protected vis-á-vis the interest that legislatively prevailed over it.[b]

b. Professor Ely argues, at 933–35, that Stone, J.'s suggestion in his famous *Carolene Products* footnote that the Court provide extraordinary constitutional protection for " 'discrete and insulate minorities' unable to form effective political alliances" does not apply to *Roe*: "Compared with men, very few women sit in our legislatures, [but] *no* fetuses sit [there]. [Stone's suggestion] was clearly intended and should be reserved for those interests which, as compared with the interests to which they have been subordinated, constitute minorities usually incapable of protecting themselves.

Compared with men, women may constitute such a 'minority'; compared with the unborn, they do not."

However, Robert Bennett, *Abortion and Judicial Review*, 75 Nw.U.L.Rev. 978, 995–96 n. 71 (1981), maintains that Professor Ely's challenge of the appropriateness of judicial intervention in *Roe* "is misguided," "because it assumes that fetuses are political actors—indeed a political minority—whose 'powerlessness' is relevant to assessing the Court's appropriate role in the abortion controversy.

"[*Roe* is] a very bad decision. [It] is bad because it is bad constitutional law, or rather because it is *not* constitutional law and gives almost no sense of an obligation to try to be. [A] neutral and durable principle may be a thing of beauty and joy forever. But if it lacks connection with any value the Constitution marks as special, it is not a constitutional principle and the Court has no business imposing it."

3. ***Is it a question of "inventing" a new right, or of the state having to justify an invasion of liberty?*** Consider the remarks of Professor Tribe in Choper, Kamisar & Tribe, *The Supreme Court: Trends and Developments 1982–83* (1984) at 215: "[The *Roe* Court] is said to have invented the right to abortion. [But once] one concedes that the word 'liberty' has substantive content in its application against the states through the Fourteenth Amendment—and it must, if any substantive provisions of the Bill of Rights are to be enforced against the states through the Fourteenth Amendment—it becomes not a question of inventing a new right, but of asking what the justification is for a state intrusion into what is indisputably an aspect of someone's personal liberty."

4. ***"Enumerated" and "unenumerated" rights.*** Although many view the distinction between enumerated and unenumerated rights as presenting the important question whether and when courts have authority to enforce rights not actually enumerated in the Constitution (e.g., the right to privacy, from which the right to an abortion is said to derive), Ronald Dworkin, *Unenumerated Rights,* 59 U.Chi.L.Rev. 381, 387–88 (1992), finds the question "unintelligible":

"The Bill of Rights * * * consists of broad and abstract principles of political morality, which together encompass, in exceptionally abstract form, all the dimensions of political morality that in our political culture can ground an individual constitutional right. The key issue in applying these abstract principles to particular political controversies is not one of reference but of *interpretation,* which is very different. [The distinction between enumerated and unenumerated rights] cannot be sustained."

ABORTION FUNDING

1. MAHER v. ROE, 432 U.S. 464 (1977) (also discussed Ch. 9, Sec. 5, V), per POWELL, J., sustained Connecticut's use of Medicaid funds to reimburse women for the costs of childbirth and "medically necessary" first trimester abortions (defined to include "psychiatric necessity"), but not for the costs of elective or nontherapeutic first trimester abortions.[a]

On "the central question"—"whether the regulation 'impinges upon a fundamental right explicitly or implicitly protected by the Constitution' "—the Court

Each political system must define, explicitly or implicitly, the universe of relevant political actors. [But] outside the abortion context there are no indications that fetuses are considered relevant political actors. [E]ven within the context of abortion-related issues, the suggestion that fetuses are a part of the larger political community appears, as in Ely's formulation, only incidentally and as part of the abortion discussion. It is, of course, possible for a legislature to take into account interests outside its own political community. [But] with fetuses, as with other interests outside the relevant universe of political actors, the legislative process can only take them into account insofar as

relevant political actors subsume those interests into their own."

a. In a companion case, *Beal v. Doe,* 432 U.S. 438 (1977), per Powell, J., held that the Medicaid Act does not require state funding of nontherapeutic first trimester abortions as a condition of participation in the joint federal-state program.

Poelker v. Doe, 432 U.S. 519 (1977), per curiam, for the reasons set forth in *Maher,* found "no constitutional violation by the city of St. Louis in electing, as a policy choice, to provide publicly financed hospital services for childbirth without providing corresponding services for nontherapeutic abortions."

held that *Roe* did not establish "an unqualified 'constitutional right to an abortion,'" but only a "right protect[ing] the woman from unduly burdensome interference with her freedom to decide whether to terminate her pregnancy. It implies no limitation on the authority of a State to make a value judgment favoring childbirth over abortion, and to implement that judgment by the allocation of public funds. [The] indigency that may make it difficult—and in some cases, perhaps, impossible—for some women to have abortions is neither created nor in any way affected by the [regulation.]"

BRENNAN, J., joined by Marshall and Blackmun, JJ., dissented, accusing the majority of "a distressing insensitivity to the plight of impoverished pregnant women." The "disparity in funding [clearly] operates to coerce indigent pregnant women to bear children they would not otherwise choose to have, and just as clearly, this coercion can only operate upon the poor, who are uniquely the victims of this form of financial pressure." *Roe* and its progeny held that "an area of privacy invulnerable to the State's intrusion surrounds the decision of a pregnant woman whether or not to carry her pregnancy to term. The Connecticut scheme clearly infringes upon that area of privacy."

2. ***The Hyde Amendment.*** Title XIX of the Social Security Act established the Medicaid program to provide federal financial assistance to states choosing to reimburse certain costs of medical treatment for needy persons. Since 1976, various versions of the so-called Hyde Amendment have limited federal funding of abortions under the Medicaid program to those necessary to save the life of the mother and certain other exceptional circumstances. HARRIS v. McRAE, 448 U.S. 297 (1980), per STEWART, J., found no constitutional violation: "The present case does differ factually from *Maher* insofar as that case involved a failure to fund nontherapeutic abortions, whereas the Hyde Amendment withholds funding of certain medically necessary abortions. [But] regardless of [how] the freedom of a woman to choose to terminate her pregnancy for health reasons [is characterized], it simply does not follow that [this freedom] carries with it a constitutional entitlement to the financial resources to avail herself of the full range of protected choices. [T]he Hyde Amendment leaves an indigent woman with at least the same range of choice in deciding whether to obtain a medically necessary abortion as she would have had if Congress had chosen to subsidize no health costs at all."

Four justices dissented—Brennan, Marshall and Blackmun, JJ. (the three *Maher* dissenters), and Stevens, J. who had joined the opinion of the Court in *Maher*. STEVENS, J., maintained that the instant case presented "[a] fundamentally different question" than the one decided in *Maher*: "This case involves the pool of benefits that Congress created by enacting [Title XIX]. Individuals who satisfy two neutral criteria—financial need and medical need—are entitled to equal access to that pool. The question is whether certain persons who satisfy those criteria may be denied access to benefits solely because they must exercise the constitutional right to have an abortion in order to obtain the medical care they need. Our prior cases plainly dictate [the answer]."

The other three dissenters wrote separately, each voicing agreement with Stevens, J.'s analysis. BRENNAN, J., joined by Marshall and Blackmun, JJ., maintained: "[W]hat the Court fails to appreciate is that it is not simply the woman's indigency that interferes with her freedom of choice, but the combination of her own poverty and the government's unequal subsidization of abortion and childbirth."

THE COURT REAFFIRMS "THE ESSENTIAL HOLDING OF *ROE*"

PLANNED PARENTHOOD OF SOUTHEASTERN PENNSYLVANIA v. CASEY

505 U.S. 833, 112 S.Ct. 2791, 120 L.Ed.2d 674 (1992).

JUSTICE O'CONNOR, JUSTICE KENNEDY, and JUSTICE SOUTER announced the judgment of the Court and delivered the opinion of the Court with respect to Parts I, II, III, V–A, V–C, and VI, an opinion with respect to Part V–E, in which JUSTICE STEVENS joins, and an opinion with respect to Parts IV, V–B, and V–D.

I. Liberty finds no refuge in a jurisprudence of doubt. Yet 19 years after our holding that the Constitution protects a woman's right to terminate her pregnancy in its early stages, *Roe v. Wade,* that definition of liberty is still questioned. Joining the respondents as amicus curiae, the United States, as it has done in five other cases in the last decade, again asks us to overrule *Roe.*

At issue in these cases are five provisions of the Pennsylvania Abortion Control Act of 1982 as amended in 1988 and 1989. [The] Act requires that a woman seeking an abortion give her informed consent prior to the abortion procedure, and specifies that she be provided with certain information at least 24 hours before the abortion is performed. For a minor to obtain an abortion, the Act requires the informed consent of one of her parents, but provides for a judicial bypass option if the minor does not wish to or cannot obtain a parent's consent. Another [provision] of the Act requires that, unless certain exceptions apply, a married woman seeking an abortion must sign a statement indicating that she has notified her husband of her intended abortion. § 3209. The Act exempts compliance with these three requirements in the event of a "medical emergency," which is defined in [§ 3203]. In addition to the above provisions regulating the performance of abortions, the Act imposes certain reporting requirements on facilities that provide abortion services.

Before any of these provisions took effect, the petitioners, who are five abortion clinics and one physician representing himself as well as a class of physicians who provide abortion services, brought this suit seeking declaratory and injunctive relief. [The District Court held all the provisions at issue unconstitutional, but the Court of Appeals sustained all of them except for the husband notification requirement.]

[At] oral argument in this Court, the attorney for the parties challenging the statute took the position that none of the enactments can be upheld without overruling *Roe.* We disagree [but] we acknowledge that our decisions after *Roe* cast doubt upon the meaning and reach of its holding. Further, the Chief Justice admits that he would overrule the central holding of *Roe* and adopt the rational relationship test as the sole criterion of constitutionality. State and federal courts as well as legislatures throughout the Union must have guidance as they seek to address this subject in conformance with the Constitution. Given these premises, we find it imperative to review once more the principles that define the rights of the woman and the legitimate authority of the State respecting the termination of pregnancies by abortion procedures.

After considering the fundamental constitutional questions resolved by *Roe,* principles of institutional integrity, and the rule of stare decisis, we are led to conclude this: the essential holding of *Roe* should be retained and once again reaffirmed.

* * * *Roe*'s essential holding, the holding we reaffirm, has three parts. First is a recognition of the right of the woman to choose to have an abortion before viability and to obtain it without undue interference from the State. Before viability, the State's interests are not strong enough to support a prohibition of abortion or the imposition of a substantial obstacle to the woman's effective right to elect the procedure. Second is a confirmation of the State's power to restrict abortions after fetal viability, if the law contains exceptions for pregnancies which endanger a woman's life or health. And third is the principle that the State has legitimate interests from the outset of the pregnancy in protecting the health of the woman and the life of the fetus that may become a child. These principles do not contradict one another; and we adhere to each.

II. Constitutional protection of the woman's decision to terminate her pregnancy derives from the Due Process Clause. [The] controlling word in the case before us is "liberty." Although a literal reading of the Clause might suggest that it governs only the procedures by which a State may deprive persons of liberty, for at least 105 years [the] Clause has been understood to contain a substantive component as well, one "barring certain government actions regardless of the fairness of the procedures used to implement them."

[It] is tempting, as a means of curbing the discretion of federal judges, to suppose that liberty encompasses no more than those rights already guaranteed to the individual against federal interference by the express provisions of the first eight amendments to the Constitution. But of course this Court has never accepted that view.

It is also tempting, for the same reason, to suppose that the Due Process Clause protects only those practices, defined at the most specific level, that were protected against government interference by other rules of law when the Fourteenth Amendment was ratified. See *Michael H. v. Gerald D.,* n. 6 [infra] (opinion of Scalia, J.). But such a view would be inconsistent with our law. It is a promise of the Constitution that there is a realm of personal liberty which the government may not enter. We have vindicated this principle before. Marriage is mentioned nowhere in the Bill of Rights and interracial marriage was illegal in most States in the 19th century, but the Court was no doubt correct in finding it to be an aspect of liberty protected against state interference by the substantive component of the Due Process Clause in *Loving v. Virginia* [Ch. 9, Sec. 2, II].

Neither the Bill of Rights nor the specific practices of States at the time of the adoption of the Fourteenth Amendment marks the outer limits of the substantive sphere of liberty which the Fourteenth Amendment protects. See U.S. Const., Amend. 9. As the second Justice Harlan recognized: "[T]he full scope of the liberty guaranteed by the Due Process Clause cannot be found in or limited by the precise terms of the specific guarantees elsewhere provided in the Constitution. This 'liberty' is not a series of isolated points pricked out in terms of the taking of property; the freedom of speech, press, and religion; the right to keep and bear arms; the freedom from unreasonable searches and seizures; and so on. It is a rational continuum which, broadly speaking, includes a freedom from all substantial arbitrary impositions and purposeless restraints * * *." *Poe v. Ullman* (Harlan, J., dissenting from dismissal on jurisdictional grounds).

Justice Harlan wrote these words in addressing an issue the full Court did not reach in *Poe,* but the Court adopted his position four Terms later in *Griswold.* [It] is settled now, as it was when the Court heard arguments in *Roe,* that the Constitution places limits on a State's right to interfere with a person's most basic decisions about family and parenthood, as well as bodily integrity. * * *

Men and women of good conscience can disagree, and we suppose some always shall disagree, about the profound moral and spiritual implications of terminating a pregnancy, even in its earliest stage. Some of us as individuals find abortion offensive to our most basic principles of morality, but that cannot control our decision. Our obligation is to define the liberty of all, not to mandate our own moral code. The underlying constitutional issue is whether the State can resolve these philosophic questions in such a definitive way that a woman lacks all choice in the matter, except perhaps [where] the pregnancy is itself a danger to her own life or health, or is the result of rape or incest. * * *

Our law affords constitutional protection to personal decisions relating to marriage, procreation, contraception, family relationships, child rearing, and education. [These] matters, involving the most intimate and personal choices a person may make in a lifetime, choices central to personal dignity and autonomy, are central to the liberty protected by the Fourteenth Amendment. At the heart of liberty is the right to define one's own concept of existence, of meaning, of the universe, and of the mystery of human life. Beliefs about these matters could not define the attributes of personhood were they formed under compulsion of the State.

These considerations begin our analysis of the woman's interest in terminating her pregnancy but cannot end it, for this reason: though the abortion decision may originate within the zone of conscience and belief, it is more than a philosophic exercise. Abortion is a unique act. It is an act fraught with consequences for others. [Though] abortion is conduct, it does not follow that the State is entitled to proscribe it in all instances. That is because the liberty of the woman is at stake in a sense unique to the human condition and so unique to the law. The mother who carries a child to full term is subject to anxieties, to physical constraints, to pain that only she must bear. That these sacrifices have from the beginning of the human race been endured by woman with a pride that ennobles her in the eyes of others and gives to the infant a bond of love cannot alone be grounds for the State to insist she make the sacrifice. Her suffering is too intimate and personal for the State to insist, without more, upon its own vision of the woman's role, however dominant that vision has been in the course of our history and our culture. The destiny of the woman must be shaped to a large extent on her own conception of her spiritual imperatives and her place in society.

[Moreover,] in some critical respects the abortion decision is of the same character as the decision to use contraception, to which [our cases] afford constitutional protection. We have no doubt as to the correctness of those decisions. They support the reasoning in *Roe* relating to the woman's liberty because they involve personal decisions concerning not only the meaning of procreation but also human responsibility and respect for it.

III. The obligation to follow precedent begins with necessity, and a contrary necessity marks its outer limit. [The] very concept of the rule of law underlying our own Constitution requires such continuity over time that a respect for precedent is, by definition, indispensable. At the other extreme, a different necessity would make itself felt if a prior judicial ruling should come to be seen so clearly as error that its enforcement was for that very reason doomed.

[When] this Court reexamines a prior holding, its judgment is customarily informed by a series of prudential and pragmatic considerations designed to test the consistency of overruling a prior decision with the ideal of the rule of law, and to gauge the respective costs of reaffirming and overruling a prior case. Thus, for example, we may ask whether the rule has proved to be intolerable simply in defying practical workability; whether the rule is subject to a kind of reliance that would lend a special hardship to the consequences of overruling and add inequity to the cost of repudiation; whether related principles of law have so far developed as to have left the old rule no more than a remnant of abandoned doctrine; or whether facts have so changed or come to be seen so differently, as to have robbed the old rule of significant application or justification.

So in this case we may inquire whether *Roe*'s central rule has been found unworkable; whether the rule's limitation on state power could be removed without serious inequity to those who have relied upon it or significant damage to the stability of the society governed by the rule in question; whether the law's growth in the intervening years has left *Roe*'s central rule a doctrinal anachronism discounted by society; and whether *Roe*'s premises of fact have so far changed in the ensuing two decades as to render its central holding somehow irrelevant or unjustifiable in dealing with the issue it addressed.

Although *Roe* has engendered opposition, it has in no sense proven "unworkable," representing as it does a simple limitation beyond which a state law is unenforceable.

[One] can readily imagine an argument stressing the dissimilarity of this case to one involving property or contract. Abortion is customarily chosen as an unplanned response to the consequence of unplanned activity or to the failure of conventional birth control, and except on the assumption that no intercourse would have occurred but for *Roe*'s holding, such behavior may appear to justify no reliance claim.

[But to eliminate the issue of reliance] would be simply to refuse to face the fact that for two decades of economic and social developments, people have organized intimate relationships and made choices that define their views of themselves and their places in society, in reliance on the availability of abortion in the event that contraception should fail. The ability of women to participate equally in the economic and social life of the Nation has been facilitated by their ability to control their reproductive lives. [While] the effect of reliance on *Roe* cannot be exactly measured, neither can the certain cost of overruling *Roe* for people who have ordered their thinking and living around that case be dismissed.

No evolution of legal principle has left *Roe*'s doctrinal footings weaker than they were in 1973. No development of constitutional law since the case was decided has implicitly or explicitly left *Roe* behind as a mere survivor of obsolete constitutional thinking.

[*Roe*] stands at an intersection of two lines of decisions, but in whichever doctrinal category one reads the case, the result for present purposes will be the same. The *Roe* Court itself placed its holding in the succession of cases most prominently exemplified by *Griswold*. When it is so seen, *Roe* is clearly in no jeopardy, since subsequent constitutional developments have neither disturbed, nor do they threaten to diminish, the scope of recognized protection accorded to the liberty relating to intimate relationships, the family, and decisions about whether or not to beget or bear a child.

Roe, however, may be seen [as] a rule (whether or not mistaken) of personal autonomy and bodily integrity, with doctrinal affinity to cases recognizing limits on governmental power to mandate medical treatment or to bar its rejection. If so, our cases since *Roe* accord with *Roe*'s view that a State's interest in the protection of life falls short of justifying any plenary override of individual liberty claims. *Cruzan* [infra].

Finally, one could classify *Roe* as sui generis. If the case is so viewed, then there clearly has been no erosion of its central determination. * * *

Nor will courts building upon *Roe* be likely to hand down erroneous decisions as a consequence. Even on the assumption that the central holding of *Roe* was in error, that error would go only to the strength of the state interest in fetal protection, not to the recognition afforded by the Constitution to the woman's liberty. The latter aspect of the decision fits comfortably within the framework of the Court's prior decisions including *Skinner, Griswold, Loving,* and *Eisenstadt,* the holdings of which are "not a series of isolated points," but mark a "rational continuum." *Poe v. Ullman* (Harlan, J., dissenting). * * *

The soundness of this prong of the *Roe* analysis is apparent from a consideration of the alternative. If indeed the woman's interest in deciding whether to bear and beget a child had not been recognized as in *Roe,* the State might as readily restrict a woman's right to choose to carry a pregnancy to term as to terminate it, to further asserted state interests in population control, or eugenics, for example. Yet *Roe* has been sensibly relied upon to counter any such suggestions. * * *

We have seen how time has overtaken some of *Roe*'s factual assumptions: advances in maternal health care allow for abortions safe to the mother later in pregnancy than was true in 1973, and advances in neonatal care have advanced viability to a point somewhat earlier. But these facts go only to the scheme of time limits on the realization of competing interests, and the divergences from the factual premises of 1973 have no bearing on the validity of *Roe*'s central holding, that viability marks the earliest point at which the State's interest in fetal life is constitutionally adequate to justify a legislative ban on nontherapeutic abortions. The soundness or unsoundness of that constitutional judgment in no sense turns on whether viability occurs at approximately 28 weeks, as was usual at the time of *Roe,* at 23 to 24 weeks, as it sometimes does today, or at some moment even slightly earlier in pregnancy, as it may if fetal respiratory capacity can somehow be enhanced in the future. [No] change in *Roe*'s factual underpinning has left its central holding obsolete, and none supports an argument for overruling it.

The sum of the precedential inquiry to this point shows *Roe*'s underpinnings unweakened in any way affecting its central holding. While it has engendered disapproval, it has not been unworkable. An entire generation has come of age free to assume *Roe*'s concept of liberty in defining the capacity of women to act in society, and to make reproductive decisions. [Within] the bounds of normal *stare decisis* analysis, [the] stronger argument is for affirming *Roe*'s central holding, with whatever degree of personal reluctance any of us may have, not for overruling it.

In a less significant case, *stare decisis* analysis could, and would, stop at the point we have reached. But the sustained and widespread debate *Roe* has provoked calls for some comparison between that case and others of comparable dimension that have responded to national controversies and taken on the impress of the controversies addressed. Only two such decisional lines from the past century present themselves for examination, and in each instance the result reached by the Court accorded with the principles we apply today.

The first example is that line of cases identified with *Lochner v. New York* (1905) [and] *Adkins v. Children's Hospital* (1923). * * * Fourteen years later, *West Coast Hotel Co. v. Parrish* (1937) signaled the demise of *Lochner* by overruling *Adkins.* In the meantime, the Depression had come and, with it, the lesson that seemed unmistakable to most people by 1937, that the interpretation of contractual freedom protected in *Adkins* rested on fundamentally false factual assumptions about the capacity of a relatively unregulated market to satisfy minimal levels of human welfare. [The] facts upon which the earlier case had premised a constitutional resolution of social controversy had proved to be untrue, and history's demonstration of their untruth not only justified but required the new choice of constitutional principle that *West Coast Hotel* announced. Of course, it was true that the Court lost something by its misperception, or its lack of prescience, and the Court-packing crisis only magnified the loss; but the clear demonstration that the facts of economic life were different from those previously assumed warranted the repudiation of the old law.

The second comparison that 20th century history invites is with the cases employing the separate-but-equal rule for applying the Fourteenth Amendment's equal protection guarantee. They began with *Plessy v. Ferguson* [Ch. 10, Sec. 2, II], holding that legislatively mandated racial segregation in public transportation works no denial of equal protection. [The] *Plessy* Court considered "the underlying fallacy of the plaintiff's argument to consist in the assumption that the enforced separation of the two races stamps the colored race with a badge of inferiority. If this be so, it is not by reason of anything found in the act, but solely because the colored race chooses to put that construction upon it." [But] this understanding of the facts and the rule it was stated to justify were repudiated in *Brown v. Board of Education* [Ch. 10, Sec. 2, II].

[The] Court in *Brown* [observed] that whatever may have been the understanding in *Plessy*'s time of the power of segregation to stigmatize those who were segregated with a "badge of inferiority," it was clear by 1954 that legally sanctioned segregation had just such an effect, to the point that racially separate public educational facilities were deemed inherently unequal. Society's understanding of the facts upon which a constitutional ruling was sought in 1954 was thus fundamentally different from the basis claimed for the decision in 1896. While we think *Plessy* was wrong the day it was decided, we must also recognize that the *Plessy* Court's explanation for its decision was so clearly at odds with the facts apparent to the Court in 1954 that the decision to reexamine *Plessy* was on this ground alone not only justified but required.

West Coast Hotel and *Brown* each rested on facts, or an understanding of facts, changed from those which furnished the claimed justifications for the earlier constitutional resolutions. [In] constitutional adjudication as elsewhere in life, changed circumstances may impose new obligations, and the thoughtful part of the Nation could accept each decision to overrule a prior case as a response to the Court's constitutional duty.

Because [neither] the factual underpinnings of *Roe*'s central holding nor our understanding of it has changed [the] Court could not pretend to be reexamining the prior law with any justification beyond a present doctrinal disposition to come out differently from the Court of 1973. To overrule prior law for no other reason than that would run counter to the view repeated in our cases, that a decision to overrule should rest on some special reason over and above the belief that a prior case was wrongly decided. * * *

The examination of the conditions justifying the repudiation of *Adkins* by *West Coast Hotel* and *Plessy* by *Brown* is enough to suggest the terrible price that would have been paid if the Court had not overruled as it did. In the present case, however, [the] terrible price would be paid for overruling. Our analysis would not be complete, however, without explaining why overruling *Roe*'s central holding would not only reach an unjustifiable result under principles of *stare decisis*, but would seriously weaken the Court's capacity to exercise the judicial power and to function as the Supreme Court of a Nation dedicated to the rule of law. [The] Court's power lies, [in] its legitimacy, a product of substance and perception that shows itself in the people's acceptance of the Judiciary as fit to determine what the Nation's law means and to declare what it demands.

The underlying substance of this legitimacy is of course the warrant for the Court's decisions in the Constitution and the lesser sources of legal principle on which the Court draws. That substance is expressed in the Court's opinions, and our contemporary understanding is such that a decision without principled justification would be no judicial act at all. But even when justification is furnished by apposite legal principle, something more is required. [The] Court's legitimacy depends on making legally principled decisions under circumstances in which their principled character is sufficiently plausible to be accepted by the Nation.

[The] country can accept some correction of error without necessarily questioning the legitimacy of the Court. In two circumstances, however, the Court would almost certainly fail to receive the benefit of the doubt in overruling prior cases. There is, first, [a] limit to the amount of error that can plausibly be imputed to prior courts. If that limit should be exceeded, disturbance of prior rulings would be taken as evidence that justifiable reexamination of principle had given way to drives for particular results in the short term. The legitimacy of the Court would fade with the frequency of its vacillation.

That first circumstance can be described as hypothetical; the second is to the point here and now. Where, in the performance of its judicial duties, the Court decides a case in such a way as to resolve the sort of intensely divisive controversy reflected in *Roe* and those rare, comparable cases, its decision has a dimension that the resolution of the normal case does not carry. It is the dimension present whenever the Court's interpretation of the Constitution calls the contending sides of a national controversy to end their national division by accepting a common mandate rooted in the Constitution.

The Court is not asked to do this very often, having thus addressed the Nation only twice in our lifetime, in the decisions of *Brown* and *Roe*. But when the Court does act in this way, its decision requires an equally rare precedential force to counter the inevitable efforts to overturn it and to thwart its implementation. [To] overrule under fire in the absence of the most compelling reason to reexamine a watershed decision would subvert the Court's legitimacy beyond any serious question.

[The] Court's duty in the present case is clear. In 1973, it confronted the already-divisive issue of governmental power to limit personal choice to undergo abortion, for which it provided a new resolution based on the due process guaranteed by the Fourteenth Amendment. Whether or not a new social consensus is developing on that issue, its divisiveness is no less today than in 1973, and pressure to overrule the decision, like pressure to retain it, has grown only more intense. A decision to overrule *Roe*'s essential holding under the existing circumstances would address error, if error there was, at the cost of both profound and unnecessary damage to the Court's legitimacy, and to the Nation's commitment to the rule of law. It is therefore imperative to adhere to the essence of *Roe*'s original decision, and we do so today.

IV. * * * We conclude that the basic decision in *Roe* was based on a constitutional analysis which we cannot now repudiate. The woman's liberty is not so unlimited, however, that from the outset the State cannot show its concern for the life of the unborn, and at a later point in fetal development the State's interest in life has sufficient force so that the right of the woman to terminate the pregnancy can be restricted.

That brings us, of course, to the point where much criticism has been directed at *Roe,* a criticism that always inheres when the Court draws a specific rule from what in the Constitution is but a general standard. [But] [l]iberty must not be extinguished for want of a line that is clear. * * *

We conclude the line should be drawn at viability, so that before that time the woman has a right to choose to terminate her pregnancy. We adhere to this principle for two reasons. First [is] the doctrine of stare decisis. [We] have twice reaffirmed [*Roe*] in the face of great opposition.

[The] second reason is that the concept of viability, as we noted in *Roe,* is the time at which there is a realistic possibility of maintaining and nourishing a life outside the womb, so that the independent existence of the second life can in reason and all fairness be the object of state protection that now overrides the rights of the woman.

[The] woman's right to terminate her pregnancy before viability is the most central principle of *Roe.* It is a rule of law and a component of liberty we cannot renounce.

On the other side of the equation is the interest of the State in the protection of potential life. [The] weight to be given this state interest, not the strength of the woman's interest, was the difficult question faced in *Roe.* We do not need to say whether each of us, had we been Members of the Court when the valuation of the State interest came before it as an original matter, would have concluded, as the *Roe* Court did, that its weight is insufficient to justify a ban on abortions prior to viability even when it is subject to certain exceptions. The matter is not before us in the first instance, and coming as it does after nearly 20 years of litigation in *Roe*'s wake we are satisfied that the immediate question is not the soundness of *Roe*'s resolution of the issue, but the precedential force that must be accorded to its holding. And we have concluded that the essential holding of *Roe* should be reaffirmed.

Yet it must be remembered that *Roe* speaks with clarity in establishing not only the woman's liberty but also the State's "important and legitimate interest in potential life." That portion [of] *Roe* has been given too little acknowledgement and implementation by the Court in its subsequent cases. Those cases decided that any regulation touching upon the abortion decision must survive strict scrutiny, to be sustained only if drawn in narrow terms to further a compelling state interest. Not all of the cases decided under that formulation can be reconciled with the holding in *Roe* itself that the State has legitimate interests in the health of the woman and in protecting the potential life within her. In resolving this tension, we choose to rely upon *Roe,* as against the later cases. * * *

We reject the trimester framework, which we do not consider to be part of the essential holding of *Roe.* Measures aimed at ensuring that a woman's choice contemplates the consequences for the fetus do not necessarily interfere with the right recognized in *Roe,* although those measures have been found to be inconsistent with the rigid trimester framework announced in that case. [The] trimester framework suffers from these basic flaws: in its formulation it misconceives the nature of the pregnant woman's interest; and in practice it undervalues the State's interest in potential life, as recognized in *Roe.*

[A] finding of an undue burden is a shorthand for the conclusion that a state regulation has the purpose or effect of placing a substantial obstacle in the path of a woman seeking an abortion of a nonviable fetus. A statute with this purpose is invalid because the means chosen by the State to further the interest in potential life must be calculated to inform the woman's free choice, not hinder it. And a statute which, while furthering the interest in potential life or some other valid state interest, has the effect of placing a substantial obstacle in the path of a woman's choice cannot be considered a permissible means of serving its legitimate ends. [In] our considered judgment, an undue burden is an unconstitutional burden. Understood another way, we answer the question, left open in previous opinions discussing the undue burden formulation, whether a law designed to further the State's interest in fetal life which imposes an undue burden on the woman's decision before fetal viability could be constitutional. The answer is no.

Some guiding principles should emerge. What is at stake is the woman's right to make the ultimate decision, not a right to be insulated from all others in doing so. Regulations which do no more than create a structural mechanism by which the State, or the parent or guardian of a minor, may express profound respect for the life of the unborn are permitted, if they are not a substantial obstacle to the woman's exercise of the right to choose. [Unless] it has that effect on her right of choice, a state measure designed to persuade her to choose childbirth over abortion will be upheld if reasonably related to that goal. Regulations designed to foster the health of a woman seeking an abortion are valid if they do not constitute an undue burden.

* * * We give this summary:

(a) To protect the central right recognized by *Roe* while at the same time accommodating the State's profound interest in potential life, we will employ the undue burden analysis as explained in this opinion. An undue burden exists, and therefore a provision of law is invalid, if its purpose or effect is to place a substantial obstacle in the path of a woman seeking an abortion before the fetus attains viability.

(b) We reject the rigid trimester framework of *Roe*. To promote the State's profound interest in potential life, throughout pregnancy the State may take measures to ensure that the woman's choice is informed, and measures designed to advance this interest will not be invalidated as long as their purpose is to persuade the woman to choose childbirth over abortion. These measures must not be an undue burden on the right.

(c) As with any medical procedure, the State may enact regulations to further the health or safety of a woman seeking an abortion. Unnecessary health regulations that have the purpose or effect of presenting a substantial obstacle to a woman seeking an abortion impose an undue burden on the right.

(d) Our adoption of the undue burden analysis does not disturb the central holding of *Roe,* and we reaffirm that holding. [A] State may not prohibit any woman from making the ultimate decision to terminate her pregnancy before viability.

(e) We also reaffirm *Roe*'s holding that "subsequent to viability, the State in promoting its interest in the potentiality of human life may, if it chooses, regulate, and even proscribe, abortion except where it is necessary, in appropriate medical judgment, for the preservation of the life or health of the mother."

These principles control our assessment of the Pennsylvania statute, and we now turn to the issue of the validity of its challenged provisions.

V. * * * A. Because it is central to the operation of various other requirements, we begin with the statute's definition of medical emergency. Under the statute, a medical emergency is "[t]hat condition which, on the basis of the physician's good faith clinical judgment, so complicates the medical condition of a pregnant woman as to necessitate the immediate abortion of her pregnancy to avert her death or for which a delay will create serious risk of substantial and irreversible impairment of a major bodily function.''

[As construed by the Court of Appeals, the statute's definition of medical emergency as] "intended to assure that compliance with [the] abortion regulations would not in any way pose a significant threat to the life or health of a woman" [imposes] no undue burden on a woman's abortion right.

B. [Except] in a medical emergency, the statute requires that at least 24 hours before performing an abortion a physician inform the woman of the nature of the procedure, the health risks of the abortion and of childbirth, and the "probable gestational age of the unborn child." The physician or a qualified nonphysician must inform the woman of the availability of printed materials published by the State describing the fetus and providing information about medical assistance for childbirth, information about child support from the father, and a list of agencies which provide adoption and other services as alternatives to abortion. An abortion may not be performed unless the woman certifies in writing that she has been informed of the availability of these printed materials and has been provided them if she chooses to view them. [This] requirement cannot be considered a substantial obstacle to obtaining an abortion, and, it follows, there is no undue burden.

[The] Pennsylvania statute also requires us to reconsider the holding in *Akron v. Akron Center for Reproductive Health (Akron I)*, 462 U.S. 416 (1983),a that the State may not require that a physician, as opposed to a qualified assistant, provide information relevant to a woman's informed consent. Since there is no evidence on this record that requiring a doctor to give the information as provided by the statute would amount in practical terms to a substantial obstacle to a woman seeking an abortion, we conclude that it is not an undue burden. * * *

Our analysis of Pennsylvania's 24–hour waiting period between the provision of the information deemed necessary to informed consent and the performance of an abortion under the undue burden standard requires us to reconsider the premise behind the decision in *Akron I* invalidating a parallel requirement. * * * We consider the [*Akron I*] conclusion to be wrong. The idea that important decisions will be more informed and deliberate if they follow some period of reflection does not strike us as unreasonable, particularly where the statute directs that important information become part of the background of the decision.

---

a. *Akron I* struck down various sections of an ordinance regulating abortion. Among the provisions invalidated was a mandatory 24–hour waiting period, which increased the cost of obtaining an abortion by requiring the woman to make two separate trips to the abortion facility; a provision requiring that after the first trimester all abortions had to be performed in a hospital, thus preventing abortions in outpatient clinics; and an "informed consent" provision that the majority characterized as "designed not to inform the woman's consent but rather to persuade her to withhold it altogether."

Akron I marked the first time the "undue burden" standard was suggested. Dissenting Justice O'Connor (joined by White and Rehnquist, JJ.), who would have upheld all the challenged regulations, maintained that the "undue burden" standard "should be applied to the challenged regulations throughout the entire pregnancy without reference to the particular 'stage' of pregnancy involved." She maintained further that if a particular regulation "does not unduly burden the fundamental right, then our evaluation of that regulation is limited to our determination that the regulation rationally relates to a legitimate state purpose."

The Court, per Powell, J., responded that the dissent adopts reasoning that, "for all practical purposes," would overrule *Roe*. Continued Powell: "[It] appears that the dissent would uphold virtually any abortion regulation under a rational-basis test. It also appears that even where heightened scrutiny is deemed appropriate, the dissent would uphold virtually any abortion-inhibiting regulation because of the State's interest in preserving human life."

[Whether] the mandatory 24–hour waiting period is nonetheless invalid because in practice it is a substantial obstacle to a woman's choice to terminate her pregnancy is a closer question. [The findings of fact indicate that for] those women who have the fewest financial resources, those who must travel long distances, and those who have difficulty explaining their whereabouts to husbands, employers, or others, the 24–hour waiting period will be "particularly burdensome."

These findings are troubling in some respects, but they do not demonstrate that the waiting period constitutes an undue burden. [Under] the undue burden standard a State is permitted to enact persuasive measures which favor childbirth over abortion, even if those measures do not further a health interest. And while the waiting period does limit a physician's discretion, that is not, standing alone, a reason to invalidate it. In light of the construction given the statute's definition of medical emergency by the Court of Appeals, and the District Court's findings, we cannot say that the waiting period imposes a real health risk.

We also disagree with the District Court's conclusion that the "particularly burdensome" effects of the waiting period on some women require its invalidation. A particular burden is not of necessity a substantial obstacle. Whether a burden falls on a particular group is a distinct inquiry from whether it is a substantial obstacle even as to the women in that group. * * *

We are left with the argument that the various aspects of the informed consent requirement are unconstitutional because they place barriers in the way of abortion on demand. Even the broadest reading of *Roe,* however, has not suggested that there is a constitutional right to abortion on demand. Rather, the right protected by *Roe* is a right to decide to terminate a pregnancy free of undue interference by the State. [The] informed consent requirement is not an undue burden on that right.

C.   Section 3209 of Pennsylvania's abortion law provides, except in cases of medical emergency, that no physician shall perform an abortion on a married woman without receiving a signed statement from the woman that she has notified her spouse that she is about to undergo an abortion. The woman has the option of providing an alternative signed statement certifying that her husband is not the man who impregnated her; that her husband could not be located; that the pregnancy is the result of spousal sexual assault which she has reported; or that the woman believes that notifying her husband will cause him or someone else to inflict bodily injury upon her. A physician who performs an abortion on a married woman without receiving the appropriate signed statement will have his or her license revoked, and is liable to the husband for damages.

[Among the findings of fact made by the District Court are that '[m]ere notification of pregnancy is frequently a flashpoint for battering and violence within the family [because the] battering husband may deny parentage and use the pregnancy as an excuse for abuse'; a woman's attempt to notify her husband pursuant to § 3209 "could accidentally disclose her whereabouts [in a shelter or safe house] to her husband"; and "[b]ecause of the nature of the battering relationship, battered women are unlikely to avail themselves of the exceptions to § 3209, regardless of whether the section applies to them."]

[Various studies of domestic violence] and the District Court's findings reinforce what common sense would suggest. In well-functioning marriages, spouses discuss important intimate decisions such as whether to bear a child. But there are millions of women in this country who are the victims of regular physical and psychological abuse at the hands of their husbands. Should these women become pregnant, they may have very good reasons for not wishing to inform their husbands of their decision to obtain an abortion.

[The]   spousal notification requirement is thus likely to prevent a significant number of women from obtaining an abortion. It does not merely make abortions a little more difficult or expensive to obtain; for many women, it will impose a substantial obstacle. We must not blind ourselves to the fact that the significant number of women who fear for their safety and the safety of their children are likely to be deterred from procuring an abortion as surely as if the Commonwealth had outlawed abortion in all cases.

[Section] 3209's real target is narrower even than the class of women seeking abortions identified by the State: it is married women seeking abortions who do not wish to notify their husbands of their intentions and who do not qualify for one of the statutory exceptions to the notice requirement. The unfortunate yet persisting conditions we document above will mean that in a large fraction of the cases in which § 3209 is relevant, it will operate as a substantial obstacle to a woman's choice to undergo an abortion. It is an undue burden, and therefore invalid.

This conclusion is in no way inconsistent with our decisions upholding parental notification or consent requirements. Those enactments, and our judgment that they are constitutional, are based on the quite reasonable assumption that minors will benefit from consultation with their parents and that children will often not realize that their parents have their best interests at heart. We cannot adopt a parallel assumption about adult women.

[It] is an inescapable biological fact that state regulation with respect to the child a woman is carrying will have a far greater impact on the mother's liberty than on the father's. The effect of state regulation on a woman's protected liberty is doubly deserving of scrutiny in such a case, as the State has touched not only upon the private sphere of the family but upon the very bodily integrity of the pregnant woman. Cf. *Cruzan*. [The] Constitution protects individuals, men and women alike, from unjustified state interference, even when that interference is enacted into law for the benefit of their spouses.

[In] keeping with our rejection of the common-law understanding of a woman's role within the family, the Court held in *Planned Parenthood v. Danforth*, 428 U.S. 52 (1976), that the Constitution does not permit a State to require a married woman to obtain her husband's consent before undergoing an abortion. The principles that guided the Court in *Danforth* should be our guides today. For the great many women who are victims of abuse inflicted by their husbands, or whose children are the victims of such abuse, a spousal notice requirement enables the husband to wield an effective veto over his wife's decision.

[The] husband's interest in the life of the child his wife is carrying does not permit the State to empower him with this troubling degree of authority over his wife. The contrary view leads to consequences reminiscent of the common law. A husband has no enforceable right to require a wife to advise him before she exercises her personal choices. * * *

Section 3209 embodies a view of marriage consonant with the common-law status of married women but repugnant to our present understanding of marriage and of the nature of the rights secured by the Constitution. Women do not lose their constitutionally protected liberty when they marry.

D.   [Except] in a medical emergency, an unemancipated young woman under 18 may not obtain an abortion unless she and one of her parents (or guardian) provides informed consent as defined above. If neither a parent nor a guardian provides consent, a court may authorize the performance of an abortion upon a determination that the young woman is mature and capable of giving informed consent and has in fact given her informed consent, or that an abortion would be in her best interests. * * *

Our cases establish, and we reaffirm today, that a State may require a minor seeking an abortion to obtain the consent of a parent or guardian, provided that there is an adequate judicial bypass procedure. * * *

E. [As for the provisions imposing certain reporting requirements on facilities that provide abortion services, in] *Danforth* we held that recordkeeping and reporting provisions "that are reasonably directed to the preservation of maternal health and that properly respect a patient's confidentiality and privacy are permissible." [Under] this standard, all the provisions at issue here except that relating to spousal notice are constitutional. Although they do not relate to the State's interest in informing the woman's choice, they do relate to health. The collection of information with respect to actual patients is a vital element of medical research, and so it cannot be said that the requirements serve no purpose other than to make abortions more difficult. Nor do we find that the requirements impose a substantial obstacle to a woman's choice. * * *

VI. Our Constitution is a covenant running from the first generation of Americans to us and then to future generations. It is a coherent succession. Each generation must learn anew that the Constitution's written terms embody ideas and aspirations that must survive more ages than one. We accept our responsibility not to retreat from interpreting the full meaning of the covenant in light of all of our precedents. We invoke it once again to define the freedom guaranteed by the Constitution's own promise, the promise of liberty. * * *

JUSTICE STEVENS, concurring in part and dissenting in part.

The portions of the Court's opinion that I have joined are more important than those with which I disagree. I shall therefore first comment on significant areas of agreement, and then explain the limited character of my disagreement.

The Court is unquestionably correct in concluding that the doctrine of stare decisis has controlling significance in a case of this kind, notwithstanding an individual justice's concerns about the merits.1 [*Roe*] was a natural sequel to the protection of individual liberty established in *Griswold*. *Roe* is an integral part of a correct understanding of both the concept of liberty and the basic equality of men and women.

Stare decisis also provides a sufficient basis for my agreement with the joint opinion's reaffirmation of *Roe*'s post-viability analysis. Specifically, I accept the proposition that "[i]f the State is interested in protecting fetal life after viability, it may go so far as to proscribe abortion during that period, except when it is necessary to preserve the life or health of the mother."

I also accept what is implicit in the Court's analysis, namely, a reaffirmation of *Roe*'s explanation of *why* the State's obligation to protect the life or health of the mother must take precedence over any duty to the unborn. The Court in *Roe* carefully considered, and rejected, the State's argument "that the fetus is a 'person' within the language and meaning of the Fourteenth Amendment."

---

1. It is sometimes useful to view the issue of stare decisis from a historical perspective. In the last nineteen years, fifteen Justices have confronted the basic issue presented in *Roe*. Of those, eleven have voted as the majority does today: Chief Justice Burger, Justices Douglas, Brennan, Stewart, Marshall, and Powell, and Justices Blackmun, O'Connor, Kennedy, Souter, and myself. Only four—all of whom happen to be on the Court today—have reached the opposite conclusion.

[From] this holding, there was no dissent; indeed, no member of the Court has ever questioned this fundamental proposition. Thus, as a matter of federal constitutional law, a developing organism that is not yet a "person" does not have what is sometimes described as a "right to life."2

My disagreement with the joint opinion begins with its understanding of the trimester framework established in *Roe*. Contrary to the suggestion of the joint opinion, it is not a "contradiction" to recognize that the State may have a legitimate interest in potential human life and, at the same time, to conclude that that interest does not justify the regulation of abortion before viability (although other interests, such as maternal health, may). The fact that the State's interest is legitimate does not tell us when, if ever, that interest outweighs the pregnant woman's interest in personal liberty. It is appropriate, therefore, to consider more carefully the nature of the interests at stake. * * *

Identifying the State's interests—which the States rarely articulate with any precision—makes clear that the interest in protecting potential life is not grounded in the Constitution. It is, instead, an indirect interest supported by both humanitarian and pragmatic concerns. Many of our citizens believe that any abortion reflects an unacceptable disrespect for potential human life and that the performance of more than a million abortions each year is intolerable; many find third-trimester abortions performed when the fetus is approaching personhood particularly offensive. The State has a legitimate interest in minimizing such offense. * * *

Weighing the State's interest in potential life and the woman's liberty interest, I agree with the joint opinion that the State may " 'expres[s] a preference for normal childbirth,' " that the State may take steps to ensure that a woman's choice "is thoughtful and informed," and that "States are free to enact laws to provide a reasonable framework for a woman to make a decision that has such profound and lasting meaning." Serious questions arise, however, when a State attempts to "persuade the woman to choose childbirth over abortion." Decisional autonomy must limit the State's power to inject into a woman's most personal deliberations its own views of what is best. The State may promote its preferences by funding childbirth, by creating and maintaining alternatives to abortion, and by espousing the virtues of family; but it must respect the individual's freedom to make such judgments.

[Under the principles established in the Court's previous cases, Justice Stevens deemed unconstitutional those sections requiring a woman to be provided with a wide range of materials "clearly designed to persuade her to choose not to undergo the abortion. But he did not find constitutionally objectionable those sections requiring the physician to inform a woman of the nature and risks of the abortion procedure and the medical risks of carrying to term for these "are neutral requirements comparable to those imposed in other medical procedures. These sections indicate no effort by the State to influence the woman's choice in any way."]

The 24–hour waiting period [raises] even more serious concerns. Such a requirement arguably furthers the State's interests in two ways, neither of which is constitutionally permissible.

First, it may be argued that the 24–hour delay is justified by the mere fact that it is likely to reduce the number of abortions, thus furthering the State's

---

2. Professor Dworkin has made this comment on the issue: "The suggestion that states are free to declare a fetus a person * * * assumes that a state can curtail some persons' constitutional rights by adding new persons to the constitutional population." * * *

interest in potential life. But such an argument would justify any form of coercion that placed an obstacle in the woman's path. * * *

Second, it can more reasonably be argued that the 24–hour delay furthers the State's interest in ensuring that the woman's decision is informed and thoughtful. But there is no evidence that the mandated delay benefits women or that it is necessary to enable the physician to convey any relevant information to the patient. The mandatory delay thus appears to rest on outmoded and unacceptable assumptions about the decisionmaking capacity of women.

[A] correct application of the "undue burden" standard leads to the same conclusion concerning the constitutionality of these requirements. A state-imposed burden on the exercise of a constitutional right is measured both by its effects and by its character: A burden may be "undue" either because the burden is too severe or because it lacks a legitimate, rational justification.

The 24–hour delay requirement fails both parts of this test. [Even] in those cases in which the delay is not especially onerous, it is, in my opinion, "undue" because there is no evidence that such a delay serves a useful and legitimate purpose.

[The] counseling provisions are similarly infirm. [The] statute requires that [information concerning alternatives to abortion, the availability of medical assistance benefits, and the possibility of child-support payments] be given to *all* women seeking abortions, including those for whom such information is clearly useless, such as those who are married, those who have undergone the procedure in the past and are fully aware of the options, and those who are fully convinced that abortion is their only reasonable option. Moreover, [information of probable gestational age] is of little decisional value in most cases, because 90% of all abortions are performed during the first trimester when fetal age has less relevance than when the fetus nears viability. * * * I conclude that [these] requirements do not serve a useful purpose and thus constitute an unnecessary— and therefore undue—burden on the woman's constitutional liberty to decide to terminate her pregnancy.

Accordingly, while I disagree with Parts IV, V–B, and V–D of the joint opinion,[8] I join the remainder of the Court's opinion.

JUSTICE BLACKMUN, concurring in part, concurring in the judgment in part, and dissenting in part.

I join parts I, II, III, V–A, V–C, and VI of the joint opinion * * *.

I do not underestimate the significance of today's joint opinion. Yet I remain steadfast in my belief that the right to reproductive choice is entitled to the full protection afforded by this Court before *Webster*. And I fear for the darkness as four Justices anxiously await the single vote necessary to extinguish the light.

Make no mistake, the joint opinion of Justices O'Connor, Kennedy, and Souter is an act of personal courage and constitutional principle. In contrast to previous decisions in which Justices O'Connor and Kennedy postponed reconsideration of *Roe,* the authors of the joint opinion today join Justice Stevens and me in concluding that "the essential holding of *Roe* should be retained and once again reaffirmed." * * *

---

8. Although I agree that a parental-consent requirement (with the appropriate bypass) is constitutional, I do not join Part V–D of the joint opinion because its approval of Pennsyl- vania's informed parental-consent requirement is based on the reasons given in Part V–B, with which I disagree.

Today, no less than yesterday, the Constitution and decisions of this Court require that a State's abortion restrictions be subjected to the strictest of judicial scrutiny. Our precedents and the joint opinion's principles require us to subject all non-de-minimis abortion regulations to strict scrutiny. Under this standard, the Pennsylvania statute's provisions requiring content-based counseling, a 24–hour delay, informed parental consent, and reporting of abortion-related information must be invalidated. [R]estrictive abortion laws force women to endure physical invasions far more substantial than those this Court has held to violate the constitutional principle of bodily integrity in other contexts.3

Further, when the State restricts a woman's right to terminate her pregnancy, it deprives a woman of the right to make her own decision about reproduction and family planning—critical life choices that this Court long has deemed central to the right to privacy. The decision to terminate or continue a pregnancy has no less an impact on a woman's life than decisions about contraception or marriage. Because motherhood has a dramatic impact on a woman's educational prospects, employment opportunities, and self-determination, restrictive abortion laws deprive her of basic control over her life.

[A] State's restrictions on a woman's right to terminate her pregnancy also implicate constitutional guarantees of gender equality. [By] restricting the right to terminate pregnancies, the State conscripts women's bodies into its service, forcing women to continue their pregnancies, suffer the pains of childbirth, and in most instances, provide years of maternal care. The State does not compensate women for their services; instead, it assumes that they owe this duty as a matter of course. This assumption—that women can simply be forced to accept the "natural" status and incidents of motherhood—appears to rest upon a conception of women's role that has triggered the protection of the Equal Protection Clause. The joint opinion recognizes that these assumptions about women's place in society "are no longer consistent with our understanding of the family, the individual, or the Constitution."

[In] my view, application of [the] analytical framework [set forth in *Roe*] is no less warranted than when it was approved by seven Members of this Court in *Roe*. [The] factual premises of the trimester framework have not been undermined and the *Roe* framework is far more administrable, and far less manipulable, than the "undue burden" standard adopted by the joint opinion. * * * *Roe*'s requirement of strict scrutiny as implemented through a trimester framework should not be disturbed. No other approach has gained a majority, and no other is more protective of the woman's fundamental right. * * * Application of the strict scrutiny standard results in the invalidation of all the challenged provisions. Indeed, as this Court has invalidated virtually identical provisions in prior cases, stare decisis requires that we again strike them down.

[The] 24–hour waiting period [is] also clearly unconstitutional. [The] District Court found that the requirement would pose especially significant burdens on women living in rural areas and those women that have difficulty explaining their whereabouts. In *Akron I* this Court invalidated a similarly arbitrary or inflexible waiting period because, as here, it furthered no legitimate state interest.8 * * * *

---

3. As the joint opinion acknowledges, this Court has recognized the vital liberty interest of persons in refusing unwanted medical treatment. *Cruzan.* Just as the Due Process Clause protects the deeply personal decision of the individual to *refuse* medical treatment, it also must protect the deeply personal decision to *obtain* medical treatment, including a woman's decision to terminate a pregnancy.

8. The Court's decision in *Hodgson v. Minnesota,* validating a 48–hour waiting period for minors seeking an abortion to permit parental involvement does not alter this conclu-

Finally, [the] statute requires every facility performing abortions to report its activities to the Commonwealth. Pennsylvania [attempts] to justify its required reports on the ground that the public has a right to know how its tax dollars are spent. A regulation designed to inform the public about public expenditures does not further the Commonwealth's interest in protecting maternal health. Accordingly, such a regulation cannot justify a legally significant burden on a woman's right to obtain an abortion.

[If] there is much reason to applaud the advances made by the joint opinion today, there is far more to fear from The Chief Justice's opinion. [His] criticism of *Roe* follows from his stunted conception of individual liberty. While recognizing that the Due Process Clause protects more than simply physical liberty, he then goes on to construe this Court's personal-liberty cases as establishing only a laundry list of particular rights, rather than a principled account of how these particular rights are grounded in a more general right of privacy. This constricted view is reinforced by The Chief Justice's exclusive reliance on tradition as a source of fundamental rights. [P]eople using contraceptives seem the next likely candidate for his list of outcasts.

Even more shocking than The Chief Justice's cramped notion of individual liberty is his complete omission of any discussion of the effects that compelled childbirth and motherhood have on women's lives. The only expression of concern with women's health is purely instrumental—for The Chief Justice, only women's *psychological* health is a concern, and only to the extent that he assumes that every woman who decides to have an abortion does so without serious consideration of the moral implications of their decision. In short, The Chief Justice's view of the State's compelling interest in maternal health has less to do with health than it does with compelling women to be maternal. * * *

CHIEF JUSTICE REHNQUIST, with whom JUSTICE WHITE, JUSTICE SCALIA, and JUSTICE THOMAS join, concurring in the judgment in part and dissenting in part.

The joint opinion, following its newly-minted variation on stare decisis, retains the outer shell of *Roe* but beats a wholesale retreat from the substance of that case. We believe that *Roe* was wrongly decided, and that it can and should be overruled consistently with our traditional approach to stare decisis in constitutional cases. We would adopt the approach of the plurality in *Webster* and uphold the challenged provisions of the Pennsylvania statute in their entirety. * * *

Unlike marriage, procreation and contraception, abortion "involves the purposeful termination of potential life." The abortion decision must therefore "be recognized as *sui generis*, different in kind from the others that the Court has protected under the rubric of personal or family privacy and autonomy." One cannot ignore the fact that a woman is not isolated in her pregnancy, and that the decision to abort necessarily involves the destruction of a fetus.

[Nor] do the historical traditions of the American people support the view that the right to terminate one's pregnancy is "fundamental." The common law which we inherited from England made abortion after "quickening" an offense. At the time of the adoption of the Fourteenth Amendment, statutory prohibitions or restrictions on abortion were commonplace; in 1868, at least 28 of the then–37 States and 8 Territories had statutes banning or limiting abortion. By the turn of the century virtually every State had a law prohibiting or restricting abortion on its books. By the middle of the present century, a liberalization trend had set in.

sion. Here the 24–hour delay is imposed on an *adult* woman. Moreover, the statute in *Hodgson* did not require any delay once the minor obtained the affirmative consent of either a parent or the court.

But 21 of the restrictive abortion laws in effect in 1868 were still in effect in 1973 when *Roe* was decided, and an overwhelming majority of the States prohibited abortion unless necessary to preserve the life or health of the mother. On this record, it can scarcely be said that any deeply rooted tradition of relatively unrestricted abortion in our history supported the classification of the right to abortion as "fundamental" under the Due Process Clause of the Fourteenth Amendment.

[The joint opinion] cannot bring itself to say that *Roe* was correct as an original matter, but [instead] contains an elaborate discussion of stare decisis. [This discussion] appears to be almost entirely dicta, because the joint opinion does not apply that principle in dealing with *Roe*. *Roe* decided that a woman had a fundamental right to an abortion. The joint opinion rejects that view. *Roe* decided that abortion regulations were to be subjected to "strict scrutiny" and could be justified only in the light of "compelling state interests." The joint opinion rejects that view. *Roe* analyzed abortion regulation under a rigid trimester framework, a framework which has guided this Court's decisionmaking for 19 years. The joint opinion rejects that framework.

[Having] failed to put forth any evidence to prove any true reliance [on *Roe*], the joint opinion's argument is based solely on generalized assertions about the national psyche, on a belief that the people of this country have grown accustomed to the *Roe* decision over the last 19 years and have "ordered their thinking and living around" it. As an initial matter, one might inquire how the joint opinion can view the "central holding" of *Roe* as so deeply rooted in our constitutional culture, when it so casually uproots and disposes of that same decision's trimester framework. Furthermore, at various points in the past, the same could have been said about this Court's erroneous decisions that the Constitution allowed "separate but equal" treatment of minorities or that "liberty" under the Due Process Clause protected "freedom of contract." [The] simple fact that a generation or more had grown used to these major decisions did not prevent the Court from correcting its errors in those cases, nor should it prevent us from correctly interpreting the Constitution here.

[The joint opinion states] that when the Court "resolve[s] the sort of intensely divisive controversy reflected in *Roe* and those rare, comparable cases," its decision is exempt from reconsideration under established principles of stare decisis in constitutional cases. [Under] this principle, when the Court has ruled on a divisive issue, it is apparently prevented from overruling that decision for the sole reason that it was incorrect, *unless opposition to the original decision has died away.*

The first difficulty with this principle [is that the] question of whether a particular issue is "intensely divisive" enough to qualify for special protection is entirely subjective and dependent on the individual assumptions of the Members of this Court. In addition, because the Court's duty is to ignore public opinion and criticism on issues that come before it, its members are in perhaps the worst position to judge whether a decision divides the Nation deeply enough to justify such uncommon protection.

[The joint opinion] agrees that the Court acted properly in rejecting the doctrine of "separate but equal" in *Brown*. In fact, the opinion lauds *Brown* in comparing it to *Roe*. This is strange, in that under the opinion's "legitimacy" principle the Court would seemingly have been forced to adhere to its erroneous decision in *Plessy* because of its "intensely divisive" character. To us, adherence to *Roe* today under the guise of "legitimacy" would seem to resemble more closely adherence to *Plessy* on the same ground. Fortunately, the Court did not choose that option in *Brown,* and instead frankly repudiated *Plessy.* [The] Court in *Brown* simply recognized, as Justice Harlan had recognized beforehand, that the Fourteenth Amendment does not permit racial segregation. The rule of *Brown* is not tied to popular opinion about the evils of segregation; it is a judgment that the Equal Protection Clause does not permit racial segregation, no matter whether the public might come to believe that it is beneficial. On that ground it stands, and on that ground alone the Court was justified in properly concluding that the *Plessy* Court had erred.

There is also a suggestion in the joint opinion that the propriety of overruling a "divisive" decision depends in part on whether "most people" would now agree that it should be overruled. [How] such agreement would be ascertained, short of a public opinion poll, the joint opinion does not say. [Even] the suggestion is totally at war with the idea of "legitimacy" in whose name it is invoked. The Judicial Branch derives its legitimacy, not from following public opinion, but from deciding by its best lights whether legislative enactments of the popular branches of Government comport with the Constitution. * * *

Roe is not this Court's only decision to generate conflict. Our decisions in some recent capital cases, and in *Bowers v. Hardwick* (1986), have also engendered demonstrations in opposition. The joint opinion's message to such protesters appears to be that they must cease their activities in order to serve their cause, because their protests will only cement in place a decision which by normal standards of stare decisis should be reconsidered. * * *

The end result of the joint opinion's paeans of praise for legitimacy is the enunciation of a brand new standard for evaluating state regulation of a woman's right to abortion—the "undue burden" standard. [While] we disagree with [*Roe's* "strict scrutiny"] standard, it at least had a recognized basis in constitutional law at the time *Roe* was decided. The same cannot be said for the "undue burden" standard, which is created largely out of whole cloth by the authors of the joint opinion. It is a standard which even today does not command the support of a majority of this Court.

* * * Because the undue burden standard is plucked from nowhere, the question of what is a "substantial obstacle" to abortion will undoubtedly engender a variety of conflicting views. For example, in the very matter before us now, the authors of the joint opinion would uphold Pennsylvania's 24–hour waiting period, concluding that a "particular burden" on some women is not a substantial obstacle. But the authors would at the same time strike down Pennsylvania's spousal notice provision, after finding that in a "large fraction" of cases the provision will be a substantial obstacle. And, while the authors conclude that the informed consent provisions do not constitute an "undue burden," Justice Stevens would hold that they do.

Furthermore, [the] "undue burden" inquiry does not in any way supply the distinction between parental consent and spousal consent which the joint opinion adopts. Despite the efforts of the joint opinion, the undue burden standard presents nothing more workable than the trimester framework which it discards today. Under the guise of the Constitution, this Court will still impart its own preferences on the States in the form of a complex abortion code.

The sum of the joint opinion's labors in the name of stare decisis and "legitimacy" is this: *Roe* stands as a sort of judicial Potemkin Village, which may be pointed out to passers by as a monument to the importance of adhering to precedent. But behind the facade, an entirely new method of analysis, without any roots in constitutional law, is imported to decide the constitutionality of state laws regulating abortion. Neither stare decisis nor "legitimacy" are truly served by such an effort.

We have stated above our belief that the Constitution does not subject state abortion regulations to heightened scrutiny. Accordingly, we think that the correct analysis is that set forth by the plurality opinion in *Webster*. A woman's interest in having an abortion is a form of liberty protected by the Due Process Clause, but States may regulate abortion procedures in ways rationally related to a legitimate state interest.

[The Chief Justice then discussed each of the challenged provisions and concluded that each should be upheld.]

JUSTICE SCALIA, with whom THE CHIEF JUSTICE, JUSTICE WHITE, and JUSTICE THOMAS join, concurring in the judgment in part and dissenting in part.

[The] issue in this case [is] not whether the power of a woman to abort her unborn child is a "liberty" in the absolute sense; or even whether it is a liberty of great importance to many women. Of course it is both. The issue is whether it is a liberty protected by the Constitution of the United States. I am sure it is not. I reach that conclusion not because of anything so exalted as my views concerning the "concept of existence, of meaning, of the universe, and of the mystery of human life." Rather, I reach it for the same reason I reach the conclusion that bigamy is not constitutionally protected—because of two simple facts: (1) the Constitution says absolutely nothing about it, and (2) the longstanding traditions of American society have permitted it to be legally proscribed.[1]

The Court destroys the proposition, evidently meant to represent my position, that "liberty" includes "only those practices, defined at the most specific level, that were protected against government interference by other rules of law when the Fourteenth Amendment was ratified" (citing *Michael H. v. Gerald D.*) (opinion of Scalia, J.). That is not, however, what *Michael H.* says; it merely observes that, in defining "liberty," we may not disregard a specific, "relevant tradition protecting, or denying protection to, the asserted right." But the Court does not wish to be fettered by any such limitation on its preferences. The Court's statement that it is "tempting" to acknowledge the authoritativeness of tradition in order to "cur[b] the discretion of federal judges" is of course rhetoric rather than reality; no government official is "tempted" to place restraints upon his own freedom of action, which is why Lord Acton did not say "Power tends to purify." The Court's temptation is in the quite opposite and more natural direction— towards systematically eliminating checks upon its own power; and it succumbs.

Beyond that brief summary of the essence of my position, I [must] respond to a few of the more outrageous arguments in today's opinion, which it is beyond human nature to leave unanswered. I shall discuss each of them under a quotation from the Court's opinion to which they pertain.

1. The Court's suggestion that adherence to tradition would require us to uphold laws against interracial marriage is entirely wrong. Any tradition in that case was contradicted *by a text*—an Equal Protection Clause that explicitly establishes racial equality as a constitutional value. [The] enterprise launched in *Roe*, by contrast, sought to *establish*—in the teeth of a clear, contrary tradition—a value found nowhere in the constitutional text.

There is, of course, no comparable tradition barring recognition of a "liberty interest" in carrying one's child to term free from state efforts to kill it. For that reason, it does not follow that the Constitution does not protect childbirth simply because it does not protect abortion. The Court's contention that the only way to protect childbirth is to protect abortion shows the utter bankruptcy of constitutional analysis deprived of tradition as a validating factor. It drives one to say that the only way to protect the right to eat is to acknowledge the constitutional right to starve oneself to death.

"The inescapable fact is that adjudication of substantive due process claims may call upon the Court in interpreting the Constitution to exercise that same capacity which by tradition courts always have exercised: reasoned judgment."

[The] whole argument of abortion opponents is that what the Court calls the fetus and what others call the unborn child *is a human life*. Thus, whatever answer *Roe* came up with after conducting its "balancing" is bound to be wrong, unless it is correct that the human fetus is in some critical sense merely potentially human. There is of course no way to determine that as a legal matter; it is in fact a value judgment. Some societies have considered newborn children not yet human, or the incompetent elderly no longer so.

[The] emptiness of the "reasoned judgment" that produced *Roe* is displayed in plain view by the fact that, after more than 19 years of effort by some of the brightest (and most determined) legal minds in the country, after more than 10 cases upholding abortion rights in this Court, and after dozens upon dozens of amicus briefs submitted in this and other cases, the best the Court can do to explain how it is that the word "liberty" *must* be thought to include the right to destroy human fetuses is to rattle off a collection of adjectives that simply decorate a value judgment and conceal a political choice. [But] it is obvious to anyone applying "reasoned judgment" that the same adjectives can be applied to many forms of conduct that this Court (including one of the Justices in today's majority, see *Bowers v. Hardwick*) has held are *not* entitled to constitutional protection—because, like abortion, they are forms of conduct that have long been criminalized in American society. Those adjectives might be applied, for example, to homosexual sodomy, polygamy, adult incest, and suicide * * *.

"Liberty finds no refuge in a jurisprudence of doubt."

One might have feared to encounter this august and sonorous phrase in an opinion defending the real *Roe*, rather than the revised version fabricated today by the authors of the joint opinion. The shortcomings of *Roe* did not include lack of clarity: Virtually all regulation of abortion before the third trimester was invalid. But to come across this phrase in the joint opinion—which calls upon federal district judges to apply an "undue burden" standard as doubtful in application as it is unprincipled in origin—is really more than one should have to bear.

[To] the extent I can discern *any* meaningful content in the "undue burden" standard as applied in the joint opinion, it appears to be that a State may not regulate abortion in such a way as to reduce significantly its incidence. The joint opinion repeatedly emphasizes that an important factor in the "undue burden" analysis is whether the regulation "prevent[s] a significant number of women from obtaining an abortion," whether a "significant number of women [are] likely to be deterred from procuring an abortion," and whether the regulation often "deters" women from seeking abortions. We are not told, however, what forms of "deterrence" are impermissible or what degree of success in deterrence is too much to be tolerated. [As] Justice Blackmun recognizes (with evident hope), the "undue burden" standard may ultimately require the invalidation of each provision upheld today if it can be shown, on a better record, that the State is too effectively "express[ing]" a preference for childbirth over abortion." Reason finds no refuge in this jurisprudence of confusion.

"While we appreciate the weight of the arguments * * * that Roe should be overruled, the reservations any of us may have in reaffirming the central holding of Roe are outweighed by the explication of individual liberty we have given combined with the force of stare decisis."

The Court's reliance upon stare decisis can best be described as contrived. It insists upon the necessity of adhering not to all of *Roe,* but only to what it calls the "central holding." It seems to me that stare decisis ought to be applied even to the doctrine of stare decisis, and I confess never to have heard of this new, keep-what-you-want-and-throw-away-the-rest version. * * * I have always thought, and I think a lot of other people have always thought, that the arbitrary trimester framework, which the Court today discards, was quite as central to *Roe* as the arbitrary viability test, which the Court today retains. * * *

"Where, in the performance of its judicial duties, the Court decides a case in such a way as to resolve the sort of intensely divisive controversy reflected in Roe * * *, its decision has a dimension that the resolution of the normal case does not carry. It is the dimension present whenever the Court's interpretation of the Constitution calls the contending sides of a national controversy to end their national division by accepting a common mandate rooted in the Constitution."

[Not] only did *Roe* not, as the Court suggests, *resolve* the deeply divisive issue of abortion; it did more than anything else to nourish it, by elevating it to the national level where it is infinitely more difficult to resolve. National politics were not plagued by abortion protests, national abortion lobbying, or abortion marches on Congress, before *Roe* was decided. Profound disagreement existed among our citizens over the issue—as it does over other issues, such as the death penalty—but that disagreement was being worked out at the state level. As with many other issues, the division of sentiment within each State was not as closely balanced as it was among the population of the Nation as a whole, meaning not only that more people would be satisfied with the results of state-by-state resolution, but also that those results would be more stable. Pre–*Roe,* moreover, political compromise was possible.

Roe's mandate for abortion-on-demand destroyed the compromises of the past, rendered compromise impossible for the future, and required the entire issue to be resolved uniformly, at the national level. At the same time, *Roe* created a vast new class of abortion consumers and abortion proponents by eliminating the moral opprobrium that had attached to the act. ("If the Constitution *guarantees* abortion, how can it be bad?"—not an accurate line of thought, but a natural one.) Many favor all of those developments, and it is not for me to say that they are wrong. But to portray *Roe* as the statesmanlike "settlement" of a divisive issue, a jurisprudential Peace of Westphalia that is worth preserving, is nothing less than Orwellian. *Roe* fanned into life an issue that has inflamed our national politics in general, and has obscured with its smoke the selection of Justices to this Court in particular, ever since. * * *

"[T]o overrule under fire [would] subvert the Court's legitimacy * * *.

"To all those who will be * * * tested by following, the Court implicitly undertakes to remain steadfast * * *. The promise of constancy, once given, binds its maker for as long as the power to stand by the decision survives [and] the commitment [is not] obsolete * * *.

"[The American people's] belief in themselves as * * * a people [who aspire to live according to the rule of law] is not readily separable from their understanding of the Court invested with the authority to decide their constitutional cases and speak before all others for their constitutional ideals. If the Court's legitimacy should be undermined, then, so would the country be in its very ability to see itself through its constitutional ideals."

The Imperial Judiciary lives. It is instructive to compare this Nietzschean vision of us unelected, life-tenured judges—leading a Volk who will be "tested by following," and whose very "belief in themselves" is mystically bound up in their "understanding" of a Court that "speak[s] before all others for their constitutional ideals"—with the somewhat more modest role envisioned for these lawyers by the Founders. * * *

I cannot agree with, indeed I am appalled by, the Court's suggestion that the decision whether to stand by an erroneous constitutional decision must be strongly influenced—*against* overruling, no less—by the substantial and continuing public opposition the decision has generated. [In] my history-book, the Court was covered with dishonor and deprived of legitimacy by *Dred Scott,* an erroneous (and widely opposed) opinion that it did not abandon, rather than by *West Coast Hotel,* which produced the famous "switch in time" from the Court's erroneous (and widely opposed) constitutional opposition to the social measures of the New Deal. (Both *Dred Scott* and one line of the cases resisting the New Deal rested upon the concept of "substantive due process" that the Court praises and employs today. Indeed, *Dred Scott* was "very possibly the first application of substantive due process in the Supreme Court, the original precedent for *Lochner* and *Roe.*" David Currie, *The Constitution in the Supreme Court* 271 (1985).)

But whether it would "subvert the Court's legitimacy" or not, the notion that we would decide a case differently from the way we otherwise would have in order to show that we can stand firm against public disapproval is frightening. [Instead] of engaging in the hopeless task of predicting public perception—a job not for lawyers but for political campaign managers—the Justices should do what is *legally* right by asking two questions: (1) Was *Roe* correctly decided? (2) Has *Roe* succeeded in producing a settled body of law? If the answer to both questions is no, *Roe* should undoubtedly be overruled.

[As] long as this Court thought (and the people thought) that we Justices were doing essentially lawyers' work up here—reading text and discerning our society's traditional understanding of that text—the public pretty much left us alone. Texts and traditions are facts to study, not convictions to demonstrate about. But if in reality our process of constitutional adjudication consists primarily of making *value judgments* [then] a free and intelligent people's attitude towards us can be expected to be (*ought* to be) quite different. The people know that their value judgments are quite as good as those taught in any law school—maybe better. * * *

There is a poignant aspect to today's opinion. Its length, and what might be called its epic tone, suggest that its authors believe they are bringing to an end a troublesome era in the history of our Nation and of our Court. "It is the dimension" of authority, they say, to "cal[l] the contending sides of national controversy to end their national division by accepting a common mandate rooted in the Constitution."

[It] is no more realistic for us in this case, than it was for [Taney, C.J.,] in [*Dred Scott*] to think that an issue of the sort they both involved—an issue involving life and death, freedom and subjugation—can be "speedily and finally settled" by the Supreme Court, as President James Buchanan in his inaugural address said the issue of slavery in the territories would be. Quite to the contrary, by foreclosing all democratic outlet for the deep passions this issue arouses, by banishing the issue from the political forum that gives all participants, even the losers, the satisfaction of a fair hearing and an honest fight, by continuing the imposition of a rigid national rule instead of allowing for regional differences, the Court merely prolongs and intensifies the anguish.

We should get out of this area, where we have no right to be, and where we do neither ourselves nor the country any good by remaining.

Commentary on Casey

1. ***The shift in approach from Roe to Casey.*** Consider Laurence H. Tribe, *Lawrence v. Texas: The "Fundamental Right" that Dare Not Speak Its Name*, 117 Harv.L.Rev. 1893, 1927–28 (2004): "[The plurality opinion in *Casey*] staked its basic agreement with *Roe* on the recognition that the women's 'bond of love,' her 'sacrifice,' and her 'suffering [are] too intimate and personal for the State to insist, without more, upon its own vision of the woman's role, however dominant that vision has been in the course of our history and our culture.'

"With that observation, the Court finally relocated its jurisprudence of reproductive liberty from a realm that, in *Roe*, had been cast in largely medical and technocratic terms, to a very different realm defined by the war against the insidious transmutation of anatomy into destiny. No longer could an analysis of liberty and of power over the unborn simply ignore the driving force of gender inequity."

2. ***The worst of all possible worlds?*** Consider Sylvia Law, *Abortion Compromise—Inevitable and Impossible,* 1992 U.Ill.L.Rev. 921, 931: "From a pro-choice point of view, one plausible assessment of the *Casey* decision is that is represents the worst of all possible worlds. The joint opinion affirmed a woman's 'fundamental constitutional right' to abortion, but simultaneously allowed the state to adopt measures that effectively curtail *many* women's exercise of the abortion right. This curtailment hits hardest those women who are most vulnerable, i.e., the poor, the unsophisticated, the young, and women who live in rural areas. The abstract recognition of a right to abortion could dampen political enthusiasm in support of reproductive choice."[a]

3. ***The alternative to an undue burden approach.*** "[T]he adoption of an expansively applied undue burden standard is hardly a panacea for the protection of fundamental rights," recognizes Alan Brownstein, *How Rights Are Infringed: The Role of Undue Burden Analysis in Constitutional Doctrine,* 45 Hast.L.J. 867, 958 (1994), for the balancing of burdens against the state's interests "is far more conducive to judicial deference to the legislature than are categorical rules of review." The alternative, however, warns Professor Brownstein, "may be even more limited and restrictive": "If the only choice is between protecting the exercise of a right against all burdens under strict scrutiny review or interpreting the interest at stake as something other than a right and providing it no constitutional protection at all, the latter option may be selected in far too many circumstances. It may be implicit in the framework offered by the critics of the 'undue burden' standard that rights are rarely recognized, although they receive aggressive protection in those few circumstances when they are found to exist."

---

a. "It is much harder to mobilize pro-choice lobbying, voting and fund-raising efforts," observes Kathleen Sullivan, *Foreword: The Justices of Rules and Standards,* 106 Harv.L.Rev. 24, 110 (1992), "if *Roe* is nickel-and-dimed away rather than frankly overruled.

* * * Why didn't pro-choice activists celebrate when five Justices reaffirmed 'the essential holding of *Roe*'? Because the Court stole their thunder by adopting a moderate, difference-splitting standard."

ANTI–ABORTION MEASURES POST-*CASEY*: ATTEMPTS TO OUTLAW "PARTIAL–BIRTH ABORTION"

GONZALES v. CARHART

550 U.S. 124, 127 S.Ct. 1610, 167 L.Ed.2d 480 (2007).

JUSTICE KENNEDY delivered the opinion of the Court.

These cases require us to consider the validity of the Partial–Birth Abortion Ban Act of 2003 (Act), a federal statute regulating abortion procedures. * * * We conclude the Act should be sustained against the objections lodged by the broad, facial attack brought against it.

[Between 85 and 90 percent of the 1.3 million abortions performed every year in the United States take place in the first trimester. The most common first-trimester abortion is vacuum aspiration (or the suction method), in which the physician vacuums out the embryonic tissue. The Act does not regulate these procedures. However, in the second trimester, when the fetus has grown too large to be removed by the suction method, different procedures are used. The usual procedure is known as "dilation and evacuation" (D&E) or "standard D&E." In this procedure, the doctor dilates the cervix and then inserts instruments into the uterus, maneuvering the instruments to grab the fetus and pull it through the cervix and vagina. The fetus is usually dismembered as it is removed. (The doctor may take 10 to 15 passes to remove the fetus in its entirety.)

[The second-trimester procedure that prompted the challenged Act (and various state statutes as well) is a variation of the standard D&E. It has several names. The Court referred to it as "intact D&E." Abortion opponents call it "partial-birth abortion."a As the Court observed, the "main difference" between standard D&E and intact D&E is that in the latter procedure, instead of dismembering the fetus, the doctor "extracts the fetus intact or largely intact with only a few passes." In this procedure, the doctor typically extracts the fetus from the uterus feet first up to the head, pierces or crushes the skull, and then extracts the whole fetus through the cervix.

[Three years before the challenged Act became law, in *Stenberg v. Carhart*, 530 U.S. 914 (2000), a 5–4 majority, per Breyer, J., struck down a Nebraska statute prohibiting "partial-birth abortion" except where "necessary to save the life of the mother. The statute defined the procedure as one in which the person performing the abortion partially delivers vaginally a living unborn child before killing it and completing the delivery. It further defined the procedure to mean deliberately and intentionally delivering into the vagina a living unborn child, *or a substantial portion thereof*, for the purpose of performing a procedure [that] will kill [and] does kill the unborn child." (Emphasis added.) The Nebraska statute was meant to ban a specific procedure called dilation and extraction (D&X) (what the Court in *Gonzales v. Carhart* was to call "intact D & E").

[*Stenberg* held the statute unconstitutional "for at least two independent reasons": (1) it lacks any exception 'for the preservation of the health of the mother,' " *Casey* (joint opinion); and (2) it imposes "an undue burden" on the womans ability to choose a more commonly used abortion procedure, D & E, "thereby unduly burdening the right to choose abortion itself": "We do not understand how one could distinguish, using [the statutory] language, between D

---

a. "The term 'partial-birth abortion,' " observed Justice Ginsburg, J., dissenting, "is neither recognized in the medical literature nor used by physicians who perform second-trimester abortions."

& E (where a foot or arm is drawn through the cervix) and D & X (where the body up to the head is drawn through the cervix). Evidence before the trial court makes clear that D & E will often involve a physician pulling 'a substantial portion' of a still living fetus, say, an arm or leg, into the vagina prior to the death of the fetus."

[O'Connor, J., concurring, observed that "if there were adequate alternative methods for a woman safely to obtain an abortion before viability, it is unlikely that prohibiting the D & X procedure alone would 'amount in practical terms to a substantial obstacle to a woman seeking an abortion.' *Casey* (joint opinion). In a dissent foreshadowing his majority opinion seven years later in *Gonzales v. Carhart*, Kennedy, J., joined by Rehnquist, C.J., maintained that the Court's decision "repudiates [the central premise of *Casey* that the States retain a critical role in legislating on the subject of abortion] by invalidating a statute advancing critical state interests, even though the law denies no woman the right to choose an abortion and places no undue burden upon the right. [The] State's brief describes its interests as including concern for the life of the unborn and 'for the partially-born,' in preserving the integrity of the medical profession, and in 'erecting a barrier to infanticide.' A review of *Casey* demonstrates the legitimacy of these policies. The Court should say so."[b]]

[The challenged Act] responded to *Stenberg* in two ways. First, Congress determined that, unlike the Supreme Court in *Stenberg*, it was not bound to accept the District Court's factual findings. Second, Congress found that a "moral and ethical consensus exists that the practice of performing a partial-birth abortion [is] a gruesome and inhumane procedure that is never medically necessary and should be prohibited." The Act provides that physicians who perform the banned procedure may face up to two years in prison.

[The district court in *Gonzales* found the Act unconstitutional because it (1) lacked an exception allowing the prohibited procedure where necessary for the mother's health and (2) covered not only intact D & E but other D & Es. The Eighth Circuit affirmed. The district court in *Planned Parenthood* found the Act unconstitutional because it (1) unduly burdened a woman's right to choose a second-trimester abortion, (2) was unduly vague, and (3) lacked a health exception. The Ninth Circuit affirmed. Both district courts enjoined the Attorney General from enforcing the Act.]

Whatever one's views concerning the *Casey* joint opinion, it is evident a premise central to its conclusion—that the government has a legitimate and substantial interest in preserving and promoting fetal life would be repudiated were the Court now to affirm the judgments of the Courts of Appeals. * * *

We assume the following principles for the purposes of this opinion. Before viability, a State "may not prohibit any woman from making the ultimate decision to terminate her pregnancy." It also may not impose upon this right an undue burden, which exists if a regulation's "purpose or effect is to place a substantial obstacle in the path of a woman seeking an abortion before the fetus attains viability." On the other hand, "[r]egulations which do no more than create a structural mechanism by which the State, or the parent or guardian of a minor, may express profound respect for the life of the unborn are permitted, if they are not a substantial obstacle to the woman's exercise of the right to choose." *Casey*, in short, struck a balance. The balance was central to its holding. We now apply its standard to the cases at bar. * * *

b. Scalia, J. dissenting, "was optimistic enough to believe that *Stenberg* will be assigned its rightful place in the history of this Court's jurisprudence beside *Korematsu* and *Dred Scott*." Thomas, J., joined by Rehnquist, C.J., and Scalia, J., also dissented.

The Act punishes "knowingly perform[ing]" a "partial-birth abortion." It defines the unlawful abortion in explicit terms. First, the person performing the abortion must "vaginally delive[r] a living fetus." [The] Act does apply both previability and postviability because, by common understanding and scientific terminology, a fetus is a living organism while within the womb, whether or not it is viable outside the womb. Second, the Act's definition of partial-birth abortion requires the fetus to be delivered "until, in the case of a head-first presentation, the entire fetal head is outside the body of the mother, or, in the case of breech presentation, any part of the fetal trunk past the naval is outside the body of the mother." [If] an abortion procedure does not involve the delivery of a living fetus to one of these "anatomical 'landmarks' " [the] prohibitions of the Act do not apply.

Third, to fall within the Act, a doctor must perform an "overt act, other than completion of the delivery, that kills the partially delivered living fetus." [Fourth,] the Act contains scienter requirements concerning all the actions involved in the prohibited abortion.

[The Act is not] unconstitutionally vague on its face. [It] provides doctors "of ordinary intelligence a reasonable opportunity to know what is prohibited." [Physicians] performing D & E will know that if they do not deliver a living fetus to an anatomical landmark they will not face criminal liability. [Respondents] likewise have failed to show that the Act should be invalidated on its face because it encourages arbitrary or discriminating enforcement. Just as the Act's anatomical landmarks provide doctors with objective standards, they also "establish minimal guidelines to govern law enforcement." The scienter requirements narrow the scope of the Act's prohibitions and limit prosecutorial discretion.

[The Court then rejected the argument that] the Act imposes an undue burden, as a facial matter, because its restrictions on second-trimester abortions are too broad. [The Act] excludes most D & Es in which the fetus is removed in pieces, not intact. If the doctor intends to remove the fetus in parts from the outset, the doctor will not have the requisite intent to incur criminal liability. [A] comparison of the Act with the Nebraska statute struck down in *Stenberg* confirms this point. [There, the] Court concluded that [the] statute encompassed D & E because "D & E will often involve a physician pulling a 'substantial portion' of a still living fetus, say, an arm or leg, into the vagina prior to the death of the fetus." * * * Congress, it is apparent, responded to these concerns because the Act departs in material ways from the statute in *Stenberg*. It adopts the phrase "delivers a living fetus" instead of "delivering [a] living unborn child, or a substantial portion thereof," [thereby targeting] extraction of an entire fetus rather than the removal of fetal pieces, [and] requir[ing] the fetus to be delivered so that it is partially "outside the body of the mother."

[By] adding an overt-act requirement Congress sought further to meet the Court's objections to the state statute considered in *Stenberg*, [making] the distinction the Nebraska statute failed to draw [by] differentiating between the overall partial-birth abortion and the distinct overt act that kills the fetus. The fatal overt act must occur after delivery to an anatomical landmark, and it must be something "other than [the] completion of delivery." This distinction matters because, unlike intact D & E, standard D & E does not involve a delivery followed by a fatal act. * * *

Contrary arguments by the respondents are unavailing. [The contention] that any D & E has the potential to violate the Act, and that a physician will not know beforehand whether the abortion will proceed in a prohibited manner [fails to] take account of the Act's intent requirements, which preclude liability from attaching to an accidental intact D & E. [The] evidence also supports a legislative determination that an intact delivery is almost always a conscious choice rather than a happenstance, [thereby belying] any claim that a standard D & E cannot be performed without intending or foreseeing an intact D & E.

[The Act,] measured by its text in this facial attack, [does not impose] a substantial obstacle to late-term, but previability, abortions.

[Congress said the following about the banned procedure:] "Implicitly approving such a brutal and inhumane procedure by choosing not to prohibit it will further coarsen society to the humanity of not only newborns, but all vulnerable and innocent human life, making it increasingly difficult to protect such life." [Furthermore,] Congress was concerned [with] the effects on the medical community and on its reputation caused by the practice of partial-birth abortion. [There] can be no doubt the government "has an interest in protecting the integrity and ethics of the medical profession." *Washington v. Glucksberg* [p. 269 infra].

[*Casey*] reaffirmed [that the] government may use its voice and its regulatory authority to show its profound respect for the life within the woman. A central premise of the opinion was that the Courts precedents after *Roe* had "undervalue[d] the State interests in potential life."

[Congress] determined that the abortion methods it proscribed had a "disturbing similarity to the killing of a newborn infant." [The] Court [has] confirmed the validity of drawing boundaries to prevent certain practices that extinguish life and are close to actions that are condemned. *Glucksberg* found reasonable the State's "fear that permitting assisted suicide will start it down the path to voluntary and perhaps even involuntary euthanasia."

Respect for human life finds an ultimate expression in the bond of love the mother has for her child. The Act recognizes this reality as well. Whether to have an abortion requires a difficult and painful moral decision. While we find no reliable data to measure the phenomenon, it seems unexceptionable to conclude some women come to regret their choice to abort the infant life they once created and sustained. Severe depression and loss of esteem can follow.

In a decision so fraught with emotional consequence some doctors may prefer not to disclose precise details of the means that will be used. [It] is, however, precisely this lack of information concerning the way in which the fetus will be killed that is of legitimate concern to the State. [The] State has an interest in ensuring so grave a choice is well informed. It is self-evident that a mother who comes to regret her choice to abort must struggle with grief more anguished and sorrow more profound when she learns, only after the event, what she once did not know: that she allowed a doctor to pierce the skull and vacuum the fast-developing brain of her unborn child, a child assuming the human form.

It is a reasonable inference that a necessary effect of the regulation and the knowledge it conveys will be to encourage some women to carry the infant to full term, thus reducing the absolute number of late-term abortions. The medical profession, furthermore, may find different and less shocking methods to abort the fetus in the second trimester, thereby accommodating legislative demand. The State's interest in respect for life is advanced by the dialogue that better informs the political and legal systems, the medical profession, expectant mothers, and society as a whole of the consequences that follow from a decision to elect a late-term abortion. * * *

Partial-birth abortion, as defined by the Act, differs from a standard D & E because the former occurs when the fetus is partially outside the mother to the point of one of the Act's anatomical landmarks. It was reasonable for Congress to think that partial-birth abortion, more than standard D & E, "undermines the public's perception of the appropriate role of a physician during the delivery process, and perverts a process during which life is brought into the world."

[The Act's failure to] allow use of the barred procedure where "necessary [for the] preservation of [the] health of the mother" [does not impose an unconstitutional burden on the abortion right]. There is documented medical disagreement whether the Act's prohibition would ever impose significant health risks on women. [The] Court's precedents instruct that [under these circumstances] the Act can survive this facial attack. The Court has given state and federal legislatures wide discretion to pass legislation in areas where there is medical and scientific uncertainty. [Such] uncertainty does not foreclose the exercise of legislative power in the abortion context any more than it does in other contexts. The medical uncertainty over whether the Act's prohibition creates significant health risks provides a sufficient basis to conclude in this facial attack that the Act does not impose an undue burden. [Moreover, if] the intact D & E procedure is truly necessary in some circumstances, it appears likely an injection that kills the fetus is an alternative under the Act that allows the doctor to perform the procedure.

[Respondents] contend that an abortion regulation must contain a health exception "if 'substantial medical authority supports the proposition that banning a particular procedure could endanger the woman's health.'" [But, a] zero tolerance policy would strike down legitimate abortion regulations, like the present one, if some part of the medical community were disinclined to follow the proscription. This is too exacting a standard to impose on the legislative power, exercised in this instance under the Commerce Clause, to regulate the medical profession. Considerations of marginal safety, including the balance of risks, are within the legislative competence when the regulation is rational and in pursuit of legitimate ends.

[The] considerations we have discussed support our further determination that these facial attacks should not have been entertained in the first instance. In these circumstances the proper means to consider exceptions is by as-applied challenge. [This] is the proper manner to protect the health of the woman if it can be shown that in discrete and well-defined instances a particular condition has or is likely to occur in which the procedure prohibited by the Act must be used. In an as-applied challenge the nature of the medical risk can be better quantified and balanced than in a facial attack. * * * ["It] would indeed be undesirable for this Court to consider every conceivable situation which might possibly arise in the application of complex and comprehensive legislation." [For] this reason, "[a]s-applied challenges are the basic building blocks of constitutional adjudication." Richard H. Fallon, Jr., *As-Applied and Facial Challenges and Third–Party Standing*, 113 Harv.L.Rev. 1321, 1328 (2000).

The Act is open to a proper as-applied challenge in a discrete case. No as-applied challenge need be brought if the prohibition in the Act threatens a woman's life because the Act already contains a life exception. * * *c

JUSTICE GINSBURG, with whom JUSTICE STEVENS, JUSTICE SOUTER, and JUSTICE BREYER join, dissenting. * * *

Today's decision is alarming. It refuses to take *Casey* and *Stenberg* seriously. It tolerates, indeed applauds, federal intervention to ban nationwide a procedure found necessary and proper in certain cases by the American College of Obstetri-

---

c. Thomas, J., joined by Scalia, J., joined the Court's opinion, but wrote separately "to reiterate my view that the Court's jurisprudence, including *Casey* and *Roe*, has no basis in the Constitution."

cians and Gynecologists (ACOG). It blurs the line, firmly drawn in *Casey*, between previability and postviability abortions. And, for the first time since *Roe*, the Court blesses a prohibition with no exception safeguarding a woman's health.

[As] *Casey* comprehended, at stake in cases challenging abortion restrictions is a woman's "control over her [own] destiny" (plurality opinion). [Thus,] legal challenges to undue restrictions on abortion procedures do not seek to vindicate some generalized notion of privacy; rather, they center on a woman's autonomy to determine her life's course, and thus to enjoy equal citizenship stature. [In] keeping with this comprehension of the right to reproductive choice, the Court has consistently required that laws regulating abortion, at any stage of pregnancy and in all cases, safeguard a woman's health. [In] *Stenberg*, we expressly held that a statute banning intact D & E was unconstitutional in part because it lacked a health exception. We noted that there existed a "division of medical opinion" about the relative safety of intact D & E, but we made clear that as long as "substantial medical authority supports the proposition that banning a particular abortion procedure could endanger women's health," a health exception is required.

[The] congressional findings on which the Partial–Birth Abortion Ban Act rests do not withstand inspection, as the lower courts have determined and this Court is obliged to concede. [Many] of the Act's recitations are incorrect. For example, Congress determined that no medical schools provide instruction on intact D & E. But in fact, numerous leading medical schools teach the procedure. [More] important, Congress claimed there was a medical consensus that the banned procedure is never necessary. But the evidence "very clearly demonstrate[d] the opposite." * * * Similarly, Congress found that "[t]here is no credible medical evidence that partial-birth abortions are safe or are safer than other abortion procedures." But the congressional record includes letters from numerous individual physicians stating that pregnant women's health would be jeopardized under the Act, as well as statements from nine professional [groups], attesting that intact D & E carries meaningful safety advantages over other methods. No comparable medical groups supported the ban. In fact, "all of the governments own witnesses disagreed with many of the specific congressional findings."

In contrast to Congress, the District Courts made findings after full trials at which all parties had the opportunity to present their best evidence. [According] to the expert testimony plaintiffs' introduced, the safety advantages of intact D & E are marked for women with certain medical conditions. [Further,] plaintiffs experts testified that intact D & E is significantly safer for women with certain pregnancy-related conditions.

[Based] on thoroughgoing review of the trial evidence and the congressional record, each of the District Courts to consider the issue rejected Congress' findings as unreasonable and not supported by the evidence. The trial courts concluded, in contrast to Congress' findings, that "significant medical authority supports the proposition that in some circumstances [intact D & E] is the safest procedure." [D]espite the District Court's appraisal of the weight of the evidence, and in undisguised conflict with *Stenberg*, the Court asserts that the Partial–Birth Abortion Ban Act can survive "[when] medical uncertainty persists." This assertion is bewildering. Not only does it defy the Courts longstanding precedent affirming the necessity of a health exception, with no carve-out for circumstances of medical uncertainty; it gives short shrift to the records before us, carefully canvassed by the District Courts. Those records indicate that "the majority of highly-qualified experts on the subject believe intact D & E to be the safest, most appropriate procedure under certain circumstances."

[The] Court offers flimsy and transparent justifications for upholding a nationwide ban on intact D & E sans any exception to safeguard a woman's health. Todays ruling, the Court declares, advances "a premise central to [*Caseys*] conclusion i.e., the Governments 'legitimate and substantial interest' in preserving and promoting fetal life." [But] the Act scarcely furthers that interest: The law saves not a single fetus from destruction, for it targets only a *method* of performing abortion.

[As] another reason for upholding the ban, the Court emphasizes that the Act does not proscribe the nonintact D & E procedure. But why not, one might ask. Nonintact D & E could equally be characterized as "brutal," involving as it does "tear[ing] [a fetus] apart" and "ripp[ing] off" its limbs. "[T]he notion that either of these two equally gruesome procedures [is] more akin to infanticide than the other, or that the State furthers any legitimate interest by banning one but not the other, is simply irrational." *Stenberg* (Stevens, J., concurring). * * *

Ultimately, the Court admits that "moral concerns" are at work, concerns that could yield prohibitions on any abortion. * * * Notably, the concerns expressed are untethered to any ground genuinely serving the Governments interest in preserving life. By allowing such concerns to carry the day and case, overriding fundamental rights, the Court dishonors our precedent [quoting from *Casey* and *Lawrence v. Texas*, p. 283 infra]. Revealing in this regard, the Court invokes an antiabortion shibboleth for which it concededly has no reliable evidence: Women who have abortions come to regret their choices, and consequently suffer from "[s]evere depression and loss of esteem."[7] Because of women's fragile emotional state and because of the "bond of love the mother has for her child," the Court worries, doctors may withhold information about the nature of the intact D & E procedure. The solution the Court approves, then, is *not* to require doctors to inform women, accurately and adequately, of the different procedures and their attendant risks. [Instead,] the Court deprives women of the right to make an autonomous choice, even at the expense of their safety. This way of thinking reflects ancient notions about women's place in the family and under the— Constitution ideas that have long since been discredited.

[In] cases on a "woman's liberty to determine whether to [continue] her pregnancy," this Court has identified viability as a critical consideration. "[T]here is no line [more workable] than viability," the Court explained in *Casey*. * * * Today, the Court blurs that line, maintaining that "[t]he Act [legitimately] appl[ies] both previability and postviability because [a] fetus is a living organism while within the womb, whether or not it is viable outside the womb." Instead of drawing the line at viability, the Court refers to Congress' purpose to differentiate "abortion and infanticide" based not on whether a fetus can survive outside the womb, but on where a fetus is anatomically located when a particular medical procedure is performed. One wonders how long a line that saves no fetus from destruction will hold in face of the Court's "moral concerns."

[The] Court further confuses our jurisprudence when it declares that "facial attacks" are not permissible in "these circumstances," i.e., where medical uncertainty exists. [This] holding is perplexing given that, in materially identical

---

7. The Court is surely correct that, for most women, abortion is a painfully difficult decision. But "neither the weight of the scientific evidence to date nor the observable reality of 33 years of legal abortion in the United States comports with the idea that having an abortion is any more dangerous to a woman's long-term mental health than delivering and parenting a child that she did not intend to have." Cohen, *Abortion and Mental Health: Myths and Realities*, 9 Guttmacher Policy Rev. 8 (2006) * * *.

circumstances we held that a statute lacking a health exception was unconstitutional on its face. *Stenberg*. [Without] attempting to distinguish *Stenberg* and earlier decisions, the majority asserts that the Act survives review because respondents have not shown that the ban on intact D & E would be unconstitutional "in a large fraction of relevant cases." But *Casey* makes clear that, in determining whether any restriction poses an undue burden on a "large fraction" of women, the relevant class is *not* "all women," nor "all pregnant women," nor even all women "seeking abortions." Rather, a provision restricting access to abortion, "must be judged by reference to those [women] for whom it is an actual rather than an irrelevant restriction." Thus the absence of a health exception burdens *all* women for whom it is relevant—women who in the judgment of their doctors, require an intact D & E because other procedures would place their health at risk. [It] makes no sense to conclude that this facial challenge fails because respondents have not shown that a health exception is necessary for a large fraction of second-trimester abortions, including those for which a health exception is unnecessary: The very purpose of a health *exception* is to protect women in *exceptional* cases.

[The] Court envisions that in an as-applied challenge, "the nature of the medical risk can be better quantified and balanced." But it should not escape notice that the record already includes hundreds and hundreds of pages of testimony identifying "discrete and well-defined instances" in which recourse to an intact D & E would better protect the health of women with particular conditions.

[Though] today's opinion does not go so far as to discard *Roe* or *Casey*, the Court, differently composed than it was when we last considered a restrictive abortion regulation, is hardly faithful to our earlier invocations of "the rule of law" and the "principles of stare decisis." Congress imposed a ban despite our clear prior holdings that the State cannot proscribe an abortion procedure when its use is necessary to protect a woman's health. Although Congress' findings could not withstand the crucible of trial, the Court defers to the legislative override of our Constitution-based rulings. A decision so at odds with our jurisprudence should not have staying power.

In sum, the notion that the Partial–Birth Abortion Ban Act furthers any legitimate governmental interest is, quite simply, irrational. The Courts defense of the statute provides no saving explanation. In candor, the Act, and the Courts defense of it, cannot be understood as anything other than an effort to chip away at a right declared again and again by this Court—and with increasing comprehension of its centrality to women's lives.

FAMILY LIVING ARRANGEMENTS, PARENTAL RIGHTS, AND THE "RIGHT TO MARRY"

As illustrated by WHALEN v. ROE, 429 U.S. 589 (1977) (sustaining a New York law that doctors disclose the names of persons obtaining certain drugs for storage in a central computer file), those attacking legislation can often cast their challenge in terms of an invasion of a constitutionally protected "zone of privacy." But the Court upheld the legislation as "a reasonable exercise of New York's broad police powers," holding that the program did not require extraordinary justification because it "does not, on its face, pose a sufficiently grievous threat" to either the "privacy" interest "in avoiding disclosure of personal matters"a or

a. The Court, however, specifically did *not* decide "any question which might be presented by the unwarranted disclosure of accumulated private data—whether intentional or unintentional—or by a system that did not contain [adequate] security provisions."

the "privacy" interest "in independence in making certain kinds of important decisions [e.g., abortion, marriage]." The cases discussed below deal with the latter "privacy" interest.

Zoning; choice of household companions; "extended family" relationships. Relying on earlier decisions sustaining local zoning regulations, Belle Terre v. Boraas, 416 U.S. 1 (1974), per DOUGLAS, J., upheld a village ordinance restricting land use to one-family dwellings (defining "family" to mean not more than two unrelated persons living together as a single housekeeping unit, and expressly excluding from the term lodging, boarding, fraternity or multiple-dwelling houses). Appellees, who had leased their houses to six unrelated college students, challenged the ordinance, inter alia, on the ground that it "trenches on the newcomers' rights of privacy." The court disagreed: "we deal with economic and social legislation where legislatures have historically drawn lines which we respect [if the law] bears 'a rational relationship to a [permissible] state objective.' "[B]oarding houses, fraternity houses, and the like present urban problems. [The] police power is not confined to elimination of filth, stench, and unhealthy places."

MARSHALL, J., dissented: The law burdened "fundamental rights of association and privacy," and thus required extraordinary justification, not a mere showing that the ordinance "bears a rational relationship to the accomplishment of legitimate governmental objectives." He viewed "the right to 'establish a home' " as an "essential part" of Fourteenth Amendment liberty and maintained that "the choice of household companions"—which "involves deeply personal considerations as to the kind and quality of intimate relationships within the home"—"surely falls within the right to privacy protected by the Constitution." The state's purposes "could be as effectively achieved by means of an ordinance that did not discriminate on the basis of constitutionally protected choices of life style."[b]

Distinguishing *Belle Terre* as involving an ordinance "affect[ing] only *unrelated* individuals," MOORE v. EAST CLEVELAND, 431 U.S. 494 (1977), invalidated a housing ordinance that limited occupancy to single families, but defined "family" so as to forbid appellant from having her two grandsons live with her. (It did not permit living arrangements if, as in this case, the grandchildren were cousins rather than brothers.)[a] POWELL, J., announcing the Court's judgment and joined by Brennan, Marshall, and Blackmun, JJ., struck down the ordinance on substantive due process grounds:

"[O]n its face [the ordinance] selects certain categories of relatives who may live together and declares that others may not. [When] a city undertakes such intrusive regulation of the family [the] usual judicial deference to the legislature is

See also *Paul v. Davis*, 424 U.S. 693 (1976), per Rehnquist, J., holding that police disclosure of a person's shoplifting arrest did not violate his right of privacy: "His claim is based not upon any challenge to the State's ability to restrict his freedom of action in a sphere contended to be 'private,' but instead on a claim that the State may not publicize a record of an official act such as an arrest. None of our substantive privacy decisions hold this or anything like this and we decline to enlarge them in this manner." Brennan, J., joined by Marshall, J., observed that "a host of state and federal courts, relying on both privacy notions and the presumption of innocence, have begun to develop a line of cases holding that there are substantive limits on the power of the Govern-

ment to disseminate unresolved arrest records outside the law enforcement [system]. I fear that after today's decision, these nascent doctrines will never have the opportunity for full growth and analysis."

b. Compare Marshall, J.'s views in *Belle Terre* with the Court's discussion of "freedom of intimate association" in *Roberts v. United States Jaycees,* p. 571 infra. See also the Court's discussion of "the freedom to enter into and carry on certain intimate of private relationships" in *Board of Directors of Rotary International v. Rotary Club of Duarte,* p. 573 infra.

a. The second grandson came to live with his grandmother after the death of his mother.

inappropriate. 'This Court has long recognized that freedom of personal choice in matters of marriage and family life is one of the liberties protected by [due process].' [When] the government intrudes on choices concerning family living arrangements, this Court must examine carefully the importance of the governmental interests advanced and the extent to which they are served by the challenged regulation [referring to Harlan, J.'s dissent in *Poe*]." "[T]hus examined, this ordinance cannot survive." Although the city's goals—preventing overcrowding, minimizing congestion and avoiding financial strain on its school system—were "legitimate," the ordinance served them "marginally at best."

"[T]he history of the *Lochner* [era] counsels caution and restraint [but] it does [not] require what the city urges here: cutting off any family rights at the first convenient, if arbitrary boundary—the boundary of the nuclear family. * * * Appropriate limits on substantive due process come not from drawing arbitrary lines but rather from careful 'respect for the teachings of history [and] solid recognition of the basic values that underlie our society.' *Griswold* (Harlan, J., concurring). Our decisions teach that the Constitution protects the sanctity of the family precisely because the institution of the family is deeply rooted in this Nation's history and tradition. [Ours] is by no means a tradition limited to respect for [the] nuclear family. The tradition of uncles, aunts, cousins, and especially grandparents sharing a household along with parents and children [especially in times of adversity] has roots equally venerable and equally deserving of constitutional recognition. [In *Pierce,* the Constitution prevented a state from] 'standardiz[ing] its children by forcing them to accept instruction from public teachers only.' By the same token the Constitution prevents East Cleveland from standardizing its children—and its adults—by forcing all to live in certain narrowly defined family patterns."**b**

STEWART, J., joined by Rehnquist, J., dissented, rejecting the argument that "the importance of the 'extended family' in American society" renders appellant's "decision to share her residence with her grandsons," like the decisions involved in bearing and raising children, "an aspect of 'family life' " entitled to substantive constitutional protection. To equate appellant's interest in sharing her residence with some of her relatives "with the fundamental decisions to marry and to bear children," he maintained, "is to extend the limited substantive contours of the Due Process Clause beyond recognition." He thought the challenged "family" definition "rationally designed to carry out the legitimate governmental purposes identified in *Belle Terre.*"

Nor could he understand why "the traditional importance of the extended family in America" need imply "that the residents of East Cleveland are constitutionally prevented from following what Justice Brennan calls the 'pattern' of

---

b. Brennan, J., joined by Marshall, J., concurred, characterizing the ordinance as "senseless," "arbitrary" and "eccentric" and as reflecting "cultural myopia" and "a distressing insensitivity toward the economic and emotional needs of a very large part of our society." He called the "extended family" "virtually a means of survival" for many poor and black families. [The] 'nuclear family' is the pattern so often found in much of white suburbia," but "the Constitution cannot * * * tolerate the imposition by government upon the rest of us of white suburbia's preference in patterns of family living." But see dissenting Justice Stewart's response, infra.

Stevens, J., concurring, thought this "unprecedented ordinance" unconstitutional even under the "limited standard of review of zoning decisions": "The city has failed totally to explain the need for a rule which would allow a homeowner to have two grandchildren live with her if they are brothers, but not if they are cousins. Since the ordinance has not been shown to have any 'substantial relation to [East Cleveland's] public health, safety, morals or general welfare' [and] since it cuts so deeply into a fundamental right normally associated with the ownership of residential property— that of an owner to decide who may reside on his or her property—it must fall [as] a taking of property without due process and without just compensation."

'white suburbia,' even though that choice may reflect 'cultural myopia.' In point of fact, East Cleveland is a predominantly Negro community, with a Negro City Manager and City Commission."c

WHITE, J., dissenting, voiced disbelief "that the interest in residing with more than one set of grandchildren is one that calls for any kind of heightened protection under the Due Process Clause." He maintained that Powell, J.'s approach—construing the Due Process Clause to protect from all but "quite important" state interests any right "that in his estimate is deeply rooted in the country's traditions"—"suggests a far too expansive charter for this Court. [What] the deeply rooted traditions of the country are is arguable; which of them deserve [due process protection] is even more debatable."d

———

The right to marry. LOVING v. VIRGINIA, 388 U.S. 1 (1967) (also at Ch. 9, Sec. 2, II), per WARREN, C.J., held that a state statutory scheme designed to prevent marriages between persons of different races not only violated the Equal Protection Clause, but deprived the Lovings of liberty without due process. The Court recalled that in *Skinner v. Oklahoma*, it had described marriage as "one of the 'basic civil rights of man.'" It "surely" is a deprivation of liberty without due process, declared the Court, "to deny this fundamental right on so unsupportable a basis as the racial classifications embodied in these statutes." Because racial discrimination played so large a role in the *Loving* case, its due process ruling was not free from ambiguity. A decade later, however, in the *Zablocki* case, discussed below, the Court confirmed that the right to marry is a fundamental right for due process purposes.

ZABLOCKI v. REDHAIL, 434 U.S. 374 (1978), invalidated a Wisconsin law forbidding marriage by any resident with minor children not in his custody whom he is under court order to support, unless he proves compliance with the support obligation and that the children "are not then and are not likely thereafter to become public charges." Appellee and the woman he desired to marry were expecting a child, but he was denied a marriage license because he had not satisfied his support obligations to his illegitimate child who had been a public charge since birth. In striking down the marriage prohibition under the "fundamental rights" branch of equal protection doctrine (Ch. 9, Sec. 4) the Court, per MARSHALL, J., observed:

"Since our past decisions make clear that the right to marry is of fundamental importance, and since the classification at issue here significantly interferes with the exercise of that right, we believe that 'critical examination' of the state's interests advanced in support of the classification is required. [Cases] subsequent to *Griswold* and *Loving* have routinely categorized the decision to marry as among the personal decisions protected by the right of privacy. [It] is not surprising that the decision to marry has been placed on the same level of importance as decisions

c. "[I]n assessing [appellant's] claim that the ordinance is 'arbitrary' and 'irrational,'" Stewart, J., considered a provision permitting her to request a variance "particularly persuasive evidence to the contrary. [The] variance procedure, a traditional part of American land-use law, bends the straight lines of East Cleveland's ordinance, shaping their contours to respond more flexibly to the hard cases that are the inevitable byproduct of legislative line-drawing."

Burger, C.J., dissented on the ground that appellant should have pursued the "plainly adequate administrative remedy" of seeking a variance, thus finding it "unnecessary to reach the difficult constitutional issue."

d. "[A]n approach grounded in history," replied Justice Powell [fn. 12], "imposes limits on the judiciary that are more meaningful than any based on [White, J.'s] abstract formula taken from *Palko*."

relating to procreation, childbirth, child rearing, and family relationships [for] it would make little sense to recognize a right of privacy with respect to other matters of family life and not with respect to the decision to enter the relationship that is the foundation of the family in our society. [If] appellee's right to procreate means anything at all, it must imply some right to enter the only relationship in which [the state] allows sexual relations legally to take place.

"By reaffirming the fundamental character of the right to marry, we do not mean to suggest that every state regulation which relates in any way to the incidents of or prerequisites for marriage must be subjected to rigorous scrutiny. [R]easonable regulations that do not significantly interfere with decisions to enter into the marital relationships may legitimately be imposed. See *Califano v. Jobst,* 434 U.S. 47 (1977), [discussed fn. 12 infra]." However, because the statute prevents any Wisconsin resident in the affected class from marrying anywhere without a court order, some in the affected class, like appellee, "are absolutely prevented from ever getting married," for "they either lack the financial means to meet their support obligations or cannot prove that their children will not become public charges"; and because "many others [will] be sufficiently burdened by having to [satisfy the statute's requirements] that they will in effect be coerced into foregoing their right to marry," this statute "clearly does interfere directly and substantially with the right to marry.12

"When a statutory classification significantly interferes with the exercise of a fundamental right, it cannot be upheld unless it is supported by sufficiently important state interests and is closely tailored to effectuate only those interests. [Assuming that the state interests said to be served by the statute—furnishing an opportunity to counsel the applicant as to the need to fulfill his prior support obligations, and protecting the welfare of the out-of-custody children—]are legitimate and substantial interests, [since] the means selected by the State for achieving these interests unnecessarily impinge on the right to marry, the statute cannot be sustained.

"[As for the argument that the statute provides incentive for the applicant to make support payments to his children], with respect to [those] unable to meet the statutory requirements, the statute merely prevents the applicant from getting married, without delivering any money at all into the hands of the [children]. More importantly, [the] State already has numerous other means for exacting compliance with support obligations, means that are at least as effective as the instant statute's and yet do not impinge upon the right to marry [such as wage assignments, civil contempt proceedings and criminal penalties]."a

STEWART, J., who concurred in the judgment, rejected the view that the Wisconsin statute violated equal protection. As he saw it, "the problem in this case is not one of discriminating classifications, but of unwarranted encroachment upon a constitutionally protected freedom." He deemed the statute unconstitu-

---

12. The directness and substantiality of the interference with the freedom to marry distinguish the instant case from *Jobst.* In *Jobst* [applying the "rationality" standard of review] we upheld sections of the Social Security Act providing, inter alia, for termination of a dependent child's benefits upon marriage to an individual not entitled to benefits under the Act. As the opinion for the Court expressly noted, the rule terminating benefits upon marriage was not "an attempt to interfere with the individual's freedom to make a decision as important as marriage." The Social Security pro-

visions placed no direct legal obstacle in the path of persons desiring to get married, [and] there was no evidence that the laws significantly discouraged, let alone made "practically impossible," any marriages. Indeed, the provisions had not deterred the individual who challenged the statute from getting married, even though he and his wife were both disabled. * * *

a. Burger, C.J., joined the Court's opinion and briefly concurred.

tional "because it exceeds the bounds of permissible state regulation of marriage." He continued:

"I do not agree [that] there is a 'right to marry' in the constitutional sense. * * * Surely, for example, a State may legitimately say that no one can marry his or her sibling, that no one can marry who is not at least 14 years old, that no one can marry without first passing an examination for venereal disease, or that no one can marry who has a living husband or wife. But, just as surely, in regulating the intimate human relationship of marriage, there is a limit beyond which a State may not constitutionally go.

"[S]ome people simply cannot afford to meet the statute's financial requirements. To deny these people permission to marry penalizes them for failing to do that which they cannot do. Insofar as it applies to indigents, the state law is an irrational means of achieving these objectives of the State. As directed against either the indigent or the delinquent parent, the law is substantially more rational if viewed as a means of assuring the financial viability of future marriages. [But] the State's legitimate concern with the financial soundness of prospective marriages must stop short of telling people they may not marry because they are too poor or because they might persist in their financial irresponsibility. [A] legislative judgment so alien to our traditions and so offensive to our shared notions of fairness offends the Due Process Clause of the Fourteenth Amendment.

"[E]qual protection doctrine has become the Court's chief instrument for invalidating state laws. Yet, in a case like this one, the doctrine is no more than substantive due process by another name. [The] message of the Court's opinion is that Wisconsin may not use its control over marriage to achieve the objectives of the state statute. Such restrictions on basic governmental power are at the heart of substantive due process. The Court is understandably reluctant to rely on substantive due process. But to embrace the essence of that doctrine under the guise of equal protection serves no purpose but obfuscation."

POWELL, J., concurred in the judgment, but wrote separately "because the majority's rationale sweeps too broadly in an area which traditionally has been subject to state regulation": "The Court apparently would subject all state regulation which 'directly and substantially' interferes with the decision to marry in a traditional family setting to 'critical examination' or 'compelling state interest' analysis. Presumably, 'reasonable regulations that do not significantly interfere with decisions to enter into the marital relationship may legitimately be imposed.' The Court does not present, however, any principled means for distinguishing between the two types of regulations. Since state regulation in this area typically takes the form of a prerequisite or barrier to marriage or divorce, the degree of 'direct' interference with the decision to marry or to divorce is unlikely to provide either guidance for state legislatures or a basis for judicial oversight.

"[State] regulation has included bans on incest, bigamy, and homosexuality, as well as various preconditions to marriage, such as blood tests. Likewise, a showing of fault on the part of one of the partners traditionally has been a prerequisite to the dissolution of an unsuccessful union. A 'compelling state purpose' inquiry would cast doubt on the network of restrictions that the States have fashioned to govern marriage and divorce.

"[The] Wisconsin measure in this case does not pass muster under either due process or equal protection standards. [As for the state's 'collection device' justification, the] vice inheres [in] the failure to make provision for those without the means to comply with child-support obligations. [As for the state interest in preserving 'the ability of marriage applicants to support their prior issue by preventing them from incurring new obligations,' the law is] so grossly underinclusive with respect to this objective, given the many ways that additional financial obligations may be incurred by the applicant quite apart from a contemplated marriage, that the classification 'does not bear a fair and substantial relation to the object of the legislation.' "

STEVENS, J., concurred: "Under this statute, a person's economic status may determine his eligibility to enter into a lawful marriage. A noncustodial parent whose children are 'public charges' may not marry even if he has met his court-ordered obligations. Thus, within the class of parents who have fulfilled their court-ordered obligations, the rich may marry and the poor may not. This type of statutory discrimination is, I believe, totally unprecedented, as well as inconsistent with our tradition of administering justice equally to the rich and to the [poor.]"**b**

In TURNER v. SAFLEY, 482 U.S. 78 (1987), a unanimous Court, per O'CONNOR, J., ruled that the right to marry, deemed to be "a fundamental right" in *Loving* and *Zablocki*, remained so in the prison setting. Thus it struck down a prison regulation that permitted inmates to marry only when the prison superintendent gave approval for "compelling reasons 'such as pregnancy or birth of a child' ": "[Although the right to marry is subject to substantial restrictions as a result of incarceration,] [m]any important attributes of marriage remain [after] taking into account the limitations imposed by prison life. First, inmate marriages, like others, are expressions of emotional support and public commitment. [In] addition, many religions recognize marriage as having spiritual significance. Third, most inmates eventually will be released [and] therefore most inmate marriages are formed in the expectation that they ultimately will be fully consummated. Finally, marital status often is a pre-condition to the receipt of government benefits, property rights, [and] other, less tangible, benefits (e.g., legitimation of children born out of wedlock). [Taken together], these remaining elements are sufficient to form a constitutionally protected marital relationship in the prison context."

Notes

Non-parental visitation rights vs. rights of parents to make decisions concerning the care, custody, and control of their children. TROXEL v. GRANVILLE, 530 U.S. 57 (2000): A Washington statute permitted "[a]ny person" to petition for visitation rights "at any time" and authorized state superior courts to grant such rights whenever "visitation may serve the best interest of the child." The Troxels petitioned for the right to visit their deceased son's two daughters. Granville, sole surviving parent of the children, and a "fit custodial mother," did not oppose all visitation, but objected to the amount sought by the girls' grandparents (two weekends of overnight visitation per month and two weeks of visitation each summer). She asked the court to order one day of visitation per month with no overnight stay. The superior court ordered more visitation than Granville desired, and she appealed.

The Washington Supreme Court struck down the statute on its face for two reasons: (1) the Constitution permits a state to interfere with the rights of parents

b. Rehnquist, J., dissented, "view[ing] this legislative judgment in the light of the traditional presumption of validity, [just as] the traditional standard of review was applied in *Jobst,* despite the claim that the statute there in question burdened [the] right to marry." He concluded that the law, "despite its imperfections, is sufficiently rational to satisfy the demands of the Fourteenth Amendment."

to rear their children only to prevent harm or potential harm to a child and the statute fails that standard "because it recognizes no threshold showing of harm"; (2) by allowing "any person" to petition for forced visitation of a child at "any time," with the only requirement being that the visitation serve "the best interest of the child," the statute sweeps too broadly. The U.S. Supreme Court affirmed, but, as Stevens, J., dissenting, noted, it did not endorse either the holding or the reasoning of the state supreme court. There was no opinion of the Court. The principal opinion was written by O'CONNOR, J., joined by Rehnquist, C.J., and Ginsburg and Breyer, JJ. The plurality found the statute "as applied in this case" unconstitutional:

"The liberty interest at issue in this case—the interests of parents in the care, custody, and control of their children—is perhaps the oldest of the fundamental liberty interests recognized by this Court. [The Court then discussed *Meyer v. Nebraska*; *Pierce*; *Prince v. Massachusetts*; *Stanley v. Illinois*, 405 U.S. 645 (1972); *Wisconsin v. Yoder* (Ch. 8, Sec. 2, I); and *Quilloin*, infra.] In light of this extensive precedent, it cannot now be doubted that the Due Process Clause of the Fourteenth Amendment protects the fundamental right of parents to make decisions concerning the care, custody, and control of their children.

"[The Washington statute], as applied to Granville and her family in this case, unconstitutionally infringes on that fundamental parental right. [The statute] is breathtakingly broad. [Its] language effectively permits any third party seeking visitation to subject any decision by a parent concerning visitation of the parent's children to state-court review. Once [the] matter is placed before a judge, a parent's decision that visitation would not be in the child's best interest is accorded no deference. [The statute] places the best-interest determination solely in the hands of the judge. [Thus,] in practical effect, in the State of Washington, a court can disregard and overturn *any* decision by a fit custodial parent concerning visitation whenever a third party affected by the decision files a visitation petition, based solely on the judge's determination of the child's best interests.

"[The] combination of several factors here compels our conclusion that [the statute], as applied, exceeded the bounds of the Due Process Clause. First, the Troxels did not allege, and no court has found, that Granville was an unfit parent. That aspect of the case is important for there is a presumption that fit parents act in the best interests of their children. [The] problem here is [that the Superior Court] gave no special weight at all to Granville's determination of her daughters' best interests. [Indeed, the] judge's remarks indicate that he [i]n effect * * * placed on Granville, the fit custodial parent, the burden of *disproving* that visitation would be in the best interest of her daughters. [Finally,] we note that there is no allegation that Granville ever sought to cut off visitation entirely. Rather, the present dispute originated when Granville informed the Troxels that she would prefer to restrict their visitation with [the girls] to one short visit per month and special holidays.

"[The] Due Process Clause does not permit a State to infringe on the fundamental right of parents to make childrearing decisions simply because a state judge believes a 'better' decision could be made. Neither the Washington [statute] generally [nor] the Superior Court in this specific case required anything more. Accordingly, we hold that [the statute], as applied in this case, is unconstitutional."a

a. Souter, J., "concur[red] in the judgment affirming the decision of the Supreme Court of Washington, whose facial invalidation of its statute is consistent with the [U.S. Supreme Court's] prior cases addressing the substantive issues at stake."

Thomas, J., also concurred in the judgment, "agree[ing] with the plurality that the Court's

STEVENS, J., dissenting, maintained that the state supreme court "erred in its federal constitutional analysis because neither the provision granting 'any person' the right to petition the court for visitation nor the absence of a provision requiring a 'threshold [finding] of harm to the child' provides a sufficient basis for holding that the statute is invalid in all its applications." He "believe[d] that a facial challenge should fail whenever a statute has 'a plainly legitimate sweep.' Under the Washington statute, there are plainly any number of cases—indeed, one suspects, the most common to arise—in which the 'person' among 'any' seeking visitation is a once-custodial caregiver, an intimate relation, or even a genetic parent."

SCALIA, J., separately dissenting, thought it "entirely compatible with the commitment to representative democracy set forth in the founding documents to argue, in legislative chambers or in electoral campaigns, that the state has *no power* to interfere with parents' authority over the rearing of their children," but did "not believe that the power which the Constitution confers upon me *as a judge* entitles me to deny legal effect to laws that (in my view) infringe upon what is (in my view) that unenumerated right."

KENNEDY, J., wrote a third dissenting opinion. His "principal concern" was that the state court's holding "seems to proceed from the assumption that the parent or parents who resist visitation have always been the child's primary caregivers and that the third parties who seek visitation have no legitimate and established relationship with the child. That idea, in turn, appears influenced by the concept that the conventional nuclear family ought to establish the visitation standard for every domestic relations case. As we all know, this is simply not the structure or prevailing condition in many households. * * *

"Cases are sure to arise—perhaps a substantial number of cases—in which a third party, by acting in a caregiving role over a significant period of time, has developed a relationship with a child which is not necessarily subject to absolute parental veto. * * * Indeed, contemporary practice should give us some pause before rejecting the best interests of the child standard in all third-party visitation cases, as the Washington court has done. The standard has been recognized for many years as a basic tool of domestic relations law in visitation proceedings. [The third-party visitation statutes enacted by all 50 states] include a variety of methods for limiting parents' exposure to third-party visitation petitions and for ensuring parental decisions are given respect. Many States limit the identity of permissible petitioners by restricting visitation petitions to grandparents or by requiring petitioners to show a substantial relationship with a child, or both.''

Adoption and rights of the natural father. QUILLOIN v. WALCOTT, 434 U.S. 246 (1978): Under Georgia law, if the natural father has not "legitimated" his offspring (appellant had not sought to do so during the 11 years between the child's birth and the adoption petition), only the mother's consent is required for the adoption of the illegitimate child. When the child was 11, the mother consented to his adoption by her husband with whom she and her son were living. Appellant attempted to block the adoption, but did not seek custody or object to the child's continuing to live with his mother and stepfather. On the basis of various findings (e.g., appellant had provided support only on an irregular basis, the child himself expressed a desire to be adopted by his stepfather who was found

recognition of a fundamental right of parents to direct the upbringing of their children resolves this case. [Here,] the State of Washington lacks even a legitimate governmental interest—to say nothing of a compelling one—in second-guessing a fit parent's decision regarding visitation with third parties."

to be fit to adopt the child), the trial court concluded that the adoption would be in the "best interests of the child."

A unanimous Court, per MARSHALL, J., affirmed: "We have recognized on numerous occasions that the relationship between parent and child is constitutionally protected, e.g., *Wisconsin v. Yoder*; *Stanley v. Illinois*, [and] [w]e have little doubt that the Due Process Clause would be offended '[i]f a State were to attempt to force the breakup of a natural family, over the objection of the parents and their children, without some showing of unfitness and for the sole reason that to do so was thought to be in the children's best interests.' *Smith v. Organization of Foster Families*, 431 U.S. 816 (1977) (Stewart, J., concurring). But this is [a case where] the result of the adoption in this case is to give full recognition to a family unit already in existence, a result desired by all concerned, except appellant. [Under these circumstances it suffices that the state found] that the adoption, and denial of legitimation, was in the 'best interests of the child.'"

Civil commitment of children by their parents. In rejecting the argument that only a formal hearing prior to parents' commitment of their minor children to a mental institution could adequately protect a child's rights, *Parham v. J.R.*, 442 U.S. 584 (1979), per Burger, C.J., applied "the traditional presumption that the parents act in the best interests of the child." That some parents may act against the interests of the child some times "is hardly a reason to discard wholesale those pages of human experience that teach that parents generally do act in the child's best interests."

MICHAEL H. v. GERALD D.

491 U.S. 110, 109 S.Ct. 2333, 105 L.Ed.2d 91 (1989).

JUSTICE SCALIA announced the judgment of the Court and delivered an opinion in which the CHIEF JUSTICE joins, and in all but footnote 6 of which JUSTICE O'CONNOR and JUSTICE KENNEDY join.

[Claiming to be the father of Victoria, the child of Carole D. and Gerald D., a married couple, Michael H. brought an action in California to establish his paternity and visitation rights. Although Gerald was listed as the father on the birth certificate and has always claimed the child as her father, blood tests showed a 98.07% probability that Michael, with whom the mother had had an adulterous affair, was the father. During the first three years of the child's life, she and her mother resided at times with Michael, who held the child out as his own. During this time, mother and child also resided at times with another man and with Gerald. [Under California law, a child born to a married woman living with her husband, who is neither impotent nor sterile, is presumed to be a child of the marriage, a presumption that may be rebutted only in very limited circumstances. Relying on this presumption, the California courts rejected Michael's claims. The U.S. Supreme Court affirmed.]

Michael contends as a matter of substantive due process that because he has established a parental relationship with Victoria, protection of Gerald's and Carole's marital union is an insufficient state interest to support termination of that relationship. This argument is, of course, predicated on the assertion that Michael has a constitutionally protected liberty interest in his relationship with Victoria. [In] an attempt to limit and guide interpretation of the [Due Process] Clause, we have insisted not merely that the interest denominated as a "liberty" be "fundamental" (a concept that, in isolation, is hard to objectify), but also that it be an interest traditionally protected by our society.2 As we have put it, the Due Process Clause affords only those protections "so rooted in the traditions and conscience of our people as to be ranked as fundamental." * * *

This insistence that the asserted liberty interest be rooted in history and tradition is evident, [in] our cases according constitutional protection to certain parental rights. Michael [reads] *Stanley v. Illinois*, invalidating an irrebuttable statutory presumption that unwed fathers are unfit parents, and such subsequent cases as *Quilloin*], as establishing that a liberty interest is created by biological fatherhood plus an established parental relationship—factors that exist in the present case as well. [As] we view [these cases], they rest not upon such isolated factors but upon the historic respect—indeed, sanctity would not be too strong a term—traditionally accorded to the relationships that develop within the unitary family.

[Thus,] the legal issue in the present case reduces to whether the relationship between persons in the situation of Michael and Victoria has been treated as a protected family unit under the historic practices of our society, or whether on any other basis it has been accorded special protection. We think it impossible to find that it has. In fact, quite to the contrary, our traditions have protected the marital family (Gerald, Carole, and the child they acknowledge to be theirs) against the sort of claim Michael asserts.4

[What] Michael asserts here is a right to have himself declared the natural father *and thereby to obtain parental prerogatives*. What he must establish, therefore, is not that our society has traditionally allowed a natural father in his circumstances to establish paternity, but that it has traditionally accorded such a father parental rights, or at least has not traditionally denied them. [What] counts is whether the States in fact award substantive parental rights to the natural father of a child conceived within and born into an extant marital union that wishes to embrace the child. We are not aware of a single case, old or new, that has done so. This is not the stuff of which fundamental rights qualifying as liberty interests are made.6 * * *

2. We do not understand what Justice Brennan has in mind by an interest "that society traditionally has thought important [without] protecting it." The protection need not take the form of an explicit constitutional provision or statutory guarantee, but it must at least exclude (all that is necessary to decide the present case) a societal tradition of enacting laws *denying* the interest. Nor do we understand why our practice of limiting the Due Process Clause to traditionally protected interests turns the clause "into a redundancy." Its purpose is to prevent future generations from lightly casting aside important traditional values—not to enable this Court to invent new ones.

4. Justice Brennan insists that in determining whether a liberty interest exists we must look at Michael's relationship with Victoria in isolation, without reference to the circumstance that Victoria's mother was married to someone else when the child was conceived, and that that woman and her husband wish to raise the child as their own. We cannot imagine what compels this strange procedure of looking at the act which is assertedly the subject of a liberty interest in isolation from its effect upon other people—rather like inquiring whether there is a liberty interest in firing a gun where the case at hand happens to involve its discharge into another person's body. The logic of Justice Brennan's position leads to the conclusion that if Michael had begotten Victoria by rape, that fact would in no way affect his possession of a liberty interest in his relationship with her.

6. Justice Brennan criticizes our methodology in using historical traditions specifically relating to the rights of an adulterous natural father, rather than inquiring more generally "whether parenthood is an interest that historically has received our attention and protection." There seems to us no basis for the contention that this methodology is "nove[l]." For example, in *Bowers v. Hardwick* [infra], we noted that at the time the Fourteenth Amendment was ratified all but 5 of the 37 States had criminal sodomy laws, that all 50 of the States had such laws prior to 1961, and that 24 States and the District of Columbia continued to have them; and we concluded from that record, regarding that very specific aspect of sexual conduct, that "to claim that a right to engage in such conduct is 'deeply rooted in this Nation's history and tradition' or 'implicit in the con-

JUSTICE O'CONNOR, with whom JUSTICE KENNEDY joins, concurring in part.

I concur in all but footnote 6 of Justice Scalia's opinion. This footnote sketches a mode of historical analysis to be used when identifying liberty interests protected by the Due Process Clause of the Fourteenth Amendment that may be somewhat inconsistent with our past decisions in this area. See *Griswold*; *Eisenstadt*. On occasion the Court has characterized relevant traditions protecting asserted rights at levels of generality that might not be "the most specific level" available [quoting from fn. 6 of Justice Scalia's opinion]. See *Loving* [and] *Turner v. Safley*. I would not foreclose the unanticipated by the prior imposition of a single mode of historical analysis. *Poe* (Harlan, J., dissenting).a

JUSTICE BRENNAN, with whom JUSTICE MARSHALL and JUSTICE BLACKMUN join, dissenting. * * *

Once we recognized that the "liberty" protected by the Due Process Clause of the Fourteenth Amendment encompasses more than freedom from bodily restraint, today's plurality opinion emphasizes, the concept was cut loose from one natural limitation on its meaning. This innovation paved the way, so the plurality hints, for judges to substitute their own preferences for those of elected officials. Dissatisfied with this supposedly unbridled and uncertain state of affairs, the plurality casts about for another limitation on the concept of liberty.

It finds this limitation in "tradition." Apparently oblivious to the fact that this concept can be as malleable and as elusive as "liberty" itself, the plurality pretends that tradition places a discernible border around the Constitution. [Yet,] as Justice White observed in his dissent in *Moore v. East Cleveland:* "What the deeply rooted traditions of the country are is arguable." [Even] if we could agree, moreover, on the content and significance of particular traditions, we still would be forced to identify the point at which a tradition becomes firm enough to be relevant to our definition of liberty and the moment at which it becomes too obsolete to be relevant any longer. The plurality supplies no objective means by which we might make these determinations.

cept of ordered liberty' is, at best, facetious." In *Roe* we spent about a fifth of our opinion negating the proposition that there was a long-standing tradition of laws proscribing abortion.

We do not understand why, having rejected our focus upon the societal tradition regarding the natural father's rights vis-à-vis a child whose mother is married to another man, Justice Brennan would choose to focus instead upon "parenthood." Why should the relevant category not be even more general—perhaps "family relationships"; or "personal relationships"; or even "emotional attachments in general"? Though the dissent has no basis for the level of generality it would select, we do: We refer to the most specific level at which a relevant tradition protecting, or denying protection to, the asserted right can be identified. If, for example, there were no societal tradition, either way, regarding the rights of the natural father of a child adulterously conceived, we would have to consult, and (if possible) reason from, the traditions regarding natural fathers in general. But there is such a more specific tradition, and it unqualifiedly denies protection to such a parent.

[Because] general traditions provide such imprecise guidance, they permit judges to dic-

tate rather than discern the society's views. The need, if arbitrary decision-making is to be avoided, to adopt the most specific tradition as the point of reference—or at least to announce, as Justice Brennan declines to do, some other criterion for selecting among the innumerable relevant traditions that could be consulted—is well enough exemplified by the fact that in the present case Justice Brennan's opinion and Justice O'Connor's opinion, which disapproves this footnote, *both* appeal to tradition, but on the basis of the tradition they select reach opposite results. Although assuredly having the virtue (if it be that) of leaving judges free to decide as they think best when the unanticipated occurs, a rule of law that binds neither by text nor by any particular, identifiable tradition, is no rule of law at all. * * *

a. Stevens, J., who concurred in the judgment, was "willing to assume for the purpose of deciding this case that Michael's relationship with Victoria is strong enough to give him a constitutional right to try to convince a trial judge that Victoria's best interest would be served by granting him visitation rights. I am satisfied, however, that the California statute, as applied in this case, gave him that opportunity."

[The plurality] does not ask whether parenthood is an interest that historically has received our attention and protection; the answer to that question is too clear for dispute. Instead, the plurality asks whether the specific variety of parenthood under consideration—a natural father's relationship with a child whose mother is married to another man—has enjoyed such protection. If we had looked to tradition with such specificity in past cases, many a decision would have reached a different result. Surely the use of contraceptives by unmarried couples, *Eisenstadt;* or even by married couples, *Griswold;* [and] even the right to raise one's natural but illegitimate children, *Stanley v. Illinois,* were not "interest[s] traditionally protected by our society" at the time of their consideration by this Court.

[The] plurality's interpretive method is more than novel; it is misguided. It ignores the good reasons for limiting the role of "tradition" in interpreting the Constitution's deliberately capacious language. In the plurality's constitutional universe, we may not take notice of the fact that the original reasons for the conclusive presumption of paternity are out of place in a world in which blood tests can prove virtually beyond a shadow of a doubt who sired a particular child and in which the fact of illegitimacy no longer plays the burdensome and stigmatizing role it once did. [By] describing the decisive question as whether Michael and Victoria's interest is one that has been "traditionally *protected by* our society" (emphasis added), rather than one that society traditionally has thought important (with or without protecting it), and by suggesting that our sole function is to "*discern* the society's views," n. 6 (emphasis added), the plurality acts as if the only purpose of the Due Process Clause is to confirm the importance of interests already protected by a majority of the States. Transforming the protection afforded by the Due Process Clause into a redundancy mocks those who, with care and purpose, wrote the Fourteenth Amendment.

In construing the Fourteenth Amendment to offer shelter only to those interests specifically protected by historical practice, moreover, the plurality ignores the kind of society in which our Constitution exists. We are not an assimilative, homogeneous society, but a facilitative, pluralistic one, in which we must be willing to abide someone else's unfamiliar or even repellant practice because the same tolerant impulse protects our own idiosyncracies. Even if we can agree, therefore, that "family" and "parenthood" are part of the good life, it is absurd to assume that we can agree on the content of those terms and destructive to pretend that we do. In a community such as ours, "liberty" must include the freedom not to conform. The plurality today squashes this freedom by requiring specific approval from history before protecting anything in the name of liberty.

The document that the plurality construes today is unfamiliar to me. It is not the living charter that I have taken to be our Constitution; it is instead a stagnant, archaic, hidebound document steeped in the prejudices and superstitions of a time long past. * * *b

---

IMPORTANCE OF TRADITION WHEN IT COMES TO SUBSTANTIVE DUE PROCESS

---

b. White, J., also dissented.

DISTRICT ATTORNEY'S OFFICE v. OSBORNE

___ U.S. ___, 129 S.Ct. 2308, 174 L.Ed.2d 38 (2009)

CHIEF JUSTICE ROBERTS delivered the opinion of the Court.

[In 1993, respondent Osborne was convicted of kidnapping and sexual assault. He claimed that at trial he had asked his attorney to seek DNA testing of biological evidence on a condom found at the scene of the crime, but she refused for various reasons, including her belief her client was guilty and that further testing would do more harm than good. There was considerable evidence of Osborne's guilt. Moreover, he confessed to the parole board, which released him after 14 years. Osborne subsequently claimed he lied to the parole board because he hoped his lie would lead to a quicker release. Osborne was recently rearrested for another crime and the state petitioned to revoke his parole.

[Osborne asked the Alaska Court of Appeals to provide the DNA testing at his own expense. The court denied relief, relying heavily on the fact that Osborne had confessed to some of his crimes in an application for parole. Osborne also brought a federal § 1983 action claiming that the Due Process Clause entitled him to a form of DNA testing more discriminating than the methods available at the time of his trial.]

DNA testing has an unparalleled ability to exonerate the wrongly convicted and to identify the guilty.a [The] Federal Government and the States have recognized this, and have developed special approaches to ensure that this evidentiary tool can be effectively incorporated into established criminal procedure–usually but not always through legislation.

Against this prompt and considered response, [respondent] would take the development [in] this area out of the hands of legislatures and state courts shaping policy in a focused manner and turn it over to federal courts applying the broad parameters of the Due Process Clause. There is no reason to constitutionalize the issue in this way. * * *

Forty-six States have already enacted statutes dealing specifically with access to DNA evidence. [The] Federal Government has also passed the Innocence Protection Act of 2004, which allows federal prisoners to move for court-ordered DNA testing under certain specified conditions. That Act also grants money to States that enact comparable statutes. * * *

Alaska is one of a handful of States yet to enact legislation [but] Alaska courts are addressing how to apply existing laws for discovery and postconviction relief to this novel technology. [Osborne] argues that access to the State's evidence is a "process" needed to vindicate his right to prove himself innocent and get out of jail. Process is not an end in itself, so a necessary premise of this argument is that he has an entitlement (what our precedents call a "liberty interest") to prove his innocence even after a fair trial has proved otherwise. We must first examine this asserted liberty interest to determine what process (if any) is due.

Osborne [does] have a liberty interest in demonstrating his innocence with new evidence under state law. As explained, Alaska law provides that those who use "newly discovered evidence" to "establis[h] by clear and convincing evidence that [they are] innocent" may obtain "vacation of [their] conviction or sentence in

---

a. According to the Innocence Project at Cardozo Law School, which represented respondent, DNA testing has played a role in 240 exonerations and in 103 of those cases the testing also identified the actual perpetrator. Adam Liptak, *Court Rejects Inmate Rights to DNA Tests*, N.Y. Times, June 19, 2009, p.1.

the interest of justice." This "state-created right can, in some circumstances, beget yet other rights to procedures essential to the realization of the parent right."

The Court of Appeals went too far, however, in concluding that the Due Process Clause requires that certain familiar preconviction trial rights be extended to protect Osborne's postconviction liberty interest. * * *

A criminal defendant proved guilty after a fair trial does not have the same liberty interests as a free man. At trial, the defendant is presumed innocent and may demand that the government prove its case beyond reasonable doubt. But "[o]nce a defendant has been afforded a fair trial and convicted of the offense for which he was charged, the presumption of innocence disappears."

[We] see nothing inadequate about the procedures Alaska has provided to vindicate its state right to postconviction relief in general, and nothing inadequate about how those procedures apply to those who seek access to DNA evidence. Alaska provides a substantive right to be released on a sufficiently compelling showing of new evidence that establishes innocence. It exempts such claims from otherwise applicable time limits.

[Osborne] asks that we recognize a freestanding right to DNA evidence untethered from the liberty interests he hopes to vindicate with it. We reject the invitation and conclude, in the circumstances of this case, that there is no such substantive due process right. "As a general matter, the Court has always been reluctant to expand the concept of substantive due process because guideposts for responsible decisionmaking in this unchartered area are scarce and open-ended." Osborne seeks access to state evidence so that he can apply new DNA-testing technology that might prove him innocent. There is no long history of such a right, and "[t]he mere novelty of such a claim is reason enough to doubt that 'substantive due process' sustains it."

And there are further reasons to doubt. The elected governments of the States are actively confronting the challenges DNA technology poses to our criminal justice systems and our traditional notions of finality, as well as the opportunities it affords. To suddenly constitutionalize this area would short-circuit what looks to be a prompt and considered legislative response. * * * "By extending constitutional protection to an asserted right or liberty interest, we, to a great extent, place the matter outside the arena of public debate and legislative action. We must therefore exercise the utmost care whenever we are asked to break new ground in this field." [*Glucksberg*, infra] We are reluctant to enlist the Federal Judiciary in creating a new constitutional code of rules for handling DNA. * * *

DNA evidence will undoubtedly lead to changes in the criminal justice system. It has done so already. The question is whether further change will primarily be made by legislative revision and judicial interpretation of the existing system, or whether the Federal Judiciary must leap ahead–revising (or even discarding) the system by creating a new constitutional right and taking over responsibility for refining it. * * * Federal courts should not presume that state criminal procedure will be inadequate to deal with technological change. * * *[b]

JUSTICE STEVENS, with whom JUSTICE GINSBURG and JUSTICE BREYER join, and with whom JUSTICE SOUTER joins as to Part I, dissenting. * * *

---

    b. Alito, J's concurring opinion, joined by   omitted.
Kennedy and Thomas, JJ. (as to Part II), is

I

[Osborne] first anchors his due process right in [Alaska's postconviction statute]. Although States are under no obligation to provide mechanisms for postconviction relief, when they choose to do so, the procedures they employ must comport with the demands of the Due Process Clause by providing litigants with fair opportunity to assert their state-created rights.

[Osborne] made full use of available state procedures in his efforts to secure access to evidence for DNA testing so that he might avail himself of the postconviction relief afforded by the State of Alaska. He was rebuffed at every turn. The manner in which the Alaska courts applied state law in this case leaves me in grave doubt about the adequacy of the procedural protections afforded to litigants under [the state's postconviction statute].

II

[Whether] framed as a "substantive liberty interest [protected] through a procedural due process right" to have evidence made available for testing, or as a substantive due process right to be free of arbitrary government action, the result is the same: On the record now before us, Osborne has established his entitlement to test the State's evidence.

The liberty protected by the Due Process Clause is not a creation of the Bill of Rights. Indeed, our Nation has long recognized that the liberty safeguarded by the Constitution has far deeper roots. [The] "most elemental" of the liberties protected by the Due Process Clause is "the interest in being free from physical detention by one's own government." *Hamdi v. Rumsfeld*, (plurality opinion) [Ch. 3, Sec. 1, III]. Our cases have recognized [that] the Due Process Clause of the Fourteenth Amendment requires States to respect certain fundamental liberties in the postconviction context. * * *

[If] the right Osborne seeks to vindicate is framed as purely substantive, the proper result is no less clear. "The touchstone of due process is protection of the individual against arbitrary action of government." When government action is so lacking in justification that it "can properly be characterized as arbitrary, or conscience shocking, in a constitutional sense," it violates the Due Process Clause. [The] arbitrariness of the State's conduct is highlighted by comparison to the private interests it denies. It seems to me obvious that if a wrongly convicted person were to produce proof of his actual innocence, no state interest would be sufficient to justify his continued punitive detention. If such proof can be readily obtained without imposing a significant burden on the State, a refusal to provide access to such evidence is wholly unjustified.

[In] this case, the State has suggested no countervailing interest that justifies its refusal to allow Osborne to test the evidence in its possession and has not provided any other nonarbitrary explanation for its conduct. * * *

JUSTICE SOUTER, dissenting.

I respectfully dissent on the ground that Alaska has failed to provide the effective procedure required by the Fourteenth Amendment for vindicating the liberty interest in demonstrating innocence that the state law recognizes. I therefore join Part I of Justice Stevens's dissenting opinion [and] would not decide Osborne's broad claim that the Fourteenth Amendment's guarantee of due process requires our recognition at this time of a substantive right of access to biological evidence for DNA analysis and comparison. [My] choice to decide this case on that procedural ground should not, therefore, be taken either as expressing skepticism that a new substantive right to test should be cognizable in some circumstances, or as implying agreement with the Court that it would necessarily be premature for the Judicial Branch to decide whether such a general right should be recognized.

There is no denying that the Court is correct when it notes that a claim of right to DNA testing, post-trial at that, is a novel one, but that only reflects the relative novelty of testing DNA, and in any event is not a sufficient reason alone to reject the right asserted. Tradition is of course one serious consideration in judging whether a challenged rule or practice, or the failure to provide a new one, should be seen as violating the guarantee of substantive due process as being arbitrary, or as falling wholly outside the realm of reasonable governmental action. See *Poe v. Ullman* (Harlan, J., dissenting). [A]s Justice Harlan pointed out, society finds reasons to modify some of its traditional practices and the accumulation of new empirical knowledge can turn yesterday's reasonable range of the government's options into a due process anomaly over time. * * *

Changes in societal understanding of the fundamental reasonableness of government actions work out in much the same way that individuals reconsider issues of fundamental belief. We can change our own inherited views just so fast, and a person is not labeled a stick-in-the-mud for refusing to endorse a new moral claim without having some time to work through it intellectually and emotionally. Just as attachment to the familiar and the limits of experience affect the capacity of an individual to see the potential legitimacy of a moral position, the broader society needs the chance to take part in the dialectic of public and political back and forth about a new liberty claim before it makes sense to declare unsympathetic state or national laws arbitrary to the point of being unconstitutional. The time required is a matter for judgment depending on the issue involved, but the need for some time to pass before a court entertains a substantive due process claim on the subject is not merely the requirement of judicial restraint as a general approach, but a doctrinal demand to be satisfied before an allegedly lagging legal regime can be held to lie beyond the discretion of reason able political judgment.

Despite my agreement with the Court on this importance of timing, though, I do not think that the doctrinal requirement necessarily stands in the way of any substantive due process consideration of a postconviction right to DNA testing, even as a right that is freestanding. Given the pace at which DNA testing has come to be recognized as potentially dispositive in many cases with biological evidence, there is no obvious argument that considering DNA testing at a general level would subject wholly intransigent legal systems to substantive due process review prematurely. But, as I said, there is no such issue before us, for Alaska does not flatly deny access to evidence for DNA testing in postconviction cases. * * *

Standing alone, the inadequacy of each of the State's reasons for denying Osborne access to the DNA evidence he seeks would not make out a due process violation. But taken as a whole the record convinces me that, while Alaska has created an entitlement of access to DNA evidence under conditions that are facially reasonable, the State has demonstrated a combination of inattentiveness and intransigence in applying those conditions that add up to procedural unfairness that violates the Due Process Clause.

IS THERE A "RIGHT TO DIE"? A RIGHT TO PHYSICIAN–ASSISTED SUICIDE? A RIGHT TO DETERMINE THE TIME AND MANNER OF ONE'S DEATH?

WASHINGTON v. GLUCKSBERG

521 U.S. 702, 117 S.Ct. 2258, 138 L.Ed.2d 772 (1997).

CHIEF JUSTICE REHNQUIST delivered the opinion of the Court.

The question presented in this case is whether Washington's prohibition against "caus[ing]" or "aid[ing]" a suicide offends the Fourteenth Amendment to the United States Constitution. We hold that it does not.

[Respondents, four physicians who declare they would assist terminally ill, suffering patients in ending their lives if not for Washington's assisted-suicide ban, and Compassion in Dying, a nonprofit organization that counsels people considering physician-assisted suicide, sought a declaration that Washington's statute is, on its face, unconstitutional. They asserted "the existence of a liberty interest protected by the Fourteenth Amendment which extends to a personal choice by a mentally competent, terminally ill adult to commit physician-assisted suicide." They relied primarily on *Casey* and *Cruzan v. Director, Missouri Dep't of Health*, 497 U.S. 261 (1990). The *Cruzan* case involved a woman (Nancy Beth Cruzan) who had been in a persistent vegetative state for many years and had virtually no chance of regaining her cognitive faculties. She was being kept alive by means of a gastrostomy tube (a feeding and hydration tube inserted into her stomach). When Nancy's parents sought to discontinue the tubal feeding, but were rebuffed by officials of the state hospital where Nancy was a patient, they turned to the courts. The state supreme court ruled that, in the absence of a "living will," they had to show "clear and convincing" evidence of Nancy's wish to be free of life support and that they had failed to do so. The U.S. Supreme Court affirmed 5–4, per Rehnquist, C.J., but assumed for purposes of the case that a *competent* person would have "a constitutionally protected right to refuse lifesaving hydration and nutrition."]

We begin, as we do in all due-process cases, by examining our Nation's history, legal traditions, and practices. In almost every State—indeed, in almost every western democracy—it is a crime to assist a suicide. The States' assisted-suicide bans are not innovations. Rather, they are longstanding expressions of the States' commitment to the protection and preservation of all human life. * * * Indeed, opposition to and condemnation of suicide—and, therefore, of assisting suicide—are consistent and enduring themes of our philosophical, legal, and cultural heritages. More specifically, for over 700 years, the Anglo–American common-law tradition has punished or otherwise disapproved of both suicide and assisting suicide.

[For] the most part, the early American colonies adopted the common-law approach. [Over] time, however, [the] colonies abolished [the] harsh common-law penalties [such as forfeiture of the suicide's property. However,] the movement away from the common law's harsh sanctions did not represent an acceptance of homicide, [but] reflected the growing consensus that it was unfair to punish the suicide's family for his wrongdoing.

[That] suicide remained a grievous, though nonfelonious, wrong is confirmed by the fact that colonial and early state legislatures and courts did not retreat from prohibiting assisting suicide. [And] the prohibitions against assisted suicide never contained exceptions for those who were near death. [In] this century, the [American Law Institute's] Model Penal Code also prohibited "aiding" suicide, prompting many States to enact or revise their assisted-suicide bans. The Code's drafters observed that "the interests in the sanctity of life that are represented by the criminal homicide laws are threatened by one who expresses a willingness to participate in taking the life of another, even though the act may be accomplished with the consent, or at the request, of the suicide victim."

Though deeply rooted, the States' assisted-suicide bans have in recent years been reexamined and, generally, reaffirmed. Because of advances in medicine and technology, Americans today are increasingly likely to die in institutions, from chronic illnesses. Public concern and democratic action are therefore sharply focused on how best to protect dignity and independence at the end of life, with the result that there have been many significant changes in state laws and in the attitudes these laws reflect. Many States, for example, now permit "living wills," surrogate health-care decisionmaking, and the withdrawal or refusal of life-sustaining medical treatment. At the same time, however, voters and legislators continue for the most part to reaffirm their States' prohibitions on assisting suicide.

The Washington statute at issue in this case was enacted in 1975 as part of a revision of that State's criminal code. Four years later, Washington passed its Natural Death Act, which specifically stated that the "withholding or withdrawal of life-sustaining treatment [shall] not, for any purpose, constitute a suicide" and that "[n]othing in this chapter shall be construed to condone, authorize, or approve mercy killing * * *." In 1991, Washington voters rejected a ballot initiative which, had it passed, would have permitted a form of physician-assisted suicide. Washington then added a provision to the Natural Death Act expressly excluding physician-assisted suicide.

California voters rejected an assisted-suicide initiative similar to Washington's in 1993. On the other hand, in 1994, voters in Oregon enacted, also through ballot initiative, that State's "Death With Dignity Act," which legalized physician-assisted suicide for competent, terminally ill adults. Since the Oregon vote, many proposals to legalize assisted-suicide have been and continue to be introduced in the States' legislatures, but none has been enacted. * * *

Thus, the States are currently engaged in serious, thoughtful examinations of physician-assisted suicide and other similar issues. For example, New York State's Task Force on Life and the Law—an ongoing, blue-ribbon commission composed of doctors, ethicists, lawyers, religious leaders, and interested laymen—was convened in 1984 and commissioned with "a broad mandate to recommend public policy on issues raised by medical advances." [After] studying physician-assisted suicide, however, the Task Force unanimously concluded that "[l]egalizing assisted suicide and euthanasia would pose profound risks to many individuals who are ill and vulnerable. [T]he potential dangers of this dramatic change in public policy would outweigh any benefit that might be achieved."

[The] Due Process Clause guarantees more than fair process, and the "liberty" it protects includes more than the absence of physical restraint. [The] Clause also provides heightened protection against government interference with certain fundamental rights and liberty interests. [We] have also assumed, and strongly suggested, that the Due Process Clause protects the traditional right to refuse unwanted lifesaving medical treatment. *Cruzan.*

But we "ha[ve] always been reluctant to expand the concept of substantive due process because guideposts for responsible decisionmaking in this unchartered area are scarce and open-ended." By extending constitutional protection to an asserted right or liberty interest, we, to a great extent, place the matter outside the arena of public debate and legislative action. We must therefore "exercise the utmost care whenever we are asked to break new ground in this field," lest the liberty protected by the Due Process Clause be subtly transformed into the policy preferences of the members of this Court.

Our established method of substantive-due-process analysis has two primary features: First, we have regularly observed that the Due Process Clause specially protects those fundamental rights and liberties which are, objectively, "deeply rooted in this Nation's history and tradition." * * * Second, we have required in substantive-due-process cases a "careful description" of the asserted fundamental liberty interest. * * *

Justice Souter, relying on Justice Harlan's dissenting opinion in *Poe v. Ullman*, would largely abandon this restrained methodology, and instead ask "whether [Washington's] statute sets up one of those 'arbitrary impositions' or 'purposeless restraints' at odds with the Due Process Clause of the Fourteenth Amendment."[17] In our view, however, the development of this Court's substantive-due-process jurisprudence, described briefly above, has been a process whereby the outlines of the "liberty" specially protected by the Fourteenth Amendment—never fully clarified, to be sure, and perhaps not capable of being fully clarified—have at least been carefully refined by concrete examples involving fundamental rights found to be deeply rooted in our legal tradition. This approach tends to rein in the subjective elements that are necessarily present in due-process judicial review. In addition, by establishing a threshold requirement—that a challenged state action implicate a fundamental right—before requiring more than a reasonable relation to a legitimate state interest to justify the action, it avoids the need for complex balancing of competing interests in every case.

"[We] have a tradition of carefully formulating the interest at stake in substantive-due-process cases. For example, although *Cruzan* is often described as a "right to die" case, we were, in fact, more precise: we assumed that the Constitution granted competent persons a "constitutionally protected right to refuse lifesaving hydration and nutrition." [The] Washington statute at issue in this case prohibits "aid[ing] another person to attempt suicide" and, thus, the question before us is whether the "liberty" specially protected by the Due Process Clause includes a right to commit suicide which itself includes a right to assistance in doing so.

We now inquire whether this asserted right has any place in our Nation's traditions. [Here,] we are confronted with a consistent and almost universal tradition that has long rejected the asserted right, and continues explicitly to reject it today, even for terminally ill, mentally competent adults. To hold for respondents, we would have to reverse centuries of legal doctrine and practice, and strike down the considered policy choice of almost every State.

[Respondents] contend that in *Cruzan* we "acknowledged that competent, dying persons have the right to direct the removal of life-sustaining medical treatment and thus hasten death" and that "the constitutional principle behind recognizing the patient's liberty to direct the withdrawal of artificial life support applies at least as strongly to the choice to hasten impending death by consuming lethal medication." [The] right assumed in *Cruzan*, however, was not simply deduced from abstract concepts of personal autonomy. Given the common-law rule

17. In Justice Souter's opinion, Justice Harlan's *Poe* dissent supplies the "modern justification" for substantive-due-process review. But although Justice Harlan's opinion has often been cited in due-process cases, we have never abandoned our fundamental-rights-based analytical method. Just four Terms ago, six of the Justices now sitting joined the Court's opinion in *Reno v. Flores*, 507 U.S. 292 (1993); *Poe* was not even cited. And in *Cruzan*, neither the Court's nor the concurring opinions relied on *Poe*; rather, we concluded that the right to refuse unwanted medical treatment was so rooted in our history, tradition, and practice as to require special protection under the Fourteenth Amendment. True, the Court relied on Justice Harlan's dissent in *Casey*, but, as *Flores* demonstrates, we did not in so doing jettison our established approach. Indeed, to read such a radical move into the Court's opinion in *Casey* would seem to fly in the face of that opinion's emphasis on stare decisis.

that forced medication was a battery, and the long legal tradition protecting the decision to refuse unwanted medical treatment, our assumption was entirely consistent with this Nation's history and constitutional traditions. The decision to commit suicide with the assistance of another may be just as personal and profound as the decision to refuse unwanted medical treatment, but it has never enjoyed similar legal protection. Indeed, the two acts are widely and reasonably regarded as quite distinct. In *Cruzan* itself, we recognized that most States outlawed assisted suicide—and even more do today—and we certainly gave no intimation that the right to refuse unwanted medical treatment could be somehow transmuted into a right to assistance in committing suicide.

Respondents also rely on *Casey*. [The] Court of Appeals, like the District Court, found *Casey* " 'highly instructive' " and " 'almost prescriptive' " for determining " 'what liberty interest may inhere in a terminally ill person's choice to commit suicide' " * * *. Similarly, respondents emphasize the statement in *Casey* that: "At the heart of liberty is the right to define one's own concept of existence, of meaning, of the universe, and of the mystery of human life. Beliefs about these matters could not define the attributes of personhood were they formed under compulsion of the State."

By choosing this language, the Court's opinion in *Casey* described, in a general way and in light of our prior cases, those personal activities and decisions that this Court has identified as so deeply rooted in our history and traditions, or so fundamental to our concept of constitutionally ordered liberty, that they are protected by the Fourteenth Amendment. [That] many of the rights and liberties protected by the Due Process Clause sound in personal autonomy does not warrant the sweeping conclusion that any and all important, intimate, and personal decisions are so protected, and *Casey* did not suggest otherwise.

The history of the law's treatment of assisted suicide in this country has been and continues to be one of the rejection of nearly all efforts to permit it. That being the case, our decisions lead us to conclude that the asserted "right" to assistance in committing suicide is not a fundamental liberty interest protected by the Due Process Clause. The Constitution also requires, however, that Washington's assisted-suicide ban be rationally related to legitimate government interests. This requirement is unquestionably met here. As the court below recognized, Washington's assisted-suicide ban implicates a number of state interests.

First, Washington has an "unqualified interest in the preservation of human life." *Cruzan*. The State's prohibition on assisted suicide, like all homicide laws, both reflects and advances its commitment to this interest.

[The] Court of Appeals also recognized Washington's interest in protecting life, but held that the "weight" of this interest depends on the "medical condition and the wishes of the person whose life is at stake." Washington, however, has rejected this sliding-scale approach and, through its assisted-suicide ban, insists that all persons' lives, from beginning to end, regardless of physical or mental condition, are under the full protection of the law. [As] we have previously affirmed, the States "may properly decline to make judgments about the 'quality' of life that a particular individual may enjoy," *Cruzan*. This remains true, as *Cruzan* makes clear, even for those who are near death.

Relatedly, all admit that suicide is a serious public-health problem, especially among persons in otherwise vulnerable groups. [Those] who attempt suicide—terminally ill or not—often suffer from depression or other mental disorders. [But research indicates] that many people who request physician-assisted suicide withdraw that request if their depression and pain are treated. The New York Task Force, however, expressed its concern that, because depression is difficult to diagnose, physicians and medical professionals often fail to respond adequately to seriously ill patients' needs. Thus, legal physician-assisted suicide could make it more difficult for the State to protect depressed or mentally ill persons, or those who are suffering from untreated pain, from suicidal impulses.

The State also has an interest in protecting the integrity and ethics of the medical profession. [The] American Medical Association, like many other medical and physicians' groups, has concluded that "[p]hysician-assisted suicide is fundamentally incompatible with the physician's role as healer." [And] physician-assisted suicide could, it is argued, undermine the trust that is essential to the doctor-patient relationship by blurring the time-honored line between healing and harming.

[Next,] the State has an interest in protecting vulnerable groups—including the poor, the elderly, and disabled persons—from abuse, neglect, and mistakes. The Court of Appeals dismissed [this] concern, [but we] have recognized [the] real risk of subtle coercion and undue influence in end-of-life situations. *Cruzan.* Similarly, the New York Task Force warned that "[l]egalizing physician-assisted suicide would pose profound risks to many individuals who are ill and vulnerable. [The] risk of harm is greatest for the many individuals in our society whose autonomy and well-being are already compromised by poverty, lack of access to good medical care, advanced age, or membership in a stigmatized social group." [If] physician-assisted suicide were permitted, many might resort to it to spare their families the substantial financial burden of end-of-life health-care costs. The State's interest here goes beyond protecting the vulnerable from coercion; it extends to protecting disabled and terminally ill people from prejudice, negative and inaccurate stereotypes, and "societal indifference."

[Finally,] the State may fear that permitting assisted suicide will start it down the path to voluntary and perhaps even involuntary euthanasia. [The] Court of Appeal's decision, and its expansive reasoning, provide ample support for the State's concerns.23 [This] concern is further supported by evidence about the practice of euthanasia in the Netherlands. The Dutch government's own [1990 study] suggests that, despite the existence of various reporting procedures, euthanasia in the Netherlands has not been limited to competent, terminally ill adults who are enduring physical suffering, and that regulation of the practice may not have prevented abuses in cases involving vulnerable persons, including severely disabled neonates and elderly persons suffering from dementia. * * * Washington, like most other States, reasonably ensures against this risk by banning, rather than regulating, assisting suicide.

We need not weigh exactly the relative strengths of these various interests. They are unquestionably important and legitimate, and Washington's ban on assisted suicide is at least reasonably related to their promotion and protection. We therefore hold that [the challenged Washington statute] does not violate the Fourteenth Amendment, either on its face or "as applied to competent, terminally

23. Justice Souter concludes that "[t]he case for the slippery slope is fairly made out here, not because recognizing one due process right would leave a court with no principled basis to avoid recognizing another, but because there is a plausible case that the right claimed would not be readily containable by reference to facts about the mind that are matters of difficult judgment, or by gatekeepers who are subject to temptation, noble or not." We agree that the case for a slippery slope has been made out, [but] we also recognize the reasonableness of the widely expressed skepticism about the lack of a principled basis for confining the right. See Brief for United States as Amicus Curiae ("Once a legislature abandons a categorical prohibition against physician-assisted suicide, there is no obvious stopping point) * * *.

ill adults who wish to hasten their deaths by obtaining medication prescribed by their doctors."24 * * *

Throughout the Nation, Americans are engaged in an earnest and profound debate about the morality, legality, and practicality of physician-assisted suicide. Our holding permits this debate to continue, as it should in a democratic society. * * *

JUSTICE O'CONNOR, concurring.*

[The] Court frames the issue in this case as whether the Due Process Clause of the Constitution protects a "right to commit suicide which itself includes a right to assistance in doing so," and concludes that our Nation's history, legal traditions, and practices do not support the existence of such a right. I join the Court's opinions because I agree that there is no generalized right to "commit suicide." But respondents urge us to address the narrower question whether a mentally competent person who is experiencing great suffering has a constitutionally cognizable interest in controlling the circumstances of his or her imminent death. I see no need to reach that question in the context of the facial challenges to the New York and Washington laws at issue here. [The] parties and *amici* agree that in these States a patient who is suffering from a terminal illness and who is experiencing great pain has no legal barriers to obtaining medication, from qualified physicians, to alleviate that suffering, even to the point of causing unconsciousness and hastening death. In this light, even assuming that we would recognize such an interest, I agree that the State's interests in protecting those who are not truly competent or facing imminent death, or those whose decisions to hasten death would not truly be voluntary, are sufficiently weighty to justify a prohibition against physician-assisted suicide.

Every one of us at some point may be affected by our own or a family member's terminal illness. There is no reason to think the democratic process will not strike the proper balance between the interests of terminally ill, mentally competent individuals who would seek to end their suffering and the State's interests in protecting those who might seek to end life mistakenly or under pressure.

[In] sum, there is no need to address the question whether suffering patients have a constitutionally cognizable interest in obtaining relief from the suffering that they may experience in the last days of their lives. There is no dispute that dying patients in Washington and New York can obtain palliative care, even when doing so would hasten their deaths. The difficulty in defining terminal illness and the risk that a dying patient's request for assistance in ending his or her life might not be truly voluntary justifies the prohibitions on assisted suicide we uphold here.

---

24. Justice Stevens states that "the Court does conceive of respondents' claim as a facial challenge—addressing not the application of the statute to a particular set of plaintiffs before it, but the constitutionality of the statute's categorical prohibition...." We emphasize that we today reject the Court of Appeals' specific holding that the statute is unconstitutional "as applied" to a particular class. Justice Stevens agrees with this holding, but would not "foreclose the possibility that an individual plaintiff seeking to hasten her death, or a doctor whose assistance was sought, could prevail in a more particularized challenge." Our opinion does not absolutely foreclose such a claim. However, given our holding that the Due Process Clause of the Fourteenth Amendment does not provide heightened protection to the asserted liberty interest in ending one's life with a physician's assistance, such a claim would have to be quite different from the ones advanced by respondents here.

* Justice Ginsberg concurs in the Court's judgments substantially for the reasons stated in this opinion. Justice Breyer joins this opinion except insofar as it joins the opinion of the Court.

[O'Connor, J.'s opinion also constitutes her concurring opinion in the companion case of *Vacco v. Quill.*]

J USTICE S TEVENS, concurring in the judgments.a

[Today,] the Court decides that Washington's statute prohibiting assisted suicide is not invalid "on its face," that is to say, in all or most cases in which it might be applied. That holding, however, does not foreclose the possibility that some applications of the statute might well be invalid. * * *

[The *Cruzan* Court] assumed that the interest in liberty protected by the Fourteenth Amendment encompassed the right of a terminally ill patient to direct the withdrawal of life-sustaining treatment. [That] assumption [was] supported by the common-law tradition protecting the individual's general right to refuse unwanted medical treatment. [However,] [g]iven the irreversible nature of her illness and the progressive character of her suffering, Nancy Cruzan's interest in refusing medical care was incidental to her more basic interest in controlling the manner and timing of her death. * * * I insist that the source of Nancy Cruzan's right to refuse treatment was not just a common-law rule. Rather, this right is an aspect of a far broader and more basic concept of freedom that is even older than the common law. This freedom embraces, not merely a person's right to refuse a particular kind of unwanted treatment, but also her interest in dignity, and in determining the character of the memories that will survive long after her death.

[Thus,] the common-law right to protection from battery, which included the right to reject medical treatment in most circumstances, did not mark "the outer limits of the substantive sphere of liberty" that supported the Cruzan family's decision to hasten Nancy's death. *Casey.* [Whatever] the outer limits of the concept may be, it definitely includes protection for matters "central to personal dignity and autonomy." *Casey.*

[The] *Cruzan* case demonstrated that some state intrusions on the right to decide how death will be encountered are also intolerable. The now-deceased plaintiffs in this action may in fact have had a liberty interest even stronger than Nancy Cruzan's because, not only were they terminally ill, they were suffering constant and severe pain. Avoiding intolerable pain and the indignity of living one's final days incapacitated and in agony is certainly "[a]t the heart of [the] liberty [to] define one's own concept of existence, of meaning, of the universe, and of the mystery of human life."

[Although] there is no absolute right to physician-assisted suicide, *Cruzan* makes it clear that some individuals who no longer have the option of deciding whether to live or to die because they are already on the threshold of death have a constitutionally protected interest that may outweigh the State's interest in preserving life at all costs. The liberty interest at stake in a case like this differs from, and is stronger than, both the common-law right to refuse medical treatment and the unbridled interest in deciding whether to live or die. It is an interest in deciding how, rather than whether, a critical threshold shall be crossed.

The state interests supporting a general rule banning the practice of physician-assisted suicide do not have the same force in all cases. First and foremost of these interests is the " 'unqualified interest in the preservation of human life,' " which is equated with " 'the sanctity of life' " * * *. Properly viewed, however, this interest is not a collective interest that should always outweigh the interests of a person who because of pain, incapacity, or sedation finds her life intolerable, but rather, an aspect of individual freedom.

[Allowing] the individual, rather than the State, to make judgments " 'about the 'quality' of life that a particular individual may enjoy' " does not mean that the lives of terminally-ill, disabled people have less value than the lives of those

a. This opinion also constitutes Stevens, J.'s concurring opinion in *Vacco v. Quill*, infra.

who are healthy. Rather, it gives proper recognition to the individual's interest in choosing a final chapter that accords with her life story, rather than one that demeans her values and poisons memories of her. See Brief for Bioethicists as Amici Curiae; see also Ronald Dworkin, *Life's Dominion* 213 (1993). * * *

Similarly, the State's legitimate interests in preventing suicide, protecting the vulnerable from coercion and abuse, and preventing euthanasia are less significant in this context. [The] State's legitimate interest in preventing abuse does not apply to an individual who is not victimized by abuse, who is not suffering from depression, and who makes a rational and voluntary decision to seek assistance in dying. * * * Encouraging the development and ensuring the availability of adequate pain treatment is of utmost importance; palliative care, however, cannot alleviate all pain and suffering. [An] individual adequately informed of the care alternatives thus might make a rational choice for assisted suicide. For such an individual, the State's interest in preventing potential abuse and mistake is only minimally implicated.

[Unlike] the Court of Appeals, I would not say as a categorical matter that [the] state interests are invalid as to the entire class of terminally ill, mentally competent patients. I do not, however, foreclose the possibility that an individual plaintiff seeking to hasten her death, or a doctor whose assistance was sought, could prevail in a more particularized challenge. Future cases will determine whether such a challenge may succeed.

JUSTICE SOUTER, concurring in the judgment.

[The] persistence of substantive due process in our cases points to the legitimacy of the modern justification for such judicial review found in Justice Harlan's dissent in *Poe*,4 [while] the acknowledged failures of some of these cases point with caution to the difficulty raised by the present claim.

[Harlan, J.'s *Poe* dissent] is important for three things that point to our responsibilities today. The first is Justice Harlan's respect for the tradition of substantive due process review itself, and his acknowledgment of the Judiciary's obligation to carry it on. * * *

[The *Poe* dissent reminds us] that the business of [substantive due process] review is not the identification of extratextual absolutes but scrutiny of a legislative resolution (perhaps unconscious) of clashing principles, each quite possibly worthy in and of itself, but each to be weighed within the history of our values as a people. It is a comparison of the relative strengths of opposing claims that informs the judicial task, not a deduction from some first premise. Thus informed, judicial review still has no warrant to substitute one reasonable resolution of the contending positions for another, but authority to supplant the balance already struck between the contenders only when it falls outside the realm of the reasonable.

[Harlan, J.,] of course assumed that adjudication under the Due Process Clauses is like any other instance of judgment dependent on common-law method, being more or less persuasive according to the usual canons of critical discourse. [When] identifying and assessing the competing interests of liberty and authority, for example, the breadth of expression that a litigant or a judge selects in stating the competing principles will have much to do with the outcome and may be dispositive. As in any process of rational argumentation, we recognize that when a generally accepted principle is challenged, the broader the attack the less likely it

---

4. The status of the Harlan dissent in *Poe v. Ullman* is shown by the Court's adoption of its result in *Griswold* and by the Court's acknowledgment of its status and adoption of its reasoning in *Casey*. * * *

is to succeed. The principle's defenders will, indeed, often try to characterize any challenge as just such a broadside, perhaps by couching the defense as if a broadside attack had occurred. [So] *Dred Scott* treated prohibition of slavery in the Territories as nothing less than a general assault on the concept of property.

Just as results in substantive due process cases are tied to the selections of statements of the competing interests, the acceptability of the results is a function of the good reasons for the selections made. It is here that the value of common-law method becomes apparent, for the usual thinking of the common law is suspicious of the all-or-nothing analysis that tends to produce legal petrification instead of an evolving boundary between the domains of old principles. Common-law method tends to pay respect instead to detail, seeking to understand old principles afresh by new examples and new counterexamples.

[So,] in *Poe,* Justice Harlan viewed it as essential to the plaintiffs' claimed right to use contraceptives that they sought to do so within the privacy of the marital bedroom. This detail in fact served two crucial and complementary functions, and provides a lesson for today. It rescued the individuals' claim from a breadth that would have threatened all state regulation of contraception or intimate relations; extramarital intimacy, no matter how privately practiced, was outside the scope of the right Justice Harlan would have recognized in that case. It was, moreover, this same restriction that allowed the interest to be valued as an aspect of a broader liberty to be free from all unreasonable intrusions into the privacy of the home and the family life within it, a liberty exemplified in constitutional provisions such as the Third and Fourth Amendments, in prior decisions of the Court involving unreasonable intrusions into the home and family life, and in the then-prevailing status of marriage as the sole lawful locus of intimate relations.[11] The individuals' interest was therefore at its peak in *Poe,* because it was supported by a principle that distinguished of its own force between areas in which government traditionally had regulated (sexual relations outside of marriage) and those in which it had not (private marital intimacies), and thus was broad enough to cover the claim at hand without being so broad as to be shot-through by exceptions.

On the other side of the balance, the State's interest in *Poe* was not fairly characterized simply as preserving sexual morality, or doing so by regulating contraceptive devices. [It] was assumed that the State might legitimately enforce limits on the use of contraceptives through laws regulating divorce and annulment, or even through its tax policy, *ibid.,* but not necessarily be justified in criminalizing the same practice in the marital bedroom, which would entail the consequence of authorizing state enquiry into the intimate relations of a married couple who chose to close their door.

* * * Constitutional recognition of the right to bodily integrity underlies the assumed right, good against the State, to require physicians to terminate artificial

---

11. Thus, as the *Poe* dissent illustrates, the task of determining whether the concrete right claimed by an individual in a particular case falls within the ambit of a more generalized protected liberty requires explicit analysis when what the individual wants to do could arguably be characterized as belonging to different strands of our legal tradition requiring different degrees of constitutional scrutiny. See also Laurence H. Tribe & Michael C. Dorf, *Levels of Generality in the Definition of Rights,* 57 U.Chi.L.Rev. 1057, 1091 (1990) (abortion might conceivably be assimilated either to the tradition regarding women's reproductive freedom in general, which places a substantial burden of justification on the State, or to the tradition regarding protection of fetuses, as embodied in laws criminalizing feticide by someone other than the mother, which generally requires only rationality on the part of the State). Selecting among such competing characterizations demands reasoned judgment about which broader principle, as exemplified in the concrete privileges and prohibitions embodied in our legal tradition, best fits the particular claim asserted in a particular case.

life support, *Cruzan,* [and] the affirmative right to obtain medical intervention to cause abortion, see *Casey.* It is, indeed, in the abortion cases that the most telling recognitions of the importance of bodily integrity and the concomitant tradition of medical assistance have occurred. [The] analogies between the abortion cases and this one are several. Even though the State has a legitimate interest in discouraging abortion, the Court recognized a woman's right to a physician's counsel and care. Like the decision to commit suicide, the decision to abort potential life can be made irresponsibly and under the influence of others, and yet the Court has held in the abortion cases that physicians are fit assistants. Without physician assistance in abortion, the woman's right would have too often amounted to nothing more than a right to self-mutilation, and without a physician to assist in the suicide of the dying, the patient's right will often be confined to crude methods of causing death, most shocking and painful to the decedent's survivors.

[Among the interests the State has put forward to justify the Washington law are the] interests in protecting patients from mistakenly and involuntarily deciding to end their lives, and in guarding against both voluntary and involuntary euthanasia. The argument is that a progression would occur, obscuring the line between the ill and the dying, and between the responsible and the unduly influenced, until ultimately doctors and perhaps others would abuse a limited freedom to aid suicides * * *. Respondents propose an answer to all this, the answer of state regulation with teeth. Legislation proposed in several States, for example, would authorize physician-assisted suicide but require two qualified physicians to confirm the patient's diagnosis, prognosis, and competence; and would mandate that the patient make repeated requests witnessed by at least two others over a specified time span; and would impose reporting requirements and criminal penalties for various acts of coercion.

But at least at this moment there are reasons for caution in predicting the effectiveness of the teeth proposed. Respondents' proposals, as it turns out, sound much like the guidelines now in place in the Netherlands, the only place where experience with physician-assisted suicide and euthanasia has yielded empirical evidence about how such regulations might affect actual practice. [There] is, however, a substantial dispute today about what the Dutch experience shows. Some commentators marshall evidence that the Dutch guidelines have in practice failed to protect patients from involuntary euthanasia and have been violated with impunity. This evidence is contested. The day may come when we can say with some assurance which side is right, but for now it is the substantiality of the factual disagreement, and the alternatives for resolving it, that matter. They are, for me, dispositive of the due process claim at this time.

I take it that the basic concept of judicial review with its possible displacement of legislative judgment bars any finding that a legislature has acted arbitrarily when the following conditions are met: there is a serious factual controversy over the feasibility of recognizing the claimed right without at the same time making it impossible for the State to engage in an undoubtedly legitimate exercise of power; facts necessary to resolve the controversy are not readily ascertainable through the judicial process; but they are more readily subject to discovery through legislative factfinding and experimentation. It is assumed in this case, and must be, that a State's interest in protecting those unable to make responsible decisions and those who make no decisions at all entitles the State to bar aid to any but a knowing and responsible person intending suicide, and to prohibit euthanasia. How, and how far, a State should act in that interest are judgments for the State, but the legitimacy of its action to deny a physician the option to aid any but the knowing and responsible is beyond question.

The capacity of the State to protect the others if respondents were to prevail is, however, subject to some genuine question, underscored by the responsible disagreement over the basic facts of the Dutch experience. This factual controversy is not open to a judicial resolution with any substantial degree of assurance at this time. [While] an extensive literature on any subject can raise the hopes for judicial understanding, the literature on this subject is only nascent. Since there is little experience directly bearing on the issue, the most that can be said is that whichever way the Court might rule today, events could overtake its assumptions, as experimentation in some jurisdictions confirmed or discredited the concerns about progression from assisted suicide to euthanasia.

Legislatures, on the other hand, have superior opportunities to obtain the facts necessary for a judgment about the present controversy. [Moreover,] their mechanisms include the power to experiment, moving forward and pulling back as facts emerge within their own jurisdictions. * * * [While] I do not decide for all time that respondents' claim should not be recognized, I acknowledge the legislative institutional competence as the better one to deal with that claim at this time.

JUSTICE GINSBURG, concurring in the judgments.

I concur in the Court's judgments in these cases substantially for the reasons stated by Justice O'Connor in her concurring opinion.

JUSTICE BREYER, concurring in the judgments.

I believe that Justice O'Connor's views, which I share, have greater legal significance than the Court's opinion suggests. I join her separate opinion, except insofar as it joins the majority. And I concur in the judgments. I shall briefly explain how I differ from the Court.

I agree with the Court in *Vacco v. Quill,* [infra] that the articulated state interests justify the distinction drawn between physician assisted suicide and withdrawal of life-support. I also agree [that] the critical question in both of the cases before us is whether "the 'liberty' specially protected by the Due Process Clause includes a right" of the sort that the respondents assert. I do not agree, however, with the Court's formulation of that claimed "liberty" interest. The Court describes it as a "right to commit suicide with another's assistance." But I would not reject the respondents' claim without considering a different formulation, for which our legal tradition may provide greater support. That formulation would use words roughly like a "right to die with dignity." But irrespective of the exact words used, at its core would lie personal control over the manner of death, professional medical assistance, and the avoidance of unnecessary and severe physical suffering—combined.

As Justice Souter points out, Justice Harlan's dissenting opinion in *Poe* offers some support for such a claim. In that opinion, Justice Harlan [recognized] that "*certain interests* require particularly careful scrutiny of the state needs asserted to justify their abridgment." The "certain interests" to which Justice Harlan referred may well be similar (perhaps identical) to the rights, liberties, or interests that the Court today, as in the past, regards as "fundamental."

Justice Harlan concluded that marital privacy was such a "special interest." He found in the Constitution a right of "privacy of the home"—with the home, the bedroom, and "intimate details of the marital relation" at its heart—by examining the protection that the law had earlier provided for related, but not identical, interests described by such words as "privacy," "home," and "family." The respondents here essentially ask us to do the same. They argue that one can find a "right to die with dignity" by examining the protection the law has provided for related, but not identical, interests relating to personal dignity, medical treatment, and freedom from state-inflicted pain.

I do not believe, however, that this Court need or now should decide whether or a not such a right is "fundamental." That is because, in my view, the avoidance of severe physical pain (connected with death) would have to comprise an essential part of any successful claim and because, as Justice O'Connor points out, the laws before us do not *force* a dying person to undergo that kind of pain. Rather, the laws of New York and of Washington do not prohibit doctors from providing patients with drugs sufficient to control pain despite the risk that those drugs themselves will kill. And under these circumstances the laws of New York and Washington would overcome any remaining significant interests and would be justified, regardless.

[Were] the legal circumstances different—for example, were state law to prevent the provision of palliative care, including the administration of drugs as needed to avoid pain at the end of life—then the law's impact upon serious and otherwise unavoidable physical pain (accompanying death) would be more directly at issue. And as Justice O'Connor suggests, the Court might have to revisit its conclusions in these cases.

———

In a companion case to *Glucksberg*, VACCO v. QUILL, 521 U.S. 793 (1997), the Court without a dissent, rejected the argument that because New York permits competent persons to refuse lifesaving medical treatment, and the refusal of such treatment is "essentially the same thing" as physician-assisted suicide, the state's assisted suicide ban violates the Equal Protection Clause. REHNQUIST, C.J., again wrote for the Court: "[The] Equal Protection Clause [embodies] a general rule that States must treat like cases alike but may treat unlike cases accordingly. If[, as here,] a legislative classification or distinction 'neither burdens a fundamental right nor targets a suspect class, we will uphold [it] so long as it bears a rational relation to some legitimate end.' *Romer v. Evans* [p. 756 infra]. [On] their faces, neither New York's ban on assisting suicide nor its statutes permitting patients to refuse medical treatment treat anyone differently than anyone else or draw any distinctions between persons. *Everyone,* regardless of physical condition, is entitled, if competent, to refuse unwanted lifesaving medical treatment; *no one* is permitted to assist a suicide.

"[The] Court of Appeals, however, concluded that some terminally ill people— those who are on life-support systems—are treated differently than those who are not, in that the former may 'hasten death' by ending treatment, but the latter may not 'hasten death' through physician-assisted suicide. This conclusion depends on the submission that ending or refusing lifesaving medical treatment 'is nothing more nor less than assisted suicide.' Unlike the Court of Appeals, we think the distinction between assisting suicide and withdrawing life-sustaining treatment, a distinction widely recognized and endorsed in the medical profession and in our legal traditions, is both important and logical; it is certainly rational.

"The distinction comports with fundamental legal principles of causation and intent. First, when a patient refuses life-sustaining medical treatment, he dies from an underlying fatal disease or pathology; but if a patient ingests lethal medication prescribed by a physician, he is killed by that medication. [Furthermore,] a physician who withdraws, or honors a patient's refusal to begin, lifesustaining medical treatment purposefully intends, or may so intend, only to respect his patient's wishes and 'to cease doing useless and futile or degrading things to the patient when [the patient] no longer stands to benefit from them.' The same is true when a doctor provides aggressive palliative care; in some cases, painkilling drugs may hasten a patient's death, but the physician's purpose and intent is, or may be, only to ease his patient's pain. A doctor who assists a suicide, however, 'must, necessarily and indubitably, intend primarily that the patient be made dead.' Similarly, a patient who commits suicide with a doctor's aid necessarily has the specific intent to end his or her own life, while a patient who refuses or discontinues treatment might not. [The] law has long used actors' intent or purpose to distinguish between two acts that may have the same result. [Put] differently, the law distinguishes actions taken 'because of' a given end from actions taken 'in spite of' their unintended but foreseen consequences.

"[Given] these general principles, it is not surprising that many courts, including New York courts, have carefully distinguished refusing life-sustaining treatment from suicide. * * * Similarly, the overwhelming majority of state legislatures have drawn a clear line between assisting suicide and withdrawing or permitting the refusal of unwanted lifesaving medical treatment by prohibiting the former and permitting the latter. * * *

New York is a case in point. [It] has acted several times to protect patients' common-law right to refuse treatment [but] reaffirmed the line between "killing' and 'letting die.' * * * More recently, the New York State Task Force on Life and the Law studied assisted suicide and euthanasia and, in 1994, unanimously recommended against legalization.

"[This] Court has also recognized, at least implicitly, the distinction between letting a patient die and making that patient die. In *Cruzan* our assumption of a right to refuse treatment was grounded not, as the Court of Appeals supposed, on the proposition that patients have a general and abstract 'right to hasten death,' but on well established, traditional rights to bodily integrity and freedom from unwanted touching. In fact, we observed that 'the majority of States in this country have laws imposing criminal penalties on one who assists another to commit suicide.' *Cruzan* therefore provides no support for the notion that refusing life-sustaining medical treatment is 'nothing more nor less than suicide.'

"For all these reasons, we disagree with respondents' claim that the distinction between refusing lifesaving medical treatment and assisted suicide is 'arbitrary' and 'irrational.'[11] [By] permitting everyone to refuse unwanted medical treatment while prohibiting anyone from assisting a suicide, New York law follows a longstanding and rational distinction.

"New York's reasons for recognizing and acting on this distinction—including prohibiting intentional killing and preserving life; preventing suicide; maintaining physicians' role as their patients' healers; protecting vulnerable people from indifference, prejudice, and psychological and financial pressure to end their lives; and avoiding a possible slide towards euthanasia—are discussed in greater detail in our opinion in *Glucksberg*. These valid and important public interests easily

---

11. Respondents also argue that the State irrationally distinguishes between physician-assisted suicide and "terminal sedation," a process respondents characterize as "induc[ing] barbiturate coma and then starv[ing] the person to death." Petitioners insist, however, that " '[a]lthough proponents of physician-assisted suicide and euthanasia contend that terminal sedation is covert physician-assisted suicide or euthanasia, the concept of sedating pharmacotherapy is based on informed consent and the principle of double effect.' " Just as a State may prohibit assisting suicide while permitting patients to refuse unwanted lifesaving treatment, it may permit palliative care related to that refusal, which may have the foreseen but unintended "double effect" of hastening the patient's death.

satisfy the constitutional requirement that a legislative classification bear a rational relation to some legitimate end.13"

STEVENS, J., concurring in the judgment, "agree[d] that the distinction between permitting death to ensue from an underlying fatal disease and causing it to occur by the administration of medication or other means provides a constitutionally sufficient basis for the State's classification." However, unlike the Court, he was "not persuaded that in all cases there will in fact be a significant difference between the intent of the physicians, the patients or the families in the two situations." He continued:

"The illusory character of any differences in intent or causation is confirmed by the fact that the American Medical Association unequivocally endorses the practice of terminal sedation—the administration of sufficient dosages of pain-killing medication to terminally ill patients to protect them from excruciating pain even when it is clear that the time of death will be advanced. [Thus,] although the differences the majority notes in causation and intent between terminating life-support and assisting in suicide support the Court's rejection of the respondents' facial challenge, these distinctions may be inapplicable to particular terminally ill patients and their doctors. Our holding today in *Quill* [just] like our holding in [*Glucksberg,*] does not foreclose the possibility that some applications of the New York statute may impose an intolerable intrusion on the patient's freedom."a

WHAT SHALL WE CALL THIS SEGMENT—THE RIGHT TO ENGAGE IN HOMOSEXUAL SODOMY? ADULT, CONSENSUAL SEXUAL CONDUCT IN THE HOME? THE AUTONOMY OF PRIVATE SEXUAL CHOICES? SEXUAL EXPRESSION AND CONTROL OF ONE'S BODY? UNCONVENTIONAL SEXUAL LIFESTYLES? THE RIGHT TO CONTROL ONE'S INTIMATE ASSOCIATIONS? THE RIGHT TO MAKE CHOICES ABOUT THE MOST INTIMATE ASPECTS OF ONE'S LIFE? THE RIGHT TO BE LET ALONE?

BOWERS v. HARDWICK, 478 U.S. 186 (1986), upheld the constitutionality of a Georgia statute criminalizing sodomy. Mr. Hardwick was charged with violating the statute by committing sodomy with another adult male in the bedroom of Hardwick's home. After a preliminary hearing, the District Attorney decided not to present the matter to a grand jury unless further evidence developed.

A 5–4 majority, per WHITE, J., rejected the argument that "the Court's prior cases have construed the Constitution to confer a right of privacy that extends to homosexual sodomy. [We] think it evident that none of the rights announced in [such cases as *Griswold* and *Roe*] bears any resemblance to the claimed constitutional right of homosexuals to engage in acts of sodomy that is asserted in this case. No connection between family, marriage, or procreation on the one hand and homosexual activity on the other has been [demonstrated]. Precedent aside,

13. Justice Stevens observes that our holding today "does not foreclose the possibility that some applications of the New York statute may impose an intolerable intrusion on the patient's freedom." This is true, but, as we observe in *Glucksberg,* a particular plaintiff hoping to show that New York's assisted-suicide ban was unconstitutional in his particular case would need to present different and considerably stronger arguments than those advanced by respondents here.

a. Souter, J., who concurred in the judgment, observed that the reasons which led him to conclude that the challenged statute in *Glucksberg* was "not arbitrary under the due process standard also support the distinction between assistance to suicide, which is banned, and practices such as termination of artificial life support and death-hastening pain medication, which are permitted." The concurring opinions of O'Connor, Ginsburg and Breyer, JJ., in *Glucksberg* also constituted their concurrences in *Vacco.*

however, respondent would have us announce [a] fundamental right to engage in homosexual sodomy. This we are quite unwilling to do." Justice White continued:

"In *Palko* it was said that [the category of rights qualifying for heightened judicial protection] includes those fundamental liberties that are 'implicit in the concept of ordered liberty,' such that 'neither liberty nor justice would exist if [they] were sacrificed.' A different description of fundamental liberties appeared in *Moore v. East Cleveland* (opinion of Powell, J.), where they are characterized as those liberties that are 'deeply rooted in this Nation's history and tradition.' It is obvious to us that neither of these formulations would extend a fundamental right to homosexuals to engage in acts of consensual sodomy.

"Nor are we inclined to take a more expansive view of our authority to discover new fundamental rights imbedded in the Due Process Clause. The Court is most vulnerable and comes nearest to illegitimacy when it deals with judge-made constitutional law having little or no cognizable roots in the language or design of the Constitution. [There] should be, therefore, great resistance to expand the substantive reach of [the due process clauses], particularly if it requires redefining the category of rights deemed to be fundamental. Otherwise, the Judiciary necessarily takes to itself further authority to govern the country without express constitutional authority. * * *

"Even if the conduct at issue here is not a fundamental right, respondent asserts that there must be a rational basis for the law and that there is none in this case other than the presumed belief of a majority of the electorate in Georgia that homosexual sodomy is immoral and unacceptable. [The] law, however, is constantly based on notions of morality, and if all laws representing essentially moral choices are to be invalidated under the Due Process Clause, the courts will be very busy indeed.

CHIEF JUSTICE BURGER, concurring, joined the Court's opinion, but also wrote separately "to underscore [his] view that in constitutional terms there is no such thing as a fundamental right to commit homosexual sodomy. [To] hold that the act of homosexual sodomy is somehow protected as a fundamental right would be to cast aside millennia of moral teaching."a

LAWRENCE v. TEXAS

539 U.S. 558, 123 S.Ct. 2472, 156 L.Ed.2d 508 (2003).

JUSTICE KENNEDY delivered the opinion of the Court.

[Responding to a reported weapons disturbance, Houston police entered petitioner's apartment and observed petitioner and another adult man, petitioner Garner, engaging in a consensual sexual act. The two men were arrested and charged with "deviate sexual intercourse, namely anal sex, with a member of the same sex (a man)." The applicable state law prohibited two persons of the same sex from engaging in "deviate sexual intercourse" and defined the crime as follows:

"(A) any contact between any part of the genitals of one person and the mouth or anus of another person; or

a. Powell, J., joined the opinion of the Court, but also wrote separately to point out that a long prison sentence for "a single private, consensual act of sodomy" (the Georgia statute authorized a prison sentence for up to 20 years for such conduct) "would create a serious Eighth Amendment issue." But in this case "respondent has not been tried, much less convicted and sentenced." Blackmun, J., joined by Brennan, Marshall and Stevens, JJ., dissented. Stevens, J., joined by Brennan and Marshall, JJ., also wrote a separate dissent.

"(B) the penetration of the genitals or the anus of another person with an object."

[Petitioners were convicted. The Texas Court of Appeals rejected their constitutional arguments, considering *Bowers* controlling.]

Liberty protects the person from unwarranted government intrusions into a dwelling or other private places. In our tradition the State is not omnipresent in the home. And there are other spheres of our lives and existence, outside the home, where the State should not be a dominant presence. Freedom extends beyond spatial bounds. Liberty presumes an autonomy of self that includes freedom of thought, belief, expressions, and certain intimate conduct. The instant case involves liberty of the person both in its spatial and more transcendent dimensions.

[Although we granted certiorari to consider whether petitioners' convictions violated the Equal Protection or Due Process Clauses or whether *Bowers* should be overruled,] [w]e conclude the case should be resolved by determining whether the petitioners were free as adults to engage in the private conduct in the exercise of their liberty under [Due Process.] For this inquiry we deem it necessary to reconsider the Court's holding in *Bowers*. [The Court then discussed *Griswold*, *Eisenstadt*, *Roe* and *Carey*.] *Roe* recognized the right of a woman to make certain fundamental decisions affecting her destiny and confirmed once more that the protection of liberty under the Due Process Clause has a substantive dimension of fundamental significance in defining the rights of the person.

[The] facts in *Bowers* had some similarities to the instant case. [One] difference between the two cases is that the Georgia statute prohibited the conduct whether or not the participants were of the same sex, while the Texas statute, as we have seen, applies only to participants of the same sex.

[The] Court began its substantive discussion in *Bowers* as follows: "The issue presented is whether the Federal Constitution confers a fundamental right upon homosexuals to engage in sodomy and hence invalidates the laws of the many States that still make such conduct illegal and have done so for a very long time." That statement, we now conclude, discloses the Court's own failure to appreciate the extent of the liberty at stake. To say that the issue in *Bowers* was simply the right to engage in certain sexual conduct demeans the claim the individual put forward, just as it would demean a married couple were it to be said marriage is simply about the right to have sexual intercourse. The laws involved in *Bowers* and here are, to be sure, statutes that purport to do no more than prohibit a particular sexual act. Their penalties and purposes, though, have more far-reaching consequences, touching upon the most private human conduct, sexual behavior, and in the most private of places, the home. The statutes do seek to control a personal relationship that, whether or not entitled to formal recognition in the law, is within the liberty of persons to choose without being punished as criminals.

This, as a general rule, should counsel against attempts by the State, or a court, to define the meaning of the relationship or to set its boundaries absent injury to a person or abuse of an institution the law protects. It suffices for us to acknowledge that adults may choose to enter upon this relationship in the confines of their homes and their own private lives and still retain their dignity as free persons. When sexuality finds overt expression in intimate conduct with another person, the conduct can be but one element in a personal bond that is more enduring. The liberty protected by the Constitution allows homosexual persons the right to make this choice.

Having misapprehended the claim of liberty there presented to it, and thus stating the claim to be whether there is a fundamental right to engage in consensual sodomy, the *Bowers* Court said: "Proscriptions against that conduct have ancient roots." In academic writings, and in many of the scholarly amici briefs filed to assist the Court in this case, there are fundamental criticisms of the historical premises relied upon by the majority and concurring opinions in *Bowers*. We need not enter this debate in the attempt to reach a definitive historical judgment, but the following considerations counsel against adopting the definitive conclusions upon which *Bowers* placed such reliance.

At the outset it should be noted that there is no longstanding history in this country of laws directed at homosexual conduct as a distinct matter. [The] absence of legal prohibitions focusing on homosexual conduct may be explained in part by noting that according to some scholars the concept of the homosexual as a distinct category of person did not emerge until the late 19th century. [Thus] early American sodomy laws were not directed at homosexuals as such but instead sought to prohibit nonprocreative sexual activity more generally. This does not suggest approval of homosexual conduct. It does tend to show that this particular form of conduct was not thought of as a separate category from like conduct between heterosexual persons.

Laws prohibiting sodomy do not seem to have been enforced against consenting adults acting in private. [Instead] of targeting relations between consenting adults in private, 19th-century sodomy prosecutions typically involved relations between men and minor girls or minor boys, relations between adults involving force, relations between adults implicating disparity in status, or relations between men and animals.

[The infrequency of prosecutions in consensual cases] makes it difficult to say that society approved of a rigorous and systematic punishment of the consensual acts committed in private and by adults. The longstanding criminal prohibition of homosexual sodomy upon which the *Bowers* decision placed such reliance is as consistent with a general condemnation of nonprocreative sex as it is with an established tradition of prosecuting acts because of their homosexual character.

[Far] from possessing "ancient roots," *Bowers,* American laws targeting same-sex couples did not develop until the last third of the 20th century. The reported decisions concerning the prosecution of consensual, homosexual sodomy between adults for the years 1880–1995 are not always clear in the details, but a significant number involved conduct in a public place. It was not until the 1970's that any State singled out same-sex relations for criminal prosecution, and only nine States have done so. [Over] the course of the last decades, States with same-sex prohibitions have moved toward abolishing them.

[In] summary, the historical grounds relied upon in *Bowers* are more complex than the majority opinion and the concurring opinion by Chief Justice Burger indicate. Their historical premises are not without doubt and, at the very least, are overstated.

It must be acknowledged, of course, that the Court in *Bowers* was making the broader point that for centuries there have been powerful voices to condemn homosexual conduct as immoral. [This does not] answer the question before us, however. The issue is whether the majority may use the power of the State to enforce these views on the whole society through operation of the criminal law. "Our obligation is to define the liberty of all, not to mandate our own moral code." *Casey.*

[In the past half century there has been] an emerging awareness that liberty gives substantial protection to adult persons in deciding how to conduct their private lives in matters pertaining to sex. "[H]istory and tradition are the starting point but not in all cases the ending point of the substantive due process inquiry." *Sacramento v. Lewis* (Kennedy J., concurring). This emerging recognition should have been apparent when *Bowers* was decided. In 1955 the American Law Institute promulgated the Model Penal Code and made clear that it did not recommend or provide for "criminal penalties for consensual sexual relations conducted in private." [In] 1961 Illinois changed its laws to conform to the Model Penal Code. Other States soon followed.

In *Bowers* the Court referred to the fact that before 1961 all 50 States had outlawed sodomy, and that at the time of the Court's decision 24 States and the District of Columbia had sodomy laws. Justice Powell pointed out that these prohibitions often were being ignored, however. Georgia, for instance, had not sought to enforce its law for decades.

[The] sweeping references by Chief Justice Burger to the history of Western civilization and to Judeo–Christian moral and ethical standards did not take account of other authorities pointing in an opposite direction. A committee advising the British Parliament recommended in 1957 repeal of laws punishing homosexual conduct. Parliament enacted the substance of those recommendations 10 years later. [Of] even more importance, almost five years before *Bowers* was decided the European Court of Human Rights considered a case with parallels to *Bowers* and to today's case. [The] court held that the laws proscribing [consensual homosexual conduct] were invalid under the European Convention on Human Rights. *Dudgeon v. United Kingdom*.

[In] our own constitutional system the deficiencies in *Bowers* became even more apparent in the years following its announcement. The 25 States with laws prohibiting the relevant conduct referenced in the *Bowers* decision are reduced now to 13, of which 4 enforce their laws only against homosexual conduct. In those States where sodomy is still proscribed, whether for same-sex or heterosexual conduct, there is a pattern of nonenforcement with respect to consenting adults acting in private. The State of Texas admitted in 1994 that as of that date it had not prosecuted anyone under those circumstances. Two principal cases decided after *Bowers* cast its holding into even more doubt. [The court then discusses *Casey* and *Romer v. Evans*, p. 756 infra.]

[As] an alternative argument in this case, counsel for the petitioners and some amici contend that *Romer* provides the basis for declaring the Texas statute invalid under the Equal Protection Clause. That is a tenable argument, but we conclude the instant case requires us to address whether *Bowers* itself has continuing validity. Were we to hold the statute invalid under the Equal Protection Clause some might question whether a prohibition would be valid if drawn differently, say, to prohibit the conduct both between same-sex and different-sex participants.

Equality of treatment and the due process right to demand respect for conduct protected by the substantive guarantee of liberty are linked in important respects, and a decision on the latter point advances both interests. If protected conduct is made criminal and the law which does so remains unexamined for its substantive validity, its stigma might remain even if it were not enforceable as drawn for equal protection reasons. When homosexual conduct is made criminal by the law of the State, that declaration in and of itself is an invitation to subject homosexual persons to discrimination both in the public and in the private spheres. The central holding of *Bowers* has been brought in question by this case, and it should be addressed. Its continuance as precedent demeans the lives of homosexual persons.

The stigma this criminal statute imposes, moreover, is not trivial. The offense, to be sure, is but [a] minor offense in the Texas legal system. Still, it remains a criminal offense with all that imports for the dignity of the persons charged. The petitioners will bear on their record the history of their criminal convictions. Just this Term we rejected various challenges to state laws requiring the registration of sex offenders. We are advised that if Texas convicted an adult for private, consensual homosexual conduct under the statute here in question the convicted person would come within the registration laws of a least four States were he or she to be subject to their jurisdiction. This underscores the consequential nature of the punishment and the state-sponsored condemnation attendant to the criminal prohibition. Furthermore, the Texas criminal conviction carries with it the other collateral consequences always following a conviction, such as notations on job application forms, to mention but one example.

The foundations of *Bowers* have sustained serious erosion from our recent decisions in *Casey* and *Romer*. When our precedent has been thus weakened, criticism from other sources is of greater significance. In the United States criticism of *Bowers* has been substantial and continuing, disapproving of its reasoning in all respects, not just as to its historical assumptions. See, e.g., Charles Fried, *Order and Law: Arguing the Reagan Revolution—A Firsthand Account* 81–84 (1991); Richard Posner, *Sex and Reason* 341–350 (1992). The courts of five different States have declined to follow it in interpreting provisions in their own state constitutions parallel to the Due Process Clause of the Fourteenth Amendment.

To the extent *Bowers* relied on values we share with a wider civilization, it should be noted that the reasoning and holding in *Bowers* have been rejected elsewhere. The European Court of Human Rights has followed not *Bowers* but its own decision in *Dudgeon v. United Kingdom*. Other nations, too, have taken action consistent with an affirmation of the protected right of homosexual adults to engage in intimate, consensual conduct. The right the petitioners seek in this case has been accepted as an integral part of human freedom in many other countries. There has been no showing that in this country the governmental interest in circumscribing personal choice is somehow more legitimate or urgent.

[In] *Casey* we noted that when a Court is asked to overrule a precedent recognizing a constitutional liberty interest, individual or societal reliance on the existence of that liberty cautions with particular strength against reversing course. [The] holding in *Bowers,* however, has not induced detrimental reliance comparable to some instances where recognized individual rights are involved. Indeed, there has been no individual or societal reliance on *Bowers* of the sort that could counsel against overturning its holding once there are compelling reasons to do so. *Bowers* itself causes uncertainty, for the precedents before and after its issuance contradict its central holding.

The rationale of *Bowers* does not withstand careful analysis. In his dissenting opinion in *Bowers* Justice Stevens came to these conclusions: "Our prior cases make two propositions abundantly clear. First, the fact that the governing majority in a State has traditionally viewed a particular practice as immoral is not a sufficient reason for upholding a law prohibiting the practice; neither history nor tradition could save a law prohibiting miscegenation from constitutional attack. Second, individual decisions by married persons, concerning the intimacies of their physical relationship, even when not intended to produce offspring, are a form of 'liberty' protected by the Due Process Clause of the Fourteenth Amendment. Moreover, this protection extends to intimate choices by unmarried as well as married persons.''

Justice Stevens' analysis, in our view, should have been controlling in *Bowers* and should control here. *Bowers* was not correct when it was decided, and it is not correct today. It ought not to remain binding precedent. *Bowers* should be and now is overruled.

[The present case] does not involve persons who might be injured or coerced or who are situated in relationships where consent might not easily be refused. It does not involve public conduct or prostitution. It does not involve whether the government must give formal recognition to any relationship that homosexual persons seek to enter. The case does involve two adults who, with full and mutual consent from each other, engaged in sexual practices common to a homosexual lifestyle. The petitioners are entitled to respect for their private lives. The State cannot demean their existence or control their destiny by making their private sexual conduct a crime. Their right to liberty under the Due Process Clause gives them the full right to engage in their conduct without intervention of the government. "It is a promise of the Constitution that there is a realm of personal liberty which the government may not enter." *Casey.* The Texas statute furthers no legitimate state interest which can justify its intrusion into the personal and private life of the individual.

Had those who drew and ratified the Due Process Clauses of the Fifth Amendment or the Fourteenth Amendment known the components of liberty in its manifold possibilities, they might have been more specific. They did not presume to have this insight. They knew times can blind us to certain truths and later generations can see that laws once thought necessary and proper in fact serve only to oppress. As the Constitution endures, persons in every generation can invoke its principles in their own search for greater freedom. * * *

JUSTICE O'CONNOR, concurring in the judgment.

[O'Connor, J., did not join the Court in overruling *Bowers*, but agreed that Texas' statute banning "same-sex sodomy" was unconstitutional, relying on the Equal Protection Clause. See p. 762 infra. At one point she observed: "That this law as applied to private, consensual conduct is unconstitutional under the Equal Protection Clause does not mean that other laws distinguishing between heterosexuals and homosexuals would similarly fail under rational basis review. Texas cannot assert any legitimate state interest here, such as national security or preserving the traditional institution of marriage."]

JUSTICE SCALIA, with whom THE CHIEF JUSTICE and JUSTICE THOMAS join, dissenting.

[N]owhere does the Court's opinion declare that homosexual sodomy is a "fundamental right" under the Due Process Clause; nor does it subject the Texas law to the standard of review that would be appropriate (strict scrutiny) if homosexual sodomy *were* a "fundamental right." Thus, while overruling the *outcome* of *Bowers,* the Court leaves strangely untouched its central legal conclusion: "[R]espondent would have us announce [a] fundamental right to engage in homosexual sodomy. This we are quite unwilling to do." Instead the Court simply describes petitioners' conduct as "an exercise of their liberty"—which it undoubtedly is—and proceeds to apply an unheard-of form of rational-basis review that will have far-reaching implications beyond this case.

* * * I do not myself believe in rigid adherence to stare decisis in constitutional cases; but I do believe that we should be consistent rather than manipulative in invoking the doctrine. Today's opinions in support of reversal do not

bother to distinguish—or indeed, even bother to mention—the paean to stare decisis coauthored by three Members of today's majority in *Casey.* There, when stare decisis meant preservation of judicially invented abortion rights, the widespread criticism of *Roe* was strong reason to *reaffirm* [it]. Today, however, the widespread opposition to *Bowers,* a decision resolving an issue as "intensely divisive" as the issue in *Roe,* is offered as a reason in favor of *overruling* it. Gone, too, is any "enquiry" (of the sort conducted in *Casey*) into whether the decision sought to be overruled has "proven 'unworkable.' "

Today's approach to stare decisis invites us to overrule an erroneously decided precedent (including an "intensely divisive" decision) *if:* (1) its foundations have been "eroded" by subsequent decisions; (2) it has been subject to "substantial and continuing" criticism; and (3) it has not induced "individual or societal reliance" that counsels against overturning. The problem is that *Roe* itself—which today's majority surely has no disposition to overrule—satisfies these conditions to at least the same degree as *Bowers.*

(1) A preliminary digressive observation with regard to the first factor: The Court's claim that *Casey* "casts some doubt" upon the holding in *Bowers* (or any other case, for that matter) does not withstand analysis. As far as its holding is concerned, *Casey* provided a *less* expansive right to abortion than did *Roe, which was already on the books when Bowers was decided.* And if the Court is referring not to the holding of *Casey,* but to the dictum of its famed sweet-mystery-of-life passage (" 'At the heart of liberty is the right to define one's own concept of existence, of meaning, of the universe, and of the mystery of human life' "): That "casts some doubt" upon either the totality of our jurisprudence or else (presumably the right answer) nothing at all. I have never heard of a law that attempted to restrict one's "right to define" certain concepts; and if the passage calls into question the government's power to regulate *actions based on* one's self-defined "concept of existence, etc.," it is the passage that ate the rule of law.

I do not quarrel with the Court's claim that *Romer* "eroded" the "foundations" of *Bowers'* rational-basis holding. But *Roe* and *Casey* have been equally "eroded" by *Washington v. Glucksberg,* which held that *only* fundamental rights which are " 'deeply rooted in this Nation's history and tradition' " qualify for anything other than rational basis scrutiny under the doctrine of "substantive due process." *Roe* and *Casey,* of course, subjected the restriction of abortion to heightened scrutiny without even attempting to establish that the freedom to abort *was* rooted in this Nation's tradition.

(2) *Bowers,* the Court says, has been subject to "substantial and continuing [criticism], disapproving of its reasoning in all respects, not just as to its historical assumptions." Exactly what those nonhistorical criticisms are, and whether the Court even agrees with them, are left unsaid, although the Court does cite two [books].1 Of course, *Roe* too (and by extension *Casey*) had been (and still is) subject to unrelenting criticism, including criticism from the two commentators cited by the Court today.

(3) That leaves, to distinguish the rock-solid, unamendable disposition of *Roe* from the readily overrulable *Bowers,* only the third factor. "[T]here has been," the Court says, "no individual or societal reliance on *Bowers* of the sort that could counsel against overturning its [holding]." It seems to me that the "societal reliance" on the principles confirmed in *Bowers* and discarded today has been overwhelming. Countless judicial decisions and legislative enactments have relied

1. [One of the *Bowers* critics cited by the majority] actually writes: "[*Bowers*] is correct nevertheless that the right to engage in homo- sexual acts is not deeply rooted in America's history and tradition." Posner, *Sex and Reason,* 343 (1992).

on the ancient proposition that a governing majority's belief that certain sexual behavior is "immoral and unacceptable" constitutes a rational basis for regulation. * * * State laws against bigamy, same-sex marriage, adult incest, prostitution, masturbation, adultery, fornication, bestiality, and obscenity are likewise sustainable only in light of *Bowers'* validation of laws based on moral choices. Every single one of these laws is called into question by today's decision. [The] impossibility of distinguishing homosexuality from other traditional "morals" offenses is precisely why *Bowers* rejected the rational-basis challenge. "The law," it said, "is constantly based on notions of morality, and if all laws representing essentially moral choices are to be invalidated under the Due Process Clause, the courts will be very busy indeed."

What a massive disruption of the current social order, therefore, the overruling of *Bowers* entails. Not so the overruling of *Roe,* which would simply have restored the regime that existed for centuries before 1973, in which the permissibility of and restrictions upon abortion were determined legislatively State-by-State. [To] tell the truth, it does not surprise me, and should surprise no one, that the Court has chosen today to revise the standards of stare decisis set forth in *Casey.* It has thereby exposed *Casey*'s extraordinary deference to precedent for the result-oriented expedient that it is.

Having decided that it need not adhere to stare decisis, the Court still must establish that *Bowers* was wrongly decided and that the Texas statute, as applied to petitioners, is unconstitutional. [The Texas law at issue] undoubtedly imposes constraints on liberty. So do laws prohibiting prostitution, recreational use of heroin, and, for that matter, working more than 60 hours per week in a bakery. But there is no right to "liberty" under the Due Process Clause, though today's opinion repeatedly makes that claim. [The] Fourteenth Amendment *expressly allows* States to deprive their citizens of "liberty," *so long as "due process of law" is provided * * *.*

Our opinions applying the doctrine known as "substantive due process" hold that the Due Process Clause prohibits States from infringing *fundamental* liberty interests, unless the infringement is narrowly tailored to serve a compelling state interest. *Glucksberg.* We have held repeatedly, in cases the Court today does not overrule, that *only* fundamental rights qualify for this so-called "heightened scrutiny" protection—that is, rights which are " 'deeply rooted in this Nation's history and tradition.' " [Scalia, J., then discusses *Reno v. Flores, Michael H. v. Gerald D., Meyer v. Nebraska* and other cases].3 All other liberty interests may be abridged or abrogated pursuant to a validly enacted state law if that law is rationally related to a legitimate state interest.

Bowers held, first, that criminal prohibitions of homosexual sodomy are not subject to heightened scrutiny because they do not implicate a "fundamental right" under the Due Process Clause. Noting that "[p]roscriptions against that conduct have ancient roots," that "[s]odomy was a criminal offense at common law and was forbidden by the laws of the original 13 States when they ratified the Bill of Rights," and that many States had retained their bans on sodomy, *Bowers*

---

3. The Court is quite right that "history and tradition are the starting point but not in all cases the ending point of the substantive due process inquiry." An asserted "fundamental liberty interest" must not only be "deeply rooted in this Nation's history and tradition," *Washington v. Glucksberg,* but it must *also* be "implicit in the concept of ordered liberty," so that "neither liberty nor justice would exist if [it] were sacrificed." Moreover, liberty interests unsupported by history and tradition, though not deserving of "heightened scrutiny," are *still* protected from state laws that are not rationally related to any legitimate state interest. As I proceed to discuss, it is this latter principle that the Court applies in the present case.

concluded that a right to engage in homosexual sodomy was not "deeply rooted in this Nation's history and tradition."

The Court today does not overrule this holding. Not once does it describe homosexual sodomy as a "fundamental right" or a "fundamental liberty interest," nor does it subject the Texas statute to strict scrutiny. Instead, [the] Court concludes that the application of Texas's statute to petitioners' conduct fails the rational-basis test, and overrules *Bowers*' holding to the contrary[:] "The Texas statute furthers no legitimate state interest which can justify its intrusion into the personal and private life of the individual."

[The] Court's description of "the state of the law" at the time of *Bowers* only confirms that *Bowers* was right. [*Griswold*] *expressly disclaimed* any reliance on the doctrine of "substantive due process," and grounded the so-called "right to privacy" in penumbras of constitutional provisions *other than* the Due Process Clause. *Eisenstadt*, likewise had nothing to do with "substantive due process"; it invalidated a Massachusetts law prohibiting the distribution of contraceptives to unmarried persons solely on the basis of the Equal Protection Clause. * * *

Roe v. Wade recognized that the right to abort an unborn child was a "fundamental right" protected by the Due Process Clause. The *Roe* Court, however, made no attempt to establish that this right was " 'deeply rooted in this Nation's history and tradition' "; instead, it based its conclusion that "the Fourteenth Amendment's concept of personal liberty [is] broad enough to encompass a woman's decision whether or not to terminate her pregnancy" on its own normative judgment that anti-abortion laws were undesirable. We have since rejected *Roe*'s holding that regulations of abortion must be narrowly tailored to serve a compelling state interest, see *Casey*, (joint opinion of O'Connor, Kennedy, and Souter, JJ.); (Rehnquist, C.J., concurring in judgment in part and dissenting in part)—and thus, by logical implication, *Roe*'s holding that the right to abort an unborn child is a "fundamental right."

[After] discussing the history of antisodomy laws, the Court proclaims that, "it should be noted that there is no longstanding history in this country of laws directed at homosexual conduct as a distinct matter." This observation in no way casts into doubt the "definitive [historical] conclusion" on which *Bowers* relied: that our Nation has a longstanding history of laws prohibiting *sodomy in general*—regardless of whether it was performed by same-sex or opposite-sex couples * * *.

It is (as *Bowers* recognized) entirely irrelevant whether the laws in our long national tradition criminalizing homosexual sodomy were "directed at homosexual conduct as a distinct matter." Whether homosexual sodomy was prohibited by a law targeted at same-sex sexual relations or by a more general law prohibiting both homosexual and heterosexual sodomy, the only relevant point is that it *was* criminalized—which suffices to establish that homosexual sodomy is not a right "deeply rooted in our Nation's history and tradition." The Court today agrees that homosexual sodomy was criminalized and thus does not dispute the facts on which Bowers *actually* relied.

Next the Court makes the claim, again unsupported by any citations, that "[l]aws prohibiting sodomy do not seem to have been enforced against consenting adults acting in private." The key qualifier here is "acting in private"—since the Court admits that sodomy laws *were* enforced against consenting adults (although the Court contends that prosecutions were "infrequent."). I do not know what "acting in private" means; surely consensual sodomy, like heterosexual intercourse, is rarely performed on stage. If all the Court means by "acting in private" is "on private premises, with the doors closed and windows covered," it is entirely unsurprising that evidence of enforcement would be hard to come by. [Surely] that lack of evidence would not sustain the proposition that consensual sodomy on private premises with the doors closed and windows covered was regarded as a "fundamental right," even though all other consensual sodomy was criminalized. [*Bowers'*] conclusion that homosexual sodomy is not a fundamental right "deeply rooted in this Nation's history and tradition" is utterly unassailable.

Realizing that fact, the Court instead says: "[W]e think that our laws and traditions in the past half century are of most relevance here. These references show *an emerging awareness* that liberty gives substantial protection to adult persons in deciding how to conduct their private lives *in matters pertaining to sex.*" (Emphasis added). [The] statement is factually false. States continue to prosecute all sorts of crimes by adults "in matters pertaining to sex": prostitution, adult incest, adultery, obscenity, and child pornography. Sodomy laws, too, have been enforced "in the past half century," in which there have been 134 reported cases involving prosecutions for consensual, adult, homosexual sodomy.

[In] any event, an "emerging awareness" is by definition not "deeply rooted in this Nation's history and tradition[s]," as we have said "fundamental right" status requires. Constitutional entitlements do not spring into existence because some States choose to lessen or eliminate criminal sanctions on certain behavior. Much less do they spring into existence, as the Court seems to believe, because *foreign nations* decriminalize conduct. The *Bowers* majority opinion *never* relied on "values we share with a wider civilization," but rather rejected the claimed right to sodomy on the ground that such a right was not " 'deeply rooted in *this Nation's* history and tradition' " (emphasis added).

I turn now to the ground on which the Court squarely rests its holding: the contention that there is no rational basis for the law here under attack. This proposition is so out of accord with our jurisprudence—indeed, with the jurisprudence of *any* society we know—that it requires little discussion.

The Texas statute undeniably seeks to further the belief of its citizens that certain forms of sexual behavior are "immoral and unacceptable," *Bowers*—the same interest furthered by criminal laws against fornication, bigamy, adultery, adult incest, bestiality, and obscenity. *Bowers* held that this *was* a legitimate state interest. The Court today reaches the opposite conclusion. [It] embraces instead Justice Stevens' declaration in his *Bowers* dissent, that "the fact that the governing majority in a State has traditionally viewed a particular practice as immoral is not a sufficient reason for upholding a law prohibiting the practice." This effectively decrees the end of all morals legislation. If, as the Court asserts, the promotion of majoritarian sexual morality is not even a *legitimate* state interest, none of the above-mentioned laws can survive rational-basis review.
* * *

Today's opinion is the product of a Court, which is the product of a law-profession culture, that has largely signed on to the so-called homosexual agenda, by which I mean the agenda promoted by some homosexual activists directed at eliminating the moral opprobrium that has traditionally attached to homosexual conduct. [The] American Association of Law Schools (to which any reputable law school *must* seek to belong) excludes from membership any school that refuses to ban from its job-interview facilities a law firm (no matter how small) that does not wish to hire as a prospective partner a person who openly engages in homosexual conduct.

One of the most revealing statements in today's opinion is the Court's grim warning that the criminalization of homosexual conduct is "an invitation to subject homosexual persons to discrimination both in the public and in the private spheres." It is clear from this that the Court has taken sides in the culture war, departing from its role of assuring, as neutral observer, that the democratic rules of engagement are observed. Many Americans do not want persons who openly engage in homosexual conduct as partners in their business, as scoutmasters for their children, as teachers in their children's schools, or as boarders in their home. They view this as protecting themselves and their families from a lifestyle that they believe to be immoral and destructive. The Court views it as "discrimination" which it is the function of our judgments to deter. So imbued is the Court with the law profession's anti-anti-homosexual culture, that it is seemingly unaware that the attitudes of that culture are not obviously "mainstream"; that in most States what the Court calls "discrimination" against those who engage in homosexual acts is perfectly legal; that proposals to ban such "discrimination" under Title VII have repeatedly been rejected by Congress; that in some cases such "discrimination" is *mandated* by federal statute, see 10 U.S.C. § 654(b)(1) (mandating discharge from the armed forces of any service member who engages in or intends to engage in homosexual acts); and that in some cases such "discrimination" is a constitutional right, see *Boy Scouts of America v. Dale*, [Ch. 7, Sec. 9, III]. Let me be clear that I have nothing against homosexuals, or any other group, promoting their agenda through normal democratic means. Social perceptions of sexual and other morality change over time, and every group has the right to persuade its fellow citizens that its view of such matters is the best. [But] persuading one's fellow citizens is one thing, and imposing one's views in absence of democratic majority will is something else. I would no more *require* a State to criminalize homosexual acts—or, for that matter, display *any* moral disapprobation of them—than I would *forbid* it to do so. What Texas has chosen to do is well within the range of traditional democratic action, and its hand should not be stayed through the invention of a brand-new "constitutional right" by a Court that is impatient of democratic change. * * *

One of the benefits of leaving regulation of this matter to the people rather than to the courts is that the people, unlike judges, need not carry things to their logical conclusion. The people may feel that their disapprobation of homosexual conduct is strong enough to disallow homosexual marriage, but not strong enough to criminalize private homosexual acts—and may legislate accordingly. The Court today pretends that it possesses a similar freedom of action, so that that we need not fear judicial imposition of homosexual marriage, as has recently occurred in Canada (in a decision that the Canadian Government has chosen not to appeal). At the end of its opinion—after having laid waste the foundations of our rational-basis jurisprudence—the Court says that the present case "does not involve whether the government must give formal recognition to any relationship that homosexual persons seek to enter." Do not believe it. More illuminating than this bald, unreasoned disclaimer is the progression of thought displayed by an earlier passage in the Court's opinion, which notes the constitutional protections afforded to "personal decisions relating to *marriage,* procreation, contraception, family relationships, child rearing, and education," and then declares that "[p]ersons in a homosexual relationship may seek autonomy for these purposes, just as heterosexual persons do" (emphasis added). Today's opinion dismantles the structure of constitutional law that has permitted a distinction to be made between heterosexual and homosexual unions, insofar as formal recognition in marriage is concerned. If moral disapprobation of homosexual conduct is "no legitimate state interest" for purposes of proscribing that conduct; and if, as the Court coos (casting aside all pretense of neutrality), "[w]hen sexuality finds overt expression in intimate conduct with another person, the conduct can be but one element in a personal bond that is more enduring"; what justification could there possibly be for denying the benefits of marriage to homosexual couples exercising "[t]he liberty protected by the Constitution"? Surely not the encouragement of procreation, since the sterile and the elderly are allowed to marry. This case "does not involve" the issue of homosexual marriage only if one entertains the belief that principle and logic have nothing to do with the decisions of this Court. Many will hope that, as the Court comfortingly assures us, this is so.a * * *

JUSTICE THOMAS, dissenting.

I join Justice Scalia's dissenting opinion. I write separately to note that the law before the Court today "is ... uncommonly silly." *Griswold* (Stewart, J., dissenting). If I were a member of the Texas Legislature, I would vote to repeal it. Punishing someone for expressing his sexual preference through noncommercial consensual conduct with another adult does not appear to be a worthy way to expend valuable law enforcement resources.

Notwithstanding this, I recognize that as a member of this Court I am not empowered to help petitioners and others similarly situated. My duty, rather, is to "decide cases 'agreeably to the Constitution and laws of the United States.' " And, just like Justice Stewart, I "can find [neither in the Bill of Rights nor any other part of the Constitution a] general right of privacy" or as the Court terms it today, the "liberty of the person both in its spatial and more transcendent dimensions."

Commentary on the Lawrence Case

1. ***The Supreme Court, the American people and the "cultural elite."*** Consider Lino A. Graglia, *Lawrence v. Texas: Our Philosopher–Kings Adopt Libertarianism as Our Official National Philosophy and Reject Traditional Morality as a Basis for Law*, 65 Ohio St.L.J. 1139, 1140–42 (2004): "[Why] do constitutional law scholars overwhelmingly favor decisionmaking on basic issues of social policy—such as the legal status of homosexuality—by the Supreme Court? The answer in a word is, of course, that it has for some time operated and, as *Lawrence* illustrates, is likely to continue to operate overwhelmingly to give them the policies they prefer and cannot get in any other way. The salient fact of American political life for the past half-century has been a deep cultural divide—in effect a 'culture war'—between the great majority of the American people and a cultural elite, made up of the 'knowledge' or 'verbal' class. This class is consisted primarily of academia, especially in elite institutions, and their progeny in the media, mainline churches, and elsewhere, whose only tools and products are words. Supreme Court Justices are almost always themselves products of the cultural elite, seeking its approval and sharing its deep distrust of the mass of their fellow citizens."

2. ***Can constitutional law proceed without making cultural judgments?*** Consider Robert C. Post, *Foreword: Fashioning the Legal Constitution: Culture, Courts and Law*, 117 Harv.L.Rev. 4, 84, 96 (2003): "[Dissenting in *Lawrence*, Scalia, J., criticized the majority] for taking 'sides in [a] culture war, departing from its role [as] neutral observer * * *.' The plausibility of Scalia's position depends upon whether constitutional law can meaningfully proceed without making cultural judgments. If, as I have argued, it cannot, then neither can constitutional law be autonomous from culture, nor can the Court be merely a 'neutral observer.'

"[*Lawrence*] unabashedly engages the values it perceives to be at stake in the case. [It] articulates the Court's own understanding of what is 'of fundamental

---

a. For portions of Scalia, J.'s dissenting opinion responding to O'Connor, J.'s concurring argument that the Texas statute violates equal protection, see p. 763 infra.

significance in defining the rights of the person.' And because it directly makes value judgments of this kind, *Lawrence* necessarily implicates itself in cultural controversy. Scalia is therefore right to accuse the Court of losing its neutrality. But this loss is an inevitable consequence of the Court's making the evaluative judgements necessary to fulfill the purpose of substantive due process doctrine, which is to identify and protect liberty interests that the Court deems constitutionally valuable."

3. ***Lawrence and the Loving case.*** In *Loving*, the Warren Court held that a state law prohibiting interracial marriage both violated the Equal Protection Clause and deprived the Lovings of liberty without due process. The Court rejected the argument that the law should be upheld if there was "any possible basis" that it "serve[d] a rational purpose," reminding Virginia that the Fourteenth Amendment has traditionally required of state laws drawn according to race "the very heavy burden of justification."

Pamela S. Karlan, *Foreword: Loving Lawrence*, 102 Mich.L.Rev. 1447, 1449–50 (2004), maintains that "*Lawrence* resembles *Loving* in important ways. Like *Loving*, *Lawrence* marks a crystallization of doctrine. Nearly forty years after *Griswold* and *Loving*, the Court has clearly established the principle that 'the substantive reach of liberty' under the Due Process Clause extends to the way individuals choose to conduct their personal relationships.' But just as *Loving* was a case about inequality that informed the jurisprudence of liberty, *Lawrence* is a case about liberty that has important implications for the jurisprudence of equality. In fact, liberty and equality are more intertwined in *Lawrence* than in *Loving*. The *Loving* Court could have rested its decision entirely on the unconstitutionality of racial subordination without looking at all at the importance of marriage; by contrast, the *Lawrence* Court's discussion of liberty would be incoherent without some underlying commitment to equality among groups."

4. ***Is same-sex marriage bound to follow?*** Yes, answers Laurence H. Tribe, *The "Fundamental Right" that Dare Not Speak Its Name*, 117 Harv.L.Rev. 1893,1945 (2004), "it is only a question of time." Professor Tribe continues: "For what, after all, could be the rationale for permitting an otherwise eligible same-sex couple to enjoy the tangible benefits and assume the legal obligations of some version of civil union but withholding from them that final measure of respect—that whole that plainly exceeds the mere sum of its component legal parts? [As] Justice Scalia rightly recognized, '"preserving the traditional institution of marriage" is just a kinder way of describing the State's *moral disapproval* of same-sex couples.'

Cf. Cass R. Sunstein, *Liberty after Lawrence*, 65 Ohio St.L.J. 1059, 1070–74 (2004): "[The] Court's effort to avoid the same-sex marriage issue was not entirely successful. Because the Court made it clear that a successful due process challenge need not be rooted in tradition, such a challenge might well be made to prohibitions on same-sex marriage under existing law. Several cases have indicated that there is a constitutional 'right to marry' under the Due Process Clause. [A] possible opinion would urge that by deeming the right to marry fundamental, the Court did not mean to suggest that it would strictly scrutinize any law that departed from the traditional idea that a marriage is between (one) woman and (one) man. It meant only to say that when a man and a woman, not members of the same family, seek to marry, the state must have exceedingly good reasons for putting significant barriers in their path. This rationale has the advantage of fitting with the results in *Loving*, *Zablocki* and *Turner*. It has the further advantage of not drawing into question bans on polygamous or incestuous marriages, or marriages between people and cats. But it does have a problem: it seems somewhat arbitrary. Why, exactly, should the right to marry be limited in this way? Why, in any case, should the definition be such as to allow the state not to recognize same-sex marriages?''

5. ***Judicial strategizing and the same-sex marriage and interracial marriage issues.*** Michael J. Klarman, *Brown and Lawrence (and Goodridge)*, 104 Mich.L.Rev. 431, 450–52 (2005): "[Just] as *Brown* led inexorably, albeit gradually, to a presumptive judicial ban on all racial classifications, so is *Lawrence* likely to lead eventually to a presumptive judicial ban on all classifications based on sexual orientation. [*Lawrence*] denies that 'moral disapproval' of homosexuality is a legitimate state interest. It is difficult, however, to identify a state interest other than moral disapproval that would convincingly justify banning same-sex marriage. The subsequent decision by the Massachusetts Supreme Court invalidating such bans confirms the difficulty of identifying plausible state interests other than moral disapproval that would justify treating gays and straights differently.[150] * * *

"Figuring out how the Court in [a same-sex marriage] case would distinguish *Lawrence* is an interesting question. Perhaps the Court would simply refuse to take such a case, much as the Justices after *Brown* managed to evade the antimiscegenation issue in [*Naim v. Naim*, 350 U.S. 891 (1955)]

"[Yet] the Court's refusal after *Brown* to extend its antidiscrimination rationale to the logical conclusion of invalidating antimiscegenation laws lasted only as long as public opinion remained overwhelmingly hostile to interracial marriage. The same is likely to be true of same-sex marriage. If public opinion on that issue becomes more tolerant—as I suggest [is] almost certain to happen—then the Court is likely to extend [*Lawrence*] and invalidate bans on same-sex marriage. The critical development in both arenas will have been changes in public opinion, not the inexorable doctrinal logic of the earlier decision."

MORE ON PRIVACY AND AUTONOMY

Personal appearance and lifestyles. KELLEY v. JOHNSON, 425 U.S. 238 (1976), per REHNQUIST, J., held that regulations directed at the style and length of male police officers' hair, sideburns and mustaches, and prohibiting beards and goatees except for medical reasons, violated no " 'liberty' interest protected by the Fourteenth Amendment": "The 'liberty' interest claimed [here] is distinguishable from [those] protected in *Roe, Eisenstadt* [and] *Griswold,* [which] involved a substantial claim of infringement on the individual's freedom of choice with respect to certain basic matters of procreation, marriage, and family life."

Assuming that "the citizenry at large has some sort of 'liberty' interest within the Fourteenth Amendment in matters of personal appearance," this assumption is insufficient to topple the regulation, for respondent has sought constitutional protection "as an employee of the county and, more particularly, as a policeman. [T]he county has chosen a mode of organization which it undoubtedly deems the most efficient in enabling its police to carry out the duties assigned to them under state and local law. Such a choice necessarily gives weight to the overall need for discipline, esprit de corps, and uniformity."

MARSHALL, J., joined by Brennan, J., dissented: "An individual's personal appearance may reflect, sustain, and nourish his personality and may well be used

---

150. *Goodridge v. Dep't of Pub. Health,* 798 N.E.2d 941 (Mass. 2003). The court in *Goodridge* rejected three interests proffered by the state to justify denying marriage to same-sex couples: (1) creating a favorable setting for procreation; (2) ensuring that childrearing takes place in "optimal" settings; (3) saving state resources by limiting the scope of the marriage "subsidy."

as a means of expressing his attitude and lifestyle. In taking control over a citizen's personal appearance, the Government forces him to sacrifice substantial elements of his integrity and identity as well. To say that the liberty guarantee of the Fourteenth Amendment does not encompass matters of personal appearance would be fundamentally inconsistent with the values of privacy, self-identity, autonomy, and personal integrity that I have always assumed the Constitution was designed to protect [referring, e.g., to *Roe* and *Griswold*]."

The substantive due process rights of involuntarily-committed mentally retarded persons. YOUNGBERG v. ROMEO, 457 U.S. 307 (1982), considered for the first time the substantive due process rights of involuntarily-committed mentally retarded persons. On his mother's petition, Romeo, a profoundly retarded 33–year-old was involuntarily committed to a Pennsylvania state institution (Pennhurst). Subsequently, concerned about injuries Romeo had suffered at Pennhurst, his mother sued institution officials claiming that her son had constitutional rights to (1) safe conditions of confinement, (2) freedom from bodily restraint, and (3) "a constitutional right to minimally adequate habilitation," i.e., minimal training and development of needed skills. (In light of his severe retardation, however, respondent conceded that no amount of training would make his release possible.) The Court, per POWELL, J., pointed out that respondent's first two claims "involve liberty interests recognized by prior decisions of this Court, interests that involuntary commitment proceedings do not extinguish," but found respondent's remaining claim "more troubling":

"Persons who have been involuntarily committed are entitled to more considerate treatment [than] criminals whose conditions of confinement are designed to punish. At the same time, the standard is lower than [a] 'compelling' or 'substantial' necessity [test for justifying restraints] that would place an undue burden on the administration of [state institutions] and also would restrict unnecessarily the exercise of professional judgment as to the needs of residents. [In] determining what is 'reasonable'—in this and in any case presenting a claim for training by a state—we emphasize that courts must show deference to the judgment exercised by a qualified professional. [The] decision, if made by a professional, is presumptively valid; liability may be imposed only when the decision by the professional is such a substantial departure from accepted professional judgment, practice or standards as to demonstrate that the person responsible actually did not base the decision on such a judgment. In an action for damages against a professional in his individual capacity, however, the professional will not be liable if he was unable to satisfy his normal professional standards because of budgetary constraints; in such a situation, good-faith immunity would bar liability."a

Blackmun, J., joined by Brennan and O'Connor, JJ., joined the Court's opinion, but concurred separately to clarify why, because of the uncertainty in the record, "that opinion properly leaves [open] difficult and important questions." Burger, C.J., concurring, agreed with much of the Court's opinion, but "would hold flatly that respondent has no constitutional right to training, or 'habilitation,' per se."

Freedom of intimate association and expressive association. See Ch. 7, Sec. 9, III.

   a. Consider, too, *DeShaney v. Winnebago County*, Ch. 10, Sec. 4.

———

SECTION 3. THE RIGHT TO KEEP AND BEAR ARMS

DISTRICT OF COLUMBIA v. HELLER

___ U.S. ___, 128 S.Ct. 2783, 171 L.Ed.2d 637 (2008).

JUSTICE SCALIA delivered the opinion of the Court.

[The District of Columbia has the strictest gun-control law in the country. It makes it a crime to carry an unregistered firearm and prohibits the registration of handguns, but authorizes the police chief to issue 1–year licenses. Moreover, residents must keep lawfully owned firearms "unloaded and disassembled or bound by a trigger lock or similar device" unless they are located in a place of business or being used for lawful recreational activities.

[Respondent, a D. C. special police officer, applied to register a handgun he wished to keep at home, but the District refused. He sued to enjoin the District from enforcing the prohibition on handgun registration, the licensing requirement (insofar as it prohibits carrying an unlicensed firearm in the home), and the trigger-lock requirement (insofar as it prohibits the use of functional firearms in the home).]

The Second Amendment provides: "A well regulated Militia, being necessary to the security of a free State, the right of the people to keep and bear Arms, shall not be infringed." In interpreting this text, we are guided by the principle that "[t]he Constitution was written to be understood by the voters; its words and phrases were used in their normal and ordinary as distinguished from technical meaning."

[The] two sides in this case have set out very different interpretations of the Amendment. Petitioners and today's dissenting Justices believe that it protects only the right to possess and carry a firearm in connection with militia service. Respondent argues that it protects an individual right to possess a firearm unconnected with service in a militia, and to use that arm for traditionally lawful purposes, such as self-defense within the home.

The Second Amendment is naturally divided into two parts: its prefatory clause and its operative clause. The former does not limit the latter grammatically, but rather announces a purpose. * * *

Putting all of [the Second Amendment's] textual elements together, we find that they guarantee the individual right to possess and carry weapons in case of confrontation. This meaning is strongly confirmed by the historical background of the Second Amendment. We look to this because it has always been widely understood that the Second Amendment, like the First and Fourth Amendments, codified a *pre-existing* right. The very text of the Second Amendment implicitly recognizes the pre-existence of the right and declares only that it "shall not be infringed."

[By] the time of the founding, the right to have arms had become fundamental for English subjects. [Blackstone's description of the right to bear arms in the English Bill of Rights] cannot possibly be thought to tie it to militia or military service.

[There] seems to us no doubt, on the basis of both text and history, that the Second Amendment conferred an individual right to keep and bear arms. Of course the right was not unlimited, just as the First Amendment's right of free speech was not. Thus, we do not read the Second Amendment to protect the right of citizens to carry arms for *any sort* of confrontation, just as we do not read the First Amendment to protect the right of citizens to speak for *any purpose*.

[Does the prefatory clause of the Second Amendment] fit with an operative clause that creates an individual right to keep and bear arms? It fits perfectly, once one knows the history that the founding generation knew and that we have described above. That history showed that the way tyrants had eliminated a militia consisting of all the able-bodied men was not by banning the militia but simply by taking away the people's arms, enabling a select militia or standing army to suppress political opponents. This is what had occurred in England that prompted codification of the right to have arms in the English Bill of Rights.

[The] prefatory clause does not suggest that preserving the militia was the only reason Americans valued the ancient right; most undoubtedly thought it even more important for self-defense and hunting. But the threat that the new Federal Government would destroy the citizens' militia by taking away their arms was the reason that right—unlike some other English rights—was codified in a written Constitution. Justice Breyer's assertion that individual self-defense is merely a "subsidiary interest" of the right to keep and bear arms is profoundly mistaken.
* * *

Justice Stevens places overwhelming reliance upon this Court's decision in *United States* v. *Miller*, 307 U.S. 174 (1939). [According to Justice Stevens, *Miller* holds that] the Second Amendment "protects the right to keep and bear arms for certain military purposes, but that it does not curtail the legislature's power to regulate the nonmilitary use and ownership of weapons."

[But] *Miller* did not hold that and cannot possibly be read to have held that. [It] upheld against a Second Amendment challenge two men's federal convictions for transporting an unregistered short-barreled shotgun [in] violation of the National Firearms Act. It is entirely clear that the Court's basis for saying that the Second Amendment did not apply was [that] the *type of weapon at issue* was not eligible for Second Amendment protection.[We] read *Miller* to say only that the Second Amendment does not protect those weapons not typically possessed by law-abiding citizens for lawful purposes, such as short-barreled shotguns. That accords with the historical understanding of the scope of the right.

[Like] most rights, the right secured by the Second Amendment is not unlimited. [For] example, the majority of the 19th-century courts to consider the question held that prohibitions on carrying concealed weapons were lawful under the Second Amendment or state analogues. Although we do not undertake an exhaustive historical analysis today of the full scope of the Second Amendment, nothing in our opinion should be taken to cast doubt on longstanding prohibitions on the possession of firearms by felons and the mentally ill, or laws forbidding the carrying of firearms in sensitive places such as schools and government buildings, or laws imposing conditions and qualifications on the commercial sale of arms.26

We also recognize another important limitation on the right to keep and carry arms. *Miller* said [that] the sorts of weapons protected were those "in common use at the time." We think that limitation is fairly supported by the historical tradition of prohibiting the carrying of "dangerous and unusual weapons."

[It] may be objected that if weapons that are most useful in military service— M–16 rifles and the like—may be banned, then the Second Amendment right is completely detached from the prefatory clause. But as we have said, the concep-

---

26. We identify these presumptively lawful regulatory measures only as examples; our list   does not purport to be exhaustive.

tion of the militia at the time of the Second Amendment's ratification was the body of all citizens capable of military service, who would bring the sorts of lawful weapons that they possessed at home to militia duty. It may well be true today that a militia, to be as effective as militias in the 18th century, would require sophisticated arms that are highly unusual in society at large. Indeed, it may be true that no amount of small arms could be useful against modern-day bombers and tanks. But the fact that modern developments have limited the degree of fit between the prefatory clause and the protected right cannot change our interpretation of the right.

We turn finally to the law at issue here. [As demonstrated earlier in this opinion,] the inherent right of self-defense has been central to the Second Amendment right. The [District's] handgun ban amounts to a prohibition of an entire class of "arms" that is overwhelmingly chosen by American society for that lawful purpose. The prohibition extends, moreover, to the home, where the need for defense of self, family, and property is most acute. Under any of the standards of scrutiny that we have applied to enumerated constitutional rights,[27] banning from the home "the most preferred firearm in the nation to 'keep' and use for protection of one's home and family" would fail constitutional muster.

It is no answer to say, as petitioners do, that it is permissible to ban the possession of handguns so long as the possession of other firearms (i.e., long guns) is allowed. It is enough to note [that] the American people have considered the handgun to be the quintessential self-defense weapon. There are many reasons that a citizen may prefer a handgun for home defense: It is easier to store in a location that is readily accessible in an emergency; it cannot easily be redirected or wrestled away by an attacker; it is easier to use for those without the upper-body strength to lift and aim a long gun; it can be pointed at a burglar with one hand while the other hand dials the police. Whatever the reason, handguns are the most popular weapon chosen by Americans for self-defense in the home, and a complete prohibition of their use is invalid.

We must also address the District's requirement (as applied to respondent's handgun) that firearms in the home be rendered and kept inoperable at all times. This makes it impossible for citizens to use them for the core lawful purpose of self-defense and is hence unconstitutional. * * *

Justice Breyer criticizes us for declining to establish a level of scrutiny for evaluating Second Amendment restrictions. He proposes, explicitly at least, none of the traditionally expressed levels (strict scrutiny, intermediate scrutiny, rational basis), but rather a judge-empowering "interest-balancing inquiry" that "asks whether the statute burdens a protected interest in a way or to an extent that is out of proportion to the statute's salutary effects upon other important governmental interests." [According to Justice Breyer:] because handgun violence is a problem, because the law is limited to an urban area, and because there were somewhat similar restrictions in the founding period (a false proposition that we have already discussed), the interest-balancing inquiry results in the constitutionality of the handgun ban. QED.

27. Justice Breyer correctly notes that this law, like almost all laws, would pass rational-basis scrutiny. But rational-basis scrutiny is a mode of analysis we have used when evaluating laws under constitutional commands that are themselves prohibitions on irrational laws. In those cases, "rational basis" is not just the standard of scrutiny, but the very substance of the constitutional guarantee. Obviously, the same test could not be used to evaluate the extent to which a legislature may regulate a specific, enumerated right, be it the freedom of speech, the guarantee against double jeopardy, the right to counsel, or the right to keep and bear arms. [If] all that was required to overcome the right to keep and bear arms was a rational basis, the Second Amendment would be redundant with the separate constitutional prohibitions on irrational laws, and would have no effect.

We know of no other enumerated constitutional right whose core protection has been subjected to a freestanding "interest-balancing" approach. The very enumeration of the right takes out of the hands of government—even the Third Branch of Government—the power to decide on a case-by-case basis whether the right is *really worth* insisting upon. A constitutional guarantee subject to future judges' assessments of its usefulness is no constitutional guarantee at all. Constitutional rights are enshrined with the scope they were understood to have when the people adopted them, whether or not future legislatures or (yes) even future judges think that scope too broad. We would not apply an "interest-balancing" approach to the prohibition of a peaceful neo-Nazi march through Skokie. See *National Socialist Party of America* v. *Skokie*, 432 U.S. 43 (1977) [see Casebook p. 732]. The First Amendment contains the freedom-of-speech guarantee that the people ratified, which included exceptions for obscenity, libel, and disclosure of state secrets, but not for the expression of extremely unpopular and wrong-headed views. The Second Amendment is no different. Like the First, it is the very *product* of an interest-balancing by the people—which Justice Breyer would now conduct for them anew. And whatever else it leaves to future evaluation, it surely elevates above all other interests the right of law-abiding, responsible citizens to use arms in defense of hearth and home. * * *

We are aware of the problem of handgun violence in this country, and we take seriously the concerns raised by [many] who believe that prohibition of handgun ownership is a solution. The Constitution leaves the District of Columbia a variety of tools for combating that problem, including some measures regulating handguns. But the enshrinement of constitutional rights necessarily takes certain policy choices off the table. These include the absolute prohibition of handguns held and used for self-defense in the home. Undoubtedly some think that the Second Amendment is outmoded in a society where our standing army is the pride of our Nation, where well-trained police forces provide personal security, and where gun violence is a serious problem. That is perhaps debatable, but what is not debatable is that it is not the role of this Court to pronounce the Second Amendment extinct. * * *

JUSTICE STEVENS, with whom JUSTICE SOUTER, JUSTICE GINSBURG, and JUSTICE BREYER join, dissenting. * * *

The Second Amendment was adopted to protect the right of the people of each of the several States to maintain a well-regulated militia. It was a response to concerns raised during the ratification of the Constitution that the power of Congress to disarm the state militias and create a national standing army posed an intolerable threat to the sovereignty of the several States. Neither the text of the Amendment nor the arguments advanced by its proponents evidenced the slightest interest in limiting any legislature's authority to regulate private civilian uses of firearms. Specifically, there is no indication that the Framers of the Amendment intended to enshrine the common-law right of self-defense in the Constitution.

In 1934, Congress enacted the National Firearms Act, the first major federal firearms law. Upholding a conviction under that Act, this Court held that, "[i]n the absence of any evidence tending to show that possession or use of a 'shotgun having a barrel of less than eighteen inches in length' at this time has some reasonable relationship to the preservation or efficiency of a well regulated militia, we cannot say that the Second Amendment guarantees the right to keep and bear such an instrument." The view of the Amendment we took in *Miller*—that it protects the right to keep and bear arms for certain military purposes, but that it does not curtail the Legislature's power to regulate the nonmilitary use and ownership of weapons—is both the most natural reading of the Amendment's text and the interpretation most faithful to the history of its adoption. * * *

The Court concludes its opinion by declaring that it is not the proper role of this Court to change the meaning of rights "enshrine[d]" in the Constitution. But the right the Court announces was not "enshrined" in the Second Amendment by the Framers; it is the product of today's law-changing decision. * * *

Until today, it has been understood that legislatures may regulate the civilian use and misuse of firearms so long as they do not interfere with the preservation of a well-regulated militia. The Court's announcement of a new constitutional right to own and use firearms for private purposes upsets that settled understanding, but leaves for future cases the formidable task of defining the scope of permissible regulations. Today judicial craftsmen have confidently asserted that a policy choice that denies a "law-abiding, responsible citize[n]" the right to keep and use weapons in the home for self-defense is "off the table." Given [the] reality that the need to defend oneself may suddenly arise in a host of locations outside the home, I fear that the District's policy choice may well be just the first of an unknown number of dominoes to be knocked off the table. * * *

JUSTICE BREYER, with whom JUSTICE STEVENS, JUSTICE SOUTER, and JUSTICE GINSBURG join, dissenting.

[The] majority's conclusion is wrong for two independent reasons. The first reason is that set forth by Justice Stevens—namely, that the Second Amendment protects militia-related, not self-defense-related, interests. These two interests are sometimes intertwined. To assure 18th-century citizens that they could keep arms for militia purposes would necessarily have allowed them to keep arms that they could have used for self-defense as well. But self-defense alone, detached from any militia-related objective, is not the Amendment's concern.

The second independent reason is that [the District's law] tailored to the urban crime problem in that it is local in scope and thus affects only a geographic area both limited in size and entirely urban; the law concerns handguns, which are specially linked to urban gun deaths and injuries, and which are the overwhelmingly favorite weapon of armed criminals; and at the same time, the law imposes a burden upon gun owners that seems proportionately no greater than restrictions in existence at the time the Second Amendment was adopted. In these circumstances, the District's law falls within the zone that the Second Amendment leaves open to regulation by legislatures.

[Respondent] proposes that the Court adopt a "strict scrutiny" test, which would require reviewing with care each gun law to determine whether it is "narrowly tailored to achieve a compelling governmental interest." But the majority implicitly, and appropriately, rejects that suggestion by broadly approving a set of laws—prohibitions on concealed weapons, forfeiture by criminals of the Second Amendment right, prohibitions on firearms in certain locales, and governmental regulation of commercial firearm sales—whose constitutionality under a strict scrutiny standard would be far from clear. * * *

I would simply adopt [an] interest-balancing inquiry explicitly. The fact that important interests lie on both sides of the constitutional equation suggests that review of gun-control regulation is not a context in which a court should effectively presume either constitutionality (as in rational-basis review) or unconstitutionality (as in strict scrutiny). Rather, [it] would take account both of the statute's effects upon the competing interests and the existence of any clearly superior less restrictive alternative. Contrary to the majority's unsupported suggestion that this sort of "proportionality" approach is unprecedented, the Court has applied it in various constitutional contexts, including election-law cases, speech cases, and due process cases.

[In] applying this kind of standard the Court normally defers to a legislature's empirical judgment in matters where a legislature is likely to have greater expertise and greater institutional factfinding capacity. Nonetheless, a court, not a legislature, must make the ultimate constitutional conclusion, exercising its "independent judicial judgment" in light of the whole record to determine whether a law exceeds constitutional boundaries.

[The record shows] a set of studies and counterstudies that, at most, could leave a judge uncertain about the proper policy conclusion. But from respondent's perspective any such uncertainty is not good enough. That is because legislators, not judges, have primary responsibility for drawing policy conclusions from empirical fact. And, given that constitutional allocation of decisionmaking responsibility, the empirical evidence presented here is sufficient to allow a judge to reach a firm *legal* conclusion.

[D]eference to legislative judgment seems particularly appropriate here, where the judgment has been made by a local legislature, with particular knowledge of local problems and insight into appropriate local solutions. [For] these reasons, I conclude that the District's statute properly seeks to further the sort of life-preserving and public-safety interests that the Court has called "compelling." [I]ts predictive judgments as to its law's tendency to achieve those objectives are adequately supported; the law does impose a burden upon any self-defense interest that the Amendment seeks to secure; and there is no clear less restrictive alternative. I turn now to the final portion of the "permissible regulation" question: Does the District's law *disproportionately* burden Amendment-protected interests? Several considerations, taken together, convince me that it does not.

First, the District law is tailored to the life-threatening problems it attempts to address. The law concerns one class of weapons, handguns, leaving residents free to possess shotguns and rifles, along with ammunition. The area that falls within its scope is totally urban. [The] urban area suffers from a serious handgun-fatality problem. The District's law directly aims at that compelling problem. And there is no less restrictive way to achieve the problem-related benefits that it seeks.

Second, the self-defense interest in maintaining loaded handguns in the home to shoot intruders is not the *primary* interest, but at most a subsidiary interest, that the Second Amendment seeks to serve. The Second Amendment's language, while speaking of a "Militia," says nothing of "self-defense."

[Further,] any self-defense interest at the time of the Framing could not have focused exclusively upon urban-crime related dangers. Two hundred years ago, most Americans, many living on the frontier, would likely have thought of self-defense primarily in terms of outbreaks of fighting with Indian tribes, rebellions, * * * marauders, and crime-related dangers to travelers on the roads, on foot-paths, or along waterways.

[Nor,] for that matter, am I aware of any evidence that *handguns* in particular were central to the Framers' conception of the Second Amendment. The lists of militia-related weapons in the late 18th-century state statutes appear primarily to refer to other sorts of weapons, muskets in particular.

[Finally,] a contrary view, as embodied in today's decision, will have unfortunate consequences. The [majority's] decision will encourage legal challenges to gun regulation throughout the Nation. Because it says little about the standards used to evaluate regulatory decisions, it will leave the Nation without clear standards for resolving those challenges. And litigation over the course of many years, or the mere specter of such litigation, threatens to leave cities without effective protection against gun violence and accidents during that time.

As important, the majority's decision threatens severely to limit the ability of more knowledgeable, democratically elected officials to deal with gun-related problems. The majority says that it leaves the District "a variety of tools for combating" such problems. It fails to list even one seemingly adequate replacement for the law it strikes down. I can understand how reasonable individuals can disagree about the merits of strict gun control as a crime-control measure, even in a totally urbanized area. But I cannot understand how one can take from the elected branches of government the right to decide whether to insist upon a handgun-free urban populace in a city now facing a serious crime problem and which, in the future, could well face environmental or other emergencies that threaten the breakdown of law and order.

The majority derides my approach as "judge-empowering." I take this criticism seriously, but I do not think it accurate. As I have previously explained, this is an approach that the Court has taken in other areas of constitutional law. Application of such an approach, of course, requires judgment, but the very nature of the approach—requiring careful identification of the relevant interests and evaluating the law's effect upon them—limits the judge's choices; and the method's necessary transparency lays bare the judge's reasoning for all to see and to criticize.

[The] majority says that that Amendment protects those weapons "typically possessed by law-abiding citizens for lawful purposes." This definition conveniently excludes machineguns, but permits handguns, which the majority describes as "the most popular weapon chosen by Americans for self-defense in the home." But what sense does this approach make? According to the majority's reasoning, if Congress and the States lift restrictions on the possession and use of machineguns, and people buy machineguns to protect their homes, the Court will have to reverse course and find that the Second Amendment *does*, in fact, protect the individual self-defense-related right to possess a machine-gun. On the majority's reasoning, if tomorrow someone invents a particularly useful, highly dangerous self-defense weapon, Congress and the States had better ban it immediately, for once it becomes popular Congress will no longer possess the constitutional authority to do so. In essence, the majority determines what regulations are permissible by looking to see what existing regulations permit. There is no basis for believing that the Framers intended such circular reasoning.

[The] majority ignores a more important question: Given the purposes for which the Framers enacted the Second Amendment, how should it be applied to modern-day circumstances that they could not have anticipated? Assume, for argument's sake, that the Framers did intend the Amendment to offer a degree of self-defense protection. Does that mean that the Framers also intended to guarantee a right to possess a loaded gun near swimming pools, parks, and playgrounds? That they would not have cared about the children who might pick up a loaded gun on their parents' bedside table? That they [would] have lacked concern for the risk of accidental deaths or suicides that readily accessible loaded handguns in urban areas might bring? Unless we believe that they intended future generations to ignore such matters, answering questions such as the questions in this case requires judgment—judicial judgment exercised within a framework for constitutional analysis that guides that judgment and which makes its exercise transparent. One cannot answer those questions by combining inconclusive historical research with judicial ipse dixit.

The argument about method, however, is by far the less important argument surrounding today's decision. Far more important are the unfortunate consequences that today's decision is likely to spawn. Not least of these [is] the fact that the decision threatens to throw into doubt the constitutionality of gun laws throughout the United States. I can find no sound legal basis for launching the courts on so formidable and potentially dangerous a mission. In my view, there simply is no untouchable constitutional right guaranteed by the Second Amendment to keep loaded handguns in the house in crime-ridden urban areas. * * *

————

Shortly after *Heller* was decided, petitioners sought a declaration that the City of Chicago's weapons ban, which effectively prohibited handgun possession by almost all private citizens residing in the City, violated the Second and Fourteenth Amendments. McDONALD v. CHICAGO, 130 S.Ct. ___ (2010), held that the Second Amendment "right to keep and bear arms for the purpose of self-defense" is "fully applicable to the States." However, the majority could not agree on what provision of the Fourteenth Amendment applied.

Alito, J.'s principal opinion recognized that "today, many legal scholars dispute the correctness of the narrow *Slaughter-House* interpretation" of the Privileges or Immunities Clause (see Casebook p. 298). But because "for many decades, the question of rights protected by the Fourteenth Amendment has been analyzed under the Due Process Clause," Alito, J., joined by Roberts, C.J., and Scalia and Kennedy, JJ., decline[d] to disturb the *Slaughter-House* holding.a

After discussing the history of the "incorporation" of the Bill of Rights provisions and Black, J.'s theory (never fully adopted) that Fourteenth Amendment Due Process "totally incorporated" all the provisions of the Bill of Rights, the Court turned to the question "whether the Second Amendment right to keep and bear arms is incorporated in the concept of due process. In answering that question [we] must decide whether [this right] is fundamental to *our* scheme of ordered liberty, *Duncan v. Louisiana* [Casebook p. 365] or [whether] this right is 'deeply rooted in this Nation's history and tradition' *Washington v. Glucksberg* [Casebook p. 471]. *Heller* points unmistakably to the answer. Self-defense is a basic right, recognized by many legal systems from ancient times to the present day, and in *Heller* we held that individual self-defense is 'the *central component*' of the Second Amendment [right.] *Heller* makes clear that this right is 'deeply rooted in this Nation's history and tradition.' *Glucksberg*."

After noting, inter alia, that in "debating the Fourteenth Amendment, the 39th Congress referred to the right to keep and bear arms as a fundamental right deserving of protection," and that "evidence from the period immediately following the ratification of the Fourteenth Amendment only confirms that the right to keep and bear arms was considered fundamental," the Court concluded: "In sum, it is clear that the Framers and ratifiers of the Fourteenth Amendment counted the right to keep and bear arms among those fundamental rights necessary to our system of ordered liberty."

As for the argument that the Second Amendment is unique among the provisions of the Bill of Rights because it concerns the right to possess a deadly implement and thus has implications for public safety, Alito, J., responded: The Second Amendment "is not the only constitutional right that has controversial public safety implications. All of the constitutional provisions that impose restric-

a. Thomas, J., who provided the fifth vote for the Court's ruling, based his opinion (infra) on the Fourteenth Amendment's Privileges or Immunities Clause.

tions on law enforcement and on the prosecution of crimes fall into the same category."

In a part of the opinion that Thomas, J., declined to join, the plurality recalled that the *Heller* Court had "made it clear [that its] holding did not cast doubt on such longstanding regulatory measures as 'prohibitions on the possession of firearms by felons and the mentally ill,' 'laws forbidding the carrying of firearms in sensitive places such as schools and government buildings, or laws imposing conditions and qualifications on the commercial sale of arms.' We repeat these assurances here."

THOMAS, J., concurring in part and in the judgment, "agree[d] with the Court that the Second Amendment right to keep and bear arms is "fully applicable to the States," and is "fundamental" to the American "scheme of ordered liberty" and "deeply rooted in the Nation's history and tradition." But he balked at utilizing the Fourteenth Amendment's Due Process Clause: "I cannot agree that the [Second Amendment] is enforceable against the States through a clause that speaks only to 'process.' Instead, the right to keep and bear arms is a privilege of American citizenship that applies to the States through the Fourteenth Amendment's Privileges or Immunities Clause": The notion that a constitutional provision that guarantees only 'process' before a person is deprived of life, liberty or property could define the substance of [rights not mentioned in the Constitution at all] strains credulity for even the most casual user of words. Moreover, this fiction is a particularly dangerous one. The one theme that links the Court's substantive due process precedents together is their lack of a guiding principle to distinguish 'fundamental' rights that warrant protection from nonfundamental rights that do not. Today's decision illustrates the point. Replaying a debate that has endured from the inception of the Court's substantive due process jurisprudence, the dissent lauds the 'flexibility' in this Court's substantive due process doctrine [while] the plurality makes yet another effort to impose principled restraints on its exercise. But neither side argues that the meaning they attribute to the Due Process Clause was consistent with public understanding at the time of its ratification."

After a long discussion of the meaning of the terms "privileges" and "immunities," the Congressional debates on the Fourteenth Amendment, what the ratifying public understood the Privileges or Immunities Clause to mean, and the civil rights legislation adopted by the 39th Congress in 1866, Thomas, J., concluded: "[T]he record makes plain that the Framers of the Privileges or Immunities Clause and the ratifying-era public understood—just as the Framers of the Second Amendment did—that the right to keep and bear arms was essential to the preservation of liberty. The record makes equally plain that they deemed this right necessary to include in the minimum baseline of federal rights that the Privileges or Immunities Clause established in the wake of the War over slavery. * * * I agree with the Court that the Second Amendment is fully applicable to the States. I do so because the right to keep and bear arms is guaranteed by the Fourteenth Amendment as a privilege of American citizenship."

BREYER, J., joined by Ginsburg and Sotomayor, JJ., dissented. After a long discussion of 18th, 19th, 20th, and 21st century history, Breyer, J., could find "nothing [that] shows a consensus that the right to private armed defense, as described in *Heller*, is 'deeply rooted in this Nation's history or tradition' or is otherwise 'fundamental.' Indeed, incorporating the right recognized in *Heller* may change the law in many of the 50 States. Read in the majority's favor, the historical evidence is at most ambiguous. And, in the absence of any other support for its conclusion, ambiguous history cannot show that the Fourteenth Amendment incorporates a private right of self-defense against the States.

"[D]etermining the constitutionality of a particular gun law requires finding answers to complex empirically based questions of a kind that legislatures are better able than courts to [make.] Suppose, for example, that after a gun regulation's adoption, the murder rate went up. Without the gun regulation would the murder rate have risen even faster? [D]oes the right to possess weapons for self-defense extend outside the home? To the car? To work? What sort of guns are necessary for self-defense? [Does] the presence of a child in the house matter? Does the presence of a convicted felon in the house matter? [When] do registration requirements become severe to the point that they amount to an unconstitutional ban? [The] difficulty of finding answers to these questions is exceeded only by the importance of doing so. Firearms cause well over 60,000 deaths and injuries in the United States each year. Those who live in urban areas, police officers, women, and children, all may be particularly at risk. And gun regulation may save their lives. Some experts have calculated, for example, that Chicago's handgun ban has saved several hundred lives, perhaps close to 1,000, since it was enacted in 1983.

"[At] the same time, the opponents of regulation cast doubt on these studies. And who is right? [Suppose] studies find more accidents and suicides where there is a handgun in the home than where there is a large gun in the home or no gun at all. To what extent do such studies justify a ban? What if opponents of the ban put forth counter studies? In answering such questions judges cannot simply refer to judicial homilies, such as Blackstone's 18th-century perception that a man's home is his castle. Nor can the plurality so simply reject, by mere assertion, the fact that 'incorporation will require judges to assess the costs and benefits of firearms restrictions.'

"[The] fact is that judges do not know the answers to the kind of empirically based questions that will often determine the need for particular forms of gun regulation. Nor do they have readily available 'tools' for finding and evaluating the technical material submitted by others."

STEVENS, J., filed a separate dissent, "agree[ing] with the plurality that there are weighty arguments supporting petitioners' [Due Process contention]. But these arguments are less compelling than the plurality suggests; they are much less compelling when applied outside the home; and their validity does not depend on the Court's holding in *Heller*. For that holding sheds no light on the meaning of the Due Process Clause. [Our] decisions construing that Clause to render various procedural guarantees in the Bill of Rights enforceable against the States likewise tell us little about the meaning of the word 'liberty' in the Clause or about the scope of its protection of nonprocedural rights. This is a substantive due process case.

"[A] key constraint on substantive due process analysis is respect for the democratic process. If a particular liberty interest is already being given careful consideration in, and subjected to ongoing calibration by, the States, judicial enforcement may not be appropriate. When the Court declined to establish a general right to physician-assisted suicide, for example, it did so in part because 'the States [were] currently engaged in serious, thoughtful examinations of physician-assisted suicide and other similar issues,' rendering judicial intervention both less necessary and potentially more disruptive. *Glucksberg*. Conversely, we have long appreciated that more 'searching' judicial review may be justified when the rights of 'discrete and insular minorities'—groups that may face systematic barriers in the political system—are at stake. *United States v. Carolene Products Co.* [Casebook p. 316].

"Recognizing a new liberty right is a momentous step. It takes that right, to a considerable extent, 'outside the arena of public debate and legislative action.' *Glucksberg*. Sometimes that momentous step must be taken; some fundamental aspects of personhood, dignity, and the like do not vary from State to State, and demand a baseline of protection. But sensitivity to the interaction between the intrinsic aspects of liberty and the practical realities of contemporary society provides an important tool for guiding judicial discretion. This sensitivity is an aspect of a deeper principle: the need to approach our work with humility and caution.

"[While] I agree with the Court that our substantive due process cases offer a principled basis for holding that petitioners have a constitutional right to possess a usable firearm in the home, I am ultimately persuaded that a better reading of our case law supports the city of Chicago. I would not foreclose the possibility that a particular plaintiff—say, an elderly widow who lives in a dangerous neighborhood and does not have the strength to operate a long gun—may have a cognizable liberty interest in possessing a handgun. But I cannot accept petitioners' broader submission. A number of factors, taken together, lead me to this conclusion.

"First, firearms have a fundamentally ambivalent relationship to liberty. Just as they can help homeowners defend their families and property from intruders, they can help thugs and insurrectionists murder innocent victims. [Amici] calculate that approximately one million Americans have been wounded or killed by gunfire in the last decade. [In] recent years, handguns were reportedly used in more than four-fifths of firearm murders and more than half of all murders nationwide.

"[The] right to possess a firearm of one's choosing is different in kind from the liberty interests we have recognized under the Due Process Clause. Despite the plethora of substantive due process cases that have been decided in the post-*Lochner* century, I have found none that holds, states, or even suggests that the term 'liberty' encompasses either the common-law right of self-defense or a right to keep and bear arms. I do not doubt for a moment that many Americans feel deeply passionate about firearms [but] it does not appear to be the case that the ability to own a handgun, or any particular type of firearm, is critical to leading a life of autonomy, dignity, or political equality. [The] liberty interest asserted by petitioners is also dissimilar from those we have recognized in its capacity to undermine the security of others. [The] handgun is itself a tool for crime; the handgun's bullets *are* the violence.

"[Although] it may be true that Americans' interest in firearm possession and state-law recognition of that interest are 'deeply rooted' in some important senses, it is equally true that the States have a long and unbroken history of regulating firearms. The idea that States may place substantial restrictions on the right to keep and bear arms short of complete disarmament is, in fact, far more entrenched than the notion that the Federal Constitution protects any such right.

"[Across] the Nation, States and localities vary significantly in the patterns and problems of gun violence they face, as well as in the traditions and cultures of lawful gun use they claim. The city of Chicago, for example, faces a pressing challenge in combating criminal street gangs. Most rural areas do not. The city of Chicago has a high population density, which increases the potential for a gunman to inflict mass terror and casualties. Most rural areas do not. The city of Chicago offers little in the way of hunting opportunities. Residents of rural communities are, one presumes, much more likely to stock the dinner table with game they have personally felled. Given that relevant background conditions diverge so much across jurisdictions, the Court ought to pay particular heed to state and legal legislatures 'right to experiment.' *New State Ice Co. v. Liebman*, 285 U.S. 262, 311 (1932). (Brandeis, J., dissenting.) So long as the regulatory measures they have chosen are not 'arbitrary, capricious, or unreasonable,' we should be allowing them to 'try novel social and economic' policies. Ibid.

"[The] strength of a liberty claim must be assessed in connection with its status in the democratic process. And in this case, no one disputes 'that opponents of [gun] control have considerable political power and do not seem to be at a systematic disadvantage in the democratic process,' or that 'the widespread commitment to an individual right to own guns [operates] as a safeguard against excessive or unjustified gun control laws.' Cass Sunstein, *Second Amendment Minimalism: Heller as Griswold*, 122 Harv.L.Rev. 246, 260 (2008). [Neither] petitioners nor those most zealously committed to their views represent a group or a claim that is liable to receive unfair treatment at the hands of the majority. On the contrary, petitioners' views are supported by powerful participants in the legislative process. * * *

"Justice Scalia's method invites not only bad history, but also bad constitutional law. [In] evaluating a claimed liberty interest (or any constitutional claim for that matter), it makes perfect sense to give history significant weight. [But] it makes little sense to give history dispositive weight in every case. And it makes *especially* little sense to answer questions like whether the right to bear arms is 'fundamental' by focusing only on the past, given that both the practical significance and the public understandings of such a right often change as society changes. What if the evidence had shown that, whereas at one time firearm possession contributed substantially to personal liberty and safety, nowadays it contributes nothing, or even tends to undermine them? Would it still have been reasonable to constitutionalize the right?

"The concern runs still deeper. Not only can historical views be less than completely clear or informative, but they can also be wrong. [It] is not the role of federal judges to be amateur historians. And it is not fidelity to the Constitution to ignore its use of deliberately capacious language, in an effort to transform foundational legal commitments into narrow rules of decision. As for 'the democratic process,' a method that looks exclusively to history can easily do more harm than good. Just consider this case. The net result of Justice Scalia's supposedly objective analysis is to vest federal judges—ultimately a majority of the judges on this Court—with unprecedented lawmaking powers in an area in which they have no special qualifications, and in which the give-and-take of the political process has functioned effectively for decades. Why this 'intrudes much less upon the democratic process' than an approach that would defer to the democratic process on the regulation of firearms is, to say the least, not self-evident."

SCALIA, J., joined the Court's opinion: "Despite my misgivings about Substantive Due Process as an original matter, I have acquiesced in the Court's interpretation of certain guarantees in the Bill of Rights 'because it is both long established and narrowly limited.' This case does not require me to reconsider that view, since straightforward application of settled doctrine suffices to decide it." He concurred separately "only to respond to some aspects of Justice Stevens' dissent":

As Scalia, J., understood Stevens, J., not all provisions of the first eight amendments are incorporated by Fourteenth Amendment Due Process, "since only '*some* fundamental aspects of personhood, dignity, and the like' are protected (emphasis added). Exactly what is covered is not clear. But whatever else is in, [Stevens, J.] *knows* that the right to keep and bear arms is out, despite its being as 'deeply rooted in this Nation's history and tradition' as a right can be, see *Heller*. I can find no other explanation for such certitude except that Justice Stevens, despite his forswearing of 'personal and private notions,' deeply believes it should be out. * * *

"Justice Stevens also argues that requiring courts to show 'respect for the democratic process' should serve as a constraint. That is true, but [he] would have them show respect in an extraordinary manner. In his view, if a right 'is already being given careful consideration in, and subjected to ongoing calibration by, the States, judicial enforcement may not be appropriate.' In other words, a right, such as the right to keep and bear arms, that has long been recognized but on which the States are considering restrictions, apparently deserves *less* protection, while a privilege the political branches (instruments of the democratic process) have withheld entirely and continue to withhold, deserves *more*. That topsy-turvy approach conveniently accomplishes the objective of ensuring that the rights this Court held protected in *Casey*, *Lawrence*, and other such cases fit the theory—but at the cost of insulting rather than respecting the democratic process.

"[Stevens, J.] offers several reasons for concluding that the Second Amendment right to keep and bear arms is not fundamental enough to be applied against the States. None is persuasive, but more pertinent to my purpose, each is either intrinsically indeterminate, would preclude incorporation of rights we have already held incorporated, or both. His approach therefore does nothing to stop a judge from arriving at any conclusion he sets out to reach. [He] begins with the odd assertion that 'firearms have a fundamentally ambivalent relationship to liberty,' since sometimes they are used to cause (or sometimes accidentally produce) injury to others. [The] criterion, [is] inherently manipulable. Surely Justice Stevens does not mean that the Clause covers only rights that have *zero* harmful effect on *anyone*. Otherwise even the First Amendment is out.

"[He] next suggests that the Second Amendment right is not fundamental because it is 'different in kind' from other rights we have recognized. [Even] though he does 'not doubt for a moment that many Americans [see firearms] as critical to their way of life as well as to their security,' he pronounces that owning a handgun is not 'critical to leading a life of autonomy, dignity, or political equality.' Who says? Deciding what is essential to an enlightened, liberty-filled life is an inherently political, moral judgment–the antithesis of an objective approach that reaches conclusions by applying neutral rules to verifiable evidence. * * *

"Justice Stevens' final reason for rejecting incorporation of the Second Amendment reveals, more clearly than any of the others, the game that is afoot. Assuming that there is a 'plausible constitutional basis' for holding that the right to keep and bear arms is incorporated, he asserts that we ought not to do so *for prudential reasons*. Even if we had the authority to withhold rights that are within the Constitution's command (and we assuredly do not), two of the reasons Justice Stevens gives for abstention show just how much power he would hand to judges. The States 'right to experiment' with solutions to the problem of gun violence, he says, is at its apex here because 'the best solution is far from clear.' That is true of most serious social problems—whether, for example, 'the best solution' for rampant crime is to admit confessions unless they are affirmatively shown to have been coerced, but see *Miranda*, or to permit jurors to impose the death penalty without a requirement that they be free to consider 'any relevant mitigating factor.'

"[The] traditional, historically focused method, [observes Justice Stevens], reposes discretion in judges as well. Historical analysis can be difficult; it sometimes requires resolving threshold questions, and making nuanced judgments about which evidence to consult and how to interpret it.

"I will stipulate to that. But the question to be decided is not whether the historically focused method is a *perfect means* of restraining aristocratic judicial Constitution-writing; but whether it is the *best means available* in an imperfect world. Or indeed, even more narrowly than that: whether it is demonstrably much better than what Justice Stevens proposes. I think it beyond all serious dispute that it is much less subjective, and intrudes much less upon the democratic process. [In] the most controversial matters brought before this Court—for example, the constitutionality of prohibiting abortion, assisted suicide, or homosexual sodomy, or the constitutionality of the death penalty—*any* historical methodology, under *any* plausible standard of proof, would lead to the same conclusion. Moreover, the methodological differences that divide historians, and the varying interpretive assumptions they bring to their work, are nothing compared to the differences among the American people (though perhaps not among graduates of prestigious law schools) with regard to the moral judgments Justice Stevens would have courts pronounce."

SECTION 4. PROCEDURAL DUE PROCESS AND THE RIGHT TO AN IMPARTIAL DECISIONMAKER

CAPERTON v. MASSEY COAL CO., 129 S.Ct. 2252 (2009) arose as follows: A West Virginia jury found Massey Coal Co. (Massey) liable for tortious interference with existing contractual relations and other torts and awarded petitioner (hereinafter Caperton) $50 million dollars in damages. After the verdict but before the appeal, West Virginia held its 2004 judicial elections. Knowing that the State Supreme Court of Appeals would consider the appeal, Massey's principal officer, Don Blankenship, supported Brent Benjamin, a judicial candidate for that court, rather than the incumbent justice seeking reelection. Blankenships $3 million in contributions exceeded the total amount spent by all other Benjamin supporters. Benjamin won by less than 50,000 votes.

Before Massey had filed its appeal to the state court of appeals, Caperton moved to disqualify now-Justice Benjamin. Justice Benjamin denied the motion. The court then overturned the $50 million verdict by a 3–2 vote, Benjamin voting with the majority. During the rehearing process, Justice Benjamin refused twice more to recuse himself. Once again, a 3–2 majority, including Justice Benjamin, reversed the jury's verdict. Four months later, Justice Benjamin filed a concurring opinion, defending the court's opinion and his own recusal decision.

KENNEDY, J., joined by STEVENS, SOUTER, GINSBURG AND BREYER, JJ., reversed because "due process requires recusal" where, as here, "the probability of actual bias on the part of the judge or decisionmaker is too high to be constitutionally tolerable":

"Justice Benjamin conducted a probing search into his actual motives and inclinations and he found none to be improper. We do no question his subjective findings of impartiality and propriety. Nor do we determine whether there was actual bias. [The] difficulties of inquiring into actual bias, and the fact that the inquiry is often a private one, simply underscore the need for objective rules. * * *

"Not every campaign contribution by a litigant or attorney creates a probability of bias that requires a judge's recusal, but this is an exceptional case. [There] is a serious risk of actual bias—based on objective and reasonable perceptions—when [one] with a personal stake in a particular case had a significant and disproportionate influence in placing the judge on the case by raising funds or directing the judge's election campaign when the case was pending or imminent. The inquiry centers on the contributions relative size in comparison to the total amount of money contributed to the campaign, the total amount spent in the election, and the apparent effect such contribution had on the outcome of the election.

"[The] failure to consider objective standards requiring recusal is not consistent with the imperatives of due process. We find that Blankenship's significant and disproportionate influence—coupled with the temporal relationship between the election and the pending case would offer a possible temptation to the average judge [which might] lead him not to hold the balance nice, clear and true.' [On] these extreme facts the probability of actual bias rises to an unconstitutional level."

ROBERTS, C.J., joined by Scalia, Thomas and Alito, JJ., dissented:

"Today, [the] Court enlists the Due Process Clause to overturn a judge's failure to recuse because of a 'probability of bias.' [The] Courts new 'rule' provides no guidance to judges and litigants about when recusal will be constitutionally required. This will inevitably lead to an increase in allegations that judges are biased, however groundless those charges may be. The end result will do far more to erode public confidence in judicial impartiality than an isolated failure to recuse in a particular case.

"[In] any given case, there are a number of factors that could give rise to a 'probability' or 'appearance' of bias: friendship with a party or lawyer, prior employment experience, membership in clubs or associations, prior speeches and writings, religious affiliation, and countless other considerations. We have never held that the Due Process Clause requires recusal for any of these reasons, even though they could be viewed as presenting a 'probability of bias.' "

Roberts, C.J., then asked *forty* questions he maintained "courts will now have to determine," including:

"1. How much money is too much money? What level of contribution or expenditure gives rise to a 'probability of bias'?

"2. How do we determine whether a given expenditure is 'disproportionate'? Disproportionate to *what*?

"3. Are independent, non-coordinated expenditures treated the same as direct contributions to a candidates campaign? What about contributions to independent outside groups supporting a candidate?

"4. Does it matter whether the litigant has contributed to other candidates or made large expenditures in connection with other elections?

"5. Does the amount at issue in the case matter? What if this case were an employment dispute with only $10,000 at stake? What if the plaintiffs only sought non-monetary relief such as an injunction or declaratory judgment? * * *

"9. What if the case involves a social or ideological issue rather than a financial one? Must a judge recuse from cases involving, say, abortion rights if he has received 'disproportionate' support from individuals who feel strongly about either side of that issue? If the supporter wants to help elect judges who are tough on crime, must the judge recuse in all criminal cases?

"10. What if the candidate draws disproportionate support from a particular racial, religious, ethnic, or other group, and the case involves an issue of particular importance to that group?"

"To its credit, the Court seems to recognize that the inherently boundless nature of its new rule poses a problem. But the majority's only answer is that the present case is an 'extreme one', so there is no need to worry about other cases. [But] this is just so much whistling past the graveyard. Claims that have little chance of success are nonetheless frequently filed. The success rate for certiorari petitions before this Court is approximately 1.1%, and yet the previous Term some 8,241 were filed. * * * Extreme cases often test the bounds of established legal principles. There is a cost to yielding to the desire to correct the extreme case, rather than adhering to the legal principle. That cost has been demonstrated so often that it is captured in a legal aphorism: 'Hard cases make bad law.' "

In a separate dissent, SCALIA, J., protested: "What above all else is eroding public confidence in the Nations judicial system is the perception that litigation is just a game, that the party with the most resourceful lawyer can play it to win, that our seemingly interminable legal proceedings are wonderfully self-perpetuating but incapable of delivering real-world justice. The Court's opinion will reinforce that perception, adding to the vast arsenal of lawyerly gambits what will come to be known as the *Caperton* claim. The facts relevant to adjudicating it will have to be litigated—and likewise the law governing it, which will be indeterminate for years to come, if not forever."

Scalia, J., then noted that "[a] Talmudic maxim instructs with respect to the Scripture: 'Turn it over, and turn it over, for all is therein.' Divinely inspired text may contain the answers to all earthly questions, but the Due Process Clause most assuredly does not. The Court today continues its quixotic quest to write all wrongs and repair all imperfections through the Constitution."

The Court was not impressed with the argument that "various adverse consequence will follow from recognizing a constitutional violation here—ranging from a flood of recusal motions to unnecessary interference with judicial elections": "The parties point to no other instance involving judicial campaign contributions that presents a potential for bias comparable to the circumstances in this case." Moreover, " '[the] Due Process Clause demarks only the outer boundaries of judicial disqualifications. Congress and the states, of course, remain free to impose more rigorous standards for judicial disqualification than those we find mandated here today.' Because the codes of judicial conduct provide more protection than due process requires, most disputes over disqualification will be resolved without resort to the Constitution. Application of the constitutional standard implicated in this case will thus be confined to rare instances."

Chapter 7

FREEDOM OF EXPRESSION
AND ASSOCIATION

SECTION 1. WHAT SPEECH IS NOT PROTECTED?

The First Amendment provides that "Congress shall make no law * * * abridging the freedom of speech, or of the press." Some have stressed that no law means NO LAW. For example, Black, J., dissenting in *Konigsberg v. State Bar,* 366 U.S. 36 (1961) argued that the "First Amendment's unequivocal command [shows] that the men who drafted our Bill of Rights did all the 'balancing' that was to be done in this field."

Laws forbidding speech, however, are commonplace. Laws against perjury, blackmail, and fraud prohibit speech. So does much of the law of contracts. Black, J., himself conceded that speech pursued as an integral part of criminal conduct was beyond First Amendment protection. Indeed no one contends that citizens are free to say anything, anywhere, at any time. As Holmes, J., observed, citizens are not free to yell "fire" falsely in a theater.

The spectre of a man crying fire falsely in the theater, however, has plagued First Amendment theory. The task is to formulate principles that separate the protected from the unprotected. But speech interacts with too many other values in too many complicated ways to expect that a single formula will prove productive.

Are advocates of illegal action, pornographers selling magazines, or publishers of defamation like that person in the theater or are they engaged in freedom of speech? Do citizens have a right to speak on government property? Which property? Is there a right of access to the print or broadcast media? Can government force private owners to grant access for speakers? Does the First Amendment offer protection for the wealthy, powerful corporations, and media conglomerates against government attempts to assure greater equality in the intellectual marketplace? Can government demand information about private political associations or reporters' confidential sources without First Amendment limits? Does the First Amendment require government to produce information it might otherwise withhold?

The Court has approached questions such as these without much attention to the language or history of the First Amendment and without a commitment to any general theory. Rather it has sought to develop principles on a case-by-case basis and has produced a complex and conflicting body of constitutional precedent. Many of the basic principles were developed in a line of cases involving the advocacy of illegal action.

I. ADVOCACY OF ILLEGAL ACTION

A. EMERGING PRINCIPLES

SCHENCK v. UNITED STATES, 249 U.S. 47 (1919): Defendants were convicted of a conspiracy to violate the 1917 Espionage Act by conspiring to cause and attempting to cause insubordination in the armed forces of the United States, and obstruction of the recruiting and enlistment service of the United States, when at war with Germany, by printing and circulating to men accepted for military service approximately fifteen thousand copies of the document described in the opinion. In affirming, HOLMES, J., said for a unanimous Court: "The document in question upon its first printed side recited the first section of the Thirteenth Amendment, said that the idea embodied in it was violated by the conscription act and that a conscript is little better than a convict. In impassioned language it intimated that conscription was despotism in its worst form and a monstrous wrong against humanity in the interest of Wall Street's chosen few. It said, 'Do not submit to intimidation,' but in form at least confined itself to peaceful measures such as a petition for the repeal of the act. The other and later printed side of the sheet was headed 'Assert Your Rights.' It stated reasons for alleging that any one violated the Constitution when he refused to recognize 'your right to assert your opposition to the draft,' and went on, 'If you do not assert and support your rights, you are helping to deny or disparage rights which it is the solemn duty of all citizens and residents of the United States to retain.' It described the arguments on the other side as coming from cunning politicians and a mercenary capitalist press, and even silent consent to the conscription law as helping to support an infamous conspiracy. It denied the power to send our citizens away to foreign shores to shoot up the people of other lands, and added that words could not express the condemnation such cold-blooded ruthlessness deserves, & c., & c., winding up, 'You must do your share to maintain, support and uphold the rights of the people of this country.' Of course the document would not have been sent unless it had been intended to have some effect, and we do not see what effect it could be expected to have upon persons subject to the draft except to influence them to obstruct the carrying of it out. The defendants do not deny that the jury might find against them on this point.

"But it is said, suppose that that was the tendency of this circular, it is protected by the First Amendment to the Constitution. [We] admit that in many places and in ordinary times the defendants in saying all that was said in the circular would have been within their constitutional rights. But the character of every act depends upon the circumstances in which it is done. The most stringent protection of free speech would not protect a man in falsely shouting fire in a theatre and causing a panic. [The] question in every case is whether the words used are used in such circumstances and are of such a nature as to create a clear and present danger that they will bring about the substantive evils that Congress has a right to prevent. It is a question of proximity and degree. When a nation is at war many things that might be said in time of peace are such a hindrance to its effort that their utterance will not be endured so long as men fight and that no Court could regard them as protected by any constitutional right. It seems to be admitted that if an actual obstruction of the recruiting service were proved, liability for words that produced that effect might be enforced. The statute of 1917 punishes conspiracies to obstruct as well as actual obstruction. If the act, (speaking, or circulating a paper), its tendency and the intent with which it is done are the same, we perceive no ground for saying that success alone warrants making the act a crime."a

———

DEBS v. UNITED STATES, 249 U.S. 211 (1919): Defendant was convicted of violating the Espionage Act for obstructing and attempting to obstruct the recruiting service and for causing and attempting to cause insubordination and disloyalty in the armed services. He was given a ten-year prison sentence on each count, to run concurrently. His criminal conduct consisted of giving the anti-war speech described in the opinion at the state convention of the Socialist Party of Ohio, held at a park in Canton, Ohio, on a June 16, 1918 Sunday afternoon before a general audience of 1,200 persons. At the time of the speech, defendant was a national political figure. In affirming, HOLMES, J., observed for a unanimous Court:

"The main theme of the speech was socialism, its growth, and a prophecy of its ultimate success. With that we have nothing to do, but if a part or the manifest intent of the more general utterances was to encourage those present to obstruct the recruiting service and if in passages such encouragement was directly given, the immunity of the general theme may not be enough to protect the speech. [Defendant had come to the park directly from a nearby jail, where he had visited three socialists imprisoned for obstructing the recruiting service. He expressed sympathy and admiration for these persons and others convicted of similar offenses, and then] said that the master class has always declared the war and the subject class has always fought the battles—that the subject class has had nothing to gain and all to lose, including their lives; [and that] 'You have your lives to lose; you certainly ought to have the right to declare war if you consider a war necessary.' [He next said of a woman serving a ten-year sentence for obstructing the recruiting service] that she had said no more than the speaker had said that afternoon; that if she was guilty so was [he].

"There followed personal experiences and illustrations of the growth of socialism, a glorification of minorities, and a prophecy of the success of [socialism], with the interjection that 'you need to know that you are fit for something better than slavery and cannon fodder.' [Defendant's] final exhortation [was] 'Don't worry about the charge of treason to your masters; but be concerned about the treason that involves yourselves.' The defendant addressed the jury himself, and while contending that his speech did not warrant the charges said 'I have been accused of obstructing the war. I admit it. Gentlemen, I abhor war. I would oppose the war if I stood alone.' The statement was not necessary to warrant the jury in finding that one purpose of the speech, whether incidental or not does not matter, was to oppose not only war in general but this war, and that the opposition was so expressed that its natural and intended effect would be to obstruct recruiting. If that was intended and if, in all the circumstances, that would be its probable effect, it would not be protected by reason of its being part of a general program and expressions of a general and conscientious belief.

"[Defendant's constitutional objections] based upon the First Amendment [were] disposed of in *Schenck*. [T]he admission in evidence of the record of the conviction [of various persons he mentioned in his speech was proper] to show

a. See also *Frohwerk v. United States*, 249 U.S. 204 (1919), where a unanimous Court, per Holmes, J., sustained a conviction for conspiracy to obstruct recruiting in violation of the Espionage Act, by means of a dozen newspaper articles praising the spirit and strength of the German nation, criticizing the decision to send American troops to France, maintaining that the government was giving false and hypocritical reasons for its course of action and implying that "the guilt of those who voted the unnatural sacrifice" is greater than the wrong of those who seek to escape by resistance.

what he was talking about, to explain the true import of his expression of sympathy and to throw light on the intent of the address. [Properly admitted, too, was an 'Anti-war Proclamation and Program' adopted the previous year, coupled with testimony that shortly before his speech defendant had stated that he approved it]. Its first recommendation was, 'continuous, active, and public opposition to the war, through demonstrations, mass petitions, and all other means within our power.' Evidence that the defendant accepted this view and this declaration of his duties at the time that he made his speech is evidence that if in that speech he used words tending to obstruct the recruiting service he meant that they should have that effect. [T]he jury were most carefully instructed that they could not find the defendant guilty for advocacy of any of his opinions unless the words used had as their natural tendency and reasonably probable effect to obstruct the recruiting service [and] unless the defendant had the specific intent to do so in his mind."

————

MASSES PUBLISHING CO. v. PATTEN, 244 Fed. 535 (S.D.N.Y.1917): The Postmaster of New York advised plaintiff that an issue of his monthly revolutionary journal, *The Masses,* would be denied the mails under the Espionage Act since it tended to encourage the enemies of the United States and to hamper the government in its conduct of the war. The Postmaster subsequently specified as objectionable several cartoons entitled, e.g., "Conscription," "Making the World Safe for Capitalism"; several articles admiring the "sacrifice" of conscientious objectors and a poem praising two persons imprisoned for conspiracy to resist the draft. Plaintiff sought a preliminary injunction against the postmaster from excluding its magazine from the mails. LEARNED HAND, D.J., granted relief:

"[The postmaster maintains] that to arouse discontent and disaffection among the people with the prosecution of the war and with the draft tends to promote a mutinous and insubordinate temper among the troops. This [is] true; men who become satisfied that they are engaged in an enterprise dictated by the unconscionable selfishness of the rich, and effectuated by a tyrannous disregard for the will of those who must suffer and die, will be more prone to insubordination than those who have faith in the cause and acquiesce in the means. Yet to interpret the word 'cause' [in the statutory language forbidding one to 'willfully cause' insubordination in the armed forces] so broadly would [necessarily involve] the suppression of all hostile criticism, and of all opinion except what encouraged and supported the existing policies, or which fell within the range of temperate argument. * * * Assuming that the power to repress such opinion may rest in Congress in the throes of a struggle for the very existence of the state, its exercise is so contrary to the use and wont of our people that only the clearest expression of such a power justifies the conclusion that it was intended.

"The defendant's position, therefore, in so far as it involves the suppression of the free utterance of abuse and criticism of the existing law, or of the policies of the war, is not, in my judgment, supported by the language of the statute. Yet there has always been a recognized limit to such expressions, incident indeed to the existence of any compulsive power of the state itself. One may not counsel or advise others to violate the law as it stands. Words are not only the keys of persuasion, but the triggers of action, and those which have no purport but to counsel the violation of law cannot by any latitude of interpretation be a part of that public opinion which is the final source of government in a democratic state. [If] one stops short of urging upon others that it is their duty or their interest to resist the law, it seems to me one should not be held to have attempted to cause its violation. If that be not the test, I can see no escape from the conclusion that under this section every political agitation which can be shown to be apt to create a seditious temper is illegal. I am confident that by such language Congress had no such revolutionary purpose in view. * * *

"[It] is plain enough that the [magazine] has the fullest sympathy for [those who resist the draft or obstruct recruiting], that it admires their courage, and that it presumptively approves their conduct. [Moreover,] these passages, it must be remembered, occur in a magazine which attacks with the utmost violence the draft and the war. That such comments have a tendency to arouse emulation in others is clear enough, but that they counsel others to follow these examples is not so plain. Literally at least they do not, and while, as I have said, the words are to be taken, not literally, but according to their full import, the literal meaning is the starting point for interpretation. One may admire and approve the course of a hero without feeling any duty to follow him. There is not the least implied intimation in these words that others are under a duty to follow. The most that can be said is that, if others do follow, they will get the same admiration and the same approval. * * *

"When the question is of a statute constituting a crime, it seems to me that there should be more definite evidence of the act. The question before me is quite the same as what would arise upon a motion to dismiss an indictment at the close of the proof: Could any reasonable man say, not that the indirect result of the language might be to arouse a seditious disposition, for that would not be enough, but that the language directly advocated resistance to the draft? I cannot think that upon such language any verdict would stand."[b]

JUSTICE HOLMES—DISSENTING IN ABRAMS v. UNITED STATES

250 U.S. 616, 624, 40 S.Ct. 17, 20, 63 L.Ed. 1173, 1178 (1919).

[In the summer of 1918, the United States sent a small body of marines to Siberia. Although the defendants maintained a strong socialist opposition to "German militarism," they opposed the "capitalist" invasion of Russia, and characterized it as an attempt to crush the Russian Revolution. Shortly thereafter, they printed two leaflets and distributed several thousand copies in New York City. Many of the copies were thrown from a window where one defendant was employed; others were passed around at radical meetings. Both leaflets supported Russia against the United States; one called upon workers to unite in a general strike. There was no evidence that workers responded to the call.

[The Court upheld the defendants' convictions for conspiring to violate two provisions of the 1918 amendments to the Espionage Act. One count prohibited language intended to "incite, provoke and encourage resistance to the United States"; the other punished those who urged curtailment of war production. As the Court interpreted the statute, an intent to interfere with efforts against a *declared* war was a necessary element of both offenses. Since the United States had not declared war upon Russia, "the main task of the government was to establish an [*intention*] *to interfere with the war with Germany*." Zechariah

---

b. In reversing, 246 Fed. 24 (1917), the Second Circuit observed: "If the natural and probable effect of what is said is to encourage resistance to a law, and the words are used in an endeavor to persuade to resistance, it is immaterial that the duty to resist is not mentioned, or the interest of the person addressed in resistance is not suggested. That one may willfully obstruct the enlistment service, without advising in direct language against enlistments, and without stating that to refrain from enlistment is a duty or in one's interest, seems to us too plain for controversy."

Chafee, *Free Speech in the United States* 115 (1941). The Court found intent on the principle that "Men must be held to have intended, and to be accountable for, the effects which their acts were likely to produce. Even if their primary purpose and intent was to aid the cause of the Russian Revolution, the plan of action which they adopted necessarily involved, before it could be realized, defeat of the war program of the United States * * *."

[HOLMES, J., dissented in an opinion with which Brandeis, J., concurred:]

[I] am aware of course that the word "intent" as vaguely used in ordinary legal discussion means no more than knowledge at the time of the act that the consequences said to be intended will ensue. [But,] when words are used exactly, a deed is not done with intent to produce a consequence unless that consequence is the aim of the deed. It may be obvious, and obvious to the actor, that the consequence will follow, and he may be liable for it even if he regrets it, but he does not do the act with intent to produce it unless the aim to produce it is the proximate motive of the specific act although there may be some deeper motive behind.

It seems to me that this statute must be taken to use its words in a strict and accurate sense. They would be absurd in any other. A patriot might think that we were wasting money on aeroplanes, or making more cannon of a certain kind than we needed, and might advocate curtailment with success, yet even if it turned out that the curtailment hindered and was thought by other minds to have been obviously likely to hinder the United States in the prosecution of the war, no one would hold such conduct a crime. * * *

I never have seen any reason to doubt that the questions of law that alone were before this Court in the cases of *Schenck, Frohwerk* and *Debs* were rightly decided. I do not doubt for a moment that by the same reasoning that would justify punishing persuasion to murder, the United States constitutionally may punish speech that produces or is intended to produce a clear and imminent danger that it will bring about forthwith certain substantive evils that the United States constitutionally may seek to prevent. The power undoubtedly is greater in time of war than in time of peace because war opens dangers that do not exist at other times.

But as against dangers peculiar to war, as against others, the principle of the right to free speech is always the same. It is only the present danger of immediate evil or an intent to bring it about that warrants Congress in setting a limit to the expression of opinion where private rights are not concerned. Congress certainly cannot forbid all effort to change the mind of the country. Now nobody can suppose that the surreptitious publishing of a silly leaflet by an unknown man, without more, would present any immediate danger that its opinions would hinder the success of the government arms or have any appreciable tendency to do so. Publishing those opinions for the very purpose of obstructing, however, might indicate a greater danger and at any rate would have the quality of an attempt. * * *

I do not see how anyone can find the intent required by the statute in any of the defendants' words. The leaflet advocating a general strike is the only one that affords even a foundation for the charge, and [its only object] is to help Russia and stop American intervention there against the popular government—not to impede the United States in the war that it was carrying on. * * *

In this case sentences of twenty years imprisonment have been imposed for the publishing of two leaflets that I believe the defendants had as much right to publish as the Government has to publish the Constitution of the United States now vainly invoked by them. [E]ven if what I think the necessary intent were shown; the most nominal punishment seems to me all that possibly could be inflicted, unless the defendants are to be made to suffer not for what the indictment alleges but for the creed that they avow—[which,] although made the subject of examination at the trial, no one has a right even to consider in dealing with the charges before the Court.

Persecution for the expression of opinions seems to me perfectly logical. If you have no doubt of your premises or your power and want a certain result with all your heart you naturally express your wishes in law and sweep away all opposition. To allow opposition by speech seems to indicate that you think the speech impotent, as when a man says that he has squared the circle, or that you do not care whole-heartedly for the result, or that you doubt either your power or your premises. But when men have realized that time has upset many fighting faiths, they may come to believe even more than they believe the very foundations of their own conduct that the ultimate good desired is better reached by free trade in ideas—that the best test of truth is the power of the thought to get itself accepted in the competition of the market, and that truth is the only ground upon which their wishes safely can be carried out. That at any rate is the theory of our Constitution. It is an experiment, as all life is an experiment. Every year if not every day we have to wager our salvation upon some prophecy based upon imperfect knowledge. While that experiment is part of our system I think that we should be eternally vigilant against attempts to check the expression of opinions that we loathe and believe to be fraught with death, unless they so imminently threaten immediate interference with the lawful and pressing purposes of the law that an immediate check is required to save the country. [Only] the emergency that makes it immediately dangerous to leave the correction of evil counsels to time warrants making any exception to the sweeping command, "Congress shall make no law * * * abridging the freedom of speech." Of course I am speaking only of expressions of opinion and exhortations, which were all that were uttered [here].

B.   STATE SEDITION LAWS

The second main group of cases in the initial development of First Amendment doctrine involved state "sedition laws" of two basic types: criminal anarchy laws, typified by the New York statute in *Gitlow,* infra, and criminal syndicalism laws similar to the California statute in *Whitney,* infra. Most states enacted anarchy and syndicalism statutes between 1917 and 1921, in response to World War I and the fear of Bolshevism that developed in its wake, but the first modern sedition law was passed by New York in 1902, soon after the assassination of President McKinley. The law, which prohibited not only actual or attempted assassinations or conspiracies to assassinate, but advocacy of anarchy as well, lay idle for nearly twenty years, until the *Gitlow* prosecution.

GITLOW v. NEW YORK, 268 U.S. 652 (1925): Defendant was a member of the Left Wing Section of the Socialist Party and a member of its National Council, which adopted a "Left Wing Manifesto," condemning the dominant "moderate Socialism" for its recognition of the necessity of the democratic parliamentary state; advocating the necessity of accomplishing the "Communist Revolution" by a militant and "revolutionary Socialism" based on "the class struggle"; and urging the development of mass political strikes for the destruction of the parliamentary state. Defendant arranged for printing and distributing, through the mails and otherwise, 16,000 copies of the Manifesto in the Left Wing's official organ, The

Revolutionary Age. There was no evidence of any effect from the publication and circulation of the Manifesto.

In sustaining a conviction under the New York "criminal anarchy" statutes, prohibiting the "advocacy, advising or teaching the duty, necessity or propriety of overthrowing or overturning organized government by force or violence" and the publication or distribution of such matter, the majority, per SANFORD, J., stated that for present purposes we may and do assume that First Amendment freedoms of expression "are among the fundamental personal rights and 'liberties' protected by the due process clause of the Fourteenth Amendment from impairment by the States," but ruled:

"By enacting the present statute the State has determined, through its legislative body, that utterances advocating the overthrow of organized government by force, violence and unlawful means, are so inimical to the general welfare and involve such danger of substantive evil that they may be penalized in the exercise of its police power. That determination must be given great weight. Every presumption is to be indulged in favor of the validity of the statute. And the case is to be considered 'in the light of the principle that the State is primarily the judge of regulations required in the interest of public safety and welfare'; and that its police 'statutes may only be declared unconstitutional where they are arbitrary or unreasonable attempts to exercise authority vested in the State in the public interest.' That utterances inciting to the overthrow of organized government by unlawful means, present a sufficient danger of substantive evil to bring their punishment within the range of legislative discretion, is clear. Such utterances, by their very nature, involve danger to the public peace and to the security of the State. They threaten breaches of the peace and ultimate revolution. And the immediate danger is none the less real and substantial, because the effect of a given utterance cannot be accurately foreseen. The State cannot reasonably be required to measure the danger from every such utterance in the nice balance of a jeweler's scale. A single revolutionary spark may kindle a fire that, smoldering for a time, may burst into a sweeping and destructive conflagration. It cannot be said that the State is acting arbitrarily or unreasonably when in the exercise of its judgment as to the measures necessary to protect the public peace and safety, it seeks to extinguish the spark without waiting until it has enkindled the flame or blazed into the conflagration. It cannot reasonably be required to defer the adoption of measures for its own peace and safety until the revolutionary utterances lead to actual disturbances of the public peace or imminent and immediate danger of its own destruction; but it may, in the exercise of its judgment, suppress the threatened danger in its incipiency.

"[It] is clear that the question in [this case] is entirely different from that involved in those cases where the statute merely prohibits certain acts involving the danger of substantive evil, without any reference to language itself, and it is sought to apply its provisions to language used by the defendant for the purpose of bringing about the prohibited results. There, if it be contended that the statute cannot be applied to the language used by the defendant because of its protection by the freedom of speech or press, it must necessarily be found, as an original question, without any previous determination by the legislative body, whether the specific language used involved such likelihood of bringing about the substantive evil as to deprive it of the constitutional protection. In such cases it has been held that the general provisions of the statute may be constitutionally applied to the specific utterance of the defendant if its natural tendency and probable effect was to bring about the substantive evil which the legislative body might prevent. *Schenck*; *Debs*. And the general statement in the *Schenck* case that the 'question in every case is whether the words are used in such circumstances and are of such a nature as to create a clear and present danger that they will bring about the substantive evils,' [was] manifestly intended, as shown by the context, to apply only in cases of this class, and has no application to those like the present, where the legislative body itself has previously determined the danger of substantive evil arising from utterances of a specified character."

Holmes, J., joined by Brandeis, J., dissented: "The general principle of free speech, it seems to me, must be taken to be included in the Fourteenth Amendment, in view of the scope that has been given to the word 'liberty' as there used, although perhaps it may be accepted with a somewhat larger latitude of interpretation than is allowed to Congress by the sweeping language that governs or ought to govern the laws of the United States. If I am right then I think that the criterion sanctioned by the full Court in *Schenck* applies. [It] is true that in my opinion this criterion was departed from in *Abrams,* but the convictions that I expressed in that case are too deep for it to be possible for me as yet to believe that it [has] settled the law. If what I think the correct test is applied it is manifest that there was no present danger of an attempt to overthrow the government by force on the part of the admittedly small minority who shared the defendant's views. It is said that this manifesto was more than a theory, that it was an incitement. Every idea is an incitement. It offers itself for belief and if believed it is acted on unless some other belief outweighs it or some failure of energy stifles the movement at its birth. The only difference between the expression of an opinion and an incitement in the narrower sense is the speaker's enthusiasm for the result. Eloquence may set fire to reason. But whatever may be thought of the redundant discourse before us it had no chance of starting a present conflagration. If in the long run the beliefs expressed in proletarian dictatorship are destined to be accepted by the dominant forces of the community, the only meaning of free speech is that they should be given their chance and have their way.

"If the publication of this document had been laid as an attempt to induce an uprising against government at once and not at some indefinite time in the future it would have presented a different question. The object would have been one with which the law might deal, subject to the doubt whether there was any danger that the publication could produce any result, or in other words, whether it was not futile and too remote from possible consequences. But the indictment alleges the publication and nothing more."

———

Cases such as *Whitney,* infra, raise questions not only about freedom of speech, but also about the right of assembly. In turn, *Whitney* raises the issue of the existence and scope of a right not mentioned in the First Amendment: freedom of association, explored in Sec. 9 infra. Several of the cases which follow are primarily characterized as speech cases because the assemblies or associations at issue were designed for the purpose of organizing future speech activity.

WHITNEY v. CALIFORNIA
274 U.S. 357, 47 S.Ct. 641, 71 L.Ed. 1095 (1927).

Justice Sanford delivered the opinion of the Court.

[Charlotte Anita Whitney was convicted of violating the 1919 Criminal Syndicalism Act of California whose pertinent provisions were]:

"Section 1. The term 'criminal syndicalism' as used in this act is hereby defined as any doctrine or precept advocating, teaching or aiding and abetting the commission of crime, sabotage (which word is hereby defined as meaning willful and malicious physical damage or injury to physical property), or unlawful acts of force and violence or unlawful methods of terrorism as a means of accomplishing a change in industrial ownership or control, or effecting any political change.

"Sec. 2. Any person who: * * * 4. Organizes or assists in organizing, or is or knowingly becomes a member of, any organization, society, group or assemblage of persons organized or assembled to advocate, teach or aid and abet criminal syndicalism; * * *

"Is guilty of a felony and punishable by imprisonment."

The first count of the information, on which the conviction was had, charged that on or about November 28, 1919, in Alameda County, the defendant, in violation of the Criminal Syndicalism Act, "did then and there unlawfully, willfully, wrongfully, deliberately and feloniously organize and assist in organizing, and was, is, and knowingly became a member of [a group] organized and assembled to advocate, teach, aid and abet criminal syndicalism." * * *

1.   While it is not denied that the evidence warranted the jury in finding that the defendant became a member of and assisted in organizing the Communist Labor Party of California, and that this was organized to advocate, teach, aid or abet criminal syndicalism as defined by the Act, it is urged that the Act, as here construed and applied, deprived the defendant of her liberty without due process of law. [Defendant's] argument is, in effect, that the character of the state organization could not be forecast when she attended the convention; that she had no purpose of helping to create an instrument of terrorism and violence; that she "took part in formulating and presenting to the convention a resolution which, if adopted, would have committed the new organization to a legitimate policy of political reform by the use of the ballot"; that it was not until after the majority of the convention turned out to be "contrary minded, and other less temperate policies prevailed" that the convention could have taken on the character of criminal syndicalism; and that as this was done over her protest, her mere presence in the convention, however violent the opinions expressed therein, could not thereby become a crime. This contention [is in effect] an effort to review the weight of the evidence for the purpose of showing that the defendant did not join and assist in organizing the Communist Labor Party of California with a knowledge of its unlawful character and purpose. This question, which is foreclosed by the verdict of the jury, [is] one of fact merely which is not open to review in this Court, involving as it does no constitutional question whatever. * * *

[That a state] may punish those who abuse [freedom of speech] by utterances inimical to the public welfare, tending to incite to crime, disturb the public peace, or endanger the foundations of organized government and threaten its overthrow by unlawful means, is not open to question. [*Gitlow*].

The essence of the offense denounced by the Act is the combining with others in an association for the accomplishment of the desired ends through the advocacy and use of criminal and unlawful methods. It partakes of the nature of a criminal conspiracy. That such united and joint action involves even greater danger to the public peace and security than the isolated utterances and acts of individuals is clear. We cannot hold that, as here applied, the Act is an unreasonable or arbitrary exercise of the police power of the State, unwarrantably infringing any right of free speech, assembly or association, or that those persons are protected from punishment by the due process clause who abuse such rights by joining and furthering an organization thus menacing the peace and welfare of the State. * * *

Affirmed.

Justice Brandeis (concurring.) * * *

The felony which the statute created is a crime very unlike the old felony of conspiracy or the old misdemeanor of unlawful assembly. The mere act of assisting in forming a society for teaching syndicalism, of becoming a member of it, or assembling with others for that purpose is given the dynamic quality of crime. There is guilt although the society may not contemplate immediate promulgation of the doctrine. Thus the accused is to be punished, not for attempt, incitement or conspiracy, but for a step in preparation, which, if it threatens the public order at all, does so only remotely. The novelty in the prohibition introduced is that the statute aims, not at the practice of criminal syndicalism, nor even directly at the preaching of it, but at association with those who propose to preach it.

Despite arguments to the contrary which had seemed to me persuasive, it is settled that the due process clause of the Fourteenth Amendment applies to matters of substantive law as well as to matters of procedure. Thus all fundamental rights comprised within the term liberty are protected by the federal Constitution from invasion by the states. The right of free speech, the right to teach and the right of assembly are, of course, fundamental rights. These may not be denied or abridged. But, although the rights of free speech and assembly are fundamental, they are not in their nature absolute. Their exercise is subject to restriction, if the particular restriction proposed is required in order to protect the state from destruction or from serious injury, political, economic or moral. That the necessity which is essential to a valid restriction does not exist unless speech would produce, or is intended to produce, a clear and imminent danger of some substantive evil which the state constitutionally may seek to prevent has been settled. See *Schenck*.

[The] Legislature must obviously decide, in the first instance, whether a danger exists which calls for a particular protective measure. But where a statute is valid only in case certain conditions exist, the enactment of the statute cannot alone establish the facts which are essential to its validity. Prohibitory legislation has repeatedly been held invalid, because unnecessary, where the denial of liberty involved was that of engaging in a particular business. The powers of the courts to strike down an offending law are no less when the interests involved are not property rights, but the fundamental personal rights of free speech and assembly.

This Court has not yet fixed the standard by which to determine when a danger shall be deemed clear; how remote the danger may be and yet be deemed present; and what degree of evil shall be deemed sufficiently substantial to justify resort to abridgment of free speech and assembly as the means of protection. To reach sound conclusions on these matters, we must bear in mind why a state is, ordinarily, denied the power to prohibit dissemination of social, economic and political doctrine which a vast majority of its citizens believes to be false and fraught with evil consequence.

Those who won our independence believed that the final end of the state was to make men free to develop their faculties, and that in its government the deliberative forces should prevail over the arbitrary. They valued liberty both as an end and as a means. They believed liberty to be the secret of happiness and courage to be the secret of liberty. They believed that freedom to think as you will and to speak as you think are means indispensable to the discovery and spread of political truth; that without free speech and assembly discussion would be futile; that with them, discussion affords ordinarily adequate protection against the dissemination of noxious doctrine; that the greatest menace to freedom is an inert people; that public discussion is a political duty; and that this should be a fundamental principle of the American government. They recognized the risks to which all human institutions are subject. But they knew that order cannot be secured merely through fear of punishment for its infraction; that it is hazardous to discourage thought, hope and imagination; that fear breeds repression; that repression breeds hate; that hate menaces stable government; that the path of safety lies in the opportunity to discuss freely supposed grievances and proposed remedies; and that the fitting remedy for evil counsels is good ones. Believing in the power of reason as applied through public discussion, they eschewed silence coerced by law—the argument of force in its worst form. Recognizing the occasional tyrannies of governing majorities, they amended the Constitution so that free speech and assembly should be guaranteed.

Fear of serious injury cannot alone justify suppression of free speech and assembly. Men feared witches and burnt women. It is the function of speech to free men from the bondage of irrational fears. To justify suppression of free speech there must be reasonable ground to fear that serious evil will result if free speech is practiced. There must be reasonable ground to believe that the danger apprehended is imminent. There must be reasonable ground to believe that the evil to be prevented is a serious one. Every denunciation of existing law tends in some measure to increase the probability that there will be violation of it. Condonation of a breach enhances the probability. Expressions of approval add to the probability. Propagation of the criminal state of mind by teaching syndicalism increases it. Advocacy of lawbreaking heightens it still further. But even advocacy of violation, however reprehensible morally, is not a justification for denying free speech where the advocacy falls short of incitement and there is nothing to indicate that the advocacy would be immediately acted on. The wide difference between advocacy and incitement, between preparation and attempt, between assembling and conspiracy, must be borne in mind. In order to support a finding of clear and present danger it must be shown either that immediate serious violence was to be expected or was advocated, or that the past conduct furnished reason to believe that such advocacy was then contemplated.

Those who won our independence by revolution were not cowards. They did not fear political change. They did not exalt order at the cost of liberty. To courageous, self-reliant men, with confidence in the power of free and fearless reasoning applied through the processes of popular government, no danger flowing from speech can be deemed clear and present, unless the incidence of the evil apprehended is so imminent that it may befall before there is opportunity for full discussion. If there be time to expose through discussion the falsehood and fallacies, to avert the evil by the processes of education, the remedy to be applied is more speech, not enforced silence. Only an emergency can justify repression. Such must be the rule if authority is to be reconciled with freedom. Such, in my opinion, is the command of the Constitution. It is therefore always open to Americans to challenge a law abridging free speech and assembly by showing that there was no emergency justifying it.

Moreover, even imminent danger cannot justify resort to prohibition of these functions essential to effective democracy, unless the evil apprehended is relatively serious. Prohibition of free speech and assembly is a measure so stringent that it would be inappropriate as the means for averting a relatively trivial harm to society. A police measure may be unconstitutional merely because the remedy, although effective as means of protection, is unduly harsh or oppressive. Thus, a state might, in the exercise of its police power, make any trespass upon the land of another a crime, regardless of the results or of the intent or purpose of the trespasser. It might, also, punish an attempt, a conspiracy, or an incitement to commit the trespass. But it is hardly conceivable that this court would hold constitutional a statute which punished as a felony the mere voluntary assembly with a society formed to teach that pedestrians had the moral right to cross uninclosed, unposted, waste lands and to advocate their doing so, even if there was imminent danger that advocacy would lead to a trespass. The fact that speech is likely to result in some violence or in destruction of property is not enough to justify its suppression. There must be the probability of serious injury to the State. Among free men, the deterrents ordinarily to be applied to prevent crime are education and punishment for violations of the law, not abridgement of the rights of free speech and assembly.

* * * Whenever the fundamental rights of free speech and assembly are alleged to have been invaded, it must remain open to a defendant to present the issue whether there actually did exist at the time a clear danger, whether the danger, if any, was imminent, and whether the evil apprehended was one so substantial as to justify the stringent restriction interposed by the Legislature. The legislative declaration, like the fact that the statute was passed and was sustained by the highest court of the State, creates merely a rebuttable presumption that these conditions have been satisfied.

Whether in 1919, when Miss Whitney did the things complained of, there was in California such clear and present danger of serious evil, might have been made the important issue in the case. She might have required that the issue be determined either by the court or the jury. She claimed below that the statute as applied to her violated the federal Constitution; but she did not claim that it was void because there was no clear and present danger of serious evil, nor did she request that the existence of these conditions of a valid measure thus restricting the rights of free speech and assembly be passed upon by the court or a jury. On the other hand, there was evidence on which the court or jury might have found that such danger existed. I am unable to assent to the suggestion in the opinion of the court that assembling with a political party, formed to advocate the desirability of a proletarian revolution by mass action at some date necessarily far in the future, is not a right within the protection of the Fourteenth Amendment. In the present case, however, there was other testimony which tended to establish the existence of a conspiracy, on the part of members of the International Workers of the World, to commit present serious crimes, and likewise to show that such a conspiracy would be furthered by the activity of the society of which Miss Whitney was a member. Under these circumstances the judgment of the State court cannot be disturbed. * * *

JUSTICE HOLMES joins in this opinion.

————

Ten years after *Whitney, De Jonge v. Oregon,* 299 U.S. 353 (1937) held that mere participation in a meeting called by the Communist party could not be made a crime. The right of peaceable assembly was declared to be "cognate to those of free speech and free press and is equally fundamental."

C. COMMUNISM AND ILLEGAL ADVOCACY

Kent Greenawalt has well described the pattern of decisions for much of the period between *Whitney* and *Dennis* infra: "[T]he clear and present danger formula emerged as the applicable standard not only for the kinds of issues with respect to which it originated but also for a wide variety of other First Amendment problems. If the Court was not always very clear about the relevance of that formula to those different problems, its use of the test, and its employment of ancillary doctrines, did evince a growing disposition to protect expression." *Speech and Crime,* 1980 Am.B.Found.Res.J. 645, 706. By 1951, however, anti-communist sentiment was a powerful theme in American politics. The Soviet Union had detonated a nuclear weapon; communists had firm control of the Chinese mainland; the Korean War had reached a stalemate; Alger Hiss had been convicted of perjury in congressional testimony concerning alleged spying activities for the Soviet Union while he was a State Department official; and Senator Joseph McCarthy of Wisconsin had created a national sensation by accusations that many "card carrying Communists" held important State Department jobs. In this context, the top leaders of the American Communist Party asked the Court to reverse their criminal conspiracy convictions.

DENNIS v. UNITED STATES

341 U.S. 494, 71 S.Ct. 857, 95 L.Ed. 1137 (1951).

CHIEF JUSTICE VINSON announced the judgment of the Court and an opinion in which JUSTICE REED, JUSTICE BURTON and JUSTICE MINTON join.

Petitioners were indicted in July, 1948, for violation of the conspiracy provisions of the Smith Act during the period of April, 1945, to July, 1948. * * * A verdict of guilty as to all the petitioners was [affirmed by the Second Circuit]. We granted certiorari, limited to the following two questions: (1) Whether either § 2 or § 3 of the Smith Act, inherently or as construed and applied in the instant case, violates the First Amendment and other provisions of the Bill of Rights; (2) whether either § 2 or § 3 of the Act, inherently or as construed and applied in the instant case, violates the First and Fifth Amendments, because of indefiniteness.

Sections 2 and 3 of the Smith Act provide as follows:

"Sec. 2.

"(a) It shall be unlawful for any person—

"(1) to knowingly or willfully advocate, abet, advise, or teach the duty, necessity, desirability, or propriety of overthrowing or destroying any government in the United States by force or violence, or by the assassination of any officer of any such government; * * *

"Sec. 3. It shall be unlawful for any person to attempt to commit, or to conspire to commit, any of the acts prohibited by the provisions [of] this title."

The indictment charged the petitioners with wilfully and knowingly conspiring (1) to organize as the Communist Party of the United States of America a society, group and assembly of persons who teach and advocate the overthrow and destruction of the Government of the United States by force and violence, and (2) knowingly and wilfully to advocate and teach the duty and necessity of overthrowing and destroying the Government of the United States by force and violence. The indictment further alleged that § 2 of the Smith Act proscribes these acts and that any conspiracy to take such action is a violation of § 3 of the Act.

The trial of the case extended over nine months, six of which were devoted to the taking of evidence, resulting in a record of 16,000 pages. Our limited grant of the writ of certiorari has removed from our consideration any question as to the sufficiency of the evidence to support the jury's determination that petitioners are guilty of the offense charged. Whether on this record petitioners did in fact advocate the overthrow of the Government by force and violence is not before us, and we must base any discussion of this point upon the conclusions stated in the opinion of the Court of Appeals, which treated the issue in great detail [and] held that the record supports the following broad conclusions: [that] the Communist Party is a highly disciplined organization, adept at infiltration into strategic positions, use of aliases, and double-meaning language; that the Party is rigidly controlled; that Communists, unlike other political parties, tolerate no dissension from the policy laid down by the guiding [forces]; that the literature of the Party and the statements and activities of its leaders, petitioners here, advocate, and the general goal of the Party was, during the period in question, to achieve a successful overthrow of the existing order by force and violence. * * *

The obvious purpose of the statute is to protect existing Government, not from change by peaceable, lawful and constitutional means, but from change by violence, revolution and terrorism. That it is within the *power* of the Congress to protect the Government of the United States from armed rebellion is a proposition which requires little discussion. Whatever theoretical merit there may be to the argument that there is a "right" to rebellion against dictatorial governments is without force where the existing structure of the government provides for peaceful and orderly change. We reject any principle of governmental helplessness in the face of preparation for revolution, which principle, carried to its logical conclusion, must lead to anarchy. No one could conceive that it is not within the power of Congress to prohibit acts intended to overthrow the Government by force and violence. The question with which we are concerned here is not whether Congress has such *power,* but whether the *means* which it has employed conflict with the First and Fifth Amendments to the Constitution.

One of the bases for the contention that the means which Congress has employed are invalid takes the form of an attack on the face of the statute on the grounds that by its terms it prohibits academic discussion of the merits of Marxism–Leninism, that it stifles ideas and is contrary to all concepts of a free speech and a free press. [This] is a federal statute which we must interpret as well as judge. Herein lies the fallacy of reliance upon the manner in which this Court has treated judgments of state courts. Where the statute as construed by the state court transgressed the First Amendment, we could not but invalidate the judgments of conviction.

The very language of the Smith Act negates the interpretation which petitioners would have us impose on that Act. It is directed at advocacy, not discussion. Thus, the trial judge properly charged the jury that they could not convict if they found that petitioners did "no more than pursue peaceful studies and discussions or teaching and advocacy in the realm of ideas." * * * Congress did not intend to eradicate the free discussion of political theories, to destroy the traditional rights of Americans to discuss and evaluate ideas without fear of governmental sanction. * * *

But although the statute is not directed at the hypothetical cases which petitioners have conjured, its application in this case has resulted in convictions for the teaching and advocacy of the overthrow of the Government by force and violence, which, even though coupled with the intent to accomplish that overthrow, contains an element of speech. For this reason, we must pay special heed to the demands of the First Amendment marking out the boundaries of speech.

[T]he basis of the First Amendment is the hypothesis that speech can rebut speech, propaganda will answer propaganda, free debate of ideas will result in the wisest governmental policies. [An] analysis of the leading cases in this Court which have involved direct limitations on speech, however, will demonstrate that both the majority of the Court and the dissenters in particular cases have recognized that this is not an unlimited, unqualified right, but that the societal value of speech must, on occasion, be subordinated to other values and considerations. * * *

Although no case subsequent to *Whitney* and *Gitlow* has expressly overruled the majority opinions in those cases, there is little doubt that subsequent opinions have inclined toward the Holmes–Brandeis rationale. * * *

In this case we are squarely presented with the application of the "clear and present danger" test, and must decide what that phrase imports. We first note that many of the cases in which this Court has reversed convictions by use of this or similar tests have been based on the fact that the interest which the State was attempting to protect was itself too insubstantial to warrant restriction of speech. * * * Overthrow of the Government by force and violence is certainly a substantial enough interest for the Government to limit speech. Indeed, this is the ultimate value of any society, for if a society cannot protect its very structure from armed internal attack, it must follow that no subordinate value can be protected. If, then, this interest may be protected, the literal problem which is presented is what has been meant by the use of the phrase "clear and present danger" of the utterances bringing about the evil within the power of Congress to punish.

Obviously, the words cannot mean that before the Government may act, it must wait until the putsch is about to be executed, the plans have been laid and the signal is awaited. If Government is aware that a group aiming at its overthrow is attempting to indoctrinate its members and to commit them to a course whereby they will strike when the leaders feel the circumstances permit, action by the Government is required. The argument that there is no need for Government to concern itself, for Government is strong, it possesses ample powers to put down a rebellion, it may defeat the revolution with ease needs no answer. For that is not the question. Certainly an attempt to overthrow the Government by force, even though doomed from the outset because of inadequate numbers or power of the revolutionists, is a sufficient evil for Congress to prevent. The damage which such attempts create both physically and politically to a nation makes it impossible to measure the validity in terms of the probability of success, or the immediacy of a successful attempt. In the instant case the trial judge charged the jury that they could not convict unless they found that petitioners intended to overthrow the Government "as speedily as circumstances would permit." This does not mean, and could not properly mean, that they would not strike until there was certainty of success. What was meant was that the revolutionists would strike when they thought the time was ripe. We must therefore reject the contention that success or probability of success is the criterion.

The situation with which Justices Holmes and Brandeis were concerned in *Gitlow* was a comparatively isolated event, bearing little relation in their minds to any substantial threat to the safety of the community. [They] were not confronted with any situation comparable to the instant one—the development of an apparatus designed and dedicated to the overthrow of the Government, in the context of world crisis after crisis.

Chief Judge Learned Hand, writing for the majority below, interpreted the phrase as follows: "In each case [courts] must ask whether the gravity of the 'evil,' discounted by its improbability, justifies such invasion of free speech as is necessary to avoid the danger." We adopt this statement of the rule. As articulated by Chief Judge Hand, it is as succinct and inclusive as any other we might devise at this time. * * *

Likewise, we are in accord with the court below, which affirmed the trial court's finding that the requisite danger existed. The mere fact that from the period 1945 to 1948 petitioners' activities did not result in an attempt to overthrow the Government by force and violence is of course no answer to the fact that there was a group that was ready to make the attempt. The formation by petitioners of such a highly organized conspiracy, with rigidly disciplined members subject to call when the leaders, these petitioners, felt that the time had come for action, coupled with the inflammable nature of world conditions, similar uprisings in other countries, and the touch-and-go nature of our relations with countries with whom petitioners were in the very least ideologically attuned, convince us that their convictions were justified on this score. And this analysis disposes of the contention that a conspiracy to advocate, as distinguished from the advocacy itself, cannot be constitutionally restrained, because it comprises only the preparation. It is the existence of the conspiracy which creates the danger. * * *

Although we have concluded that the finding that there was a sufficient danger to warrant the application of the statute was justified on the merits, there remains the problem of whether the trial judge's treatment of the issue was correct. He charged the jury, in relevant part, as follows:

"In further construction and interpretation of the statute I charge you that it is not the abstract doctrine of overthrowing or destroying organized government by unlawful means which is denounced by this law, but the teaching and advocacy of action for the accomplishment of that purpose, by language reasonably and ordinarily calculated to incite persons to such action. Accordingly, you cannot find the defendants or any of them guilty of the crime charged unless you are satisfied beyond a reasonable doubt that they conspired to organize a society, group and assembly of persons who teach and advocate the overthrow or destruction of the Government of the United States by force and violence and to advocate and teach the duty and necessity of overthrowing or destroying the Government of the United States by force and violence, with the intent that such teaching and advocacy be of a rule or principle of action and by language reasonably and ordinarily calculated to incite persons to such action, all with the intent to cause the overthrow or destruction of the Government of the United States by force and violence as speedily as circumstances would permit. * * *

"If you are satisfied that the evidence establishes beyond a reasonable doubt that the defendants, or any of them, are guilty of a violation of the statute, as I have interpreted it to you, I find as matter of law that there is sufficient danger of a substantive evil that the Congress has a right to prevent to justify the application of the statute under the First Amendment of the Constitution. This is matter of law about which you have no concern. * * * "

It is thus clear that he reserved the question of the existence of the danger for his own determination, and the question becomes whether the issue is of such a nature that it should have been submitted to the jury.

[When] facts are found that establish the violation of a statute, the protection against conviction afforded by the First Amendment is a matter of law. The doctrine that there must be a clear and present danger of a substantive evil that Congress has a right to prevent is a judicial rule to be applied as a matter of law by the courts. The guilt is established by proof of facts. Whether the First Amendment protects the activity which constitutes the violation of the statute must depend upon a judicial determination of the scope of the First Amendment applied to the circumstances of the case.

[In] *Schenck* this Court itself examined the record to find whether the requisite danger appeared, and the issue was not submitted to a jury. And in every later case in which the Court has measured the validity of a statute by the "clear and present danger" test, that determination has been by the court, the question of the danger not being submitted to the jury. * * * Petitioners intended to overthrow the Government of the United States as speedily as the circumstances would permit. Their conspiracy to organize the Communist Party and to teach and advocate the overthrow of the Government of the United States by force and violence created a "clear and present danger" of an attempt to overthrow the Government by force and violence. They were properly and constitutionally convicted * * *.

Affirmed.

JUSTICE CLARK took no part in the consideration or decision of this case.

JUSTICE FRANKFURTER, concurring in affirmance of the judgment.

[The] demands of free speech in a democratic society as well as the interest in national security are better served by candid and informed weighing of the competing interests, within the confines of the judicial process, than by announcing dogmas too inflexible for the non-Euclidian problems to be solved.

But how are competing interests to be assessed? Since they are not subject to quantitative ascertainment, the issue necessarily resolves itself into asking, who is to make the adjustment?—who is to balance the relevant factors and ascertain which interest is in the circumstances to prevail? Full responsibility for the choice cannot be given to the courts. Courts are not representative bodies. They are not designed to be a good reflex of a democratic society. Their judgment is best informed, and therefore most dependable, within narrow limits. Their essential quality is detachment, founded on independence. History teaches that the independence of the judiciary is jeopardized when courts become embroiled in the passions of the day and assume primary responsibility in choosing between competing political, economic and social pressures.

Primary responsibility for adjusting the interests which compete in the situation before us of necessity belongs to the Congress. [We] are to set aside the judgment of those whose duty it is to legislate only if there is no reasonable basis for [it]. Free-speech cases are not an exception to the principle that we are not legislators, that direct policy-making is not our province. How best to reconcile competing interests is the business of legislatures, and the balance they strike is a judgment not to be displaced by ours, but to be respected unless outside the pale of fair judgment. [A] survey of the relevant decisions indicates that the results which we have reached are on the whole those that would ensue from careful weighing of conflicting interests. The complex issues presented by regulation of speech in public places by picketing, and by legislation prohibiting advocacy of crime have been resolved by scrutiny of many factors besides the imminence and gravity of the evil threatened. The matter has been well summarized by a reflective student of the Court's work. "The truth is that the clear-and-present-danger test is an oversimplified judgment unless it takes account also of a number of other factors: the relative seriousness of the danger in comparison with the value of the occasion for speech or political activity; the availability of more moderate controls than those which the state has imposed; and perhaps the specific intent with which the speech or activity is launched. No matter how rapidly we utter the phrase 'clear and present danger,' or how closely we hyphenate the words, they are not a substitute for the weighing of values. They tend to convey a delusion of certitude when what is most certain is the complexity of the strands in the web of freedoms which the judge must disentangle." Paul Freund, *On Understanding the Supreme Court* 27–28 [1949]. * * *

To make validity of legislation depend on judicial reading of events still in the womb of time—a forecast, that is, of the outcome of forces at best appreciated only with knowledge of the topmost secrets of nations—is to charge the judiciary with duties beyond its equipment. * * *

Even when moving strictly within the limits of constitutional adjudication, judges are concerned with issues that may be said to involve vital finalities. The too easy transition from disapproval of what is undesirable to condemnation as unconstitutional, has led some of the wisest judges to question the wisdom of our scheme in lodging such authority in courts. But it is relevant to remind that in sustaining the power of Congress in a case like this nothing irrevocable is done. The democratic process at all events is not impaired or restricted. Power and responsibility remain with the people and immediately with their representation. All the Court says is that Congress was not forbidden by the Constitution to pass this enactment and that a prosecution under it may be brought against a conspiracy such as the one before us. * * *

JUSTICE JACKSON, concurring.

[E]ither by accident or design, the Communist stratagem outwits the anti-anarchist pattern of statute aimed against "overthrow by force and violence" if qualified by the doctrine that only "clear and present danger" of accomplishing that result will sustain the prosecution.

The "clear and present danger" test was an innovation by Mr. Justice Holmes in the *Schenck* case, reiterated and refined by him and Mr. Justice Brandeis in later cases, all arising before the era of World War II revealed the subtlety and efficacy of modernized revolutionary techniques used by totalitarian parties. In those cases, they were faced with convictions under so-called criminal syndicalism statutes aimed at anarchists but which, loosely construed, had been applied to punish socialism, pacifism, and left-wing ideologies, the charges often resting on farfetched inferences which, if true, would establish only technical or trivial violations. They proposed "clear and present danger" as a test for the sufficiency of evidence in particular cases.

I would save it, unmodified, for application as a "rule of reason" in the kind of case for which it was devised. When the issue is criminality of a hotheaded speech on a street corner, or circulation of a few incendiary pamphlets, or parading by some zealots behind a red flag, or refusal of a handful of school children to salute our flag, it is not beyond the capacity of the judicial process to gather, comprehend, and weigh the necessary materials for decision whether it is a clear and present danger of substantive evil or a harmless letting off of steam. It is not a prophecy, for the danger in such cases has matured by the time of trial or it was never present. The test applies and has meaning where a conviction is sought to be based on a speech or writing which does not directly or explicitly advocate a crime but to which such tendency is sought to be attributed by construction or by implication from external circumstances. The formula in such cases favors freedoms that are vital to our society, and, even if sometimes applied too generously, the consequences cannot be grave. But its recent expansion has extended, in particular to Communists, unprecedented immunities. Unless we are to hold our Government captive in a judge-made verbal trap, we must approach the problem of a well-organized, nation-wide conspiracy, such as I have described, as realistically as our predecessors faced the trivialities that were being prosecuted until they were checked with a rule of reason.

I think reason is lacking for applying that test to this case.

If we must decide that this Act and its application are constitutional only if we are convinced that petitioner's conduct creates a "clear and present danger" of violent overthrow, we must appraise imponderables, including international and national phenomena which baffle the best informed foreign offices and our most experienced politicians. We would have to foresee and predict the effectiveness of Communist propaganda, opportunities for infiltration, whether, and when, a time will come that they consider propitious for action, and whether and how fast our existing government will deteriorate. And we would have to speculate as to whether an approaching Communist coup would not be anticipated by a national-istic fascist movement. No doctrine can be sound whose application requires us to make a prophecy of that sort in the guise of a legal decision. The judicial process simply is not adequate to a trial of such far-flung issues. The answers given would reflect our own political predilections and nothing more.

The authors of the clear and present danger test never applied it to a case like this, nor would I. If applied as it is proposed here, it means that the Communist plotting is protected during its period of incubation; its preliminary stages of organization and preparation are immune from the law; the Government can move only after imminent action is manifest, when it would, of course, be too late.

The highest degree of constitutional protection is due to the individual acting without conspiracy. But even an individual cannot claim that the Constitution protects him in advocating or teaching overthrow of government by force or violence. I should suppose no one would doubt that Congress has power to make such attempted overthrow a crime. But the contention is that one has the constitutional right to work up a public desire and will to do what it is a crime to attempt. I think direct incitement by speech or writing can be made a crime, and I think there can be a conviction without also proving that the odds favored its success by 99 to 1, or some other extremely high ratio. * * *

What really is under review here is a conviction of conspiracy, after a trial for conspiracy, on an indictment charging conspiracy, brought under a statute outlaw-ing conspiracy. With due respect to my colleagues, they seem to me to discuss anything under the sun except the law of conspiracy. * * *

The Constitution does not make conspiracy a civil right. [Although] I consider criminal conspiracy a dragnet device capable of perversion into an instrument of injustice in the hands of a partisan or complacent judiciary, it has an established place in our system of law, and no reason appears for applying it only to concerted action claimed to disturb interstate commerce and withholding it from those claimed to undermine our whole Government. * * *

I do not suggest that Congress could punish conspiracy to advocate some-thing, the doing of which it may not punish. Advocacy or exposition of the doctrine of communal property ownership, or any political philosophy unassociated with advocacy of its imposition by force or seizure of government by unlawful means could not be reached through conspiracy prosecution. But it is not forbidden to put down force or violence, it is not forbidden to punish its teaching or advocacy, and the end being punishable, there is no doubt of the power to punish conspiracy for the purpose. * * *

JUSTICE BLACK, dissenting. * * *

So long as this Court exercises the power of judicial review of legislation, I cannot agree that the First Amendment permits us to sustain laws suppressing freedom of speech and press on the basis of Congress' or our own notions of mere "reasonableness." Such a doctrine waters down the First Amendment so that it amounts to little more than an admonition to Congress. The Amendment as so construed is not likely to protect any but those "safe" or orthodox views which rarely need its protection. I must also express my objection to the holding because, as Mr. Justice Douglas' dissent shows, it sanctions the determination of a crucial issue of fact by the judge rather than by the jury. * * *

Public opinion being what it now is, few will protest the conviction of these Communist petitioners. There is hope, however, that in calmer times, when present pressures, passions and fears subside, this or some later Court will restore the First Amendment liberties to the high preferred place where they belong in a free society.

JUSTICE DOUGLAS, dissenting.

If this were a case where those who claimed protection under the First Amendment were teaching the techniques of sabotage, the assassination of the President, the filching of documents from public files, the planting of bombs, the art of street warfare, and the like, I would have no doubts. The freedom to speak is not absolute; the teaching of methods of terror and other seditious conduct should be beyond the pale along with obscenity and immorality. This case was argued as if those were the facts. The argument imported much seditious conduct into the record. That is easy and it has popular appeal, for the activities of Communists in plotting and scheming against the free world are common knowledge. But the fact is that no such evidence was introduced at the trial. There is a statute which makes a seditious conspiracy unlawful. Petitioners, however, were not charged with a "conspiracy to overthrow" the Government. They were charged with a conspiracy to form a party and groups and assemblies of people who teach and advocate the overthrow of our Government by force or violence and with a conspiracy to advocate and teach its overthrow by force and violence. It may well be that indoctrination in the techniques of terror to destroy the Government would be indictable under either statute. But the teaching which is condemned here is of a different character.

So far as the present record is concerned, what petitioners did was to organize people to teach and themselves teach the Marxist–Leninist doctrine contained chiefly in four books: *Foundations of Leninism* by Stalin (1924); *The Communist Manifesto* by Marx and Engels (1848); *State and Revolution* by Lenin (1917); *History of the Communist Party of the Soviet Union* (B.) (1939).

Those books are to Soviet Communism what *Mein Kampf* was to Nazism. If they are understood, the ugliness of Communism is revealed, its deceit and cunning are exposed, the nature of its activities becomes apparent, and the chances of its success less likely. That is not, of course, the reason why petitioners chose these books for their classrooms. They are fervent Communists to whom these volumes are gospel. They preached the creed with the hope that some day it would be acted upon.

The opinion of the Court does not outlaw these texts nor condemn them to the fire, as the Communists do literature offensive to their creed. But if the books themselves are not outlawed, if they can lawfully remain on library shelves, by what reasoning does their use in a classroom become a crime? It would not be a crime under the Act to introduce these books to a class, though that would be teaching what the creed of violent overthrow of the Government is. The Act, as construed, requires the element of intent—that those who teach the creed believe in it. The crime then depends not on what is taught but on who the teacher is. That is to make freedom of speech turn not on *what is said,* but on the *intent* with which it is said. Once we start down that road we enter territory dangerous to the liberties of every citizen. * * *

The vice of treating speech as the equivalent of overt acts of a treasonable or seditious character is emphasized by a concurring opinion, which by invoking the law of conspiracy makes speech do service for deeds which are dangerous to society. [N]ever until today has anyone seriously thought that the ancient law of conspiracy could constitutionally be used to turn speech into seditious conduct. Yet that is precisely what is suggested. I repeat that we deal here with speech alone, not with speech *plus* acts of sabotage or unlawful conduct. Not a single seditious act is charged in the indictment. To make a lawful speech unlawful because two men conceive it is to raise the law of conspiracy to appalling proportions. * * *

There comes a time when even speech loses its constitutional immunity. Speech innocuous one year may at another time fan such destructive flames that it must be halted in the interests of the safety of the Republic. That is the meaning of the clear and present danger test. When conditions are so critical that there will be no time to avoid the evil that the speech threatens, it is time to call a halt. Otherwise, free speech which is the strength of the Nation will be the cause of its destruction.

Yet free speech is the rule, not the exception. The restraint to be constitutional must be based on more than fear, on more than passionate opposition against the speech, on more than a revolted dislike for its contents. There must be some immediate injury to society that is likely if speech is allowed. * * *

I had assumed that the question of the clear and present danger, being so critical an issue in the case, would be a matter for submission to the jury. [The] Court, I think, errs when it treats the question as one of law.

Yet, whether the question is one for the Court or the jury, there should be evidence of record on the issue. This record, however, contains no evidence whatsoever showing that the acts charged viz., the teaching of the Soviet theory of revolution with the hope that it will be realized, have created any clear and present danger to the Nation. The Court, however, rules to the contrary. [The majority] might as well say that the speech of petitioners is outlawed because Soviet Russia and her Red Army are a threat to world peace.

The nature of Communism as a force on the world scene would, of course, be relevant to the issue of clear and present danger of petitioners' advocacy within the United States. But the primary consideration is the strength and tactical position of petitioners and their converts in this country. On that there is no evidence in the record. If we are to take judicial notice of the threat of Communists within the nation, it should not be difficult to conclude that *as a political party* they are of little consequence. Communists in this country have never made a respectable or serious showing in any election. I would doubt that there is a village, let alone a city or county or state, which the Communists could carry. Communism in the world scene is no bogeyman; but Communism as a political faction or party in this country plainly is. Communism has been so thoroughly exposed in this country that it has been crippled as a political force. Free speech has destroyed it as an effective political party. It is inconceivable that those who went up and down this country preaching the doctrine of revolution which petitioners espouse would have any success. In days of trouble and confusion, when bread lines were long, when the unemployed walked the streets, when people were starving, the advocates of a short-cut by revolution might have a chance to gain adherents. But today there are no such conditions. The country is not in despair; the people know Soviet Communism; the doctrine of Soviet revolution is exposed in all of its ugliness and the American people want none of it.

[Unless] and until extreme and necessitous circumstances are shown our aim should be to keep speech unfettered and to allow the processes of law to be invoked only when the provocateurs among us move from speech to action. * * *

Note

Dennis distinguished. In 1954, Senator McCarthy was censured by the United States Senate for acting contrary to its ethics and impairing its dignity. In 1957, when the convictions of 14 "second string" communist leaders reached the Supreme Court in YATES v. UNITED STATES, 354 U.S. 298 (1957), McCarthy had died, and so had McCarthyism. Although strong anti-communist sentiment persisted, the political atmosphere in *Yates'* 1957 was profoundly different from that of *Dennis'* 1951. HARLAN, J., distinguishing *Dennis,* construed the Smith Act narrowly: "[The] essence of the *Dennis* holding was that indoctrination of a group in preparation for future violent action, as well as exhortation to immediate action, by advocacy found to be directed to 'action for the accomplishment' of forcible overthrow, to violence as 'a rule or principle of action,' and employing 'language of incitement,' is not constitutionally protected when the group is of sufficient size and cohesiveness, is sufficiently oriented towards action, and other circumstances are such as reasonably to justify apprehension that action will occur. This is quite a different thing from the view of the District Court here that mere doctrinal justification of forcible overthrow, if engaged in with the intent to accomplish overthrow, is punishable per se under the Smith Act. [T]he trial court's statement that the proscribed advocacy must include the 'urging,' 'necessity,' and 'duty' of forcible overthrow, and not merely its 'desirability' and 'propriety,' may not be regarded as a sufficient substitute for charging that the Smith Act reaches only advocacy of action for the overthrow of government by force and violence. The essential distinction is that those to whom the advocacy is addressed must be urged to *do* something, now or in the future, rather than merely to *believe* in something." Applying this standard, Harlan J., acquitted 5 defendants and remanded to the lower court for proceedings against the remaining defendants.[a]

After *Yates,* the government sought to prosecute communists for being members of an organization advocating the overthrow of the government by force and violence. The Court in *Scales v. United States,* 367 U.S. 203 (1961) and *Noto v. United States,* 367 U.S. 290 (1961) interpreted the membership clause to require that the organization engage in advocacy of the sort described in *Yates* and that the members be active with knowledge of the organization's advocacy and the specific intent to bring about violent overthrow as speedily as circumstances permit. These were demanding standards. Similarly, *Bond v. Floyd,* 385 U.S. 116 (1966) found ambiguity in expressions of support for those unwilling to respond to the draft that earlier opinions would have characterized as clear advocacy of illegal action. Even before *Bond,* the Justice Department abandoned its prosecutions of the communists.

a. Burton, J., concurred. Black, joined by Douglas, JJ., dissenting, would have acquitted all defendants. Clark, J., dissenting, would have affirmed the convictions of all defendants. Brennan and Whittaker, JJ., took no part. On remand, the government requested dismissal of the indictments, explaining that it could not meet *Yates'* evidentiary requirements.

D. A MODERN "RESTATEMENT"

BRANDENBURG v. OHIO

395 U.S. 444, 89 S.Ct. 1827, 23 L.Ed.2d 430 (1969).

PER CURIAM.

The appellant, a leader of a Ku Klux Klan group, was convicted under [a 1919] Ohio Criminal Syndicalism statute of "advocat[ing] the duty, necessity, or propriety of crime, sabotage, violence, or unlawful methods of terrorism as a means of accomplishing industrial or political reform" and of "voluntarily assembl[ing] with any society, group or assemblage of persons formed to teach or advocate the doctrines of criminal syndicalism." He was fined $1,000 and sentenced to one to 10 years' imprisonment. * * *

The record shows that a man, identified at trial as the appellant, telephoned an announcer-reporter on the staff of a Cincinnati television station and invited him to come to a Ku Klux Klan "rally" to be held at a farm in Hamilton County. With the cooperation of the organizers, the reporter and a cameraman attended the meeting and filmed the events. Portions of the films were later broadcast on the local station and on a national network.

The prosecution's case rested on the films and on testimony identifying the appellant as the person who communicated with the reporter and who spoke at the rally. The State also introduced into evidence several articles appearing in the film, including a pistol, a rifle, a shotgun, ammunition, a Bible, and a red hood worn by the speaker in the films.

One film showed 12 hooded figures, some of whom carried firearms. They were gathered around a large wooden cross, which they burned. No one was present other than the participants and the newsmen who made the film. Most of the words uttered during the scene were incomprehensible when the film was projected, but scattered phrases could be understood that were derogatory of Negroes and, in one instance, of Jews. Another scene on the same film showed the appellant, in Klan regalia, making a speech. The speech, in full, was as follows:

"This is an organizers' meeting. We have had quite a few members here today which are—we have hundreds, hundreds of members throughout the State of Ohio. I can quote from a newspaper clipping from the Columbus Ohio Dispatch, five weeks ago Sunday morning. The Klan has more members in the State of Ohio than does any other organization. We're not a revengent organization, but if our President, our Congress, our Supreme Court, continues to suppress the white, Caucasian race, it's possible that there might have to be some revengence taken.

"We are marching on Congress July the Fourth, four hundred thousand strong. From there we are dividing into two groups, one group to march on St. Augustine, Florida, the other group to march into Mississippi. Thank you."

The second film showed six hooded figures one of whom, later identified as the appellant, repeated a speech very similar to that recorded on the first film. The reference to the possibility of "revengence" was omitted, and one sentence was added: "Personally, I believe the nigger should be returned to Africa, the Jew returned to Israel." Though some of the figures in the films carried weapons, the speaker did not.

[*Whitney*] sustained the constitutionality of California's Criminal Syndicalism Act, the text of which is quite similar to that of the laws of Ohio. The Court upheld the statute on the ground that, without more, "advocating" violent means to effect political and economic change involves such danger to the security of the State that the State may outlaw it. But *Whitney* has been thoroughly discredited by later decisions [such as *Dennis* which] have fashioned the principle that the constitutional guarantees of free speech and free press do not permit a State to forbid or proscribe advocacy of the use of force or of law violation except where such advocacy is directed to inciting or producing imminent lawless action and is likely to incite or produce such action.2 As we said in *Noto*, "the mere abstract teaching [of] the moral propriety or even moral necessity for a resort to force and violence, is not the same as preparing a group for violent action and steeling it to such action." See also *Bond v. Floyd*. A statute which fails to draw this distinction impermissibly intrudes upon the freedoms guaranteed by the First and Fourteenth Amendments. It sweeps within its condemnation speech which our Constitution has immunized from governmental control. Cf. *Yates* * * *.

Measured by this test, Ohio's Criminal Syndicalism Act cannot be sustained. The Act punishes persons who "advocate or teach the duty, necessity, or propriety" of violence "as a means of accomplishing industrial or political reform"; or who publish or circulate or display any book or paper containing such advocacy; or who "justify" the commission of violent acts "with intent to exemplify, spread or advocate the propriety of the doctrines of criminal syndicalism"; or [who] "voluntarily assemble" with a group formed "to teach or advocate the doctrines of criminal syndicalism." Neither the indictment nor the trial judge's instructions to the jury in any way refined the statute's bald definition of the crime in terms of mere advocacy not distinguished from incitement to imminent lawless action.3

Accordingly, we are here confronted with a statute which, by its own words and as applied, purports to punish mere advocacy and to forbid, on pain of criminal punishment, assembly with others merely to advocate the described type of action.4 Such a statute falls within the condemnation of the First and Fourteenth Amendments. The contrary teaching of *Whitney* cannot be supported, and that decision is therefore overruled.

Reversed.

JUSTICE BLACK, concurring.

I agree with the views expressed by Mr. Justice Douglas in his concurring opinion in this case that the "clear and present danger" doctrine should have no place in the interpretation of the First Amendment. I join the Court's opinion, which, as I understand it, simply cites *Dennis*, but does not indicate any agreement on the Court's part with the "clear and present danger" doctrine on which *Dennis* purported to rely.

JUSTICE DOUGLAS, concurring.

While I join the opinion of the Court, I desire to enter a caveat.

[Whether] the war power—the greatest leveler of them all—is adequate to sustain [the "clear and present danger"] doctrine is debatable. The dissents in *Abrams* [and other cases] show how easily "clear and present danger" is manipulated to crush what Brandeis called "the fundamental right of free men to strive for better conditions through new legislation and new institutions" by argument

---

2. It was on the theory that the Smith Act embodied such a principle and that it had been applied only in conformity with it that this Court sustained the Act's constitutionality. That this was the basis for *Dennis* was emphasized in *Yates*, in which the Court overturned convictions for advocacy of the forcible overthrow of the Government under the Smith Act, because the trial judge's instructions had allowed conviction for mere advocacy, unrelated to its tendency to produce forcible action.

3. The first count of the indictment charged that appellant "did unlawfully by word of mouth advocate the necessity, or propriety of crime, violence, or unlawful methods

of terrorism as a means of accomplishing political reform * * *." The second count charged that appellant "did unlawfully voluntarily assemble with a group or assemblage of persons formed to advocate the doctrines of criminal syndicalism * * *." The trial judge's charge merely followed the language of the indictment. * * *

4. Statutes affecting the right of assembly, like those touching on freedom of speech, must observe the established distinctions between mere advocacy and incitement to lawless action * * *.

and discourse even in time of war. Though I doubt if the "clear and present danger" test is congenial to the First Amendment in time of a declared war, I am certain it is not reconcilable with the First Amendment in days of peace. * * *

Mr. Justice Holmes, though never formally abandoning the "clear and present danger" test, moved closer to the First Amendment ideal when he said in dissent in *Gitlow* [quoting the passage beginning, "Every idea is an incitement."] We have never been faithful to the philosophy of that dissent.

"[In *Dennis,* we distorted] the 'clear and present danger' test beyond recognition. [I] see no place in the regime of the First Amendment for any 'clear and present danger' test whether strict and tight as some would make it or free-wheeling as the Court in *Dennis* rephrased it.

———

The *Brandenburg* "inciting or producing imminent lawless action" standard was the basis for reversal of a disorderly conduct conviction in HESS v. INDIANA, 414 U.S. 105 (1973) (per curiam). After antiwar demonstrators on the Indiana University campus had blocked a public street, police moved them to the curbs on either side. As an officer passed him, appellant stated loudly, "We'll take the fucking street later [or again]," which led to his disorderly conduct conviction. His statement, observed the Court, "was not addressed to any person or group in particular" and "his tone, although loud, was no louder than that of the other people in the area. [At] best, [the] statement could be taken as counsel for present moderation; at worst, it amounted to nothing more than advocacy of illegal action at some indefinite future time." This was insufficient, under *Brandenburg,* to punish appellant's words, as the State had, on the ground that they had a "tendency to produce violence." It could not be said that appellant "was advocating, in the normal sense, any action" and there was "no evidence" that "his words were intended to produce, and likely to produce, *imminent* disorder."

REHNQUIST, J., joined by Burger, C.J., and Blackmun, J., dissented: "The simple explanation for the result in this case is that the majority has interpreted the evidence differently from the courts below." The dissenters quarreled with the Court's conclusion that appellant's advocacy "was not directed towards inciting imminent action. [T]here are surely possible constructions of the statement which would encompass more or less immediate and continuing action against the police. They should not be rejected out of hand because of an unexplained preference for other acceptable alternatives."

In another potentially important development, COMMUNIST PARTY OF INDIANA v. WHITCOMB, 414 U.S. 441 (1974), invalidated an Indiana statute denying a political party or its candidates access to the ballot unless the party filed an affidavit that it "does not advocate the overthrow of local, state or national government by force or violence." The Court, per BRENNAN J., maintained that the required oath (which had been interpreted to include advocacy of abstract doctrine) violated the principle of *Brandenburg* and stated that the principle applied not only to attempted denials of public employment, bar licensing, and tax exemption, but also to ballot access denials. The flaw with the state's position was that it furnished access to the ballot "not because the Party urges others 'to *do* something now *or in the future* [but] merely to believe in something,' [*Yates*]" (second emphasis added).

Congress prohibits providing material support or resources to any organization designated by the Secretary of State to be a foreign terrorist organization. Plaintiffs sought to provide support to two such organizations: the Kurdistan Workers Party ("PKK") and the Liberation Tigers of Tamil Eelam ("LTTE"). They wished to support training members of the PKK to use law to peacefully resolve disputes; to teach PKK how to petition representative bodies such as the United Nations for relief; and/or to engage in political advocacy on behalf of Kurds who live in Turkey or on behalf of the LTTE. HOLDER v. HUMANITARIAN LAW PROJECT, 130 S.Ct.___ (2010), per ROBERTS, C.J., held that the congressional prohibition could constitutionally be applied to training and expert advice for peaceful speech activities even if the provision of such support was not intended to assist in the unlawful activities of the organization. Roberts, C.J., emphasized that the statute does not cover independent advocacy on behalf of such organizations or even membership in such organizations.a Rather it covers support including training, expert advice, or speech under the direction of or in coordination with an organization designated as terrorist in character.

Roberts, C.J., did not deny that the support offered was a form of presumptively protected speech, but deferred to the findings of the congressional and executive branches that the organizations were "so tainted by their criminal conduct that any contribution to such an organization facilitates that conduct." He reasoned that support frees up other resources, helps to legitimize such organizations, and strains U.S. relationships with its allies. The skills taught could be used in manipulative ways and might gain further monetary gains for such organizations. Roberts, C.J., concluded that the prohibitions were necessary to further an urgent objective of the highest order.

BREYER, J., joined by Ginsburg and Sotomayor, JJ., dissenting, argued that the decision interfered with centrally important peaceful speech activities. He argued that peaceful advocacy should ordinarily be protected whether or not it was coordinated with a designated terrorist organization: "I believe the Court has failed to examine the Government's justification with sufficient care. It has failed to insist upon specific evidence, rather than general assertion. It has failed to require tailoring of means to fit compelling ends. And ultimately it deprives the individuals before us of the protection that the First Amendment demands."

II. REPUTATION AND PRIVACY

In an important article, Harry Kalven coined the phrase "two level theory," *The Metaphysics of the Law of Obscenity,* 1960 Sup.Ct.Rev. 1, 11. As he described it, *Beauharnais, infra,* and other cases employed a First Amendment methodology that classified speech at two levels. Some speech—libel, obscenity, "fighting words"—was thought to be so bereft of social utility as to be beneath First Amendment protection. At the second level, speech of constitutional value was thought to be protected unless it presented a clear and present danger of a substantive evil.

In considering libel and privacy, we will witness the collapse of "two level theory." The purpose is not a detailed examination of libel and privacy law. Our interests include the initial exclusion of defamation from First Amendment protection, the themes and methods contributing to the erosion of that exclusion, and the articulation of basic First Amendment values having implications and applications beyond defamation and the right to privacy.

a. Roberts, C.J., stated that the record did not disclose whether the plaintiffs sought to engage in independent or coordinated advocacy.

A. GROUP LIBEL

BEAUHARNAIS v. ILLINOIS, 343 U.S. 250 (1952), per FRANKFURTER, J., sustained a statute prohibiting exhibition in any public place of any publication portraying "depravity, criminality, unchastity, or lack of virtue of a class of citizens, of any race, color, creed or religion [which exposes such citizens] to contempt, derision or obloquy or which is productive of breach of the peace or riots." The Court affirmed a conviction for organizing the distribution of a leaflet which petitioned the Mayor and City Council of Chicago "to halt the further encroachment, harassment and invasion of white people, their property, neighborhoods and persons by the Negro"; called for "one million self respecting white people in Chicago to unite"; and warned that if "the need to prevent the white race from becoming mongrelized by the Negro will not unite us, then the [aggressions], rapes, robberies, knives, guns, and marijuana of the Negro, surely will.":

"Today every American jurisdiction [punishes] libels directed at individuals. '[There] are certain well-defined and narrowly limited classes of speech, the prevention and punishment of which have never been thought to raise any constitutional problem. These include the lewd and obscene, the profane, the libelous, and the insulting or "fighting" words—those which by their very utterance inflict injury or tend to incite to an immediate breach of the peace. It has been well observed that such utterances are no essential part of any exposition of ideas, and are of such slight social value as a step to truth that any benefit that may be derived from them is clearly outweighed by the social interest in order and morality. "Resort to epithets or personal abuse is not in any proper sense communication of information or opinion safeguarded by the Constitution, and its punishment as a criminal act would raise no question under that instrument." *Cantwell v. Connecticut,* [Ch. 8, Sec. 2].' Such were the views of a unanimous Court in *Chaplinsky v. New Hampshire,* Sec. 1, IV, A infra.6

"No one will gainsay that it is libelous falsely to charge another with being a rapist, robber, carrier of knives and guns, and user of marijuana. The [question is whether the fourteenth amendment] prevents a State from punishing such libels—as criminal libel has been defined, limited and constitutionally recognized time out of mind—directed at designated collectivities and flagrantly disseminated. [I]f an utterance directed at an individual may be the object of criminal sanctions, we cannot deny to a State power to punish the same utterance directed at a defined group, unless we can say that this is a wilful and purposeless restriction unrelated to the peace and well-being of the State.

"Illinois did not have to look beyond her own borders to await the tragic experience of the last three decades to conclude that wilful purveyors of falsehood concerning racial and religious groups promote strife and tend powerfully to obstruct the manifold adjustments required for free, orderly life in a metropolitan, polyglot community. From the murder of the abolitionist Lovejoy in 1837 to the Cicero riots of 1951, Illinois has been the scene of exacerbated tension between races, often flaring into violence and destruction. In many of these outbreaks, utterances of the character here in question, so the Illinois legislature could conclude, played a significant [part].

"In the face of this history and its frequent obligato of extreme racial and religious propaganda, we would deny experience to say that the Illinois legislature

---

6. In all but five States, the constitutional guarantee of free speech to every person is explicitly qualified by holding him "responsible for the abuse of that right." * * *

was without reason in seeking ways to curb false or malicious defamation of racial and religious groups, made in public places and by means calculated to have a powerful emotional impact on those to whom it was presented.

"[It would] be arrant dogmatism, quite outside the scope of our authority [, for] us to deny that the Illinois Legislature may warrantably believe that a man's job and his educational opportunities and the dignity accorded him may depend as much on the reputation of the racial and religious group to which he willynilly belongs, as on his own merits. This being so, we are precluded from saying that speech concededly punishable when immediately directed at individuals cannot be outlawed if directed at groups with whose position and esteem in society the affiliated individual may be inextricably involved. * * *18

"As to the defense of truth, Illinois in common with many States requires a showing not only that the utterance state the facts, but also that the publication be made 'with good motives and for justifiable ends'. Both elements are necessary if the defense is to prevail. [The] teaching of a century and a half of criminal libel prosecutions in this country would go by the board if we were to hold that Illinois was not within her rights in making this combined requirement. Assuming that defendant's offer of proof directed to a part of the defense was adequate, it did not satisfy the entire requirement which Illinois could exact."

The Court ruled that the trial court properly declined to require the jury to find a "clear and present danger": "Libelous utterances not being within the area of constitutionally protected speech, it is unnecessary, either for us or for the State courts, to consider the issues behind the phrase 'clear and present danger.' Certainly no one would contend that obscene speech, for example, may be punished only upon a showing of such circumstances. Libel, as we have seen, is in the same class."

BLACK, J., joined by Douglas, J., dissented: "[The Court] acts on the bland assumption that the First Amendment is wholly irrelevant. [Today's] case degrades First Amendment freedoms to the 'rational basis' level. [We] are cautioned that state legislatures must be left free to 'experiment' and to make legislative judgments. [State] experimentation in curbing freedom of expression is startling and frightening doctrine in a country dedicated to self-government by its people.

"[As] 'constitutionally recognized,' [criminal libel] has provided for punishment of false, malicious, scurrilous charges against individuals, not against huge groups. This limited scope of the law of criminal libel is of no small importance. It has confined state punishment of speech and expression to the narrowest of areas involving nothing more than private feuds. Every expansion of the law of criminal libel so as to punish discussion of matters of public concern means a corresponding invasion of the area dedicated to free expression by the First Amendment.

"[If] there be minority groups who hail this holding as their victory, they might consider the possible relevancy of this ancient remark: 'Another such victory and I am undone.' "

REED, J., joined by Douglas, J., dissenting, argued that the statute was unconstitutionally vague: "These words—'virtue,' 'derision,' and 'obloquy'—have neither general nor special meanings well enough known to apprise those within their reach as to limitations on speech. Philosophers and poets, thinkers of high and low degree from every age and race have sought to expound the meaning of

---

18. [If] a statute sought to outlaw libels of political parties, quite different problems not now before us would be raised. For one thing, the whole doctrine of fair comment as indispensable to the democratic political process would come into play. Political parties, like public men, are, as it were, public property.

virtue. [Are] the tests of the Puritan or the Cavalier to be applied, those of the city or the farm, the Christian or non-Christian, the old or the young?''

DOUGLAS, J., dissented: "Hitler and his Nazis showed how evil a conspiracy could be which was aimed at destroying a race by exposing it to contempt, derision, and obloquy. I would be willing to concede that such conduct directed at a race or group in this country could be made an indictable offense. For such a project would be more than the exercise of free speech. [It] would be free speech plus.

"I would also be willing to concede that even without the element of conspiracy there might be times and occasions when the legislative or executive branch might call a halt to inflammatory talk, such as the shouting of 'fire' in a school or a theatre.

"My view is that if in any case other public interests are to override the plain command of the First Amendment, the peril of speech must be clear and present, leaving no room for argument, raising no doubts as to the necessity of curbing speech in order to prevent disaster.''

JACKSON, J., dissenting, argued that the fourteenth amendment does not incorporate the first, as such, but permits the states more latitude than the Congress. He concluded, however, that due process required the trier of fact to evaluate the evidence as to the truth and good faith of the speaker and the clarity and presence of the danger. He was unwilling to assume danger from the tendency of the words and felt that the trial court had precluded the defendant's efforts to show truth and good motives.

The First Amendment refers to a right to petition for redress of grievances. Nothing was made of it in *Beauharnais,* and *McDonald v. Smith,* 472 U.S. 479 (1985) ultimately denied any special First Amendment status for the Petition Clause.

B. PUBLIC OFFICIALS AND SEDITIOUS LIBEL

NEW YORK TIMES CO. v. SULLIVAN

376 U.S. 254, 84 S.Ct. 710, 11 L.Ed.2d 686 (1964).

JUSTICE BRENNAN delivered the opinion of the Court.

[Sullivan, the Montgomery, Ala. police commissioner, sued the New York Times and four black Alabama clergymen for alleged libelous statements in a paid, full-page fund-raising advertisement signed by a "Committee to defend Martin Luther King and the struggle for freedom in the South." The advertisement stated that "truckloads of police armed with shotguns and tear-gas ringed Alabama State College Campus" in Montgomery, and that "the Southern violators [have] bombed [Dr. King's] home, assaulted his person [and] arrested him seven times." In several respects the statements were untrue. Several witnesses testified that they understood the statements to refer to Sullivan because he supervised Montgomery police. Sullivan proved he did not participate in the events described. He offered no proof of pecuniary loss.[3] Pursuant to Alabama law, the trial court

----

3. Approximately 394 copies of the edition of the Times containing the advertisement were circulated in Alabama. Of these, about 35 copies were distributed in Montgomery County. The total circulation of the Times for that day was approximately 650,000 copies.

submitted the libel issue to the jury, giving general and punitive damages instructions. It returned a $500,000 verdict for Sullivan against all of the defendants.] We hold that the rule of law applied by the Alabama courts is constitutionally deficient for failure to provide the safeguards for freedom of speech and of the press that are required by the First and Fourteenth Amendments in a libel action brought by a public official against critics of his official conduct.4 We further hold that under the proper safeguards the evidence presented in this case is constitutionally insufficient to support the judgment for respondent.

I. [The] publication here [communicated] information, expressed opinion, recited grievances, protested claimed abuses, and sought financial support on behalf of a movement whose existence and objectives are matters of the highest public interest and concern. That the Times was paid for publishing the advertisement is as immaterial in this connection as is the fact that newspapers and books are sold. *Smith v. California*, Sec. 1, III, B infra. Any other conclusion would discourage newspapers from carrying "editorial advertisements" of this type, and so might shut off an important outlet for the promulgation of information and ideas by persons who do not themselves have access to publishing facilities.

II. Under Alabama law [once] "libel per se" has been established, the defendant has no defense as to stated facts unless he can persuade the jury that they were true in all their particulars. [His] privilege of "fair comment" for expressions of opinion depends on the truth of the facts upon which the comment is based. [Unless] he can discharge the burden of proving truth, general damages are presumed, and may be awarded without proof of pecuniary injury.

[Respondent] relies heavily, as did the Alabama courts, on statements of this Court to the effect that the Constitution does not protect libelous publications. Those statements do not foreclose our inquiry here. None of the cases sustained the use of libel laws to impose sanctions upon expression critical of the official conduct of public officials. [L]ibel can claim no talismanic immunity from constitutional limitations. It must be measured by standards that satisfy the First Amendment.

The First Amendment, said Judge Learned Hand, "presupposes that right conclusions are more likely to be gathered out of a multitude of tongues, than through any kind of authoritative selection. To many this is, and always will be, folly; but we have staked upon it our all." [Thus] we consider this case against the background of a profound national commitment to the principle that debate on public issues should be uninhibited, robust, and wide-open, and that it may well include vehement, caustic, and sometimes unpleasantly sharp attacks on government and public officials. The present advertisement, as an expression of grievance and protest on one of the major public issues of our time, would seem clearly to qualify for the constitutional protection. The question is whether it forfeits that protection by the falsity of some of its factual statements and by its alleged defamation of respondent.

4. [The] Times contends that the assumption of jurisdiction over its corporate person by the Alabama courts overreaches the territorial limits of the Due Process Clause. The latter claim is foreclosed from our review by the ruling of the Alabama courts that the Times entered a general appearance in the action and thus waived its jurisdictional objection. * * *

[Since *New York Times* the Court has upheld expansive personal jurisdiction against media defendants. *Calder v. Jones*, 465 U.S. 783 (1984); *Keeton v. Hustler*, 465 U.S. 770 (1984). *Calder* rejected the suggestion that First Amendment concerns enter into jurisdictional analysis. It feared complicating the inquiry and argued that because First Amendment concerns are taken into account in limiting the substantive law of defamation, "to reintroduce those concerns at the jurisdictional stage would be a form of double counting."]

Authoritative interpretations of the First Amendment guarantees have consistently refused to recognize an exception for any test of truth—whether administered by judges, juries, or administrative officials—and especially not one that puts the burden of proving truth on the speaker. [E]rroneous statement is inevitable in free debate, and [it] must be protected if the freedoms of expression are to have the "breathing space" that they "need [to] survive."

[Injury] to official reputation affords no more warrant for repressing speech that would otherwise be free than does factual error. Where judicial officers are involved, this Court has held that concern for the dignity and reputation of the courts does not justify the punishment as criminal contempt of criticism of the judge or his decision. This is true even though the utterance contains "half-truths" and "misinformation." Such repression can be justified, if at all, only by a clear and present danger of the obstruction of justice. If judges are to be treated as "men of fortitude, able to thrive in a hardy climate," surely the same must be true of other government officials, such as elected city commissioners. Criticism of their official conduct does not lose its constitutional protection merely because it is effective criticism and hence diminishes their official reputations.

If neither factual error nor defamatory content suffices to remove the constitutional shield from criticism of official conduct, the combination of the two elements is no less inadequate. This is the lesson to be drawn from the great controversy over the Sedition Act of 1798, 1 Stat. 596, which first crystallized a national awareness of the central meaning of the First Amendment. [Although] the Sedition Act was never tested in this Court, the attack upon its validity has carried the day in the court of history. Fines levied in its prosecution were repaid by Act of Congress on the ground that it was unconstitutional. * * * Jefferson, as President, pardoned those who had been convicted and sentenced under the Act and remitted their fines. [Its] invalidity [has] also been assumed by Justices of this Court. [These] views reflect a broad consensus that the Act, because of the restraint it imposed upon criticism of government and public officials, was inconsistent with the First Amendment. * * *

What a State may not constitutionally bring about by means of a criminal statute is likewise beyond the reach of its civil law of libel. The fear of damage awards under a rule such as that invoked by the Alabama courts here may be markedly more inhibiting than the fear of prosecution under a criminal statute. [The] judgment awarded in this case—without the need for any proof of actual pecuniary loss—was one thousand times greater than the maximum fine provided by the Alabama criminal [libel law], and one hundred times greater than that provided by the Sedition Act. And since there is no double-jeopardy limitation applicable to civil lawsuits, this is not the only judgment that may be awarded against petitioners for the same publication.18 Whether or not a newspaper can survive a succession of such judgments, the pall of fear and timidity imposed upon those who would give voice to public criticism is an atmosphere in which the First Amendment freedoms cannot [survive].

The state rule of law is not saved by its allowance of the defense of truth. A defense for erroneous statements honestly made is no less essential here than was the requirement of proof of guilty knowledge which, in *Smith v. California,* we held indispensable to a valid conviction of a bookseller for possessing obscene writings for [sale].

---

18. The Times states that four other libel suits based on the advertisement have been filed against it by [others]; that another $500,000 verdict has been awarded in [one]; and that the damages sought in the other three total $2,000,000.

A rule compelling the critic of official conduct to guarantee the truth of all his factual assertions—and to do so on pain of libel judgments virtually unlimited in amount—leads to a comparable "self-censorship." Allowance of the defense of truth, with the burden of proving it on the defendant, does not mean that only false speech will be deterred.19 [Under] such a rule, would-be critics of official conduct may be deterred from voicing their criticism, even though it is believed to be true and even though it is in fact true, because of doubt whether it can be proved in court or fear of the expense of having to do so. They tend to make only statements which "steer far wider of the unlawful zone." The rule thus dampens the vigor and limits the variety of public [debate].

The constitutional guarantees require, we think, a federal rule that prohibits a public official from recovering damages for a defamatory falsehood relating to his official conduct unless he proves that the statement was made with "actual malice"—that is, with knowledge that it was false or with reckless disregard of whether it was false or [not].a

Such a privilege for criticism of official conduct is appropriately analogous to the protection accorded a public official when *he* is sued for libel by a private citizen. In *Barr v. Matteo,* 360 U.S. 564, 575 (1959), this Court held the utterance of a federal official to be absolutely privileged if made "within the outer perimeter" of his duties. The States accord the same immunity to statements of their highest officers, although some differentiate their lesser officials and qualify the privilege they enjoy. But all hold that all officials are protected unless actual malice can be proved. The reason for the official privilege is said to be that the threat of damage suits would otherwise "inhibit the fearless, vigorous, and effective administration of policies of government" and "dampen the ardor of all but the most resolute, or the most irresponsible, in the unflinching discharge of their duties." *Barr.* Analogous considerations support the privilege for the citizen-critic of government. It is as much his duty to criticize as it is the official's duty to administer. [It] would give public servants an unjustified preference over the public they serve, if critics of official conduct did not have a fair equivalent of the immunity granted to the officials themselves. We conclude that such a privilege is required by the First and Fourteenth Amendments.23

III. [W]e consider that the proof presented to show actual malice lacks the convincing clarityb which the constitutional standard demands, and hence that it would not constitutionally sustain the judgment for respondent under the proper rule of law. [T]here is evidence that the Times published the advertisement without checking its accuracy against the news stories in the Times' own files.

---

19. Even a false statement may be deemed to make a valuable contribution to the public debate, since it brings about "the clearer perception and livelier impression of truth, produced by its collision with error." Mill, *On Liberty* 15 (1955).

a. Compare *St. Amant v. Thompson,* 390 U.S. 727 (1968) (publishing while "in fact entertain[ing] serious doubts about the truth of the publication" satisfies standard) with *Garrison v. Louisiana,* 379 U.S. 64 (1964) (standard requires "high degree of awareness of probable falsity"). See also *Masson v. New Yorker Magazine, Inc.,* 501 U.S. 496 (1991) ("a deliberate alteration of the words uttered by a plaintiff does not equate with knowledge of falsity [unless] the alteration results in a material change of meaning conveyed by the statement").

23. We have no occasion here to determine how far down into the lower ranks of government employees the "public official" designation would extend for purposes of this rule, or otherwise to specify categories of persons who would or would not be included. [Nor] need we here determine the boundaries of the "official conduct" concept. * * *

b. Compare *Bose Corp. v. Consumers Union,* 466 U.S. 485 (1984) (appellate courts "must exercise independent judgment and determine whether the record establishes actual malice with convincing clarity."). Accord *Harte–Hanks Communications, Inc. v. Connaughton,* 491 U.S. 657 (1989). See also *Anderson v. Liberty Lobby, Inc.,* 477 U.S. 242 (1986) (same standard at summary judgment).

The mere presence of the stories in the files does [not] establish that the Times "knew" the advertisement was false, since the state of mind required for actual malice would have to be brought home to the persons in the Times' organization having responsibility for the publication of the advertisement. With respect to the failure of those persons to make the check, the record shows that they relied upon their knowledge of the good reputation of many [whose] names were listed as sponsors of the advertisement, and upon the letter from A. Philip Randolph, known to them as a responsible individual, certifying that the use of the names was authorized. There was testimony that the persons handling the advertisement saw nothing in it that would render it unacceptable under the Times' policy of rejecting advertisements containing "attacks of a personal character"; their failure to reject it on this ground was not unreasonable. We think the evidence against the Times supports at most a finding of negligence in failing to discover the misstatements, and is constitutionally insufficient to show the recklessness that is required for a finding of actual malice.

[T]he evidence was constitutionally defective in another respect: it was incapable of supporting the jury's finding that the allegedly libelous statements were made "of and concerning" respondent. [On this point, the Supreme Court of Alabama] based its ruling on the proposition that: "[The] average person knows that municipal agents, such as police and firemen, and others, are under the control and direction of the city governing body, and more particularly under the direction and control of a single commissioner. In measuring the performance or deficiencies of such groups, praise or criticism is usually attached to the official in complete control of the body."

This proposition has disquieting implications for criticism of governmental conduct. [It would transmute] criticism of government, however impersonal it may seem on its face, into personal criticism, and hence potential libel, of the officials of whom the government is composed. [Raising] as it does the possibility that a good-faith critic of government will be penalized for his criticism, the proposition relied on by the Alabama courts strikes at the very center of the constitutionally protected area of free expression. We hold that such a proposition may not constitutionally be utilized to establish that an otherwise impersonal attack on governmental operations was a libel of an official responsible for those operations. Since it was relied on exclusively here, and there was no other evidence to connect the statements with respondent, the evidence was constitutionally insufficient to support a finding that the statements referred to respondent. * * *c

JUSTICE BLACK, with whom JUSTICE DOUGLAS joins (concurring).

* * * "Malice," even as defined by the Court, is an elusive, abstract concept, hard to prove and hard to disprove. The requirement that malice be proved provides at best an evanescent protection for the right critically to discuss public affairs and certainly does not measure up to the sturdy safeguard embodied in the First Amendment. Unlike the Court, therefore, I vote to reverse exclusively on the ground that the Times and the individual defendants had an absolute, unconditional constitutional right to publish in the Times advertisement their criticisms of the Montgomery agencies and [officials].

The half-million-dollar verdict [gives] dramatic proof [that] state libel laws threaten the very existence of an American press virile enough to publish unpopular views on public affairs and bold enough to criticize the conduct of

---

c. For a similar ruling that impersonal criticism of a government operation cannot be the basis for defamation "of and concerning" the supervisor of the operation, see *Rosenblatt v.* *Baer,* 383 U.S. 75 (1966): "[T]antamount to a demand for recovery based on libel of government."

public officials. [B]riefs before us show that in Alabama there are now pending eleven libel suits by local and state officials against the Times seeking $5,600,000, and five such suits against the Columbia Broadcasting System seeking $1,700,000. Moreover, this technique for harassing and punishing a free press—now that it has been shown to be possible—is by no means limited to cases with racial overtones; it can be used in other fields where public feelings may make local as well as out-of-state newspapers easy prey for libel verdict seekers.

In my opinion the Federal Constitution has dealt with this deadly danger to the press in the only way possible without leaving the press open to destruction—by granting the press an absolute immunity for criticism of the way public officials do their public duty.

[This] Nation, I suspect, can live in peace without libel suits based on public discussions of public affairs and public officials. But I doubt that a country can live in freedom where its people can be made to suffer physically or financially for criticizing their government, its actions, or its officials. * * *d

Notes

1. ***Public officials.*** *New York Times,* fn. 23 left open "how far down into the lower ranks of governmental employees" the rule would extend, and *Rosenblatt v. Baer,* 383 U.S. 75 (1966) suggested the rule might apply to the supervisor of a publicly owned ski resort, saying it applies among other things to those who "appear to the public to [have] substantial responsibility for or control over the conduct of government affairs."

2. ***Private conduct of public officials and candidates.*** *Garrison v. Louisiana,* 379 U.S. 64 (1964) extended *New York Times* to "anything which might touch on an official's fitness for office," even if the defamation did not concern official conduct in office. Invoking that standard, *Monitor Patriot Co. v. Roy,* 401 U.S. 265 (1971) applied *New York Times* to a news column describing a candidate for public office as a "former small-time bootlegger."

3. ***Public figures.*** In CURTIS PUB. CO. v. BUTTS and ASSOCIATED PRESS v. WALKER, 388 U.S. 130 (1967), HARLAN, J., contended that because public figures were not subject to the restraints of the political process, any criticism of them was not akin to seditious libel and was, therefore, a step removed from the central meaning of the First Amendment. Nonetheless, he argued that public figure actions should not be left entirely to the vagaries of state defamation law and would have required that public figures show "highly unreasonable conduct constituting an extreme departure from the standards of investigation and reporting ordinarily adhered to by responsible publishers" as a prerequisite to recovery. In response, WARREN, C.J., argued that the inapplicability of the restraints of the political process to public figures underscored the importance for uninhibited debate about their activities since "public opinion may be the only instrument by which society can attempt to influence their conduct." He observed that increasingly "the distinctions between governmental and private sectors are blurred," that public figures, like public officials, "often play an influential role in ordering society," and as a class have a ready access to the mass media "both to influence policy and to counter criticism of their views and activities." He accordingly concluded that the *New York Times* rule should be

d. Goldberg, J., joined by Douglas, J., concurring, also asserted for "the citizen and [the] press an absolute unconditional privilege to criticize official conduct," but maintained that the imposition of liability for "[p]urely private defamation" did not abridge the First Amendment because it had "little to do with the political ends of a self-governing society."

extended to public figures. Four other justices in *Butts* and *Walker* were willing to go at least as far as Warren, C.J., and subsequent cases have settled on the position that public figures must meet the *New York Times* requirements in order to recover in a defamation action. The critical issues are how to define the concept of public figure and how to apply it in practice. See *Gertz,* infra.

4. ***Private plaintiffs and public issues.*** Without deciding whether any First Amendment protection should extend to matters not of general or public interest, a plurality led by BRENNAN, J., joined by Burger, C.J., and Blackmun, J., argued in ROSENBLOOM v. METROMEDIA, INC., 403 U.S. 29 (1971), that the *New York Times* rule should be extended to defamatory statements involving matters of public or general interest "without regard to whether the persons involved are famous or anonymous." Black, J., would have gone further, opining that the First Amendment "does not permit the recovery of libel judgments against the news media even when statements are broadcast with knowledge they are false," and Douglas, J., shared Black, J.'s approach (at least with respect to matters of public interest, although he did not participate in *Rosenbloom*.) WHITE, J., felt that the *New York Times* rule should apply to reporting on the official actions of public servants and to reporting on those involved in or affected by their official action. That principle was broad enough to cover Rosenbloom, a distributor of nudist magazines who had been arrested by the Philadelphia police for distributing obscene materials. The defamatory broadcast wrongly assumed his guilt. Dissenting, Harlan, Stewart and Marshall, JJ., counseled an approach similar to that taken in *Gertz,* infra.

After *Rosenbloom* the lower courts rather uniformly followed the approach taken by the plurality. By 1974, however, the composition of the Court had changed and so had the minds of some of the justices.

C. PRIVATE INDIVIDUALS AND PUBLIC FIGURES

GERTZ v. ROBERT WELCH, INC.

418 U.S. 323, 94 S.Ct. 2997, 41 L.Ed.2d 789 (1974).

JUSTICE POWELL delivered the opinion of the Court.

[Respondent published *American Opinion,* a monthly outlet for the John Birch Society. It published an article falsely stating that Gertz, a lawyer, was the "architect" in a "communist frameup" of a policeman convicted of murdering a youth whose family Gertz represented in resultant civil proceedings, and that Gertz had a "criminal record" and had been an officer in a named "Communist-fronter" organization that advocated violent seizure of our government. In Gertz' libel action there was evidence that *Opinion*'s managing editor did not know the statements were false and had relied on the reputation of the article's author and prior experience with the accuracy of his articles. After a $50,000 verdict for Gertz, the trial court entered judgment n.o.v., concluding that the *New York Times* rule applied to any discussion of a "public issue." The court of appeals affirmed, ruling that the publisher did not have the requisite "awareness of probable falsity." The Court held that *New York Times* did not apply to defamation of private individuals, but remanded for a new trial "because the jury was allowed to impose liability without fault [and] to presume damages without proof of injury."]

II. The principal issue in this case is whether a newspaper or broadcaster that publishes defamatory falsehoods about an individual who is neither a public official nor a public figure may claim a constitutional privilege against liability for the injury inflicted by those statements. * * *

In his opinion for the plurality in *Rosenbloom,* Mr. Justice Brennan took the *Times* privilege one step further [than *Butts* and *Walker*]. He concluded that its protection should extend to defamatory falsehoods relating to private persons if the statements concerned matters of general or public interest. He abjured the suggested distinction between public officials and public figures on the one hand and private individuals on the other. He focused instead on society's interest in learning about certain issues: "If a matter is a subject of public or general interest, it cannot suddenly become less so merely because a private individual is involved or because in some sense the individual did not choose to become involved." Thus, under the plurality opinion, a private citizen involuntarily associated with a matter of general interest has no recourse for injury to his reputation unless he can satisfy the demanding requirements of the *Times* [test].

III. [Under] the First Amendment there is no such thing as a false idea. However pernicious an opinion may seem, we depend for its correction not on the conscience of the judges and juries but on the competition of other ideas.a But there is no constitutional value in false statements of fact. Neither the intentional lie nor the careless error materially advances society's interest in "uninhibited, robust, and wide-open" debate on public issues. * * *

Although the erroneous statement of fact is not worthy of constitutional protection, it is nevertheless inevitable in free debate. [P]unishment of error runs the risk of inducing a cautious and restrictive exercise of the constitutionally guaranteed freedoms of speech and press. [The] First Amendment requires that we protect some falsehood in order to protect speech that matters.

The need to avoid self-censorship by the news media is, however, not the only societal value at issue. [The] legitimate state interest underlying the law of libel is the compensation of individuals for the harm inflicted on them by defamatory falsehoods. We would not lightly require the State to abandon this purpose, for, as Mr. Justice Stewart has reminded us, the individual's right to the protection of his own good name "reflects no more than our basic concept of the essential dignity and worth of every human being—a concept at the root of any decent system of ordered liberty. * * * " *Rosenblatt*.b

Some tension necessarily exists between the need for a vigorous and uninhibited press and the legitimate interest in redressing wrongful injury. [In] our continuing effort to define the proper accommodation between these competing concerns, we have been especially anxious to assure to the freedoms of speech and press that "breathing space" essential to their fruitful exercise. To that end this Court has extended a measure of strategic protection to defamatory falsehood.

The *New York Times* standard defines the level of constitutional protection appropriate to the context of defamation of [public figures and those who hold governmental office]. Plainly many deserving plaintiffs, including some intentionally subjected to injury, will be unable to surmount the barrier of the *New York Times* test. [For] the reasons stated below, we conclude that the state interest in

a. For many years the lower courts took this language seriously and deemed opinion to be absolutely protected (see, e.g., *Ollman v. Evans,* 750 F.2d 970 (D.C.Cir.1984)), but *Milkovich v. Lorain Journal Co.,* 497 U.S. 1 (1990), per Rehnquist, C.J., ultimately denied that there is any "wholesale defamation exception for anything that might be labeled 'opinion.'"

b. Stewart J., continued: "The protection of private personality, like the protection of life itself, is left primarily to the individual States under the Ninth and Tenth Amendments. But this does not mean that the right is entitled to any less recognition by this Court as a basic of our constitutional system."

compensating injury to the reputation of private individuals requires that a different rule should obtain with respect to them.

[W]e have no difficulty in distinguishing among defamation plaintiffs. The first remedy of any victim of defamation is self-help—using available opportunities to contradict the lie or correct the error and thereby to minimize its adverse impact on reputation. Public officials and public figures usually enjoy significantly greater access to the channels of effective communication and hence have a more realistic opportunity to counteract false statements than private individuals normally enjoy.[9] Private individuals are therefore more vulnerable to injury, and the state interest in protecting them is correspondingly greater.

More important than the likelihood that private individuals will lack effective opportunities for rebuttal, there is a compelling normative consideration underlying the distinction between public and private defamation plaintiffs. An individual who decides to seek governmental office must accept certain necessary consequences of that involvement in public affairs. He runs the risk of closer public scrutiny than might otherwise be the case. [Those] classed as public figures stand in a similar [position.]

Even if the foregoing generalities do not obtain in every instance, the communications media are entitled to act on the assumption that public officials and public figures have voluntarily exposed themselves to increased risk of injury from defamatory falsehoods concerning them. No such assumption is justified with respect to a private individual. He has not accepted public office nor assumed an "influential role in ordering society." *Butts.* He has relinquished no part of his interest in the protection of his own good name, and consequently he has a more compelling call on the courts for redress of injury inflicted by defamatory falsehood. Thus, private individuals are not only more vulnerable to injury than public officials and public figures; they are also more deserving of recovery.

For these reasons we conclude that the States should retain substantial latitude in their efforts to enforce a legal remedy for defamatory falsehood injurious to the reputation of a private individual. The extension of the *Times* test proposed by the *Rosenbloom* plurality would abridge this legitimate state interest to a degree that we find unacceptable. And it would occasion the additional difficulty of forcing state and federal judges to decide on an ad hoc basis which publications address issues of "general or public interest" and which do not—to determine, in the words of Mr. Justice Marshall, "what information is relevant to self-government." *Rosenbloom.* We doubt the wisdom of committing this task to the conscience of judges. [The] "public or general interest" test for determining the applicability of the *Times* standard to private defamation actions inadequately serves both of the competing values at stake. On the one hand, a private individual whose reputation is injured by defamatory falsehood that does concern an issue of public or general interest has no recourse unless he can meet the rigorous requirements of *Times.* This is true despite the factors that distinguish the state interest in compensating private individuals from the analogous interest involved in the context of public persons. On the other hand, a publisher or broadcaster of a defamatory error which a court deems unrelated to an issue of public or general interest may be held liable in damages even if it took every reasonable precaution to ensure the accuracy of its assertions. And liability may far exceed compensation for any actual injury to the plaintiff, for the jury may be

9. Of course, an opportunity for rebuttal seldom suffices to undo harm of defamatory falsehood. Indeed, the law of defamation is rooted in our experience that the truth rarely catches up with a lie. But the fact that the self-help remedy of rebuttal, standing alone, is inadequate to its task does not mean that it is irrelevant to our inquiry.

permitted to presume damages without proof of loss and even to award punitive damages.

We hold that, so long as they do not impose liability without fault, the States may define for themselves the appropriate standard of liability for a publisher or broadcaster of defamatory falsehood injurious to a private individual. This approach provides a more equitable boundary between the competing concerns involved here. It recognizes the strength of the legitimate state interest in compensating private individuals for wrongful injury to reputation, yet shields the press and broadcast media from the rigors of strict liability for defamation. At least this conclusion obtains where, as here, the substance of the defamatory statement "makes substantial danger to reputation apparent." *Butts.* This phrase places in perspective the conclusion we announce today. Our inquiry would involve considerations somewhat different from those discussed above if a State purported to condition civil liability on a factual misstatement whose content did not warn a reasonably prudent editor or broadcaster of its defamatory potential. Cf. *Time, Inc. v. Hill* [Part D infra]. Such a case is not now before us, and we intimate no view as to its proper resolution.

IV. [T]he strong and legitimate state interest in compensating private individuals for injury to reputation [extends] no further than compensation for actual injury. For the reasons stated below, we hold that the States may not permit recovery of presumed or punitive damages, at least when liability is not based on a showing of knowledge of falsity or reckless disregard for the truth.

The common law of defamation is an oddity of tort [law]. Juries may award substantial sums as compensation for supposed damage to reputation without any proof that such harm actually occurred. [This] unnecessarily compounds the potential of any system of liability for defamatory falsehood to inhibit the vigorous exercise of First Amendment freedoms [and] invites juries to punish unpopular opinion rather than to compensate individuals for injury sustained by the publication of a false fact. More to the point, the States have no substantial interest in securing for plaintiffs such as this petitioner gratuitous awards of money damages far in excess of any actual injury.

We would not, of course, invalidate state law simply because we doubt its wisdom, but here we are attempting to reconcile state law with a competing interest grounded in the constitutional command of the First Amendment. It is therefore appropriate to require that state remedies for defamatory falsehood reach no farther than is necessary to protect the legitimate interest involved. It is necessary to restrict defamation plaintiffs who do not prove knowledge of falsity or reckless disregard for the truth to compensation for actual injury. We need not define "actual injury," as trial courts have wide experience in framing appropriate jury instructions in tort action. Suffice it to say that actual injury is not limited to out-of-pocket loss. Indeed, the more customary types of actual harm inflicted by defamatory falsehood include impairment of reputation and standing in the community, personal humiliation, and mental anguish and suffering. Of course, juries must be limited by appropriate instructions, and all awards must be supported by competent evidence concerning the injury, although there need be no evidence which assigns an actual dollar value to the injury.

We also find no justification for allowing awards of punitive damages against publishers and broadcasters held liable under state-defined standards of liability for defamation. In most jurisdictions jury discretion over the amounts awarded is limited only by the gentle rule that they not be excessive. Consequently, juries assess punitive damages in wholly unpredictable amounts bearing no necessary relation to the actual harm caused. And they remain free to use their discretion selectively to punish expressions of unpopular views. [J]ury discretion to award punitive damages unnecessarily exacerbates the danger of media self-censorship; [punitive] damages are wholly irrelevant to the state interest that justifies a negligence standard for private defamation actions. They are not compensation for injury. Instead, they are private fines levied by civil juries to punish reprehensible conduct and to deter its future occurrence. In short, the private defamation plaintiff who establishes liability under a less demanding standard than that stated by *Times* may recover only such damages as are sufficient to compensate him for actual injury.c

V. Notwithstanding our refusal to extend the *New York Times* privilege to defamation of private individuals, respondent contends that we should affirm the judgment below on the ground that petitioner is [a] public figure. [That] designation may rest on either of two alternative bases. In some instances an individual may achieve such pervasive fame or notoriety that he becomes a public figure for all purposes and in all contexts. More commonly, an individual voluntarily injects himself or is drawn into a particular public controversy and thereby becomes a public figure for a limited range of issues. In either case such persons assume special prominence in the resolution of public questions.

Petitioner has long been active in community and professional affairs. He has served as an officer of local civic groups and of various professional organizations, and he has published several books and articles on legal subjects. Although petitioner was consequently well known in some circles, he had achieved no general fame or notoriety in the community. None of the prospective jurors called at the trial had ever heard of petitioner prior to this litigation, and respondent offered no proof that this response was atypical of the local population. We would not lightly assume that a citizen's participation in community and professional affairs rendered him a public figure for all purposes. Absent clear evidence of general fame or notoriety in the community, and pervasive involvement in the affairs of society, an individual should not be deemed a public personality for all aspects of his life. It is preferable to reduce the public-figure question to a more meaningful context by looking to the nature and extent of an individual's participation in the particular controversy giving rise to the defamation.

In this context it is plain that petitioner was not a public figure. He played a minimal role at the coroner's inquest, and his participation related solely to his representation of a private client. He took no part in the criminal prosecution of Officer Nuccio. Moreover, he never discussed either the criminal or civil litigation with the press and was never quoted as having done so. He plainly did not thrust himself into the vortex of this public issue, nor did he engage the public's attention in an attempt to influence its outcome. We are persuaded that the trial court did not err in refusing to characterize petitioner as a public figure for the purpose of this litigation.

We therefore conclude that the *New York Times* standard is inapplicable to this case and that the trial court erred in entering judgment for respondent. Because the jury was allowed to impose liability without fault and was permitted to presume damages without proof of injury, a new trial is necessary.d

c. On remand, Gertz was awarded $100,000 in compensatory damages and $300,000 in punitive damages. In the prior trial, he had been awarded only $50,000 in damages.

d. Blackmun, J., concurred: "[Although I joined Brennan, J.'s plurality opinion in *Rosenbloom,* from which the Court's opinion in the present case departs, I join] the Court's opinion and its judgment for two reasons:

"1. By removing the spectres of presumed and punitive damages in the absence of *Times* malice, the Court eliminates significant and powerful motives for self-censorship that otherwise are present in the traditional libel ac-

JUSTICE BRENNAN, dissenting.

[While the Court's] arguments are forcefully and eloquently presented, I cannot accept them for the reasons I stated in *Rosenbloom:* "The *New York Times* standard was applied to libel of a public official or public figure to give effect to the Amendment's function to encourage ventilation of public issues, not because the public official has any less interest in protecting his reputation than an individual in private life. [In] the vast majority of libels involving public officials or public figures, the ability to respond through the media will depend on the same complex factor on which the ability of a private individual depends: the unpredictable event of the media's continuing interest in the story. Thus the unproved, and highly improbable, generalization that an as yet [not fully defined] class of 'public figures' involved in matters of public concern will be better able to respond through the media than private individuals also involved in such matters seems too insubstantial a reed on which to rest a constitutional distinction."

[Adoption], by many States, of a reasonable care standard in cases where private individuals are involved in matters of public interest—the probable result of today's decision—[will] lead to self-censorship since publishers will be required carefully to weigh a myriad of uncertain factors before publication. The reasonable care standard is "elusive," *Time, Inc. v. Hill;* it saddles the press with "the intolerable burden of guessing how a jury might assess the reasonableness of steps taken by it to verify the accuracy of every reference to a name, picture or portrait." Ibid. Under a reasonable care regime, publishers and broadcasters will have to make pre-publication judgments about juror assessment of such diverse considerations as the size, operating procedures, and financial condition of the news gathering system, as well as the relative costs and benefits of instituting less frequent and more costly reporting at a higher level of accuracy. [And] most hazardous, the flexibility which inheres in the reasonable care standard will create the danger that a jury will convert it into "an instrument for the suppression of those 'vehement, caustic, and sometimes unpleasantly sharp attacks,' [which] must be protected if the guarantees of the First and Fourteenth Amendments are to prevail." *Monitor Patriot Co.*

[A] jury's latitude to impose liability for want of due care poses a far greater threat of suppressing unpopular views than does a possible recovery of presumed or punitive damages. Moreover, the Court's broad-ranging examples of "actual injury" [allow] a jury bent on punishing expression of unpopular views a formidable weapon for doing so. [E]ven a limitation of recovery to "actual injury"— however much it reduces the size or frequency of recoveries—will not provide the necessary elbow room for First Amendment expression. "[The] very possibility of having to engage in litigation, an expensive and protracted process, is threat enough to cause discussion and debate to 'steer far wider of the unlawful zone' thereby keeping protected discussion from public cognance. * * * " *Rosenbloom.*

[I] reject the argument that my *Rosenbloom* view improperly commits to judges the task of determining what is and what is not an issue of "general or public interest."3 I noted in *Rosenbloom* that performance of this task would not

tion. By so doing, the Court leaves what should prove to be sufficient and adequate breathing space for a vigorous press. What the Court has done, I believe, will have little, if any, practical effect on the functioning of responsible journalism.

"2. The Court was sadly fractionated in *Rosenbloom*. A result of that kind inevitably leads to uncertainty. I feel that it is of profound importance for the Court to come to rest in the defamation area and to have a clearly defined majority position that eliminates the unsureness engendered by *Rosenbloom's* diversity. If my vote were not needed to create a majority, I would adhere to my prior view. A definitive ruling, however, is paramount."

3. The Court, taking a novel step, would not limit application of First Amendment pro-

always be easy. But surely the courts, the ultimate arbiters of all disputes concerning clashes of constitutional values, would only be performing one of their traditional functions in undertaking this duty. [The] public interest is necessarily broad; any residual self-censorship that may result from the uncertain contours of the "general or public interest" concept should be of far less concern to publishers and broadcasters than that occasioned by state laws imposing liability for negligent falsehood. * * *e

JUSTICE WHITE, dissenting.

[T]he Court, in a few printed pages, has federalized major aspects of libel law by declaring unconstitutional in important respects the prevailing defamation law in all or most of the 50 States. * * *

I. [These] radical changes in the law and severe invasions of the prerogatives of the States [should] at least be shown to be required by the First Amendment or necessitated by our present circumstances. Neither has been [demonstrated.]

The central meaning of *New York Times,* and for me the First Amendment as it relates to libel laws, is that seditious libel—criticism of government and public officials—falls beyond the police power of the State. In a democratic society such as ours, the citizen has the privilege of criticizing his government and its officials. But neither *New York Times* nor its progeny suggest that the First Amendment intended in all circumstances to deprive the private citizen of his historic recourse to redress published falsehoods damaging to reputation or that, contrary to history and precedent, the amendment should now be so interpreted. Simply put, the First Amendment did not confer a "license to defame the citizen." Douglas, *The Right of the People* 38 (1958).

[T]he law has heretofore put the risk of falsehood on the publisher where the victim is a private citizen and no grounds of special privilege are invoked. The Court would now shift this risk to the victim, even though he has done nothing to invite the calumny, is wholly innocent of fault, and is helpless to avoid his injury. I doubt that jurisprudential resistance to liability without fault is sufficient ground for employing the First Amendment to revolutionize the law of libel, and in my view, that body of legal rules poses no realistic threat to the press and its service

tection to private libels involving issues of general or public interest, but would forbid the States from imposing liability without fault in any case where the substance of the defamatory statement made substantial danger to reputation apparent. As in *Rosenbloom,* I would leave open the question of what constitutional standard, if any, applies when defamatory falsehoods are published or broadcast concerning either a private or public person's activities not within the scope of the general or public interest.

Parenthetically, my Brother White argues that the Court's view and mine will prevent a plaintiff—unable to demonstrate some degree of fault—from vindicating his reputation by securing a judgment that the publication was false. This argument overlooks the possible enactment of statutes, not requiring proof of fault, which provide for an action for retraction or for publication of a court's determination of falsity if the plaintiff is able to demonstrate that false statements have been published concerning his activities. Although it may be that questions could be raised concerning the constitutionality of such statutes, certainly noth-

ing I have said today (and, as I read the Court's opinion, nothing said there) should be read to imply that a private plaintiff, unable to prove fault, must inevitably be denied the opportunity to secure a judgment upon the truth or falsity of statements published about him.

e. Douglas, J., dissented, objecting to "continued recognition of the possibility of state libel suits for public discussion of public issues" as diluting First Amendment protection. He added: "Since this case involves a discussion of public affairs, I need not decide at this point whether the First Amendment prohibits all libel actions. 'An unconditional right to say what one pleases about public affairs is what I consider to be *the minimum guarantee* of the First Amendment.' *New York Times* (Black, J., concurring) (emphasis added). But 'public affairs' includes a great deal more than merely political affairs. Matters of science, economics, business, art, literature, etc., are all matters of interest to the general public. Indeed, any matter of sufficient general interest to prompt media coverage may be said to be a public affair. Certainly police killings, 'Communist conspiracies,' and the like qualify."

to the public. The press today is vigorous and robust. To me, it is quite incredible to suggest that threats of libel suits from private citizens are causing the press to refrain from publishing the truth. I know of no hard facts to support that proposition, and the Court furnishes none.

[I]f the Court's principal concern is to protect the communications industry from large libel judgments, it would appear that its new requirements with respect to general and punitive damages would be ample protection. Why it also feels compelled to escalate the threshold standard of liability I cannot fathom, particularly when this will eliminate in many instances the plaintiff's possibility of securing a judicial determination that the damaging publication was indeed false, whether or not he is entitled to recover money damages. [I] find it unacceptable to distribute the risk in this manner and force the wholly innocent victim to bear the injury; for, as between the two, the defamer is the only culpable party. It is he who circulated a falsehood that he was not required to publish. * * *f

V. [I] fail to see how the quality or quantity of public debate will be promoted by further emasculation of state libel laws for the benefit of the news media.41 If anything, this trend may provoke a new and radical imbalance in the communications process. Cf. Jerome Barron, *Access to the Press—A New First Amendment Right,* 80 Harv.L.Rev. 1641, 1657 (1967). It is not at all inconceivable that virtually unrestrained defamatory remarks about private citizens will discourage them from speaking out and concerning themselves with social problems. This would turn the First Amendment on its head. * * *g

---

Public figures. TIME, INC. v. FIRESTONE, 424 U.S. 448 (1976), per REHNQUIST, J., declared that persons who have not assumed a role of especial prominence in the affairs of society are not public figures unless they have " 'thrust themselves to the forefront of particular public controversies in order to influence the resolution of the issues involved.' " It held that a divorce proceeding involving one of America's wealthiest industrial families and containing testimony concerning the extramarital sexual activities of the parties did not involve a "public controversy," "even though the marital difficulties of extremely wealthy individuals may be of interest to some portion of the reading public." Nor was the filing of a divorce suit, or the holding of press conferences ("to satisfy inquiring reporters") thought to be freely publicizing the issues in order to influence their outcome.

f. White, J., also argued strongly against the Court's rulings on presumed and punitive damages.

41. Cf. Willard Pedrick, *Freedom of the Press and the Law of Libel: The Modern Revised Translation,* 49 Cornell L.Q. 581, 601–02 (1964): "A great many forces in our society operate to determine the extent to which men are free in fact to express their ideas. Whether there is a privilege for good faith defamatory misstatements on matters of public concern or whether there is strict liability for such statements may not greatly affect the course of public discussion. How different has life been in those states which heretofore followed the majority rule imposing strict liability for mis-

statements of fact defaming public figures from life in the minority states where the good faith privilege held sway?"

g. Burger, C.J., also dissented: "I am frank to say I do not know the parameters of a 'negligence' doctrine as applied to the news media. [I] would prefer to allow this area of law to continue to evolve as it has up to now with respect to private citizens rather then embark on a new doctrinal theory which has no jurisprudential ancestry. [I would remand] for reinstatement of the verdict of the jury and the entry of an appropriate judgment on that verdict."

D. EMOTIONAL DISTRESS

HUSTLER MAGAZINE v. FALWELL, 485 U.S. 46 (1988), per REHNQUIST, C.J., held that public figures and public officials offended by a mass media parody could not recover for the tort of intentional infliction of emotional distress without a showing of *New York Times* malice. Parodying a series of liquor advertisements in which celebrities speak about their "first time," the editors of *Hustler* chose plaintiff Jerry Falwell (a nationally famous minister, host of a nationally syndicated television show, and founder of the Moral Majority political organization) "as the featured celebrity and drafted an alleged 'interview' with him in which he states that his 'first time' was during a drunken incestuous rendezvous with his mother in an outhouse. The *Hustler* parody portrays [Falwell] and his mothera 'as drunk and immoral,' and suggests that [Falwell] is a hypocrite who preaches only when he is drunk. In small print at the bottom of the page, the ad contains the disclaimer, 'ad parody—not to be taken seriously.' The magazine's table of contents also lists the ad as 'Fiction; Ad and Personality Parody.' * * *

"We must decide whether a public figure may recover damages for emotional harm caused by the publication of an ad parody offensive to him, and doubtless gross and repugnant in the eyes of most.3 [Falwell] would have us find that a State's interest in protecting public figures from emotional distress is sufficient to deny First Amendment protection to speech that is patently offensive and is intended to inflict emotional injury, even when that speech could not reasonably have been interpreted as stating actual facts about the public figure involved. * * *

"Generally speaking the law does not regard the intent to inflict emotional distress as one which should receive much solicitude, and it is quite understandable that most if not all jurisdictions have chosen to make it civilly culpable where the conduct in question is sufficiently 'outrageous.' But in the world of debate about public affairs, many things done with motives that are less than admirable are protected by the First Amendment. '[Debate] on public issues will not be uninhibited if the speaker must run the risk that it will be proved in court that he spoke out of hatred; even if he did speak out of hatred, utterances honestly believed contribute to the free interchange of ideas and the ascertainment of truth.' *Garrison*. Thus while such a bad motive may be deemed controlling for purposes of tort liability in other areas of the law, we think the First Amendment prohibits such a result in the area of public debate about public figures.

"Were we to hold otherwise, there can be little doubt that political cartoonists and satirists would be subjected to damage awards without any showing that their work falsely defamed its subject. * * *

"There is no doubt that the caricature of [Falwell] and his mother published in Hustler is at best a distant cousin of [traditional] political cartoons [and] a rather poor relation at that. If it were possible by laying down a principled standard to separate the one from the other, public discourse would probably suffer little or no harm. But we doubt that there is any such standard, and we are quite sure that the pejorative description 'outrageous' does not supply one. 'Outrageousness' in the area of political and social discourse has an inherent subjectiveness about it which would allow a jury to impose liability on the basis of the jurors' tastes or views, or perhaps on the basis of their dislike of a particular expression.

a. Falwell's mother was not a plaintiff.

3. Under Virginia law, in an action for intentional infliction of emotional distress a plaintiff must show that the defendant's conduct (1) is intentional or reckless; (2) offends generally accepted standards of decency or morality; (3) is causally connected with the plaintiff's emotional distress; and (4) caused emotional distress that was severe.

"We conclude that public figures and public officials may not recover for the tort of intentional infliction of emotional distress by reason of publications such as the one here at issue without showing in addition that the publication contains a false statement of fact which was made with 'actual malice,' i.e., with knowledge that the statement was false or with reckless disregard as to whether or not it was true."b

———

Time Inc. v. Hill, 385 U.S. 374 (1967) applied the *New York Times* knowing and reckless falsity standard to a right of privacy action for publishing an erroneous but not defamatory report about private individuals involved in an incident of public interest. The Court maintained that "[N]egligence would be a most elusive standard, especially when the content of the speech itself affords no warning of prospective harm to another through falsity. A negligence test would place on the press the intolerable burden of guessing how a jury might assess the reasonableness of steps taken by it to verify the accuracy of every reference to a name, picture or [portrait]."

Compare *Hill* with ZACCHINI v. SCRIPPS–HOWARD BROADCASTING CO., 433 U.S. 562 (1977): Zacchini performed as a "human cannonball," being shot from a cannon into a net some 200 feet away. Without Zacchini's permission to film or broadcast his act, Scripps–Howard obtained and broadcast the tape of his "shot" on the news. The Ohio Supreme Court held the telecast was protected under *Time, Inc. v. Hill* as a newsworthy event. The Court, per WHITE, J., reversed. *Hill* was distinguishable because Zacchini's claim was based not on privacy or reputation but "in protecting the proprietary interest," an interest "closely analogous to the goals of patent and copyright law." Unlike *Hill,* the issue was not whether Zacchini's act would be available to the public: "[T]he only question is who gets to do the publishing."c

E.   DISCLOSURE OF PRIVATE FACTS

FLORIDA STAR v. B.J.F.

491 U.S. 524, 109 S.Ct. 2603, 105 L.Ed.2d 443 (1989).

JUSTICE MARSHALL delivered the opinion of the Court.

Florida Stat. § 794.03 (1987) makes it unlawful to "print, publish, or broadcast [in] any instrument of mass communication" the name of the victim of a sexual offense. Pursuant to this statute, appellant The Florida Star was found civilly liable for publishing the name of a rape victim which it had obtained from a publicly released police report. [B.J.F.] testified that she had suffered emotional distress from the publication of her name. She stated that she had heard about the article from fellow workers and acquaintances; that her mother had received several threatening phone calls from a man who stated that he would rape B.J.F. again; and that these events had forced B.J.F. to change her phone number and residence, to seek police protection, and to obtain mental health counseling. [The

b. White, J., concurred, but stated that *New York Times* was irrelevant because of the jury's finding that the parody contained no assertion of fact. Kennedy, J., took no part.

c. Powell, J., joined by Brennan and Marshall, JJ., dissented, observing that there was

no showing that the broadcast was a "subterfuge or cover for private or commercial exploitation." Stevens, J., dissented on procedural grounds.

jury] awarded B.J.F. $75,000 in compensatory damages and $25,000 in punitive damages. * * *

[We do not] accept appellant's invitation to hold broadly that truthful publication may never be punished consistent with the First Amendment. Our cases have carefully eschewed reaching this ultimate question, mindful that the future may bring scenarios which prudence counsels our not resolving anticipatorily. See, e.g., *Near v. Minnesota,* [Section 4, I, B] (hypothesizing "publication of the sailing dates of transports or the number and location of troops"); see also *Garrison v. Louisiana* (endorsing absolute defense of truth "where discussion of public affairs is concerned," but leaving unsettled the constitutional implications of truthfulness "in the discrete area of purely private libels"). Indeed, in [*Cox Broadcasting v. Cohn,* 420 U.S. 469 (1975)], we pointedly refused to answer even the less sweeping question "whether truthful publications may ever be subjected to civil or criminal liability" for invading "an area of privacy" defined by the State. [We] continue to believe that the sensitivity and significance of the interests presented in clashes between First Amendment and privacy rights counsel relying on limited principles that sweep no more broadly than the appropriate context of the instant case.

In our view, this case is appropriately analyzed with reference to such a limited First Amendment principle. It is the one, in fact, which we articulated in *Smith v. Daily Mail Pub. Co.,* [Section 5, I] in our synthesis of prior cases involving attempts to punish truthful publication: "[I]f a newspaper lawfully obtains truthful information about a matter of public significance then state officials may not constitutionally punish publication of the information, absent a need to further a state interest of the highest order." * * *

Applied to the instant case, the *Daily Mail* principle clearly commands reversal. The first inquiry is whether the newspaper "lawfully obtain[ed] truthful information about a matter of public significance." It is undisputed that the news article describing the assault on B.J.F. was accurate. In addition, appellant lawfully obtained B.J.F.'s name. Appellee's argument to the contrary is based on the fact that under Florida law, police reports which reveal the identity of the victim of a sexual offense are not among the matters of "public record" which the public, by law, is entitled to inspect. But the fact that state officials are not required to disclose such reports does not make it unlawful for a newspaper to receive them when furnished by the government. Nor does the fact that the Department apparently failed to fulfill its obligation under § 794.03 not to "cause or allow to [be] published" the name of a sexual offense victim make the newspaper's ensuing receipt of this information unlawful. Even assuming the Constitution permitted a State to proscribe *receipt* of information, Florida has not taken this step. It is, clear, furthermore, that the news article concerned "a matter of public significance[.]" That is, the article generally, as opposed to the specific identity contained within it, involved a matter of paramount public import: the commission, and investigation, of a violent crime which had been reported to authorities.

The second inquiry is whether imposing liability on appellant pursuant to § 794.03 serves "a need to further a state interest of the highest order." Appellee argues that a rule punishing publication furthers three closely related interests: the privacy of victims of sexual offenses; the physical safety of such victims, who may be targeted for retaliation if their names become known to their assailants; and the goal of encouraging victims of such crimes to report these offenses without fear of exposure.

At a time in which we are daily reminded of the tragic reality of rape, it is undeniable that these are highly significant interests. [We] accordingly do not rule out the possibility that, in a proper case, imposing civil sanctions for publication of the name of a rape victim might be so overwhelmingly necessary to advance these interests as to satisfy the *Daily Mail* standard. For three independent reasons, however, imposing liability for publication under the circumstances of this case is too precipitous a means of advancing these interests to convince us that there is a "need" within the meaning of the *Daily Mail* formulation for Florida to take this extreme step.

First is the manner in which appellant obtained the identifying information in question. [B.J.F.'s] identity would never have come to light were it not for the erroneous, if inadvertent, inclusion by the Department of her full name in an incident report made available in a press room open to the public. [Where] as here, the government has failed to police itself in disseminating information, it is clear [that] the imposition of damages against the press for its subsequent publication can hardly be said to be a narrowly tailored means of safeguarding anonymity.

That appellant gained access to the information in question through a government news release makes it especially likely that, if liability were to be imposed, self-censorship would result. Reliance on a news release is a paradigmatically "routine newspaper reporting techniqu[e]." The government's issuance of such a release, without qualification, can only convey to recipients that the government considered dissemination lawful, and indeed expected the recipients to disseminate the information further. Had appellant merely reproduced the news release prepared and released by the Department, imposing civil damages would surely violate the First Amendment. The fact that appellant converted the police report into a news story by adding the linguistic connecting tissue necessary to transform the report's facts into full sentences cannot change this result.

A second problem with Florida's imposition of liability for publication is the broad sweep of the negligence per se standard applied under the civil cause of action implied from § 794.03. Unlike claims based on the common law tort of invasion of privacy, civil actions based on § 794.03 require no case-by-case findings that the disclosure of a fact about a person's private life was one that a reasonable person would find highly offensive. On the contrary, under the per se theory of negligence adopted by the courts below, liability follows automatically from publication. This is so regardless of whether the identity of the victim is already known throughout the community; whether the victim has voluntarily called public attention to the offense; or whether the identity of the victim has otherwise become a reasonable subject of public concern—because, perhaps, questions have arisen whether the victim fabricated an assault by a particular person. Nor is there a scienter requirement of any kind under § 794.03, engendering the perverse result that truthful publications challenged pursuant to this cause of action are less protected by the First Amendment than even the least protected defamatory falsehoods: those involving purely private figures, where liability is evaluated under a standard, usually applied by a jury, of ordinary negligence. See *Gertz.* * * *

Third, and finally, the facial underinclusiveness of § 794.03 raises serious doubts about whether Florida is, in fact, serving, with this statute, the significant interests which appellee invokes in support of affirmance. Section 794.03 prohibits the publication of identifying information only if this information appears in an "instrument of mass communication," a term the statute does not define. Section 794.03 does not prohibit the spread by other means of the identities of victims of sexual offenses. An individual who maliciously spreads word of the identity of a rape victim is thus not covered, despite the fact that the communication of such information to persons who live near, or work with, the victim may have consequences equally devastating as the exposure of her name to large numbers of strangers.

When a State attempts the extraordinary measure of punishing truthful publication in the name of privacy, it must demonstrate its commitment to advancing this interest by applying its prohibition evenhandedly, to the small-time disseminator as well as the media giant. Where important First Amendment interests are at stake, the mass scope of disclosure is not an acceptable surrogate for injury. Without more careful and inclusive precautions against alternative forms of dissemination, we cannot conclude that Florida's selective ban on publication by the mass media satisfactorily accomplishes its stated purpose.

Our holding today is limited. We do not hold that truthful publication is automatically constitutionally protected, or that there is no zone of personal privacy within which the State may protect the individual from intrusion by the press, or even that a State may never punish publication of the name of a victim of a sexual offense. We hold only that where a newspaper publishes truthful information which it has lawfully obtained, punishment may lawfully be imposed, if at all, only when narrowly tailored to a state interest of the highest order, and that no such interest is satisfactorily served by imposing liability under § 794.03 to appellant under the facts of this case. * * *

JUSTICE SCALIA, concurring in part and concurring in the judgment.

I think it sufficient to decide this case to rely upon the third ground set forth in the Court's opinion: that a law cannot be regarded as protecting an interest "of the highest order" and thus as justifying a restriction upon truthful speech, when it leaves appreciable damage to that supposedly vital interest unprohibited. In the present case, I would anticipate that the rape victim's discomfort at the dissemination of news of her misfortune among friends and acquaintances would be at least as great as her discomfort at its publication by the media to people to whom she is only a name. Yet the law in question does not prohibit the former in either oral or written form. Nor is it at all clear, as I think it must be to validate this statute, that Florida's general privacy law would prohibit such gossip. Nor, finally, is it credible that the interest meant to be served by the statute is the protection of the victim against a rapist still at large—an interest that arguably would extend only to mass publication. There would be little reason to limit a statute with that objective to rape alone; or to extend it to all rapes, whether or not the felon has been apprehended and confined. In any case, the instructions here did not require the jury to find that the rapist was at large.

This law has every appearance of a prohibition that society is prepared to impose upon the press but not upon itself. Such a prohibition does not protect an interest "of the highest order." For that reason, I agree that the judgment of the court below must be reversed.

JUSTICE WHITE, with whom THE CHIEF JUSTICE and JUSTICE O'CONNOR join, dissenting.

"Short of homicide, [rape] is the 'ultimate violation of self.'" *Coker v. Georgia,* [433 U.S. 584 (1977)] (opinion of White, J.). For B.J.F., however, the violation she suffered at a rapist's knife-point marked only the beginning of her ordeal. [Yet] today, the Court holds that a jury award of $75,000 to compensate B.J.F. for the harm she suffered due to the Star's negligence is at odds with the First Amendment. I do not accept this result.

[T]he three "independent reasons" the Court cites for reversing the judgment for B.J.F. [do not] support its result.

The first of these reasons [is] the fact "appellant gained access to [B.J.F.'s name] through a government news release." [But the] "release" of information provided by the government was not, as the Court says, "without qualification." As the Star's own reporter conceded at trial, the crime incident report that inadvertently included B.J.F.'s name was posted in a room that contained signs making it clear that the names of rape victims were not matters of public record, and were not to be published. The Star's reporter indicated that she understood that she "[was not] allowed to take down that information" (i.e., B.J.F.'s name) and that she "[was] not supposed to take the information from the police department." Thus, by her own admission the posting of the incident report did not convey to the Star's reporter the idea that "the government considered dissemination lawful"; the Court's suggestion to the contrary is inapt. * * *

Unfortunately, as this case illustrates, mistakes happen: even when States take measures to "avoid" disclosure, sometimes rape victim's names are found out. As I see it, it is not too much to ask the press, in instances such as this, to respect simple standards of decency and refrain from publishing a victim's name, address, and/or phone number.

Second, the Court complains [that] a newspaper might be found liable under the Florida courts' negligence per se theory without regard to a newspaper's scienter or degree of fault. The short answer to this complaint is that whatever merit the Court's argument might have, it is wholly inapposite here, where the jury found that appellant acted with "reckless indifference towards the rights of others," a standard far higher than the *Gertz* standard the Court urges as a constitutional minimum today.

But even taking the Court's concerns in the abstract, they miss the mark. [The] Court says that negligence per se permits a plaintiff to hold a defendant liable without a showing that the disclosure was "of a fact about a person's private life [that] a reasonable person would find highly offensive." But the point here is that the legislature—reflecting popular sentiment—has determined that disclosure of the fact that a person was raped is categorically a revelation that reasonable people find offensive. And as for the Court's suggestion that the Florida courts' theory permits liability without regard for whether the victim's identity is already known, or whether she herself has made it known—these are facts that would surely enter into the calculation of damages in such a case. In any event, none of these mitigating factors was present [here].

Third, the Court faults the Florida criminal statute for being underinclusive. [But] our cases which have struck down laws that limit or burden the press due to their underinclusiveness have involved situations where a legislature has singled out one segment of the news media or press for adverse treatment. Here, the Florida law evenhandedly covers all "instrument[s] of mass communication" no matter their form, media, content, nature or purpose. It excludes neighborhood gossips because presumably the Florida Legislature has determined that neighborhood gossips do not pose the danger and intrusion to rape victims that "instrument[s] of mass communication" do. Simply put: Florida wanted to prevent the widespread distribution of rape victim's names, and therefore enacted a statute tailored almost as precisely as possible to achieving that end. * * *

At issue in this case is whether there is any information about people, which—though true—may not be published in the press. [The] Court accepts appellant's invitation to obliterate one of the most note-worthy legal inventions of the 20th–Century: the tort of the publication of private facts. William Prosser,

John Wade, & Victor Schwartz, *Torts* 951–952 (8th ed. 1988). Even if the Court's opinion does not say as much today, such obliteration will follow inevitably from the Court's conclusion here. [The] Court's ruling has been foreshadowed. In *Time, Inc. v. Hill,* we observed that—after a brief period early in this century where Brandeis' view was ascendant—the trend in "modern" jurisprudence has been to eclipse an individual's right to maintain private any truthful information that the press wished to publish. More recently, in *Cox Broadcasting,* we acknowledged the possibility that the First Amendment may prevent a State from ever subjecting the publication of truthful but private information to civil liability. Today, we hit the bottom of the slippery slope.

I would find a place to draw the line higher on the hillside: a spot high enough to protect B.J.F.'s desire for privacy and peace-of-mind in the wake of a horrible personal tragedy. There is no public interest in publishing the names, addresses, and phone numbers of persons who are the victims of crime—and no public interest in immunizing the press from liability in the rare cases where a State's efforts to protect a victim's privacy have failed. Consequently, I respectfully dissent.5

———

During the course of a cell phone conversation, the president of a local teacher's union, Kane, told his chief labor negotiator, Bartnicki: "If they're not gonna move for three percent, we're gonna have to go to their, their homes * * * To blow off their front porches, we'll have to do some work on some of those guys. (PAUSES). Really, uh, really and truthfully because this is, you know, this is bad news." The conversation was illegally intercepted by an unknown person and was sent to the head of a local taxpayer's organization, Yocum, who in turn, shared it with school board members and a local broadcaster, Vopper. Vopper played the tape on his radio show. Bartnicki and Kane brought an action against Yocum and Vopper invoking state and federal laws prohibiting the disclosure of material known to be unlawfully intercepted.

BARTNICKI v. VOPPER, 532 U.S. 514 (2001), per STEVENS, J., held the statutes unconstitutional as applied to circumstances in which the defendants played no role in the illegal acquisition of the material, their access to the conversation was obtained lawfully, and the conversation was about a public issue: "We agree with petitioners that 18 U.S.C. § 2511(1)(c), as well as its Pennsylvania analog, is in fact a content-neutral law of general applicability. [In] this case, the basic purpose of the statute at issue is to 'protec[t] the privacy of wire[, electronic,] and oral communications.' S.Rep. No. 1097, 90th Cong., 2d Sess., 66 (1968). The statute does not distinguish based on the content of the intercepted conversations, nor is it justified by reference to the content of those conversations. Rather, the communications at issue are singled out by virtue of the fact that they were illegally intercepted—by virtue of the source, rather than the subject matter.

"On the other hand, the naked prohibition against disclosures is fairly characterized as a regulation of pure speech. Unlike the prohibition against the 'use' of the contents of an illegal interception in § 2511(1)(d), subsection (c) is not a regulation of conduct. It is true that the delivery of a tape recording might be regarded as conduct, but given that the purpose of such a delivery is to provide

---

5. The Court does not address the distinct constitutional questions raised by the award of punitive damages in this case. Consequently, I do not do so either. That award is more troublesome than the compensatory award discussed above. Cf. Note, *Punitive Damages and Libel Law,* 98 Harv.L.Rev. 847 (1985).

the recipient with the text of recorded statements, it is like the delivery of a handbill or a pamphlet, and as such, it is the kind of 'speech' that the First Amendment protects.

"[As] a general matter, 'state action to punish the publication of truthful information seldom can satisfy constitutional standards.' *Daily Mail.* [The] Government identifies two interests served by the statute—first, the interest in removing an incentive for parties to intercept private conversations, and second, the interest in minimizing the harm to persons whose conversations have been illegally intercepted. We assume that those interests adequately justify the prohibition in § 2511(1)(d) against the interceptor's own use of information that he or she acquired by violating § 2511(1)(a), but it by no means follows that punishing disclosures of lawfully obtained information of public interest by one not involved in the initial illegality is an acceptable means of serving those ends.

"The normal method of deterring unlawful conduct is to impose an appropriate punishment on the person who engages in it. If the sanctions that presently attach to a violation of § 2511(1)(a) do not provide sufficient deterrence, perhaps those sanctions should be made more severe. But it would be quite remarkable to hold that speech by a law-abiding possessor of information can be suppressed in order to deter conduct by a non-law-abiding third party.[a]

"[With] only a handful of exceptions, the violations of § 2511(1)(a) that have been described in litigated cases have been motivated by either financial gain or domestic disputes. In virtually all of those cases, the identity of the person or persons intercepting the communication has been known. Moreover, petitioners cite no evidence that Congress viewed the prohibition against disclosures as a response to the difficulty of identifying persons making improper use of scanners and other surveillance devices and accordingly of deterring such conduct, and there is no empirical evidence to support the assumption that the prohibition against disclosures reduces the number of illegal interceptions.

"Although this case demonstrates that there may be an occasional situation in which an anonymous scanner will risk criminal prosecution by passing on information without any expectation of financial reward or public praise, surely this is the exceptional case. Moreover, there is no basis for assuming that imposing sanctions upon respondents will deter the unidentified scanner from continuing to engage in surreptitious interceptions. Unusual cases fall far short of a showing that there is a 'need of the highest order' for a rule supplementing the traditional means of deterring antisocial conduct. The justification for any such novel burden on expression must be 'far stronger than mere speculation about serious harms.' Accordingly, the Government's first suggested justification for applying § 2511(1)(c) to an otherwise innocent disclosure of public information is plainly insufficient.[19]

"The Government's second argument, however, is considerably stronger. Privacy of communication is an important interest, [and] the fear of public disclosure of private conversations might well have a chilling effect on private

---

a. The Court recognized some exceptional cases, but stated the speech implicated was of minimal value, *New York v. Ferber,* Sec. 1, VI, A, infra (child pornography), or did not involve a prohibition of speech (possession or receipt of stolen mail or other property).

19. Our holding, of course, does not apply to punishing parties for obtaining the relevant information unlawfully. "It would be frivolous to assert—and no one does in these cases—that

the First Amendment, in the interest of securing news or otherwise, confers a license on either the reporter or his news sources to violate valid criminal laws. Although stealing documents or private wiretapping could provide newsworthy information, neither reporter nor source is immune from conviction for such conduct, whatever the impact on the flow of news." *Branzburg.*

speech. [Accordingly], it seems to us that there are important interests to be considered on both sides of the constitutional calculus. In considering that balance, we acknowledge that some intrusions on privacy are more offensive than others, and that the disclosure of the contents of a private conversation can be an even greater intrusion on privacy than the interception itself. As a result, there is a valid independent justification for prohibiting such disclosures by persons who lawfully obtained access to the contents of an illegally intercepted message, even if that prohibition does not play a significant role in preventing such interceptions from occurring in the first place.

"We need not decide whether that interest is strong enough to justify the application of § 2511(c) to disclosures of trade secrets or domestic gossip or other information of purely private concern. In other words, the outcome of the case does not turn on whether § 2511(1)(c) may be enforced with respect to most violations of the statute without offending the First Amendment. The enforcement of that provision in this case, however, implicates the core purposes of the First Amendment because it imposes sanctions on the publication of truthful information of public concern.

"In this case, privacy concerns give way when balanced against the interest in publishing matters of public importance. [The] months of negotiations over the proper level of compensation for teachers at the Wyoming Valley West High School were unquestionably a matter of public concern, and respondents were clearly engaged in debate about that concern. That debate may be more mundane than the Communist rhetoric that inspired Justice Brandeis' classic opinion in *Whitney v. California*, but it is no less worthy of constitutional protection."

BREYER, J., joined by O'Connor, J., concurred: "I write separately to explain why, in my view, the Court's holding does not imply a significantly broader constitutional immunity for the media.

"[As] a general matter, despite the statutes' direct restrictions on speech, the Federal Constitution must tolerate laws of this kind because of the importance of these privacy and speech-related objectives. [Nonetheless], looked at more specifically, the statutes, as applied in these circumstances, do not reasonably reconcile the competing constitutional objectives. Rather, they disproportionately interfere with media freedom. For one thing, the broadcasters here engaged in no unlawful activity other than the ultimate publication of the information another had previously obtained. [For] another thing, the speakers had little or no legitimate interest in maintaining the privacy of the particular conversation. That conversation involved a suggestion about 'blow[ing] off ... front porches' and 'do[ing] some work on some of these guys,' thereby raising a significant concern for the safety of others. Where publication of private information constitutes a wrongful act, the law recognizes a privilege allowing the reporting of threats to public safety. [Even] where the danger may have passed by the time of publication, that fact cannot legitimize the speaker's earlier privacy expectation. Nor should editors, who must make a publication decision quickly, have to determine present or continued danger before publishing this kind of threat.

"Further, the speakers themselves, the president of a teacher's union and the union's chief negotiator, were 'limited public figures,' for they voluntarily engaged in a public controversy. They thereby subjected themselves to somewhat greater public scrutiny and had a lesser interest in privacy than an individual engaged in purely private affairs. [This] is not to say that the Constitution requires anyone, including public figures, to give up entirely the right to private communication, i.e., communication free from telephone taps or interceptions. But the subject matter of the conversation at issue here is far removed from that in situations where the media publicizes truly private matters.

"Thus, in finding a constitutional privilege to publish unlawfully intercepted conversations of the kind here at issue, the Court does not create a 'public interest' exception that swallows up the statutes' privacy-protecting general rule. Rather, it finds constitutional protection for publication of intercepted information of a special kind. Here, the speakers' legitimate privacy expectations are unusually low, and the public interest in defeating those expectations is unusually high."

REHNQUIST, C.J., joined by Scalia and Thomas, JJ., dissented: "Technology now permits millions of important and confidential conversations to occur through a vast system of electronic networks. These advances, however, raise significant privacy concerns. We are placed in the uncomfortable position of not knowing who might have access to our personal and business e-mails, our medical and financial records, or our cordless and cellular telephone conversations. In an attempt to prevent some of the most egregious violations of privacy, the United States, the District of Columbia, and 40 States have enacted laws prohibiting the intentional interception and knowing disclosure of electronic communications. The Court holds that all of these statutes violate the First Amendment insofar as the illegally intercepted conversation touches upon a matter of 'public concern,' an amorphous concept that the Court does not even attempt to define. But the Court's decision diminishes, rather than enhances, the purposes of the First Amendment: chilling the speech of the millions of Americans who rely upon electronic technology to communicate each day. * * *

"The Court correctly observes that these are 'content-neutral law[s] of general applicability' which serve recognized interests of the 'highest order': 'the interest in individual privacy [and] in fostering private speech.' It nonetheless subjects these laws to the strict scrutiny normally reserved for governmental attempts to censor different viewpoints or ideas. There is scant support, either in precedent or in reason, for the Court's tacit application of strict scrutiny.

"[Here], Congress and the Pennsylvania Legislature have acted 'without reference to the content of the regulated speech.' There is no intimation that these laws seek 'to suppress unpopular ideas or information or manipulate the public debate' or that they 'distinguish favored speech from disfavored speech on the basis of the ideas or views expressed.' [As] the concerns motivating strict scrutiny are absent, these content-neutral restrictions upon speech need pass only intermediate scrutiny.

"[I]t is obvious that the *Daily Mail* cases upon which the Court relies do not address the question presented here. Our decisions themselves made this clear: 'The *Daily Mail* principle does not settle the issue whether, in cases where information has been acquired unlawfully by a newspaper or by a source, the government may ever punish not only the unlawful acquisition, but the ensuing publication as well.' *Florida Star*. [Undaunted], the Court places an inordinate amount of weight upon the fact that the receipt of an illegally intercepted communication has not been criminalized. But this hardly renders those who knowingly receive and disclose such communications 'law-abiding,' and it certainly does not bring them under the *Daily Mail* principle. The transmission of the intercepted communication from the eavesdropper to the third party is itself illegal; and where, as here, the third party then knowingly discloses that communication, another illegal act has been committed. The third party in this situation cannot be likened to the reporters in the *Daily Mail* cases, who lawfully obtained their information through consensual interviews or public documents. * * *

"The 'dry up the market' theory, which posits that it is possible to deter an illegal act that is difficult to police by preventing the wrongdoer from enjoying the fruits of the crime, is neither novel nor implausible. It is a time-tested theory that undergirds numerous laws, such as the prohibition of the knowing possession of stolen goods. See 2 W. LaFave & A. Scott, *Substantive Criminal Law* § 8.10(a), p. 422 (1986) ("Without such receivers, theft ceases to be profitable. It is obvious that the receiver must be a principal target of any society anxious to stamp out theft in its various forms"). We ourselves adopted the exclusionary rule based upon similar reasoning, believing that it would 'deter unreasonable searches,' *Oregon v. Elstad*, 470 U.S. 298, 306 (1985), by removing an officer's 'incentive to disregard [the Fourth Amendment],' *Elkins v. United States*, 364 U.S. 206, 217 (1960). * * * Reliance upon the 'dry up the market' theory is both logical and eminently reasonable, and our precedents make plain that it is 'far stronger than mere speculation.'

"These statutes also protect the important interests of deterring clandestine invasions of privacy and preventing the involuntary broadcast of private communications. [These] statutes undeniably protect this venerable right of privacy. * * * The Court concludes that the private conversation between Gloria Bartnicki and Anthony Kane is somehow a 'debate * * * worthy of constitutional protection.' Perhaps the Court is correct that '[i]f the statements about the labor negotiations had been made in a public arena—during a bargaining session, for example—they would have been newsworthy.' The point, however, is that Bartnicki and Kane had no intention of contributing to a public 'debate' at all, and it is perverse to hold that another's unlawful interception and knowing disclosure of their conversation is speech 'worthy of constitutional protection.' * * *

"The Constitution should not protect the involuntary broadcast of personal conversations. Even where the communications involve public figures or concern public matters, the conversations are nonetheless private and worthy of protection. Although public persons may have forgone the right to live their lives screened from public scrutiny in some areas, it does not and should not follow that they also have abandoned their right to have a private conversation without fear of it being intentionally intercepted and knowingly disclosed."

III. OBSCENITY

A. THE SEARCH FOR A RATIONALE

Roth v. United States, 354 U.S. 476 (1957) held that obscenity was "not within the area of constitutionally protected speech or press" because, drawing from *Chaplinsky*, such utterances were "*no essential part of any exposition of ideas, and are of such slight social value as a step to truth that any benefit that may be derived from them is clearly outweighed by the social interest in order and morality.*" [Emphasis in original]. The Court determined that sexually explicit material was not necessarily obscene. Instead the question was "whether to the average person, applying contemporary community standards, the dominant theme of the material taken as a whole appeals to prurient interest." Such material, according to the Court, was "utterly without redeeming social importance."

Despite *Roth*'s view that obscene speech had no First Amendment value, *Stanley v. Georgia*, 394 U.S. 557 (1969) concluded that the First Amendment protected the possession of obscene material in the home. The Court argued that the constitutional right "to receive information and ideas, regardless of their social worth, is fundamental to our free society." The Court distinguished the public distribution of obscene materials on the ground that there was a greater danger that such material might fall into the hands of children or "intrude on the sensibilities or privacy of the general public."

Many commentators believed that *Roth* and *Stanley* left the law in an unstable position. *Roth* had insufficiently supported the view that obscenity was without constitutional value and, as interpreted, had offered an approach to defining obscenity that was difficult for prosecutors; *Stanley's* logic went further and seemed to suggest that public showings of obscene material might be constitutional if children were excluded and if individuals were not exposed to the material without informed consent. *Paris Adult Theatre,* infra, attempted to provide a rationale for the regulation of obscenity that would prevent the showing of obscene material in public theaters; *Miller,* infra, sought to loosen the definition of obscenity.

PARIS ADULT THEATRE I v. SLATON

413 U.S. 49, 93 S.Ct. 2628, 37 L.Ed.2d 446 (1973).

CHIEF JUSTICE BURGER delivered the opinion of the Court.

[The entrance to Paris Adult Theatres I & II was conventional and inoffensive without any pictures. Signs read: "Adult Theatre—You must be 21 and able to prove it. If viewing the nude body offends you, Please Do Not Enter." The District Attorney, nonetheless, had brought an action to enjoin the showing of two films that the Georgia Supreme Court described as "hard core pornography" leaving "little to the imagination." The Georgia Supreme Court assumed that the adult theaters in question barred minors and gave a full warning to the general public of the nature of the films involved, but held that the showing of the films was not constitutionally protected.]

[We] categorically disapprove the theory [that] obscene, pornographic films acquire constitutional immunity from state regulation simply because they are exhibited for consenting adults only. [Although we have] recognized the high importance of the state interest in regulating the exposure of obscene materials to juveniles and unconsenting adults, this Court has never declared these to be the only legitimate state interests permitting regulation of obscene material.

[W]e hold that there are legitimate state interests at stake in stemming the tide of commercialized obscenity, even assuming it is feasible to enforce effective safeguards against exposure to juveniles and to the passerby.7 [These] include the interest of the public in the quality of life and the total community environment, the tone of commerce in the great city centers, and, possibly, the public safety itself. The Hill–Link Minority Report of the Commission on Obscenity and Pornography indicates that there is at least an arguable correlation between obscene material and crime. Quite apart from sex crimes, however, there remains one problem of large proportions aptly described by Professor Bickel: "It concerns the tone of the society, the mode, or to use terms that have perhaps greater

---

7. It is conceivable that an "adult" theatre can—if it really insists—prevent the exposure of its obscene wares to juveniles. An "adult" bookstore, dealing in obscene books, magazines, and pictures, cannot realistically make this claim. The Hill–Link Minority Report of the Commission on Obscenity and Pornography emphasizes evidence (the Abelson National Survey of Youth and Adults) that, although most pornography may be bought by elders, "the heavy users and most highly exposed peo-

ple to pornography are adolescent females (among women) and adolescent and young males (among men)." *The Report of the Commission on Obscenity* 401 (1970). The legitimate interest in preventing exposure of juveniles to obscene materials cannot be fully served by simply barring juveniles from the immediate physical premises of "adult" bookstores, when there is a flourishing "outside business" in these materials.

currency, the style and quality of life, now and in the future. A man may be entitled to read an obscene book in his room, or expose himself indecently there. [We] should protect his privacy. But if he demands a right to obtain the books and pictures he wants in the market, and to foregather in public places—discreet, if you will, but accessible to all—with others who share his tastes, *then to grant him his right is to affect the world about the rest of us, and to impinge on other privacies.* Even supposing that each of us can, if he wishes, effectively avert the eye and stop the ear (which, in truth, we cannot), what is commonly read and seen and heard and done intrudes upon us all, want it or not." 22 *The Public Interest* 25, 25–26 (Winter, 1971). (Emphasis supplied.) [T]here is a "right of the Nation and of the States to maintain a decent [society]," *Jacobellis* (Warren, C.J., dissenting).

But, it is argued, there is no scientific data which conclusively demonstrates that exposure to obscene materials adversely affects men and women or their society. It is urged [that], absent such a demonstration, any kind of state regulation is "impermissible." We reject this argument. It is not for us to resolve empirical uncertainties underlying state legislation, save in the exceptional case where that legislation plainly impinges upon rights protected by the Constitution itself. [Although] there is no conclusive proof of a connection between antisocial behavior and obscene material, the legislature of Georgia could quite reasonably determine that such a connection does or might exist. In deciding *Roth,* this Court implicitly accepted that a legislature could legitimately act on such a conclusion to protect "*the social interest in order and morality.*"

From the beginning of civilized societies, legislators and judges have acted on various unprovable assumptions. Such assumptions underlie much lawful state regulation of commercial and business affairs. The same is true of the federal securities, antitrust laws and a host of other federal regulations. [Likewise], when legislatures and administrators act to protect the physical environment from pollution and to preserve our resources of forests, streams and parks, they must act on such imponderables as the impact of a new highway near or through an existing park or wilderness area. [The] fact that a congressional directive reflects unprovable assumptions about what is good for the people, including imponderable aesthetic assumptions, is not a sufficient reason to find that statute unconstitutional.

If we accept the unprovable assumption that a complete education requires certain books, and the well nigh universal belief that good books, plays, and art lift the spirit, improve the mind, enrich the human personality and develop character, can we then say that a state legislature may not act on the corollary assumption that commerce in obscene books,[a] or public exhibitions focused on obscene conduct, have a tendency to exert a corrupting and debasing impact leading to antisocial behavior? [The] sum of experience, including that of the past two decades, affords an ample basis for legislatures to conclude that a sensitive, key relationship of human existence, central to family life, community welfare, and the development of human personality, can be debased and distorted by crass commercial exploitation of sex. Nothing in the Constitution prohibits a State from

---

a. The only case after *Roth* in which the Court upheld a conviction based upon books was in *Mishkin* [Sec. 1, III, B infra] and most, if not all, of those books were illustrated. *Kaplan v. California,* 413 U.S. 115 (1973) held that books without pictures can be legally obscene "in the sense of being unprotected by the First Amendment." It observed that books are "passed hand to hand, and we can take note of the tendency of widely circulated books of this category to reach the impressionable young and have a continuing impact. A State could reasonably regard the 'hard core' conduct described by *Suite 69* as capable of encouraging or causing antisocial behavior, especially in its impact on young people."

reaching such a conclusion and acting on it legislatively simply because there is no conclusive evidence or empirical data.

[Nothing] in this Court's decisions intimates that there is any "fundamental" privacy right "implicit in the concept of ordered liberty" to watch obscene movies in places of public accommodation. [W]e have declined to equate the privacy of the home relied on in *Stanley* with a "zone" of "privacy" that follows a distributor or a consumer of obscene materials wherever he goes.b

[W]e reject the claim that Georgia is here attempting to control the minds or thoughts of those who patronize theatres. Preventing unlimited display or distribution of obscene material, which by definition lacks any serious literary, artistic, political, or scientific value as communication, is distinct from a control of reason and the intellect. Cf. John Finnis, *"Reason and Passion": The Constitutional Dialectic of Free Speech and Obscenity,* 116 U.Pa.L.Rev. 222, 229–230, 241–243 (1967).

[Finally], petitioners argue that conduct which directly involves "consenting adults" only has, for that sole reason, a special claim to constitutional protection. Our Constitution establishes a broad range of conditions on the exercise of power by the States, but for us to say that our Constitution incorporates the proposition that conduct involving consenting adults only is always beyond state regulation,[14] is a step we are unable to take.[15] [The] issue in this context goes beyond whether someone, or even the majority, considers the conduct depicted as "wrong" or "sinful." The States have the power to make a morally neutral judgment that public exhibition of obscene material, or commerce in such material, has a tendency to injure the community as a whole, to endanger the public safety, or to jeopardize, in Mr. Chief Justice Warren's words, the States' "right [to] maintain a decent society." *Jacobellis* (dissenting). * * *

JUSTICE BRENNAN, with whom JUSTICE STEWART and JUSTICE MARSHALL join, dissenting.

[I] am convinced that the approach initiated 15 years ago in *Roth* and culminating in the Court's decision today, cannot bring stability to this area of the law without jeopardizing fundamental First Amendment values, and I have concluded that the time has come to make a significant departure from that [approach.]

b. In a series of cases, the Court limited *Stanley* strictly to its facts. It held that Stanley did not apply to the possession of child pornography even in the home. *Osborne v. Ohio,* 495 U.S. 103 (1990). It held that *Stanley* did not protect the mailing of obscene material to consenting adults, *United States v. Reidel,* 402 U.S. 351 (1971) or the transporting or importing of obscene materials for private use, *United States v. Orito,* 413 U.S. 139 (1973) (transporting); *United States v. 12 200-Ft. Reels,* 413 U.S. 123 (1973) (importing). Dissenting in *Reels,* Douglas, J., argued that *Stanley* rights could legally be realized "only if one wrote or designed a tract in his attic and printed or processed it in his basement, so as to be able to read it in his study."

For the declaration that *Stanley's* "privacy of the home" principle is "firmly grounded" in the First Amendment while resisting the principle's expansion to protect consensual adult homosexual sodomy in the home, see *Bowers v. Hardwick,* Ch. 6, Sec. 2. But see Blackmun, J., joined by Brennan, Marshall, and Stevens, JJ., dissenting in *Bowers* ("*Stanley* rested as much on the Court's understanding of the Fourth Amendment as it did on the First").

14. Cf. John Stuart Mill, *On Liberty* 13 (1955).

15. The state statute books are replete with constitutionally unchallenged laws against prostitution, suicide, voluntary self-mutilation, brutalizing "bare fist" prize fights, and duels, although these crimes may only directly involve "consenting adults." Statutes making bigamy a crime surely cut into an individual's freedom to associate, but few today seriously claim such statutes violate the First Amendment or any other constitutional provision.

[The] decision of the Georgia Supreme Court rested squarely on its conclusion that the State could constitutionally suppress these films even if they were displayed only to persons over the age of 21 who were aware of the nature of their contents and who had consented to viewing them. [I] am convinced of the invalidity of that conclusion [and] would therefore vacate the [judgment]. I have no occasion to consider the extent of State power to regulate the distribution of sexually oriented materials to juveniles or to unconsenting [adults.] [*Stanley*] reflected our emerging view that the state interests in protecting children and in protecting unconsenting adults may stand on a different footing from the other asserted state interests. It may well be, as one commentator has argued, that "exposure to [erotic material] is for some persons an intense emotional experience. A communication of this nature, imposed upon a person contrary to his wishes, has all the characteristics of a physical assault. [And it] constitutes an invasion of his [privacy]." [But] whatever the strength of the state interests in protecting juveniles and unconsenting adults from exposure to sexually oriented materials, those interests cannot be asserted in defense of the holding of the Georgia Supreme Court, [which] assumed for the purposes of its decision that the films in issue were exhibited only to persons over the age of 21 who viewed them willingly and with prior knowledge of the nature of their contents. [The] justification for the suppression must be found, therefore, in some independent interest in regulating the reading and viewing habits of consenting [adults].

In *Stanley* we pointed out that "[t]here appears to be little empirical basis for" the assertion that "exposure to obscene materials may lead to deviant sexual behavior or crimes of sexual violence." In any event, we added that "if the State is only concerned about printed or filmed materials inducing antisocial conduct, we believe that in the context of private consumption of ideas and information we should adhere to the view that '[a]mong free men, the deterrents ordinarily to be applied to prevent crime are education and punishment for violations of the [law].'"

Moreover, in *Stanley* we rejected as "wholly inconsistent with the philosophy of the First Amendment," the notion that there is a legitimate state concern in the "control [of] the moral content of a person's thoughts." [The] traditional description of state police power does embrace the regulation of morals as well as the health, safety, and general welfare of the citizenry. [But] the State's interest in regulating morality by suppressing obscenity, while often asserted, remains essentially unfocused and ill-defined. And, since the attempt to curtail unprotected speech necessarily spills over into the area of protected speech, the effort to serve this speculative interest through the suppression of obscene material must tread heavily on rights protected by the First Amendment. * * *

In short, while I cannot say that the interests of the State—apart from the question of juveniles and unconsenting adults—are trivial or nonexistent, I am compelled to conclude that these interests cannot justify the substantial damage to constitutional rights and to this Nation's judicial machinery that inevitably results from state efforts to bar the distribution even of unprotected material to consenting adults.c

Justice Douglas, dissenting. * * *

"Obscenity" at most is the expression of offensive ideas. There are regimes in the world where ideas "offensive" to the majority (or at least to those who control the majority) are suppressed. There life proceeds at a monotonous pace. Most of us would find that world offensive. One of the most offensive experiences in my life

---

c. For the portion of Brennan, J.'s dissent addressing the difficulties of formulating an acceptable constitutional standard, see *Miller v. California*, infra.

was a visit to a nation where bookstalls were filled only with books on mathematics and books on religion.

I am sure I would find offensive most of the books and movies charged with being obscene. But in a life that has not been short, I have yet to be trapped into seeing or reading something that would offend me. I never read or see the materials coming to the Court under charges of "obscenity," because I have thought the First Amendment made it unconstitutional for me to act as a censor. * * *

Ideas and the First Amendment. KINGSLEY INT'L PICTURES CORP. v. REGENTS, 360 U.S. 684 (1959), per STEWART, J., underlined the distinction between obscenity and non-obscene "portrayal of sex" in art and literature. *Kingsley* held invalid New York's denial of a license to exhibit the film *Lady Chatterley's Lover* pursuant to a statute requiring such denial when a film "portrays acts of sexual immorality [as] desirable, acceptable or proper patterns of behavior": "[What] New York has done, [is] to prevent the exhibition of a motion picture because that picture advocates an idea—that adultery under certain circumstances may be proper behavior. Yet the First Amendment's basic guarantee is of freedom to advocate ideas. The State, quite simply, has thus struck at the very heart of constitutionally protected liberty."

B. A REVISED STANDARD

MILLER v. CALIFORNIA

413 U.S. 15, 93 S.Ct. 2607, 37 L.Ed.2d 419 (1973).

CHIEF JUSTICE BURGER delivered the opinion of the Court. [The Court remanded, "for proceedings not inconsistent" with the opinion's obscenity standard, Miller's conviction under California's obscenity law for mass mailing of unsolicited pictorial advertising brochures depicting men and women in a variety of group sexual activities.]

This is one of a group of "obscenity-pornography" cases being reviewed by the Court in a re-examination of standards enunciated in earlier cases involving what Mr. Justice Harlan called "the intractable obscenity problem." [I]n this context[a] [we] are called on to define the standards which must be used to identify obscene material that a State may [regulate].

[Nine years after *Roth*], in *Memoirs v. Massachusetts*, 383 U.S. 413 (1966), the Court veered sharply away from the Roth concept and, with only three Justices in the plurality opinion, articulated a new test of obscenity. The plurality held that under the Roth definition "as elaborated in subsequent cases, three elements must coalesce: it must be established that (a) the dominant theme of the material taken as a whole appeals to a prurient interest in sex; (b) the material is patently offensive because it affronts contemporary community standards relating to the description or representation of sexual matters; and (c) the material is utterly without redeeming social value." * * *

---

a. The "context" was that in *Miller* "sexually explicit materials have been thrust by aggressive sales action upon unwilling recipients." But nothing in *Miller* limited the revised standard to that context, and the companion case, *Paris Adult Theatre,* applied the same standard to dissemination limited to consenting adults.

While *Roth* presumed "obscenity" to be "utterly without redeeming social importance," *Memoirs* required that to prove obscenity it must be affirmatively established that the material is *"utterly* without redeeming social value."

Thus, even as they repeated the words of *Roth,* the *Memoirs* plurality produced a drastically altered test that called on the prosecution to prove a negative, i.e., that the material was *"utterly* without redeeming social value"—a burden virtually impossible to discharge under our criminal standards of proof. [Apart] from the initial formulation in *Roth,* no majority of the Court has at any given time been able to agree on a standard to determine what constitutes obscene, pornographic material subject to regulation under the States' police power. See, e.g., *Redrup v. New York*, 386 U.S. 767 (1967).3 This is not remarkable, for in the area of freedom of speech and press the courts must always remain sensitive to any infringement on genuinely serious literary, artistic, political, or scientific expression. * * *

II.　This much has been categorically settled by the Court, that obscene material is unprotected by the First Amendment. [We] acknowledge, however, the inherent dangers of undertaking to regulate any form of expression. State statutes designed to regulate obscene materials must be carefully limited. As a result, we now confine the permissible scope of such regulation to works which depict or describe sexual conduct. That conduct must be specifically defined by the applicable state law, as written or authoritatively construed.6 A state offense must also be limited to works which, taken as a whole, appeal to the prurient interest in sex, which portray sexual conduct in a patently offensive way, and which, taken as a whole, do not have serious literary, artistic, political, or scientific value.

The basic guidelines for the trier of fact must be: (a) whether "the average person, applying contemporary community standards" would find that the work, taken as a whole, appeals to the prurient interest, (b) whether the work depicts or describes, in a patently offensive way, sexual conduct specifically defined by the applicable state law, and (c) whether the work, taken as a whole, lacks serious literary, artistic, political, or scientific value. We do not adopt as a constitutional standard the *"utterly* without redeeming social value" test of *Memoirs;* that concept has never commanded the adherence of more than three Justices at one time.7 If a state law that regulates obscene material is thus limited, as written or construed, the First Amendment values applicable to the States [are] adequately

---

3.　In the absence of a majority view, this Court was compelled to embark on the practice of summarily reversing convictions for the dissemination of materials that at least five members of the Court, applying their separate tests, found to be protected by the First Amendment. *Redrup.* [Beyond] the necessity of circumstances, however, no justification has ever been offered in support of the *Redrup* "policy." The *Redrup* procedure has cast us in the role of an unreviewable board of censorship for the 50 States, subjectively judging each piece of material brought before us.

6.　See, e.g., Oregon Laws 1971, c. 743, Art. 29, §§ 255–262, and Hawaii Penal Code, Tit. 37, §§ 1210–1216, 1972 Hawaii Session Laws, pp. 126–129, Act 9, Pt. II, as examples of state laws directed at depiction of defined physical conduct, as opposed to expression. [We] do not hold, as Mr. Justice Brennan intimates, that all States other than Oregon must now enact new obscenity statutes. Other existing state stat-

utes, as construed heretofore or hereafter, may well be adequate.

7.　"[We] also reject, as a constitutional standard, the ambiguous concept of 'social importance'." [*Hamling v. United States*, 418 U.S. 87 (1974) upheld a conviction in which the jury had been instructed to find that the material was "utterly without redeeming social value." Defendant argued that the latter phrase was unconstitutionally vague and cited *Miller.* The Court rejected the vagueness challenge: "[O]ur opinion in *Miller* plainly indicates that we rejected the '[social] value' formulation, not because it was so vague as to deprive criminal defendants of adequate notice, but instead because it represented a departure from [*Roth*], and because in calling on the prosecution to 'prove a negative,' it imposed a '[prosecutorial] burden virtually impossible to discharge' and which was not constitutionally required."]

protected by the ultimate power of appellate courts to conduct an independent review of constitutional claims when necessary.

We emphasize that it is not our function to propose regulatory schemes for the States. [It] is possible, however, to give a few plain examples of what a state statute could define for regulation under the second part (b) of the standard announced in this opinion, supra:

(a) Patently offensive representations or descriptions of ultimate sexual acts, normal or perverted, actual or simulated.

(b) Patently offensive representations or descriptions of masturbation, excretory functions, and lewd exhibition of the genitals.**b**

Sex and nudity may not be exploited without limit by films or pictures exhibited or sold in places of public accommodation any more than live sex and nudity can be exhibited or sold without limit in such public places.8 At a minimum, prurient,**c** patently offensive depiction or description of sexual conduct must have serious literary, artistic, political, or scientific value to merit First Amendment protection. For example, medical books for the education of physicians and related personnel necessarily use graphic illustrations and descriptions of human anatomy. In resolving the inevitably sensitive questions of fact and law, we must continue to rely on the jury system, accompanied by the safeguards that judges, rules of evidence, presumption of innocence and other protective features [provide].

Mr. Justice Brennan [has] abandoned his former positions and now maintains that no formulation of this Court, the Congress, or the States can adequately distinguish obscene material unprotected by the First Amendment from protected expression, *Paris Adult Theatre I v. Slaton* (Brennan, J., dissenting). Paradoxically, Mr. Justice Brennan indicates that suppression of unprotected obscene material is permissible to avoid exposure to unconsenting adults, as in this case, and to juveniles, although he gives no indication of how the division between protected and nonprotected materials may be drawn with greater precision for these purposes than for regulation of commercial exposure to consenting adults only. Nor does he indicate where in the Constitution he finds the authority to distin-

b. *Jenkins v. Georgia,* 418 U.S. 153 (1974) held the film *Carnal Knowledge* not obscene because it did not " ' "depict or describe patently offensive "hard core" sexual conduct' " as required by *Miller:* "[While there] are scenes in which sexual conduct including 'ultimate sexual acts' is to be understood to be taking place, the camera does not focus on the bodies of the actors at such times. There is no exhibition whatever of the actors' genitals, lewd or otherwise, during these scenes. There are occasional scenes of nudity, but nudity alone is not enough to make material legally obscene under the *Miller* standards." *Ward v. Illinois,* 431 U.S. 767 (1977) held that it was not necessary for the legislature or the courts to provide an "exhaustive list of the sexual conduct [the] description of which may be held obscene." It is enough that a state adopt *Miller's* explanatory examples. Stevens, J., joined by Brennan, Stewart and Marshall, JJ., dissented: "[I]f the statute need only describe the 'kinds' of proscribed sexual conduct, it adds no protection to what the Constitution itself creates. [The]

specificity requirement as described in *Miller* held out the promise of a principled effort to respond to [the vagueness] argument. By abandoning that effort today, the Court withdraws the cornerstone of the *Miller* [structure]."

8. Although we are not presented here with the problem of regulating lewd public conduct itself, the States have greater power to regulate nonverbal, physical conduct than to suppress depictions or descriptions of the same behavior. * * *

c. *Brockett v. Spokane Arcades, Inc.,* 472 U.S. 491 (1985) held that appeals to prurient interest could not be taken to include appeals to "normal" interests in sex. Only appeals to a "shameful or morbid interest in sex" are prurient. Although the Court was resolute in its position that appeals to "good, old fashioned, healthy" interests in sex were constitutionally protected, it did not further specify how "normal" sex was to be distinguished from the "shameful" or "morbid."

guish between a willing "adult" one month past the state law age of majority and a willing "juvenile" one month younger.d

Under the holdings announced today, no one will be subject to prosecution for the sale or exposure of obscene materials unless these materials depict or describe patently offensive "hard core" sexual conduct specifically defined by the regulating state law, as written or construed. We are satisfied that these specific prerequisites will provide fair notice to a dealer in such materials that his public and commercial activities may bring prosecution. If the inability to define regulated materials with ultimate, god-like precision altogether removes the power of the States or the Congress to regulate, then "hard core" pornography may be exposed without limit to the juvenile, the passerby, and the consenting adult alike, as indeed, Mr. Justice Douglas contends.

[N]o amount of "fatigue" should lead us to adopt a convenient "institutional" rationale—an absolutist, "anything goes" view of the First Amendment—because it will lighten our burdens. [Nor] should we remedy "tension between state and federal courts" by arbitrarily depriving the States of a power reserved to them under the Constitution, a power which they have enjoyed and exercised continuously from before the adoption of the First Amendment to this day. See *Roth.* "Our duty admits of no 'substitute for facing up to the tough individual problems of constitutional judgment involved in every obscenity case.'" *Jacobellis* (opinion of Brennan, J.).

III. Under a national Constitution, fundamental First Amendment limitations on the powers of the States do not vary from community to community, but this does not mean that there are, or should or can be, fixed, uniform national standards of precisely what appeals to the "prurient interest" or is "patently offensive." These are essentially questions of fact, and our nation is simply too big and too diverse for this Court to reasonably expect that such standards could be articulated for all 50 States in a single formulation, even assuming the prerequisite consensus exists. When triers of fact are asked to decide whether "the average person, applying contemporary community standards" would consider certain materials "prurient," it would be unrealistic to require that the answer be based on some abstract formulation. The adversary system, with lay jurors as the usual ultimate fact finders in criminal prosecutions, has historically permitted triers-of-fact to draw on the standards of their community, guided always by limiting instructions on the law. To require a State to structure obscenity proceedings around evidence of a *national* "community standard" would be an exercise in [futility].

We conclude that neither the State's alleged failure to offer evidence of "national standards," nor the trial court's charge that the jury consider state

---

d. The suggestion that the same book may be obscene in some contexts but not in others has been endorsed in several different contexts. *Butler v. Michigan,* 352 U.S. 380 (1957) held that the state could not ban sales to the general public of material unsuitable for children: "The State insists that [by] quarantining the general reading public against books not too rugged for grown men and women in order to shield juvenile innocence, it is exercising its power to promote the general welfare. Surely, this is to burn the house to roast the pig. [The] incidence of this enactment is to reduce the adult population of Michigan to reading only what is fit for children." *Ginsberg v. New York,* 390 U.S. 629 (1968), however, held that the state could bar the distribution to children of books that were suitable for adults, the Court recognizing it was adopting a "variable" concept of obscenity. See also *Ginzburg v. United States,* 383 U.S. 463 (1966) ("pandering" method of marketing supports obscenity conviction even though the materials might not otherwise have been considered obscene); *Mishkin v. New York,* 383 U.S. 502 (1966) (material designed for and primarily disseminated to deviant sexual group can meet prurient appeal requirement even if the material lacks appeal to an average member of the general public; appeal is to be tested with reference to the sexual interests of the intended and probable recipient group).

community standards, were constitutional errors. Nothing in the First Amendment requires that a jury must consider hypothetical and unascertainable "national standards" when attempting to determine whether certain materials are obscene as a matter of [fact].

It is neither realistic nor constitutionally sound to read the First Amendment as requiring that the people of Maine or Mississippi accept public depiction of conduct found tolerable in Las Vegas, or New York City. People in different States vary in their tastes and attitudes, and this diversity is not to be strangled by the absolutism of imposed uniformity. As the Court made clear in *Mishkin,* the primary concern with requiring a jury to apply the standard of "the average person, applying contemporary community standards" is to be certain that, so far as material is not aimed at a deviant group, it will be judged by its impact on an average person, rather than a particularly susceptible or sensitive person—or indeed a totally insensitive one.**e** [We] hold the requirement that the jury evaluate the materials with reference to "contemporary standards of the State of California" serves this protective purpose and is constitutionally adequate.**f** * * *

In sum we (a) reaffirm the *Roth* holding that obscene material is not protected by the First Amendment, (b) hold that such material can be regulated by the States, subject to the specific safeguards enunciated above, without a showing that the material is "*utterly* without redeeming social value," and (c) hold that obscenity is to be determined by applying "contemporary community standards," not "national standards." * * *

JUSTICE DOUGLAS, dissenting. * * *

My contention is that until a civil proceeding has placed a tract beyond the pale, no criminal prosecution should be sustained. For no more vivid illustration of vague and uncertain laws could be designed than those we have fashioned. [If] a specific book [or] motion picture has in a civil proceeding been condemned as obscene and review of that finding has been completed, and thereafter a person publishes [or] displays that particular book or film, then a vague law has been made specific. There would remain the underlying question whether the First Amendment allows an implied exception in the case of obscenity. I do not think it does and my views on the issue have been stated over and again. But at least a criminal prosecution brought at that juncture would not violate the time-honored void-for-vagueness test.8

e. *Pinkus v. United States,* 436 U.S. 293 (1978) upheld a jury instruction stating "you are to judge these materials by the standard of the hypothetical average person in the community, but in determining this average standard you must include the *sensitive and the insensitive,* in other words, [everyone] in the community." On the other hand, in the absence of evidence that "children were the intended recipients" or that defendant "had reason to know children were likely to receive the materials," it was considered erroneous to instruct the jury that children were part of the relevant community. *Butler.* When the evidence would support such a charge, the Court stated that prurient appeal to deviant sexual groups could be substituted for appeal to the average person; moreover, the jury was entitled to take pandering into account. *Ginzburg.*

f. *Jenkins,* fn. b supra, stated that a judge may instruct a jury to apply "contemporary community standards" without any further specification. Alternatively, the state may choose "to define the standards in more precise geographic terms, as was done by California in *Miller.*" *Hamling,* fn. 7 supra, interpreted a federal obscenity statute to make the relevant community the one from which the jury was drawn. The judge's instruction to consider the "community standards of the 'nation as a whole' delineated a wider geographical area than would be warranted by [*Miller*]" or the Court's construction of the statute, but the error was regarded as harmless under the circumstances. See also *Sable Communications v. FCC,* Sec. 8, II, infra ("dial-a-porn" company bears burden of complying with congressional obscenity ban despite diverse local community standards).

8. The Commission on Obscenity and Pornography has advocated such a procedure. [See] *Report of the Commission on Obscenity and Pornography* 70–71 (1970).

No such protective procedure has been designed by California in this case. Obscenity—which even we cannot define with precision—is a hodge-podge. To send men to jail for violating standards they cannot understand, construe, and apply is a monstrous thing to do in a Nation dedicated to fair trials and due process. * * *

JUSTICE BRENNAN, with whom JUSTICE STEWART and JUSTICE MARSHALL join, dissenting.

In my dissent in *Paris Adult Theatre,* decided this date, I noted that I had no occasion to consider the extent of state power to regulate the distribution of sexually oriented material to juveniles or the offensive exposure of such material to unconsenting adults. [I] need not now decide whether a statute might be drawn to impose, within the requirements of the First Amendment, criminal penalties for the precise conduct at issue here. For it is clear that under my dissent in *Paris Adult Theatre,* the statute under which the prosecution was brought is unconstitutionally overbroad, and therefore invalid on its face. * * *

[In his *Paris Adult Theatre* dissent, Brennan, J., joined by Stewart and Marshall, JJ., argued that the state interests in regulating obscenity were not strong enough to justify the degree of vagueness. He criticized not only the Court's standard in *Miller,* but also a range of alternatives:]

II.   [The] essence of our problem [is] that we have been unable to provide "sensitive tools" to separate obscenity from other sexually oriented but constitutionally protected speech, so that efforts to suppress the former do not spill over into the suppression of the latter. [The dissent traced the Court's experience with *Roth* and its progeny.]

III.   Our experience with the *Roth* approach has certainly taught us that the outright suppression of obscenity cannot be reconciled with the fundamental principles of the First and Fourteenth Amendments. For we have failed to formulate a standard that sharply distinguishes protected from unprotected speech, and out of necessity, we have resorted to the *Redrup* approach, which resolves cases as between the parties, but offers only the most obscure guidance to legislation, adjudication by other courts, and primary conduct. [T]he vagueness problem would be largely of our own creation if it stemmed primarily from our failure to reach a consensus on any one standard. But after 15 years of experimentation and debate I am reluctantly forced to the conclusion that none of the available formulas, including the one announced today, can reduce the vagueness to a tolerable level while at the same time striking an acceptable balance between the protections of the First and Fourteenth Amendments, on the one hand, and on the other the asserted state interest in regulating the dissemination of certain sexually oriented materials. Any effort to draw a constitutionally acceptable boundary on state power must resort to such indefinite concepts as "prurient interest," "patent offensiveness," "serious literary value," and the like. The meaning of these concepts necessarily varies with the experience, outlook, and even idiosyncracies of the person defining them. Although we have assumed that obscenity does exist and that we "know it when [we] see it," *Jacobellis* (Stewart, J., concurring), we are manifestly unable to describe it in advance except by reference to concepts so elusive that they fail to distinguish clearly between protected and unprotected speech.

[Added to the inherent vagueness of standards] is the further complication that the obscenity of any particular item may depend upon nuances of presentation and the context of its dissemination. See *Ginzburg.* [N]o one definition, no matter how precisely or narrowly drawn, can possibly suffice for all situations, or carve out fully suppressible expression from all media without also creating a substantial risk of encroachment upon the guarantees of the Due Process Clause and the First Amendment.

[The] resulting level of uncertainty is utterly intolerable, not alone because it makes "[b]ookselling [a] hazardous profession," *Ginsberg* (Fortas, J., dissenting), but as well because it invites arbitrary and erratic enforcement of the law. [We] have indicated that "stricter standards of permissible statutory vagueness may be applied to a statute having a potentially inhibiting effect on speech; a man may the less be required to act at his peril here, because the free dissemination of ideas may be the loser." * * *

The problems of fair notice and chilling protected speech are very grave standing alone. But [a] vague statute in this area creates a third [set] of problems. These [concern] the institutional stress that inevitably results where the line separating protected from unprotected speech is excessively vague. [Almost] every obscenity case presents a constitutional question of exceptional difficulty. [As] a result of our failure to define standards with predictable application to any given piece of material, there is no probability of regularity in obscenity decisions by state and lower federal courts. [O]ne cannot say with certainty that material is obscene until at least five members of this Court, applying inevitably obscure standards, have pronounced it [so].

We have managed the burden of deciding scores of obscenity cases by relying on per curiam reversals or denials of certiorari—a practice which conceals the rationale of decision and gives at least the appearance of arbitrary action by this Court. More important, [the] practice effectively censors protected expression by leaving lower court determinations of obscenity intact even though the status of the allegedly obscene material is entirely unsettled until final review here. In addition, the uncertainty of the standards creates a continuing source of tension between state and federal [courts].

The severe problems arising from the lack of fair notice, from the chill on protected expression, and from the stress imposed on the state and federal judicial machinery persuade me that a significant change in direction is urgently required. I turn, therefore, to the alternatives that are now open.

IV. 1. The approach requiring the smallest deviation from our present course would be to draw a new line between protected and unprotected speech, still permitting the States to suppress all material on the unprotected side of the line. In my view, clarity cannot be obtained pursuant to this approach except by drawing a line that resolves all doubts in favor of state power and against the guarantees of the First Amendment. We could hold, for example, that any depiction or description of human sexual organs, irrespective of the manner or purpose of the portrayal, is outside the protection of the First Amendment and therefore open to suppression by the States. That formula would, no doubt, offer much fairer notice [and] give rise to a substantial probability of regularity in most judicial determinations under the standard. But such a standard would be appallingly overbroad, permitting the suppression of a vast range of literary, scientific, and artistic masterpieces. Neither the First Amendment nor any free community could possibly tolerate such a standard.

2. [T]he Court today recognizes that a prohibition against any depiction or description of human sexual organs could not be reconciled with the guarantees of the First Amendment. But the Court [adopts] a restatement of the *Roth–Memoirs* definition of obscenity [that] permits suppression if the government can prove that the materials lack "*serious* literary, artistic, political or scientific value." [In] *Roth* we held that certain expression is obscene, and thus outside the protection of the First Amendment, precisely *because* it lacks even the slightest redeeming

social value. [The] Court's approach necessarily assumes that some works will be deemed obscene—even though they clearly have *some* social value—because the State was able to prove that the value, measured by some unspecified standard, was not sufficiently "serious" to warrant constitutional protection. That result [is] nothing less than a rejection of the fundamental First Amendment premises and rationale of the *Roth* opinion and an invitation to widespread suppression of sexually oriented speech. Before today, the protections of the First Amendment have never been thought limited to expressions of *serious* literary or political value. *Gooding v. Wilson*; *Cohen v. California*; *Terminiello v. Chicago* [Part IV infra].

[T]he Court's approach [can] have no ameliorative impact on the cluster of problems that grow out of the vagueness of our current standards. Indeed, even the Court makes no argument that the reformulation will provide fairer notice to booksellers, theatre owners, and the reading and viewing public. Nor does the Court contend that the approach will provide clearer guidance to law enforcement officials or reduce the chill on protected expression [or] mitigate [the] institutional [problems].

Of course, the Court's restated *Roth* test does limit the definition of obscenity to depictions of physical conduct and explicit sexual acts. And that limitation may seem, at first glance, a welcome and clarifying addition to the *Roth–Memoirs* formula. But just as the agreement in *Roth* on an abstract definition of obscenity gave little hint of the extreme difficulty that was to follow in attempting to apply that definition to specific material, the mere formulation of a "physical conduct" test is no assurance that it can be applied with any greater facility. [The] Court surely demonstrates little sensitivity to our own institutional problems, much less the other vagueness-related difficulties, in establishing a system that requires us to consider whether a description of human genitals is sufficiently "lewd" to deprive it of constitutional protection; whether a sexual act is "ultimate"; whether the conduct depicted in materials before us fits within one of the categories of conduct whose depiction the state or federal governments have attempted to suppress; and a host of equally pointless inquiries. * * *

If the application of the "physical conduct" test to pictorial material is fraught with difficulty, its application to textual material carries the potential for extraordinary abuse. Surely we have passed the point where the mere written description of sexual conduct is deprived of First Amendment protection. Yet the test offers no guidance to us, or anyone else, in determining which written descriptions of sexual conduct are protected, and which are not.

Ultimately, the reformulation must fail because it still leaves in this Court the responsibility of determining in each case whether the materials are protected by the First Amendment. * * *

3. I have also considered the possibility of reducing our own role, and the role of appellate courts generally, in determining whether particular matter is obscene. Thus, [we] might adopt the position that where a lower federal or state court has conscientiously applied the constitutional standard, its finding of obscenity will be no more vulnerable to reversal by this Court than any finding of fact. [E]ven if the Constitution would permit us to refrain from judging for ourselves the alleged obscenity of particular materials, that approach would solve at best only a small part of our problem. For while it would mitigate the institutional stress, [it] would neither offer nor produce any cure for the other vices of vagueness. Far from providing a clearer guide to permissible primary conduct, the approach would inevitably lead to even greater uncertainty and the consequent due process problems of fair notice. And the approach would expose

much protected, sexually oriented expression to the vagaries of jury determinations. Plainly, the institutional gain would be more than offset by the unprecedented infringement of First Amendment rights.

4. Finally, I have considered the view, urged so forcefully since 1957 by our Brothers Black and Douglas, that the First Amendment bars the suppression of any sexually oriented expression. That position would effect a sharp reduction, although perhaps not a total elimination, of the uncertainty that surrounds our current approach. Nevertheless, I am convinced that it would achieve that desirable goal only by stripping the States of power to an extent that cannot be justified by the commands of the Constitution, at least so long as there is available an alternative approach that strikes a better balance between the guarantee of free expression and the States' legitimate interests.

* * * I would hold, therefore, that at least in the absence of distribution to juveniles or obtrusive exposure to unconsenting adults, the First and Fourteenth Amendments prohibit the state and federal governments from attempting wholly to suppress sexually oriented materials on the basis of their allegedly "obscene" contents.g Nothing in this approach precludes those governments from taking action to serve what may be strong and legitimate interests through regulation of the manner of distribution of sexually oriented material.

VI. * * * I do not pretend to have found a complete and infallible [answer]. Difficult questions must still be faced, notably in the areas of distribution to juveniles and offensive exposure to unconsenting adults. Whatever the extent of state power to regulate in those areas,29 it should be clear that the view I espouse today would introduce a large measure of clarity to this troubled area, would reduce the institutional pressure on this Court and the rest of the State and Federal judiciary, and would guarantee fuller freedom of expression while leaving room for the protection of legitimate governmental interests. * * *

Notes

1. **Serious value.** *Pope v. Illinois,* 481 U.S. 497 (1987) declared that: "The proper inquiry is not whether an ordinary member of any given community would find serious literary, artistic, political, or scientific value[,] but whether a reasonable person would find such value in the material taken as a whole."

2. **Scienter.** *Smith v. California,* 361 U.S. 147 (1959) invalidated an ordinance that dispensed with any requirement that a seller of an obscene book have knowledge of its contents, but did not decide what sort of mental element was needed to prosecute. *Hamling v. United States,* supra, stated that it was constitutionally sufficient to show that a distributor of an advertising collage of pictures of sexual acts "had knowledge of the contents of the materials [and] that he knew the character and nature of the materials."

C. VAGUENESS AND OVERBREADTH: AN OVERVIEW

In *Paris Adult Theatre,* Brennan, J., dissents on the ground that the obscenity statute is unconstitutionally vague. He envisions the possibility that an obscenity

---

g. For the portion of Brennan, J.'s dissent addressing the strength and legitimacy of the state interests, see *Paris Adult Theatre,* supra.

29. The Court erroneously states, *Miller,* that the author of this opinion "indicates that suppression of unprotected obscene material is permissible to avoid exposure to unconsenting adults [and] to juveniles * * *." I defer expression of my views as to the scope of state power in these areas until cases squarely presenting these questions are before the Court.

statute might overcome his vagueness objection if it were tailored to combat distribution to unconsenting adults or to children. In *Miller,* the materials were in fact distributed to unconsenting adults. There Brennan, J., does not reach the vagueness question but objects on the ground that the statute is overbroad,—i.e., it is not confined to the protection of unconsenting adults and children, but also prohibits distribution of obscene materials to consenting adults. In Brennan, J.'s view, even if the particular conduct at issue in *Miller* might be constitutionally prohibited by a narrower statute, it cannot be reached under a statute that sweeps so much protected speech within its terms.

The doctrines of "vagueness" and "overbreadth" referred to in Brennan, J.'s dissents are deeply embedded in First Amendment jurisprudence. At first glance, the doctrines appear discrete. A statute that prohibits the use of the words "kill" and "President" in the same sentence may not be vague, but it is certainly overbroad even though some sentences using those words may be unprotected. Conversely, a vague statute may not be overbroad; it may not pertain to First Amendment freedoms at all, or it may clearly be intended to exclude all protected speech from its prohibition but use vague language to accomplish that purpose.

Ordinarily, however, the problems of "vagueness" and "overbreadth" are closely related. An Airport Commissioners resolution banning all "First Amendment activities" in the Los Angeles International Airport was declared overbroad in *Board of Airport Commissioners v. Jews for Jesus,* 482 U.S. 569 (1987). Literally read the statute would have prevented anyone from talking or reading in the airport. But if the language literally covers a variety of constitutionally protected activities, it *cannot be read literally.* If the statute cannot be read according to its terms, however, problems of vagueness will often emerge. To be sure, statutes may be interpreted in ways that will avoid vagueness or overbreadth difficulties. See, e.g., *Scales v. United States,* Sec. 1, I, D supra. It is established doctrine, for example, that an attack based either upon vagueness or overbreadth will be unsuccessful in federal court if the statute in question is "readily subject to a narrowing construction by the state courts." *Young v. American Mini Theatres, Inc.*; *Erznoznik v. Jacksonville,* Sec. 3, I infra. Moreover, "[f]or the purpose of determining whether a state statute is too vague and indefinite to constitute valid legislation [the Court takes] 'the statute as though it read precisely as the highest court of the State has interpreted it.'" *Wainwright v. Stone,* 414 U.S. 21 (1973). Under this policy, a litigant can be prosecuted successfully for violating a statute that by its terms appears vague or overbroad but is interpreted by the state court in the same prosecution to mean something clearer or narrower than its literal language would dictate. *Cox v. New Hampshire,* Sec. 6, I, A infra. The harshness of this doctrine is mitigated somewhat by the fact that "unexpected" or "unforeseeable" judicial constructions in such contexts violate due process. See *Marks v. United States,* 430 U.S. 188 (1977).

Somewhat more complicated is the issue of when general attacks on a statute are permitted. Plainly litigants may argue that statutes are vague as to their own conduct or that their own speech is protected. In other words, litigants are always free to argue that a statute is invalid "as applied" to their own conduct. The dispute concerns when litigants can attack a statute without reference to their own conduct, an attack sometimes called "on its face."

A separate question is: when should such attacks result in partial or total invalidation of a statute? The terminology here has become as confused as the issues. The Court has frequently referred to facial attacks on statutes in a way that embraces attempts at either partial or total invalidation. In some opinions, however, including those quoted below, it uses the term "facial attack" or "on its face" to refer only to arguments seeking total invalidation of a statute.

Terminology aside, one of the recurrent questions has been the extent to which litigants may argue that a statute is unconstitutionally overbroad even though their own conduct would not otherwise be constitutionally protected. This is often characterized as a standing issue. Ordinarily litigants do not have standing to raise the rights of others. But it has been argued that litigants should have standing to challenge overbroad statutes even if their own conduct would be otherwise unprotected in order to prevent a chilling effect on freedom of speech. Alternatively, it has been argued that no standing problem is genuinely presented because "[u]nder 'conventional' standing principles, a litigant has always had the right to be judged in accordance with a constitutionally valid rule of law." Henry Monaghan, *Overbreadth,* 1981 S.Ct.Rev. 1, 3. On this view, if a statute is unconstitutionally overbroad, it is not a valid rule of law, and any defendant prosecuted under the statute has standing to make that claim. However the issue may be characterized, White, J., contended for many years that a litigant whose own conduct is unprotected should not prevail on an overbreadth challenge without a showing that the statute's overbreadth is "real and substantial." After much litigation, White, J., finally prevailed. The "substantial" overbreadth doctrine now burdens all litigants who argue that a statute should be declared overbroad when their own conduct would otherwise be unprotected. *Brockett v. Spokane Arcades, Inc.; New York v. Ferber,* Sec. 1, V, A infra.

Less clear are the circumstances in which a litigant whose conduct *is* protected can go beyond a claim that the statute is unconstitutional "as applied." Again, litigants are always free to argue that their own conduct is protected. Moreover, the Court has stated that "[t]here is no reason to limit challenges to case-by-case 'as applied' challenges when the statute [in] all its applications falls short of constitutional demands." *Secretary of State of Maryland v. Joseph H. Munson Co.,* 467 U.S. 947 (1984). How far beyond this the Court will go is unclear. In *Brockett v. Spokane Arcades, Inc.,* Sec. 1, III, B supra, it referred to the "normal rule that partial, rather than facial invalidation" of statutes is to be preferred and observed that: "[A]n individual whose own speech or expressive conduct may validly be prohibited or sanctioned is permitted to challenge a statute on its face because it also threatens others not before the court—those who desire to engage in legally protected expression but who may refrain from doing so rather than risk prosecution or undertake to have the law declared partially invalid. If the overbreadth is 'substantial,' the law may not be enforced against anyone, including the party before the court, until it is narrowed to reach only unprotected activity, whether by legislative action or by judicial construction or partial invalidation.

"It is otherwise where the parties challenging the statute are those who desire to engage in protected speech that the overbroad statute purports to punish, or who seek to publish both protected and unprotected material. There is then no want of a proper party to challenge the statute, no concern that an attack on the statute will be unduly delayed or protected speech discouraged. The statute may forthwith be declared invalid to the extent that it reaches too far, but otherwise left intact."

Brockett takes the view that it must give standing to the otherwise unprotected to raise an overbreadth challenge, in order to secure the rights of those whose speech should be protected. But it sees no purpose in giving standing to the protected in order to secure rights for those whose speech should not be protected. This position is not without its ironies. In some circumstances, a litigant whose speech is unprotected will be in a better position than one whose speech is protected, at least if the litigant's goal is completely to stop enforcement of a statute.

Finally, what of the cases when it is uncertain whether the litigant's speech is protected? Should courts consider as applied attacks before proceeding to overbreadth attacks? *Board of Trustees v. Fox,* Sec. 3, II infra, declared it "not the usual judicial practice" and "generally undesirable" to proceed to an overbreadth challenge without first determining whether the statute would be valid as applied. Yet the Court has frequently (see, e.g., Sec. 1, IV, C infra (fighting words cases; *Jews For Jesus*)) declared statutes overbroad without an as applied determination. The Court has yet systematically to detail the considerations relevant to separating the "usual" judicial practice from the unusual.

The issues with respect to vagueness challenges are similar. White, J., maintained that vagueness challenges should be confined to "as applied" attacks unless a statute were vague in all of its applications. Accordingly, if a statute clearly proscribed the conduct of a particular defendant, to allow that defendant to challenge a statute for vagueness would in his view have been "to confound vagueness and overbreadth." *Kolender v. Lawson,* 461 U.S. 352 (1983) (White, J., dissenting). In response, the Court stated that a facial attack upon a statute need not depend upon a showing of vagueness in all of a statute's applications: "[W]e permit a facial challenge if a law reaches 'a substantial amount of constitutionally protected conduct,'" *Kolender.* Moreover, the Court has previously allowed litigants to raise the vagueness issue "even though there is no uncertainty about the impact of the ordinances on their own rights." *Young.* But see, e.g., *Broadrick v. Oklahoma,* Sec. 1, VI, A infra, in which White, J., writing for the Court suggested that standing to raise the vagueness argument should not be permitted in this situation.

Much less clear are the circumstances in which litigants whose conduct is *not* clearly covered by a statute can go beyond an "as applied" attack. One approach would be to apply the same rule to all litigants, e.g., allowing total invalidation of statutes upon a showing of a "substantial" vagueness. In *Kolender,* the Court made no determination whether the statute involved was vague as to the defendant's own conduct; arguably, the opinion implied that it made no difference. Another approach would analogize to the approach suggested in *Brockett* for overbreadth challenges. Thus, a court might refrain from total invalidation of a statute and confine itself to striking the vague part insofar as the vague part seems to cover protected speech, leaving the balance of the statute intact. *Kolender* itself recites that the Court has "traditionally regarded vagueness and overbreadth as logically related and similar doctrines," but the Court's attitudes toward vagueness remain unclear. The questions of what standards should govern challenges to statutes that go beyond the facts before the Court, who should be able to raise the challenges, and under what circumstances have not been systematically and consistently addressed.

IV. "FIGHTING WORDS," OFFENSIVE WORDS AND HOSTILE AUDIENCES

A.   FIGHTING WORDS

CHAPLINSKY v. NEW HAMPSHIRE, 315 U.S. 568 (1942): In the course of proselytizing on the streets, appellant, a Jehovah's Witness, denounced organized religion. Despite the city marshal's warning to "go slow" because his listeners were upset with his attacks on religion, appellant continued and a disturbance occurred. At this point, a police officer led appellant toward the police station, without arresting him. While en route, appellant again encountered the city marshal who had previously admonished him. Appellant then said to the marshal (he claimed, but the marshal denied, in response to the marshal's cursing him): "You are a God damned racketeer" and "a damned Fascist and the whole government of Rochester are Fascists or agents of Fascists."**a** He was convicted of violating a state statute forbidding anyone to address "any offensive, derisive or annoying word to any other person who is lawfully in any [public place] [or] call[ing] him by any offensive or derisive name." The Court, per MURPHY, J., upheld the conviction:

"There are certain well-defined and narrowly limited classes of speech, the prevention and punishment of which have never been thought to raise any Constitutional problem. These include the lewd and obscene, the profane, the libelous, and the insulting or 'fighting' words—those which by their very utterance inflict injury or tend to incite an immediate breach of the peace. [S]uch utterances are no essential part of any exposition of ideas, and are of such slight social value as a step to truth that any benefit that may be derived from them is clearly outweighed by the social interest in order and morality. * * *

"On the authority of its earlier decisions, the state court declared that the statute's purpose was to preserve the public peace, no words being 'forbidden except such as have a direct tendency to cause acts of violence by the person to whom, individually, the remark is addressed'. It was further said: 'The word "offensive" is not to be defined in terms of what a particular addressee thinks. [The] test is what men of common intelligence would understand would be words likely to cause an average addressee to fight. [The] English language has a number of words and expressions which by general consent are "fighting words" when said without a disarming smile. [Such] words, as ordinary men know, are likely to cause a fight. So are threatening, profane or obscene revilings. Derisive and annoying words can be taken as coming within the purview of the statute as heretofore interpreted only when they have this characteristic of plainly tending to excite the addressee to a breach of the peace. [The] statute, as construed, does no more than prohibit the face-to-face words plainly likely to cause a breach of the peace by the addressee, words whose speaking constitute a breach of the peace by the speaker—including "classical fighting words", words in current use less "classical" but equally likely to cause violence, and other disorderly words, including profanity, obscenity and threats.'

"[A] statute punishing verbal acts, carefully drawn so as not unduly to impair liberty of expression, is not too vague for a criminal law. * * *8

"Nor can we say that the application of the statute to the facts disclosed by the record substantially or unreasonably impinges upon the privilege of free speech. Argument is unnecessary to demonstrate that the appellations 'damn

---

a. The Supreme Court's version of the facts is sanitized. Bowering, the city marshall, stood by as a companion named Bowman punched Chaplinsky and later used a flagstaff as a spear in an effort to impale him. Without intervention from Bowering, the crowd demanded that Chaplinsky salute the flag and assaulted him when he refused. When Chaplinsky asked Bowering to arrest those who had committed violence against him, Bowering called him a damned bastard and demanded that he come along. Then Chaplinsky responded with epithets.

8. [Even] if the interpretative gloss placed on the statute by the court below be disregarded, the statute had been previously construed as intended to preserve the public peace by punishing conduct, the direct tendency of which was to provoke the person against whom it was directed to acts of violence.

Appellant need not therefore have been a prophet to understand what the statute condemned.

racketeer' and 'damn Fascist' are epithets likely to provoke the average person to retaliation, and thereby cause a breach of the peace.

"The refusal of the state court to admit evidence of provocation and evidence bearing on the truth or falsity of the utterances is open to no Constitutional objection. Whether the facts sought to be proved by such evidence constitute a defense to the charge or may be shown in mitigation are questions for the state court to determine. Our function is fulfilled by a determination that the challenged statute, on its face and as applied, does not contravene the Fourteenth Amendment."

B. HOSTILE AUDIENCES

TERMINIELLO v. CHICAGO, 337 U.S. 1 (1949): Petitioner "vigorously, if not viciously" criticized various political and racial groups and condemned "a surging, howling mob" gathered in protest outside the auditorium in which he spoke. He called his adversaries "slimy scum," "snakes," "bedbugs," and the like. Those inside the hall could hear those on the outside yell, "Fascists, Hitlers!" The crowd outside tried to tear the clothes off those who entered. About 28 windows were broken; stink bombs were thrown. But in charging the jury, the trial court defined "breach of the peace" to include speech which "stirs the public to anger, *invites dispute,* [or] brings about a condition of unrest (emphasis added)." A 5–4 majority, per DOUGLAS, J., struck down the breach of peace ordinance as thus construed: "[A] function of free speech under our system of government is to invite dispute. It may indeed best serve its high purpose when it induces a condition of unrest, creates dissatisfaction with conditions as they are, or even stirs people to anger. [That] is why freedom of speech, though not absolute, *Chaplinsky,* is nevertheless protected against censorship or punishment, unless shown likely to produce a clear and present danger of a serious substantive evil that rises far above public inconvenience, annoyance, or unrest."

FEINER v. NEW YORK, 340 U.S. 315 (1951): Petitioner made a speech on a street corner in a predominantly black residential section of Syracuse, N.Y. A crowd of 75 to 80 persons, black and white, gathered around him, and several pedestrians had to go into the highway in order to pass by. A few minutes after he started, two police officers arrived and observed the rest of the meeting. In the course of his speech, publicizing a meeting of the Young Progressives of America to be held that evening in a local hotel and protesting the revocation of a permit to hold the meeting in a public school auditorium, petitioner referred to the President as a "bum," to the American Legion as "a Nazi Gestapo," and to the Mayor of Syracuse as a "champagne-sipping bum" who "does not speak for the Negro people." He also indicated in an excited manner: "The Negroes don't have equal rights; they should rise up in arms and fight for them."

These statements "stirred up a little excitement." One man indicated that if the police did not get that "S * * * O * * * B* * *" off the stand, he would do so himself. There was not yet a disturbance, but according to police testimony "angry muttering and pushing." In the words of the arresting officer whose testimony was accepted by the trial judge, he "stepped in to prevent it from resulting in a fight." After disregarding two requests to stop speaking, petitioner was arrested and convicted for disorderly conduct. The Court, per VINSON, C.J., affirmed: "The language of *Cantwell* is appropriate here. '[Nobody would] suggest that the principle of freedom of speech sanctions incitement to riot or that religious liberty connotes the privilege to exhort others to physical attack upon those belonging to another sect. When clear and present danger of riot, disorder, interference with traffic upon the public street or other immediate threat to public safety, peace, or order, appears, the power of the State to prevent or punish is obvious.'

"[It] is one thing to say that the police cannot be used as an instrument for the suppression of unpopular views, and another to say that, when as here the speaker passes the bounds of argument or persuasion and undertakes incitement to riot, they are powerless to prevent a breach of the peace. Nor in this case can we condemn the considered judgment of three New York courts approving the means which the police, faced with a crisis, used in the exercise of their power and duty to preserve peace and order."

BLACK, J., dissented: "The Court's opinion apparently rests on this reasoning: The policeman, under the circumstances detailed, could reasonably conclude that serious fighting or even riot was imminent; therefore he could stop petitioner's speech to prevent a breach of peace; accordingly, it was 'disorderly conduct' for petitioner to continue speaking in disobedience of the officer's request. As to the existence of a dangerous situation on the street corner, it seems far-fetched to suggest that the 'facts' show any imminent threat of riot or uncontrollable disorder. It is neither unusual nor unexpected that some people at public street meetings mutter, mill about, push, shove, or disagree, even violently, with the speaker. Indeed, it is rare where controversial topics are discussed that an outdoor crowd does not do some or all of these things. Nor does one isolated threat to assault the speaker forebode disorder. Especially should the danger be discounted where, as here, the person threatening was a man whose wife and two small children accompanied him and who, so far as the record shows, was never close enough to petitioner to carry out the threat.

"Moreover, assuming that the 'facts' did indicate a critical situation, I reject the implication of the Court's opinion that the police had no obligation to protect petitioner's constitutional right to talk. The police of course have power to prevent breaches of the peace. But if, in the name of preserving order, they ever can interfere with a lawful public speaker, they first must make all reasonable efforts to protect him. Here the policemen did not even pretend to try to protect petitioner. According to the officers' testimony, the crowd was restless but there is no showing of any attempt to quiet it; pedestrians were forced to walk into the street, but there was no effort to clear a path on the sidewalk; one person threatened to assault petitioner but the officers did nothing to discourage this when even a word might have sufficed. Their duty was to protect petitioner's right to talk, even to the extent of arresting the man who threatened to interfere. Instead, they shirked that duty and acted only to suppress the right to speak.

"Finally, I cannot agree with the Court's statement that petitioner's disregard of the policeman's unexplained request amounted to such 'deliberate defiance' as would justify an arrest or conviction for disorderly conduct. On the contrary, I think that the policeman's action was a 'deliberate defiance' of ordinary official duty as well as of the constitutional right of free speech. For at least where time allows, courtesy and explanation of commands are basic elements of good official conduct in a democratic society. Here petitioner was 'asked' then 'told' then 'commanded' to stop speaking, but a man making a lawful address is certainly not required to be silent merely because an officer directs it. Petitioner was entitled to know why he should cease doing a lawful act. Not once was he told."

Douglas, J., joined by Minton, J., dissented: "A speaker may not, of course, incite a riot any more than he may incite a breach of the peace by the use of 'fighting words'. But this record shows no such extremes. It shows an unsympathetic audience and the threat of one man to haul the speaker from the stage. It is against that kind of threat that speakers need police protection. If they do not receive it and instead the police throw their weight on the side of those who would break up the meetings, the police become the new censors of speech. Police censorship has all the vices of the censorship from city halls which we have repeatedly struck down."

———

Edwards v. South Carolina, 372 U.S. 229 (1963) reversed a breach of the peace conviction of civil rights demonstrators who refused to disperse within 15 minutes of a police command. The Court maintained that the 200 to 300 onlookers did not threaten violence and that the police protection was ample. It described the situation as a "far cry from [*Feiner*]." Clark, J., dissenting, pointed to the racially charged atmosphere ("200 youthful Negro demonstrators were being aroused to a 'fever pitch' before a crowd of some 300 people who undoubtedly were hostile.") and concluded that city officials in good faith believed that disorder and violence were imminent.

C. OFFENSIVE WORDS

COHEN v. CALIFORNIA

403 U.S. 15, 91 S.Ct. 1780, 29 L.Ed.2d 284 (1971).

Justice Harlan delivered the opinion of the Court.

[Defendant was convicted of violating that part of a general California disturbing-the-peace statute which prohibits "maliciously and willfully disturb[ing] the peace or quiet of any neighborhood or person" by "offensive conduct." He had worn a jacket bearing the plainly visible words "Fuck the Draft" in a Los Angeles courthouse corridor, where women and children were present. He testified that he did so as a means of informing the public of the depth of his feelings against the Vietnam War and the draft. He did not engage in, nor threaten, any violence, nor was anyone who saw him violently aroused. Nor was there any evidence that he uttered any sound prior to his arrest. In affirming, the California Court of Appeal construed "offensive conduct" to mean "behavior which has a tendency to provoke *others* to acts of violence or to in turn disturb the peace" and held that the state had proved this element because it was "reasonably foreseeable" that defendant's conduct "might cause others to rise up to commit a violent act against [him] or attempt to forceably remove his jacket."]

In order to lay hands on the precise issue which this case involves, it is useful first to canvass various matters which this record does *not* present.

The conviction quite clearly rests upon the asserted offensiveness of the *words* Cohen used to convey his message to the public. The only "conduct" which the State sought to punish is the fact of communication. Thus, we deal here with a conviction resting solely upon "speech," not upon any separately identifiable conduct which allegedly was intended by Cohen to be perceived by others as expressive of particular views but which, on its face, does not necessarily convey any message and hence arguably could be regulated without effectively repressing Cohen's ability to express himself. Cf. *United States v. O'Brien* [Sec. 2 infra].

Further, the State certainly lacks power to punish Cohen for the underlying content of the message the inscription conveyed. At least so long as there is no showing of an intent to incite disobedience to or disruption of the draft, Cohen could not, consistently with the First and Fourteenth Amendments, be punished for asserting the evident position on the inutility or immorality of the draft his jacket reflected. *Yates*.

Appellant's conviction, then, rests squarely upon his exercise [of] "freedom of speech" [and] can be justified, if at all, only as a valid regulation of the manner in which he exercised that freedom, not as a permissible prohibition on the substantive message it conveys. This does not end the inquiry, of course, for the First and Fourteenth Amendments have never been thought to give absolute protection to every individual to speak whenever or wherever he pleases, or to use any form of address in any circumstances that he chooses. In this vein, too, however, we think it important to note that several issues typically associated with such problems are not presented here.

In the first place, Cohen was tried under a statute applicable throughout the entire State. Any attempt to support this conviction on the ground that the statute seeks to preserve an appropriately decorous atmosphere in the courthouse where Cohen was arrested must fail in the absence of any language in the statute that would have put appellant on notice that certain kinds of otherwise permissible speech or conduct would nevertheless, under California law, not be tolerated in certain places. No fair reading of the phrase "offensive conduct" can be said sufficiently to inform the ordinary person that distinctions between certain locations are thereby created.3

In the second place, as it comes to us, this case cannot be said to fall within those relatively few categories of instances where prior decisions have established the power of government to deal more comprehensively with certain forms of individual expression simply upon a showing that such a form was employed. This is not, for example, an obscenity case. Whatever else may be necessary to give rise to the States' broader power to prohibit obscene expression, such expression must be, in some significant way, erotic. *Roth*. It cannot plausibly be maintained that this vulgar allusion to the Selective Service System would conjure up such psychic stimulation in anyone likely to be confronted with Cohen's crudely defaced jacket.

This Court has also held that the States are free to ban the simple use, without a demonstration of additional justifying circumstances, of so-called "fighting words," those personally abusive epithets which, when addressed to the ordinary citizen, are, as a matter of common knowledge, inherently likely to provoke violent reaction. *Chaplinsky*. While the four-letter word displayed by Cohen in relation to the draft is not uncommonly employed in a personally provocative fashion, in this instance it was clearly not "directed to the person of the hearer." No individual actually or likely to be present could reasonably have regarded the words on appellant's jacket as a direct personal insult. Nor do we have here an instance of the exercise of the State's police power to prevent a speaker from intentionally provoking a given group to hostile reaction. Cf. *Feiner*; *Terminiello*. There is, as noted above, no showing that anyone who saw Cohen was in fact violently aroused or that appellant intended such a result.

3. It is illuminating to note what transpired when Cohen entered a courtroom in the building. He removed his jacket and stood with it folded over his arm. Meanwhile, a policeman sent the presiding judge a note suggesting that Cohen be held in contempt of court. The judge declined to do so and Cohen was arrested by the officer only after he emerged from the courtroom.

[T]he mere presumed presence of unwitting listeners or viewers does not serve automatically to justify curtailing all speech capable of giving offense. While this Court has recognized that government may properly act in many situations to prohibit intrusion into the privacy of the home of unwelcome views and ideas which cannot be totally banned from the public dialogue, we have at the same time consistently stressed that "we are often 'captives' outside the sanctuary of the home and subject to objectionable speech." The ability of government, consonant with the Constitution, to shut off discourse solely to protect others from hearing it is, in other words, dependent upon a showing that substantial privacy interests are being invaded in an essentially intolerable manner. Any broader view of this authority would effectively empower a majority to silence dissidents simply as a matter of personal predilections.

[Given] the subtlety and complexity of the factors involved if Cohen's "speech" was otherwise entitled to constitutional protection, we do not think the fact that some unwilling "listeners" in a public building may have been briefly exposed to it can serve to justify this breach of the peace conviction where, as here, there was no evidence that persons powerless to avoid appellant's conduct did in fact object to it, and where [unlike another portion of the same statute barring the use of "vulgar, profane or indecent language within [the] hearing of women or children, in a loud and boisterous manner"], the [challenged statutory provision] evinces no concern [with] the special plight of the captive auditor, but, instead, indiscriminately sweeps within its prohibitions all "offensive conduct" that disturbs "any neighborhood or person."

Against this background, the issue flushed by this case stands out in bold relief. It is whether California can excise, as "offensive conduct," one particular scurrilous epithet from the public discourse, either upon the theory of the court below that its use is inherently likely to cause violent reaction or upon a more general assertion that the States, acting as guardians of public morality, may properly remove this offensive word from the public vocabulary.

The rationale of the California court is plainly untenable. At most it reflects an "undifferentiated fear or apprehension of disturbance [which] is not enough to overcome the right to freedom of expression." *Tinker* [Sec. 7, II infra]. We have been shown no evidence that substantial numbers of citizens are standing ready to strike out physically at whoever may assault their sensibilities with execrations like that uttered by Cohen. There may be some persons about with such lawless and violent proclivities, but that is an insufficient base upon which to erect, consistently with constitutional values, a governmental power to force persons who wish to ventilate their dissident views into avoiding particular forms of expression. The argument amounts to little more than the self-defeating proposition that to avoid physical censorship of one who has not sought to provoke such a response by a hypothetical coterie of the violent and lawless, the States may more appropriately effectuate that censorship themselves.

Admittedly, it is not so obvious that the First and Fourteenth Amendments must be taken to disable the States from punishing public utterance of this unseemly expletive in order to maintain what they regard as a suitable level of discourse within the body politic. We think, however, that examination and reflection will reveal the shortcomings of a contrary viewpoint.

[The] constitutional right of free expression is powerful medicine in a society as diverse and populous as ours. It is designed and intended to remove governmental restraints from the arena of public discussion, putting the decision as to what views shall be voiced largely into the hands of each of us, in the hope that use of such freedom will ultimately produce a more capable citizenry and more perfect polity and in the belief that no other approach would comport with the premise of individual dignity and choice upon which our political system rests.

To many, the immediate consequence of this freedom may often appear to be only verbal tumult, discord, and even offensive utterance. These are, however, within established limits, in truth necessary side effects of the broader enduring values which the process of open debate permits us to achieve. That the air may at times seem filled with verbal cacophony is, in this sense not a sign of weakness but of strength. We cannot lose sight of the fact that, in what otherwise might seem a trifling and annoying instance of individual distasteful abuse of a privilege, these fundamental societal values are truly implicated. * * *

Against this perception of the constitutional policies involved, we discern certain more particularized considerations that peculiarly call for reversal of this conviction. First, the principle contended for by the State seems inherently boundless. How is one to distinguish this from any other offensive word? Surely the State has no right to cleanse public debate to the point where it is grammatically palatable to the most squeamish among us. Yet no readily ascertainable general principle exists for stopping short of that result were we to affirm the judgment below. For, while the particular four-letter word being litigated here is perhaps more distasteful than most others of its genre, it is nevertheless often true that one man's vulgarity is another's lyric. Indeed, we think it is largely because governmental officials cannot make principled distinctions in this area that the Constitution leaves matters of taste and style so largely to the individual.

Additionally, we cannot overlook the fact, because it is well illustrated by the episode involved here, that much linguistic expression serves a dual communicative function: it conveys not only ideas capable of relatively precise, detached explication, but otherwise inexpressible emotions as well. In fact, words are often chosen as much for their emotive as their cognitive force. We cannot sanction the view that the Constitution, while solicitous of the cognitive content of individual speech, has little or no regard for that emotive function which, practically speaking, may often be the more important element of the overall message sought to be communicated. * * *

Finally, and in the same vein, we cannot indulge the facile assumption that one can forbid particular words without also running a substantial risk of suppressing ideas in the process. Indeed, governments might soon seize upon the censorship of particular words as a convenient guise for banning the expression of unpopular views. We have been able [to] discern little social benefit that might result from running the risk of opening the door to such grave results.

It is, in sum, our judgment that, absent a more particularized and compelling reason for its actions, the State may not, consistently with the First and Fourteenth Amendments, make the simple public display here involved of this single four-letter expletive a criminal offense. * * *

[BLACKMUN, J., joined by Burger, C.J., and Black, J., dissented for two reasons: (1) "Cohen's absurd and immature antic [was] mainly conduct and little speech" and the case falls "well within the sphere of *Chaplinsky*"; (2) although it declined to review the state court of appeals' decision in *Cohen,* the California Supreme Court subsequently narrowly construed the breach-of-the-peace statute in another case and *Cohen* should be remanded to the California Court of Appeal in the light of this subsequent construction. White, J., concurred with the dissent on the latter ground.]

A series of cases in the early 1970s reversed convictions involving abusive language. *Gooding v. Wilson,* 405 U.S. 518 (1972), invalidated a Georgia ordinance primarily because it had been previously applied to "utterances where there was no likelihood that the person addressed would make an immediate violent response." *Lewis v. New Orleans*, 415 U.S. 130 (1974), ruled that vulgar or offensive speech was protected under the First Amendment. Because the statute punished "opprobrious language," it was deemed by the Court to embrace words that do not " 'by their very utterance inflict injury or tend to invite an immediate breach of the peace.' "

Although *Gooding* seemed to require a danger of immediate violence, *Lewis* recited that infliction of injury was sufficient. Dissenting in both cases, BURGER, C.J., and Blackmun and Rehnquist, JJ., complained that the majority invoked vagueness and overbreadth analysis "indiscriminately without regard to the nature of the speech in question, the possible effect the statute or ordinance has upon such speech, the importance of the speech in relation to the exposition of ideas, or the purported or asserted community interest in preventing that speech." The dissenters focused upon the facts of the cases (e.g., Gooding to a police officer: "White son of a bitch, I'll kill you," "You son of a bitch, I'll choke you to death," and "You son of a bitch, if you ever put your hands on me again, I'll cut you to pieces."). They complained that the majority had relegated the facts to "footnote status, conveniently distant and in less disturbing focus." In *Gooding, Lewis,* and the other cases, POWELL, J., insisted upon the importance of context in decision making. Dissenting in *Rosenfeld v. New Jersey,* 408 U.S. 901 (1972), he suggested that *Chaplinsky* be extended to the "wilful use of scurrilous language calculated to offend the sensibilities of an unwilling audience"; concurring in *Lewis,* he maintained that allowing prosecutions for offensive language directed at police officers invited law enforcement abuse. Finally, he suggested in *Rosenfeld* that whatever the scope of the "fighting words" doctrine, overbreadth analysis was inappropriate in such cases. He doubted that such statutes deter others from exercising First Amendment rights.

V. OWNERSHIP OF SPEECH

Former President Ford had contracted with Harper & Row and Readers Digest to publish his memoirs and granted them the right to license prepublication excerpts concentrating on his pardon of former President Nixon. Some weeks before a licensed article in Time was to appear, an unknown person presented the editor of The Nation with an unauthorized copy of the 200,000 word Ford manuscript from which the editor wrote a 2,250 word article entitled, "The Ford Memoirs—Behind the Nixon Pardon." The article included 26 verbatim quotations totaling 300 words of Ford's copyrighted expression and was timed to scoop Time. Accordingly, Time cancelled its article and refused to pay the publishers the remaining half of its $25,000 contract price.

In defense against the publishers' copyright claim, The Nation maintained that its publication was protected by the fair use provision of the Copyright Revision Act of 1976, 17 U.S.C. § 107 and by the First Amendment. HARPER & ROW v. NATION ENTERPRISES, 471 U.S. 539 (1985), per O'CONNOR, J., concluded that neither defense was viable and that the fair use provision properly accommodated the relevant First Amendment interests: "Article I, § 8, of the Constitution provides that: 'The Congress shall have Power * * * to Promote the Progress of Science and useful Arts, by securing for limited Times to Authors and Inventors the exclusive Right to their respective Writings and Discoveries.' '[This] limited grant is a means by which an important public purpose may be achieved.

It is intended to motivate the creative activity of authors and inventors by the provision of a special reward, and to allow the public access to the products of their genius after the limited period of exclusive control has expired.' The monopoly created by copyright thus rewards the individual author in order to benefit the public. This principle applies equally to works of fiction and nonfiction. The book at issue here, for example, was two years in the making, and began with a contract giving the author's copyright to the publishers in exchange for their services in producing and marketing the work. In preparing the book, Mr. Ford drafted essays and word portraits of public figures and participated in hundreds of taped interviews that were later distilled to chronicle his personal viewpoint. It is evident that the monopoly granted by copyright actively served its intended purpose of inducing the creation of new material of potential historical value.

"Section 106 of the Copyright Act confers a bundle of exclusive rights to the owner of the copyright. [T]hese rights—to publish, copy, and distribute the author's work—vest in the author of an original work from the time of its creation. In practice, the author commonly sells his rights to publishers who offer royalties in exchange for their services in producing and marketing the author's work. The copyright owner's rights, however, are subject to certain statutory exceptions. Among these is § 107 which codifies the traditional privilege of other authors to make 'fair use' of an earlier writer's work.1 In addition, no author may copyright facts or ideas. § 102. The copyright is limited to those aspects of the work—termed 'expression'—that display the stamp of the author's originality.

"[T]here is no dispute that the unpublished manuscript of 'A Time to Heal,' as a whole, was protected by § 106 from unauthorized reproduction. Nor do respondents dispute that verbatim copying of excerpts of the manuscript's original form of expression would constitute infringement unless excused as fair use. Yet copyright does not prevent subsequent users from copying from a prior author's work those constituent elements that are not original—for example, quotations borrowed under the rubric of fair use from other copyrighted works, facts, or materials in the public domain—as long as such use does not unfairly appropriate the author's original contributions. Perhaps the controversy between the lower courts in this case over copyrightability is more aptly styled a dispute over whether The Nation's appropriation of unoriginal and uncopyrightable elements encroached on the originality embodied in the work as a whole. Especially in the realm of factual narrative, the law is currently unsettled regarding the ways in which uncopyrightable elements combine with the author's original contributions to form protected expression.

"We need not reach these issues, however, as The Nation has admitted to lifting verbatim quotes of the author's original language [constituting] some 13% of The Nation article. [To thereby] lend authenticity to its account of the forthcoming memoirs, The Nation effectively arrogated to itself the right of first publication, an important marketable subsidiary right. For the reasons set forth below, we find that this use of the copyrighted manuscript, even stripped to the

---

1. Section 107 states: "Notwithstanding the provisions of section 106, the fair use of a copyrighted work [for] purposes such as criticism, comment, news reporting, teaching (including multiple copies for classroom use), scholarship, or research, is not an infringement of copyright. In determining whether the use made of a work in any particular case is a fair use the factors to be considered shall include—

"(1) the purpose and character of the use, including whether such use is of a commercial nature or is for nonprofit educational purposes;

"(2) the nature of the copyrighted work;

"(3) the amount and substantiality of the portion used in relation to the copyrighted work as a whole; and

"(4) the effect of the use upon the potential market for or value of the copyrighted work."

verbatim quotes conceded by The Nation to be copyrightable expression, was not a fair use within the meaning of the Copyright Act.

"[The] nature of the interest at stake is highly relevant to whether a given use is fair. [The] right of first publication implicates a threshold decision by the author whether and in what form to release his work. First publication is inherently different from other § 106 rights in that only one person can be the first publisher; as the contract with Time illustrates, the commercial value of the right lies primarily in exclusivity. [Under] ordinary circumstances, the author's right to control the first public appearance of his undisseminated expression will outweigh a claim of fair use.

"Respondents, however, contend that First Amendment values require a different rule under the circumstances of this case. [Respondents] advance the substantial public import of the subject matter of the Ford memoirs as grounds for excusing a use that would ordinarily not pass muster as a fair use—the piracy of verbatim quotations for the purpose of 'scooping' the authorized first serialization. Respondents explain their copying of Mr. Ford's expression as essential to reporting the news story it claims the book itself represents. In respondents' view, not only the facts contained in Mr. Ford's memoirs, but 'the precise manner in which [he] expressed himself was as newsworthy as what he had to say.' Respondents argue that the public's interest in learning this news as fast as possible outweighs the right of the author to control its first publication.

"The Second Circuit noted, correctly, that copyright's idea/expression dichotomy 'strike[s] a definitional balance between the First Amendment and the Copyright Act by permitting free communication of facts while still protecting an author's expression.' No author may copyright his ideas or the facts he narrates.

"Respondents' theory, however, would expand fair use to effectively destroy any expectation of copyright protection in the work of a public figure. Absent such protection, there would be little incentive to create or profit in financing such memoirs and the public would be denied an important source of significant historical information. The promise of copyright would be an empty one if it could be avoided merely by dubbing the infringement a fair use 'news report' of the book. * * *

"In our haste to disseminate news, it should not be forgotten that the Framers intended copyright itself to be the engine of free expression. By establishing a marketable right to the use of one's expression, copyright supplies the economic incentive to create and disseminate ideas. * * *

"Moreover, freedom of thought and expression 'includes both the right to speak freely and the right to refrain from speaking at all.' We do not suggest this right not to speak would sanction abuse of the copyright owner's monopoly as an instrument to suppress facts. [But] 'the essential thrust of the First Amendment is to prohibit improper restraints on the *voluntary* public expression of ideas; it shields the man who wants to speak or publish when others wish him to be quiet. There is necessarily, and within suitably defined areas, a concomitant freedom *not* to speak publicly, one which serves the same ultimate end as freedom of speech in its affirmative aspect.' *Estate of Hemingway v. Random House, Inc.,* 23 N.Y.2d 341, 348, 296 N.Y.S.2d 771, 776, 244 N.E.2d 250, 255 (1968). * * *

"In view of the First Amendment protections already embodied in the Copyright Act's distinction between copyrightable expression and uncopyrightable facts and ideas, and the latitude for scholarship and comment traditionally afforded by fair use, we see no warrant for expanding the doctrine of fair use to create what amounts to a public figure exception to copyright. Whether verbatim copying from a public figure's manuscript in a given case is or is not fair must be judged according to the traditional equities of fair use."

In assessing the equities, the Court found the purpose of the article to count against fair use, noting that the publication "went beyond simply reporting uncopyrightable information" and made "a 'news event' out of its unauthorized first publication," that the publication was "commercial as opposed to non-profit," that The Nation intended to supplant the "right of first publication," and that it acted in bad faith, for it "knowingly exploited a purloined manuscript." In considering the nature of the copyrighted work, the Court found it significant not only that Ford's work was yet unpublished, but also that The Nation had focused "on the most expressive elements of the work" in a way that exceeded "that necessary to disseminate the facts" and in a "clandestine" fashion that afforded no "opportunity for creative or quality control" by the copyright holder. In evaluating the amount and substantiality of the portion used, the Court cited the district court finding that "The Nation took what was essentially the heart of the book" and pointed to the "expressive value of the excerpts and their key role in the infringing work." Finally, the Court observed that the effect of the use on the market for the copyrighted work was the most important element. It found the Time contract cancellation to be "clear cut evidence of actual damage."

BRENNAN, J., joined by White and Marshall, JJ., dissented: "When The Nation was not quoting Mr. Ford, [its] efforts to convey the historical information in the Ford manuscript did not so closely and substantially track Mr. Ford's language and structure as to constitute an appropriation of literary form.

"[The] Nation is thus liable in copyright only if the quotation of 300 words infringed any of Harper & Row's exclusive rights under § 106 of the Act. [Limiting] the inquiry to the propriety of a subsequent author's use of the copyright owner's literary form is not easy in the case of a work of history. Protection against only substantial appropriation of literary form does not ensure historians a return commensurate with the full value of their labors. The literary form contained in works like 'A Time to Heal' reflects only a part of the labor that goes into the book. It is the labor of collecting, sifting, organizing and reflecting that predominates in the creation of works of history such as this one. The value this labor produces lies primarily in the information and ideas revealed, and not in the particular collocation of words through which the information and ideas are expressed. Copyright thus does not protect that which is often of most value in a work of history and courts must resist the tendency to reject the fair use defense on the basis of their feeling that an author of history has been deprived of the full value of his or her labor. A subsequent author's taking of information and ideas is in no sense piratical because copyright law simply does not create any property interest in information and ideas.

"The urge to compensate for subsequent use of information and ideas is perhaps understandable. An inequity seems to lurk in the idea that much of the fruit of the historian's labor may be used without compensation. This, however, is not some unforeseen by-product of a statutory scheme intended primarily to ensure a return for works of the imagination. Congress made the affirmative choice that the copyright laws should apply in this way: 'Copyright does not preclude others from using the ideas or information revealed by the author's work. It pertains to the literary [form] in which the author expressed intellectual concepts.' This distinction is at the essence of copyright. The copyright laws serve as the 'engine of free expression,' only when the statutory monopoly does not choke off multifarious indirect uses and consequent broad dissemination of information and ideas. To ensure the progress of arts and sciences and the integrity of First Amendment values, ideas and information must not be freighted with claims of proprietary right.13

"In my judgment, the Court's fair use analysis has fallen to the temptation to find copyright violation based on a minimal use of literary form in order to provide compensation for the appropriation of information from a work of history."

Since news reporting is ordinarily conducted for profit and marked by attempts to "scoop" the opposition and by attempts to create "news events," Brennan, J., found the drawing of any negative implications from these factors to be inconsistent with congressional recognition in § 107 that news reporting is a prime example of fair use. He found reliance on bad faith to be equally unwarranted: "No court has found that The Nation possessed the Ford manuscript illegally or in violation of any common law interest of Harper & Row; all common law causes of action have been abandoned or dismissed in this case. Even if the manuscript had been 'purloined' by someone, nothing in this record imputes culpability to The Nation. On the basis of the record in this case, the most that can be said is that The Nation made use of the contents of the manuscript knowing the copyright owner would not sanction the use.

"[T]he Court purports to rely on [the] factual findings that The Nation had taken 'the heart of the book.' This reliance is misplaced, and would appear to be another result of the Court's failure to distinguish between information and literary form. When the District Court made this finding, it was evaluating not the quoted words at issue here but the 'totality' of the information and reflective commentary in the Ford work. The vast majority of what the District Court considered the heart of the Ford work, therefore, consisted of ideas and information The Nation was free to use. It may well be that, as a qualitative matter, most of the value of the manuscript did lie in the information and ideas the Nation used. But appropriation of the 'heart' of the manuscript in this sense is irrelevant to copyright analysis because copyright does not preclude a second author's use of information and ideas.

"At least with respect to the six particular quotes of Mr. Ford's observations and reflections about President Nixon, I agree with the Court's conclusion that The Nation appropriated some literary form of substantial quality. I do not agree, however, that the substantiality of the expression taken was clearly excessive or inappropriate to The Nation's news reporting purpose.

"Had these quotations been used in the context of a critical book review of the Ford work, there is little question that such a use would be fair use within the meaning of § 107 of the Act. The amount and substantiality of the use—in both quantitative and qualitative terms—would have certainly been appropriate to the purpose of such a use. It is difficult to see how the use of these quoted words in a news report is less appropriate.

"The Nation's publication indisputably precipitated Time's eventual cancellation. But that does not mean that The Nation's use of the 300 quoted words caused this injury to Harper & Row. Wholly apart from these quoted words, The Nation published significant information and ideas from the Ford manuscript. [If] The Nation competed with Time, the competition was not for a share of the

---

13. This congressional limitation on the scope of copyright does not threaten the production of history. That this limitation results in significant diminution of economic incentives is far from apparent. In any event non-economic incentives motivate much historical research and writing. For example, former public officials often have great incentive to "tell their side of the story." And much history is the product of academic scholarship. Perhaps most importantly, the urge to preserve the past is as old as human kind.

market in excerpts of literary form but for a share of the market in the new information in the Ford work. * * *

"Because The Nation was the first to convey the information in this case, it did perhaps take from Harper & Row some of the value that publisher sought to garner for itself through the contractual arrangement with Ford and the license to Time. Harper & Row had every right to seek to monopolize revenue from that potential market through contractual arrangements but it has no right to set up copyright [as] a shield from competition in that market because copyright does not protect information. The Nation had every right to seek to be the first to publish that information. * * *

"The Court's exceedingly narrow approach to fair use permits Harper & Row to monopolize information. This holding 'effect[s] an important extension of property rights and a corresponding curtailment in the free use of knowledge and of ideas.' The Court has perhaps advanced the ability of the historian—or at least the public official who has recently left office—to capture the full economic value of information in his or her possession. But the Court does so only by risking the robust debate of public issues that is the 'essence of self-government.' *Garrison.* The Nation was providing the grist for that robust debate. The Court imposes liability upon The Nation for no other reason than that The Nation succeeded in being the first to provide certain information to the public."

––––––––

The 1976 Copyright Act generally provided copyright protection until 50 years after an author's death. The Copyright Term Extension Act of 1998 ("CTEA") extended the term to 70 years for new and existing copyrights. ELDRED v. ASHCROFT, 537 U.S. 186 (2003), per GINSBURG, J., upheld the Act against a claim that the extended copyright protection to already existing intellectual property was unconstitutional: "Petitioners [argue] that the CTEA is a content-neutral regulation of speech that fails heightened judicial review under the First Amendment. We reject petitioners' plea for imposition of uncommonly strict scrutiny on a copyright scheme that incorporates its own speech-protective purposes and safeguards. The Copyright Clause and First Amendment were adopted close in time. This proximity indicates that, in the Framers' view, copyright's limited monopolies are compatible with free speech principles. Indeed, copyright's purpose is to *promote* the creation and publication of free expression. * * *

"In addition to spurring the creation and publication of new expression, copyright law contains built-in First Amendment accommodations. First, it distinguishes between ideas and expression and makes only the latter eligible for copyright protection. [Due] to this distinction, every idea, theory, and fact in a copyrighted work becomes instantly available for public exploitation at the moment of publication. * * *

"Second, the 'fair use' defense allows the public to use not only facts and ideas contained in a copyrighted work, but also expression itself in certain circumstances. [The] fair use defense affords considerable 'latitude for scholarship and comment,' and even for parody. The CTEA itself supplements these traditional First Amendment safeguards. First, it allows libraries, archives, and similar institutions to 'reproduce' and 'distribute, display, or perform in facsimile or digital form' copies of certain published works 'during the last 20 years of any term of copyright [for] purposes of preservation, scholarship, or research' if the work is not already being exploited commercially and further copies are unavailable at a reasonable price. Second, Title II of the CTEA, known as the Fairness in

Music Licensing Act of 1998, exempts small businesses, restaurants, and like entities from having to pay performance royalties on music played from licensed radio, television, and similar facilities. * * *

"The First Amendment securely protects the freedom to make—or decline to make—one's own speech; it bears less heavily when speakers assert the right to make other people's speeches. To the extent such assertions raise First Amendment concerns, copyright's built-in free speech safeguards are generally adequate to address them. [W]hen, as in this case, Congress has not altered the traditional contours of copyright protection, further First Amendment scrutiny is unnecessary."

BREYER, J., dissented: "The Copyright Clause and the First Amendment seek related objectives—the creation and dissemination of information. When working in tandem, these provisions mutually reinforce each other, the first serving as an 'engine of free expression,' the second assuring that government throws up no obstacle to its dissemination. At the same time, a particular statute that exceeds proper Copyright Clause bounds may set Clause and Amendment at cross-purposes, thereby depriving the public of the speech-related benefits that the Founders, through both, have promised. [The] majority [invokes] the 'fair use' exception, and it notes that copyright law itself is restricted to protection of a work's expression, not its substantive content. Neither the exception nor the restriction, however, would necessarily help those who wish to obtain from electronic databases material that is not there—say, teachers wishing their students to see albums of Depression Era photographs, to read the recorded words of those who actually lived under slavery, or to contrast, say, Gary Cooper's heroic portrayal of Sergeant York with filmed reality from the battlefield of Verdun. Such harm, and more, will occur despite the 1998 Act's exemptions and despite the other 'First Amendment safeguards' in which the majority places its trust. The statute falls outside the scope of legislative power that the Copyright Clause, read in light of the First Amendment, grants to Congress."a

VI. SHOULD NEW CATEGORIES BE CREATED?

Suppose a legislature were to outlaw speech whose dominant theme appeals to a morbid interest in violence, that is patently offensive to contemporary community standards, and that lacks serious literary, artistic, political or scientific value. Constitutional? One approach would be to contend that speech is protected unless it falls into already established categorical exceptions to First Amendment protection. Another would be to argue by analogy, e.g., if obscenity is beneath First Amendment protection, this speech should (or should not) be beneath such protection. Similarly, one could argue that exceptions to First Amendment protection has been fashioned by resort to a balancing methodology and that balancing

a. Although the majority argued that the act created incentives for the copyright holders to further invest in and disseminate their property, Breyer, J., rejoined: "This claim cannot justify this statute, however, because the rationale is inconsistent with the basic purpose of the Copyright Clause—as understood by the Framers and by this Court. The Clause assumes an initial grant of monopoly, designed primarily to encourage creation, followed by termination of the monopoly grant in order to promote dissemination of already-created works. It assumes that it is the *disappearance* of the monopoly grant, not its *perpetuation*, that will, on balance, promote the dissemination of works already in existence. This view of the Clause does not deny the empirical possibility that grant of a copyright monopoly to the heirs or successors of a long-dead author could *on occasion* help publishers resurrect the work, say, of a long-lost Shakespeare. But it does deny Congress the Copyright Clause power to base its actions primarily upon that empirical possibility—lest copyright grants become perpetual, lest on balance they restrict dissemination, lest too often they seek to bestow benefits that are solely retroactive." Stevens, J., also dissented.

the relevant interests is the right approach. Alternatively, one could proceed from a particular substantive vision of the First Amendment, such as the Meiklejohn view.

New York v. Ferber, infra, is interesting because it involves the question of whether to create a new category.

A.   HARM TO CHILDREN AND THE OVERBREADTH DOCTRINE

NEW YORK v. FERBER, 458 U.S. 747 (1982), per WHITE, J., upheld conviction of a seller of films depicting young boys masturbating, under N.Y.Penal Law § 263.15, for "promoting[a] a sexual performance," defined as "any performance [which] includes sexual conduct[b] by a child" under 16. The Court addressed the "single question": " 'To prevent the abuse of children who are made to engage in sexual conduct for commercial purposes, could the New York State Legislature, consistent with the First Amendment, prohibit the dissemination of material which shows children engaged in sexual conduct, regardless of whether such material is obscene?'[c] * * *

"The *Miller* standard, like its predecessors, was an accommodation between the state's interests in protecting the 'sensibilities of unwilling recipients' from exposure to pornographic material and the dangers of censorship inherent in unabashedly content-based laws. Like obscenity statutes, laws directed at the dissemination of child pornography run the risk of suppressing protected expression by allowing the hand of the censor to become unduly heavy. For the following reasons, however, we are persuaded that the States are entitled to greater leeway in the regulation of pornographic depictions of children.

"First. [The] prevention of sexual exploitation and abuse of children constitutes a government objective of surpassing importance. The legislative findings accompanying passage of the New York laws reflect this concern. * * *

"We shall not second-guess this legislative judgment. Respondent has not intimated that we do so. Suffice it to say that virtually all of the States and the United States have passed legislation proscribing the production of or otherwise combating 'child pornography.' The legislative judgment, as well as the judgment found in the relevant literature, is that the use of children as subjects of pornographic materials is harmful to the physiological, emotional, and mental health of the child. That judgment, we think, easily passes muster under the First Amendment.

"Second. The distribution of photographs and films depicting sexual activity by juveniles is intrinsically related to the sexual abuse of children in at least two ways. First, the materials produced are a permanent record of the children's

---

a. "Promote" was defined to include all aspects of production, distribution, exhibition and sale.

b. Sec. 263.3 defined "sexual conduct" as "actual or simulated sexual intercourse, deviate sexual intercourse, sexual bestiality, masturbation, sado-masochistic abuse, or lewd exhibition of the genitals."

c. The opinion gave the background for such legislation: "In recent years, the exploitive use of children in the production of pornography has become a serious national problem. The federal government and forty-seven States have sought to combat the problem with statutes specifically directed at the production of child pornography. At least half of such statutes do not require that the materials produced be legally obscene. Thirty-five States and the United States Congress have also passed legislation prohibiting the distribution of such materials; twenty States prohibit the distribution of material depicting children engaged in sexual conduct without requiring that the material be legally obscene. New York is one of the twenty."

participation and the harm to the child is exacerbated by their circulation. Second, the distribution network for child pornography must be closed if the production of material which requires the sexual exploitation of children is to be effectively controlled. Indeed, there is no serious contention that the legislature was unjustified in believing that it is difficult, if not impossible, to halt the exploitation of children by pursuing only those who produce the photographs and movies. While the production of pornographic materials is a low-profile, clandestine industry, the need to market the resulting products requires a visible apparatus of distribution. The most expeditious if not the only practical method of law enforcement may be to dry up the market for this material by imposing severe criminal penalties on persons selling, advertising, or otherwise promoting the product. Thirty-five States and Congress have concluded that restraints on the distribution of pornographic materials are required in order to effectively combat the problem, and there is a body of literature and testimony to support these legislative conclusions.

"[The] *Miller* standard, like all general definitions of what may be banned as obscene, does not reflect the State's particular and more compelling interest in prosecuting those who promote the sexual exploitation of children. Thus, the question under the *Miller* test of whether a work, taken as a whole, appeals to the prurient interest of the average person bears no connection to the issue of whether a child has been physically or psychologically harmed in the production of the work. Similarly, a sexual explicit depiction need not be 'patently offensive' in order to have required the sexual exploitation of a child for its production. In addition, a work which, taken on the whole, contains serious literary, artistic, political, or scientific value may nevertheless embody the hardest core of child pornography. 'It is irrelevant to the child [who has been abused] whether or not the material [has] a literary, artistic, political, or social value.' We therefore cannot conclude that the *Miller* standard is a satisfactory solution to the child pornography problem.

"Third. The advertising and selling of child pornography provides an economic motive for and is thus an integral part of the production of such materials, an activity illegal throughout the nation. 'It rarely has been suggested that the constitutional freedom for speech and press extends its immunity to speech or writing used as an integral part of conduct in violation of a valid criminal statute.' * * *

"Fourth. The value of permitting live performances and photographic reproductions of children engaged in lewd sexual conduct is exceedingly modest, if not de minimis. We consider it unlikely that visual depictions of children performing sexual acts or lewdly exhibiting their genitals would often constitute an important and necessary part of a literary performance or scientific or educational work. As the trial court in this case observed, if it were necessary for literary or artistic value, a person over the statutory age who perhaps looked younger could be utilized. * * *

"Fifth. Recognizing and classifying child pornography as a category of material outside the protection of the First Amendment is not incompatible with our earlier decisions. 'The question whether speech is, or is not protected by the First Amendment often depends on the content of the speech.' *Young v. American Mini Theatres, Inc.* [Sec. 3, I infra]. '[I]t is the content of an utterance that determines whether it is a protected epithet or [an] unprotected "fighting comment". Leaving aside the special considerations when public officials are the target, *New York Times Co. v. Sullivan,* a libelous publication is not protected by the Constitution. *Beauharnais.* [It] is not rare that a content-based classification of speech has been accepted because it may be appropriately generalized that within the confines of the given classification, the evil to be restricted so overwhelmingly outweighs the expressive interests, if any, at stake, that no process of case-by-case adjudication is required. When a definable class of material, such as that covered by § 263.15, bears so heavily and pervasively on the welfare of children engaged in its production, we think the balance of competing interests is clearly struck and that it is permissible to consider these materials as without the protection of the First Amendment.

"There are, of course, limits on the category of child pornography which, like obscenity, is unprotected by the First Amendment. As with all legislation in this sensitive area, the conduct to be prohibited must be adequately defined by the applicable state law, as written or authoritatively construed. Here the nature of the harm to be combated requires that the state offense be limited to works that *visually* depict sexual conduct by children below a specified age. The category of 'sexual conduct' proscribed must also be suitably limited and described.

"The test for child pornography is separate from the obscenity standard enunciated in *Miller,* but may be compared to it for purpose of clarity. The *Miller* formulation is adjusted in the following respects: A trier of fact need not find that the material appeals to the prurient interest of the average person; it is not required that sexual conduct portrayed be done so in a patently offensive manner; and the material at issue need not be considered as a whole. We note that the distribution of descriptions or other depictions of sexual conduct, not otherwise obscene, which do not involve live performance or photographic or other visual reproduction of live performances, retains First Amendment protection. As with obscenity laws, criminal responsibility may not be imposed without some element of scienter on the part of the defendant. * * *

"It remains to address the claim that the New York statute is unconstitutionally overbroad because it would forbid the distribution of material with serious literary, scientific, or educational value or material which does not threaten the harms sought to be combated by the State. * * *

"The traditional rule is that a person to whom a statute may constitutionally be applied may not challenge that statute on the ground that it may conceivably be applied unconstitutionally to others in situations not before the Court. *Broadrick v. Oklahoma,* 413 U.S. 601 (1973). In *Broadrick,* we recognized that this rule reflects two cardinal principles of our constitutional order: the personal nature of constitutional rights and prudential limitations on constitutional adjudication.[20] [By] focusing on the factual situation before us, and similar cases necessary for development of a constitutional rule,[21] we face 'flesh-and-blood' legal problems with data 'relevant and adequate to an informed judgment.' This practice also fulfills a valuable institutional purpose: it allows state courts the opportunity to construe a law to avoid constitutional infirmities.

"What has come to be known as the First Amendment overbreadth doctrine is one of the few exceptions to this principle and must be justified by weighty countervailing policies. The doctrine is predicated on the sensitive nature of protected expression: persons whose expression is constitutionally protected may well refrain from exercising their rights for fear of criminal sanctions by a statute susceptible of application to protected expression. * * *

20. In addition to prudential restraints, the traditional rule is grounded in Art. III limits on the jurisdiction of federal courts to actual cases and controversies. * * *

21. Overbreadth challenges are only one type of facial attack. A person whose activity may be constitutionally regulated nevertheless may argue that the statute under which he is convicted or regulated is invalid on its face. See, e.g., *Terminiello.* See generally Henry Monaghan, *Overbreadth,* 1981 S.Ct.Rev. 1, 10–14.

"In *Broadrick,* we explained [that]: '[T]he plain import of our cases is, at the very least, that facial overbreadth adjudication is an exception to our traditional rules of practice and that its function, a limited one at the outset, attenuates as the otherwise unprotected behavior that it forbids the State to sanction moves from "pure speech" toward conduct and that conduct—even if expressive—falls within the scope of otherwise valid criminal laws that reflect legitimate state interests in maintaining comprehensive controls over harmful, constitutionally unprotected conduct. * * * '

"[*Broadrick*] examined a regulation involving restrictions on political campaign activity, an area not considered 'pure speech,' and thus it was unnecessary to consider the proper overbreadth test when a law arguably reaches traditional forms of expression such as books and films. As we intimated in *Broadrick,* the requirement of substantial overbreadth extended 'at the very least' to cases involving conduct plus speech. This case, which poses the question squarely, convinces us that the rationale of *Broadrick* is sound and should be applied in the present context involving the harmful employment of children to make sexually explicit materials for distribution.

"The premise that a law should not be invalidated for overbreadth unless it reaches a substantial number of impermissible applications is hardly novel.d On most occasions involving facial invalidation, the Court has stressed the embracing sweep of the statute over protected expression.26 Indeed, Justice Brennan observed in his dissenting opinion in *Broadrick*: 'We have never held that a statute should be held invalid on its face merely because it is possible to conceive of a single impermissible application, and in that sense a requirement of substantial overbreadth is already implicit in the doctrine.'

"The requirement of substantial overbreadth is directly derived from the purpose and nature of the doctrine. While a sweeping statute, or one incapable of limitation, has the potential to repeatedly chill the exercise of expressive activity by many individuals, the extent of deterrence of protected speech can be expected to decrease with the declining reach of the regulation. This observation appears equally applicable to the publication of books and films as it is to activities, such as picketing or participation in election campaigns, which have previously been categorized as involving conduct plus speech. We see no appreciable difference between the position of a publisher or bookseller in doubt as to the reach of New York's child pornography law and the situation faced by the Oklahoma state employees with respect to the State's restriction on partisan political activity.e * * *

"Applying these principles, we hold that § 263.15 is not substantially overbroad. We consider this the paradigmatic case of a state statute whose legitimate reach dwarfs its arguably impermissible applications. [While] the reach of the statute is directed at the hard core of child pornography, the Court of Appeals was understandably concerned that some protected expression, ranging from medical textbooks to pictorials in the National Geographic would fall prey to the statute.

d. Scalia, J., dissenting in *Chicago v. Morales,* 527 U.S. 41 (1999), argues that in order to avoid advisory opinions, federal courts should limit themselves to as applied attacks, but that if they insist on considering facial attacks, they should insist that a statute be unconstitutional in all its applications before declaring it unconstitutional.

26. In *Gooding v. Wilson,* the Court's invalidation of a Georgia statute making it a misdemeanor to use " 'opprobrious words or abusive language, tending to cause a breach of the peace' " followed from state judicial decisions indicating that "merely to speak words offensive to some who hear them" could constitute a "breach of the peace." * * *

e. *Brockett v. Spokane Arcades, Inc.,* Sec. 1, III, B supra, stated: "The Court of Appeals erred in holding that the *Broadrick* substantial overbreadth requirement is inapplicable where pure speech rather than conduct is at issue. *Ferber* specifically held to the contrary."

How often, if ever, it may be necessary to employ children to engage in conduct clearly within the reach of § 263.15 in order to produce educational, medical, or artistic works cannot be known with certainty. Yet we seriously doubt, and it has not been suggested, that these arguably impermissible applications of the statute amount to more than a tiny fraction of the materials within the statute's reach."f

Notes

1. *Absence of children.* SIMON & SCHUSTER, INC. v. MEMBERS OF NEW YORK STATE CRIME VICTIMS BD., 502 U.S. 105 (1991), per O'CONNOR, J., struck down a law requiring that income derived from works in which individuals admit to crime involving victims be used to compensate the victims: "[T]he State has a compelling interest in compensating victims from the fruits of the crime, but little if any interest in limiting such compensation to the proceeds of the wrongdoer's speech about the crime."g

2. *Overbreadth without a chilling effect?* Massachusetts prohibited adults from posing or exhibiting nude children for purposes of photographs, publications, or pictures, moving or otherwise. Bona fide scientific or medical purposes were excepted as were educational or cultural purposes for a bona fide school, museum, or library. Douglas Oakes was prosecuted for taking 10 color photographs of his 14–year–old stepdaughter in a state of nudity covered by the statute. The Massachusetts Supreme Judicial Court declared the statute over-broad. After certiorari was granted in MASSACHUSETTS v. OAKES, 491 U.S. 576 (1989), Massachusetts added a "lascivious intent" requirement to the statute and eliminated the exemptions. O'CONNOR, J., joined by Rehnquist, C.J., and White and Kennedy, JJ., accordingly refused to entertain the overbreadth challenge and voted to remand the case for determination of the statute's constitutionality as applied: "Because it has been repealed, the former version of [the Massachusetts law] cannot chill protected speech."

f. Brennan, J., joined by Marshall, J., agreed "with much of what is said in the Court's opinion. [This] special and compelling interest (in protecting the well-being of the State's youth), and the particular vulnerability of children, afford the State the leeway to regulate pornographic material, the promotion of which is harmful to children, even though the State does not have such leeway when it seeks only to protect consenting adults from exposure to such materials. * * * I also agree with the Court that the 'tiny fraction' of material of serious artistic, scientific or educational value that could conceivably fall within the reach of the statute is insufficient to justify striking the statute on grounds of over-breadth." But the concurrence stated that application of the statute to such materials as "do have serious artistic, scientific or medical value would violate the First Amendment."

On that issue O'Connor, J., wrote a short concurrence: "Although I join the Court's opinion, I write separately to stress that the Court does not hold that New York must except 'material with serious literary, scientific or educational value' from its statute. The Court merely holds that, even if the First Amendment shelters such material, New York's current statute is not sufficiently overbroad to support respondent's facial attack. The compelling interests identified in today's opinion suggest that the Constitution might in fact permit New York to ban knowing distribution of works depicting minors engaged in explicit sexual conduct, regardless of the social value of the depictions. For example, a 12–year–old child photographed while masturbating surely suffers the same psychological harm whether the community labels the photograph 'edifying' or 'tasteless.' The audience's appreciation of the depiction is simply irrelevant to New York's asserted interest in protecting children from psychological, emotional, and mental harm."

Stevens, J., also concurred in the judgment in a short opinion that noted his conclusion that the films in the case were not entitled to First Amendment protection, and his view that overbreadth analysis should be avoided by waiting until the hypothetical case actually arises.

Blackmun, J., concurred in the result without opinion.

g. Kennedy, J., concurring, would have stricken the statute without reference to the compelling state interest test which he condemned as ad hoc balancing. Blackmun, J., also concurred. Thomas, J., did not participate.

SCALIA, J., joined by Blackmun, Brennan, Marshall, and Stevens, JJ., disagreed:h "It seems to me strange judicial theory that a conviction initially invalid can be resuscitated by postconviction alteration of the statute under which it was obtained. [Even as a policy matter, the] overbreadth doctrine serves to protect constitutionally legitimate speech not merely *ex post,* that is, after the offending statute is enacted, but also *ex ante,* that is, when the legislature is contemplating what sort of statute to enact. If the promulgation of overbroad laws affecting speech was cost free[,] if *no* conviction of constitutionally proscribable conduct would be lost, so long as the offending statute was narrowed before the final appeal—then legislatures would have significantly reduced incentive to stay within constitutional bounds in the first place. [More] fundamentally, however, [it] seems to me that we are only free to pursue policy objectives through the modes of action traditionally followed by the courts and by the law. [I] have heard of a voidable contract, but never of a voidable law. The notion is bizarre."

3. ***How substantial is substantial overbreadth?*** Five justices addressed the overbreadth question in *Oakes,* but the substantive issue was not resolved. BRENNAN, J., joined by Marshall and Stevens, JJ., objected that the statute would make it criminal for parents "to photograph their infant children or toddlers in the bath or romping naked on the beach." More generally, he argued that the First Amendment "blocks the prohibition of nude posing by minors in connection with the production of works of art not depicting lewd behavior. [Many] of the world's great artists—Degas, Renoir, Donatello, to name but a few—have worked from models under 18 years of age, and many acclaimed photographs have included nude or partially clad minors."

SCALIA, J., joined by Blackmun, J., disagreed: "[G]iven the known extent of the kiddie-porn industry[,] I would estimate that the legitimate scope [of the statute] vastly exceeds the illegitimate. [Even] assuming that proscribing artistic depictions of preadolescent genitals and postadolescent breasts is impermissible,2 the body of material that would be covered is, as far as I am aware, insignificant compared with the lawful scope of the statute. That leaves the family photos. [Assuming] that it is unconstitutional (as opposed to merely foolish) to prohibit such photography, I do not think it so common as to make the statute *substantially* overbroad. [My] perception differs, for example, from Justice Brennan's belief that there is an 'abundance of baby and child photographs taken every day' depicting genitals."

4. ***Digital child pornography.*** The Child Pornography Act of 1996 (the "CPPA") in addition to outlawing child pornography involving minors, extends its coverage to prohibit images that "appear to be, of a minor engaging in sexually explicit conduct" or marketed in a way that "conveys the impression" that it depicts a "minor engaging in sexually explicit conduct." ASHCROFT v. FREE SPEECH COALITION, 535 U.S. 234 (2002), per KENNEDY, J., declared these

h. Although these five justices agreed that the overbreadth challenge should be entertained, they divided on the merits of the challenge. Scalia, J., joined by Blackmun, J., found no merit in the overbreadth claim (see note 5 infra) and voted to reverse and to remand for determination of the statute's constitutionality as applied. The three remaining justices (see note 5 infra) agreed with the overbreadth challenge and voted to affirm the judgment below. O'Connor, J.'s opinion, therefore, became the plurality opinion, and the Court's judgment was to vacate the judgment below and to remand. In the end, six justices voted against the overbreadth challenge: four because it was moot; two because it did not meet the requirement of substantial overbreadth.

2. [Most] adults, I expect, would not hire themselves out as nude models, whatever the intention of the photographer or artist, and however unerotic the pose. There is no cause to think children are less sensitive. It is not unreasonable, therefore, for a State to regard parents' using (or permitting the use) of their children as nude models, or other adults' use of consenting minors, as a form of child exploitation.

provisions to be unconstitutional: "The CPPA [extends] to images that appear to depict a minor engaging in sexually explicit activity without regard to the *Miller* requirements. [T]he Government says that the possibility of producing images by using computer imaging makes it very difficult for it to prosecute those who produce pornography by using real children. Experts, we are told, may have difficulty in saying whether the pictures were made by using real children or by using computer imaging. The necessary solution, the argument runs, is to prohibit both kinds of images. The argument, in essence, is that protected speech may be banned as a means to ban unprotected speech. This analysis turns the First Amendment upside down. The Government may not suppress lawful speech as the means to suppress unlawful speech."i

THOMAS, J., concurred: "In my view, the Government's most persuasive asserted interest [is] the prosecution rationale that persons who possess and disseminate pornographic images of real children may escape conviction by claiming that the images are computer-generated, thereby raising a reasonable doubt as to their guilt. At this time, however, the Government asserts only that defendants raise such defenses, not that they have done so successfully. In fact, the Government points to no case in which a defendant has been acquitted based on a computer-generated images defense. While this speculative interest cannot support the broad reach of the CPPA, technology may evolve to the point where it becomes impossible to enforce actual child pornography laws because the Government cannot prove that certain pornographic images are of real children. * * *

"The Court suggests that the Government's interest in enforcing prohibitions against real child pornography cannot justify prohibitions on virtual child pornography, because 'this analysis turns the First Amendment upside down.' [But] if technological advances thwart prosecution of unlawful speech, the Government may well have a compelling interest in barring or otherwise regulating some narrow category of lawful speech in order to enforce effectively laws against pornography made through the abuse of real children."

O'CONNOR, J., concurring in part and dissenting in part, agreed that the act's attempt to ban sexually explicit images of adults that appear to be children was overbroad, but, in a portion of her opinion joined by Rehnquist, C.J., and Scalia, J., she argued that the prohibitions of computer generated sexually explicit images appearing to be children or conveying that impression were constitutional: "[D]efendants indicted for the production, distribution, or possession of actual-child pornography may evade liability by claiming that the images attributed to them are in fact computer-generated. Respondents may be correct that no defendant has successfully employed this tactic. But, given the rapid pace of advances in computer-graphics technology, the Governments concern is reasonable. Computer-generated images lodged with the Court bear a remarkable likeness to actual human beings. [T]his Court's cases do not require Congress to wait for harm to occur before it can legislate against it.

"The Court concludes that the CPPAs ban on virtual-child pornography is overbroad. The basis for this holding is unclear. [Respondents] provide no examples of films or other materials that are wholly computer-generated and contain images that 'appea[r] to be' of minors engaging in indecent conduct, but that have serious value or do not facilitate child abuse."

---

i. In overthrowing the "conveys the impression provision," Kennedy, J., argued that it applied to a substantial amount of material that could not be reached by anti-pandering obscenity law and wrongfully proscribed possession of material that was distributed in a manner conveying a false impression even when the possessor knew the material was mislabeled.

REHNQUIST, C.J., joined in part by Scalia, J.,j dissenting, would have construed the statute to apply to "visual depictions of youthful looking adult actors engaged in actual sexual activity; mere suggestions of sexual activity, such as youthful looking adult actors squirming under a blanket, are more akin to written descriptions than visual depictions, and thus fall outside the purview of the statute. The reference to simulated has been part of the definition of sexually explicit conduct since the statute was first passed. But the inclusion of simulated conduct, alongside actual conduct, does not change the hard core nature of the image banned. The reference to simulated conduct simply brings within the statute's reach depictions of hard core pornography that are made to look genuine including the main target of the CPPA, computer generated images virtually indistinguishable from real children engaged in sexually explicit conduct. Neither actual conduct nor simulated conduct, however, is properly construed to reach depictions such as those in a film portrayal of Romeo and Juliet which are far removed from the hard core pornographic depictions that Congress intended to reach.

"To the extent the CPPA prohibits possession or distribution of materials that convey the impression of a child engaged in sexually explicit conduct, that prohibition can and should be limited to reach the sordid business of pandering which lies outside the bounds of First Amendment protection. [The] First Amendment may protect the video shopowner or film distributor who promotes material as 'entertaining' or 'acclaimed' regardless of whether the material contains depictions of youthful looking adult actors engaged in nonobscene but sexually suggestive conduct. The First Amendment does not, however, protect the panderer. Thus, materials promoted as conveying the impression that they depict actual minors engaged in sexually explicit conduct do not escape regulation merely because they might warrant First Amendment protection if promoted in a different manner. * * *

"In sum, while potentially impermissible applications of the CPPA may exist, I doubt that they would be substantial in relation to the statute's plainly legitimate sweep."

UNITED STATES v. WILLIAMS, 553 U.S. 285 (2008), per SCALIA, J., held that "offers to provide or requests to obtain child pornography are categorically excluded from the First Amendment" even if the material offered is not actually child pornography. *Free Speech Coalition* was distinguished on the ground that it "went *beyond* pandering to prohibit possession of material that could not otherwise be proscribed."k

B. HARM TO WOMEN: FEMINISM AND PORNOGRAPHY

Catharine MacKinnon and Andrea Dworkin drafted an anti-pornography ordinance that was considered in a number of jurisdictions.a Pornography was defined as the graphic sexually explicit subordination of women through pictures and/or words that also includes one or more of the following: (i) women are presented dehumanized as sexual objects, things or commodities; or (ii) women are presented as sexual objects who enjoy pain or humiliation; or (iii) women are

---

j. Scalia, J., did not join a portion of Rehnquist, C.J.'s opinion discussing the statute's legislative history.

k. Stevens, J., joined by Breyer, J., concurred. Souter, J., joined by Ginsburg, J., dissented.

a. The ordinance was first considered in Minneapolis. Different versions of the ordinance were passed in Indianapolis, Indiana and Bellingham, Washington Both versions were declared unconstitutional.

presented as sexual objects who experience sexual pleasure in being raped; or (iv) women are presented as sexual objects tied up or cut up or mutilated or bruised or physically hurt; or (v) women are presented in postures of sexual submission, servility, or display; or (vi) women's body parts—including but not limited to vaginas, breasts, or buttocks—are exhibited such that women are reduced to those parts; or (vii) women are presented as whores by nature; or (viii) women are presented as being penetrated by objects or animals; or (ix) women are presented in scenarios of degradation, injury, torture, shown as filthy or inferior, bleeding, bruised or hurt in a context that makes these conditions sexual.

The Indianapolis version of the anti-pornography civil rights ordinance was struck down in AMERICAN BOOKSELLERS ASS'N v. HUDNUT, 771 F.2d 323 (7th Cir.1985), affirmed, 475 U.S. 1001 (1986). The Seventh Circuit, per EASTER-BROOK, J., ruled that the definition of pornography infected the entire ordinance (including provisions against trafficking, coercion into pornography, forcing por-nography on a person, and assault or physical attack due to pornography) because it impermissibly discriminated on the basis of point of view: "Indianapolis enacted an ordinance defining 'pornography' as a practice that discriminates against women. * * *

"The Indianapolis ordinance does not refer to the prurient interest, to offensiveness, or to the standards of the community. It demands attention to particular depictions, not to the work judged as a whole. It is irrelevant under the ordinance whether the work has literary, artistic, political, or scientific value. The City and many amici point to these omissions as virtues. They maintain that pornography influences attitudes, and the statute is a way to alter the socializa-tion of men and women rather than to vindicate community standards of offen-siveness. And as one of the principal drafters of the ordinance has asserted, 'if a woman is subjected, why should it matter that the work has other value?' Catharine MacKinnon, *Pornography, Civil Rights, and Speech,* 20 Harv.Civ.Rts.—Civ.Lib.L.Rev. 1, 21 (1985).

"Civil rights groups and feminists have entered this case as amici on both sides. Those supporting the ordinance say that it will play an important role in reducing the tendency of men to view women as sexual objects, a tendency that leads to both unacceptable attitudes and discrimination in the workplace and violence away from it. Those opposing the ordinance point out that much radical feminist literature is explicit and depicts women in ways forbidden by the ordinance and that the ordinance would reopen old battles. It is unclear how Indianapolis would treat works from James Joyce's *Ulysses* to Homer's *Iliad;* both depict women as submissive objects for conquest and domination.

"We do not try to balance the arguments for and against an ordinance such as this. The ordinance discriminates on the ground of the content of the speech. Speech treating women in the approved way—in sexual encounters 'premised on equality' (MacKinnon, supra, at 22)—is lawful no matter how sexually explicit. Speech treating women in the disapproved way—as submissive in matters sexual or as enjoying humiliation—is unlawful no matter how significant the literary, artistic, or political qualities of the work taken as a whole. The state may not ordain preferred viewpoints in this way. The Constitution forbids the state to declare one perspective right and silence opponents. [Under] the First Amend-ment the government must leave to the people the evaluation of ideas. Bald or subtle, an idea is as powerful as the audience allows it to be. A belief may be pernicious—the beliefs of Nazis led to the death of millions, those of the Klan to the repression of millions. A pernicious belief may prevail. Totalitarian govern-ments today rule much of the planet, practicing suppression of billions and spreading dogma that may enslave others. One of the things that separates our society from theirs is our absolute right to propagate opinions that the government finds wrong or even hateful. * * *

"Under the ordinance graphic sexually explicit speech is 'pornography' or not depending on the perspective the author adopts. Speech that 'subordinates' women and also, for example, presents women as enjoying pain, humiliation, or rape, or even simply presents women in 'positions of servility or submission or display' is forbidden, no matter how great the literary or political value of the work taken as a whole. Speech that portrays women in positions of equality is lawful, no matter how graphic the sexual content. This is thought control. It establishes an 'approved' view of women, of how they may react to sexual encounters, of how the sexes may relate to each other. Those who espouse the approved view may use sexual images; those who do not, may not.

"Indianapolis justifies the ordinance on the ground that pornography affects thoughts. Men who see women depicted as subordinate are more likely to treat them so. Pornography is an aspect of dominance. It does not persuade people so much as change them. It works by socializing, by establishing the expected and the permissible. In this view pornography is not an idea; pornography is the injury.

"There is much to this perspective. Beliefs are also facts. People often act in accordance with the images and patterns they find around them. People raised in a religion tend to accept the tenets of that religion, often without independent examination. People taught from birth that black people are fit only for slavery rarely rebelled against that creed; beliefs coupled with the self-interest of the masters established a social structure that inflicted great harm while enduring for centuries. Words and images act at the level of the subconscious before they persuade at the level of the conscious. Even the truth has little chance unless a statement fits within the framework of beliefs that may never have been subjected to rational study.

"Therefore we accept the premises of this legislation. Depictions of subordination tend to perpetuate subordination. The subordinate status of women in turn leads to affront and lower pay at work, insult and injury at home, battery and rape on the streets.2 * * *

"Yet this simply demonstrates the power of pornography as speech. All of these unhappy effects depend on mental intermediation. Pornography affects how people see the world, their fellows, and social relations. If pornography is what pornography does, so is other speech. Hitler's orations affected how some Germans saw Jews. Communism is a world view, not simply a *Manifesto* by Marx and Engels or a set of speeches. Efforts to suppress communist speech in the United States were based on the belief that the public acceptability of such ideas would

2. MacKinnon's article collects empirical work that supports this proposition. The social science studies are very difficult to interpret, however, and they conflict. Because much of the effect of speech comes through a process of socialization, it is difficult to measure incremental benefits and injuries caused by particular speech. Several psychologists have found, for example, that those who see violent, sexually explicit films tend to have more violent thoughts. But how often does this lead to actual violence? National commissions on obscenity here, in the United Kingdom, and in Canada have found that it is not possible to demonstrate a direct link between obscenity and rape or exhibitionism. The opinions in *Miller* discuss the U.S. commission. See also *Report of the Committee on Obscenity and Film Censorship* 61–95 (Home Office, Her Majesty's Stationery Office, 1979); 1 *Pornography and Prostitution in Canada* 71–73, 95–103. In saying that we accept the finding that pornography as the ordinance defines it leads to unhappy consequences, we mean only that there is evidence to this effect, that this evidence is consistent with much human experience, and that as judges we must accept the legislative resolution of such disputed empirical questions.

increase the likelihood of totalitarian government. [Many] people believe that the existence of television, apart from the content of specific programs, leads to intellectual laziness, to a penchant for violence, to many other ills. The Alien and Sedition Acts passed during the administration of John Adams rested on a sincerely held belief that disrespect for the government leads to social collapse and revolution—a belief with support in the history of many nations. Most governments of the world act on this empirical regularity, suppressing critical speech. In the United States, however, the strength of the support for this belief is irrelevant. Seditious libel is protected speech unless the danger is not only grave but also imminent. See *New York Times*; cf. *Brandenburg*.

"Racial bigotry, anti-semitism, violence on television, reporters' biases—these and many more influence the culture and shape our socialization. None is directly answerable by more speech, unless that speech too finds its place in the popular culture. Yet all is protected as speech, however insidious. Any other answer leaves the government in control of all of the institutions of culture, the great censor and director of which thoughts are good for us.

"Sexual responses often are unthinking responses, and the association of sexual arousal with the subordination of women therefore may have a substantial effect. But almost all cultural stimuli provoke unconscious responses. Religious ceremonies condition their participants. Teachers convey messages by selecting what not to cover; the implicit message about what is off limits or unthinkable may be more powerful than the messages for which they present rational argument. Television scripts contain unarticulated assumptions. People may be conditioned in subtle ways. If the fact that speech plays a role in a process of conditioning were enough to permit governmental regulation, that would be the end of freedom of speech. * * *

"Much of Indianapolis's argument rests on the belief that when speech is 'unanswerable,' and the metaphor that there is a 'marketplace of ideas' does not apply, the First Amendment does not apply either. The metaphor is honored; Milton's *Aeropagitica* and John Stuart Mill's *On Liberty* defend freedom of speech on the ground that the truth will prevail, and many of the most important cases under the First Amendment recite this position. The Framers undoubtedly believed it. As a general matter it is true. But the Constitution does not make the dominance of truth a necessary condition of freedom of speech. To say that it does would be to confuse an outcome of free speech with a necessary condition for the application of the amendment.

"A power to limit speech on the ground that truth has not yet prevailed and is not likely to prevail implies the power to declare truth. At some point the government must be able to say (as Indianapolis has said): 'We know what the truth is, yet a free exchange of speech has not driven out falsity, so that we must now prohibit falsity.' If the government may declare the truth, why wait for the failure of speech? Under the First Amendment, however, there is no such thing as a false idea, *Gertz,* so the government may not restrict speech on the ground that in a free exchange truth is not yet dominant. * * *

"We come, finally, to the argument that pornography is 'low value' speech, that it is enough like obscenity that Indianapolis may prohibit it. Some cases hold that speech far removed from politics and other subjects at the core of the Framers' concerns may be subjected to special regulation. E.g., *FCC v. Pacifica Foundation* [Sec. 8, II infra]; *Young v. American Mini Theatres*; *Chaplinsky*. These cases do not sustain statutes that select among viewpoints, however. In *Pacifica* the FCC sought to keep vile language off the air during certain times. The Court held that it may; but the Court would not have sustained a regulation prohibiting scatological descriptions of Republicans but not scatological descriptions of Democrats, or any other form of selection among viewpoints.

"At all events, pornography is not low value speech within the meaning of these cases. Indianapolis seeks to prohibit certain speech because it believes this speech influences social relations and politics on a grand scale, that it controls attitudes at home and in the legislature. This precludes a characterization of the speech as low value. True, pornography and obscenity have sex in common. But Indianapolis left out of its definition any reference to literary, artistic, political, or scientific value. The ordinance applies to graphic sexually explicit subordination in works great and small.3 The Court sometimes balances the value of speech against the costs of its restriction, but it does this by category of speech and not by the content of particular works. See John Hart Ely, *Flag Desecration: A Case Study in the Roles of Categorization and Balancing in First Amendment Analysis,* 88 Harv.L.Rev. 1482 (1975); Geoffrey Stone, *Restrictions of Speech Because of its Content: The Strange Case of Subject–Matter Restrictions,* 46 U.Chi.L.Rev. 81 (1978). Indianapolis has created an approved point of view and so loses the support of these cases.

"Any rationale we could imagine in support of this ordinance could not be limited to sex discrimination. Free speech has been on balance an ally of those seeking change. Governments that want stasis start by restricting speech. Culture is a powerful force of continuity; Indianapolis paints pornography as a part of the culture of power. Change in any complex system ultimately depends on the ability of outsiders to challenge accepted views and the reigning institutions. Without a strong guarantee of freedom of speech, there is no effective right to challenge what is."**b**

C. RACIST SPEECH REVISITED: THE NAZIS

"What do you want to sell in the marketplace? What idea? The idea of murder?"

*Erna Gans, a concentration camp survivor and active leader in the Skokie B'nai B'rith.*a

COLLIN v. SMITH, 578 F.2d 1197 (7th Cir.), cert. denied, 439 U.S. 916 (1978), per PELL, J., struck down a Village of Skokie "Racial Slur" Ordinance, making it a misdemeanor to disseminate any material (defined to include "public

---

3. Indianapolis briefly argues that *Beauharnais,* which allowed a state to penalize "group libel," supports the ordinance. In *Collin v. Smith,* [Sec. 1, V, C infra], we concluded that cases such as *New York Times v. Sullivan* had so washed away the foundations of *Beauharnais* that it could not be considered authoritative. If we are wrong in this, however, the case still does not support the ordinance. It is not clear that depicting women as subordinate in sexually explicit ways, even combined with a depiction of pleasure in rape, would fit within the definition of a group libel. The well received film *Swept Away* used explicit sex, plus taking pleasure in rape, to make a political statement, not to defame. Work must be an insult or slur for its own sake to come within the ambit of *Beauharnais,* and a work need not be scurrilous at all to be pornography under the ordinance.

b. The balance of the opinion suggested ways that parts of the ordinance might be salvaged, if redrafted. It suggested, for example, that the city might forbid coerced participation in any film or in "any film containing explicit sex." If the latter were adopted, would it make a difference if the section applied to persons coerced into participation in such films without regard to whether they were forced into explicit sex scenes? Swygert, J., concurring, joined part of Easterbrook, J.'s opinion for the court, but objected both to the "questionable and broad assertions regarding how human behavior can be conditioned" and to the "advisory" opinion on how parts of the ordinance might be redrafted.

a. Quoted in Fred Friendly & Martha Elliot, *The Constitution: That Delicate Balance* 83 (1984).

display of markings and clothing of symbolic significance") promoting and inciting racial or religious hatred. The Village would apparently apply this ordinance to the display of swastikas and military uniforms by the NSPA, a "Nazi organization" which planned to peacefully demonstrate for some 20–30 minutes in front of the Skokie Village Hall.

Although there was some evidence that some individuals "might have difficulty restraining their reactions to the Nazi demonstration," the Village "does not rely on a fear of responsive violence to justify the ordinance, and does not even suggest that there will be any physical violence if the march is held. This confession takes the case out of the scope of *Brandenburg* and *Feiner*. [It] also eliminates any argument based on the fighting words doctrine of *Chaplinsky*, [which] applied only to words with a direct tendency to cause violence by the persons to whom, individually, the words were addressed."

The court rejected, inter alia, the argument that the Nazi march, with its display of swastikas and uniforms, "will create a substantive evil that it has a right to prohibit: the infliction of psychic trauma on resident holocaust survivors [some 5,000] and other Jewish residents. [The] problem with engrafting an exception on the First Amendment for such situations is that they are indistinguishable in principle from speech that 'invite[s] dispute [or] induces a condition of unrest [or] even stirs people to anger,' *Terminiello*. Yet these are among the 'high purposes' of the First Amendment. [Where,] as here, a crime is made of a silent march, attended only by symbols and not by extrinsic conduct offensive in itself, we think the words of *Street v. New York* [Sec. 2 infra] are very much on point: '[A]ny shock effect [must] be attributed to the content of the ideas expressed. [P]ublic expression of ideas may not be prohibited merely because the ideas are themselves offensive to some of their hearers.' "

Nor was the court impressed with the argument that the proposed march was "not speech, [but] rather an invasion, intensely menacing no matter how peacefully conducted" (most of Skokie's residents are Jewish): "There *need be* no captive audience, as Village residents may, if they wish, simply avoid the Village Hall for thirty minutes on a Sunday afternoon, which no doubt would be their normal course of conduct on a day when the Village Hall was not open in the regular course of business. Absent such intrusion or captivity, there is no justifiable substantial privacy interest to save [the ordinance], when it attempts, by fiat, to declare the entire Village, at all times, a privacy zone that may be sanitized from the offensiveness of Nazi ideology and symbols."

D. ANIMAL CRUELTY AND THE FLIGHT FROM NEW CATEGORIES

18 U.S.C. § 48 criminalizes knowing creation, sale, or possession of a depiction of animal cruelty, if done for commercial gain in interstate or foreign commerce. A depiction of animal cruelty is defined as one "in which a living animal is intentionally maimed, mutilated, tortured, wounded, or killed," if that conduct violates federal or state law where "the creation, sale, or possession takes place." The law exempts any depiction "that has serious religious, political, scientific, educational, journalistic, historical, or artistic value." Respondent was convicted under the statute for selling videos of dog fighting, but argued that the statute violated the First Amendment on its face. UNITED STATES v. STEVENS, per ROBERTS, C.J., rejected this contention and held that the statute was substantially overbroad, but it left room for Congress to pass a more narrowly drawn statute: "The Government's primary submission is that [the] banned

depictions of animal cruelty, as a class, are categorically unprotected by the First Amendment. We disagree.

" * * * 'From 1791 to the present,' [the] First Amendment has 'permitted restrictions upon the content of speech in a few limited areas,' and has never 'include[d] a freedom to disregard these traditional limitations.' These 'historic and traditional categories long familiar to the bar,'—including obscenity, *Roth*, defamation, *Beauharnais*, fraud, *Virginia Bd.*, incitement, *Brandenburg*, and speech integral to criminal conduct, *Giboney v. Empire Storage & Ice Co.*, 336 U.S. 490 (1949)—are 'well-defined and narrowly limited classes of speech, the prevention and punishment of which have never been thought to raise any Constitutional problem.' *Chaplinsky.*

"The Government argues that 'depictions of animal cruelty' should be added to the list. It contends that depictions of 'illegal acts of animal cruelty' that are 'made, sold, or possessed for commercial gain' necessarily 'lack expressive value,' and may accordingly 'be regulated as *unprotected* speech.' * * *

"The Government contends that 'historical evidence' about the reach of the First Amendment is not 'a necessary prerequisite for regulation today,' and that categories of speech may be exempted from the First Amendment's protection without any long-settled tradition of subjecting that speech to regulation. Instead, the Government points to Congress's 'legislative judgment that ... depictions of animals being intentionally tortured and killed [are] of such minimal redeeming value as to render [them] unworthy of First Amendment protection,' and asks the Court to uphold the ban on the same basis. The Government thus proposes that a claim of categorical exclusion should be considered under a simple balancing test: 'Whether a given category of speech enjoys First Amendment protection depends upon a categorical balancing of the value of the speech against its societal costs.'

"As a free-floating test for First Amendment coverage, that sentence is startling and dangerous. The First Amendment's guarantee of free speech does not extend only to categories of speech that survive an ad hoc balancing of relative social costs and benefits. The First Amendment itself reflects a judgment by the American people that the benefits of its restrictions on the Government outweigh the costs. * * *

"To be fair to the Government, its view did not emerge from a vacuum. As the Government correctly notes, this Court has often *described* historically unprotected categories of speech as being 'of such slight social value as a step to truth that any benefit that may be derived from them is clearly outweighed by the social interest in order and morality.' In *Ferber,* we noted that within these categories of unprotected speech, 'the evil to be restricted so overwhelmingly outweighs the expressive interests, if any, at stake, that no process of case-bycase adjudication is required,' because 'the balance of competing interests is clearly struck,' The Government derives its proposed test from these descriptions in our precedents.

"But such descriptions are just that—descriptive. They do not set forth a test that may be applied as a general matter to permit the Government to imprison any speaker so long as his speech is deemed valueless or unnecessary, or so long as an ad hoc calculus of costs and benefits tilts in a statute's favor. When we have identified categories of speech as fully outside the protection of the First Amendment, it has not been on the basis of a simple cost-benefit analysis. In *Ferber,* for example, we classified child pornography as such a category. We noted that the State of New York had a compelling interest in protecting children from abuse, and that the value of using children in these works (as opposed to simulated conduct or adult actors) was de minimis. But our decision did not rest on this 'balance of competing interests' alone. We made clear that *Ferber* presented a special case: The market for child pornography was 'intrinsically related' to the underlying abuse, and was therefore 'an integral part of the production of such materials, an activity illegal throughout the Nation.' As we noted, '[i]t rarely has been suggested that the constitutional freedom for speech and press extends its immunity to speech or writing used as an integral part of conduct in violation of a valid criminal statute.' (quoting *Giboney*). *Ferber* thus grounded its analysis in a previously recognized, long-established category of unprotected speech * * *.

"Our decisions in *Ferber* and other cases cannot be taken as establishing a freewheeling authority to declare new categories of speech outside the scope of the First Amendment. Maybe there are some categories of speech that have been historically unprotected, but have not yet been specifically identified or discussed as such in our case law. But if so, there is no evidence that 'depictions of animal cruelty' is among them. We need not foreclose the future recognition of such additional categories to reject the Government's highly manipulable balancing test as a means of identifying them."

Roberts, C.J., thereafter argued that the statute was substantially overbroad. Depictions of maiming, mutilating, and torture convey cruelty, he said, but not depictions of wounding or killing, and he did not interpret the statute to apply exclusively to instances of animal cruelty. Nor was the illegality of the underlying activity a proxy for cruelty, he suggested, because many laws involving the proper treatment of animals are not related to cruelty. And the serious value section of the statute did not resolve the overbreadth issue because depictions of hunting might be protected even if they did not have *serious* value.

"Our construction of § 48 decides the constitutional question; the Government makes no effort to defend [its constitutionality] as applied beyond crush videos and depictions of animal fighting. It argues that those particular depictions are intrinsically related to criminal conduct or are analogous to obscenity (if not themselves obscene), and that the ban on such speech is narrowly tailored to reinforce restrictions on the underlying conduct, prevent additional crime arising from the depictions, or safeguard public mores. But the Government nowhere attempts to extend these arguments to depictions of any other activities—depictions that are presumptively protected by the First Amendment but that remain subject to the criminal sanctions of § 48.

"However 'growing' and 'lucrative' the markets for crush videos and dogfighting depictions might be, they are dwarfed by the market for other depictions, such as hunting magazines and videos. We therefore need not and do not decide whether a statute limited to crush videos or other depictions of extreme animal cruelty would be constitutional. We hold only that § 48 is not so limited but is instead substantially overbroad, and therefore invalid under the First Amendment."

ALITO, J., dissented: "The Court strikes down in its entirety a valuable statute that was enacted not to suppress speech, but to prevent horrific acts of animal cruelty—in particular, the creation and commercial exploitation of 'crush videos,' a form of depraved entertainment that has no social value. [A] sample crush video, which has been lodged with the Clerk, records the following event:

'[A] kitten, secured to the ground, watches and shrieks in pain as a woman thrusts her high-heeled shoe into its body, slams her heel into the kitten's eye socket and mouth loudly fracturing its skull, and stomps repeatedly on the animal's head. The kitten hemorrhages blood, screams blindly in pain, and is ultimately left dead in a moist pile of blood-soaked hair and bone.'

"It is undisputed that the *conduct* depicted in crush videos may constitutionally be prohibited. All 50 States and the District of Columbia have enacted statutes prohibiting animal cruelty. But before the enactment of § 48 the underlying conduct depicted in crush videos was nearly impossible to prosecute. These videos, which 'often appeal to persons with a very specific sexual fetish,' were made in secret, generally without a live audience, and 'the faces of the women inflicting the torture in the material often were not shown, nor could the location of the place where the cruelty was being inflicted or the date of the activity be ascertained from the depiction.' Thus, law enforcement authorities often were not able to identify the parties responsible for the torture. * * *

"In light of the practical problems thwarting the prosecution of the creators of crush videos under state animal cruelty laws, Congress concluded that the only effective way of stopping the underlying criminal conduct was to prohibit the commercial exploitation of the videos of that conduct. And Congress' strategy appears to have been vindicated. We are told that '[b]y 2007, sponsors of § 48 declared the crush video industry dead. Even overseas Websites shut down in the wake of § 48. Now, after the Third Circuit's decision [facially invalidating the statute], crush videos are already back online.'

Alito, J., argued that the principles of *Ferber* lead easily to the conclusion that crush and dog fight videos were constitutionally unprotected though he conceded that the government interest was more significant in *Ferber*. He dissented from the Court's conclusion that the statute was overbroad: "I would hold that § 48 does not apply to depictions of hunting. First, because § 48 targets depictions of 'animal cruelty,' I would interpret that term to apply only to depictions involving acts of animal cruelty as defined by applicable state or federal law, not to depictions of acts that happen to be illegal for reasons having nothing to do with the prevention of animal cruelty. Virtually all state laws prohibiting animal cruelty either expressly define the term "animal" to exclude wildlife or else specifically exempt lawful hunting activities, so the statutory prohibition [may] reasonably be interpreted not to reach most if not all hunting depictions. * * *

Second, even if the hunting of wild animals were otherwise covered[,] I would hold that hunting depictions fall within the exception [for] depictions that have 'serious' (*i.e.*, not 'trifling') 'scientific,' 'educational,' or 'historical' value. [Thus,] it is widely thought that hunting has 'scientific' value in that it promotes conservation, 'historical' value in that it provides a link to past times when hunting played a critical role in daily life, and 'educational' value in that it furthers the understanding and appreciation of nature and our country's past and instills valuable character traits. And if hunting itself is widely thought to serve these values, then it takes but a small additional step to conclude that depictions of hunting make a non-trivial contribution to the exchange of ideas. Accordingly, I would hold that hunting depictions fall comfortably within the exception * * *.

"I do not have the slightest doubt that Congress, in enacting § 48, had no intention of restricting the creation, sale, or possession of depictions of hunting. Proponents of the law made this point clearly. [But] even if § 48 did impermissibly reach the sale or possession of depictions of hunting in a few unusual situations (for example, the sale in Oregon of a depiction of hunting with a crossbow in Virginia or the sale in Washington State of the hunting of a sharp-tailed grouse in Idaho, those isolated applications would hardly show that § 48 bans a substantial amount of protected speech."

After making similar arguments with other examples put forth by Roberts, C.J., Alito, J., concluded that the statute "has a substantial core of constitutionally permissible applications'' and that the respondent had not met his burden of demonstrating that any impermissible applications of the statute were substantial.

SECTION 2. DISTINGUISHING BETWEEN CONTENT REGULATION AND MANNER REGULATION: UNCONVENTIONAL FORMS OF COMMUNICATION

Special First Amendment questions are often said to arise by regulation of the time, place, and manner of speech as opposed to regulation of its content. But the two types of regulation are not mutually exclusive. It is possible to regulate time, place, manner, and content in the same regulation. For example, in *Linmark*, Sec. 3, II infra, the township outlawed signs (but not leaflets) advertising a house for sale (but not other advertisements or other messages) on front lawns (but not other places).

Further, the terms, manner and content are strongly contested concepts. Indeed, an issue recurring in this section is whether the regulations in question are of manner or content. To the extent this section is about manner regulation, it is not exhaustive—much comes later. Most of the cases in this section involve unconventional forms of expression. Speakers claim protection for burning draft cards, wearing armbands, mutilating flags, nude dancing, wearing long hair. Fact patterns such as these fix renewed attention on the question of how ''speech'' should be defined. It may be a nice question as to whether obscenity is not speech within the First Amendment lexicon, whether it is such speech but has been balanced into an unprotected state, or whether it is not *freedom* of speech or *the* freedom of speech. But assassinating a public figure, even to send a message, raises no First Amendment problem. Robbing a bank does not raise a free speech issue. What does? How do we decide?

The fact patterns in this section also invite scrutiny of other issues that appear in succeeding sections. Should it make a difference if the state's interest in regulating speech is unrelated to what is being said? Suppose the state's concern arises from the non-communicative impact of the speech act—from its manner. Should that distinction make a constitutional difference, and, if so, how much? These questions become more complicated because in context it is often difficult to determine what the state interest is and sometimes difficult to determine whether there is a meaningful distinction between what is said and how it is said.

Even when the distinction between the manner of the speech and the content of the speech is clear, further doctrinal complications abound. Sometimes the regulation considered by the Court is described as one regulating the ''time, place, or manner'' of speech, and the Court employs the ''time, place, or manner test'' which is itself differently phrased in different cases. On other occasions the regulation is described as having an ''incidental'' impact on freedom of speech, and the Court turns to a different test. These different tests are sometimes described by the Court as functional equivalents.

Finally, in this and succeeding sections the question arises of the extent to which freedom of speech should require special sensitivity to the methods and communications needs of the less powerful.

UNITED STATES v. O'BRIEN

391 U.S. 367, 88 S.Ct. 1673, 20 L.Ed.2d 672 (1968).

CHIEF JUSTICE WARREN delivered the opinion of the Court.

On the morning of March 31, 1966, David Paul O'Brien and three companions burned their Selective Service registration certificates on the steps of the South Boston Courthouse. A sizable crowd, including several [FBI agents] witnessed the event. Immediately after the burning, members of the crowd began attacking O'Brien [and he was ushered to safety by an FBI agent.] O'Brien stated to FBI agents that he had burned his registration certificate because of his beliefs, knowing that he was violating federal law.

[For this act, O'Brien was convicted in federal court.] He [told] the jury that he burned the certificate publicly to influence others to adopt his antiwar beliefs, as he put it, "so that other people would reevaluate their positions with Selective Service, with the armed forces, and reevaluate their place in the culture of today, to hopefully consider my position."

The indictment upon which he was tried charged that he "_estricti and knowingly did mutilate, destroy, and change by burning [his] Registration Certificate; in violation of [§ 462(b)(3) of the Universal Military Training and Service Act of 1948], amended by Congress in 1965 (adding the words italicized below), so that at the time O'Brien burned his certificate an offense was committed by any person, "who forges, alters, *knowingly destroys, knowingly mutilates,* or in any manner changes any such certificate * * *." (Italics supplied.)

[On appeal, the] First Circuit held the 1965 Amendment unconstitutional as a law abridging freedom of speech. At the time the Amendment was enacted, a regulation of the Selective Service System required registrants to keep their registration certificates in their "personal possession at all times." Wilful violations of regulations promulgated pursuant to the Universal Military Training and Service Act were made criminal by statute. The Court of Appeals, therefore, was of the opinion that conduct punishable under the 1965 Amendment was already punishable under the nonpossession regulation, and consequently that the Amendment served no valid purpose; further, that in light of the prior regulation, the Amendment must have been "directed at public as distinguished from private destruction." On this basis, the Court concluded that the 1965 Amendment ran afoul of the First Amendment by singling out persons engaged in protests for special treatment. * * *

When a male reaches the age of 18, he is required by the Universal Military Training and Service Act to register with a local draft board. He is assigned a Selective Service number, and within five days he is issued a registration certificate. Subsequently, and based on a questionnaire completed by the registrant, he is assigned a classification denoting his eligibility for induction, and "[a]s soon as practicable" thereafter he is issued a Notice of Classification. * * *

Both the registration and classification certificates bear notices that the registrant must notify his local board in writing of every change in address, physical condition, and occupational, marital, family, dependency, and military status, and of any other fact which might change his classification. Both also contain a notice that the registrant's Selective Service number should appear on all communications to his local board.

[The 1965] Amendment does not distinguish between public and private destruction, and it does not punish only destruction engaged in for the purpose of expressing views. A law prohibiting destruction of Selective Service certificates no more abridges free speech on its face than a motor vehicle law prohibiting the destruction of drivers' licenses, or a tax law prohibiting the destruction of books and records.

O'Brien nonetheless argues [first] that the 1965 Amendment is unconstitutional [as] applied to him because his act of burning his registration certificate was protected "symbolic speech" within the First Amendment. [He claims that] the First Amendment guarantees include all modes of "communication of ideas by conduct," and that his conduct is within this definition because he did it in "demonstration against the war and against the draft."

We cannot accept the view that an apparently limitless variety of conduct can be labeled "speech" whenever the person engaging in the conduct intends thereby to express an idea. However, even on the assumption that the alleged communicative element in O'Brien's conduct is sufficient to bring into play the First Amendment, it does not necessarily follow that the destruction of a registration certificate is constitutionally protected activity. This Court has held that when "speech" and "nonspeech" elements are combined in the same course of conduct, a sufficiently important governmental interest in regulating the nonspeech element can justify incidental limitations on First Amendment freedoms. To characterize the quality of the governmental interest which must appear, the Court has employed a variety of descriptive terms: compelling; substantial; subordinating; paramount; cogent; strong. [W]e think it clear that a government regulation is sufficiently justified if it is within the constitutional power of the government; if it furthers an important or substantial governmental interest; if the governmental interest is unrelated to the suppression of free expression; and if the incidental restriction on alleged First Amendment freedom is no greater than is essential to the furtherance of that interest. We find that the 1965 Amendment meets all of these requirements, and consequently that O'Brien can be constitutionally convicted for violating it. [Pursuant to its power to classify and conscript manpower for military service], Congress may establish a system of registration for individuals liable for training and service, and may require such individuals within reason to cooperate in the registration system. The issuance of certificates indicating the registration and eligibility classification of individuals is a legitimate and substantial administrative aid in the functioning of this system. And legislation to insure the continuing availability of issued certificates serves a legitimate and substantial purpose in the system's administration.

[O'Brien] essentially adopts the position that [Selective Service] certificates are so many pieces of paper designed to notify registrants of their registration or classification, to be retained or tossed in the wastebasket according to the convenience or taste of the registrant. Once the registrant has received notification, according to this view, there is no reason for him to retain the certificates. [However, the registration and classification certificates serve] purposes in addition to initial notification. Many of these purposes would be defeated by the certificates' destruction or mutilation. Among these are [simplifying verification of the registration and classification of suspected delinquents, evidence of availability for induction in the event of emergency, ease of communication between registrants and local boards, continually reminding registrants of the need to notify local boards of changes in status].

The many functions performed by Selective Service certificates establish beyond doubt that Congress has a legitimate and substantial interest in preventing their wanton and unrestrained destruction and assuring their continuing availability by punishing people who knowingly and wilfully destroy or mutilate them. And we are unpersuaded that the pre-existence of the nonpossession regulations in any way negates this interest.

In the absence of a question as to multiple punishment, it has never been suggested that there is anything improper in Congress providing alternative statutory avenues of prosecution to assure the effective protection of one and the same interest. Here, the pre-existing avenue of prosecution was not even statutory. Regulations may be modified or revoked from time to time by administrative discretion. Certainly, the Congress may change or supplement a regulation.

[The] gravamen of the offense defined by the statute is the deliberate rendering of certificates unavailable for the various purposes which they may serve. Whether registrants keep their certificates in their personal possession at all times, as required by the regulations, is of no particular concern under the 1965 Amendment, as long as they do not mutilate or destroy the certificates so as to render them unavailable. [The 1965 amendment] is concerned with abuses involving *any* issued Selective Service certificates, not only with the registrant's own certificates. The knowing destruction or mutilation of someone else's certificates would therefore violate the statute but not the nonpossession regulations.

We think it apparent that the continuing availability to each registrant of his Selective Service certificates substantially furthers the smooth and proper functioning of the system that Congress has established to raise armies. * * *

It is equally clear that the 1965 Amendment specifically protects this substantial governmental interest. We perceive no alternative means that would more precisely and narrowly assure the continuing availability of issued Selective Service certificates than a law which prohibits their wilful mutilation or destruction. The 1965 Amendment prohibits such conduct and does nothing more. [The] governmental interest and the scope of the 1965 Amendment are limited to preventing a harm to the smooth and efficient functioning of the Selective Service System. When O'Brien deliberately rendered unavailable his registration certificate, he wilfully frustrated this governmental interest. For this noncommunicative impact of his conduct, and for nothing else, he was convicted.* * *

O'Brien finally argues that the 1965 Amendment is unconstitutional as enacted because what he calls the "purpose" of Congress was "to suppress freedom of speech." We reject this argument because under settled principles the purpose of Congress, as O'Brien uses that term, is not a basis for declaring this legislation unconstitutional.

It is a familiar principle of constitutional law that this Court will not strike down an otherwise constitutional statute on the basis of an alleged illicit legislative motive.

[I]f we were to examine legislative purpose in the instant case, we would be obliged to consider not only [the statements of the three members of Congress who addressed themselves to the amendment, all viewing draft-card burning as a brazen display of unpatriotism] but also the more authoritative reports of the Senate and House Armed Services Committees. [B]oth reports make clear a concern with the "defiant" destruction of so-called "draft cards" and with "open" encouragement to others to destroy their cards, [but they] also indicate that this concern stemmed from an apprehension that unrestrained destruction of cards would disrupt the smooth functioning of the Selective Service System. * * *

Reversed.a

Justice Harlan concurring. * * *

a. Marshall, J., took no part.

I wish to make explicit my understanding that [the Court's analysis] does not foreclose consideration of First Amendment claims in those rare instances when an "incidental" restriction upon expression, imposed by a regulation which furthers an "important or substantial" governmental interest and satisfies the Court's other criteria, in practice has the effect of entirely preventing a "speaker" from reaching a significant audience with whom he could not otherwise lawfully communicate. This is not such a case, since O'Brien manifestly could have conveyed his message in many ways other than by burning his draft card.

JUSTICE DOUGLAS, dissenting.

[Douglas, J., thought that "the underlying and basic problem in this case" was the constitutionality of a draft "in the absence of a declaration of war" and that the case should be put down for reargument on this question. The following Term, concurring in *Brandenburg*, he criticized *O'Brien* on the merits. After recalling that the Court had rejected O'Brien's First Amendment argument on the ground that "legislation to insure the continuing availability of issued certificates serves a legitimate and substantial purpose in the [selective service] system's administration," he commented: "But O'Brien was not prosecuted for not having his draft card available when asked for by a federal agent. He was indicted, tried, and convicted for burning the card. And this Court's affirmance [was not] consistent with the First Amendment." He observed, more generally in *Brandenburg*:

["Action is often a method of expression and within the protection of the First Amendment. Suppose one tears up his own copy of the Constitution in eloquent protest to a decision of this Court. May he be indicted? Suppose one rips his own Bible to shreds to celebrate his departure from one 'faith' and his embrace of atheism. May he be indicted? * * *

["The act of praying often involves body posture and movement as well as utterances. It is nonetheless protected by the Free Exercise Clause. Picketing [is] 'free speech plus.' [Therefore], it can be regulated when it comes to the 'plus' or 'action' side of the protest. It can be regulated as to the number of pickets and the place and hours, because traffic and other community problems would otherwise suffer. But none of these considerations are implicated in the symbolic protest of the Vietnam war in the burning of a draft card."]

TEXAS v. JOHNSON

491 U.S. 397, 109 S.Ct. 2533, 105 L.Ed.2d 342 (1989).

JUSTICE BRENNAN delivered the opinion of the Court.

[Gregory] Lee Johnson was convicted of desecrating a flag in violation of Texas law.[1]

I.   While the Republican National Convention was taking place in Dallas in 1984, respondent Johnson participated in a political demonstration dubbed the "Republican War Chest Tour." [The] demonstration ended in front of Dallas City

---

1.   Tex.Penal Code Ann. § 42.09 (1989) provides in full: "§ 42.09. Desecration of Venerated Object

"(a) A person commits an offense if he intentionally or knowingly desecrates:

"(1) a public monument;

"(2) a place of worship or burial; or

"(3) a state or national flag.

"(b) For purposes of this section, 'desecrate' means deface, damage, or otherwise physically mistreat in a way that the actor knows will seriously offend one or more persons likely to observe or discover his action.

"(c) An offense under this section is a Class A misdemeanor."

Hall, where Johnson unfurled the American flag, doused it with kerosene, and set it on fire. While the flag burned, the protestors chanted, "America, the red, white, and blue, we spit on you." [No] one was physically injured or threatened with injury, though several witnesses testified that they had been seriously offended by the flag-burning. * * *

II. Johnson was convicted of flag desecration for burning the flag rather than for uttering insulting words.2 [We] must first determine whether Johnson's burning of the flag constituted expressive conduct, permitting him to invoke the First Amendment in challenging his conviction. If his conduct was expressive, we next decide whether the State's regulation is related to the suppression of free expression. *O'Brien.* If the State's regulation is not related to expression, then the less stringent standard we announced in *O'Brien* for regulations of noncommunicative conduct controls. If it is, then we are outside of *O'Brien*'s test, and we must ask whether this interest justifies Johnson's conviction under a more demanding standard.3 A third possibility is that the State's asserted interest is simply not implicated on these facts, and in that event the interest drops out of the picture. * * *

In deciding whether particular conduct possesses sufficient communicative elements to bring the First Amendment into play, we have asked whether "[a]n intent to convey a particularized message was present, and [whether] the likelihood was great that the message would be understood by those who viewed it." [In] *Spence v. Washington,* 418 U.S. 405 (1974), for example, we emphasized that Spence's taping of a peace sign to his flag was "roughly simultaneous with and concededly triggered by the Cambodian incursion and the Kent State tragedy." The State of Washington had conceded, in fact, that Spence's conduct was a form of communication, and we stated that "the State's concession is inevitable on this record."

III. In order to decide whether *O'Brien*'s test [applies] we must decide whether Texas has asserted an interest in support of Johnson's conviction that is unrelated to the suppression of expression.

IV. Texas claims that its interest in preventing breaches of the peace justifies Johnson's conviction for flag desecration.4 However, no disturbance of the

2. Because the prosecutor's closing argument observed that Johnson had led the protestors in chants denouncing the flag while it burned, Johnson suggests that he may have been convicted for uttering critical words rather than for burning the flag. He relies on *Street v. New York,* 394 U.S. 576 (1969), in which we reversed a conviction obtained under a New York statute that prohibited publicly defying or casting contempt on the flag "either by words or act" because we were persuaded that the defendant may have been convicted for his words alone. Unlike the law we faced in *Street,* however, the Texas flag-desecration statute does not on its face permit conviction for remarks critical of the flag, as Johnson himself admits. Nor was the jury in this case told that it could convict Johnson of flag desecration if it found only that he had uttered words critical of the flag and its referents. * * *

3. [Johnson] has raised a facial challenge to Texas' flag-desecration [statute]. Section 42.09 regulates only physical conduct with respect to the flag, not the written or spoken word, and

although one violates the statute only if one "knows" that one's physical treatment of the flag "will seriously offend one or more persons likely to observe or discover his action," this fact does not necessarily mean that the statute applies only to *expressive* conduct protected by the First Amendment. A tired person might, for example, drag a flag through the mud, knowing that this conduct is likely to offend others, and yet have no thought of expressing any idea; neither the language nor the Texas courts' interpretations of the statute precludes the possibility that such a person would be prosecuted for flag desecration. Because the prosecution of a person who had not engaged in expressive conduct would pose a different case, and because we are capable of disposing of this case on narrower grounds, we address only Johnson's claim that § 42.09 as applied to political expression like his violates the First Amendment.

4. Relying on our decision in *Boos v. Barry,* Johnson argues [that] the violent reaction to flag-burning feared by Texas would be the re-

peace actually occurred or threatened to occur because of Johnson's burning of the flag. [The] only evidence offered by the State at trial to show the reaction to Johnson's actions was the testimony of several persons who had been seriously offended by the flag-burning.

The State's position, therefore, amounts to a claim that an audience that takes serious offense at particular expression is necessarily likely to disturb the peace and that the expression may be prohibited on this basis. [W]e have not permitted the Government to assume that every expression of a provocative idea will incite a riot, but have instead required careful consideration of the actual circumstances surrounding such expression, asking whether the expression "is directed to inciting or producing imminent lawless action and is likely to incite or produce such action." *Brandenburg*. To accept Texas' arguments that it need only demonstrate "the potential for a breach of the peace," and that every flag-burning necessarily possesses that potential, would be to eviscerate our holding in *Brandenburg*. This we decline to do.

Nor does Johnson's expressive conduct fall within that small class of "fighting words" that are "likely to provoke the average person to retaliation, and thereby cause a breach of the peace." *Chaplinsky*. No reasonable onlooker would have regarded Johnson's generalized expression of dissatisfaction with the policies of the Federal Government as a direct personal insult or an invitation to exchange fisticuffs.

We thus conclude that the State's interest in maintaining order is not implicated on these facts. * * *

B.   The State also asserts an interest in preserving the flag as a symbol of nationhood and national unity. [The] State, apparently, is concerned that such conduct will lead people to believe either that the flag does not stand for nationhood and national unity, but instead reflects other, less positive concepts, or that the concepts reflected in the flag do not in fact exist, that is, we do not enjoy unity as a Nation. These concerns blossom only when a person's treatment of the flag communicates some message, and thus are related "to the suppression of free expression" within the meaning of *O'Brien*. We are thus outside of *O'Brien*'s test altogether.

IV.   It remains to consider whether the State's interest in preserving the flag as a symbol of nationhood and national unity justifies Johnson's conviction. [If Johnson] had burned the flag as a means of disposing of it because it was dirty or torn, he would not have been convicted of flag desecration under this Texas law: federal law designates burning as the preferred means of disposing of a flag "when it is in such condition that it is no longer a fitting emblem for display," 36 U.S.C. § 176(k), and Texas has no quarrel with this means of disposal. The Texas law is thus not aimed at protecting the physical integrity of the flag in all circumstances, but is designed instead to protect it only against impairments that would cause serious offense to others.6

sult of the message conveyed by them, and that this fact connects the State's interest to the suppression of expression. This view has found some favor in the lower courts. Johnson's theory may overread *Boos* insofar as it suggests that a desire to prevent a violent audience reaction is "related to expression" in the same way that a desire to prevent an audience from being offended is "related to expression." Because we find that the State's interest in preventing breaches of the peace is not implicated

on these facts, however, we need not venture further into this area.

6.   *Cf. Smith v. Goguen*, 415 U.S. 566 (1974) (Blackmun, J., dissenting) (emphasizing that lower court appeared to have construed state statute so as to protect physical integrity of the flag in all circumstances); id. (Rehnquist, J., dissenting) (same). [In *Goguen*, Blackmun, J., argued that "Goguen's punishment was constitutionally permissible for harming the physical integrity of the flag by wearing it affixed to the

Whether Johnson's treatment of the flag violated Texas law thus depended on the likely communicative impact of his expressive conduct. Our decision in *Boos v. Barry*, 485 U.S. 312 (1988), tells us that this restriction on Johnson's expression is content-based. In *Boos,* we considered the constitutionality of a law prohibiting "the display of any sign within 50 feet of a foreign embassy if that sign tends to bring that foreign government into 'public odium' or 'public disrepute.' " Rejecting the argument that the law was content-neutral because it was justified by "our international law obligation to shield diplomats from speech that offends their dignity," we held that "[t]he emotive impact of speech on its audience is not a 'secondary effect' " unrelated to the content of the expression itself.

According to the principles announced in *Boos,* Johnson's political expression was restricted because of the content of the message he conveyed. We must therefore subject the State's asserted interest in preserving the special symbolic character of the flag to "the most exacting scrutiny." *Boos.*8 * * *

If there is a bedrock principle underlying the First Amendment, it is that the Government may not prohibit the expression of an idea simply because society finds the idea itself offensive or disagreeable. [We] have not recognized an exception to this principle even where our flag has been involved. [We] never before have held that the Government may ensure that a symbol be used to express only one view of that symbol or its referents. Indeed, in *Schacht v. United States*, 398 U.S. 58 (1970), we invalidated a federal statute permitting an actor portraying a member of one of our armed forces to " 'wear the uniform of that armed force if the portrayal does not tend to discredit that armed force.' " This proviso, we held, "which leaves Americans free to praise the war in Vietnam but can send persons like Schacht to prison for opposing it, cannot survive in a country which has the First Amendment."

We perceive no basis on which to hold that the principle underlying our decision in *Schacht* does not apply to this case. To conclude that the Government may permit designated symbols to be used to communicate only a limited set of messages would be to enter territory having no discernible or defensible boundaries. Could the Government, on this theory, prohibit the burning of state flags? Of copies of the Presidential seal? Of the Constitution? In evaluating these choices under the First Amendment, how would we decide which symbols were sufficiently special to warrant this unique status? To do so, we would be forced to consult our own political preferences, and impose them on the citizenry, in the very way that the First Amendment forbids us to do.

There is, moreover, no indication—either in the text of the Constitution or in our cases interpreting it—that a separate judicial category exists for the American flag alone. Indeed, we would not be surprised to learn that the persons who framed our Constitution and wrote the Amendment that we now construe were not known for their reverence for the Union Jack. The First Amendment does not guarantee that other concepts virtually sacred to our Nation as a whole—such as the principle that discrimination on the basis of race is odious and destructive—will go unquestioned in the marketplace of ideas. See *Brandenburg.* We decline,

seat of his pants" and emphasized that such punishment would not be for "speech—a communicative element."].

8. Our inquiry is, of course, bounded by the particular facts of this case and by the statute under which Johnson was convicted. There was no evidence that Johnson himself stole the flag he burned, nor did the prosecution or the arguments urged in support of it depend on the theory that the flag was stolen. [Thus] nothing in our opinion should be taken to suggest that one is free to steal a flag so long as one later uses it to communicate an idea. We also emphasize that Johnson was prosecuted *only* for flag desecration—not for trespass, disorderly conduct, or arson.

therefore, to create for the flag an exception to the joust of principles protected by the First Amendment.

It is not the State's ends, but its means, to which we object. It cannot be gainsaid that there is a special place reserved for the flag in this Nation, and thus we do not doubt that the Government has a legitimate interest in making efforts to "preserv[e] the national flag as an unalloyed symbol of our country." We reject the suggestion, urged at oral argument by counsel for Johnson, that the Government lacks "any state interest whatsoever" in regulating the manner in which the flag may be displayed. Congress has, for example, enacted precatory regulations describing the proper treatment of the flag, see 36 U.S.C. §§ 173–177, and we cast no doubt on the legitimacy of its interest in making such recommendations. To say that the Government has an interest in encouraging proper treatment of the flag, however, is not to say that it may criminally punish a person for burning a flag as a means of political protest. "National unity as an end which officials may foster by persuasion and example is not in question. The problem is whether under our Constitution compulsion as here employed is a permissible means for its achievement."

[W]e submit that nobody can suppose that this one gesture of an unknown man will change our Nation's attitude towards its flag. See *Abrams* (Holmes, J., dissenting). Indeed, Texas' argument that the burning of an American flag " 'is an act having a high likelihood to cause a breach of the peace,' " and its statute's implicit assumption that physical mistreatment of the flag will lead to "serious offense," tend to confirm that the flag's special role is not in danger; if it were, no one would riot or take offense because a flag had been burned.

We are tempted to say, in fact, that the flag's deservedly cherished place in our community will be strengthened, not weakened, by our holding today. Our decision is a reaffirmation of the principles of freedom and inclusiveness that the flag best reflects, and of the conviction that our toleration of criticism such as Johnson's is a sign and source of our strength. Indeed, one of the proudest images of our flag, the one immortalized in our own national anthem, is of the bombardment it survived at Fort McHenry. It is the Nation's resilience, not its rigidity, that Texas sees reflected in the flag—and it is that resilience that we reassert today.

The way to preserve the flag's special role is not to punish those who feel differently about these matters. It is to persuade them that they are wrong. [We] can imagine no more appropriate response to burning a flag than waving one's own, no better way to counter a flag-burner's message than by saluting the flag that burns, no surer means of preserving the dignity even of the flag that burned than by—as one witness here did—according its remains a respectful burial. * * *

JUSTICE KENNEDY, concurring. * * *

Our colleagues in dissent advance powerful arguments why respondent may be convicted for his expression, reminding us that among those who will be dismayed by our holding will be some who have had the singular honor of carrying the flag in battle. And I agree that the flag holds a lonely place of honor in an age when absolutes are distrusted and simple truths are burdened by unneeded apologetics.

With all respect to those views, I do not believe the Constitution gives us the right to rule as the dissenting members of the Court urge, however painful this judgment is to announce. Though symbols often are what we ourselves make of them, the flag is constant in expressing beliefs Americans share, beliefs in law and peace and that freedom which sustains the human spirit. The case here today forces recognition of the costs to which those beliefs commit us. It is poignant but fundamental that the flag protects those who hold it in contempt.

For all the record shows, this respondent was not a philosopher and perhaps did not even possess the ability to comprehend how repellent his statements must be to the Republic itself. But whether or not he could appreciate the enormity of the offense he gave, the fact remains that his acts were speech, in both the technical and the fundamental meaning of the Constitution. So I agree with the Court that he must go free.

CHIEF JUSTICE REHNQUIST, with whom JUSTICE WHITE and JUSTICE O'CONNOR join, dissenting.

In holding this Texas statute unconstitutional, the Court ignores Justice Holmes' familiar aphorism that "a page of history is worth a volume of logic." *New York Trust Co. v. Eisner,* 256 U.S. 345 (1921). * * *

The American flag [throughout] more than 200 years of our history, has come to be the visible symbol embodying our Nation.a It does not represent the views of any particular political party, and it does not represent any particular political philosophy. The flag is not simply another "idea" or "point of view" competing for recognition in the marketplace of ideas. Millions and millions of Americans regard it with an almost mystical reverence regardless of what sort of social, political, or philosophical beliefs they may have. I cannot agree that the First Amendment invalidates the Act of Congress, and the laws of 48 of the 50 States, which make criminal the public burning of the flag.

More than 80 years ago in *Halter v. Nebraska* [205 U.S. 34 (1907)], this Court upheld the constitutionality of a Nebraska statute that forbade the use of representations of the American flag for advertising purposes upon articles of merchandise. The Court there said: "For that flag every true American has not simply an appreciation but a deep affection. [Hence,] it has often occurred that insults to a flag have been the cause of war, and indignities put upon it, in the presence of those who revere it, have often been resented and sometimes punished on the spot."

Only two Terms ago, in *San Francisco Arts & Athletics, Inc. v. United States Olympic Committee,* [483 U.S. 522 (1987)], the Court held that Congress could grant exclusive use of the word "Olympic" to the United States Olympic Committee. The Court thought that this "restriction on expressive speech properly [was] characterized as incidental to the primary congressional purpose of encouraging and rewarding the USOC's activities." As the Court stated, "when a word [or symbol] acquires value 'as the result of organization and the expenditure of labor, skill, and money' by an entity, that entity constitutionally may obtain a limited property right in the word [or symbol]." Surely Congress or the States may recognize a similar interest in the flag.b

a. Rehnquist, C.J., invoked a legacy of prose, poetry, and law in honor of flags in general and the American flag in particular both in peace and in war, quoting from, among others, Ralph Waldo Emerson and John Greenleaf Whittier. Emerson's poem referred to the Union Jack, but he did not always speak warmly of the American flag. After passage of the Fugitive Slave Law Emerson wrote, "We sneak about with the infamy of crime in the streets, & cowardice in ourselves and frankly once for all the Union is sunk, the flag is hateful, and shall be hissed." *Emerson in His Journals* 421 (Joel Porte ed. 1982).

b. In response, Brennan, J., observed that *Halter* was decided "nearly twenty years" before the First Amendment was applied to the states and "[m]ore important" that *Halter* involved "purely commercial rather than political speech." Similarly, he stated that the authorization "to prohibit certain commercial and promotional uses of the word 'Olympic' [does not] even begin to tell us whether the Government may criminally punish physical conduct towards the flag engaged in as a means of political protest."

[T]he public burning of the American flag by Johnson was no essential part of any exposition of ideas, and at the same time it had a tendency to incite a breach of the peace. Johnson was free to make any verbal denunciation of the flag that he wished; indeed, he was free to burn the flag in private. He could publicly burn other symbols of the Government or effigies of political leaders. He did lead a march through the streets of Dallas, and conducted a rally in front of the Dallas City Hall. He engaged in a "die-in" to protest nuclear weapons. He shouted out various slogans during the march, including: "Reagan, Mondale which will it be? Either one means World War III"; "Ronald Reagan, killer of the hour, Perfect example of U.S. power"; and "red, white and blue, we spit on you, you stand for plunder, you will go under." For none of these acts was he arrested or prosecuted. [As] with "fighting words," so with flag burning, for purposes of the First Amendment: It is "no essential part of any exposition of ideas, and [is] of such slight social value as a step to truth that any benefit that may be derived from [it] is clearly outweighed" by the public interest in avoiding a probable breach of the peace. * * *

The result of the Texas statute is obviously to deny one in Johnson's frame of mind one of many means of "symbolic speech." Far from being a case of "one picture being worth a thousand words," flag burning is the equivalent of an inarticulate grunt or roar that, it seems fair to say, is most likely to be indulged in not to express any particular idea, but to antagonize others. [The] Texas statute [left Johnson] with a full panoply of other symbols and every conceivable form of verbal expression to express his deep disapproval of national policy. Thus, in no way can it be said that Texas is punishing him because his hearers—or any other group of people—were profoundly opposed to the message that he sought to convey. Such opposition is no proper basis for restricting speech or expression under the First Amendment. It was Johnson's use of this particular symbol, and not the idea that he sought to convey by it or by his many other expressions, for which he was punished. * * *

The Court concludes its opinion with a regrettably patronizing civics lecture, presumably addressed to the Members of both Houses of Congress, the members of the 48 state legislatures that enacted prohibitions against flag burning, and the troops fighting under that flag in Vietnam who objected to its being burned: "The way to preserve the flag's special role is not to punish those who feel differently about these matters. It is to persuade them that they are wrong." The Court's role as the final expositor of the Constitution is well established, but its role as a platonic guardian admonishing those responsible to public opinion as if they were truant school children has no similar place in our system of government. * * *

Uncritical extension of constitutional protection to the burning of the flag risks the frustration of the very purpose for which organized governments are instituted. The Court decides that the American flag is just another symbol, about which not only must opinions pro and con be tolerated, but for which the most minimal public respect may not be enjoined. The government may conscript men into the Armed Forces where they must fight and perhaps die for the flag, but the government may not prohibit the public burning of the banner under which they fight. I would uphold the Texas statute as applied in this case.[2]

---

2. In holding that the Texas statute as applied to Johnson violates the First Amendment, the Court does not consider Johnson's claims that the statute is unconstitutionally vague or overbroad. I think those claims are without merit. [By] defining "desecrate" as "deface," "damage" or otherwise "physically mistreat" in a manner that the actor knows will "seriously offend" others, § 42.09 only prohibits flagrant acts of physical abuse and destruction of the flag of the sort at issue here—soaking a flag with lighter fluid and igniting it in public—and not any of the exam-

JUSTICE STEVENS, dissenting. * * *

Even if flag burning could be considered just another species of symbolic speech under the logical application of the rules that the Court has developed in its interpretation of the First Amendment in other contexts, this case has an intangible dimension that makes those rules inapplicable.

A country's flag is a symbol of more than "nationhood and national unity." [T]he American flag [is] more than a proud symbol of the courage, the determination, and the gifts of nature that transformed 13 fledgling Colonies into a world power. It is a symbol of freedom, of equal opportunity, of religious tolerance, and of goodwill for other peoples who share our aspirations. The symbol carries its message to dissidents both at home and abroad who may have no interest at all in our national unity or survival.

The value of the flag as a symbol cannot be measured. Even so, I have no doubt that the interest in preserving that value for the future is both significant and legitimate. Conceivably that value will be enhanced by the Court's conclusion that our national commitment to free expression is so strong that even the United States as ultimate guarantor of that freedom is without power to prohibit the desecration of its unique symbol. But I am unpersuaded. The creation of a federal right to post bulletin boards and graffiti on the Washington Monument might enlarge the market for free expression, but at a cost I would not pay. Similarly, in my considered judgment, sanctioning the public desecration of the flag will tarnish its value—both for those who cherish the ideas for which it waves and for those who desire to don the robes of martyrdom by burning it. That tarnish is not justified by the trivial burden on free expression occasioned by requiring that an available, alternative mode of expression—including uttering words critical of the flag be employed.

It is appropriate to emphasize certain propositions that are not implicated by this case. [The] statute does not compel any conduct or any profession of respect for any idea or any symbol. [Nor] does the statute violate "the government's paramount obligation of neutrality in its regulation of protected communication." The content of respondent's message has no relevance whatsoever to the case. The concept of "desecration" does not turn on the substance of the message the actor intends to convey, but rather on whether those who view the act will take serious offense. Accordingly, one intending to convey a message of respect for the flag by burning it in a public square might nonetheless be guilty of desecration if he knows that others—perhaps simply because they misperceive the intended message—will be seriously offended. Indeed, even if the actor knows that all possible witnesses will understand that he intends to send a message of respect, he might still be guilty of desecration if he also knows that this understanding does not lessen the offense taken by some of those witnesses. The case has nothing to do with "disagreeable ideas." It involves disagreeable conduct that, in my opinion, diminishes the value of an important national asset.

[Had respondent] chosen to spray paint—or perhaps convey with a motion picture projector—his message of dissatisfaction on the façade of the Lincoln Memorial, there would be no question about the power of the Government to prohibit his means of expression. The prohibition would be supported by the legitimate interest in preserving the quality of an important national asset. Though the asset at stake in this case is intangible, given its unique value, the same interest supports a prohibition on the desecration of the American flag.*

ples of improper flag etiquette cited in Respondent's brief.

* The Court suggested that a prohibition against flag desecration is not content-neutral

The ideas of liberty and equality have been an irresistible force in motivating leaders like Patrick Henry, Susan B. Anthony, and Abraham Lincoln, schoolteachers like Nathan Hale and Booker T. Washington, the Philippine Scouts who fought at Bataan, and the soldiers who scaled the bluff at Omaha Beach. If those ideas are worth fighting for—and our history demonstrates that they are—it cannot be true that the flag that uniquely symbolizes their power is not itself worthy of protection from unnecessary desecration.

———

In response to *Johnson,* Congress passed the Flag Protection Act of 1989, which attached criminal penalties to the knowing mutilation, defacement, burning, maintaining on the floor or ground, or trampling upon any flag of the United States. UNITED STATES v. EICHMAN, 496 U.S. 310 (1990), per BRENNAN, J., invalidated the statute: "Although the Flag Protection Act contains no explicit content-based limitation on the scope of prohibited conduct, it is nevertheless clear that the Government's asserted *interest* is 'related "to the suppression of free expression" and concerned with the content of such expression. The Government's interest in protecting the "physical integrity" of a privately owned flag rests upon a perceived need to preserve the flag's status as a symbol of our Nation and certain national ideals. But the mere destruction or disfigurement of a particular physical manifestation of the symbol, without more, does not diminish or otherwise affect the symbol itself in any way. For example, the secret destruction of a flag in one's own basement would not threaten the flag's recognized meaning. Rather, the Government's desire to preserve the flag as a symbol for certain national ideals is implicated "only when a person's treatment of the flag communicates [a] message" to others that is inconsistent with those ideals.' "

STEVENS, J., joined by Rehnquist, C.J., White and O'Connor, JJ., dissenting, argued that the government's "legitimate interest in protecting the symbolic value of the American flag" outweighed the free speech interest. In describing the flag's symbolic value he stated that the flag "inspires and motivates the average citizen to make personal sacrifices in order to achieve societal goals of overriding importance; at all times, it serves as a reminder of the paramount importance of pursuing the ideals that characterize our society. * * * [T]he communicative value of a well-placed bomb in the Capital does not entitle it to the protection of the First Amendment. Burning a flag is not, of course, equivalent to burning a public building. Assuming that the protester is burning his own flag, it causes no physical harm to other persons or to their property. The impact is purely symbolic, and it is apparent that some thoughtful persons believe that impact far

because this form of symbolic speech is only used by persons who are critical of the flag or the ideas it represents. In making this suggestion the Court does not pause to consider the far-reaching consequences of its introduction of disparate impact analysis into our First Amendment jurisprudence. It seems obvious that a prohibition against the desecration of a gravesite is content-neutral even if it denies some protesters the right to make a symbolic statement by extinguishing the flame in Arlington Cemetery where John F. Kennedy is buried while permitting others to salute the flame by bowing their heads. Few would doubt that a protester who extinguishes the flame has desecrated the gravesite, regardless of whether he prefaces that act with a speech explaining that his purpose is to express deep admiration or unmitigated scorn for the late President. Likewise, few would claim that the protester who bows his head has desecrated the gravesite, even if he makes clear that his purpose is to show disrespect. In such a case, as in a flag burning case, the prohibition against desecration has absolutely nothing to do with the content of the message that the symbolic speech is intended to convey.

from depreciating the value of the symbol, will actually enhance its meaning. I most respectfully disagree.''

———

Community for Creative Non–Violence (CCNV) sought to conduct a winter-time demonstration near the White House in Lafayette Park and the Mall to dramatize the plight of the homeless. The National Park Service authorized the erection of two symbolic tent cities for purposes of the demonstration, but denied CCNV's request that demonstrators be permitted to sleep in the tents. National Park Service regulations permit camping (the "use of park land for living accommodation purposes such as sleeping activities") in National Parks only in campgrounds designated for that purpose.

CLARK v. COMMUNITY FOR CREATIVE NON–VIOLENCE, 468 U.S. 288 (1984), per WHITE, J., rejected CCNV's claim that the regulations could not be constitutionally applied against its demonstration: "We need not differ with the view of the Court of Appeals that overnight sleeping in connection with the demonstration is expressive conduct protected to some extent by the First Amendment.5 We assume for present purposes, but do not decide, that such is the case, cf. *O'Brien*, but this assumption only begins the inquiry. Expression, whether oral or written or symbolized by conduct, is subject to reasonable time, place, or manner restrictions. We have often noted that restrictions of this kind are valid provided that they are justified without reference to the content of the regulated speech, that they are narrowly tailored to serve a significant governmental interest, and that they leave open ample alternative channels for communication of the information.

"It is also true that a message may be delivered by conduct that is intended to be communicative and that, in context, would reasonably be understood by the viewer to be communicative. Symbolic expression of this kind may be forbidden or regulated if the conduct itself may constitutionally be regulated, if the regulation is narrowly drawn to further a substantial governmental interest, and if the interest is unrelated to the suppression of free speech. *O'Brien*.

"[That] sleeping, like the symbolic tents themselves, may be expressive and part of the message delivered by the demonstration does not make the ban any less a limitation on the manner of demonstrating, for reasonable time, place, or manner regulations normally have the purpose and direct effect of limiting expression but are nevertheless valid. Neither does the fact that sleeping, arguendo, may be expressive conduct, rather than oral or written expression, render the sleeping prohibition any less a time, place, or manner regulation. To the contrary, the Park Service neither attempts to ban sleeping generally nor to ban it everywhere in the parks. It has established areas for camping and forbids it elsewhere, including Lafayette Park and the Mall. Considered as such, we have very little trouble concluding that the Park Service may prohibit overnight sleeping in the parks involved here.

"The requirement that the regulation be content-neutral is clearly satisfied. The courts below accepted that view, and it is not disputed here that the prohibition on camping, and on sleeping specifically, is content-neutral and is not

5. We reject the suggestion of the plurality below, however, that the burden on the demonstrators is limited to "the advancement of a plausible contention" that their conduct is expressive. Although it is common to place the burden upon the Government to justify im-pingements on First Amendment interests, it is the obligation of the person desiring to engage in assertedly expressive conduct to demonstrate that the First Amendment even applies. To hold otherwise would be to create a rule that all conduct is presumptively expressive.

being applied because of disagreement with the message presented.a Neither was the regulation faulted, nor could it be, on the ground that without overnight sleeping the plight of the homeless could not be communicated in other ways. The regulation otherwise left the demonstration intact, with its symbolic city, signs, and the presence of those who were willing to take their turns in a day-and-night vigil. Respondents do not suggest that there was, or is, any barrier to delivering to the media, or to the public by other means, the intended message concerning the plight of the homeless.

"It is also apparent to us that the regulation narrowly focuses on the Government's substantial interest in maintaining the parks in the heart of our Capital in an attractive and intact condition, readily available to the millions of people who wish to see and enjoy them by their presence. To permit camping— using these areas as living accommodations—would be totally inimical to these purposes, as would be readily understood by those who have frequented the National Parks across the country and observed the unfortunate consequences of the activities of those who refuse to confine their camping to designated areas.

"It is urged by [CCNV] that if the symbolic city of tents was to be permitted and if the demonstrators did not intend to cook, dig, or engage in aspects of camping other than sleeping, the incremental benefit to the parks could not justify the ban on sleeping, which was here an expressive activity said to enhance the message concerning the plight of the poor and homeless. We cannot agree. In the first place, we seriously doubt that the First Amendment requires the Park Service to permit a demonstration in Lafayette Park and the Mall involving a 24–hour vigil and the erection of tents to accommodate 150 people. Furthermore, although we have assumed for present purposes that the sleeping banned in this case would have an expressive element, it is evident that its major value to this demonstration would be facilitative. Without a permit to sleep, it would be difficult to get the poor and homeless to participate or to be present at all.

"Beyond this, however, it is evident from our cases that the validity of this regulation need not be judged solely by reference to the demonstration at hand. Absent the prohibition on sleeping, there would be other groups who would demand permission to deliver an asserted message by camping in Lafayette Park. Some of them would surely have as credible a claim in this regard as does CCNV, and the denial of permits to still others would present difficult problems for the Park Service. With the prohibition, however, as is evident in the case before us, at least some around-the-clock demonstrations lasting for days on end will not materialize, others will be limited in size and duration, and the purposes of the regulation will thus be materially served. Perhaps these purposes would be more effectively and not so clumsily achieved by preventing tents and 24–hour vigils entirely in the core areas. But the Park Service's decision to permit nonsleeping demonstrations does not, in our view, impugn the camping prohibition as a valuable, but perhaps imperfect, protection to the parks. If the Government has a legitimate interest in ensuring that the National Parks are adequately protected, which we think it has, and if the parks would be more exposed to harm without the sleeping prohibition than with it, the ban is safe from invalidation under the First Amendment as a reasonable regulation of the manner in which a demonstration may be carried out. * * *

a. Marshall, J., dissenting, observed that CCNV had held a demonstration the previous winter in which it set up nine tents and slept in Lafayette Park. The D.C. Circuit held that the regulations did not preclude such a demonstration. According to Marshall, J., "The regulations at issue in this case were passed in direct response" to that holding.

"[The] foregoing analysis demonstrates that the Park Service regulation is sustainable under the four-factor standard of *O'Brien*, for validating a regulation of expressive conduct, which, in the last analysis is little, if any, different from the standard applied to time, place, or manner restrictions.8 No one contends that aside from its impact on speech a rule against camping or overnight sleeping in public parks is beyond the constitutional power of the Government to enforce. And for the reasons we have discussed above, there is a substantial Government interest in conserving park property, an interest that is plainly served by, and requires for its implementation, measures such as the proscription of sleeping that are designed to limit the wear and tear on park properties. That interest is unrelated to suppression of expression.

"We are unmoved by the Court of Appeals' view that the challenged regulation is unnecessary, and hence invalid, because there are less speech-restrictive alternatives that could have satisfied the Government interest in preserving park lands. [The] Court of Appeals' suggestions that the Park Service minimize the possible injury by reducing the size, duration, or frequency of demonstrations would still curtail the total allowable expression in which demonstrators could engage, whether by sleeping or otherwise, and these suggestions represent no more than a disagreement with the Park Service over how much protection the core parks require or how an acceptable level of preservation is to be attained. We do not believe, however, that either *United States v. O'Brien* or the time, place, or manner decisions assign to the judiciary the authority to replace the Park Service as the manager of the Nation's parks or endow the judiciary with the competence to judge how much protection of park lands is wise and how that level of conservation is to be [attained.]"

BURGER, C.J., joined in the Court's opinion, adding: "[CCNV's] attempt at camping in the park is a form of 'picketing'; it is conduct, not speech. [It] trivializes the First Amendment to seek to use it as a shield in the manner asserted here."

MARSHALL, J., joined by Brennan, J., dissented: "The majority assumes, without deciding, that the respondents' conduct is entitled to constitutional protection. The problem with this assumption is that the Court thereby avoids examining closely the reality of respondents' planned expression. The majority's approach denatures respondents' asserted right and thus makes all too easy identification of a Government interest sufficient to warrant its abridgment.

"[Missing] from the majority's description is any inkling that Lafayette Park and the Mall have served as the sites for some of the most rousing political demonstrations in the Nation's history.[2] [The] primary purpose for making *sleep* an integral part of the demonstration was 'to re-enact the central reality of homelessness' and to impress upon public consciousness, in as dramatic a way as

---

8. Reasonable time, place, or manner restrictions are valid even though they directly limit oral or written expression. It would be odd to insist on a higher standard for limitations aimed at regulable conduct and having only an incidental impact on speech. Thus, if the time, place, or manner restriction on expressive sleeping, if that is what is involved in this case, sufficiently and narrowly serves a substantial enough governmental interest to escape First Amendment condemnation, it is untenable to invalidate it under *O'Brien* on the ground that the governmental interest is insufficient to warrant the intrusion on First Amendment concerns or that there is an inade-

quate nexus between the regulation and the interest sought to be served. We note that only recently, in a case dealing with the regulation of signs, the Court framed the issue under *O'Brien* and then based a crucial part of its analysis on the time, place, or manner cases.

2. At oral argument, the Government informed the Court "that on any given day there will be an average of three or so demonstrations going on" in the Mall–Lafayette Park area. Respondents accurately describe Lafayette Park "as the American analogue to 'Speaker's Corner' in Hyde Park."

possible, that homelessness is a widespread problem, often ignored, that confronts its victims with life-threatening deprivations. As one of the homeless men seeking to demonstrate explained: 'Sleeping in Lafayette Park or on the Mall, for me, is to show people that conditions are so poor for the homeless and poor in this city that we would actually sleep *outside* in the winter to get the point across.' * * * Here respondents clearly intended to protest the reality of homelessness by sleeping outdoors in the winter in the near vicinity of the magisterial residence of the President of the United States. In addition to accentuating the political character of their protest by their choice of location and mode of communication, respondents also intended to underline the meaning of their protest by giving their demonstration satirical names. Respondents planned to name the demonstration on the Mall 'Congressional Village,' and the demonstration in Lafayette Park, 'Reaganville II.' * * *

"Although sleep in the context of this case is symbolic speech protected by the First Amendment, it is nonetheless subject to reasonable time, place, and manner restrictions. I agree with the standard enunciated by the majority.6 I conclude, however, that the regulations at issue in this case, as applied to respondents, fail to satisfy this [standard].

"[T]here are no substantial Government interests advanced by the Government's regulations as applied to respondents. All that the Court's decision advances are the prerogatives of a bureaucracy that over the years has shown an implacable hostility toward citizens' exercise of First Amendment [rights].

"The disposition of this case impels me to make two additional observations. First, in this case, as in some others involving time, place, and manner restrictions, the Court has dramatically lowered its scrutiny of governmental regulations once it has determined that such regulations are content-neutral. The result has been the creation of a two-tiered approach to First Amendment cases: while regulations that turn on the content of the expression are subjected to a strict form of judicial review, regulations that are aimed at matters other than expression receive only a minimal level of scrutiny. [The] Court has seemingly overlooked the fact that content-neutral restrictions are also capable of unnecessarily restricting protected expressive activity. [The] Court [has] transformed the ban against content distinctions from a floor that offers all persons at least equal liberty under the First Amendment into a ceiling that restricts persons to the protection of First Amendment equality—but nothing more.14 The consistent imposition of silence upon all may fulfill the dictates of an evenhanded content-neutrality. But it offends our 'profound national commitment to the principle that debate on public issues should be uninhibited, robust, and wide-open'. *New York Times v. Sullivan.*

"Second, the disposition of this case reveals a mistaken assumption regarding the motives and behavior of Government officials who create and administer content-neutral regulations. The Court's salutary skepticism of governmental decisionmaking in First Amendment matters suddenly dissipates once it deter-

6. I also agree with the majority that no substantial difference distinguishes the test applicable to time, place, and manner restrictions and the test articulated in *O'Brien.*

14. Furthermore, [a] content-neutral regulation that restricts an inexpensive mode of communication will fall most heavily upon relatively poor speakers and to points of view that such speakers typically espouse. This sort of latent inequality is very much in evidence in this case, for respondents lack the financial means necessary to buy access to more conventional modes of persuasion.

A disquieting feature about the disposition of this case is that it lends credence to the charge that judicial administration of the First Amendment, in conjunction with a social order marked by large disparities of wealth and other sources of power, tends systematically to discriminate against efforts by the relatively disadvantaged to convey their political ideas. * * *

mines that a restriction is not content-based. The Court evidently assumes that the balance struck by officials is deserving of deference so long as it does not appear to be tainted by content discrimination. What the Court fails to recognize is that public officials have strong incentives to overregulate even in the absence of an intent to censor particular views. This incentive stems from the fact that of the two groups whose interests officials must accommodate—on the one hand, the interests of the general public and, on the other, the interests of those who seek to use a particular forum for First Amendment activity—the political power of the former is likely to be far greater than that of the latter."

———

The "time, place, or manner" test set out in *Clark* is differently stated in different cases. For example, *U.S. Postal Service v. Council of Greenburgh,* 453 U.S. 114 (1981), speaks of "adequate" as opposed to "ample" alternative channels of communication, and *Renton v. Playtime Theatres, Inc.,* Sec. 3, I infra, transcends the difference by requiring that the restriction not "unreasonably limit" alternative channels of communication. Beyond these differences, a number of cases state that the regulation must serve a significant government interest without stating that it must be "narrowly tailored" to serve a significant government interest. See e.g., *Heffron v. International Soc. For Krishna Consciousness,* Sec. 6, I, A infra. But see *Ward v. Rock Against Racism,* Sec. 6, I, A infra (reaffirming and defining narrowly tailored requirement).

———

New York Public Health law authorizes the forced closure of a building for one year if it has been used for the purpose of "lewdness, assignation or prostitution." A civil complaint alleged that prostitution solicitation and sexual activities by patrons were occurring at an adult bookstore within observation of the proprietor. Accordingly, the complaint called for the closure of the building for one year. There was no claim that any books in the store were obscene. The New York Court of Appeals held that the closure remedy violated the First Amendment because it was broader than necessary to achieve the restriction against illicit sexual activities. It reasoned that an injunction against the alleged sexual conduct could further the state interest without infringing on First Amendment values. ARCARA v. CLOUD BOOKS, INC., 478 U.S. 697 (1986), per BURGER, C.J., reversed, holding that the closure remedy did not require any First Amendment scrutiny: "This Court has applied First Amendment scrutiny to a statute regulating conduct which has the incidental effect of burdening the expression of a particular political opinion. *O'Brien.* * * *

"We have also applied First Amendment scrutiny to some statutes which, although directed at activity with no expressive component, impose a disproportionate burden upon those engaged in protected First Amendment activities. In *Minneapolis Star & Tribune v. Minnesota Commissioner of Revenue,* 460 U.S. 575 (1983), we struck down a tax imposed on the sale of large quantities of newsprint and ink because the tax had the effect of singling out newspapers to shoulder its burden. [Even] while striking down the tax in *Minneapolis Star,* we emphasized: 'Clearly, the First Amendment does not prohibit all regulation of the press. It is beyond dispute that the States and the Federal Government can subject newspapers to generally applicable economic regulations without creating constitutional problems.'

"The New York Court of Appeals held that the *O'Brien* test for permissible governmental regulation was applicable to this case because the closure order sought by petitioner would also impose an incidental burden upon respondents' bookselling activities. [But] unlike the symbolic draft card burning in *O'Brien,* the sexual activity carried on in this case manifests absolutely no element of protected expression.a In *Paris Adult Theatre,* we underscored the fallacy of seeking to use the First Amendment as a cloak for obviously unlawful public sexual conduct by the diaphanous device of attributing protected expressive attributes to that conduct. First Amendment values may not be invoked by merely linking the words 'sex' and 'books.'

"Nor does the distinction drawn by the New York Public Health Law inevitably single out bookstores or others engaged in First Amendment protected activities for the imposition of its burden, as did the tax struck down in *Minneapolis Star.* [If] the city imposed closure penalties for demonstrated Fire Code violations or health hazards from inadequate sewage treatment, the First Amendment would not aid the owner of premises who had knowingly allowed such violations to persist. * * *

"It is true that the closure order in this case would require respondents to move their bookselling business to another location. Yet we have not traditionally subjected every criminal and civil sanction imposed through legal process to 'least restrictive means' scrutiny simply because each particular remedy will have some effect on the First Amendment activities of those subject to sanction.4"b

O'CONNOR, J., joined by Stevens, J., concurred: "I agree that the Court of Appeals erred in applying a First Amendment standard of review where, as here, the government is regulating neither speech nor an incidental, non-expressive effect of speech. Any other conclusion would lead to the absurd result that any government action that had some conceivable speech-inhibiting consequences, such as the arrest of a newscaster for a traffic violation, would require analysis under the First Amendment."

BLACKMUN, J., joined by Brennan and Marshall, JJ., dissented: "Until today, this Court has never suggested that a State may suppress speech as much as it likes, without justification, so long as it does so through generally applicable regulations that have 'nothing to do with any expressive conduct.' * * *

"At some point, of course, the impact of state regulation on First Amendment rights become so attenuated that it is easily outweighed by the state interest. But when a State directly and substantially impairs First Amendment activities, such as by shutting down a bookstore, I believe that the State must show, at a

---

a. In an earlier section of the opinion, Burger, C.J., stated that, "petitioners in *O'Brien* had, as respondents here do not, at least the semblance of expressive activity in their claim that the otherwise unlawful burning of a draft card was to 'carry a message' of the actor's opposition to the draft."

4. [T]here is no suggestion on the record before us that the closure of respondents' bookstore was sought under the public health nuisance statute as a pretext for the suppression of First Amendment protected material. Were respondents able to establish the existence of such a speech suppressive motivation or policy on the part of the District Attorney, they might have a claim of selective prosecution. Respondents in this case made no such assertion before the trial court.

b. On remand, the New York Court of Appeals held that, in the absence of a showing that the state had chosen a course no broader than necessary to accomplish its purpose, any forced closure of the bookstore would unduly impair the bookseller's rights of free expression under the New York State constitution. From New York's perspective, the question is not "who is aimed at but who is hit." *People ex rel. Arcara v. Cloud Books, Inc.,* 68 N.Y.2d 553, 510 N.Y.S.2d 844, 503 N.E.2d 492 (1986). New York has since retreated. See also *Alexander v. United States,* 509 U.S. 544 (1993)(confiscation and destruction of protected materials for distribution of obscene materials does not violate First Amendment).

minimum, that it has chosen the least restrictive means of pursuing its legitimate objectives. The closure of a bookstore can no more be compared to a traffic arrest of a reporter than the closure of a church could be compared to the traffic arrest of its clergyman.

"A State has a legitimate interest in forbidding sexual acts committed in public, including a bookstore. An obvious method of eliminating such acts is to arrest the patron committing them. But the statute in issue does not provide for that. Instead, it imposes absolute liability on the bookstore simply because the activity occurs on the premises. And the penalty—a mandatory 1–year closure—imposes an unnecessary burden on speech. Of course 'linking the words 'sex' and 'books' is not enough to extend First Amendment protection to illegal sexual activity, but neither should it suffice to remove First Amendment protection from books situated near the site of such activity. The State's purpose in stopping public lewdness cannot justify such a substantial infringement of First Amendment rights. * * *

"Petitioner has not demonstrated that a less restrictive remedy would be inadequate to abate the nuisance. The Court improperly attempts to shift to the bookseller the responsibility for finding an alternative site. But surely the Court would not uphold a city ordinance banning all public debate on the theory that the residents could move somewhere else.

Notes

1. **Generally applicable laws.** A newspaper published the name of a confidential source who it believed had misled it for political reasons. The source sued for breach of contract and prevailed in the Minnesota Supreme Court. COHEN v. COWLES MEDIA CO., 501 U.S. 663 (1991), per White, J., affirmed, dismissing the First Amendment claim with the observation that "generally applicable laws do not offend the First Amendment simply because their enforcement against the press has incidental effects on its ability to gather and report the news."c

2. **Arcara extended?** The Richmond Redevelopment and Housing Authority barred Hicks from trespassing on property where public low income housing existed in the absence of permission from the manager of the housing project. VIRGINIA v. HICKS, 539 U.S. 113 (2003), per Scalia, J., held that the bar was not substantially overbroad since it prevented a wide range of conduct, and that even if Hicks wanted to enter the property to speak or leaflet, the bar would properly be applied: "Neither the basis for the barment sanction (the prior trespass) nor its purpose (preventing prior trespasses) has anything to do with the First Amendment."d

SECTION 3. IS SOME PROTECTED SPEECH LESS EQUAL THAN OTHER PROTECTED SPEECH?

I. NEAR OBSCENE SPEECH

RENTON v. PLAYTIME THEATRES, INC., 475 U.S. 41 (1986), per Rehnquist, J., upheld a zoning ordinance that prohibited adult motion picture theaters

---

c. Blackmun, J., joined by Marshall & Souter, JJ., dissented; Souter, J., joined by Marshall, Blackmun, & O'Connor, JJ., and dissented.

d. Souter, J., joined by Breyer, J., concurred.

from locating within 1,000 feet of any residential zone, church, park, or school. The effect was to exclude such theaters from approximately 94% of the land in the city. Of the remaining 520 acres, a substantial part was occupied by a sewage disposal and treatment plant, a horse racing track and environs, a warehouse and manufacturing facilities, a Mobil Oil tank farm, and a fully-developed shopping center: "[T]he resolution of this case is largely dictated by our decision in *Young v. American Mini Theatres, Inc.,* 427 U.S. 50 (1976). There, although five Members of the Court did not agree on a single rationale for the decision, we held that the city of Detroit's zoning ordinance, which prohibited locating an adult theater within 1,000 feet of any two other 'regulated uses' or within 500 feet of any residential zone, did not violate the First and Fourteenth amendments. The Renton ordinance, like the one in *Young,* does not ban adult theaters altogether, but merely provides that such theaters may not be located within 1,000 feet of any residential zone, single- or multiple-family dwelling, church, park, or school. The ordinance is therefore properly analyzed as a form of time, place, and manner regulation.

"This Court has long held that regulations enacted for the purpose of restraining speech on the basis of its content presumptively violate the First Amendment. See *Chicago Police Dept. v. Mosley,* Sec. 6, I, B infra.a On the other hand, so-called 'content-neutral' time, place, and manner regulations are acceptable so long as they are designed to serve a substantial governmental interest and do not unreasonably limit alternative avenues of communication.

"At first glance, the Renton ordinance, like the ordinance in *Young,* does not appear to fit neatly into either the 'content-based' or the 'content-neutral' category. To be sure, the ordinance treats theaters that specialize in adult films differently from other kinds of theaters. Nevertheless, [the] City Council's '*predominate* concerns' were with the secondary effects of adult theaters, and not with the content of adult films themselves. * * *

"[This] finding as to 'predominate' intent is more than adequate to establish that the city's pursuit of its zoning interests here was unrelated to the suppression of free expression.b The ordinance by its terms is designed to prevent crime, protect the city's retail trade, maintain property values, and generally 'protec[t] and preserv[e] the quality of [the city's] neighborhoods, commercial districts, and the quality of urban life,' not to suppress the expression of unpopular views. As Justice Powell observed in *Young,* '[i]f [the city] had been concerned with restricting the message purveyed by adult theaters, it would have tried to close them or restrict their number rather than circumscribe their choice as to location.'

"In short, the [ordinance] does not contravene the fundamental principle that underlies our concern about 'content-based' speech regulations: that 'government may not grant the use of a forum to people whose views it finds acceptable, but

a. *Mosley* involved an ordinance that banned picketing near a school building except the "peaceful picketing of any school involved in a labor dispute." The Court stated: "The regulation '[slips] from the neutrality of time, place, and circumstance into a concern about content.' This is never permitted."

b. The Court interpreted the court of appeals opinion to require the invalidation of the ordinance if a "motivating factor" to restrict the exercise of First Amendment rights was present "apparently no matter how small a part this motivating factor may have played in

the City Council's decision." This view of the law, the Court continued, "was rejected in *O'Brien:* 'It is a familiar principle of constitutional law that this Court will not strike down an otherwise constitutional statute on the basis of an alleged illicit legislative motive. [What] motivates one legislator to make a speech about a statute is not necessarily what motivates scores of others to enact it, and the stakes are sufficiently high for us to eschew guesswork.' "

deny use to those wishing to express less favored or more controversial views.'
Mosley.

"It was with this understanding in mind that, in *Young,* a majority of this
Court decided that at least with respect to businesses that purvey sexually explicit
materials,c zoning ordinances designed to combat the undesirable secondary
effects of such businesses are to be reviewed under the standards applicable to
'content-neutral' time, place, and manner regulations.2

"The appropriate inquiry in this case, then, is whether the Renton ordinance
is designed to serve a substantial governmental interest and allows for reasonable
alternative avenues of communication."

After concluding that the ordinance was designed to serve substantial government interests, the Court ruled that the Renton ordinance allowed "for reasonable
alternative avenues of communication": "[W]e note that the ordinance leaves
some 520 acres, or more than five percent of the entire land area of Renton, open
to use as adult theater sites. [Respondents] argue, however, that some of the land
in question is already occupied by existing businesses, that 'practically none' of
the undeveloped land is currently for sale or lease, and that in general there are
no 'commercially viable' adult theater sites within the 520 acres left open by the
Renton ordinance. The Court of Appeals accepted these arguments. * * *

"We disagree. [That] respondents must fend for themselves in the real estate
market, on an equal footing with other prospective purchasers and lessees, does
not give rise to a First Amendment violation. And although we have cautioned
against the enactment of zoning regulations that have 'the effect of suppressing,
or greatly restricting access to, lawful speech,' *Young* (plurality opinion), we have
never suggested that the First Amendment compels the Government to ensure
that adult theaters, or any other kinds of speech-related businesses for that
matter, will be able to obtain sites at bargain prices. [T]he First Amendment
requires only that Renton refrain from effectively denying respondents a reasonable opportunity to open and operate an adult theater within the city, and the
ordinance before us easily meets this requirement. * * *4"d

BRENNAN, J., joined by Marshall, J., dissented: "The fact that adult movie
theaters may cause harmful 'secondary' land use effects may arguably give Renton
a compelling reason to regulate such establishments; it does not mean, however,
that such regulations are content-neutral. * * *

"The ordinance discriminates on its face against certain forms of speech
based on content. Movie theaters specializing in 'adult motion pictures' may not

c. The secondary effects justification was
deemed to distinguish *Erznoznik v. City of
Jacksonville,* 422 U.S. 205 (1975) (invalidating
ordinance prohibiting drive-in theaters from
showing films containing nudity) and *Schad v.
Mount Ephraim,* 452 U.S. 61 (1981) (invalidating ordinance prohibiting live entertainment,
as applied to nude dancing, in commercial
zone).

2. See *Young* (plurality opinion) ("[I]t is
manifest that society's interest in protecting
this type of expression is of a wholly different,
and lesser, magnitude than the interest in untrammeled political debate * * *."). [Eds. note:
The plurality opinion in *Young* stated that
"[f]ew of us would march our sons and daughters off to war to see 'Specified Sexual Activities' exhibited in the theaters of our choice."]

4. [We] reject respondents' "vagueness" argument for the same reasons that led us to
reject a similar challenge in *Young.* There, the
Detroit ordinance applied to theaters "used to
present material distinguished or characterized
by an emphasis on [sexually explicit matter]."
We held that "even if there may be some
uncertainty about the effect of the ordinances
on other litigants, they are unquestionably applicable to these respondents." We also held
that the Detroit ordinance created no "significant deterrent effect" that might justify invocation of the First Amendment "overbreadth"
doctrine.

d. Blackmun, J., concurred in the result
without opinion.

be located within 1,000 feet of any residential zone, single-or multiple-family dwelling, church, park, or school. Other motion picture theaters, and other forms of 'adult entertainment,' such as bars, massage parlors, and adult bookstores, are not subject to the same restrictions. This selective treatment strongly suggests that Renton was interested not in controlling the 'secondary effects' associated with adult businesses, but in discriminating against adult theaters based on the content of the films they exhibit. [Moreover,] [a]s the Court of Appeals observed, '[b]oth the magistrate and the district court recognized that many of the stated reasons for the ordinance were no more than expressions of dislike for the subject matter.'3 That some residents may be offended by the *content* of the films shown at adult movie theaters cannot form the basis for state regulation of speech. See *Terminiello.*

"Some of the 'findings' [do] relate to supposed 'secondary effects' associated with adult movie theaters4 [but they were added by the City Council only after this law suit was filed and the Court should not] accept these post-hoc statements at face value. [As] the Court of Appeals concluded, '[t]he record presented by Renton to support its asserted interest in enacting the zoning ordinance is very thin.' 5 * * *7

"Even assuming that the ordinance should be treated like a content-neutral time, place, and manner restriction, I would still find it unconstitutional. [T]he ordinance is invalid because it does not provide for reasonable alternative avenues of communication.e [R]espondents do not ask Renton to guarantee low-price sites for their businesses, but seek, only a reasonable opportunity to operate adult theaters in the city. By denying them this opportunity, Renton can effectively ban

3. For example, "finding" number 2 states that "[l]ocation of adult entertainment land uses on the main commercial thoroughfares of the City gives an impression of legitimacy to, and causes a loss of sensitivity to the adverse effect of pornography upon children, established family relations, respect for marital relationship and for the sanctity of marriage relations of others, and the concept of nonaggressive, consensual sexual relations."

"Finding" number 6 states that "[l]ocation of adult land uses in close proximity to residential uses, churches, parks, and other public facilities, and schools, will cause a degradation of the community standard of morality. Pornographic material has a degrading effect upon the relationship between spouses."

4. For example, "finding" number 12 states that "[l]ocation of adult entertainment land uses in proximity to residential uses, churches, parks and other public facilities, and schools, may lead to increased levels of criminal activities, including prostitution, rape, incest and assaults in the vicinity of such adult entertainment land uses."

5. As part of the amendment passed after this lawsuit commenced, the City Council added a statement that it had intended to rely on the Washington Supreme Court's opinion in *Northend Cinema, Inc. v. Seattle,* 90 Wash.2d 709, 585 P.2d 1153 (1978), cert. denied, 441 U.S. 946 (1979), which upheld Seattle's zoning regulations against constitutional attack.

Again, despite the suspicious coincidental timing of the amendment, the Court holds that "Renton was entitled to rely [on] the 'detailed findings' summarized in [the] *Northend Cinema* opinion." In *Northend Cinema,* the court noted that "[t]he record is replete with testimony regarding the effects of adult movie theater locations on residential neighborhoods." The opinion however, does not explain the evidence it purports to summarize, and provided no basis for determining whether Seattle's experience is relevant to Renton's.

7. As one commentator has noted: "[A]nyone with any knowledge of human nature should naturally assume that the decision to adopt almost any content-based restriction might have been affected by an antipathy on the part of at least some legislators to the ideas or information being suppressed. The logical assumption, in other words, is not that there is not improper motivation but, rather, because legislators are only human, that there is a substantial risk that an impermissible consideration has in fact colored the deliberative process." Geoffrey Stone, *Restrictions on Speech Because of its Content: The Peculiar Case of Subject–Matter Restrictions,* 46 U.Chi. L.Rev. 81, 106 (1978).

e. Brennan, J., argued that the ordinance also failed as an acceptable time, place, and manner restriction because it was not narrowly tailored to serve a significant governmental interest.

a form of protected speech from its borders. The ordinance 'greatly restrict[s] access to, lawful speech,' *Young*, and is plainly unconstitutional."

Notes

1. **Primary effects.** *Renton's* "secondary effects" notion was revisited by several justices in BOOS v. BARRY, Sec. 2, supra: A District of Columbia ordinance banned the display of any sign within 500 feet of a foreign embassy that would tend to bring the embassy into "public odium" or "public disrepute." O'CONNOR, J., joined by Stevens and Scalia, JJ., distinguished *Renton*: "Respondents and the United States do not point to the 'secondary effects' of picket signs in front of embassies. They do not point to congestion, to interference with ingress or egress, to visual clutter, or to the need to protect the security of embassies. Rather, they rely on the need to protect the dignity of foreign diplomatic personnel by shielding them from speech that is critical of their governments. This justification focuses *only* on the content of the speech and the direct impact that speech has on its listeners. The emotive impact of speech on its audience is not a 'secondary effect.'f Because the display clause regulates speech due to its potential primary impact, we conclude it must be considered content-based."g

BRENNAN, J., joined by Marshall, J., agreed with the conclusion that the ordinance was content-based, but objected to O'Connor, J.'s "assumption that the *Renton* analysis applies not only outside the context of businesses purveying sexually explicit materials but even to political speech."h

2. ***The nature of content regulation reconsidered.*** LOS ANGELES v. ALAMEDA BOOKS, 535 U.S. 425 (2002), per O'CONNOR, J., reaffirmed *Renton* and found a sufficient showing of secondary effects to permit Los Angeles not only to disperse adult businesses, but also to prohibit more than one adult entertainment business within the same building, i.e., a company could not have an adult bookstore and an adult video arcade in the same building.

SCALIA, J., concurring, would have gone further: "[I]n a case such as this our First Amendment traditions make secondary effects analysis quite unnecessary. The Constitution does not prevent those communities that wish to do so from regulating, or indeed entirely suppressing, the business of pandering sex."

Four justices expressed doubts about the conception of "content" employed in *Renton*. KENNEDY, J., concurring, criticized *Renton's* conception of "content":

f. See *Forsyth County v. The Nationalist Movement,* 505 U.S. 123 (1992)("Listener's reaction to speech is not a content-neutral basis for regulation,"—not secondary effects).

g. In an earlier passage O'Connor, J., responded to the argument that the ordinance was not content-based on the theory that the government was not selecting between viewpoints. The argument was instead that "the permissible message on a picket sign is determined solely by the policies of a foreign government. We reject this contention, although we agree the provision is not viewpoint-based. The display clause determines which viewpoint is acceptable in a neutral fashion by looking to the policies of foreign governments. While this prevents the display clause from being directly viewpoint-based, a label with potential First Amendment ramifications of its own, it does not render the statute content-neutral. Rather,

we have held that a regulation that 'does not favor either side of a political controversy' is nonetheless impermissible because the 'First Amendment's hostility to content-based regulation extends [to] prohibition of public discussion of an entire topic.' Here the government has determined that an entire category of speech—signs or displays critical of foreign governments—is not to be permitted."

h. Rehnquist, J., joined by White and Blackmun, JJ., voted to uphold the ordinance on the basis of Bork, J.'s opinion below in *Finzer v. Barry,* 798 F.2d 1450 (D.C.Cir.1986). Bork, J., stated that the need to adhere to principles of international law might constitute a secondary effect under *Renton* but was not "entirely sure" whether *Renton* alone could dictate that result and did not resolve the issue. Id. at 1469–70 n. 15.

"*Renton* described a similar ordinance as "content neutral," and I agree with the dissent that the designation is imprecise. [T]he ordinance in *Renton* 'treat[ed] theaters that specialize in adult films differently from other kinds of theaters.' The fiction that this sort of ordinance is content neutral—or 'content neutral'—is perhaps more confusing than helpful, as Justice Souter demonstrates. [These] ordinances are content based, and we should call them so."

Nonetheless, Kennedy, J., adhered to the "intermediate scrutiny" of *Renton* and required a city to "advance some basis to show that its regulation has the purpose and effect of suppressing secondary effects, while leaving the quantity and accessibility of speech substantially intact. The ordinance may identify the speech based on content, but only as a shorthand for identifying the secondary effects outside. A city may not assert that it will reduce secondary effects by reducing speech in the same proportion. [The] rationale of the ordinance must be that it will suppress secondary effects and not by suppressing speech." Kennedy, J., found that Los Angeles ordinance met this burden.

SOUTER, J., joined by Stevens and Ginsburg, and in part by Breyer, JJ., dissented:i "[W]hile it may be true that an adult business is burdened only because of its secondary effects, it is clearly burdened only if its expressive products have adult content. Thus, the Court has recognized that this kind of regulation, though called content neutral, occupies a kind of limbo between full-blown, content-based restrictions and regulations that apply without any reference to the substance of what is said.

"It would in fact make sense to give this kind of zoning regulation a First Amendment label of its own, and if we called it content correlated, we would not only describe it for what it is, but keep alert to a risk of content-based regulation that it poses. The risk lies in the fact that when a law applies selectively only to speech of particular content, the more precisely the content is identified, the greater is the opportunity for government censorship. Adult speech refers not merely to sexually explicit content, but to speech reflecting a favorable view of being explicit about sex and a favorable view of the practices it depicts; a restriction on adult content is thus also a restriction turning on a particular viewpoint, of which the government may disapprove.

"This risk of viewpoint discrimination is subject to a relatively simple safeguard, however. If combating secondary effects of property devaluation and crime is truly the reason for the regulation, it is possible to show by empirical evidence that the effects exist, that they are caused by the expressive activity subject to the zoning, and that the zoning can be expected either to ameliorate them or to enhance the capacity of the government to combat them (say, by concentrating them in one area), without suppressing the expressive activity itself. This capacity of zoning regulation to address the practical problems without eliminating the speech is, after all, the only possible excuse for speaking of secondary-effects zoning as akin to time, place, or manner regulations." Souter, J., argued that Los Angeles had not met this burden.

3. **Nude dancing.** Erie, Pennsylvania forbade knowingly or intentionally appearing in a public "state of nudity." The preamble to the ordinance stated a concern with limiting a recent increase in nude live entertainment within the City which led to prostitution and other crime. Pap's A.M., operated "Kandyland," featuring nude erotic dancing by women. To comply with the ordinance, these dancers had to minimally wear "pasties" and a "G-string." Pap's sought an injunction against the ordinance's enforcement. In ERIE v. PAP'S A.M., 529 U.S.

---

i. Breyer, J., joined this section of the opinion, but not the portion quoted here.

277 (2000), the plurality per O'CONNOR, J., joined by Rehnquist, C.J., and Kennedy and Breyer, JJ., upheld application of the ordinance to prevent nude dancing: "Being 'in a state of nudity' is not an inherently expressive condition. [N]ude dancing of the type at issue here is expressive conduct, although we think that it falls only within the outer ambit of the First Amendment's protection. [G]overnment restrictions on public nudity such as the ordinance at issue here should be evaluated under the framework set forth in *O'Brien* for content-neutral restrictions on symbolic speech. * * *

"The ordinance [bans] all public nudity, regardless of whether that nudity is accompanied by expressive activity [and] updates provisions of an 'Indecency and Immorality' ordinance that has been on the books since 1866, predating the prevalence of nude dancing establishments such as Kandyland. * * *

"[E]ven if Erie's public nudity ban has some minimal effect on the erotic message by muting that portion of the expression that occurs when the last stitch is dropped, [a]ny effect on the overall expression is de minimis. And as Justice Stevens eloquently stated for the plurality in *Young*, 'even though we recognize that the First Amendment will not tolerate the total suppression of erotic materials that have some arguably artistic value, it is manifest that society's interest in protecting this type of expression is of a wholly different, and lesser, magnitude than the interest in untrammeled political debate.' * * *

"As to [whether] the regulation furthers the government interest—it is evident that, since crime and other public health and safety problems are caused by the presence of nude dancing establishments like Kandyland, a ban on such nude dancing would further Erie's interest in preventing such secondary effects. To be sure, requiring dancers to wear pasties and G-strings may not greatly reduce these secondary effects, but *O'Brien* requires only that the regulation further the interest in combating such effects. [It may] be true that a pasties and G-string requirement would not be as effective as, for example, a requirement that the dancers be fully clothed, but the city must balance its efforts to address the problem with the requirement that the restriction be no greater than necessary to further the city's interest. [The] requirement that dancers wear pasties and G-strings is a minimal restriction in furtherance of the asserted government interests, and the restriction leaves ample capacity to convey the dancer's erotic message. Justice Souter points out that zoning is an alternative means of addressing this problem. It is far from clear, however, that zoning imposes less of a burden on expression than the minimal requirement implemented here. In any event, since this is a content-neutral restriction, least restrictive means analysis is not required."

SCALIA, J., joined by Thomas., J., concurring, voted to uphold the ordinance: " 'not because it survives some lower level of First Amendment scrutiny, but because, as a general law regulating conduct and not specifically directed at expression, it is not subject to First Amendment scrutiny at all.' Erie's ordinance, too, by its terms prohibits not merely nude dancing, but the act—irrespective of whether it is engaged in for expressive purposes—of going nude in public. The [fact] that a preamble to the ordinance explains that its purpose, in part, is to 'limi[t] a recent increase in nude live entertainment,' * * * simply reflect[s] the fact that Erie had recently been having a public nudity problem not with streakers, sunbathers or hot-dog vendors, but with lap dancers."

SOUTER, J., concurred in part and dissented in part: "I [agree] with the analytical approach that the plurality employs in deciding this case. [But] intermediate scrutiny requires a regulating government to make some demonstration of an evidentiary basis for the harm it claims to flow from the expressive activity, and for the alleviation expected from the restriction imposed. [What] is clear is that the evidence of reliance must be a matter of demonstrated fact, not speculative supposition. By these standards, the record before us today is deficient."

STEVENS, J., joined by Ginsburg, J., dissented: "[Never] before have we approved the use of ['the so-called 'secondary effects' test'] to justify a total ban on protected First Amendment expression. On the contrary, we have been quite clear that the doctrine would not support that end. * * * The reason we have limited our secondary effects cases to zoning and declined to extend their reasoning to total bans is clear and straightforward: A dispersal that simply limits the places where speech may occur is a minimal imposition whereas a total ban is the most exacting of restrictions. * * *

"[T]he plurality concedes that 'requiring dancers to wear pasties and G-strings may not greatly reduce these secondary effects.' To believe that the mandatory addition of pasties and a G-string will have *any* kind of noticeable impact on secondary effects requires nothing short of a titanic surrender to the implausible."

II. COMMERCIAL SPEECH

VIRGINIA STATE BOARD OF PHARMACY v. VIRGINIA CITIZENS CONSUMER COUNCIL

425 U.S. 748, 96 S.Ct. 1817, 48 L.Ed.2d 346 (1976).

JUSTICE BLACKMUN delivered the opinion of the Court.

[The Court held invalid a Virginia statute that made advertising the prices of prescription drugs "unprofessional conduct," subjecting pharmacists to license suspension or revocation. Prescription drug prices strikingly varied within the same locality, in Virginia and nationally, sometimes by several hundred percent. Such drugs were dispensed exclusively by licensed pharmacists but 95% were prepared by manufacturers, not compounded by the pharmacists.]

[Appellants] contend that the advertisement of prescription drug prices is outside the protection of the First Amendment because it is "commercial speech." There can be no question that in past decisions the Court has given some indication that commercial speech is unprotected.a

Last Term, in *Bigelow v. Virginia*, 421 U.S. 809 (1975), the notion of unprotected "commercial speech" all but passed from the scene. We reversed a conviction for violation of a Virginia statute that made the circulation of any publication to encourage or promote the processing of an abortion in Virginia a misdemeanor. The defendant had published in his newspaper the availability of abortions in New York. The advertisement in question, in addition to announcing that abortions were legal in New York, offered the services of a referral agency in that State. [We] concluded that "the Virginia courts erred in their assumptions that advertising, as such, was entitled to no First Amendment protection," and we observed that the "relationship of speech to the marketplace of products or of services does not make it valueless in the marketplace of ideas."

Some fragment of hope for the continuing validity of a "commercial speech" exception arguably might have persisted because of the subject matter of the advertisement in *Bigelow*. We noted that in announcing the availability of legal abortions in New York, the advertisement "did more than simply propose a

---

a. Starting with *Valentine v. Chrestensen,* 316 U.S. 52 (1942), the opinion summarized   the decisions and dicta that gave such "indication."

commercial transaction. It contained factual material of clear 'public interest.'" And, of course, the advertisement related to activity with which, at least in some respects, the State could not interfere. See *Roe v. Wade*. Indeed, we observed: "We need not decide in this case the precise extent to which the First Amendment permits regulation of advertising that is related to activities the State may legitimately regulate or even prohibit."

Here, [the] question whether there is a First Amendment exception for "commercial speech" is squarely before us. Our pharmacist does not wish to editorialize on any subject, cultural, philosophical, or political. He does not wish to report any particularly newsworthy fact, or to make generalized observations even about commercial matters. The "idea" he wishes to communicate is simply this: "I will sell you the X prescription drug at the Y price." Our question, then, is whether this communication is wholly outside the protection of the First Amendment.

V. [Speech] does not lose its First Amendment protection because money is spent to project it, as in a paid advertisement of one form or another. *New York Times Co. v. Sullivan*. Speech likewise is protected even though it is carried in a form that is "sold" for profit. *Smith v. California*. [Our] question is whether speech which does "no more than propose a commercial transaction," is so removed from any "exposition of ideas," and from "truth, science, morality, and arts in general, in its diffusion of liberal sentiments on the administration of Government", *Roth*, that it lacks all protection. Our answer is that it is not.

Focusing first on the individual parties to the transaction that is proposed in the commercial advertisement, we may assume that the advertiser's interest is a purely economic one. That hardly disqualifies him for protection under the First Amendment. The interests of the contestants in a labor dispute are primarily economic, but it has long been settled that both the employee and the employer are protected by the First Amendment when they express themselves on the merits of the dispute in order to influence its outcome. * * *17

As to the particular consumer's interest in the free flow of commercial information, that interest may be as keen, if not keener by far, than his interest in the day's most urgent political debate. Appellees' case in this respect is a convincing one. Those whom the suppression of prescription drug price information hits the hardest are the poor, the sick, and particularly the aged. A disproportionate amount of their income tends to be spent on prescription drugs; yet they are the least able to learn, by shopping from pharmacist to pharmacist, where their scarce dollars are best spent. When drug prices vary as strikingly as they do, information as to who is charging what becomes more than a convenience. It could mean the alleviation of physical pain or the enjoyment of basic necessities.

Generalizing, society also may have a strong interest in the free flow of commercial information. Even an individual advertisement, though entirely "commercial," may be of general public interest. The facts of decided cases furnish illustrations: advertisements stating that referral services for legal abortions are available, *Bigelow;* that a manufacturer of artificial furs promotes his product as an alternative to the extinction by his competitors of fur-bearing mammals, see

---

17. The speech of labor disputants, of course, is subject to a number of restrictions. The Court stated in *NLRB v. Gissel Packing Co.*, 395 U.S., at 618 (1969), for example, that an employer's threats of retaliation for the labor actions of his employees are "without the protection of the First Amendment." The con- stitutionality of restrictions upon speech in the special context of labor disputes is not before us here. We express no views on that complex subject, and advert to cases in the labor field only to note that in some circumstances speech of an entirely private and economic character enjoys the protection of the First Amendment.

Fur Information & Fashion Council, Inc. v. E.F. Timme & Son, 364 F.Supp. 16 (S.D.N.Y.1973); and that a domestic producer advertises his product as an alternative to imports that tend to deprive American residents of their jobs, cf. *Chicago Joint Board v. Chicago Tribune Co.,* 435 F.2d 470 (C.A.7 1970), cert. denied, 402 U.S. 973 (1971). Obviously, not all commercial messages contain the same or even a very great public interest element. There are few to which such an element, however, could not be added. Our pharmacist, for example, could cast himself as a commentator on store-to-store disparities in drug prices, giving his own and those of a competitor as proof. We see little point in requiring him to do so, and little difference if he does not.

Moreover, there is another consideration that suggests that no line between publicly "interesting" or "important" commercial advertising and the opposite kind could ever be drawn. Advertising, however tasteless and excessive it sometimes may seem, is nonetheless dissemination of information as to who is producing and selling what product, for what reason, and at what price. So long as we preserve a predominantly free enterprise economy, the allocation of our resources in large measure will be made through numerous private economic decisions. It is a matter of public interest that those decisions, in the aggregate, be intelligent and well informed. To this end, the free flow of commercial information is indispensable. And if it is indispensable to the proper allocation of resources in a free enterprise system, it is also indispensable to the formation of intelligent opinions as to how that system ought to be regulated or altered. Therefore, even if the First Amendment were thought to be primarily an instrument to enlighten public decision making in a democracy, we could not say that the free flow of information does not serve that goal.

Arrayed against these substantial individual and societal interests are a number of justifications for the advertising ban. These have to do principally with maintaining a high degree of professionalism on the part of licensed pharmacists. [Price] advertising, it is argued, will place in jeopardy the pharmacist's expertise and, with it, the customer's health. It is claimed that the aggressive price competition that will result from unlimited advertising will make it impossible for the pharmacist to supply professional services in the compounding, handling, and dispensing of prescription drugs. Such services are time-consuming and expensive; if competitors who economize by eliminating them are permitted to advertise their resulting lower prices, the more painstaking and conscientious pharmacist will be forced either to follow suit or to go out of business. [It] is further claimed that advertising will lead people to shop for their prescription drugs among the various pharmacists who offer the lowest prices, and the loss of stable pharmacist-customer relationships will make individual [attention] impossible. Finally, it is argued that damage will be done to the professional image of the pharmacist. This image, that of a skilled and specialized craftsman, attracts talent to the profession and reinforces the better habits of those who are in [it].

The strength of these proffered justifications is greatly undermined by the fact that high professional standards, to a substantial extent, are guaranteed by the close regulation to which pharmacists in Virginia are subject. [At] the same time, we cannot discount the Board's justifications entirely. [The Court regarded justifications of this type sufficient to sustain the advertising bans challenged on due process and equal protection grounds].**b**

b. The Court referred here to cases upholding bans on advertising prices for eyeglass frames and optometrist and dental services.

The challenge now made, however, is based on the First Amendment. This casts the Board's justifications in a different light, for on close inspection it is seen that the State's protectiveness of its citizens rests in large measure on the advantages of their being kept in ignorance. The advertising ban does not directly affect professional standards one way or the other. It affects them only through the reactions it is assumed people will have to the free flow of drug price information. There is no claim that the advertising ban in any way prevents the cutting of corners by the pharmacist who is so inclined. That pharmacist is likely to cut corners in any event. The only effect the advertising ban has on him is to insulate him from price competition and to open the way for him to make a substantial, and perhaps even excessive, profit in addition to providing an inferior service. The more painstaking pharmacist is also protected but, again, it is a protection based in large part on public ignorance.

It appears to be feared that if the pharmacist who wishes to provide low cost, and assertedly low quality, services is permitted to advertise, he will be taken up on his offer by too many unwitting customers. They will choose the low-cost, low-quality service and drive the "professional" pharmacist out of business. [They] will go from one pharmacist to another, following the discount, and destroy the pharmacist-customer relationship. They will lose respect for the profession because it advertises. All this is not in their best interests, and all this can be avoided if they are not permitted to know who is charging what.

[A]n alternative to this highly paternalistic approach [is] to assume that this information is not in itself harmful, that people will perceive their own best interests if only they are well enough informed, and that the best means to that end is to open the channels of communication rather than to close them. If they are truly open, nothing prevents the "professional" pharmacist from marketing his own assertedly superior product, and contrasting it with that of the low-cost, high-volume prescription drug retailer. But the choice among these alternative approaches is not ours to make or the Virginia General Assembly's. It is precisely this kind of choice, between the dangers of suppressing information, and the dangers of its misuse if it is freely available, that the First Amendment makes for [us].

VI. In concluding that commercial speech, like other varieties, is protected, we of course do not hold that it can never be regulated in any way. Some forms of commercial speech regulation are surely permissible. We mention a few. [There] is no claim, for example, that the prohibition on prescription drug price advertising is a mere time, place, and manner restriction. We have often approved restrictions of that kind provided that they are justified without reference to the content of the regulated speech, that they serve a significant governmental interest, and that in so doing they leave open ample alternative channels for communication of the information. Whatever may be the proper bounds of time, place, and manner restrictions on commercial speech, they are plainly exceeded by this Virginia statute, which singles out speech of a particular content and seeks to prevent its dissemination completely.

Nor is there any claim that prescription drug price advertisements are forbidden because they are false or misleading in any way. Untruthful speech, commercial or otherwise, has never been protected for its own sake. *Gertz.* Obviously much commercial speech is not provably false, or even wholly false, but only deceptive or misleading. We foresee no obstacle to a State's dealing effectively with this problem.24 The First Amendment, as we construe it today, does not

24. [C]ommon sense differences between speech that does "no more than propose a commercial transaction," *Pittsburgh Press* and other varieties [suggest] that a different degree

prohibit the State from insuring that the stream of commercial information flows cleanly as well as freely.

Also, there is no claim that the transactions proposed in the forbidden advertisements are themselves illegal in any way. Finally, the special problems of the electronic broadcast media are likewise not in this case.

What is at issue is whether a State may completely suppress the dissemination of concededly truthful information about entirely lawful activity, fearful of that information's effect upon its disseminators and its recipients. Reserving other questions,25 we conclude that the answer to this one is in the [negative].

JUSTICE STEWART, concurring.c

[I] write separately to explain why I think today's decision does not preclude [governmental regulation of false or deceptive advertising]. The Court has on several occasions addressed the problems posed by false statements of fact in libel cases. [Factual] errors are inevitable in free debate, and the imposition of liability for [such errors] can "dampe[n] the vigor and limi[t] the variety of public debate" by inducing "self-censorship." [In] contrast to the press, which must often attempt to assemble the true facts from sketchy and sometimes conflicting sources under the pressure of publication deadlines, the commercial advertiser generally knows the product or service he seeks to sell and is in a position to verify the accuracy of his factual representations before he disseminates them. The advertiser's access to the truth about his product and its price substantially eliminates any danger that governmental regulation of false or misleading price or product advertising will chill accurate and nondeceptive commercial [expression].

Since the factual claims contained in commercial price or product advertisements relate to tangible goods or services, they may be tested empirically and corrected to reflect the truth without in any manner jeopardizing the free dissemination of thought. Indeed, the elimination of false and deceptive claims serves to promote the one facet of commercial price and product advertising that warrants First Amendment protection—its contribution to the flow of accurate and reliable information relevant to public and private decision making.

JUSTICE REHNQUIST, dissenting.

of protection is necessary to insure that the flow of truthful and legitimate commercial information is unimpaired. The truth of commercial speech, for example, may be more easily verifiable by its disseminator than, let us say, news reporting or political commentary, in that ordinarily the advertiser seeks to disseminate information about a specific product or service that he himself provides and presumably knows more about than anyone else. Also, commercial speech may be more durable than other kinds. Since advertising is the sine qua non of commercial profits, there is little likelihood of its being chilled by proper regulation and foregone entirely.

Attributes such as these, the greater objectivity and hardiness of commercial speech, may make it less necessary to tolerate inaccurate statements for fear of silencing the speaker. They may also make it appropriate to require that a commercial message appear in such a form, or include such additional information, warnings and disclaimers, as are necessary to prevent its being deceptive. They may also make inapplicable the prohibition on prior restraints. Compare *New York Times v. United States* [Sec. 4, III infra] with *Donaldson v. Read Magazine,* 333 U.S. 178 (1948).

25. We stress that we have considered in this case the regulation of commercial advertising by pharmacists. Although we express no opinion as to other professions, the distinctions, historical and functional, between professions, may require consideration of quite different factors. Physicians and lawyers, for example, do not dispense standardized products; they render professional *services* of almost infinite variety and nature, with the consequent enhanced possibility for confusion and deception if they were to undertake certain kinds of advertising.

c. Burger, C.J., separately concurring, stressed the reservation in fn. 25 of the opinion with respect to advertising by attorneys and physicians. Stevens, J., took no part.

[Under] the Court's opinion the way will be open not only for dissemination of price information but for active promotion of prescription drugs, liquor, cigarettes and other products the use of which it has previously been thought desirable to discourage. Now, however, such promotion is protected by the First Amendment so long as it is not misleading or does not promote an illegal product or [enterprise].

The Court speaks of the consumer's interest in the free flow of commercial information. [This] should presumptively be the concern of the Virginia Legislature, which sits to balance [this] and other claims in the process of making laws such as the one here under attack. The Court speaks of the importance in a "predominantly free enterprise economy" of intelligent and well-informed decisions as to allocation of resources. While there is again much to be said for the Court's observation as a matter of desirable public policy, there is certainly nothing in the United States Constitution which requires the Virginia Legislature to hew to the teachings of Adam Smith in its legislative decisions regulating the pharmacy profession. E.g., *Nebbia v. New York*; *Olsen v. Nebraska*.

[There] are undoubted difficulties with an effort to draw a bright line between "commercial speech" on the one hand and "protected speech" on the other, and the Court does better to face up to these difficulties than to attempt to hide them under labels. In this case, however, the Court has unfortunately substituted for the wavering line previously thought to exist between commercial speech and protected speech a no more satisfactory line of its own—that between "truthful" commercial speech, on the one hand, and that which is "false and misleading" on the other. The difficulty with this line is not that it wavers, but on the contrary that it is simply too Procrustean to take into account the congeries of factors which I believe could, quite consistently with the First and Fourteenth Amendments, properly influence a legislative decision with respect to commercial advertising.

[S]uch a line simply makes no allowance whatever for what appears to have been a considered legislative judgment in most States that while prescription drugs are a necessary and vital part of medical care and treatment, there are sufficient dangers attending their widespread use that they simply may not be promoted in the same manner as hair creams, deodorants, and toothpaste. The very real dangers that general advertising for such drugs might create in terms of encouraging, even though not sanctioning, illicit use of them by individuals for whom they have not been prescribed, or by generating patient pressure upon physicians to prescribe them are simply not dealt with in the Court's [opinion].

OHRALIK v. OHIO STATE BAR ASS'N, 436 U.S. 447 (1978), upheld the indefinite suspension of an attorney for violating the anti-solicitation provisions of the Ohio Code of Professional Responsibility. Those provisions generally do not allow lawyers to recommend themselves to anyone who has not sought "their advice regarding employment of a lawyer." Albert Ohralik had approached two young accident victims to solicit employment—Carol McClintock in a hospital room where she lay in traction and Wanda Lou Holbert on the day she came home from the hospital. He employed a concealed tape recorder with Holbert, apparently to insure he would have evidence of her assent to his representation. The next day, when Holbert's mother informed Ohralik that she and her daughter did not want to have appellant represent them, he insisted that the daughter had entered into a binding agreement. McClintock also discharged Ohralik, and Ohralik sued her for breach of contract. The Court ruled, per POWELL, J., that a state may forbid in-person solicitation of clients by lawyers for pecuniary gain:

"Expression concerning purely commercial transactions has come within the ambit of the Amendment's protection only recently. In rejecting the notion that such speech is wholly outside the protection of the First Amendment, *Virginia Pharmacy,* we were careful not to hold that it is wholly undifferentiable from other forms of speech.

"We have not discarded the common sense distinction between speech proposing a commercial transaction, which occurs in an area traditionally subject to government regulation, and other varieties of speech. To require a parity of constitutional protection for commercial and noncommercial speech alike could invite dilution, simply by a leveling process, of the force of the Amendment's guarantee with respect to the latter kind of speech. Rather than subject the First Amendment to such a devitalization, we instead have afforded commercial speech a limited measure of protection, commensurate with its subordinate position in the scale of First Amendment values, while allowing modes of regulation that might be impermissible in the realm of noncommercial expression.

"Moreover, 'it has never been deemed an abridgment of freedom of speech or press to make a course of conduct illegal merely because the conduct was in part initiated, evidenced, or carried out by means of language, either spoken, written, or printed.' *Giboney v. Empire Storage & Ice Co.,* 336 U.S. 490, 502 (1949). Numerous examples could be cited of communications that are regulated without offending the First Amendment, such as the exchange of information about securities, *SEC v. Texas Gulf Sulphur Co.,* 401 F.2d 833 (C.A.2 1968), cert. denied, 394 U.S. 976 (1969), corporate proxy statements, *Mills v. Electric Auto–Lite Co.,* 396 U.S. 375 (1970), the exchange of price and production information among competitors, *American Column & Lumber Co. v. United States,* 257 U.S. 377 (1921), and employers' threats of retaliation for the labor activities of employees, *NLRB v. Gissel Packing Co.,* 395 U.S. 575, 618 (1969). [These examples [illustrate] that the State does not lose its power to regulate commercial activity deemed harmful to the public whenever speech is a component of that activity. Neither *Virginia Pharmacy* nor *Bates* purported to cast doubt on the permissibility of these kinds of commercial regulation.

"In-person solicitation by a lawyer of remunerative employment is a business transaction in which speech is an essential but subordinate component. While this does not remove the speech from the protection of the First Amendment, as was held in *Bates* and *Virginia Pharmacy,* it lowers the level of appropriate judicial scrutiny. [A] lawyer's procurement of remunerative employment is a subject only marginally affected with First Amendment concerns. It falls within the State's proper sphere of economic and professional regulation. While entitled to some constitutional protection, appellant's conduct is subject to regulation in furtherance of important state [interests].

" 'The interest of the States in regulating lawyers is especially great since lawyers are essential to the primary function of administering justice and have historically been officers of the courts' [and] act 'as trusted agents of their clients and as assistants to the court in search of a just solution to disputes.'

"[The] substantive evils of solicitation have been stated over the years in sweeping terms: stirring up litigation, assertion of fraudulent claims, debasing the legal profession, and potential harm to the solicited client in the form of overreaching, overcharging, underrepresentation, and misrepresentation." In providing information about the availability and terms of proposed legal services "inperson solicitation serves much the same function as the advertisement at issue in

Bates. But there are significant differences as well. Unlike a public advertisement, which simply provides information and leaves the recipient free to act upon it or not, in-person solicitation may exert pressure and often demands an immediate response, without providing an opportunity for comparison or reflection. The aim and effect of in-person solicitation may be to provide a one-sided presentation and to encourage speedy and perhaps uninformed decision making; there is no opportunity for intervention or counter-education by agencies of the Bar, supervisory authorities, or persons close to the solicited individual. The admonition that 'the fitting remedy for evil counsels is good ones' is of little value when the circumstances provide no opportunity for any remedy at all. In-person solicitation is as likely as not to discourage persons needing counsel from engaging in a critical comparison of the 'availability, nature, and prices' of legal services; it actually may disserve the individual and societal interest, identified in *Bates,* in facilitating 'informed and reliable decision making.'

"[Appellant's argument that none of the evils of solicitation was found in his case] misconceives the nature of the State's interest. The rules prohibiting solicitation are prophylactic measures whose objective is the prevention of harm before it occurs. The rules were applied in this case to discipline a lawyer for soliciting employment for pecuniary gain under circumstances likely to result in the adverse consequences the State seeks to avert. In such a situation, which is inherently conducive to overreaching and other forms of misconduct, the State has a strong interest in adopting and enforcing rules of conduct designed to protect the public from harmful solicitation by lawyers whom it has [licensed].

"The efficacy of the State's effort to prevent such harm to prospective clients would be substantially diminished if, having proved a solicitation in circumstances like those of this case, the State were required in addition to prove actual injury. Unlike the advertising in *Bates,* in-person solicitation is not visible or otherwise open to public scrutiny. Often there is no witness other than the lawyer and the lay person whom he has solicited, rendering it difficult or impossible to obtain reliable proof of what actually took place. This would be especially true if the lay person were so distressed at the time of the solicitation that he or she could not recall specific details at a later date. If appellant's view were sustained, in-person solicitation would be virtually immune to effective oversight and regulation by the State or by the legal profession, in contravention of the State's strong interest in regulating members of the Bar in an effective, objective, and self-enforcing manner. It therefore is not unreasonable, or violative of the Constitution, for a State to respond with what in effect is a prophylactic rule."a

Notes

1. ***Companion case.*** IN RE PRIMUS, 436 U.S. 412 (1978), per POWELL, J., held that a state could not constitutionally discipline an ACLU "cooperating lawyer" who, after advising a gathering of allegedly illegally sterilized women of their rights, initiated further contact with one of the women by writing her a letter informing her of the ACLU's willingness to provide free legal representation for women in her situation and of the organization's desire to file a lawsuit on her behalf. "South Carolina's action in punishing appellant for soliciting a prospective litigant by mail, on behalf of ACLU, must withstand the 'exacting scrutiny applicable to limitations on core First Amendment rights.' [Where] political

a. Marshall and Rehnquist, JJ., each separately concurred in the judgment. Brennan, J., did not participate.

expression or association is at issue, this Court has not tolerated the degree of imprecision that often characterizes government regulation of the conduct of commercial affairs. The approach we adopt today in *Ohralik* that the State may proscribe in-person solicitation for pecuniary gain under circumstances likely to result in adverse consequences, cannot be applied to appellant's activity on behalf of the ACLU. Although a showing of potential danger may suffice in the former context, appellant may not be disciplined unless her activity in fact involved the type of misconduct at which South Carolina's broad prohibition is said to be directed. The record does not support appellee's contention that undue influence, overreaching, misrepresentation, or invasion of privacy actually occurred in this case."

2. ***Related cases.*** *Edenfield v. Fane,* 507 U.S. 761 (1993) held that direct personal solicitation of prospective business clients by Certified Public Accountants is protected under the First Amendment,[b] but *Florida Bar v. Went For It, Inc.,* 515 U.S. 618 (1995) held that targeted direct-mail solicitations by personal injury attorneys to victims and their relatives for thirty days following an accident were not protected under the First Amendment. See also *Tennessee Secondary School Athletic Assn v. Brentwood Academy,* 551 U.S. 291 (2007) (five justices maintain that *Ohralik* does not apply to rules designed to protect chidren from recruitment solicitations by high school coaches).

3. ***Muddying the hierarchy.*** Cincinnati permitted 1,500–2,000 news racks throughout the city for publications not classified as commercial speech, but refused to allow an additional 62 news racks that contained two publications classified as commercial speech. CINCINNATI v. DISCOVERY NETWORK, 507 U.S. 410 (1993), per STEVENS, J., held that this discrimination violated the First Amendment: "The major premise supporting the city's argument is the proposition that commercial speech has only a low value. Based on that premise, the city contends that the fact that assertedly more valuable publications are allowed to use news racks does not undermine its judgment that its esthetic and safety interests are stronger than the interest in allowing commercial speakers to have similar access to the reading public. [In] our view, the city's argument attaches more importance to the distinction between commercial and non-commercial speech than our cases warrant and seriously underestimates the value of commercial speech.20"c

b. Blackmun, J., concurred; O'Connor, J., dissented. Compare *Ibanez v. Florida Dep't of Business and Professional Regulation,* 512 U.S. 136 (1994) (attorney's references in advertising, business cards and stationery to her credentials as a CPA and a Certified Financial Planner are not deceptive or misleading and are protected commercial speech); Accord, *Peel v. Attorney Registration and Disciplinary Comm'n,* 496 U.S. 91 (1990) (reference on letterhead to prestigious certification is protected speech).

20. *Metromedia, Inc. v. San Diego,* 453 U.S. 490 (1981), upon which the city heavily relies, is not to the contrary. In that case, a plurality of the Court found as a permissible restriction on commercial speech a city ordinance that, for the most part, banned outdoor "offsite" advertising billboards, but permitted "onsite" advertising signs identifying the owner of the premises and the goods sold or manufactured on the site. Unlike this case, which involves discrimination between commercial and noncommer-

cial speech, the "offsite-onsite" distinction involved disparate treatment of two types of commercial speech. Only the onsite signs served both the commercial and public interest in guiding potential visitors to their intended destinations; moreover, the plurality concluded that a "city may believe that offsite advertising, with its periodically changing content, presents a more acute problem than does onsite advertising." Neither of these bases has any application to the disparate treatment of news racks in this case.

The Chief Justice is correct that seven Justices in the Metromedia case were of the view that San Diego could completely ban offsite commercial billboards for reasons unrelated to the content of those billboards. Those seven Justices did not say, however, that San Diego could distinguish between commercial and noncommercial offsite billboards that cause the same esthetic and safety concerns. That question was not presented in Metromedia, for the

4. ***The reach of Discovery Network.*** (a) In MARTIN v. STRUTHERS, 319 U.S. 141 (1943), a city forbade knocking on the door or ringing the doorbell of a resident in order to deliver handbills (in an industrial community where many worked night shifts and slept during the day). In striking down the ordinance, the Court, per BLACK, J., pointed out that the city's objectives could be achieved by means of a law making it an offense for any person to ring the doorbell of a householder who has "appropriately indicated that he is unwilling to be disturbed. This or any similar regulation leaves the decision as to whether distributors of literature may lawfully call at a home where it belongs—with the homeowner himself." By contrast, *Breard v. Alexandria,* 341 U.S. 622 (1951) upheld an ordinance forbidding the practice of going door to door to solicit orders for the sale of goods.

(b) Compare *Schneider,* Sec. 6, I, A infra (prohibition against leaflet distribution on streets unconstitutional) with *Valentine,* Sec. 3, II supra (prohibition against distribution of commercial leaflets upheld). Does (should) the *holding* of *Valentine* survive *Virginia Pharmacy?* Does *Discovery Network* settle the issue?

(c) *Linmark* held it unconstitutional for a locality to prohibit "For Sale" signs on residential property. Similarly, the Court has held it unconstitutional to permit property owners to display "For Sale" signs while prohibiting most other signs including those with political, religious or personal messages. *Ladue v. Gilleo,* 512 U.S. 43 (1994).

———

In CENTRAL HUDSON GAS & ELEC. CORP. v. PUBLIC SERV. COMM'N, 447 U.S. 557 (1980), the Court, per POWELL, J., characterized the prior commercial speech cases as embracing a special test: "In commercial speech cases, then, a four-part analysis has developed. At the outset, we must determine whether the expression is protected by the First Amendment. For commercial speech to come within that provision, it at least must concern lawful activity and not be misleading. Next, we ask whether the asserted governmental interest is substantial. If both inquiries yield positive answers, we must determine whether the regulation directly advances the governmental interest asserted, and whether it is not more extensive than is necessary to serve that interest."

LORILLARD TOBACCO CO. v. REILLY

533 U.S. 525, 121 S.Ct. 2404, 150 L.Ed.2d 532 (2001).

JUSTICE O'CONNOR delivered the opinion of the Court.

In January 1999, the Attorney General of Massachusetts promulgated comprehensive regulations governing the advertising and sale of cigarettes, smokeless tobacco, and cigars. Petitioners, a group of cigarette, smokeless tobacco, and cigar manufacturers and retailers, filed suit in Federal District Court claiming that the regulations violate federal law and the United States Constitution.

I. [The Court observed that the purpose of the restrictions was "to eliminate deception and unfairness in the way cigarettes and smokeless tobacco products are

regulation at issue in that case did not draw a distinction between commercial and noncommercial offsite billboards; with a few exceptions, it essentially banned all offsite billboards.

c. Rehnquist, C.J., joined by White & Thomas, JJ., dissented.

marketed, sold and distributed in Massachusetts in order to address the incidence of cigarette smoking and smokeless tobacco use by children under legal age [and] to prevent access to such products by underage consumers. The similar purpose of the cigar regulations is 'to eliminate [the] false perception that cigars are a safe alternative to cigarettes [and] to prevent access to such products by underage consumers.' " Among other things the restrictions prohibited outdoor advertising, "including advertising in enclosed stadiums and advertising from within a retail establishment that is directed toward or visible from the outside of the establishment, in any location that is within a 1,000 foot radius of any public playground, playground area in a public park, elementary school or secondary school."].a

II. [The Court concluded that the Federal Cigarette Labeling and Advertising Act of 1965 as amended, prevented states and localities from regulating the location of cigarette advertising.]

III. By its terms, the FCLAA's pre-emption provision only applies to cigarettes. Accordingly, we must evaluate the smokeless tobacco and cigar petitioners' First Amendment challenges to the State's outdoor and point-of-sale advertising regulations. The cigarette petitioners did not raise a pre-emption challenge to the sales practices regulations. Thus, we must analyze the cigarette as well as the smokeless tobacco and cigar petitioners' claim that certain sales practices regulations for tobacco products violate the First Amendment.

A. [Petitioners] urge us to reject the *Central Hudson* analysis and apply strict scrutiny. [S]everal Members of the Court have expressed doubts about the *Central Hudson* analysis and whether it should apply in particular cases. See, e.g., *44 Liquormart, Inc. v. Rhode Island*, 517 U.S. 484, 501 (1996) (joint opinion of Stevens, Kennedy, and Ginsburg, JJ.)(Scalia, J. concurring in part and concurring in judgment)(Thomas, J., concurring in part and concurring in judgment). [But] we see "no need to break new ground. *Central Hudson*, as applied in our more recent commercial speech cases, provides an adequate basis for decision."

Only the last two steps of *Central Hudson*'s four-part analysis are at issue here. The Attorney General has assumed for purposes of summary judgment that petitioners' speech is entitled to First Amendment protection. With respect to the second step, none of the petitioners contests the importance of the State's interest in preventing the use of tobacco products by minors.

The third step of *Central Hudson* [requires] that "the speech restriction directly and materially advanc[e] the asserted governmental interest. 'This burden is not satisfied by mere speculation or conjecture; rather, a governmental body seeking to sustain a restriction on commercial speech must demonstrate that the harms it recites are real and that its restriction will in fact alleviate them to a material degree.' " We do not, however, require that "empirical data [come] accompanied by a surfeit of background information. [W]e have permitted litigants to justify speech restrictions by reference to studies and anecdotes pertaining to different locales altogether, or even, in a case applying strict scrutiny, to justify restrictions based solely on history, consensus, and 'simple common sense.' "

a. The regulations also banned such advertising at the point of sale if they were within five feet of the floor of the retail establishment and within a 1000 feet radius of the places identified in the outdoor advertising restrictions. O'Connor, J., found that these regulations violated the third and fourth prongs of *Central Hudson*. Stevens, J., joined by Ginsburg and Breyer, JJ., dissenting, found these restrictions to be "little more than an adjunct" to rules prohibiting the placement of the products within the reach of customers and of only slight impact on the ability of adults to purchase "a poisonous product and may save some children from taking the first step on the road to addiction."

The last step of the *Central Hudson* analysis "complements" the third step, "asking whether the speech restriction is not more extensive than necessary to serve the interests that support it." We have made it clear that "the least restrictive means" is not the standard; instead, the case law requires a reasonable " 'fit between the legislature's ends and the means chosen to accomplish those ends, [a] means narrowly tailored to achieve the desired objective.' " * * *

B.   [1.] The smokeless tobacco and cigar petitioners [maintain] that although the Attorney General may have identified a problem with underage cigarette smoking, he has not identified an equally severe problem with respect to underage use of smokeless tobacco or cigars. The smokeless tobacco petitioner emphasizes the "lack of parity" between cigarettes and smokeless tobacco. The cigar petitioners catalogue a list of differences between cigars and other tobacco products, including the characteristics of the products and marketing strategies. The petitioners finally contend that the Attorney General cannot prove that advertising has a causal link to tobacco use such that limiting advertising will materially alleviate any problem of underage use of their products.

In previous cases, we have acknowledged the theory that product advertising stimulates demand for products, while suppressed advertising may have the opposite effect. *United States v. Edge Broadcasting Co.*, 509 U.S. 418, 434 (1993). The Attorney General cites numerous studies to support this theory in the case of tobacco products [, providing] ample documentation of the problem with underage use of smokeless tobacco and cigars. In addition, we disagree with petitioners' claim that there is no evidence that preventing targeted campaigns and limiting youth exposure to advertising will decrease underage use of smokeless tobacco and cigars. On this record and in the posture of summary judgment, we are unable to conclude that the Attorney General's decision to regulate advertising of smokeless tobacco and cigars in an effort to combat the use of tobacco products by minors was based on mere "speculation [and] conjecture."

2.   Whatever the strength of the Attorney General's evidence to justify the outdoor advertising regulations, however, we conclude that the regulations do not satisfy the fourth step of the *Central Hudson* analysis. * * *

The outdoor advertising regulations prohibit any smokeless tobacco or cigar advertising within 1,000 feet of schools or playgrounds. In the District Court, petitioners maintained that this prohibition would prevent advertising in 87% to 91% of Boston, Worcester, and Springfield. The 87% to 91% figure appears to include not only the effect of the regulations, but also the limitations imposed by other generally applicable zoning restrictions. The Attorney General disputed petitioners' figures but "concede[d] that the reach of the regulations is substantial." * * *

In some geographical areas, these regulations would constitute nearly a complete ban on the communication of truthful information about smokeless tobacco and cigars to adult consumers. The breadth and scope of the regulations, and the process by which the Attorney General adopted the regulations, do not demonstrate a careful calculation of the speech interests involved. * * *

The Attorney General apparently selected the 1,000–foot distance based on the FDA's decision to impose an identical 1,000–foot restriction when it attempted to regulate cigarette and smokeless tobacco advertising. But [the] degree to which speech is suppressed—or alternative avenues for speech remain available—under a particular regulatory scheme tends to be case specific [for] although a State or locality may have common interests and concerns about underage smoking and the effects of tobacco advertisements, the impact of a restriction on speech will undoubtedly vary from place to place. The FDA's regulations would have had widely disparate effects nationwide. Even in Massachusetts, the effect of the Attorney General's speech regulations will vary based on whether a locale is rural, suburban, or urban. The uniformly broad sweep of the geographical limitation demonstrates a lack of tailoring. * * *

The State's interest in preventing underage tobacco use is substantial, and even compelling, but it is no less true that the sale and use of tobacco products by adults is a legal activity. We must consider that tobacco retailers and manufacturers have an interest in conveying truthful information about their products to adults, and adults have a corresponding interest in receiving truthful information about tobacco products. [In] some instances, Massachusetts' outdoor advertising regulations would impose particularly onerous burdens on speech. For example, we disagree with the Court of Appeals' conclusion that because cigar manufacturers and retailers conduct a limited amount of advertising in comparison to other tobacco products, "the relative lack of cigar advertising also means that the burden imposed on cigar advertisers is correspondingly small." If some retailers have relatively small advertising budgets, and use few avenues of communication, then the Attorney General's outdoor advertising regulations potentially place a greater, not lesser, burden on those retailers' speech. * * *

JUSTICE KENNEDY, with whom JUSTICE SCALIA joins, concurring in part and concurring in the judgment.

The obvious overbreadth of the outdoor advertising restrictions suffices to invalidate them under the fourth part of the test in *Central Hudson*. [My] continuing concerns that the test gives insufficient protection to truthful, nonmisleading commercial speech require me to refrain from expressing agreement with the Court's application of the third part of *Central Hudson*. With the exception of Part III–B–1, then, I join the opinion of the Court.

JUSTICE THOMAS, concurring in part and concurring in the judgment

I join the opinion of the Court (with the exception of Part III–B–1). * * *

I have observed previously that there is no "philosophical or historical basis for asserting that 'commercial' speech is of 'lower value' than 'noncommercial' speech." Indeed, I doubt whether it is even possible to draw a coherent distinction between commercial and noncommercial speech.2

It should be clear that if these regulations targeted anything other than advertising for commercial products—if, for example, they were directed at billboards promoting political candidates—all would agree that the restrictions should be subjected to strict scrutiny. In my view, an asserted government interest in keeping people ignorant by suppressing expression "is per se illegitimate and can no more justify regulation of 'commercial' speech than it can justify regulation of 'noncommercial' speech." That is essentially the interest asserted here. * * *

[R]espondents [argue] that the regulations target deceptive and misleading speech. Second, they argue that the regulations restrict speech that promotes an illegal transaction—i.e., the sale of tobacco to minors. Neither theory is properly before the Court. For purposes of summary judgment, respondents were willing to assume "that the tobacco advertisements at issue here are truthful, nonmisleading speech about a lawful activity." [E]ven if we were to entertain these arguments, neither is persuasive. Respondents suggest that tobacco advertising is

---

2. Tobacco advertising provides a good illustration. The sale of tobacco products is the subject of considerable political controversy, and not surprisingly, some tobacco advertisements both promote a product and take a stand in this political debate. A recent cigarette advertisement, for example, displayed a brand logo next to text reading, "Why do politicians smoke cigars while taxing cigarettes?"

misleading because "its youthful imagery [and] sheer ubiquity" leads children to believe "that tobacco use is desirable and pervasive." This justification is belied, however, by the sweeping overinclusivity of the regulations. Massachusetts has done nothing to target its prohibition to advertisements appealing to "excitement, glamour, and independence"; the ban applies with equal force to appeals to torpor, homeliness, and servility. It has not focused on "youthful imagery"; smokers depicted on the sides of buildings may no more play shuffleboard than they may ride skateboards. * * *

[Viewed] as an effort to proscribe solicitation to unlawful conduct, these regulations clearly fail the *Brandenburg* test. [Even] if Massachusetts could prohibit advertisements reading, "Hey kids, buy cigarettes here," these regulations sweep much more broadly than that. They cover "[any] statement or representation [the] purpose or effect of which is to promote the use or sale" of tobacco products, whether or not the statement is directly or indirectly addressed to minors. [It] is difficult to see any stopping point to a rule that would allow a State to prohibit all speech in favor of an activity in which it is illegal for minors to engage. Presumably, the State could ban car advertisements in an effort to enforce its restrictions on underage driving. It could regulate advertisements urging people to vote, because children are not permitted to vote. * * *

Underlying many of the arguments of respondents and their amici is the idea that tobacco is in some sense sui generis [so] that application of normal First Amendment principles should be suspended. [Nevertheless], it seems appropriate to point out that to uphold the Massachusetts tobacco regulations would be to accept a line of reasoning that would permit restrictions on advertising for a host of other products.

Tobacco use is, we are told, "the single leading cause of preventable death in the United States." The second largest contributor to mortality rates in the United States is obesity. [A] significant factor has been the increased availability of large quantities of high-calorie, high-fat foods. Such foods, of course, have been aggressively marketed and promoted by fast food companies. Respondents say that tobacco companies are covertly targeting children in their advertising. Fast food companies do so openly. Moreover, there is considerable evidence that they have been successful in changing children's eating behavior. * * *

To take another example, the third largest cause of preventable deaths in the United States is alcohol. [Although] every State prohibits the sale of alcohol to those under age 21, much alcohol advertising is viewed by children. Not surprisingly, there is considerable evidence that exposure to alcohol advertising is associated with underage drinking. * * *

Respondents have identified no principle of law or logic that would preclude the imposition of restrictions on fast food and alcohol advertising similar to those they seek to impose on tobacco advertising. In effect, they seek a "vice" exception to the First Amendment. No such exception exists. If it did, it would have almost no limit, for "any product that poses some threat to public health or public morals might reasonably be characterized by a state legislature as relating to 'vice activity.' "

No legislature has ever sought to restrict speech about an activity it regarded as harmless and inoffensive. [It] is therefore no answer for the State to say that the makers of cigarettes are doing harm: perhaps they are. But in that respect they are no different from the purveyors of other harmful products, or the advocates of harmful ideas. When the State seeks to silence them, they are all entitled to the protection of the First Amendment. * * *

JUSTICE SOUTER, concurring in part and dissenting in part.

I join Parts I, II–C, II–D, III–A, III–B–1, III–C, and III–D of the Court's opinion. I join Part I of the opinion of Justice Stevens concurring in the judgment in part and dissenting in part. I respectfully dissent from Part III–B–2 of the opinion of the Court, and like Justice Stevens would remand for trial on the constitutionality of the 1,000–foot limit.

JUSTICE STEVENS, with whom JUSTICE GINSBURG and JUSTICE BREYER join, and with whom JUSTICE SOUTER joins as to Part I, concurring in part, concurring in the judgment in part, and dissenting in part. * * *

I. [Stevens, J., argued that the Federal Cigarette Labeling and Advertising Act of 1965 did not preclude state and local regulation of the location of cigarette advertising.]

II. *The 1,000–Foot Rule.* I am in complete accord with the Court's analysis of the importance of the interests served by the advertising restrictions. As the Court lucidly explains, few interests are more "compelling," than ensuring that minors do not become addicted to a dangerous drug before they are able to make a mature and informed decision as to the health risks associated with that substance. [Nevertheless,] noble ends do not save a speech-restricting statute whose means are poorly tailored. Such statutes may be invalid for two different reasons. First, the means chosen may be insufficiently related to the ends they purportedly serve. Alternatively, the statute may be so broadly drawn that, while effectively achieving its ends, it unduly restricts communications that are unrelated to its policy aims.

To my mind, the 1,000–foot rule does not present a tailoring problem of the first type. For reasons cogently explained in our prior opinions and in the opinion of the Court, we may fairly assume that advertising stimulates consumption and, therefore, that regulations limiting advertising will facilitate efforts to stem consumption. Furthermore, if the government's intention is to limit consumption by a particular segment of the community—in this case, minors—it is appropriate, indeed necessary, to tailor advertising restrictions to the areas where that segment of the community congregates—in this case, the area surrounding schools and playgrounds.

However, I share the majority's concern as to whether the 1,000–foot rule unduly restricts the ability of cigarette manufacturers to convey lawful information to adult consumers. This, of course, is a question of line-drawing. [E]fforts to protect children from exposure to harmful material will undoubtedly have some spillover effect on the free speech rights of adults. [Though] many factors plausibly enter the equation when calculating whether a child-directed location restriction goes too far in regulating adult speech, one crucial question is whether the regulatory scheme leaves available sufficient "alternative avenues of communication." Because I do not think the record contains sufficient information to enable us to answer that question, I would vacate the award of summary judgment upholding the 1,000–foot rule and remand for trial on that issue.

[For example,] depending on the answers to empirical questions on which we lack data, the ubiquity of print advertisements hawking particular brands of cigarettes might suffice to inform adult consumers of the special advantages of the respective brands. Similarly, print advertisements, circulars mailed to people's homes, word of mouth, and general information may or may not be sufficient to imbue the adult population with the knowledge that particular stores, chains of stores, or types of stores sell tobacco products.

I note, moreover, that the alleged "overinclusivity" of the advertising regulations while relevant to whether the regulations are narrowly tailored, does not "beli[e]" the claim that tobacco advertising imagery misleads children into believing that smoking is healthy, glamorous, or sophisticated. For purposes of summary judgment, the State conceded that the tobacco companies' advertising concerns lawful activity and is not misleading. Under the Court's disposition of the case today, the State remains free to proffer evidence that the advertising is in fact misleading. * * *

III.   Because I strongly disagree with the Court's conclusion on the preemption issue, I dissent from Parts II–A and II–B of its opinion. Though I agree with much of what the Court has to say about the First Amendment, I ultimately disagree with its disposition or its reasoning on each of the regulations before us.12

Notes

1.   Federal law permits compounding of drugs for the needs of specific patients without resort to FDA approval, so long as advertising of such drugs is not involved. The government rationale is that advertising would be indicative of mass manufacture rather than tailoring to the specific needs of individual patients. THOMPSON v. WESTERN STATES MEDICAL CENTER, 535 U.S. 357 (2002), per O'CONNOR, J., invalidated these restrictions in part by concluding that the government did not meet its burden to show that less restrictive alternatives were unavailable.

BREYER, J., joined by Rehnquist, C.J., and Stevens and Ginsburg, JJ., dissenting, argued that the Court's approach to such issues should be flexible. He contended that the Court rightly applied the less demanding *Central Hudson* test because "it has concluded that, from a constitutional perspective, commercial speech does not warrant application of the Court's strictest speech-protective tests. And it has reached this conclusion in part because restrictions on commercial speech do not often repress individual self-expression; they rarely interfere with the functioning of democratic political processes; and they often reflect a democratically determined governmental decision to regulate a commercial venture in order to protect, for example, the consumer, the public health, individual safety, or the environment. [The] Court, in my view, gives insufficient weight to the Government's regulatory rationale, and too readily assumes the existence of practical alternatives. It thereby applies the commercial speech doctrine too strictly. [A]n overly rigid commercial speech doctrine will transform what ought to be a legislative or regulatory decision about the best way to protect the health and safety of the American public into a constitutional decision prohibiting the legislature from enacting necessary protections. As history in respect to the Due Process Clause shows, any such transformation would involve a tragic constitutional misunderstanding."

2.   *Defining commercial speech.* In 1996 Nike, Inc. was confronted with allegations that it underpaid and otherwise mistreated workers at foreign facilities. Nike attempted to answer these charges with press releases, letters to editors, university presidents and athletic directors, and with a commissioned report by Andrew Young about working conditions in its factories. Kasky, a California resident, sued as a private attorney general under a California statute

---

12.   Reflecting my partial agreement with the Court, I join Parts I, II–C, II–D, and III–B–   1 and concur in the judgment reflected in Part III–D.

prohibiting unfair and deceptive practices.b Kasky alleged that in order to boost sales, Nike made a number of false statements and/or material omissions of fact. Assume that some of Nike's communications went to customers and that some did not. Are any of the communications "commercial speech"? All of them? Compare *Kasky v. Nike, Inc.*, 27 Cal.4th 939, 119 Cal.Rptr.2d 296, 45 P.3d 243 (2002) with *Nike, Inc. v. Kasky*, 539 U.S. 654 (2003) (Breyer, J., joined by O'Connor, J., dissenting from dismissal of the writ as improvidently granted).

III. PRIVATE SPEECH

Before studying *Dun & Bradstreet*, below, review *Gertz*, Sec. 1, II, C supra.

Dun & Bradstreet, Inc., a credit reporting agency, falsely and negligently reported to five of its subscribers that Greenmoss Builders, Inc. had filed a petition for bankruptcy and also negligently misrepresented Greenmoss' assets and liabilities. In the ensuing defamation action, Greenmoss recovered $50,000 in compensatory damages and $300,000 in punitive damages. Dun & Bradstreet argued that, under *Gertz,* its First Amendment rights had been violated because presumed and punitive damages had been imposed without instructions requiring a showing of *New York Times* malice. Greenmoss argued that the *Gertz* protections did not extend to non-media defendants and, in any event, did not extend to commercial speech. DUN & BRADSTREET, INC. v. GREENMOSS BUILDERS, INC., 472 U.S. 749 (1985), rejected Dun & Bradstreet's contention, but there was no opinion of the Court. The common theme of the five justices siding with Greenmoss was that the First Amendment places less value on "private" speech than upon "public" speech.

POWELL, J., joined by Rehnquist and O'Connor, JJ., noted that the Vermont Supreme Court below had held "as a matter of federal constitutional law" that "the media protections outlined in *Gertz* are inapplicable to nonmedia defamation actions." In affirming, Powell, J., stated that his reasons were "different from those relied upon by the Vermont Supreme Court": "Like every other case in which this Court has found constitutional limits to state defamation laws, *Gertz* involved expression on a matter of undoubted public concern. * * *

"We have never considered whether the *Gertz* balance obtains when the defamatory statements involve no issue of public concern. To make this determination, we must employ the approach approved in *Gertz* and balance the State's interest in compensating private individuals for injury to their reputation against the First Amendment interest in protecting this type of expression. This state interest is identical to the one weighed in *Gertz.* * * *

"The First Amendment interest, on the other hand, is less important than the one weighed in *Gertz.* We have long recognized that not all speech is of equal First Amendment importance.5 It is speech on 'matters of public concern' that is 'at the

---

b. The Solicitor General argued that the private attorneys general provision should have doomed the statute on First Amendment grounds because of the potential chilling effect wholly apart from the status of the speech as commercial or political.

5. This Court on many occasions has recognized that certain kinds of speech are less central to the interests of the First Amendment than others. Obscene speech and "fighting words" long have been accorded no protection. *Roth*; *Chaplinsky*. In the area of protected speech, the most prominent example of re-

duced protection for certain kinds of speech concerns commercial speech. Such speech, we have noted, occupies a "subordinate position in the scale of First Amendment values." *Ohralik.* * * *

Other areas of the law provide further examples. In *Ohralik* we noted that there are "[n]umerous examples [of] communications that are regulated without offending the First Amendment, such as the exchange of information about securities, * * * corporate proxy statements, [the] exchange of price and production

heart of the First Amendment's protection.' [In] contrast, speech on matters of purely private concern is of less First Amendment concern. As a number of state courts, including the court below, have recognized, the role of the Constitution in regulating state libel law is far more limited when the concerns that activated *New York Times* and *Gertz* are absent.6 In such a case, '[t]here is no threat to the free and robust debate of public issues; there is no potential interference with a meaningful dialogue of ideas concerning self-government; and there is no threat of liability causing a reaction of self-censorship by the press. The facts of the present case are wholly without the First Amendment concerns with which the Supreme Court of the United States has been struggling.' *Harley-Davidson Motorsports, Inc. v. Markley,* 279 Or. 361, 366, 568 P.2d 1359, 1363 (1977).

"While such speech is not totally unprotected by the First Amendment, see *Connick v. Myers* [Sec. 9, III infra], its protections are less stringent. [In] light of the reduced constitutional value of speech involving no matters of public concern, we hold that the state interest adequately supports awards of presumed and punitive damages—even absent a showing of 'actual malice.'7

"The only remaining issue is whether petitioner's credit report involved a matter of public concern. In a related context, we have held that '[w]hether [speech] addresses a matter of public concern must be determined by [the expression's] content, form, and context [as] revealed by the whole record.' *Connick*. These factors indicate that petitioner's credit report concerns no public issue.8 It was speech solely in the individual interest of the speaker and its specific business audience. Cf. *Central Hudson*. This particular interest warrants no special protection when—as in this case—the speech is wholly false and clearly damaging to the victim's business reputation. Moreover, since the credit report was made available to only five subscribers, who, under the terms of the subscription agreement, could not disseminate it further, it cannot be said that the report involves any 'strong interest in the free flow of commercial information.' *Virginia*

information among competitors, [and] employers' threats of retaliation for the labor activities of employees." Yet similar regulation of political speech is subject to the most rigorous scrutiny. Likewise, while the power of the State to license lawyers, psychiatrists, and public school teachers—all of whom speak for a living—is unquestioned, this Court has held that a law requiring licensing of union organizers is unconstitutional under the First Amendment. *Thomas v. Collins*, [Sec. 4, I, A infra]; see also *Rosenbloom v. Metromedia* (opinion of Brennan, J.) ("the determinant whether the First Amendment applies to state libel actions is whether the utterance involved concerns an issue of public or general concern").

6. As one commentator has remarked with respect to "the case of a commercial supplier of credit information that defames a person applying for credit"—the case before us today— "If the First Amendment requirements outlined in *Gertz* apply, there is something clearly wrong with the First Amendment or with *Gertz*." Steven Shiffrin, *The First Amendment and Economic Regulation: Away From a General Theory of the First Amendment,* 78 Nw. L.Rev. 1212, 1268 (1983).

7. The dissent, purporting to apply the same balancing test that we do today, concludes that even speech on purely private mat-

ters is entitled to the protections of *Gertz*. * * *

The dissent's "balance" [would] lead to the protection of all libels—no matter how attenuated their constitutional interest. If the dissent were the law, a woman of impeccable character who was branded a "whore" by a jealous neighbor would have no effective recourse unless she could prove "actual malice" by clear and convincing evidence. This is not malice in the ordinary sense, but in the more demanding sense of *New York Times*. The dissent would, in effect, constitutionalize the entire common law of libel.

8. The dissent suggests that our holding today leaves all credit reporting subject to reduced First Amendment protection. This is incorrect. The protection to be accorded a particular credit report depends on whether the report's "content, form, and context" indicate that it concerns a public matter. We also do not hold, as the dissent suggests we do, that the report is subject to reduced constitutional protection because it constitutes economic or commercial speech. We discuss such speech, along with advertising, only to show how many of the same concerns that argue in favor of reduced constitutional protection in those areas apply here as well.

Pharmacy. There is simply no credible argument that this type of credit reporting requires special protection to ensure that 'debate on public issues [will] be uninhibited, robust, and wide-open.' *New York Times.*

"In addition, the speech here, like advertising, is hardy and unlikely to be deterred by incidental state regulation. See *Virginia Pharmacy.* It is solely motivated by the desire for profit, which, we have noted, is a force less likely to be deterred than others. Arguably, the reporting here was also more objectively verifiable than speech deserving of greater protection. In any case, the market provides a powerful incentive to a credit reporting agency to be accurate, since false credit reporting is of no use to creditors. Thus, any incremental 'chilling' effect of libel suits would be of decreased significance.

"We conclude that permitting recovery of presumed and punitive damages in defamation cases absent a showing of 'actual malice' does not violate the First Amendment when the defamatory statements do not involve matters of public concern."

Although expressing the view that *Gertz* should be overruled and that the *New York Times* malice definition should be reconsidered, BURGER, C.J., concurring, stated that: "The single question before the Court today is whether *Gertz* applies to this case. The plurality opinion holds that *Gertz* does not apply because, unlike the challenged expression in *Gertz,* the alleged defamatory expression in this case does not relate to a matter of public concern. I agree that *Gertz* is limited to circumstances in which the alleged defamatory expression concerns a matter of general public importance, and that the expression in question here relates to a matter of essentially private concern. I therefore agree with the plurality opinion to the extent that it holds that *Gertz* is inapplicable in this case for the two reasons indicated. No more is needed to dispose of the present case."

WHITE, J., who had dissented in *Gertz,* was prepared to overrule that case or to limit it, but he disagreed with Powell, J.'s, suggestion that the plurality's resolution of the case was faithful to *Gertz:* "It is interesting that Justice Powell declines to follow the *Gertz* approach in this case. I had thought that the decision in *Gertz* was intended to reach cases that involve any false statements of fact injurious to reputation, whether the statement is made privately or publicly and whether or not it implicates a matter of public importance. Justice Powell, however, distinguishes *Gertz* as a case that involved a matter of public concern, an element absent here. Wisely, in my view, Justice Powell does not rest his application of a different rule here on a distinction drawn between media and non-media defendants. On that issue, I agree with Justice Brennan that the First Amendment gives no more protection to the press in defamation suits than it does to others exercising their freedom of speech. None of our cases affords such a distinction; to the contrary, the Court has rejected it at every turn. It should be rejected again, particularly in this context, since it makes no sense to give the most protection to those publishers who reach the most readers and therefore pollute the channels of communication with the most misinformation and do the most damage to private reputation. If *Gertz* is to be distinguished from this case, on the ground that it applies only where the allegedly false publication deals with a matter of general or public importance, then where the false publication does not deal with such a matter, the common-law rules would apply whether the defendant is a member of the media or other public disseminator or a non-media individual publishing privately. Although Justice Powell speaks only of the inapplicability of the *Gertz* rule with respect to presumed and punitive damages, it must be that the *Gertz* requirement of some kind of fault on the part of the defendant is also inapplicable in cases such as this. * * *

"The question before us is whether *Gertz* is to be applied in this case. For either of two reasons, I believe that it should not. First, I am unreconciled to the *Gertz* holding and believe that it should be overruled. Second, as Justice Powell indicates, the defamatory publication in this case does not deal with a matter of public importance."

BRENNAN, J., joined by Marshall, Blackmun and Stevens, JJ., dissented: "This case involves a difficult question of the proper application of *Gertz* to credit reporting—a type of speech at some remove from that which first gave rise to explicit First Amendment restrictions on state defamation law—and has produced a diversity of considered opinions, none of which speaks for the Court. Justice Powell's plurality opinion affirming the judgment below would not apply the *Gertz* limitations on presumed and punitive damages [because] the speech involved a subject of purely private concern and was circulated to an extremely limited audience. * * * Justice White also would affirm; he would not apply *Gertz* to this case on the ground that the subject matter of the publication does not deal with a matter of general or public importance. The Chief Justice apparently agrees with Justice White. The four who join this opinion would reverse the judgment of the Vermont Supreme Court. We believe that, although protection of the type of expression at issue is admittedly not the 'central meaning of the First Amendment,' *Gertz* makes clear that the First Amendment nonetheless requires restraints on presumed and punitive damage awards for this expression. * * *

"[Respondent urged that *Gertz* be restricted] to cases in which the defendant is a 'media' entity. Such a distinction is irreconcilable with the fundamental First Amendment principle that '[t]he inherent worth [of] speech in terms of its capacity for informing the public does not depend upon the identity of its source, whether corporation, association, union, or individual.' *First National Bank v. Bellotti* [Sec. 10 infra]. First Amendment difficulties lurk in the definitional questions such an approach would generate. And the distinction would likely be born an anachronism.7 Perhaps most importantly, the argument that *Gertz* should be limited to the media misapprehends our cases. We protect the press to ensure the vitality of First Amendment guarantees. This solicitude implies no endorsement of the principle that speakers other than the press deserve lesser First Amendment protection. * * *

"The free speech guarantee gives each citizen an equal right to self-expression and to participation in self-government. [Accordingly,] at least six Members of this Court (the four who join this opinion and Justice White and The Chief Justice) agree today that, in the context of defamation law, the rights of the institutional media are no greater and no less than those enjoyed by other individuals or organizations engaged in the same activities.10 * * *

"Purporting to 'employ the approach approved in *Gertz,*' Justice Powell balances the state interest in protecting private reputation against the First Amendment interest in protecting expression on matters not of public concern.11

7. Owing to transformations in the technological and economic structure of the communications industry, there has been an increasing convergence of what might be labeled "media" and "nonmedia."

10. Justice Powell's opinion does not expressly reject the media/nonmedia distinction, but does expressly decline to apply that distinction to resolve this case.

11. One searches *Gertz* in vain for a single word to support the proposition that limits on presumed and punitive damages obtained only when speech involved matters of public concern. *Gertz* could not have been grounded in such a premise. Distrust of placing in the courts the power to decide what speech was of public concern was precisely the rationale *Gertz* offered for rejecting the *Rosenbloom* plurality approach. * * *

"The five Members of the Court voting to affirm the damage award in this case have provided almost no guidance as to what constitutes a protected 'matter of public concern.' Justice White offers nothing at all, but his opinion does indicate that the distinction turns on solely the subject matter of the expression and not on the extent or conditions of dissemination of that expression. Justice Powell adumbrates a rationale that would appear to focus primarily on subject matter.12 The opinion relies on the fact that the speech at issue was 'solely in the individual interest of the speaker and its *business* audience.' Analogizing explicitly to advertising, the opinion also states that credit reporting is 'hardy' and 'solely motivated by the desire for profit.' These two strains of analysis suggest that Justice Powell is excluding the subject matter of credit reports from 'matters of public concern' because the speech is predominantly in the realm of matters of economic concern."

Brennan, J., pointed to precedents (particularly labor cases) protecting speech on economic matters and argued that, "the breadth of this protection evinces recognition that freedom of expression is not only essential to check tyranny and foster self-government but also intrinsic to individual liberty and dignity and instrumental in society's search for truth."

Moreover, he emphasized the importance of credit reporting: "The credit reporting of Dun & Bradstreet falls within any reasonable definition of 'public concern' consistent with our precedents. Justice Powell's reliance on the fact that Dun & Bradstreet publishes credit reports 'for profit' is wholly unwarranted. Time and again we have made clear that speech loses none of its constitutional protection 'even though it is carried in a form that is "sold" for profit.' *Virginia Pharmacy.* More importantly, an announcement of the bankruptcy of a local company is information of potentially great concern to residents of the community where the company is [located]. And knowledge about solvency and the effect and prevalence of bankruptcy certainly would inform citizen opinions about questions of economic regulation. It is difficult to suggest that a bankruptcy is not a subject matter of public concern when federal law requires invocation of judicial mechanisms to effectuate it and makes the fact of the bankruptcy a matter of public record. * * *

"Even if the subject matter of credit reporting were properly considered—in the terms of Justice White and Justice Powell—as purely a matter of private discourse, this speech would fall well within the range of valuable expression for which the First Amendment demands protection. Much expression that does not directly involve public issues receives significant protection. Our cases do permit some diminution in the degree of protection afforded one category of speech about economic or commercial matters. 'Commercial speech'—defined as advertisements that 'do no more than propose a commercial transaction'—may be more closely

12. Justice Powell also appears to rely in part on the fact that communication was limited and confidential. Given that his analysis also relies on the subject matter of the credit report, it is difficult to decipher exactly what role the nature and extent of dissemination plays in Justice Powell's analysis. But because the subject matter of the expression at issue is properly understood as a matter of public concern, it may well be that this element of confidentiality is crucial to the outcome as far as Justice Powell's opinion is concerned. In other words, it may be that Justice Powell thinks this particular expression could not contribute to public welfare because the public generally does not receive it. This factor does not suffice to save the analysis. See n. 18 infra.

[In fn. 18, Brennan, J., indicated that, "Dun & Bradstreet doubtless provides thousands of credit reports to thousands of subscribers who receive the information pursuant to the same strictures imposed on the recipients in this case. As a systemic matter, therefore, today's decision diminishes the free flow of information because Dun & Bradstreet will generally be made more reticent in providing information to all its subscribers."]

regulated than other types of speech. [Credit] reporting is not 'commercial speech' as this Court has defined the term.

"[In] *every* case in which we have permitted more extensive state regulation on the basis of a commercial speech rationale—the speech being regulated was pure advertising—an offer to buy or sell goods and services or encouraging such buying and selling. Credit reports are not commercial advertisements for a good or service or a proposal to buy or sell such a product. We have been extremely chary about extending the 'commercial speech' doctrine beyond this narrowly circumscribed category of advertising because often vitally important speech will be uttered to advance economic interests and because the profit motive making such speech hardy dissipates rapidly when the speech is not advertising."[a]

Finally, Brennan, J., argued that even if credit reports were characterized as commercial speech, "unrestrained" presumed and punitive damages would violate the commercial speech requirement that "the regulatory means chosen be narrowly tailored so as to avoid any unnecessary chilling of protected expression. [Accordingly,] Greenmoss Builders should be permitted to recover for any actual damage it can show resulted from Dun & Bradstreet's negligently false credit report, but should be required to show actual malice to receive presumed or punitive damages."

IV. CONCEIVING AND RECONCEIVING THE STRUCTURE OF FIRST AMENDMENT DOCTRINE: HATE SPEECH REVISITED—AGAIN

R.A.V. v. ST. PAUL

505 U.S. 377, 112 S.Ct. 2538, 120 L.Ed.2d 305 (1992).

JUSTICE SCALIA delivered the opinion of the Court.

In the predawn hours of June 21, 1990, petitioner and several other teenagers allegedly assembled a crudely-made cross by taping together broken chair legs. They then allegedly burned the cross inside the fenced yard of a black family that lived across the street from the house where petitioner was staying. Although this conduct could have been punished under any of a number of laws, one of the two provisions under which respondent city of St. Paul chose to charge petitioner (then a juvenile) was the St. Paul Bias–Motivated Crime Ordinance, which provides: "Whoever places on public or private property a symbol, object, appellation, characterization or graffiti, including, but not limited to, a burning cross or Nazi swastika, which one knows or has reasonable grounds to know arouses anger, alarm or resentment in others on the basis of race, color, creed, religion or gender commits disorderly conduct and shall be guilty of a misdemeanor." * * *

I. [W]e accept the Minnesota Supreme Court's authoritative statement that the ordinance reaches only those expressions that constitute "fighting words" within the meaning of Chaplinsky. [W]e nonetheless conclude that the ordinance is facially unconstitutional in that it prohibits otherwise permitted speech solely on the basis of the subjects the speech addresses.

[From] 1791 to the present, our society, like other free but civilized societies, has permitted restrictions upon the content of speech in a few limited areas, which are "of such slight social value as a step to truth that any benefit that may

---

a. Brennan, J., cited *Consolidated Edison Co. v. Public Service Comm'n,* 447 U.S. 530 (1980), which invalidated a regulation that prohibited a utility company from inserting its views on "controversial issues of public policy" into its monthly electrical bill mailings. The mailing that prompted the regulation advocated nuclear power.

be derived from them is clearly outweighed by the social interest in order and morality." *Chaplinsky.* * * *

We have sometimes said that these categories of expression are "not within the area of constitutionally protected speech," *Roth*; *Beauharnais*; *Chaplinsky;* or that the "protection of the First Amendment does not extend" to them, *Sable Communications of Cal., Inc. v. FCC* [Sec. 8, II infra]. Such statements must be taken in context, however, and are no more literally true than is the occasionally repeated shorthand characterizing obscenity "as not being speech at all," Cass Sunstein, *Pornography and the First Amendment,* 1986 Duke L.J. 589, 615, n. 146. What they mean is that these areas of speech can, consistently with the First Amendment, be regulated *because of their constitutionally proscribable content* (obscenity, defamation, etc.)—not that they are categories of speech entirely invisible to the Constitution, so that they may be made the vehicles for content discrimination unrelated to their distinctively proscribable content. Thus, the government may proscribe libel; but it may not make the further content discrimination of proscribing *only* libel critical of the government. * * *

Our cases surely do not establish the proposition that the First Amendment imposes no obstacle whatsoever to regulation of particular instances of such proscribable expression, so that the government "may regulate [them] freely," (White, J., concurring in judgment). That would mean that a city council could enact an ordinance prohibiting only those legally obscene works that contain criticism of the city government or, indeed, that do not include endorsement of the city government. Such a simplistic, all-or-nothing-at-all approach to First Amendment protection is at odds with common sense and with our jurisprudence as well.1 It is not true that "fighting words" have at most a "de minimis" expressive content or that their content is *in all respects* "worthless and undeserving of constitutional protection"; sometimes they are quite expressive indeed. We have not said that they constitute *"no* part of the expression of ideas," but only that they constitute "no *essential* part of any exposition of ideas." *Chaplinsky.*

The proposition that a particular instance of speech can be proscribable on the basis of one feature (e.g., obscenity) but not on the basis of another (e.g., opposition to the city government) is commonplace, and has found application in many contexts. We have long held, for example, that nonverbal expressive activity can be banned because of the action it entails, but not because of the ideas it expresses—so that burning a flag in violation of an ordinance against outdoor fires could be punishable, whereas burning a flag in violation of an ordinance against dishonoring the flag is not. See *Johnson.* See also *Barnes* (Scalia, J., concurring in judgment) (Souter, J., concurring in judgment); *O'Brien.* Similarly, we have upheld reasonable "time, place, or manner" restrictions, but only if they are "justified without reference to the content of the regulated speech." *Ward;* see also *Clark* (noting that the *O'Brien* test differs little from the standard applied to time, place, or manner restrictions). And just as the power to proscribe particular speech on the basis of a noncontent element (e.g., noise) does not entail the power to proscribe the same speech on the basis of a content element; so also, the power

---

1. Justice White concedes that a city council cannot prohibit only those legally obscene works that contain criticism of the city government, but asserts that to be the consequence, not of the First Amendment, but of the Equal Protection Clause. Such content-based discrimination would not, he asserts, "be rationally related to a legitimate government interest." But of course the only *reason* that government interest is not a "legitimate" one is that it violates the First Amendment. This Court itself has occasionally fused the First Amendment into the Equal Protection Clause in this fashion, but at least with the acknowledgment (which Justice White cannot afford to make) that the First Amendment underlies its analysis. * * *

to proscribe it on the basis of *one* content element (e.g., obscenity) does not entail the power to proscribe it on the basis of *other* content elements.

In other words, the exclusion of "fighting words" from the scope of the First Amendment simply means that, for purposes of that Amendment, the unprotected features of the words are, despite their verbal character, essentially a "non-speech" element of communication. Fighting words are thus analogous to a noisy sound truck: Each [is,] a "mode of speech,"; both can be used to convey an idea; but neither has, in and of itself, a claim upon the First Amendment. As with the sound truck, however, so also with fighting words: The government may not regulate use based on hostility—or favoritism—towards the underlying message expressed.

The concurrences describe us as setting forth a new First Amendment principle that prohibition of constitutionally proscribable speech cannot be "underinclusiv[e]" (White, J., concurring in judgment)—a First Amendment "absolutism" whereby "within a particular 'proscribable' category of expression, [a] government must either proscribe *all* speech or no speech at all" (Stevens, J., concurring in judgment). That easy target is of the concurrences' own invention. In our view, the First Amendment imposes not an "underinclusiveness" limitation but a "content discrimination" limitation upon a State's prohibition of proscribable speech. There is no problem whatever, for example, with a State's prohibiting obscenity (and other forms of proscribable expression) only in certain media or markets, for although that prohibition would be "underinclusive," it would not discriminate on the basis of content. See, e.g., *Sable Communications* (upholding 47 U.S.C. § 223(b)(1) (1988), which prohibits obscene *telephone* communications).

Even the prohibition against content discrimination that we assert the First Amendment requires is not absolute. It applies differently in the context of proscribable speech than in the area of fully protected speech. The rationale of the general prohibition, after all, is that content discrimination "rais[es] the specter that the Government may effectively drive certain ideas or viewpoints from the marketplace," *Simon & Schuster,* [Sec. 1, V, A infra]. But content discrimination among various instances of a class of proscribable speech often does not pose this threat.

When the basis for the content discrimination consists entirely of the very reason the entire class of speech at issue is proscribable, no significant danger of idea or viewpoint discrimination exists. Such a reason, having been adjudged neutral enough to support exclusion of the entire class of speech from First Amendment protection, is also neutral enough to form the basis of distinction within the class. To illustrate: A State might choose to prohibit only that obscenity which is the most patently offensive *in its prurience*—i.e., that which involves the most lascivious displays of sexual activity. But it may not prohibit, for example, only that obscenity which includes offensive *political* messages. And the Federal Government can criminalize only those threats of violence that are directed against the President, see 18 U.S.C. § 871—since the reasons why threats of violence are outside the First Amendment (protecting individuals from the fear of violence, from the disruption that fear engenders, and from the possibility that the threatened violence will occur) have special force when applied to the person of the President. See *Watts* [Sec. 1, I, D supra] (upholding the facial validity of § 871 because of the "overwhelmin[g] interest in protecting the safety of [the] Chief Executive and in allowing him to perform his duties without interference from threats of physical violence"). But the Federal Government may not criminalize only those threats against the President that mention his policy on aid to inner cities. And to take a final example (one mentioned by Justice Stevens), a

State may choose to regulate price advertising in one industry but not in others, because the risk of fraud (one of the characteristics of commercial speech that justifies depriving it of full First Amendment protection) is in its view greater there. Cf. *Morales v. Trans World Airlines, Inc.,* 504 U.S. 374 (1992) (state regulation of airline advertising); *Ohralik* (state regulation of lawyer advertising). But a State may not prohibit only that commercial advertising that depicts men in a demeaning fashion.

Another valid basis for according differential treatment to even a content-defined subclass of proscribable speech is that the subclass happens to be associated with particular "secondary effects" of the speech, so that the regulation is *"justified* without reference to the content of [the] speech," *Renton.* A State could, for example, permit all obscene live performances except those involving minors. Moreover, since words can in some circumstances violate laws directed not against speech but against conduct (a law against treason, for example, is violated by telling the enemy the nation's defense secrets), a particular content-based subcategory of a proscribable class of speech can be swept up incidentally within the reach of a statute directed at conduct rather than speech. Thus, for example, sexually derogatory "fighting words," among other words, may produce a violation of Title VII's general prohibition against sexual discrimination in employment practices. Where the government does not target conduct on the basis of its expressive content, acts are not shielded from regulation merely because they express a discriminatory idea or philosophy.

These bases for distinction refute the proposition that the selectivity of the restriction is "even arguably 'conditioned upon the sovereign's agreement with what a speaker may intend to say.'" There may be other such bases as well. Indeed, to validate such selectivity (where totally proscribable speech is at issue) it may not even be necessary to identify any particular "neutral" basis, so long as the nature of the content discrimination is such that there is no realistic possibility that official suppression of ideas is afoot. (We cannot think of any First Amendment interest that would stand in the way of a State's prohibiting only those obscene motion pictures with blue-eyed actresses.) Save for that limitation, the regulation of "fighting words," like the regulation of noisy speech, may address some offensive instances and leave other, equally offensive, instances alone. See *Posadas.*[2]

II.   [Although] the phrase in the ordinance, "arouses anger, alarm or resentment in others," has been limited by the Minnesota Supreme Court's construction to reach only those symbols or displays that amount to "fighting words," the remaining, unmodified terms make clear that the ordinance applies only to "fighting words" that insult, or provoke violence, "on the basis of race, color, creed, religion or gender." Displays containing abusive invective, no matter how vicious or severe, are permissible unless they are addressed to one of the specified disfavored topics. Those who wish to use "fighting words" in connection with other ideas—to express hostility, for example, on the basis of political affiliation, union membership, or homosexuality—are not covered. The First Amendment does not permit St. Paul to impose special prohibitions on those speakers who express views on disfavored subjects.

2. Justice Stevens cites a string of opinions as supporting his assertion that "selective regulation of speech based on content" is not presumptively invalid. [A]ll that their contents establish is what we readily concede: that presumptive invalidity does not mean invariable invalidity, leaving room for such exceptions as reasonable and viewpoint-neutral content-based discrimination in nonpublic forums, or with respect to certain speech by government employees.

In its practical operation, moreover, the ordinance goes even beyond mere content discrimination, to actual viewpoint discrimination. Displays containing some words—odious racial epithets, for example—would be prohibited to proponents of all views. But "fighting words" that do not themselves invoke race, color, creed, religion, or gender—aspersions upon a person's mother, for example—would seemingly be usable ad libitum in the placards of those arguing *in favor* of racial, color, etc. tolerance and equality, but could not be used by that speaker's opponents. One could hold up a sign saying, for example, that all "anti-Catholic bigots" are misbegotten; but not that all "papists" are, for that would insult and provoke violence "on the basis of religion." St. Paul has no such authority to license one side of a debate to fight freestyle, while requiring the other to follow Marquis of Queensbury Rules.

What we have here, it must be emphasized, is not a prohibition of fighting words that are directed at certain persons or groups (which would be *facially* valid if it met the requirements of the Equal Protection Clause); but rather, a prohibition of fighting words that contain (as the Minnesota Supreme Court repeatedly emphasized) messages of "bias-motivated" hatred and in particular, as applied to this case, messages "based on virulent notions of racial supremacy." One must wholeheartedly agree with the Minnesota Supreme Court that "[i]t is the responsibility, even the obligation, of diverse communities to confront such notions in whatever form they appear," but the manner of that confrontation cannot consist of selective limitations upon speech. St. Paul's brief asserts that a general "fighting words" law would not meet the city's needs because only a content-specific measure can communicate to minority groups that the "group hatred" aspect of such speech "is not condoned by the majority." The point of the First Amendment is that majority preferences must be expressed in some fashion other than silencing speech on the basis of its content. * * *

[T]he reason why fighting words are categorically excluded from the protection of the First Amendment is not that their content communicates any particular idea, but that their content embodies a particularly intolerable (and socially unnecessary) *mode* of expressing *whatever* idea the speaker wishes to convey. St. Paul has not singled out an especially offensive mode of expression—it has not, for example, selected for prohibition only those fighting words that communicate ideas in a threatening (as opposed to a merely obnoxious) manner. Rather, it has proscribed fighting words of whatever manner that communicate messages of racial, gender, or religious intolerance. Selectivity of this sort creates the possibility that the city is seeking to handicap the expression of particular ideas.

* * * St. Paul argues that the ordinance [is] aimed only at the "secondary effects" of the speech, see *Renton*. According to St. Paul, the ordinance is intended, "not to impact on [sic] the right of free expression of the accused," but rather to "protect against the victimization of a person or persons who are particularly vulnerable because of their membership in a group that historically has been discriminated against." Even assuming that an ordinance that completely proscribes, rather than merely regulates, a specified category of speech can ever be considered to be directed only to the secondary effects of such speech, it is clear that the St. Paul ordinance is not directed to secondary effects within the meaning of *Renton*. As we said in *Boos* "[l]isteners' reactions to speech are not the type of 'secondary effects' we referred to in *Renton*." * * *7

7. St. Paul has not argued in this case that the ordinance merely regulates that subclass of fighting words which is most likely to provoke a violent response. But even if one assumes (as appears unlikely) that the categories selected may be so described, that would not justify selective regulation under a "secondary effects" theory. The only reason why such ex-

Finally, St. Paul [asserts] that the ordinance helps to ensure the basic human rights of members of groups that have historically been subjected to discrimination, including the right of such group members to live in peace where they wish. We do not doubt that these interests are compelling, and that the ordinance can be said to promote them. But the "danger of censorship" presented by a facially content-based statute requires that that weapon be employed only where it is "*necessary* to serve the asserted [compelling] interest". The existence of adequate content-neutral alternatives thus "undercut[s] significantly" any defense of such a statute, casting considerable doubt on the government's protestations that "the asserted justification is in fact an accurate description of the purpose and effect of the law." [An] ordinance not limited to the favored topics, for example, would have precisely the same beneficial effect. In fact the only interest distinctively served by the content limitation is that of displaying the city council's special hostility towards the particular biases thus singled out. That is precisely what the First Amendment forbids. The politicians of St. Paul are entitled to express that hostility—but not through the means of imposing unique limitations upon speakers who (however benightedly) disagree. * * *

Let there be no mistake about our belief that burning a cross in someone's front yard is reprehensible. But St. Paul has sufficient means at its disposal to prevent such behavior without adding the First Amendment to the fire. * * *

JUSTICE WHITE, with whom JUSTICE BLACKMUN and JUSTICE O'CONNOR join, and with whom JUSTICE STEVENS joins except as to Part I(A), concurring in the judgment. * * *

I.A. [T]he majority holds that the First Amendment protects those narrow categories of expression long held to be undeserving of First Amendment protection—at least to the extent that lawmakers may not regulate some fighting words more strictly than others because of their content. [Should] the government want to criminalize certain fighting words, the Court now requires it to criminalize all fighting words.

To borrow a phrase, "Such a simplistic, all-or-nothing-at-all approach to First Amendment protection is at odds with common sense and with our jurisprudence as well." It is inconsistent to hold that the government may proscribe an entire category of speech because the content of that speech is evil, but that the government may not treat a subset of that category differently without violating the First Amendment; the content of the subset is by definition worthless and undeserving of constitutional protection.

The majority's observation that fighting words are "quite expressive indeed," is no answer. Fighting words are not a means of exchanging views, rallying supporters, or registering a protest; they are directed against individuals to provoke violence or to inflict injury. Therefore, a ban on all fighting words or on a subset of the fighting words category would restrict only the social evil of hate speech, without creating the danger of driving viewpoints from the marketplace.

Therefore, the Court's insistence on inventing its brand of First Amendment underinclusiveness puzzles me.3 [T]he Court's new "underbreadth" creation [invites] the continuation of expressive conduct that in this case is evil and

pressive conduct would be especially correlated with violence is that it conveys a particularly odious message; because the "chain of causation" thus *necessarily* "run[s] through the persuasive effect of the expressive component" of the conduct, it is clear that the St. Paul ordinance regulates on the basis of the "primary"

effect of the speech—i.e., its persuasive (or repellent) force.

3. The assortment of exceptions the Court attaches to its rule belies the majority's claim that its new theory is truly concerned with content discrimination. See Part I(C), infra (discussing the exceptions).

worthless in First Amendment terms until the city of St. Paul cures the under-breadth by adding to its ordinance a catch-all phrase such as "and all other fighting words that may constitutionally be subject to this ordinance."

Any contribution of this holding to First Amendment jurisprudence is surely a negative one, since it necessarily signals that expressions of violence, such as the message of intimidation and racial hatred conveyed by burning a cross on someone's lawn, are of sufficient value to outweigh the social interest in order and morality that has traditionally placed such fighting words outside the First Amendment.4 Indeed, by characterizing fighting words as a form of "debate" the majority legitimates hate speech as a form of public discussion. * * *

B. [Although] the First Amendment does not apply to categories of unpro-tected speech, such as fighting words, the Equal Protection Clause requires that the regulation of unprotected speech be rationally related to a legitimate govern-ment interest. A defamation statute that drew distinctions on the basis of political affiliation or "an ordinance prohibiting only those legally obscene works that contain criticism of the city government" would unquestionably fail rational basis review.9

Turning to the St. Paul ordinance and assuming arguendo, as the majority does, that the ordinance is not constitutionally overbroad (but see Part II, infra), there is no question that it would pass equal protection review. The ordinance [reflects] the City's judgment that harms based on race, color, creed, religion, or gender are more pressing public concerns than the harms caused by other fighting words. In light of our Nation's long and painful experience with discrimination, this determination is plainly reasonable. Indeed, as the majority concedes, the interest is compelling.

C. The Court has patched up its argument with an apparently nonexhaust-ive list of ad hoc exceptions, in what can be viewed either as an attempt to confine the effects of its decision to the facts of this case, or as an effort to anticipate some of the questions that will arise from its radical revision of First Amendment law. * * *

To save the statute [making it illegal to threaten the life of the President], the majority has engrafted the following exception onto its newly announced First Amendment rule: Content-based distinctions may be drawn within an unprotected category of speech if the basis for the distinctions is "the very reason the entire class of speech at issue is proscribable." * * *

The exception swallows the majority's rule. Certainly, it should apply to the St. Paul ordinance, since "the reasons why [fighting words] are outside the First Amendment [have] special force when applied to [groups that have historically been subjected to discrimination]."

To avoid the result of its own analysis, the Court suggests that fighting words are simply a mode of communication, rather than a content-based category, and

---

4. This does not suggest, of course, that cross burning is always unprotected. Burning a cross at a political rally would almost certainly be protected expression. Cf. *Brandenburg*. But in such a context, the cross burning could not be characterized as a "direct personal insult or an invitation to exchange fisticuffs," *Texas v. Johnson*, to which the fighting words doctrine, see Part II, infra, applies.

9. The majority is mistaken in stating that a ban on obscene works critical of government would fail equal protection review only because the ban would violate the First Amendment.

While decisions such as *Mosley* recognize that First Amendment principles may be relevant to an equal protection claim challenging distinc-tions that impact on protected expression, there is no basis for linking First and Four-teenth Amendment analysis in a case involving unprotected expression. Certainly, one need not resort to First Amendment principles to conclude that the sort of improbable legislation the majority hypothesizes is based on senseless distinctions.

that the St. Paul ordinance has not singled out a particularly objectionable mode of communication. Again, the majority confuses the issue. A prohibition on fighting words is not a time, place, or manner restriction; it is a ban on a class of speech that conveys an overriding message of personal injury and imminent violence, a message that is at its ugliest when directed against groups that have long been the targets of discrimination. Accordingly, the ordinance falls within the first exception to the majority's theory.

As its second exception, the Court posits that certain content-based regulations will survive under the new regime if the regulated subclass "happens to be associated with particular 'secondary effects' of the speech" which the majority treats as encompassing instances in which "words [can] violate laws directed not against speech but against conduct."11 Again, there is a simple explanation for the Court's eagerness to craft an exception to its new First Amendment rule: Under the general rule the Court applies in this case, Title VII hostile work environment claims would suddenly be unconstitutional.

Title VII * * * regulations covering hostile workplace claims forbid "sexual harassment," which includes "[u]nwelcome sexual advances, requests for sexual favors, and other verbal or physical conduct of a sexual nature" which creates "an intimidating, hostile, or offensive working environment." The regulation does not prohibit workplace harassment generally; it focuses on what the majority would characterize as the "disfavored topi[c]" of sexual harassment. In this way, Title VII is similar to the St. Paul ordinance that the majority condemns because it "impose[s] special prohibitions on those speakers who express views on disfavored subjects." * * *

Hence, the majority's second exception, which the Court indicates would insulate a Title VII hostile work environment claim from an underinclusiveness challenge because "sexually derogatory 'fighting words' [may] produce a violation of Title VII's general prohibition against sexual discrimination in employment practices." But application of this exception to a hostile work environment claim does not hold up under close examination.

First, the hostile work environment regulation is not keyed to the presence or absence of an economic quid pro quo, but to the impact of the speech on the victimized worker. Consequently, the regulation would no more fall within a secondary effects exception than does the St. Paul ordinance. Second, the majority's focus on the statute's general prohibition on discrimination glosses over the language of the specific regulation governing hostile working environment, which reaches beyond any "incidental" effect on speech. If the relationship between the broader statute and specific regulation is sufficient to bring the Title VII regulation within *O'Brien,* then all St. Paul need do to bring its ordinance within this exception is to add some prefatory language concerning discrimination generally.

As the third exception to the Court's theory for deciding this case, the majority concocts a catchall exclusion to protect against unforeseen problems. [It] would apply in cases in which "there is no realistic possibility that official suppression of ideas is afoot." As I have demonstrated, this case does not concern the official suppression of ideas. The majority discards this notion out-of-hand. * * *

II.   * * * I would decide the case on overbreadth grounds. * * *

11. The consequences of the majority's conflation of the rarely-used secondary effects standard and the *O'Brien* test for conduct incorporating "speech" and "nonspeech" elements, see generally *O'Brien,* present another question that I fear will haunt us and the lower courts in the aftermath of the majority's opinion.

In construing the St. Paul ordinance, [I understand the Minnesota Supreme Court] to have ruled that St. Paul may constitutionally prohibit expression that "by its very utterance" causes "anger, alarm or resentment."

Our fighting words cases have made clear, however, that [t]he mere fact that expressive activity causes hurt feelings, offense, or resentment does not render the expression unprotected. See *Eichman*; *Texas v. Johnson*; *Falwell.* * * *13 The ordinance is therefore fatally overbroad and invalid on its face.

JUSTICE BLACKMUN, concurring in the judgment.

[B]y deciding that a State cannot regulate speech that causes great harm unless it also regulates speech that does not (setting law and logic on their heads), the Court seems to abandon the categorical approach, and inevitably to relax the level of scrutiny applicable to content-based laws. [The] simple reality is that the Court will never provide child pornography or cigarette advertising the level of protection customarily granted political speech. If we are forbidden from categorizing, as the Court has done here, we shall reduce protection across the board. * * *

[There] is the possibility that this case will not significantly alter First Amendment jurisprudence, but, instead, will be regarded as an aberration—a case where the Court manipulated doctrine to strike down an ordinance whose premise it opposed, namely, that racial threats and verbal assaults are of greater harm than other fighting words. I fear that the Court has been distracted from its proper mission by the temptation to decide the issue over "politically correct speech" and "cultural diversity," neither of which is presented here. If this is the meaning of today's opinion, it is perhaps even more regrettable.

I see no First Amendment values that are compromised by a law that prohibits hoodlums from driving minorities out of their homes by burning crosses on their lawns, but I see great harm in preventing the people of Saint Paul from specifically punishing the race-based fighting words that so prejudice their community. * * *

JUSTICE STEVENS, with whom JUSTICE WHITE and JUSTICE BLACKMUN join as to Part I, concurring in the judgment. * * *

I. [Our] First Amendment decisions have created a rough hierarchy in the constitutional protection of speech. Core political speech occupies the highest, most protected position; commercial speech and nonobscene, sexually explicit speech are regarded as a sort of second-class expression; obscenity and fighting words receive the least protection of all. Assuming that the Court is correct that this last class of speech is not wholly "unprotected," it certainly does not follow that fighting words and obscenity receive the *same* sort of protection afforded core political speech. Yet in ruling that proscribable speech cannot be regulated based on subject matter, the Court does just that. Perversely, this gives fighting words *greater* protection than is afforded commercial speech. If Congress can prohibit false advertising directed at airline passengers without also prohibiting false advertising directed at bus passengers and if a city can prohibit political advertisements in its buses while allowing other advertisements, it is ironic to hold that a city cannot regulate fighting words based on "race, color, creed, religion or gender" while leaving unregulated fighting words based on "union membership or

---

13. Although the First Amendment protects offensive speech, it does not require us to be subjected to such expression at all times, in all settings. We have held that such expression may be proscribed when it intrudes upon a "captive audience." And expression may be limited when it merges into conduct. *O'Brien*. However, because of the manner in which the Minnesota Supreme Court construed the St. Paul ordinance, those issues are not before us in this case.

homosexuality." * * * Perhaps because the Court recognizes these perversities, it quickly offers some ad hoc limitations on its newly extended prohibition on content-based regulations.**a**

[T]he Court recognizes that a State may regulate advertising in one industry but not another because "the risk of fraud (one of the characteristics that justifies depriving [commercial speech] of full First Amendment protection)" in the regulated industry is "greater" than in other industries. "[O]ne of the characteristics that justifies" the constitutional status of fighting words is that such words "by their very utterance inflict injury or tend to incite an immediate breach of the peace." *Chaplinsky.* Certainly a legislature that may determine that the risk of fraud is greater in the legal trade than in the medical trade may determine that the risk of injury or breach of peace created by race-based threats is greater than that created by other threats.

Similarly, it is impossible to reconcile the Court's analysis of the St. Paul ordinance with its recognition that "a prohibition of fighting words that are directed at certain persons or groups [would] be facially valid." A selective proscription of unprotected expression designed to protect "certain persons or groups" (for example, a law proscribing threats directed at the elderly) would be constitutional if it were based on a legitimate determination that the harm created by the regulated expression differs from that created by the unregulated expression (that is, if the elderly are more severely injured by threats than are the nonelderly). Such selective protection is no different from a law prohibiting minors (and only minors) from obtaining obscene publications. St. Paul has determined—reasonably in my judgment—that fighting-word injuries "based on race, color, creed, religion or gender" are qualitatively different and more severe than fighting-word injuries based on other characteristics. Whether the selective proscription of proscribable speech is defined by the protected target ("certain persons or groups") or the basis of the harm (injuries "based on race, color, creed, religion or gender") makes no constitutional difference: what matters is whether the legislature's selection is based on a legitimate, neutral, and reasonable distinction. * * *

III. [Unlike] the Court, I do not believe that all content-based regulations are equally infirm and presumptively invalid; unlike Justice White, I do not believe that fighting words are wholly unprotected by the First Amendment. To the contrary, I believe our decisions establish a more complex and subtle analysis, one that considers the content and context of the regulated speech, and the nature and scope of the restriction on speech. * * * Whatever the allure of absolute doctrines, it is just too simple to declare expression "protected" or "unprotected" or to proclaim a regulation "content-based" or "content-neutral."

In applying this analysis to the St. Paul ordinance, I assume arguendo—as the Court does—that the ordinance regulates *only* fighting words and therefore is *not*

---

a. In an earlier passage and footnote of his opinion, Stevens, J., argued: "[W]hile the Court rejects the 'all-or-nothing-at-all' nature of the categorical approach, it promptly embraces an absolutism of its own: within a particular 'proscribable' category of expression, the Court holds, a government must either proscribe all speech or no speech at all. The Court disputes this characterization because it has crafted two exceptions, one for 'certain media or markets' and the other for content discrimination based upon 'the very reason that the entire class of speech at issue is proscribable.' These exceptions are, at best, ill-

defined. The Court does not tell us whether, with respect to the former, fighting words such as cross-burning could be proscribed only in certain neighborhoods where the threat of violence is particularly severe, or whether, with respect to the second category, fighting words that create a particular risk of harm (such as a race riot) would be proscribable. The hypothetical and illusory category of these two exceptions persuades me that either my description of the Court's analysis is accurate or that the Court does not in fact mean much of what it says in its opinion."

overbroad. Looking to the content and character of the regulated activity, two things are clear. First, by hypothesis the ordinance bars only low-value speech, namely, fighting words. * * * Second, the ordinance regulates "expressive conduct [rather] than [the] written or spoken word."

Looking to the context of the regulated activity, it is again significant that the statute (by hypothesis) regulates *only* fighting words. Whether words are fighting words is determined in part by their context. Fighting words are not words that merely cause offense; fighting words must be directed at individuals so as to "by their very utterance inflict injury." By hypothesis, then, the St. Paul ordinance restricts speech in confrontational and potentially violent situations. The case at hand is illustrative. The cross-burning in this case—directed as it was to a single African–American family trapped in their home—was nothing more than a crude form of physical intimidation. That this cross-burning sends a message of racial hostility does not automatically endow it with complete constitutional protection.

Significantly, the St. Paul ordinance regulates speech not on the basis of its subject matter or the viewpoint expressed, but rather on the basis of the *harm* the speech causes. * * * Contrary to the Court's suggestion, the ordinance regulates only a subcategory of expression that causes *injuries based on* "race, color, creed, religion or gender," not a subcategory that involves *discussions* that concern those characteristics.9 * * *

Finally, it is noteworthy that the St. Paul ordinance is, as construed by the Court today, quite narrow. The St. Paul ordinance does not ban all "hate speech," nor does it ban, say, all cross-burnings or all swastika displays. Rather it only bans a subcategory of the already narrow category of fighting words. Such a limited ordinance leaves open and protected a vast range of expression on the subjects of racial, religious, and gender equality. As construed by the Court today, the ordinance certainly does not " 'raise the specter that the Government may effectively drive certain ideas or viewpoints from the marketplace.' " Petitioner is free to burn a cross to announce a rally or to express his views about racial supremacy, he may do so on private property or public land, at day or at night, so long as the burning is not so threatening and so directed at an individual as to "by its very [execution] inflict injury." Such a limited proscription scarcely offends the First Amendment. * * *

Notes

1.   At the capital sentencing phase of a murder case, the prosecution sought to introduce evidence that the defendant was a member of the Aryan Brotherhood which was stipulated to be a "white racist gang." DAWSON v. DELAWARE, 503 U.S. 159 (1992), per REHNQUIST, C.J., held that its admission violated the First Amendment: "Even if the Delaware group to which Dawson allegedly belongs is

9. The Court contends that this distinction is "wordplay," reasoning that "[w]hat makes [the harms caused by race-based threats] distinct from [the harms] produced by other fighting words [is] the fact that [the former are] caused by a *distinctive idea.*" In this way, the Court concludes that regulating speech based on the injury it causes is no different from regulating speech based on its subject matter. This analysis fundamentally miscomprehends the role of "race, color, creed, religion [and] gender" in contemporary American society. One need look no further than the recent so- cial unrest in the Nation's cities to see that race-based threats may cause more harm to society and to individuals than other threats. Just as the statute prohibiting threats against the President is justifiable because of the place of the President in our social and political order, so a statute prohibiting race-based threats is justifiable because of the place of race in our social and political order. * * * [S]uch a place and is so incendiary an issue, until the Nation matures beyond that condition, laws such as St. Paul's ordinance will remain reasonable and justifiable.

racist, those beliefs, so far as we can determine, had no relevance to the sentencing proceeding in this case. For example, the Aryan Brotherhood evidence was not tied in any way to the murder of Dawson's [white] victim. [Moreover], we conclude that Dawson's First Amendment rights were violated by the admission of the Aryan Brotherhood evidence in this case, because the evidence proved nothing more than Dawson's abstract beliefs. [Delaware] might have avoided this problem if it had presented evidence showing more than mere abstract beliefs on Dawson's part, but on the present record one is left with the feeling that the Aryan Brotherhood evidence was employed simply because the jury would find these beliefs morally reprehensible."

THOMAS, J., dissented: "Dawson introduced mitigating character evidence that he had acted kindly toward his family. The stipulation tended to undercut this showing by suggesting that Dawson's kindness did not extend to members of other racial groups. Although we do not sit in judgment of the morality of particular creeds, we cannot bend traditional concepts of relevance to exempt the antisocial."

2. *Wisconsin v. Mitchell*, 508 U.S. 476 (1993) found no First Amendment violation when Wisconsin permitted a sentence for aggravated battery to be enhanced on the ground that the white victim had been selected because of his race. The Court observed that, unlike *R.A.V.*, the Wisconsin statute was aimed at conduct, not speech, that a chilling effect on speech was unlikely, that the focus on motive was no different from that employed in anti-discrimination statutes, and that bias-inspired conduct is more likely "to provoke retaliatory crimes, inflict distinct emotional harms on their victims, and incite community unrest."

3. In 1952, Virginia declared it a felony publicly to burn a cross with the intent of intimidating any person or group of persons. In 1968, Virginia added a provision that any such burning shall be prima facie evidence of an intent to intimidate. Barry Black led a Ku Klux Klan rally in which a cross was burned after a series of speeches marked by racial hostility, including one speaker saying that he "would love to take a .30/.30 and just random[ly] shoot the blacks." Forty to fifty cars passed the site during the rally, and eight to ten houses were located in its vicinity. The trial court used a Virginia Model Instruction that "the burning of a cross by itself is sufficient evidence from which you may infer the required intent."

The Virginia Supreme Court declared the statute unconstitutional in light of *R.A.V.* and overturned the conviction of Black. VIRGINIA v. BLACK, 538 U.S. 343 (2003), per O'CONNOR, J., upheld the cross burning with intent to intimidate provision, but struck down the prima facie evidence provision as interpreted by the jury instruction in the Black case, and, thereby, affirmed the dismissal of Black's prosecution while remanding for further proceedings in a companion case where the state was required to prove intent: "[T]he First Amendment [permits] a State to ban a 'true threat.' *Watts.* * * * Intimidation in the constitutionally proscribable sense of the word is a type of true threat. [T]he First Amendment permits Virginia to outlaw cross burnings done with the intent to intimidate because burning a cross is a particularly virulent form of intimidation." In a section of the opinion joined by Rehnquist, C.J., Stevens and Breyer, JJ., O'Connor, J., addressed the prima facie evidence provision: "[As] construed by the jury instruction, the prima facie provision strips away the very reason why a State may ban cross burning with the intent to intimidate. The prima facie evidence provision permits a jury to convict in every cross-burning case in which defendants exercise their constitutional right not to put on a defense. And even where a defendant like Black presents a defense, the prima facie evidence provision makes it more likely that the jury will find an intent to intimidate regardless of the particular facts of the case. The provision permits the Commonwealth to arrest, prosecute, and convict a person based solely on the fact of cross burning itself.''

SCALIA, J., joined by Thomas, J., concurring and dissenting, agreed that the cross burning/intimidation portion of the statute was constitutional, but he denied that the prima facie evidence aspect of the statute was necessarily unconstitutional. In his view the Virginia Supreme Court had yet to provide an authoritative construction of that provision.

SOUTER, J., joined by Kennedy and Ginsburg, JJ., concurring in part and dissenting in part, argued that both the cross burning/intimidation section and the prima facie evidence section were unconstitutional: ''The question here is * * * the claim of a clearly content-based statute to an exception from the general prohibition of content-based proscriptions, an exception that is not warranted if the statute's terms show that suppression of ideas may be afoot. Accordingly, the way to look at the prima facie evidence provision is to consider it for any indication of what is afoot. And if we look at the provision for this purpose, it has a very obvious significance as a mechanism for bringing within the statute's prohibition some expression that is doubtfully threatening though certainly distasteful.''

THOMAS, J., dissenting, maintained that the statute was constitutional: ''Although I agree with the majority's conclusion that it is constitutionally permissible to 'ban . . . cross burning carried out with intent to intimidate,' I believe that the majority errs in imputing an expressive component to the activity in question. In my view, whatever expressive value cross burning has, the legislature simply wrote it out by banning only intimidating conduct undertaken by a particular means. A conclusion that the statute prohibiting cross burning with intent to intimidate sweeps beyond a prohibition on certain conduct into the zone of expression overlooks not only the words of the statute but also reality. * * *

''Strengthening [my] conclusion, that the legislature sought to criminalize terrorizing *conduct* is the fact that at the time the statute was enacted, racial segregation was not only the prevailing practice, but also the law in Virginia. And, just two years after the enactment of this statute, Virginia's General Assembly embarked on a campaign of 'massive resistance' in response to *Brown v. Board of Education*. It strains credulity to suggest that a state legislature that adopted a litany of segregationist laws self-contradictorily intended to squelch the segregationist message. ''[Even] assuming that the statute implicates the First Amendment, in my view, the fact that the statute permits a jury to draw an inference of intent to intimidate from the cross burning itself presents no constitutional problems. [The] inference is rebuttable and, as the jury instructions given in this case demonstrate, Virginia law still requires the jury to find the existence of each element, including intent to intimidate, beyond a reasonable doubt.''

SECTION 4. PRIOR RESTRAINTS

Prior restraint is a technical term in First Amendment law. A criminal statute prohibiting all advocacy of violent action would *restrain* speech and would have been enacted *prior* to any restrained communication. The statute would be overbroad, but it would not be a prior restraint. A prior restraint refers only to closely related, distinctive methods of regulating expression that are said to have in common their own peculiar set of evils and problems, in addition to those that accompany most any governmental interference with free expression. ''The issue is not whether the government may impose a particular restriction of substance in an area of public expression, such as forbidding obscenity in newspapers, but whether it may do so by a particular method, such as advance screening of newspaper copy. In other words, restrictions which could be validly imposed when enforced by subsequent punishment are, nevertheless, forbidden if attempted by prior restraint." Thomas Emerson, *The Doctrine of Prior Restraint*, 20 Law and Contemp.Prob. 648 (1955).

The classic prior restraints were the English licensing laws which required a license in advance to print any material or to import or to sell any book. One of the questions raised in this chapter concerns the types of government conduct beyond the classic licensing laws that should be characterized as prior restraints. Another concerns the question of when government licensing of speech, press, or assembly should be countenanced. Perhaps, most important, the Section explores the circumstances in which otherwise protected speech may be restrained on an ad hoc basis.

I. FOUNDATION CASES

A. LICENSING

LOVELL v. GRIFFIN, 303 U.S. 444 (1938), per HUGHES, C.J., invalidated an ordinance prohibiting the distribution of handbooks, advertising or literature within the city of Griffin, Georgia without obtaining written permission of the City Manager: "[T]he ordinance is invalid on its face. Whatever the motive which induced its adoption, its character is such that it strikes at the very foundation of the freedom of the press by subjecting it to license and censorship. The struggle for the freedom of the press was primarily directed against the power of the licensor. It was against that power that John Milton directed his assault by his 'Appeal for the Liberty of Unlicensed Printing.' And the liberty of the press became initially a right to publish '*without* a license what formerly could be published only *with* one.' While this freedom from previous restraint upon publication cannot be regarded as exhausting the guaranty of liberty, the prevention of that restraint was a leading purpose in the adoption of the constitutional provision. Legislation of the type of the ordinance in question would restore the system of license and censorship in its baldest form.

"The liberty of the press is not confined to newspapers and periodicals. It necessarily embraces pamphlets and leaflets. These indeed have been historic weapons in the defense of liberty, as the pamphlets of Thomas Paine and others in our own history abundantly attest. The press in its historic connotation comprehends every sort of publication which affords a vehicle of information and opinion. * * *

"The ordinance cannot be saved because it relates to distribution and not to publication. 'Liberty of circulating is as essential to that freedom as liberty of publishing; indeed, without the circulation, the publication would be of little value.' *Ex parte Jackson*, 96 U.S. (6 Otto) 727, 733 (1877).

"[As] the ordinance is void on its face, it was not necessary for appellant to seek a permit under it. She was entitled to contest its validity in answer to the charge against her."a

Notes

1. **Beyond press content.** The prior restraint doctrine is not confined to restraints on press content. It has, for example, been applied to films. Times Film

---

a. Cardozo, J., took no part.

Corp. v. Chicago, 365 U.S. 43 (1961). It has also been applied to a licensing ordinance that otherwise forbids soliciting membership in organizations that exact fees of their members. *Staub v. Baxley,* 355 U.S. 313 (1958), to a licensing ordinance that otherwise prohibits attempts to secure contributions for charitable or religious causes. *Cantwell v. Connecticut,* 310 U.S. 296 (1940); *Riley v. National Federation of the Blind*, 487 U.S. 781 (1988) and to an ordinance granting a Mayor the power to grant or deny annual permits to place newsracks on public property. *Lakewood v. Plain Dealer Publishing Co.,* 486 U.S. 750 (1988). See also *Thomas v. Collins,* 323 U.S. 516 (1945) (registration requirement for paid union organizers invalid prior restraint); *Talley v. California,* 362 U.S. 60 (1960) (ban on anonymous handbills "void on its face," noting that the "obnoxious press licensing law of England, which was also enforced on the Colonies was due in part to the knowledge that exposure of the names of printers, writers and distributors would lessen the circulation of literature critical of the government").

2. **Absence of discretion.** *Hynes v. Mayor,* 425 U.S. 610 (1976), per Burger, C.J., stated in dictum that a municipality could regulate house to house soliciting by requiring advance notice to the police department in order to protect its citizens from crime and undue annoyance: "A narrowly drawn ordinance, that does not vest in municipal officials the undefined power to determine what messages residents will hear, may serve these important interests without running afoul of the First Amendment." *Hynes v. Mayor,* 425 U.S. 610 (1976), per Burger, C.J., stated in dictum that a municipality could regulate house to house soliciting by requiring advance notice to the police department in order to protect its citizens from crime and undue annoyance: "A narrowly drawn ordinance, that does not vest in municipal officials the undefined power to determine what messages residents will hear, may serve these important interests without running afoul of the First Amendment." But *Watchtower Bible & Tract Society v. Stratton*, 536 U.S. 150 (2002) held to the contrary: "It is offensive—not only to the values protected by the First Amendment, but to the very notion of a free society—that in the context of everyday public discourse a citizen must first inform the government of her desire to speak to her neighbors and then obtain a permit to do so. Even if the issuance of permits by the mayor's office is a ministerial task that is performed promptly and at no cost to the applicant, a law requiring a permit to engage in such speech constitutes a dramatic departure from our national heritage and constitutional tradition."

B. INJUNCTIONS

NEAR v. MINNESOTA

283 U.S. 697, 51 S.Ct. 625, 75 L.Ed. 1357 (1931).

CHIEF JUSTICE HUGHES delivered the opinion of the Court.

[The *Saturday Press* published articles charging that through graft and incompetence named public officials failed to expose and punish gangsters responsible for gambling, bootlegging, and racketeering in Minneapolis. It demanded a special grand jury and special prosecutor to deal with the situation and to investigate an alleged attempt to assassinate one of its publishers. Under a statute that authorized abatement of a "malicious, scandalous and defamatory newspaper" the state secured, and its supreme court affirmed, a court order that "abated" the Press and perpetually enjoined the defendants from publishing or circulating "any publication whatsoever which is a malicious, scandalous or defamatory newspaper." The order did not restrain the defendants from operating a newspaper "in harmony with the general welfare."]

The object of the statute is not punishment, in the ordinary sense, but suppression of the offending newspaper. [In] the case of public officers, it is the reiteration of charges of official misconduct, and the fact that the newspaper [is] principally devoted to that purpose, that exposes it to suppression. [T]he operation and effect of the statute [is] that public authorities may bring the owner or publisher of a newspaper or periodical before a judge upon a charge of conducting a business of publishing scandalous and defamatory matter—in particular that the matter consists of charges against public officers of official dereliction—and, unless the owner or publisher is able and disposed to bring competent evidence to satisfy the judge that the charges are true and are published with good motives and for justifiable ends, his newspaper or periodical is suppressed and further publication is made punishable as a contempt. This is of the essence of censorship.

The question is whether a statute authorizing such proceedings [is] consistent with the conception of the liberty of the press as historically conceived and guaranteed. [I]t has been generally, if not universally, considered that it is the chief purpose of the guaranty to prevent previous restraints upon publication. The struggle in England, directed against the legislative power of the licenser, resulted in renunciation of the censorship of the press. The liberty deemed to be established was thus described by Blackstone: "The liberty of the press is indeed essential to the nature of a free state; but this consists in laying no *previous* restraints upon publications, and not in freedom from censure for criminal matter when published. Every freeman has an undoubted right to lay what sentiments he pleases before the public; to forbid this, is to destroy the freedom of the press; but if he publishes what is improper, mischievous or illegal, he must take the consequence of his own temerity." [The] criticism upon Blackstone's statement has not been because immunity from previous restraint upon publication has not been regarded as deserving of special emphasis, but chiefly because that immunity cannot be deemed to exhaust the conception of the liberty guaranteed by State and Federal Constitutions.

[T]he protection even as to previous restraint is not absolutely unlimited. But the limitation has been recognized only in exceptional cases. [N]o one would question but that a government might prevent actual obstruction to its recruiting service or the publication of the sailing dates of transports or the number and location of troops. On similar grounds, the primary requirements of decency may be enforced against obscene publications. The security of the community life may be protected against incitements to acts of violence and the overthrow by force of orderly [government]. * * *

The fact that for approximately one hundred and fifty years there has been almost an entire absence of attempts to impose previous restraints upon publications relating to the malfeasance of public officers is significant of the deep-seated conviction that such restraints would violate constitutional right. Public officers, whose character and conduct remain open to debate and free discussion in the press, find their remedies for false accusations in actions under libel laws providing for redress and punishment, and not in proceedings to restrain the publication of newspapers and periodicals. [The] fact that the liberty of the press may be abused by miscreant purveyors of scandal does not make any the less necessary the immunity of the press from previous restraint in dealing with official misconduct. Subsequent punishment for such abuses as may exist is the appropriate remedy, consistent with constitutional [privilege].

The statute in question cannot be justified by reason of the fact that the publisher is permitted to show, before injunction issues, that the matter published is true and is published with good motives and for justifiable ends. If such a statute, authorizing suppression and injunction on such a basis, is constitutionally valid, it would be equally permissible for the Legislature to provide that at any time the publisher of any newspaper could be brought before a court, or even an administrative officer (as the constitutional protection may not be regarded as resting on mere procedural details), and required to produce proof of the truth of his publication, or of what he intended to publish and of his motives, or stand enjoined. If this can be done, the Legislature may provide machinery for determining in the complete exercise of its discretion what are justifiable ends and restrain publication accordingly. And it would be but a step to a complete system of censorship.

[For] these reasons we hold the statute, so far as it authorized the proceedings in this action, [to] be an infringement of the liberty of the press guaranteed by the Fourteenth Amendment. * * *

JUSTICE BUTLER (dissenting).

[T]he *previous restraints* referred to by [Blackstone] subjected the press to the arbitrary will of an administrative officer. [The] Minnesota statute does not operate as a *previous* restraint on publication within the proper meaning of that phrase. It does not authorize administrative control in advance such as was formerly exercised by the licensers and censors, but prescribes a remedy to be enforced by a suit in equity. In this case [t]he business and publications unquestionably constitute an abuse of the right of free press. [A]s stated by the state Supreme Court [they] threaten morals, peace, and good order. [The] restraint authorized is only in respect of continuing to do what has been duly adjudged to constitute a nuisance. [It] is fanciful to suggest similarity between the granting or enforcement of the decree authorized by this statute to prevent *further* publication of malicious, scandalous, and defamatory articles and the *previous restraint* upon the press by licensers as referred to by Blackstone and described in the history of the times to which he alludes. * * *

It is well known, as found by the state supreme court, that existing libel laws are inadequate effectively to suppress evils resulting from the kind of business and publications that are shown in this case. The doctrine [of this decision] exposes the peace and good order of every community and the business and private affairs of every individual to the constant and protracted false and malicious assaults of any insolvent publisher who may have purpose and sufficient capacity to contrive and put into effect a scheme or program for oppression, blackmail or extortion. * * *

JUSTICE VAN DEVANTER, JUSTICE MCREYNOLDS, and JUSTICE SUTHERLAND concur in this opinion.

Notes

1. ***The collateral bar rule.*** The collateral bar rule provides "that a court order must be obeyed until it is set aside, and that persons subject to the order who disobey it may not defend against the ensuing charge of criminal contempt on the ground that the order was erroneous or even unconstitutional." WALKER v. BIRMINGHAM, 388 U.S. 307 (1967) upheld the rule against a First Amendment challenge in affirming the contempt conviction of defendants for violating an ex parte injunction issued by an Alabama court enjoining them from engaging in street parades without a municipal permit issued pursuant to the city's parade ordinance. The Court, per STEWART, J., (Warren, C.J., Brennan, Douglas, and Fortas, JJ., dissenting) held that because the petitioners neither moved to dissolve the injunction nor sought to comply with the city's parade ordinance, their claim

that the injunction and ordinance were unconstitutional[a] did not need to be considered: "This Court cannot hold that the petitioners were constitutionally free to ignore all the procedures of the law and carry their battle to the streets. [R]espect for judicial process is a small price to pay for the civilizing hand of law, which alone can give abiding meaning to constitutional freedom." Although *Walker* suggested that its holding might be different if the court issuing the injunction lacked jurisdiction or if the injunction were "transparently invalid or had only a frivolous pretense to validity," it held that Alabama's invocation of the collateral bar rule was not itself unconstitutional. Cf. *Poulos v. New Hampshire,* 345 U.S. 395 (1953) (claim of arbitrary refusal to issue license for open air meeting need not be entertained when a licensing statute is considered to be valid on its face in circumstance where speaker fails to seek direct judicial relief and proceeds without a license).[b]

2. **Time, place, and manner regulations.** *Madsen v. Women's Health Center,* 512 U.S. 753 (1994) maintained that in evaluating a content neutral injunction, the standard is whether the injunction burdened substantially more speech than necessary. It stated that the ordinary rules governing time, place, and manner regulations are insufficiently rigorous.

3. **Enjoining speech determined to be obscene or otherwise unprotected.** Kingsley Books, Inc. v. Brown, 354 U.S. 436 (1957) upheld an injunction against the distribution of materials that the lower court had determined to be obscene. *Near* was distinguished on the ground that the injunction there applied to future publications (without an assessment of their content) because of prior newspaper content. And Pittsburgh Press Co. v. Pittsburgh Comm'n on Human Relations, 413 U.S. 376 (1973) upheld an order forbidding Pittsburgh Press to carry sex-designated "help wanted" ads, except for exempt jobs.

4. ***Procedural safeguards.*** FREEDMAN v. MARYLAND, 380 U.S. 51 (1965), per BRENNAN, J., set out procedural safeguards designed to reduce the dangers associated with prior restraints of films. It required that the procedure must "assure a prompt final judicial decision, to minimize the deterrent effect of an interim and possibly erroneous denial of a license," that the censor must promptly institute the proceedings, that the burden of proof to show that the speech in question is unprotected must rest on the censor, and that the proceedings be adversarial. The *Freedman* standards have been applied in other contexts. *Blount v. Rizzi,* 400 U.S. 410 (1971) (postal stop orders of obscene materials); *United States v. Thirty–Seven Photographs,* 402 U.S. 363 (1971) (customs seizure of obscene materials); *Southeastern Promotions, Ltd. v. Conrad,* 420 U.S. 546 (1975) (denial of permit to use municipal theater for the musical, Hair); *Carroll v. President and Commissioners,* 393 U.S. 175 (1968) (10 day restraining order against particular rallies or meetings invalid because *ex parte*); *City of Littleton v. Z.J. Gifts D–4,* 541 U.S. 774 (2004) (adult business licensing ordinances including the assurance of speedy court decisions); But see *Thomas v. Chicago Park Dist.,* 534 U.S. 316 (2002) (*Freedman* does not apply to content neutral licensing requirement granting authorities for assemblies involving more than fifty persons in public park even when ordinance as a matter of course grants authorities fourteen days to decide whether permit should be issued). Cf. *FW/PBS v. Dallas,* 493 U.S. 215 (1990) (suggesting that partial application of *Freedman* standards

---

a. Indeed, the ordinance in question was declared unconstitutional two years later. *Shuttlesworth v. Birmingham,* 394 U.S. 147 (1969) (ordinance conferring unbridled discretion to prohibit any parade or demonstration is unconstitutional prior restraint).

b. For consideration of when licensing statutes for assemblies are valid, see *Cox v. New Hampshire,* Sec. 6, I, A infra.

(dispensing with burden of going to court and burden of proof, but retaining assurance of timely decision making by licensor and prompt judicial review) to ordinance licensing sexually oriented businesses ostensibly without regard to content of films or books would be appropriate).

5. **Beyond injunctions.** BANTAM BOOKS, INC. v. SULLIVAN, 372 U.S. 58 (1963), per BRENNAN, J., (Harlan, J. dissenting) held unconstitutional the activities of a government commission that would identify "objectionable" books (some admittedly not obscene), notify the distributor in writing, inform the distributor of the Commission's duty to recommend obscenity prosecutions to the Attorney General and that the Commission's list of objectionable books was distributed to local police departments. The Commission thanked distributors in advance for their "cooperation," and a police officer usually visited the distributor to learn what action had been taken. In characterizing these practices as a system of prior administrative restraints, rather than mere legal advice, the Court observed that it did not mean to foreclose private consultation between law enforcement officers and distributors so long as such consultations were "genuinely undertaken with the purpose of aiding the distributor to comply" with the laws and avoid prosecution.

II. PRIOR RESTRAINTS AND NATIONAL SECURITY

NEW YORK TIMES CO. v. UNITED STATES [THE PENTAGON PAPERS CASE]

403 U.S. 713, 91 S.Ct. 2140, 29 L.Ed.2d 822 (1971).

PER CURIAM.

We granted certiorari in these cases in which the United States seeks to enjoin the *New York Times* and the *Washington Post* from publishing the contents of a classified study entitled "History of U.S. Decision–Making Process on Viet Nam Policy."a

"Any system of prior restraints of expression comes to this Court bearing a heavy presumption against its constitutional validity." *Bantam Books;* see also *Near.* The Government "thus carries a heavy burden of showing justification for the enforcement of such a restraint." [The district court in the *Times* case and both lower federal courts] in the *Post* case held that the Government had not met that burden. We agree. [T]he stays entered [by this Court five days previously] are vacated. * * *

JUSTICE BLACK, with whom JUSTICE DOUGLAS joins, concurring.

I adhere to the view that the Government's case against the *Post* should have been dismissed and that the injunction against the *Times* should have been vacated without oral argument when the cases were first presented to this Court. I believe that every moment's continuance of the injunctions against these newspapers amounts to a flagrant, indefensible, and continuing violation of the First Amendment. Furthermore, after oral arguments, I agree [with] the reasons stated by my Brothers Douglas and Brennan. In my view it is unfortunate that some of my Brethren are apparently willing to hold that the publication of news

a. On June 12–14, 1971 the *New York Times* and on June 18 the *Washington Post* published portions of this "top secret" Pentagon study. Government actions seeking temporary restraining orders and injunctions pro- gressed through two district courts and two courts of appeals between June 15–23. After a June 26 argument, ten Supreme Court opinions were issued on June 30, 1971.

may sometimes be enjoined. Such a holding would make a shambles of the First Amendment.

[F]or the first time in the 182 years since the founding of the Republic, the federal courts are asked to hold that the First Amendment does not mean what it says, but rather means that the Government can halt the publication of current news of vital importance to the people of this country. * * *

The Government does not even attempt to rely on any act of Congress. Instead it makes the bold and dangerously far-reaching contention that the courts should take it upon themselves to "make" a law abridging freedom of the press in the name of equity, presidential power and national security, even when the representatives of the people in Congress have adhered to the command of the First Amendment and refused to make such a law. To find that the President has "inherent power" to halt the publication of news by resort to the courts would wipe out the First Amendment and destroy the fundamental liberty and security of the very people the Government hopes to make "secure." [The] word "security" is a broad, vague generality whose contours should not be invoked to abrogate the fundamental law embodied in the First Amendment. * * *

JUSTICE DOUGLAS, with whom JUSTICE BLACK joins, concurring.

While I join the opinion of the Court I believe it necessary to express my views more fully.

[The First Amendment leaves] no room for governmental restraint on the press. There is, moreover, no statute barring the publication by the press of the material which the *Times* and *Post* seek to use. [These] disclosures may have a serious impact. But that is no basis for sanctioning a previous restraint on the press * * *.

The dominant purpose of the First Amendment was to prohibit the widespread practice of governmental suppression of embarrassing information. [A] debate of large proportions goes on in the Nation over our posture in Vietnam. That debate antedated the disclosure of the contents of the present documents. The latter are highly relevant to the debate in progress.

Secrecy in government is fundamentally anti-democratic, perpetuating bureaucratic errors. Open debate and discussion of public issues are vital to our national health. [The] stays in these cases that have been in effect for more than a week constitute a flouting of the principles of the First Amendment as interpreted in *Near*.

JUSTICE BRENNAN, concurring.

I write separately [to] emphasize what should be apparent: that our judgment in the present cases may not be taken to indicate the propriety, in the future, of issuing temporary stays and restraining orders to block the publication of material sought to be suppressed by the Government. So far as I can determine, never before has the United States sought to enjoin a newspaper from publishing information in its possession. * * *

The entire thrust of the Government's claim throughout these cases has been that publication of the material sought to be enjoined "could," or "might," or "may" prejudice the national interest in various ways. But the First Amendment tolerates absolutely no prior judicial restraints of the press predicated upon surmise or conjecture that untoward consequences may result.* Our cases, it is

---

* *Freedman* and similar cases regarding temporary restraints of allegedly obscene materials are not in point. For those cases rest upon the proposition that "obscenity is not protected by the freedoms of speech and press." *Roth*. Here there is no question but that the material

true, have indicated that there is a single, extremely narrow class of cases in which the First Amendment's ban on prior judicial restraint may be overridden. Our cases have thus far indicated that such cases may arise only when the Nation "is at war," [*Schenck*]. Even if the present world situation were assumed to be tantamount to a time of war, or if the power of presently available armaments would justify even in peacetime the suppression of information that would set in motion a nuclear holocaust, in neither of these actions has the Government presented or even alleged that publication of items from or based upon the material at issue would cause the happening of an event of that nature. [Thus,] only governmental allegation and proof that publication must inevitably, directly and immediately cause the occurrence of an event kindred to imperiling the safety of a transport already at sea can support even the issuance of an interim restraining order. In no event may mere conclusions be sufficient: for if the Executive Branch seeks judicial aid in preventing publication, it must inevitably submit the basis upon which that aid is sought to scrutiny by the judiciary. And therefore, every restraint issued in this case, whatever its form, has violated the First Amendment—and not less so because that restraint was justified as necessary to afford the courts an opportunity to examine the claim more thoroughly. Unless and until the Government has clearly made out its case, the First Amendment commands that no injunction may issue.

JUSTICE STEWART, with whom JUSTICE WHITE joins, concurring.

[I]n the cases before us we are asked neither to construe specific regulations nor to apply specific laws. [We] are asked, quite simply, to prevent the publication by two newspapers of material that the Executive Branch insists should not, in the national interest, be published. I am convinced that the Executive is correct with respect to some of the documents involved. But I cannot say that disclosure of any of them will surely result in direct, immediate, and irreparable damage to our Nation or its people. That being so, there can under the First Amendment be but one judicial resolution of the issues before us. I join the judgments * * *.

JUSTICE WHITE, with whom JUSTICE STEWART joins, concurring.

I concur in today's judgments, but only because of the concededly extraordinary protection against prior restraints enjoyed by the press under our constitutional system. I do not say that in no circumstances would the First Amendment permit an injunction against publishing information about government plans or operations. Nor, after examining the materials the Government characterizes as the most sensitive and destructive, can I deny that revelation of these documents will do substantial damage to public interests. Indeed, I am confident that their disclosure will have that result. But I nevertheless agree that the United States has not satisfied the very heavy burden which it must meet to warrant an injunction against publication in these cases, at least in the absence of express and appropriately limited congressional authorization for prior restraints in circumstances such as these.

The Government's position is simply stated: The responsibility of the Executive for the conduct of the foreign affairs and for the security of the Nation is so basic that the President is entitled to an injunction against publication of a newspaper story whenever he can convince a court that the information to be revealed threatens "grave and irreparable" injury to the public interest; and the injunction should issue whether or not the material to be published is classified, whether or not publication would be lawful under relevant criminal statutes

sought to be suppressed is within the protection of the First Amendment; the only question is whether, notwithstanding that fact, its publication may be enjoined for a time because of the presence of an overwhelming national interest. * * *

enacted by Congress and regardless of the circumstances by which the newspaper came into possession of the information.

At least in the absence of legislation by Congress, based on its own investigations and findings, I am quite unable to agree that the inherent powers of the Executive and the courts reach so far as to authorize remedies having such sweeping potential for inhibiting publications by the press. [To] sustain the Government in these cases would start the courts down a long and hazardous road that I am not willing to travel at least without congressional guidance and direction.

* * * Prior restraints require an unusually heavy justification under the First Amendment; but failure by the Government to justify prior restraints does not measure its constitutional entitlement to a conviction for criminal publication. That the Government mistakenly chose to proceed by injunction does not mean that it could not successfully proceed in another way.

* * * Congress has addressed itself to the problems of protecting the security of the country and the national defense from unauthorized disclosure of potentially damaging information. It has not, however, authorized the injunctive remedy against threatened publication. It has apparently been satisfied to rely on criminal sanctions and their deterrent effect on the responsible as well as the irresponsible press. * * *

JUSTICE HARLAN, with whom THE CHIEF JUSTICE and JUSTICE BLACKMUN join, dissenting. * * *

With all respect, I consider that the Court has been almost irresponsibly feverish in dealing with these cases. Both [the] Second Circuit and [the] District of Columbia Circuit rendered judgment on June 23. [This] Court's order setting a hearing before us on June 26 at 11 a.m., a course which I joined only to avoid the possibility of even more peremptory action by the Court, was issued less than 24 hours before. The record in the *Post* case was filed with the Clerk shortly before 1 p.m. on June 25; the record in the *Times* case did not arrive until 7 or 8 o'clock that same night. The briefs of the parties were received less than two hours before argument on June 26.

This frenzied train of events took place in the name of the presumption against prior restraints created by the First Amendment. Due regard for the extraordinarily important and difficult questions involved in these litigations should have led the Court to shun such a precipitate timetable. In order to decide the merits of these cases properly, some or all of the following questions should have been faced: * * *

2. Whether the First Amendment permits the federal courts to enjoin publication of stories which would present a serious threat to national security. See *Near* (dictum). * * *

4. Whether the unauthorized disclosure of any of these particular documents would seriously impair the national security.

5. What weight should be given to the opinion of high officers in the Executive Branch of the Government with respect to [question 4]. * * *

7. Whether the threatened harm to the national security or the Government's possessory interest in the documents justifies the issuance of an injunction against publication in light of—

a. The strong First Amendment policy against prior restraints on publication; b. The doctrine against enjoining conduct in violation of criminal statutes;

and c. The extent to which the materials at issue have apparently already been otherwise disseminated.

These are difficult questions of fact, of law, and of judgment; the potential consequences of erroneous decision are enormous. The time which has been available to us, to the lower courts, and to the parties has been wholly inadequate for giving these cases the kind of consideration they deserve. It is a reflection on the stability of the judicial process that these great issues—as important as any that have arisen during my time on the Court—should have been decided under the pressures engendered by the torrent of publicity that has attended these litigations from their inception.

Forced as I am to reach the merits of these cases, I dissent from the opinion and judgments of the Court. Within the severe limitations imposed by the time constraints under which I have been required to operate, I can only state my reasons in telescoped form, even though in different circumstances I would have felt constrained to deal with the cases in the fuller sweep indicated above.

[It] is plain to me that the scope of the judicial function in passing upon the activities of the Executive Branch of the Government in the field of foreign affairs is very narrowly restricted. This view is, I think, dictated by the concept of separation of powers upon which our constitutional system [rests.] I agree that, in performance of its duty to protect the values of the First Amendment against political pressures, the judiciary must review the initial Executive determination to the point of satisfying itself that the subject matter of the dispute does lie within the proper compass of the President's foreign relations power. Constitutional considerations forbid "a complete abandonment of judicial control." Moreover, the judiciary may properly insist that the determination that disclosure of the subject matter would irreparably impair the national security be made by the head of the Executive Department concerned—here the Secretary of State or the Secretary of Defense—after actual personal consideration by that officer. This safeguard is required in the analogous area of executive claims of privilege for secrets of state.

But in my judgment the judiciary may not properly go beyond these two inquiries and redetermine for itself the probable impact of disclosure on the national security. "[T]he very nature of executive decisions as to foreign policy is political, not judicial. Such decisions are wholly confided by our Constitution to the political departments of the government, Executive and Legislative. They are delicate, complex, and involve large elements of prophecy. They are and should be undertaken only by those directly responsible to the people whose welfare they advance or imperil. They are decisions of a kind for which the judiciary has neither aptitude, facilities nor responsibility and which has long been held to belong in the domain of political power not subject to judicial intrusion or inquiry." *Chicago & S. Air Lines v. Waterman S.S. Corp.* (Jackson, J.), 333 U.S. 103 (1948).

Even if there is some room for the judiciary to override the executive determination, it is plain that the scope of review must be exceedingly narrow. I can see no indication in the opinions of either the District Court or the Court of Appeals in the *Post* litigation that the conclusions of the Executive were given even the deference owing to an administrative agency, much less that owing to a co-equal branch of the Government operating within the field of its constitutional prerogative. * * *

Pending further hearings in each case conducted under the appropriate ground rules, I would continue the restraints on publication. I cannot believe that the doctrine prohibiting prior restraints reaches to the point of preventing courts from maintaining the status quo long enough to act responsibly in matters of such national importance as those involved here.

JUSTICE BLACKMUN, dissenting.

[The First Amendment] is only one part of an entire Constitution. Article II of the great document vests in the Executive Branch primary power over the conduct of foreign affairs and places in that branch the responsibility for the Nation's safety. Each provision of the Constitution is important, and I cannot subscribe to a doctrine of unlimited absolutism for the First Amendment at the cost of downgrading other provisions. First Amendment absolutism has never commanded a majority of this Court. What is needed here is a weighing, upon properly developed standards, of the broad right of the press to print and of the very narrow right of the Government to prevent. Such standards are not yet developed. The parties here are in disagreement as to what those standards should be. But even the newspapers concede that there are situations where restraint is in order and is constitutional. Mr. Justice Holmes gave us a suggestion when he said in *Schenck,* "It is a question of proximity and degree. When a nation is at war many things that might be said in time of peace are such a hindrance to its effort that their utterance will not be endured so long as men fight and that no Court could regard them as protected by any constitutional right."

I therefore would remand these cases to be developed expeditiously, of course, but on a schedule permitting the orderly presentation of evidence from both sides [and] with the preparation of briefs, oral argument and court opinions of a quality better than has been seen to this point. [T]hese cases and the issues involved and the courts, including this one, deserve better than has been produced thus far. * * *b

Notes

1. UNITED STATES v. PROGRESSIVE, INC., 467 F.Supp. 990 (W.D.Wis.) (preliminary injunction issued Mar. 28, 1979), request for writ of mandamus den. sub nom. *Morland v. Sprecher,* 443 U.S. 709 (1979), case dismissed, 610 F.2d 819 (7th Cir.1979).a *The Progressive* planned to publish an article. "The H–Bomb Secret—How We Got It, Why We're Telling It," maintaining that the article would contribute to informed opinion about nuclear weapons and demonstrate the inadequacies of a system of secrecy and classification. Although the government conceded that at least some of the information contained in the article was "in the public domain" or had been "declassified," it argued that "national security" permitted it to censor information originating in the public domain "if when drawn together, synthesized and collated, such information acquires the character of presenting immediate, direct and irreparable harm to the interests of the United States." The Secretary of State stated that publication would increase thermonuclear proliferation and that this would "irreparably impair the national security of the United States." The Secretary of Defense maintained that dissemi-

b. Marshall, J., concurring, did not deal with First Amendment issues but only with separation of powers—the government's attempt to secure through the Court injunctive relief that Congress had refused to authorize.

Burger, C.J., dissenting, complained that because of "unseemly haste," "we do not know the facts of this case. [W]e literally do not know what we are acting on." He expressed no views on the merits, apart from his joinder in

Harlan, J.'s opinion, and a statement that he would have continued the temporary restraints in effect while returning the cases to the lower courts for more thorough exploration of the facts and issues.

a. The government's action against *The Progressive* was abandoned after information similar to that it sought to enjoin was published elsewhere.

nation of the Morland article would lead to a substantial increase in the risk of thermonuclear proliferation and to use or threats that would "adversely affect the national security of the United States."

Although recognizing that this constituted "the first instance of prior restraint against a publication in this fashion in the [nation's history]," the district court enjoined defendants, pending final resolution of the litigation, from publishing or otherwise disclosing any information designated by the government as "restricted data" within the meaning of The Atomic Energy Act of 1954: "What is involved here is information dealing with the most destructive weapon in the history of mankind, information of sufficient destructive potential to nullify the right to free speech and to endanger the right to life itself. [Faced] with a stark choice between upholding the right to continued life and the right to freedom of the press, most jurists would have no difficulty in opting for the chance to continue to breathe and function as they work to achieve perfect freedom of expression.

"[A] mistake in ruling against *The Progressive* will seriously infringe cherished First Amendment rights. [A] mistake in ruling against the United States could pave the way for thermonuclear annihilation for us all. In that event, our right to life is extinguished and the right to publish becomes moot.

"[W]ar by foot soldiers has been replaced in large part by machines and bombs. No longer need there be any advance warning or any preparation time before a nuclear war could be commenced. [In light of these factors] publication of the technical information on the hydrogen bomb contained in the article is analogous to publication of troop movements or locations in time of war and falls within the extremely narrow exception to the rule against prior restraint [recognized in *Near*].

"The government has met its burden under § 2274 of The Atomic Energy Act [which authorizes injunctive relief against one who would communicate or disclose restricted data 'with reason to believe such data will be utilized to injure the United States or to secure an advantage to any foreign nation.'] [I]t has also met the test enunciated by two Justices in *Pentagon Papers,* namely grave, direct, immediate and irreparable harm to the United States."

The court distinguished *Pentagon Papers*: "[T]he study involved [there] contained historical data relating to events some three to twenty years previously. Secondly, the Supreme Court agreed with the lower court that no cogent reasons were advanced by the government as to why the article affected national security except that publication might cause some embarrassment to the United States. A final and most vital difference between these two cases is the fact that a specific statute is involved here [§ 2274 of The Atomic Energy Act]."

2. *CIA secrecy agreement.* The Central Intelligence Agency requires employees to sign a "secrecy agreement" as a condition of employment, an agreement committing the employee not to reveal classified information nor to publish any information obtained during the course of employment without prior approval of the Agency. In SNEPP v. UNITED STATES, 444 U.S. 507 (1980), Snepp had published a book called *Decent Interval* about certain CIA activities in South Vietnam based on his experiences as an agency employee without seeking prepublication review. At least for purposes of the litigation, the government conceded that Snepp's book divulged no confidential information. The Court, per curiam (Stevens, J., joined by Brennan and Marshall, JJ., dissenting) held that Snepp's failure to submit the book was a breach of trust and the government was entitled to a constructive trust on the proceeds of the book: "[E]ven in the absence of an express agreement, the CIA could have acted to protect substantial government

interests by imposing reasonable restrictions on employee activities that in other contexts might be protected by the First Amendment. The Government has a compelling interest in protecting both the secrecy of information important to our national security and the appearance of confidentiality so essential to the effective operation of our foreign intelligence service."**b**

SECTION 5.   JUSTICE AND NEWSGATHERING

This section explores three problems connected with the fair administration of justice or with newsgathering or with both. The first problem involves pre-trial publicity. The government seeks to deter or punish speech by the press that it fears will threaten the fair administration of justice, but speech of that character falls into no recognized category of unprotected speech. Thus, the courts must consider whether absolute protection is called for, or, alternatively, whether new categories or ad hoc determinations are appropriate, and whether prior restraints are permissible. Alternatively, if the press cannot be prevented from speaking about trials, can prosecutors, defense attorneys, litigants and potential witnesses be prevented from speaking to the press?

In the second problem the government seeks to fairly administer the justice system by forcing reporters to reveal their confidential sources. The press maintains that any such authorized compulsion would have a chilling effect on its ability to gather the news.

In the final problem, government seeks not to punish speech, but to administer justice in private. It refuses to let the public or press witness its handling of prisoners, or its conduct of trial or pre-trial proceedings. The question is whether the First Amendment can serve as a sword allowing the press or citizen-critics to gather information. Assuming it can, what are its limits within the justice system? Does any right of access reach beyond the justice system? Does the First Amendment require that the press be granted access not afforded the public? Does the First Amendment permit differential access? If so, what are the limits on how government defines the press?

I. PUBLICITY ABOUT TRIALS

In a number of cases, defendants have asserted that their rights to a fair trial have been abridged by newspaper publicity. SHEPPARD v. MAXWELL, 384 U.S. 333 (1966), is probably the most notorious "trial by newspaper" case. The Court, per CLARK, J., (Black, J. dissenting) agreed with the "finding" of the Ohio Supreme Court that the atmosphere of defendant's murder trial was that of a " 'Roman holiday' for the news media." The courtroom was jammed with reporters. And in the corridors outside the courtroom, "a host of photographers and television personnel" photographed witnesses, counsel and jurors as they entered and left the courtroom. Throughout the trial, there was a deluge of publicity, much of which contained information never presented at trial, yet the jurors were not sequestered until the trial was over and they had begun their deliberations.

The Court placed the primary blame on the trial judge. He could "easily" have prevented "the carnival atmosphere of the trial" since "the courtroom and courthouse premises" were subject to his control. For example, he should have

---

b. Compare *Haig v. Agee,* 453 U.S. 280 (1981), stating that "repeated disclosures of intelligence operations and names of intelligence personnel" for the "purpose of obstruct-ing intelligence operations and the recruiting of intelligence personnel" are "clearly not protected by the Constitution."

provided privacy for the jury, insulated witnesses from the media, instead of allowing them to be interviewed at will, and "made some effort to control the release of leads, information, and gossip to the press by police officers, witnesses, and the counsel for both sides." No one "coming under the jurisdiction of the court should be permitted to frustrate its function."

The Court recognized that "there is nothing that proscribes the press from reporting events that transpire in the courtroom. But where there is a reasonable likelihood that prejudicial news prior to trial will prevent a fair trial, the judge should continue the case until the threat abates, or transfer it to another county not so permeated with publicity. In addition, sequestration of the jury was something the judge should have raised sua sponte with counsel. If publicity during the proceedings threatens the fairness of the trial, a new trial should be ordered. But we must remember that reversals are but palliatives; the cure lies in those remedial measures that will prevent the prejudice at its inception."

The Court, however, reiterated its extreme reluctance "to place any direct limitations on the freedom traditionally exercised by the news media for '[w]hat transpires in the courtroom is public property.'" The press "does not simply publish information about trials but guards against the miscarriage of justice by subjecting the police, prosecutors, and judicial processes to extensive public scrutiny and criticism."

In anticipation of the trial of Simants for a mass murder which had attracted widespread news coverage, the county court prohibited everyone in attendance from, inter alia, releasing or authorizing for publication "any testimony given or evidence adduced." Simants' preliminary hearing (open to the public) was held the same day, subject to the restrictive order. Simants was bound over for trial. Respondent Nebraska state trial judge then entered an order which, as modified by the state supreme court, restrained the press and broadcasting media from reporting any confessions or incriminating statements made by Simants to law enforcement officers or third parties, except members of the press, and from reporting other facts "strongly implicative" of the defendant. The order expired when the jury was impaneled.

NEBRASKA PRESS ASS'N v. STUART, 427 U.S. 539 (1976), per BURGER, C.J., struck down the state court order: "To the extent that the order prohibited the reporting of evidence adduced at the open preliminary hearing, it plainly violated settled principles: 'There is nothing that proscribes the press from reporting events that transpire in the courtroom.' *Sheppard*."a To the extent that the order prohibited publication "based on information gained from other sources, [the] heavy burden imposed as a condition to securing a prior restraint was not met." The portion of the order regarding "implicative" information was also "too vague and too broad" to survive scrutiny of restraints on First Amendment rights.

"[P]retrial publicity—even pervasive, adverse publicity—does not inevitably lead to an unfair trial. The capacity of the jury eventually impaneled to decide the case fairly is influenced by the tone and extent of the publicity, which is in part, and often in large part, shaped by what attorneys, police and other officials do to precipitate news coverage. [T]he measures a judge takes or fails to take to mitigate the effects of pretrial publicity—the measures described in *Sheppard*—

a. The Court added, however, that the county court "could not know that closure of the preliminary hearing was an alternative open to it until the Nebraska Supreme Court so construed state law."

may well determine whether the defendant receives a trial consistent [with] due process.

"[The] Court has interpreted [First Amendment] guarantees to afford special protection against orders that prohibit the publication or broadcast of particular information or commentary—orders that impose [a] 'prior' restraint on speech. None of our decided cases on prior restraint involved restrictive orders entered to protect a defendant's right to a fair and impartial jury, but [they] have a common thread relevant to this case. * * *

"The thread running through [*Near* and *Pentagon Papers*], is that prior restraints on speech and publication are the most serious and the least tolerable infringement on First Amendment rights. A criminal penalty or a judgment in a defamation case is subject to the whole panoply of protections afforded by deferring the impact of the judgment until all avenues of appellate review have been exhausted. [But] a prior restraint [has] an immediate and irreversible sanction. If it can be said that a threat of criminal or civil sanctions after publication 'chills' speech, prior restraint 'freezes' it at least for the time.

"[I]f the authors of [the first and sixth amendments], fully aware of the potential conflicts between them, were unwilling or unable to resolve the issue by assigning to one priority over the other, it is not for us to rewrite the Constitution by undertaking what they declined. [Yet] it is nonetheless clear that the barriers to prior restraint remain high unless we are to abandon what the Court has said for nearly a quarter of our national existence and implied throughout all of [it.]

"We turn now to the record in this case to determine whether, as Learned Hand put it, 'the gravity of the 'evil,' discounted by its improbability, justifies such invasion of free speech as is necessary to avoid the danger,' *Dennis* [2d Cir.], aff'd. To do so, we must examine the evidence before the trial judge when the order was entered to determine (a) the nature and extent of pretrial news coverage; (b) whether other measures would be likely to mitigate the effects of unrestrained pretrial publicity; (c) how effectively a restraining order would operate to prevent the threatened danger. The precise terms of the restraining order are also important. We must then consider whether the record supports the entry of a prior restraint on publication, one of the most extraordinary remedies known to our jurisprudence."

As to (a), although the trial judge was justified in concluding there would be extensive pretrial publicity concerning this case, he "found only 'a clear and present danger that pretrial publicity *could* impinge upon the defendant's right to a fair trial.' [Emphasis added by the Court]. His conclusion as to the impact of such publicity on prospective jurors was of necessity speculative, dealing as he was with factors unknown and unknowable."

As to (b), "there is no finding that alternative means [e.g., change of venue, postponement of trial to allow public attention to subside, searching questions of prospective jurors] would not have protected Simants' rights, and the Nebraska Supreme Court did no more than imply that such measures might not be adequate. Moreover, the record is lacking in evidence to support such a finding."

As to (c), in view of such practical problems as the limited territorial jurisdiction of the trial court issuing the order, the difficulties of predicting what information "will in fact undermine the impartiality of jurors," the problem of drafting an order that will "effectively keep prejudicial information from prospective jurors," and that the events "took place in a community of only 850 people"—throughout which, "it is reasonable to assume," rumors that "could well be more damaging than reasonably accurate news accounts" would "travel swiftly by word of mouth"—"it is far from clear that prior restraint on publication would have protected Simants' rights."

"[It] is significant that when this Court has reversed a state conviction because of prejudicial publicity, it has carefully noted that some course of action short of prior restraint would have made a critical difference. However difficult it may be, we need not rule out the possibility of showing the kind of threat to fair trial rights that would possess the requisite degree of certainty to justify restraint. [We] reaffirm that the guarantees of freedom of expression are not an absolute prohibition under all circumstances, but the barriers to prior restraint remain high and the presumption against its use continues intact. We hold that, with respect to the order entered in this case [the] heavy burden imposed as a condition to securing a prior restraint was not [met]."

BRENNAN, J., joined by Stewart and Marshall, JJ., concurring, would hold that "resort to prior restraints on the freedom of the press is a constitutionally impermissible method for enforcing [the right to a fair trial by a jury]; judges have at their disposal a broad spectrum of devices for ensuring that fundamental fairness is accorded the accused without necessitating so drastic an incursion on the equally fundamental and salutary constitutional mandate that discussion of public affairs in a free society cannot depend on the preliminary grace of judicial censors": " * * * Settled case law concerning the impropriety and constitutional invalidity of prior restraints on the press compels the conclusion that there can be no prohibition on the publication by the press of any information pertaining to pending judicial proceedings or the operation of the criminal justice system, no matter how shabby the means by which the information is obtained.15 This does not imply, however, any subordination of Sixth Amendment rights, for an accused's right to a fair trial may be adequately assured through methods that do not infringe First Amendment values.

"[The narrow national security exception mentioned in *Near* and *Pentagon Papers*] does not mean [that] prior restraints can be justified on an ad hoc balancing approach that concludes that the 'presumption' must be overcome in light of some perceived 'justification.' Rather, this language refers to the fact that, as a matter of procedural safeguards and burden of proof, prior restraints even within a recognized exception to the rule against prior restraints will be extremely difficult to justify; but as an initial matter, the purpose for which a prior restraint is sought to be imposed 'must fit within one of the narrowly defined exceptions to the prohibition against prior restraints.' Indeed, two Justices in [*Pentagon Papers*] apparently controverted the existence of even a limited 'military security' exception to the rule against prior restraints on the publication of otherwise protected material. (Black, J., concurring); (Douglas, J., concurring). And a majority of the other Justices who expressed their views on the merits made it clear that they would take cognizance only of a 'single, extremely narrow class of cases in which the First Amendment's ban on prior judicial restraint may be overridden.' (Brennan, J., concurring). * * *

"The only exception that has thus far been recognized even in dictum to the blanket prohibition against prior restraints against publication of material which would otherwise be constitutionally shielded was the 'military security' situation addressed in [*Pentagon Papers*]. But unlike the virtually certain, direct, and immediate harm required for such a restraint [the] harm to a fair trial that might

---

15. Of course, even if the press cannot be enjoined from reporting certain information, that does not necessarily immunize it from civil liability for libel or invasion of privacy or from criminal liability for transgressions of general criminal laws during the course of obtaining that information.

otherwise eventuate from publications which are suppressed pursuant to orders such as that under review must inherently remain speculative."

Although they joined the Court's opinion, White and Powell, JJ., also filed brief concurrences. WHITE, J., expressed "grave doubts" that these types of restrictive orders "would ever be justifiable." POWELL, J., "emphasize[d] the unique burden" resting upon one who "undertakes to show the necessity for prior restraint on pretrial publicity." In his judgment, a prior restraint "requires a showing that (i) there is a clear threat to the fairness of trial, (ii) such a threat is posed by the actual publicity to be restrained, and (iii) no less restrictive alternatives are available. Notwithstanding such a showing, a restraint may not issue unless it also is shown that previous publicity or publicity from unrestrained sources will not render the restraint inefficacious. [A]ny restraint must comply with the standards of specificity always required in the First Amendment context."

STEVENS, J., concurred in the judgment. He agreed with Brennan, J., that the "judiciary is capable of protecting the defendant's right to a fair trial without enjoining the press from publishing information in the public domain, and that it may not do so." But he reserved judgment, until further argument, on "[w]hether the same absolute protection would apply no matter how shabby or illegal the means by which the information is obtained, no matter how serious an intrusion on privacy might be involved, no matter how demonstrably false the information might be, no matter how prejudicial it might be to the interests of innocent persons, and no matter how perverse the motivation for publishing it." He indicated that "if ever required to face the issue squarely" he "may well accept [Brennan, J.'s] ultimate conclusion."

Notes

1. **Obstructing justice.** A series of cases have held that the First Amendment greatly restricts contempt sanctions against persons whose comments on pending cases were alleged to have created a danger of obstruction of the judicial process. "Such repression can be justified, if at all, only by a clear and present danger of the obstruction of justice." *New York Times.* In *Bridges v. California,* 314 U.S. 252 (1941), union leader Bridges had caused publication or acquiesced in publication of a telegram threatening a strike if an "outrageous" California state decision involving Bridges' dock workers were enforced. The Court reversed Bridges' contempt citation. Cf. *Wood v. Georgia,* 370 U.S. 375 (1962) (open letter to press and grand jury—contempt citation reversed). But cf. *Cox v. Louisiana,* 379 U.S. 559 (1965) (statute forbidding parades near courthouse with intent to interfere with administration of justice upheld): ("[W]e deal not with the contempt power [but] a statute narrowly drawn to punish" not a pure form of speech but expression mixed with conduct "that infringes a substantial state interest in protecting the judicial process.").

2. **Confidentiality and privacy.** Many cases have rebuffed state efforts to protect confidentiality or privacy by prohibiting publication. *Cox Broadcasting Corp. v. Cohn,* Sec. 1, II, F supra (state could not impose liability for public dissemination of the name of rape victim derived from public court documents); *Oklahoma Pub. Co. v. District Court,* 430 U.S. 308 (1977) (pretrial order enjoining press from publishing name or picture of 11-year-old boy accused of murder invalid when reporters had been lawfully present at a prior public hearing and had photographed him en route from the courthouse); *Landmark Communications, Inc. v. Virginia,* 435 U.S. 829 (1978) (statute making it a crime to publish information about particular confidential proceedings invalid as applied to non-

participant in the proceedings, at least when the information had been lawfully acquired); *Smith v. Daily Mail Pub. Co.,* 443 U.S. 97 (1979) (statute making it a crime for newspapers (but not broadcasters) to publish the name of any youth charged as a juvenile offender invalid as applied to information lawfully acquired from private sources). But cf. *Seattle Times Co. v. Rhinehart,* 467 U.S. 20 (1984) (order enjoining newspaper from disseminating information acquired as a litigant in pretrial discovery valid so long as order is entered on a showing of good cause and does not restrict the dissemination of the information if gained from other sources).

II. NEWSGATHERING

A. PROTECTION OF CONFIDENTIAL SOURCES

BRANZBURG v. HAYES

408 U.S. 665, 92 S.Ct. 2646, 33 L.Ed.2d 626 (1972).

JUSTICE WHITE delivered the opinion of the Court.

[Branzburg, a Kentucky reporter, wrote articles describing his observations of local hashish-making and other drug violations. He refused to testify before a grand jury regarding his information. The state courts rejected his claim of a First Amendment privilege.

[Pappas, a Massachusetts TV newsman-photographer, was allowed to enter and remain inside a Black Panther headquarters on condition he disclose nothing. When an anticipated police raid did not occur, he wrote no story. Summoned before a local grand jury, he refused to answer any questions about what had occurred inside the Panther headquarters or to identify those he had observed. The state courts denied his claim of a First Amendment privilege.

[Caldwell, a N.Y. Times reporter covering the Black Panthers, was summoned to appear before a federal grand jury investigating Panther activities. A federal court issued a protective order providing that although he had to divulge information given him "for publication," he could withhold "confidential" information "developed or maintained by him as a professional journalist." Maintaining that absent a specific need for his testimony he should be excused from attending the grand jury altogether, Caldwell disregarded the order and was held in contempt. The Ninth Circuit reversed, holding that absent "compelling reasons" Caldwell could refuse even to attend the grand jury, because of the potential impact of such an appearance on the flow of news to the public.]

[Petitioners' First Amendment claims] may be simply put: that to gather news it is often necessary to agree either not to identify [sources] or to publish only part of the facts revealed, or both; that if the reporter is nevertheless forced to reveal these confidences to a grand jury, the source so identified and other confidential sources of other reporters will be measurably deterred from furnishing publishable information, all to the detriment of the free flow of information protected by the First Amendment. Although petitioners do not claim an absolute privilege [they] assert that the reporter should not be forced either to appear or to testify before a grand jury or at trial until and unless sufficient grounds are shown for believing that the reporter possesses information relevant to a crime the grand jury is investigating, that the information the reporter has is unavailable from other sources, and that the need for the information is sufficiently compelling to override the claimed invasion of First Amendment interests occasioned by the disclosure. [The] heart of the claim is that the burden on news gathering resulting from compelling reporters to disclose confidential information outweighs any public interest in obtaining the information.

[We agree] that news gathering [qualifies] for First Amendment protection; without some protection for seeking out the news, freedom of the press could be eviscerated. But this case involves no intrusions upon speech [and no] command that the press publish what it prefers to withhold. [N]o penalty, civil or criminal, related to the content of published material is at issue here. The use of confidential sources by the press is not forbidden or restricted; reporters remain free to seek news from any source by means within the law. No attempt is made to require the press to publish its sources of information or indiscriminately to disclose them on request.

The sole issue before us is the obligation of reporters to respond to grand jury subpoenas as other citizens do and to answer questions relevant to an investigation into the commission of crime.

[T]he First Amendment does not guarantee the press a constitutional right of special access to information not available to the public generally. [Although] news gathering may be hampered, the press is regularly excluded from grand jury proceedings, our own conferences, the meetings of other official bodies gathered in executive session, and the meetings of private organizations. Newsmen have no constitutional right of access to the scenes of crime or disaster when the general public is excluded, and they may be prohibited from attending or publishing information about trials if such restrictions are necessary to assure a defendant a fair trial before an impartial tribunal. [It] is thus not surprising that the great weight of authority is that newsmen are not exempt from the normal duty of appearing before a grand jury and answering questions relevant to a criminal investigation.

[Because] its task is to inquire into the existence of possible criminal conduct and to return only well-founded indictments, [the grand jury's] investigative powers are necessarily broad. [T]he long standing principle that "the public has a right to every man's evidence," except for those persons protected by a constitutional, common law, or statutory privilege, is particularly applicable to grand jury proceedings.

A [number] of States have provided newsmen a statutory privilege of varying breadth, [but] none has been provided by federal statute. [We decline to create one] by interpreting the First Amendment to grant newsmen a testimonial privilege that other citizens do not enjoy. [On] the records now before us, we perceive no basis for holding that the public interest in law enforcement and in ensuring effective grand jury proceedings is insufficient to override the consequential, but uncertain, burden on news gathering which is said to result from insisting that reporters, like other citizens, respond to relevant questions put to them in the course of a valid grand jury investigation or criminal trial.

This conclusion [does not] threaten the vast bulk of confidential relationships between reporters and their sources. Grand juries address themselves to the issues of whether crimes have been committed and who committed them. Only where news sources themselves are implicated in crime or possess information relevant to the grand jury's task need they or the reporter be concerned about grand jury subpoenas. Nothing before us indicates that a large number or percentage of *all* confidential news sources fall into either category and would in any way be deterred by [our holding]. * * *33

33. In his *Press Subpoenas: An Empirical and Legal Analysis* 6–12 (1971), Prof. Blasi found that slightly more than half of the 975 reporters questioned said that they relied on

Accepting the fact, however, that an undetermined number of informants not themselves implicated in crime will nevertheless, for whatever reason, refuse to talk to newsmen if they fear identification by a reporter in an official investigation, we cannot accept the argument that the public interest in possible future news about crime from undisclosed, unverified sources must take precedence over the public interest in pursuing and prosecuting those crimes reported to the press by informants and in thus deterring the commission of such crimes in the future. * * *

[The] privilege claimed here is conditional, not absolute; given the suggested preliminary showings and compelling need, the reporter would be required to testify. [If] newsmen's confidential sources are as sensitive as they are claimed to be, the prospect of being unmasked whenever a judge determines the situation justifies it is hardly a satisfactory solution to the problem. For them, it would appear that only an absolute privilege would suffice.

We are unwilling to embark the judiciary on a long and difficult journey to such an uncertain destination. The administration of a constitutional newsman's privilege would present practical and conceptual difficulties of a high order. Sooner or later, it would be necessary to define those categories of newsmen who qualified for the privilege, a questionable procedure in light of the traditional doctrine that liberty of the press is the right of the lonely pamphleteer who uses carbon paper or a mimeograph just as much as of the large metropolitan publisher who utilizes the latest photocomposition methods. [The] informative function asserted by representatives of the organized press in the present cases is also performed by lecturers, political pollsters, novelists, academic researchers, and dramatists. Almost any author may quite accurately assert that he is contributing to the flow of information to the public, that he relies on confidential sources of information, and that these sources will be silenced if he is forced to make disclosures before a grand jury.

In each instance where a reporter is subpoenaed to testify, the courts would also be embroiled in preliminary factual and legal determinations with respect to whether the proper predicate had been laid for the reporters' appearance. [I]n the end, by considering whether enforcement of a particular law served a "compelling" governmental interest, the courts would be inextricably involved in distinguishing between the value of enforcing different criminal laws. By requiring testimony from a reporter in investigations involving some crimes but not in others, they would be making a value judgment which a legislature had declined to [make.]

At the federal level, Congress has freedom to determine whether a statutory newsman's privilege is necessary and desirable and to fashion standards and rules as narrow or broad as deemed necessary [and], equally important, to re-fashion those rules as experience from time to time may dictate. There is also merit in leaving state legislatures free, within First Amendment limits, to fashion their own standards in light of the conditions and problems with respect to the relations between law enforcement officials and press in their own [areas]. * * *

[G]rand jury investigations if instituted or conducted other than in good faith, would pose wholly different issues for resolution under the First Amendment. Official harassment of the press undertaken not for purposes of law enforcement

regular confidential sources for at least 10% of their stories. Of this group of reporters, only 8% were able to say with some certainty that their professional functioning had been adversely affected by the threat of subpoena; another 11% were not certain whether or not they had been adversely affected. [See also Vincent Blasi, *The Newsman's Privilege: An Empirical Study,* 70 Mich.L.Rev. 229 (1971).]

but to disrupt a reporter's relationship with his news sources would have no justification. Grand juries are subject to judicial control and subpoenas to motions to quash. We do not expect courts will forget that grand juries must operate within the limits of the First Amendment as well as the Fifth.

We turn, therefore, to the disposition of the cases before us. [*Caldwell*] must be reversed. If there is no First Amendment privilege to refuse to answer the relevant and material questions asked during a good-faith grand jury investigation, then it is a fortiori true that there is no privilege to refuse to appear before such a grand jury until the Government demonstrates some "compelling need" for a newsman's testimony. [*Branzburg*] must be affirmed. [P]etitioner refused to answer questions that directly related to criminal conduct which he had observed and written about. [If] what petitioner wrote was true, he had direct information to provide the grand jury concerning the commission of serious crimes. [In *Pappas,* we] affirm [and] hold that petitioner must appear before the grand jury to answer the questions put to him, subject, of course, to the supervision of the presiding judge as to "the propriety, purposes, and scope of the grand jury inquiry and the pertinence of the probable testimony."

JUSTICE POWELL, concurring in the opinion of the Court.

I add this brief statement to emphasize what seems to me to be the limited nature of the Court's holding. The Court does not hold that newsmen, subpoenaed to testify before a grand jury, are without constitutional rights with respect to the gathering of news or in safeguarding their sources. [As] indicated in the concluding portion of the opinion, the Court states that no harassment of newsmen will be tolerated. If a newsman believes that the grand jury investigation is not being conducted in good faith he is not without remedy. Indeed, if the newsman is called upon to give information bearing only a remote and tenuous relationship to the subject of the investigation, or if he has some other reason to believe that his testimony implicates confidential source relationships without a legitimate need of law enforcement, he will have access to the Court on a motion to quash and an appropriate protective order may be entered. The asserted claim to privilege should be judged on its facts by the striking of a proper balance between freedom of the press and the obligation of all citizens to give relevant testimony with respect to criminal conduct. The balance of these vital constitutional and societal interests on a case-by-case basis accords with the tried and traditional way of adjudicating such questions.*

In short, the courts will be available to newsmen under circumstances where legitimate First Amendment interests require protection.

JUSTICE DOUGLAS, dissenting.

[T]here is no "compelling need" that can be shown [by the Government] which qualifies the reporter's immunity from appearing or testifying before a grand jury, unless the reporter himself is implicated in a crime. His immunity in

---

* It is to be remembered that Caldwell asserts a constitutional privilege not even to appear before the grand jury unless a court decides that the government has made a showing that meets the three preconditions specified in [Stewart, J.'s dissent]. To be sure, this would require a "balancing" of interests by the Court, but under circumstances and constraints significantly different from the balancing that will be appropriate under the Court's decision. The newsman witness, like all other witnesses, will have to appear; he will not be in a position to litigate at the threshold the State's very authority to subpoena him. Moreover, absent the constitutional preconditions that [the dissent] would impose as heavy burdens of proof to be carried by the State, the court—when called upon to protect a newsman from improper or prejudicial questioning—would be free to balance the competing interests on their merits in the particular case. The new constitutional rule endorsed by [the dissent] would, as a practical matter, defeat such a fair balancing and the essential societal interest in the detection and prosecution of crime would be heavily subordinated.

my view is therefore quite complete, for absent his involvement in a crime, the First Amendment protects him against an appearance before a grand jury and if he is involved in a crime, the Fifth Amendment stands as a barrier. Since in my view there is no area of inquiry not protected by a privilege, the reporter need not appear for the futile purpose of invoking one to each [question.]

Two principles which follow from [Alexander Meiklejohn's] understanding of the First Amendment are at stake here. One is that the people, the ultimate governors, must have absolute freedom of and therefore privacy of their individual opinions and beliefs regardless of how suspect or strange they may appear to others. Ancillary to that principle is the conclusion that an individual must also have absolute privacy over whatever information he may generate in the course of testing his opinions and beliefs. In this regard, Caldwell's status as a reporter is less relevant than is his status as a student who affirmatively pursued empirical research to enlarge his own intellectual viewpoint. The second principle is that effective self-government cannot succeed unless the people are immersed in a steady, robust, unimpeded, and uncensored flow of opinion and reporting which are continuously subjected to critique, rebuttal, and re-examination. In this respect, Caldwell's status as a newsgatherer and an integral part of that process becomes critical. * * *

Sooner or later any test which provides less than blanket protection to beliefs and associations will be twisted and relaxed so as to provide virtually no protection at [all]. Perceptions of the worth of state objectives will change with the composition of the Court and with the intensity of the politics of the [times.]

JUSTICE STEWART, with whom JUSTICE BRENNAN and JUSTICE MARSHALL join, dissenting.

The Court's crabbed view of the First Amendment reflects a disturbing insensitivity to the critical role of an independent press in our society. [While] Mr. Justice Powell's enigmatic concurring opinion gives some hope of a more flexible view in the future, the Court in these cases holds that a newsman has no First Amendment right to protect his sources when called before a grand jury. The Court thus invites state and federal authorities to undermine the historic independence of the press by attempting to annex the journalistic profession as an investigative arm of government. Not only will this decision impair performance of the press' constitutionally protected functions, but it will, I am convinced, in the long run, harm rather than help the administration of justice.

[As] private and public aggregations of power burgeon in size and the pressures for conformity necessarily mount, there is obviously a continuing need for an independent press to disseminate a robust variety of information and opinion through reportage, investigation and criticism, if we are to preserve our constitutional tradition of maximizing freedom of choice by encouraging diversity of expression. * * *

A corollary of the right to publish must be the right to gather news. [This right] implies, in turn, a right to a confidential relationship between a reporter and his source. This proposition follows as a matter of simple logic once three factual predicates are recognized: (1) newsmen require informants to gather news; (2) confidentiality—the promise or understanding that names or certain aspects of communications will be kept off-the-record—is essential to the creation and maintenance of a news-gathering relationship with informants; and (3) the existence of an unbridled subpoena power—the absence of a constitutional right protecting, in *any* way, a confidential relationship from compulsory process—will either deter sources from divulging information or deter reporters from gathering and publishing information. * * *

After today's decision, the potential informant can never be sure that his identity or off-the-record communications will not subsequently be revealed through the compelled testimony of a newsman. A public spirited person inside government, who is not implicated in any crime, will now be fearful of revealing corruption or other governmental wrong-doing, because he will now know he can subsequently be identified by use of compulsory process. The potential source must, therefore, choose between risking exposure by giving information or avoiding the risk by remaining silent.

The reporter must speculate about whether contact with a controversial source or publication of controversial material will lead to a subpoena. In the event of a subpoena, under today's decision, the newsman will know that he must choose between being punished for contempt if he refuses to testify, or violating his profession's ethics[10] and impairing his resourcefulness as a reporter if he discloses confidential information. * * *

The impairment of the flow of news cannot, of course, be proven with scientific precision, as the Court seems to demand. [But] we have never before demanded that First Amendment rights rest on elaborate empirical studies demonstrating beyond any conceivable doubt that deterrent effects exist; we have never before required proof of the exact number of people potentially affected by governmental action, who would actually be dissuaded from engaging in First Amendment activity. * * *

We cannot await an unequivocal—and therefore unattainable—imprimatur from empirical studies. We can and must accept the evidence developed in the record, and elsewhere, that overwhelmingly supports the premise that deterrence will occur with regularity in important types of newsgathering relationships. Thus, we cannot escape the conclusion that when neither the reporter nor his source can rely on the shield of confidentiality against unrestrained use of the grand jury's subpoena power, valuable information will not be published and the public dialogue will inevitably be impoverished.

[W]hen a reporter is asked to appear before a grand jury and reveal confidences, I would hold that the government must (1) show that there is probable cause to believe that the newsman has information which is clearly relevant to a specific probable violation of law; (2) demonstrate that the information sought cannot be obtained by alternative means less destructive of First Amendment rights; and (3) demonstrate a compelling and overriding interest in the information. * * *

Both the "probable cause" and "alternative means" requirements [would] serve the vital function of mediating between the public interest in the administration of justice and the constitutional protection of the full flow of information. These requirements would avoid a direct conflict between these competing concerns, and they would generally provide adequate protection for newsmen. No doubt the courts would be required to make some delicate judgments in working out this accommodation. But that, after all, is the function of courts of law. Better such judgments, however difficult, than the simplistic and stultifying absolutism adopted by the Court in denying any force to the First Amendment in these cases.[36] * * *

---

10. The American Newspaper Guild has adopted the following rule as part of the newsman's code of ethics: "Newspaper men shall refuse to reveal confidences or disclose sources of confidential information in court or before other judicial or investigative bodies."

36. The disclaimers in Mr. Justice Powell's concurring opinion leave room for the hope that in some future case the Court may take a less absolute position in this area.

[In Stewart, J.'s view, the Ninth Circuit correctly ruled that in the circumstances of the case, Caldwell need not divulge confidential information and, moreover, that in this case Caldwell had established that "his very appearance [before] the grand jury would jeopardize his relationship with his sources, leading to a severance of the news gathering relationship and impairment of the flow of news to the public." But because "only in very rare circumstances would a confidential relationship between a reporter and his source be so sensitive [as to preclude] his mere appearance before the grand jury," Stewart, J., would confine "*this* aspect of the *Caldwell* judgment [to] its own facts." Thus, he would affirm in *Caldwell* and remand the other cases for further proceedings not inconsistent with his views.]

Notes

1. ***State "shield laws" and a criminal defendant's right to compulsory process.*** Most states and the District of Columbia have enacted "shield" laws. Some protect only journalists' sources; some (including New Jersey) protect undisclosed information obtained in the course of a journalist's professional activities as well as sources.

IN RE FARBER, 78 N.J. 259, 394 A.2d 330 (1978), cert. denied, 439 U.S. 997 (1978): New York Times investigative reporter Myron Farber wrote a series of articles claiming that an unidentified "Doctor X" had caused the death of several patients by poisoning. This led to the indictment and eventual prosecution of Dr. Jascalevich for murder. (He was ultimately acquitted.) In response to the defendant's request, the trial court demanded the disclosure of Farber's sources and the production of his interview notes and other information for his in camera inspection. Relying on the First Amendment and the state shield law, Farber refused to comply with the subpoenas. After White, J., and then Marshall, J., had denied stays, each deeming it unlikely that four justices would grant certiorari at this stage of the case, Farber was jailed for civil contempt and the *Times* heavily fined.

The state supreme court (5–2) upheld civil and criminal convictions of the *Times* and Farber. Under the circumstances, it ruled, the First Amendment did not protect Farber against disclosure. Nor did the New Jersey shield law, for Farber's statutory rights had to yield to Dr. Jascalevich's sixth amendment right "to have compulsory process for obtaining witnesses in his favor."

2. **Searching newspapers.** ZURCHER v. STANFORD DAILY, 436 U.S. 547 (1978), again declined to afford the press special protection—dividing very much as in *Branzburg*.a A student newspaper that had published articles and photographs of a clash between demonstrators and police brought this federal action, claiming that a search of its offices for film and pictures showing events at the scene of the police-demonstrators clash (the newspaper was not involved in the unlawful acts) had violated its first and fourth amendment rights. A 5–3 majority, per WHITE, J., held that the fourth amendment does not prevent the government from issuing a search warrant (based on reasonable cause to believe that the "things" to be searched for are located on the property) simply because

---

a. In both cases, White, J., joined by Burger, C.J., Blackmun, Powell and Rehnquist, JJ., delivered the opinion of the Court and in both cases the "fifth vote"—Powell, J.,—also wrote a separate opinion which seemed to meet the concerns of the dissent part way. In both cases Stewart, J., dissented, maintaining that the Court's holding would seriously impair "newsgathering." Stevens, J., who had replaced Douglas, J., also dissented in Zurcher, as had Douglas in *Branzburg*. Brennan, J., who had joined Stewart, J.'s dissent in *Branzburg,* did not participate in *Zurcher*.

the owner or possessor of the place to be searched is not reasonably suspected of criminal involvement. The Court also rejected the argument that "whatever may be true of third-party searches generally, where the third party is a newspaper, there are additional [First Amendment factors justifying] a nearly per se rule forbidding the search warrant and permitting only the subpoena duces tecum. The general submission is that searches of newspaper offices for evidence of crime reasonably believed to be on the premises will seriously threaten the ability of the press to gather, analyze, and disseminate news.

"[Although] [a]ware of the long struggle between Crown and press and desiring to curb unjustified official intrusions, [the Framers] did not forbid warrants where the press was involved, did not require special showing that subpoenas would be impractical, and did not insist that the owner of the place to be searched, if connected with the press, must be shown to be implicated in the offense being investigated. Further, the prior cases do no more than insist that the courts apply the warrant requirements with particular exactitude when First Amendment interests would be endangered by the search. [N]o more than this is required where the warrant requested is for the seizure of criminal evidence reasonably believed to be on the premises occupied by a newspaper. Properly administered, the preconditions for a warrant—probable cause, specificity [as to] place [and] things to be seized and overall reasonableness—should afford [the press] sufficient protection * * *.

"[R]espondents and amici have pointed to only a very few instances [since] 1971 involving [newspaper office searches]. This reality hardly suggests abuse, and if abuse occurs, there will be time enough to deal with it. Furthermore, the press [is] not easily intimidated—nor should it be."

POWELL, J., concurring, rejected Stewart, J.'s dissenting view that the press is entitled to "a special procedure, not available to others," when the government requires evidence in its possession, but added: "This is not to say [that a warrant] sufficient to support the search of an apartment or an automobile would be reasonable in supporting the search of a newspaper office. [While] there is no justification for the establishment of a separate Fourth Amendment procedure for the press, a magistrate asked to issue a warrant for the search of press offices can and should take cognizance of the independent values protected by the First Amendment—such as those highlighted by [Stewart, J., dissenting]—when he weighs such factors."b

STEWART, joined by Marshall, J., dissented: "A search warrant allows police officers to ransack the files of a newspaper, reading each and every document until they have found the one named in the warrant, while a subpoena would permit the newspaper itself to produce only the specific documents requested. A search, unlike a subpoena, will therefore lead to the needless exposure of confidential information completely unrelated to the purpose of the investigation. The knowledge that police officers can make an unannounced raid on a newsroom is thus bound to have a deterrent effect on the availability of confidential news sources. [The result] will be a diminishing flow of potentially important information to the public.

"[Here, unlike *Branzburg*, the newspaper does] not claim that any of the evidence sought was privileged[, but] only that a subpoena would have served equally well to produce that evidence. Thus, we are not concerned with the

---

b. Powell, J., noted that his *Branzburg* concurrence may "properly be read as supporting the view expressed in the text above, and in the Court's [*Zurcher*] opinion," that under the warrant requirement "the magistrate should consider the values of a free press as well as the societal interest in enforcing the criminal laws."

principle, central to *Branzburg,* that " 'the public [has] a right to everyman's evidence,' " but only with whether any significant social interest would be impaired if the police were generally required to obtain evidence from the press by means of a subpoena rather than a search. * * *

"Perhaps as a matter of abstract policy a newspaper office should receive no more protection from unannounced police searches than, say, the office of a doctor or the office of a bank. But we are here to uphold a Constitution. And our Constitution does not explicitly protect the practice of medicine or the business of banking from all abridgement by government. It does explicitly protect the freedom of the press."**c**

B. ACCESS TO TRIALS AND OTHER GOVERN-MENTALLY CONTROLLED INFORMATION AND INSTITUTIONS

By 1978, no Supreme Court holding contradicted Burger, C.J.'s contention for the plurality in *Houchins v. KQED,* 438 U.S. 1 (1978) that, "neither the First Amendment nor the Fourteenth Amendment mandates a right of access to government information or sources of information within the government's control." Or as Stewart, J., put it in an often-quoted statement, "The Constitution itself is neither a Freedom of Information Act nor an Official Secrets Act." *"Or of the Press,"* 26 Hast.L.J. 631, 636 (1975). *Richmond Newspapers,* infra, constitutes the Court's first break with its past denials of First Amendment rights to information within governmental control.

RICHMOND NEWSPAPERS, INC. v. VIRGINIA

448 U.S. 555, 100 S.Ct. 2814, 65 L.Ed.2d 973 (1980).

[At the commencement of his fourth trial on a murder charge (his first conviction having been reversed and two subsequent retrials having ended in mistrials), defendant moved, without objection by the prosecutor or two reporters present, that the trial be closed to the public—defense counsel stating that he did not "want any information being shuffled back and forth when we have a recess as [to] who testified to what." The trial judge granted the motion, stating that "the statute gives me that power specifically." He presumably referred to Virginia Code § 19.2–266, providing that in all criminal trials "the court may, in its discretion, exclude [any] persons whose presence would impair the conduct of a fair trial, provided that the [defendant's right] to a public trial shall not be violated." Later the same day the trial court granted appellants' request for a hearing on a motion to vacate the closure order. At the closed hearing, appellants observed that prior to the entry of its closure order the court had failed to make any evidentiary findings or to consider any other, less drastic measures to ensure a fair trial. Defendant stated that he "didn't want information to leak out," be published by the media, perhaps inaccurately, and then be seen by the jurors. Noting inter alia that "having people in the Courtroom is distracting to the jury" and that if "the rights of the defendant are infringed in any way [and if his closure motion] doesn't completely override all rights of everyone else, then I'm inclined to go along with" the defendant, the court denied the motion to vacate the closure order. Defendant was subsequently found not guilty.]

CHIEF JUSTICE BURGER announced the judgment of the Court and delivered an opinion in which JUSTICE WHITE and JUSTICE STEVENS joined.

---

c. Stevens, J., dissented on the general Fourth Amendment issue.

[T]he precise issue presented here has not previously been before this Court for decision. [*Gannett Co. v. DePasquale,* 443 U.S. 368 (1979)] was not required to decide whether a right of access to *trials,* as distinguished from hearings on *pre*trial motions, was constitutionally guaranteed. The Court held that the Sixth Amendment's guarantee to the accused of a public trial gave neither the public nor the press an enforceable right of access to a *pre*trial suppression hearing. One concurring opinion specifically emphasized that "a hearing on a motion before trial to suppress evidence is not a *trial.*" (Burger, C.J., concurring). Moreover, the Court did not decide whether the First and Fourteenth Amendments guarantee a right of the public to attend trials; nor did the dissenting opinion reach this issue. [H]ere for the first time the Court is asked to decide whether a criminal trial itself may be closed to the public upon the unopposed request of a defendant, without any demonstration that closure is required to protect the defendant's superior right to a fair trial, or that some other overriding consideration requires closure.

[T]he historical evidence demonstrates conclusively that at the time when our organic laws were adopted, criminal trials both here and in England had long been presumptively open[, thus giving] assurance that the proceedings were conducted fairly to all concerned, [and] discourag[ing] perjury, the misconduct of participants, and decisions based on secret bias or partiality. [Moreover, the] early history of open trials in part reflects the widespread acknowledgment [that] public trials had significant therapeutic value. [When] a shocking crime occurs, a community reaction of outrage and public protest often follows. Thereafter the open processes of justice serve an important prophylactic purpose, providing an outlet for community concern, hostility, and emotion.

[The] crucial prophylactic aspects of the administration of justice cannot function in the dark; no community catharsis can occur if justice is "done in a corner [or] in any covert manner." [To] work effectively, it is important that society's criminal process "satisfy the appearance of justice," and the appearance of justice can best be provided by allowing people to observe it.

[From] this unbroken, uncontradicted history, supported by reasons as valid today as in centuries past, we are bound to conclude that a presumption of openness inheres in the very nature of a criminal trial under our system of criminal justice. [Nevertheless,] the State presses its contention that neither the Constitution nor the Bill of Rights contains any provision which by its terms guarantees to the public the right to attend criminal trials. Standing alone, this is correct, but there remains the question whether, absent an explicit provision, the Constitution affords protection against exclusion of the public from criminal trials.

[The] expressly guaranteed [First Amendment] freedoms share a common core purpose of assuring freedom of communication on matters relating to the functioning of government. Plainly it would be difficult to single out any aspect of government of higher concern and importance to the people than the manner in which criminal trials are conducted * * *.

The Bill of Rights was enacted against the backdrop of the long history of trials being presumptively open. [In] guaranteeing freedoms such as those of speech and press, the First Amendment can be read as protecting the right of everyone to attend trials so as to give meaning to those explicit guarantees. * * * Free speech carries with it some freedom to listen. "In a variety of contexts this Court has referred to a First Amendment right to 'receive information and ideas.' " *Kleindienst v. Mandel,* 408 U.S. 753 (1972).a What this means in the

---

a. *Mandel* held that the Executive had plenary power to exclude a Belgium journalist from the country, at least so long as it operated on the basis of a facially legitimate and bona

context of trials is that the First Amendment guarantees of speech and press, standing alone, prohibit government from summarily closing courtroom doors which had long been open to the public at the time that amendment was adopted.

[It] is not crucial whether we describe this right to attend criminal trials to hear, see, and communicate observations concerning them as a "right of access," cf. *Gannett* (Powell, J., concurring); *Saxbe v. Washington Post Co.,* 417 U.S. 843 (1974); *Pell v. Procunier,* 417 U.S. 817 (1974),11 or a "right to gather information," for we have recognized that "without some protection for seeking out the news, freedom of the press could be eviscerated." *Branzburg v. Hayes.* The explicit, guaranteed rights to speak and to publish concerning what takes place at a trial would lose much meaning if access to observe the trial could, as it was here, be foreclosed arbitrarily.

The right of access to places traditionally open to the public, as criminal trials have long been, may be seen as assured by the amalgam of the First Amendment guarantees of speech and press; and their affinity to the right of assembly is not without relevance. From the outset, the right of assembly was regarded not only as an independent right but also as a catalyst to augment the free exercise of the other First Amendment rights with which it was deliberately linked by the draftsmen. [Subject] to the traditional time, place, and manner restrictions, streets, sidewalks, and parks are places traditionally open, where First Amendment rights may be exercised [see generally Sec. 6 infra]; a trial courtroom also is a public place where the people generally—and representatives of the media—have a right to be present, and where their presence historically has been thought to enhance the integrity and quality of what takes place.

* * * Notwithstanding the appropriate caution against reading into the Constitution rights not explicitly defined, the Court has acknowledged that certain unarticulated rights are implicit in enumerated guarantees [referring, inter alia, to the rights of association and of privacy and the right to travel. [T]hese important but unarticulated rights [have] been found to share constitutional protection in common with explicit guarantees. The concerns expressed by Madison and others have thus been [resolved].**b**

We hold that the right to attend criminal trials17 is implicit in the guarantees of the First Amendment; without the freedom to attend such trials, which people have exercised for centuries, important aspects of freedom of speech and "of the press could be eviscerated." *Branzburg.*

[In the present case,] the trial court made no findings to support closure; no inquiry was made as to whether alternative solutions would have met the need to ensure fairness; there was no recognition of any right under the Constitution for the public or press to attend the trial. In contrast to the pretrial proceeding dealt

---

fide reason for exclusion. Although the Court decided ultimately not to balance the government's particular justification against the First Amendment interest, it recognized that those who sought personal communication with the excluded alien did have a First Amendment interest at stake. The Court apparently assumed that the excluded speaker had no rights at stake, and none were asserted on his behalf.

11. *Procunier* and *Saxbe* are distinguishable in the sense that they were concerned with penal institutions which, by definition, are not "open" or public places. [See] also *Greer v. Spock* (military bases).

b. The Chief Justice noted "the perceived need" of the Constitution's draftsmen "for some sort of constitutional 'saving clause' [which] would serve to foreclose application to the Bill of Rights of the maxim that the affirmation of particular rights implies a negation of those not expressly defined. Madison's efforts, culminating in the Ninth Amendment, served to allay the fears of those who were concerned that expressing certain guarantees could be read as excluding others."

17. Whether the public has a right to attend [civil trials is] not raised by this case, but we note that historically both civil and criminal trials have been presumptively open.

with in *Gannett,* there exist in the context of the trial itself various tested alternatives to satisfy the constitutional demands of fairness. [For example, there was nothing] to indicate that sequestration of the jurors would not have guarded against their being subjected to any improper information. [Absent] an overriding interest articulated in findings, the trial of a criminal case must be open to the public. * * *

Reversed.c

JUSTICE BRENNAN, with whom JUSTICE MARSHALL joins, concurring in the judgment.

[*Gannett*] held that the Sixth Amendment right to a public trial was personal to the accused, conferring no right of access to pretrial proceedings that is separately enforceable by the public or the press. [This case] raises the question whether the First Amendment, of its own force and as applied to the States through the Fourteenth Amendment, secures the public an independent right of access to trial proceedings. Because I believe that [it does secure] such a public right of access, I agree [that], without more, agreement of the trial judge and the parties cannot constitutionally close a trial to the public.1

While freedom of expression is made inviolate by the First Amendment, and with only rare and stringent exceptions, may not be suppressed, the First Amendment has not been viewed by the Court in all settings as providing an equally categorical assurance of the correlative freedom of access to information.2 Yet the Court has not ruled out a public access component to the First Amendment in every circumstance. Read with care and in context, our decisions must therefore be understood as holding only that any privilege of access to governmental information is subject to a degree of restraint dictated by the nature of the information and countervailing interests in security or confidentiality. [Cases such as *Houchins, Saxbe* and *Pell*] neither comprehensively nor absolutely deny that public access to information may at times be implied by the First Amendment and the principles which animate it.

The Court's approach in right of access cases simply reflects the special nature of a claim of First Amendment right to gather information. Customarily, First Amendment guarantees are interposed to protect communication between speaker and listener. When so employed against prior restraints, free speech protections are almost insurmountable. See generally Brennan, *Address,* 32 Rutg. L.Rev. 173, 176 (1979). But the First Amendment embodies more than a commitment to free expression and communicative interchange for their own sakes; it has a *structural* role to play in securing and fostering our republican system of self-government. Implicit in this structural role is not only "the principle that debate

---

c. Powell, J., took no part. In *Gannett,* he took the position that a First Amendment right of access applied to courtroom proceedings, albeit subject to overriding when justice so demanded or when confidentiality was necessary.

1. Of course, the Sixth Amendment remains the source of the *accused's* own right to insist upon public judicial proceedings. *Gannett.*

That the Sixth Amendment explicitly establishes a public trial right does not impliedly foreclose the derivation of such a right from other provisions of the Constitution. The Constitution was not framed as a work of carpentry, in which all joints must fit snugly without overlapping. * * *

2. A conceptually separate, yet related, question is whether the media should enjoy greater access rights than the general public. But no such contention is at stake here. Since the media's right of access is at least equal to that of the general public, this case is resolved by a decision that the state statute unconstitutionally restricts public access to trials. As a practical matter, however, the institutional press is the likely, and fitting, chief beneficiary of a right of access because it serves as the "agent" of interested citizens, and funnels information about trials to a large number of individuals.

on public issues should be uninhibited, robust, and wide-open," but the antecedent assumption that valuable public debate—as well as other civic behavior—must be informed. The structural model links the First Amendment to that process of communication necessary for a democracy to survive, and thus entails solicitude not only for communication itself, but for the indispensable conditions of meaningful communication.

[A]n assertion of the prerogative to gather information must [be] assayed by considering the information sought and the opposing interests invaded. This judicial task is as much a matter of sensitivity to practical necessities as it is of abstract reasoning. But at least two helpful principles may be sketched. First, the case for a right of access has special force when drawn from an enduring and vital tradition of public entree to particular proceedings or information. Such a tradition commands respect in part because the Constitution carries the gloss of history. More importantly, a tradition of accessibility implies the favorable judgment of experience. Second, the value of access must be measured in specifics. Analysis is not advanced by rhetorical statements that all information bears upon public issues; what is crucial in individual cases is whether access to a particular government process is important in terms of that very process.

[This Court has] persistently defended the public character of the trial process. *In re Oliver*, 333 U.S. 257 (1948), established that [fourteenth amendment due process] forbids closed criminal trials [and] acknowledged that open trials are indispensable to First Amendment political and religious freedoms.

By the same token, a special solicitude for the public character of judicial proceedings is evident in the Court's rulings upholding the right to report about the administration of justice. While these decisions are impelled by the classic protections afforded by the First Amendment to pure communication, they are also bottomed upon a keen appreciation of the structural interest served in opening the judicial system to public inspection. So, in upholding a privilege for reporting truthful information about judicial misconduct proceedings, *Landmark* emphasized that public scrutiny of the operation of a judicial disciplinary body implicates a major purpose of the First Amendment—"discussion of governmental affairs." Again, *Nebraska Press* noted that the traditional guarantee against prior restraint "should have particular force as applied to reporting of criminal proceedings." And *Cox Broadcasting* instructed that "[w]ith respect to judicial proceedings in particular, the function of the press serves to guarantee the fairness of trials and to bring to bear the beneficial effects of public scrutiny upon the administration of justice."

[Open] trials play a fundamental role in furthering the efforts of our judicial system to assure the criminal defendant a fair and accurate adjudication of guilt or innocence. But, as a feature of our governing system of justice, the trial process serves other, broadly political, interests, and public access advances these objectives as well. To that extent, trial access possesses specific structural significance.

[For] a civilization founded upon principles of ordered liberty to survive and flourish, its members must share the conviction that they are governed equitably. That necessity * * * mandates a system of justice that demonstrates the fairness of the law to our citizens. One major function of the trial is to make that demonstration.

Secrecy is profoundly inimical to this demonstrative [purpose]. Public access is essential, therefore, if trial adjudication is to achieve the objective of maintaining public confidence in the administration of justice. But the trial [also] plays a pivotal role in the entire judicial process, and, by extension, in our form of government. Under our system, judges are not mere umpires, but, in their own sphere, lawmakers—a coordinate branch of *government*. [Thus], so far as the trial is the mechanism for judicial factfinding, as well as the initial forum for legal decisionmaking, it is a genuine governmental proceeding.

[More] importantly, public access to trials acts as an important check, akin in purpose to the other checks and balances that infuse our system of government. "The knowledge that every criminal trial is subject to contemporaneous review in the forum of public opinion is an effective restraint on possible abuse of judicial power," *Oliver*—an abuse that, in many cases, would have ramifications beyond the impact upon the parties before the court. * * *

Popular attendance at trials, in sum, substantially furthers the particular public purposes of that critical judicial proceeding. In that sense, public access is an indispensable element of the trial process itself. Trial access, therefore, assumes structural importance in our "government of laws."

As previously noted, resolution of First Amendment public access claims in individual cases must be strongly influenced by the weight of historical practice and by an assessment of the specific structural value of public access in the circumstances. With regard to the case at hand, our ingrained tradition of public trials and the importance of public access to the broader purposes of the trial process, tip the balance strongly toward the rule that trials be open.23 What countervailing interests might be sufficiently compelling to reverse this presumption of openness need not concern us now,24 for the statute at stake here authorizes trial closures at the unfettered discretion of the judge and parties.25 [Thus it] violates the First and Fourteenth Amendments * * *.

Justice Stewart, concurring in the judgment.

Whatever the ultimate answer [may] be with respect to pretrial suppression hearings in criminal cases, the First and Fourteenth Amendments clearly give the press and the public a right of access to trials themselves, civil as well as criminal. * * *

In conspicuous contrast to a military base, *Greer*; a jail, *Adderley v. Florida*, 385 U.S. 39 (1966); or a prison, *Pell*, a trial courtroom is a public place. Even more than city streets, sidewalks, and parks as areas of traditional First Amendment activity, a trial courtroom is a place where representatives of the press and of the public are not only free to be, but where their presence serves to assure the integrity of what goes on.

But this does not mean that the First Amendment right of members of the public and representatives of the press to attend civil and criminal trials is absolute. Just as a legislature may impose reasonable time, place and manner restrictions upon the exercise of First Amendment freedoms, so may a trial judge impose reasonable limitations upon the unrestricted occupation of a courtroom by representatives of the press and members of the public. Moreover, [there] may be

---

23. The presumption of public trials is, of course, not at all incompatible with reasonable restrictions imposed upon courtroom behavior in the interests of decorum. Thus, when engaging in interchanges at the bench, the trial judge is not required to allow public or press intrusion upon the huddle. Nor does this opinion intimate that judges are restricted in their ability to conduct conferences in chambers, inasmuch as such conferences are distinct from trial proceedings.

24. For example, national security concerns about confidentiality may sometimes warrant closures during sensitive portions of trial proceedings, such as testimony about state secrets.

25. Significantly, closing a trial lacks even the justification for barring the door to pretrial hearings: the necessity of preventing dissemination of suppressible prejudicial evidence to the public before the jury pool has become, in a practical sense, finite and subject to sequestration.

occasions when not all who wish to attend a trial may do so.3 And while there exist many alternative ways to satisfy the constitutional demands of a fair trial, those demands may also sometimes justify limitations upon the unrestricted presence of spectators in the courtroom.5

Since in the present case the trial judge appears to have given no recognition to the right [of] the press and [the] public to be present at [the] murder trial over which he was presiding, the judgment under review must be [reversed.]

JUSTICE WHITE, concurring.

This case would have been unnecessary had *Gannett* construed the Sixth Amendment to forbid excluding the public from criminal proceedings except in narrowly defined circumstances. But the Court there rejected the submission of four of us to this effect, thus requiring that the First Amendment issue involved here be addressed. On this issue, I concur in the opinion of the Chief Justice.

JUSTICE BLACKMUN, concurring in the judgment.

My opinion and vote in partial dissent [in] *Gannett* compels my vote to reverse the judgment. [It] is gratifying [to] see the Court now looking to and relying upon legal history in determining the fundamental public character of the criminal trial. * * *

The Court's ultimate ruling in *Gannett,* with such clarification as is provided by the opinions in this case today, apparently is now to the effect that there is no *Sixth* Amendment right on the part of the public—or the press—to an open hearing on a motion to suppress. I, of course, continue to believe that *Gannett* was in error, both in its interpretation of the Sixth Amendment generally, and in its application to the suppression hearing, for I remain convinced that the right to a public trial is to be found where the Constitution explicitly placed it—in the Sixth Amendment.

[But] with the Sixth Amendment set to one side in this case, I am driven to conclude, as a secondary position, that the First Amendment must provide some measure of protection for public access to the trial. The opinion in partial dissent in *Gannett* explained that the public has an intense need and a deserved right to know about the administration of justice in general; about the prosecution of local crimes in particular; about the conduct of the judge, the prosecutor, defense counsel, police officers, other public servants, and all the actors in the judicial arena; and about the trial itself. It is clear and obvious to me, on the approach the Court has chosen to take, that, by closing this criminal trial, the trial judge abridged these First Amendment interests of the public. * * *

JUSTICE STEVENS, concurring.

This is a watershed case. Until today the Court has accorded virtually absolute protection to the dissemination of information or ideas, but never before has it squarely held that the acquisition of newsworthy matter is entitled to any constitutional protection whatsoever. An additional word of emphasis is therefore appropriate.

Twice before, the Court has implied that any governmental restriction on access to information, no matter how severe and no matter how unjustified, would

---

3. In such situations, representatives of the press must be assured access, *Houchins* (concurring opinion).

5. This is not to say that only constitutional considerations can justify such restrictions. The preservation of trade secrets, for example, might justify the exclusion of the public from at least some segments of a civil trial. And the sensibilities of a youthful prosecution witness, for example, might justify similar exclusion in a criminal trial for rape, so long as the defendant's Sixth Amendment right to a public trial were not impaired.

be constitutionally acceptable so long as it did not single out the press for special disabilities not applicable to the public at large. In a dissent joined by [Brennan and Marshall, JJ.] in *Saxbe,* Justice Powell unequivocally rejected [that conclusion.] And in *Houchins,* I explained at length why [Brennan, Powell, JJ.] and I were convinced that "[a]n official prison policy of concealing * * * knowledge from the public by arbitrarily cutting off the flow of information at its source abridges [First Amendment freedoms]." Since [Marshall and Blackmun, JJ.] were unable to participate in that case, a majority of the Court neither accepted nor rejected that conclusion or the contrary conclusion expressed in the prevailing opinions. Today, however, for the first time, the Court unequivocally holds that an arbitrary interference with access to important information is an abridgment of the freedoms of speech and of the press protected by the First Amendment.

It is somewhat ironic that the Court should find more reason to recognize a right of access today than it did in *Houchins.* For *Houchins* involved the plight of a segment of society least able to protect itself, an attack on a longstanding policy of concealment, and an absence of any legitimate justification for abridging public access to information about how government operates. In this case we are protecting the interests of the most powerful voices in the community, we are concerned with an almost unique exception to an established tradition of openness in the conduct of criminal trials, and it is likely that the closure order was motivated by the judge's desire to protect the individual defendant from the burden of a fourth criminal trial.[2]

In any event, for the reasons stated [in] my *Houchins* opinion, as well as those stated by the Chief Justice today, I agree that the First Amendment protects the public and the press from abridgment of their rights of access to information about the operation of their government, including the Judicial Branch; given the total absence of any record justification for the closure order entered in this case, that order violated the First Amendment * * *.

JUSTICE REHNQUIST, dissenting.

[I] do not believe that [anything in the Constitution] require[s] that a State's reasons for denying public access to a trial, where both [the prosecution and defense] have consented to [a court-approved closure order], are subject to any additional constitutional review at our hands.

[The] issue here is not whether the "right" to freedom of the press * * * overrides the defendant's "right" to a fair trial, [but] whether any provision in the Constitution may fairly be read to prohibit what the [trial court] did in this case. Being unable to find any such prohibition in the First, Sixth, Ninth, or any other Amendments [or] in the Constitution itself, I dissent.

Notes

1. ***Closing trials.*** To overcome either the First Amendment or the Sixth Amendment right to a public trial, the Court has required that the party seeking to close the proceedings "must advance an overriding interest that is likely to be prejudiced, the closure must be no broader than necessary to protect that interest, the trial court must consider reasonable alternatives to closing the proceeding,

---

2. Neither that likely motivation nor facts showing the risk that a fifth trial would have been necessary without closure of the fourth are disclosed in this record, however. The absence of any articulated reason for the closure order is a sufficient basis for distinguishing this case from *Gannett.* The decision today is in no way inconsistent with the perfectly unambiguous holding in *Gannett* that the rights guaranteed by the Sixth Amendment are rights that may be asserted by the accused rather than members of the general public. * * *

and it must make findings adequate to support the closure." *Waller v. Georgia,* 467 U.S. 39 (1984). See *Globe Newspaper Co. v. Superior Court,* 457 U.S. 596 (1982) (routine exclusion of press and public during testimony of minor victim of sex offense unconstitutional); *Press-Enterprise Co. v. Superior Court,* 464 U.S. 501 (1984) (extending *Richmond Newspapers* to voir dire examination of jurors).

2. ***Electronic access.*** Access to trials need not mean electronic access, but such access may be permitted. *Chandler v. Florida,* 449 U.S. 560 (1981) held that subject to certain safeguards a state may *permit* electronic media and still photography coverage of public criminal proceedings over the objection of the accused.

SECTION 6. GOVERNMENT PROPERTY AND THE PUBLIC FORUM

The case law treating the question of when persons can speak on public property has come to be known as public forum doctrine. But "[t]he public forum saga began, and very nearly ended," Geoffrey Stone, *Fora Americana: Speech in Public Places,* 1974 Sup.Ct.Rev. 233, 236, with an effort by Holmes, J., then on the Supreme Judicial Court of Massachusetts, "to solve a difficult First Amendment problem by simplistic resort to a common-law concept," Vincent Blasi, *Prior Restraints on Demonstrations,* 68 Mich.L.Rev. 1482, 1484 (1970). For holding religious meetings on the Boston Common, a preacher was convicted under an ordinance prohibiting "any public address" upon publicly-owned property without a permit from the mayor. In upholding the permit ordinance Holmes, J., observed: "For the legislature absolutely or conditionally to forbid public speaking in a highway or public park is no more an infringement of rights of a member of the public than for the owner of a private house to forbid it in the house." *Massachusetts v. Davis,* 162 Mass. 510, 511, 39 N.E. 113, 113 (1895). On appeal, a unanimous Supreme Court adopted the Holmes position, 167 U.S. 43 (1897): "[T]he right to absolutely exclude all right to use [public property], necessarily includes the authority to determine under what circumstances such use may be availed of, as the greater power contains the lesser."

This view survived until HAGUE v. CIO, 307 U.S. 496 (1939), which rejected Jersey City's claim that its ordinance requiring a permit for an open air meeting was justified by the "plenary power" rationale of *Davis.* In rejecting the implications of the *Davis* dictum, ROBERTS, J., in a plurality opinion, uttered a famous "counter dictum," which has played a central role in the evolution of public forum theory: "Wherever the title of streets and parks may rest, they have immemorially been held in trust for the use of the public and, time out of mind, have been used for purposes of assembly, communicating thoughts between citizens, and discussing public questions. Such use of the streets and public places has, from ancient times, been a part of the privileges, immunities, rights, and liberties of citizens. [This privilege of a citizen] is not absolute, but relative, and must be exercised in subordination to the general comfort and convenience, and in consonance with peace and good order; but it must not, in the guise of regulation, be abridged or denied." Eight months later, the *Hague* dictum was given impressive content by Roberts, J., for the Court, in *Schneider* infra.

I. FOUNDATION CASES

A. MANDATORY ACCESS

SCHNEIDER v. IRVINGTON, 308 U.S. 147 (1939), per ROBERTS, J., invalidated several ordinances prohibiting leafleting on public streets or other public places: "Municipal authorities, as trustees for the public, have the duty to keep their communities' streets open and available for movement of people and property, the primary purpose to which the streets are dedicated. So long as legislation to this end does not abridge the constitutional liberty of one rightfully upon the street to impart information through speech or the distribution of literature, it may lawfully regulate the conduct of those using the streets. For example, a person could not exercise this liberty by taking his stand in the middle of a crowded street, contrary to traffic regulations, and maintain his position to the stoppage of all traffic; a group of distributors could not insist upon a constitutional right to form a cordon across the street and to allow no pedestrian to pass who did not accept a tendered leaflet; nor does the guarantee of freedom of speech or of the press deprive a municipality of power to enact regulations against throwing literature broadcast in the streets. Prohibition of such conduct would not abridge the constitutional liberty since such activity bears no necessary relationship to the freedom to speak, write, print or distribute information or opinion. * * *

"In *Lovell* [Sec. 4, I, A supra] this court held void an ordinance which forbade the distribution by hand or otherwise of literature of any kind without written permission from the city manager. [Similarly] in *Hague v. C.I.O.*, an ordinance was held void on its face because it provided for previous administrative censorship of the exercise of the right of speech and assembly in appropriate public places." The [ordinances] under review do not purport to license distribution but all of them absolutely prohibit it in the streets and, one of them, in other public places as well.

"The motive of the legislation under attack in Numbers 13, 18 and 29 is held by the courts below to be the prevention of littering of the streets and, although the alleged offenders were not charged with themselves scattering paper in the streets, their convictions were sustained upon the theory that distribution by them encouraged or resulted in such littering. We are of opinion that the purpose to keep the streets clean and of good appearance is insufficient to justify an ordinance which prohibits a person rightfully on a public street from handing literature to one willing to receive it. Any burden imposed upon the city authorities in cleaning and caring for the streets as an indirect consequence of such distribution results from the constitutional protection of the freedom of speech and press. This constitutional protection does not deprive a city of all power to prevent street littering. There are obvious methods of preventing littering. Amongst these is the punishment of those who actually throw papers on the streets.

"It is suggested that [the] ordinances are valid because their operation is limited to streets and alleys and leaves persons free to distribute printed matter in other public places. But, as we have said, the streets are natural and proper places for the dissemination of information and opinion; and one is not to have the exercise of his liberty of expression in appropriate places abridged on the plea that it may be exercised in some other place."

McREYNOLDS, J., "is of opinion that the judgment in each case should be affirmed."

Notes

1. **Beyond leaflets.** *Cox v. New Hampshire*, 312 U.S. 569 (1941) upheld convictions of sixty-eight Jehovah's Witnesses for parading without a permit. They had marched in four or five groups (with perhaps twenty others) along the sidewalk in single file carrying signs and handing out leaflets: "A municipality

undoubtedly has authority to control the use of its public streets for parades or processions."

2. ***Charging for use of public forum.*** *Cox* said there was nothing "contrary to the Constitution" in the exaction of a fee " 'incident to the administration of the [licensing] Act and to the maintenance of public order in the matter licensed.' " But see *Forsyth County v. The Nationalist Movement,* 505 U.S. 123 (1992)(speech cannot be financially burdened for expenses associated with hostile audience in a licensing context).

3. ***Reasonable time, place, and manner regulations.*** As *Cox* reveals, a right of access to a public forum does not guarantee immunity from reasonable time, place, and manner regulations. *Heffron v. International Soc. for Krishna Consciousness,* 452 U.S. 640 (1981), for example, upheld a state fair rule prohibiting the distribution of printed material or the solicitation of funds except from a duly licensed booth on the fairgrounds. The Court noted that consideration of a forum's special attributes is relevant to the determination of reasonableness, and the test of reasonableness is whether the restrictions "are justified without reference to the content of the regulated speech, that they serve a significant governmental interest, and that in doing so they leave open ample alternative channels for communication of the information."

WARD v. ROCK AGAINST RACISM, 491 U.S. 781 (1989) also commented on time, place, and manner regulations in the context of a public forum. It maintained that the *O'Brien* test is little different from the time, place, and manner test, and then stated: "[A] regulation of the time, place, or manner of protected speech must be narrowly tailored to serve the government's legitimate content-neutral interests but [it] need not be the least-restrictive or least-intrusive means of doing so. Rather, the requirement of narrow tailoring is satisfied 'so long as [the] regulation promotes a substantial government interest that would be achieved less effectively absent the regulation.' To be sure, this standard does not mean that a time, place, or manner regulation may burden substantially more speech than is necessary to further the government's legitimate interests. Government may not regulate expression in such a manner that a substantial portion of the burden on speech does not serve to advance its goals.

B.   EQUAL ACCESS

CHICAGO POLICE DEPT. v. MOSLEY, 408 U.S. 92 (1972), invalidated an ordinance banning all picketing within 150 feet of a school building while the school is in session and one half-hour before and afterwards, except "the peaceful picketing of any school involved in a labor dispute." The suit was brought by a federal postal employee who, for seven months prior to enactment of the ordinance, had frequently picketed a high school in Chicago. "During school hours and usually by himself, Mosley would walk the public sidewalk adjoining the school, carrying a sign that read: 'Jones High School practices black discrimination. Jones High School has a black quota.' His lonely crusade was always peaceful, orderly, and [quiet]." The Court, per MARSHALL, J., viewed the ordinance as drawing "an impermissible distinction between labor picketing and other peaceful picketing": "The central problem with Chicago's ordinance is that it describes permissible picketing in terms of its subject matter. Peaceful picketing on the subject of a school's labor-management dispute is permitted, but all other peaceful picketing is prohibited. The operative distinction is the message on a picket sign. But, above all else, the First Amendment means that government has no power to restrict expression because of its message, its ideas, its subject matter, or its content.

"[U]nder the Equal Protection Clause, not to mention the First Amendment itself,a government may not grant the use of a forum to people whose views it finds acceptable, but deny use to those wishing to express less favored or more controversial views. And it may not select which issues are worth discussing or debating in public facilities. There is an 'equality of status in the field of ideas,' and government must afford all points of view an equal opportunity to be heard. Once a forum is opened up to assembly or speaking by some groups, government may not prohibit others from assembling or speaking on the basis of what they intend to say. Selective exclusions from a public forum may not be based on content alone, and may not be justified by reference to content alone.

"[Not] all picketing must always be allowed. We have continually recognized that reasonable 'time, place and manner' regulations of picketing may be necessary to further significant governmental interests. Similarly, under an equal protection analysis, there may be sufficient regulatory interests justifying selective exclusions or distinctions among picketers. [But] [b]ecause picketing plainly involves expressive conduct within the protection of the First Amendment, discriminations among picketers must be tailored to serve a substantial governmental interest. In this case, the ordinance itself describes impermissible picketing not in terms of time, place and manner, but in terms of subject matter. The regulation 'thus slip[s] from the neutrality of time, place and circumstance into a concern about content.' This is never permitted. * * *

"Although preventing school disruption is a city's legitimate concern, Chicago itself has determined that peaceful labor picketing during school hours is not an undue interference with school. Therefore, under the Equal Protection clause, Chicago may not maintain that other picketing disrupts the school unless that picketing is clearly more disruptive than the picketing Chicago already permits. If peaceful labor picketing is permitted, there is no justification for prohibiting all nonlabor picketing, both peaceful and nonpeaceful. 'Peaceful' labor picketing, however the term 'peaceful' is defined, is obviously no less disruptive than 'peaceful' nonlabor picketing. But Chicago's ordinance permits the former and prohibits the latter.

"[We also] reject the city's argument that, although it permits peaceful labor picketing, it may prohibit all nonlabor picketing because, as a class, nonlabor picketing is more prone to produce violence than labor picketing. Predictions about imminent disruption from picketing involve judgments appropriately made on an individualized basis, not by means of broad classifications, especially those based on subject matter. Freedom of expression, and its intersection with the guarantee of equal protection, would rest on a soft foundation indeed if government could distinguish among picketers on such a wholesale and categorical basis. '[I]n our system, undifferentiated fear or apprehension of disturbance is not enough to overcome the right to freedom of expression.' *Tinker*. Some labor picketing is peaceful, some disorderly; the same is true for picketing on other themes. No labor picketing could be more peaceful or less prone to violence than Mosley's solitary vigil. In seeking to restrict nonlabor picketing which is clearly more disruptive than peaceful labor picketing, Chicago may not prohibit all nonlabor picketing at the school forum."b

a. *Consolidated Edison Co. v. Public Service Comm'n*, abandoned equal protection and cited *Mosley* as a First Amendment case: "The First Amendment's hostility to content-based regulation extends not only to restrictions on particular viewpoints, but also to prohibition of public discussion of an entire topic." But see, e.g., *Minnesota State Board v. Knight*, 465 U.S. 271 (1984) (stating that *Mosley* is an equal protection case).

b. Burger, C.J., joined the Court's opinion, but also concurred. Blackmun and Rehnquist, JJ., concurred in the result.

Note

Residential picketing. An Illinois statute prohibited picketing residences or dwellings—except when the dwelling is "used as a place of business," or is "a place of employment involved in a labor dispute or the place of holding a meeting [on] premises commonly used to discuss subjects of general public interest," or when a "person is picketing his own [dwelling]. *Carey v. Brown,* 447 U.S. 455 (1980) found the statute 'constitutionally indistinguishable' from the ordinance struck down in *Mosley.*

II. NEW FORUMS

Are First Amendment rights on government property confined to streets and parks? "[W]hat about other publicly owned property, ranging from the grounds surrounding a public building, to the inside of a welfare office, publicly run bus, or library, to a legislative gallery?" Stone, *Fora Americana,* supra, at 245.

INTERNATIONAL SOCIETY FOR KRISHNA CONSCIOUSNESS, INC. v. LEE

505 U.S. 672, 112 S.Ct. 2701, 120 L.Ed.2d 541 (1992).

CHIEF JUSTICE REHNQUIST delivered the opinion of the Court.

* * * Petitioner International Society for Krishna Consciousness, Inc. (ISK-CON) is a not-for-profit religious corporation whose members perform a ritual known as sankirtan. The ritual consists of " 'going into public places, disseminating religious literature and soliciting funds to support the religion.' " The primary purpose of this ritual is raising funds for the movement.

Respondent [was] the police superintendent of the Port Authority of New York and New Jersey and was charged with enforcing the regulation at issue. The Port Authority owns and operates three major airports in the greater New York City area [which] collectively form one of the world's busiest metropolitan airport complexes. By decade's end they are expected to serve at least 110 million passengers annually. * * *

The Port Authority has adopted a regulation forbidding within the terminals the repetitive solicitation of money or distribution of literature [but permitting] solicitation and distribution on the sidewalks outside the terminal buildings. The regulation effectively prohibits petitioner from performing sankirtan in the terminals. * * *

It is uncontested that the solicitation at issue in this case is a form of speech protected under the First Amendment.[3] But it is also well settled that the government need not permit all forms of speech on property that it owns and controls. *United States Postal Service v. Council of Greenburgh Civic Assns.,* 453 U.S. 114, 129 (1981);[a] *Greer v. Spock,* 424 U.S. 828 (1976).[b] Where the govern-

---

3. We deal here only with [ISKCON's] claim raising the permissibility of solicitation. Respondent's cross-petition concerning the leafletting ban is disposed of in the companion case, *Lee v. International Society for Krishna Consciousness, Inc.,* infra.

a. *Greenburgh* held that the post office could prevent individuals from placing un-stamped material in residential mail boxes.

b. *Greer* held that the military could bar a presidential candidate from speaking on a military base even though members of the public were free to visit the base, the President had spoken on the base, and other speakers (e.g.,

ment is acting as a proprietor, managing its internal operations, rather than acting as lawmaker with the power to regulate or license, its action will not be subjected to the heightened review to which its actions as a lawmaker may be subject. Thus, we have upheld a ban on political advertisements in city-operated transit vehicles, *Lehman v. City of Shaker Heights,* 418 U.S. 298 (1974), even though the city permitted other types of advertising on those vehicles. Similarly, we have permitted a school district to limit access to an internal mail system used to communicate with teachers employed by the district. *Perry Education Assn. v. Perry Local Educators' Ass'n,* 460 U.S. 37 (1983).c

These cases reflect, either implicitly or explicitly, a "forum-based" approach for assessing restrictions that the government seeks to place on the use of its property. *Cornelius v. NAACP Legal Defense and Educational Fund, Inc.,* 473 U.S. 788, 800 (1985).d Under this approach, regulation of speech on government property that has traditionally been available for public expression is subject to the highest scrutiny. Such regulations survive only if they are narrowly drawn to achieve a compelling state interest. *Perry.* The second category of public property is the designated public forum, whether of a limited or unlimited character— property that the state has opened for expressive activity by part or all of the public. Id.e Regulation of such property is subject to the same limitations as that governing a traditional public forum. Finally, there is all remaining public property. Limitations on expressive activity conducted on this last category of property must survive only a much more limited review. The challenged regula-

entertainers and anti-drug speakers) had spoken by invitation on the base.

c. *Perry* held it permissible to deny access to the mailboxes for a competing union despite permitting access for the duly elected union and access for various community groups such as the cub scouts, the YMCA, and other civic and church organizations. *Mosley* and *Carey* were distinguished: "[The] key to those decisions [was] the presence of a public forum." Compare *Lamb's Chapel v. Center Moriches Union Free School Dist.,* 508 U.S. 384 (1993) (school could not exclude religious groups from access to school property for after school meetings so long as it held the property generally open for meetings by social, civic, and recreation groups). *Good News Club v. Milford Central School,* 533 U.S. 98 (2001)(viewpoint discrimination to refuse access to elementary school classrooms after school for group engaging in religious instruction and prayer to discuss morals and character while permitting access to groups who would discuss the development of character and morals in other ways).

d. *Cornelius* upheld an executive order that included organizations providing direct health and welfare services to individuals or their families in a charity drive in the federal workplace while excluding legal defense and political advocacy organizations.

A 4–3 majority, per O'Connor, J., determined that "government does not create a public forum by inaction or by permitting limited discourse, but only by intentionally opening a non-traditional forum for public discourse." Observing that the Court will look to the policy and practice of the government, the nature of the property and its compatibility with expressive activity in discerning intent, O'Connor, J., insisted that "we will not find that a public forum has been created in the face of clear evidence of a contrary intent, nor will we infer that the Government intended to create a public forum when the nature of the property is inconsistent with expressive activity."

Blackmun, J., dissented: "If the Government does not create a limited public forum unless it intends to provide an 'open forum' for expressive activity, and if the exclusion of some speakers is evidence that the Government did not intend to create such a forum, no speaker challenging denial of access will ever be able to prove that the forum is a limited public forum. The very fact that the Government denied access to the speaker indicates that the Government did not intend to provide an open forum for expressive activity, and [that] fact alone would demonstrate that the forum is not a limited public forum."

e. In interpreting this approach, *Perry* also stated in footnote 7 that: "a public forum may be created for a limited purpose such as use by certain groups, e.g., *Widmar v. Vincent* [Ch. 8, Sec. 1, III] (student groups), or for discussion of certain subjects, e.g., *Madison Joint School District v. Wisconsin Employ. Relat. Comm'n,* 429 U.S. 167 (1976) (school board business)". On this approach, the exclusion of a student group or statement concerning school board business would be subject to strict scrutiny, but the exclusion of persons or topics falling outside the limited purpose would be subject to a reasonableness test.

tion need only be reasonable, as long as the regulation is not an effort to suppress the speaker's activity due to disagreement with the speaker's view.

[Our] precedents foreclose the conclusion that airport terminals are public fora. Reflecting the general growth of the air travel industry, airport terminals have only recently achieved their contemporary size and character. [Moreover,] even within the rather short history of air transport, it is only "[i]n recent years [that] it has become a common practice for various religious and non-profit organizations to use commercial airports as a forum for the distribution of literature, the solicitation of funds, the proselytizing of new members, and other similar activities." 45 Fed.Reg. 35314 (1980). Thus, the tradition of airport activity does not demonstrate that airports have historically been made available for speech activity. Nor can we say that these particular terminals, or airport terminals generally, have been intentionally opened by their operators to such activity; the frequent and continuing litigation evidencing the operators' objections belies any such claim. * * *

Petitioner attempts to circumvent the history and practice governing airport activity by pointing our attention to the variety of speech activity that it claims historically occurred at various "transportation nodes" such as rail stations, bus stations, wharves, and Ellis Island. Even if we were inclined to accept petitioner's historical account[,] we think that such evidence is of little import for two reasons. First, much of the evidence is irrelevant to *public* fora analysis, because sites such as bus and rail terminals traditionally have had *private* ownership. The development of privately owned parks that ban speech activity would not change the public fora status of publicly held parks. But the reverse is also true. The practices of privately held transportation centers do not bear on the government's regulatory authority over a publicly owned airport.

Second, the relevant unit for our inquiry is an airport, not "transportation nodes" generally. When new methods of transportation develop, new methods for accommodating that transportation are also likely to be needed. And with each new step, it therefore will be a new inquiry whether the transportation necessities are compatible with various kinds of expressive activity. [The] "security magnet," for example, is an airport commonplace that lacks a counterpart in bus terminals and train stations. And public access to air terminals is also not infrequently restricted—just last year the Federal Aviation Administration required airports for a 4–month period to limit access to areas normally publicly accessible. To blithely equate airports with other transportation centers, therefore, would be a mistake. [T]he record demonstrates that Port Authority management considers the purpose of the terminals to be the facilitation of passenger air travel, not the promotion of expression. Even if we look beyond the intent of the Port Authority to the manner in which the terminals have been operated, the terminals have never been dedicated (except under the threat of court order) to expression in the form sought to be exercised [here]. Thus, we think that neither by tradition nor purpose can the terminals be described as satisfying the standards we have previously set out for identifying a public forum.

The restrictions here challenged, therefore, need only satisfy a requirement of reasonableness. * * *

We have on many prior occasions noted the disruptive effect that solicitation may have on business. "Solicitation requires action by those who would respond: The individual solicited must decide whether or not to contribute (which itself might involve reading the solicitor's literature or hearing his pitch), and then, having decided to do so, reach for a wallet, search it for money, write a check, or produce a credit card." *United States v. Kokinda*, 497 U.S. 720 (1990). Passengers who wish to avoid the solicitor may have to alter their path, slowing both themselves and those around them. The result is that the normal flow of traffic is impeded. This is especially so in an airport, where "air travelers, who are often weighted down by cumbersome baggage [may] be hurrying to catch a plane or to arrange ground transportation." Delays may be particularly costly in this setting, as a flight missed by only a few minutes can result in hours worth of subsequent inconvenience.

In addition, face to face solicitation presents risks of duress that are an appropriate target of regulation. The skillful, and unprincipled, solicitor can target the most vulnerable, including those accompanying children or those suffering physical impairment and who cannot easily avoid the solicitation. The unsavory solicitor can also commit fraud through concealment of his affiliation or through deliberate efforts to shortchange those who agree to purchase. Compounding this problem is the fact that, in an airport, the targets of such activity frequently are on tight schedules. This in turn makes such visitors unlikely to stop and formally complain to airport authorities. As a result, the airport faces considerable difficulty in achieving its legitimate interest in monitoring solicitation activity to assure that travelers are not interfered with unduly.

[T]he sidewalk areas outside the terminals [are] frequented by an overwhelming percentage of airport users. [W]e think it would be odd to conclude that the Port Authority's terminal regulation is unreasonable despite the Port Authority having otherwise assured access to an area universally traveled. * * *

Moreover, "[if] petitioner is given access, so too must other groups. "Obviously, there would be a much larger threat to the State's interest in crowd control if all other religious, nonreligious, and noncommercial organizations could likewise move freely." As a result, we conclude that the solicitation ban is reasonable. * * *

JUSTICE O'CONNOR, concurring in 91–155 [on the solicitation issue] and concurring in the judgment in 91–339 [on the distribution of literature issue]. * * *

I concur in the Court's opinion in No. 91–155 and agree that publicly owned airports are not public fora.

[This], however, does not mean that the government can restrict speech in whatever way it likes. * * *

"The reasonableness of the Government's restriction [on speech in a nonpublic forum] must be assessed in light of the purpose of the forum and all the surrounding circumstances." *Cornelius.* " '[C]onsideration of a forum's special attributes is relevant to the constitutionality of a regulation since the significance of the governmental interest must be assessed in light of the characteristic nature and function of the particular forum involved.' " *Kokinda.* In this case, the "special attributes" and "surrounding circumstances" of the airports operated by the Port Authority are determinative. Not only has the Port Authority chosen *not* to limit access to the airports under its control, it has created a huge complex open to travelers and nontravelers alike. The airports house restaurants, cafeterias, snack bars, coffee shops, cocktail lounges, post offices, banks, telegraph offices, clothing shops, drug stores, food stores, nurseries, barber shops, currency exchanges, art exhibits, commercial advertising displays, bookstores, newsstands, dental offices and private clubs. The International Arrivals Building at JFK Airport even has two branches of BloomingFirst Amendment's.

We have said that a restriction on speech in a nonpublic forum is "reasonable" when it is "consistent with the [government's] legitimate interest in 'preserv[ing] the property [for] the use to which it is lawfully dedicated.' " *Perry.*

[The] reasonableness inquiry, therefore, is not whether the restrictions on speech are "consistent [with] preserving the property" for air travel, but whether they are reasonably related to maintaining the multipurpose environment that the Port Authority has deliberately created.

Applying that standard, I agree with the Court in No. 91–155 that the ban on solicitation is reasonable. * * *

In my view, however, the regulation banning leafletting [cannot] be upheld as reasonable on this record. I therefore concur in the judgment in No. 91–339 striking down that prohibition. [W]e have expressly noted that leafletting does not entail the same kinds of problems presented by face-to-face solicitation. Specifically, "[o]ne need not ponder the contents of a leaflet or pamphlet in order mechanically to take it out of someone's [hand]. 'The distribution of literature does not require that the recipient stop in order to receive the message the speaker wishes to convey; instead the recipient is free to read the message at a later time.' " With the possible exception of avoiding litter, it is difficult to point to any problems intrinsic to the act of leafletting that would make it naturally incompatible with a large, multipurpose forum such as those at issue here. * * *

Of course, it is still open for the Port Authority to promulgate regulations of the time, place, and manner of leafletting which are "content-neutral, narrowly tailored to serve a significant government interest, and leave open ample alternative channels of communication." For example, during the many years that this litigation has been in progress, the Port Authority has not banned sankirtan completely from JFK International Airport, but has restricted it to a relatively uncongested part of the airport terminals, the same part that houses the airport chapel. In my view, that regulation meets the standards we have applied * * *.

JUSTICE KENNEDY, with whom JUSTICE BLACKMUN, JUSTICE STEVENS, and JUSTICE SOUTER join as to Part I, concurring in the judgment.

I. [The Court] leaves the government with almost unlimited authority to restrict speech on its property by doing nothing more than articulating a non-speech-related purpose for the area, and it leaves almost no scope for the development of new public forums absent the rare approval of the government. The Court's error [in] analysis is a classification of the property that turns on the government's own definition or decision, unconstrained by an independent duty to respect the speech its citizens can voice there. The Court acknowledges as much, by reintroducing today into our First Amendment law a strict doctrinal line between the proprietary and regulatory functions of government which I thought had been abandoned long ago. *Schneider; Grayned v. Rockford,* 408 U.S. 104 (1972).f

[Public] places are of necessity the locus for discussion of public issues, as well as protest against arbitrary government action. At the heart of our jurisprudence lies the principle that in a free nation citizens must have the right to gather and speak with other persons in public places. The recognition that certain government-owned property is a public forum provides open notice to citizens that their freedoms may be exercised there without fear of a censorial government, adding tangible reinforcement to the idea that we are a free people. * * *

The Court's analysis rests on an inaccurate view of history. The notion that traditional public forums are property which have public discourse as their

f. *Grayned* stated that: "The crucial question is whether the manner of expression is basically incompatible with the normal activity of a particular place at a particular time." Applying that test, the Court held constitutional an ordinance forbidding the making of noise which disturbs or tends to disturb the peace or good order of a school session.

principal purpose is a most doubtful fiction. The types of property that we have recognized as the quintessential public forums are streets, parks, and sidewalks. It would seem apparent that the principal purpose of streets and sidewalks, like airports, is to facilitate transportation, not public discourse. [Similarly,] the purpose for the creation of public parks may be as much for beauty and open space as for discourse. Thus under the Court's analysis, even the quintessential public forums would appear to lack the necessary elements of what the Court defines as a public forum. * * *

One of the places left in our mobile society that is suitable for discourse is a metropolitan airport [because] in these days an airport is one of the few government-owned spaces where many persons have extensive contact with other members of the public. Given that private spaces of similar character are not subject to the dictates of the First Amendment, it is critical that we preserve these areas for protected speech. [If] the objective, physical characteristics of the property at issue and the actual public access and uses which have been permitted by the government indicate that expressive activity would be appropriate and compatible with those uses, the property is a public forum. [The] possibility of some theoretical inconsistency between expressive activities and the property's uses should not bar a finding of a public forum, if those inconsistencies can be avoided through simple and permitted regulations.

The second category of the Court's jurisprudence, the so-called designated forum, provides little, if any, additional protection for speech. [I] do not quarrel with the fact that speech must often be restricted on property of this kind to retain the purpose for which it has been designated. And I recognize that when property has been designated for a particular expressive use, the government may choose to eliminate that designation. But this increases the need to protect speech in other places, where discourse may occur free of such restrictions. In some sense the government always retains authority to close a public forum, by selling the property, changing its physical character, or changing its principal use. Otherwise the State would be prohibited from closing a park, or eliminating a street or sidewalk, which no one has understood the public forum doctrine to require. The difference is that when property is a protected public forum the State may not by fiat assert broad control over speech or expressive activities; it must alter the objective physical character or uses of the property, and bear the attendant costs, to change the property's forum status.

Under this analysis, it is evident that the public spaces of the Port Authority's airports are public forums. First, the District Court made detailed findings [that] show that the public spaces in the airports are broad, public thoroughfares full of people and lined with stores and other commercial activities. An airport corridor is of course not a street, but that is not the proper inquiry. The question is one of physical similarities, sufficient to suggest that the airport corridor should be a public forum for the same reasons that streets and sidewalks have been treated as public forums by the people who use them.

Second, the airport areas involved here are open to the public without restriction. Plaintiffs do not seek access to the secured areas of the airports, nor do I suggest that these areas would be public forums. And while most people who come to the Port Authority's airports do so for a reason related to air travel, [this] does not distinguish an airport from streets or sidewalks, which most people use for travel. * * *

Third, and perhaps most important, it is apparent from the record, and from the recent history of airports, that when adequate time, place, and manner regulations are in place, expressive activity is quite compatible with the uses of major airports. The Port Authority [argues] that the problem of congestion in its airports' corridors makes expressive activity inconsistent with the airports' primary purpose, which is to facilitate air travel. The First Amendment is often inconvenient. But that is besides the point. Inconvenience does not absolve the government of its obligation to tolerate speech. * * *

[A] grant of plenary power allows the government to tilt the dialogue heard by the public, to exclude many, more marginal voices. [We] have long recognized that the right to distribute flyers and literature lies at the heart of the liberties guaranteed by the Speech and Press Clauses of the First Amendment. The Port Authority's rule, which prohibits almost all such activity, is among the most restrictive possible of those liberties. The regulation is in fact so broad and restrictive of speech, Justice O'Connor finds it void even under the standards applicable to government regulations in nonpublic forums. I have no difficulty deciding the regulation cannot survive the far more stringent rules applicable to regulations in public forums. The regulation is not drawn in narrow terms and it does not leave open ample alternative channels for communication. * * *

II.   It is my view, however, that the Port Authority's ban on the "solicitation and receipt of funds" [may] be upheld as either a reasonable time, place, and manner restriction, or as a regulation directed at the nonspeech element of expressive conduct. The two standards have considerable overlap in a case like this one. * * *

I am in full agreement with the statement of the Court that solicitation is a form of protected speech. If the Port Authority's solicitation regulation prohibited all speech which requested the contribution of funds, I would conclude that it was a direct, content-based restriction of speech in clear violation of the First Amendment. The Authority's regulation does not prohibit all solicitation, however; it prohibits the "solicitation and receipt of funds." [It] reaches only personal solicitations for immediate payment of money. [The] regulation does not cover, for example, the distribution of preaddressed envelopes along with a plea to contribute money to the distributor or his organization. As I understand the restriction it is directed only at the physical exchange of money, which is an element of conduct interwoven with otherwise expressive solicitation.

[T]he government interest in regulating the sales of literature[, however,] is not as powerful as in the case of solicitation. The danger of a fraud arising from such sales is much more limited than from pure solicitation, because in the case of a sale the nature of the exchange tends to be clearer to both parties. Also, the Port Authority's sale regulation is not as narrowly drawn as the solicitation rule, since it does not specify the receipt of money as a critical element of a violation. And perhaps most important, the flat ban on sales of literature leaves open fewer alternative channels of communication than the Port Authority's more limited prohibition on the solicitation and receipt of funds. Given the practicalities and ad hoc nature of much expressive activity in the public forum, sales of literature must be completed in one transaction to be workable. Attempting to collect money at another time or place is a far less plausible option in the context of a sale than when soliciting donations, because the literature sought to be sold will under normal circumstances be distributed within the forum. * * *

Against all of this must be balanced the great need, recognized by our precedents, to give the sale of literature full First Amendment protection. We have long recognized that to prohibit distribution of literature for the mere reason that it is sold would leave organizations seeking to spread their message without funds to operate. "It should be remembered that the pamphlets of Thomas Paine were not distributed free of charge." *Murdock v. Pennsylvania,* 319 U.S. 105 (1943).

The effect of a rule of law distinguishing between sales and distribution would be to close the marketplace of ideas to less affluent organizations and speakers, leaving speech as the preserve of those who are able to fund themselves. One of the primary purposes of the public forum is to provide persons who lack access to more sophisticated media the opportunity to speak. [And] while the same arguments might be made regarding solicitation of funds, the answer is that the Port Authority has not prohibited all solicitation, but only a narrow class of conduct associated with a particular manner of solicitation. * * *

JUSTICE SOUTER, with whom JUSTICE BLACKMUN and JUSTICE STEVENS join, concurring in the judgment in No. 91–339 [on the distribution of literature issue] and dissenting in No. 91–155 [on the solicitation issue].

[R]espondent comes closest to justifying the [total ban on solicitation of money for immediate payment] as one furthering the government's interest in preventing coercion and fraud.1 [While] a solicitor can be insistent, a pedestrian on the street or airport concourse can simply walk [away]. Since there is here no evidence of any type of coercive conduct, over and above the merely importunate character of the open and public solicitation, that might justify a ban, the regulation cannot be sustained to avoid coercion.

As for fraud, our cases do not provide government with plenary authority to ban solicitation just because it could be [fraudulent.] The evidence of fraudulent conduct here is virtually nonexistent. It consists of one affidavit describing eight complaints, none of them substantiated, "involving some form of fraud, deception, or larceny" over an entire 11–year period between 1975 and 1986, during which the regulation at issue here was, by agreement, not enforced. [B]y the Port Authority's own calculation, there has not been a single claim of fraud or misrepresentation since 1981. * * *

Even assuming a governmental interest adequate to justify some regulation, the present ban would fall when subjected to the requirement of narrow tailoring. Thus, in *Schaumburg v. Citizens for a Better Environment,* 444 U.S. 620 (1980), we said: "The Village's legitimate interest in preventing fraud can be better served by measures less intrusive than a direct prohibition on solicitation. Fraudulent misrepresentations can be prohibited and the penal laws used to punish such conduct directly."

[Finally,] I do not think the Port Authority's solicitation ban leaves open the "ample" channels of communication required of a valid content-neutral time, place and manner restriction. A distribution of preaddressed envelopes is unlikely to be much of an alternative. The practical reality of the regulation, which this Court can never ignore, is that it shuts off a uniquely powerful avenue of communication for organizations like the International Society for Krishna Consciousness, and may, in effect, completely prohibit unpopular and poorly funded groups from receiving funds in response to protected solicitation. * * *

---

1. Respondent also attempts to justify its regulation on the alternative basis of "interference with air travelers," referring in particular to problems of "annoyance," and "congestion." The First Amendment inevitably requires people to put up with annoyance and uninvited persuasion. Indeed, in such cases we need to scrutinize restrictions on speech with special care. In their degree of congestion, most of the public spaces of these airports are probably more comparable to public streets than to the fairground as we described it in *Heffron.* Consequently, the congestion argument, which was held there to justify a regulation confining solicitation to a fixed location, should have less force here. Be that as it may, the conclusion of a majority of the Court today that the Constitution forbids the ban on the sale as well as the distribution, of leaflets puts to rest respondent's argument that congestion justifies a total ban on solicitation. While there may, of course, be congested locations where solicitation could severely compromise the efficient flow of pedestrians, the proper response would be to tailor the restrictions to those choke points.

LEE v. INTERNATIONAL SOCIETY FOR KRISHNA CONSCIOUSNESS, INC.

505 U.S. 830, 112 S.Ct. 2709, 120 L.Ed.2d 669 (1992).

PER CURIAM.

For the reasons expressed in the opinions of Justice O'Connor, Justice Kennedy, and Justice Souter in *ISKCON v. Lee,* the judgment of the Court of Appeals holding that the ban on distribution of literature in the Port Authority airport terminals is invalid under the First Amendment is affirmed.

CHIEF JUSTICE REHNQUIST, with whom JUSTICE WHITE, JUSTICE SCALIA and JUSTICE THOMAS join, dissenting.

Leafletting [must] be evaluated against a backdrop of the substantial congestion problem facing the Port Authority and with an eye to the cumulative impact that will result if all groups are permitted terminal access. Viewed in this light, I conclude that the distribution ban, no less than the solicitation ban, is reasonable.

[The] weary, harried, or hurried traveler may have no less desire and need to avoid the delays generated by having literature foisted upon him than he does to avoid delays from a financial solicitation. And while a busy passenger perhaps may succeed in fending off a leafletter with minimal disruption to himself by agreeing simply to take the proffered material, this does not completely ameliorate the dangers of congestion flowing from such leafletting. Others may choose not simply to accept the material but also to stop and engage the leafletter in debate, obstructing those who follow. Moreover, those who accept material may often simply drop it on the floor once out of the leafletter's range, creating an eyesore, a safety hazard, and additional cleanup work for airport staff. See *Los Angeles City Council v. Taxpayers for Vincent,* 466 U.S. 789 (1984) (aesthetic interests may provide basis for restricting speech).

[Under] the regime that is today sustained, the Port Authority is obliged to permit leafletting. But monitoring leafletting activity in order to ensure that it is *only* leafletting that occurs, and not also soliciting, may prove little less burdensome than the monitoring that would be required if solicitation were permitted. At a minimum, therefore, I think it remains open whether at some future date the Port Authority may be able to reimpose a complete ban, having developed evidence that enforcement of a differential ban is overly burdensome. * * *

Note

Several cases have upheld the denial of access to public property on the basis of content or prohibitions of particular speech on public property. Prior to *Lee* or *Perry,* LEHMAN V. SHAKER HEIGHTS, 418 U.S. 298 (1974), held that a public transit system could sell commercial advertising space for cards on its vehicles while refusing to sell space for "political" or "public issue" advertising. BLACKMUN, J., joined by Burger, C.J., White and Rehnquist, JJ., ruled that card space was not a public forum and found the city's decision reasonable because it minimized "chances of abuse, the appearance of favoritism, and the risk of imposing upon a captive audience." DOUGLAS, J., concurring, maintained that political messages and commercial messages were both offensive and intrusive to captive audiences, noted that the commercial advertising policy was not before the Court, and voted to deny a right to spread a political message to a captive audience. BRENNAN, J., joined by Stewart, Marshall, and Powell, JJ., dissenting, observed that the "city's solicitous regard for 'captive riders' [has] a hollow ring in the present case where [it] has opened its rapid transit system as a forum for communication."

BURSON v. FREEMAN, 504 U.S. 191 (1992), upheld a statute prohibiting the soliciting of votes and the display or distribution of campaign materials within 100 feet of the entrance to a polling place In order to prevent voter intimidation and election fraud. BLACKMUN, J., joined by Rehnquist, C.J., and White and Kennedy, J.J., argued that the 100 foot zone was a public forum, that the regulation was based on the content of the speech, that the state was required to show that its statute was necessary to achieve a compelling state interest and narrowly drawn to achieve that end, and determined that this was the "rare case" in which strict scrutiny against content regulation could be satisfied.g

SCALIA, J., agreed with Blackmun, J., that the regulation was justified, but maintained that the area around a polling place was not a public forum: "If the category of 'traditional public forum' is to be a tool of analysis rather than a conclusory label, it must remain faithful to its name and derive its content from *tradition*. Because restrictions on speech around polling places are as venerable a part of the American tradition as the secret ballot, [Tennessee's statute] does not restrict speech in a traditional public forum. [I] believe that the [statute] though content-based, is constitutional because it is a reasonable, viewpoint-neutral regulation of a non-public forum."

STEVENS, J., joined by O'Connor and Souter, JJ., dissenting, did not address the question of whether the area around a polling place was a public forum, but agreed with Blackmun, J., that the regulation could not be upheld without showing that it was necessary to serve a compelling state interest by means narrowly tailored to that end. He contended that the existence of the secret ballot was a sufficient safeguard against intimidation and that the fear of fraud from last minute campaigning could not be reconciled with *Mills v. Alabama,* 384 U.S. 214 (1966)(prohibition on election day editorials unconstitutional). In addition, Stevens, J., argued that the prohibition disproportionately affected candidates with "fewer resources, candidates from lesser visibility offices, and 'grassroots' candidates" who specially profit from "last-minute campaigning near the polling place. [The] hubbub of campaign workers outside a polling place may be a nuisance, but it is also the sound of a vibrant democracy."

Finally, HILL v. COLORADO, 530 U.S. 703 (2000), per STEVENS, J., upheld a state statute making it unlawful, within 100 feet of the entrance to any health care facility, for any person to "knowingly approach" within eight feet of another person, without that person's consent, "for the purpose of passing a leaflet or handbill to, displaying a sign to, or engaging in oral protest, education, or counseling with such other person": "The Colorado statute's regulation [places] no restrictions on—and clearly does not prohibit—either a particular viewpoint or any subject matter that may be discussed by a speaker. Rather, it simply establishes a minor place restriction on an extremely broad category of communications with unwilling listeners. Instead of drawing distinctions based on the subject that the approaching speaker may wish to address, the statute applies equally to used car salesmen, animal rights activists, fundraisers, environmentalists, and missionaries.

"Here, the statute's restriction seeks to protect those who enter a health care facility from the harassment, the nuisance, the persistent importuning, the following, the dogging, and the implied threat of physical touching that can accompany an unwelcome approach within eight feet of a patient by a person

---

g. Kennedy, J., concurring, reaffirmed the views he had put forward in *Simon and Schuster,* but noted that the First Amendment must appropriately give way in some cases where other constitutional rights are at stake. Thomas, J., took no part.

wishing to argue vociferously face-to-face and perhaps thrust an undesired hand-bill upon her."**h**

Scalia, J., joined by Thomas, J., dissented: "[The] Court's confident assurance that the statute poses no special threat to First Amendment freedoms because it applies alike to "used car salesmen, animal rights activists, fundraisers, environ-mentalists, and missionaries," is a wonderful replication (except for its lack of sarcasm) of Anatole France's observation that "[t]he law, in its majestic equality, forbids the rich as well as the poor to sleep under bridges." [We] know what the Colorado legislators, by their careful selection of content ('protest, education, and counseling'), were taking aim at, for they set it forth in the statute itself: the 'right to protest or counsel against certain medical procedures' on the sidewalks and streets surrounding health care facilities."

SECTION 7. GOVERNMENT SUPPORT OF SPEECH

Public forum doctrine recognizes that government is obligated to permit some of its property to be used for communicative purposes without content discrimina-tion, but public forum doctrine also allows other government property to be restricted to some speakers or for talk about selected subjects. In short, in some circumstances government can provide resources for some speech while denying support for other speech. Indeed, government is a significant actor in the market-place of ideas. Sometimes the government speaks as government; sometimes it subsidizes speech without purporting to claim that the resulting message is its own. It supports speech in many ways: official government messages; statements of public officials at publicly subsidized press conferences; artistic, scientific, or political subsidies; even the classroom communications of public school teachers.

If content distinctions are suspect when government acts as censor, they are the norm when government speaks or otherwise subsidizes speech. Government makes editorial judgments; it decides that some content is appropriate for the occasion and other content is not. The public museum curator makes content decisions in selecting exhibits; the librarian in selecting books; the public board in selecting recipients for research grants; the public official in composing press releases.

The line between support for speech and censorship of speech is not always bright, however. In any event, the Constitution limits the choices government may make in supporting speech. For example, government support of religious speech is limited under the establishment clause. See Ch. 8. This section explores the extent to which the speech clause or constitutional conceptions of equality should limit government discretion in supporting speech.

I. SUBSIDIES OF SPEECH

Pleasant Grove, Utah permitted private groups to place a number of perma-nent monuments in its Pioneer Park including a Ten Commandments monument provided by the Fraternal Order of Eagles. Summum, a religious organization, requested permission to erect a monument containing Seven Aphorisms which it believes were presented by God to Moses. Summum challenged the city's refusal on the ground that the city was engaging in unacceptable content discrimination in a public forum.

h. Souter, J., joined by O'Connor, Gins-   dissented.
burg, and Breyer, JJ. concurred. Kennedy, J.,

PLEASANT GROVE CITY v. SUMMUM, 129 S.Ct. 1125 (2009), per Alito, J., upheld the city: "[A]lthough a park is a traditional public forum for speeches and other transitory expressive acts, the display of a permanent monument in a public park is not a form of expression to which forum analysis applies. Instead, the placement of a permanent monument in a public park is best viewed as a form of government speech and is therefore not subject to scrutiny under the Free Speech Clause. [If] government entities must maintain viewpoint neutrality in their selection of donated monuments, they must either brace themselves for an influx of clutter or face the pressure to remove longstanding and cherished monuments. Every jurisdiction that has accepted a donated war memorial may be asked to provide equal treatment for a donated monument questioning the cause for which the veterans fought. New York City, having accepted a donated statue of one heroic dog (Balto, the sled dog who brought medicine to Nome, Alaska, during a diphtheria epidemic) may be pressed to accept monuments for other dogs who are claimed to be equally worthy of commemoration. The obvious truth of the matter is that if public parks were considered to be traditional public forums for the purpose of erecting privately donated monuments, most parks would have little choice but to refuse all such donations." Earlier in the opinion, the Court noted: "This does not mean that there are no restraints on government speech. For example, government speech must comport with the Establishment Clause. The involvement of public officials in advocacy may be limited by law, regulation, or practice. And of course, a government entity is ultimately 'accountable to the electorate and the political process for its advocacy.' 'If the citizenry objects, newly elected officials later could espouse some different or contrary position.' "a

RUST v. SULLIVAN
500 U.S. 173, 111 S.Ct. 1759, 114 L.Ed.2d 233 (1991).

CHIEF JUSTICE REHNQUIST delivered the opinion of the Court.

These cases concern a facial challenge to Department of Health and Human Services (HHS) regulations which limit the ability of Title X fund recipients to engage in abortion-related activities. * * *

A. In 1970, Congress enacted Title X of the Public Health Service Act (Act), 84 Stat. 1506, as amended, 42 U.S.C. §§ 300–300a–41, which provides federal funding for family-planning services. The Act authorizes the Secretary to "make grants to and enter into contracts with public or nonprofit private entities to assist in the establishment and operation of voluntary family planning projects which shall offer a broad range of acceptable and effective family planning methods and services." 42 U.S.C. § 300(a). Grants and contracts under Title X must "be made in accordance with such regulations as the Secretary may promulgate." 42 U.S.C. § 300a–4. Section 1008 of the Act, however, provides that "[n]one of the funds appropriated under this subchapter shall be used in programs where abortion is a method of family planning." 42 U.S.C. § 300a–6. * * *

a. The Court recognized that there might be situations where it is difficult to tell whether government is speaking or providing a forum for private speech. Stevens, J., joined by Ginsburg, J., concurring, doubted that it made a difference whether the city's acceptance of the Ten Commandment's monument was deemed to be government speech or implicit endorsement of the donor's message. Scalia, J., joined by Thomas J., concurring, expressed the view that the city's action did not violate the Establishment Clause (although the issue was not presented). Breyer, J., concurring, expressed the view that the phrase, "government speech" needed to be applied not as a label, but with an eye toward the category's purpose. He did not think the government action disproportionately burdened Summum's speech. Souter, J., concurring in the judgment, applied a reasonable observer test to determine that the Ten Commandment's monument was government speech. He thought it premature to decide Establishment Clause issues.

In 1988, the Secretary promulgated new regulations designed to provide " 'clear and operational guidance' to grantees about how to preserve the distinction between Title X programs and abortion as a method of family planning." 53 Fed.Reg. 2923–2924 (1988). * * *

The regulations attach three principal conditions on the grant of federal funds for Title X projects. First, the regulations specify that a "Title X project may not provide counseling concerning the use of abortion as a method of family planning or provide referral for abortion as a method of family planning." 42 CFR § 59.8(a)(1) (1989). Because Title X is limited to preconceptional services, the program does not furnish services related to childbirth. Only in the context of a referral out of the Title X program is a pregnant woman given transitional information. § 59.8(a)(2). Title X projects must refer every pregnant client "for appropriate prenatal and/or social services by furnishing a list of available providers that promote the welfare of the mother and the unborn child." Id. The list may not be used indirectly to encourage or promote abortion, "such as by weighing the list of referrals in favor of health care providers which perform abortions, by including on the list of referral providers health care providers whose principal business is the provision of abortions, by excluding available providers who do not provide abortions, or by 'steering' clients to providers who offer abortion as a method of family planning." § 59.8(a)(3). The Title X project is expressly prohibited from referring a pregnant woman to an abortion provider, even upon specific request. One permissible response to such an inquiry is that "the project does not consider abortion an appropriate method of family planning and therefore does not counsel or refer for abortion." § 59.8(b)(5).

Second, the regulations broadly prohibit a Title X project from engaging in activities that "encourage, promote or advocate abortion as a method of family planning." § 59.10(a). Forbidden activities include lobbying for legislation that would increase the availability of abortion as a method of family planning, developing or disseminating materials advocating abortion as a method of family planning, providing speakers to promote abortion as a method of family planning, using legal action to make abortion available in any way as a method of family planning, and paying dues to any group that advocates abortion as a method of family planning as a substantial part of its activities. Id.

Third, the regulations require that Title X projects be organized so that they are "physically and financially separate" from prohibited abortion activities. § 59.9. To be deemed physically and financially separate, "a Title X project must have an objective integrity and independence from prohibited activities. Mere bookkeeping separation of Title X funds from other monies is not sufficient." Id. The regulations provide a list of nonexclusive factors for the Secretary to consider in conducting a case-by-case determination of objective integrity and independence, such as the existence of separate accounting records and separate personnel, and the degree of physical separation of the project from facilities for prohibited activities. Id.

[Petitioners] are Title X grantees and doctors who supervise Title X funds suing on behalf of themselves and their patients. Respondent is the Secretary of the Department of Health and Human Services. [Petitioners] contend that the regulations violate the First Amendment by impermissibly discriminating based on viewpoint because they prohibit "all discussion about abortion as a lawful option—including counseling, referral, and the provision of neutral and accurate information about ending a pregnancy—while compelling the clinic or counselor to provide information that promotes continuing a pregnancy to term." They assert that the regulations violate the "free speech rights of private health care organizations that receive Title X funds, of their staff, and of their patients" by impermissibly imposing "viewpoint-discriminatory conditions on government subsidies" and thus "penaliz[e] speech funded with non-Title X monies." Because "Title X continues to fund speech ancillary to pregnancy testing in a manner that is not even-handed with respect to views and information about abortion, it invidiously discriminates on the basis of viewpoint." Relying on *Regan v. Taxation with Representation of Washington,* 461 U.S. 540 (1983)a and *Arkansas Writers' Project, Inc. v. Ragland,* 481 U.S. 221 (1987),b petitioners also assert that while the Government may place certain conditions on the receipt of federal subsidies, it may not "discriminate invidiously in its subsidies in such a way as to 'ai[m] at the suppression of dangerous ideas.' " *Regan.*

There is no question but that the statutory prohibition contained in § 1008 is constitutional. [The] Government can, without violating the Constitution, selectively fund a program to encourage certain activities it believes to be in the public interest, without at the same time funding an alternate program which seeks to deal with the problem in another way.c In so doing, the Government has not discriminated on the basis of viewpoint; it has merely chosen to fund one activity to the exclusion of the other. "[A] legislature's decision not to subsidize the exercise of a fundamental right does not infringe the right." *Regan.* * * *

The challenged regulations implement the statutory prohibition by prohibiting counseling, referral, and the provision of information regarding abortion as a method of family planning. They are designed to ensure that the limits of the federal program are observed. The Title X program is designed not for prenatal care, but to encourage family planning. A doctor who wished to offer prenatal care to a project patient who became pregnant could properly be prohibited from doing so because such service is outside the scope of the federally funded program. The regulations prohibiting abortion counseling and referral are of the same ilk; "no funds appropriated for the project may be used in programs where abortion is a method of family planning," and a doctor employed by the project may be prohibited in the course of his project duties from counseling abortion or referring for abortion. This is not a case of the Government "suppressing a dangerous idea," but of a prohibition on a project grantee or its employees from engaging in activities outside of its scope.

To hold that the Government unconstitutionally discriminates on the basis of viewpoint when it chooses to fund a program dedicated to advance certain permissible goals, because the program in advancing those goals necessarily discourages alternate goals, would render numerous government programs constitutionally suspect. When Congress established a National Endowment for Democracy to encourage other countries to adopt democratic principles, 22 U.S.C. § 4411(b), it was not constitutionally required to fund a program to encourage

a. *Regan* upheld tax code provisions that permitted contributions to veteran's organizations to be deductible even if they engaged in substantial lobbying while denying deductions for contributions to other religious, charitable, scientific, or educational organizations if they engaged in substantial lobbying.

b. *Arkansas Writers' Project* held it unconstitutional to impose a sales tax on general interest magazines while exempting newspapers, religious, professional, trade, and sports journals. Discriminatory taxation against the press or segments of it has generally been invalidated. *Minneapolis Star & Tribune v. Minnesota Comm. of Rev.,* 460 U.S. 575 (1983)

(some press treated more favorably and press treated differently from other enterprises); *Grosjean v. American Press Co.,* 297 U.S. 233 (1936) (same). But see *Leathers v. Medlock,* 499 U.S. 439 (1991) (upholding general sales tax extension to cable that was not applicable to the print media on the grounds that it did not suppress ideas and that the tax did not target a small group of speakers).

c. The Court cited *Maher v. Roe,* 432 U.S. 464 (1977) (constitutional for government to subsidize childbirth without subsidizing abortions) and *Harris v. McRae,* 448 U.S. 297 (1980) (accord).

competing lines of political philosophy such as Communism and Fascism. Petitioners' assertions ultimately boil down to the position that if the government chooses to subsidize one protected right, it must subsidize analogous counterpart rights. But the Court has soundly rejected that proposition. Within far broader limits than petitioners are willing to concede, when the government appropriates public funds to establish a program it is entitled to define the limits of that program.

We believe that petitioners' reliance upon our decision in *Arkansas Writers' Project* is misplaced. That case involved a state sales tax which discriminated between magazines on the basis of their content. Relying on this fact, and on the fact that the tax "targets a small group within the press," contrary to our decision in *Minneapolis Star,* the Court held the tax invalid. But we have here not the case of a general law singling out a disfavored group on the basis of speech content, but a case of the Government refusing to fund activities, including speech, which are specifically excluded from the scope of the project funded.

Petitioners rely heavily on their claim that the regulations would not, in the circumstance of a medical emergency, permit a Title X project to refer a woman whose pregnancy places her life in imminent peril to a provider of abortions or abortion-related services. This case, of course, involves only a facial challenge to the regulations, and we do not have before us any application by the Secretary to a specific fact situation. On their face, we do not read the regulations to bar abortion referral or counseling in such circumstances. * * *

Petitioners also contend that the restrictions on the subsidization of abortion-related speech contained in the regulations are impermissible because they condition the receipt of a benefit, in this case Title X funding, on the relinquishment of a constitutional right, the right to engage in abortion advocacy and counseling.

[H]ere the government is not denying a benefit to anyone, but is instead simply insisting that public funds be spent for the purposes for which they were authorized. The Secretary's regulations do not force the Title X grantee to give up abortion-related speech; they merely require that the grantee keep such activities separate and distinct from Title X activities. Title X expressly distinguishes between a Title X *grantee* and a Title X *project.* The grantee, which normally is a health care organization, may receive funds from a variety of sources for a variety of purposes. The grantee receives Title X funds, however, for the specific and limited purpose of establishing and operating a Title X project. 42 U.S.C. § 300(a). The regulations govern the scope of the Title X *project's* activities, and leave the grantee unfettered in its other activities. The Title X *grantee* can continue to perform abortions, provide abortion-related services, and engage in abortion advocacy; it simply is required to conduct those activities through programs that are separate and independent from the project that receives Title X funds.

In contrast, our "unconstitutional conditions" cases involve situations in which the government has placed a condition on the *recipient* of the subsidy rather than on a particular program or service, thus effectively prohibiting the recipient from engaging in the protected conduct outside the scope of the federally funded program. [By] requiring that the Title X grantee engage in abortion-related activity separately from activity receiving federal funding, Congress has, consistent with our teachings in *League of Women Voters*, [Sec. 8, II infra], and *Regan,* not denied it the right to engage in abortion-related activities. Congress has merely refused to fund such activities out of the public fisc, and the Secretary has simply required a certain degree of separation from the Title X project in order to ensure the integrity of the federally funded program.

The same principles apply to petitioners' claim that the regulations abridge the free speech rights of the grantee's staff. Individuals who are voluntarily employed for a Title X project must perform their duties in accordance with the regulation's restrictions on abortion counseling and referral. The employees remain free, however, to pursue abortion-related activities when they are not acting under the auspices of the Title X project. The regulations, which govern solely the scope of the Title X project's activities, do not in any way restrict the activities of those persons acting as private individuals. The employees' freedom of expression is limited during the time that they actually work for the project; but this limitation is a consequence of their decision to accept employment in a project, the scope of which is permissibly restricted by the funding authority.

This is not to suggest that funding by the Government, even when coupled with the freedom of the fund recipients to speak outside the scope of the Government-funded project, is invariably sufficient to justify government control over the content of expression. For example, this Court has recognized that the existence of a Government "subsidy," in the form of Government-owned property, does not justify the restriction of speech in areas that have "been traditionally open to the public for expressive activity," or have been "expressly dedicated to speech activity." Similarly, we have recognized that the university is a traditional sphere of free expression so fundamental to the functioning of our society that the Government's ability to control speech within that sphere by means of conditions attached to the expenditure of Government funds is restricted by the vagueness and overbreadth doctrines of the First Amendment, *Keyishian v. Board of Regents*. It could be argued by analogy that traditional relationships such as that between doctor and patient should enjoy protection under the First Amendment from government regulation, even when subsidized by the Government. We need not resolve that question here, however, because the Title X program regulations do not significantly impinge upon the doctor-patient relationship. Nothing in them requires a doctor to represent as his own any opinion that he does not in fact hold. Nor is the doctor-patient relationship established by the Title X program sufficiently all-encompassing so as to justify an expectation on the part of the patient of comprehensive medical advice. The program does not provide post-conception medical care, and therefore a doctor's silence with regard to abortion cannot reasonably be thought to mislead a client into thinking that the doctor does not consider abortion an appropriate option for her. The doctor is always free to make clear that advice regarding abortion is simply beyond the scope of the program. In these circumstances, the general rule that the Government may choose not to subsidize speech applies with full force. * * *

JUSTICE BLACKMUN, with whom JUSTICE MARSHALL joins, with whom JUSTICE STEVENS joins as to Parts II,d and III,e and with whom JUSTICE O'CONNOR joins as to Part I,f dissenting. * * *

II.   A. Until today, the Court never has upheld viewpoint-based suppression of speech simply because that suppression was a condition upon the acceptance of public funds. Whatever may be the Government's power to condition the receipt of its largess upon the relinquishment of constitutional rights, it surely does not extend to a condition that suppresses the recipient's cherished freedom of speech based solely upon the content or viewpoint of that speech. * * *

It cannot seriously be disputed that the counseling and referral provisions at issue in the present cases constitute content-based regulation of speech. Title X

d. Part II discussed freedom of speech and portions of it are set out below.

e. Part III argued that the regulations violated the fifth amendment due process clause.

f. Part I contended that the regulations were not authorized by the statute. O'Connor, and Stevens, JJ., each filed separate dissents advancing the same contention.

grantees may provide counseling and referral regarding any of a wide range of family planning and other topics, save abortion.

The Regulations are also clearly viewpoint-based. While suppressing speech favorable to abortion with one hand, the Secretary compels anti-abortion speech with the other. For example, the Department of Health and Human Services' own description of the Regulations makes plain that "Title X projects are *required* to facilitate access to prenatal care and social services, including adoption services, that might be needed by the pregnant client to promote her well-being and that of her child, while making it abundantly clear that the project is not permitted to promote abortion by facilitating access to abortion through the referral process." 53 Fed.Reg. 2927 (1988) (emphasis added).

Moreover, the Regulations command that a project refer for prenatal care each woman diagnosed as pregnant, irrespective of the woman's expressed desire to continue or terminate her pregnancy. 42 CFR § 59.8(a)(2) (1990). If a client asks directly about abortion, a Title X physician or counselor is required to say, in essence, that the project does not consider abortion to be an appropriate method of family planning. § 59.8(b)(4). Both requirements are antithetical to the First Amendment. See *Wooley v. Maynard*.

The Regulations pertaining to "advocacy" are even more explicitly viewpoint-based. These provide: "A Title X project may not *encourage, promote or advocate* abortion as a method of family planning." § 59.10 (emphasis added). They explain: "This requirement prohibits actions to *assist* women to obtain abortions or *increase* the availability or accessibility of abortion for family planning purposes." § 59.10(a) (emphasis added). The Regulations do not, however, proscribe or even regulate anti-abortion advocacy. These are clearly restrictions aimed at the suppression of "dangerous ideas."

Remarkably, the majority concludes that "the Government has not discriminated on the basis of viewpoint; it has merely chosen to fund one activity to the exclusion of another." But the majority's claim that the Regulations merely limit a Title X project's speech to preventive or preconceptional services rings hollow in light of the broad range of nonpreventive services that the Regulations authorize Title X projects to provide.2 By refusing to fund those family-planning projects that advocate abortion *because* they advocate abortion, the Government plainly has targeted a particular viewpoint. The majority's reliance on the fact that the Regulations pertain solely to funding decisions simply begs the question. Clearly, there are some bases upon which government may not rest its decision to fund or not to fund. For example, the Members of the majority surely would agree that government may not base its decision to support an activity upon considerations of race. As demonstrated above, our cases make clear that ideological viewpoint is a similarly repugnant ground upon which to base funding decisions.

The majority's reliance upon *Regan* in this connection is [misplaced]. That case stands for the proposition that government has no obligation to subsidize a private party's efforts to petition the legislature regarding its views. Thus, if the challenged Regulations were confined to non-ideological limitations upon the use of Title X funds for lobbying activities, there would exist no violation of the First Amendment. The advocacy Regulations at issue here, however, are not limited to lobbying but extend to all speech having the effect of encouraging, promoting, or

---

2. In addition to requiring referral for prenatal care and adoption services, the Regulations permit general health services such as physical examinations, screening for breast cancer, treatment of gynecological problems, and treatment for sexually transmitted diseases. 53 Fed.Reg. 2927 (1988). None of the latter are strictly preventive, preconceptional services.

advocating abortion as a method of family planning. § 59.10(a). Thus, in addition to their impermissible focus upon the viewpoint of regulated speech, the provisions intrude upon a wide range of communicative conduct, including the very words spoken to a woman by her physician. By manipulating the content of the doctor/patient dialogue, the Regulations upheld today force each of the petitioners "to be an instrument for fostering public adherence to an ideological point of view [he or she] finds unacceptable." *Wooley v. Maynard.* This type of intrusive, ideologically based regulation of speech goes far beyond the narrow lobbying limitations approved in *Regan,* and cannot be justified simply because it is a condition upon the receipt of a governmental benefit.3

B.   The Court concludes that the challenged Regulations do not violate the First Amendment rights of Title X staff members because any limitation of the employees' freedom of expression is simply a consequence of their decision to accept employment at a federally funded project. Ante, at 22. But it has never been sufficient to justify an otherwise unconstitutional condition upon public employment that the employee may escape the condition by relinquishing his or her job.

The majority attempts to circumvent this principle by emphasizing that Title X physicians and counselors "remain free [to] pursue abortion-related activities when they are not acting under the auspices of the Title X project." "The regulations," the majority explains, "do not in any way restrict the activities of those persons acting as private individuals." Under the majority's reasoning, the First Amendment could be read to tolerate *any* governmental restriction upon an employee's speech so long as that restriction is limited to the funded workplace. This is a dangerous proposition, and one the Court has rightly rejected in the past.

In *Abood,* it was no answer to the petitioners' claim of compelled speech as a condition upon public employment that their speech outside the workplace remained unregulated by the State.g Nor was the public employee's First Amendment claim in *Rankin v. McPherson,* 483 U.S. 378 (1987), derogated because the communication that her employer sought to punish occurred during business hours.h At the least, such conditions require courts to balance the speaker's interest in the message against those of government in preventing its dissemination.

In the cases at bar, the speaker's interest in the communication is both clear and vital. In addressing the family-planning needs of their clients, the physicians and counselors who staff Title X projects seek to provide them with the full range

---

3. The majority attempts to obscure the breadth of its decision through its curious contention that "the Title X program regulations do not significantly impinge upon the doctor-patient relationship." That the doctor-patient relationship is substantially burdened by a rule prohibiting the dissemination by the physician of pertinent medical information is beyond serious dispute. This burden is undiminished by the fact that the relationship at issue here is not an "all-encompassing" one. A woman seeking the services of a Title X clinic has every reason to expect, as do we all, that her physician will not withhold relevant information regarding the very purpose of her visit. To suggest otherwise is to engage in uninformed fantasy. Further, to hold that the doctor-patient relationship is somehow incomplete where a patient lacks the resources to seek

comprehensive healthcare from a single provider is to ignore the situation of a vast number of Americans. As Justice Marshall has noted in a different context: "It is perfectly proper for judges to disagree about what the Constitution requires. But it is disgraceful for an interpretation of the Constitution to be premised upon unfounded assumptions about how people live." *United States v. Kras,* 409 U.S. 434 (1973) (dissenting opinion).

g. *Abood v. Detroit Board of Education,* Sec. 9, II infra (compelled funding of ideological activities of union violates freedom of speech).

h. *Rankin* (expressed hope that assassination attempt of president be successful is protected speech when uttered in private to fellow employee during working hours).

of information and options regarding their health and reproductive freedom. Indeed, the legitimate expectations of the patient and the ethical responsibilities of the medical profession demand no less. "The patient's right of self-decision can be effectively exercised only if the patient possesses enough information to enable an intelligent choice. * * * The physician has an ethical obligation to help the patient make choices from among the therapeutic alternatives consistent with good medical practice." Current Opinions, the Council on Ethical and Judicial Affairs of the American Medical Association ¶ 8.08 (1989). * * *

The Government's articulated interest in distorting the doctor/patient dialogue—ensuring that federal funds are not spent for a purpose outside the scope of the program—falls far short of that necessary to justify the suppression of truthful information and professional medical opinion regarding constitutionally protected conduct.4 Moreover, the offending Regulation is not narrowly tailored to serve this interest. For example, the governmental interest at stake could be served by imposing rigorous bookkeeping standards to ensure financial separation or adopting content-neutral rules for the balanced dissemination of family-planning and health information. By failing to balance or even to consider the free speech interests claimed by Title X physicians against the Government's asserted interest in suppressing the speech, the Court falters in its duty to implement the protection that the First Amendment clearly provides for this important message.

C.   Finally, it is of no small significance that the speech the Secretary would suppress is truthful information regarding constitutionally protected conduct of vital importance to the listener. One can imagine no legitimate governmental interest that might be served by suppressing such information. * * *

Notes

1. **Refusals to subsidize.** (a) Idaho law prohibits state and local government entities from employing payroll deductions for political activities even if agreed to by employees and their government employer. At the same time payroll deductions for union dues are permissible. A group of unions contended that the prohibition on payroll deductions for political purposes as applied to local government entities violated the First Amendment. YSURSA v. POCATELLO EDUCATION ASS'N, 129 S.Ct. 1093 (2009), per ROBERTS, C.J., upheld the prohibition. He argued that local governments were mere instrumentalities of the state, that publicly administered payroll deductions were government subsidies, that government had no obligation to subsidize, that the presence of existing subsidies did not confer tenure upon them, and that the refusal to subsidize was justified by the interest in avoiding favoritism or entanglement with partisan politics.i

BREYER, J., concurring and dissenting in part, would remand to the lower court to determine whether the deduction prohibition "applied even handedly among similar politically related contributions. [A] restriction that applies to the political activities of unions alone would seem unlikely to further the government's justifying objective, namely providing the appearance of political neutrality. And in that case, the provision could well bring about speech-related harm that is disproportionate to the statute's tendency to further the government's 'neutrality' objective."j

---

4. It is to be noted that the Secretary has made no claim that the Regulations at issue reflect any concern for the health or welfare of Title X clients.

i. Ginsburg, J., concurred in the judgment. Stevens, J., dissented on the ground that the legislation "was intended to target union political activity" in a discriminatory way.

j. Breyer, J., argued for a middle level form

b. ***Rust distinguished.*** The University of Virginia subsidized the printing costs of a wide variety of student organizations, but refused to fund religious activities (those that "primarily promote or manifest a particular belief in or about a deity or an ultimate reality"). ROSENBERGER v. UNIVERSITY OF VIRGINIA, 515 U.S. 819 (1995), per KENNEDY, J., also set forth Ch. 8, Sec. I infra held that the refusal to fund religious speech violated the free speech clause: "[In *Rust*] the government did not create a program to encourage private speech but instead used private speakers to transmit specific information pertaining to its own program. We recognized that when the government appropriates public funds to promote a particular policy of its own it is entitled to say what it wishes.

"It does not follow [that] viewpoint-based restrictions are proper when the University does not itself speak or subsidize transmittal of a message it favors but instead expends funds to encourage a diversity of views from private speakers."k

SOUTER, J., joined by Stevens, Ginsburg and Breyer, JJ., dissented: "If the Guidelines were written or applied so as to limit only such Christian advocacy and no other evangelical efforts that might compete with it, the discrimination would be based on viewpoint. But that is not what the regulation authorizes; it applies to Muslim and Jewish and Buddhist advocacy as well as to Christian. And since it limits funding to activities promoting or manifesting a particular belief not only 'in' but 'about' a deity or ultimate reality, it applies to agnostics and atheists as well as it does to deists and theists. The Guidelines [thus] do not skew debate by funding one position but not its competitors. [T]hey simply deny funding for hortatory speech that 'primarily promotes or manifests' any view on the merits of religion; they deny funding for the entire subject matter of religious apologetics."

2. **Funding arts and sciences.** Clearly the government may fund or not fund artistic and scientific projects on the basis of their perceived merit. The extent to which government may make further content judgments in such decisions and the role that political actors may play in the process was debated in *National Endowment for the Arts v. Finley*, 524 U.S. 569 (1998), but not resolved.

II. GOVERNMENT AS EDUCATOR AND EDITOR

Many problems involved with government speech have arisen in the school setting. Government can compel children to attend schools, but it may not compel children to attend public schools. *Pierce v. Society of Sisters*, 268 U.S. 510 (1925) held that compulsory public education violated parental substantive due process rights though government may require that basic educational requirements be met even in private schools. In public schools there are limits to which the institution may be an exclusive enclave for government messages. *Tinker v. Des Moines School District*, 393 U.S. 503 (1969) upheld the rights of school children to wear black armbands in a classroom in protest of the Vietnam War. Moreover, there are constitutional limits on the government's power to shield students from ideas by removing books from a school library. *Board of Educ. v. Pico*, 457 U.S.

of scrutiny, "namely whether the statute imposes a burden on speech that is disproportionate in light of the other interests the government seeks to achieve." He observed that such an approach would be consistent with several other Supreme Court cases and with the approach taken by constitutional courts in Canada, Israel, South Africa, and the European Court of Human Rights.

k. O'Connor, J., and Thomas, J., filed concurring opinions. *Rust* was also distinguished in *Legal Services Corp. v. Velazquez*, 531 U.S. 533 (2001). The Court struck down a restriction preventing the the Legal Services Corporation from distributing federal funds to challenge the constitutionality or the statutory validity of existing welfare laws. It concluded that the speech of lawyers on behalf of indigent clients was not government speech.

853 (1982).a On the other hand, school authorities have been granted broad editorial control over the school curriculum including school-sponsored publications, theatrical productions, and other expressive activities.

HAZELWOOD SCHOOL DISTRICT v. KUHLMEIER

484 U.S. 260, 108 S.Ct. 562, 98 L.Ed.2d 592 (1988).

JUSTICE WHITE delivered the opinion of the Court. * * *

Petitioners are the Hazelwood School District in St. Louis County, Missouri; various school officials; Robert Eugene Reynolds, the principal of Hazelwood East High School, and Howard Emerson, a teacher in the school district. Respondents are three former Hazelwood East students who were staff members of Spectrum, the school newspaper. * * *

The practice at Hazelwood East during the spring 1983 semester was for the journalism teacher to submit page proofs of each Spectrum issue to Principal Reynolds for his review prior to publication. On May 10, Emerson delivered the proofs of the May 13 edition to Reynolds, who objected to two of the articles scheduled to appear in that edition. One of the stories described three Hazelwood East students' experiences with pregnancy; the other discussed the impact of divorce on students at the school.

Reynolds was concerned that, although the pregnancy story used false names "to keep the identity of these girls a secret," the pregnant students still might be identifiable from the text. He also believed that the article's references to sexual activity and birth control were inappropriate for some of the younger students at the school. In addition, Reynolds was concerned that a student identified by name in the divorce story had complained [about] her father * * *. Reynolds believed that the student's parents should have been given an opportunity to respond to these remarks or to consent to their publication. He was unaware that Emerson had deleted the student's name from the final version of the article.

Reynolds believed that there was no time to make the necessary changes in the stories before the scheduled press run and that the newspaper would not appear before the end of the school year if printing were delayed to any significant extent. He concluded that his only options under the circumstances were to publish a four-page newspaper instead of the planned six-page newspaper, eliminating the two pages on which the offending stories appeared, or to publish no newspaper at all. Accordingly, he directed Emerson to withhold from publication the two pages containing the stories on pregnancy and divorce.1 He informed his superiors of the decision, and they concurred. * * *

[T]he First Amendment rights of students in the public schools "are not automatically coextensive with the rights of adults in other settings," *Bethel School District No. 403 v. Fraser,* 478 U.S. 675 (1986), and must be "applied in light of the special characteristics of the school environment." *Tinker.* A school

---

a. But see *United States v. American Library Association, Inc.,* 539 U.S. 194 (2003)(constitutional to condition federal funding on the adoption of "a policy of Internet safety for minors that includes the operation of a technology protection measure [that] protects against access" by all persons to "visual depictions" that constitute "obscenity" or "child pornography," and that protects against access by minors to "visual depictions" that are "harmful to minors.")

1. The two pages deleted from the newspaper also contained articles on teenage marriage, runaways, and juvenile delinquents, as well as a general article on teenage pregnancy. Reynolds testified that he had no objection to these articles and that they were deleted only because they appeared on the same pages as the two objectionable articles.

need not tolerate student speech that is inconsistent with its "basic educational mission," *Fraser,* even though the government could not censor similar speech outside the school. Accordingly, we held in *Fraser* that a student could be disciplined for having delivered a speech that was "sexually explicit" but not legally obscene at an official school [assembly]. We thus recognized that "[t]he determination of what manner of speech in the classroom or in school assembly is inappropriate properly rests with the school board," rather than with the federal courts. * * *

We deal first with the question whether Spectrum may appropriately be characterized as a forum for public expression. [T]he evidence relied upon by the Court of Appeals fails to demonstrate the "clear intent to create a public forum," *Cornelius,* that existed in cases in which we found public forums to have been created. School [officials] "reserve[d] the forum for its intended purpos[e]," *Perry,* as a supervised learning experience for journalism students. Accordingly, school officials were entitled to regulate the contents of Spectrum in any reasonable manner. * * *

The question whether the First Amendment requires a school to tolerate particular student speech—the question that we addressed in *Tinker*—is different from the question whether the First Amendment requires a school affirmatively to promote particular student speech. The former question addresses educators' ability to silence a student's personal expression that happens to occur on the school premises. The latter question concerns educators' authority over school-sponsored publications, theatrical productions, and other expressive activities that students, parents, and members of the public might reasonably perceive to bear the imprimatur of the school. These activities may fairly be characterized as part of the school curriculum, whether or not they occur in a traditional classroom setting, so long as they are supervised by faculty members and designed to impart particular knowledge or skills to student participants and audiences.

[A] school may in its capacity as publisher of a school newspaper or producer of a school play "disassociate itself," *Fraser,* not only from speech that would "substantially interfere with [its] work [or] impinge upon the rights of other students," *Tinker,* but also from speech that is, for example, ungrammatical, poorly written, inadequately researched, biased or prejudiced, vulgar or profane, or unsuitable for immature audiences.4 A school must be able to set high standards for the student speech that is disseminated under its auspices—standards that may be higher than those demanded by some newspaper publishers or theatrical producers in the "real" world—and may refuse to disseminate student speech that does not meet those standards. [Otherwise,] the schools would be unduly constrained from fulfilling their role as "a principal instrument in awakening the child to cultural values, in preparing him for later professional training, and in helping him to adjust normally to his environment." *Brown v. Board of Education.*

Accordingly, we conclude that the standard articulated in *Tinker* for determining when a school may punish student expression need not also be the standard for determining when a school may refuse to lend its name and resources

---

4. [The] decision in *Fraser* rested on the "vulgar," "lewd," and "plainly offensive" character of a speech delivered at an official school assembly rather than on any propensity of the speech to "materially disrupt[ ] classwork or involve[ ] substantial disorder or invasion of the rights of others." Indeed, the *Fraser* Court cited as "especially relevant" a portion of Justice Black's dissenting opinion in *Tinker* "disclaim[ing] any purpose [to] hold that the Federal Constitution compels the teachers, parents and elected school officials to surrender control of the American public school system to public school students." Of course, Justice Black's observations are equally relevant to the instant case.

to the dissemination of student expression. Instead, we hold that educators do not offend the First Amendment by exercising editorial control over the style and content of student speech in school-sponsored expressive activities so long as their actions are reasonably related to legitimate pedagogical concerns.7 * * *a

JUSTICE BRENNAN, with whom JUSTICE MARSHALL and JUSTICE BLACKMUN join, dissenting.

[Under] *Tinker,* school officials may censor only such student speech as would "materially disrup[t]" a legitimate curricular function. Manifestly, student speech is more likely to disrupt a curricular function when it arises in the context of a curricular activity—one that "is designed to teach" something—than when it arises in the context of a noncurricular activity. Thus, under *Tinker,* the school may constitutionally punish the budding political orator if he disrupts calculus class but not if he holds his tongue for the cafeteria. That is not because some more stringent standard applies in the curricular context. (After all, this Court applied the same standard whether the Tinkers wore their armbands to the "classroom" or the "cafeteria.") It is because student speech in the noncurricular context is less likely to disrupt materially any legitimate pedagogical purpose.

I fully agree with the Court that the First Amendment should afford an educator the prerogative not to sponsor the publication of a newspaper article that is "ungrammatical, poorly written, inadequately researched, biased or prejudiced," or that falls short of the "high standards [for] student speech that is disseminated under [the school's] auspices." But we need not abandon *Tinker* to reach that conclusion; we need only apply it. The enumerated criteria reflect the skills that the curricular newspaper "is designed to teach." The educator may, under *Tinker,* constitutionally "censor" poor grammar, writing, or research because to reward such expression would "materially disrup[t]" the newspaper's curricular purpose. * * *

The Court relies on bits of testimony to portray the principal's conduct as a pedagogical lesson to Journalism II students who "had not sufficiently mastered those portions of [the] curriculum that pertained to the treatment of controversial issues and personal attacks, the need to protect the privacy of individuals [and] 'the legal, moral, and ethical restrictions imposed upon journalists * * *.' "

But the principal never consulted the students before censoring their work. [T]hey learned of the deletions when the paper was released. [Further,] he explained the deletions only in the broadest of generalities. In one meeting called at the behest of seven protesting Spectrum staff members (presumably a fraction of the full class), he characterized the articles as " 'too sensitive' for 'our immature audience of readers,' " and in a later meeting he deemed them simply "inappropriate, personal, sensitive and unsuitable for the newspaper." The Court's supposition that the principal intended (or the protesters understood) those generalities as a lesson on the nuances of journalistic responsibility is

---

7. A number of lower federal courts have similarly recognized that educators' decisions with regard to the content of school sponsored newspapers, dramatic productions, and other expressive activities are entitled to substantial deference. We need not now decide whether the same degree of deference is appropriate with respect to school-sponsored expressive activities at the college and university level.

a. White, J., concluded that Principal Reynolds acted reasonably in requiring deletion of the pages from the newspaper. In addition to concerns about privacy and failure to contact persons discussed in the stories, it was "not unreasonable for the principal to have concluded that [frank talk about sexual histories, albeit not graphic, with comments about use or nonuse of birth control] was inappropriate in a school-sponsored publication distributed to 14–year–old freshmen and presumably taken home to be read by students' even younger brothers and sisters."

utterly incredible. If he did, a fact that neither the District Court nor the Court of Appeals found, the lesson was lost on all but the psychic Spectrum staffer.

The Court's second excuse for deviating from precedent is the school's interest in shielding an impressionable high school audience from material whose substance is "unsuitable for immature audiences." [*Tinker*] teaches us that the state educator's undeniable, and undeniably vital, mandate to inculcate moral and political values is not a general warrant to act as "thought police" stifling discussion of all but state-approved topics and advocacy of all but the official position. [The] mere fact of school sponsorship does not, as the Court suggests, license such thought control in the high school, whether through school suppression of disfavored viewpoints or through official assessment of topic sensitivity. [Moreover, the] State's prerogative to dissolve the student newspaper entirely (or to limit its subject matter) no more entitles it to dictate which viewpoints students may express on its pages, than the State's prerogative to close down the schoolhouse entitles it to prohibit the nondisruptive expression of antiwar sentiment within its gates.

Official censorship of student speech on the ground that it addresses "potentially sensitive topics" is, for related reasons, equally impermissible. I would not begrudge an educator the authority to limit the substantive scope of a school-sponsored publication to a certain, objectively definable topic, such as literary criticism, school sports, or an overview of the school year. Unlike those determinate limitations, "potential topic sensitivity" is a vaporous nonstandard [that] invites manipulation to achieve ends that cannot permissibly be achieved through blatant viewpoint discrimination and chills student speech to which school officials might not object. * * *b

Notes

1. MORSE v. FREDERICK, 551 U.S. 393 (2007), per ROBERTS, C.J., upheld the suspension of a high school student for refusing to take down a banner at a school sponsored event that read "BONG HiTS 4 JESUS": "The concern is not that Fredericks speech is offensive, but that it was reasonably viewed as promoting illegal drug use."

ALITO, J., joined by Kennedy, J., concurring, joined the Court's opinion on the understanding that it "goes no further than to hold that a public school may restrict speech that a reasonable observer would interpret as advocating illegal drug use" and provides no support for restricting comments on political or social issues including "the wisdom of the war on drugs or legalizing marijuana for medicinal use."a

THOMAS, J., concurring, would overrule *Tinker*: "In light of the history of American public education, it cannot be seriously suggested that the First Amendment 'freedom of speech' encompasses a student's right to speak in public schools. Early public schools gave total control to teachers, who expected obedience and respect from students."

STEVENS, J., joined by Souter and Ginsburg, JJ., dissenting, thought it was not reasonable to conclude that the message on the banner advocated drug use or that it would persuade students to use drugs.

b. Brennan, J. further argued that the material deleted was not conceivably tortious and that less restrictive alternatives, such as more precise deletions, were readily available.

a. Breyer, J., concurring in part and dissenting in part would not have reached the First Amendment issue except to maintain that it was close enough that the high school principal could not be held liable for monetary damages.

2.   GARCETTI v. CEBALLOS, 547 U.S. 410 (2006) ruled that government employees had no First Amendment claim if penalized for speech uttered as a part of their official duties (as opposed to speech they might make as a citizen on a matter of public concern). The Court indicated that, "There is some argument that expression related to academic scholarship or classroom instruction implicates additional constitutional interests that are not fully accounted for by this Court's customary employee-speech jurisprudence."

SECTION 8.   THE ELECTRONIC MEDIA

The mass media are not invariably the most effective means of communication. For example, the right to place messages on utility poles concerning a lost dog may be more important than access to a radio or a television station. In some circumstances, picketing outside a school or placing leaflets in teachers' mailboxes may be the most effective communications medium. Moreover, the rise of the internet and various computer applications has contributed to newspaper closings, declines in audiences for broadcasters, and layoffs in the print and broadcast media. Nonetheless, the impact of the print and broadcast media remains important. Newspaper readership in the U.S. reaches about 100 million people daily. Network newscasts alone reach 20 to 30 million people every day. See Lee C. Bollinger, *Uninhibited, Robust, and Wide–Open* 85–86 (2010). This section considers first, cases in which government seeks to force newspapers and broadcasters to grant access and cases in which the First Amendment is claimed to demand access. Second, this section considers cases involving content regulation of the electronic media, particularly those where government seeks otherwise to regulate content in broadcasting, cable, and on the internet particularly with respect to sexually oriented material.

I.   ACCESS TO THE MASS MEDIA

MIAMI HERALD PUB. CO. v. TORNILLO, 418 U.S. 241 (1974), per BURGER, C.J., unanimously struck down a Florida "right of reply" statute, which required any newspaper that "assails" the personal character or official record of a candidate in any election to print, on demand, free of cost, any reply the candidate may make to the charges, in as conspicuous a place and the same kind of type, provided the reply takes up no more space than the charges. The opinion carefully explained the aim of the statute to "ensure that a wide variety of views reach the public" even though "chains of newspapers, national newspapers, national wire and news services, and one-newspaper towns, are the dominant features of a press that has become noncompetitive and enormously powerful and influential in its capacity to manipulate popular opinion and change the course of events," placing "in a few hands the power to inform the American people and shape public opinion."

Nonetheless, the Court concluded that to require the printing of a reply violated the First Amendment: "Compelling editors or publishers to publish that which "reason" tells them should not be published' is what is at issue in this case. The Florida statute operates as a command in the same sense as a statute or regulation forbidding appellant from publishing specified matter. [The] Florida statute exacts a penalty on the basis of the content of a newspaper. The first phase of the penalty resulting from the compelled printing of a reply is exacted in terms of the cost in printing and composing time and materials and in taking up space that could be devoted to other material the newspaper may have preferred to print. It is correct, as appellee contends, that a newspaper is not subject to the finite technological limitations of time that confront a broadcaster but it is not correct to say that, as an economic reality, a newspaper can proceed to infinite expansion of its column space to accommodate the replies that a government agency determines or a statute commands the readers should have available.

"Faced with the penalties that would accrue to any newspaper that published news or commentary arguably within the reach of the right of access statute, editors might well conclude that the safe course is to avoid controversy and that, under the operation of the Florida statute, political and electoral coverage would be blunted or reduced. Government enforced right of access inescapably 'dampens the vigor and limits the variety of public debate,' *New York Times.*

"Even if a newspaper would face no additional costs to comply with a compulsory access law and would not be forced to forego publication of news or opinion by the inclusion of a reply, the Florida statute fails to clear the barriers of the First Amendment because of its intrusion into the function of editors. A newspaper is more than a passive receptacle or conduit for news, comment, and advertising. The choice of material to go into a newspaper, and the decisions made as to limitations on the size of the paper, and content, and treatment of public issues and public officials—whether fair or unfair—constitutes the exercise of editorial control and judgment. It has yet to be demonstrated how governmental regulation of this crucial process can be exercised consistent with First Amendment guarantees of a free press as they have evolved to this time."a

---

The Federal Communications Commission for many years imposed on radio and television broadcasters the "fairness doctrine"—requiring that stations (1) devote a reasonable percentage of broadcast time to discussion of public issues and (2) assure fair coverage for each side. At issue in RED LION BROADCASTING CO. v. FCC, 395 U.S. 367 (1969), were the application of the fairness doctrine to a particular broadcastb and two specific access regulations promulgated under the doctrine: (1) the "political editorial" rule, requiring that when a broadcaster, in an editorial, "endorses or opposes" a political candidate, it must notify the candidate opposed, or the rivals of the candidate supported, and afford them a "reasonable opportunity" to respond; (2) the "personal attack" rule, requiring

a. Brennan, J., joined by Rehnquist, J., joined the Court's opinion in a short statement to express the understanding that it "implies no view upon the constitutionality of 'retraction' statutes affording plaintiffs able to prove defamatory falsehoods a statutory action to require publication of a retraction."

White, J., concurred. After agreeing that "prior compulsion by government in matters going to the very nerve center of a newspaper—the decision as to what copy will or will not be included in any given edition—collides with the First Amendment," he returned to his attack on *Gertz,* decided the same day: "Reaffirming the rule that the press cannot be forced to print an answer to a personal attack made by it [throws] into stark relief the consequences of the new balance forged by the Court in the companion case also announced today. *Gertz* goes far toward eviscerating the effectiveness of the ordinary libel action, which has long been the only potent response avail-

able to the private citizen libeled by the press. [To] me it is a near absurdity to so deprecate individual dignity, as the Court does in *Gertz,* and to leave the people at the complete mercy of the press, at least in this stage of our history when the press, as the majority in this case so well documents, is steadily becoming more powerful and much less likely to be deterred by threats of libel suits."

b. *Red Lion* grew out of a series of radio broadcasts by fundamentalist preacher Billy James Hargis, who had attacked Fred J. Cook, author of an article attacking Hargis and "hate clubs of the air." When Cook heard about the broadcast, he demanded that the station give him an opportunity to reply. Cook refused to pay for his "reply time" and the FCC ordered the station to give Cook the opportunity to reply whether or not he would pay for it. The Supreme Court upheld the order of free reply time.

that "when, during the presentation of views on a controversial issue of public importance, an attack is made on the honesty, character [or] integrity [of] an identified person or group," the person or group attacked must be given notice, a transcript of the attack, and an opportunity to respond.c "[I]n view of [the] scarcity of broadcast frequencies, the Government's role in allocating those frequencies, and the legitimate claims of those unable without government assistance to gain access to those frequencies for expression of their views," a 7–0 majority, per WHITE, J., upheld both access regulations:d

"[The broadcasters] contention is that the First Amendment protects their desire to use their allotted frequencies continuously to broadcast whatever they choose, and to exclude whomever they choose from ever using that frequency. No man may be prevented from saying or publishing what he thinks, or from refusing in his speech or other utterances to give equal weight to the views of his opponents. This right, they say, applies equally to broadcasters.

"Although broadcasting is clearly a medium affected by a First Amendment interest, differences in the characteristics of new media justify differences in the First Amendment standards applied to [them]. Just as the Government may limit the use of sound-amplifying equipment potentially so noisy that it drowns out civilized private speech, so may the Government limit the use of broadcast equipment. The right of free speech of a broadcaster, the user of a sound truck, or any other individual does not embrace a right to snuff out the free speech of [others].

"Where there are substantially more individuals who want to broadcast than there are frequencies to allocate, it is idle to posit an unabridgeable First Amendment right to broadcast comparable to the right of every individual to speak, write, or publish. [It] would be strange if the First Amendment, aimed at protecting and furthering communications, prevented the Government from making radio communication possible by requiring licenses to broadcast and by limiting the number of licenses so as not to overcrowd the spectrum. * * *

"By the same token, as far as the First Amendment is concerned those who are licensed stand no better than those to whom licenses are refused. A license permits broadcasting, but the licensee has no constitutional right [to] monopolize a radio frequency to the exclusion of his fellow citizens. There is nothing in the First Amendment which prevents the Government from requiring a licensee to share his frequency with others and to conduct himself as a proxy or fiduciary with obligations to present those views and voices which are representative of his community and which would otherwise, by necessity, be barred from the airwaves.

"[The] people as a whole retain their interest in free speech by radio and their collective right to have the medium function consistently with the ends and purposes of the First Amendment. It is the right of the viewers and listeners, not the right of the broadcasters, which is paramount. [It] is the purpose of the First Amendment to preserve an uninhibited marketplace of ideas in which truth will ultimately prevail, rather than to countenance monopolization of that market, whether it be by the Government itself or a private licensee. [It] is the right of the public to receive suitable access to social, political, esthetic, moral, and other ideas and experiences which is crucial [here.]

c. Excepted were "personal attacks [by] legally qualified candidates [on] other such candidates" and "bona fide newscasts, bona fide news interviews, and on-the-spot coverage of a bona fide news event."

d. Surprisingly, none of the justices joining White, J.'s opinion felt the need to make additional remarks, but Douglas, J., who did not participate in *Red Lion,* expressed his disagreement with it in the *CBS* case, infra.

"In terms of constitutional principle, and as enforced sharing of a scarce resource, the personal attack and political editorial rules are indistinguishable from the equal-time provision of § 315 [of the Communications Act], a specific enactment of Congress requiring [that stations allot equal time to qualified candidates for public office] and to which the fairness doctrine and these constituent regulations are important complements. [Nor] can we say that it is inconsistent with the First Amendment goal of producing an informed public capable of conducting its own affairs to require a broadcaster to permit answers to personal attacks occurring in the course of discussing controversial issues, or to require that the political opponents of those endorsed by the station be given a chance to communicate with the public. Otherwise, station owners and a few networks would have unfettered power to make time available only to the highest bidders, to communicate only their own views on public issues, people and candidates, and to permit on the air only those with whom they agreed. There is no sanctuary in the First Amendment for unlimited private censorship operating in a medium not open to all.

"[It is contended] that if political editorials or personal attacks will trigger an obligation in broadcasters to afford the opportunity for expression to speakers who need not pay for time and whose views are unpalatable to the licensees, then broadcasters will be irresistibly forced to self-censorship and their coverage of controversial public issues will be eliminated or at least rendered wholly ineffective. Such a result would indeed be a serious matter, [but] that possibility is at best speculative. [If these doctrines turn out to have this effect], there will be time enough to reconsider the constitutional implications. The fairness doctrine in the past has had no such overall effect. That this will occur now seems unlikely, however, since if present licensees should suddenly prove timorous, the Commission is not powerless to insist that they give adequate and fair attention to public issues. It does not violate the First Amendment to treat licensees given the privilege of using scarce radio frequencies as proxies for the entire community, obligated to give suitable time and attention to matters of great public concern. To condition the granting or renewal of licenses on a willingness to present representative community views on controversial issues is consistent with the ends and purposes of those constitutional provisions forbidding the abridgment of freedom of speech and freedom of the press."e

"Like many equal protection issues," observes Kenneth Karst, *Equality as a Central Principle in the First Amendment*, 43 U. Chi. L. Rev. 20, 45 (1975), "the media-access problem should be approached from two separate constitutional directions. First, what does the Constitution *compel* government to do in the way of equalizing? Second, what does the Constitution *permit* government to do in equalizing by statute?" *Red Lion* and *Miami Herald* presented the second question; the first is raised by COLUMBIA BROADCASTING SYSTEM, INC. v. DEMOCRATIC NAT'L COMMITTEE, 412 U.S. 94 (1973) (*CBS*): The FCC rejected the claims of Business Executives' Move for Vietnam Peace (BEM) and the Democratic National Committee (DNC) that "responsible" individuals and

---

e. The Court noted that it "need not deal with the argument that even if there is no longer a technological scarcity of frequencies limiting the number of broadcasters, there nevertheless is an economic scarcity in the sense that the Commission could or does limit entry to the broadcasting market on economic grounds and license no more stations than market will support. Hence, it is said, the fairness doctrine or its equivalent is essential to satisfy the claims of those excluded and of the public generally. A related argument, which we also put side, is that quite apart from scarcity of frequencies, technological or economic, Congress does not abridge freedom of speech or press by legislation directly or indirectly multiplying the voices and views presented to the public through time sharing, fairness doctrines, or other devices which limit or dissipate the power of those who sit astride the channels of communication with the general public."

groups are entitled to purchase advertising time to comment on public issues, even though the broadcaster has complied with the fairness doctrine. The District of Columbia Circuit held that "a flat ban on paid public issue announcements" violates the First Amendment "at least when other sorts of paid announcements are accepted," and remanded to the FCC to develop "reasonable procedures and regulations determining which and how many 'editorial advertisements' will be put on the air." The Supreme Court, per BURGER, C.J., reversed, holding that neither the "public interest" standard of the Communications Act (which draws heavily from the First Amendment) nor the First Amendment itself—assuming that refusal to accept such advertising constituted "governmental action" for First Amendment purposesa—requires broadcasters to accept paid editorial announcements. As pointed out in Vincent Blasi, *The Checking Value in First Amendment Theory*, 1977 Am.B.Found.Res.J. 521, 613–14 although the Chief Justice "built to some extent" on *Red Lion,* his opinion "evinced a most important change of emphasis. For whereas White, J., based his argument in *Red Lion* on the premise that broadcasters are mere 'proxies' or 'fiduciaries' for the general public, the Chief Justice's opinion [in *CBS*] invoked a concept of 'journalistic independence' or 'journalistic discretion,' the essence of which is that broadcasters do indeed have special First Amendment interests which have to be considered in the constitutional calculus."

Observed the Chief Justice: "[From various provisions of the Communications Act of 1934] it seems clear that Congress intended to permit private broadcasting to develop with the widest journalistic freedom consistent with its public obligations. Only when the interests of the public are found to outweigh the private journalistic interests of the broadcasters will government power be asserted within the framework of the Act. License renewal proceedings, in which the listening public can be heard, are a principal means of such regulation.

"[W]ith the advent of radio a half century ago, Congress was faced with a fundamental choice between total Government ownership and control of the new medium—the choice of most other countries—or some other alternative. Long before the impact and potential of the medium was realized, Congress opted for a system of private broadcasters licensed and regulated by Government. The legislative history suggests that this choice was influenced not only by traditional attitudes toward private enterprise, but by a desire to maintain for licensees, so far as consistent with necessary regulation, a traditional journalistic [role.]

"The regulatory scheme evolved slowly, but very early the licensee's role developed in terms of a 'public trustee' charged with the duty of fairly and impartially informing the public audience. In this structure the Commission acts in essence as an 'overseer,' but the initial and primary responsibility for fairness, balance, and objectivity rests with the licensee. This role of the Government as an overseer and ultimate arbiter and guardian of the public interest and the role of the licensee as a journalistic 'free agent' call for a delicate balancing of competing interests. The maintenance of this balance for more than 40 years has called on both the regulators and the licensees to walk a 'tightrope' to preserve the First Amendment values written into the Radio Act and its successor, the Communications Act.

a. Burger, C.J., joined by Stewart and Rehnquist, JJ., concluded that a broadcast licensee's refusal to accept an advertisement was not "governmental action" for First Amendment purposes. Although White, Blackmun and Powell, JJ., concurred in parts of the Chief Justice's opinion, they did not decide this question for, *assuming* governmental action, they found that the challenged ban did not violate the First Amendment. Douglas, J., who concurred in the result, assumed *no* governmental action. Dissenting, Brennan, J., joined by Marshall, J., found that the challenged ban did constitute "governmental action."

"The tensions inherent in such a regulatory structure emerge more clearly when we compare a private newspaper with a broadcast licensee. The power of a privately owned newspaper to advance its own political, social, and economic views is bounded by only two factors: first, the acceptance of a sufficient number of readers—and hence advertisers—to assure financial success; and, second, the journalistic integrity of its editors and publishers. A broadcast licensee has a large measure of journalistic freedom but not as large as that exercised by a newspaper. A licensee must balance what it might prefer to do as a private entrepreneur with what it is required to do as a 'public trustee.' To perform its statutory duties, the Commission must oversee without censoring. This suggests something of the difficulty and delicacy of administering the Communications Act—a function calling for flexibility and the capacity to adjust and readjust the regulatory mechanism to meet changing problems and needs.

"The licensee policy challenged in this case is intimately related to the journalistic role of a licensee for which it has been given initial and primary responsibility by Congress. The licensee's policy against accepting editorial advertising cannot be examined as an abstract proposition, but must be viewed in the context of its journalistic role. It does not help to press on us the idea that editorial ads are 'like' commercial ads, for the licensee's policy against editorial spot ads is expressly based on a journalistic judgment that 10– to 60–second spot announcements are ill-suited to intelligible and intelligent treatment of public issues; the broadcaster has chosen to provide a balanced treatment of controversial questions in a more comprehensive form. Obviously, the licensee's evaluation is based on its own journalistic judgment of priorities and newsworthiness.

"Moreover, the Commission has not fostered the licensee policy challenged here; it has simply declined to command particular action because it fell within the area of journalistic discretion. [The] Commission's reasoning, consistent with nearly 40 years of precedent, is that so long as a licensee meets its 'public trustee' obligation to provide balanced coverage of issues and events, it has broad discretion to decide how that obligation will be met. We do not reach the question whether the First Amendment or the Act can be read to preclude the Commission from determining that in some situations the public interest requires licensees to re-examine their policies with respect to editorial advertisements.b The Commission has not yet made such a determination; it has, for the present at least, found the policy to be within the sphere of journalistic discretion which Congress has left with the licensee.

"[I]t must constantly be kept in mind that the interest of the public is our foremost concern. With broadcasting, where the available means of communication are limited in both space and time, [Meiklejohn's admonition] that '[w]hat is essential is not that everyone shall speak, but that everything worth saying shall be said' is peculiarly appropriate.

"[Congress] has time and again rejected various legislative attempts that would have mandated a variety of forms of individual access. [It] has chosen to leave such questions with the Commission, to which it has given the flexibility to experiment with new ideas as changing conditions require. In this case, the

---

b. *Columbia Broadcasting System, Inc. v. FCC,* 453 U.S. 367 (1981), upheld FCC administration of a statutory provision guaranteeing "reasonable" access to the airwaves for federal election candidates. The Court, per Burger, C.J., observed that "the Court has never approved a *general* right of access to the media.

Miami Herald; *CBS v. DNC*. Nor do we do so today." But it found that the limited right of access "properly balances the First Amendment rights of federal candidates, the public, and broadcasters." White, J., joined by Rehnquist and Stevens, JJ., dissented on statutory grounds.

Commission has decided that on balance the undesirable effects of the right of access urged by respondents would outweigh the asserted [benefits.]

"The Commission was justified in concluding that the public interest in providing access to the marketplace of 'ideas and experiences' would scarcely be served by a system so heavily weighted in favor of the financially affluent, or those with access to wealth. Even under a first-come-first-served system [the] views of the affluent could well prevail over those of others, since they would have it within their power to purchase time more frequently. Moreover, there is the substantial danger [that] the time allotted for editorial advertising could be monopolized by those of one political persuasion.

"These problems would not necessarily be solved by applying the Fairness Doctrine, including the *Cullman* doctrine [requiring broadcasters to provide free time for the presentation of opposing views if a paid sponsor is unavailable], to editorial advertising. If broadcasters were required to provide time, free when necessary, for the discussion of the various shades of opinion on the issue discussed in the advertisement, the affluent could still determine in large part the issues to be discussed. Thus, the very premise of the Court of Appeals' holding— that a right of access is necessary to allow individuals and groups the opportunity for self-initiated speech—would have little meaning to those who could not afford to purchase time in the first instance.

"If the Fairness Doctrine were applied to editorial advertising, there is also the substantial danger that the effective operation of that doctrine would be jeopardized. To minimize financial hardship and to comply fully with its public responsibilities a broadcaster might well be forced to make regular programming time available to those holding a view different from that expressed in an editorial advertisement. [The] result would be a further erosion of the journalistic discretion of broadcasters in the coverage of public issues, and a transfer of control over the treatment of public issues from the licensees who are accountable for broadcast performance to private individuals who are not. The public interest would no longer be 'paramount' but rather subordinate to private whim especially since, under the Court of Appeals' decision, a broadcaster would be largely precluded from rejecting editorial advertisements that dealt with matters trivial or insignificant or already fairly covered by the broadcaster. If the Fairness Doctrine and the *Cullman* doctrine were suspended to alleviate these problems, as respondents suggest might be appropriate, the question arises whether we would have abandoned more than we have gained. Under such a regime the congressional objective of balanced coverage of public issues would be seriously threatened.

"Nor can we accept the Court of Appeals' view that every potential speaker is "he best judge' of what the listening public ought to hear or indeed the best judge of the merits of his or her views. All journalistic tradition and experience is to the contrary. For better or worse, editing is what editors are for; and editing is selection and choice of material. That editors—newspaper or broadcast—can and do abuse this power is beyond doubt, but that is not reason to deny the discretion Congress provided. Calculated risks of abuse are taken in order to preserve higher values. The presence of these risks is nothing new; the authors of the Bill of Rights accepted the reality that these risks were evils for which there was no acceptable remedy other than a spirit of moderation and a sense of responsibility—and civility—on the part of those who exercise the guaranteed freedoms of expression.

"It was reasonable for Congress to conclude that the public interest in being informed requires periodic accountability on the part of those who are entrusted with the use of broadcast frequencies, scarce as they are. In the delicate balancing historically followed in the regulation of broadcasting Congress and the Commission could appropriately conclude that the allocation of journalistic priorities should be concentrated in the licensee rather than diffused among many. This policy gives the public some assurance that the broadcaster will be answerable if he fails to meet their legitimate needs. No such accountability attaches to the private individual, whose only qualifications for using the broadcast facility may be abundant funds and a point of view. To agree that debate on public issues should be 'robust, and wide-open' does not mean that we should exchange 'public trustee' broadcasting, with all its limitations, for a system of self-appointed editorial commentators.

"[T]he risk of an enlargement of Government control over the content of broadcast discussion of public issues [is] inherent in the Court of Appeals' remand requiring regulations and procedures to sort out requests to be heard—a process involving the very editing that licensees now perform as to regular programming. [Under] a constitutionally commanded and government supervised right-of-access system urged by respondents and mandated by the Court of Appeals, the Commission would be required to oversee far more of the day-to-day operations of broadcasters' conduct, deciding such questions as whether a particular individual or group has had sufficient opportunity to present its viewpoint and whether a particular viewpoint has already been sufficiently aired. Regimenting broadcasters is too radical a therapy for the ailment respondents complain of. * * *

"The Commission is also entitled to take into account the reality that in a very real sense listeners and viewers constitute a 'captive audience.' [It] is no answer to say that because we tolerate pervasive commercial advertisement [we] can also live with its political counterparts.

"The rationale for the Court of Appeals' decision imposing a constitutional right of access on the broadcast media was that the licensee impermissibly discriminates by accepting commercial advertisements while refusing editorial advertisements. The court relied on [lower court cases] holding that state-supported school newspapers and public transit companies were forbidden by the First Amendment from excluding controversial editorial advertisements in favor of commercial advertisements.c The court also attempted to analogize this case to some of our decisions holding that States may not constitutionally ban certain protected speech while at the same time permitting other speech in public areas [citing e.g., *Grayned* and *Mosley,* Sec. 6 supra].

"These decisions provide little guidance, however, in resolving the question whether the First Amendment required the Commission to mandate a private right of access to the broadcast media. In none of those cases did the forum sought for expression have an affirmative and independent statutory obligation to provide full and fair coverage of public issues, such as Congress has imposed on all broadcast licensees. In short, there is no 'discrimination' against controversial speech present in this case. The question here is not whether there is to be discussion of controversial issues of public importance on the broadcast media, but rather who shall determine what issues are to be discussed by whom, and when."

Douglas, J., concurred in the result, but "for quite different reasons." Because the Court did not decide whether a broadcast licensee is "a federal agency within the context of this case," he assumed that it was not. He "fail[ed] to see," then "how constitutionally we can treat TV and the radio differently than we treat newspapers": "I did not participate in [*Red Lion* and] would not support it. The Fairness Doctrine has no place in our First Amendment regime. It puts the head

---

c. But see *Lehman v. Shaker Heights,* Sec.   6, II supra.

of the camel inside the tent and enables administration after administration to toy with TV or radio in order to serve its sordid or its benevolent ends. [The uniqueness of radio and TV] is due to engineering and technical problems. But the press in a realistic sense is likewise not available to all. [T]he daily newspapers now established are unique in the sense that it would be virtually impossible for a competitor to enter the field due to the financial exigencies of this era. The result is that in practical terms the newspapers and magazines, like the TV and radio, are available only to a select few. [That] may argue for a redefinition of the responsibilities of the press in First Amendment terms. But I do not think it gives us carte blanche to design systems of supervision and control nor empower [the government to] make 'some' laws 'abridging' freedom of the press. * * *

"Licenses are, of course, restricted in time and while, in my view, Congress has the power to make each license limited to a fixed term and nonreviewable, there is no power to deny renewals for editorial or ideological reasons [for] the First Amendment gives no preference to one school of thought over the others.

"The Court in today's decision by endorsing the Fairness Doctrine sanctions a federal saddle on broadcast licensees that is agreeable to the traditions of nations that never have known freedom of press and that is tolerable in countries that do not have a written constitution containing prohibitions as absolute as those in the First Amendment."d

BRENNAN, J., joined by Marshall, J., dissented, viewing "the *absolute* ban on the sale of air time for the discussion of controversial issues" as "governmental action" violating the First Amendment: "As a practical matter, the Court's reliance on the Fairness Doctrine as an 'adequate' alternative to editorial advertising seriously overestimates the ability—or willingness—of broadcasters to expose the public to the 'widest possible dissemination of information from diverse and antagonistic sources.' [Indeed,] in light of the strong interest of broadcasters in maximizing their audience, and therefore their profits, it seems almost naive to expect the majority of broadcasters to produce the variety and controversiality of material necessary to reflect a full spectrum of viewpoints. Stated simply, angry customers are not good customers and, in the commercial world of mass communications, it is simply 'bad business' to espouse—or even to allow others to espouse—the heterodox or the controversial. As a result, even under the Fairness Doctrine, broadcasters generally tend to permit only established—or at least moderated—views to enter the broadcast world's 'marketplace of ideas.'24

"Moreover, the Court's reliance on the Fairness Doctrine as the *sole* means of informing the public seriously misconceives and underestimates the public's interest in receiving ideas and information directly from the advocates of those ideas without the interposition of journalistic middlemen. Under the Fairness Doctrine, broadcasters decide what issues are 'important,' how 'fully' to cover them, and what format, time and style of coverage are 'appropriate.' The retention of such *absolute* control in the hands of a few government licensees is inimical to the First Amendment, for vigorous, free debate can be attained only when members of the public have at least *some* opportunity to take the initiative and editorial control into their own hands.

"[S]tanding alone, [the Fairness Doctrine] simply cannot eliminate the need for a further, complementary airing of controversial views through the limited availability of editorial advertising. Indeed, the availability of at least *some* opportunity for editorial advertising is imperative if we are ever to attain the 'free

---

d. Noting that his views "closely approach those expressed by Mr. Justice Douglas," Stewart, J., also concurred.

24. [Citing many secondary sources to support this statement.]

and general discussion of public matters [that] seems absolutely essential to prepare the people for an intelligent exercise of their rights as citizens.'

"Moreover, a proper balancing of the competing First Amendment interests at stake in this controversy must consider, not only the interests of broadcasters and of the listening and viewing public, but also the independent First Amendment interest of groups and individuals in effective self-expression. [I]n a time of apparently growing anonymity of the individual in our society, it is imperative that we take special care to preserve the vital First Amendment interest in assuring 'self-fulfillment [of expression] for each individual.' For our citizens may now find greater than ever the need to express their own views directly to the public, rather than through a governmentally appointed surrogate, if they are to feel that they can achieve at least some measure of control over their own destinies.

"[F]reedom of speech does not exist in the abstract. [It] can flourish only if it is allowed to operate in an effective forum—whether it be a public park, a schoolroom, a town meeting hall, a soapbox, or a radio and television frequency. For in the absence of an effective means of communication, the right to speak would ring hollow indeed. And, in recognition of these principles, we have consistently held that the First Amendment embodies not only the abstract right to be free from censorship, but also the right of an individual to utilize an appropriate and effective medium for the expression of his views.

"[W]ith the assistance of the Federal Government, the broadcast industry has become what is potentially the most efficient and effective 'marketplace of ideas' ever devised. [Thus], although 'full and free discussion' of ideas may have been a reality in the heyday of political pamphleteering, modern technological developments in the field of communications have made the soapbox orator and the leafleteer virtually obsolete. And, in light of the current dominance of the electronic media as the most effective means of reaching the public, any policy that *absolutely* denies citizens access to the airwaves necessarily renders even the concept of 'full and free discussion' practically meaningless.

"[T]he challenged ban can be upheld only if it is determined that such editorial advertising would unjustifiably impair the broadcaster's assertedly overriding interest in exercising *absolute* control over 'his' frequency. Such an analysis, however, hardly reflects the delicate balancing of interests that this sensitive question demands. Indeed, this 'absolutist' approach wholly disregards the competing First Amendment rights of all 'nonbroadcaster' citizens, ignores the teachings of our recent decision in *Red Lion,* and is not supported by the historical purposes underlying broadcast regulation in this Nation. [T]here is simply no overriding First Amendment interest of broadcasters that can justify the *absolute* exclusion of virtually all of our citizens from the most effective 'marketplace of ideas' ever devised.

"[T]his case deals *only* with the allocation of *advertising* time—airtime that broadcasters regularly relinquish to others without the retention of significant editorial control. Thus, we are concerned here not with the speech of broadcasters themselves but, rather, with their 'right' to decide which *other* individuals will be given an opportunity to speak in a forum that has already been opened to the public.

"Viewed in this context, the *absolute* ban on editorial advertising seems particularly offensive because, although broadcasters refuse to sell any airtime whatever to groups or individuals wishing to speak out on controversial issues of public importance, they make such airtime readily available to those 'commercial' advertisers who seek to peddle their goods and services to the public. [Yet an] individual seeking to discuss war, peace, pollution, or the suffering of the poor is denied this right to speak. Instead, he is compelled to rely on the beneficence of a corporate 'trustee' appointed by the Government to argue his case for him.

"It has been long recognized, however, that although access to public forums may be subjected to reasonable 'time, place, and manner' regulations, '[s]elective exclusions from a public forum, may not be based on *content* alone.' *Mosley* (emphasis added). Here, of course, the differential treatment accorded 'commercial' and 'controversial' speech clearly violates that principle. Moreover, and not without some irony, the favored treatment given 'commercial' speech under the existing scheme clearly reverses traditional First Amendment priorities. For it has generally been understood that 'commercial' speech enjoys *less* First Amendment protection than speech directed at the discussion of controversial issues of public importance."

Notes

1. ***The fairness doctrine repealed.*** The FCC concluded a 15 month administrative proceeding with an official denunciation of the fairness doctrine, pointing in particular to the marked increase in the information services marketplace since *Red Lion* and the effects of the doctrine in application. FCC, [*General*] *Fairness Doctrine Obligations of Broadcast Licensees*, 102 F.C.C.2d 143 (1985). *Syracuse Peace Council*, 2 FCC Rcd 5043 (1987) held that "under the constitutional standard established by *Red Lion* and its progeny, the fairness doctrine contravenes the First Amendment and its enforcement is no longer in the public interest."a

2. ***Candidate debates on public television.*** A third party candidate was excluded from a debate sponsored by a public television station on the ground that he had little popular support. He claimed a right of access. *Arkansas Educational Television Comm'n v. Forbes*, 523 U.S. 666 (1998), concluded that a candidate debate sponsored by a state-owned public television broadcaster was a nonpublic forum subject to constitutional restraints (because the views expressed were those of the candidates, not the broadcaster and because of the importance of such debates to the political process), but that the broadcaster's decision to exclude a particular candidate was reasonable.

3. ***Cable Television.*** The Cable Television and Consumer Protection and Competition Act of 1992 required cable television systems to devote a portion of their channels to local broadcasters including commercial stations and public broadcast stations.b Congress was concerned about the monopolistic character of

---

a. *Syracuse Peace Council v. FCC*, 867 F.2d 654 (D.C.Cir.1989), affirmed the FCC's determination that the fairness doctrine no longer serves the public interest without reaching constitutional issues. On June 20, 1987, President had vetoed congressional legislation designed to preserve the fairness doctrine on the ground that the legislation was unconstitutional. *Radio-Television News Directors Assoc. v. FCC*, 229 F.3d 269 (D.C.Cir.2000), ordered the FCC to vacate the personal attack rules with the understanding that the rules might be reinstituted if the Commission conducted a new rule-making proceeding to determine whether the public interest, consistent with the First Amendment, required them.

b. It also required that they be placed in the same numerical position as when broadcast over the air. *Los Angeles v. Preferred Communications, Inc.*, 476 U.S. 488 (1986), per REHNQUIST, J., upheld the refusal to dismiss a complaint brought by a cable company demanding access to a city's utility poles and asserting a right to be free of government-mandated channels: "Cable television partakes of some of the aspects of speech and the communication of ideas as do the traditional enterprises of newspapers and [book publishers]. Respondent's proposed activities would seem to implicate First Amendment interests as do the activities of wireless broadcasters, which were found to fall within the ambit of the First Amendment in [*Red Lion*]. Of course, ['Even] protected

cable operations in most localities and the economic incentives for cable operators to favor their own programming. It also pointed to the importance of maintaining local broadcasting. TURNER BROADCASTING SYSTEM, INC. v. FCC, 512 U.S. 622 (1994), per KENNEDY, J., joined by Rehnquist, C.J., and Blackmun and Souter, JJ., upheld the requirement so long as the Government could demonstrate on remand that in the absence of legislation, a large number of broadcast stations would not be carried or would be adversely repositioned, that such stations would be at serious risk of financial difficulty, that the cable operators' programming selections (as opposed to using unused channel capacity) would not be excessively affected, and that no less restrictive alternative means existed.c

After remand, TURNER BROADCASTING SYSTEM, INC. v. FCC, 520 U.S. 180 (1997), per KENNEDY, J., joined by Rehnquist, C.J., Stevens, and Souter, JJ., upheld the must-carry provisions. Applying the *O'Brien* test, he emphasized the importance of deferring to Congress so long as it had "drawn reasonable inferences based upon substantial evidence." He found that the legislation was narrowly tailored to preserve the benefits of local broadcast television, to promote widespread dissemination of information from a multiplicity of sources, and to promote fair competition.

BREYER, J., concurring, joined Kennedy, J.'s opinion except for his discussion and conclusion regarding the fair competition rationale:d "Whether or not the statute does or does not sensibly compensate for some significant market defect, it undoubtedly seeks to provide over-the-air viewers who *lack* cable with a rich mix of over-the-air programming by guaranteeing the over-the-air stations that provide such programming with the extra dollars that an additional cable audience will generate. I believe that this purpose-to assure the over-the-air public 'access to a multiplicity of information sources,' provides sufficient basis for rejecting appellants' First Amendment claim.

"I do not deny that the compulsory carriage that creates the 'guarantee' extracts a serious First Amendment price. It interferes with the protected interests of the cable operators to choose their own programming; it prevents displaced cable program providers from obtaining an audience; and it will sometimes prevent some cable viewers from watching what, in its absence, would have been their preferred set of programs. This 'price' amounts to a 'suppression of speech.'"

Breyer, J., observed that a cable system, physically dependent upon the availability of space along city streets, at present (perhaps less in the future) typically faces little competition, that it therefore constitutes a kind of bottleneck that controls the range of viewer choice (whether or not it uses any consequent economic power for economically predatory purposes), and that *some* degree—at least a limited degree of governmental intervention and control through regulation can prove appropriate when justified under *O'Brien* (at least when not 'content based'). Cf. *Red Lion*. Breyer, J., concluded that the statute survived

---

speech is not equally permissible in all places and at all times.' *Cornelius*. Moreover, where speech and conduct are joined in a single course of action, the First Amendment values must be balanced against competing societal interests. See, e.g., *Vincent*; *O'Brien*." The Court postponed fuller discussion of any cable rights until a factual record had been developed.

c. Blackmun, J., concurring, emphasized the importance of deferring to Congress during the new proceedings. Stevens, J., concurring, reluctantly joined the order to remand; he would have preferred to affirm the must-carry legislation without further proceedings. O'Connor, joined by Scalia, Thomas, and Ginsburg, voted to invalidate the legislation.

d. Stevens, J., also filed a concurring opinion.

" 'intermediate scrutiny,' whether or not the statute [was] properly tailored to Congress' purely economic objectives."

O'CONNOR, J., joined by Scalia, Thomas, and Ginsburg, JJ., dissenting, argued again that strict scrutiny should apply, agreed that deference was owed to Congress "in its predictive judgments and its evaluation of complex economic questions," but maintained that even under intermediate scrutiny, the Court had an independent duty to examine with care the Congressional interests, the findings, and the fit between the goals and consequences. She criticized the Court for being too deferential even on the assumption that the legislation was content neutral. On her analysis, the record did not support either the conclusion that cable posed a significant threat to local broadcast markets or that the act was narrowly tailored to deal with anti-competitive conduct.

II. THE ELECTRONIC MEDIA AND CONTENT REGULATION

FCC v. PACIFICA FOUNDATION

438 U.S. 726, 98 S.Ct. 3026, 57 L.Ed.2d 1073 (1978).

JUSTICE STEVENS delivered the opinion of the Court (Parts I, II, III, and IV–C) and an opinion in which CHIEF JUSTICE BURGER and JUSTICE REHNQUIST joined (Parts IV–A and IV–B).

[In an early afternoon weekday broadcast which was devoted that day to contemporary attitudes toward the use of language, respondent's New York radio station aired a 12–minute selection called "Filthy Words," from a comedy album by a satiric humorist, George Carlin. The monologue, which had evoked frequent laughter from a live theater audience, began by referring to Carlin's thought about the seven words you can't say on the public airwaves, "the ones you definitely wouldn't say ever." He then listed the words ("shit," "piss," "fuck," "motherfucker," "cocksucker," "cunt," and "tits"), "the ones that will curve your spine, grow hair on your hands and (laughter) maybe, even bring us, God help us, peace without honor (laughter) um, and a bourbon (laughter)," and repeated them over and over in a variety of colloquialisms. Immediately prior to the monologue, listeners were advised that it included sensitive language which some might regard as offensive. Those who might be offended were advised to change the station and return in fifteen minutes.

[The FCC received a complaint from a man stating that while driving in his car with his young son he had heard the broadcast of the Carlin monologue. The FCC issued an order to be "associated with the station's license file, and in the event that subsequent complaints are received, the Commission will then decide whether it should utilize any of the available sanctions it has been granted by Congress."]

The Commission characterized the language used in the Carlin monologue as "patently offensive," though not necessarily obscene, and expressed the opinion that it should be regulated by principles analogous to those found in the law of nuisance where the "law generally speaks to *channeling* behavior more than actually prohibiting [it]."5

Applying these considerations to the language used in the monologue as broadcast by respondent, the Commission concluded that certain words depicted sexual and excretory activities in a patently offensive manner, noted that they

---

5. Thus, the Commission suggested, if an offensive broadcast had literary, artistic, political or scientific value, and were preceded by warnings, it might not be indecent in the late evening, but would be so during the day, when children are in the audience.

"were broadcast at a time when children were undoubtedly in the audience (i.e., in the early afternoon)," and that the prerecorded language, with these offensive words "repeated over and over," was "deliberately broadcast." In summary, the Commission stated: "We therefore hold that the language as broadcast was indecent [under 18 U.S.C. 1464]."

IV. Pacifica [argues] that the Commission's construction of the statutory language broadly encompasses so much constitutionally protected speech that reversal is required even if Pacifica's broadcast of the "Filthy Words" monologue is not itself protected by the First Amendment. * * *

A. The first argument fails because our review is limited to the question whether the Commission has the authority to proscribe this particular broadcast. As the Commission itself emphasized, its order was "issued in a specific factual context." That approach is appropriate for courts as well as the Commission when regulation of indecency is at stake, for indecency is largely a function of context—it cannot be adequately judged in the abstract. * * *

It is true that the Commission's order may lead some broadcasters to censor themselves. At most, however, the Commission's definition of indecency will deter only the broadcasting of patently offensive references to excretory and sexual organs and activities.[18] While some of these references may be protected, they surely lie at the periphery of First Amendment concern. * * * Invalidating any rule on the basis of its hypothetical application to situations not before the Court is "strong medicine" to be applied "sparingly and only as a last resort." *Broadrick* [Sec. I, 5 supra]. We decline to administer that medicine to preserve the vigor of patently offensive sexual and excretory speech.

B. [The] words of the Carlin monologue are unquestionably "speech" within the meaning of the First Amendment. [The] question in this case is whether a broadcast of patently offensive words dealing with sex and excretion may be regulated because of its content.[20] Obscene materials have been denied the protection of the First Amendment because their content is so offensive to contemporary moral standards. *Roth.* But the fact that society may find speech offensive is not a sufficient reason for suppressing it. Indeed, if it is the speaker's opinion that gives offense, that consequence is a reason for according it constitutional protection. For it is a central tenet of the First Amendment that the government must remain neutral in the marketplace of ideas. If there were any reason to believe that the Commission's characterization of the Carlin monologue as offensive could be traced to its political content—or even to the fact that it satirized contemporary attitudes about four letter words[22]—First Amendment protection might be required. But that is simply not this case. These words offend for the same reasons that obscenity offends. Their place in the hierarchy of First

---

18. A requirement that indecent language be avoided will have its primary effect on the form, rather than the content, of serious communication. There are few, if any, thoughts that cannot be expressed by the use of less offensive language.

[*FCC v. Fox Television Stations, Inc.*, 129 S.Ct. 1800 (2009), per Scalia, J., observed that "any chilled references to excretory and sexual material 'surely lie at the periphery of First Amendment concern.'"]

20. Although neither Justice Powell nor Justice Brennan directly confronts this question, both have answered it affirmatively, the latter explicitly, at fn. 3, infra, and the former

implicitly by concurring in a judgment that could not otherwise stand.

22. The monologue does present a point of view; it attempts to show that the words it uses are "harmless" and that our attitudes toward them are "essentially silly." The Commission objects, not to this point of view, but to the way in which it is expressed. The belief that these words are harmless does not necessarily confer a First Amendment privilege to use them while proselytizing just as the conviction that obscenity is harmless does not license one to communicate that conviction by the indiscriminate distribution of an obscene leaflet.

Amendment values was aptly sketched by Justice Murphy when he said, "such utterances are no essential part of any exposition of ideas, and are of such slight social value as a step to truth that any benefit that may be derived from them is clearly outweighed by the social interest in order and morality." *Chaplinsky.*

Although these words ordinarily lack literary, political, or scientific value, they are not entirely outside the protection of the First Amendment. Some uses of even the most offensive words are unquestionably protected. Indeed, we may assume, arguendo, that this monologue would be protected in other contexts. [It] is a characteristic of speech such as this that both its capacity to offend and its "social value," to use Justice Murphy's term, vary with the circumstances. Words that are commonplace in one setting are shocking in another. To paraphrase Justice Harlan, one occasion's lyric is another's vulgarity. Cf. *Cohen v. California.*25

In this case it is undisputed that the content of Pacifica's broadcast was "vulgar," "offensive," and "shocking." Because content of that character is not entitled to absolute constitutional protection under all circumstances, we must consider its context in order to determine whether the Commission's action was constitutionally permissible.

C. We have long recognized that each medium of expression presents special First Amendment problems. And of all forms of communication, it is broadcasting that has received the most limited First Amendment [protection.]

The reasons for these distinctions are complex, but two have relevance to the present case. First, the broadcast media have established a uniquely pervasive presence in the lives of all Americans. Patently offensive, indecent material presented over the airwaves confronts the citizen, not only in public, but also in the privacy of the home, where the individual's right to be let alone plainly outweighs the First Amendment rights of an intruder. *Rowan v. Post Office Dept.,* 397 U.S. 728. Because the broadcast audience is constantly tuning in and out, prior warnings cannot completely protect the listener or viewer from unexpected program content. To say that one may avoid further offense by turning off the radio when he hears indecent language is like saying that the remedy for an assault is to run away after the first blow.27 * * *

Second, broadcasting is uniquely accessible to children, even those too young to read. Although Cohen's written message might have been incomprehensible to a first grader, Pacifica's broadcast could have enlarged a child's vocabulary in an instant. Other forms of offensive expression may be withheld from the young without restricting the expression at its source. Bookstores and motion picture theaters, for example, may be prohibited from making indecent material available to children. We held in *Ginsberg* [Sec. 1, III, B supra] that the government's interest in the "well being of its youth" and in supporting "parents' claim to

25. The importance of context is illustrated by the *Cohen* case. [So] far as the evidence showed no one in the courthouse was offended by [Cohen's jacket.]

In holding that criminal sanctions could not be imposed on Cohen for his political statement in a public place, the Court rejected the argument that his speech would offend unwilling viewers; it noted that "there was no evidence that persons powerless to avoid [his] conduct did in fact object to it." In contrast, in this case the Commission was responding to a listener's strenuous complaint, and Pacifica does not question its determination that this afternoon broadcast was likely to offend listeners. It should be noted that the Commission imposed a far more moderate penalty on Pacifica than the state court imposed on Cohen. Even the strongest civil penalty at the Commission's command does not include criminal prosecution.

27. Outside the home, the balance between the offensive speaker and the unwilling audience may sometimes tip in favor of the speaker, requiring the offended listener to turn away. See *Erznoznik.* * * *

authority in their own household" justified the regulation of otherwise protected expression.28 * * *

It is appropriate, in conclusion, to emphasize the narrowness of our holding. This case does not involve a two-way radio conversation between a cab driver and a dispatcher, or a telecast of an Elizabethan comedy. We have not decided that an occasional expletive in either setting would justify any sanction or, indeed, that this broadcast would justify a criminal prosecution. The Commission's decision rested entirely on a nuisance rationale under which context is all-important.

[R]eversed.

JUSTICE POWELL, with whom JUSTICE BLACKMUN joins, concurring.

[T]he language employed is, to most people, vulgar and offensive. It was chosen specifically for this quality, and it was repeated over and over as a sort of verbal shock treatment. [In] essence, the Commission sought to "channel" the monologue to hours when the fewest unsupervised children would be exposed to it. In my view, this consideration provides strong support for the Commission's holding.

[The] Commission properly held that the speech from which society may attempt to shield its children is not limited to that which appeals to the youthful prurient interest. The language involved in this case is as potentially degrading and harmful to children as representations of many erotic acts.

In most instances, the dissemination of this kind of speech to children may be limited without also limiting willing adults' access to it. Sellers of printed and recorded matter and exhibitors of motion pictures and live performances may be required to shut their doors to children, but such a requirement has no effect on adults' access. See *Ginsberg*. The difficulty is that [d]uring most of the broadcast hours, both adults and unsupervised children are likely to be in the broadcast audience, and the broadcaster cannot reach willing adults without also reaching children. This, as the Court emphasizes, is one of the distinctions between the broadcast and other media to which we often have adverted as justifying a different treatment of the broadcast media for First Amendment purposes. In my view, the Commission was entitled to give substantial weight to this difference in reaching its decision in this case.

[Another difference] is that broadcasting—unlike most other forms of communication—comes directly into the home, the one place where people ordinarily have the right not to be assaulted by uninvited and offensive sights and sounds. *Erznoznik*; *Cohen*; *Rowan*. * * * "That we are often 'captives' outside the sanctuary of the home and subject to objectionable speech and other sound does not mean we must be captives everywhere." *Rowan*. The Commission also was entitled to give this factor appropriate weight in the circumstances of the instant case. This is not to say, however, that the Commission has an unrestricted license to decide what speech, protected in other media, may be banned from the airwaves in order to protect unwilling adults from momentary exposure to it in their homes.2 * * *

28. The Commission's action does not by any means reduce adults to hearing only what is fit for children. Cf. *Butler v. Michigan* [Sec. 1, III, B supra]. Adults who feel the need may purchase tapes and records or go to theatres and nightclubs to hear these words. In fact, the Commission has not unequivocally closed even broadcasting to speech of this sort; whether broadcast audiences in the late evening contain so few children that playing this monologue would be permissible is an issue neither the Commission nor this Court has decided.

2. It is true that the radio listener quickly may tune out speech that is offensive to him. In addition, broadcasters may preface potentially offensive programs with warnings. But such warnings do not help the unsuspecting listener who tunes in at the middle of a pro-

[M]y views are generally in accord with what is said in Part IV(C) of opinion. I therefore join that portion of his opinion. I do not join Part IV(B), however, because I do not subscribe to the theory that the Justices of this Court are free generally to decide on the basis of its content which speech protected by the First Amendment is most "valuable" and hence deserving of the most protection, and which is less "valuable" and hence deserving of less protection.3 In my view, the result in this case does not turn on whether Carlin's monologue, viewed as a whole, or the words that comprise it, have more or less "value" than a candidate's campaign speech. This is a judgment for each person to make, not one for the judges to impose upon him.4

The result turns instead on the unique characteristics of the broadcast media, combined with society's right to protect its children from speech generally agreed to be inappropriate for their years, and with the interest of unwilling adults in not being assaulted by such offensive speech in their homes. Moreover, I doubt whether today's decision will prevent any adult who wishes to receive Carlin's message in Carlin's own words from doing so, and from making for himself a value judgment as to the merit of the message and words. These are the grounds upon which I join the judgment of the Court as to Part IV.

JUSTICE BRENNAN, with whom JUSTICE MARSHALL joins, dissenting.

[T]he Court refuses to embrace the notion, completely antithetical to basic First Amendment values, that the degree of protection the First Amendment affords protected speech varies with the social value ascribed to that speech by five Members of this Court. See opinion of Justice Powell. Moreover, [all] Members of the Court agree that [the monologue] does not fall within one of the categories of speech, such as "fighting words," or obscenity, that is totally without First Amendment protection. [Yet] a majority of the Court1 nevertheless finds that, on the facts of this case, the FCC is not constitutionally barred from imposing sanctions on Pacifica for its airing of the Carlin monologue. * * *

[A]n individual's actions in switching on and listening to communications transmitted over the public airways and directed to the public at-large do not implicate fundamental privacy interests, even when engaged in within the home. Instead, because the radio is undeniably a public medium, these actions are more properly viewed as a decision to take part, if only as a listener, in an ongoing public discourse. Although an individual's decision to allow public radio communications into his home undoubtedly does not abrogate all of his privacy interests, the residual privacy interests he retains vis-à-vis the communication he voluntari-

---

gram. In this respect, too, broadcasting appears to differ from books and records, which may carry warnings on their faces, and from motion pictures and live performances, which may carry warnings on their marquees.

3. The Court has, however, created a limited exception to this rule in order to bring commercial speech within the protection of the First Amendment. See *Ohralik* [Sec. 3, II supra].

4. For much the same reason, I also do not join Part IV(A). I had not thought that the application vel non of overbreadth analysis should depend on the Court's judgment as to the value of the protected speech that might be deterred. Except in the context of commercial speech, see *Bates* [Sec. 3, II supra], it has not

in the past. See, e.g., *Lewis v. New Orleans*; *Gooding*.

As Justice Stevens points out, however, the Commission's order was limited to the facts of this case; "it did not purport to engage in formal rulemaking or in the promulgation of any regulations." In addition, since the Commission may be expected to proceed cautiously, as it has in the past, I do not foresee an undue "chilling" effect on broadcasters' exercise of their rights. I agree, therefore, that respondent's overbreadth challenge is meritless.

1. Where I refer without differentiation to the actions of "the Court," my reference is to this majority, which consists of my Brothers Powell and Stevens and those Members of the Court joining their separate opinions.

ly admits into his home are surely no greater than those of the people present in the corridor of the Los Angeles courthouse in [Cohen].

Even if an individual who voluntarily opens his home to radio communications retains privacy interests of sufficient moment to justify a ban on protected speech if those interests are "invaded in an essentially intolerable manner," *Cohen,* the very fact that those interests are threatened only by a radio broadcast precludes any intolerable invasion of privacy; for unlike other intrusive modes of communication, such as sound trucks, "[t]he radio can be turned off"—and with a minimum of effort. [Whatever] the minimal discomfort suffered by a listener who inadvertently tunes into a program he finds offensive during the brief interval before he can simply extend his arm and switch stations or flick the "off" button, it is surely worth the candle to preserve the broadcaster's right to send, and the right of those interested to receive, a message entitled to full First Amendment protection. * * *

The Court's balance, of necessity, fails to accord proper weight to the interests of listeners who wish to hear broadcasts the FCC deems offensive. It permits majoritarian tastes completely to preclude a protected message from entering the homes of a receptive, unoffended minority. No decision of this Court supports such a result. Where the individuals comprising the offended majority may freely choose to reject the material being offered, we have never found their privacy interests of such moment to warrant the suppression of speech on privacy grounds. [In] *Rowan,* the Court upheld a statute, permitting householders to require that mail advertisers stop sending them lewd or offensive materials and remove their names from mailing lists. Unlike the situation here, householders who wished to receive the sender's communications were not prevented from doing so. Equally important, the determination of offensiveness vel non under the statute involved in *Rowan* was completely within the hands of the individual householder; no governmental evaluation of the worth of the mail's content stood between the mailer and the householder. In contrast, the visage of the censor is all too discernable here. * * *

Because the Carlin monologue is obviously not an erotic appeal to the prurient interests of children, the Court, for the first time, allows the government to prevent minors from gaining access to materials that are not obscene, and are therefore protected, as to them.2 It thus ignores our recent admonition that "[s]peech that is neither obscene as to youths nor subject to some other legitimate proscription cannot be suppressed solely to protect the young from ideas or images that a legislative body thinks unsuitable for them." *Erznoznik.*3 The Court's refusal to follow its own pronouncements is especially lamentable since it has the anomalous subsidiary effect, at least in the radio context at issue here, of making completely unavailable to adults material which may not constitutionally be kept even from children. * * * *Yoder* and *Pierce,* hold that parents, *not* the govern-

2. Even if the monologue appealed to the prurient interest of minors, it would not be obscene as to them unless, as to them, "the work, taken as a whole, lacks serious literary, artistic, political, or scientific value." *Miller.*

3. It may be that a narrowly drawn regulation prohibiting the use of offensive language on broadcasts directed specifically at younger children constitutes one of the "other legitimate proscription[s]" alluded to in *Erznoznik.* This is so both because of the difficulties inherent in adapting the *Miller* formulation to communications received by young children, and because such children are "not possessed of

that full capacity for individual choice which is the presupposition of the First Amendment guarantees." *Ginsberg.* (Stewart, J., concurring). I doubt, as my Brother Stevens suggests, that such a limited regulation amounts to a regulation of speech based on its content, since, by hypothesis, the only persons at whom the regulated communication is directed are incapable of evaluating its content. To the extent that such a regulation is viewed as a regulation based on content, it marks the outermost limits to which content regulation is permissible.

ment, have the right to make certain decisions regarding the upbringing of their children. As surprising as it may be to individual Members of this Court, some parents may actually find Mr. Carlin's unabashed attitude towards the seven "dirty words" healthy, and deem it desirable to expose their children to the manner in which Mr. Carlin defuses the taboo surrounding the words. Such parents may constitute a minority of the American public, but the absence of great numbers willing to exercise the right to raise their children in this fashion does not alter the right's nature or its existence. Only the Court's regrettable decision does that.

As demonstrated above, neither of the factors relied on by both [Powell and Stevens, JJ.]—the intrusive nature of radio and the presence of children in the listening audience—can, when taken on its own terms, support the FCC's disapproval of the Carlin monologue. [N]either of the opinions comprising the Court serve to clarify the extent to which the FCC may assert the privacy and children-in-the-audience rationales as justification for expunging from the airways protected communications the Commission finds offensive. Taken to their logical extreme, these rationales would support the cleansing of public radio of any "four-letter words" whatsoever, regardless of their context. The rationales could justify the banning from radio of a myriad of literary works, novels, poems, and plays by the likes of Shakespeare, Joyce, Hemingway, Ben Jonson, Henry Fielding, Robert Burns, and Chaucer; they could support the suppression of a good deal of political speech, such as the Nixon tapes; and they could even provide the basis for imposing sanctions for the broadcast of certain portions of the Bible.

In order to dispel the spectre of the possibility of so unpalatable a degree of censorship, and to defuse Pacifica's overbreadth challenge, the FCC insists that it desires only the authority to reprimand a broadcaster on facts analogous to those present in this case. [Powell and Stevens, JJ.] take the FCC at its word, and consequently do no more than permit the Commission to censor the afternoon broadcast of the "sort of verbal shock treatment" involved [here]. I would place the responsibility and the right to weed worthless and offensive communications from the public airways where it belongs and where, until today, it resided: in a public free to choose those communications worthy of its attention from a marketplace unsullied by the censor's hand. * * *

My Brother Stevens [finds] solace in his conviction that "[t]here are few, if any, thoughts that cannot be expressed by the use of less offensive language." The idea that the content of a message and its potential impact on any who might receive it can be divorced from the words that are the vehicle for its expression is transparently fallacious. A given word may have a unique capacity to capsule an idea, evoke an emotion, or conjure up an image. Indeed, for those of us who place an appropriately high value on our cherished First Amendment rights, the word "censor" is such a word. Justice Harlan, speaking for the Court, recognized the truism that a speaker's choice of words cannot surgically be separated from the ideas he desires to express when he warned that "we cannot indulge the facile assumption that one can forbid particular words without also running a substantial risk of suppressing ideas in the process."

[Stevens, J.] also finds relevant to his First Amendment analysis the fact that "[a]dults who feel the need may purchase tapes and records or go to theatres and nightclubs to hear [the tabooed] words." [Powell, J.,] agrees. [The] opinions of my Brethren display both a sad insensitivity to the fact that these alternatives involve the expenditure of money, time, and effort that many of those wishing to hear Mr. Carlin's message may not be able to afford, and a naive innocence of the reality that in many cases, the medium may well be the message.

The Court apparently believes that the FCC's actions here can be analogized to the zoning ordinances upheld in *American Mini Theatres.* For two reasons, it is wrong. First, the zoning ordinances found to pass constitutional muster [had] valid goals other than the channeling of protected speech. No such goals are present here. Second, [the] ordinances did not restrict the access of distributors or exhibitors to the market or impair the viewing public's access to the regulated material. Again, this is not the situation here.

[T]here runs throughout the opinions of my Brothers Powell and Stevens [a] depressing inability to appreciate that in our land of cultural pluralism, there are many who think, act, and talk differently from the Members of this Court, and who do not share their fragile sensibilities. It is only an acute ethnocentric myopia that enables the Court [to blink at] persons who do not share the Court's view as to which words or expressions are acceptable and who, for a variety of reasons, including a conscious desire to flout majoritarian conventions, express themselves using words that may be regarded as offensive by those from different socio-economic backgrounds.8 In this context, the Court's decision may be seen for what, in the broader perspective, it really is: another of the dominant culture's inevitable efforts to force those groups who do not share its mores to conform to its way of thinking, acting, and speaking. * * *a

Notes

1. ***Telephonic "indecency" compared.*** SABLE COMMUNICATIONS v. FCC, 492 U.S. 115 (1989), per WHITE, J., invalidated a congressional ban on "indecent" interstate commercial telephone messages, i.e., "dial-a-porn."b The Court thought *Pacifica* was "readily distinguishable from this case, most obviously because it did not involve a total ban on broadcasting indecent material. [Second,] there is no 'captive audience' problem here; callers will generally not be unwilling listeners. [Third,] the congressional record contains no legislative findings that would justify us in concluding that there is no constitutionally acceptable less restrictive means, short of a total ban, to achieve the Government's interest in protecting minors."

2. ***Internet "indecency" compared.*** (a) Two provisions of the Communications Decency Act ("CDA") sought to protect minors from indecent or patently offensive material on the Internet. 47 U.S.C. § 223(a) prohibited the knowing transmission of indecent messages to any recipient under 18 years of age. 47 U.S.C. § 223(d) prohibited the knowing sending or displaying of patently offensive messages in a manner that is available to a person under 18 years of age. Patently offensive was defined as any "image or other communication that in context, depicts or describes, in terms patently offensive as measured by contemporary community standards, sexual or excretory activities or organs * * *." RENO v.

---

8. Under the approach taken by my Brother Powell, the availability of broadcasts *about* groups whose members comprise such audiences might also be affected. Both news broadcasts about activities involving these groups and public affairs broadcasts about their concerns are apt to contain interviews, statements, or remarks by group leaders and members which may contain offensive language to an extent my Brother Powell finds unacceptable.

a. Stewart, J., joined by Brennan, White, and Marshall, JJ., dissenting maintained that the Commission lacked statutory authority to issue its order and did not reach the constitutional question.

b. The Court upheld a ban on "obscene" interstate commercial telephonic messages. Scalia, J., concurring, noted: "[W]hile we hold the Constitution prevents Congress from banning indecent speech in this fashion, we do not hold that the Constitution requires public utilities to carry it." Brennan, J., joined by Marshall and Stevens, JJ., concurred on the indecency issue and dissented on the obscenity issue.

AMERICAN CIVIL LIBERTIES UNION, 521 U.S. 844 (1997), invalidated both provisions: "The breadth of the CDA's coverage is wholly unprecedented. Unlike the regulations upheld in *Ginsberg* and *Pacifica,* the scope of the CDA is not limited to commercial speech or commercial entities. [The] general, undefined terms 'indecent' and 'patently offensive' cover large amounts of nonpornographic material with serious educational or other value."

(b).   The Child Online Protection Act prohibits any person with commercial purposes from knowingly causing material that is obscene for children to be placed on the World Wide Web.c It is a defense under the act that the defendant has required proof of age by credit card or adult verification screens, or any reasonable measure that is feasible under available technology. The federal district court issued a preliminary injunction against the enforcement of COPA, finding it likely that the statute was unconstitutional. The Third Circuit found no abuse of discretion in the issuance of the preliminary injunction. ASHCROFT v. AMERICAN CIVIL LIBERTIES UNION (II), 542 U.S. 656 (2004), per KENNEDY, J., affirmed on the ground that plausible less restrictive alternatives appeared to be available: "Blocking and filtering software is an alternative that is less restrictive than COPA, and, in addition, likely more effective as a means of restricting children's access to materials harmful to [them]."

————

Cable operators are required under federal law to reserve channels for commercial lease ("leased access channels"). For some years federal law prevented cable operators from employing any editorial control over the content of leased access. The Cable Television Consumer Protection and Competition of 1992, however, permitted cable operators to prohibit the broadcast of material that the cable operator "reasonably believes describes or depicts sexual or excretory activities or organs in a patently offensive manner" on leased access channels (47 U.S.C.§ 10(a)).

DENVER AREA EDUCATIONAL TELECOMMUNICATIONS CONSOR-TIUM, INC. v. FCC, 518 U.S. 727 (1996), upheld the constitutionality of § 10(a).a BREYER, J., joined by Stevens, O'Connor, and Souter, JJ., argued that the statute was sufficiently tailored to address a significant problem: "Justices Kennedy and Thomas would have us decide this case simply by transferring and applying literally categorical standards this Court has developed in other contexts. For Justice Kennedy, leased access channels are like a common carrier, cablecast is a protected medium, strict scrutiny applies, § 10(a) fails this test, and, therefore, § 10(a) is invalid. For Justice Thomas, the case is simple because the cable operator who owns the system over which access channels are broadcast, like a bookstore owner with respect to what it displays on the shelves, has a predomi-

---

c. *Ashcroft v. American Civil Liberties Union (I)*, 535 U.S. 564 (2002), per Thomas, J., held that the Child Online Protection Act's requirement that prurient interest to children and patent offensiveness for children be determined by reference to "community standards" did not by itself render the statute substantially overbroad.

a. O'Connor, J's concurring opinion is omitted. The Court also struck down (1) a provision permitting a cable operator to prohibit indecent speech on public access channels, distinguishing leased access channels in part because the presence of other supervisory mechanisms for public access channels made the provision seem less needed; (2) a provision requiring that a cable operator scramble or otherwise block any indecent speech permitted on leased access channels allowing for unscrambling on written request; and (3) a similar provision blocking provision for channels primarily dedicated to sexual programming. With respect to the blocking requirements, the Court was troubled by the inconsistent treatment between channels and the breadth of the restrictions.

nant First Amendment interest. Both categorical approaches suffer from the same flaws: they import law developed in very different contexts into a new and changing environment, and they lack the flexibility necessary to allow government to respond to very serious practical problems without sacrificing the free exchange of ideas the First Amendment is designed to protect. * * *

"Over the years, this Court has restated and refined [basic] First Amendment principles, adopting them more particularly to the balance of competing interests and the special circumstances of each field of application. [This] tradition teaches that the First Amendment embodies an overarching commitment to protect speech from Government regulation through close judicial scrutiny, thereby enforcing the Constitution's constraints, but without imposing judicial formulae so rigid that they become a straightjacket that disables Government from responding to serious problems. This Court, in different contexts, has consistently held that the Government may directly regulate speech to address extraordinary problems, where its regulations are appropriately tailored to resolve those problems without imposing an unnecessarily great restriction on speech. Justices Kennedy and Thomas would have us further declare which, among the many applications of the general approach that this Court has developed over the years, we are applying here. But no definitive choice among competing analogies (broadcast, common carrier, bookstore) allows us to declare a rigid single standard, good for now and for all future media and purposes. That is not to say that we reject all the more specific formulations of the standard—they appropriately cover the vast majority of cases involving Government regulation of speech. Rather, aware as we are of the changes taking place in the law, the technology, and the industrial structure, related to telecommunications, we believe it unwise and unnecessary definitively to pick one analogy or one specific set of words now.

"[W]e can decide this case more narrowly, by closely scrutinizing § 10(a) to assure that it properly addresses an extremely important problem, without imposing, in light of the relevant interests, an unnecessarily great restriction on speech. The importance of the interest at stake here—protecting children from exposure to patently offensive depictions of sex; the accommodation of the interests of programmers in maintaining access channels and of cable operators in editing the contents of their channels; the similarity of the problem and its solution to those at issue in *Pacifica*, and the flexibility inherent in an approach that permits private cable operators to make editorial decisions, lead us to conclude that § 10(a) is a sufficiently tailored response to an extraordinarily important problem. * * *

"[W]e part company with Justice Kennedy on two issues. First, Justice Kennedy's focus on categorical analysis forces him to disregard the cable system operators' interests. We, on the other hand, recognize that in the context of cable broadcast that involves an access requirement (here, its partial removal), and unlike in most cases where we have explicitly required 'narrow tailoring,' the expressive interests of cable operators do play a legitimate role. Cf. *Turner*. While we cannot agree with Justice Thomas that everything turns on the rights of the cable owner, we also cannot agree with Justice Kennedy that we must ignore the expressive interests of cable operators altogether. Second, Justice Kennedy's application of a very strict 'narrow tailoring' test depends upon an analogy with a category ('the public forum cases'), which has been distilled over time from the similarities of many cases. Rather than seeking an analogy to a category of cases, however, we have looked to the cases themselves. And, [we find] that *Pacifica* provides the closest analogy. * * *

"The Court's distinction in *Turner*, [between] cable and broadcast television, relied on the inapplicability of the spectrum scarcity problem to cable. While that distinction was relevant in *Turner* to the justification for structural regulations at issue there (the 'must carry' rules), it has little to do with a case that involves the effects of television viewing on children. Those effects are the result of how parents and children view television programming, and how pervasive and intrusive that programming is. In that respect, cable and broadcast television differ little, if at all.

"[I]f one wishes to view the permissive provisions before us through a 'public forum' lens, one should view those provisions as limiting the otherwise totally open nature of the forum that leased access channels provide for communication of other than patently offensive sexual material—taking account of the fact that the limitation was imposed in light of experience gained from maintaining a totally open 'forum.' One must still ask whether the First Amendment forbids the limitation. But unless a label alone were to make a critical First Amendment difference (and we think here it does not), the features of this case that we have already discussed—the government's interest in protecting children, the 'permissive' aspect of the statute, and the nature of the medium—sufficiently justify the 'limitation' on the availability of this forum."

STEVENS, J., concurring, agreed with Breyer, J., that it was unwise to characterize leased channels as public fora: "When the Federal Government opens cable channels that would otherwise be left entirely in private hands, it deserves more deference than a rigid application of the public forum doctrine would allow. At this early stage in the regulation of this developing industry, Congress should not be put to an all or nothing-at-all choice in deciding whether to open certain cable channels to programmers who would otherwise lack the resources to participate in the marketplace of ideas."

SOUTER, J., concurred: "All of the relevant characteristics of cable are presently in a state of technological and regulatory flux. Recent and far-reaching legislation not only affects the technical feasibility of parental control over children's access to undesirable material but portends fundamental changes in the competitive structure of the industry and, therefore, the ability of individual entities to act as bottlenecks to the free flow of information. As cable and telephone companies begin their competition for control over the single wire that will carry both their services, we can hardly settle rules for review of regulation on the assumption that cable will remain a separable and useful category of First Amendment scrutiny. And as broadcast, cable, and the cyber-technology of the Internet and the World Wide Web approach the day of using a common receiver, we can hardly assume that standards for judging the regulation of one of them will not have immense, but now unknown and unknowable, effects on the others.
* * *

"The upshot of appreciating the fluidity of the subject that Congress must regulate is simply to accept the fact that not every nuance of our old standards will necessarily do for the new technology, and that a proper choice among existing doctrinal categories is not obvious. Rather than definitively settling the issue now, Justice Breyer wisely reasons by direct analogy rather than by rule, concluding that the speech and the restriction at issue in this case may usefully be measured against the ones at issue in *Pacifica*. If that means it will take some time before reaching a final method of review for cases like this one, there may be consolation in recalling that 16 years passed, from *Roth* to *Miller*, before the modern obscenity rule jelled; that it took over 40 years, from *Hague v. CIO* to *Perry*, for the public forum category to settle out; and that a round half-century passed before the clear and present danger of *Schenck* evolved into the modern incitement rule of *Brandenburg*.

"I cannot guess how much time will go by until the technologies of communication before us today have matured and their relationships become known. But until a category of indecency can be defined both with reference to the new technology and with a prospect of durability, the job of the courts will be just what Justice Breyer does today: recognizing established First Amendment interests through a close analysis that constrains the Congress, without wholly incapacitating it in all matters of the significance apparent here, maintaining the high value of open communication, measuring the costs of regulation by exact attention to fact, and compiling a pedigree of experience with the changing subject. These are familiar judicial responsibilities in times when we know too little to risk the finality of precision, and attention to them will probably take us through the communications revolution. Maybe the judicial obligation to shoulder these responsibilities can itself be captured by a much older rule, familiar to every doctor of medicine: 'First, do no harm.' "

KENNEDY, J., joined by Ginsburg, J., concurring in part and dissenting in part, faulted the plurality opinion for upholding § 10(a): "The plurality opinion, insofar as it upholds § 10(a) [is] adrift. The opinion treats concepts such as public forum, broadcaster, and common carrier as mere labels rather than as categories with settled legal significance; it applies no standard, and by this omission loses sight of existing First Amendment doctrine. When confronted with a threat to free speech in the context of an emerging technology, we ought to have the discipline to analyze the case by reference to existing elaborations of constant First Amendment principles. This is the essence of the case-by-case approach to ensuring protection of speech under the First Amendment, even in novel settings. * * *

"The plurality begins its flight from standards with a number of assertions nobody disputes. I agree, of course, that it would be unwise 'to declare a rigid single standard, good for now and for all future media and purposes.' I do think it necessary, however, to decide what standard applies to discrimination against indecent programming on cable access channels in the present state of the industry. We owe at least that much to public and leased access programmers whose speech is put at risk nationwide by these laws. * * *

"The plurality claims its resistance to standards is in keeping with our case law, where we have shown a willingness to be flexible in confronting novel First Amendment problems. [W]e have developed specialized or more or less stringent standards when certain contexts demanded them; we did not avoid the use of standards altogether. Indeed, the creation of standards and adherence to them, even when it means affording protection to speech unpopular or distasteful, is the central achievement of our First Amendment jurisprudence. Standards are the means by which we state in advance how to test a law's validity, rather than letting the height of the bar be determined by the apparent exigencies of the day. They also provide notice and fair warning to those who must predict how the courts will respond to attempts to suppress their speech. Yet formulations like strict scrutiny, used in a number of constitutional settings to ensure that the inequities of the moment are subordinated to commitments made for the long run mean little if they can be watered down whenever they seem too strong. They mean still less if they can be ignored altogether when considering a case not on all fours with what we have seen before.

"The plurality seems distracted by the many changes in technology and competition in the cable industry. The laws challenged here, however, do not retool the structure of the cable industry. [The] straightforward issue here is whether the Government can deprive certain speakers, on the basis of the content of their speech, of protections afforded all others. There is no reason to discard our existing First Amendment jurisprudence in answering this question.

"While it protests against standards, the plurality does seem to favor one formulation of the question in this case: namely, whether the Act 'properly addresses an extremely important problem, without imposing, in light of the relevant interests, an unnecessarily great restriction on speech.' [This] description of the question accomplishes little, save to clutter our First Amendment case law by adding an untested rule with an uncertain relationship to the others we use to evaluate laws restricting speech. * * *

"Justice Souter recommends to the Court the precept 'First, do no harm.' The question, though, is whether the harm is in sustaining the law or striking it down. If the plurality is concerned about technology's direction, it ought to begin by allowing speech, not suppressing it. We have before us an urgent claim for relief against content-based discrimination, not a dry run.

"The constitutionality under *Turner Broadcasting* of requiring a cable operator to set aside leased access channels is not before us. For purposes of this case, we should treat the cable operator's rights in these channels as extinguished, and address the issue these petitioners present: namely, whether the Government can discriminate on the basis of content in affording protection to certain programmers. I cannot agree with Justice Thomas that the cable operator's rights inform this analysis.

"Laws requiring cable operators to provide leased access are the practical equivalent of making them common carriers, analogous in this respect to telephone companies: They are obliged to provide a conduit for the speech of others. [Laws] removing common-carriage protection from a single form of speech based on its content should be reviewed under the same standard as content-based restrictions on speech in a public forum. Making a cable operator a common carrier does not create a public forum in the sense of taking property from private control and dedicating it to public use; rather, regulations of a common carrier dictate the manner in which private control is exercised. A common-carriage mandate, nonetheless, serves the same function as a public forum. It ensures open, nondiscriminatory access to the means of communication.

"*Pacifica* did not purport, however, to apply a special standard for indecent broadcasting. Emphasizing the narrowness of its holding, the Court in *Pacifica* conducted a context-specific analysis of the FCC's restriction on indecent programming during daytime hours. It relied on the general rule that 'broadcasting [has] received the most limited First Amendment protection.' We already have rejected the application of this lower broadcast standard of review to infringements on the liberties of cable operators, even though they control an important communications medium. *Turner.* * * *

"[Indecency] often is inseparable from the ideas and viewpoints conveyed, or separable only with loss of truth or expressive power. Under our traditional First Amendment jurisprudence, factors perhaps justifying some restriction on indecent cable programming may all be taken into account without derogating this category of protected speech as marginal.

"Congress does have, however, a compelling interest in protecting children from indecent speech. So long as society gives proper respect to parental choices, it may, under an appropriate standard, intervene to spare children exposure to material not suitable for minors. This interest is substantial enough to justify some regulation of indecent speech even under, I will assume, the [strict scrutiny standard].

"[Section 10(a) nonetheless is] not narrowly tailored to protect children from indecent programs on access channels. First, to the extent some operators may allow indecent programming, children in localities those operators serve will be left unprotected. Partial service of a compelling interest is not narrow tailoring. Put another way, the interest in protecting children from indecency only at the caprice of the cable operator is not compelling. Perhaps Congress drafted the law this way to avoid the clear constitutional difficulties of banning indecent speech * * *, but the First Amendment does not permit this sort of ill fit between a law restricting speech and the interest it is said to serve.

"Second, to the extent cable operators prohibit indecent programming on access channels, not only children but adults will be deprived of it."

THOMAS, J., joined by Rehnquist, C.J., and Scalia, J., concurring in part and dissenting in part, argued that § 10(a) validly protected the constitutional rights of cable operators: "It is one thing to compel an operator to carry leased [access] speech, in apparent violation of *Tornillo*, but it is another thing altogether to say that the First Amendment forbids Congress to give back part of the operators' editorial discretion, which all recognize as fundamentally protected, in favor of a broader access right. It is no answer to say that leased [is] content neutral and that [§ 10(a) is] not, for that does not change the fundamental fact, which petitioners never address, that it is the operators' journalistic freedom that is infringed, whether the challenged restrictions be content neutral or content based.

"Because the access provisions are part of a scheme that restricts the free speech rights of cable operators, and expands the speaking opportunities of access programmers, who have no underlying constitutional right to speak through the cable medium, I do not believe that access programmers can challenge the scheme, or a particular part of it, as an abridgment of their 'freedom of speech.' Outside the public forum doctrine, government intervention that grants access programmers an opportunity to speak that they would not otherwise enjoy—and which does not directly limit programmers' underlying speech rights—cannot be an abridgment of the same programmers' First Amendment rights, even if the new speaking opportunity is content-based.

"The permissive nature of [§] 10(a) is important in this regard. If Congress had forbidden cable operators to carry indecent programming on leased * * * channels, that law would have burdened the programmer's right, recognized in *Turner* to compete for space on an operator's system. The Court would undoubtedly strictly scrutinize such a law."

————

§ 505 of the Telecommunications Act of 1996 requires that cable television operators who provide channels "primarily dedicated to sexually-oriented programming" either "fully scramble or otherwise fully block" the channels so that non-subscribers to the programming would not be able to hear or see it. The art of scrambling has not been perfected, however. "Signal bleed" occurs on many channels, allowing some of the visual and audio aspects of the programming to be heard or seen. In the case of signal bleed, the act requires that the programming be blocked except during hours when children are unlikely to be viewing. The FCC's regulations provide that those hours are between 10 p.m. and 6 a.m ("the safe harbor provision"). § 504 of the same act required operators to block other programming upon a subscriber's request. A cable television programmer challenged § 505. *United States v. Playboy Entertainment Group*, 529 U.S. 803 (2000) declared the restriction to be content-based with a serious impact on protected speech and held that it did not survive strict scrutiny. The Court doubted that signal bleed was sufficiently substantial to imperil children and argued that the government had not demonstrated that a requirement to block upon request with notice of the option provided to the subscriber could not be an effective, but less restrictive alternative.

SECTION 9.   THE RIGHT NOT TO SPEAK, THE RIGHT TO ASSOCIATE, AND THE RIGHT NOT TO ASSOCIATE

NAACP v. Alabama ex rel. Patterson, 357 U.S. 449 (1958), per Harlan, J., held that the First Amendment barred Alabama from compelling production of NAACP membership lists. The opinion used the phrase freedom of association repeatedly, "elevat[ing] freedom of association to an independent right, possessing an equal status with the other rights specifically enumerated in the First Amendment." Thomas Emerson, *Freedom of Association and Freedom of Expression*, 74 Yale L.J. 1, 2 (1964).

From the materials on advocacy of illegal action (Sec. 1, 1 supra) onward, it has been evident that individuals have rights to join with others for expressive purposes. This section explores other aspects of the freedom to associate and its corollary, the freedom not to associate. First, we explore cases which the Court bases on a right not to speak, but might better be understood as establishing a right not to be associated with particular ideas. Second, instead of persons resisting forced membership in a group, we confront groups resisting members.

I.   THE RIGHT NOT TO BE ASSOCIATED WITH PARTICULAR IDEAS

WEST VIRGINIA STATE BD. OF EDUC. v. BARNETTE, 319 U.S. 624 (1943), per JACKSON, J., upheld the right of public school students to refuse to salute the flag:a "To sustain the compulsory flag salute we are required to say that a Bill of Rights which guards the individual's right to speak his own mind, left it open to public authorities to compel him to utter what is not in his mind. * * * Struggles to coerce uniformity of sentiment in support of some end thought essential to their time and country have been waged by many good as well as by evil men. [Ultimate] futility of such attempts to compel coherence is the lesson of every such effort from the Roman drive to stamp out Christianity as a disturber of its pagan unity, the Inquisition, as a means to religious and dynastic unity, the Siberian exiles as a means to Russian unity, down to the fast failing efforts of our present totalitarian enemies. Those who begin coercive elimination of dissent soon find themselves exterminating dissenters. Compulsory unification of opinion achieves only the unanimity of the graveyard. * * *

"If there is any fixed star in our constitutional constellation, it is that no official, high or petty, can prescribe what shall be orthodox in politics, nationalism, religion, or other matters of opinion or force citizens to confess by word or act their faith therein. If there are any circumstances which permit an exception, they do not now occur to us. We think the action of the local authorities in compelling the flag salute and pledge transcends constitutional limitations on their power and

---

a. The Court observed that it was constitutional to otherwise involve students in the reci-tation of the pledge (which at that time did not include "Under God") during a school day.

invades the sphere of intellect and spirit which it is the purpose of the First Amendment to our Constitution to reserve from all official control."[b]

———

New Hampshire required that noncommercial vehicles bear license plates embossed with the state motto, "Live Free or Die." "Refus[ing] to be coerced by the State into advertising a slogan which I find morally, ethically, religiously and politically abhorrent," appellee, a Jehovah's Witness, covered up the motto on his license plate, a misdemeanor under state law. After being convicted several times of violating the misdemeanor statute, appellee sought federal injunctive and declaratory relief. WOOLEY v. MAYNARD, 430 U.S. 705 (1977), per Burger, C.J., held that requiring appellee to display the motto on his license plates violated his First Amendment right to "refrain from speaking": "[T]he freedom of thought protected by the First Amendment [includes] both the right to speak freely and the right to refrain from speaking at all. See *Barnette.* The right to speak and the right to refrain from speaking are complementary components of the broader concept of 'individual freedom of mind.' This is illustrated [by] *Miami Herald* [infra], where we held unconstitutional a Florida statute placing an affirmative duty upon newspapers to publish the replies of political candidates whom they had criticized.

" * * * Compelling the affirmative act of a flag salute [the situation in *Barnette*] involved a more serious infringement upon personal liberties than the passive act of carrying the state motto on a license plate, but the difference is essentially one of degree. Here, as in *Barnette,* we are faced with a state measure which forces an individual as part of his daily life—indeed constantly while his automobile is in public view—to be an instrument for fostering public adherence to an ideological point of view he finds unacceptable. In doing so, the State 'invades the sphere of intellect and spirit which it is the purpose of the First Amendment [to] reserve from all official control.' *Barnette.*

"New Hampshire's statute in effect requires that appellees use their private property as a 'mobile billboard' for the State's ideological message—or suffer a penalty, as Maynard already has. [The] fact that most individuals agree with the thrust of [the] motto is not the test; most Americans also find the flag salute acceptable. The First Amendment protects the right of individuals to hold a point of view different from the majority and to refuse to foster, in the way New Hampshire commands, an idea they find morally objectionable."

The Court next considered whether "the State's countervailing interest" was "sufficiently compelling" to justify appellees to display the motto on their license plates. The two interests claimed by the state were (1) facilitating the identification of state license plates from those of similar colors of other states and (2) promoting "appreciation of history, state pride, [and] individualism." As to (1), the record revealed that these state license plates were readily distinguishable from others without reference to the state motto and, in any event, the state's purpose could be achieved by "less drastic means," i.e., by alternative methods less restrictive of First Amendment freedoms. As to (2), where the State's interest is to communicate an "official view" as to history and state pride or to dissemi-

---

b. Black and Douglas, JJ., concurred, abandoning their position taken in a recent flag salute case *Minersville School Dist. v. Gobitis,* 310 U.S. 586 (1940), which the Court reconsidered in *Barnette*; Roberts and Reed, JJ., citing their position in *Gobitis,* and Frankfurter, J., taking a position on the judicial role similar to that which he had expressed in *Dennis,* dissented.

nate any other "ideology," "such interest cannot outweigh an individual's First Amendment right to avoid becoming the courier for such message."

REHNQUIST, J., joined by Blackmun, J., dissented, not only agreeing with what he called "the Court's implicit recognition that there is no protected 'symbolic speech' in this case," but maintaining that "that conclusion goes far to undermine the Court's ultimate holding that there is an element of protected expression here. The State has not forced appellees to 'say' anything; and it has not forced them to communicate ideas with nonverbal actions reasonably likened to 'speech,' such as wearing a lapel button promoting a political candidate or waving a flag as a symbolic gesture. The State has simply required that *all* noncommercial automobiles bear license tags with the state motto. [Appellees] have not been forced to affirm or reject that motto; they are simply required by the State [to] carry a state auto license tag for identification and registration purposes. [The] issue, unconfronted by the Court, is whether appellees, in displaying, as they are required to do, state license tags, the format of which is known to all as having been prescribed by the State, would be considered to be advocating political or ideological views.

"[H]aving recognized the rather obvious differences between [*Barnette* and this case], the Court does not explain why the same result should obtain. The Court suggests that the test is whether the individual is forced 'to be an instrument for fostering public adherence to an ideological point of view he finds unacceptable,' [but] these are merely conclusory words. [For] example, were New Hampshire to erect a multitude of billboards, each proclaiming 'Live Free or Die,' and tax all citizens for the cost of erection and maintenance, clearly the message would be 'fostered' by the individual citizen-taxpayers and just as clearly those individuals would be 'instruments' in that communication. Certainly, however, that case would not fall within the ambit of *Barnette*. In that case, as in this case, there is no *affirmation* of belief. For First Amendment principles to be implicated, the State must place the citizen in the position of either appearing to, or actually, 'asserting as true' the message. This was the focus of *Barnette,* and clearly distinguishes this case from that one."c

Notes

1. *Use of private property as a forum for the speech of others*. (a) Appellees sought to enjoin a shopping center from denying them access to the center's central courtyard in order to solicit signatures from passersby for petitions opposing a U.N. resolution. The California Supreme Court held they were entitled to conduct their activity at the center, construing the state constitution to protect "speech and petitioning, reasonably exercised, in shopping centers, even [when] privately owned." PRUNEYARD SHOPPING CENTER v. ROBINS, 447 U.S. 74 (1980), per REHNQUIST, J., held that the shopping center's First Amendment rights were not violated: "[In *Wooley,*] the government itself prescribed the message, required it to be displayed openly on appellee's personal property that was used 'as part of his daily life,' and refused to permit him [to] cover up the motto even though the Court found that the display of the motto served no important state interest. Here, by contrast, [the center] is not limited to the personal use of appellants, [but is] a business establishment that is open to the public to come and go as they please. The views expressed by members of the public in passing out pamphlets or seeking signatures for a petition thus will not likely be identified with those of the owner. Second, no specific message is dictated

c. White, J., joined by Blackmun and Rehnquist, JJ., dissented on procedural grounds.

by the State to be displayed on appellants' property. There consequently is no danger of government discrimination for or against a particular message. Finally, [it appears] appellants can expressly disavow any connection with the message by simply posting signs in the area where the speakers or handbillers stand."

Unlike *Barnette,* appellants "are not [being] compelled to affirm their belief in any governmentally prescribed position or view, and they are free to publicly dissociate themselves from the views of the speakers or handbillers. [*Miami Herald*] rests on the principle that the State cannot tell a newspaper what it must print. [There was also a danger that the statute requiring a newspaper to publish a political candidate's reply to previously published criticism would deter] editors from publishing controversial political [statements]. Thus, the statute was found to be an 'intrusion into the function of editors.' These concerns obviously are not present here."

POWELL, J., joined by White, J., concurring in the judgment, maintained that "state action that transforms privately owned property into a forum for the expression of the public's views could raise serious First Amendment questions": "I do not believe that the result in *Wooley* would have changed had [the state] directed its citizens to place the slogan 'Live Free or Die' in their shop windows rather than on their automobiles. [*Wooley*] protects a person who refuses to allow use of his property as a market place for the ideas of others. [One] who has merely invited the public onto his property for commercial purposes cannot fairly be said to have relinquished his right 'to decline to be an instrument for fostering public adherence to an ideological point of view he finds unacceptable.' *Wooley.*

"[E]ven when [as here] no particular message is mandated by the State, First Amendment interests are affected by state action that forces a property owner to admit third-party speakers. [A] right of access [may be] no less intrusive than speech compelled by the State itself. [A] law requiring that a newspaper permit others to use its columns imposes an unacceptable burden upon the newspaper's First Amendment right to select material for publication. *Miami Herald.*

"[If] a state law mandated public access to the bulletin board of a freestanding store [or] small shopping center [or allowed soliciting or pamphleteering in the entrance area of a store,] customers might well conclude that the messages reflect the view of the proprietor. [He] either could permit his customers to receive a mistaken impression [or] disavow the messages. Should he take the first course, he effectively has been compelled to affirm someone else's belief. Should he choose the second, he has been forced to speak when he would prefer to remain silent. In short, he has lost control over his freedom to speak or not to speak on certain issues. The mere fact that he is free to dissociate himself from the views expressed on his property cannot restore his 'right to refrain from speaking at all.' *Wooley.*

"A property owner may also be faced with speakers who wish to use his premises as a platform for views that he finds morally repugnant[, for example, a] minority-owned business confronted with leafleteers from the American Nazi Party or the Ku Klux Klan, [or] a church-operated enterprise asked to host demonstrations in favor of abortion. [The] pressure to respond is particularly apparent [in the above cases, but] an owner who strongly objects to some of the causes to which the state-imposed right of access would extend may oppose ideological activities 'of *any* sort' that are not related to the purposes for which he has invited the public onto his property. See *Abood.* To require the owner to specify the particular ideas he finds objectionable enough to compel a response would force him to relinquish his 'freedom to maintain his own beliefs without public disclosure.' *Abood.* * * *

"[On this record] I cannot say that customers of this vast center [occupying several city blocks and containing more than 65 shops] would be likely to assume that appellees' limited speech activity expressed the views of [the center]. [Moreover, appellants] have not alleged that they object to [appellees' views, nor asserted] that some groups who reasonably might be expected to speak at [the center] will express views that are so objectionable as to require a response even when listeners will not mistake their source. [Thus,] I join the judgment of the Court, [but] I do not interpret our decision today as a blanket approval for state efforts to transform privately owned commercial property into public forums."

(b) *Pacific Gas & Electric Co. v. Public Utilities Comm'n*, 475 U.S. 1 (1986), per Powell, J., joined by Burger, C.J., and Brennan and O'Connor, JJ., (together with Marshall, J., concurring), struck down a commission requirement that a private utility company include in its billing envelope materials supplied by a public interest group that were critical of some of the company's positions.**d**

(c) The Solomon Amendment provides that if any part of an institution of higher education denies military recruiters access equal to that afforded to other recruiters, the entire institution would be deprived of federal funds. A consortium of law schools filed suit, alleging that the Amendment violated the First Amendment. RUMSFELD v. FORUM FOR ACADEMIC AND INSTITUTIONAL RIGHTS, INC., 547 U.S. 47 (2006), per ROBERTS, C.J., did not unduly burden freedom of speech or association: "The Solomon Amendment neither limits what law schools may say nor requires them to say anything. Law schools remain free under the statute to express whatever views they may have on the military's congressionally mandated employment policy, all the while retaining eligibility for federal funds. See Tr. of Oral Arg. 25 (Solicitor General acknowledging that law schools "could put signs on the bulletin board next to the door, they could engage in speech, they could help organize student protests"). As a general matter, the Solomon Amendment regulates conduct, not speech. It affects what law schools must *do*—afford equal access to military recruiters—not what they may or may not *say*. * * *

"Compelling a law school that sends scheduling e-mails for other recruiters to send one for a military recruiter is simply not the same as forcing a student to pledge allegiance, or forcing a Jehovah's Witness to display the motto 'Live Free or Die,' and it trivializes the freedom protected in *Barnette* and *Wooley* to suggest that it is." **e**

2. ***Paraders' rights***. Boston authorized the South Boston Allied War Veterans Council to conduct the St. Patrick's Day–Evacuation parade (commemorating the evacuation of British troops from the city in 1776). The Veterans Council refused to let the Irish–American Gay, Lesbian and Bisexual Group of Boston march in the parade, but the Massachusetts courts ruled that the Council's refusal violated a public accommodations law in that the parade was an "open recreational event." HURLEY v. IRISH–AMERICAN GAY, LESBIAN AND BISEXUAL GROUP OF BOSTON, 515 U.S. 557 (1995), per SOUTER, J., held that "[t]his use of the State's power violates the fundamental rule of protection under the First Amendment, that a speaker has the autonomy to choose the content of his own message. * * *

"[The Council's] claim to the benefit of this principle of autonomy to control one's own speech is as sound as the South Boston parade is expressive. Rather like

d. Burger, C.J., filed a concurring opinion; Rehnquist, J., joined by White and Stevens, JJ., dissented; Stevens, J., filed a separate dissent; Blackmun, J., took no part.

e. Alito, J., took no part.

a composer, the Council selects the expressive units of the parade from potential participants, and though the score may not produce a particularized message, each contingent's expression in the Council's eyes comports with what merits celebration on that day. Even if this view gives the Council credit for a more considered judgment than it actively made, the Council clearly decided to exclude a message it did not like from the communication it chose to make, and that is enough to invoke its right as a private speaker to shape its expression by speaking on one subject while remaining silent on another. * * *

"Unlike the programming offered on various channels by a cable network, the parade does not consist of individual, unrelated segments that happen to be transmitted together for individual selection by members of the audience. Although each parade unit generally identifies itself, each is understood to contribute something to a common theme, and accordingly there is no customary practice whereby private sponsors disavow any 'identity of viewpoint' between themselves and the selected participants. Practice follows practicability here, for such disclaimers would be quite curious in a moving parade. [*PruneYard* found] that the proprietors were running 'a business establishment that is open to the public to come and go as they please,' that the solicitations would 'not likely be identified with those of the owner,' and that the proprietors could 'expressly disavow any connection with the message by simply posting signs in the area where the speakers or handbillers stand.' "

4. ***Economic pressure to engage in political activity***. NAACP v. CLAIBORNE HARDWARE CO., 458 U.S. 886 (1982): The NAACP had organized a consumer boycott whose principal objective was, according to the lower court, "to force the white merchants [to] bring pressure upon [the government] to grant defendants' demands or, in the alternative, to suffer economic ruin." Mississippi characterized the boycott as a tortious and malicious interference with the plaintiffs' businesses. The Court, per STEVENS, J., held for the NAACP: Although labor boycotts organized for economic ends had long been subject to prohibition, "speech to protest racial discrimination" was "essential political speech lying at the core of the First Amendment" and was therefore distinguishable.

5. ***Orthodoxy and commercial advertising***. ZAUDERER v. OFFICE OF DISCIPLINARY COUNSEL, 471 U.S. 626 (1985), per WHITE, J., upheld an Ohio requirement that an attorney advertising availability on a contingency basis must disclose in the ad whether the clients would have to pay costs if their lawsuits should prove unsuccessful: "[T]he interests at stake in this case are not of the same order as those discussed in *Wooley*, *Miami Herald,* and *Barnette*. Ohio has not attempted to 'prescribe what shall be orthodox in politics, nationalism, religion, or other matters of opinion or force citizens to confess by word or act their faith therein.' The State has attempted only to prescribe what shall be orthodox in commercial advertising [regarding] purely factual and uncontroversial information about the terms under which his services will be available. Because the extension of First Amendment protection to commercial speech is justified principally by the value to consumers of the information such speech provides, *Virginia Pharmacy,* appellant's constitutionally protected interest in *not* providing any particular factual information in his advertising is minimal. [We] recognize that unjustified or unduly burdensome disclosure requirements might offend the First Amendment by chilling protected commercial speech. But we hold that an advertiser's rights are adequately protected as long as disclosure requirements are reasonably related to the State's interest in preventing deception of consumers."

The Court stated that the First Amendment interests "implicated by disclosure requirements are substantially weaker than those at stake when speech is actually suppressed." Accordingly it rejected any requirement that the advertisement in question be shown to be deceptive absent the disclosure or that the state meet a "least restrictive means" analysis.

Brennan, J., joined by Marshall, J., dissenting on this issue, conceded that the distinction between disclosure and suppression "supports some differences in analysis," but thought the Court had exaggerated the importance of the distinction: "[A]n affirmative publication requirement 'operates as a command in the same sense as a statute or regulation forbidding [someone] to publish specified matter,' and that [a] compulsion to publish that which 'reason tells [one] should not be published' therefore raises substantial First Amendment concerns. *Miami Herald.*" Accordingly, he would have required a demonstration that the advertising was inherently likely to deceive or record evidence that the advertising was in fact deceptive, or a showing that another substantial interest was directly [advanced]. Applying this standard, Brennan, J., agreed with the Court that a state may require an advertising attorney to include a costs disclaimer, but concluded that the state had provided Zauderer with inadequate notice of what he was required to include in the advertisement.

6. ***Compelled monetary subsidies***. A series of cases have invalidated government forced monetary contributions for support of speech opposed by the contributors. *Abood v. Detroit Bd. of Educ.*, 431 U.S. 209 (1977)(members of public employee bargaining unit who are not members of a union can be compelled to pay service fees to union, but rebates must be provided if they object to the union's support of political candidates or political views unrelated to the union's duties as exclusive bargaining representative); *Davenport v. Washington Education Ass'n*, 551 U.S. 177 (2007)(public-sector unions may be required to receive affirmative authorization from a nonmember before spending that person's compelled fees for election purposes, though nonmembers fees need not be commingled with members' fees); *Keller v. State Bar of California*, 496 U.S. 1 (1990) (compulsory bar dues could only be used if "reasonably incurred for the purpose of regulating the legal profession or improving the quality of the legal service available to the people of the State" not to endorse or advance a gun control or nuclear weapons freeze initiative); *United States v. United Foods, Inc.*, 533 U.S. 405 (2001)(objecting mushroom handlers can not be compelled to fund generic advertisements supporting mushroom sales).**f** But see *Glickman v. Wileman Bros. & Elliott, Inc.*, 521 U.S. 457 (1997) (tree fruit producers can be compelled to pay assessments for advertising). Nonetheless, taxpayers routinely fund speech activities to which they are opposed without First Amendment rights being violated.

This paradox was addressed in a case involving beef subsidies. Pursuant to the Beef Promotion and Research Act, the Secretary of Agriculture established a beef promotion and research board funded by government compelled contributions from the sales and importation of cattle. More than 1 billion dollars has been collected, much of it used to promote the sale of beef employing the slogan, "Beef: It's What's for Dinner." Many of the promotional messages state that they are funded by America's beef producers. Plaintiffs brought suit maintaining that compelled financial support of generic advertisements for beef impeded their efforts to promote the superiority of American beef, grain-fed beef, or certified Angus or Hereford beef, and violated the First Amendment.

f. Despite ideological objections, compulsory exactions might be justified by the strength of the government interest. See *Abood* (forced support of union collective bargaining activities permissible despite ideological objection); *Board of Regents v. Southworth*, 529 U.S. 217 (2000) (no refund appropriate of mandatory student fee so long as allocation of funding is viewpoint neutral because the interest in stimulating diverse ideas on campus outweighs the interests of objecting students).

JOHANNS v. LIVESTOCK MARKETING ASSOCIATION, 544 U.S. 550 (2005), per Scalia, J., concluded that compelled support of private speech raised First Amendment issues, that such compelled support of government speech did not raise First Amendment issues, and that the beef promotional messages were government speech: "We have sustained First Amendment challenges to allegedly compelled expression in two categories of cases: true 'compelled speech' cases, in which an individual is obliged personally to express a message he disagrees with, imposed by the government; and 'compelled subsidy' cases, in which an individual is required by the government to subsidize a message he disagrees with, expressed by a private entity. We have not heretofore considered the First Amendment consequences of government-compelled subsidy of the government's own speech.

"Our compelled-subsidy cases have consistently respected the principle that '[c]ompelled support of a private association is fundamentally different from compelled support of government.' ['The] government, as a general rule, may support valid programs and policies by taxes or other exactions binding on protesting parties. Within this broader principle it seems inevitable that funds raised by the government will be spent for speech and other expression to advocate and defend its own policies.' We have generally assumed, though not yet squarely held, that compelled funding of government speech does not alone raise First Amendment concerns. * * *

"Respondents [assert] that the challenged promotional campaigns differ dispositively from the type of government speech that, our cases suggest, is not susceptible to First Amendment challenge. They point to the role of the Beef Board and its Operating Committee in designing the promotional campaigns, and to the use of a mandatory assessment on beef producers to fund the advertising. * * *

"The Secretary of Agriculture does not write ad copy himself. Rather, the Beef Board's promotional campaigns are designed by the Beef Board's Operating Committee. [Nonetheless, the] message set out in the beef promotions is from beginning to end the message established by the Federal Government.[5]

"Congress has directed the implementation of a 'coordinated program' of promotion, 'including paid advertising, to advance the image and desirability of beef and beef products.' * * * Congress and the Secretary have set out the overarching message and some of its elements, and they have left the development of the remaining details to an entity whose members are answerable to the Secretary (and in some cases appointed by him as well).

"Moreover, the record demonstrates that the Secretary exercises final approval authority over every word used in every promotional campaign. All proposed promotional messages are reviewed by Department officials both for substance and for wording, and some proposals are rejected or rewritten by the Department. * * *

"The compelled-*subsidy* analysis is altogether unaffected by whether the funds for the promotions are raised by general taxes or through a targeted assessment. Citizens may challenge compelled support of private speech, but have no First Amendment right not to fund government speech. And that is no less

---

5. The principal dissent suggests that if this is so, then the Government has adopted at best a mixed message, because it also promulgates dietary guidelines that, if followed, would discourage excessive consumption of beef. Even if we agreed that the protection of the government-speech doctrine must be forfeited when- ever there is inconsistency in the message, we would nonetheless accord the protection here. The beef promotions are perfectly compatible with the guidelines' message of moderate consumption—the ads do not insist that beef is also What's for Breakfast, Lunch, and Midnight Snack.

true when the funding is achieved through targeted assessments devoted exclusively to the program to which the assessed citizens object.

"[R]espondents' contend that crediting the advertising to 'America's Beef Producers' impermissibly uses not only their money but also their seeming endorsement to promote a message with which they do not agree. Communications cannot be 'government speech,' they argue, if they are attributed to someone other than the government; and the person to whom they are attributed, when he is, by compulsory funding, made the unwilling instrument of communication, may raise a First Amendment objection.

"We need not determine the validity of this argument—which relates to compelled *speech* rather than compelled *subsidy*—with regard to respondents' facial challenge. Since neither the Beef Act nor the Beef Order requires attribution, neither can be the cause of any possible First Amendment harm. The District Court's order enjoining the enforcement of the Act and the Order thus cannot be sustained on this theory.

"[This theory might form] the basis for an as-applied challenge—if it were established, that is, that individual beef advertisements were attributed to respondents. [Whether] the *individual* respondents who are beef producers would be associated with speech labeled as coming from 'America's Beef Producers' is a question on which the trial record is altogether silent. We have only the funding tagline itself, a trademarked term that, standing alone, is not sufficiently specific to convince a reasonable factfinder that any particular beef producer, or all beef producers, would be tarred with the content of each trademarked ad."a

BREYER, J., concurred: "The beef checkoff program in these cases is virtually identical to the mushroom checkoff program in which the Court struck down on First Amendment grounds. The 'government speech' theory the Court adopts today was not before us in *United Foods* [where I dissented] based on my view that the challenged assessments involved a form of economic regulation, not speech. * * *

"I remain of the view that the assessments in these cases are best described as a form of economic regulation. However, I recognize that a majority of the Court does not share that view. Now that we have had an opportunity to consider the 'government speech' theory, I accept it as a solution to the problem presented by these cases."

GINSBURG, J., concurred in the judgment: "I resist ranking the promotional messages funded under the Beef Promotion and Research Act of 1985 as government speech, given the message the Government conveys in its own name [discouraging the consumption of trans fatty acids found in cattle and sheep]. I remain persuaded, however, that the assessments in these cases qualify as permissible economic regulation."

SOUTER, J., joined by Stevens and Kennedy, JJ., dissented: "I take the view that if government relies on the government-speech doctrine to compel specific groups to fund speech with targeted taxes, it must make itself politically accountable by indicating that the content actually is a government message, not just the statement of one self-interested group the government is currently willing to invest with power. Sometimes, as in these very cases, government can make an effective disclosure only by explicitly labeling the speech as its own.

"[T]he requirement of effective public accountability means the ranchers ought to prevail, it being clear that the Beef Act does not establish an advertising

---

a. Thomas, J. concurred. Kennedy, J., dissented.

scheme subject to effective democratic checks. The reason for this is simple: the ads are not required to show any sign of being speech by the Government, and experience under the Act demonstrates how effectively the Government has masked its role in producing the ads. Most obviously, many of them include the tag line, '[f]unded by America's Beef Producers,' which all but ensures that no one reading them will suspect that the message comes from the National Government. But the tag line just underscores the point that would be true without it, that readers would most naturally think that ads urging people to have beef for dinner were placed and paid for by the beef producers who stand to profit when beef is on the table. No one hearing a commercial for Pepsi or Levi's thinks Uncle Sam is the man talking behind the curtain. Why would a person reading a beef ad think Uncle Sam was trying to make him eat more steak? Given the circumstances, it is hard to see why anyone would suspect the Government was behind the message unless the message came out and said so."

7. *A right not to speak?* *Wooley* and succeeding cases establish a right not to be associated with ideas to which one is ideologically opposed. Yet individuals are forced to speak in a wide variety of situations. *See e.g., Barenblatt v. United States,* 360 U.S. 109 (1959)(witness can be compelled before Congress to testify about his political connections with the Communist Party if he does not invoke the fifth amendment). Other cases are more sympathetic to those who choose to remain silent.

(a) *Anonymous political speech.* McINTYRE v. OHIO ELECTIONS COMM'N, 514 U.S. 334 (1995), per STEVENS, J., held that Ohio's prohibition against the distribution of anonymous campaign literature was unconstitutional: "Under our Constitution, anonymous pamphleteering is not a pernicious, fraudulent practice, but an honorable tradition of advocacy and of dissent. [The] State may and does punish fraud directly. But it cannot seek to punish fraud indirectly by indiscriminately outlawing a category of speech, based on its content, with no necessary relationship to the danger sought to be prevented."[b]

THOMAS, J., concurred, but argued that instead of asking whether " 'an honorable tradition' of free speech has existed throughout American history. [We] should seek the original understanding when we interpret the Speech and Press clauses, just as we do when we read the Religion Clauses of the First Amendment." According to Thomas, J., the original understanding approach also protected anonymous speech.

SCALIA, joined by Rehnquist, C.J., dissenting, asserted that it was the "Court's (and society's) traditional view that the Constitution bears its original meaning and is unchanging." Applying that approach, he concluded that anonymous political speech is not protected under the First Amendment.

(b) *Compelled election disclosures.* BROWN v. SOCIALIST WORKERS, 459 U.S. 87 (1982), per MARSHALL, J., held that an Ohio statute requiring every political party to report the names and addresses of campaign contributors and recipients of campaign disbursements could not be applied to the Socialist Workers Party. Citing *Buckley v. Valeo,* Sec. 10 infra, the Court held that the " 'evidence offered [by a minor party] need show only a reasonable probability that the compelled disclosure [of] names will subject them to threats, harassment, or reprisals from either Government officials or private parties.' "

b. Ginsburg, J., concurred. *See also Buckley v. American Constitutional Law Foundation,* 525 U.S. 182 (1999), per Ginsburg, J., which held unconstitutional a Colorado statute requiring that circulators of initiatives wear identification badges bearing their names and that sponsors of the initiative report the names and addresses of all paid circulators. By contrast, the Court was satisfied that the requirement of the filing of an affidavit containing the name and address of the circulator of petitions was consistent with the First Amendment.

II. INTIMATE ASSOCIATION AND EXPRESSIVE ASSOCIATION

ROBERTS v. UNITED STATES JAYCEES, 468 U.S. 609 (1984): Appellee U.S. Jaycees, a nonprofit national membership corporation whose objective is to pursue educational and charitable purposes that promote the growth and development of young men's civic organizations, limits regular membership to young men between the ages of 18 and 35. Associate membership is available to women and older men. An associate member may not vote or hold local or national office. Two local chapters in Minnesota violated appellee's bylaws by admitting women as regular members. When they learned that revocation of their charters was to be considered, members of both chapters filed discrimination charges with the Minnesota Department of Human Rights, alleging that the exclusion of women from full membership violated the Minnesota Human Rights Act (Act), which makes it an "unfair discriminatory practice" to deny anyone "the full and equal enjoyment of goods, services, facilities, privileges, advantages, and accommodations of a place of public accommodation" because, inter alia, of sex.

Before a hearing on the state charge took place, appellee brought federal suit, alleging that requiring it to accept women as regular members would violate the male members' constitutional "freedom of association." A state hearing officer decided against appellee and the federal district court certified to the Minnesota Supreme Court the question whether appellee is "a place of public accommodation" within the meaning of the Act. With the record of the administrative hearing before it, the state Supreme Court answered that question in the affirmative. The U.S. Court of Appeals held that application of the Act to appellee's membership policies would violate its freedom of association.a

In rejecting appellee's claims,b the Court, per BRENNAN, J., pointed out that the Constitution protects " 'freedom of association' in two distinct senses," what might be called "freedom of intimate association" and "freedom of expressive association": "In one line of decisions, the Court has concluded that choices to enter into and maintain certain intimate human relationships must be secured against undue intrusion by the State because of the role of such relationships in safeguarding the individual freedom that is central to our constitutional scheme. In this respect, freedom of association receives protection as a fundamental element of personal liberty. In another set of decisions, the Court has recognized a right to associate for the purpose of engaging in those activities protected by the First Amendment—speech, assembly, petition for the redress of grievances, [and] religion. The Constitution guarantees freedom of association of this kind as an indispensable means of preserving other individual liberties."

The freedom of intimate association was deemed important because, "certain kinds of personal bonds have played a critical role in the culture and traditions of the Nation by cultivating and transmitting shared ideals and beliefs; they thereby foster diversity and act as critical buffers between the individual and the power of the State. Moreover, the constitutional shelter afforded such relationships reflects the realization that individuals draw much of their emotional enrichment from

---

a. When the state supreme court held that appellee was "a place of public accommodation" within the meaning of the Act, it suggested that, unlike appellee, the Kiwanis Club might be sufficiently "private" to be outside the scope of the Act. Appellee then amended its complaint to allege that the state court's interpretation of the Act rendered it unconstitutionally vague. The Eighth Circuit so held, but the Supreme Court reversed.

b. There was no dissent. Rehnquist, J., concurred in the judgment. O'Connor, J., joined part of the Court's opinion and concurred in the judgment. See infra. Burger, C.J., and Blackmun, J., took no part.

close ties with others. Protecting these relationships from unwarranted state interference therefore safeguards the ability independently to define one's identity that is central to any concept of liberty.

"The personal affiliations that exemplify these considerations [are] distinguished by such attributes as relative smallness, a high degree of selectivity in decisions to begin and maintain the affiliation, and seclusion from others in critical aspects of the relationship. [A]n association lacking these qualities—such as a large business enterprise—seems remote from the concerns giving rise to this constitutional protection. * * *

"Between these poles, of course, lies a broad range of human relationships that may make greater or lesser claims to constitutional protection from particular incursions by the State. [We] need not mark the potentially significant points on this terrain with any precision. We note only that factors that may be relevant include size, purpose, policies, selectivity, congeniality, and other characteristics that in a particular case may be pertinent. In this case, however, several features of the Jaycees clearly place the organization outside of the category of relationships worthy of this kind of constitutional protection.

"[T]he local chapters of the Jaycees are large and basically unselective groups. [Apart] from age and sex, neither the national organization nor the local chapters employs any criteria for judging applicants for membership, and new members are routinely recruited and admitted with no inquiry into their backgrounds. In fact, a local officer testified that he could recall no instance in which an applicant had been denied membership on any basis other than age or sex. [Furthermore], numerous non-members of both genders regularly participate in a substantial portion of activities central to the decision of many members to associate with one another, including many of the organization's various community programs, awards ceremonies, and recruitment meetings.

"[We] turn therefore to consider the extent to which application of the Minnesota statute to compel the Jaycees to accept women infringes the group's freedom of expressive association. * * *

"Government actions that may unconstitutionally infringe upon [freedom of expressive association] can take a number of forms. Among other things, government may seek to impose penalties or withhold benefits from individuals because of their membership in a disfavored group; it may attempt to require disclosure of the fact of membership in a group seeking anonymity; and it may try to interfere with the internal organization or affairs of the group. [There] can be no clearer example of an intrusion into the internal structure or affairs of an association than a regulation that forces the group to accept members it does not desire. Such a regulation may impair the ability of the original members to express only those views that brought them together. Freedom of association therefore plainly presupposes a freedom not to associate. See *Abood.*

"The right to associate for expressive purposes is not, however, absolute. Infringements on that right may be justified by regulations adopted to serve compelling state interests, unrelated to the suppression of ideas, that cannot be achieved through means significantly less restrictive of associational freedoms.

"[I]n upholding Title II of the Civil Rights Act of 1964, which forbids race discrimination in public accommodations, we emphasized that its 'fundamental object [was] to vindicate "the deprivation of personal dignity that surely accompanies denials of equal access to public establishments."' *Heart of Atlanta Motel,* [Ch. 2, Sec. 2, III]. That stigmatizing injury, and the denial of equal opportunities that accompanies it, is surely felt as strongly by persons suffering discrimination on the basis of their sex as by those treated differently because of their race.

"Nor is the state interest in assuring equal access limited to the provision of purely tangible goods and services. A State enjoys broad authority to create rights of public access on behalf of its citizens. *PruneYard.* Like many States and municipalities, Minnesota has adopted a functional definition of public accommodations that reaches various forms of public, quasi-commercial conduct. This expansive definition reflects a recognition of the changing nature of the American economy and of the importance, both to the individual and to society, of removing the barriers to economic advancement and political and social integration that have historically plagued certain disadvantaged groups, including women. * * *

"In applying the Act to the Jaycees, the State has advanced those interests through the least restrictive means of achieving its ends. Indeed, the Jaycees have failed to demonstrate that the Act imposes any serious burdens on the male members' freedom of expressive association. See *Hishon v. King & Spalding,* 467 U.S. 69 (1984) (law firm 'has not shown how its ability to fulfill [protected] function[s] would be inhibited by a requirement that it consider [a woman lawyer] for partnership on her merits'). To be sure, a 'not insubstantial part' of the Jaycees' activities constitutes protected expression on political, economic, cultural, and social affairs. [There] is, however, no basis in the record for concluding that admission of women as full voting members will impede the organization's ability to engage in these protected activities or to disseminate its preferred views. The Act requires no change in the Jaycees' creed of promoting the interests of young men, and it imposes no restrictions on the organization's ability to exclude individuals with ideologies or philosophies different from those of its existing members. Moreover, the Jaycees already invite women to share the group's views and philosophy and to participate in much of [its] activities. Accordingly, any claim that admission of women as full voting members will impair a symbolic message conveyed by the very fact that women are not permitted to vote is attenuated at best.

"[In] claiming that women might have a different attitude about such issues as the federal budget, school prayer, voting rights, and foreign relations, or that the organization's public positions would have a different effect if the group were not 'a purely young men's association,' the Jaycees rely solely on unsupported generalizations about the relative interests and perspectives of men and women. Although such generalizations may or may not have a statistical basis in fact with respect to particular positions adopted by the Jaycees, we have repeatedly condemned legal decisionmaking that relies uncritically on such assumptions. In the absence of a showing far more substantial than that attempted by the Jaycees, we decline to indulge in the sexual stereotyping [of appellees].

"In any event, even if enforcement of the Act causes some incidental abridgement of the Jaycees' protected speech, that effect is no greater than is necessary to accomplish the State's legitimate purposes. [A]cts of invidious discrimination in the distribution of publicly available goods, services, and other advantages cause unique evils that government has a compelling interest to prevent—wholly apart from the point of view such conduct may transmit. Accordingly, like violence or other types of potentially expressive activities that produce special harms distinct from their communicative impact, such practices are entitled to no constitutional protection."c

c. For cases following or extending *Roberts,* see *Board of Directors of Rotary International v. Rotary Club of Duarte,* 481 U.S. 537 (1987); *New York State Club Ass'n v. New York,* 487 U.S. 1 (1988) (upholding city ordinance against facial challenge that prohibits discrimination

O'Connor, J., concurring, joined the Court's opinion except for its analysis of freedom of expressive association: "[T]he Court has adopted a test that unadvisedly casts doubt on the power of States to pursue the profoundly important goal of ensuring nondiscriminatory access to commercial opportunities" yet "accords insufficient protection to expressive associations and places inappropriate burdens on groups claiming the protection of the First Amendment":

"[The] Court declares that the Jaycees' right of association depends on the organization's making a 'substantial' showing that the admission of unwelcome members 'will change the message communicated by the group's speech.' [S]uch a requirement, especially in the context of the balancing-of-interests test articulated by the Court, raises the possibility that certain commercial associations, by engaging occasionally in certain kinds of expressive activities, might improperly gain protection for discrimination. The Court's focus raises other problems as well. [W]ould the Court's analysis of this case be different if, for example, the Jaycees membership had a steady history of opposing public issues thought (by the Court) to be favored by women? It might seem easy to conclude, in the latter case, that the admission of women to the Jaycees' ranks would affect the content of the organization's message, but I do not believe that should change the outcome of this case. Whether an association is or is not constitutionally protected in the selection of its membership should not depend on what the association says or why its members say it.

"The Court's readiness to inquire into the connection between membership and message reveals a more fundamental flaw in its analysis. The Court pursues this inquiry as part of its mechanical application of a 'compelling interest' test, [and] entirely neglects to establish at the threshold that the Jaycees is an association whose activities or purposes should engage the strong protections that the First Amendment extends to expressive associations.

"On the one hand, an association engaged exclusively in protected expression enjoys First Amendment protection of both the content of its message and the choice of its members. * * * Protection of the association's right to define its membership derives from the recognition that the formation of an expressive association is the creation of a voice, and the selection of members is the definition of that voice. [A] ban on specific group voices on public affairs violates the most basic guarantee of the First Amendment—that citizens, not the government, control the content of public discussion.

"On the other hand, there is only minimal constitutional protection of the freedom of *commercial* association. There are, of course, some constitutional protections of commercial speech—speech intended and used to promote a commercial transaction with the speaker. But the State is free to impose any rational regulation on the commercial transaction itself. The Constitution does not guarantee a right to choose employees, customers, suppliers, or those with whom one engages in simple commercial transactions, without restraint from the State.

"[A]n association should be characterized as commercial, and therefore subject to rationally related state regulation of its membership and other associational activities, when, and only when, the association's activities are not predominantly of the type protected by the First Amendment. It is only when the association is predominantly engaged in protected expression that state regulation

based on race, creed, or sex by institutions (except benevolent orders or religious corporations) with more than 400 members that provide regular meal service and receive payment from nonmembers for the furtherance of trade or business); *Dallas v. Stanglin*, 490 U.S. 19 (1989) (upholding ordinance restricting admission to certain dance halls to persons between the ages of 14 and 18).

of its membership will necessarily affect, change, dilute, or silence one collective voice that would otherwise be heard. An association must choose its market. Once it enters the marketplace of commerce in any substantial degree it loses the complete control over its membership that it would otherwise enjoy if it confined its affairs to the marketplace of ideas.

"[N]otwithstanding its protected expressive activities, [appellee] is, first and foremost, an organization that, at both the national and local levels, promotes and practices the art of solicitation and management. The organization claims that the training it offers its members gives them an advantage in business, and business firms do indeed sometimes pay the dues of individual memberships for their employees. Jaycees members hone their solicitation and management skills, under the direction and supervision of the organization, primarily through their active recruitment of new members. [The] 'not insubstantial' volume of protected Jaycees activity found by the Court of Appeals is simply not enough to preclude state regulation of the Jaycees' commercial activities. The State of Minnesota has a legitimate interest in ensuring nondiscriminatory access to the commercial opportunity presented by membership in the Jaycees."

James Dale's position as an assistant scoutmaster of a New Jersey troop of the Boy Scouts of America was revoked. The Scouts had learned that he was gay, and that as the co-President of the Rutgers University Lesbian/Gay Alliance, he had been publicly quoted on the importance in his own life on the need for gay role models. Dale sued, and the New Jersey Supreme Court ultimately held that New Jersey's anti-discrimination public accommodation law required that the Scouts readmit him.

BOY SCOUTS OF AMERICA v. DALE, 530 U.S. 640 (2000), per REHNQUIST, C.J., held that the New Jersey law violated the expressive association rights of the Boy Scouts: "The First Amendment's protection of expressive association is not reserved for advocacy groups. But to come within its ambit, a group must engage in some form of expression, whether it be public or private.

"Because this is a First Amendment case where the ultimate conclusions of law are virtually inseparable from findings of fact, we are obligated to independently review the factual record.

"The Boy Scouts [says] that it 'teach[es] that homosexual conduct is not morally straight' * * *. We need not inquire further to determine the nature of the Boy Scouts' expression with respect to homosexuality. But because the record before us contains written evidence of the Boy Scouts' viewpoint, we look to it as instructive, if only on the question of the sincerity of the professed beliefs."

After exploring some of the written evidence, Rehnquist, C.J., stated that "[A]ssociations do not have to associate for the 'purpose' of disseminating a certain message in order to be entitled to the protections of the First Amendment. An association must merely engage in expressive activity that could be impaired in order to be entitled to protection. For example, the purpose of the St. Patrick's Day parade in Hurley was not to espouse any views about sexual orientation, but we held that the parade organizers had a right to exclude certain participants nonetheless. * * *

"We recognized in cases such as *Roberts* and *Duarte* that States have a compelling interest in eliminating discrimination against women in public accommodations. But in each of these cases we went on to conclude that the enforcement of these statutes would not materially interfere with the ideas that the organization sought to express. * * * New Jersey's public accommodations law directly and immediately affects associational rights, in this case associational rights that enjoy First Amendment protection. Thus, *O'Brien*['s] intermediate standard of review [is] inapplicable."

STEVENS, J., joined by Souter, Ginsburg, and Breyer, JJ., dissented: "[At] a minimum, a group seeking to prevail over an antidiscrimination law must adhere to a clear and unequivocal view. * * *

"Several principles are made perfectly clear by *Jaycees* and *Rotary Club*. First, to prevail on a claim of expressive association in the face of a State's antidiscrimination law, it is not enough simply to engage in *some kind* of expressive activity. Both the Jaycees and the Rotary Club engaged in expressive activity protected by the First Amendment, yet that fact was not dispositive. Second, it is not enough to adopt an openly avowed exclusionary membership policy. Both the Jaycees and the Rotary Club did that as well. Third, it is not sufficient merely to articulate *some* connection between the group's expressive activities and its exclusionary policy. The Rotary Club, for example, justified its male-only membership policy by pointing to the 'aspect of fellowship ... that is enjoyed by the [exclusively] male membership' and by claiming that only with an exclusively male membership could it 'operate effectively' in foreign countries.

"Rather, in *Jaycees*, we asked whether Minnesota's Human Rights Law requiring the admission of women 'impose[d] any *serious burdens*' on the group's 'collective effort on behalf of [its] *shared goals*.' Notwithstanding the group's obvious publicly stated exclusionary policy, we did not view the inclusion of women as a 'serious burden' on the Jaycees' ability to engage in the protected speech of its choice. Similarly, in *Rotary Club*, we asked whether California's law would 'affect in any *significant* way the existing members' ability' to engage in their protected speech, or whether the law would require the clubs 'to abandon their basic goals.' * * *

"The evidence before this Court makes it exceptionally clear that BSA has, at most, simply adopted an exclusionary membership policy and has no shared goal of disapproving of homosexuality [or] collective effort to foster a belief about homosexuality at all—let alone one that is significantly burdened by admitting homosexuals." Stevens, J., argued that the deference afforded to the litigants statements of their expressive commitments was inappropriate in the absence of record evidence. With respect to GLIB, he maintained: "[W]e found it relevant that GLIB's message 'would likely be perceived' as the parade organizers' own speech. That was so because '[p]arades and demonstrations [are] not understood to be so neutrally presented or selectively viewed' as, say, a broadcast by a cable operator, who is usually considered to be 'merely 'a conduit' for the speech' produced by others. * * *

"Dale's inclusion in the Boy Scouts [sends] no cognizable message to the Scouts or to the world. Unlike GLIB, Dale did not carry a banner or a sign; he did not distribute any fact sheet; and he expressed no intent to send any message. If there is any kind of message being sent, then, it is by the mere act of joining the Boy Scouts. [S]ome acts are so imbued with symbolic meaning that they qualify as 'speech' under the First Amendment. [But], if merely joining a group did constitute symbolic speech; and such speech were attributable to the group being joined; and that group has the right to exclude that speech (and hence, the right to exclude that person from joining), then the right of free speech effectively becomes a limitless right to exclude for every organization, whether or not it engages in any expressive activities. That cannot be, and never has been, the law."

————

CHRISTIAN LEGAL SOCIETY v. MARTINEZ, 130 S.Ct. ___ (2010), per GINSBURG, J., held that Hastings Law School could condition official recognition of a student group—and the resulting eligibility for financial resources and access to certain facilities—on its agreement to open its membership and eligibility for access to leadership positions to all students ("all-comers" policy). a The Christian Legal Society restricted membership to Christians and denied access to those who "engage in unrepentant homosexual conduct." Ginsburg, J., concluded that the policy, denying the Society access to a limited public forum, was viewpoint neutral; indeed it drew no distinction between groups based on their message or perspective; it regulated conduct, not speech.

She also maintained that the policy was "reasonable." It ensured that students were afforded leadership, educational, and social opportunities, that Hastings students are not forced through student fees to fund a group that would reject them as members, helped Hastings enforce its anti-discrimination policy (and state anti-discrimination laws) without the necessity of determining the basis for membership restrictions, and by bringing together people of diverse backgrounds encouraged toleration, cooperation, and learning. Any claim that hostile students would take over an organization was contrary to the experience of the school and unduly speculative.

The reasonableness of the policy was also indicated by its measured character. The school offered the Society access to school facilities to conduct meetings and the use of chalkboards and some bulletin boards, and it could take advantage of electronic media and social networking sites. "It is beyond dissenter's license * * * constantly to maintain that nonrecognition of a group is equivalent to prohibiting its members from speaking."

Nor did the policy impinge on the Society's freedom of association right to choose its members. Although the Society had a right to be selective in its membership, it had no right for the state to subsidize its selectivity. Finally, the Court rejected claims that the policy had been applied in a discriminatory way and that it was a pretext to single out the Christian Legal Society for special treatment. Ginsburg, J., maintained that such claims were not before the Court because the parties stipulated that Hastings current policy was an all-comers policy and that it applied equally to religious and political groups. The Court remanded to permit the lower court to explore claims of pretext if they were still open to the plaintiffs.

STEVENS, J., concurring, argued that Hastings' exclusion of the Society from its limited public forum would have been justified even under a policy that only excluded groups discriminating on the basis of race, gender, religion, and sexual orientation: Hastings "excludes students who will not sign its Statement of Faith or who engage in 'unrepentant homosexual conduct.' [Other] groups may exclude or mistreat Jews, blacks and women—or those who do not share their contempt for Jews, blacks and women. A free society may tolerate such groups. It need not

---

a. The Hastings brief observed that recognized student organizations can require students to pay dues, maintain good attendance, refrain from gross misconduct, or to pass a skill-based test, such as the writing competitions administered by the law journals. The dissent stated that this admission transformed the all-comers policy into a some-comers policy.

subsidize them, give them its official imprimatur, or grant them equal access to law school facilities."b

ALITO, J., joined by Roberts, C.J., Scalia and Thomas, JJ., dissented, mostly disagreeing with the majority's reading of the record. Alito, J., argued that the Hastings policy shifted over the years, that it had been applied in a discriminatory way (including the denial of access to facilities), that it was ultimately pretextual, and that such issues were rightly before the Court, and that the decision was a "serious setback for freedom of expression in this country."

As to the all-comers policy, even applied in a non-discriminatory way, he argued that it was unreasonable in large part because it impinged on freedom of association by denying access to needed facilities, and that subsidies were a minor part of the case. Respecting freedom of association also promoted leadership, educational, and social opportunities. He denied that the difficulty of enforcing a nondiscrimination policy was greater than other policies it sought to enforce and denied that California law called into question that right of religious groups to discriminate on the basis of religion. He maintained that furthering toleration, cooperation, and learning skills was consistent with pluralism. Alito, J., also denied that the all-comers policy was viewpoint neutral in that it opened the door for hostile groups to take over organizations and because of his view of discriminatory purpose and treatment.

———

In the *Rumsfeld* case, note 1(c) supra, FAIR, citing *Dale,* argued that the Solomon Amendment violated law schools' freedom of expressive association. But the Court disagreed: "To comply with the statute, law schools must allow military recruiters on campus and assist them in whatever way the school chooses to assist other employers. Law schools therefore 'associate' with military recruiters in the sense that they interact with them. But recruiters are not part of the law school. Recruiters are, by definition, outsiders who come onto campus for the limited purpose of trying to hire students—not to become members of the school's expressive association. This distinction is critical. Unlike the public accommodations law in *Dale,* the Solomon Amendment does not force a law school 'to accept members it does not desire.' "

SECTION 10.   WEALTH AND THE POLITICAL PROCESS: CONCERNS FOR EQUALITY

The idea of equality has loomed large throughout this chapter. Some feel it should be a central concern of the First Amendment. Equality has been championed by those who seek access to government property and to media facilities. It has been invoked in support of content regulation and against it. This section considers government efforts to prevent the domination of the political process by wealthy individuals and business corporations. In the end, it would be appropriate to reconsider the arguments for and against a marketplace conception of the First Amendment, to ask whether the Court's interpretations overall (e.g., taking the public forum materials, the media materials, and the election materials together)

---

b. Kennedy, J., concurring, argued that Hastings could reasonably believe that the process of learning how to create arguments in a "convincing, rational, and respectful manner and to express doubt and disagreement in a professional way" is best enhanced when dialogue is "vibrant" which cannot occur if "students wall themselves off from opposing points of view."

have adequately considered the interest in equality, and to inquire generally about the relationship between liberty and equality in the constitutional scheme.

BUCKLEY v. VALEO

424 U.S. 1, 96 S.Ct. 612, 46 L.Ed.2d 659 (1976).

PER CURIAM.

[In this portion of a lengthy opinion dealing with the validity of the Federal Election Campaign Act of 1971, as amended in 1974, the Court considers those parts of the Act limiting *contributions* to a candidate for federal office (all sustained), and those parts limiting *expenditures* in support of such candidacy (all held invalid).]

A. *General Principles.* The Act's contribution and expenditure limitations operate in an area of the most fundamental First Amendment activities. Discussion of public issues and debate on the qualifications of candidates are integral to the operation of the system of government established by our Constitution.

[Appellees] contend that what the Act regulates is conduct, and that its effect on speech and association is incidental at most. Appellants respond that contributions and expenditures are at the very core of political speech, and that the Act's limitations thus constitute restraints on First Amendment liberty that are both gross and [direct.]

We cannot share the view [that] the present Act's contribution and expenditure limitations are comparable to the restrictions on conduct upheld in *O'Brien* [Sec. 2 supra]. The expenditure of money simply cannot be equated with such conduct as destruction of a draft card. Some forms of communication made possible by the giving and spending of money involve speech alone, some involve conduct primarily, and some involve a combination of the two. Yet this Court has never suggested that the dependence of a communication on the expenditure of money operates itself to introduce a non-speech element or to reduce the exacting scrutiny required by the First Amendment. * * *

Even if the categorization of the expenditure of money as conduct were accepted, the limitations challenged here would not meet the *O'Brien* test because the governmental interests advanced in support of the Act involve "suppressing communication." The interests served by the Act include restricting the voices of people and interest groups who have money to spend and reducing the overall scope of federal election campaigns. [Unlike] *O'Brien,* where [the] interest in the preservation of draft cards was wholly unrelated to their use as a means of communication, it is beyond dispute that the interest in regulating the alleged "conduct" of giving or spending money "arises in some measure because the communication allegedly integral to the conduct is itself thought to be harmful."

Nor can the Act's contribution and expenditure limitations be sustained, as some of the parties suggest, by reference to the constitutional principles reflected in such decisions as *Adderley* and *Kovacs,* 336 U.S. 77 (1949) [Sec. 5 II, B and Sec. 6, III supra]. [The] critical difference between this case and those time, place and manner cases is that the present Act's contribution and expenditure limitations impose direct quantity restrictions on political communication and association by persons, groups, candidates and political parties in addition to any reasonable time, place, and manner regulations otherwise imposed.

A restriction on the amount of money a person or group can spend on political communication during a campaign necessarily reduces the quantity of expression by restricting the number of issues discussed, the depth of their exploration, and the size of the audience reached. This is because virtually every means of communicating ideas in today's mass society requires the expenditure of [money].

The expenditure limitations contained in the Act represent substantial rather than merely theoretical restraints on the quantity and diversity of political speech. The $1,000 ceiling on spending "relative to a clearly identified candidate," 18 U.S.C. § 608(e)(1), would appear to exclude all citizens and groups except candidates, political parties and the institutional press from any significant use of the most effective modes of communication.20 * * *

By contrast with a limitation upon expenditures for political expression, a limitation [on] the amount of money a person may give to a candidate or campaign organization [involves] little direct restraint on his political communication, for it permits the symbolic expression of support evidenced by a contribution but does not in any way infringe the contributor's freedom to discuss candidates and issues. While contributions may result in political expression if spent by a candidate or an association to present views to the voters, the transformation of contributions into political debate involves speech by someone other than the contributor.

[There] is no indication [that] the contribution limitations imposed by the Act would have any dramatic adverse effect on the funding of campaigns and political associations.23 The overall effect of the Act's contribution ceilings is merely to require candidates and political committees to raise funds from a greater number of persons and to compel people who would otherwise contribute amounts greater than the statutory limits to expend such funds on direct political expression, rather than to reduce the total amount of money potentially available to promote political expression. * * *

In sum, although the Act's contribution and expenditure limitations both implicate fundamental First Amendment interests, its expenditure ceilings impose significantly more severe restrictions on protected freedoms of political expression and association than do its limitations on financial contributions.

B. *Contribution Limitations.* [Section] 608(b) provides, with certain limited exceptions, that "no person shall make contributions to any candidate with respect to any election for Federal office which, in the aggregate, exceeds $1,000."a* * *

Appellants contend that the $1,000 contribution ceiling unjustifiably burdens First Amendment freedoms, employs overbroad dollar limits, and discriminates against candidates opposing incumbent officeholders and against minor-party candidates in violation of the Fifth Amendment.

[In] view of the fundamental nature of the right to associate, governmental "action which may have the effect of curtailing the freedom to associate is subject

20. The record indicates that, as of January 1, 1975, one full-page advertisement in a daily edition of a certain metropolitan newspaper costs $6,971.04—almost seven times the annual limit on expenditures "relative to" a particular candidate imposed on the vast majority of individual citizens and associations by § 608(e)(1).

23. Statistical findings agreed to by the parties reveal that approximately 5.1% of the $73,483,613 raised by the 1161 candidates for Congress in 1974 was obtained in amounts in excess of $1,000. In 1974, two major-party senatorial candidates, Ramsey Clark and Senator Charles Mathias, Jr., operated large-scale cam-

paigns on contributions raised under a voluntarily imposed $100 contribution limitation.

a. As defined, "person" includes "an individual, partnership, committee, association, corporation or any other organization or group." The limitation applies to: (1) anything of value, such as gifts, loans, advances, and promises to give, (2) contributions made direct to the candidate or to an intermediary, or a committee authorized by the candidate, (3) the aggregate amounts contributed to the candidate for each election, treating primaries, runoff elections and general elections separately and all Presidential primaries within a single calendar year as one election.

to the closest scrutiny." Yet, it is clear that "[n]either the right to associate nor the right to participate in political activities is absolute." Even a " 'significant interference' with protected rights of political association" may be sustained if the State demonstrates a sufficiently important interest and employs means closely drawn to avoid unnecessary abridgment of associational freedoms. * * *

It is unnecessary to look beyond the Act's primary purpose—to limit the actuality and appearance of corruption resulting from large individual financial contributions—in order to find a constitutionally sufficient justification for the $1,000 contribution limitation. [The] increasing importance of the communications media and sophisticated mass mailing and polling operations to effective campaigning make the raising of large sums of money an ever more essential ingredient of an effective candidacy. To the extent that large contributions are given to secure political quid pro quos from current and potential office holders, the integrity of our system of representative democracy is undermined. Although the scope of such pernicious practices can never be reliably ascertained, the deeply disturbing examples surfacing after the 1972 election demonstrate that the problem is not an illusory one.

Of almost equal concern as the danger of actual quid pro quo arrangements is the impact of the appearance of corruption stemming from public awareness of the opportunities for abuse inherent in a regime of large individual financial contributions. In *Letter Carriers,* the Court found that the danger to "fair and effective government" posed by partisan political conduct on the part of federal employees charged with administering the law was a sufficiently important concern to justify broad restrictions on the employees' right of partisan political association. Here, as there, Congress could legitimately conclude that the avoidance of the appearance of improper influence "is also critical [if] confidence in the system of representative Government is not to be eroded to a disastrous extent."29

Appellants contend that the contribution limitations must be invalidated because bribery laws and narrowly-drawn disclosure requirements constitute a less restrictive means of dealing with "proven and suspected quid pro quo arrangements." But laws [against] bribes deal with only the most blatant and specific attempts of those with money to influence governmental action. [And] Congress was surely entitled to conclude that disclosure was only a partial measure, and that contribution ceilings were a necessary legislative concomitant to deal with the reality or appearance of corruption inherent in a system permitting unlimited financial contributions, even when the identities of the contributors and the amounts of their contributions are fully disclosed.

The Act's $1,000 contribution limitation focuses precisely on the problem of large campaign contributions—the narrow aspect of political association where the actuality and potential for corruption have been identified—while leaving persons free to engage in independent political expression, to associate actively through volunteering their services. [The] Act's contribution limitations [do] not undermine to any material degree the potential for robust and effective discussion of candidates and campaign [issues].

We find that, under the rigorous standard of review established by our prior decisions, the weighty interests served by restricting the size of financial contribu-

29. Although the Court in *Letter Carriers* found that this interest was constitutionally sufficient to justify legislation prohibiting federal employees from engaging in certain parti-san political activities, it was careful to emphasize that the limitations did not restrict an employee's right to express his views on political issues and candidates.

tions to political candidates are sufficient to justify the limited effect upon First Amendment freedoms caused by the $1,000 contribution ceiling.**b**

C. *Expenditure Limitations.* [1.] Section 608(e)(1) provides that "[n]o person may make any expenditure [relative] to a clearly identified candidate during a calendar year which, when added to all other expenditures made by such person during the year advocating the election or defeat of such candidate, exceeds $1,000." [Its] plain effect [is] to prohibit all individuals, who are neither candidates nor owners of institutional press facilities, and all groups, except political parties and campaign organizations, from voicing their views "relative to a clearly identified candidate" through means that entail aggregate expenditures of more than $1,000 during a calendar year. The provision, for example, would make it a federal criminal offense for a person or association to place a single one-quarter page advertisement "relative to a clearly identified candidate" in a major metropolitan newspaper.

[Although] "expenditure," "clearly identified," and "candidate" are defined in the Act, there is no definition clarifying what expenditures are "relative to" a candidate. [But the "when" clause in § 608(e)(1)] clearly permits, if indeed it does not require, the phrase "relative to" a candidate to be read to mean "advocating the election or defeat of" a candidate.

But while such a construction of § 608(e)(1) refocuses the vagueness question, [it hardly] eliminates the problem of unconstitutional vagueness altogether. For the distinction between discussion of issues and candidates and advocacy of election or defeat of candidates may often dissolve in practical application. Candidates, especially incumbents, are intimately tied to public issues involving legislative proposals and governmental actions. Not only do candidates campaign on the basis of their positions on various public issues, but campaigns themselves generate issues of public interest.

[Constitutionally deficient uncertainty which "compels the speaker to hedge and trim"] can be avoided only by reading § 608(e)(1) as limited to communications that include explicit words of advocacy of election or defeat of a candidate, much as the definition of "clearly identified" in § 608(e)(2) requires that an explicit and unambiguous reference to the candidate appear as part of the communication. This is the reading of the provision suggested by the nongovernmental appellees in arguing that "[f]unds spent to propagate one's views on issues without expressly calling for a candidate's election or defeat are thus not covered." We agree that in order to preserve the provision against invalidation on vagueness grounds, § 608(e)(1) must be construed to apply only to expenditures

---

b. The Court rejected the challenges that the $1,000 limit was overbroad because (1) most large contributors do not seek improper influence over a candidate, and (2) much more than $1,000 would still not be enough to influence improperly a candidate or office holder. With respect to (1), "Congress was justified in concluding that the interest in safeguarding against the appearance of impropriety requires that the opportunity for abuse inherent in the process of raising large monetary contributions be eliminated." With respect to (2), "As the Court of Appeals observed, '[a] court has no scalpel to probe, whether, say, a $2,000 ceiling might not serve as well as $1,000.' Such distinctions in degree become significant only when they can be said to amount to differences in kind."

The Court also rejected as without support in the record the claims that the contribution limitations worked invidious discrimination between incumbents and challengers to whom the same limitations applied.

The Court then upheld (1) exclusion from the $1,000 limit of the value of unpaid volunteer services and of certain expenses paid by the volunteer up to a maximum of $500; (2) the higher limit of $5,000 for contributions to a candidate by established, registered political committees with at least 50 contributing supporters and fielding at least five candidates for federal office; and (3) the $25,000 limit on total contributions to all candidates by one person in one calendar year.

for communications that in express terms advocate the election or defeat of a clearly identified candidate for federal office.

We turn then to the basic First Amendment question—whether § 608(e)(1), even as thus narrowly and explicitly construed, impermissibly burdens the constitutional right of free expression. * * *

We find that the governmental interest in preventing corruption and the appearance of corruption is inadequate to justify § 608(e)(1)'s ceiling on independent expenditures. First, assuming arguendo that large independent expenditures pose the same dangers of actual or apparent quid pro quo arrangements as do large contributions, § 608(e)(1) does not provide an answer that sufficiently relates to the elimination of those dangers. Unlike the contribution limitations' total ban on the giving of large amounts of money to candidates, § 608(e)(1) prevents only some large expenditures. So long as persons and groups eschew expenditures that in express terms advocate the election or defeat of a clearly identified candidate, they are free to spend as much as they want to promote the candidate and his views. The exacting interpretation of the statutory language necessary to avoid unconstitutional vagueness thus undermines the limitation's effectiveness as a loophole-closing provision by facilitating circumvention by those seeking to exert improper influence upon a candidate or office-holder. It would naively underestimate the ingenuity and resourcefulness of persons and groups desiring to buy influence to believe that they would have much difficulty devising expenditures that skirted the restriction on express advocacy of election or defeat but nevertheless benefitted the candidate's campaign. * * *

Second, [the] independent advocacy restricted by the provision does not presently appear to pose dangers of real or apparent corruption comparable to those identified with large campaign contributions. The parties defending § 608(e)(1) contend that it is necessary to prevent would-be contributors from avoiding the contribution limitations by the simple expedient of paying directly for media advertisements or for other portions of the candidate's campaign activities. [Section] 608(b)'s contribution ceilings rather than § 608(e)(1)'s independent expenditure limitation prevent attempts to circumvent the Act through prearranged or coordinated expenditures amounting to disguised contributions.53 By contrast, § 608(e)(1) limits expenditures for express advocacy of candidates made totally independently of the candidate and his campaign. [The] absence of prearrangement and coordination of an expenditure with the candidate or his agent not only undermines the value of the expenditure to the candidate, but also alleviates the danger that expenditures will be given as a quid pro quo for improper commitments from the candidate. Rather than preventing circumvention of the contribution limitations, § 608(e)(1) severely restricts all independent advocacy despite its substantially diminished potential for abuse.

While the independent expenditure ceiling thus fails to serve any substantial governmental interest in stemming the reality or appearance of corruption in the electoral process, it heavily burdens core First Amendment expression. [Advocacy]

---

53. Section 608(e)(1) does not apply to expenditures "on behalf of a candidate within the meaning of" § 608(2)(B). That section provides that expenditures "authorized or requested by the candidate, an authorized committee of the candidate, or an agent of the candidate" are to be treated as expenditures of the candidate and contributions by the person or group making the expenditure. [In] view of [the] legislative history and the purposes of the Act, we find that the "authorized or requested" standard of the Act operates to treat all expenditures placed in cooperation with or with the consent of a candidate, his agents, or an authorized committee of the candidate as contributions subject to the limitations set forth in § 608(b). [Eds. Subsequent cases have held that group expenditures on behalf of a candidate that are not coordinated with the candidate may not constitutionally be restricted. FEC v. National Conservative Political Action Comm., 470 U.S. 480 (1985)].

of the election or defeat of candidates for federal office is no less entitled to protection under the First Amendment than the discussion of political policy generally or advocacy of the passage or defeat of legislation.

It is argued, however, that the ancillary governmental interest in equalizing the relative ability of individuals and groups to influence the outcome of elections serves to justify the limitation on express advocacy of the election or defeat of candidates imposed by § 608(e)(1)'s expenditure ceiling. But the concept that government may restrict the speech of some elements of our society in order to enhance the relative voice of others is wholly foreign to the First Amendment, which was designed "to secure 'the widest possible dissemination of information from diverse and antagonistic sources,'" and "'to assure unfettered interchange of ideas for the bringing about of political and social changes desired by the people.'" *New York Times Co. v. Sullivan.* The First Amendment's protection against governmental abridgement of free expression cannot properly be made to depend on a person's financial ability to engage in public discussion.**55**

* * * *Mills v. Alabama,* 384 U.S. 214 (1966), held that legislative restrictions on advocacy of the election or defeat of political candidates are wholly at odds with the guarantees of the First Amendment. [Yet] the prohibition on election day editorials invalidated in *Mills* is clearly a lesser intrusion on constitutional freedom than a $1,000 limitation on the amount of money any person or association can spend *during an entire election year* in advocating the election or defeat of a candidate for public office.

For the reasons stated, we conclude that § 608(e)(1)'s independent expenditure limitation is unconstitutional under the First Amendment. * * * *c

2. [The] Act also sets limits on expenditures by a candidate "from his personal funds, or the personal funds of his immediate family, in connection with his campaigns during any calendar year." § 608(a)(1).**d**

The ceiling on personal expenditures by candidates on their own behalf [imposes] a substantial restraint on the ability of persons to engage in protected First Amendment expression. The candidate, no less than any other person, has a First Amendment right to engage in the discussion of public issues and vigorously and tirelessly to advocate his own election and the election of other candidates. Indeed, it is of particular importance that candidates have the unfettered opportunity to make their views known so that the electorate may intelligently evaluate the candidates' personal qualities and their positions on vital public issues before choosing among them on election day. [Section] 608(a)'s ceiling on personal

55. Neither the voting rights cases nor the Court's decision upholding the FCC's fairness doctrine lends support to appellees' position that the First Amendment permits Congress to abridge the rights of some persons to engage in political expression in order to enhance the relative voice of other segments of our [society].

c. The Court invalidated restrictions on the amount of personal funds candidates could spend on their own behalf and on the amount of overall campaign expenditures by federal candidates. The anti-corruption rationale did not apply in the former instance and was already served by the Act's contribution and disclosure provisions. Building on this rationale, *Davis v. FEC,* 128 S.Ct. 2759 (2008), held that Congress could not increase the contribution limits for a candidate whose opponent had achieved a specified spending advantage by virtue of his or her personal funds. The Court maintained that the anti-corruption rationale did not apply and that the goal of equalizing electoral opportunities was not a sufficient interest to override First Amendment rights. It did indicate that Congress could raise contribution limits for *both* candidates if concerns of advantages gained by personal wealth were present. Moreover, the *Buckley* Court stated that Congress could engage in public financing of election campaigns and condition acceptance of public funds on an agreement by the candidate to accept expenditure limitations.

d. $50,000 for Presidential or Vice Presidential candidates; $35,000 for Senate candidates; $25,000 for most candidates for the House of Representatives.

expenditures by a candidate in furtherance of his own candidacy thus clearly and directly interferes with constitutionally protected freedoms.

The primary governmental interest served by the Act—the prevention of actual and apparent corruption of the political process—does not support the limitation on the candidate's expenditure of his own personal funds. [Indeed], the use of personal funds reduces the candidate's dependence on outside contributions and thereby counteracts the coercive pressures and attendant risks of abuse to which the Act's contribution limitations are directed.

The ancillary interest in equalizing the relative financial resources of candidates competing for elective office, therefore, provides the sole relevant rationale for Section 608(a)'s expenditure ceiling. That interest is clearly not sufficient to justify the provision's infringement of fundamental First Amendment rights. First, the limitation may fail to promote financial equality among candidates. [Indeed], a candidate's personal wealth may impede his [fundraising efforts]. Second, and more fundamentally, the First Amendment simply cannot tolerate § 608(a)'s restriction upon the freedom of a candidate to speak without legislative limit on behalf of his own candidacy. We therefore hold that § 608(a)'s restrictions on a candidate's personal expenditures is unconstitutional.

3. [Section] 608(c) of the Act places limitations on overall campaign expenditures by candidates [seeking] election to federal office. [For Presidential candidates the ceiling is $10,000,000 in seeking nomination and $20,000,000 in the general election campaign; for House of Representatives candidates it is $70,000 for each campaign—primary and general; for candidates for Senator the ceiling depends on the size of the voting age population.]

No governmental interest that has been suggested is sufficient to justify [these restrictions] on the quantity of political expression. [The] interest in alleviating the corrupting influence of large contributions is served by the Act's contribution limitations and disclosure provisions rather than by § 608(c)'s campaign expenditure ceilings. [There] is no indication that the substantial criminal penalties for violating the contribution ceilings combined with the political repercussion of such violations will be insufficient to police the contribution provisions. Extensive reporting, auditing, and disclosure requirements applicable to both contributions and expenditures by political campaigns are designed to facilitate the detection of illegal contributions. * * *

The interest in equalizing the financial resources of candidates competing for federal office is no more convincing a justification for restricting the scope of federal election campaigns. Given the limitation on the size of outside contributions, the financial resources available to a candidate's campaign, like the number of volunteers recruited, will normally vary with the size and intensity of the candidate's support. There is nothing invidious, improper, or unhealthy in permitting such funds to be spent to carry the candidate's message to the electorate. Moreover, the equalization of permissible campaign expenditures might serve not to equalize the opportunities of all candidates but to handicap a candidate who lacked substantial name recognition or exposure of his views before the start of the campaign.

The campaign expenditure ceilings appear to be designed primarily to serve the governmental interests in reducing the allegedly skyrocketing costs of political campaigns. [But the] First Amendment denies government the power to determine that spending to promote one's political views is wasteful, excessive, or unwise. In the free society ordained by our Constitution it is not the government but the people individually as citizens and candidates and collectively as associations and political committees who must retain control over the quantity and range of debate on public issues in a political campaign.65

For these reasons we hold that § 608(c) is constitutionally invalid. * * *

CHIEF JUSTICE BURGER, concurring in part and dissenting in part.

[I] agree fully with that part of the Court's opinion that holds unconstitutional the limitations the Act puts on campaign expenditures. [Yet] when it approves similarly stringent limitations on contributions, the Court ignores the reasons it finds so persuasive in the context of expenditures. For me contributions and expenditures are two sides of the same First Amendment coin.

[Limiting] contributions, as a practical matter, will limit expenditures and will put an effective ceiling on the amount of political activity and debate that the Government will permit to take place.5

The Court attempts to separate the two communicative aspects of political contributions—the "moral" support that the gift itself conveys, which the Court suggests is the same whether the gift is of $10 or $10,000,6 and the fact that money translates into communication. The Court dismisses the effect of the limitations on the second aspect of contributions: "[T]he transformation of contributions into political debate involves speech by someone other than the contributor." On this premise—that contribution limitations restrict only the speech of "someone other than the contributor"—rests the Court's justification for treating contributions differently from expenditures. The premise is demonstrably flawed; the contribution limitations will, in specific instances, limit exactly the same political activity that the expenditure ceilings limit, and at least one of the "expenditure" limitations the Court finds objectionable operates precisely like the "contribution" limitations.8

The Court's attempt to distinguish the communication inherent in political *contributions* from the speech aspects of political *expenditures* simply will not wash. We do little but engage in word games unless we recognize that people—candidates and contributors—spend money on political activity because they wish to communicate ideas, and their constitutional interest in doing so is precisely the same whether they or someone else utter the words.

[T]he restrictions are hardly incidental in their effect upon particular campaigns. Judges are ill-equipped to gauge the precise impact of legislation, but a law that impinges upon First Amendment rights requires us to make the attempt. It is

---

65. [Congress] may engage in public financing of election campaigns and may condition acceptance of public funds on an agreement by the candidate to abide by specified expenditure limitations. Just as a candidate may voluntarily limit the size of the contributions he chooses to accept he may decide to forgo private fundraising and accept public funding.

5. The Court notes that 94.9% of the funds raised by congressional candidates in 1974 came in contributions of less than $1,000, n. 27, and suggests that the effect of the contribution limitations will be minimal. This logic ignores the disproportionate influence large contributions may have when they are made early in a campaign; "seed money" can be essential, and the inability to obtain it may effectively end some candidacies before they begin. Appellants have excerpted from the record data on nine campaigns to which large, initial contributions were critical. Campaigns

such as these will be much harder, and perhaps impossible, to mount under the Act.

6. Whatever the effect of the limitation, it is clearly arbitrary—Congress has imposed the same ceiling on contributions to a New York or California senatorial campaign that it has put on House races in Alaska or Wyoming. Both the strength of support conveyed by the gift of $1,000 *and* the gift's potential for corruptly influencing the recipient will vary enormously from place to place. * * *

8. The Court treats the Act's provisions limiting a candidate's spending from his *personal resources* as *expenditure* limits, as indeed the Act characterizes them, and holds them unconstitutional. As Mr. Justice Marshall points out, infra, by the Court's logic these provisions could as easily be treated as limits on *contributions*, since they limit what the candidate can give to his own campaign.

not simply speculation to think that the limitations on contributions will foreclose some candidacies.9 The limitations will also alter the nature of some electoral contests drastically.10

[In] striking down the limitations on campaign expenditures, the Court relies in part on its conclusion that other means—namely, disclosure and contribution ceilings—will adequately serve the statute's aim. It is not clear why the same analysis is not also appropriate in weighing the need for contribution ceilings in addition to disclosure requirements. Congress may well be entitled to conclude that disclosure was a "partial measure," but I had not thought until today that Congress could enact its conclusions in the First Amendment area into laws immune from the most searching review by this Court. * * *e

JUSTICE WHITE, concurring in part and dissenting in part. * * *

I [agree] with the Court's judgment upholding the limitations on contributions. I dissent [from] the Court's view that the expenditure limitations [violate] the First Amendment. [This] case depends on whether the nonspeech interests of the Federal Government in regulating the use of money in political campaigns are sufficiently urgent to justify the incidental effects that the limitations visit upon the First Amendment interests of candidates and their supporters.

[The Court] accepts the congressional judgment that the evils of unlimited contributions are sufficiently threatening to warrant restriction regardless of the impact of the limits on the contributor's opportunity for effective speech and in turn on the total volume of the candidate's political communications by reason of his inability to accept large sums from those willing to give.

The congressional judgment, which I would also accept, was that other steps must be taken to counter the corrosive effects of money in federal election campaigns. One of these steps is § 608(e), which [limits] what a contributor may independently spend in support or denigration of one running for federal office. Congress was plainly of the view that these expenditures also have corruptive potential; but the Court strikes down the provision, strangely enough claiming more insight as to what may improperly influence candidates than is possessed by the majority of Congress that passed this Bill and the President who signed it. Those supporting the Bill undeniably included many seasoned professionals who have been deeply involved in elective processes and who have viewed them at close range over many years.

It would make little sense to me, and apparently made none to Congress, to limit the amounts an individual may give to a candidate or spend with his approval but fail to limit the amounts that could be spent on his behalf. Yet the Court permits the former while striking down the latter limitation. [I] would take the word of those who know—that limiting independent expenditures is essential to prevent transparent and widespread evasion of the contribution limits. * * *

9. Candidates who must raise large initial contributions in order to appeal for more funds to a broader audience will be handicapped. See n. 5, supra. It is not enough to say that the contribution ceilings "merely require candidates [to] raise funds from a greater number of persons," where the limitations will effectively prevent candidates without substantial personal resources from doing just that.

10. Under the Court's holding, candidates with personal fortunes will be free to contribute to their own campaigns as much as they like, since the Court chooses to view the Act's provisions in this regard as unconstitutional "expenditure" limitations rather than "contribution" limitations. See n. 8, supra.

e. Blackmun, J., also dissented separately from that part of the Court's opinion upholding the Act's restrictions on campaign contributions, unpersuaded that "a principled constitutional distinction" could be made between the contribution and expenditure limitations involved.

The Court also rejects Congress' judgment manifested in § 608(c) that the federal interest in limiting total campaign expenditures by individual candidates justifies the incidental effect on their opportunity for effective political speech. I disagree both with the Court's assessment of the impact on speech and with its narrow view of the values the limitations will serve.

[M]oney is not always equivalent to or used for speech, even in the context of political campaigns. [There are] many expensive campaign activities that are not themselves communicative or remotely related to speech. Furthermore, campaigns differ among themselves. Some seem to spend much less money than others and yet communicate as much or more than those supported by enormous bureaucracies with unlimited financing. The record before us no more supports the conclusion that the communicative efforts of congressional and Presidential candidates will be crippled by the expenditure limitations than it supports the contrary. The judgment of Congress was that reasonably effective campaigns could be conducted within the limits established by the Act and that the communicative efforts of these campaigns would not seriously suffer. In this posture of the case, there is no sound basis for invalidating the expenditure limitations, so long as the purposes they serve are legitimate and sufficiently substantial, which in my view they are.

[E]xpenditure ceilings reinforce the contribution limits and help eradicate the hazard of corruption. [Without] limits on total expenditures, campaign costs will inevitably and endlessly escalate. Pressure to raise funds will constantly build and with it the temptation to resort in "emergencies" to those sources of large sums, who, history shows, are sufficiently confident of not being caught to risk flouting contribution [limits.]

The ceiling on candidate expenditures represents the considered judgment of Congress that elections are to be decided among candidates none of whom has overpowering advantage by reason of a huge campaign war chest. At least so long as the ceiling placed upon the candidates is not plainly too low, elections are not to turn on the difference in the amounts of money that candidates have to spend. This seems an acceptable purpose and the means chosen a common sense way to achieve [it.]

I also disagree with the Court's judgment that § 608(a), which limits the amount of money that a candidate or his family may spend on his campaign, violates the Constitution. Although it is true that this provision does not promote any interest in preventing the corruption of candidates, the provision does, nevertheless, serve salutary purposes related to the integrity of federal campaigns. By limiting the importance of personal wealth, § 608(a) helps to assure that only individuals with a modicum of support from others will be viable candidates. This in turn would tend to discourage any notion that the outcome of elections is primarily a function of money. Similarly, § 608(a) tends to equalize access to the political arena, encouraging the less wealthy, unable to bankroll their own campaigns, to run for political office.f

––––––––

f. Marshall, J., dissented from that part of the Court's opinion invalidating the limitation on the amount a candidate or his family may spend on his campaign. He considered "the interest in promoting the reality and appearance of equal access to the political arena" sufficient to justify the limitation: "[T]he wealthy candidate's immediate access to a substantial personal fortune may give him an initial advantage that his less wealthy opponent can never overcome. [With the option of large contributions removed by § 608(b)], the less wealthy candidate is without the means to match the large initial expenditures of money of which the wealthy candidate is capable. In short, the limitations on contributions put a premium on a candidate's personal wealth. [Section 608(a) then] emerges not simply as a

Notes

Vitality of Buckley. Vermont's 1997 campaign finance statute limited the amount that state candidates could spend on their campaigns and the amounts that individuals, organizations, and parties could contribute to those campaigns. RANDALL v. SORRELL, 548 U.S. 230 (2006) struck down both the expenditure limitations and the contribution limitations with a diversity of views concerning the authority of *Buckley*. BREYER, J., announced the judgment of the Court and delivered an opinion joined by Roberts, C.J., and, in part, by Alito, J. He determined that the expenditure provision was unconstitutional on the strength of *Buckley*. On the basis of *stare decisis,* he declined what he perceived to be an invitation to overrule *Buckley's* ruling on candidate expenditure limits,[a] and he rejected the view that *Buckley* could be distinguished on the ground that it failed to consider the argument that such limitations are justified because they help to prevent candidates from spending too much time raising money. With respect to the contribution limits, Breyer, J., maintained that they were too restrictive, noting, for example, that the limit on contributions for governor (adjusted for inflation) was slightly more than one-twentieth of the limit on contributions to federal office before the Court in *Buckley*. He also determined that Vermont's per election contribution limit was the lowest in the nation. Breyer, J., concluded that such limits would impair the ability of some candidates running against incumbent officeholder to mount an effective challenge.

THOMAS, J., joined by Scalia, J., concurred in the judgment. He demanded strict scrutiny in examining expenditure and contributions limitations.[b] He also argued that the plurality's attempt to distinguish permissible from impermissible contribution limits could not be administered in a principled way: "[T]he plurality's determination that this statute clearly lies on the *impermissible* side of the constitutional line gives no assistance in drawing this line, and it is clear that no such line can be drawn rationally. There is simply no way to calculate just how much money a person would need to receive before he would be corrupt or perceived to be corrupt (and such a calculation would undoubtedly vary by person). Likewise, there is no meaningful way of discerning just how many resources must be lost before speech is 'disproportionately burden[ed].' "

STEVENS, J., dissenting, would depart from *Buckley's* strict scrutiny of candidate expenditure limits. He would uphold such limits "so long as the purposes they serve are legitimate and sufficiently substantial": "The interest in freeing candidates from the fundraising straitjacket is * * * compelling. Without expenditure limits, fundraising devours the time and attention of political leaders, leaving them too busy to handle their public responsibilities effectively. That fact was well recognized by backers of the legislation reviewed in *Buckley*, by the Court of Appeals judges who voted to uphold the expenditure limitations in that statute, and by Justice White—who not incidentally had personal experience as an active participant in a Presidential campaign. The validity of their judgment has surely been confirmed by the mountains of evidence that has been accumulated in recent years concerning the time that elected officials spend raising money for future

device to reduce the natural advantage of the wealthy candidate, but as a provision providing some symmetry to a regulatory scheme that otherwise enhances the natural advantage of the wealthy."

a. Alito, J., concurring in part and in judgment, argued that the question whether to overrule *Buckley's* standard on expenditure limits was not properly presented to the Court and should not have been reached.

b. Kennedy, J., who has also maintained that *Buckley's* standard regarding contributions is too relaxed, concurred in the judgment.

campaigns and the adverse effect of fundraising on the performance of their official duties."

SOUTER, J., joined by Ginsburg, JJ., and, on the contributions issue, by Stevens, J., dissented. He argued that the question whether to relax Buckley's standard on expenditure requirements was not properly before the Court. He voted to affirm the Court of Appeals decision to remand on the expenditures issue to determine if the record met the requirements of *Buckley*. He voted to uphold the contribution limits: "I believe the Court of Appeals correctly rejected the challenge to the contribution limits. Low though they are, one cannot say that 'the contribution limitation[s are] so radical in effect as to render political association ineffective, drive the sound of a candidate's voice below the level of notice, and render contributions pointless.' *Nixon* v. *Shrink Missouri Government PAC*, 528 U.S. 377 (2000). The limits set by Vermont are not remarkable departures either from those previously upheld by this Court or from those lately adopted by other States. The plurality concedes that on a per-citizen measurement Vermont's limit for statewide elections 'is slightly more generous,' than the one set by the Missouri statute approved by this Court in *Shrink*.c

CITIZENS UNITED v. FEC

___ U.S. ___, 130 S.Ct. 876, ___ L.Ed.2d ___ (2010).

JUSTICE KENNEDY delivered the opinion of the Court.

[In January 2008, Citizens United, a nonprofit corporation that accepts a small portion of its funds from for-profit companies, released a film entitled *Hillary: The Movie*. The film was a documentary arguing that Senator Hilary Clinton was an unsuitable candidate for President. Citizens United had released its film in theaters and on DVD, but it also wished to make the film available through video-on-demand on cable and to promote the film with ads on broadcast and cable television.]

Federal law prohibits corporations and unions from using their general treasury funds to make independent expenditures for speech defined as an "electioneering communication" or for speech expressly advocating the election or defeat of a candidate. Federal Election Campaign Act of 1971, 2 U.S.C. § 441b. Limits on electioneering communications were upheld in *McConnell v. Federal Election Comm'n*, (2003). The holding of *McConnell* rested to a large extent on an earlier case, *Austin v. Michigan Chamber of Commerce*, 494 U.S. 652 (1990). *Austin* had held that political speech may be banned based on the speaker's corporate identity.

In this case we are asked to reconsider *Austin* and, in effect, *McConnell*. * * * We [hold] that stare decisis does not compel the continued acceptance of *Austin*. The Government may regulate corporate political speech through disclaimer and disclosure requirements, but it may not suppress that speech altogether.

Before the Bipartisan Campaign Reform Act of 2002 (BCRA), federal law prohibited—and still does prohibit—corporations and unions from using general treasury funds to make direct contributions to candidates or independent expenditures that expressly advocate the election or defeat of a candidate, through any form of media, in connection with certain qualified federal elections. BCRA § 203 amended § 441b to prohibit any "electioneering communication" as [well,] de-

---

c. In response, Breyer, J., argued: "[T]his does not necessarily mean that Vermont's limits are less objectionable than the limit upheld in *Shrink*. A campaign for state auditor is likely to be less costly than a campaign for governor; campaign costs do not automatically increase or decrease in precise proportion to the size of an electoral district."

fined as "any broadcast, cable, or satellite communication" that "refers to a clearly identified candidate for a Federal office" and is made [well] within 30 days of a primary or 60 days of a general [election.]a Corporations and [may] unions establish, however, a "separate segregated fund" (known as a political action committee, or PAC) for these purposes. The moneys received by the segregated fund are limited to donations from stockholders and employees of the corporation or, in the case of unions, members of the union. * * *

[T]he following acts would all be felonies under § 441b: The Sierra Club runs an ad, within the crucial phase of 60 days before the general election, that exhorts the public to disapprove of a Congressman who favors logging in national forests; the National Rifle Association publishes a book urging the public to vote for the challenger because the incumbent U.S. Senator supports a handgun ban; and the American Civil Liberties Union creates a Web site telling the public to vote for a Presidential candidate in light of that candidate's defense of free speech. These prohibitions are classic examples of censorship.

[A] PAC is a separate association from the corporation. So the PAC exemption from § 441b's expenditure ban does not allow corporations to speak. Even if a PAC could somehow allow a corporation to speak—and it does not—the option to form PACs does not alleviate the First Amendment problems with § 441b. PACs are burdensome alternatives; they are expensive to administer and subject to extensive regulations. For example, every PAC must appoint a treasurer, forward donations to the treasurer promptly, keep detailed records of the identities of the persons making donations, preserve receipts for three years, and file an organization statement and report changes to this information within 10 days. * * *

By taking the right to speak from some and giving it to others, the Government deprives the disadvantaged person or class of the right to use speech to strive to establish worth, standing, and respect for the speaker's voice. The Government may not by these means deprive the public of the right and privilege to determine for itself what speech and speakers are worthy of consideration. The First Amendment protects speech and speaker, and the ideas that flow from each.

The Court has upheld a narrow class of speech restrictions that operate to the disadvantage of certain persons, but these rulings were based on an interest in allowing governmental entities to perform their functions. See, e.g., *Bethel School Dist. No. 403 v. Fraser,* 478 U.S. 675, 683 (1986) (protecting the "function of public school education"); *Jones v. North Carolina Prisoners' Labor Union, Inc.,* 433 U.S. 119, 129 (furthering "the legitimate penological objectives of the corrections system"); *Parker v. Levy,* 417 U.S. 733, 759 (1974) (ensuring "the capacity of the Government to discharge its [military] responsibilities"); *Civil Service Comm'n v. Letter Carriers,* 413 U.S. 548, 557 (1973) ("[F]ederal service should depend upon meritorious performance rather than political service"). The corporate independent expenditures at issue in this case, however, would not interfere with governmental functions, so these cases are inapposite. These precedents stand only for the proposition that there are certain governmental functions that cannot operate without some restrictions on particular kinds of speech. By contrast, it is inherent in the nature of the political process that voters must be free to obtain information from diverse sources in order to determine how to cast their votes. At least before *Austin,* the Court had not allowed the exclusion of a class of speakers from the general public dialogue.

a. The law exempted any news story, commentary, or editorial distributed through the facilities of any broadcasting station, newspaper, magazine, or other periodical publication, unless such facilities are owned or controlled by any political party, political committee, or candidate.

[Laws] that burden political speech are "subject to strict scrutiny," which requires the Government to prove that the restriction "furthers a compelling interest and is narrowly tailored to achieve that interest." *Austin* identified a new governmental interest in limiting political speech: an antidistortion interest. *Austin* found a compelling governmental interest in preventing "the corrosive and distorting effects of immense aggregations of wealth that are accumulated with the help of the corporate form and that have little or no correlation to the public's support for the corporation's political ideas." [As] for *Austin*'s antidistortion rationale, the Government does little to defend it. * * *

If the First Amendment has any force, it prohibits Congress from fining or jailing citizens, or associations of citizens, for simply engaging in political speech. If the antidistortion rationale were to be accepted, however, it would permit Government to ban political speech simply because the speaker is an association that has taken on the corporate form. The Government contends that *Austin* permits it to ban corporate expenditures for almost all forms of communication stemming from a corporation. If *Austin* were correct, the Government could prohibit a corporation from expressing political views in media beyond those presented here, such as by printing books. The Government responds "that the FEC has never applied this statute to a book," and if it did, "there would be quite [a] good as-applied challenge." This troubling assertion of brooding governmental power cannot be reconciled with the confidence and stability in civic discourse that the First Amendment must secure. * * *

Austin sought to defend the antidistortion rationale as a means to prevent corporations from obtaining "an unfair advantage in the political marketplace" by using "resources amassed in the economic marketplace." But *Buckley* rejected the premise that the Government has an interest "in equalizing the relative ability of individuals and groups to influence the outcome of elections." *Buckley* was specific in stating that "the skyrocketing cost of political campaigns" could not sustain the governmental prohibition. The First Amendment's protections do not depend on the speaker's "financial ability to engage in public discussion."

[*Austin*] undertook to distinguish wealthy individuals from corporations on the ground that "[s]tate law grants corporations special advantages—such as limited liability, perpetual life, and favorable treatment of the accumulation and distribution of assets." This does not suffice, however, to allow laws prohibiting speech. "It is rudimentary that the State cannot exact as the price of those special advantages the forfeiture of First Amendment rights."

It is irrelevant for purposes of the First Amendment that corporate funds may "have little or no correlation to the public's support for the corporation's political ideas." All speakers, including individuals and the media, use money amassed from the economic marketplace to fund their speech. The First Amendment protects the resulting speech, even if it was enabled by economic transactions with persons or entities who disagree with the speaker's ideas.

Austin's antidistortion rationale would produce the dangerous, and unacceptable, consequence that Congress could ban political speech of media corporations [now] exempt from § 441b's ban on corporate expenditures. Yet media corporations accumulate wealth with the help of the corporate form, the largest media corporations have "immense aggregations of wealth," and the views expressed by media corporations often "have little or no correlation to the public's support" for those views. Thus, under the Government's reasoning, wealthy media corporations could have their voices diminished to put them on par with other media entities. There is no precedent for permitting this [nor any] precedent supporting laws that attempt to distinguish between corporations which are deemed to be exempt as media corporations and those which are not. "We have consistently rejected the proposition that the institutional press has any constitutional privilege beyond that of other speakers." * * *

[T]he Government falls back on the argument that corporate political speech can be banned in order to prevent corruption or its appearance. In *Buckley,* the Court found this interest "sufficiently important" to allow limits on contributions but did not extend that reasoning to expenditure limits. * * *

With regard to large direct contributions, *Buckley* reasoned that they could be given "to secure a political quid pro quo," and that "the scope of such pernicious practices can never be reliably ascertained." The practices *Buckley* noted would be covered by bribery laws if a quid pro quo arrangement were proved. The Court, in consequence, has noted that restrictions on direct contributions are preventative, because few if any contributions to candidates will involve quid pro quo arrangements. The *Buckley* Court, nevertheless, sustained limits on direct contributions in order to ensure against the reality or appearance of corruption. That case did not extend this rationale to independent expenditures, and the Court does not do so here. * * *

When *Buckley* identified a sufficiently important governmental interest in preventing corruption or the appearance of corruption, that interest was limited to quid pro quo corruption. The fact that speakers may have influence over or access to elected officials does not mean that these officials are corrupt: "[It] is in the nature of an elected representative to favor certain policies, and, by necessary corollary, to favor the voters and contributors who support those policies. It is well understood that a substantial and legitimate reason, if not the only reason, to cast a vote for, or to make a contribution to, one candidate over another is that the candidate will respond by producing those political outcomes the supporter favors. Democracy is premised on responsiveness." Reliance on a "generic favoritism or influence theory . . . is at odds with standard First Amendment analyses because it is unbounded and susceptible to no limiting principle."

The appearance of influence or access, furthermore, will not cause the electorate to lose faith in our democracy. By definition, an independent expenditure is political speech presented to the electorate that is not coordinated with a candidate. The fact that a corporation, or any other speaker, is willing to spend money to try to persuade voters presupposes that the people have the ultimate influence over elected officials. This is inconsistent with any suggestion that the electorate will refuse "to take part in democratic governance" because of additional political speech made by a corporation or any other speaker.

The *McConnell* record was "over 100,000 pages" long, yet it "does not have any direct examples of votes being exchanged for . . . expenditures," This confirms *Buckley*'s reasoning that independent expenditures do not lead to, or create the appearance of, quid pro quo corruption. In fact, there is only scant evidence that independent expenditures even ingratiate. Ingratiation and access, in any event, are not corruption. The BCRA record establishes that certain donations to political parties, called "soft money," were made to gain access to elected officials. This case, however, is about independent expenditures, not soft money. [If] elected officials succumb to improper influences from independent expenditures; if they surrender their best judgment; and if they put expediency before principle, then surely there is cause for concern. We must give weight to attempts by Congress to seek to dispel either the appearance or the reality of these influences. The remedies enacted by law, however, must comply with the First Amendment; and, it is our law and our tradition that more speech, not less, is the governing rule.

The Government contends further that corporate independent expenditures can be limited because of its interest in protecting dissenting shareholders from being compelled to fund corporate political speech. This asserted interest, like *Austin*'s antidistortion rationale, would allow the Government to ban the political speech even of media corporations. Assume, for example, that a shareholder of a corporation that owns a newspaper disagrees with the political views the newspaper expresses. Under the Government's view, that potential disagreement could give the Government the authority to restrict the media corporation's political speech. The First Amendment does not allow that power. There is, furthermore, little evidence of abuse that cannot be corrected by shareholders "through the procedures of corporate democracy."

Those reasons are sufficient to reject this shareholder-protection interest; and, moreover, the statute is both underinclusive and overinclusive. As to the first, if Congress had been seeking to protect dissenting shareholders, it would not have banned corporate speech in only certain media within 30 or 60 days before an election. A dissenting shareholder's interests would be implicated by speech in any media at any time. As to the second, the statute is overinclusive because it covers all corporations, including nonprofit corporations and for-profit corporations with only single shareholders. As to other corporations, the remedy is not to restrict speech but to consider and explore other regulatory mechanisms. The regulatory mechanism here, based on speech, contravenes the First Amendment.

[441b] is not limited to corporations or associations that were created in foreign countries or funded predominately by foreign shareholders. Section 441b therefore would be overbroad even if we assumed, arguendo, that the Government has a compelling interest in limiting foreign influence over our political process.

Austin is overruled, [thus] "effectively invalidate[ing] not only BCRA Section 203, but also 441b's prohibition on the use of corporate treasury funds for express advocacy." Section 441b's restrictions on corporate independent expenditures are therefore invalid and cannot be applied to *Hillary*.

Given our conclusion we are further required to overrule the part of *McConnell* that upheld BCRA § 203's extension of § 441b's restrictions on corporate independent expenditures. * * *b

JUSTICE STEVENS, with whom JUSTICE GINSBURG, JUSTICE BREYER, and JUSTICE SOTOMAYOR join, concurring in partc and dissenting in part.

Pervading the Court's analysis is the ominous image of a "categorical ba[n]" on corporate speech. [But our] cases have repeatedly pointed out that, "[c]ontrary to the [majority's] critical assumptions," the statutes upheld in *Austin* and *McConnell* do "not impose an *absolute* ban on all forms of corporate political spending." For starters, both statutes provide exemptions for PACs, separate segregated funds established by a corporation for political purposes. "The ability to form and administer separate segregated funds," we observed in *McConnell*, "has provided corporations and unions with a constitutionally sufficient opportunity to engage in express advocacy. That has been this Court's unanimous view."

A significant and growing number of corporations avail themselves of this option; during the most recent election cycle, corporate and union PACs raised

b. Thomas, J., joined the opinion of Kennedy, J., except for a section upholding disclosure requirements. Roberts, C.J., joined by Alito, J., concurring argued that the principle of stare decisis did not apply. Scalia, J., joined by Alito, J., and Thomas, J., in part, concurring, argued that the Stevens, J., dissent did not properly assess the original understanding of the First Amendment.

c. Stevens, J., joined by Ginsburg, Breyer, and Sotomayor, JJ., joined that part of the Court's opinion upholding disclosure requirements.

nearly a billion dollars. Administering a PAC entails some administrative burden, but so does complying with the disclaimer, disclosure, and reporting requirements that the Court today upholds, and no one has suggested that the burden is severe for a sophisticated for-profit corporation. To the extent the majority is worried about this issue, it is important to keep in mind that we have no record to show how substantial the burden really is, just the majority's own unsupported factfinding.

The laws upheld in *Austin* and *McConnell* leave open many additional avenues for corporations' political speech. Consider the statutory provision we are ostensibly evaluating in this case, BCRA § 203. It has no application to genuine issue advertising—a category of corporate speech Congress found to be far more substantial than election-related advertising or to Internet, telephone, and print advocacy. * * * It also allows corporations to spend unlimited sums on political communications with their executives and shareholders, to fund additional PAC activity through trade associations, to distribute voting guides and voting records, to underwrite voter registration and voter turnout activities, to host fundraising events for candidates within certain limits, and to publicly endorse candidates through a press release and press conference. * * *

In many ways, then, § 203 functions as a source restriction or a time, place, and manner restriction. It applies in a viewpoint-neutral fashion to a narrow subset of advocacy messages about clearly identified candidates for federal office, made during discrete time periods through discrete channels. In the case at hand, all Citizens United needed to do to broadcast *Hillary* right before the primary was to abjure business contributions or use the funds in its PAC, which by its own account is "one of the most active conservative PACs in America."

[Laws] such as § 203 target a class of communications that is especially likely to corrupt the political process, that is at least one degree removed from the views of individual citizens, and that may not even reflect the views of those who pay for it. Such laws burden political speech, and that is always a serious matter, demanding careful scrutiny. But the majority's incessant talk of a "ban" aims at a straw man. * * *

The second pillar of the Court's opinion is its assertion that "the Government cannot restrict political speech based on the speaker's . . . identity." [Yet] in a variety of contexts, we have held that speech can be regulated differentially on account of the speaker's identity, when identity is understood in categorical or institutional terms. The Government routinely places special restrictions on the speech rights of students, prisoners, members of the Armed Forces, foreigners, and its own employees. When such restrictions are justified by a legitimate governmental interest, they do not necessarily raise constitutional problems. [T]he Court, of course, is right that the First Amendment closely guards political speech. But in [the election] context, too, the authority of legislatures to enact viewpoint-neutral regulations based on content and identity is well settled. We have, for example, allowed state-run broadcasters to exclude independent candidates from televised debates. We have upheld statutes that prohibit the distribution or display of campaign materials near a polling place. Although we have not reviewed them directly, we have never cast doubt on laws that place special restrictions on campaign spending by foreign nationals. And we have consistently approved laws that bar Government employees, but not others, from contributing to or participating in political [activities].

* * * Undergirding the majority's approach to the merits is the claim that the only "sufficiently important governmental interest in preventing corruption or the appearance of corruption" is one that is "limited to quid pro quo corruption."

[On] numerous occasions we have recognized Congress' legitimate interest in preventing the money that is spent on elections from exerting an "undue influence on an officeholder's judgment" and from creating "the appearance of such influence," beyond the sphere of quid pro quo relationships. Corruption can take many forms. Bribery may be the paradigm case. But the difference between selling a vote and selling access is a matter of degree, not kind. And selling access is not qualitatively different from giving special preference to those who spent money on one's behalf. Corruption operates along a spectrum, and the majority's apparent belief that quid pro quo arrangements can be neatly demarcated from other improper influences does not accord with the theory or reality of politics. It certainly does not accord with the record Congress developed in passing BCRA, a record that stands as a remarkable testament to the energy and ingenuity with which corporations, unions, lobbyists, and politicians may go about scratching each other's backs-and which amply supported Congress' determination to target a limited set of especially destructive practices.

Stevens, J., then quoted the district court: "The factual findings of the Court illustrate that corporations and labor unions routinely notify Members of Congress as soon as they air electioneering communications relevant to the Members' elections. The record also indicates that Members express appreciation to organizations for the airing of these election-related advertisements. Indeed, Members of Congress are particularly grateful when negative issue advertisements are run by these organizations, leaving the candidates free to run positive advertisements and be seen as 'above the fray.' Political consultants testify that campaigns are quite aware of who is running advertisements on the candidate's behalf, when they are being run, and where they are being run. Likewise, a prominent lobbyist testifies that these organizations use issue advocacy as a means to influence various Members of Congress. [Finally], a large majority of Americans (80%) are of the view that corporations and other organizations that engage in electioneering communications, which benefit specific elected officials, receive special consideration from those officials when matters arise that affect these corporations and organizations."

[When] private interests are seen to exert outsized control over officeholders solely on account of the money spent on (or withheld from) their campaigns, the result can depart so thoroughly "from what is pure or correct" in the conduct of Government that it amounts to a "subversion ... of the electoral process." [Starting] today, corporations with large war chests to deploy on electioneering may find democratically elected bodies becoming much more attuned to their interests. * * *

The fact that corporations are different from human beings might seem to need no elaboration, except that the majority opinion almost completely elides it. *Austin* set forth some of the basic differences. Unlike natural persons, corporations have "limited liability" for their owners and managers, "perpetual life," separation of ownership and control, "and favorable treatment of the accumulation and distribution of assets ... that enhance their ability to attract capital and to deploy their resources in ways that maximize the return on their shareholders' investments." [It] might also be added that corporations have no consciences, no beliefs, no feelings, no thoughts, no desires. Corporations help structure and facilitate the activities of human beings, to be sure, and their "personhood" often serves as a useful legal fiction. But they are not themselves members of "We the People" by whom and for whom our Constitution was established. * * *

It is an interesting question "who" is even speaking when a business corporation places an advertisement that endorses or attacks a particular candidate. Presumably it is not the customers or employees, who typically have no say in such matters. It cannot realistically be said to be the shareholders, who tend to be far removed from the day-to-day decisions of the firm and whose political preferences may be opaque to management. Perhaps the officers or directors of the corporation have the best claim to be the ones speaking, except their fiduciary duties generally prohibit them from using corporate funds for personal ends. * * *

In critiquing *Austin*'s antidistortion rationale and campaign finance regulation more generally, our colleagues place tremendous weight on the example of media corporations. Yet it is not at all clear that *Austin* would permit § 203 to be applied to them. The press plays a unique role not only in the text, history, and structure of the First Amendment but also in facilitating public discourse * * *. Our colleagues have raised some interesting and difficult questions about Congress' authority to regulate electioneering by the press, and about how to define what constitutes the press. *But that is not the case before us.* Section 203 does not apply to media corporations, and even if it did, Citizens United is not a media corporation. * * *

Interwoven with *Austin*'s concern to protect the integrity of the electoral process is a concern to protect the rights of shareholders from a kind of coerced speech: electioneering expenditures that do not "reflec[t] [their] support." When corporations use general treasury funds to praise or attack a particular candidate for office, it is the shareholders, as the residual claimants, who are effectively footing the bill. Those shareholders who disagree with the corporation's electoral message may find their financial investments being used to undermine their political convictions.

The PAC mechanism, by contrast, helps assure that those who pay for an electioneering communication actually support its content and that managers do not use general treasuries to advance personal agendas. [The] shareholder protection rationale has been criticized as underinclusive, in that corporations also spend money on lobbying and charitable contributions in ways that any particular shareholder might disapprove. But those expenditures do not implicate the selection of public officials, an area in which "the interests of unwilling . . . corporate shareholders [in not being] forced to subsidize that speech" "are at their zenith." And in any event, the question is whether shareholder protection provides a basis for regulating expenditures in the weeks before an election, not whether additional types of corporate communications might similarly be conditioned on voluntariness.

Recognizing the limits of the shareholder protection rationale, the *Austin* Court did not hold it out as an adequate and independent ground for sustaining the statute in question. Rather, the Court applied it to reinforce the antidistortion rationale, in two main ways. First, the problem of dissenting shareholders shows that even if electioneering expenditures can advance the political views of some members of a corporation, they will often compromise the views of others. Second, it provides an additional reason, beyond the distinctive legal attributes of the corporate form, for doubting that these "expenditures reflect actual public support for the political ideas espoused." * * *

While American democracy is imperfect, few outside the majority of this Court would have thought its flaws included a dearth of corporate money in politics.

Notes

1.   The practical impact of *Citizens United* may not be substantial. PACs were already permitted, and the Court had already held that non-profit corporations not involved in business and formed for the purpose of advocacy were as free as individuals to engage in campaign spending so long as they had no shareholders with claims on its assets and earnings and did not receive contributions from business corporations or unions. *Federal Election Commission v. Massachusetts Citizens for Life*, 479 U.S. 238 (1986). Even more important, the Court had already narrowed the limitation on electioneering ads in ways that provided substantial leeway for business corporations. Wisconsin Right to Life, Inc., a non-profit advocacy corporation, ran three broadcast ads from its treasury funds, which included contributions of $50,000 from business corporations, for the ads. Wisconsin Right to Life had previously campaigned against Senator Feingold, and one of its concerns was his support of filibustering of judicial nominees. The ads spoke out against filibustering and asked citizens to contact Senators Feingold and McCain without referring to Feingold's position on the issue (though his position was well known in Wisconsin). The ads appeared to violate BCRA § 203.

FEC v. WISCONSIN RIGHT TO LIFE, INC., 551 U.S. 449 (2007), per ROBERTS, C.J., joined only by Alito, J., concluded that § 203 was constitutional only as applied to ads that are "susceptible of no reasonable interpretation other than as an appeal to vote for or against a specific candidate." Because of the importance of political speech, any doubt on the matter was to be resolved in favor of the ads. Neither the intent nor the effect of the ads counted in the determination. Roberts, C.J., found Wisconsin Right to Life's ads to be protected under the First Amendment.a

SOUTER, J., joined by Stevens, Ginsburg, and Breyer, JJ., dissenting, found it hard to imagine that the Chief Justice would ever find an ad unprotected unless it contained words of express advocacy.

2.   As interpreted, the Federal Election Campaign Act of 1971 ("FECA") distinguishes between hard and soft money. Hard money is contributed money that falls at or under the specified contribution limits and complies with certain source limitations. Soft money encompasses contributions not subject to those restrictions which are for the most part ostensibly designed to encourage party-building activities benefitting the political parties in general, but not specific candidates. Under FECA, as interpreted, however, wealthy donors were able to use soft money directly or indirectly in ways that benefited federal candidates.

BCRA sought to close the soft money loophole. BCRA forbids national party committees from soliciting, receiving, or directing the use of soft-money; it prohibits state and local party committees from using soft money (although it permits their use of hard money and some additional funding) for activities affecting federal elections, including voter registration activity during the 120 days before a federal election and get-out-the-vote drives conducted in connection with an election in which a federal candidate appears on the ballot; it forbids the use of soft money by state and local party committees or state and local candidates and officeholders for any public communication that supports or attacks a federal candidate, whether or not the communication specifically asks for a vote for or against a particular candidate.

a. Alito, J., concurring, observed that the Court would presumably be asked to reconsider its holding that § 203 is facially constitutional. Scalia, J., joined by Kennedy and Thomas, JJ., concurring in the judgment, would have overruled *McConnell's* upholding of § 203.

McCONNELL v. FEDERAL ELECTION COMMISSION, per STEVENS and O'CONNOR, JJ., joined by Souter, Ginsburg and Breyer, JJ. (the "Joint Opinion"), upheld the soft money provisions of the Act against a facial constitutional challenge: "Of the two major parties' total spending, soft money accounted for 5% ($21.6 million) in 1984, 11% ($45 million) in 1988, 16% ($80 million) in 1992, 30% ($272 million) in 1996, and 42% ($498 million) in 2000. The national parties transferred large amounts of their soft money to the state parties, which were allowed to use a larger percentage of soft money to finance mixed-purpose activities under FEC rules. In the year 2000, for example, the national parties diverted $280 million—more than half of their soft money—to state parties.

"Many contributions of soft money were dramatically larger than the contributions of hard money permitted by FECA. For example, in 1996 the top five corporate soft-money donors gave, in total, more than $9 million in nonfederal funds to the two national party committees. In the most recent election cycle the political parties raised almost $300 million—60% of their total soft-money fundraising—from just 800 donors, each of which contributed a minimum of $120,000. Moreover, the largest corporate donors often made substantial contributions to both parties. Such practices corroborate evidence indicating that many corporate contributions were motivated by a desire for access to candidates and a fear of being placed at a disadvantage in the legislative process relative to other contributors, rather than by ideological support for the candidates and parties."

Despite the fact that many of the soft money restrictions regulated spending, the Joint Opinion concluded that the less than strict scrutiny applied to the contribution limits in *Buckley* and *Nixon v. Shrink Missouri Government PAC*, 528 U.S. 377 (2000), was appropriately applied to the soft money restrictions: "The relevant inquiry is whether the mechanism adopted to implement the contribution limit, or to prevent circumvention of that limit, burdens speech in a way that a direct restriction on the contribution itself would not. That is not the case here." Applying the *Buckley* contribution limits standard, it concluded that the soft money restrictions were "closely drawn to match the important governmental interests of preventing corruption and the appearance of corruption"[b]

The dissents employed themes about incumbent protection, the failure to show quid pro *quo* corruption, lack of precision, and deep invasion of treasured First Amendment rights.[c]

b. The Joint Opinion argued that the application of soft money restrictions to minor parties was permissible because the corruption and appearance of corruption interests were not a function of the number of legislators elected and that an as-applied challenge could be brought if the act prevented the massing of sufficient resources for effective advocacy. The Court had previously held that limitations on independent expenditures of the major parties were unconstitutional, *Colorado Republican Fed. Campaign Comm. v. FEC*, 518 U.S. 604 (1996), but prohibitions of expenditures coordinated with a candidate were constitutional. *FEC v. Colorado Republican Fed. Campaign Comm.*, 533 U.S. 431 (2001).

c. Scalia, J., dissented. Thomas, J., joined in part by Scalia, J., dissented. Kennedy, joined Rehnquist, C.J., and in part by Scalia and Thomas, JJ., dissented. Rehnquist, C.J., joined by Scalia and Kennedy, JJ., dissented.

Chapter 8

FREEDOM OF RELIGION

This chapter concerns the "Religion Clauses" of the First Amendment, commonly known as the "Establishment Clause" (forbidding laws "respecting an establishment of religion") and the "Free Exercise Clause" (forbidding laws "prohibiting the free exercise thereof"). It is difficult to explore either clause in isolation from the other. The extent to which the clauses interact may be illustrated by the matter of public financial aid to parochial schools, Sec. 1, II. On one hand, does such aid violate the Establishment Clause? On the other, does a state's failure to provide such aid violate the Free Exercise Clause? Another example of the potential conflict between the clauses—also considered in the materials below—is whether, on one hand, a state's exemption of church buildings from property taxes contravenes the Establishment Clause or whether, on the other, a state's taxing these buildings contravenes the Free Exercise Clause.

Despite this interrelationship of the two clauses, Sec. 1 deals almost exclusively with the Establishment Clause. Sec. 2, I then considers conventional problems under the Free Exercise Clause. Sec. 2, II examines the complex issues of defining "religion" for purposes of the First Amendment and determining the bona fides of an asserted "religious" belief—both matters usually presumed in the cases decided by the Supreme Court and the former never specifically addressed by a majority of the justices. Issues under each clause having been explored in some detail, Sec. 3 presents the subject of preference among religions that has both establishment and free exercise ramifications, and, finally, Sec. 4 discusses problems presented by government action that attempts to accommodate the seemingly opposing demands of the two religion clauses.

SECTION 1. ESTABLISHMENT CLAUSE

I. INTRODUCTION

It is generally agreed that the Establishment Clause seeks to assure the separation of church and state in a nation characterized by religious pluralism. Prior to 1947, only two decisions concerning the Establishment Clause produced any significant consideration by the Court. *Bradfield v. Roberts,* 175 U.S. 291 (1899), upheld federal appropriations to a hospital in the District of Columbia, operated by the Catholic Church, for ward construction and care of indigent patients. *Quick Bear v. Leupp,* 210 U.S. 50 (1908), upheld federal disbursement of funds, held in trust for the Sioux Indians, to Catholic schools designated by the Sioux for payment of tuition costs.

In the Court's first modern decision, *Everson v. Board of Educ.* (1947), Part II infra, Rutledge, J., observed that "no provision of the Constitution is more closely tied to or given content by its generating history than the religious clause of the First Amendment." Black, J., writing for the majority, recounted that the Religion Clauses "reflected in the minds of early Americans a vivid mental picture of conditions and practices which they fervently wished to stamp out in order to preserve liberty for themselves and for their posterity." Black, J., detailed the history of religious persecution in Europe "before and contemporaneous with the colonization of America" and the "repetition of many of the old world practices" in the colonies. For example, in Massachusetts, Quakers, Baptists, and other religious minorities suffered harshly and were taxed for the established Congregational Church. In 1776, the Maryland "Declaration of Rights" stated that "only persons professing the Christian religion" were entitled to religious freedom, and not until 1826 were Jews permitted to hold public office. The South Carolina Constitution of 1778 stated that "the Christian Protestant religion shall be deemed [the] established religion of this state." Black, J., explained that "abhorrence" of these practices "reached its dramatic climax in Virginia in 1785–86" when "Madison wrote his great Memorial and Remonstrance" against renewal of "Virginia's tax levy for support of the established church" and the Virginia Assembly "enacted the famous 'Virginia Bill for Religious Liberty' originally written by Thomas Jefferson. [T]he provisions of the First Amendment, in the drafting and adoption of which Madison and Jefferson played such leading roles, had the same objective and were intended to provide the same protection against governmental intrusion on religious liberty as the Virginia statute."

Still, the specific historical record suggests that rather than disclosing a coherent "intent of the Framers," those who influenced the framing of the First Amendment were animated by several distinct and sometimes conflicting goals. Thus, Jefferson believed that the integrity of government could be preserved only by erecting "a wall of separation" between church and state. A sharp division of authority was essential, in his view, to insulate the democratic process from ecclesiastical depradations and excursions. Madison shared this view, but also perceived church-state separation as benefiting religious institutions. Even more strongly, Roger Williams, one of the earliest colonial proponents of religious freedom, posited an evangelical theory of separation, believing it vital to protect the sanctity of the church's "garden" from the "wilderness" of the state. Finally, there is evidence that one purpose of the Establishment Clause was to protect the existing state-established churches from the newly ordained national government.a (Indeed, although disestablishment was then well under way, the epoch of state-sponsored churches did not close until 1833 when Massachusetts separated church and state.)

The varied ideologies that prompted the founders do, however, disclose a dominant theme: constitutional status for the integrity of individual conscience. Moreover, as revealed in Virginia's Bill for Religious Liberty, a practice seen by many as anathema to religious freedom was forcing the people to support religion through compulsory taxation, although there was a division of opinion as to whether non-preferential aid to religion violated liberty of conscience.b

a. In *Elk Grove Unified School Dist. v. Newdow*, Part IV infra, Thomas, J., stated that "text and history * * * strongly suggest" that the Establishment Clause is only "a federalism provision."

b. The view that it did not do so was endorsed by Rehnquist, J., in *Wallace v. Jaffree*, Part III, and Thomas, J., found "much to commend" this position in *Rosenberger v. University of Virginia*, Part II infra.

A final matter involving the history of the Establishment Clause concerns *Everson*'s unanimous ruling that it was "made applicable to the states" by the Fourteenth Amendment.

II. AID TO RELIGION

EVERSON v. BOARD OF EDUC., 330 U.S. 1 (1947), involved one of the major areas of controversy under the Establishment Clause: public financial assistance to church-related institutions (mainly parochial schools). A New Jersey township reimbursed parents for the cost of sending their children "on regular buses operated by the public transportation system," to and from schools, including nonprofit private and parochial schools. The Court, per BLACK, J., rejected a municipal taxpayer's contention that payment for Catholic parochial school students violated the Establishment Clause:

"The 'establishment of religion' clause of the First Amendment means at least this: Neither a state nor the Federal Government can set up a church. Neither can pass laws which aid one religion, aid all religions, or prefer one religion over another. Neither can force nor influence a person to go to or to remain away from church against his will or force him to profess a belief or disbelief in any religion. No person can be punished for entertaining or professing religious beliefs or disbeliefs, for church attendance or non-attendance. No tax in any amount, large or small can be levied to support any religious activities or institutions, whatever they may be called, or whatever form they may adopt to teach or practice religion. Neither a state nor the Federal Government can, openly or secretly, participate in the affairs of any religious organizations or groups and vice versa. In the words of Jefferson, the clause against establishment of religion by law was intended to erect 'a wall of separation between Church and State.'

"We must [not invalidate the New Jersey statute] if it is within the state's constitutional power even though it approaches the verge of that power. New Jersey [cannot] contribute tax-raised funds to the support of an institution which teaches the tenets and faith of any church. On the other hand, other language of the amendment commands that New Jersey cannot hamper its citizens in the free exercise of their own religion. Consequently, it cannot exclude individual Catholics, Lutherans, Mohammedans, Baptists, Jews, Methodists, Non-believers, Presbyterians, or the members of any other faith, *because of their faith, or lack of it,* from receiving the benefits of public welfare legislation. While we do not mean to intimate that a state could not provide transportation only to children attending public schools, we must be careful, in protecting the citizens of New Jersey against state-established churches, to be sure that we do not inadvertently prohibit New Jersey from extending its general State law benefits to all its citizens without regard to their religious belief."

Noting that "the New Jersey legislature has decided that a public purpose will be served" by having children "ride in public buses to and from schools rather than run the risk of traffic and other hazards incident to walking or 'hitchhiking,'" the Court conceded "that children are helped to get to church schools. There is even a possibility that some of the children might not be sent to the church schools if the parents were compelled to pay their children's bus fares out of their own pockets when transportation to a public school would have been paid for by the State. [But] state-paid policemen, detailed to protect children going to and from church schools from the very real hazards of traffic, would serve much the same [purpose]. Similarly, parents might be reluctant to permit their children to attend schools which the state had cut off from such general government services as ordinary police and fire protection, connections for sewage disposal, public highways and sidewalks. Of course, cutting off church schools from these services, so separate and so indisputably marked off from the religious function, would make it far more difficult for the schools to operate. But such is obviously not the purpose of the First Amendment. That Amendment requires the state to be a neutral in its relations with groups of religious believers and non-believers; it does not require the state to be their adversary. * * *

"This Court had said that parents may, in the discharge of their duty under state compulsory education laws, send their children to a religious rather than a public school if the school meets the secular educational requirements which the state has power to impose. See *Pierce v. Society of Sisters,* [Ch. 7, Sec. 7, II]. It appears that these parochial schools meet New Jersey's requirements. The State contributes no money to the schools. [Its] legislation, as applied, does no more than provide a general program to help parents get their children, regardless of their religion, safely and expeditiously to and from accredited schools.

"The First Amendment has erected a wall between church and state. That wall must be kept high and impregnable. We could not approve the slightest breach. New Jersey has not breached it here."

RUTLEDGE, J., joined by Frankfurter, Jackson and Burton, JJ., filed the principal dissent, arguing that the statute aided children "in a substantial way to get the very thing which they are sent to the particular school to secure, namely, religious training and [teaching.] Commingling the religious with the secular teaching does not divest the whole of its religious permeation and emphasis or make them of minor part, if proportion were material. Indeed, on any other view, the constitutional prohibition always could be brought to naught by adding a modicum of the secular. [Transportation] cost is as much a part of the total expense, except at times in amount, as the cost of textbooks, of school lunches, of athletic equipment, of writing and other [materials]. Payment of transportation is [no] less essential to education, whether religious or secular, than payment for tuitions, for teachers' salaries, for buildings, equipment and necessary materials. [Now], as in Madison's time, not the amount but the principle of assessment is wrong.

" * * * Public money devoted to payment of religious costs, educational or other, brings the quest for more. It brings too the struggle of sect against sect for the larger share or for any. Here one by numbers alone will benefit most, there another. That is precisely the history of societies which have had an established religion and dissident groups. It is the very thing Jefferson and Madison experienced and sought to guard [against]. The end of such strife cannot be other than to destroy the cherished liberty. The dominating group will achieve the dominant benefit; or all will embroil the state in their dissensions. [Nor] is the case comparable to one of furnishing fire or police protection, or access to public highways. These things are matters of common right, part of the general need for safety. Certainly the fire department must not stand idly by while the church burns."

The Court did not again confront the subject of aid to parochial schools for more than two decades.a During the intervening years, however, the Court continued to develop its Establishment Clause rationale in cases involving other issues, emphasizing the "purpose and primary effect" of the challenged government action (see Part III infra).

a. See *Board of Educ. v. Allen* (1968), discussed by Souter, J., in *Zelman*, infra.

WALZ v. TAX COM'N, 397 U.S. 664 (1970), per BURGER, C.J., upheld state tax exemption for "real or personal property used exclusively for religious, educational or charitable purposes": "The legislative purpose of a property tax exemption is neither the advancement nor the inhibition of religion; it is neither sponsorship nor hostility. New York, in common with the other states, has determined that certain entities that exist in a harmonious relationship to the community at large, and that foster its 'moral or mental improvement,' should not be inhibited in their activities by property taxation or the hazard of loss of those properties for nonpayment of taxes. It [has] granted exemption to all houses of religious worship within a broad class of property owned by nonprofit, quasi-public corporations which include hospitals, libraries, playgrounds, scientific, professional, historical and patriotic groups. * * * We must also be sure that the end result—the effect—is not an excessive government entanglement with religion. The test is inescapably one of degree. * * * Elimination of exemption would tend to expand the involvement of government by giving rise to tax valuation of church property, tax liens, tax foreclosures, and the direct confrontations and conflicts that follow in the train of those legal processes. * * *

"It is obviously correct that no one acquires a vested or protected right in violation of the Constitution by long use * * *. Yet an unbroken practice of according the exemption to churches [is] not something to be lightly cast aside." Douglas, J., dissented.

Note

"Neutrality" and "endorsement." TEXAS MONTHLY, INC. v. BULLOCK, 489 U.S. 1 (1989), held violative of the Establishment Clause a Texas sales tax exemption for books and "periodicals that are published or distributed by a religious faith and that consist wholly of writings promulgating the teaching of the faith." BRENNAN, J., joined by Marshall and Stevens, JJ., referred to several important themes in the Court's developing Establishment Clause rationale: "[*Walz*] emphasized that the benefits derived by religious organizations flowed to a large number of nonreligious groups as [well]. However, when government directs a subsidy exclusively to religious organizations [that] either burdens nonbeneficiaries markedly or cannot reasonably be seen as removing a significant state-imposed deterrent to the free exercise of religion, as Texas has done, it 'provide[s] unjustifiable awards of assistance to religious organizations' and cannot but 'conve[y] a message of endorsement' to slighted members of the community. This is particularly true where, as here, the subsidy is targeted at writings that *promulgate* the teachings of religious faiths. It is difficult to view Texas' narrow exemption as anything but state sponsorship of religious belief [which] lacks a secular objective." Scalia, J., joined by Rehnquist, C.J., and Kennedy, J., dissented from Brennan, J.'s distinction of *Walz*.

———

In 1971, LEMON v. KURTZMAN, 403 U.S. 602, per BURGER C.J., which invalidated state salary supplements to teachers of secular subjects in nonpublic schools, articulated a three-part test for judging Establishment Clause issues. This test is most frequently invoked by the lower courts: "First, the statute must have a secular legislative purpose; second, its principal or primary effect must be one that neither advances nor inhibits religion, finally, the statute must not foster "an excessive government entanglement with religion." During the next fifteen years, the Court, using the *Lemon* test, invalidated a large number of aid programs for elementary and secondary schools, even though it found that virtually all had a "secular" purpose.b The *Lemon* Court began with a critical premise: the mission of church related elementary and secondary schools is to teach religion, and all subjects are, or carry the potential of being, permeated with religion. Thus, states would have to engage in a "comprehensive, discriminating, and continuing state surveillance" to prevent misuse of tax funds for religious purposes, which would be impermissibly entangling, and "pregnant with dangers of excessive government direction of church schools and hence of churches."c Furthermore, state assistance risked another sort of entanglement: "divisive political potential" along religious lines.

————

Zelman v. Simmons–Harris, infra, is the most recent case on the subject. It is preceded by *Mitchell v. Helms* because of its strong emphasis of the "neutrality" theme. Both review the important decisions since *Lemon*.

MITCHELL v. HELMS, 530 U.S. 793 (2000), involved a federal program that lends "secular, neutral and nonideological" educational materials (mainly for libraries and computers)—which may not "supplant funds from non-Federal sources"—to elementary and secondary schools, both public and private. THOMAS, J., joined by Rehnquist, C.J., and Scalia and Kennedy, JJ., upheld the program, overruling *Meek v. Pittenger*, 421 U.S. 349 (1975) and *Wolman v. Walter*, 433 U.S. 229 (1977), "in which we held unconstitutional programs that provided many of the same sorts of materials and equipment," and noting that *Agostini v. Felton*, 521 U.S. 203 (1997), "in which we approved a program [that] provided public employees to teach remedial classes at private schools, including religious schools, [had] overruled *Aguilar v. Felton*, 473 U.S. 402 (1985), and partially overruled *School Dist. of Grand Rapids v. Ball*, 473 U.S. 373 (1985), both of which had involved such a program": "[W]e have consistently turned to the principle of neutrality. [I]f the government, seeking to further some legitimate secular purpose, offers aid on the same terms, without regard to religion, to all who adequately further that purpose, then it is fair to say that any aid going to a religious recipient only has the effect of furthering that secular purpose.

"[T]here was a period [when] whether a school that receives aid [was] pervasively sectarian [mattered, particularly if it] was a primary or secondary school. But that period [is] thankfully long past. [The] religious nature of a recipient should not matter to the constitutional analysis, so long as the recipient

b. "This reflects, at least in part, our reluctance to attribute unconstitutional motives to the states, particularly when a plausible secular purpose for the state's program may be discerned from the face of the statute." *Mueller v. Allen*, discussed infra. *Mueller* added: "A state's decision to defray the cost of educational expenses incurred by parents—regardless of the type of schools their children attend—evidences a purpose that is both secular and understandable. An educated populace is essential to the political and economic health of any community, and a state's efforts to assist parents in meeting the rising cost of educational expenses plainly serves this secular purpose of ensuring that the state's citizenry is well-educated. Similarly, [states] could conclude that there is a strong public interest in assuring the continued financial health of private schools, both sectarian and non-sectarian. By educating a substantial number of students such schools relieve public schools of a correspondingly great burden—to the benefit of all taxpayers. In addition, private schools may serve as a benchmark for public schools."

c. White, J., dissenting in *Lemon*, accused the Court of "creat[ing] an insoluble paradox for the State and the parochial schools. The State cannot finance secular instruction if it permits religion to be taught in the same classroom; but if it exacts a promise that religion not be so taught—a promise the school and its teachers are quite willing and on this record able to give—and enforces it, it is then entangled in the 'no entanglement' aspect of the Court's Establishment Clause jurisprudence."

adequately furthers the government's secular purpose. [T]he inquiry into the recipient's religious views required by a focus on whether a school is pervasively sectarian is not only unnecessary but also offensive. It is well established [that] courts should refrain from trolling through a person's or institution's religious beliefs * * *.

"Finally, hostility to aid to pervasively sectarian schools has a shameful pedigree * * *. Opposition to aid to 'sectarian' schools acquired prominence in the 1870's with Congress's consideration (and near passage) of the Blaine Amendment, which would have amended the Constitution to bar any aid to sectarian institutions. Consideration of the amendment arose at a time of pervasive hostility to the Catholic Church and to Catholics in general, and it was an open secret that 'sectarian' was code for 'Catholic.' [When the Court coined the term 'pervasively sectarian,' it] could be applied almost exclusively to Catholic parochial schools [and] even today's dissent exemplifies chiefly by reference to such schools."

O'CONNOR, J., joined by Breyer, J., concurred only in the result: "[W]e have never held that a government-aid program passes constitutional muster solely because of the neutral criteria it employs as a basis for distributing aid." Rather, under *Agostini*, "we [ask] whether the program results in governmental indoctrination [that] could reasonably be attributed to governmental action."

SOUTER, J., joined by Stevens and Ginsburg, JJ., dissented: "[I]f we looked no further than evenhandedness, and failed to ask what activities the aid might support, or in fact did support, religious schools could be blessed with government funding as massive as expenditures made for the benefit of their public school counterparts, and religious missions would thrive on public money."

ZELMAN v. SIMMONS–HARRIS

536 U.S. 639, 122 S.Ct. 2460, 153 L.Ed.2d 604 (2002).

CHIEF JUSTICE REHNQUIST delivered the opinion of the Court.

* * * Cleveland's public schools have been among the worst performing public schools in the Nation. In 1995, a Federal District Court declared a "crisis of magnitude" and placed the entire Cleveland school district under state control. Shortly thereafter, the state auditor found that Cleveland's public schools [had] failed to meet any of the 18 state standards for minimal acceptable performance. Only 1 in 10 ninth graders could pass a basic proficiency examination, and students at all levels performed at a dismal rate compared with students in other Ohio public schools. More than two-thirds of high school students either dropped or failed out before graduation. [Of] those students who did graduate, few could read, write, or compute at levels comparable to their counterparts in other cities.

It is against this backdrop that Ohio enacted, among other initiatives, its Pilot Project Scholarship Program [which] provides financial assistance to families in any Ohio school district that is or has been "under federal court order requiring supervision and operational management of the district by the state superintendent." Cleveland is the only Ohio school district to fall within that category.

[First,] the program provides tuition aid for students [to] attend a participating public or private school of their parent's choosing. Second, the program provides tutorial aid for students who choose to remain enrolled in public school.

[Any] private school, whether religious or nonreligious, may participate in the tuition aid portion of [the] program [so] long as the school is located within the boundaries of a covered district and meets statewide educational standards. Participating private schools must agree not to discriminate on the basis of race, religion, or ethnic background, or to "advocate or foster unlawful behavior or teach hatred of any person or group on the basis of race, ethnicity, national origin, or religion." Any public school located in a school district adjacent to the covered district may also participate [and is] eligible to receive a $2,250 tuition grant for each program student accepted in addition to the full amount of per-pupil state funding attributable to each additional student.

Tuition aid is distributed to parents according to financial need. Families with incomes below 200% of the poverty line are given priority [and] receive 90% of private school tuition up to $2,250. For these lowest-income families, participating private schools may not charge a parental co-payment greater than $250. For all other families, the program pays 75% of tuition costs, up to $1,875, with no co-payment cap. [If] parents choose a private school, checks are made payable to the parents who then endorse the checks over to the chosen school.

[In] the 1999–2000 school year, 56 private schools participated in the program, 46 (or 82%) of which had a religious affiliation. None of the public schools in districts adjacent to Cleveland have elected to participate. More than 3,700 students participated in the scholarship program, most of whom (96%) enrolled in religiously affiliated schools. Sixty percent of these students were from families at or below the poverty line. * * *

The program is part of a broader undertaking by the State to enhance the educational options of Cleveland's schoolchildren in response to the 1995 takeover. That undertaking includes programs governing community and magnet schools. Community schools are funded under state law but are run by their own school boards, not by local school districts. These schools enjoy academic independence to hire their own teachers and to determine their own curriculum. They can have no religious affiliation and are required to accept students by lottery. During the 1999–2000 school year, there were 10 start-up community schools in the Cleveland City School District with more than 1,900 students enrolled. For each child enrolled in a community school, the school receives state funding of $4,518, twice the funding a participating program school may receive.

Magnet schools are public schools operated by a local school board that emphasize a particular subject area, teaching method, or service to students. For each student enrolled in a magnet school, the school district receives $7,746, including state funding of $4,167, the same amount received per student enrolled at a traditional public school. As of 1999, parents in Cleveland were able to choose from among 23 magnet schools, which together enrolled more than 13,000 students in kindergarten through eighth grade. These schools provide specialized teaching methods, such as Montessori, or a particularized curriculum focus, such as foreign language, computers, or the arts.

[There] is no dispute that the program challenged here was enacted for the valid secular purpose of providing educational assistance to poor children in a demonstrably failing public school system. Thus, the question presented is whether the Ohio program nonetheless has the forbidden "effect" of advancing or inhibiting religion.

To answer that question, our decisions have drawn a consistent distinction between government programs that provide aid directly to religious schools, *Mitchell*; *Rosenberger v. University of Virginia*, 515 U.S. 819, 842 (1995),a and

---

a. The *Rosenberger* majority, Ch. 7, Sec. 7, I, which consisted of the *Mitchell* plurality and O'Connor, J., held that the Establishment Clause permits a public university to fund a student newspaper that proselytized a Christian perspective as part of a program that generally funded student publications. Although recognizing "special Establishment

programs of true private choice, in which government aid reaches religious schools only as a result of the genuine and independent choices of private individuals. While our jurisprudence with respect to the constitutionality of direct aid programs has "changed significantly" over the past two decades, our jurisprudence with respect to true private choice programs has remained consistent and unbroken. Three times we have confronted Establishment Clause challenges to neutral government programs that provide aid directly to a broad class of individuals, who, in turn, direct the aid to religious schools or institutions of their own choosing. Three times we have rejected such challenges.

In *Mueller v. Allen,* 463 U.S. 388 (1983), we rejected an Establishment Clause challenge to a Minnesota program authorizing tax deductions for various educational expenses, including private school tuition costs, even though the great majority of the program's beneficiaries (96%) were parents of children in religious schools. [In] *Witters v. Washington Dept. of Servs. for Blind,* 474 U.S. 481 (1986), we used identical reasoning to reject an Establishment Clause challenge to a vocational scholarship program that provided tuition aid to a student studying at a religious institution to become a pastor. [Finally,] in *Zobrest v. Catalina Foothills School Dist.*, 509 U.S. 1 (1993), we applied *Mueller* and *Witters* to reject an Establishment Clause challenge to a federal program that permitted sign-language interpreters to assist deaf children enrolled in religious schools. * * *

Mueller, Witters, and *Zobrest* thus make clear that where a government aid program is neutral with respect to religion, and provides assistance directly to a broad class of citizens who, in turn, direct government aid to religious schools wholly as a result of their own genuine and independent private choice, the program is not readily subject to challenge under the Establishment Clause. [The] incidental advancement of a religious mission, or the perceived endorsement of a religious message, is reasonably attributable to the individual recipient, not to the government, whose role ends with the disbursement of benefits [citing the opinions of the plurality and O'Connor, J., in *Mitchell*].b [It] is precisely for these reasons that we have never found a program of true private choice to offend the Establishment Clause.

Clause dangers" in direct aid to religious entities, the plurality noted that its decision "cannot be read as addressing an expenditure from a general tax fund." Rather, the money came from a "special student activities fund from which any group of students with [recognized] status can draw for purposes consistent with the University's educational mission." As in *Lamb's Chapel v. Center Moriches Union Free School Dist.*, 508 U.S. 384 (1993), holding that a school district did not violate the Establishment Clause in permitting a church's after-hours use of school facilities to show a religiously oriented film series on family values when the school district also permitted presentation of views on the subject by nonreligious groups, "a public university may maintain its own computer facility and give student groups access to that facility, including the use of the printers, on a religion neutral, say first-come-first-served, basis." This is no different than "a school paying a third-party contractor to operate the facility on its behalf. The latter occurs here." Since the University made payments for publication costs directly to the printing companies, "we do not confront a case where, even under a neutral program that includes nonsectarian recipients, the government is making direct money payments to an institution or group that is engaged in religious activity."

b. O'Connor, J. reasoned: "In terms of public perception, a government program of direct aid to religious schools based on the number of students attending each school differs meaningfully from the government distributing aid directly to individual students who, in turn, decide to use the aid at the same religious schools. In the former example, if the religious school uses the aid to inculcate religion [, the] reasonable observer would naturally perceive the aid program as *government* support for the advancement of religion. That the amount of aid received by the school is based on the school's enrollment does not separate the government from the endorsement of the religious message. [In] contrast, when government aid supports a school's religious mission only because of independent decisions made by numerous individuals to guide their secular aid to that [school,] endorsement of the religious message is reasonably attributed to the individuals who select the path of the aid."

We believe that the program challenged here is a program of true private choice. [It] is neutral in all respects toward religion. It is part of a general and multifaceted undertaking by the State of Ohio to provide educational opportunities to the children of a failed school district. It confers educational assistance directly to a broad class of individuals defined without reference to religion. [The] program permits the participation of *all* schools within the district, religious or nonreligious. Adjacent public schools also may participate and have a financial incentive to do so. [The] only preference stated anywhere in the program is a preference for low-income families* * *.

There are no "financial incentive[s]" that "ske[w]" the program toward religious schools. *Witters*. Such incentives "[are] not present [where] the aid is allocated on the basis of neutral, secular criteria that neither favor nor disfavor religion, and is made available to both religious and secular beneficiaries on a nondiscriminatory basis." *Agostini*. The program here in fact creates financial *dis*incentives for religious schools, with private schools receiving only half the government assistance given to community schools and one-third the assistance given to magnet schools. Adjacent public schools, should any choose to accept program students, are also eligible to receive two to three times the state funding of a private religious [school]. Parents that choose to participate in the scholarship program and then to enroll their children in a private school (religious or nonreligious) must copay a portion of the school's tuition. Families that choose a community school, magnet school, or traditional public school pay nothing. Although such features of the program are not necessary to its constitutionality, they clearly dispel the claim that the program "creates * * * financial incentive[s] for parents to choose a sectarian school." *Zobrest*.22

[Any] objective observer familiar with the full history and context of the Ohio program would reasonably view it as one aspect of a broader undertaking to assist poor children in failed schools, not as an endorsement of religious schooling in general.

There also is no evidence that the program fails to provide genuine opportunities for Cleveland parents to select secular educational options for their school-age children. Cleveland schoolchildren [may] remain in public school as before, remain in public school with publicly funded tutoring aid, obtain a scholarship and choose a religious school, obtain a scholarship and choose a nonreligious private school, enroll in a community school, or enroll in a magnet school. That 46 of the 56 private schools now participating in the program are religious schools does not condemn it as [t]he Establishment Clause question is whether Ohio is coercing parents into sending their children to religious schools, and that question must be answered by evaluating *all* options * * *.

Justice Souter speculates that because more private religious schools currently participate in the program, the program itself must somehow discourage the participation of private nonreligious schools.23 But Cleveland's preponderance of

22. Justice Souter suggests the program is not "neutral" because program students cannot spend scholarship vouchers at traditional public schools. This objection is mistaken: Public schools in Cleveland already receive $7,097 in public funding per pupil—$4,167 of which is attributable to the State. Program students who receive tutoring aid and remain enrolled in traditional public schools therefore direct almost twice as much state funding to their chosen school as do program students who

receive a scholarship and attend a private school.* * *

23. Justice Souter appears to base this claim on the unfounded assumption that capping the amount of tuition charged to low-income students (at $2,500) favors participation by religious schools. [But] the record [shows] that nonreligious private schools operating in Cleveland also seek and receive substantial third-party contributions. Indeed, the actual operation of the program refutes Justice

religiously affiliated private schools certainly did not arise as a result of the program; it is a phenomenon common to many American cities. Indeed, by all accounts the program has captured a remarkable cross-section of private schools, religious and nonreligious. It is true that 82% of Cleveland's participating private schools are religious schools, but it is also true that 81% of private schools in Ohio are religious schools. To attribute constitutional significance to this figure, more-over, would lead to the absurd result that a neutral school-choice program might [be] constitutional in some States, such as Maine or Utah, where less than 45% of private schools are religious schools, but not in other States, such as Nebraska or Kansas, where over 90% of private schools are religious schools.

Respondents and Justice Souter claim [that] we should attach constitutional significance to the fact that 96% of scholarship recipients have enrolled in religious schools. They claim that this alone proves parents lack genuine choice, even if no parent has ever said so. We need not consider this argument in detail, since it was flatly rejected in *Mueller*, where we found it irrelevant that 96% of parents taking deductions for tuition expenses paid tuition at religious schools. [The] constitutionality of a neutral educational aid program simply does not turn on whether and why, in a particular area, at a particular time, most private schools are run by religious organizations, or most recipients choose to use the aid at a religious school. As we said in *Mueller*, "[s]uch an approach would scarcely provide the certainty that this field stands in need of, nor can we perceive principled standards by which such statistical evidence might be evaluated."

This point is aptly illustrated here. The 96% figure upon which respondents and Justice Souter rely discounts entirely (1) the more than 1,900 Cleveland children enrolled in alternative community schools, (2) the more than 13,000 children enrolled in alternative magnet schools, and (3) the more than 1,400 children enrolled in traditional public schools with tutorial assistance. Including some or all of these children in the denominator of children enrolled in nontraditional schools during the 1999–2000 school year drops the percentage enrolled in religious schools from 96% to under 20%. The 96% figure also represents but a snapshot of one particular school year. In the 1997–1998 school year, by contrast, only 78% of scholarship recipients attended religious schools. The difference was attributable to two private nonreligious schools that had accepted 15% of all scholarship students electing instead to register as community schools, in light of larger per-pupil funding for community schools and the uncertain future of the scholarship program generated by this litigation.24 Many of the students enrolled

Souter's [argument]: Ten secular private schools operated within the Cleveland City School District when the program was adopted. All 10 chose to participate in the program and have continued to participate to this day. And while no religious schools have been created in response to the program, several *nonreligious* schools have been created in spite of the fact that a principal barrier to entry of new private schools is the uncertainty caused by protracted litigation which has plagued the program since its inception. See also 234 F.3d 945, 970 (CA6 2000) ("There is not a scintilla of evidence in this case that any school, public or private, has been discouraged from participating in the school voucher program because it cannot 'afford' to do so") (Ryan, J., concurring in part and dissenting in part). Similarly mistaken is Justice Souter's reliance on the low enrollment of scholarship students in nonreligious schools during the 1999–2000 school year. These fig-

ures ignore the fact that the number of program students enrolled in nonreligious schools has widely varied from year to year, underscoring why the constitutionality of a neutral choice program does not turn on annual tallies of private decisions made in any given year by thousands of individual aid recipients.

24. The fluctuations seen in the Cleveland program are hardly atypical. Experience in Milwaukee, which since 1991 has operated an educational choice program similar to the Ohio program, demonstrates that the mix of participating schools fluctuates significantly from year to year based on a number of factors, one of which is the uncertainty caused by persistent litigation. Since the Wisconsin Supreme Court declared the Milwaukee program constitutional in 1998, several nonreligious private schools have entered the Milwaukee market, and now represent 32% of all participating

in these schools as scholarship students remained enrolled as community school students, thus demonstrating the arbitrariness of counting one type of school but not the other to assess primary effect.25 * * *

Respondents finally claim that we should look to *Committee for Public Ed. & Religious Liberty v. Nyquist*, 413 U.S. 756 (1973) [involving a state partial tuition tax credit to parents who sent their children to nonpublic schools; for parents too poor to be liable for income taxes and therefore unable to benefit from a tax credit, the state gave an outright grant of up to fifty percent of tuition] to decide these cases. We disagree for two reasons. First, the program in *Nyquist* was quite different from the program challenged [here.] Although the program was enacted for ostensibly secular purposes, we found that its "function" was "unmistakably to provide desired financial support for nonpublic, sectarian institutions." Its genesis, we said, was that private religious schools faced "increasingly grave fiscal problems." [It] provided tax benefits "unrelated to the amount of money actually expended by any parent on tuition," ensuring a windfall to parents of children in religious schools. It similarly provided tuition reimbursements designed explicitly to "offe[r] an incentive to parents to send their children to sectarian schools." Indeed, the program flatly prohibited the participation of any public school, or parent of any public school enrollee. Ohio's program shares none of these features.

Second, [we] expressly reserved judgment with respect to "a case involving some form of public assistance (e.g., scholarships) made available generally without regard to the sectarian-nonsectarian, or public-nonpublic nature of the institution benefited." That, of course, is the very question now before us, and it has since been answered [in *Mueller*, *Witters*, and *Zobrest*].26

The judgment of the Court of Appeals is reversed.

JUSTICE O'CONNOR, concurring. * * *

These cases are different from prior indirect aid cases in part because a significant portion of the funds appropriated for the voucher program reach religious schools without restrictions on the use of these funds. The share of public resources that reach religious schools is not, however, as significant as respondents suggest. [Even if] all voucher students came from low-income families and that each voucher student used up the entire $2,250 voucher, at most $8.2 million of public funds flowed to religious schools under the voucher program in 1999–2000. Although just over one-half as many students attended community schools as religious private schools on the state fisc, the State spent over $1 million more [on] students in community schools than on students in religious private schools because per-pupil aid to community schools is more than double the per-pupil aid to private schools under the voucher program. Moreover, the amount spent on religious private schools is minor compared to the $114.8 million the State spent on students in the Cleveland magnet schools.

schools. [There] are currently 34 nonreligious private schools participating in the Milwaukee program, a nearly a five-fold increase from the 7 nonreligious schools that participated when the program began in 1990. * * *

25. Justice Souter and Justice Stevens claim that community schools and magnet schools are separate and distinct from program schools, simply because the program itself does not include community and magnet school options. But none of the dissenting opinions explain how there is any perceptible difference between scholarship schools, community schools, or magnet schools from the perspec-

tive of Cleveland parents looking to choose the best educational option for their school-age children.* * *

26. Justice Breyer would raise the invisible specters of "divisiveness" and "religious strife" to find the program unconstitutional [but] the program has ignited no "divisiveness" or "strife" other than this litigation. * * * We quite rightly have rejected the claim that some speculative potential for divisiveness bears on the constitutionality of educational aid programs. *Mitchell.*

Although $8.2 million is no small sum, it pales in comparison to the amount of funds that federal, state, and local governments already provide religious institutions. Religious organizations may qualify for exemptions from the federal corporate income tax, the corporate income tax in many States, and property taxes in all 50 States, and clergy qualify for a federal tax break on income used for housing expenses. In addition, the Federal Government provides [a] tax deduction for charitable contributions to qualified religious groups. Finally, the Federal Government and certain state governments provide tax credits for educational expenses, many of which are spent on education at religious schools.

[The] state property tax exemptions for religious institutions alone amount to very large sums annually. For example, available data suggest [that] Wisconsin's exemption lowers revenues by approximately $122 million. [As] for the Federal Government, the tax deduction for charitable contributions reduces federal tax revenues by nearly $25 billion annually, and it is reported that over 60 percent of household charitable contributions go to religious charities. [Federal] dollars also reach religiously affiliated organizations through public health programs such as Medicare and Medicaid, through educational programs such as the Pell Grant program and the G. I. Bill of Rights, and through child care programs such as the Child Care and Development Block Grant Program. [A] significant portion of the funds appropriated for these programs reach religiously affiliated institutions, typically without restrictions on its subsequent use.c

JUSTICE SOUTER, with whom JUSTICE STEVENS, JUSTICE GINSBURG, and JUSTICE BREYER join, dissenting.

[In] the city of Cleveland the overwhelming proportion of large appropriations for voucher money must be spent on religious schools if it is to be spent at all, and will be spent in amounts that cover almost all of tuition. The money will thus pay for eligible students' instruction not only in secular subjects but in religion as well, in schools that can fairly be characterized as founded to teach religious doctrine and to imbue teaching in all subjects with a religious dimension.2 * * *

The majority's statements of Establishment Clause doctrine cannot be appreciated without some historical perspective on the Court's announced limitations on government aid to religious education, and its repeated repudiation of limits previously set. My object here [is] to set out the broad doctrinal stages covered in the modern era, and to show that doctrinal bankruptcy has been reached today.

Viewed with the necessary generality, the cases can be categorized in three groups. In the period from 1947 to 1968, the basic principle of no aid to religion through school benefits was unquestioned. Thereafter for some 15 years, the Court termed its efforts as attempts to draw a line against aid that would be divertible to support the religious, as distinct from the secular, activity of an institutional beneficiary. Then, starting in 1983, concern with divertibility was gradually lost in favor of approving aid in amounts unlikely to afford substantial benefits to religious schools, when offered evenhandedly without regard to a recipient's religious character, and when channeled to a religious institution only

c. The concurring opinion of Thomas, J.—questioning whether the Establishment Clause should be applied to the states (see his opinion in *Van Orden v. Perry*, Sec. IV infra), and rejecting use of the fourteenth amendment "to oppose neutral programs of school choice through the incorporation of the Establishment Clause"—is omitted.

2. See, e.g., App. (Saint Jerome School Parent and Student Handbook 1999–2000, p. 1)

("FAITH must dominate the entire educational process so that the child can make decisions according to Catholic values and choose to lead a Christian life"); id., (Westside Baptist Christian School Parent–Student Handbook, p. 7) ("Christ is the basis of all learning. All subjects will be taught from the Biblical perspective that all truth is God's truth").

by the genuinely free choice of some private individual. Now, the three stages are succeeded by a fourth, in which the substantial character of government aid is held to have no constitutional significance, and the espoused criteria of neutrality in offering aid, and private choice in directing it, are shown to be nothing but examples of verbal formalism.

[Souter, J., began with *Everson* and continued with *Board of Educ. v. Allen*, 392 U.S. 236 (1968), upholding a program for lending state approved secular textbooks to all schoolchildren, including those attending church-related schools.] The Court relied [on] the theory that the in-kind aid could only be used for secular educational purposes, and found it relevant that "no funds or books are furnished [directly] to parochial schools, and the financial benefit is to parents and children, not to schools.4" * * *

Allen recognized the reality that "religious schools pursue two goals, religious instruction and secular education;" if state aid could be restricted to serve the second, it might be permissible under the Establishment Clause. But in the retrenchment that followed, the Court saw that the two educational functions were so intertwined in religious primary and secondary schools that aid to secular education could not readily be segregated, and the intrusive monitoring required to enforce the line itself raised Establishment Clause concerns about the entanglement of church and state. See *Lemon*. To avoid the entanglement, the Court's focus in the post-*Allen* cases was on the principle of divertibility. [The] greater the risk of diversion to religion (and the monitoring necessary to avoid it), the less legitimate the aid scheme was under the no-aid principle. On the one hand, the Court tried to be practical, and when the aid recipients were not so "pervasively sectarian" that their secular and religious functions were inextricably intertwined, the Court generally upheld aid earmarked for secular use. See, e.g., *Roemer v. Board of Public Works*, 426 U.S. 736 (1976); *Hunt v. McNair*, 413 U.S. 734 (1973); *Tilton v. Richardson*, 403 U.S. 672 (1971).d But otherwise the principle of nondivertibility was enforced strictly, with its violation being presumed in most cases, even when state aid seemed secular on its face. Compare, e.g., *Levitt v. Committee for Public Ed. & Religious Liberty*, 413 U.S. 472 (1973) (striking down state program reimbursing private schools' administrative costs for teacher-prepared tests in compulsory secular subjects), with *Wolman* (upholding similar program using standardized tests [and] permitting state aid for diagnostic speech, hearing, and psychological testing).

The fact that the Court's suspicion of divertibility reflected a concern with the substance of the no-aid principle is apparent in its rejection of stratagems invented to dodge it. [The] *Nyquist* Court dismissed warranties of a "statistical guarantee," that the scheme provided at most 15% of the total cost of an

---

4. The Court noted that "the record contains no evidence that any of the private schools ... previously provided textbooks for their students," and "[t]here is some evidence that at least some of the schools did not." This was a significant distinction: if the parochial schools provided secular textbooks to their students, then the State's provision of the same in their stead might have freed up church resources for allocation to other uses, including, potentially, religious indoctrination.

d. These cases all involved higher education. *Tilton* and *Roemer* upheld direct government grants to church-related colleges and universities as part of general programs for construction of buildings and other activities not involving sectarian activities. *Tilton* noted:

"The 'affirmative, if not dominant, policy' of the instruction in pre-college church-schools is 'to assure future adherents to a particular faith by having control of their total education at an early age.' There is substance to the contention that college students are less impressionable and less susceptible to religious indoctrination. [Further], by their very nature, college and postgraduate courses tend to limit the opportunities for sectarian influence by virtue of their own internal disciplines. Many church-related colleges and universities are characterized by a high degree of academic freedom and seek to evoke free and critical responses from their students."

education at a religious school which could presumably be matched to a secular 15% of a child's education at the school. And it rejected the idea that the path of state aid to religious schools might be dispositive: "far from providing a per se immunity from examination of the substance of the State's program, the fact that aid is disbursed to parents rather than to the schools is only one among many factors to be considered." The point was that "the effect of the aid is unmistakably to provide desired financial support for nonpublic, sectarian institutions." [The Court's object] had always been a realistic assessment of facts aimed at respecting the principle of no aid. In *Mueller*, however, that object began to fade, for *Mueller* started down the road from realism to formalism.

[If] regular, public schools (which can get no voucher payments) "participate" in a voucher scheme with schools that can, and public expenditure is still predominantly on public schools, then the majority's reasoning would find neutrality in a scheme of vouchers available for private tuition in districts with no secular private schools at all. "Neutrality" as the majority employs the term is, literally, verbal and nothing more. * * *

The majority addresses the issue of choice the same way it addresses neutrality, by asking whether recipients or potential recipients of voucher aid have a choice of public schools among secular alternatives to religious schools. [But this] ignores the whole point of the choice test: it is a criterion for deciding whether indirect aid to a religious school is legitimate because it passes through private hands that can spend or use the aid in a secular school. [The] majority now has transformed this question about private choice in channeling aid into a question about selecting from examples of state spending (on education) including direct spending on magnet and community public schools that goes through no private hands and could never reach a religious school under any circumstance. [And] because it is unlikely that any participating private religious school will enroll more pupils than the generally available public system, it will be easy to generate numbers suggesting that aid to religion is not the significant intent or effect of the voucher scheme.* * *

If, contrary to the majority, we ask the right question about genuine choice to use the vouchers, the answer shows that something is influencing choices in a way that aims the money in a religious direction: * * * 96.6% of all voucher recipients go to religious schools, only 3.4% to nonreligious [ones.] One answer to these statistics, for example, which would be consistent with the genuine choice claimed to be operating, might be that 96.6% of families choosing to avail themselves of vouchers choose to educate their children in schools of their own religion. This would not, in my view, render the scheme constitutional, but it would speak to the majority's choice criterion. Evidence shows, however, that almost two out of three families using vouchers to send their children to religious schools did not embrace the religion of those schools. The families made it clear they had not chosen the schools because they wished their children to be proselytized in a religion not their own, or in any religion, but because of educational opportunity.

Even so, [that] some 2,270 students chose to apply their vouchers to schools of other religions might be consistent with true choice if the students "chose" their religious schools over a wide array of private nonreligious options, or if it could be shown [that] Ohio's program had no effect on educational choices and thus no impermissible effect of advancing religious education. But both possibilities are contrary to fact. First, even if all existing nonreligious private schools in Cleveland were willing to accept large numbers of voucher students, only a few more than the 129 currently enrolled in such schools would be able to attend, as the total enrollment at all nonreligious private schools in Cleveland for kindergarten through eighth grade is only 510 children, and there is no indication that these schools have many open seats.13 Second, the $2,500 cap that the program places on tuition for participating low-income pupils has the effect of curtailing the participation of nonreligious schools: "nonreligious schools with higher tuition (about $4,000) stated that they could afford to accommodate just a few voucher students."14 By comparison, the average tuition at participating Catholic schools in Cleveland in 1999–2000 was $1,592, almost $1,000 below the cap.

Of course, the obvious fix would be to increase the value of vouchers so that existing nonreligious private and non-Catholic religious schools would be able to enroll more voucher students, and to provide incentives for educators to create new such schools given that few presently exist. [But] it is simply unrealistic to presume that parents of elementary and middle schoolchildren in Cleveland will have a range of secular and religious choices even arguably comparable to the statewide program for vocational and higher education in *Witters*. And to get to that hypothetical point would require that such massive financial support be made available to religion as to disserve every objective of the Establishment Clause even more than the present scheme does.

[And] contrary to the majority's assertion, public schools in adjacent districts hardly have a financial incentive to participate in the Ohio voucher program, and none has.17 [It] is entirely irrelevant that the State did not deliberately design the network of private schools for the sake of channeling money into religious institutions. The criterion is one of genuinely free choice on the part of the private individuals who choose, and a Hobson's choice is not a choice, whatever the reason for being Hobsonian. * * *

The scale of the aid to religious schools approved today is unprecedented, both in the number of dollars and in the proportion of systemic school expenditure supported. Each measure has received attention in previous cases. [In] paying for practically the full amount of tuition for thousands of qualifying students, the scholarships purchase everything that tuition purchases, be it instruction in math or indoctrination in faith. [T]he majority makes no pretense that substantial amounts of tax money are not systematically underwriting religious practice and indoctrination.

It is virtually superfluous to point out that every objective underlying the prohibition of religious establishment is betrayed by this scheme, but something has to be said about the enormity of the violation. [The first objective is] respect for freedom of conscience. Jefferson described it as the idea that no one "shall be compelled [to] support any religious worship, place, or ministry whatsoever."

13. Justice O'Connor points out that "there is no record evidence that any voucher-eligible student was turned away from a nonreligious private school in the voucher program." But there is equally no evidence to support her assertion that "many parents with vouchers selected nonreligious private schools over religious alternatives," and in fact the evidence is to the contrary, as only 129 students used vouchers at private nonreligious schools.

14. Of the 10 nonreligious private schools that "participate" in the Cleveland voucher program, 3 currently enroll no voucher students. And of the remaining seven schools, one enrolls over half of the 129 students [while] only two others enroll more than 8 voucher students. Such schools can charge full tuition to students whose families do not qualify as "low income," but unless the number of vouchers are drastically increased, it is unlikely that these students will constitute a large fraction of voucher recipients, as the program gives preference in the allocation of vouchers to low-income children.

17. As the Court points out, an out-of-district public school that participates will receive a $2,250 voucher for each Cleveland student on top of its normal state funding. The basic state funding, though, is a drop in the bucket as compared to the cost of educating that student, as much of the cost (at least in relatively affluent areas with presumptively better academic standards) is paid by local income and property taxes. * * *

As for the second objective, to save religion from its own corruption, [t]he risk is already being realized. In Ohio, for example, a condition of receiving government money under the program is that [the] school may not give admission preferences to children who are members of the patron faith. [In addition], a participating religious school may well be forbidden to choose a member of its own clergy to serve as teacher or principal over a layperson of a different religion claiming equal qualification for the job. Indeed, a separate condition that "[t]he school [not] teach hatred of any person or group on the basis [of] religion," could be understood (or subsequently broadened) to prohibit religions from teaching traditionally legitimate articles of faith as to the error, sinfulness, or ignorance of [others].

For perspective on this foot-in-the-door of religious regulation, it is well to remember that the money has barely begun to flow. [T]here is no question that religious schools in Ohio are on the way to becoming bigger businesses with budgets enhanced to fit their new stream of tax-raised income. See, e.g., People for the American Way Foundation, A Painful Price 5, 9, 11 (Feb. 14, 2002) (of 91 schools participating in the Milwaukee program, 75 received voucher payments in excess of tuition, 61 of those were religious and averaged $185,000 worth of overpayment per school, justified in part to "raise low salaries"). [A] move in the Ohio State Senate [would] raise the current maximum value of a school voucher from $2,250 to the base amount of current state spending on each public school student ($4,814 for the 2001 fiscal year). Ohio, in fact, is merely replicating the experience in Wisconsin, where a similar increase in the value of educational vouchers in Milwaukee has induced the creation of some 23 new private schools, some of which, we may safely surmise, are religious. New schools have presumably pegged their financial prospects to the government from the start, and the odds are that increases in government aid will bring the threshold voucher amount closer to the tuition at even more expensive religious schools. * * *

JUSTICE BREYER, with whom JUSTICE STEVENS and JUSTICE SOUTER join, dissenting.

[T]he Court's 20th century Establishment Clause cases—both those limiting the practice of religion in public schools and those limiting the public funding of private religious education—focused directly upon social conflict, potentially created when government becomes involved in religious education. [The] Court appreciated the religious diversity of contemporary American society. [It] understood the Establishment Clause to prohibit (among other things) [favoring some religions at the expense of others]. Yet *how* did the Clause achieve that objective? Did it simply require the government to give each religion an equal chance to introduce religion into the primary schools? [T]he Court concluded that the Establishment Clause required "separation," in part because an "equal opportunity" approach was not workable. With respect to religious activities in the public schools, [i]n many places there were too many religions, too diverse a set of religious practices, too many whose spiritual beliefs denied the virtue of formal religious training. * * *

With respect to government aid to private education, did not history show that efforts to obtain equivalent funding for the private education of children whose parents did not hold popular religious beliefs only exacerbated religious strife? * * * America boasts more than 55 different religious groups and subgroups with a significant number of members. [V]oucher programs finance the religious education of the young. And, if widely adopted, they may well provide billions of dollars that will do so. Why will different religions not become concerned about, and seek to influence, the criteria used to channel this money to religious schools? Why will they not want to examine the implementation of the programs that provide this money—to determine, for example, whether implementation has biased a program toward or against particular sects, or whether recipient religious schools are adequately fulfilling a program's criteria? If so, just how is the State to resolve the resulting controversies without provoking legitimate fears of the kinds of religious favoritism that, in so religiously diverse a Nation, threaten social dissension? * * *

I concede that the Establishment Clause currently permits States to channel various forms of assistance to religious schools, for example, transportation costs for students, computers, and secular texts. [V]oucher programs differ, however, in both *kind* and *degree* from aid programs upheld in the past. They differ in kind because they direct financing to a core function of the church: the teaching of religious truths to young [children]. History suggests, not that such private school teaching of religion is undesirable, but that *government funding* of this kind of religious endeavor is far more contentious than providing funding for secular textbooks, computers, vocational training, or even funding for adults who wish to obtain a college education at a religious university. [H]istory also shows that government involvement in religious primary education is far more divisive than state property tax exemptions for religious institutions or tax deductions for charitable contributions, both of which come far closer to exemplifying the neutrality that distinguishes, for example, fire protection on the one hand from direct monetary assistance on the other. * * *

I do not believe that the "parental choice" aspect of the voucher program sufficiently offsets the concerns I have mentioned. Parental choice cannot help the taxpayer who does not want to finance the religious education of children. It will not always help the parent who may see little real choice between inadequate nonsectarian public education and adequate education at a school whose religious teachings are contrary to his own. It will not satisfy religious minorities unable to participate because they are too few in number to support the creation of their own private schools. It will not satisfy groups whose religious beliefs preclude them from participating in a government-sponsored program, and who may well feel ignored as government funds primarily support the education of children in the doctrines of the dominant religions. And it does little to ameliorate the entanglement problems or the related problems of social division * * *.e

III. RELIGION AND PUBLIC SCHOOLS

WALLACE v. JAFFREE

472 U.S. 38, 105 S.Ct. 2479, 86 L.Ed.2d 29 (1985).

JUSTICE STEVENS delivered the opinion of the Court.

[In 1978, Alabama enacted § 16–1–20 authorizing a one-minute period of silence in all public schools "for meditation"; in 1981, it enacted § 16–1–20.1 authorizing a period of silence "for meditation or voluntary prayer." Appellees] have not questioned the holding that § 16–1–20 is valid. Thus, the narrow question for decision [concerns § 16–1–20.1].

[T]he Court has unambiguously concluded that the individual freedom of conscience protected by the First Amendment embraces the right to select any religious faith or none at all. * * *

[Under Lemon,] even though a statute that is motivated in part by a religious purpose may satisfy the first criterion, the First Amendment requires that a

e. Stevens, J.'s brief separate dissent—stating that "whenever we remove a brick from the wall that was designed to separate religion and government, we increase the risk of religious strife and weaken the foundation of our democracy"—is omitted.

statute must be invalidated if it is entirely motivated by a purpose to advance religion. In applying the purpose test, it is appropriate to ask "whether government's actual purpose is to endorse or disapprove of religion."[42] In this case, the answer to that question is dispositive.* * *

The sponsor of the bill that became § 16–1–20.1, Senator Donald Holmes, inserted into the legislative record—apparently without dissent—a statement indicating that the legislation was an "effort to return voluntary prayer" to the public schools. Later Senator Holmes confirmed this purpose before the District Court. In response to the question whether he had any purpose for the legislation other than returning voluntary prayer to public schools, he stated: "No, I did not have no other purpose in mind." The State did not present evidence of *any* secular purpose. * * *

The legislative intent to return prayer to the public schools is, of course, quite different from merely protecting every student's right to engage in voluntary prayer during an appropriate moment of silence during the schoolday. The 1978 statute already protected that right, containing nothing that prevented any student from engaging in voluntary prayer during a silent minute of meditation. [The] legislature enacted § 16–1–20.1, despite the existence of § 16–1–20 for the sole purpose of expressing the State's endorsement of prayer activities for one minute at the beginning of each schoolday. The addition of "or voluntary prayer" indicates that the State intended to characterize prayer as a favored practice. Such an endorsement is not consistent with the established principle that the government must pursue a course of complete neutrality toward religion.

The importance of that principle does not permit us to treat this as an inconsequential case involving nothing more than a few words of symbolic speech on behalf of the political majority.[51] For whenever the State itself speaks on a religious subject, one of the questions [is] "whether the government intends to convey a message of endorsement or disapproval of religion." * * *

JUSTICE O'CONNOR concurring in the judgment.

* * * Although a distinct jurisprudence has enveloped each of [the Religion] Clauses, their common purpose is to secure religious liberty. On these principles the Court has been and remains unanimous. [O]ur goal should be "to frame a principle for constitutional adjudication that is not only grounded in the history and language of the first amendment, but one that is also capable of consistent application to the relevant problems." Jesse H. Choper, *Religion in the Public Schools: A Proposed Constitutional Standard,* 47 Minn.L.Rev. 329, 332–333

---

42. *Lynch v. Donnelly,* [Part IV infra] (O'Connor, J., concurring) ("The purpose prong of the *Lemon* test asks whether government's actual purpose is to endorse or disapprove of religion. The effect prong asks whether, irrespective of government's actual purpose, the practice under review in fact conveys a message of endorsement or disapproval. An affirmative answer to either question should render the challenged practice invalid").

51. As this Court stated in *Engel v. Vitale,* [infra]: "The Establishment Clause, unlike the Free Exercise Clause, does not depend upon any showing of direct governmental compulsion and is violated by the enactment of laws which establish an official religion whether those laws operate directly to coerce nonobserving individuals or not." Moreover, this

Court has noted that "[w]hen the power, prestige and financial support of government is placed behind a particular religious belief, the indirect coercive pressure upon religious minorities to conform to the prevailing officially approved religion is plain." Id. This comment has special force in the public-school context where attendance is mandatory. Justice Frankfurter acknowledged this reality in *McCollum v. Board of Education,* [note 1(a) infra] (concurring opinion): "That a child is offered an alternative may reduce the constraint; it does not eliminate the operation of influence by the school in matters sacred to conscience and outside the school's domain. The law of imitation operates, and non-conformity is not an outstanding characteristic of children." * * *

(1963). Last Term, I proposed a refinement of the *Lemon* test with this goal in mind. *Lynch v. Donnelly* (concurring opinion).

The *Lynch* concurrence suggested that the religious liberty protected by the Establishment Clause is infringed when the government makes adherence to religion relevant to a person's standing in the political community. Direct government action endorsing religion or a particular religious practice is invalid under this approach because it "sends a message to nonadherents that they are outsiders, not full members of the political community, and an accompanying message to adherents that they are insiders, favored members of the political community." [In] this country, church and state must necessarily operate within the same community. Because of this coexistence, it is inevitable that the secular interests of government and the religious interests of various sects and their adherents will frequently intersect, conflict, and combine. A statute that ostensibly promotes a secular interest often has an incidental or even a primary effect of helping or hindering a sectarian belief. Chaos would ensue if every such statute were invalid under the Establishment Clause. For example, the State could not criminalize murder for fear that it would thereby promote the Biblical command against killing.a The task for the Court is to sort out those statutes and government practices whose purpose and effect go against the grain of religious liberty protected by the First Amendment.

The endorsement test does not preclude government from acknowledging religion or from taking religion into account in making law and policy. It does preclude government from conveying or attempting to convey a message that religion or a particular religious belief is favored or preferred. Such an endorsement infringes the religious liberty of the nonadherent * * *.

Twenty-five states permit or require public school teachers to have students observe [a] moment of silence at the beginning of the schoolday during which students may meditate, pray, or reflect on the activities of the day. * * * Relying on this Court's decisions disapproving vocal prayer and Bible reading in the public schools, see *School Dist. v. Schempp,* 374 U.S. 203 (1963); *Engel v. Vitale,* 370 U.S. 421 (1962), the courts that have struck down the moment of silence statutes generally conclude that their purpose and effect are to encourage prayer in public schools.

The *Engel* and *Schempp* decisions are not dispositive. [In] *Engel,* a New York statute required teachers to lead their classes in a vocal prayer.b The Court concluded that "it is no part of the business of government to compose official prayers for any group of the American people to recite as part of a religious program carried on by the government." In *Schempp,* the Court addressed Pennsylvania and Maryland statutes that authorized morning Bible readings in public schools. The Court reviewed the purpose and effect of the statutes, concluded that they required religious exercises, and therefore found them to

a. On this analysis, *McGowan v. Maryland,* 366 U.S. 420 (1961), per Warren, C.J., upheld Maryland's Sunday Closing Laws. Although "the original laws which dealt with Sunday labor were motivated by religious forces," the Court showed that secular emphases in language and interpretation have come about, that recent "legislation was supported by labor groups and trade associations," and that "secular justifications have been advanced for making Sunday a day of rest, a day when people may recover from the labors of the week just passed and may physically and mentally prepare for the week's work to come. [It] would seem unrealistic for enforcement purposes and perhaps detrimental to the general welfare to require a State to choose a common day of rest other than that which most persons would select of their own accord." Douglas, J., dissented.

b. The prayer, composed by the N.Y. Board of Regents, provided: "Almighty God, we acknowledge our dependence upon Thee, and we beg Thy blessings upon us, our parents, our teachers and our country."

violate the Establishment Clause. Under all of these statutes, a student who did not share the religious beliefs expressed in the course of the exercise was left with the choice of participating, thereby compromising the nonadherent's beliefs, or withdrawing, thereby calling attention to his or her nonconformity. The decisions acknowledged the coercion implicit under the statutory schemes, see *Engel*,**c** but they expressly turned only on the fact that the government was sponsoring a manifestly religious exercise.**d**

A state-sponsored moment of silence in the public schools is different from state-sponsored vocal prayer or Bible reading. First, a moment of silence [unlike] prayer or Bible reading, need not be associated with a religious exercise. Second, [d]uring a moment of silence, a student who objects to prayer is left to his or her own thoughts, and is not compelled to listen to the prayers or thoughts of others. [It] is difficult to discern a serious threat to religious liberty from a room of silent, thoughtful schoolchildren.

By mandating a moment of silence, a State does not necessarily endorse any activity that might occur during the period. Even if a statute specifies that a student may choose to pray silently during a quiet moment, the State has not thereby encouraged prayer over other specified alternatives. Nonetheless, it is also possible that a moment of silence statute, either as drafted or as actually implemented, could effectively favor the child who prays over the child who does not. For example, the message of endorsement would seem inescapable if the teacher exhorts children to use the designated time to pray. Similarly, the fact of the statute or its legislative history may clearly establish that it seeks to encourage or promote voluntary prayer over other alternatives, rather than merely provide a quiet moment that may be dedicated to prayer by those so inclined. The crucial question is whether the State has conveyed or attempted to convey the message that children should use the moment of silence for prayer.[2] This question cannot be answered in the abstract, but instead requires courts to examine the history, language, and administration of a particular statute to determine whether it operates as an endorsement of religion.

[T]he inquiry into the purpose of the legislature in enacting a moment of silence law should be deferential and limited. In determining whether the government intends a moment of silence statute to convey a message of endorsement or disapproval of religion, a court has no license to psychoanalyze the legislators. If a legislature expresses a plausible secular purpose for a moment of silence statute in either the text or the legislative history, or if the statute disclaims an intent to encourage prayer over alternatives during a moment of silence, then courts should generally defer to that stated intent. It is particularly troublesome to denigrate an expressed secular purpose due to postenactment testimony by particular legisla-

---

c. See fn. 51 in the Court's opinion, supra.

d. *Engel* distinguished "the fact that school children and others are officially encouraged to express love for our country by reciting historical documents such as the Declaration of Independence which contain references to the Deity or by singing officially espoused anthems which include the composer's professions of faith in a Supreme Being, or with the fact that there are many manifestations in our public life of belief in God. Such patriotic or ceremonial occasions bear no true resemblance to the unquestioned religious exercise that the State of New York has sponsored in this instance."

2. Appellants argue that *Zorach v. Clauson,* [note 1(b) infra], suggests there is no constitu-

tional infirmity in a State's encouraging a child to pray during a moment of silence. [There] the Court stated that "[w]hen the state encourages religious instruction—*[by] adjusting the schedule of public events to sectarian needs,* it follows the best of our traditions." When the State provides a moment of silence during which prayer may occur at the election of the student, it can be said to be adjusting the schedule of public events to sectarian needs. But when the State also encourages the student to pray during a moment of silence, it converts an otherwise inoffensive moment of silence into an effort by the majority to use the machinery of the State to encourage the minority to participate in a religious exercise.

tors or by interested persons who witnessed the drafting of the statute.**e** Even if the text and official history of a statute express no secular purpose, the statute should be held to have an improper purpose only if it is beyond purview that endorsement of religion or a religious belief "was and is the law's reason for existence." *Epperson v. Arkansas,* [note 3(b) infra]. Since there is arguably a secular pedagogical value to a moment of silence in public schools, courts should find an improper purpose behind such a statute only if the statute on its face, in its official legislative history, or in its interpretation by a responsible administrative agency suggests it has the primary purpose of endorsing prayer.

[It is] possible that a legislature will enunciate a sham secular purpose for a statute. I have little doubt that our courts are capable of distinguishing a sham secular purpose from a sincere one, or that the *Lemon* inquiry into the effect of an enactment would help decide those close cases where the validity of an expressed secular purpose is in doubt. [T]he *Lynch* concurrence suggested that the effect of a moment of silence law is not entirely a question of [fact]. The relevant issue is whether an objective observer, acquainted with the text, legislative history, and implementation of the statute, would perceive it as a state endorsement of prayer in public schools. A moment of silence law that is clearly drafted and implemented so as to permit prayer, meditation, and reflection within the prescribed period, without endorsing one alternative over the others, should pass this test.

[M]oment of silence laws in many States should pass Establishment Clause scrutiny because they do not favor the child who chooses to pray during a moment of silence over the child who chooses to meditate or reflect. § 16–1–20.1 does not stand on the same footing. However deferentially one examines its text and legislative history, however objectively one views the message attempted to be conveyed to the public, the conclusion is unavoidable that the purpose of the statute is to endorse prayer in public schools.* * *

CHIEF JUSTICE BURGER dissenting.

* * * Today's decision recalls the observations of Justice Goldberg: "[U]ntutored devotion to the concept of neutrality can lead to invocation or approval of results which partake not simply of that noninterference and noninvolvement with the religious which the Constitution commands, but of a brooding and pervasive dedication to the secular and a passive, or even active, hostility to the religious. Such results are not only not compelled by the Constitution, but, it seems to me, are prohibited by it." *Schempp* (concurring opinion). * * *

Curiously, the opinions do not mention that *all* of the sponsor's statements relied upon—including the statement "inserted" into the Senate Journal—were made *after* the legislature had passed the statute; [there] is not a shred of evidence that the legislature as a whole shared the sponsor's motive or that a majority in either house was even aware of the sponsor's view of the bill when it was [passed.]

The several preceding opinions conclude that the principal difference between § 16–1–20.1 and its predecessor statute proves that the sole purpose behind the inclusion of the phrase "or voluntary prayer" in § 16–1–20.1 was to endorse and promote prayer. This reasoning is simply a subtle way of focusing exclusively on the religious component of the statute rather than examining the statute as a whole. Such logic—if it can be called that—would lead the Court to hold, for example, that a state may enact a statute that provides reimbursement for bus transportation to the parents of all schoolchildren, but may not *add* parents of parochial school students to an existing program providing reimbursement for parents of public school students.

---

e. For further discussion of this point, see Burger, C.J.'s opinion infra.

* * * Without pressuring those who do not wish to pray, the statute simply creates an opportunity to think, to plan, or to pray if one wishes—as Congress does by providing chaplains and chapels. [If] the government may not accommodate religious needs when it does so in a wholly neutral and noncoercive manner, the "benevolent neutrality" that we have long considered the correct constitutional standard will quickly translate into the "callous indifference" that the Court has consistently held the Establishment Clause does not require. * * *

JUSTICE REHNQUIST, dissenting.

[There] is simply no historical foundation for the proposition that the Framers intended to build the "wall of separation" that was constitutionalized in *Everson*. [And the "purpose and effect" tests] are in no way based on either the language or intent of the drafters. [If] the purpose prong is intended to void those aids to sectarian institutions accompanied by a stated legislative purpose to aid religion, the prong will condemn nothing so long as the legislature utters a secular purpose and says nothing about aiding religion. [I]f the purpose prong is aimed to void all statutes enacted with the intent to aid sectarian institutions, whether stated or not, then most statutes providing any aid, such as textbooks or bus rides for sectarian school children, will fail because one of the purposes behind every statute, whether stated or not, is to aid the target of its largesse. * * *

If a constitutional theory has no basis in the history of the amendment it seeks to interpret, is difficult to apply and yields unprincipled results, I see little use in it. [It] would come as much of a shock to those who drafted the Bill of Rights as it will to a large number of thoughtful Americans today to learn that the Constitution [prohibits] the Alabama Legislature from "endorsing" prayer. George Washington himself, at the request of the very Congress which passed the Bill of Rights, proclaimed a day of "public thanksgiving and prayer, to be observed by acknowledging with grateful hearts the many and signal favors of Almighty God." History must judge whether it was the Father of his Country in 1789, [the] Court today, which has strayed from the meaning of the Establishment Clause. * * *

Notes

1. ***Released time.*** (a) McCOLLUM v. BOARD OF EDUC., 333 U.S. 203 (1948), per BLACK, J., held that a public school released time program violated the Establishment Clause. Privately employed religious teachers held weekly classes, on public school premises, in their respective religions, for students whose parents signed request cards, while non-attending students pursued secular studies in other parts of the building: "[N]ot only are the state's tax-supported public school buildings used for the dissemination of religious doctrines. The State also affords sectarian groups an invaluable aid in that it helps to provide pupils for their religious classes through use of the state's compulsory public school machinery." Reed, J., dissented.

(b) ZORACH v. CLAUSON, 343 U.S. 306 (1952), per DOUGLAS, J., upheld a released time program when the religious classes were held in church buildings: "[This] involves neither religious instruction in public school classrooms nor the expenditure of public funds. All costs, including the application blanks, are paid by the religious organizations. The case is therefore unlike *McCollum*.* * *

"We are a religious people whose institutions presuppose a Supreme Being. We guarantee the freedom to worship as one chooses. [When] the state encourages religious instruction or cooperates [by] adjusting the schedule of public events to sectarian needs, [it] respects the religious nature of our people and accommodates the public service to their spiritual needs. To hold that it may not would [be] preferring those who believe in no religion over those who do believe. [The] problem, like many problems in constitutional law, is one of degree." Black, Frankfurter, and Jackson, JJ., dissented.

2. *Secular purpose.* Several decisions, in addition to *Jaffree,* have invalidated public school practices because their "purpose" has been found to be "religious":

(a) STONE v. GRAHAM, 449 U.S. 39 (1980), per curiam, held that a Kentucky statute—requiring "the posting of a copy of the Ten Commandments, purchased with private contributions, on the wall of each public classroom in the State," with the notation at the bottom that "The secular application of the Ten Commandments is clearly seen in its adoption as the fundamental legal code of Western Civilization and the Common Law of the United States"—had "no secular legislative purpose." Burger, C.J., and Stewart, Rehnquist, and Blackmun, JJ., dissented.

(b) EPPERSON v. ARKANSAS, 393 U.S. 97 (1968), per FORTAS, J., held that an "anti-evolution" statute, forbidding public school teachers "to teach the theory or doctrine that mankind ascended or descended from a lower order of animals," violated both religion clauses: "Arkansas' law selects from the body of knowledge a particular segment which it proscribes for the sole reason that it is deemed to conflict with a particular religious doctrine."

(c) EDWARDS v. AGUILLARD, 482 U.S. 578 (1987), per BRENNAN, J., held that a Louisiana statute, barring "teaching of the theory of evolution in public schools unless accompanied by instruction in 'creation science,'" had "no clear secular purpose": "True, the Act's stated purpose is to protect academic freedom. [While] the Court is normally deferential to a State's articulation of a secular purpose, it is required that the statement of such purpose be sincere and not a sham. [The] legislative history documents that the Act's primary purpose was to change the science curriculum of public schools in order to provide persuasive advantage to a particular religious doctrine that rejects the factual basis of evolution in its entirety [and that] embodies the religious belief that a supernatural creator was responsible for the creation of humankind. [T]eaching a variety of scientific theories about the origins of humankind to school children might be validly done with the clear secular intent of enhancing the effectiveness of science instruction. But because the primary purpose of the Creationism Act is to endorse a particular religious doctrine, the Act furthers religion in violation of the Establishment Clause."

SCALIA, J., joined by Rehnquist, C.J., dissented: The legislature did not care *whether* the topic of origins was taught; it simply wished to ensure that *when* the topic was taught, [it] be 'taught as a theory, rather than as proven scientific fact' and that scientific evidence inconsistent with the theory of evolution (viz., 'creation science') be taught as well. [The law] treats the teaching of creation the same way. [A] valid secular purpose is not rendered impermissible simply because its pursuit is prompted by concern for religious sensitivities."

3. *Purpose, primary effect, and "neutrality".* (a) BOARD OF EDUC. v. MERGENS, 496 U.S. 226 (1990), interpreted the Equal Access Act, passed by Congress, to apply to public secondary schools that (a) receive federal financial assistance, and (b) give official recognition to noncurriculum related student groups (e.g., chess club and scuba diving club in contrast to Latin club and math club) in such ways as allowing them to meet on school premises during noninstructional time. O'CONNOR, J., joined by Rehnquist, C.J., and White and Blackmun, JJ., held that the Establishment Clause did not forbid Westside High School

from including within its thirty recognized student groups a Christian club "to read and discuss the Bible, to have fellowship and to pray together": "In *Widmar v. Vincent,* 454 U.S. 263 (1981), we applied the three-part *Lemon* test to hold that an 'equal access' policy, at the university level, does not violate the Establishment Clause. We concluded that 'an open-forum policy, including nondiscrimination against religious speech, would have a secular purpose,' and would in fact *avoid* entanglement with religion. See id. ("[T]he University would risk greater 'entanglement' by attempting to enforce its exclusion of 'religious worship' and 'religious speech' "). We also found that although incidental benefits accrued to religious groups who used university facilities, this result did not amount to an establishment of religion. First, we stated that a university's forum does not 'confer any imprimatur of state approval on religious sects or practices.' Indeed, the message is one of neutrality rather than endorsement; if a State refused to let religious groups use facilities open to others, then it would demonstrate not neutrality but hostility toward religion. Second, we noted that '[t]he [University's] provision of benefits to [a] broad spectrum of groups'—both nonreligious and religious speakers—was 'an important index of secular effect.'

"We think the logic of *Widmar* applies. [There] is a crucial difference between *government* speech endorsing religion, which the Establishment Clause forbids, and *private* speech endorsing religion, which the Free Speech and Free Exercise Clauses protect. We think that secondary school students are mature enough and are likely to understand that a school does not endorse or support student speech that it merely permits on a nondiscriminatory basis." Stevens, J., dissented.

(b) GOOD NEWS CLUB v. MILFORD CENTRAL SCHOOL, 533 U.S. 98 (2001), per THOMAS, J., used similar analysis to find no Establishment Clause violation for a public school's permitting a Christian organization to use schoolrooms for weekly after school meetings, which involved religious instruction and worship, when the school allowed such use by other groups for "the moral and character development of children." Stevens and Souter, JJ., dissented.a

IV.   OFFICIAL ACKNOWLEDGMENT OF RELIGION

ALLEGHENY COUNTY v. ACLU

492 U.S. 573, 109 S.Ct. 3086, 106 L.Ed.2d 472 (1989).

JUSTICE BLACKMUN announced the judgment of the Court and delivered the opinion of the Court with respect to Parts III–A, IV, and V, an opinion with respect to Parts I and II, in which JUSTICE O'CONNOR and JUSTICE STEVENS join, an opinion with respect to Part III–B, in which JUSTICE STEVENS joins, and an opinion with respect to Part VI.

This litigation concerns the constitutionality of two recurring holiday displays located on public property in downtown Pittsburgh. The first is a crèche placed on the Grand Staircase of the Allegheny County Courthouse. The second is a Chanukah menorah placed just outside the City–County Building, next to a Christmas tree and a sign saluting liberty. * * *

I.A. [The] crèche [is] a visual representation of the scene in the manger in Bethlehem shortly after the birth of Jesus, as described in the Gospels of Luke and Matthew. The crèche includes [an] angel bearing a banner that proclaims "Gloria in Excelsis Deo!"

a. The most recent decisions on Religion and Public Schools are considered in Part IV infra.

[III.A.] Although "the myriad, subtle ways in which Establishment Clause values can be eroded," are not susceptible to a single verbal formulation, this Court has attempted to encapsulate the essential precepts. [Thus,] in *Everson,* the Court gave this often-repeated summary [stating the second ¶ in Part II supra]. In *Lemon,* the Court sought to refine these principles by focusing on three "tests." [In] recent years, we have paid particularly close attention to whether the challenged governmental practice either has the purpose or effect of "endorsing" religion. [See] *Lynch* (O'Connor, J., concurring).

B. [In *Lynch,*] we considered whether the city of Pawtucket, R.I., had violated the Establishment Clause by including a crèche in its annual Christmas display, located in a private park within the downtown shopping district.a By a 5–4 decision[,] the Court [held] that the inclusion of the crèche did not have the impermissible effect of advancing or promoting religion. [First,] the opinion states that the inclusion of the crèche in the display was "no more an advancement or endorsement of religion" than other "endorsements" this Court has approved in the past—but the opinion offers no discernible measure for distinguishing between permissible and impermissible endorsements. Second, the opinion observes that any benefit the government's display of the crèche gave to religion was no more than "indirect, remote, and incidental"—without saying how or why. * * * Justice O'Connor['s] concurrence [provides] a sound analytical framework for evaluating governmental use of religious symbols.

First and foremost, the concurrence [recognizes] any endorsement of religion as "invalid," because it "sends a message to nonadherents that they are outsiders, not full members of the political community, and an accompanying message to adherents that they are insiders, favored members of the political community."

Second, [it] articulates a method for determining whether the government's use of an object with religious meaning has the effect of endorsing religion[:] the question is "what viewers may fairly understand to be the purpose of the display." That inquiry, of necessity, turns upon the context in which the contested object appears: "a typical museum setting, though not neutralizing the religious content of a religious painting, negates any message of endorsement of that content." * * *

The concurrence applied this mode of analysis to the Pawtucket crèche, seen in the context of that city's holiday celebration as a whole. In addition to the crèche the city's display contained: a Santa Claus House with a live Santa distributing candy; reindeer pulling Santa's sleigh; a live 40–foot Christmas tree strung with lights; statues of carolers in old-fashioned dress; candy-striped poles; a "talking" wishing well; a large banner proclaiming "SEASONS GREETINGS"; a miniature "village" with several houses and a church, and various "cut-out" figures, including those of a clown, a dancing elephant, a robot, and a teddy bear. The concurrence concluded that both because the crèche is "a traditional symbol" of Christmas, a holiday with strong secular elements, and because the crèche was "displayed along with purely secular symbols," the crèche's setting "changes what viewers may fairly understand to be the purpose of the display" and "negates any message of endorsement" of "the Christian beliefs represented by the crèche."

The four *Lynch* dissenters agreed with [O'Connor, J.'s approach but] concluded that the other elements of the Pawtucket display did not negate the endorsement of Christian faith caused by the presence of the crèche. [Thus,] despite

---

a. "[Ten years ago], when [the] crèche was acquired, it cost the City $1365; it now is valued at $200. The erection and dismantling of the crèche costs the City about $20 per year; nominal expenses are incurred in lighting the crèche. No money has been expended on its maintenance for the past 10 years."

divergence at the bottom line, the five Justices in concurrence and dissent in *Lynch* agreed upon the relevant constitutional principles [which] are sound, and have been adopted by the Court in subsequent cases. [*Grand Rapids.*]

IV. We turn first to the county's crèche display. [U]nlike *Lynch*, nothing in the context of the display detracts from the crèche's religious message. [T]he crèche sits on the Grand Staircase, the "main" and "most beautiful part" of the building that is the seat of county government. No viewer could reasonably think that it occupies this location without the support and approval of the government [which] has chosen to celebrate Christmas in a way that has the effect of endorsing a patently Christian message: Glory to God for the birth of Jesus Christ. * * *

V. Justice Kennedy and the three Justices who join him would [uphold] display of the crèche. [The] reasons for deciding otherwise are so far-reaching in their implications that they require a response in some depth:

A. In *Marsh v. Chambers*, 463 U.S. 783 (1983) [upholding the practice of legislative prayer], the Court relied specifically on the fact that Congress authorized legislative prayer at the same time that it produced the Bill of Rights.b Justice Kennedy, however, argues that *Marsh* legitimates all "practices with no greater potential for an establishment of religion" than those "accepted traditions dating back to the Founding." Otherwise, the Justice asserts, such practices as our national motto ("In God We Trust") and our Pledge of Allegiance (with the phrase "under God," added in 1954) are in danger of invalidity.

Our previous opinions have considered in dicta the motto and the pledge, characterizing them as consistent with the proposition that government may not communicate an endorsement of religious belief. We need not return to the subject of "ceremonial deism,"c because there is an obvious distinction between crèche displays and references to God in the motto and the pledge. However history may affect the constitutionality of nonsectarian references to religion by the government,52 history cannot legitimate practices that demonstrate the government's allegiance to a particular sect or creed. [The] history of this Nation, it is perhaps sad to say, contains numerous examples of official acts that endorsed Christianity specifically [but] this heritage of official discrimination against non-Christians has no place in the jurisprudence of the Establishment Clause. * * *

C. Although Justice Kennedy repeatedly accuses the Court of harboring a "latent hostility" or "callous indifference" toward religion, nothing could be further from the truth. [The] government does not discriminate against any citizen on the basis of the citizen's religious faith if the government is secular in

b. *Marsh* also pointed, inter alia, to the practice in the colonies (including Virginia after adopting its Declaration of Rights which has been "considered the precursor of both the Free Exercise and Establishment Clauses"), to the opening invocations in federal courts (including the Supreme Court), and in the Continental Congress and First Congress: "[T]he practice of opening sessions with prayer has continued without interruption ever since that early session of Congress. It has also been followed consistently in most of the states." Brennan, Marshall and Stevens, JJ., dissented.

c. Brennan, J., joined by Marshall, Blackmun and Stevens, JJ., dissenting in *Lynch* "suggest[ed] that such practices as the designation of 'In God We Trust' as our national motto, or the references to God contained in the Pledge of Allegiance can best be understood [as] a form of 'ceremonial deism,' protected from Establishment Clause scrutiny chiefly because they have lost through rote repetition any significant religious content."

52. It is worth noting that just because *Marsh* sustained the validity of legislative prayer, it does not necessarily follow that practices like proclaiming a National Day of Prayer are constitutional. Legislative prayer does not urge citizens to engage in religious practices, and on that basis could well be distinguishable from an exhortation from government to the people that they engage in religious conduct. But, as this practice is not before us, we express no judgment about its constitutionality.

its functions and operations. On the contrary, the Constitution mandates that the government remain secular, rather than affiliating itself with religious beliefs or institutions, precisely in order to avoid discriminating among citizens on the basis of their religious faiths. A secular state, it must be remembered, is not the same as an atheistic or antireligious state. A secular state establishes neither atheism nor religion as its official creed. * * *59

VI.   The display of the Chanukah menorah in front of the City–County Building may well present a closer [issue. The] question for Establishment Clause purposes is whether the combined display of the tree, the sign, and the menorah has the effect of endorsing both Christian and Jewish faiths, or rather simply recognizes that both Christmas and Chanukah are part of the same winter-holiday season, which has attained a secular status in our society. Of the two interpretations of this particular display, the latter seems far more plausible* * *.64

The Christmas tree, unlike the menorah, is not itself a religious symbol. [The] widely accepted view of the Christmas tree as the preeminent secular symbol of the Christmas holiday season serves to emphasize the secular component of the message communicated by other elements of an accompanying holiday display, including the Chanukah menorah.66 The tree, moreover, is clearly the predominant element in the city's display. The 45–foot tree occupies the central position [in] the City–County Building; the 18–foot menorah is positioned to one side. Given this configuration, it is much more sensible to interpret the meaning of the menorah in light of the tree, rather than vice versa. [While] an adjudication of the display's effect must take into account the perspective of one who is neither Christian nor Jewish, as well as of those who adhere to either of these religions, the constitutionality of its effect must also be judged according to the standard of a "reasonable observer." When measured against this standard, the menorah need not be excluded from this particular display.

The conclusion [here] does not foreclose the possibility that the display of the menorah might violate either the "purpose" or "entanglement" prong of the *Lemon* analysis. These issues [may] be considered [on] remand. * * *

JUSTICE KENNEDY, with whom THE CHIEF JUSTICE, JUSTICE WHITE, and JUSTICE SCALIA join, concurring in the judgment in part and dissenting in part. * * *

I.   In keeping with the usual fashion of recent years, the majority applies the *Lemon* [test]. Persuasive criticism of *Lemon* has emerged. * * *

---

59. In his attempt to legitimate the display of the crèche on the Grand Staircase, Justice Kennedy repeatedly characterizes it as an "accommodation" of religion. But an accommodation of religion, in order to be permitted under the Establishment Clause, must lift "an identifiable burden *on the exercise of religion*." *Corporation of Presiding Bishop v. Amos,* [Sec. 4 infra]. Prohibiting the display of a crèche at this location [does] not impose a burden on the practice of Christianity (except to the extent some Christian sect seeks to be an officially approved religion), and therefore permitting the display is not an "accommodation" of religion in the conventional sense.

["Accommodation" of religion and the relationship between the Establishment and Free Exercise Clauses is considered in Sec. 3 infra.]

64. [The] conclusion that Pittsburgh's combined Christmas–Chanukah display cannot be

interpreted as endorsing Judaism alone does not mean, however, that it is implausible, as a general matter, for a city like Pittsburgh to endorse a minority faith. The display of a menorah alone might well have that effect.

66. Although the Christmas tree represents the secular celebration of Christmas, its very association with Christmas (a holiday with religious dimensions) makes it conceivable that the tree might be seen as representing Christian religion when displayed next to an object associated with Jewish religion. For this reason, I agree with Justice Brennan and Justice Stevens that one must ask whether the tree and the menorah together endorse the *religious* beliefs of Christians and Jews. For the reasons stated in the text, however, I conclude the city's overall display does not have this impermissible effect.

Rather than requiring government to avoid any action that acknowledges or aids religion, the Establishment Clause permits government some latitude in recognizing and accommodating the central role religion plays in our society. *Lynch*; *Walz*. Any approach less sensitive to our heritage would border on latent hostility toward religion, as it would require government in all its multifaceted roles to acknowledge only the secular. [A] categorical approach would install federal courts as jealous guardians of an absolute "wall of separation," sending a clear message of disapproval. In this century, as the modern administrative state expands to touch the lives of its citizens in such diverse ways and redirects their financial choices through programs of its own, it is difficult to maintain the fiction that requiring government to avoid all assistance to religion can in fairness be viewed as serving the goal of neutrality. * * *

The ability of the organized community to recognize and accommodate religion in a society with a pervasive public sector requires diligent observance of the border between accommodation and establishment. Our cases disclose two limiting principles: government may not coerce anyone to support or participate in any religion or its exercise; and it may not, in the guise of avoiding hostility or callous indifference, give direct benefits to religion in such a degree that it in fact "establishes a [state] religion or religious faith, or tends to do so." *Lynch*. These two principles, while distinct, are not unrelated, for it would be difficult indeed to establish a religion without some measure of more or less subtle coercion, be it in the form of taxation to supply the substantial benefits that would sustain a state-established faith, direct compulsion to observance, or governmental exhortation to religiosity that amounts in fact to proselytizing.

[The] freedom to worship as one pleases without government interference or oppression is the great object of both the Establishment and the Free Exercise Clauses. Barring all attempts to aid religion through government coercion goes far toward attainment of this object. [S]ome of our recent cases reject the view that coercion is the sole touchstone of an Establishment Clause violation. See *Engel* (dictum) [see fn. 53 in *Jaffree*]; *Schempp*; *Nyquist*. That may be true if by "coercion" is meant *direct* coercion in the classic sense of an establishment of religion that the Framers knew. But coercion need not be a direct tax in aid of religion or a test oath. Symbolic recognition or accommodation of religious faith may violate the Clause in an extreme case.1 I doubt not, for example, that the Clause forbids a city to permit the permanent erection of a large Latin cross on the roof of city hall. This is not because government speech about religion is per se suspect, as the majority would have it, but because such an obtrusive year-round religious display would place the government's weight behind an obvious effort to proselytize on behalf of a particular religion. * * * Absent coercion, the risk of infringement of religious liberty by passive or symbolic accommodation is minimal. [In] determining whether there exists an establishment, or a tendency toward one, we refer to the other types of church-state contacts that have existed unchallenged throughout our history, or that have been found permissible in our caselaw [discussing *Lynch* and *Marsh*].

II.   These principles are not difficult to apply to the facts of the case before us. [If] government is to participate in its citizens' celebration of a holiday that contains both a secular and a religious component, enforced recognition of only the secular aspect would signify the callous indifference toward religious faith that

---

1. [The] prayer invalidated in *Engel* was unquestionably coercive in an indirect manner, as the *Engel* Court itself recognized * * *.

[*Marsh* noted that "here, the individual claiming injury by the practice is an adult, presumably not readily susceptible to 'religious indoctrination,' see *Tilton*, or peer pressure, compare *Schempp* (Brennan, J., concurring)."]

our cases and traditions do not require; [the] government would be refusing to acknowledge [the] historical reality, that many of its citizens celebrate its religious aspects as well. [The] Religion Clauses do not require government to acknowledge these holidays or their religious component; but our strong tradition of government accommodation and acknowledgment permits government to do so.

There is no suggestion here that the government's power to coerce has been used to further the interests of Christianity or Judaism in any way. No one was compelled to observe or participate in any religious ceremony or activity. Neither the city nor the county contributed significant amounts of tax money to serve the cause of one religious faith. The crèche and the menorah are purely passive symbols of religious holidays. Passersby who disagree with the message conveyed by these displays are free to ignore them, or even to turn their backs, just as they are free to do when they disagree with any other form of government speech.

[Crucial to the decision in *Lynch* was] the simple fact that, when displayed by government during the Christmas season, a crèche presents no realistic danger of moving government down the forbidden road toward an establishment of religion. Whether the crèche be surrounded by poinsettias, talking wishing wells, or carolers, the conclusion remains the same, for the relevant context is not the items in the display itself but the season as a whole. * * *

[III.] Even if *Lynch* did not control, I would not commit this Court to [the] notion that cases arising under the Establishment Clause should be decided by an inquiry into whether a " 'reasonable observer' " may " 'fairly understand' " government action to " 'sen[d] a message to nonadherents that they are outsiders, not full members of the political community.' " [This is a] most unwelcome, addition to our tangled Establishment Clause jurisprudence. * * *

[A.] *Marsh* stands for the proposition, not that specific practices common in 1791 are an exception to the otherwise broad sweep of the Establishment Clause, but rather that the meaning of the Clause is to be determined by reference to historical practices and understandings.7 Whatever test we choose to apply must permit not only legitimate practices two centuries old but also any other practices with no greater potential for an establishment of religion. [Few] can withstand scrutiny under a faithful application [the endorsement test].

Some examples suffice to make plain my concerns. Since the Founding of our Republic, American Presidents have issued Thanksgiving Proclamations establishing a national day of celebration and prayer. The first such proclamation was issued by President Washington at the request of the First Congress [and] the forthrightly religious nature of these proclamations has not waned with the years. President Franklin D. Roosevelt went so far as to "suggest a nationwide reading of the Holy Scriptures during the period from Thanksgiving Day to Christmas" so that "we may bear more earnest witness to our gratitude to Almighty God." It requires little imagination to conclude that these proclamations would cause nonadherents to feel excluded.* * *.9

The Executive has not been the only Branch of our Government to recognize the central role of religion in our society. [T]his Court opens its sessions with the request that "God save the United States and this honorable Court." [The] Legislature has gone much further, not only employing legislative chaplains, but

---

7. [T]he relevant historical practices are those conducted by governmental units which were subject to the constraints of the Establishment Clause. Acts of "official discrimination against non-Christians" perpetrated in the eighteenth and nineteenth centuries by States and municipalities are of course irrelevant to this inquiry, but the practices of past Congresses and Presidents are highly informative.

9. Similarly, our presidential inaugurations have traditionally opened with a request for divine blessing. * * *

also setting aside a special prayer room in the Capitol for use by Members of the House and Senate. The room is decorated with a large stained glass panel that depicts President Washington kneeling in prayer; around him is etched the first verse of the 16th Psalm: "Preserve me, O God, for in Thee do I put my trust." * * * Congress has directed the President to "set aside and proclaim a suitable day each year [as] a National Day of Prayer, on which the people of the United States may turn to God in prayer and meditation at churches, in groups, and as individuals." [Also] by statute, the Pledge of Allegiance to the Flag describes the United States as "one Nation under God." To be sure, no one is obligated to recite this phrase, see *West Virginia State Bd. of Educ. v. Barnette*, [Sec. 2, I infra] but it borders on sophistry to suggest that the " 'reasonable' " atheist would not feel less than a " 'full membe[r] of the political community' " every time his fellow Americans recited, as part of their expression of patriotism and love for country, a phrase he believed to be false. Likewise, our national motto, "In God we trust," which is prominently engraved in the wall above the Speaker's dias in the Chamber of the House of Representatives and is reproduced on every coin minted and every dollar printed by the Federal Government, must have the same effect.

If the intent of the Establishment Clause is to protect individuals from mere feelings of exclusion, then legislative prayer cannot escape invalidation. It has been argued that "[these] government acknowledgments of religion serve, in the only ways reasonably possible in our culture, the legitimate secular purposes of solemnizing public occasions, expressing confidence in the future, and encouraging the recognition of what is worthy of appreciation in society." *Lynch* (O'Connor, J., concurring). I fail to see why prayer is the only way to convey these messages; appeals to patriotism, moments of silence, and any number of other approaches would be as effective, were the only purposes at issue the ones described by the *Lynch* concurrence. [No] doubt prayer is "worthy of appreciation," but that is most assuredly not because it is secular. Even accepting the secular-solemnization explanation at face value, moreover, it seems incredible to suggest that the average observer of legislative prayer who either believes in no religion or whose faith rejects the concept of God would not receive the clear message that his faith is out of step with the political norm.[10]

[IV.] The case before us is admittedly a troubling one. It must be conceded that, however neutral the purpose of the city and county, the eager proselytizer may seek to use these symbols for his own ends. The urge to use them to teach or to taunt is always present. It is also true that some devout adherents of Judaism or Christianity may be as offended by the holiday display as are nonbelievers, if not more so. To place these religious symbols in a common hallway or sidewalk, where they may be ignored or even insulted, must be distasteful to many who cherish their meaning. For these reasons, I might have voted against installation [were] I a local legislative official. But [the] principles of the Establishment Clause and our Nation's historic traditions of diversity and pluralism allow communities to make reasonable judgments respecting the accommodation or acknowledgment of holidays with both cultural and religious aspects. No constitutional violation

---

10. If the majority's test were to be applied logically, it would lead to the elimination of all nonsecular Christmas caroling in public buildings or, presumably, anywhere on public property. It is difficult to argue that lyrics like "Good Christian men, rejoice," "Joy to the world! the Savior reigns," "This, this is Christ the King," "Christ, by highest heav'n adored," and "Come and behold Him, Born the King of angels," have acquired such a secular nature that nonadherents would not feel "left out" by a government-sponsored or approved program that included these carols. [Like] Thanksgiving Proclamations, the reference to God in the Pledge of Allegiance, and invocations to God in sessions of Congress and of this Court, they constitute practices that the Court will not proscribe, but that the Court's reasoning today does not explain.

occurs when they do so by displaying a symbol of the holiday's religious origins. * * *

JUSTICE O'CONNOR with whom JUSTICE BRENNAN and JUSTICE STEVENS join as to Part II, concurring in part and concurring in the judgment. * * *

II. In his separate opinion, Justice Kennedy asserts that the endorsement test "is flawed in its fundamentals and unworkable in practice." * * *

An Establishment Clause standard that prohibits only "coercive" practices or overt efforts at government proselytization, but fails to take account of the numerous more subtle ways that government can show favoritism to particular beliefs or convey a message of disapproval to others, would [not] adequately protect the religious liberty or respect the religious diversity of the members of our pluralistic political community. Thus, this Court has never relied on coercion alone as the touchstone of Establishment Clause analysis. To require a showing of coercion, even indirect coercion, as an essential element of an Establishment Clause violation would make the Free Exercise Clause a redundancy. [Moreover,] as even Justice Kennedy recognizes, any Establishment Clause test limited to "*direct* coercion" clearly would fail to account for forms of "[s]ymbolic recognition or accommodation of religious faith" that may violate the Establishment Clause.

[To] be sure, the endorsement test depends on a sensitivity to the unique circumstances and context of a particular challenged practice and, like any test that is sensitive to context, it may not always yield results with unanimous agreement at the margins. But that is true of many standards in constitutional law, and even the modified coercion test offered by Justice Kennedy involves judgment and hard choices at the margin.* * *

Justice Kennedy submits that the endorsement test [would] invalidate many traditional practices. [But] historical acceptance of a practice does not in itself validate that practice under the Establishment Clause if the practice violates the values protected by that Clause, just as historical acceptance of racial or gender based discrimination does not immunize such practices from scrutiny under the 14th Amendment.**d** [On] the contrary, the "history and ubiquity" of a practice is relevant because it provides part of the context in which a reasonable observer evaluates whether a challenged governmental practice conveys a message of endorsement of religion. [Thus,] the celebration of Thanksgiving as a public holiday, despite its religious origins, is now generally understood as a celebration of patriotic values rather than particular religious beliefs.**e** * * *

III. For reasons which differ somewhat from those set forth in Part VI of Justice Blackmun's opinion, I also conclude [that] Pittsburgh's combined holiday display [does] not have the effect of conveying an endorsement of religion. * * *

---

d. In contending that "specific historical practice should [not] override [the] clear constitutional imperative," Brennan, J., joined by Marshall, J., dissenting in *Marsh,* noted that "the sort of historical argument made by the Court should be advanced with some hesitation in light of certain other skeletons in the congressional closet. See, e.g., An Act for the Punishment of certain Crimes against the United States (1790) (enacted by the First Congress and requiring that persons convicted of certain theft offenses 'be publicly whipped, not exceeding thirty-nine stripes'); Act of July 23, 1866 (reaffirming the racial segregation of the public schools in the District of Columbia; enacted exactly one week after Congress proposed Fourteenth Amendment to the States)."

Brennan, J., concurring in *Schempp,* further observed that "today the Nation is far more heterogeneous religiously, including as it does substantial minorities not only of Catholics and Jews but as well of those who worship according to no version of the Bible and those who worship no God at all. In the face of such profound changes, practices which may have been objectionable to no one in the time of Jefferson and Madison may today be highly offensive to many persons, the deeply devout and the non-believers alike. [Thus], our use of the history of their time must limit itself to broad purposes, not specific practices."

e. Brennan, J.'s dissent in *Lynch* expressed a similar view.

JUSTICE BRENNAN, with whom JUSTICE MARSHALL and JUSTICE STEVENS join, concurring in part and dissenting in part.

* * * I continue to believe that the display of an object that "retains a specifically Christian [or other] religious meaning," is incompatible with the separation of church and state demanded by our Constitution. I therefore agree with the Court that Allegheny County's display of a crèche at the county courthouse signals an endorsement of the Christian faith in violation of the Establishment Clause, and join Parts III–A, IV, and V of the Court's opinion. I cannot agree, however, [with] the decision as to the menorah [which] rests on three premises: the Christmas tree is a secular symbol; Chanukah is a holiday with secular dimensions, symbolized by the menorah; and the government may promote pluralism by sponsoring or condoning displays having strong religious associations on its property. None of these is sound. * * *

Justice Blackmun, in his acceptance of the city's message of "diversity," and, even more so, Justice O'Connor, in her approval of the "message of pluralism and freedom to choose one's own beliefs," appear to believe that, where seasonal displays are concerned, more is better. * * * I know of no principle under the Establishment Clause, however, that permits us to conclude that governmental promotion of religion is acceptable so long as one religion is not favored. We have, on the contrary, interpreted that Clause to require neutrality, not just among religions, but between religion and nonreligion. [The] uncritical acceptance of a message of religious pluralism also ignores the extent to which even that message may offend. Many religious faiths are hostile to each other, and indeed, refuse even to participate in ecumenical services designed to demonstrate the very pluralism Justices Blackmun and O'Connor extol. * * *

JUSTICE STEVENS, with whom JUSTICE BRENNAN and JUSTICE MARSHALL join, concurring in part and dissenting in part. * * *

In my opinion the Establishment Clause should be construed to create a strong presumption against the display of religious symbols on public property. There is always a risk that such symbols will offend nonmembers of the faith being advertised as well as adherents who consider the particular advertisement disrespectful. [Even] though "[p]assersby who disagree with the message conveyed by these displays are free to ignore them, or even turn their backs," displays of this kind inevitably have a greater tendency to emphasize sincere and deeply felt differences among individuals than to achieve an ecumenical goal. The Establishment Clause does not allow public bodies to foment such disagreement.

Application of a strong presumption [will not] "require a relentless extirpation of all contact between government and religion," (Kennedy, J., concurring and dissenting), for it will prohibit a display only when its message, evaluated in the context in which it is presented, is nonsecular. For example, a carving of Moses holding the Ten Commandments, if that is the only adornment on a courtroom wall, conveys an equivocal message, perhaps of respect for Judaism, for religion in general, or for law. The addition of carvings depicting Confucius and Mohammed may honor religion, or particular religions, to an extent that the First Amendment does not tolerate any more than it does "the permanent erection of a large Latin cross on the roof of city hall." Placement of secular figures such as Caesar Augustus, William Blackstone, Napoleon Bonaparte, and John Marshall alongside these three religious leaders, however, signals respect not for great proselytizers but for great lawgivers. It would be absurd to exclude such a fitting message from a courtroom,[13] as it would to exclude religious paintings by Italian

---

13. All these leaders, of course, appear in friezes on the walls of our courtroom.

Renaissance masters from a public museum.f Far from "border[ing] on latent hostility toward religion," this careful consideration of context gives due regard to religious and nonreligious members of our society. * * *

Notes

1. ***Secular purpose.*** *(a) Lynch* found that "Pawtucket has *a* secular purpose for its display": "The City [has] principally taken note of a significant historical religious event long celebrated in the Western World. [Were] the test that the government must have 'exclusively secular' objectives, much of the conduct and legislation this Court has approved in the past would have been invalidated." Brennan, J.'s dissent in *Lynch,* reasoned: "When government decides to recognize Christmas day as a public holiday, it does no more than accommodate the calendar of public activities to the plain fact that many Americans will expect on that day to spend time visiting with their families, attending religious services, and perhaps enjoying some respite from preholiday activities. [If] public officials go further and participate in the *secular* celebration of Christmas—by, for example, decorating public places with such secular images as wreaths, garlands or Santa Claus figures—they move closer to the limits of their constitutional power but nevertheless remain within the boundaries set by the Establishment Clause. But when those officials participate in or appear to endorse the distinctively religious elements of this otherwise secular event, they encroach upon First Amendment freedoms. [The] Court seems to assume that forbidding Pawtucket from displaying a crèche would be tantamount to forbidding a state college from including the Bible or Milton's *Paradise Lost* in a course on English literature. But in those cases the religiously-inspired materials are being considered solely as literature. [In] this case, by contrast, the crèche plays no comparable secular role. [It] would be another matter if the crèche were displayed in a museum setting, in the company of other religiously-inspired artifacts, as an example, among many, of the symbolic representation of religious myths. In that setting, we would have objective guarantees that the crèche could not suggest that a particular faith had been singled out for public favor and recognition."

(b) Two cases in 2005 involving the Ten Commandments further considered the issue of secular purpose. *McCreary*, below, was the first since *Allegheny County* to invalidate a public acknowledgment of religion outside the context of the public schools.

McCREARY COUNTY v. ACLU, 545 U.S. 844 (2005), per Souter, J. held that posting copies of the Ten Commandments in two Kentucky county courthouses violated the Establishment Clause because of a "predominantly religious purpose": "When government acts with the ostensible and predominant purpose of advancing religion, it violates that central Establishment Clause value of official religious neutrality, [even though] given its generality as a principle, an appeal to neutrality alone cannot possibly lay every issue to rest, or tell us what issues on the margins are substantial enough for constitutional significance * * *.

"Examination of purpose is a staple of statutory interpretation [and] governmental purpose is a key element of a good deal of constitutional doctrine, e.g., *Washington v. Davis*, [Ch. 9, Sec. 2, III] (discriminatory purpose required for Equal Protection violation); *Hunt v. Washington State Apple Advertising Comm'n,*

---

f. As an example of government "reference to our religious heritage," *Lynch* noted that "the National Gallery in Washington, maintained with Government support [has] long exhibited masterpieces with religious messages, notably the Last Supper, and paintings depicting the Birth of Christ, the Crucifixion, and the Resurrection, among many others with explicit Christian themes and messages."

[Ch. 4, Sec. 2, I] (discriminatory purpose relevant to dormant Commerce Clause claim); *Church of Lukumi Babalu Aye, Inc. v. Hialeah,* [Sec. 2, I infra] (discriminatory purpose raises level of scrutiny required by free exercise claim). [S]crutinizing purpose does make practical sense, [where] an understanding of official objective emerges from readily discoverable fact, without any judicial psychoanalysis of a drafter's heart of hearts [, and when "openly available data supported a common-sense conclusion that a religious objective permeated the government's action."] The eyes that look to purpose belong to an 'objective observer,' one who takes account of the traditional external signs that show up in the 'text, legislative history, and implementation of the statute,' or comparable official act. *Santa Fe Ind. School Dist.* [note 3 infra]. [A]lthough a legislature's stated reasons will generally get deference, the secular purpose required has to be genuine, not a sham, and not merely secondary to a religious objective.[13]"

The Court's detailed examination of the record showed that the counties first posted only the Ten Commandments. When suit was filed, the counties adopted "resolutions reciting that the Ten Commandments are 'the precedent legal code upon which the civil and criminal codes [of] Kentucky are founded,' and stating several grounds for taking that position," most of which were related to religion. The displays were expanded to include "eight other documents in smaller frames, each either having a religious theme or excerpted to highlight a religious element," including the Preamble to the Constitution, the Mayflower Compact, and Presidential Proclamations. After a preliminary injunction was issued, the counties installed another display, "the third within a year," entitled "The Foundations of American Law and Government Display," made up "of nine framed documents of equal size" including the Bill of Rights and a picture of Lady Justice, all [with] statements about their historical and legal significance.

"[T]he Commandments 'are undeniably a sacred text in the Jewish and Christian faiths' [*Stone v. Graham*]. This is not to deny that the Commandments have had influence on civil or secular law; [but where] the text is set out, the insistence of the religious message is hard to avoid in the absence of a context plausibly suggesting a message going beyond an excuse to promote the religious point of view.a [W]e do not decide that the Counties' past actions forever taint any effort on their part to deal with the subject matter. [But] a conclusion that centuries-old purposes may no longer be operative says nothing about the relevance of recent evidence of purpose. [Nor] do we have occasion here to hold that a sacred text can never be integrated constitutionally into a governmental display on the subject of law, or American history. * * *

"The dissent, however, puts forward a limitation on the application of the neutrality principle [to] show that the Framers understood the ban on establishment of religion as sufficiently narrow to allow the government to espouse submission to the divine will [and] that government may espouse a tenet of traditional monotheism. [This] apparently means that government should be free to approve the core beliefs of a favored religion over the tenets of others, a view that should trouble anyone who prizes religious liberty. [But] there is also evidence supporting the proposition that the Framers intended the Establishment

13. The dissent nonetheless maintains that the purpose test is satisfied so long as any secular purpose for the government action is apparent. [While] heightened deference to legislatures is appropriate for the review of economic legislation, an approach that credits any valid purpose, no matter how trivial, has not been the way the Court has approached government action that implicates establishment.

a. As for *Marsh* and *Lynch*, "créches placed with holiday symbols and prayers by legislators do not insistently call for religious action on the part of citizens; the history of posting the Commandments expressed a purpose to urge citizens to act in prescribed ways as a personal response to divine authority."

Clause to require governmental neutrality in matters of religion, including neutrality in statements acknowledging religion."

SCALIA, joined by Rehnquist, C.J. and Kennedy and Thomas, JJ., dissented: "[B]oth historical fact [pointing to actions beginning with President Washington and the First Congress to Congress's unanimous action in 2002 approving "under God" in the Pledge of Allegiance] and current practice ["federal, state and local governments across the Nation" have displayed the Ten Commandments] [contradict] the demonstrably false principle that the government cannot favor religion over irreligion. [T]he principle that the government cannot favor one religion over another [is valid] where public aid or assistance to religion [or] where the free exercise of religion is at issue, but it necessarily applies in a more limited sense to public acknowledgment of the Creator. [Nothing] stands behind the Court's assertion that governmental affirmation of the society's belief in God is unconstitutional except the Court's own say-so, citing as support only the unsubstantiated say-so of earlier Courts going back no farther than the mid–20th [century.] Publicly honoring the Ten Commandments cannot be reasonably understood as a government endorsement of a particular religious viewpoint. [We must] recognize that in the context of public acknowledgments of God there are legitimate *competing* interests: On the one hand, the interest of that minority in not feeling 'excluded'; but on the other, the interest of the overwhelming majority of religious believers in being able to give God thanks and supplication *as a people,* and with respect to our national endeavors. [T]he legitimacy of a government action with a wholly secular effect [cannot] turn on the *misperception* of an imaginary observer that the government officials behind the action had the intent to advance religion.

"[The] constitutional problem, the Court says, is with the Counties' *purpose* in erecting the Foundations Displays, not the displays themselves. The Court [adds]: 'One consequence of taking account of the purpose underlying past actions is that the same government action may be constitutional if taken in the first instance and unconstitutional if it has a sectarian heritage.' This inconsistency may be explicable in theory, but I suspect that the 'objective observer' with whom the Court is so concerned will recognize its absurdity in [practice.] Displays erected in silence (and under the direction of good legal advice) are permissible, while those hung after discussion and debate are deemed unconstitutional. Reduction of the Establishment Clause to such minutiae trivializes the Clause's protection against religious establishment; indeed, it may inflame religious passions by making the passing comments of every government official the subject of endless litigation.

"In any event, the Court's conclusion that the Counties exhibited the Foundations Displays with the purpose of promoting religion is doubtful. [If,] as discussed above, the Commandments have a proper place in our civic history, even placing them by themselves can be civically motivated—especially when they are placed [in] a courthouse. [What] Justice Kennedy said of the crèche in *Allegheny County* is equally true of the Counties' original Ten Commandments displays [quoting the second ¶ in Part II of his opinion]. [They] are assuredly a religious symbol, but they are not so closely associated with a single religious belief that their display can reasonably be understood as preferring one religious sect over another. The Ten Commandments are recognized by Judaism, Christianity, and Islam alike as divinely given. [The] Court may well be correct in identifying the third displays as the fruit of a desire to display the Ten Commandments, but neither our cases nor our history support its assertion that such a desire renders the fruit poisonous."

————

VAN ORDEN v. PERRY, 545 U.S. 677 (2005), upheld the display of a monument, donated by the Eagles, inscribed with the Ten Commandments on the Texas State Capitol grounds "between the Capitol and the Supreme Court building. [The] 22 acres contain 17 monuments and 21 historical markers commemorating the 'people, ideals, and events that compose Texan identity.'a [A]n eagle grasping the American flag, an eye inside of a pyramid, and two small tablets with what appears to be an ancient script are carved above the text of the Ten Commandments. Below the text are two Stars of David and the superimposed Greek letters Chi and Rho, which represent Christ. The bottom of the monument bears the inscription 'PRESENTED TO THE PEOPLE AND YOUTH OF TEXAS BY THE FRATERNAL ORDER OF EAGLES OF TEXAS 1961.'" REHNQUIST, C.J., joined by Scalia, Kennedy, and Thomas, JJ. wrote the plurality opinion: "Our institutions presuppose a Supreme Being, yet these institutions must not press religious observances upon their citizens. Reconciling [these] requires that we neither abdicate our responsibility to maintain a division between church and state nor evince a hostility to religion by disabling the government from in some ways recognizing our religious heritage. * * *

"Whatever may be the fate of the *Lemon* test in the larger scheme of Establishment Clause jurisprudence, we think it not useful in dealing with the sort of passive monument that Texas has erected on its Capitol grounds. Instead, our analysis is driven both by the nature of the monument and by our Nation's history. As we explained in *Lynch,* 'There is an unbroken history of official acknowledgment by all three branches of government of the role of religion in American life from at least 1789.' * * * Recognition of the role of God in our Nation's heritage has also been reflected in our decisions. We have acknowledged, for example, that 'religion has been closely identified with our history and government,' *Schempp,* and that '[t]he history of man is inseparable from the history of religion,' *Engel*. This recognition has led us to hold that the Establishment Clause permits a state legislature to open its daily sessions with a prayer by a chaplain paid by the State. *Marsh*.8 Such a practice, we thought, was 'deeply embedded in the history and tradition of this country.' [In] this case we are faced with a display of the Ten Commandments on government property outside the Texas State Capitol. [Such] acknowledgments [are] common throughout America [and] can be seen throughout a visitor's tour of our Nation's Capital. * * *

"Of course, the Ten Commandments are religious. [According] to Judeo–Christian belief, the Ten Commandments were given to Moses by God on Mt. Sinai. But Moses was a lawgiver as well as a religious leader. And the Ten Commandments have an undeniable historical meaning, as the foregoing examples demonstrate. Simply having religious content or promoting a message consistent with a religious doctrine does not run afoul of the Establishment Clause. There are, of course, limits to the display of religious messages or symbols. [*Stone*] stands as an example of the fact that we have 'been particularly vigilant in monitoring compliance with the Establishment Clause in elementary and secondary schools.' [The] placement of the Ten Commandments monument on the Texas State Capitol grounds is a far more passive use of those texts than was the case in *Stone,* where the text confronted elementary school students every day."

a. The monuments are: Heroes of the Alamo, Hood's Brigade, Confederate Soldiers, Volunteer Fireman, Terry's Texas Rangers, Texas Cowboy, Spanish–American War, Texas National Guard, Ten Commandments, Tribute to Texas School Children, Texas Pioneer Woman, The Boy Scouts' Statue of Liberty Replica, Pearl Harbor Veterans, Korean War Veterans, Soldiers of World War I, Disabled Veterans, and Texas Peace Officers.

8. Indeed, [i]n *Marsh,* the prayers were often explicitly Christian, but the chaplain removed all references to Christ the year after the suit was filed.

SCALIA, J. also concurred briefly: "I would prefer to reach the same result by adopting an Establishment Clause jurisprudence that is in accord with our Nation's past and present practices, and that can be consistently applied. [See] *McCreary* (Scalia, J., dissenting)."

THOMAS, J., also concurred: Attempting "to balance out its willingness to consider almost any acknowledgment of religion an establishment, in other cases Members of this Court have concluded that the term or symbol at issue has no religious meaning by virtue of its ubiquity or rote ceremonial invocation. [Even] when this Court's precedents recognize the religious meaning of symbols or words, that recognition fails to respect fully religious belief or disbelief. [R]ather than trying to suggest meaninglessness where there is meaning, the Chief Justice rightly recognizes that the monument has 'religious significance.' " Preferably, however, the Court should "return to the views of the Framers" and hold that the Establishment Clause does not apply to the states, or even if it does, the Court should "adopt coercion as the touchstone for our Establishment Clause inquiry."

BREYER, J. concurred only in the judgment: "[T]he Establishment Clause does not compel the government to purge from the public sphere all that in any way partakes of the religious. Such absolutism is not only inconsistent with our national traditions, but would also tend to promote the kind of social conflict the Establishment Clause seeks to avoid. Thus, [the] Court has found no single mechanical formula that can accurately draw the constitutional line in every case. [T]ests designed to measure 'neutrality' alone are insufficient, both because it is sometimes difficult to determine when a legal rule is 'neutral,' and because 'untutored devotion to the concept of neutrality can lead to invocation or approval of results which partake not simply of that noninterference and noninvolvement with the religious which the Constitution commands, but of a brooding and pervasive devotion to the secular and a passive, or even active, hostility to the religious.' * * *

"If the relation between government and religion is one of separation, but not of mutual hostility and suspicion, one will inevitably find difficult borderline cases. And in such cases, I see no test-related substitute for the exercise of legal judgment. That judgment is not a personal judgment. Rather, as in all constitutional cases, it must reflect and remain faithful to the underlying purposes of the Clauses, and it must take account of context and consequences measured in light of those purposes. While the Court's prior tests provide useful guideposts—and might well lead to the same result the Court reaches today—no exact formula can dictate a resolution to such fact-intensive cases. [In] certain contexts, a display of the tablets of the Ten Commandments can convey not simply a religious message but also a secular moral message (about proper standards of social conduct). And in certain contexts, a display of the tablets can also convey a historical message (about a historic relation between those standards and the law)—a fact that helps to explain the display of those tablets in dozens of courthouses throughout the Nation, including the Supreme Court of the United States.

"Here [t]he group that donated the monument, the Fraternal Order of Eagles, a private civic (and primarily secular) organization, while interested in the religious aspect of the Ten Commandments, sought to highlight the Commandments' role in shaping civic morality as part of that organization's efforts to combat juvenile delinquency. [The] monument sits in a large park containing 17 monuments and 21 historical markers, all designed to illustrate the 'ideals' of those who settled in Texas and of those who have lived there since that time. The setting does not readily lend itself to meditation or any other religious activity. [T]he context suggests that the State intended the display's moral message—an illustrative message reflecting the historical 'ideals' of Texans—to predominate. [The] 40 years [that] passed in which the presence of this monument, legally speaking, went unchallenged suggest [that] the public visiting the capitol grounds has considered the religious aspect of the tablets' message as part of what is a broader moral and historical message reflective of a cultural heritage. [This] case also differs from *McCreary County*, where the short (and stormy) history of the courthouse Commandments' displays demonstrates the substantially religious objectives of those who mounted them, and the effect of this readily apparent objective upon those who view them. [This] display has stood apparently uncontested for nearly two generations. That experience helps us understand that as a practical matter of *degree* this display is unlikely to prove divisive. And this matter of degree is, I believe, critical in a borderline case such as this one.

"At the same time, to reach a contrary conclusion [would], I fear, lead the law to exhibit a hostility toward religion [that] might well encourage disputes concerning the removal of longstanding depictions of the Ten Commandments from public buildings across the Nation. And it could thereby create the very kind of religiously based divisiveness that the Establishment Clause seeks to avoid."

STEVENS, J., joined by Ginsburg, J., dissented: "Viewed on its face, Texas' display has no purported connection to God's role in the formation of Texas or the founding of our Nation; nor does it provide the reasonable observer with any basis to guess that it was erected to honor any individual or organization. The message transmitted by Texas' chosen display is quite plain: This State endorses the divine code of the 'Judeo–Christian' God. [In] my judgment, at the very least, the Establishment Clause has created a strong presumption against the display of religious symbols on public property. [We] have repeatedly reaffirmed that neither a State nor the Federal Government 'can constitutionally pass laws or impose requirements which aid all religions as against non-believers, and neither can aid those religions based on a belief in the existence of God as against those religions founded on different beliefs.' I do not discount the importance of avoiding an overly strict interpretation of [this principle]. This Court has often recognized 'an unbroken history of official acknowledgment [of] the role of religion in American life.' [This] case, however, is not about historic preservation or the mere recognition of religion. [This] Nation's resolute commitment to neutrality with respect to religion is flatly inconsistent with the plurality's wholehearted validation of an official state endorsement of the message that there is one, and only one, God.

"When the Ten Commandments monument was donated to the State of Texas in 1961, it was not for the purpose of commemorating a noteworthy event in Texas history. [B]y disseminating the 'law of God'—directing fidelity to God and proscribing murder, theft, and adultery—the Eagles hope that this divine guidance will help wayward youths conform their behavior and improve their lives. In my judgment, the significant secular by-products that are intended consequences of religious instruction—indeed, of the establishment of most religions—are not the type of 'secular' purposes that justify government promulgation of sacred religious messages. [The] State may admonish its citizens not to lie, cheat or steal, to honor their parents and to respect their neighbors' property; and it may do so by printed words, in television commercials, or on granite monuments in front of its public buildings. Moreover, the State may provide its schoolchildren and adult citizens with educational materials that explain the important role that our forebears' faith in God played. [The] message at issue in this case, however, is fundamentally different from either a bland admonition to observe generally accepted rules of behavior or a general history lesson. [It] cannot be analogized to an appendage to a common article of commerce ('In God we Trust') or an incidental part of a familiar recital ('God save the United States and this honorable Court'). [Attempts] to secularize what is unquestionably a sacred text defy credibility and disserve people of faith.

"Even if [the] message of the monument, despite the inscribed text, fairly could be said to represent the belief system of all Judeo–Christians, it would still run afoul of the Establishment Clause by prescribing a compelled code of conduct from one God, namely a Judeo–Christian God, that is rejected by prominent polytheistic sects, such as Hinduism, as well as nontheistic religions, such as Buddhism. * * * Critical examination of the Decalogue's prominent display at the seat of Texas government, rather than generic citation to the role of religion in American life, unmistakably reveals on which side of the 'slippery slope,' (Breyer, J., concurring in judgment), this display must fall. * * *

"The speeches and rhetoric characteristic of the founding era [do] not answer the question before us. [W]hen public officials deliver public speeches, we recognize that their words are not exclusively a transmission from *the* government because those oratories have embedded within them the inherently personal views of the speaker as an individual member of the polity. The permanent placement of a textual religious display on state property is different in kind; it amalgamates otherwise discordant individual views into a collective statement of government approval. [T]here is another critical nuance lost in the plurality's portrayal of history. Simply put, many of the Founders who are often cited as authoritative expositors of the Constitution's original meaning understood the Establishment Clause to stand for a *narrower* proposition than the plurality [is] willing to accept. Namely, many of the Framers understood the word 'religion' in the Establishment Clause to encompass only the various sects of Christianity. [Scalia, J.'s] inclusion of Judaism and Islam [in his *McCreary* dissent] is a laudable act of religious tolerance, but it is one that is unmoored from the Constitution's history and text, and moreover one that is patently arbitrary in its inclusion of some, but exclusion of other (e.g., Buddhism), widely practiced non-Christian religions. * * *

"A reading of the First Amendment dependent on [the] purported original meanings [would] eviscerate the heart of the Establishment Clause. [It] would permit States to construct walls of their own choosing—Baptists inside, Mormons out; Jewish Orthodox inside, Jewish Reform out. [As] we have said in the context of statutory interpretation, legislation 'often [goes] beyond the principal evil [at which the statute was aimed] to cover reasonably comparable evils, and it is ultimately the provisions of our laws rather than the principal concerns of our legislators by which we are governed.' In similar fashion, we have construed the Equal Protection Clause [to] prohibit segregated schools, even though those who drafted [the Fourteenth] Amendment evidently thought that separate was not unequal. We have held that the same Amendment prohibits discrimination against individuals on account of their gender, despite the fact that the contemporaries of the Amendment 'doubt[ed] very much whether any action of a State not directed by way of discrimination against the negroes as a class, or on account of their race, will ever be held to come within the purview of this provision,' And we have construed 'evolving standards of decency' to make impermissible practices that were not considered 'cruel and unusual' at the founding. * * *

"The principle that guides my analysis is neutrality.35 [As] religious pluralism has expanded, so has our acceptance of what constitutes valid belief systems. The

35. Justice Thomas contends that the Establishment Clause [reaches] only the governmental coercion of individual belief or disbelief. In my view, [that] cannot be the full extent of the provision's reach. [Thomas, J.'s] "coercion view," [would] not prohibit explicit state endorsements of religious orthodoxies of particular sects, actions that lie at the heart of what the Clause was meant to regulate. The government could, for example, take out television

evil of discriminating today against atheists, "polytheists[,] and believers in unconcerned deities," *McCreary County*, (Scalia, J., dissenting), is in my view a direct descendent of the evil of discriminating among Christian sects. The Establishment Clause thus forbids it and, in turn, forbids Texas from displaying the Ten Commandments monument the plurality so casually affirms."

SOUTER, J., joined by Stevens and Ginsburg, JJ., also dissented:**b** "A governmental display of an obviously religious text cannot be squared with neutrality, except in a setting that plausibly indicates that the statement is not placed in view with a predominant purpose on the part of government either to adopt the religious message or to urge its acceptance by others.**1**

"[A] pedestrian happening upon the monument at issue here needs no training in religious doctrine to realize that the statement of the Commandments, quoting God himself, proclaims that the will of the divine being is the source of obligation to obey the rules, including the facially secular ones. [To] ensure that the religious nature of the monument is clear to even the most casual passerby, the word 'Lord' appears in all capital letters (as does the word 'am'), so that the most eye-catching segment of the quotation is the declaration 'I AM the LORD thy God.' [It] would therefore be difficult to miss the point that the government of Texas is telling everyone who sees the monument to live up to a moral code because God requires it, with both code and conception of God being rightly understood as the inheritances specifically of Jews and Christians. [It] stands in contrast to any number of perfectly constitutional depictions of [the Commandments], the frieze of our own Courtroom providing a good example, where the figure of Moses stands among history's great lawgivers. [N]o one looking at the lines of figures in marble relief is likely to see a religious purpose behind the assemblage or take away a religious message from it. [T]he viewers may just as naturally see the tablets of the Commandments (showing the later ones, forbidding things like killing and theft, but without the divine preface) as background from which the concept of law emerged. [But] 17 monuments with no common appearance, history, or esthetic role scattered over 22 acres is not a museum, and anyone strolling around the lawn would surely take each memorial on its own terms without any dawning sense that some purpose held the miscellany together more coherently than fortuity and the edge of the grass.[6]

"To be sure, Kentucky's compulsory-education law [in *Stone*] meant that the schoolchildren were forced to see the display every day, whereas many see the monument by choice, and those who customarily walk the Capitol grounds can presumably avoid it if they choose. But in my judgment [this] distinction should make no difference. The monument in this case sits on the grounds of the Texas State Capitol[,] the civic home of every one of the State's citizens. If neutrality in religion means something, any citizen should be able to visit that civic home without having to confront religious expressions clearly meant to convey an

advertisements lauding Catholicism as the only pure religion. [T]hose programs would not be coercive because the viewer could simply turn off the television or ignore the ad.

Further, [e]nshrining coercion as the Establishment Clause touchstone fails to eliminate the difficult judgment calls regarding "the form that coercion must take." * * *

b. O'Connor, J., dissented, "for essentially the reasons given by Justice Souter."

1. [In this] case, the religious purpose was evident on the part of the donating organiza-

tion. [I]t was not just the terms of the moral code, but the proclamation that the terms of the code were enjoined by God, that the Eagles put forward in the monuments they donated.

6. [A]lthough the nativity scene in *Allegheny County* was donated by the Holy Name Society, we concluded that "[n]o viewer could reasonably think that [the scene] occupies [its] location [at the seat of county government] without the support and approval of the government."

official religious position that may be at odds with his own religion, or with rejection of religion.

"Finally, though this too is a point on which judgment will vary, I do not see a persuasive argument for constitutionality in the plurality's observation that Van Orden's lawsuit comes '[f]orty years after the monument's erection.' [We] have approved framing-era practices because they must originally have been understood as constitutionally permissible, e.g., *Marsh*, and we have recognized that Sunday laws have grown recognizably secular over time, *McGowan*. There is also an analogous argument, not yet evaluated, that ritualistic religious expression can become so numbing over time that its initial Establishment Clause violation becomes at some point too diminished for notice. [But] other explanations may do better in accounting for the late resort to the courts. Suing a State over religion puts nothing in a plaintiff's pocket and can take a great deal out, and even with volunteer litigators to supply time and energy, the risk of social ostracism can be powerfully deterrent."

2. ***Differing interpretations of the "coercion" test.*** (a) LEE v. WEISMAN, 505 U.S. 577 (1992), per KENNEDY, J., held violative of the Establishment Clause the practice of public school officials inviting members of the clergy to offer invocation and benediction prayers at graduation ceremonies: "[The] school district's supervision and control of a high school graduation ceremony places public pressure, as well as peer pressure, on attending students to stand as a group or, at least, maintain respectful silence during the Invocation and Benediction. This pressure, though subtle and indirect, can be as real as any overt compulsion. * * * Research in psychology supports the common assumption that adolescents are often susceptible to pressure from their peers towards conformity, and that the influence is strongest in matters of social convention. [I]n our society and in our culture high school graduation is one of life's most significant occasions. * * * Attendance may not be required by official decree, yet it is apparent that a student is not free to absent herself from the graduation exercise in any real sense of the term 'voluntary,' for absence would require forfeiture of these intangible benefits which have motivated the student through youth and all her high school years."

SCALIA, J., joined by Rehnquist, C.J., and White and Thomas, JJ., dissented: "[Since] the Court does not dispute that students exposed to prayer at graduation ceremonies retain (despite 'subtle coercive pressures,') the free will to sit, there is absolutely no basis for the Court's decision. [The] coercion that was a hallmark of historical establishments of religion was coercion of religious orthodoxy and of financial support by force of *law and threat of penalty*. [The] Court relies on our 'school prayer' cases, *Engel* and *Schempp*. But whatever the merit of those cases, they do not support, much less compel, the Court's ["ersatz, 'peer-pressure' psycho-coercion"] journey. In the first place, *Engel* and *Schempp* do not constitute an exception to the rule, distilled from historical practice, that public ceremonies may include prayer; rather, they simply do not fall within the scope of the rule (for the obvious reason that school instruction is not a public ceremony). Second, we have made clear our understanding that school prayer occurs within a framework in which legal coercion to attend school (i.e., coercion under threat of penalty) provides the ultimate backdrop. * * * Voluntary prayer at graduation—a one-time ceremony at which parents, friends and relatives are present—can hardly be thought to raise the same concerns."

(b) ELK GROVE UNIFIED SCHOOL DIST. v. NEWDOW, 542 U.S. 1 (2004), reversed the Ninth Circuit's decision that daily classroom recitation by the teacher of the Pledge of Allegiance, with the words "Under God" added in 1954 by

Congress, violates the Establishment Clause. The Court held that the father of the schoolgirl had no standing, see Ch. 12, Sec. 2, I. Three justices reached the merits and would reverse. REHNQUIST, C.J., joined by O'Connor, J., did "not believe that the phrase 'under God' in the Pledge converts its recital into a 'religious exercise' of the sort described in *Lee*. [It is] in no sense a prayer, nor an endorsement of any religion. [It] is a patriotic exercise, not a religious one; participants promise fidelity to our flag and our Nation, not to any particular God, faith, or church."

O'CONNOR, J., added: "For centuries, we have marked important occasions or pronouncements with references to God and invocations of divine assistance. [These] can serve to solemnize an occasion instead of to invoke divine provenance. The reasonable observer [,] fully aware of our national history and the origins of such practices, would not perceive these [as] signifying a government endorsement of any specific religion, or even of religion over non-religion. * * *

"This case requires us to determine whether the appearance of the phrase 'under God' in the Pledge of Allegiance constitutes an instance of such ceremonial deism. Although it is a close question, I conclude that it [does.] "The Pledge complies with [the] requirement [that "no religious acknowledgment could claim to be an instance of ceremonial deism if it explicitly favored one particular religious belief system over another"]. It does not refer to a nation 'under Jesus' or 'under Vishnu,' but instead acknowledges religion in a general way: a simple reference to a generic 'God.' Of course, some religions—Buddhism, for instance— are not based upon a belief in a separate Supreme Being. But one would be hard pressed to imagine a brief solemnizing reference to religion that would adequately encompass every religious belief expressed by any citizen of this Nation."

THOMAS, J., also concurred: "Adherence to *Lee* would require us to strike down the Pledge policy, which, in most respects, poses more serious difficulties. [I] believe, however, that *Lee* was wrongly decided. [The] kind of coercion implicated by the Religion Clauses is that accomplished *by force of law and threat of penalty*." *Lee* (Scalia, J., dissenting). Peer pressure, unpleasant as it may be, is not coercion."

3. ***Prayer at other school activities***. SANTA FE IND. SCHOOL DIST. v. DOE, 530 U.S. 290 (2000), per STEVENS, J., relied on *Lee* to hold that a school policy titled "Prayer at Football Games," authorizing a student election on (a) whether to have a student "invocation or statement" before each varsity game "to solemnize the event," and (b) to select the student to deliver it and to decide its content, violates the Establishment Clause. Unlike student speeches at an open public forum, this policy's purpose was found to encourage religious messages, and its authorization of only one student for the entire football season results in the majoritarian process silencing minority views. Although the informal pressure on students to attend is not as strong as at graduation, many high school students do feel "immense social pressure" to be involved in such events.

4. ***Differing interpretations of the "endorsement" test***. (a) CAPITOL SQUARE REVIEW & ADVISORY BOARD v. PINETTE, 515 U.S. 753 (1995), per SCALIA, J., relying on *Widmar* and *Lamb's Chapel,* held that petitioner's permitting the Ku Klux Klan to place a Latin cross in Capitol Square—"A 10–acre, state-owned plaza surrounding the Statehouse in Columbus, Ohio"—when it had also permitted such other unattended displays as "a State-sponsored lighted tree during the Christmas season, a privately-sponsored menorah during Chanukah, a display showing the progress of a United Way fundraising campaign, and booths and exhibits during an arts festival," did not violate the Establishment Clause: "The State did not sponsor respondents' expression, the expression was made on government property that had been opened to the public for speech, and permis-

sion was requested through the same application process [for] other private groups."

The seven-justice majority divided, however, on the scope of the "endorsement" test. SCALIA, J., joined by Rehnquist, C.J., and Kennedy and Thomas, JJ., rejected petitioners' claim based on "the forum's proximity to the seat of government, which, they contend, may produce the perception that the cross bears the State's approval": "[W]e have consistently held that it is no violation for government to enact neutral policies that happen to benefit religion. Where we have tested for endorsement of religion, the subject of the test was either expression by the government itself, *Lynch,* or else government action alleged to discriminate in favor of private religious expression or activity, *Allegheny County.* [O]ne can conceive of a case in which a governmental entity manipulates its administration of a public forum close to the seat of government (or within a government building) in such a manner that only certain religious groups take advantage of it, creating an impression of endorsement that is in fact accurate. But those situations, which involve governmental favoritism, do not exist here. * * *

"The contrary view, most strongly espoused by Justice Stevens [infra], but endorsed by Justice Souter and Justice O'Connor [and Breyer, J.] as well, [infra], exiles private religious speech to a realm of less-protected expression. [It] is no answer to say that the Establishment Clause tempers religious speech. By its terms that Clause applies only to the words and acts of government. It [has] never been read by this Court to serve as an impediment to purely private religious speech connected to the State only through its occurrence in a public forum."

O'CONNOR, J., joined by Souter and Breyer, JJ., concurred in part: "Where the government's operation of a public forum has the effect of endorsing religion, even if the governmental actor neither intends nor actively encourages that result, the Establishment Clause is violated [because] the State's own actions (operating the forum in a particular manner and permitting the religious expression to take place therein), and their relationship to the private speech at issue, actually convey a message of endorsement."c

STEVENS, J., dissented: "[If] a reasonable person could perceive a government endorsement of religion from a private display, then the State may not allow its property to be used as a forum for that display. No less stringent rule can adequately protect non-adherents from a well-grounded perception that their sovereign supports a faith to which they do not subscribe.d, 5

---

c. Souter, J., joined by O'Connor and Breyer, JJ., concurred "in large part because of the possibility of affixing a sign to the cross adequately disclaiming any government sponsorship or endorsement of it."

"[As] long as the governmental entity does not 'manipulat[e]' the forum in such a way as to exclude all other speech, the plurality's opinion would seem to [invite] government encouragement [of religion], even when the result will be the domination of the forum by religious displays and religious speakers. [Something] of the sort, in fact, may have happened here. Immediately after the District Court issued the injunction ordering petitioners to grant the Klan's permit, a local church council [invited] all local churches to erect crosses, and the Board granted 'blanket permission' for 'all churches friendly to or affiliated with' the council to do so. The end result was that a part of the square was strewn with crosses, and

while the effect in this case may have provided more embarrassment than suspicion of endorsement, the opportunity for the latter is clear."

d. O'Connor, J., responded: "Under such an approach, a religious display is necessarily precluded so long as some passersby would perceive a governmental endorsement thereof. [But the] reasonable observer in the endorsement inquiry must be deemed aware of the history and context of the community and forum in which the religious display appears. [An] informed member of the community will know how the public space in question has been used in the past—and it is that fact, not that the space may meet the legal definition of a public forum, which is relevant to the endorsement inquiry."

5. [O'Connor, J.'s] 'reasonable person' comes off as a well-schooled jurist, a being finer than the tort-law model. With respect, I

"[The] 'reasonable observer' of any symbol placed unattended in front of any capitol in the world will normally assume that the sovereign [has] sponsored and facilitated its message. [Even] if the disclaimer at the foot of the cross (which stated that the cross was placed there by a private organization) were legible, that inference would remain, because a property owner's decision to allow a third party to place a sign on her property conveys the same message of endorsement as if she had erected it herself. [This] clear image of endorsement was lacking in *Widmar* and *Lamb's Chapel,* in which the issue was access to government facilities. Moreover, there was no question in those cases of an unattended display; private speakers, who could be distinguished from the state, were present."

GINSBURG, J., also dissented, reserving the question of whether an unequivocal disclaimer, "legible from a distance," "that Ohio did not endorse the display's message" would suffice: "Near the stationary cross were the government's flags and the government's statues. No human speaker was present to disassociate the religious symbol from the State. No other private display was in sight. No plainly visible sign informed the public that the cross belonged to the Klan and that Ohio's government did not endorse the display's message."

(b) SALAZAR v. BUONO, 130 S.Ct. 1803 (2010): In 1934, members of the Veterans of Foreign Wars placed a Latin cross on federal land to honor American soldiers who died in World War I. Easter services have been regularly held there over the years. After a federal court held this violative of the Establishment Clause, Congress prohibited spending governmental funds to remove the cross and directed the Secretary of the Interior to transfer the cross and land to VFW in exchange for privately owned land elsewhere in the Preserve. The statute provided that the property would revert to the Government if not maintained "as a memorial commemorating United States participation in World War I and honoring the American veterans of that war." A splintered 5–4 majority reversed on grounds of (1) rules pertaining to the law of injunctions or (2) standing. Four justices reached the constitutional issue but their discussion was somewhat influenced by their view of injunction doctrine.

ALITO, J., who was part of the majority, would uphold the statute: "Assuming that it is appropriate to apply the so-called 'endorsement test,' [the 'reasonable observer'] would be familiar with the origin and history of the monument and would also know both that the land on which the monument is located is privately owned and that the new owner is under no obligation preserve the monument's present design. [A] well-informed observer would appreciate that the transfer represents an effort by Congress to address a unique situation and to find a solution that best accommodates conflicting concerns [to] commemorate our Nation's war dead and to avoid the disturbing symbolism that would have been created by the destruction of the monument."a

STEVENS, J., joined by Ginsburg and Sotomayor, JJ., dissented: "[I]t is undisputed that the Latin cross is the preeminent symbol of Christianity. It is exclusively a Christian symbol, and not a symbol of any other religion. * * * I

think this enhanced tort-law standard is singularly out of place in the Establishment Clause context. It strips of constitutional protection every reasonable person whose knowledge happens to fall below some 'ideal' standard. * * * Justice O'Connor's argument that 'there is always someone' who will feel excluded by any particular governmental action, ignores the requirement that such an apprehension be objectively reasonable. A person who views an exotic cow at the zoo as a symbol of the Government's approval of the Hindu religion cannot survive this test.

a. Alito, J.'s analysis generally conforms to the discussion in the plurality opinion by Kennedy, J., joined by Roberts, C.J., and Alito, J., which based its conclusion on the law of injunctions. Breyer, J., also relied on the law of injunctions, but dissented. Scalia, J., joined by Thomas, J., concurred in the judgment on the ground that respondent had no standing.

certainly agree that the Nation should memorialize the service of those who fought and died in World War I, but it cannot lawfully do so by continued endorsement of a starkly sectarian message.

"[T]he transfer [statute] would not end government endorsement of the cross for two independently sufficient reasons. First, after the transfer it would continue to appear to any reasonable observer that the Government has endorsed the cross, notwithstanding that the name has changed on the title to a small patch of underlying land. This is particularly true because the Government has designated the cross as a national memorial, and that endorsement continues regardless of whether the cross sits on public or private land. Second, the transfer continues the existing government endorsement of the cross because the purpose of the transfer is to preserve its display. Congress' intent to preserve the display of the cross maintains the Government's endorsement of the cross."

SECTION 2.   FREE EXERCISE CLAUSE AND RELATED PROBLEMS

I. CONFLICT WITH STATE REGULATION

The most common problem respecting free exercise of religion has involved a generally applicable government regulation, whose purpose is nonreligious, that either makes illegal (or otherwise burdens) conduct that is dictated by some religious belief, or requires (or otherwise encourages) conduct that is forbidden by some religious belief. REYNOLDS v. UNITED STATES, 98 U.S. 145 (1878), the first major decision on the Free Exercise Clause, upheld a federal law making polygamy illegal as applied to a Mormon whose religious duty was to practice polygamy: "Congress was deprived of all legislative power over mere opinion, but was left free to reach actions which were in violation of social duties or subversive of good order." CANTWELL v. CONNECTICUT, 310 U.S. 296 (1940), reemphasized this distinction between religious opinion or belief, on the one hand, and action taken because of religion, on the other, although the Court this time spoke more solicitously about the latter: "Freedom of conscience and freedom to adhere to such religious organization or form of worship as the individual may choose cannot be restricted by law. [Free exercise] embraces two concepts,—freedom to believe and freedom to act. The first is absolute but, in the nature of things, the second cannot be. [The] freedom to act must have appropriate definition to preserve the enforcement of that protection [although] the power to regulate must be so exercised as not, in attaining a permissible end, unduly to infringe the protected freedom."

Beginning with *Cantwell*—which first held that the Fourteenth Amendment made the free exercise guarantee applicable to the states—a number of cases invalidated application of state laws to conduct undertaken pursuant to religious beliefs. Like *Cantwell,* these decisions, a number of which are set forth in Ch. 7,[a] rested in whole or in part on the freedom of expression protections of the First and Fourteenth Amendments. Similarly, WEST VIRGINIA STATE BD. OF EDUC. v. BARNETTE, 319 U.S. 624 (1943), held that compelling a flag salute by public school children whose religious scruples forbade it violated the First Amendment: "[The] freedoms of speech and of press, of assembly, and of worship [are] susceptible of restriction only to prevent grave and immediate danger to interests which the state may lawfully protect. [The] freedom asserted by these

---

a. E.g., *Schneider v. Irvington,* Ch.7, Sec.6, I, A; *Lovell v. Griffin,* Ch. 7, Sec. 4, I, A supra   (involving distribution of religious literature). See also *Marsh v. Alabama,* Ch. 10, Sec. 2.

appellees does not bring them into collision with rights asserted by any other individual. It is such conflicts which most frequently require intervention of the State to determine where the rights of one end and those of another begin. [T]he compulsory flag salute and pledge requires *affirmation of a belief* and an *attitude of mind*. [If] there is any fixed star in our constitutional constellation, it is that no official, high or petty, can prescribe what shall be orthodox in politics, nationalism or other matters of opinion or force citizens to confess by word or act their faith therein."

It was not until 1963 that the Court held conduct protected by the Free Exercise Clause alone. SHERBERT v. VERNER, 374 U.S. 398 (1963), per BRENNAN, J., held that South Carolina's denial of unemployment compensation benefits to a Sabbatarian, who refused to work on Saturdays because of sincerely held religious convictions, violated the Free Exercise Clause: The State's disqualification of Sherbert "forced her to choose between following the precepts of her religion and forfeiting benefits, on the one hand, and abandoning one of the precepts of her religion in order to accept work, on the other hand. Governmental imposition of such a choice puts the same kind of burden upon the free exercise of religion as would a fine imposed against [her] for her Saturday worship." The principle that "such infringements must be subjected to strict scrutiny and could be justified only by proof by the State of a compelling interest," and that it was "incumbent upon the [state] to demonstrate that no alternative forms of regulation would [satisfy its interests] without infringing First Amendment rights," was reaffirmed several times in respect to denial of unemployment compensation benefits, see *Thomas v. Review Board*, 450 U.S. 707 (1981); *Hobbie v. Unemployment Appeals Com'n*, 480 U.S. 136 (1987), and was also applied in *Wisconsin v. Yoder*, 406 U.S. 205 (1972), which invalidated a law compelling school attendance to age 16 as applied to Amish parents who refused on religious grounds to send their children to high school.

Notes

Rejections of free exercise claims. (a) *Taxation.* (i) JIMMY SWAGGART MINISTRIES v. BOARD OF EQUAL., 493 U.S. 378 (1990), per O'CONNOR, J., unanimously held that the Free Exercise Clause does not prohibit imposing a sales and use tax on sale of religious materials by a religious organization. The Court distinguished *Murdock v. Pennsylvania,* 319 U.S. 105 (1943) and *Follett v. McCormick,* 321 U.S. 573 (1944), which had invalidated license taxes for sellers as applied to Jehovah's Witnesses who went from house to house selling religious pamphlets, because of the "particular nature of the challenged taxes—flat license taxes that operated as a prior restraint on the exercise of religious liberty": "[T]o the extent that imposition of a generally applicable tax merely decreases the amount of money appellant has to spend on its religious activities, any such burden is not constitutionally significant. [B]ecause appellant's religious beliefs do not forbid payment of the sales and use tax, appellant's reliance on *Sherbert* and its progeny is misplaced. [Although] it is of course possible to imagine that a more onerous tax, even if generally applicable, might effectively choke off an adherent's religious practices, cf. *Murdock* (the burden of a flat tax could render itinerant evangelism 'crushed and closed out by the sheer weight of the toll or tribute which is exacted town by town'), we face no such situation in this case."

(ii) UNITED STATES v. LEE, 455 U.S. 252 (1982), per BURGER, C.J., held that the Free Exercise Clause does not require an exemption for members of the Old Order Amish from payment of social security taxes even though "both payment and receipt of social security benefits is forbidden by the Amish faith":

"The state may justify a limitation on religious liberty by showing that it is essential to accomplish an overriding governmental interest [and] mandatory participation is indispensable to the fiscal vitality of the social security system. [To] maintain an organized society that guarantees religious freedom to a great variety of faiths requires that some religious practices yield to the common good. [The] tax system could not function if denominations were allowed to challenge the tax system because tax payments were spent in a manner that violates their religious belief."

(b) *Conscription.* (i) GILLETTE v. UNITED STATES, 401 U.S. 437 (1971), per MARSHALL, J., held that the Free Exercise Clause does not forbid Congress from "conscripting persons who oppose a particular war on grounds of conscience and religion. * * *23": "The conscription laws [are] not designed to interfere with any religious ritual or practice, and do not work a penalty against any theological position. The incidental burdens felt by [petitioners] are strictly justified by substantial governmental interests that relate directly to the very impacts questioned. And more broadly [is] the Government's interest in procuring the manpower necessary for military purposes * * *." Douglas, J., dissented.

(ii) In JOHNSON v. ROBISON, 415 U.S. 361 (1974), a federal statute granted educational benefits for veterans who served on active duty but disqualified conscientious objectors who performed alternate civilian service. The Court, per BRENNAN, J., found a "rational basis" for the classification and thus no violation of equal protection, because the "disruption caused by military service is quantitatively greater [and] qualitatively different." Further, the statute "involves only an incidental burden upon appellee's free exercise of religion—if, indeed, any burden exists at [all.]19 Government's substantial interest in raising and supporting armies is of 'a kind and weight' clearly sufficient to sustain the challenged legislation, for the burden upon appellee's free exercise [is] not nearly of the same order or magnitude as" in *Gillette*. Douglas, J., dissented.

(c) *Tax exemption.* BOB JONES UNIV. v. UNITED STATES, 461 U.S. 574 (1983), per BURGER, C.J., held that IRS denial of tax exempt status to private schools that practice racial discrimination on the basis of sincerely held religious beliefs does not violate the Free Exercise Clause: "[T]he Government has a fundamental, overriding interest in eradicating racial discrimination in education [which] substantially outweighs whatever burden denial of tax benefits places on petitioners' exercise of their religious beliefs. The interests asserted by petitioners cannot be accommodated with that compelling governmental interest, see *Lee;* and no 'less restrictive means' are available to achieve the governmental interest."a

(d) *Internal government affairs.* LYNG v. NORTHWEST INDIAN CEMETERY PROTECTIVE ASS'N, 485 U.S. 439 (1988), per O'CONNOR, J., held the federal government's building a road [in] a national forest did not violate the free

---

23. We are not faced with the question whether the Free Exercise Clause itself would require exemption of any class other than objectors to particular wars. * * * We note that the Court has previously suggested that relief for conscientious objectors is not mandated by the Constitution. See *Hamilton v. Regents,* 293 U.S. 245 (1934); *United States v. Macintosh,* 283 U.S. at 623–24 (1931).

19. * * * Congress has bestowed relative benefits upon conscientious objectors by permitting them to perform their alternate service obligation as civilians. Thus, [to] grant educational benefits to military servicemen might arguably be viewed as an attempt to equalize

the burdens of military service and civilian alternate service, rather than an effort [to] place a relative burden upon a conscientious objector's free exercise of religion.

a. Four justices also rejected the claim that Nebraska's denial of a driver's license to a person whose sincerely held religious beliefs—pursuant to the Second Commandment prohibition of "graven images"—forbade her to be photographed, violated the Free Exercise Clause. *Quaring v. Peterson,* 728 F.2d 1121 (8th Cir.1984) (free exercise violation), affirmed by an equally divided Court, 472 U.S. 478 (1985).

exercise rights of American Indian tribes even though this would "virtually destroy the Indians' ability to practice their religion" because it would irreparably damage "sacred areas which are an integral and necessary part of [their] belief systems": "In *Bowen v. Roy*, we considered a challenge to a federal statute that required the States to use Social Security numbers in administering certain welfare programs. Two applicants [contended] that their religious beliefs prevented them from acceding to the use of a Social Security number [that had been assigned to] their two-year-old daughter because the use of a numerical identifier would' " rob the spirit" of [their] daughter and prevent her from attaining greater spiritual power.' [The] Court rejected [this]: 'The Free Exercise Clause simply cannot be understood to require the Government to conduct its own internal affairs in ways that comport with the religious beliefs of particular citizens. Just as the Government may not insist that [the Roys] engage in any set form of religious observance, so [they] may not demand that the Government join in their chosen religious practices by refraining from using a number to identify their daughter. [The] Free Exercise Clause affords an individual protection from certain forms of governmental compulsion; it does not afford an individual a right to dictate the conduct of the Government's internal procedures.' " Brennan, J., joined by Marshall and Blackmun, JJ., dissented: Kennedy, J., did not participate.

EMPLOYMENT DIVISION v. SMITH

494 U.S. 872, 110 S.Ct. 1595, 108 L.Ed.2d 876 (1990).

JUSTICE SCALIA delivered the opinion of the Court. * * *

Respondents [were] fired from their jobs with a private drug rehabilitation organization because they ingested peyote for sacramental purposes at a ceremony of the Native American Church, of which both are members. When respondents applied to petitioner [for] unemployment compensation, they were determined to be ineligible for benefits because they had been discharged for work-related "misconduct." [We believe] that "if a State has prohibited through its criminal laws certain kinds of religiously motivated conduct without violating the First Amendment, it certainly follows that it may impose the lesser burden of denying unemployment compensation benefits to persons who engage in that conduct."

[The] free exercise of religion means, first and foremost, the right to believe and profess whatever religious doctrine one desires. Thus, the First Amendment obviously excludes all "governmental regulation of religious *beliefs* as such." The government may not compel affirmation of religious belief, see *Torcaso v. Watkins,* [Part II infra], punish the expression of religious doctrines it believes to be false, *United States v. Ballard,* [Part II infra], impose special disabilities on the basis of religious views or religious status, see *McDaniel v. Paty,* 435 U.S. 618 (1978) [state rule disqualifying clergy from being legislators]; cf. *Larson v. Valente,* [Sec. 3 infra] or lend its power to one or the other side in controversies over religious authority or dogma, see *Presbyterian Church v. Hull Church,* [Sec. 3 infra].

But the "exercise of religion" often involves not only belief and profession but the performance of (or abstention from) physical acts: assembling with others for a worship service, participating in sacramental use of bread and wine, proselytizing, abstaining from certain foods or certain modes of transportation. It would be true, we think (though no case of ours has involved the point), that a state would be "prohibiting the free exercise [of religion]" if it sought to ban such acts or abstentions only when they are engaged in for religious reasons, or only because of the religious belief that they display. It would doubtless be unconstitutional, for example, to ban the casting of "statues that are to be used for worship purposes," or to prohibit bowing down before a golden calf.

Respondents [seek] to carry the meaning of "prohibiting the free exercise [of religion]" one large step further. They contend that their religious motivation for using peyote places them beyond the reach of a criminal law that is not specifically directed at their religious practice, and that is concededly constitutional as applied to those who use the drug for other reasons. [As] a textual matter, we do not think the words must be given that meaning. It is no more necessary to regard the collection of a general tax, for example, as "prohibiting the free exercise [of religion]" by those citizens who believe support of organized government to be sinful, than it is to regard the same tax as "abridging the freedom [of] the press" of those publishing companies that must pay the tax as a condition of staying in business. It is a permissible reading of the text [to] say that if prohibiting the exercise of religion (or burdening the activity of printing) is not the object of the tax but merely the incidental effect of a generally applicable and otherwise valid provision, the First Amendment has not been offended. Compare *Citizen Publishing Co. v. United States,* 394 U.S. 131 (1969) (upholding application of antitrust laws to press), with *Grosjean v. American Press Co.,* [Ch. 7, Sec. 7, I] (striking down license tax applied only to newspapers with weekly circulation above a specified level); see generally *Minneapolis Star & Tribune Co. v. Minnesota Commissioner of Revenue* [Ch. 7, Sec. 7, I].

Our decisions reveal that the latter reading is the correct one. We have never held that an individual's religious beliefs excuse him from compliance with an otherwise valid law prohibiting conduct that the State is free to regulate. [In] *Prince v. Massachusetts,* 321 U.S. 158 (1944), we held that a mother could be prosecuted under the child labor laws for using her children to dispense literature in the streets, her religious motivation notwithstanding. [The opinion also discusses *Braunfeld, Gillette,* and *Lee.*]

The only decisions in which we have held that the First Amendment bars application of a neutral, generally applicable law to religiously motivated action have involved [the] Free Exercise Clause in conjunction with other constitutional protections, such as freedom of speech and of the press, see *Cantwell* (invalidating a licensing system for religious and charitable solicitations under which the administrator had discretion to deny a license to any cause he deemed nonreligious); *Murdock; Follett,* or the right of parents, acknowledged in *Pierce v. Society of Sisters* [Sec. 2 supra] to direct the education of their children, see *Yoder.*1 Some of our cases prohibiting compelled expression, decided exclusively upon free speech grounds, have also involved freedom of religion, cf. *Wooley v. Maynard* [Ch. 7, Sec. 9, I] (invalidating compelled display of a license plate slogan that offended individual religious beliefs); *Barnette.* And it is easy to envision a case in which a challenge on freedom of association grounds would likewise be reinforced by Free Exercise Clause concerns. Cf. *Roberts v. United States Jaycees* [Ch. 7, Sec. 9, III] ("An individual's freedom to speak, to worship, and to petition the government for the redress of grievances could not be vigorously protected from interference by the State [if] a correlative freedom to engage in group effort toward those ends were not also guaranteed."). * * *

Respondents argue that [the] claim for a religious exemption must be evaluated under the balancing test set forth in *Sherbert*[:] governmental actions that

---

1. [*Yoder*] said that "[*Pierce*] stands as a charter of the rights of parents to direct the religious upbringing of their children. And, when the interests of parenthood are combined with a free exercise claim of the nature revealed by this record, more than merely a 'reasonable relation to some purpose within the competency of the State' is required to sustain the validity of the State's requirement under the First Amendment."

substantially burden a religious practice must be justified by a compelling governmental interest. [We] have never invalidated any governmental action on the basis of the *Sherbert* test except the denial of unemployment compensation. Although we have sometimes purported to apply the *Sherbert* test in contexts other than that, we have always found the test satisfied, see *Lee, Gillette*. In recent years we have abstained from applying the *Sherbert* test (outside the unemployment compensation field) at all [discussing *Roy* and *Lyng*]. In *Goldman v. Weinberger*, 475 U.S. 503 (1986), we rejected application of the *Sherbert* test to military dress regulations that forbade the wearing of yarmulkes. In *O'Lone v. Shabazz*, 482 U.S. 342 (1987), we sustained, without mentioning the *Sherbert* test, a prison's refusal to excuse inmates from work requirements to attend worship services.

[The] *Sherbert* test [was] developed in a context that lent itself to individualized governmental assessment of the reasons for the relevant conduct. [O]ur decisions in the unemployment cases stand for the proposition that where the State has in place a system of individual exemptions, it may not refuse to extend that system to cases of "religious hardship" without compelling reason.

Whether or not the decisions are that limited, they at least have nothing to do with an across-the-board criminal prohibition on a particular form of conduct. [T]he sounder approach, and the approach in accord with the vast majority of our precedents, is to hold the test inapplicable to such challenges. [To] make an individual's obligation to obey such a law contingent upon the law's coincidence with his religious beliefs, except where the State's interest is "compelling"—permitting him, by virtue of his beliefs, "to become a law unto himself," *Reynolds*—contradicts both constitutional tradition and common sense.2

The "compelling government interest" requirement seems benign, because it is familiar from other fields. But using it as the standard that must be met before the government may accord different treatment on the basis of race, see [Ch. 9, Sec. 2, I], or before the government may regulate the content of speech, is not remotely comparable to using it for the purpose asserted here. What it produces in those other fields—equality of treatment, and an unrestricted flow of contending speech—are constitutional norms; what it would produce here—a private right to ignore generally applicable laws—is a constitutional anomaly.3

Nor is it possible to limit the impact of respondents' proposal by requiring a "compelling state interest" only when the conduct prohibited is "central" to the individual's religion. It is no more appropriate for judges to determine the "centrality" of religious beliefs [than] it would be for them to determine the "importance" of ideas before applying the "compelling interest" test in the free speech field. What principle of law or logic can be brought to bear to contradict a believer's assertion that a particular act is "central" to his personal faith? [I]n

2. Justice O'Connor seeks to distinguish *Lyng* and *Roy* on the ground that those cases involved the government's conduct of "its own internal affairs." [But] it is hard to see any reason in principle or practicality why the government should have to tailor its health and safety laws to conform to the diversity of religious belief, but should not have to tailor its management of public lands, *Lyng*, or its administration of welfare programs, *Roy*.

3. [Just] as we subject to the most exacting scrutiny laws that make classifications based on race or on the content of speech, so too we strictly scrutinize governmental classifications based on religion, see *McDaniel*; see also *Tor-*caso. But we have held that race-neutral laws that have the *effect* of disproprotionately disadvantaging a particular racial group do not thereby become subject to compelling-interest analysis under the Equal Protection Clause, see *Washington v. Davis* [Ch. 9, Sec. 2, III] (police employment examination); and we have held that generally applicable laws unconcerned with regulating speech that have the *effect* of interfering with speech do not thereby become subject to compelling-interest analysis under the First Amendment, see *Citizen Publishing Co. v. United States* (antitrust laws). Our conclusion [today] is the only approach compatible with these precedents.

many different contexts, we have warned that courts must not presume to determine the place of a particular belief in a religion or the plausibility of a religious claim. See, e.g., *Thomas* [Part II infra]; *Jones v. Wolf,* 443 U.S. 595 (1979); *Ballard.*4

If the "compelling interest" test is to be applied at all, then, it must be applied across the board, to all actions thought to be religiously commanded. Moreover, if "compelling interest" really means what it says (and watering it down here would subvert its rigor in the other fields where it is applied), many laws will not meet the test. Any society adopting such a system would be courting anarchy, but that danger increases in direct proportion to the society's diversity of religious [beliefs]. Precisely because "we are a cosmopolitan nation made up of people of almost every conceivable religious preference," and precisely because we value and protect that religious divergence, we cannot afford the luxury of deeming *presumptively invalid,* as applied to the religious objector, every regulation of conduct that does not protect an interest of the highest order. The rule respondents favor would open the prospect of constitutionally required religious exemptions from civic obligations of almost every conceivable kind—ranging from compulsory military service, see, e.g., *Gillette,* to the payment of taxes, see, e.g., *Lee,* to health and safety regulation such as manslaughter and child neglect laws, compulsory vaccination laws, drug laws, and traffic laws, to social welfare legislation such as minimum wage laws, see *Tony and Susan Alamo Foundation v. Secretary of Labor,* 471 U.S. 290 (1985), child labor laws, see *Prince;* animal cruelty laws, see, e.g., *Church of the Lukumi Babalu Aye Inc. v. Hialeah,* [note 1 infra], environmental protection laws, and laws providing for equality of opportunity for the races, see e.g., *Bob Jones University.* The First Amendment's protection of religious liberty does not require this.5

[A] number of States have made an exception to their drug laws for sacramental peyote use. But to say that a nondiscriminatory religious-practice exemption is permitted, or even that it is desirable, is not to say that it is constitutionally required, and that the appropriate occasions for its creation can be discerned by the courts. It may fairly be said that leaving accommodation to the political process will place at a relative disadvantage those religious practices that are not widely engaged in; but that unavoidable consequence of democratic government must be preferred to a system in which each conscience is a law unto itself or in which judges weigh the social importance of all laws against the centrality of all religious beliefs. * * *

JUSTICE O'CONNOR, with whom JUSTICE BRENNAN, JUSTICE MARSHALL, and JUSTICE BLACKMUN join as to [Part II], concurring in the judgment. * * *

4. [In] any case, dispensing with a "centrality" inquiry is utterly unworkable. It would require, for example, the same degree of "compelling state interest" to impede the practice of throwing rice at church weddings as to impede the practice of getting married in church. There is no way out of the difficulty that, if general laws are to be subjected to a "religious practice" exception, *both* the importance of the law at issue *and* the centrality of the practice at issue must reasonably be considered. * * *

5. Justice O'Connor contends that the "parade of horribles" in the text only "demonstrates [that] courts have been quite capable of strik[ing] sensible balances between religious liberty and competing state interests." But the cases we cite have struck "sensible balances" only because they have all applied the general laws, despite the claims for religious exemption. In any event, Justice O'Connor mistakes the purpose of our parade: it is not to suggest that courts would necessarily permit harmful exemptions from these laws (though they might), but to suggest that courts would constantly be in the business of determining whether the "severe impact" of various laws on religious practice (to use Justice Blackmun's terminology) or the "constitutiona[l] significan[ce]" of the "burden on the particular plaintiffs" (to use Justice O'Connor's terminology) suffices to permit us to confer an exemption. It [is] horrible to contemplate that federal judges will regularly balance against the importance of general laws the significance of religious practice.

II.   [A] law that prohibits certain conduct—conduct that happens to be an act of worship for someone—manifestly does prohibit that person's free exercise of his religion [regardless] of whether the law prohibits the conduct only when engaged in for religious reasons, only by members of that religion, or by all persons.

[If] the First Amendment is to have any vitality, it ought not be construed to cover only the extreme and hypothetical situation in which a State directly targets a religious practice. [*Yoder*] expressly rejected the interpretation the Court now adopts: "[T]o agree that religiously grounded conduct must often be subject to the broad police power of the State is not to deny that there are areas of conduct protected by the Free Exercise Clause [and] thus beyond the power of the State to control, *even under regulations of general applicability.* [A] regulation neutral on its face may, in its application, nonetheless offend the constitutional requirement for government neutrality if it unduly burdens the free exercise of religion."

The Court endeavors to escape from our decisions in *Cantwell* and *Yoder* by labeling them "hybrid" decisions but there is no denying that both cases expressly relied on the Free Exercise Clause. [I]n each of the other cases cited by the Court to support its categorical rule, we rejected the particular constitutional claims before us only after carefully weighing the competing interests. [That] we rejected the free exercise claims in those cases hardly calls into question the applicability of First Amendment doctrine.

[W]e have never distinguished between cases in which a State conditions receipt of a benefit on conduct prohibited by religious beliefs and cases in which a State affirmatively prohibits such conduct. The *Sherbert* compelling interest test applies in both kinds of cases. [A] neutral criminal law prohibiting conduct that a State may legitimately regulate is, if anything, *more* burdensome than a neutral civil statute placing legitimate conditions on the award of a state benefit.

[Even] if, as an empirical matter, a government's criminal laws might usually serve a compelling interest in health, safety, or public order, the First Amendment at least requires a case-by-case determination of the question, sensitive to the facts of each particular claim. Given the range of conduct that a State might legitimately make criminal, we cannot assume, merely because a law carries criminal sanctions and is generally applicable, that the First Amendment *never* requires the State to grant a limited exemption for religiously motivated conduct.

Moreover, we have not "rejected" or "declined to apply" the compelling interest test in our recent cases. See, e.g., *Hobbie*. The cases cited by the Court signal no retreat from our consistent adherence to the compelling interest test. In both *Roy* and *Lyng,* for example, we expressly distinguished *Sherbert* on the ground that the First Amendment does not "require the Government *itself* to behave in ways that the individual believes will further his or her spiritual development. * * * " This distinction makes sense because "the Free Exercise Clause is written in terms of what the government cannot do to the individual, not in terms of what the individual can exact from the government." *Sherbert* (Douglas, J., concurring). Because [this case] plainly falls into the former category, I would apply those established precedents to the facts of this case.

Similarly, the other cases cited by the Court for the proposition that we have rejected application of the *Sherbert* test outside the unemployment compensation field are distinguishable because they arose in the narrow, specialized contexts in which we have not traditionally required the government to justify a burden on religious conduct by articulating a compelling interest. See *Goldman v. Weinberger* ("Our review of military regulations challenged on First Amendment grounds is far more deferential than constitutional review of similar laws or regulations designed for civilian society"); *O'Lone v. Shabazz* ("[P]rison regulations alleged to infringe constitutional rights are judged under a 'reasonableness' test less restrictive than that ordinarily applied to alleged infringements of fundamental constitutional rights"). That we did not apply the compelling interest test in these cases says nothing about whether the test should continue to apply in paradigm free exercise cases such as the one presented here.

[As] the language of the Clause itself makes clear, an individual's free exercise of religion is a preferred constitutional activity. A law that makes criminal such an activity therefore [triggers] heightened judicial scrutiny. [Our] free speech cases similarly recognize that neutral regulations that affect free speech values are subject to a balancing, rather than categorical, approach. See, e.g., *United States v. O'Brien*, [Ch. 7, Sec. 2]; *Renton v. Playtime Theatres, Inc.*, [Ch. 7, Sec. 3, I]; cf. *Anderson v. Celebrezze*, 460 U.S. 780 (1983) (generally applicable laws may impinge on free association concerns). * * *

Finally, the Court today suggests that the disfavoring of minority religions is an "unavoidable consequence" under our system of government and that accommodation of such religions must be left to the political process. In my view, however, the First Amendment was enacted precisely to protect the rights of those whose religious practices are not shared by the majority and may be viewed with hostility. The history of our free exercise doctrine amply demonstrates the harsh impact majoritarian rule has had on unpopular or emerging religious groups such as the Jehovah's Witnesses and the Amish. [The] compelling interest test reflects the First Amendment's mandate of preserving religious liberty to the fullest extent possible in a pluralistic society. For the Court to deem this command a "luxury" is to denigrate "[t]he very purpose of a Bill of Rights."

III.   The Court's holding today [is] unnecessary to this case. I would reach the same result applying our established free exercise jurisprudence.

There is no dispute that Oregon's criminal prohibition of peyote places a severe burden on the ability of respondents to freely exercise their religion. Peyote is a sacrament of the Native American Church and is regarded as vital to respondents' ability to practice their religion. * * *

There is also no dispute that Oregon has a significant interest in enforcing laws that control the possession and use of controlled substances by its citizens. [Indeed,] under federal law (incorporated by Oregon law in relevant part), peyote is specifically regulated as a Schedule I controlled substance, which means that Congress has found that it has a high potential for abuse, that there is no currently accepted medical use, and that there is a lack of accepted safety for use of the drug under medical supervision. In light of our recent decisions holding that the governmental interests in the collection of income tax, *Hernandez v. Commissioner*, [Sec. 3 infra], a comprehensive social security system, see *Lee*, and military conscription, see *Gillette*, are compelling, respondents do not seriously dispute that Oregon has a compelling interest in prohibiting the possession of peyote. [Although] the question is close, I would conclude that uniform application of Oregon's criminal prohibition is "essential to accomplish," *Lee*, its overriding interest in preventing the physical harm caused by the use of a Schedule I controlled substance. [Because] the health effects caused by the use of controlled substances exist regardless of the motivation of the user, [use] for religious purposes, violates the very purpose of the laws that prohibit them. Moreover, in view of the societal interest in preventing trafficking[,] uniform application of the criminal prohibition at issue is essential to the effectiveness of Oregon's stated interest in preventing any possession of peyote. * * *

Respondents contend that any incompatibility is belied by the fact that the Federal Government and several States provide exemptions for the religious use of peyote. But other governments may surely choose to grant an exemption without Oregon, with its specific asserted interest in uniform application of its drug laws, being *required* to do so by the First Amendment. Respondents also note that the sacramental use of peyote is central to the tenets of the Native American Church, but I agree with the Court [that] "[i]t is not within the judicial ken to question the centrality of particular beliefs or practices to a faith." [This] does not mean [that] courts may not make factual findings as to whether a claimant holds a sincerely held religious belief that conflicts with [the] challenged law. The distinction between questions of centrality and questions of sincerity and burden is admittedly fine, but it is one that is an established part of our free exercise doctrine * * *.a

JUSTICE BLACKMUN, with whom JUSTICE BRENNAN and JUSTICE MARSHALL join, dissenting.

This Court over the years painstakingly has developed a consistent and exacting standard to test the constitutionality of a state statute that burdens the free exercise of religion. Such a statute may stand only if the law in general, and the State's refusal to allow a religious exemption in particular, are justified by a compelling interest that cannot be served by less restrictive means.

[I]t is important to articulate in precise terms the state interest involved. It is not the State's broad interest in fighting the critical "war on drugs" that must be weighed against respondents' claim, but the State's narrow interest in refusing to make an exception for the religious, ceremonial use of peyote. [The] State cannot plausibly assert that unbending application of a criminal prohibition is essential to fulfill any compelling interest, if it does not, in fact, attempt to enforce that prohibition. * * * Oregon has never sought to prosecute respondents, and does not claim that it has made significant enforcement efforts against other religious users of peyote. The State's asserted interest thus amounts only to the symbolic preservation of an unenforced prohibition. * * *

Similarly, this Court's prior decisions have not allowed a government to rely on mere speculation about potential harms, but have demanded evidentiary support for a refusal to allow a religious exception. [In] this case, the State [offers] no evidence that the religious use of peyote has ever harmed anyone. The factual findings of other courts cast doubt on the State's assumption that religious use of peyote is harmful. See *State v. Whittingham,* 19 Ariz.App. 27, 30, 504 P.2d 950, 953 (1973) ("the State failed to prove that the quantities of peyote used in the sacraments of the Native American Church are sufficiently harmful to the health and welfare of the participants * * * "); *People v. Woody,* 61 Cal.2d 716, 722–723, 40 Cal.Rptr. 69, 74, 394 P.2d 813, 818 (1964) ("as the Attorney General [admits,] the opinion of scientists and other experts is 'that peyote [works] no permanent deleterious injury to the Indian' ").

[The] Federal Government [does] not find peyote so dangerous as to preclude an exemption for religious use.2 Moreover, other Schedule I drugs have lawful uses. See *Olsen v. Drug Enforcement Administration,* 878 F.2d 1458 (D.C.Cir. 1989) (medical and research uses of marijuana).

a. In *Boerne v. Flores,* Ch. 11, Sec. 2, O'Connor, J., joined by Breyer, J., argued that "the historical evidence [bears] out the conclusion that, at the time the Bill of Rights was ratified, it was accepted that government should, when possible, accommodate religious practice." Scalia, J., joined by Stevens, J., disagreed: "The historical evidence put forward by the dissent does nothing to undermine the conclusion we reached in *Smith.*"

2. [Moreover,] 23 States, including many that have significant Native American populations, have statutory or judicially crafted exemptions in their drug laws for religious [use].

The carefully circumscribed ritual context in which respondents used peyote is far removed from the irresponsible and unrestricted recreational use of unlawful drugs.3 * * *4 [J]ust as in *Yoder,* the values and interests of those seeking a religious exemption in this case are congruent, to a great degree, with those the State seeks to promote through its drug laws. See *Yoder* (since the Amish accept formal schooling up to 8th grade, and then provide "ideal" vocational education, State's interest in enforcing its law against the Amish is "less substantial than [for] children generally"). Not only does the Church's doctrine forbid nonreligious use of peyote; it also generally advocates self-reliance, familial responsibility, and abstinence from alcohol. There is considerable evidence that the spiritual and social support provided by the Church has been effective in combatting the tragic effects of alcoholism on the Native American population. * * *

The State also seeks to support its refusal to make an exception [by] invoking its interest in abolishing drug trafficking. There is, however, practically no illegal traffic in peyote. * * *

Finally, the State argues that, [if] it grants an exemption for religious peyote use, a flood of other claims to religious exemptions will follow. [But almost] half the States, and the Federal Government, have maintained an exemption for religious peyote use for many years, and apparently have not found themselves overwhelmed by claims to other religious exemptions.5 [The] unusual circumstances that make the religious use of peyote compatible with the State's interests in health and safety and in preventing drug trafficking would not apply to other religious claims. Some religions, for example, might not restrict drug use to a limited ceremonial context, as does the Native American Church. See, e.g., *Olsen* ("the Ethiopian Zion Coptic Church [teaches] that marijuana is properly smoked 'continually all day' "). Some religious claims involve drugs such as marijuana and heroin, in which there is significant illegal traffic, [so] that it would be difficult to grant a religious exemption without seriously compromising law enforcement efforts.6 [Though] the State must treat all religions equally, and not favor one over another, this obligation is fulfilled by the uniform application of the "compelling interest" *test* to all free exercise claims, not by reaching uniform *results* as to all claims. * * *

Respondents believe, and their sincerity has *never* been at issue, that the peyote plant embodies their deity, and eating it is an act of worship and communion. Without peyote, they could not enact the essential ritual of their religion. [This] potentially devastating impact must be viewed in light of the federal policy—reached in reaction to many years of religious persecution and intolerance—of protecting the religious freedom of Native Americans. See American Indian Religious Freedom Act. * * *b

3. In this respect, respondents' use of peyote seems closely analogous to the sacramental use of wine by the Roman Catholic Church. During Prohibition, the Federal Government exempted such use of wine from its general [ban]. However compelling the Government's then general interest in prohibiting the use of alcohol may have been, it could not plausibly have asserted an interest sufficiently compelling to outweigh Catholics' right to take communion.

4. The use of peyote is, to some degree, self-limiting. [It] is extremely bitter, and eating it is an unpleasant experience, which would tend to discourage casual or recreational use.

5. [V]arious sects have raised free exercise claims regarding drug use. In no reported case, except those involving claims of religious peyote use, has the claimant prevailed.

6. Thus, this case is distinguishable from *Lee,* in which the Court concluded that there was "no principled way" to distinguish other exemption claims, and the "tax system could not function if denominations were allowed to challenge the tax system because tax payments were spent in a manner that violates their religious belief."

b. In 1993, Congress passed the Religious Freedom Restoration Act which effectively reinstated the *Sherbert–Yoder* test for generally applicable laws that burden religious practices.

Notes

1. ***Discrimination.*** (a) CHURCH OF THE LUKUMI BABALU AYE, INC. v. HIALEAH, 508 U.S. 520 (1993), per KENNEDY, J., held that city ordinances barring ritual animal sacrifice violated the Free Exercise Clause: "[I]f the object of a law is to infringe upon or restrict practices because of their religious motivation, the law is not neutral, see *Smith;* and it is invalid unless it is justified by a compelling interest and is narrowly tailored to advance that interest. [The] ordinances had as their object the suppression of [the Santeria] religion. The [record] discloses animosity to Santeria adherents and their religious practices; the ordinances by their own terms target this religious exercise; the texts of the ordinances were gerrymandered with care to proscribe religious killings of animals but to exclude almost all secular killings; and the ordinances suppress much more religious conduct than is necessary in order to achieve the legitimate ends asserted in their defense. [A] law that targets religious conduct for distinctive treatment or advances legitimate governmental interests only against conduct with a religious motivation will survive strict scrutiny only in rare cases. [T]hese ordinances cannot withstand this scrutiny." SOUTER, J., concurred specially stating that the Court should re-examine *Smith*.

(b) LOCKE v. DAVEY, 540 U.S. 712 (2004), per REHNQUIST, C.J., held that the exclusion (as required by the state constitution) from Washington's postsecondary education Promise Scholarship Program to assist academically gifted students, of pursuit of a devotional theology degree (i.e., one "designed to induce religious faith"), did not violate the Free Exercise clause: "[W]e have long said that 'there is room for play in the points' between [the religion clauses]. *Walz*. In other words, there are some state actions permitted by the Establishment Clause but not required by the Free Exercise Clause. [And] there is no doubt that the State could, consistent with the Federal Constitution, permit Promise Scholars to pursue a degree in devotional theology, see *Witters* * * *.

"[Respondent] contends that [under] *Lukumi*, the program is presumptively unconstitutional because it is not facially neutral with respect to religion. [But here], the State's disfavor of religion (if it can be called that) is of a far milder kind [than in *Lukumi*]. It imposes neither criminal nor civil sanctions on any type of religious service or rite. It does not deny to ministers the right to participate in the political affairs of the community. See *McDaniel*. And it does not require students to choose between their religious beliefs and receiving a government benefit.4 See *Hobbie*; *Sherbert*. The State has merely chosen not to fund a distinct category of instruction.

"[M]ajoring in devotional theology is akin to a religious calling as well as an academic pursuit. [T]he interest that [the Washington constitution] seeks to further is scarcely novel. In fact, we can think of few areas in which a State's antiestablishment interests come more into play. Since the founding of our country, there have been popular uprisings against procuring taxpayer funds to support church leaders, which was one of the hallmarks of an 'established' religion. * * *

Most States that sought to avoid such an establishment around the time of the founding placed in their constitutions formal prohibitions against using tax

RFRA was held unconstitutional in *Boerne v. Flores*, Ch. 11, Sec. 2.

4. Promise Scholars may still use their scholarship to pursue a secular degree at a different institution from where they are studying devotional theology.

funds to support the ministry. [T]hat early state constitutions saw no problem in explicitly excluding *only* the ministry from receiving state dollars reinforces the conclusion that religious instruction is of a different ilk.

"Far from evincing the hostility toward religion which was manifest in *Lukumi*, we believe that the entirety of the Promise Scholarship Program goes a long way toward including religion in its benefits.8 The program permits students to attend pervasively religious schools, so long as they are accredited [and] students are still eligible to take devotional theology courses."

SCALIA, J., joined by Thomas, J., dissented, finding *Lukumi* "irreconcilable with today's decision": "When the State makes a public benefit generally available, that benefit becomes part of the baseline against which burdens on religion are measured; and when the State withholds that benefit from some individuals solely on the basis of religion, it violates the Free Exercise Clause no less than if it had imposed a special tax.

"[No] field of study but religion is singled out for disfavor. [The history relied on by the Court] involved not the inclusion of religious ministers in public benefits programs like the one at issue here, but laws that singled them out for financial aid. [No] one would seriously contend, for example, that the Framers would have barred ministers from using public roads on their way to church.1

"[T]he State already has all the play in the joints it needs. There are any number of ways it could respect both its unusually sensitive concern for the conscience of its taxpayers *and* the Federal Free Exercise Clause. It could make the scholarships redeemable only at public universities (where it sets the curriculum), or only for select courses of study. Either option would replace a program that facially discriminates against religion with one that just happens not to subsidize it.

"[T]he interest to which the Court defers is not fear of a conceivable Establishment Clause violation, budget constraints, avoidance of endorsement, or substantive neutrality—none of these. It is a pure philosophical preference: the State's opinion that it would violate taxpayers' freedom of conscience *not* to discriminate against candidates for the ministry. This sort of protection of 'freedom of conscience' has no logical limit and can justify the singling out of religion for exclusion from public programs in virtually any context.c The Court never says whether it deems this interest compelling (the opinion is devoid of any mention of standard of review) but, self-evidently, it is not.2

"The Court makes no serious attempt to defend the program's neutrality, and instead identifies two features thought to render its discrimination less offensive. The first is the lightness of Davey's burden. The Court offers no authority for approving facial discrimination against religion simply because its material consequences are not severe. I might understand such a test if we were still in the

8. Washington has also been solicitous in ensuring that its constitution is not hostile towards religion, and at least in some respects, its constitution provides greater protection of religious liberties than the Free Exercise Clause (rejecting standard in *Smith*) * * *.

1. No State [with] a constitutional provision [that] prohibited the use of tax funds to support the ministry [has,] so far as I know, ever prohibited the hiring of public employees who use their salary to conduct ministries, or excluded ministers from generally available disability or unemployment benefits. * * *

c. The Court responded that "the only interest at issue here is the State's interest in not funding the religious training of clergy."

2. [If] religious discrimination required only a rational basis, the Free Exercise Clause would impose no constraints other than those the Constitution already imposes on all government action. The question is not whether theology majors are different, but whether the differences are substantial enough to justify a discriminatory financial penalty that the State inflicts on no other major. Plainly they are not. * * *

business of reviewing facially neutral laws that merely happen to burden some individual's religious exercise, but we are not. See *Smith*. Discrimination *on the face of a statute* is something else. The indignity of being singled out for special burdens on the basis of one's religious calling is so profound that the concrete harm produced can never be dismissed as insubstantial. The Court has not required proof of 'substantial' concrete harm with other forms of discrimination, see, e.g., *Brown v. Board of Education,* and it should not do so here. * * *

"The other reason the Court thinks this particular facial discrimination less offensive is that the scholarship program was not motivated by animus toward religion. [If] a State deprives a citizen of trial by jury or passes an ex post facto law, we do not pause to investigate whether it was actually trying to accomplish the evil the Constitution prohibits. It is sufficient that the citizen's rights have been infringed. [We] do sometimes look to legislative intent to smoke out more subtle instances of discrimination, but we do so as a *supplement* to the core guarantee of facially equal treatment, not as a replacement for it.

"[This] case is about discrimination against a religious minority. Most citizens of this country identify themselves as professing some religious belief, but [t]hose the statutory exclusion actually affects—those whose belief in their religion is so strong that they dedicate their study and their lives to its ministry—are a far narrower set. One need not delve too far into modern popular culture to perceive a trendy disdain for deep religious conviction."

II. UNUSUAL RELIGIOUS BELIEFS AND PRACTICES

1. *Validity and sincerity.* UNITED STATES v. BALLARD, 322 U.S. 78 (1944), per DOUGLAS, J., held that the First Amendment forbids courts (or juries) from finding that any person's asserted religious beliefs are untrue—since many of the most traditional and accepted religious beliefs could not be proved today. But courts *can* determine whether a person *sincerely believes* the asserted religious tenets.a

2. *What is "religion"?* Religious beliefs need not be theistic to qualify for constitutional protection. TORCASO v. WATKINS, per BLACK, J., 367 U.S. 488 (1961), invalidated a Maryland provision requiring a declaration of belief in God as a test for public office, noting that "among religions [that] do not teach what would generally be considered a belief in the existence of God are Buddhism, Taoism, Ethical Culture, Secular Humanism and others." But the Court has said in *Yoder* that religious beliefs must constitute more than merely a philosophic rejection of contemporary secular values.

UNITED STATES v. SEEGER, 380 U.S. 163 (1965), interpreted § 6(j) of the Universal Military Training and Service Act, which exempted from combat any person "who, by reason of religious training and belief, is conscientiously opposed to participation in war in any form. Religious training and belief in this [means] an individual's belief in a relation to a Supreme Being involving duties superior to those arising from any human relation, but does not include essentially political, sociological or philosophical views or a merely personal moral code." The Court, per CLARK, J., avoided constitutional questions and perhaps suggested a constitutional definition: The belief must occupy a place in the believer's life parallel to that occupied by orthodox religious beliefs. Such a belief may be internally derived, but it must be something beyond a merely political or philosophical view.

---

a. *Thomas v. Review Board,* Part I supra, held that courts must respect sincerely held religious beliefs even though they may not appear to be logical, consistent, or comprehensible to others.

SECTION 3. PREFERENCE AMONG RELIGIONS

In BOARD OF EDUC. OF KIRYAS JOEL v. GRUMET, 512 U.S. 687 (1994), a New York statute constituted the Village of Kiryas Joel—"a religious enclave of Satmar Hasidim, practitioners of a strict form of Judaism"—as a separate school district. Most of the children attend pervasively religious private schools. The newly created district "currently runs only a special education program for handicapped [Satmar] children" who reside both inside and outside the village. The statute was passed "to enable the village's handicapped children to receive a secular, public-school education" because when they previously attended public schools in the larger school district outside the village, they suffered "panic, fear and trauma [in] leaving their own community and being with people whose ways were so different." The Court, per SOUTER, J., invoked "a principle at the heart of the Establishment Clause, that government should not prefer one religion to another. [Because] Kiryas Joel did not receive its new governmental authority simply as one of many communities eligible for equal treatment under a general law, we have no assurance that the next similarly situated group seeking a school district of its own will receive one; [and] a legislature's failure to enact a special law is itself unreviewable.a [Here] the benefit flows only to a single sect, [and] therefore crosses the line from permissible accommodation to impermissible establishment."b

---

LARSON v. VALENTE, 456 U.S. 228 (1982), involved a challenge by the Unification Church ("Moonies") to "a Minnesota statute, imposing certain registration and reporting requirements upon only those religious organizations that solicit more than fifty per cent of their funds from nonmembers." The Court, per BRENNAN, J., held that the statute violated the Establishment Clause because it did not survive "strict scrutiny." Assuming that the state's "valid secular purpose [in] protecting its citizens from abusive practices in the solicitation of funds for charity" is "compelling," the state "failed to demonstrate that the fifty per cent rule [is] 'closely fitted' " to furthering that interest.

WHITE, J., joined by Rehnquist, J., dissented, disagreeing with the Court's view "that the rule [is] an explicit and deliberate preference for some religious beliefs over others": "The rule [names] no churches or denominations. [Some] religions will qualify and some will not, but this depends on the source of their contributions, not on their brand of religion." Burger, C.J. and White and O'Connor, JJ., also dissented on the ground that the church had no standing.

---

a. Kennedy, J., disagreed: if another religious community were denied legislative help, it "could sue the State of New York, contending that New York's discriminatory treatment of the two religious communities violated the Establishment Clause. [T]he court would have only to determine whether the community does indeed bear the same burden on its religious practice as [did] Kiryas Joel." Nonetheless, "whether or not the purpose is accommodation and whether or not the government provides similar gerrymanders to people of all religious faiths, the Establishment Clause forbids the government to use religion [as] a criterion to draw political or electoral lines."

b. Souter, J., joined by Blackmun, Stevens and Ginsburg, JJ., found an additional ground for invalidating the statute: "delegating the State's discretionary authority over public schools to a group defined by its character as a religious community, in a legal and historical context that gives no assurance that governmental power has been or will be exercised neutrally." They relied on *Larkin v. Grendel's Den, Inc.*, 459 U.S. 116 (1982), which held that a Massachusetts law (§ 16C), giving churches and schools the power "to veto applications for liquor licenses within a five hundred foot radius of the church or school, violates the Establishment Clause."

HERNANDEZ v. COMMISSIONER, 490 U.S. 680 (1989), per MARSHALL, J., found no violation of the Establishment Clause in not permitting federal taxpayers to deduct as "charitable contributions" payments to the Church of Scientology for "auditing" and "training" sessions. A central tenet of the Church requires "fixed donations" for these sessions to study the faith's tenets and to increase spiritual awareness. The proceeds are the Church's primary source of income. *Larson* was distinguished on the ground that IRS disallowance for payments made "with some expectation of a quid pro quo in terms of goods or services [makes] no 'explicit and deliberate distinctions between different religious organizations.'"

O'CONNOR, J., joined by Scalia, J., dissented: "In exchange for their payment of pew rents, Christians receive particular seats during worship services. Similarly, in some synagogues attendance at the worship services for Jewish High Holy Days is often predicated upon the purchase of a general admission ticket or a reserved seat ticket. * * * Mormons must tithe ten percent of their income as a necessary but not sufficient condition to obtaining a 'temple recommend,' i.e., the right to be admitted into the temple. [Thus, the case] involves the differential application of a standard based on constitutionally impermissible differences drawn by the Government among religions." Brennan and Kennedy, JJ., did not participate.

SECTION 4. CONFLICT BETWEEN THE CLAUSES

The decision in *Employment Division v. Smith* appeared to have relieved some of the tension that had existed between the doctrines that the Court had developed under the Establishment and Free Exercise Clauses. But substantial questions remained, e.g., do (a) the decisions in *Sherbert (Thomas, Hobbie), Yoder* and *Roy,* and (b) statutes granting religious exemptions from laws of general applicability violate the Establishment Clause because they impermissibly aid religion?

CORPORATION OF THE PRESIDING BISHOP OF THE CHURCH OF JESUS CHRIST OF LATTER–DAY SAINTS v. AMOS

483 U.S. 327, 107 S.Ct. 2862, 97 L.Ed.2d 273 (1987).

JUSTICE WHITE delivered the opinion of the Court.

Section 702 of the Civil Rights Act of 1964 exempts religious organizations from Title VII's prohibition against discrimination in employment on the basis of religion. [The] Deseret Gymnasium (Gymnasium) in Salt Lake City, Utah, is a nonprofit facility, open to the public, run by [an] unincorporated religious association sometimes called the Mormon or LDS Church. Appellee Mayson worked at the Gymnasium for some 16 years as an assistant building engineer and then building engineer. He was discharged in 1981 because he failed to qualify for a temple recommend, that is, a certificate that he is a member of the Church and eligible to attend its temples. Mayson [contended that] § 702 violates the Establishment Clause. * * *

"This Court has long recognized that the government may (and sometimes must) accommodate religious practices [without] violating the Establishment Clause." It is well established, too, that "[t]he limits of permissible state accommodation to religion are by no means co-extensive with the noninterference mandated by the Free Exercise Clause." *Walz.* [At] some point, accommodation may devolve into "an unlawful fostering of religion," but this is not such a [case].

Lemon requires [a] "secular legislative purpose." This does not mean that the law's purpose must be unrelated to religion. [Rather,] *Lemon*'s "purpose" requirement aims at preventing the relevant governmental decisionmaker—in this case, Congress—from abandoning neutrality and acting with the intent of promoting a particular point of view in religious matters.

Under the *Lemon* analysis, it is a permissible legislative purpose to alleviate significant governmental interference with the ability of religious organizations to define and carry out their religious missions. Appellees argue that there is no such purpose here because § 702 provided adequate protection for religious employers prior to the 1972 amendment, when it exempted only the religious activities of such employers from the statutory ban on religious discrimination. We may assume for the sake of argument that the pre–1972 exemption was adequate in the sense that the Free Exercise Clause required no more. Nonetheless, it is a significant burden on a religious organization to require it, on pain of substantial liability, to predict which of its activities a secular court will consider religious. The line is hardly a bright one, and an organization might understandably be concerned that a judge would not understand its religious tenets [and] affect the way an organization carried out what it understood to be its religious mission. * * *

The second requirement under *Lemon* is that the law in question have "a principal or primary effect [that] neither advances nor inhibits religion." Undoubtedly, religious organizations are better able now to advance their purposes than they were prior to the 1972 amendment to § 702. But religious groups have been better able to advance their purposes on account of many laws that have passed constitutional muster: for example, the property tax exemption at issue in *Walz,* or the loans of school books to school children, including parochial school students, upheld in *Allen.* A law is not unconstitutional simply because it *allows* churches to advance religion, which is their very purpose. For a law to have forbidden "effects" under *Lemon,* it must be fair to say that the *government itself* has advanced religion through its own activities and influence. [Moreover,] we find no persuasive evidence in the record before us that the Church's ability to propagate its religious doctrine through the Gymnasium is any greater now than it was prior to the passage of the Civil Rights Act in 1964. In such circumstances, we do not see how any advancement of religion achieved by the Gymnasium can be fairly attributed to the Government, as opposed to the Church.15

We find unpersuasive [that] § 702 singles out religious entities for a benefit. [The Court] has never indicated that statutes that give special consideration to religious groups are per se invalid. That would run contrary to [our] cases that there is ample room for accommodation of religion under the Establishment Clause. Where, as here, government acts with the proper purpose of lifting a regulation that burdens the exercise of religion, we see no reason to require that the exemption come packaged with benefits to secular [entities.] *Larson* indicates that laws discriminating *among* religions are subject to strict scrutiny, and that laws "affording a uniform benefit to *all* religions" should be analyzed under *Lemon.* In a case such as this, where a statute is neutral on its face and motivated by a permissible purpose of limiting governmental interference with the exercise of religion, we see no justification for applying strict scrutiny to a statute that passes the *Lemon* [test.] § 702 is rationally related to the legitimate purpose of alleviating significant governmental interference with the ability of religious organizations to define and carry out their religious missions. * * *

15. Undoubtedly, Mayson's freedom of choice in religious matters was impinged upon, but it was the Church [and] not the Government, who put him to the choice of changing his religious practices or losing his job. * * *

JUSTICE BRENNAN, with whom JUSTICE MARSHALL joins, concurring in the judgment.

[Any] exemption from Title VII's proscription on religious discrimination [says] that a person may be put to the choice of either conforming to certain religious tenets or losing a job opportunity. [The] potential for coercion created by such a provision is in serious tension with our commitment to individual freedom of conscience in matters of religious belief.

At the same time, religious organizations have an interest in autonomy in ordering their internal affairs * * *. Determining that certain activities are in furtherance of an organization's religious mission, and that only those committed to that mission should conduct them, is thus a means by which a religious community defines itself. Solicitude for a church's ability to do so reflects the idea that furtherance of the autonomy of religious organizations often furthers individual religious freedom as well. * * *

This rationale suggests that, ideally, religious organizations should be able to discriminate on the basis of religion *only* with respect to religious activities [because] the infringement on religious liberty that results from conditioning performance of *secular* activity upon religious belief cannot be defended as necessary for the community's self-definition. Furthermore, the authorization of discrimination in such circumstances is not an accommodation that simply enables a church to gain members by the normal means of prescribing the terms of membership for those who seek to participate in furthering the mission of the community. Rather, it puts at the disposal of religion the added advantages of economic leverage in the secular realm. * * *

What makes the application of a religious-secular distinction difficult is that the character of an activity is not self-evident [and] requires a searching case-by-case analysis. This results in considerable ongoing government entanglement in religious affairs [and] raises concern that a religious organization may be chilled in its Free Exercise activity. * * *

Sensitivity to individual religious freedom dictates that religious discrimination be permitted only with respect to employment in religious activities. Concern for the autonomy of religious organizations demands that we avoid the entanglement and the chill on religious expression that a case-by-case determination would produce. We cannot escape the fact that these aims are in tension. Because of the nature of nonprofit activities, I believe that a categorical exemption for such enterprises appropriately balances these competing concerns. * * *

JUSTICE O'CONNOR, concurring in the judgment.a * * *

In *Jaffree,* I noted [that, "on] the one hand, a rigid application of the *Lemon* test would invalidate legislation exempting religious observers from generally applicable government obligations. By definition, such legislation has a religious purpose and effect in promoting the free exercise of religion.b On the other hand, judicial deference to all legislation that purports to facilitate the free exercise of religion would completely vitiate the Establishment Clause. Any statute pertaining to religion can be viewed as an 'accommodation' of free exercise rights."c

a. Blackmun, J., concurred in the judgment, "essentially for the reasons set forth in Justice O'Connor's opinion."

b. In her *Jaffree* concurrence, O'Connor, J., added: "Indeed, the statute at issue in *Lemon* [can] be viewed as an accommodation of the religious beliefs of parents who choose to send their children to religious schools."

c. In *Jaffree,* O'Connor, J. added: "It [is] difficult to square any notion of 'complete neutrality' with the mandate of the Free Exercise Clause that government must sometimes exempt a religious observer from an otherwise

In my view, the opinion for the Court leans toward the second of the two unacceptable options described [above.] Almost any government benefit to religion could be recharacterized as simply "allowing" a religion to better advance itself, unless perhaps it involved actual proselytization by government agents. In nearly every case of a government benefit to religion, the religious mission would not be advanced if the religion did not take advantage of the benefit; even a direct financial subsidy to a religious organization would not advance religion if for some reason the organization failed to make any use of the funds. * * *

The necessary first step in evaluating an Establishment Clause challenge to a government action lifting from religious organizations a generally applicable regulatory burden is to recognize that such government action *does* have the effect of advancing religion. The necessary second step is to separate those benefits to religion that constitutionally accommodate the free exercise of religion from those that provide unjustifiable awards of assistance to religious organizations. As I have suggested in earlier opinions, the inquiry framed by the *Lemon* test should be "whether government's purpose is to endorse religion and whether the statute actually conveys a message of endorsement." [T]he relevant issue is how it would be perceived by an objective observer, acquainted with the text, legislative history, and implementation of the statute.d [This] case involves a government decision to lift from a nonprofit activity of a religious organization the burden of demonstrating that the particular nonprofit activity is religious as well as the burden of refraining from discriminating on the basis of religion. Because there is a probability that a nonprofit activity of a religious organization will itself be involved in the organization's religious mission, in my view the objective observer should perceive the government action as an accommodation of the exercise of religion rather than as a government endorsement of religion.

[U]nder the holding of the Court, [the] constitutionality of the § 702 exemption as applied to for-profit activities of religious organizations remains open.

Notes

1. **Draft exemption**. Did the statute in *Gillette*, exempting only "religious" conscientious objectors, impermissibly prefer religion over nonreligion? In WELSH v. UNITED STATES, Sec. 2, II supra, WHITE, J., joined by Burger, C.J., and Stewart, J., found it valid: "First, § 6(j) may represent a purely practical judgment that religious objectors, however admirable, would be of no more use in combat than many others unqualified for military service. [On] this basis, the exemption has neither the primary purpose nor the effect of furthering religion. [Second], Congress may have [believed that] to deny the exemption would violate the Free Exercise Clause or at least raise grave problems in this respect."

HARLAN, J., disagreed, believing that "having chosen to exempt, [Congress] cannot draw the line between theistic or nontheistic religious beliefs on the one

---

generally applicable obligation. [The] solution [lies] in identifying workable limits to the Government's license to promote the free exercise of religion. [O]ne can plausibly assert that government pursues free exercise clause values when it lifts a government-imposed burden on the free exercise of religion. [T]hen the standard Establishment Clause test should be modified accordingly. [T]he Court should simply acknowledge that the religious purpose of such a statute is legitimated by the Free Exercise Clause."

d. In *Jaffree*, O'Connor, J., added: "[C]ourts should assume that the 'objective observer,' is acquainted with the Free Exercise Clause and the values it promotes. Thus individual perceptions, or resentment that a religious observer is exempted from a particular government requirement, would be entitled to little weight if the Free Exercise Clause strongly supported the exemption."

hand and secular beliefs on the other. [I]t must encompass the class of individuals it purports to exclude, those whose beliefs emanate from a purely moral, ethical, or philosophical source.9 The common denominator must be the intensity of moral [conviction]. *Everson, McGowan* and *Allen,* all sustained legislation on the premise that it was neutral [notwithstanding] that it may have assisted religious groups by giving them the same benefits accorded to nonreligious groups.12 To the extent that *Zorach* and *Sherbert* stand for the proposition that the Government may (*Zorach*), or must (*Sherbert*), shape its secular programs to accommodate the beliefs and tenets of religious groups, I think these cases unsound.13"

2. ***Unemployment compensation.*** (a) In THOMAS v. REVIEW BD., Sec. 2 supra, REHNQUIST, J., dissented, finding the result "inconsistent with many of our prior Establishment Clause cases"2: "If Indiana were to legislate [an] unemployment compensation law which permitted benefits to be granted to those persons who quit their jobs for religious reasons—the statute would 'plainly' violate the Establishment Clause as interpreted in such cases as [*Lemon*]. First, [the] proviso would clearly serve only a religious purpose. It would grant financial benefits for the sole purpose of accommodating religious beliefs. Second, [the] primary effect of the proviso would be to 'advance' religion by facilitating the exercise of religious belief. Third, [it] would surely 'entangle' the State in religion. [By] granting financial benefits to persons solely on the basis of their religious beliefs, the State must necessarily inquire whether the claimant's belief is 'religious' and whether it is sincerely [held.] I believe that Justice Stewart, dissenting in *Schempp,* accurately stated the reach of the Establishment Clause [as] limited to 'government support of proselytizing activities of religious sects by throwing the weight of secular authorities behind the dissemination of religious tenets.' See *McCollum* (Reed, J., dissenting) (impermissible aid is only 'purposeful assistance directly to the church itself or to some religious [group] performing ecclesiastical functions'). Conversely, governmental assistance which does not have the effect of 'inducing' religious belief, but instead merely 'accommodates' or implements an independent religious choice does not impermissibly involve the government in religious choices and therefore does not violate the Establishment [Clause]. I would think that in

9. * * * I suggested [in *Sherbert*] that a State could constitutionally create exceptions to its program to accommodate religious scruples. [But] any such exception in order to satisfy the Establishment Clause [would] have to be sufficiently broad so as to be religiously neutral. This would require creating an exception for anyone who, as a matter of conscience, could not comply with the statute. * * *

12. [I] fail to see how [§ 6(j)] has "any substantial legislative purpose" apart from honoring the conscience of individuals who oppose war on only religious grounds. * * *

13. [At] the very least the Constitution requires that the State not excuse students early for the purpose of receiving religious instruction when it does not offer to nonreligious students the opportunity to use school hours for spiritual or ethical instruction of a nonreligious nature. Moreover, whether a released-time program cast in terms of improving "conscience" to the exclusion of artistic or cultural pursuits, would be "neutral" and consistent with the requirement of "voluntarism," is by no means an easy question. * * *

2. To the extent *Sherbert* was correctly decided, it might be argued that cases such as *McCollum, Engel, Schempp, Lemon,* and *Ny-*

quist were wrongly decided. The "aid" rendered to religion in these latter cases may not be significantly different, in kind or degree, than the "aid" afforded Mrs. Sherbert or Thomas. For example, if the State in *Sherbert* could not deny compensation to one refusing work for religious reasons, it might be argued that a State may not deny reimbursement to students who choose for religious reasons to attend parochial schools. The argument would be that although a State need not allocate any funds to education, once it has done so, it may not require any person to sacrifice his religious beliefs in order to obtain an equal education. There can be little doubt that to the extent secular education provides answers to important moral questions without reference to religion or teaches that there are no answers, a person in one sense sacrifices his religious belief by attending secular schools. And even if such "aid" were not constitutionally compelled by the Free Exercise Clause, Justice Harlan may well be right in *Sherbert* when he finds sufficient flexibility in the Establishment Clause to permit the States to voluntarily choose to grant such benefits to individuals.

this case, as in *Sherbert,* had the state voluntarily chosen to pay unemployment compensation benefits to persons who left their jobs for religious reasons, such aid would be constitutionally permissible because it redounds directly to the benefit of the individual."

(b) ***Breadth of exemption.*** In TEXAS MONTHLY, INC. v. BULLOCK, Sec. 1, II supra, SCALIA, J., joined by Rehnquist, C.J., and Kennedy, J., charged that according to Brennan, J.'s plurality opinion, "no law is constitutional whose 'benefits [are] confined to religious organizations,' except, of course, those laws that are unconstitutional *unless* they contain benefits confined to religious organizations. [But] 'the limits of permissible state accommodation to religion are by no means co-extensive with the noninterference mandated by the Free Exercise Clause.' Breadth of coverage is essential to constitutionality whenever a law's benefiting of religious activity [is] defended [as] merely the incidental consequence of seeking to benefit *all* activity that achieves a particular secular goal. But that is a different rationale—more commonly invoked than accommodation of religion [but] not preclusive of it. Where accommodation of religion is the justification, by definition religion is being singled out." Finally, "the proper lesson to be drawn from" the fact that the Free Exercise Clause may not require the Texas sales tax exemption and "that *Murdock* and *Follett* are narrowly distinguishable" is that "if the exemption comes so close to being a constitutionally required accommodation, there is no doubt that it is at least a permissible one."

BRENNAN, J., joined by Marshall and Stevens, JJ., responded: "[W]e in no way suggest that *all* benefits conferred exclusively upon religious groups or upon individuals on account of their religious beliefs are forbidden by the Establishment Clause unless they are mandated by the Free Exercise Clause. Our decisions in *Zorach* and *Amos* offer two examples. Similarly, if the Air Force provided a sufficiently broad exemption from its dress requirements for servicemen whose religious faiths commanded them to wear certain headgear, [see] *Goldman v. Weinberger,* that exemption presumably would not be invalid under the Establishment Clause even though this Court has not found it to be required by the Free Exercise Clause.

"All of these cases, however, involve legislative exemptions that did not or would not impose substantial burdens on nonbeneficiaries while allowing others to act according to their religious [beliefs]. New York City's decision to release students from public schools so that they might obtain religious instruction elsewhere, which we upheld in *Zorach,* was found not to coerce students who wished to remain behind to alter their religious beliefs, nor did it impose monetary costs on their parents or other taxpayers who opposed or were indifferent to the religious instruction given to students who were released. The hypothetical Air Force uniform exemption also would not place a monetary burden on those required to conform to the dress code or subject them to any appreciable privation. And the application of Title VII's exemption for religious organizations that we approved in *Amos,* though it had some adverse effect on those holding or seeking employment with those organizations (if not on taxpayers generally), prevented potentially serious encroachments on protected religious freedoms.

"Texas' tax exemption, by contrast, does not remove a demonstrated and possible grave imposition on religious activity sheltered by the Free Exercise Clause. Moreover, it burdens nonbeneficiaries by increasing their tax bills by whatever amount is needed to offset the benefit bestowed on subscribers to religious publications."

3. ***Sabbath observance.*** THORNTON v. CALDOR, INC., 472 U.S. 703 (1985), per BURGER, C.J., held that a Connecticut law—"that those who observe a

Sabbath any day of the week as a matter of religious conviction must be relieved of the duty to work on that day, no matter what burden or inconvenience this imposes on the employer or fellow workers"—"has a primary effect that impermissibly advances a particular religious practice" and thus violates the Establishment Clause: "The statute arms Sabbath observers with an absolute and unqualified right not to work on whatever day they designate as their Sabbath [and thus] goes beyond having an incidental or remote effect of advancing religion."

O'CONNOR, J., joined by Marshall, J., concurred, distinguishing "the religious accommodation provisions of Title VII of the Civil Rights Act [which] require private employers to reasonably accommodate the religious practices of employees unless to do so would cause undue hardship to the employer's business": "Since Title VII calls for reasonable rather than absolute accommodation and extends [to] all religious beliefs and practices rather than protecting only the Sabbath observance, I believe an objective observer would perceive it as an anti-discrimination law rather than an endorsement of religion or a particular religious practice." Rehnquist, J., dissented.

In *Kiryas Joel,* Sec. 3 supra, SCALIA, J., joined by Rehnquist, C.J., and Thomas, J., disagreed with the Court's conclusion that New York had impermissibly preferred one religion: "[M]ost efforts at accommodation seek to solve a problem that applies [to] only one or a few religions. Not every religion uses wine in its sacraments, but that does not make an exemption from Prohibition for sacramental wine-use impermissible, nor does it require the State granting such an exemption to explain [how] it will treat every other claim for dispensation from its controlled-substances laws. Likewise, not every religion uses peyote in its services, but we have suggested that legislation which exempts the sacramental use of peyote from generally applicable drug laws is not only permissible, but desirable, see *Smith,* without any suggestion that some 'up front' legislative guarantee of equal treatment for sacramental substances used by other sects must be provided." Kennedy, J., expressed a similar view: "It is normal for legislatures to respond to problems as they [arise.] Most accommodations cover particular religious practices."

4. ***Unanimous approval.*** CUTTER v. WILKINSON, 544 U.S. 709 (2005), per GINSBURG, J., relying on *Amos* and language in *Smith,* held that the Religious Land Use and Institutionalized Persons Act of 2000—"No government shall impose a substantial burden on the religious exercise of a person residing [in] an institution," unless the burden furthers "a compelling governmental interest," and does so by "the least restrictive means"—does not violate the Establishment Clause:

RLUIPA "does not, on its face, exceed the limits of permissible government accommodation [because] it alleviates exceptional government-created burdens on private religious exercise. [Further], the Act [does] not founder on shoals the Court's prior decisions have identified: Properly applying RLUIPA, courts must take adequate account of the burdens a requested accommodation may impose on nonbeneficiaries, see *Caldor,* and they must be satisfied that the Act's prescriptions [are] administered neutrally among different faiths, see *Kiryas Joel.*8 [It] covers state-run institutions—mental hospitals, prisons, and the like—in which the government exerts a degree of control unparalleled in civilian society and severely disabling to private religious exercise.9 * * *10 * * *

8. Directed at obstructions institutional arrangements place on religious observances, RLUIPA does not require a State to pay for an inmate's devotional accessories.

9. See, e.g., *Charles v. Verhagen,* 348 F.3d 601 (C.A.7 2003) (prison's regulation prohibited Muslim prisoner from possessing ritual cleansing oil); *Young v. Lane,* 922 F.2d 370,

"[RLUIPA's sponsors] anticipated that courts would apply the Act's standard with 'due deference to the experience and expertise of prison and jail administrators in establishing necessary regulations and procedures to maintain good order, security and discipline, consistent with consideration of costs and limited resources.' "

5. ***School prayer.*** In *Jaffree,* O'CONNOR, J., applied her "solution"a to Alabama's moment of silence law: "No law prevents a student who is so inclined from praying silently in public schools. [Of] course, the State might argue that § 16–1–20.1 protects not silent prayer, but rather group silent prayer under State sponsorship. Phrased in these terms, the burden lifted by the statute is not one imposed by the State of Alabama, but by the Establishment Clause as interpreted in *Engel* and *Schempp.* In my view, it is beyond the authority of the State of Alabama to remove burdens imposed by the Constitution itself."

375–376 (C.A.7 1991) (prison's regulation restricted wearing of yarmulkes); *Hunafa v. Murphy,* 907 F.2d 46, 47–48 (C.A.7 1990) (noting instances in which Jewish and Muslim prisoners were served pork, with no substitute available).

10. Respondents argue [that RLUIPA] advances religion by encouraging prisoners to "get religion." [While] some accommodations of religious observance, notably the opportunity to assemble in worship services, might attract joiners seeking a break in their closely guarded day, we doubt that all accommodations would be perceived as "benefits." For example, congressional hearings on RLUIPA revealed that one state corrections system served as its kosher diet "a fruit, a vegetable, a granola bar, and a liquid nutritional supplement—each and every meal." The argument, in any event, founders on the fact that Ohio already facilitates religious services for mainstream faiths. The State provides chaplains, allows inmates to possess religious items, and permits assembly for worship.

a. See fn. c in *Amos.*

Chapter 9

EQUAL PROTECTION

Virtually no legislation applies universally and treats all persons equally; all laws classify (or "discriminate") by imposing special burdens (or granting exemptions from such burdens) or by conferring benefits on some people and not others. To take uncontroversial examples, only those who can pass an examination and possess good eyesight qualify for driver's licenses. Those with expensive homes frequently must pay higher taxes than those with less expensive homes. People who are not high school graduates typically are denied admission to state universities. Under what circumstances do legislative classifications violate the Fourteenth Amendment's command that no state shall "deny to any person within its jurisdiction the equal protection of the laws"?a

Although the language of the Equal Protection Clause is not confined to racial discrimination, the *Slaughter-House Cases,* Ch. 5, Sec. 1, III (the first decision interpreting the Civil War amendments), "doubt[ed] very much whether any action of a state not directed by way of discrimination against the negroes as a class, or on account of their race, will ever be held to come within the purview of this provision." At least as early as 1897, however, the Court invoked the Equal Protection Clause to invalidate a commonplace economic regulation that obligated railroad defendants (but not others) to pay the attorneys' fees of successful plaintiffs. The Court acknowledged that "as a general proposition, [it] is undeniably true [that] it is not within the scope of the Fourteenth Amendment to withhold from States the power of classification." But, the Court continued, "it must appear" that a classification is "based upon some reasonable ground—some difference which bears a just and proper relation to the attempted classification—and is not a mere arbitrary selection." *Gulf, C. & S. F. Ry. v. Ellis,* 165 U.S. 150 (1897).b

a. By its terms, the Equal Protection Clause does not apply to the federal government. Nonetheless, at least since its 1954 decision in *Bolling v. Sharpe,* Sec. 2, II infra, the Court has held that the Due Process Clause incorporates equal protection norms binding on the federal government. Although its pattern of decisions has not been perfectly consistent, the Court has generally insisted that the "approach to Fifth Amendment equal protection claims [is] precisely the same as to equal protection claims under the Fourteenth Amendment." *Weinberger v. Wiesenfeld,* Sec. 3 infra; see also *Adarand Constructors, Inc. v.*

Pena, Sec. 2, VI infra. The principal exception to this general rule of "congruence" involves the treatment of aliens. Current doctrine subjects state discriminations against aliens to more searching judicial scrutiny than federal discriminations against aliens—a disparity considered in Sec. 4, I infra.

b. For an even earlier invocation of the Equal Protection Clause to invalidate a classification of transportation rates, see *Reagan v. Farmers' Loan & Trust Co.,* 154 U.S. 362 (1894).

Sec. 1 of this Chapter considers this "traditional approach" under the Equal Protection Clause to general economic and social welfare regulations. Sec. 2 then deals with the "strict scrutiny" given to explicit racial and ethnic classifications, which the Court has deemed "suspect," as well as with related issues involving race. Sec. 3 reviews the Court's treatment of gender-based classifications. Sec. 4 addresses the use of a nondeferential standard of review for governmental action that disadvantages several other groups. Finally, Sec. 5 examines standards for equal protection review of classifications affecting what the Court classifies as "fundamental" rights.

SECTION 1.   TRADITIONAL APPROACH

As seen in Ch. 5, the Due Process Clause was the usual provision invoked by the Court in the first third of the twentieth century to overturn a great many economic and social welfare regulations. But despite Holmes, J.'s dismissive reference to the Equal Protection Clause as "the usual last resort of constitutional arguments,"c the Court held during this period that approximately twenty state and local laws violated equal protection. For the most part, the Court at least purported to take a deferential approach that granted the states "a broad discretion in classification in the exercise of [their] power of regulation" and interposed the "constitutional guaranty of equal protection" only "against discriminations that are entirely arbitrary."d The materials that follow concern the Court's equal protection scrutiny of economic and social welfare regulations since the late 1930s, when it abandoned active substantive due process review of such legislation.

RAILWAY EXPRESS AGENCY v. NEW YORK

336 U.S. 106, 69 S.Ct. 463, 93 L.Ed. 533 (1949).

JUSTICE DOUGLAS delivered the opinion of the Court.

[T]he Traffic Regulations of the City of New York [provide]: "No person shall operate [on] any street an advertising vehicle; [except for] business notices upon business delivery vehicles, so long as such vehicles are engaged in the usual business [of] the owner and not used merely or mainly for advertising."

Appellant [operates] about 1,900 trucks in New York City and sells the space on the exterior sides of these trucks for advertising [for] the most part unconnected with its own business. It was convicted * * *.

The court [below] concluded that advertising on [vehicles] constitutes a distraction to vehicle drivers and to pedestrians alike and therefore affects the safety of the public in the use of the streets. We do not sit to weigh evidence on the due process issue in order to determine whether the regulation is sound or appropriate; nor is it our function to pass judgment on its wisdom. See *Olsen v. Nebraska* [Ch. 5, Sec. 3]. We would be trespassing on one of the most intensely local and specialized of all municipal problems if we held that this regulation had no relation to the traffic problem of New York City. It is the judgment of the local authorities that it does have such a relation.

[The] question of equal protection of the laws is pressed more strenuously on us. [It] is said, for example, that one of appellant's trucks carrying the advertisement of a commercial house would not cause any greater distraction of pedestrians and vehicle drivers than if the commercial house carried the same advertise-

---

c.   *Buck v. Bell,* 274 U.S. 200 (1927).   d.   *Smith v. Cahoon,* 283 U.S. 553 (1931).

ment on its own truck. Yet the regulation allows the latter to do what the former is forbidden from doing. It is therefore contended that the classification which the regulation makes has no relation to the traffic problem since a violation turns not on what kind of advertisements are carried on trucks but on whose trucks they are carried.

That, however, is a superficial way of analyzing the [problem]. The local authorities may well have concluded that those who advertised their own wares on their trucks do not present the same traffic problem in view of the nature or extent of the advertising which they use. * * *

We cannot say that that judgment is not an allowable one. Yet if it is, the classification has relation to the purpose for which it is made and does not contain the kind of discrimination against which the Equal Protection Clause affords protection. It is by such practical considerations based on experience rather than by theoretical inconsistencies that the question of equal protection is to be answered. And the fact that New York City sees fit to eliminate from traffic this kind of distraction but does not touch what may be even greater ones in a different category, such as the vivid displays on Times Square, is immaterial. It is no requirement of equal protection that all evils of the same genus be eradicated or none at all. * * *

Affirmed.

JUSTICE RUTLEDGE acquiesces in the Court's opinion and judgment, dubitante on the question of equal protection of the laws.

JUSTICE JACKSON, concurring. * * *

The burden should rest heavily upon one who would persuade us to use the Due Process Clause to strike down a substantive [law]. Even its provident use against municipal regulations frequently disables all government—state, municipal and federal—from dealing with the conduct in question because the requirement of due process is also applicable to State and Federal Governments. * * *

Invocation of the Equal Protection Clause, on the other hand, does not disable any governmental body from dealing with the subject at hand. It merely means that the prohibition or regulation must have a broader impact. I regard it as a salutary doctrine that cities, states and the Federal Government must exercise their powers so as not to discriminate between their inhabitants except upon some reasonable differentiation fairly related to the object of regulation. [T]here is no more effective practical guaranty against arbitrary and unreasonable government than to require that the principles of law which officials would impose upon a minority must be imposed generally. Conversely, nothing opens the door to arbitrary action so effectively as to allow those officials to pick and choose only a few to whom they will apply legislation and thus to escape the political retribution that might be visited upon them if larger numbers were affected. Courts can take no better measure to assure that laws will be just than to require that laws be equal in operation. * * *

In this case, if the City of New York should assume that display of any advertising on vehicles tends and intends to distract the attention of persons using the highways and to increase the dangers of its traffic, I should think it fully within its constitutional powers to forbid it all. [Instead], however, the City seeks to reduce the hazard only by saying that while some may, others may not exhibit such appeals. The same display, for example, advertising cigarettes, which this appellant is forbidden to carry on its trucks, may be carried on the trucks of a cigarette dealer. [The] courts of New York have declared that the sole nature and purpose of the regulation before us is to reduce traffic hazards. There is not even a pretense here that the traffic hazard created by the advertising which is forbidden is in any manner or degree more hazardous than that which is permitted. * * *

* * * I do not think differences of treatment under law should be approved on classification because of differences unrelated to the legislative purpose. The Equal Protection Clause ceases to assure either equality or protection if it is avoided by any conceivable difference that can be pointed out between those bound and those left free. This Court has often announced the principle that the differentiation must have an appropriate relation to the object of the [legislation].

The question in my mind comes to this. Where individuals contribute to an evil or danger in the same way and to the same degree, may those who do so for hire be prohibited, while those who do so for their own commercial ends but not for hire be allowed to continue? I think the answer has to be that the hireling may be put in a class by himself and may be dealt with differently than those who act on their own. But this is not merely because such a discrimination will enable the lawmaker to diminish the evil. That might be done by many classifications, which I should think wholly unsustainable. It is rather because there is a real difference between doing in self-interest and doing for hire, so that it is one thing to tolerate action from those who act on their own and it is another thing to permit the same action to be promoted for a price. * * *

NEW ORLEANS v. DUKES

427 U.S. 297, 96 S.Ct. 2513, 49 L.Ed.2d 511 (1976).

PER CURIAM.

[A 1972 New Orleans ordinance banned all pushcart food vendors in the French Quarter ("Vieux Carre") except those who had continuously operated there for eight or more years. Two vendors had done so for twenty or more years and qualified under the "grandfather clause." Appellee, who had operated a pushcart for only two years, attacked the ordinance.]

When local economic regulation is challenged solely as violating the Equal Protection Clause, this Court consistently defers to legislative determinations as to the desirability of particular statutory discriminations. Unless a classification trammels fundamental personal rights or is drawn upon inherently suspect distinctions such as race, religion, or alienage, our decisions presume the constitutionality of the statutory discriminations and require only that the classification challenged be rationally related to a legitimate state interest. States are accorded wide latitude in the regulation of their local economies under their police powers, and rational distinctions may be made with substantially less than mathematical exactitude. Legislatures may implement their program step by step in such economic areas, adopting regulations that only partially ameliorate a perceived evil and deferring complete elimination of the evil to future regulations. See, e.g., *Williamson v. Lee Optical Co.*a In short, the judiciary may not sit as a superlegislature to judge the wisdom or desirability of legislative policy determinations made

---

a. In *Lee Optical,* Ch. 5, Sec. 3, a statute that otherwise prohibited the fitting of eyeglasses without a prescription exempted businesses that sold ready-to-wear glasses. The Court found no violation of equal protection: "Evils in the same field may be of different dimensions and proportions, requiring different remedies. Or so the legislature may think. Or the reform may take one step at a time, addressing itself to the phase of the problem which seems most acute to the legislative mind. The legislature may select one phase of one field and apply a remedy there, neglecting the others. [For] all this record shows, the ready-to-wear branch of this business may not loom large in Oklahoma or may present problems of regulation distinct from the other branch."

in areas that neither affect fundamental rights nor proceed along suspect lines; in the local economic sphere, it is only the invidious discrimination, the wholly arbitrary act, which cannot stand consistently with the Fourteenth Amendment. See, e.g., *Ferguson v. Skrupa.*5

[New Orleans'] classification rationally furthers the purpose which [the] city had identified as its objective in enacting the provision, that is, as a means "to preserve the appearance and custom valued by the Quarter's residents and attractive to tourists." The legitimacy of that objective is obvious. The City Council plainly could further that objective by making the reasoned judgment that street peddlers and hawkers tend to interfere with the charm and beauty of an historic area [and] that to ensure the economic vitality of that area, such businesses should be substantially curtailed in the Vieux Carre, if not totally banned.

It is suggested that the "grandfather provision" [was] a totally arbitrary and irrational method of achieving the city's purpose. But rather than proceeding by the immediate and absolute abolition of all pushcart food vendors, the city could rationally [decide] that newer businesses were less likely to have built up substantial reliance interests in continued operation in the Vieux Carre and that the two vendors who qualified under the "grandfather clause" [had] themselves become part of the distinctive character and charm that distinguishes the Vieux Carre. We cannot say that these judgments so lack rationality that they constitute a constitutionally impermissible denial of equal protection. * * *

Reversed.

JUSTICE MARSHALL concurs in the judgment.

JUSTICE STEVENS took no part in [the] case.

————

NEW YORK CITY TRANSIT AUTH. v. BEAZER, 440 U.S. 568 (1979), per STEVENS, J., upheld the exclusion of all methadone users from any Transit Authority (TA) employment. It reversed the federal district court's conclusion that, because about 75% of "patients who have been on methadone maintenance for at least a year are free from illicit drug use" and because the exclusion applied to non-safety sensitive jobs, it had "no rational relation to the demands of the job to be performed": "[T]he District Court * * * concluded that employment in nonsensitive jobs could not be denied to methadone users who had progressed satisfactorily with their treatment for one year, and who, when examined individually, satisfied the TA's employment criteria. In short, having recognized that the disparate treatment of methadone users simply because they are methadone users is permissible [the] District Court construed the Equal Protection Clause as requiring TA to adopt additional and more precise special rules for that special class.

"But any special rule short of total exclusion that TA might adopt is likely to be less precise—and will assuredly be more costly—than the one that it currently enforces. If eligibility is marked at any intermediate point—whether after one year of treatment or later—the classification will inevitably discriminate between employees or applicants equally or almost equally apt to achieve full recovery. [By]

---

5. *Ferguson* [Ch. 5, Sec. 3] presented an analogous situation. There, a Kansas statute excepted lawyers from the prohibition of a statute making it a misdemeanor for any per-son to engage in the business of debt adjusting. We held that the exception of lawyers was not a denial of [equal protection].

contrast, the 'no drugs' policy now enforced by TA is supported by the legitimate inference that as long as a treatment program (or other drug use) continues, a degree of uncertainty persists.* * *

"[T]he District Court's conclusion was that TA's rule is broader than necessary to exclude those methadone users who are not actually qualified to work for TA. We may assume [that] it is probably unwise for a large employer like TA to rely on a general rule instead of individualized consideration of every job applicant. But these assumptions concern matters of personnel policy that do not implicate the principle safeguarded by the Equal Protection Clause. As the District Court recognized, the special classification created by TA's rule serves the general objectives of safety and efficiency. Moreover, the exclusionary line challenged by respondents [does] not circumscribe a class of persons characterized by some unpopular trait or affiliation, it does not create or reflect any special likelihood of bias on the part of the ruling majority. Under these circumstances, it is of no constitutional significance that the degree of rationality is not as great with respect to certain ill-defined subparts of the classification as it is with respect to the classification as a whole."a

WHITE, J., joined by Marshall, J., dissented: Both courts below "found that those who have been maintained on methadone for at least a year and who are free from the use of illicit drugs and alcohol can easily be identified through normal personnel procedures and, for a great many jobs, are as employable as and present no more risk than applicants from the general population. [On] the facts as found [one] can reach the Court's result only if [equal protection] imposes no real constraint at all in this situation. * * *

"Of course, the District Court's order permitting total exclusion of all methadone users maintained for less than one year, whether successfully or not, would still exclude some employables and would to this extent be overinclusive. [But although] many of those who have not been successfully maintained for a year are employable, as a class they, unlike the protected group, are not as employable as the general population. Thus, even assuming the bad risks could be identified, serving the end of employability would require unusual efforts to determine those more likely to revert. But that legitimate secondary goal is not fulfilled by excluding the protected [class]. Accordingly, the rule's classification of successfully maintained persons as dispositively different from the general population is left without any justification and, with its irrationality and invidiousness thus uncovered, must fall before the Equal Protection Clause."

White, J., added in a footnote: "I have difficulty also with the Court's easy conclusion that the challenged rule was '[q]uite plainly' not motivated 'by any special animus against a specific group of persons.' Heroin addiction is a special problem of the poor, and the addict population is composed largely of racial minorities that the Court has previously recognized as politically powerless and historical subjects of majoritarian neglect. Persons on methadone maintenance have few interests in common with members of the majority, and thus are unlikely to have their interests protected, or even considered, in governmental decisionmaking. Indeed, petitioners stipulated that '[o]ne of the reasons for [the] drug policy is the fact that [petitioners] feel[ ] an adverse public reaction would

---

a. See also *Vance v. Bradley*, 440 U.S. 93 (1979), per White, J., (sustaining mandatory retirement at age 60 for federal Foreign Service personnel), conceding that the classification was "to some extent both under-and over-inclusive" but holding that "perfection is by no means required. [In] an equal protection case of this type, [those] challenging the legislative judgment must convince the court that the legislative facts on which the classification is apparently based could not reasonably be conceived to be true by the governmental decisionmaker."

result if it were generally known that [petitioners] employed persons with a prior history of drug abuse, including persons participating in methadone maintenance programs.' It is hard for me to reconcile that stipulation of animus against former addicts with our past holdings that 'a bare [desire] to harm a politically unpopular group cannot constitute a *legitimate* governmental interest.' *U.S. Dept. of Agriculture v. Moreno*, [p. 677 infra]. On the other hand, the afflictions to which petitioners are more sympathetic, such as alcoholism and mental illness, are shared by both white and black, rich and poor.

"Some weight should also be given to the history of the rule. Petitioners admit that it was not the result of a reasoned policy decision and stipulated that they had never studied the ability of those on methadone maintenance to perform petitioners' jobs. Petitioners are not directly accountable to the public, are not the type of official body that normally makes legislative judgments of fact such as those relied upon by the majority today, and are by nature more concerned with business efficiency than with other public policies for which they have no direct responsibility. Both the State and City of New York, which do exhibit those democratic characteristics, hire persons in methadone programs for similar jobs.

"These factors together strongly point to a conclusion of invidious discrimination. * * * "

UNITED STATES R.R. RETIREMENT BD. v. FRITZ

449 U.S. 166, 101 S.Ct. 453, 66 L.Ed.2d 368 (1980).

JUSTICE REHNQUIST delivered the opinion of the Court.

The United States District Court [held violative of the "equal protection component of the Fifth Amendment" § 231b(h)] of the Railroad Retirement Act of 1974. [Under the] Act's predecessor statute, a person who worked for both railroad and nonrailroad employers and who qualified for railroad retirement benefits and social security benefits received retirement benefits under both systems and an accompanying "windfall" benefit. [Congress] determined to place the system on a "sound financial basis" by eliminating future accruals of those benefits. Congress also enacted various transitional provisions [which] expressly preserved windfall benefits for some classes of employees.

* * * First, those employees who lacked the requisite 10 years of railroad employment to qualify for railroad retirement benefits as of January 1, 1975, the changeover date, would have their retirement benefits computed under the new system and would not receive any windfall benefit. Second, those individuals already retired and already receiving dual benefits [would] continue to receive a windfall benefit. Third, those employees who had qualified for both railroad and social security benefits as of the changeover date, but who had not yet retired as of that date (and thus were not yet receiving dual benefits), were entitled to windfall benefits if they had (1) performed some railroad service in 1974 or (2) had a "current connection" with the railroad industry as of December 31, 1974,[6] or (3) completed 25 years of railroad service as of December 31, 1974. * * *

Thus, an individual who, as of the changeover date, was unretired and had 11 years of railroad employment and sufficient nonrailroad employment to qualify for social security benefits is eligible for the full windfall amount if he worked for the railroad in 1974 or had a current connection with the railroad as of December 31, 1974, or his later retirement date. But an unretired individual with 24 years of

---

6. The term "current connection" is defined [to] mean, in general, employment in the railroad industry in 12 of the preceding 30 calendar months.

railroad service and sufficient nonrailroad service to qualify for social security benefits is not eligible for a full windfall amount unless he worked for the railroad in 1974, or had a current connection with the railroad as of December 31, 1974 or his later retirement date. * * *

The District Court agreed with appellees that a differentiation based solely on whether an employee was "active" in the railroad business as of 1974 was not "rationally related" to the congressional purposes of insuring the solvency of the railroad retirement system and protecting vested benefits. We disagree and reverse.

[The] plain language of § 231b(h) marks the beginning and end of our inquiry. There Congress determined that some of those who in the past received full windfall benefits would not continue to do so. Because Congress could have eliminated windfall benefits for all classes of employees, it is not constitutionally impermissible for Congress to have drawn lines between groups of employees for the purpose of phasing out those benefits. *Dukes.*

The only remaining question is whether Congress achieved its purpose in a patently arbitrary or irrational way. [Congress] could properly conclude that persons who had actually acquired statutory entitlement to windfall benefits while still employed in the railroad industry had a greater equitable claim to those benefits than the members of appellees' class who were no longer in railroad employment when they became eligible for dual benefits. [Furthermore,] Congress could assume that those who had a current connection with the railroad industry when the Act was passed in 1974, or who returned to the industry before their retirement, were more likely than those who had left the industry prior to 1974 and who never returned, to be among the class of persons who pursue careers in the railroad industry, the class for whom the Railroad Retirement Act was designed.

Where, as here, there are plausible reasons for Congress' action, our inquiry is at an end. It is, of course, "constitutionally irrelevant whether this reasoning in fact underlay the legislative decision," because this Court has never insisted that a legislative body articulate its reasons for enacting a statute. This is particularly true where the legislature must necessarily engage in a process of line drawing. The "task of classifying persons for [benefits] inevitably requires that some persons who have an almost equally strong claim to favorite treatment be placed on different sides of the line," *Mathews v. Diaz,* [Sec. 4, III infra], and the fact the line might have been drawn differently at some points is a matter for legislative, rather than judicial consideration.

Finally, we disagree with the District Court's conclusion that Congress was unaware of what it accomplished or that it was misled by the groups that appeared before it. If this test were applied literally to every member of any legislature that ever voted on a law, there would be very few laws which would survive it. The language of the statute is clear, and we have historically assumed that Congress intended what it enacted. To be sure, appellees lost a political battle in which they had a strong interest, but this is neither the first nor the last time that such a result will occur in the legislative forum. * * *a

JUSTICE BRENNAN, with whom JUSTICE MARSHALL joins, dissenting.

[When] faced with a challenge to a legislative classification under the rational basis test, the court should ask, first, what the purposes of the statute are, and second, whether the classification is rationally related to achievement of those purposes. The purposes of the Railroad Retirement Act of 1974 are clear, because

---

a.   Stevens, J., concurred in the judgment.

Congress has commendably stated them in the House and Senate reports accompanying the Act. A section of the reports is entitled "Principal Purpose of the Bill." It notes generally that "[t]he bill provides for a complete restructuring of the Railroad Retirement Act of 1937, and will place it on a sound financial basis," and then states: "Persons who already have vested rights under both the Railroad Retirement and the Social Security systems will in the future be permitted to receive benefits computed under both systems just as is true under existing law."3 Moreover, Congress explained that this purpose was based on considerations of fairness and the legitimate expectations of the retirees. [The] classification at issue here, which deprives some retirees of vested dual benefits that they had earned prior to 1974, directly conflicts with Congress' stated purpose. As such, the classification is not only rationally unrelated to the congressional purpose; it is inimical to it. * * *

A. The Court states that "the plain language of § 231b(h) marks the beginning and end of our inquiry." [Since] the Act deprives appellees of their vested earned dual benefits, the Court apparently assumes that Congress must have *intended* that result. But by presuming purpose from result, the Court reduces analysis to tautology. It may always be said that Congress intended to do what it in fact did. If that were the extent of our analysis, we would find every statute, no matter how arbitrary or irrational, perfectly tailored to achieve its purpose. But equal protection scrutiny under the rational basis test requires the courts first to deduce the independent objectives of the statute, usually from statements of purpose and other evidence in the statute and legislative history, and second to analyze whether the challenged classification rationally furthers achievement of those objectives. The Court's tautological approach will not suffice.

B. The Court analyzes the rationality of § 231b(h) in terms of a justification suggested by Government attorneys, but never adopted by Congress. [But] this Court has frequently recognized that the actual purposes of Congress, rather than the post hoc justifications offered by Government attorneys, must be the primary basis for analysis under the rational basis test. * * *

The Court argues that Congress chose to discriminate against appellees for reasons of equity, [but, as] I have shown, Congress expressed the view that it would be inequitable to deprive any retirees of any portion of the benefits they had been promised and that they had earned under prior law. The Court is unable to cite even one statement in the legislative history by a Representative or Senator that makes the equitable judgment it imputes to Congress. * * *

[L]abor representatives demanded that benefits be increased for their current members, the cost to be offset by divesting the appellee class of a portion of the benefits they had earned under prior law. [In] fact, the [management and labor representatives] and Railroad Retirement Board members who testified at congressional hearings perpetuated the inaccurate impression that all retirees with earned vested dual benefits under prior law would retain their benefits unchanged. * * *

Of course, a misstatement or several misstatements by witnesses before Congress would not ordinarily lead us to conclude that Congress misapprehended what it was doing. In this instance, however, where complex legislation was drafted by outside parties and Congress relied on them to explain it, where the misstatements are frequent and unrebutted, and where no Member of Congress

---

3. Several pages later, the reports make clear that persons with vested rights to earned dual benefits would retain [them]. Only in technical discussions and in the section-by- section analyses do the reports reflect the actual consequences of the Act on the appellee class. * * *

can be found to have stated the effect of the classification correctly, we are entitled to suspect that Congress may have been misled. As the District Court found: "At no time during the hearings did Congress even give a hint that it understood that the bill by its language eliminated an earned benefit of plaintiff's class."

Therefore, I do not think that this classification was rationally related to an *actual* governmental purpose.

[Because] the Court is willing to accept a tautological analysis of congressional purpose, an assertion of "equitable" considerations contrary to the expressed judgment of Congress, and a classification patently unrelated to achievement of the identified purpose, it succeeds in effectuating neither equity nor congressional intent. * * *

Despite the highly deferential approach exhibited in most equal protection cases involving rational basis review, there are some notable exceptions, including a few cases in which the Court has found that the legislature acted for an impermissible purpose. UNITED STATES DEPT. OF AGRICULTURE v. MORENO, 413 U.S. 528 (1973), per BRENNAN, J., applying " 'traditional' equal protection analysis," held that a provision of the Food Stamp Act—excluding "any household containing an individual who is unrelated to any other member of the household"—was "wholly without any rational basis": The exclusion "is clearly irrelevant to the stated purposes of the Act [to] raise levels of nutrition among low-income households. [Thus], the challenged classification must rationally further some legitimate governmental interest other than those specifically stated in the Congressional 'Declaration of Policy.'

"[The] little legislative history [that] does exist" indicates that the provision "was intended to [prevent] 'hippie communes' from participating in the food stamp program. [But equal protection] at the very least mean[s] that a bare congressional desire to harm a politically unpopular group cannot constitute a *legitimate* governmental interest." Nor does the classification "operate so as rationally to further the prevention of fraud" because, under the Act, "two *unrelated* persons living together" may "avoid the 'unrelated person' exclusion simply by altering their living arrangements so as [to] create two separate 'households,' both of which are eligible for assistance. [Thus], in practical operation, the [provision] excludes from participation [not] those persons who are 'likely to abuse the program' but, rather, only those persons who are so desperately in need of aid that they cannot even afford to alter their living arrangements so as to retain their eligibility."

DOUGLAS, J., concurred: "I could not say that [this] provision has no 'rational' relation to control of fraud. We deal here, however, with the right of association, protected by the First Amendment." Thus, the classification "can be sustained only on a showing of a 'compelling' governmental interest."

REHNQUIST, J., joined by Burger, C.J., dissented: "Congress attacked the problem with a rather blunt instrument, [b]ut I do not think it is unreasonable for Congress to conclude that the basic unit which it was willing to support [with] food stamps is some variation on the family as we know it—a household consisting of related individuals. This unit provides a guarantee which is not provided by households containing unrelated individuals that the household exists for some purpose other than to collect federal food stamps.

"Admittedly, [the] limitation will make ineligible many households which have not been formed for the purpose of collecting federal food stamps, and will [not] wholly deny food stamps to those households which may have been formed in large part to take advantage of the program. But, as the Court concedes, 'traditional' equal protection analysis does not require that every classification be drawn with precise mathematical nicety."

———

Other cases finding equal protection violations, purportedly pursuant to a rational basis test, based on judicial findings that the state acted for impermissible purposes are *Romer v. Evans*, Sec. 4, II infra (involving "animus" against homosexuals), and *Cleburne v. Cleburne Living Center, Inc.*, Sec. 4, III infra (invalidating action predicated on "irrational prejudice against the mentally retarded"). See also *Village of Willowbrook v. Olech*, 528 U.S. 562 (2000) (finding that a plaintiff constituting a "class of one" could bring an actionable equal protection complaint based on allegations that "she has been treated differently from others similarly situated" and declining to consider an alternative theory of "subjective ill will").**b**

———

Even apart from cases involving impermissible purposes, there are at least a few modern cases in which the Court, although employing the traditional "rational basis" standard, has held laws violative of equal protection.

For example, ALLEGHENY PITTSBURGH COAL CO. v. COUNTY COMM'N, 488 U.S. 336 (1989), per REHNQUIST, C.J., unanimously found an equal protection violation when a West Virginia county tax assessor "valued petitioners' real property on the basis of its recent purchase price, but made only minor modifications in the assessments of land which had not been recently sold," producing the result that "petitioners' property has been assessed at roughly 8 to 35 times more than comparable neighboring property, and these discrepancies have continued for more than 10 years with little change." The Court held that the county assessor's practice was not "rationally related" to West Virginia's rule "that all property of the kind held by petitioners shall be taxed at a rate uniform throughout the state according to its estimated market value."

But compare NORDLINGER v. HAHN, 505 U.S. 1 (1992), per BLACKMUN, J., which held that California's "acquisition value" system for initially assessing property (Proposition 13) "rationally furthers the State's ['legitimate'] interests in neighborhood stability and the protection of property owners' reliance interests." As in *Allegheny*, Proposition 13 "resulted in dramatic disparities in taxation of properties of comparable value." But "the Equal Protection Clause is satisfied so long as there is a plausible policy reason for the classification, *Fritz*, [and] *Allegheny* was the rare case where the facts precluded any plausible inference that the reason for the unequal assessment practice was to achieve the benefits of an acquisition-value tax scheme. By contrast, Proposition 13 was enacted precisely to achieve the benefits."

b. But see *Engquist v. Oregon Dept. of Agriculture*, 553 U.S. 591 (2008) (holding that "the class-of-one theory of equal protection does not apply in the public employment context" because it would be untenable if "any personnel action in which a wronged employee [could] conjure up a claim of differential treatment" provided the basis for a constitutional case).

THOMAS, J., concurred in upholding Proposition 13 but would have "confronted [*Allegheny*] directly": "Even if the assessor did violate West Virginia law, she would not have violated the Equal Protection Clause. A violation of state law does not by itself constitute a violation of the Federal Constitution."

SECTION 2. RACE AND ETHNIC ANCESTRY

I. HISTORICAL BACKGROUND

Racism and practices of race discrimination are deeply embedded in American constitutional history. At least six of the thirteen original colonies—Maryland, Delaware, Virginia, the Carolinas, and Georgia—gave express legal support to slavery. At the Constitutional Convention, the existence of slavery was accepted as a political fact; there was no serious discussion of the Constitution forbidding slavery. On the contrary, at least three provisions of the original Constitution recognized and arguably countenanced slavery: Art. I, § 2, which based a state's representation in the House of Representatives on its free population and three-fifths of "all other Persons" within its territory; Art. 1, § 9, which barred Congress from abolishing the slave trade before 1808; and Art. 4, § 2, which provided that "no Person held to Service or Labor" under the laws of one state could escape that status upon flight to another state but, on the contrary, "shall be delivered up on the Claim of the Party to whom such Service or Labour may be due." Even in many "free" states, at the time of the Constitutional Convention and thereafter African–Americans were denied the vote, excluded from jury service, and separated from whites in most public conveyances.

In the antebellum years, the Supreme Court decided major cases involving the African slave trade,[a] the return of fugitive slaves,[b] slavery in the federal territories, and the rights of slaves in transit through free states—virtually all in a manner accepting slavery's basic lawfulness. The most notorious of the antebellum decisions involving slavery came in the *Dred Scott* case.

The plaintiff/appellant in DRED SCOTT v. SANDFORD, 60 U.S. (19 How.) 393 (1857), was born in slavery in Virginia but, in the company of his master, later traveled in the free state of Illinois and the free territory of Wisconsin, where slavery was prohibited by the Missouri Compromise. Following his return to Missouri, a slave state, Dred Scott was sold as a slave to Sandford. Scott thereupon brought suit against Sandford in federal court, arguing that he had attained his freedom under the law of Illinois and the law of Wisconsin (the "free" status of which was established by the Missouri Compromise). Scott predicated his claim of federal jurisdiction on diversity of citizenship, alleging that he was a citizen of Missouri and Sandford a citizen of New York. The Court, per TANEY, C.J., dismissed the suit. It held that Scott was incapable of becoming a "citizen" of Missouri eligible to invoke federal diversity jurisdiction; that Congress's effort in the Missouri Compromise to abolish slavery in federal territories was unconstitutional; and that whatever Scott's status in Illinois, after he had returned volun-

a. See, e.g., *The Antelope,* 23 U.S. (10 Wheat.) 66 (1825) (recognizing the right of foreigners to engage in the slave trade, if the laws of their nation permitted them to do so, but upholding prosecutions against American slave traders).

b. See *Prigg v. Pennsylvania,* 41 U.S. (16 Pet.) 539 (1842) (upholding the federal Fugitive Slave Act of 1793, which established federal procedures for the capture and return of runaway slaves, and invalidating a Pennsylvania law creating impediments to recapture of slaves).

tarily to Missouri, his status was governed by the law of Missouri, which treated him as a slave:

"The question before us is, whether the class of persons described in the plea in abatement [are 'citizens' capable of invoking federal jurisdiction based on diversity of citizenship]. We think they are not, and that they are not included, and were not intended to be included, under the word 'citizens' in the Constitution, and can therefore claim none of the rights and privileges which that instrument provides for and secures to citizens of the United States. On the contrary, they were at that time considered as a subordinate and inferior class of beings, who had been subjugated by the dominant race, and, whether emancipated or not, yet remained subject to their authority, and had no rights or privileges but such as those who held the power and the Government might choose to grant them. [It] is difficult at this day to realize the state of public opinion in relation to that unfortunate race, which prevailed in the civilized and enlightened portions of the world at the time of the Declaration of Independence, and when the Constitution of the United States was framed and adopted. But the public history of every European nation displays it in a manner too plain to be mistaken. [Negroes] had for more than a century before been regarded as beings of inferior order, and altogether unfit to associate with the white race, either in social or political relations; and so far inferior, that they had no rights which the white man was bound to respect; and that the negro might justly and lawfully be reduced to slavery for his benefit. He was bought and sold, and treated as an ordinary article of merchandise and traffic, whenever a profit could be made by it. This opinion was at that time fixed and universal in the civilized portion of the white race. It was regarded as an axiom in morals as well as in politics, which no one thought of disputing, or supposed to be open to dispute; and men in every grade and position in society daily and habitually acted upon it in their private pursuits, as well as in matters of public concern, without doubting for a moment the correctness of this opinion.

"But it is too clear for dispute, that the enslaved African race were not intended to be included, and formed no part of the people who framed and adopted this declaration; for if the language, as understood in that day, would embrace them, the conduct of the distinguished men who framed the Declaration of Independence would have been utterly and flagrantly inconsistent with the principles they asserted; and instead of the sympathy of mankind, to which they so confidently appealed, they would have deserved and received universal rebuke and reprobation.

"Yet the men who framed this declaration were great men—high in literary acquirements—high in their sense of honor, and incapable of asserting principles inconsistent with those on which they were acting. They perfectly understood the meaning of the language they used, and how it would be understood by others; and they knew that it would not in any part of the civilized world be supposed to embrace the negro race, which, by common consent, had been excluded from civilized Governments and the family of nations, and doomed to slavery. They spoke and acted according to the then established doctrines and principles, and in the ordinary language of the day, no one misunderstood them. The unhappy black race were separated from the white by indelible marks, and laws long before established, and were never thought of or spoken of except as property, and when the claims of the owner or the profit of the trader were supposed to need protection. * * *

"No one, we presume, supposes that any change in public opinion or feeling, in relation to this unfortunate race, in the civilized nations of Europe or in this country, should induce the court to give to the words of the Constitution a more liberal construction in their favor than they were intended to bear when the instrument was framed and adopted. Such an argument would be altogether inadmissible in any tribunal called on to interpret it. If any of its provisions are deemed unjust, there is a mode prescribed in the instrument itself by which it may be amended; but while it remains unaltered, it must be construed now as it was understood at the time of its adoption. [Any] other rule of construction would abrogate the judicial character of this court, and make it the mere reflex of the popular opinion or passion of the day. This court was not created by the Constitution for such purposes. Higher and graver trusts have been confided to it, and it must not falter in the path of duty. * * *

"[Nor does Article IV, § 3, cl. 2, which empowers Congress to "make all needful Rules and Regulations respecting the Territory and other Property of the United States," authorize Congress to prohibit slavery in the territories.] These powers, and others, in relation to rights of person, which it is not necessary here to enumerate, are, in express and positive terms, denied to the General Government; and the rights of private property have been guarded with equal care. Thus the rights of property are united with the rights of persons, and placed on the same ground by the fifth amendment to the Constitution, which provides that no person shall be deprived of life, liberty, and property, without due process of law. And an act of Congress which deprives a citizen of the United States of his liberty or property merely because he came himself or brought his property into a particular Territory of the United States, and who had committed no offence against the laws, could hardly be dignified with the name of due process of law.

"[The] powers of the Government, and the rights of the citizen under it, are positive and practical regulations plainly written down. [It] has no power over the person or property of a citizen but what the citizens of the United States have granted. And no laws or usages of other nations, or reasoning of statesmen or jurists upon the relations of master and slave, can enlarge the powers of the Government, or take from the citizens the rights they have reserved. And if the Constitution recognizes the right of property of the master in a slave, and makes no distinction between that description of property and other property owned by a citizen, no tribunal, acting under the authority of the United States, whether it be legislative, executive, or judicial, has a right to draw such a distinction, or deny to it the benefit of the provisions and guarantees which have been provided for the protection of private property against the encroachments of the Government.

"Now, as we have already said in an earlier part of this opinion, upon a different point, the right of property in a slave is distinctly and expressly affirmed in the Constitution. The right to traffic in it, like an ordinary article of merchandise and property, was guarantied to the citizens of the United States, in every State that might desire it, for twenty years. And the Government in express terms is pledged to protect it in all future time, if the slave escapes from his owner. This is done in plain words—too plain to be misunderstood. And no word can be found in the Constitution which gives Congress a greater power over slave property, or which entitles property of that kind to less protection than property of any other description. The only power conferred is the power coupled with the duty of guarding and protecting the owner in his rights.

"Upon these considerations, it is the opinion of the court that the act of Congress which prohibited a citizen from holding and owning property of this kind in the territory of the United States north of the line therein mentioned, is not warranted by the Constitution, and is therefore void; and that neither Dred Scott himself, nor any of his family, were made free by being carried into this territory;

even if they had been carried there by the owner, with the intention of becoming a permanent resident.''

II. DISCRIMINATION AGAINST RACIAL AND ETHNIC MINORITIES

The "evil to be remedied" by the Equal Protection Clause, declared the *Slaughter-House Cases*, was "the existence of laws in the States where the newly emancipated negroes resided, which discriminated with gross injustice and hardship against them as a class." STRAUDER v. WEST VIRGINIA, 100 U.S. (10 Otto) 303 (1880)—the first post-Civil War race discrimination case to reach the Court—per STRONG, J., invalidated the state murder conviction of an African-American on the ground that state law forbade blacks from serving on grand or petit juries. In the course of its opinion, the Court observed that "the true spirit and meaning" of the Civil War amendments was "securing to a race recently emancipated [the] enjoyment of all the civil rights that under the law are enjoyed by [whites]. What is [equal protection but] that all persons, whether colored or white, shall stand equal before the laws of the States, and, in regard to the colored race, for whose protection the amendment was primarily designed, that no discrimination shall be made against them by law because of their color? The words of the amendment [contain] a positive immunity or right, most valuable to the colored race,—the right to exemption from unfriendly legislation against them distinctively as colored,—exemption from legal discriminations, implying inferiority in civil society, lessening the security of their enjoyment of the rights which others enjoy, and discriminations which are steps towards reducing them to the condition of a subject race.

"That the West Virginia statute respecting juries [is] such a discrimination ought not to be doubted. [And if] in those States where the colored people constitute a majority of the entire population a law should be enacted excluding all white men from jury service, [we] apprehend no one would be heard to claim that it would not be a denial to white men of the equal protection of the laws. Nor if a law should be passed excluding all naturalized Celtic Irishmen, would there be any doubt of its inconsistency with the spirit of the amendment. * * *

"We do not say that within the limits from which it is not excluded by the amendment a State may not prescribe the qualifications of its jurors, and in so doing make discriminations. It may confine the selection to males, to freeholders, to citizens, to persons within certain ages, or to persons having educational qualifications. We do not believe the Fourteenth Amendment was ever intended to prohibit this. Looking at its history, it is clear it had no such purpose. Its aim was against discrimination because of race or color."

PLESSY v. FERGUSON

163 U.S. 537, 16 S.Ct. 1138, 41 L.Ed. 256 (1896).

JUSTICE BROWN delivered the opinion of the Court.

[An 1890 Louisiana law required that railway passenger cars have "equal but separate accommodations for the white, and colored races." Plessy, alleging that he "was seven-eighths Caucasian and one-eighth African blood; that the mixture of colored blood was not discernible in him; and that he was entitled to every right [of] the white race," was arrested for refusing to vacate a seat in a coach for whites.]

That [the challenged statute] does not conflict with the Thirteenth Amendment [is] too clear for argument. Slavery implies involuntary servitude,—a state of bondage * * *. This amendment [was] regarded by the statesmen of that day as insufficient to protect the colored race from certain laws [imposing] onerous disabilities and burdens, and curtailing their rights in the pursuit of life, liberty, and property to such an extent that their freedom was of little value; [and] the Fourteenth Amendment was devised to meet this exigency. * * *

The object of the amendment was undoubtedly to enforce the absolute equality of the two races before the law, but, in the nature of things, it could not have been intended to abolish distinctions based upon color, or to enforce social, as distinguished from political equality, or a commingling of the two races upon terms unsatisfactory to either. Laws permitting, and even requiring, their separation, in places where they are liable to be brought into contact do not necessarily imply the inferiority of either race to the other, and have been generally, if not universally, recognized as within the competency of the state legislatures in the exercise of their police power. The most common instance of this is connected with the establishment of separate schools for white and colored children, which have been [upheld] even by courts of states where the political rights of the colored race have been longest and most earnestly enforced [citing cases from Mass., Ohio, Mo., Cal., La., N.Y., Ind., and Ky.].

Laws forbidding the intermarriage of the two races may be said in a technical sense to interfere with the freedom of contract, and yet have been universally recognized as within the police power of the state. The distinction between laws interfering with the political equality of the negro and those requiring the separation of the two races in schools, theatres and railway carriages have been frequently drawn by this court. Thus in *Strauder v. West Virginia* it was held that a law of West Virginia [forbidding blacks to serve on juries] was a discrimination which implied a legal inferiority in civil society, which lessened the security of the colored race, and was a step toward reducing them to a condition of servility.

[S]tatutes for the separation of the two races upon public conveyances were held to be constitutional in [federal decisions and cases from Pa., Mich., Ill., Tenn. and N.Y. Almost] directly on point is [a Mississippi case] wherein the railway company was indicted for a violation of a statute of Mississippi, enacting that all railroads carrying passengers should provide equal, but separate, accommodations for the white and colored races. [It is suggested] that the same argument that will justify the state legislature in requiring railways to provide separate accommodations for the two races will also authorize them to require separate cars to be provided for people whose hair is of a certain color, or who are aliens, or who belong to certain nationalities, or to enact laws requiring colored people to walk upon one side of the street, and white people upon the other, or requiring white men's houses to be painted white, and colored men's black, or their vehicles or business signs to be of different colors, upon the theory that one side of the street is as good as the other, or that a house or vehicle of one color is as good as one of another color. The reply to all this is that every exercise of the police power must be reasonable, and extend only to such laws as are enacted in good faith for the promotion of the public good, and not for the annoyance or oppression of a particular class. [In] determining the question of reasonableness, [the state] is at liberty to act with reference to the established usages, customs, and traditions of the people, and with a view to the promotion of their comfort, and the preservation of the public peace and good order. Gauged by this standard, we cannot say [this law] is unreasonable, or more obnoxious to the Fourteenth Amendment than the [acts] requiring separate schools for colored children in the District of Columbia, the constitutionality of which does not seem to have been questioned, or the corresponding acts of state legislatures.

We consider the underlying fallacy of the plaintiff's argument to consist in the assumption that the enforced separation of the two races stamps the colored race with a badge of inferiority. If this be so, it is not by reason of anything found in the act, but solely because the colored race chooses to put that construction upon it. [The] argument also assumes that social prejudices may be overcome by legislation, and that equal rights cannot be secured to the negro except by an enforced commingling of the two races. We cannot accept this proposition. If the two races are to meet upon terms of social equality, it must be the result [of] voluntary consent of individuals. * * * Legislation is powerless to eradicate racial instincts, or to abolish distinctions based upon physical differences, and the attempt to do so can only result in accentuating the difficulties of the present situation. If the civil and political rights of both races be equal, one cannot be inferior to the other civilly or politically. If one race be inferior to the other socially, the Constitution of the United States cannot put them on the same plane. * * *

JUSTICE BREWER did [not] participate in the decision of this case.

JUSTICE HARLAN dissenting.

[No] legislative body or judicial tribunal may have regard to the race of citizens when the civil rights of those citizens are involved. * * *

It was said in argument that the statute of Louisiana does not discriminate against either race, but prescribes a rule applicable alike to white and colored citizens. But [e]very one knows that [it] had its origin in the purpose, not so much to exclude white persons from railroad cars occupied by blacks, as to exclude colored people from coaches occupied by or assigned to white persons. [The] fundamental objection, therefore, to the statute is that it interferes with the personal freedom of citizens. * * *

The white race deems itself to be the dominant race in this country. And so it is, in prestige, in achievements, in education, in wealth, and in power. So, I doubt not, it will continue to be for all time, if it remains true to its great heritage, and holds fast to the principles of constitutional liberty. But in view of the constitution, in the eye of the law, there is in this country no superior, dominant, ruling class of citizens. There is no caste here. Our constitution is color-blind * * *.

In my opinion, the judgment this day rendered will, in time, prove to be quite as pernicious as the decision made by this tribunal in the *Dred Scott Case.* [What] can more certainly arouse race hate, what more certainly create and perpetuate a feeling of distrust between these races, than state enactments which, in fact, proceed on the ground that colored citizens are so inferior and degraded that they cannot be allowed to sit in public coaches occupied by white citizens? [The] thin disguise of "equal" accommodations for passengers in railroad coaches will not mislead any one, nor atone for the wrong this day done. * * *

I do not deem it necessary to review the decisions of state courts to which reference was made in argument. Some [are] inapplicable, because rendered prior to the adoption of the last amendments of the [Constitution]. Others were made at a time [when] race prejudice was, practically, the supreme law of the land. Those decisions cannot be guides in the era introduced by the recent amendments of the supreme law, which established universal civil freedom * * *.

KOREMATSU v. UNITED STATES

323 U.S. 214, 65 S.Ct. 193, 89 L.Ed. 194 (1944).

JUSTICE BLACK delivered the opinion of the Court.

[Following the Japanese attack on Pearl Harbor, President Franklin Roosevelt signed Executive Order 9066, which gave military officials the legal authority to exclude any or all persons from designated areas on the west coast in order to insure against sabotage and espionage. Congress implicitly ratified the Executive Order by providing that the violation of an implementing order by a military commander constituted a misdemeanor punishable by fine or imprisonment. Under the authority of the Executive Order, the War Relocation Authority subjected all persons of Japanese ancestry on the west coast to a curfew, excluded them from their homes, detained them in assembly centers, and then evacuated them to "relocation centers" in California, Idaho, Utah, Arizona, Wyoming, Colorado, and Arkansas. By the end of 1942, roughly 112,000 persons—over 65,000 of whom were U.S. citizens—had been involuntarily removed to relocation centers.]

The petitioner, an American citizen of Japanese descent, was convicted in a federal district court for remaining in San Leandro, California, a "Military Area," contrary to Civilian Exclusion Order No. 34 of the Commanding General of the Western Command, U.S. Army, which directed that after May 9, 1942, all persons of Japanese ancestry should be excluded from that area. No question was raised as to petitioner's loyalty to the United States. * * *

[A]ll legal restrictions which curtail the civil rights of a single racial group are immediately suspect. That is not to say that all such restrictions are unconstitutional. It is to say that courts must subject them to the most rigid scrutiny. Pressing public necessity may sometimes justify the existence of such restrictions; racial antagonism never can. * * *

Exclusion Order No. 34 [was] one of a number of military orders. [In] *Hirabayashi v. United States,* 320 U.S. 81 (1943), we sustained a conviction [for] violation of [a] curfew order [applicable only to persons of Japanese ancestry as] an exercise of the power [to] take steps necessary to prevent espionage and sabotage in an area threatened by Japanese attack.

In the light of the principles we announced in the *Hirabayashi* case, we are unable to conclude that it was beyond the war power of Congress and the Executive to exclude those of Japanese ancestry from the West Coast war area at the time they did. [Nothing] short of apprehension by the proper military authorities of the gravest imminent danger to the public safety can constitutionally justify either. But exclusion from a threatened area, no less than curfew, has a definite and close relationship to the prevention of espionage and sabotage. * * *

Here, as in *Hirabayashi,* "we cannot reject as unfounded the judgment of the military authorities and of Congress that there were disloyal members of that population, whose number and strength could not be precisely and quickly ascertained. We cannot say that the war-making branches of the Government did not have ground for believing that in a critical hour such persons could not readily be isolated and separately dealt with, and constituted a menace to the national defense and safety, which demanded that prompt and adequate measures be taken to guard against it."

[This] answers the contention that the exclusion was in the nature of group punishment based on antagonism to those of Japanese origin. That there were members of the group who retained loyalties to Japan has been confirmed by investigations made subsequent to the exclusion. Approximately five thousand American citizens of Japanese ancestry refused to swear unqualified allegiance to the United States [and] several thousand evacuees requested repatriation to Japan.

[H]ardships are part of war, and war is an aggregation of hardships. [E]xclusion of large groups of citizens from their homes, except under circumstances of direst emergency and peril, is inconsistent with our basic governmental institutions. But when under conditions of modern warfare our shores are threatened by hostile forces, the power to protect must be commensurate with the threatened danger. * * *

It is said that we are dealing here with the case of imprisonment of a citizen in a concentration camp solely because of his ancestry, without evidence or inquiry concerning his loyalty and good disposition towards the United States. [But] we are dealing specifically with nothing but an exclusion order. To cast this case into outlines of racial prejudice, without reference to the real military dangers which were presented, merely confuses the issue. Korematsu was not excluded from the Military Area because of hostility to him or his race. He was excluded because we are at war with the Japanese Empire, because the properly constituted military authorities feared an invasion of our West Coast and felt constrained to take proper security measures, because they decided that the military urgency of the situation demanded that all citizens of Japanese ancestry be segregated from the West Coast temporarily, and finally, because Congress, reposing its confidence in this time of war in our military leaders—as inevitably it must—determined that they should have the power to do just this. There was evidence of disloyalty on the part of some, the military authorities considered the need for action was great, and time was short. We cannot—by availing ourselves of the calm perspective of hindsight—now say that at that time these actions were unjustified.

Affirmed.

Justice Frankfurter [who joined the Court's opinion], concurring.

[To] find that the Constitution does not forbid the military measures now complained of does not carry with it approval of that which Congress and the Executive did. That is their business, not ours.

Justice Murphy, dissenting.

[T]he exclusion, either temporarily or permanently, of all persons with Japanese blood in their veins [must] rely for its reasonableness upon the assumption that *all* persons of Japanese ancestry may have a dangerous tendency to commit sabotage and espionage and [it] is difficult to believe that reason, logic or experience could be marshalled in support of such an assumption. [The] reasons appear, instead, to be largely an accumulation of much of the misinformation, half-truths and insinuations that for years have been directed against Japanese Americans by people with racial and economic prejudices—the same people who have been among the foremost advocates of the evacuation. A military judgment based upon such racial and sociological considerations is not entitled to the great weight ordinarily given the judgments based upon strictly military considerations. Especially is this so when every charge relative to race, religion, culture, geographical location, and legal and economic status has been substantially discredited by independent studies made by experts in these matters. * * *

Moreover, there was no adequate proof that the FBI and the military and naval intelligence services did not have the espionage and sabotage situation well in hand during this long period. Nor is there any denial of the fact that not one person of Japanese ancestry was accused or convicted of espionage or sabotage after Pearl Harbor while they were still free, a fact which is some evidence of the loyalty of the vast majority of these individuals and of the effectiveness of the established methods of combatting these evils. It seems incredible that under these circumstances it would have been impossible to hold loyalty hearings for the mere 112,000 persons involved—or at least for the 70,000 American citizens— especially when a large part of this number represented children and elderly men and women. Any inconvenience that may have accompanied an attempt to conform to procedural due process cannot be said to justify violations of constitutional [rights].

JUSTICE JACKSON, dissenting.

Korematsu was born on our soil, of parents born in Japan. [Had] Korematsu been one of four—the others being, say, a German alien enemy, an Italian alien enemy, and a citizen of American-born ancestors, convicted of treason but out on parole—only Korematsu's presence would have violated the order. The difference between their innocence and his crime would result, not from anything he did, said, or thought, different than they, but only in that he was born of different racial stock.

Now, if any fundamental assumption underlies our system, it is that guilt is personal and not inheritable. [If] Congress in peace-time legislation should enact such a criminal law, I should suppose this Court would refuse to enforce it.

But [it] would be impracticable and dangerous idealism to expect or insist that each specific military command in an area of probable operations will conform to conventional tests of constitutionality. When an area is so beset that it must be put under military control at all, the paramount consideration is that its measures be successful, rather than legal. * * * I cannot say, from any evidence before me, that the orders of General DeWitt were not reasonably expedient military precautions, nor could I say that they were. But even if they were permissible military procedures, I deny that it follows that they are constitutional. If, as the Court holds, it does follow, then we may as well say that any military order will be constitutional and have done with it.

The limitation under which courts always will labor in examining the necessity for a military order are illustrated by this case. How does the Court know that these orders have a reasonable basis in necessity? No evidence whatever on that subject has been taken by this or any other court. There is sharp controversy as to the credibility of the DeWitt report. So the Court, having no real evidence before it, has no choice but to accept General DeWitt's own unsworn, self-serving statement, untested by any cross-examination, that what he did was reasonable. And thus it will always be when courts try to look into the reasonableness of a military order. * * *

[A] judicial construction of the Due Process Clause that will sustain this order is a far more subtle blow to liberty than the promulgation of the order itself. A military order, however unconstitutional, is not apt to last longer than the military emergency. [But] once a judicial opinion rationalizes [the] Constitution to show that the Constitution sanctions such an order, the Court for all time has validated the principle of racial discrimination in criminal procedure and of transplanting American citizens. The principle then lies about like a loaded weapon ready for the hand of any authority that can bring forward a plausible claim of an urgent need. * * *

My duties as a justice as I see them do not require me to make a military judgment as to whether General DeWitt's evacuation and detention program was a reasonable military necessity. I do not suggest that the courts should have attempted to interfere with the Army in carrying out its task. But I do not think they may be asked to execute a military expedient that has no place in law under the Constitution. I would reverse the judgment and discharge the prisoner.a

BROWN v. BOARD OF EDUCATION

347 U.S. 483, 74 S.Ct. 686, 98 L.Ed. 873 (1954).

CHIEF JUSTICE WARREN delivered the opinion of the Court.

These cases come to us from the States of Kansas, South Carolina, Virginia, and Delaware. * * *

In each of the cases, minors of the Negro race [seek] the aid of the courts in obtaining admission to the public schools of their community on a nonsegregated basis. [In] each of the cases other than the Delaware case, a three-judge federal district court denied relief to the plaintiffs on the so-called "separate but equal" doctrine announced by this Court in [Plessy]. In the Delaware case, the Supreme Court of Delaware adhered to that doctrine, but ordered that the plaintiffs be admitted to the white schools because of their superiority to the Negro schools.

* * * Argument was heard in the 1952 Term, and reargument was heard this Term on certain questions propounded by the Court.

Reargument was largely devoted to the circumstances surrounding the adoption of the Fourteenth Amendment in 1868. It covered exhaustively consideration of the Amendment in Congress, ratification by the states, then existing practices in racial segregation, and the views of proponents and opponents of the Amendment. This discussion and our own investigation convince us that, although these sources cast some light, it is not enough to resolve the problem with which we are faced. At best, they are inconclusive. The most avid proponents of the post-War Amendments undoubtedly intended them to remove all legal distinctions among "all persons born or naturalized in the United States." Their opponents, just as certainly, were antagonistic to both the letter and the spirit of the Amendments and wished them to have the most limited effect. What others in Congress and the state legislatures had in mind cannot be determined with any degree of certainty.

An additional reason for the inconclusive nature of the Amendment's history, with respect to segregated schools, is the status of public education at that time. In the South, the movement toward free common schools, supported by general taxation, had not yet taken hold. Education of white children was largely in the hands of private groups. Education of Negroes was almost nonexistent, and practically all of the race were illiterate. In fact, any education of Negroes was forbidden by law in some states. Today, in contrast, many Negroes have achieved outstanding success in the arts and sciences as well as in the business and professional world. It is true that public school education at the time of the Amendment had advanced further in the North, but the effect of the Amendment on Northern States was generally ignored in the congressional debates. Even in the North, the conditions of public education did not approximate those existing today. The curriculum was usually rudimentary; ungraded schools were common in rural areas; the school term was but three months a year in many states; and compulsory school attendance was virtually unknown. As a consequence, it is not

a. The dissenting opinion of Roberts, J., is omitted.

surprising that there should be so little in the history of the Fourteenth Amendment relating to its intended effect on public education.

In the first cases in this Court construing the Fourteenth Amendment, decided shortly after its adoption, the Court interpreted it as proscribing all state-imposed discriminations against the Negro race.6 The doctrine of "separate but equal" did not make its appearance in this Court until 1896 in *Plessy,* involving not education but transportation. [In] this Court, there have been six cases involving the "separate but equal" doctrine in the field of public education. In *Cumming v. Board of Education,* 175 U.S. 528, and *Gong Lum v. Rice,* 275 U.S. 78, the validity of the doctrine itself was not challenged.8 In more recent cases, all on the graduate school level, inequality was found in that specific benefits enjoyed by white students were denied to Negro students of the same educational qualifications. *Missouri ex rel. Gaines v. Canada,* 305 U.S. 337a; *Sipuel v. Oklahoma,* 332 U.S. 631; *Sweatt v. Painter,* 339 U.S. 629b; *McLaurin v. Oklahoma State Regents,* 339 U.S. 637.c In none of these cases was it necessary to re-examine the doctrine to grant relief to the Negro plaintiff. And in *Sweatt,* the Court expressly reserved decision on the question whether *Plessy* should be held inapplicable to public education.

In the instant cases, that question is directly presented. [T]here are findings below that the Negro and white schools involved have been equalized, or are being equalized, with respect to buildings, curricula, qualifications and salaries of teachers, and other "tangible" factors. Our decision, therefore, cannot turn on merely a comparison of these tangible factors in the Negro and white schools involved in each of the cases. We must look instead to the effect of segregation itself on public education.

In approaching this problem, we cannot turn the clock back to 1868 when the Amendment was adopted, or even to 1896 when *Plessy* was written. We must consider public education in the light of its full development and its present place in American life throughout the Nation. Only in this way can it be determined if segregation in public schools deprives these plaintiffs of the equal protection of the laws.

Today, education is perhaps the most important function of state and local governments. Compulsory school attendance laws and the great expenditures for education both demonstrate our recognition of the importance of education to our

---

6. *Slaughter–House Cases; Strauder.* See also *Virginia v. Rives,* 1879, 100 U.S. 313, 318.

8. In *Cumming,* Negro taxpayers sought an injunction requiring the defendant school board to discontinue the operation of a high school for white children until the board resumed operation of a high school for Negro children. Similarly, in *Gong Lum,* the plaintiff, a child of Chinese descent, contended only that state authorities had misapplied the doctrine by classifying him with Negro children and requiring him to attend a Negro school.

a. *Gaines,* in 1938, invalidated the refusal to admit blacks to the University of Missouri School of Law, despite the state's offer to pay petitioner's tuition at an out-of-state law school pending establishment of a state law school for African–Americans.

b. *Sweatt,* in 1950, required admission of African–Americans to the University of Texas Law School, despite the recent establishment of a state law school for blacks: "In terms of

number of the faculty, variety of courses and opportunity for specialization, size of the student body, scope of the library, availability of law review and similar activities, the University of Texas Law School is superior. [Equally troubling is that the] law school to which Texas is willing to admit petitioner excludes from its student body members of the racial groups which number 85% of the population of the State and include most of the lawyers, witnesses, jurors, judges and other officials with whom petitioner will inevitably be dealing when he becomes a member of the Texas Bar."

c. *McLaurin,* in 1950, held violative of equal protection requirements that African–American graduate students at the University of Oklahoma sit at separate desks adjoining the classrooms and separate tables outside the library reading room, and eat at separate times in the school cafeteria.

democratic society. It is required in the performance of our most basic public responsibilities, even service in the armed forces. It is the very foundation of good citizenship. Today it is a principal instrument in awakening the child to cultural values, in preparing him for later professional training, and in helping him to adjust normally to his environment. In these days, it is doubtful that any child may reasonably be expected to succeed in life if he is denied the opportunity of an education. Such an opportunity, where the state has undertaken to provide it, is a right which must be made available to all on equal terms.

We come then to the question presented: Does segregation of children in public schools solely on the basis of race, even though the physical facilities and other "tangible" factors may be equal, deprive the children of the minority group of equal educational opportunities? We believe that it does.

In *Sweatt,* in finding that a segregated law school for Negroes could not provide them equal educational opportunities, this Court relied in large part on "those qualities which are incapable of objective measurement but which make for greatness in a law school." In *McLaurin,* the Court, in requiring that a Negro admitted to a white graduate school be treated like all other students, again resorted to intangible considerations: "[his] ability to study, to engage in discussions and exchange views with other students, and in general, to learn his profession." Such considerations apply with added force to children in grade and high schools. To separate them from others of similar age and qualifications solely because of their race generates a feeling of inferiority as to their status in the community that may affect their hearts and minds in a way unlikely ever to be undone. The effect of this separation on their educational opportunities was well stated by a finding in the Kansas case by a court which nevertheless felt compelled to rule against the Negro plaintiffs: "Segregation of white and colored children in public schools has a detrimental effect upon the colored children. The impact is greater when it has the sanction of the law; for the policy of separating the races is usually interpreted as denoting the inferiority of the Negro group. A sense of inferiority affects the motivation of a child to learn. Segregation with the sanction of law, therefore, has a tendency to [retard] the educational and mental development of Negro children and to deprive them of some of the benefits they would receive in a racial[ly] integrated school system."[10] Whatever may have been the extent of psychological knowledge at the time of *Plessy,* this finding is amply supported by modern authority.[11] Any language in *Plessy* contrary to this finding is rejected.

We conclude that in the field of public education the doctrine of "separate but equal" has no place. Separate educational facilities are inherently unequal. Therefore, we hold that the plaintiffs and others similarly situated for whom the actions have been brought are, by reason of the segregation complained of, deprived of [equal protection].

10. A similar finding was made in the Delaware case: "I conclude from the testimony that in our Delaware society, State-imposed segregation in education itself results in the Negro children, as a class, receiving educational opportunities which are substantially inferior to those available to white children otherwise similarly situated."

11. Kenneth B. Clark, *Effect of Prejudice and Discrimination on Personality Development* (Midcentury White House Conference on Children and Youth, 1950); Helen L. Witmer and Ruth Kotinsky, *Personality in the Making* (1952), c. VI; Max Deutscher and Isidor Chein, *The Psychological Effects of Enforced Segregation: A Survey of Social Science Opinion,* 26 J.Psychol. 259 (1948); Chein, *What are the Psychological Effects of Segregation Under Conditions of Equal Facilities?,* 3 Int.J. Opinion and Attitude Res. 229 (1949); Theodore Brameld, *Educational Costs in Discrimination and National Welfare* (MacIver, ed., 1949), 44–48; Frazier, *The Negro in the United States* (1949), 674–681. And, see generally Gunnar Myrdal, *An American Dilemma* (1944).

Because these are class actions, because of the wide applicability of this decision, and because of the great variety of local conditions, the formulation of decrees in these cases presents problems of considerable complexity. On reargument, the consideration of appropriate relief was necessarily subordinated to the primary question—the constitutionality of segregation in public education. We have now announced that such segregation is a denial of the equal protection of the laws. In order that we may have the full assistance of the parties in formulating decrees, the cases will be restored to the docket, and the parties are requested to present further argument on Questions 4 and 5 previously propounded by the Court for the reargument this Term.13 * * *

———

BOLLING v. SHARPE, 347 U.S. 497 (1954), per WARREN, C.J., held—on the same day as *Brown*—that public school segregation in the District of Columbia "constitutes an arbitrary deprivation [of] liberty in violation of the Due Process Clause" of the Fifth Amendment: "The Fifth Amendment [does] not contain an Equal Protection Clause as does the Fourteenth Amendment which applies only to the states. But the concepts of equal protection and due process, both stemming from our American ideal of fairness, are not mutually exclusive. The 'equal protection of the laws' is a more explicit safeguard of prohibited unfairness than 'due process of law,' and, therefore, we do not imply that the two are always interchangeable phrases. But, as this Court has recognized, discrimination may be so unjustifiable as to be violative of due process.

"Classifications based solely upon race must be scrutinized with particular care, since they are contrary to our traditions and hence constitutionally suspect. ['Liberty'] extends to the full range of conduct which the individual is free to pursue, and it cannot be restricted except for a proper governmental objective. Segregation in public education is not reasonably related to any proper governmental objective * * *.

"In view of our decision that the Constitution prohibits the states from maintaining racially segregated public schools, it would be unthinkable that the same Constitution would impose a lesser duty on the Federal Government."

---

13. "4. Assuming it is decided that segregation in public schools violates the Fourteenth Amendment

"(a) would a decree necessarily follow providing that, within the limits set by normal geographic school districting, Negro children should forthwith be admitted to schools of their choice, or

"(b) may this Court, in the exercise of its equity powers, permit an effective gradual adjustment to be brought about from existing segregated systems to a system not based on color distinctions?

"5. On the assumption on which questions 4(a) and (b) are based, and assuming further that this Court will exercise its equity powers to the end described in question 4(b),

"(a) should this Court formulate detailed decrees in these cases;

"(b) if so, what specific issues should the decrees reach;

"(c) should this Court appoint a special master to hear evidence with a view to recommending specific terms for such decrees;

"(d) should this Court remand to the courts of first instance with directions to frame decrees in these cases, and if so what general directions should the decrees of this Court include and what procedures should the courts of first instance follow in arriving at the specific terms of more detailed decrees?"

BROWN v. BOARD OF EDUCATION (II)

349 U.S. 294, 75 S.Ct. 753, 99 L.Ed. 1083 (1955).

CHIEF JUSTICE WARREN delivered the opinion of the Court.

These cases were decided on May 17, 1954. [There] remains for consideration the manner in which relief is to be accorded. * * *

Full implementation of these constitutional principles may require solution of varied local school problems. School authorities have the primary responsibility for elucidating, assessing, and solving [them]; courts will have to consider whether the action of school authorities constitutes good faith implementation of the governing constitutional principles. Because of their proximity to local conditions and the possible need for further hearings, the courts which originally heard these cases can best perform this judicial appraisal. Accordingly, we believe it appropriate to remand the cases to those courts.

In fashioning and effectuating the decrees, the courts will be guided by equitable principles. Traditionally, equity has been characterized by a practical flexibility in shaping its remedies and by a facility for adjusting and reconciling public and private needs. [A]t stake is the personal interest of the plaintiffs in admission to public schools as soon as practicable on a nondiscriminatory basis. To effectuate this interest may call for elimination of a variety of obstacles in making the transition to school systems operated in accordance with the constitutional principles set forth in our May 17, 1954, decision. Courts of equity may properly take into account the public interest in the elimination of such obstacles in a systematic and effective manner. But it should go without saying that the vitality of these constitutional principles cannot be allowed to yield simply because of disagreement with them.

While giving weight to these public and private considerations, the courts will require that the defendants make a prompt and reasonable start toward full compliance with our May 17, 1954, ruling. Once such a start has been made, the courts may find that additional time is necessary to carry out the ruling in an effective manner. The burden rests upon the defendants to establish that such time is necessary in the public interest and is consistent with good faith compliance at the earliest practicable date. To that end, the courts may consider problems related to administration, arising from the physical condition of the school plant, the school transportation system, personnel, revision of school districts and attendance areas into compact units to achieve a system of determining admission to the public schools on a nonracial basis, and revision of local laws and regulations which may be necessary in solving the foregoing problems. They will also consider the adequacy of any plans the defendants may propose to meet these problems and to effectuate a transition to a racially nondiscriminatory school system. During this period of transition, the courts will retain jurisdiction of these cases.

The [cases are remanded] to take such proceedings and enter such orders and decrees consistent with this opinion as are necessary and proper to admit to public schools on a racially nondiscriminatory basis with all deliberate speed the parties to these cases. * * *

LOVING v. VIRGINIA

388 U.S. 1, 87 S.Ct. 1817, 18 L.Ed.2d 1010 (1967).

CHIEF JUSTICE WARREN delivered the opinion of the Court.

This case presents a constitutional question never addressed by this Court: whether a statutory scheme adopted by Virginia to prevent marriages between persons solely on the basis of racial classifications violates [the] Fourteenth

Amendment. [Appellants, a black woman and white man, were married in the District of Columbia, returned to reside in Virginia, and were convicted under the state antimiscegenation statute.]

Virginia is now one of 16 States which prohibit and punish marriages on the basis of racial classifications.5 [The] state court concluded that the State's legitimate purposes were "to preserve the racial integrity of its citizens," and to prevent "the corruption of blood," "a mongrel breed of citizens," and "the obliteration of racial pride," obviously an endorsement of the doctrine of White Supremacy. [T]he State [argues] that the meaning of the Equal Protection Clause, as illuminated by the statements of the Framers, is only that state penal laws containing an interracial element as part of the definition of the offense must apply equally to whites and Negroes in the sense that members of each race are punished to the same degree. * * *

Because we reject the notion that the mere "equal application" of a statute containing racial classifications is enough to remove the classifications from the Fourteenth Amendment's proscription of all invidious racial discriminations, we do not accept the State's contention that these statutes should be upheld if there is any possible basis for concluding that they serve a rational purpose. [Here], we deal with statutes containing racial classifications, and the fact of equal application does not immunize the statute from the very heavy burden of justification which the Fourteenth Amendment has traditionally required of state statutes drawn according to race.

The State argues that statements in the Thirty-ninth Congress about the time of the passage of the Fourteenth Amendment indicate that the Framers did not intend the Amendment to make unconstitutional state miscegenation laws. Many of the statements [have] some relevance to the intention of Congress in submitting the Fourteenth Amendment, [but] it must be understood that they pertained to the passage of specific statutes and not to the broader, organic purpose of a constitutional amendment. As for the various statements directly concerning the Fourteenth Amendment, we have said in connection with a related problem, that although these historical sources "cast some light" they are not sufficient to resolve the problem; "[a]t best, they are inconclusive." *Brown.* We have rejected the proposition that the debates in the Thirty-ninth Congress or in the state legislatures which ratified the Fourteenth Amendment supported the theory [that equal protection] is satisfied by penal laws defining offenses based on racial classifications so long as white and Negro participants in the offense were similarly punished. *McLaughlin v. Florida,* 379 U.S. 184 (1964).a

The State finds support for its "equal application" theory [in] *Pace v. Alabama,* 106 U.S. 583 (1883). In that case, the Court upheld a conviction under an Alabama statute forbidding adultery or fornication between a white person and a Negro which imposed a greater penalty than that of a statute proscribing similar conduct by members of the same race. The Court reasoned that the statute could not be said to discriminate against Negroes because the punishment for each participant in the offense was the same. However, as recently as the 1964 Term, in rejecting the reasoning of that case, we stated "*Pace* represents a limited view of the Equal Protection Clause which has not withstood analysis in the subsequent decisions of this Court." *McLaughlin.* [The] clear and central purpose of the Fourteenth Amendment was to eliminate all official state sources of invidious racial discrimination in the States. [At] the very least, the Equal Protection

5. [Over] the past 15 years, 14 States have repealed laws outlawing interracial marriages * * *.

a. *McLaughlin* invalidated a statute making interracial cohabitation a crime.

Clause demands that racial classifications, especially suspect in criminal statutes, be subjected to the "most rigid scrutiny," and, if they are ever to be upheld, they must be shown to be necessary to the accomplishment of some permissible state objective, independent of the racial discrimination which it was the object of the Fourteenth Amendment to eliminate.**b** Indeed, two [justices] have already stated that they "cannot conceive of a valid legislative purpose [which] makes the color of a person's skin the test of whether his conduct is a criminal offense." *McLaughlin* (Stewart, J., joined by Douglas, J., concurring).

There is patently no legitimate overriding purpose independent of invidious racial discrimination which justifies this classification. The fact that Virginia only prohibits interracial marriages involving white persons demonstrates that the racial classifications must stand on their own justification, as measures designed to maintain White Supremacy.11 We have consistently denied the constitutionality of measures which restrict the rights of citizens on account of race. There can be no doubt that restricting the freedom to marry solely because of racial classifications violates the central meaning of the Equal Protection Clause.

These statutes also deprive the Lovings of liberty without [due process].

Marriage is one of the "basic civil rights of man," fundamental to our very existence and survival. *Skinner v. Oklahoma* [Ch. 6, Sec. 2]. To deny this fundamental freedom on so unsupportable a basis as the racial classifications embodied in these statutes [surely denies due process].

Reversed.

JUSTICE STEWART, concurring.

I have previously expressed the belief that "it is simply not possible for a state law to be valid under our Constitution which makes the criminality of an act depend upon the race of the actor." *McLaughlin* (concurring opinion). Because I adhere to that belief, I concur in the judgment of the Court.

PALMORE v. SIDOTI, 466 U.S. 429 (1984), per BURGER, C.J., held that Florida's denial of child custody to a white mother because her new husband was black violated equal protection: "There is a risk that a child living with a step-parent of a different race may be subject to a variety of pressures and stresses not present if the child were living with parents of the same racial or ethnic origin. [But the] effects of racial prejudice, however real, cannot justify a racial classification removing an infant child from the custody of its natural mother found to be an appropriate person to have such custody."

---

b. *McLaughlin* also stated that racial classifications were " 'in most circumstances irrelevant' to any constitutionally acceptable legislative purpose." Harlan, J., concurring, added that "necessity, not mere reasonable relationship, is the proper test"; this "test which developed to protect free speech against state infringement should be equally applicable in a case involving state racial discrimination—prohibition of which lies at the very heart of the Fourteenth Amendment."

11. [While] Virginia prohibits whites from marrying any nonwhite (subject to the exception for the descendants of Pocahontas), Ne-

groes, Orientals and any other racial class may intermarry without statutory interference. Appellants contend that this distinction renders Virginia's miscegenation statutes arbitrary and unreasonable even assuming the constitutional validity of an official purpose to preserve "racial integrity." We need not reach this contention because we find the racial classifications in these statutes repugnant to the Fourteenth Amendment, even assuming an evenhanded state purpose to protect the "integrity" of all races.

JOHNSON v. CALIFORNIA, 543 U.S. 499 (2005), held that the "strict scrutiny" test developed in prior race discrimination cases (under which racial classifications will be upheld only if proven to be "narrowly tailored" to further "compelling governmental interests") applied to a policy of the California Department of Corrections (CDC) to assign newly arrived prisoners to temporary cells "based on a number of factors, [but] predominantly race." The Court, per O'CONNOR, J., rejected arguments for applying "the deferential standard of review articulated in *Turner v. Safley*, 482 U.S. 78 (1987)," under which courts will ordinarily uphold any prison regulation that is "reasonably related" to "legitimate penological interests." Unlike burdens on prisoners' rights to privacy, speech, and religion, "[t]he right not to be discriminated against based on one's race is not susceptible to the logic of *Turner*. It is not a right that need necessarily be compromised for the sake of proper prison administration."

Although Stevens, J., agreed with the majority about the applicable standard of review, he dissented from the Court's decision to remand the case to the district court to apply the compelling interest test and would have held squarely that the challenged policy violated the Equal Protection Clause. Thomas, J., joined by Scalia, J., dissented. In light of the threats of race-based prison violence and the general needs of prison administration, he would have upheld the CDC's policy on the basis of *Turner*.

III. DE JURE vs. DE FACTO DISCRIMINATION

Part II of this Section involved laws that explicitly discriminated against racial and ethnic minorities. But intentional (or "de jure") discrimination may exist even though the law in question is racially "neutral" on its face: the law may be deliberately administered in a discriminatory way; or the law, although neutral in its language and applied in accordance with its terms, may have been enacted with a purpose (or motive) to disadvantage a "suspect" class. This section begins by considering these additional types of "de jure" discrimination. It then examines the Court's response to government action that is racially neutral in its terms, administration, and purpose but has a discriminatory effect or impact.

YICK WO v. HOPKINS

118 U.S. 356, 6 S.Ct. 1064, 30 L.Ed. 220 (1886).

JUSTICE MATTHEWS delivered the opinion of the Court.

[A San Francisco ordinance made it unlawful to operate a laundry without the consent of the board of supervisors except in a brick or stone building. Yick Wo, a Chinese alien who had operated a laundry for 22 years, had certificates from the health and fire authorities, but was refused consent by the board. It was admitted that "there were about 320 laundries in the city [and] about 240 were owned [by] subjects of China, and of the whole number, viz., 320, about 310 were constructed of wood"; that "petitioner, and more than 150 of his countrymen, have been arrested" for violating the ordinance "while those who are not subjects of China, and who are conducting 80 odd laundries under similar conditions, are left unmolested."]

[T]he facts shown establish an administration directed so exclusively against a particular class of persons as to warrant and require the conclusion that, whatever may have been the intent of the ordinances as adopted, they are applied [with] a mind so unequal and oppressive as to amount to a practical denial by the State of [equal protection]. Though the law itself be fair on its face and impartial in appearance, yet, if it is applied and administered by public authority with an evil eye and an unequal hand, so as practically to make unjust and illegal discriminations between persons in similar circumstances, material to their rights, the denial of equal justice is still within the prohibition of the Constitution. [The] fact of this discrimination is admitted. No reason for it is shown, and the conclusion cannot be resisted that no reason for it exists except hostility to [Yick Wo's] race and nationality * * *.

WASHINGTON v. DAVIS

426 U.S. 229, 96 S.Ct. 2040, 48 L.Ed.2d 597 (1976).

JUSTICE WHITE delivered the opinion of the Court.

This case involves the validity of a qualifying test administered to applicants for positions as police officers in the District of Columbia. [T]he police recruit was required to satisfy certain physical and character standards, to be a high school graduate or its equivalent and to receive a grade of at least 40 out of 80 on "Test 21," which is "an examination that is used generally throughout the federal service," which "was developed by the Civil Service Commission, not the Police Department," and which was "designed to test verbal ability, vocabulary, reading and comprehension."

[The evidence showed that roughly four times as many blacks as whites failed Test 21. Apart from the test, however, the Police Department had systematically and affirmatively sought to enroll black officers. As a result, 44% of new police force recruits had been black in the years immediately preceding the litigation. There was, accordingly, no allegation that the Department had acted with discriminatory intent—only that a test with a substantially discriminatory impact could not be used, at least in the absence of a showing that performance on Test 21 bore a substantial and demonstrated relationship to performance on the job.]

[The] District Court rejected the assertion that Test 21 was culturally slanted to favor whites and was "satisfied that the undisputable facts prove the test to be reasonably and directly related to the requirements of the police recruit training program and that it is neither so designed nor operates to discriminate against otherwise qualified blacks." [The Court of Appeals held] that lack of discriminatory intent in designing and administering Test 21 was irrelevant; the critical fact was rather [that] four times as many [blacks] failed the test than did whites. This disproportionate impact [was] held sufficient to establish a constitutional violation, absent proof by petitioners that the test was an adequate measure of job performance in addition to being an indicator of probable success in the training program, a burden which the court ruled petitioners had failed to discharge. * * *

The central purpose of the Equal Protection Clause [is] the prevention of official conduct discriminating on the basis of race. It is also true that the Due Process Clause of the Fifth Amendment contains an equal protection component prohibiting the United States from invidiously discriminating between individuals or groups. But our cases have not embraced the proposition that a law or other official act, without regard to whether it reflects a racially discriminatory purpose, is unconstitutional *solely* because it has a racially disproportionate impact.

Almost 100 years ago, *Strauder* established that the exclusion of Negroes from grand and petit juries in criminal proceedings violated the Equal Protection Clause, but the fact that a particular jury or a series of juries does not statistically reflect the racial composition of the community does not in itself make out an invidious discrimination forbidden by the Clause. "A purpose to discriminate must be present which may be proven by systematic exclusion of eligible jurymen of the prescribed race or by an unequal application of the law to such an extent as to show intentional discrimination." * * *

The school desegregation cases have also adhered to the basic equal protection principle that the invidious quality of a law claimed to be racially discriminatory must ultimately be traced to a racially discriminatory purpose. That there are both predominantly black and predominantly white schools in a community is not alone violative of the Equal Protection Clause. The essential element ["differentiating] between de jure segregation and so-called de facto segregation [is] *purpose* or *intent* to segregate."

This is not to say that the necessary discriminatory racial purpose must be express or appear on the face of the statute, or that a law's disproportionate impact is irrelevant. [A] statute, otherwise neutral on its face, must not be applied so as invidiously to discriminate on the basis of race. *Yick Wo.* It is also clear from the cases dealing with racial discrimination in the selection of juries that [a] prima facie case of discriminatory purpose may be proved [by] the absence of Negroes on a particular jury combined with the failure of the jury commissioners to be informed of eligible Negro jurors in a community, or with racially non-neutral selection procedures. With a prima facie case made out, "the burden of proof shifts to the State to rebut the presumption of unconstitutional action by showing that permissible racially neutral selection criteria and procedures have produced the monochromatic result."

Necessarily, an invidious discriminatory purpose may often be inferred from the totality of the relevant facts, including [that] the law bears more heavily on one race than another. It is also not infrequently true that the discriminatory impact—in the jury cases for example, the total or seriously disproportionate exclusion of Negroes from jury venires—may for all practical purposes demonstrate unconstitutionality because in various circumstances the discrimination is very difficult to explain on nonracial grounds. Nevertheless, we have not held that a law, neutral on its face and serving ends otherwise within the power of government to pursue, is invalid under the Equal Protection Clause simply because it may affect a greater proportion of one race than of another. Disproportionate impact is not irrelevant, but it is not the sole touchstone of an invidious racial discrimination forbidden by the Constitution. Standing alone, it does not trigger the rule that racial classifications are to be subjected to the strictest scrutiny and are justifiable only by the weightiest of considerations.

There are some indications to the contrary in our cases. In *Palmer v. Thompson,* 403 U.S. 217 (1971), the city of Jackson, Miss., following a court decree to this effect, desegregated all of its public facilities save five swimming pools which [were] closed by ordinance pursuant to a determination by the city council that closure was necessary to preserve peace and order and that integrated pools could not be economically operated. [T]his Court rejected the argument that [the] otherwise seemingly permissible ends served by the ordinance could be impeached by demonstrating that racially invidious motivations had prompted the city council's action. [W]hatever dicta the opinion may contain, the decision did not involve, much less invalidate, a statute or ordinance having neutral purposes but disproportionate racial consequences.11

11. To the extent that *Palmer* suggests a generally applicable proposition that legislative purpose is irrelevant in constitutional adjudication, our prior cases—as indicated in the text—are to the contrary; and very shortly after *Palmer,* all Members of the Court majority in that case [joined] *Lemon v. Kurtzman,* [Ch. 8, Sec. 1, II], [which held that determining] the validity of public aid to church-related schools includes close inquiry into the purpose of the challenged statute.

[Test 21] seeks to ascertain whether those who take it have acquired a particular level of verbal skill; and it is untenable that the Constitution prevents the government from seeking modestly to upgrade the communicative abilities of its employees rather than to be satisfied with some lower level of competence, particularly where the job requires special ability to communicate orally and in writing. Respondents, as Negroes, could no more successfully claim that the test denied them equal protection than could white applicants who also failed. The conclusion would not be different in the face of proof that more Negroes than whites had been disqualified by Test 21. * * *

Nor on the facts of the case before us would the disproportionate impact of Test 21 warrant the conclusion that it is a purposeful device to discriminate against Negroes. [T]he test is neutral on its face and rationally may be said to serve a purpose the government is constitutionally empowered to pursue. Even agreeing with the District Court that the differential racial effect of Test 21 called for further inquiry, we think the District Court correctly held that the affirmative efforts of the Metropolitan Police Department to recruit black officers, the changing racial composition of the recruit classes and of the force in general, and the relationship of the test to the training program negated any inference that the Department discriminated on the basis of race * * *.

Under Title VII [of the Civil Rights Act of 1964], Congress provided that when hiring and promotion practices disqualifying substantially disproportionate numbers of blacks are challenged, discriminatory purpose need not be proved, and that it is an insufficient response to demonstrate some rational basis for the challenged practices. It is necessary, in addition, that they be "validated" in terms of job performance * * *. However this process proceeds, it involves a more probing judicial review of, and less deference to, the seemingly reasonable acts of administrators and executives than is appropriate under the Constitution where special racial impact, without discriminatory purpose, is claimed. We are not disposed to adopt this more rigorous standard for the purposes of applying the Fifth and the Fourteenth Amendments in cases such as this.

A rule that a statute designed to serve neutral ends is nevertheless invalid, absent compelling justification, if in practice it benefits or burdens one race more than another would be far-reaching and would raise serious questions about, and perhaps invalidate, a whole range of tax, welfare, public service, regulatory, and licensing statutes that may be more burdensome to the poor and to the average black than to the more affluent white.14

Given that rule, such consequences would perhaps be likely to follow. However, in our view, extension of the rule beyond those areas where it is already applicable by reason of statute, such as in the field of public employment, should await legislative prescription. * * *a

JUSTICE STEVENS [who joined the Court's opinion] concurring. * * *

The requirement of purposeful discrimination is a common thread running through the cases summarized [by the Court. But] in each of these contexts, the

---

14. Frank I. Goodman, *De Facto School Segregation: A Constitutional and Empirical Analysis,* 60 Calif.L.Rev. 275, 300 (1972), suggests that disproportionate-impact analysis might invalidate "tests and qualifications for voting, draft deferment, public employment, jury service, and other government-conferred [benefits]; [s]ales taxes, bail schedules, utility rates, bridge tolls, license fees, and other state-imposed charges." It has also been argued that minimum wage and usury laws as well as

professional licensing requirements would require major modifications in light of the unequal-impact rule.

a. The Court also found no violation of the relevant statutory provisions. Stewart, J., joined only the constitutional aspects of the Court's opinion. Brennan, J., joined by Marshall, J., did not address the constitutional questions but dissented on statutory grounds.

burden of proving a prima facie case may well involve differing evidentiary considerations. The extent of deference that one pays to the trial court's determination of the factual issue, and indeed, the extent to which one characterizes the intent issue as a question of fact or a question of law, will vary in different contexts.

Frequently the most probative evidence of intent will be objective evidence of what actually happened rather than evidence describing the subjective state of mind of the actor. For normally the actor is presumed to have intended the natural consequences of his deeds. This is particularly true in the case of governmental action which is frequently the product of compromise, of collective decisionmaking, and of mixed motivation. It is unrealistic, on the one hand, to require the victim of alleged discrimination to uncover the actual subjective intent of the decisionmaker or conversely, to invalidate otherwise legitimate action simply because an improper motive affected the deliberation of a participant in the decisional process. A law conscripting clerics should not be invalidated because an atheist voted for it.

My point [is] to suggest that the line between discriminatory purpose and discriminatory impact is not nearly as bright, and perhaps not quite as critical, as the reader of the Court's opinion might assume. I agree [that] a constitutional issue does not arise every time some disproportionate impact is shown. On the other hand, when the disproportion is as dramatic as in *Gomillion v. Lightfoot,* 364 U.S. 339 (1960),b or *Yick Wo,* it really does not matter whether the standard is phrased in terms of purpose or effect. * * *

There are two reasons why I am convinced that the challenge to Test 21 is insufficient. First, the test serves the neutral and legitimate purpose of requiring all applicants to meet a uniform minimum standard of literacy. Reading ability is manifestly relevant to the police function, there is no evidence that the required passing grade was set at an arbitrarily high level, and there is sufficient disparity among high schools and high school graduates to justify the use of a separate uniform test. Second, the same test is used throughout the federal service. The applicants for employment in the District of Columbia Police Department represent such a small fraction of the total number of persons who have taken the test that their experience is of minimal probative value [to] overcome the presumption that a test which is this widely used by the Federal Government is in fact neutral in its effect as well as its "purpose" as that term is used in constitutional adjudication. * * *

The Court strongly suggested that discriminatory impact alone (in the absence of a showing of discriminatory intent) will not establish a Fifteenth Amendment violation in *Mobile v. Bolden,* Sec. V, I, D infra. The Court considered the requisites for establishing a Thirteenth Amendment violation in MEMPHIS v. GREENE, 451 U.S. 100 (1981). At the behest of citizens of Hein Park, a white residential district, the city closed West Drive, a street that traversed Hein Park

b. In *Gomillion,* an Alabama statute changed the Tuskegee city boundaries from a square to a 28–sided figure, allegedly removing "all save only four or five of its 400 Negro voters while not removing a single white voter or resident." The Court held that the complaint "amply alleges a claim of racial discrimination" in violation of the Fifteenth Amendment: "If these allegations upon a trial remained uncontradicted or unqualified, the conclusion would be irresistible, tantamount for all practical purposes to a mathematical demonstration, that the legislation is solely concerned with segregating white and colored voters by fencing Negro citizens out of town so as to deprive them of their pre-existing municipal vote."

and was used mainly by African–Americans living nearby, in part to reduce "traffic pollution," described as "noise, litter, [and] interruption of community living." The Court, per STEVENS, J., agreeing that "the adverse impact on blacks was greater than on whites," found no violation of 42 U.S.C.A. § 1982 [quoted in Ch. 11, Sec. 1 infra] or the Thirteenth Amendment: "[T]he critical facts established by the record are these: The city's decision to close West Drive was motivated by its interest in protecting the safety and tranquility of a residential neighborhood. The procedures followed in making the decision were fair and were not affected by any racial or other impermissible factors. The city has conferred a benefit on certain white property owners but there is no reason to believe that it would refuse to confer a comparable benefit on black property owners. The closing has not affected the value of property owned by black citizens, but it has caused some slight inconvenience to black motorists.

"[T]he record discloses no racially discriminatory motive on the part of the City Council [and] a review of the justification for the official action challenged in this case demonstrates that its disparate impact on black citizens could not [be] fairly characterized as a badge or incident of slavery.

"[To] decide the narrow constitutional question presented by this record we need not speculate about the sort of impact on a racial group that might be prohibited by the Amendment itself. We merely hold that the impact of the closing of West Drive on nonresidents of Hein Park [does] not reflect a violation of the Thirteenth Amendment."

MARSHALL, J., joined by Brennan and Blackmun, JJ., dissented: "The majority treats this case as involving nothing more than a dispute over a city's race-neutral decision to place a barrier across a road. My own examination of the record suggests [a] white community disgruntled over sharing its streets with Negroes, taking legal measures to keep out the 'undesirable traffic,' and of a city, heedless to the harm to its Negro citizens, acquiescing in the plan.

"I [do] not mean to imply that all municipal decisions that affect Negroes adversely and benefit whites are prohibited by the Thirteenth Amendment. I would, however, insist that the government carry a heavy burden of justification before I would sustain against Thirteenth Amendment challenge conduct as egregious as erection of a barrier to prevent predominantly-Negro traffic from entering a historically all-white neighborhood. [I] do not believe that the city has discharged that burden in this case, and for that reason I would hold that the erection of the barrier at the end of West Drive amounts to a badge or incident of slavery forbidden by the Thirteenth Amendment."

Although *Washington v. Davis* rejected the "disparate impact" theory and held that a facially neutral statute violates the Equal Protection Clause only if motivated by a discriminatory purpose, the Court did not address in detail what counts as a discriminatory purpose. The leading case addressing that issue involved gender, not race, but the Court's approach to identifying forbidden intent or purposes appears to be the same. PERSONNEL ADMINISTRATOR v. FEENEY, 442 U.S. 256 (1979), per STEWART, J., upheld Massachusetts' "absolute lifetime preference to veterans" for state civil service positions, even though "the preference operates overwhelmingly to the advantage of males": "When a statute gender-neutral on its face is challenged on the ground that its effects upon women are disproportionately adverse, a two-fold inquiry [is] appropriate. The first question is whether the statutory classification is indeed neutral * * *. If the classification itself, covert or overt, is not based upon gender, the second question is whether the adverse effect reflects invidious gender-based discrimination. In this second inquiry, impact provides an 'important starting point,' but purposeful discrimination is 'the condition that offends the Constitution.' "

As to the first question, "The District Court [found] first, that ch. 31 serves legitimate and worthy purposes; second, that the absolute preference was not established for the purpose of discriminating against women. [Thus,] the distinction between veterans and nonveterans drawn by ch. 31 is not a pretext for gender discrimination. * * *

"If the impact of this statute could not be plausibly explained on a neutral ground, impact itself would signal that the real classification made by the law was in fact not neutral. But there can be but one answer to the question whether this veteran preference excludes significant numbers of women from preferred state jobs because they are women or because they are nonveterans. [Although] few women benefit from the preference, * * * significant numbers of nonveterans are men, and all nonveterans—male as well as female—are placed at a disadvantage. Too many men are affected by ch. 31 to permit the inference that the statute is but a pretext for preferring men over women. * * *

"The dispositive question, then, is whether the appellee has shown that a gender-based discriminatory purpose has, at least in some measure, shaped [ch. 31. Her] contention that this veterans' preference is 'inherently non-neutral' or 'gender-biased' presumes that the State, by favoring veterans, intentionally incorporated into its public employment policies the panoply of sex-based and assertedly discriminatory federal laws that have prevented all but a handful of women from becoming veterans. There are two serious difficulties with this argument. First, it is wholly at odds with the District Court's central finding that Massachusetts has not offered a preference to veterans for the purpose of discriminating against women. Second, [t]o the extent that the status of veteran is one that few women have been enabled to achieve, every hiring preference for veterans, however modest or extreme, is inherently gender-biased. If Massachusetts by offering such a preference can be said intentionally to have incorporated into its state employment policies the historical gender-based federal military personnel practices, the degree of the preference would or should make no constitutional difference. Invidious discrimination does not become less so because the discrimination accomplished is of a lesser magnitude.[23] Discriminatory intent is simply not amenable to calibration. It either is a factor that has influenced the legislative choice or it is not. The District Court's conclusion that the absolute veterans' preference was not originally enacted or subsequently reaffirmed for the purpose of giving an advantage to males as such necessarily compels the conclusion that the State intended nothing more than to prefer 'veterans.' * * *

"To be sure, this case is unusual in that it involves a law that by design is not neutral. [As] opposed to the written test at issue in *Davis*, it does not purport to define a job related characteristic. To the contrary, it confers upon a specifically described group—perceived to be particularly deserving—a competitive head start. But the District Court found, and the appellee has not disputed, that this legislative choice was legitimate. [Thus, it] must be analyzed as is any other neutral law that casts a greater burden upon women as a group than upon men as a group. The enlistment policies of the armed services may well have discrimi-

23. This is not to say that the degree of impact is irrelevant to the question of intent. But it is to say that a more modest preference, while it might well lessen impact and, as the State argues, might lessen the effectiveness of the statute in helping veterans, would not be any more or less "neutral" in the constitutional sense.

nated on the basis of sex. But the history of discrimination against women in the military is not on trial in this case.

"The appellee's ultimate argument rests upon the presumption, common to the criminal and civil law, that a person intends the natural and foreseeable consequences of his voluntary actions. * * *

" 'Discriminatory purpose,' however, implies more than intent as volition or intent as awareness of consequences. It implies that the decisionmaker, in this case a state legislature, selected or reaffirmed a particular course of action at least in part 'because of,' not merely 'in spite of,' its adverse effects upon an identifiable group.25 Yet nothing in the record demonstrates that this preference for veterans was originally devised or subsequently re-enacted because it would accomplish the collateral goal of keeping women in a stereotypic and predefined place in the Massachusetts Civil Service."

STEVENS, J., joined by White, J., concurred in the Court's opinion, adding: "[F]or me the answer is largely provided by the fact that the number of males disadvantaged by Massachusetts' Veterans Preference (1,867,000) is sufficiently large—and sufficiently close to the number of disadvantaged females (2,954,000)— to refute the claim that the rule was intended to benefit males as a class over females as a class."

MARSHALL, J., joined by Brennan, J., dissented: "In my judgment, [ch. 31] evinces purposeful gender-based discrimination. * * *

"That a legislature seeks to advantage one group does not, as a matter of logic or of common sense, exclude the possibility that it also intends to disadvantage another. Individuals in general and lawmakers in particular frequently act for a variety of reasons. [S]ince reliable evidence of subjective intentions is seldom obtainable, resort to inference based on objective factors is generally unavoidable. To discern the purposes underlying facially neutral policies, this Court has therefore considered the degree, inevitability, and foreseeability of any disproportionate impact as well as the alternatives reasonably available.

"[T]he impact of the Massachusetts statute on women is undisputed. Any veteran with a passing grade on the civil service exam must be placed ahead of a nonveteran, regardless of their respective scores. [Because] less than 2% of the women in Massachusetts are veterans, the absolute preference formula has rendered desirable state civil service employment an almost exclusively male prerogative. [Where] the foreseeable impact of a facially neutral policy is so disproportionate, the burden should rest on the State to establish that sex-based considerations played no part in the choice of the particular legislative scheme.

"Clearly, that burden was not sustained here. The legislative history of the statute reflects the Commonwealth's patent appreciation of the impact the preference system would have on women, and an equally evident desire to mitigate that impact only with respect to certain traditionally female occupations. Until 1971, the statute [and] regulations exempted from operation of the preference any job requisitions 'especially calling for women.' In practice, this exemption, coupled with the absolute preference for veterans, has created a gender-based civil service

---

25. This is not to say that the inevitability or foreseeability of consequences of a neutral rule has no bearing upon the existence of discriminatory intent. Certainly, when the adverse consequences of a law upon an identifiable group are as inevitable as the gender-based consequences of ch. 31, a strong inference that the adverse effects were desired can reasonably be drawn. But in this inquiry— made as it is under the Constitution—an inference is a working tool, not a synonym for proof. When as here, the impact is essentially an unavoidable consequence of a legislative policy that has in itself always been deemed to be legitimate, and when, as here, the statutory history and all of the available evidence affirmatively demonstrate the opposite, the inference simply fails to ripen into proof.

hierarchy, with women occupying low grade clerical and secretarial jobs and men holding more responsible and remunerative positions. [Particularly] when viewed against the range of less discriminatory alternatives available to assist veterans,[2] Massachusetts's choice of a formula that so severely restricts public employment opportunities for women cannot reasonably be thought gender-neutral. The Court's conclusion to the contrary—that 'nothing in the record' evinces a 'collateral goal of keeping women in a stereotypic and predefined place in the Massachusetts Civil Service'—displays a singularly myopic view of the facts established below.[3]"

IV. AFFIRMATIVE ACTION AND "BENIGN" DISCRIMINATION

A. AFFIRMATIVE ACTION IN EDUCATION

The first major affirmative action case to be decided by the Supreme Court on the merits, REGENTS OF UNIV. OF CALIFORNIA v. BAKKE, 438 U.S. 265 (1978), presented a challenge to the affirmative action program of the Medical School of the University of California at Davis, which reserved 16 out of 100 places in its entering class for members of minority groups, apparently defined as "Blacks," "Chicanos," "Asians," and "American Indians." The constitutionality of the program was challenged by Allan Bakke, a white male applicant who was rejected, even though some applicants were admitted under the affirmative action program who had "significantly lower" grade point averages and test scores than he did. The issues presented by the case divided the Court almost literally down the middle. Four Justices—Burger, C.J., and Stewart, Rehnquist, and Stevens, JJ.—believed that a federal statute, Title VI of the 1964 Civil Rights Act, forbade schools receiving federal funds from taking any account of race in their admissions processes. Four other Justices—Brennan, White, Marshall, and Blackmun—concluded that all aspects of the Medical School's policy passed muster under a level of judicial scrutiny less searching than "strict scrutiny." With the Court thus divided, the determining vote lay with Justice Lewis Powell, who sought to stake out an intermediate position in an opinion that was not joined in some critical sections by even a single other Justice.

In a part of his opinion joined by Brennan, White, Marshall, and Blackmun, JJ., POWELL, J., first found that Title VI of the Civil Rights Act of 1964—which provides that "No person in the United States shall, on the ground of race, color, or national origin, be excluded from participation in, be denied the benefits of, or be subjected to, discrimination under any program or activity receiving Federal financial assistance"—proscribes "only those racial classifications that would violate the Equal Protection Clause or the Fifth Amendment." Then, writing mostly only for himself, he turned to the equal protection arguments: "[P]etitioner argues that the court below erred in applying strict scrutiny to the special admissions program because white males, such as respondent, are not a 'discrete and insular minority' requiring extraordinary protection from the majoritarian political process. *Carolene Products Co.,* n. 4 [p. 173 supra. These] characteristics may be relevant in deciding whether or not to add new types of classifications to

---

2. Only four States afford a preference comparable in [scope]. Other States and the Federal Government grant point or tie-breaking preferences that do not foreclose opportunities for women.

3. Although it is relevant that the preference statute also disadvantages a substantial group of men, it is equally pertinent that 47%

of Massachusetts men over 18 are veterans, as compared to 0.8% of Massachusetts women. Given this disparity, and the indicia of intent noted supra, the absolute number of men denied preference cannot be dispositive, especially since they have not faced the barriers to achieving veteran status confronted by women.

the list of 'suspect' categories or whether a particular classification survives close examination. Racial and ethnic classifications, however, are subject to stringent examination without regard to these additional characteristics.

"[This] perception of racial and ethnic distinctions is rooted in our Nation's constitutional and demographic history. [T]he white 'majority' itself is composed of various minority groups, most of which can lay claim to a history of prior discrimination at the hands of the State and private individuals. [It] is the individual who is entitled to judicial protection against classifications based upon his racial or ethnic background. [When legal classifications] touch upon an individual's race or ethnic background, he is entitled to a judicial determination that the burden he is asked to bear on that basis is precisely tailored to serve a compelling governmental interest.

"[The] special admissions program purports to serve the purposes of: (i) 'reducing the historic deficit of traditionally disfavored minorities in medical schools and the medical profession,' (ii) countering the effects of societal discrimination; (iii) increasing the number of physicians who will practice in communities currently undeserved; and (iv) obtaining the educational benefits that flow from an ethnically diverse student body.

"[If] petitioner's purpose is to assure within its student body some specified percentage of a particular group merely because of its race or ethnic origin, such a preferential purpose must be rejected not as insubstantial but as facially invalid. Preferring members of any one group for no reason other than race or ethnic origin is discrimination for its own sake. This the Constitution forbids. E.g., *Loving*; *Brown*.

"The State certainly has a legitimate and substantial interest in ameliorating, or eliminating where feasible, the disabling effects of identified discrimination. [That] goal [is] far more focused than the remedying of the effects of 'societal discrimination,' an amorphous concept of injury that [would *not* provide a compelling justification for affirmative action]. We have never approved a classification that aids persons perceived as members of relatively victimized groups at the expense of other innocent individuals in the absence of judicial, legislative, or administrative findings of constitutional or statutory violations. [Without] such findings of constitutional or statutory violations, [which have not been made in this case,] it cannot be said that the government has any greater interest in helping one individual than in refraining from harming another. [To] hold otherwise would be to convert a remedy heretofore reserved for violations of legal rights into a privilege that all institutions throughout the Nation could grant at their pleasure to whatever groups are perceived as victims of societal discrimination.

"Petitioner identifies, as another purpose of its program, improving the delivery of health-care services to communities currently undeserved. It may be assumed that in some situations a State's interest in facilitating the health care of its citizens is sufficiently compelling to support the use of a suspect classification. But there is virtually no evidence in the record indicating that petitioner's special admissions program is either needed or geared to promote that goal. The court below addressed this failure of proof: 'The University concedes it cannot assure that minority doctors who entered under the program, all of whom express an 'interest' in participating in a disadvantaged community, will actually do so.'

"[The] fourth goal asserted by petitioner is the attainment of a diverse student body. This is clearly a permissible goal for an institution of higher education. Academic freedom, though not a specifically enumerated constitutional right, long has been viewed as a special concern of the First Amendment. [Thus,] in arguing that its universities must be accorded the right to select those students who will contribute the most to the robust exchange of ideas, petitioner invokes a countervailing constitutional interest, [and] must be viewed as seeking to achieve a goal that is of paramount importance in the fulfillment of its mission. * * *

"Ethnic diversity, however, is only one element in a range of factors a university properly may consider in attaining the goal of a heterogeneous student body. Although a university must have wide discretion in making the sensitive judgments as to who should be admitted, constitutional limitations protecting individual rights may not be disregarded. [As] the interest of diversity is compelling in the context of a university's admissions program, the question remains whether the program's racial classification is necessary to promote this interest.

"[P]etitioner's argument that this is the only effective means of serving the interest of diversity is seriously flawed. [The] diversity that furthers a compelling state interest encompasses a far broader array of qualifications and characteristics of which racial or ethnic origin is but a single though important element. Petitioner's special admissions program, focused *solely* on ethnic diversity, would hinder rather than further attainment of genuine diversity. * * * "

Powell, J., then referred favorably to the Harvard College admissions program, under which, "when the Committee on Admissions reviews the large middle group of applicants who are 'admissible' and deemed capable of doing good work in their courses, the race of an applicant may tip the balance in his favor just as geographic origin or a life spent on a farm may tip the balance in other candidates' cases. * * * This kind of program treats each applicant as an individual in the admissions process. The applicant who loses out [to] another candidate receiving a 'plus' on the basis of ethnic background will not have been foreclosed from all consideration simply because he was not the right color or had the wrong surname. It would mean only that his combined qualifications, which may have included similar nonobjective factors, did not outweigh those of the other applicant. His qualifications would have been weighed fairly and competitively and he would have no basis to complain of unequal treatment under the Fourteenth Amendment."

Because the Medical School had applied a quota system, Powell, J., found it invalid, despite his recognition that a properly tailored affirmative action program designed to promote diversity could survive strict judicial scrutiny.

In a joint opinion, Brennan, White, Marshall, and Blackmun, JJ., concurred in part and dissented in part: "[C]laims that law must be 'color-blind' or that the datum of race is no longer relevant to public policy must be seen as aspiration rather than as description of reality. [We] cannot [let] color blindness become myopia which masks the reality that many 'created equal' have been treated within our lifetimes as inferior both by the law and by their fellow citizens.

"[A] government practice or statute which [contains] 'suspect classifications' is to be subjected to 'strict scrutiny.' [But] whites as a class [do not] have any of the 'traditional indicia of suspectness: the class is not saddled with such disabilities, or subjected to such a history of purposeful unequal treatment, or relegated to such a position of political powerlessness as to command extraordinary protection from the majoritarian political process.'

"[On] the other hand, the fact that this case does not fit neatly into our prior analytic framework for race cases does not mean that it should be analyzed by applying the very loose rational-basis [standard]. Instead, a number of considerations—developed in gender discrimination cases but which carry even more force when applied to racial classifications—lead us to conclude that racial classifications designed to further remedial purposes 'must serve important governmental objectives and must be substantially related to achievement of those objectives.' *Craig v. Boren,* [Sec. 3, I infra].

"[Davis'] articulated purpose of remedying the effects of past societal discrimination is, under our cases, sufficiently important to justify the use of race-conscious admissions programs where there is a sound basis for concluding that minority underrepresentation is substantial and chronic, and that the handicap of past discrimination is impeding access of minorities to the medical school.

"[Davis] had a sound basis for believing that the problem of underrepresentation of minorities was substantial and chronic and that the problem was attributable to handicaps imposed on minority applicants by past and present racial discrimination. [For] example, the entering classes in 1968 and 1969 [included] only 1 Chicano and 2 Negroes out of the 50 admittees for each year. [A]s petitioner argues, there are no practical means by which it could achieve its ends in the foreseeable future without the use of race-conscious measures. With respect to any factor (such as poverty or family educational background) that may be used as a substitute for race as an indicator of past discrimination, whites greatly outnumber racial minorities simply because whites make up a far larger percentage of the total population and therefore far outnumber minorities in absolute terms at every socio-economic level. * * *

"Finally, Davis' special admissions program cannot be said to violate the Constitution simply because it has set aside a predetermined number of places for qualified minority applicants rather than using minority status as a positive factor to be considered in evaluating the applications of disadvantaged minority applicants. For purposes of constitutional adjudication, there is no difference between the two approaches. In any admissions program which accords special consideration to disadvantaged racial minorities, a determination of the degree of preference to be given is unavoidable, and any given preference that results in the exclusion of a white candidate is no more or less constitutionally acceptable than a program such as that at Davis."

MARSHALL, J., also wrote a separate opinion: "[I]t must be remembered that, during most of the past 200 years, the Constitution as interpreted by this Court did not prohibit the most ingenious and pervasive forms of discrimination against the Negro. Now, when a State acts to remedy the effects of that legacy of discrimination, I cannot believe that this same Constitution stands as a barrier. [In] light of the sorry history of discrimination and its devastating impact on the lives of Negroes, bringing the Negro into the mainstream of American life should be a state interest of the highest order. To fail to do so is to ensure that America will forever remain a divided society. * * *

"Since the Congress that considered and rejected the objections to the 1866 Freedmen's Bureau Act concerning special relief to Negroes also proposed the Fourteenth Amendment, it is inconceivable that the Fourteenth Amendment was intended to prohibit all race-conscious relief measures. [T]o hold that it barred state action to remedy the effects [of] discrimination [would] pervert the intent of the framers by substituting abstract equality for the genuine equality the amendment was intended to achieve."

In an additional separate opinion, BLACKMUN, J., wrote: "I yield to no one in my earnest hope that the time will come when an 'affirmative action' program is unnecessary. [In the meantime, however, it] is somewhat ironic to have us so deeply disturbed over a program where race is an element of consciousness, and yet be aware of the fact [that] institutions of higher learning [have] given conceded preferences [to] those possessed of athletic skills, to the children of alumni, to the affluent who may bestow largesse on the institutions, and to those having connections with celebrities, the famous, and the powerful.

"I suspect that it would be impossible to arrange an affirmative action program in a racially neutral way and have it successful. To ask this is to demand the impossible. In order to get beyond racism, we must first take account of race. There is no other way. And in order to treat some persons equally, we must treat them differently. We cannot—we dare not—let the Equal Protection Clause perpetuate racial supremacy."

STEVENS, J, with whom Burger, C.J. and Stewart and Rehnquist, JJ., joined, did not reach any constitutional issue. He thought that the specific admissions program challenged in the case was illegal under Title VI and that "the question whether race can ever be used as a factor in an admissions decision" was "not an issue in this case" nor one appropriate for the Court to consider under the circumstances.

GRUTTER v. BOLLINGER

539 U.S. 306, 123 S.Ct. 2325, 156 L.Ed.2d 304 (2003).

JUSTICE O'CONNOR delivered the opinion of the Court.

This case requires us to decide whether the use of race as a factor in student admissions by the University of Michigan Law School (Law School) is unlawful.

I A. The Law School ranks among the Nation's top law schools. It receives more than 3,500 applications each year for a class of around 350 students. The hallmark of [the Law School's admission] policy is its focus on academic ability coupled with a flexible assessment of applicants' talents, experiences, and potential "to contribute to the learning of those around them." [In] reviewing an applicant's file, admissions officials must consider the applicant's undergraduate grade point average (GPA) and Law School Admissions Test (LSAT) score because they are important (if imperfect) predictors of academic success in law school. [But] so-called "soft variables" such as "the enthusiasm of recommenders, the quality of the undergraduate institution, the quality of the applicant's essay, and the areas and difficulty of undergraduate course selection" are all brought to bear in assessing an "applicant's likely contributions to the intellectual and social life of the institution."

[The] policy aspires to "achieve that diversity which has the potential to enrich everyone's education and thus make a law school class stronger than the sum of its parts." [By] enrolling a "critical mass of [underrepresented] minority students," the Law School seeks to "ensur[e] their ability to make unique contributions to the character of the Law School."

B. Petitioner Barbara Grutter is a white Michigan resident who applied to the Law School in 1996 with a 3.8 grade point average and 161 LSAT score. The Law School initially placed petitioner on a waiting list, but subsequently rejected her application. [She then filed suit alleging that University officials] discriminated against her on the basis of race in violation of the Fourteenth Amendment [and civil rights statutes including the 1964 Civil Rights Act].

[During] the 15–day bench trial, the parties introduced extensive evidence concerning the Law School's use of race in the admissions process. [A former admissions director] testified that at the height of the admissions season, he would frequently consult the so-called "daily reports" that kept track of the racial and ethnic composition of the class (along with other information such as residency status and gender). This was done, [he] testified, to ensure that a critical mass of underrepresented minority students would be reached so as to realize the educational benefits of a diverse student body. [The current admissions director Erica Munzel] testified that "critical mass" means "meaningful numbers" or "meaningful representation," which she understood to mean a number that encourages underrepresented minority students to participate in the classroom and not feel isolated. Munzel stated there is no number, percentage, or range of numbers or percentages that constitute critical mass. Munzel also asserted that she must consider the race of applicants because a critical mass of underrepresented minority students could not be enrolled if admissions decisions were based primarily on undergraduate GPAs and LSAT scores.

[An expert witness of the Law School,] Dr. Stephen Raudenbush, [testified] that in 2000, [when] 35 percent of underrepresented minority applicants were admitted, [if] race were not considered, only 10 percent of those applicants would have been admitted. Under this scenario, underrepresented minority students would have comprised 4 percent of the entering class in 2000 instead of the actual figure of 14.5 percent. * * *

II A. We last addressed the use of race in public higher education over 25 years ago [in] the landmark *Bakke* case. [Since then,] Justice Powell's opinion announcing the judgment of the Court has served as the touchstone for constitutional analysis of race-conscious admissions policies. Public and private universities across the Nation have modeled their own admissions programs on Justice Powell's views on permissible race-conscious policies. [Justice] Powell approved the university's use of race to further only one interest: "the attainment of a diverse student body." * * *

B. [Because] the Fourteenth Amendment "protect[s] *persons*, not *groups*," all "governmental action based on race—a group classification long recognized as in most circumstances irrelevant and therefore prohibited—should be subjected to detailed judicial inquiry to ensure that the *personal* right to equal protection of the laws has not been infringed." *Adarand Constructors, Inc. v. Pena*, [p. 732 infra]. We have held that all racial classifications imposed by government "must be analyzed by a reviewing court under strict scrutiny." [We] apply strict scrutiny to all racial classifications to " 'smoke out' illegitimate uses of race by assuring that [government] is pursuing a goal important enough to warrant use of a highly suspect tool." *Richmond v. J.A. Croson Co.* Strict scrutiny is not "strict in theory, but fatal in fact." *Adarand*. [When] race-based action is necessary to further a compelling governmental interest, such action does not violate the constitutional guarantee of equal protection so long as the narrow-tailoring requirement is also satisfied.

III A. [R]espondents assert only one justification for their use of race in the admissions process: obtaining "the educational benefits that flow from a diverse student body." [We] first wish to dispel the notion that the Law School's argument has been foreclosed, either expressly or implicitly, by our affirmative-action cases decided since *Bakke*. It is true that some language in those opinions might be read to suggest that remedying past discrimination is the only permissible justification for race-based governmental action. But we have never held that the only governmental use of race that can survive strict scrutiny is remedying past discrimination.

[Today], we hold that the Law School has a compelling interest in attaining a diverse student body. The Law School's educational judgment that such diversity is essential to its educational mission is one to which we defer. * * *

As part of its goal of "assembling a class that is both exceptionally academically qualified and broadly diverse," the Law School seeks to "enroll a 'critical mass' of minority students." The Law School's interest is not simply "to assure within its student body some specified percentage of a particular group merely because of its race or ethnic origin." That would amount to outright racial balancing, which is patently unconstitutional. Rather, the Law School's concept of critical mass is defined by reference to the educational benefits that diversity is designed to produce. These benefits are substantial. As the District Court emphasized, the Law School's admissions policy promotes "cross-racial understanding," helps to break down racial stereotypes, and "enables [students] to better understand persons of different races." These benefits are "important and laudable," because "classroom discussion is livelier, more spirited, and simply more enlightening and interesting" when the students have "the greatest possible variety of backgrounds." [Numerous] studies show that student body diversity promotes learning outcomes, and "better prepares students for an increasingly diverse workforce and society, and better prepares them as professionals."

These benefits are not theoretical but real, as major American businesses have made clear that the skills needed in today's increasingly global marketplace can only be developed through exposure to widely diverse people, cultures, ideas, and viewpoints. What is more, high-ranking retired officers and civilian leaders of the United States military assert that, "[b]ased on [their] decades of experience," a "highly qualified, racially diverse officer corps is essential to the military's ability to fulfill its principle mission to provide national security." The primary sources for the Nation's officer corps are the service academies and the Reserve Officers Training Corps (ROTC), the latter comprising students already admitted to participating colleges and universities. At present, "the military cannot achieve an officer corps that is *both* highly qualified *and* racially diverse unless the service academies and the ROTC used limited race-conscious recruiting and admissions policies." To fulfill its mission, the military "must be selective in admissions for training and education for the officer corps, and it must train and educate a highly qualified, racially diverse officer corps in a racially diverse setting." Ibid. We agree that "[i]t requires only a small step from this analysis to conclude that our country's other most selective institutions must remain both diverse and selective."

[U]niversities, and in particular, law schools, represent the training ground for a large number of our Nation's leaders. *Sweatt v. Painter*. [In] order to cultivate a set of leaders with legitimacy in the eyes of the citizenry, it is necessary that the path to leadership be visibly open to talented and qualified individuals of every race and ethnicity. All members of our heterogeneous society must have confidence in the openness and integrity of the educational institutions that provide this training. As we have recognized, law schools "cannot be effective in isolation from the individuals and institutions with which the law interacts." See *Sweatt*. Access to legal education (and thus the legal profession) must be inclusive of talented and qualified individuals of every race and ethnicity, so that all members of our heterogeneous society may participate in the educational institutions that provide the training and education necessary to succeed in America.

The Law School does not premise its need for critical mass on "any belief that minority students always (or even consistently) express some characteristic minority viewpoint on any issue." To the contrary, diminishing the force of such stereotypes is both a crucial part of the Law School's mission, and one that it cannot accomplish with only token numbers of minority students. Just as growing up in a particular region or having particular professional experiences is likely to affect an individual's views, so too is one's own, unique experience of being a racial minority in a society, like our own, in which race unfortunately still matters. The Law School has determined, based on its experience and expertise, that a "critical mass" of underrepresented minorities is necessary to further its compelling interest in securing the educational benefits of a diverse student body.

B. Even in the limited circumstance when drawing racial distinctions is permissible to further a compelling state interest, government is still "constrained in how it may pursue that end." [A] university may consider race or ethnicity only as a " 'plus' in a particular applicant's file," without "insulat[ing] the individual from comparison with all other candidates for the available seats." [We] find that the Law School's admissions program bears the hallmarks of a narrowly tailored plan. [The] Law School's goal of attaining a critical mass of underrepresented minority students does not transform its program into a quota. [Nor] does the Law School's consultation of the "daily reports," which keep track of the racial and ethnic composition of the class (as well as of residency and gender), "sugges[t] there was no further attempt at individual review save for race itself" during the final stages of the admissions process. To the contrary, the Law School's admissions officers testified without contradiction that they never gave race any more or less weight based on the information contained in these reports. Moreover, [between] 1993 and 1998, the number of African–American, Latino, and Native–American students in each class at the Law School varied from 13.5 to 20.1 percent, a range inconsistent with a quota.

[Petitioner] and the United States argue that the Law School's plan is not narrowly tailored because race-neutral means exist to obtain the educational benefits of student body diversity that the Law School seeks. We disagree. Narrow tailoring does not require exhaustion of every conceivable race-neutral alternative. Nor does it require a university to choose between maintaining a reputation for excellence or fulfilling a commitment to provide educational opportunities to members of all racial groups. [The] District Court took the Law School to task for failing to consider race-neutral alternatives such as "using a lottery system" or "decreasing the emphasis for all applicants on undergraduate GPA and LSAT scores." But these alternatives would require a dramatic sacrifice of diversity, the academic quality of all admitted students, or both. [The] United States advocates "percentage plans," recently adopted by public undergraduate institutions in Texas, Florida, and California to guarantee admission to all students above a certain class-rank threshold in every high school in the State. The United States does not, however, explain how such plans could work for graduate and professional schools.

[We] acknowledge that "there are serious problems of justice connected with the idea of preference itself." [We] are mindful, [too], that "[a] core purpose of the Fourteenth Amendment was to do away with all governmentally imposed discrimination based on race." Accordingly, race-conscious admissions policies must be limited in time. This requirement reflects that racial classifications, however compelling their goals, are potentially so dangerous that they may be employed no more broadly than the interest demands. In the context of higher education, the durational requirement can be met by sunset provisions in race-conscious admissions policies and periodic reviews to determine whether racial preferences are still necessary to achieve student body diversity. [We] take the Law School at its word that it would "like nothing better than to find a race-neutral admissions formula" and will terminate its race-conscious admissions program as soon as practicable. It has been 25 years since Justice Powell first approved the use of race to further an interest in student body diversity in the context of public higher education. Since that time, the number of minority applicants with high grades and test scores has indeed increased. We expect that 25 years from now, the use of racial preferences will no longer be necessary to further the interest approved today.

JUSTICE GINSBURG, with whom JUSTICE BREYER joins, concurring.

[It] was only 25 years before *Bakke* that this Court declared public school segregation unconstitutional, a declaration that, after prolonged resistance, yielded an end to a law-enforced racial caste system, itself the legacy of centuries of slavery. [Today, it] is well documented that conscious and unconscious race bias, even rank discrimination based on race, remain alive in our land, impeding realization of our highest values and ideals. As to public education, data for the years 2000–2001 show that 71.6% of African–American children and 76.3% of Hispanic children attended a school in which minorities made up a majority of the student body. And schools in predominantly minority communities lag far behind others measured by the educational resources available to them. [Despite] these inequalities, some minority students are able to meet the high threshold requirements set for admission to the country's finest undergraduate and graduate educational institutions. As lower school education in minority communities improves, an increase in the number of such students may be anticipated. From today's vantage point, one may hope, but not firmly forecast, that over the next generation's span, progress toward nondiscrimination and genuinely equal opportunity will make it safe to sunset affirmative action.

CHIEF JUSTICE REHNQUIST, with whom JUSTICE SCALIA, JUSTICE KENNEDY, and JUSTICE THOMAS join, dissenting.

I agree with the Court that, "in the limited circumstance when drawing racial distinctions is permissible," the government must ensure that its means are narrowly tailored to achieve a compelling state interest. I do not believe, however, that the University of Michigan Law School's (Law School) means are narrowly tailored to the interest it asserts. [Stripped] of its "critical mass" veil, the Law School's program is revealed as a naked effort to achieve racial balancing.

[From] 1995 through 2000, the Law School admitted between 1,130 and 1,310 students. Of those, between 13 and 19 were Native American, between 91 and 108 were African–Americans, and between 47 and 56 were Hispanic. If the Law School is admitting between 91 and 108 African–Americans in order to achieve "critical mass," thereby preventing African–American students from feeling "isolated or like spokespersons for their race," one would think that a number of the same order of magnitude would be necessary to accomplish the same purpose for Hispanics and Native Americans. Similarly, even if all of the Native American applicants admitted in a given year matriculate, which the record demonstrates is not at all the case,1 how can this possibly constitute a "critical mass" of Native Americans in a class of over 350 students? * * *

These different numbers, moreover, come only as a result of substantially different treatment among the three underrepresented minority groups. [For] example, in 2000, 12 Hispanics who scored between a 159–160 on the LSAT and earned a GPA of 3.00 or higher applied for admission and only 2 were admitted. Meanwhile, 12 African–Americans in the same range of qualifications applied for admission and all 12 were admitted. Likewise, that same year, 16 Hispanics who scored between a 151–153 on the LSAT and earned a 3.00 or higher applied for admission and only 1 of those applicants was admitted. Twenty-three similarly qualified African–Americans applied for admission and 14 were admitted.

Only when the "critical mass" label is discarded does a likely explanation for these numbers emerge. [The] correlation between the percentage of the Law School's pool of applicants who are members of the three minority groups and the

---

1. Indeed, during this 5–year time period, enrollment of Native American students dropped to as low as three such students. Any assertion that such a small group constituted a "critical mass" of Native Americans is simply absurd.

percentage of the admitted applicants who are members of these same groups is far too precise to be dismissed as merely the result of the school paying "some attention to [the] numbers." As the tables below show, from 1995 through 2000 the percentage of admitted applicants who were members of these minority groups closely tracked the percentage of individuals in the school's applicant pool who were from the same groups.

For example, in 1995, when 9.7% of the applicant pool was African–American, 9.4% of the admitted class was African–American. By 2000, only 7.5% of the applicant pool was African–American, and 7.3% of the admitted class was African–American. [The] tight correlation between the percentage of applicants and admittees of a given race, therefore, must result from careful race based planning by the Law School. It suggests a formula for admission based on the aspirational assumption that all applicants are equally qualified academically, and therefore that the proportion of each group admitted should be the same as the proportion of that group in the applicant pool. [This] is precisely the type of racial balancing that the Court itself calls "patently unconstitutional."

JUSTICE KENNEDY, dissenting.

The opinion by Justice Powell in *Bakke*, in my view, states the correct rule for resolving this case. The Court, however, does not apply strict scrutiny. By trying to say otherwise, it undermines both the test and its own controlling precedents. [At] the very least, the constancy of admitted minority students and the close correlation between the racial breakdown of admitted minorities and the composition of the applicant pool, [require] the Law School either to produce a convincing explanation or to show it has taken adequate steps to ensure individual assessment. The Law School does neither. * * *

JUSTICE SCALIA, with whom JUSTICE THOMAS joins, concurring in part and dissenting in part.

The "educational benefit" that the University of Michigan seeks to achieve by racial discrimination consists, according to the Court, of "cross-racial understanding," and "better prepar[ation of] students for an increasingly diverse workforce and society," all of which is necessary not only for work, but also for good "citizenship." This is not, of course, an "educational benefit" on which students will be graded on their Law School transcript (Works and Plays Well with Others: B+) or tested by the bar examiners (Q: Describe in 500 words or less your cross-racial understanding). For it is a lesson of life rather than law—essentially the same lesson taught to (or rather learned by, for it cannot be "taught" in the usual sense) people three feet shorter and twenty years younger than the full-grown adults at the University of Michigan Law School, in institutions ranging from Boy Scout troops to public-school kindergartens. If properly considered an "educational benefit" at all, it is surely not one that is either uniquely relevant to law school or uniquely "teachable" in a formal educational setting. *And therefore*: If it is appropriate for the University of Michigan Law School to use racial discrimination for the purpose of putting together a "critical mass" that will convey generic lessons in socialization and good citizenship, surely it is no less appropriate— indeed, *particularly* appropriate—for the civil service system of the State of Michigan to do so. There, also, those exposed to "critical masses" of certain races will presumably become better Americans, better Michiganders, better civil servants. And surely private employers cannot be criticized—indeed, should be praised—if they also "teach" good citizenship to their adult employees through a patriotic, all-American system of racial discrimination in hiring. The nonminority individuals who are deprived of a legal education, a civil service job, or any job at all by reason of their skin color will surely understand.

Unlike a clear constitutional holding that racial preferences in state educational institutions are impermissible, or even a clear anticonstitutional holding that racial preferences in state educational institutions are OK, today's [decision in *Grutter*, when coupled with the Court's decision in *Gratz*, which follows immediately,] seems perversely designed to prolong the controversy and the litigation. Some future lawsuits will presumably focus on whether the discriminatory scheme in question contains enough evaluation of the applicant "as an individual," and sufficiently avoids "separate admissions tracks" [to be constitutionally permissible]. Some will focus on whether a university has gone beyond the bounds of a " 'good faith effort' " and has so zealously pursued its "critical mass" as to make it an unconstitutional de facto quota system, rather than merely " 'a permissible goal.' " Other lawsuits may focus on whether, in the particular setting at issue, any educational benefits flow from racial diversity. (That issue was not contested in *Grutter*; and while the opinion accords "a degree of deference to a university's academic decisions," "deference does not imply abandonment or abdication of judicial review.") Still other suits may challenge the bona fides of the institution's expressed commitment to the educational benefits of diversity that immunize the discriminatory scheme in *Grutter*. (Tempting targets, one would suppose, will be those universities that talk the talk of multiculturalism and racial diversity in the courts but walk the walk of tribalism and racial segregation on their campuses—through minority-only student organizations, separate minority housing opportunities, separate minority student centers, even separate minority-only graduation ceremonies.) And still other suits may claim that the institution's racial preferences have gone below or above the mystical *Grutter*-approved "critical mass." Finally, litigation can be expected on behalf of minority groups intentionally short changed in the institution's composition of its generic minority "critical mass." I do not look forward to any of these cases. The Constitution proscribes government discrimination on the basis of race, and state-provided education is no exception.

JUSTICE THOMAS, with whom JUSTICE SCALIA joins as to Parts I–VII, concurring in part and dissenting in part.

Frederick Douglass, speaking to a group of abolitionists almost 140 years ago, delivered a message lost on today's majority: "[I]n regard to the colored people, there is always more that is benevolent, I perceive, than just, manifested towards us. What I ask for the negro is not benevolence, not pity, not sympathy, but simply *justice*.... And if the negro cannot stand on his own legs, let him fall.... All I ask is, give him a chance to stand on his own legs! Let him alone! [Y]our interference is doing him positive injury." [Like] Douglass, I believe blacks can achieve in every avenue of American life without the meddling of university administrators. Because I wish to see all students succeed whatever their color, I share, in some respect, the sympathies of those who sponsor the type of discrimination advanced by the University of Michigan Law School. [The] Constitution does not, however, tolerate institutional devotion to the status quo in admissions policies when such devotion ripens into racial discrimination. Nor does the Constitution countenance the unprecedented deference the Court gives to the Law School, an approach inconsistent with the very concept of "strict scrutiny."

II. Unlike the majority, I seek to define with precision the interest being asserted by the Law School before determining whether that interest is so compelling as to justify racial discrimination. The Law School maintains that it wishes to obtain "educational benefits that flow from student body diversity." This statement must be evaluated carefully, because it implies that both "diversity" and "educational benefits" are components of the Law School's compelling state interest. [The] Law School [apparently] believes that only a racially mixed student body can lead to the educational benefits it seeks. How, then, is the Law School's interest in these allegedly unique educational "benefits" *not* simply the forbidden interest in "racial balancing" that the majority expressly rejects? A distinction between these two ideas (unique educational benefits based on racial aesthetics and race for its own sake) is purely sophistic—so much so that the majority uses them interchangeably.

III.   [Justice] Powell's opinion in *Bakke* and the Court's decision today rest on the fundamentally flawed proposition that racial discrimination can be contextualized so that a goal, such as classroom aesthetics, can be compelling in one context but not in another. [Under] the proper standard, there is no pressing public necessity in maintaining a public law school at all and, it follows, certainly not an elite law school. Likewise, marginal improvements in legal education do not qualify as a compelling state interest. * * *

IV.   [With] the adoption of different admissions methods, such as accepting all students who meet minimum qualifications, the Law School could achieve its vision of the racially aesthetic student body without the use of racial discrimination. The Law School concedes this, but the Court holds, implicitly and under the guise of narrow tailoring, that the Law School has a compelling state interest in doing what it wants to do. I cannot agree. First, under strict scrutiny, the Law School's assessment of the benefits of racial discrimination and devotion to the admissions status quo are not entitled to any sort of deference, grounded in the First Amendment or anywhere else. Second, even if its "academic selectivity" must be maintained at all costs along with racial discrimination, the Court ignores the fact that other top law schools have succeeded in meeting their aesthetic demands without racial discrimination.

[The] Court relies heavily on social science evidence to justify its deference. The Court never acknowledges, however, the growing evidence that racial (and other sorts) of heterogeneity actually impairs learning among black students. See, e.g., Flowers & Pascarella, *Cognitive Effects of College Racial Composition on African American Students After 3 Years of College*, 40 J. of College Student Development 669, 674 (1999) (concluding that black students experience superior cognitive development at Historically Black Colleges (HBCs) and that, even among blacks, "a substantial diversity moderates the cognitive effects of attending an HBC"); Allen, *The Color of Success: African–American College Student Outcomes at Predominantly White and Historically Black Public Colleges and Universities*, 62 Harv. Educ. Rev. 26, 35 (1992) (finding that black students attending HBCs report higher academic achievement than those attending predominantly white colleges). * * *

VI.   [I] believe what lies beneath the Court's decision today are the benighted notions that one can tell when racial discrimination benefits (rather than hurts) minority groups, and that racial discrimination is necessary to remedy general societal ills. [I] must contest the notion that the Law School's discrimination benefits those admitted as a result of it. The Court spends considerable time discussing the impressive display of amicus support for the Law School in this case from all corners of society. But nowhere in any of the filings in this Court is any evidence that the purported "beneficiaries" of this racial discrimination prove themselves by performing at (or even near) the same level as those students who receive no preferences. Cf. Thernstrom & Thernstrom, *Reflections on the Shape of the River*, 46 UCLA L. Rev. 1583, 1605–1608 (1999) (discussing the failure of defenders of racial discrimination in admissions to consider the fact that its "beneficiaries" are underperforming in the classroom).

[The] Law School tantalizes unprepared students with the promise of a University of Michigan degree and all of the opportunities that it offers. These overmatched students take the bait, only to find that they cannot succeed in the cauldron of competition. And this mismatch crisis is not restricted to elite institutions. See T. Sowell, *Race and Culture* 176–177 (1994) ("Even if most minority students are able to meet the normal standards at the 'average' range of colleges and universities, the systematic mismatching of minority students begun at the top can mean that such students are generally overmatched throughout all levels of higher education"). [While] these students may graduate with law degrees, there is no evidence that they have received a qualitatively better legal education (or become better lawyers) than if they had gone to a less "elite" law school for which they were better prepared.

[It] is uncontested that each year, the Law School admits a handful of blacks who would be admitted in the absence of racial discrimination. Who can differentiate between those who belong and those who do not? The majority of blacks are admitted to the Law School because of discrimination, and because of this policy all are tarred as undeserving. This problem of stigma does not depend on determinacy as to whether those stigmatized are actually the "beneficiaries" of racial discrimination. When blacks take positions in the highest places of government, industry, or academia, it is an open question today whether their skin color played a part in their advancement. The question itself is the stigma—because either racial discrimination did play a role, in which case the person may be deemed "otherwise unqualified," or it did not, in which case asking the question itself unfairly marks those blacks who would succeed without discrimination.

GRATZ v. BOLLINGER

539 U.S. 244, 123 S.Ct. 2411, 156 L.Ed.2d 257 (2003).

CHIEF JUSTICE REHNQUIST delivered the opinion of the Court.

[Petitioner Gratz was a Caucasian resident of Michigan who was denied admission to the University of Michigan's (University) College of Literature, Science, and the Arts ("LSA"). She subsequently filed suit challenging the constitutionality of the University's undergraduate affirmative action policies.]

The University changed its admissions guidelines a number of times during the period relevant to this litigation, [but the version in place at the time of the Court's decision, introduced during the 1998 academic year, employed] a "selection index," on which an applicant could score a maximum of 150 points. This index was divided linearly into ranges generally calling for admissions dispositions as follows: 100–150 (admit); 95–99 (admit or postpone); 90–94 (postpone or admit); 75–89 (delay or postpone); 74 and below (delay or reject). Each application received points based on high school grade point average, standardized test scores, academic quality of an applicant's high school, strength or weakness of high school curriculum, in-state residency, alumni relationship, personal essay, and personal achievement or leadership. Of particular significance here, under a "miscellaneous" category, an applicant was entitled to 20 points based upon his or her membership in an underrepresented racial or ethnic minority group. [Under the same category, 20 points could also be awarded based upon socioeconomic status, upon status as a recruited athlete, or upon a designation by the provost.]

[Starting] in 1999, [the] University established an Admissions Review Committee (ARC), to provide an additional level of consideration for some applications. Under the new system, counselors may, in their discretion, "flag" an application for the ARC to review after determining that the applicant (1) is academically prepared to succeed at the University, (2) has achieved a minimum selection index score, and (3) possesses a quality or characteristic important to the University's composition of its freshman class, such as high class rank, unique life experiences, challenges, circumstances, interests or talents, socioeconomic disadvantage, and underrepresented race, ethnicity, or geography. After reviewing "flagged" applications, the ARC determines whether to admit, defer, or deny each applicant.

II. [Petitioners' argument that the Fourteenth Amendment categorically prohibits the use of racial preferences to promote educational diversity fails under the holding of *Grutter*. But] the University's policy, which automatically distributes 20 points, or one-fifth of the points needed to guarantee admission, to every single "underrepresented minority" applicant solely because of race, is not narrowly tailored to achieve the interest in educational diversity that respondents claim justifies their program.

In *Bakke*, Justice Powell reiterated that "[p]referring members of any one group for no reason other than race or ethnic origin is discrimination for its own sake." [His opinion] emphasized the importance of considering each particular applicant as an individual, assessing all of the qualities that individual possesses, and in turn, evaluating that individual's ability to contribute to the unique setting of higher education. [The] current LSA policy does not provide such individualized consideration. The LSA's policy automatically distributes 20 points to every single applicant from an "underrepresented minority" group, as defined by the University. The only consideration that accompanies this distribution of points is a factual review of an application to determine whether an individual is a member of one of these minority groups. Moreover, unlike Justice Powell's example, where the race of a "particular black applicant" could be considered without being decisive, the LSA's automatic distribution of 20 points has the effect of making "the factor of race * * * decisive" for virtually every minimally qualified underrepresented minority applicant.

Also instructive in our consideration of the LSA's system is the example provided in the description of the Harvard College Admissions Program, which Justice Powell both discussed in, and attached to, his opinion in *Bakke*. The example was included to "illustrate the kind of significance attached to race" under the Harvard College program. It provided as follows: "The Admissions Committee, with only a few places left to fill, might find itself forced to choose between A, the child of a successful black physician in an academic community with promise of superior academic performance, and B, a black who grew up in an inner-city ghetto of semi-literate parents whose academic achievement was lower but who had demonstrated energy and leadership as well as an apparently abiding interest in black power. If a good number of black students much like A but few like B had already been admitted, the Committee might prefer B; and vice versa. If C, a white student with extraordinary artistic talent, were also seeking one of the remaining places, his unique quality might give him an edge over both A and B. Thus, the critical criteria are often individual qualities or experience *not dependent upon race but sometimes associated with it.*"

This example further demonstrates the problematic nature of the LSA's admissions system. Even if student C's "extraordinary artistic talent" rivaled that of Monet or Picasso, the applicant would receive, at most, five points under the LSA's system. At the same time, every single underrepresented minority applicant, including students A and B, would automatically receive 20 points for submitting an application. Clearly, the LSA's system does not offer applicants the individualized selection process described in Harvard's example.

[Respondents] emphasize the fact that the LSA has created the possibility of an applicant's file being flagged for individualized consideration by the ARC. We think that the flagging program only emphasizes the flaws of the University's system as a whole when compared to that described by Justice Powell. Again, students A, B, and C illustrate the point. First, student A would never be flagged. This is because, as the University has conceded, the effect of automatically awarding 20 points is that virtually every qualified underrepresented minority applicant is admitted. Student A, an applicant "with promise of superior academic performance," would certainly fit this description. Thus, the result of the automatic distribution of 20 points is that the University would never consider student A's individual background, experiences, and characteristics to assess his individual "potential contribution to diversity." Instead, every applicant like student A would simply be admitted.

It is possible that students B and C would be flagged and considered as individuals. This assumes that student B was not already admitted because of the automatic 20–point distribution, and that student C could muster at least 70 additional points. But the fact that the "review committee can look at the applications individually and ignore the points," once an application is flagged is of little comfort under our strict scrutiny analysis. The record does not reveal precisely how many applications are flagged for this individualized consideration, but it is undisputed that such consideration is the exception and not the rule in the operation of the LSA's admissions program. Additionally, this individualized review is only provided after admissions counselors automatically distribute the University's version of a "plus" that makes race a decisive factor for virtually every minimally qualified underrepresented minority applicant.

Respondents contend that "[t]he volume of applications and the presentation of applicant information make it impractical for [LSA] to use [the] admissions system" upheld by the Court today in *Grutter*. But the fact that the implementation of a program capable of providing individualized consideration might present administrative challenges does not render constitutional an otherwise problematic system. Nothing in Justice Powell's opinion in *Bakke* signaled that a university may employ whatever means it desires to achieve the stated goal of diversity without regard to the limits imposed by our strict scrutiny analysis.

JUSTICE O'CONNOR, with whom JUSTICE BREYER joins except as to the last sentence, concurring.

Unlike the law school admissions policy the Court upholds today in *Grutter v. Bollinger*, the procedures employed by the University of Michigan's Office of Undergraduate Admissions do not provide for a meaningful individualized review of applicants. [Although] the Office of Undergraduate Admissions does assign 20 points to some "soft" variables other than race, the points available for other diversity contributions, such as leadership and service, personal achievement, and geographic diversity, are capped at much lower levels. [The] only potential source of individualized consideration appears to be the Admissions Review Committee. The evidence in the record, however, reveals very little about how the review committee actually functions. And what evidence there is indicates that the committee is a kind of afterthought, rather than an integral component of a system of individualized review. [As] a result, I join the Court's opinion * * *.

JUSTICE THOMAS, concurring.

I join the Court's opinion because I believe it correctly applies our precedents, including today's decision in *Grutter*. For similar reasons to those given in my separate opinion in that case, however, I would hold that a State's use of racial discrimination in higher education admissions is categorically prohibited by the Equal Protection Clause.

JUSTICE BREYER, concurring in the judgment.

[I] join Justice O'Connor's opinion except insofar as it joins that of the Court. [I] agree with Justice Ginsburg that, in implementing the Constitution's equality instruction, government decisionmakers may properly distinguish between policies of inclusion and exclusion, for the former are more likely to prove consistent with the basic constitutional obligation that the law respect each individual equally.

JUSTICE STEVENS, with whom JUSTICE SOUTER joins, dissenting.

[Because the case should be dismissed for lack of standing,] I respectfully dissent.

JUSTICE SOUTER, with whom JUSTICE GINSBURG joins as to Part II, dissenting.

II. The cases now contain two pointers toward the line between the valid and the unconstitutional in race-conscious admissions schemes. *Grutter* reaffirms the permissibility of individualized consideration of race to achieve a diversity of students, at least where race is not assigned a preordained value in all cases. On the other hand, Justice Powell's opinion in *Bakke* rules out a racial quota or set-aside, in which race is the sole fact of eligibility for certain places in a class. Although the freshman admissions system here is subject to argument on the merits, I think it is closer to what *Grutter* approves than to what *Bakke* condemns, and should not be held unconstitutional on the current record.

The record does not describe a system with a quota like the one struck down in *Bakke*, which "insulate[d]" all nonminority candidates from competition from certain seats. [Although] membership in an underrepresented minority is given a weight of 20 points on the 150–point scale[,] this assignment of specific points does not set race apart from all other weighted considerations. Nonminority students may receive 20 points for athletic ability, socioeconomic disadvantage, attendance at a socioeconomically disadvantaged or predominantly minority high school, or at the Provost's discretion; they may also receive 10 points for being residents of Michigan, 6 for residence in an underrepresented Michigan county, 5 for leadership and service, and so on.

[The] very nature of a college's permissible practice of awarding value to racial diversity means that race must be considered in a way that increases some applicants' chances for admission. [It] suffices for me that there are no *Bakke*-like set-asides and that consideration of an applicant's whole spectrum of ability is no more ruled out by giving 20 points for race than by giving the same points for athletic ability or socioeconomic disadvantage.

JUSTICE GINSBURG, with whom JUSTICE SOUTER joins, dissenting.

I. [A]s I see it, government decisionmakers may properly distinguish between policies of exclusion and inclusion. [Our] jurisprudence ranks race a "suspect" category, "not because [race] is inevitably an impermissible classification, but because it is one which usually, to our national shame, has been drawn for the purpose of maintaining racial inequality." But where race is considered "for the purpose of achieving equality," no automatic proscription is in order. * * *

II. [The] racial and ethnic groups to which the College accords special consideration (African–Americans, Hispanics, and Native–Americans) historically have been relegated to inferior status by law and social practice; their members continue to experience class-based discrimination to this day. There is no suggestion that the College adopted its current policy in order to limit or decrease enrollment by any particular racial or ethnic group, and no seats are reserved on the basis of race. Nor has there been any demonstration that the College's program unduly constricts admissions opportunities for students who do not receive special consideration based on race.

The stain of generations of racial oppression is still visible in our society, and the determination to hasten its removal remains vital. One can reasonably anticipate, therefore, that colleges and universities will seek to maintain their minority enrollment—and the networks and opportunities thereby opened to minority graduates—whether or not they can do so in full candor through adoption of affirmative action plans of the kind here at issue. Without recourse to such plans, institutions of higher education may resort to camouflage. For example, schools may encourage applicants to write of their cultural traditions in the essays they submit, or to indicate whether English is their second language. Seeking to improve their chances for admission, applicants may highlight the minority group associations to which they belong, or the Hispanic surnames of their mothers or grandparents. In turn, teachers' recommendations may emphasize who a student is as much as what he or she has accomplished. If honesty is the best policy, surely Michigan's accurately described, fully disclosed College affirmative action program is preferable to achieving similar numbers through winks, nods, and disguises.

PARENTS INVOLVED IN COMMUNITY SCHOOLS
v. SEATTLE SCHOOL DIST. NO. 1

551 U.S. 701, 127 S.Ct. 2738, 168 L.Ed.2d 508 (2007).

ROBERTS, C.J., announced the judgment of the Court, and delivered the opinion of the Court with respect to Parts I, II, III–A, and III–C, and an opinion with respect to Parts III–B and IV, in which JUSTICES SCALIA, THOMAS, and ALITO join.

The school districts in these cases [involving Seattle, Washington, and Jefferson County, Kentucky] voluntarily adopted student assignment plans that rely upon race to determine which public schools certain children may attend. * * *

I. Both cases present the same underlying legal question—whether a public school that had not operated legally segregated schools or has been found to be unitary may choose to classify students by race and rely upon that classification in making school assignments.

[The Seattle School District was never officially segregated by law, but racial imbalances led to threatened and actual lawsuits in the 1960s and 1970s and to a series of steps to settle those lawsuits that once included mandatory busing, despite the fact that official discrimination was never proved nor admitted. In 1998, the district] adopted the plan at issue in this case for assigning students to [its ten high] schools. The plan allows incoming ninth graders to choose from among any of the district's high schools, ranking however many schools they wish in order of preference. [If] too many students list the same school as their first choice, the district employs a series of "tiebreakers" to determine who will fill the open slots at the oversubscribed school. The first tiebreaker selects for admission students who have a sibling currently enrolled in the chosen school. The next tiebreaker depends upon the racial composition of the particular school and the race of the individual student. [This second tiebreaker comes into play if a school's enrollment deviates by more than 10% from the districts overall balance of approximately 41% white and 59% nonwhite students.]

Jefferson County Public Schools operates the public school system in metropolitan Louisville, Kentucky. In 1973 a federal court found that Jefferson County had maintained a segregated school system, and in 1975 the District Court entered a desegregation decree. Jefferson County operated under this decree until 2000, when the District Court dissolved the decree after finding that the district had achieved unitary status by eliminating "[t]o the greatest extent practicable" the vestiges of its prior policy of segregation.

In 2001, after the decree had been dissolved, Jefferson County adopted the voluntary student assignment plan at issue in this case. [That plan, which covers 97,000 students—roughly 34% of whom are black and the remaining 66% of whom are mostly white—] requires all nonmagnet schools to maintain a minimum black enrollment of 15 percent, and a maximum black enrollment of 50 percent. [The requirements can sometimes block initial assignments and transfers, including assignments and transfers to neighborhood schools, that would otherwise occur.]

III.   A. It is well established that when the government distributes burdens or benefits on the basis of individual racial classifications, that action is reviewed under strict scrutiny. *Johnson* v. *California*, [Sec. 2, II]; *Grutter*. As the Court recently reaffirmed, " 'racial classifications are simply too pernicious to permit any but the most exact connection between justification and classification.' " *Gratz*. In order to satisfy this searching standard of review, the school districts must demonstrate that the use of individual racial classifications in the assignment plans here under review is "narrowly tailored" to achieve a "compelling" government interest.

[O]ur prior cases, in evaluating the use of racial classifications in the school context have recognized two interests that qualify as compelling. The first is [remedying] the effects of past intentional discrimination. See *Freeman* v. *Pitts*, 503 U.S. 467, 494 (1992). Yet the Seattle public schools have not shown that they were ever segregated by law, and were not subject to court-ordered desegregation decrees. The Jefferson County public schools [have been found to have] "eliminated the vestiges associated with [its] former policy of segregation and its pernicious effects" and thus [to have] achieved "unitary" status. Jefferson County accordingly does not rely upon an interest in remedying the effects of past intentional discrimination in defending its present use of race in assigning students. Nor could it. We have emphasized [that] "the Constitution is not violated by racial imbalance in the schools, without more." *Milliken* v. *Bradley*, 433 U.S. 267, 280 n. 14 (1977).

[The] second government interest we have recognized as compelling for purposes of strict scrutiny is the interest in diversity in higher education upheld in *Grutter*. The specific interest found compelling in *Grutter* was student body diversity "in the context of higher education." The diversity interest was not focused on race alone but encompassed "all factors that may contribute to student body diversity." [The] entire gist of the analysis in *Grutter* was that the admissions program at issue there focused on each applicant as an individual, and not simply as a member of a particular racial group. [In] the present cases, by contrast, race is not considered as part of a broader effort to achieve "exposure to widely diverse people, cultures, ideas, and viewpoints"; race, for some students, is determinative standing alone. [Even] when it comes to race, the plans here employ only a limited notion of diversity, viewing race exclusively in white/nonwhite terms in Seattle and black/"other" terms in Jefferson County. [Under] the Seattle plan, a school with 50 percent Asian–American students and 50 percent white students but no African–American, Native–American, or Latino students would qualify as balanced, while a school with 30 percent Asian–American, 25 percent African–American, 25 percent Latino, and 20 percent white students would not. [The] present cases are not governed by Grutter.

B. Each school district argues that educational and broader socialization benefits flow from a racially diverse learning environment, and each contends that because the diversity they seek is racial diversity—not the broader diversity at issue in *Grutter*—it makes sense to promote that interest directly by relying on race alone. The parties and their amici dispute whether racial diversity in schools in fact has a marked impact on test scores and other objective yardsticks or achieves intangible socialization benefits. The debate is not one we need to resolve, however, because it is clear that the racial classifications employed by the districts are not narrowly tailored to the goal of achieving the educational and social benefits asserted to flow from racial diversity. In design and operation, the plans are directed only to racial balance, pure and simple, an objective this Court has repeatedly condemned as illegitimate. [The] districts offer no evidence that the level of racial diversity necessary to achieve the asserted educational benefits happens to coincide with the racial demographics of the respective school districts—or rather the white/nonwhite or black/"other" balance of the districts, since that is the only diversity addressed by the plans. * * *

[It is a further constitutional defect that] in each case the extreme measure of relying on race in assignments is unnecessary to achieve the stated goals, even as defined by the districts. For example, at Franklin High School in Seattle, the racial tiebreaker was applied because nonwhite enrollment exceeded 69 percent, and resulted in an incoming ninth-grade class in 2000–2001 that was 30.3 percent Asian–American, 21.9 percent African–American, 6.8 percent Latino, 0.5 percent Native–American, and 40.5 percent Caucasian. Without the racial tiebreaker, the class would have been 39.6 percent Asian–American, 30.2 percent African–American, 8.3 percent Latino, 1.1 percent Native–American, and 20.8 percent Caucasian. When the actual racial breakdown is considered, enrolling students without regard to their race yields a substantially diverse student body under any definition of diversity.

C. The districts assert, as they must, that the way in which they have employed individual racial classifications is necessary to achieve their stated ends. The minimal effect these classifications have on student assignments, however, suggests that other means would be effective. Seattle's racial tiebreaker results, in the end, only in shifting a small number of students between schools. Approximately 307 student assignments were affected by the racial tiebreaker in 2000–2001, [and of] these, 209 were assigned to a school that was one of their choices, 87 of whom were assigned to the same school to which they would have been assigned without the racial tiebreaker. Eighty-four students were assigned to schools that they did not list as a choice, but 29 of those students would have been assigned to their respective school without the racial tiebreaker, and 3 were able to attend one of the oversubscribed schools due to waitlist and capacity adjustments. In over one-third of the assignments affected by the racial tiebreaker, then, the use of race in the end made no difference, and the district could identify only 52 students who were ultimately affected adversely by the racial tiebreaker in that it resulted in assignment to a school they had not listed as a preference and to which they would not otherwise have been assigned. [Similarly,] Jefferson County's use of racial classifications has only a minimal effect on the assignment of students. * * * Jefferson County estimates that the racial guidelines account for only 3 percent of assignments. While we do not suggest that *greater* use of race would be preferable, the minimal impact of the districts' racial classifications on school enrollment casts doubt on the necessity of using racial classifications. In *Grutter*, the consideration of race was viewed as indispensable in more than tripling minority representation at the law school-from 4 to 14.5 percent.

[The] districts have also failed to show that they considered methods other than explicit racial classifications to achieve their stated goals. Narrow tailoring requires "serious, good faith consideration of workable race-neutral alternatives." *Grutter*.

IV. Justice Breyer's dissent [fails] to ground the result it would reach in law. [It] seeks to justify the plans at issue under our precedents recognizing the compelling interest in remedying past intentional discrimination. [But the] distinction between segregation by state action and racial imbalance caused by other factors has been central to our jurisprudence in this area for generations. [The dissent also relies heavily on dicta, especially from *Swann v. Charlotte–Mecklenburg Bd. of Ed.*, 402 U.S. 1 (1971), but it is well settled that the Court is not bound by dicta on points that were not fully debated. In any event, Swann and the other cases relied on by the dissent to establish once-prevailing legal assumptions were decided "before this Court definitively determined that 'all racial classifications [must] be analyzed by a reviewing court under strict scrutiny.' " *Adarand Constructors, Inc. v. Pena*, Part IV, B infra.]

In Brown v. Board of Education, we held that segregation deprived black children of equal educational opportunities regardless of whether school facilities and other tangible factors were equal, because government classification and separation on grounds of race themselves denoted inferiority. [The] parties and their amici debate which side is more faithful to the heritage of *Brown*, but the position of the plaintiffs in *Brown* was spelled out in their brief and could not have been clearer: "[T]he Fourteenth Amendment prevents states from according differential treatment to American children on the basis of their color or race." Before *Brown*, schoolchildren were told where they could and could not go to school based on the color of their skin. The school districts in these cases have not carried the heavy burden of demonstrating that we should allow this once again— even for very different reasons. For schools that never segregated on the basis of race, such as Seattle, or that have removed the vestiges of past segregation, such as Jefferson County, the way "to achieve a system of determining admission to the public schools on a nonracial basis," is to stop assigning students on a racial basis. The way to stop discrimination on the basis of race is to stop discriminating on the basis of race.

JUSTICE THOMAS, concurring.

* * * I wholly concur in The Chief Justices opinion. I write separately to address several of the contentions in Justice Breyer's dissent. * * *

Disfavoring a color-blind interpretation of the Constitution, the dissent would give school boards a free hand to make decisions on the basis of race—an approach reminiscent of that advocated by the segregationists in *Brown*. This approach is just as wrong today as it was a half-century ago. [The] dissent repeatedly claims that the school districts are threatened with resegregation and that they will succumb to that threat if these plans are declared unconstitutional. [But racial] imbalance is not segregation, and the mere incantation of terms like resegregation and remediation cannot make up the difference. [Although] there is arguably a danger of racial imbalance in schools in Seattle and Louisville, there is no danger of resegregation. * * *

The dissent points to data that indicate that "black and white students in desegregated schools are less racially prejudiced than those in segregated schools." [But] it is unclear whether increased interracial contact improves racial attitudes and relations. [Some] studies have even found that a deterioration in racial attitudes seems to result from racial mixing in schools.* * *

Most of the dissent's criticisms of today's result can be traced to its rejection of the color-blind Constitution. [The] dissent appears to pin its interpretation of the Equal Protection Clause to current societal practice and expectations, deference to local officials, likely practical consequences, and reliance on previous statements from this and other courts. Such a view was ascendant [in] *Plessy*, where the Court asked whether a state law providing for segregated railway cars was "a reasonable regulation." [In] place of the color-blind Constitution, the dissent would permit measures to keep the races together and proscribe measures to keep the races apart. Although no such distinction is apparent in the Fourteenth Amendment, the dissent would constitutionalize today's faddish social theories that embrace that distinction. The Constitution is not that malleable. [Can] we really be sure that the racial theories that motivated *Dred Scott* and *Plessy* are a relic of the past or that future theories will be nothing but beneficent and progressive? That is a gamble I am unwilling to take, and it is one the Constitution does not allow.

JUSTICE KENNEDY, concurring in part and concurring in the judgment.

I.   * * * Diversity, depending on its meaning and definition, is a compelling educational goal a school district may pursue. [But the] government bears the burden of justifying its use of individual racial classifications. As part of that burden it must establish, in detail, how decisions based on an individual student's race are made in a challenged governmental program. The Jefferson County Board of Education fails to meet this threshold mandate.

Petitioner Crystal Meredith challenges the districts decision to deny her son Joshua McDonald a requested transfer for his kindergarten enrollment. The district concedes it denied his request "under the guidelines," which is to say, on the basis of Joshua's race. Yet the district also maintains that the guidelines do not apply to "kindergartens," and it fails to explain the discrepancy. Resort to the record, including the parties' Stipulation of Facts, further confuses the matter. [The] discrepancy identified is not some simple and straightforward error that touches only upon the peripheries of the district's use of individual racial classifications. To the contrary, Jefferson County [fails] to make clear [who] makes the decisions; what if any oversight is employed; the precise circumstances in which an assignment decision will or will not be made on the basis of race; or how it is determined which of two similarly situated children will be subjected to a given race-based decision. * * *

As for the Seattle case, the school district has gone further in describing the methods and criteria used to determine assignment decisions on the basis of individual racial classifications. The district, nevertheless, has failed to make an adequate showing in at least one respect. It has failed to explain why, in a district composed of a diversity of races, with fewer than half of the students classified as "white," it has employed the crude racial categories of "white" and "non-white" as the basis for its assignment decisions. [Other] problems are evident in Seattle's system, but there is no need to address them now. As the district fails to account for the classification system it has chosen, despite what appears to be its ill fit, Seattle has not shown its plan to be narrowly tailored to achieve its own ends; and thus it fails to pass strict scrutiny.

II.   [Parts] of the opinion by The Chief Justice imply an all-too-unyielding insistence that race cannot be a factor in instances when, in my view, it may be taken into account. The plurality opinion is too dismissive of the legitimate interest government has in ensuring all people have equal opportunity regardless of their race. [Fifty] years of experience since *Brown v. Board of Education* should teach us that the problem before us defies so easy a solution. School districts can seek to reach *Brown's* objective of equal educational opportunity. The plurality opinion is at least open to the interpretation that the Constitution requires school districts to ignore the problem of de facto resegregation in schooling. I cannot endorse that conclusion. To the extent the plurality opinion suggests the Constitution mandates that state and local school authorities must accept the status quo of racial isolation in schools, it is, in my view, profoundly mistaken.

[In] the administration of public schools by the state and local authorities it is permissible to consider the racial makeup of schools and to adopt general policies to encourage a diverse student body, one aspect of which is its racial composition. Cf. *Grutter* (Kennedy, J., dissenting). If school authorities are concerned that the student-body compositions of certain schools interfere with the objective of offering an equal educational opportunity to all of their students, they are free to devise race-conscious measures to address the problem in a general way and without treating each student in different fashion solely on the basis of a systematic, individual typing by race.

School boards may pursue the goal of bringing together students of diverse backgrounds and races through other means, including strategic site selection of new schools; drawing attendance zones with general recognition of the demographics of neighborhoods; allocating resources for special programs; recruiting students and faculty in a targeted fashion; and tracking enrollments, performance, and other statistics by race. These mechanisms are race conscious but do not lead to different treatment based on a classification that tells each student he or she is to be defined by race, so it is unlikely any of them would demand strict scrutiny to be found permissible. See *Bush v. Vera*, [Sec. 5, I, D infra] (plurality opinion). Executive and legislative branches, which for generations now have considered these types of policies and procedures, should be permitted to employ them with candor and with confidence that a constitutional violation does not occur whenever a decisionmaker considers the impact a given approach might have on students of different races. Assigning to each student a personal designation according to a crude system of individual racial classifications is quite a different matter; and the legal analysis changes accordingly.

Each respondent has asserted that its assignment of individual students by race is permissible because there is no other way to avoid racial isolation in the school districts. Yet, as explained, each has failed to provide the support necessary for that proposition. [In] the cases before us it is noteworthy that the number of students whose assignment depends on express racial classifications is limited. I join Part III–C of the Court's opinion because I agree that in the context of these plans, the small number of assignments affected suggests that the schools could have achieved their stated ends through different means. These include the facially race-neutral means set forth above or, if necessary, a more nuanced, individual evaluation of school needs and student characteristics that might include race as a component. The latter approach would be informed by *Grutter*, though of course the criteria relevant to student placement would differ based on the age of the students, the needs of the parents, and the role of the schools.

III. [The] dissent [relies on lower court opinions that have upheld explicitly race-conscious student-assignment plans by reasoning, to] oversimplify the matter a bit, [as follows]: If it is legitimate for school authorities to work to avoid racial isolation in their schools, must they do so only by indirection and general policies? Does the Constitution mandate this inefficient result? Why may the authorities not recognize the problem in candid fashion and solve it altogether through resort to direct assignments based on student racial classifications? So, the argument proceeds, if race is the problem, then perhaps race is the solution.

The argument ignores the dangers presented by individual classifications, dangers that are not as pressing when the same ends are achieved by more indirect means. When the government classifies an individual by race, it must first define what it means to be of a race. Who exactly is white and who is nonwhite? To be forced to live under a state-mandated racial label is inconsistent with the dignity of individuals in our society. And it is a label that an individual is powerless to change. Governmental classifications that command people to march in different directions based on racial typologies can cause a new divisiveness. The practice can lead to corrosive discourse, where race serves not as an element of our diverse heritage but instead as a bargaining chip in the political process. On the other hand, race-conscious measures that do not rely on differential treatment based on individual classifications present these problems to a lesser degree. * * *

Justice Stevens, dissenting.

While I join Justice Breyer's eloquent and unanswerable dissent in its entirety, it is appropriate to add these words. There is a cruel irony in The Chief Justices reliance on our decision in *Brown*. This [reliance] reminds me of Anatole France's observation: "[T]he majestic equality of the la[w], forbid[s] rich and poor alike to sleep under bridges, to beg in the streets, and to steal their bread."

[If] we look at cases decided during the interim between *Brown* and *Adarand*, we can see how [the Courts] rigid adherence to tiers of scrutiny obscures Brown's clear message. Perhaps the best example is provided by our approval of the decision of the Supreme Judicial Court of Massachusetts in 1967 upholding a state statute mandating racial integration in that State's school system. See *School Comm. of Boston v. Board of Education*, 352 Mass. 693, 227 N. E. 2d 729. [Our] ruling on the merits simply stated that the appeal was "dismissed for want of a substantial federal question." School Comm. of Boston v. Board of Education, 389 U. S. 572 (1968) (per curiam). The Court has changed significantly since it decided *School Comm. of Boston* in 1968. It was then more faithful to Brown and more respectful of our precedent than it is today. It is my firm conviction that no Member of the Court that I joined in 1975 would have agreed with today's decision.

Justice Breyer, with whom Justice Stevens, Justice Souter, and Justice Ginsburg, join, dissenting.

[The Court's opinion] reverses [the path of the law since Brown] and reaches the wrong conclusion. In doing so, it distorts precedent, it misapplies the relevant constitutional principles, it announces legal rules that will obstruct efforts by state and local governments to deal effectively with the growing resegregation of public schools, it threatens to substitute for present calm a disruptive round of race-related litigation, and it undermines *Brown*'s promise of integrated primary and secondary education that local communities have sought to make a reality. * * *

I.   The historical and factual context in which these cases arise is critical. In *Brown*, this Court held that the government's segregation of schoolchildren by race violates the Constitution's promise of equal protection. [In] dozens of subsequent cases, this Court told school districts previously segregated by law what they must do at a minimum to comply with *Brown*'s constitutional holding. The measures required by those cases often included race-conscious practices, such as mandatory busing and race-based restrictions on voluntary transfers. Beyond those minimum requirements, the Court left much of the determination of how to achieve integration to the judgment of local communities. Thus, in respect to race-conscious desegregation measures that the Constitution *permitted*, but did not *require* (measures similar to those at issue here), this Court unanimously stated: "School authorities are traditionally charged with broad power to formulate and implement educational policy and might well conclude, for example, that in order to prepare students to live in a pluralistic society each school should have a prescribed ratio of Negro to white students reflecting the proportion for the district as a whole. *To do this as an educational policy is within the broad discretionary powers of school authorities." Swann* (emphasis added).

As a result [of this and similar signals from the Court], different districts—some acting under court decree, some acting in order to avoid threatened lawsuits, some seeking to comply with federal administrative orders, some acting purely voluntarily—adopted, modified, and experimented with hosts of different kinds of plans, including race-conscious plans, all with a similar objective: greater racial integration of public schools. [Overall] these efforts brought about considerable racial integration. More recently, however, progress has stalled. Between 1968 and 1980, the number of black children attending a school where minority children constituted more than half of the school fell from 77% to 63% in the Nation (from 81% to 57% in the South) but then reversed direction by the year 2000, rising from 63% to 72% in the Nation (from 57% to 69% in the South). Similarly, between 1968 and 1980, the number of black children attending schools that were more than 90% minority fell from 64% to 33% in the Nation (from 78% to 23% in the South), but that too reversed direction, rising by the year 2000 from 33% to 37% in the Nation (from 23% to 31% in the South). [In] light of the evident risk of a return to school systems that are in fact (though not in law) resegregated, many school districts have felt a need to maintain or to extend their integration efforts.

[Breyer, J., here offered a lengthy recitation of the historical context in Seattle and Louisville as "typical" of "school integration stories" throughout the country. His account of events in Seattle emphasized that although there was never a formal finding of school segregation, a 1956 school board memo spoke of discriminatory policies making it difficult for blacks to transfer from one city school to another, and many of the school district's desegregation efforts in the 1960s and 1970s occurred in response to threatened and actual litigation. More generally, his account emphasized ongoing, adaptive efforts by the Seattle and Louisville school districts to achieve meaningful integration through politically acceptable mechanisms.]

[These histories] make clear the futility of looking simply to whether earlier school segregation was de jure or de facto in order to draw firm lines separating the constitutionally permissible from the constitutionally forbidden use of "race-conscious" criteria. [No] one here disputes that Louisville's segregation was de jure. But what about Seattle's? Was it de facto? De jure? A mixture? Opinions differed. Or is it that a prior federal court had not adjudicated the matter? Does that make a difference? Is Seattle free on remand to say that its schools were de jure segregated, just as in 1956 a memo for the School Board admitted? The plurality does not seem confident as to the answer. * * *

Moreover, Louisville's history makes clear that a community under a court order to desegregate might submit a race-conscious remedial plan *before* the court dissolved the order, but with every intention of following that plan even *after* dissolution. How could such a plan be lawful the day before dissolution but then become unlawful the very next day? On what legal ground can the majority rest its contrary view? * * *

II. A longstanding and unbroken line of legal authority tells us that the Equal Protection Clause permits local school boards to use race-conscious criteria to achieve positive race-related goals, even when the Constitution does not compel it. [The plain dicta of *Swann*, supra, established] a basic principle of constitutional law—a principle of law that has found "wide acceptance in the legal culture." [In] fact, without being exhaustive, I have counted 51 federal statutes that use racial classifications. I have counted well over 100 state statutes that similarly employ racial classifications. Presidential administrations for the past half-century have used and supported various race-conscious measures. And during the same time, hundreds of local school districts have adopted student assignment plans that use race-conscious criteria.

That *Swann*'s legal statement should find such broad acceptance is not surprising. [There] is reason to believe that those who drafted [the Fourteenth Amendment] would have understood the legal and practical difference between the use of race-conscious criteria [to] keep the races apart, and the use of race-conscious criteria to [bring] the races together.

[No] case—not *Adarand, Gratz, Grutter*, or any other—has ever held that the test of "strict scrutiny" means that all racial classifications—no matter whether they seek to include or exclude—must in practice be treated the same. [Here], the context is one in which school districts seek to advance or to maintain racial integration in primary and secondary schools. It is a context, as *Swann* makes clear, where history has required special administrative remedies. [It] is *not* a context that involves the use of race to decide who will receive goods or services that are normally distributed on the basis of merit and which are in short supply. It is not one in which race-conscious limits stigmatize or exclude. * * *

These and related considerations convinced one Ninth Circuit judge in the Seattle case to apply a standard of constitutionality review that is less than "strict," and to conclude that this Court's precedents do not require the contrary. [In] my view, this contextual approach to scrutiny is altogether fitting. [Nonetheless,] in light of *Grutter* and other precedents, I shall [apply] the version of strict scrutiny that those cases embody. * * *

III.   The principal interest advanced in these cases to justify the use of race-based criteria goes by various names. Sometimes a court refers to it as an interest in achieving racial "diversity." Other times a court, like the plurality here, refers to it as an interest in racial "balancing." [Regardless] of its name, however, the interest at stake possesses three essential elements. First, there is a historical and remedial element: an interest in setting right the consequences of prior conditions of segregation. This refers back to a time when public schools were highly segregated, often as a result of legal or administrative policies that facilitated racial segregation in public schools. It is an interest in continuing to combat the remnants of segregation caused in whole or in part by these school-related policies, which have often affected not only schools, but also housing patterns, employment practices, economic conditions, and social attitudes. It is an interest in maintaining hard-won gains. And it has its roots in preventing what gradually may become the de facto resegregation of America's public schools.

Second, there is an educational element: an interest in overcoming the adverse educational effects produced by and associated with highly segregated schools. Studies suggest that children taken from those schools and placed in integrated settings often show positive academic gains. Other studies reach different conclusions. But the evidence supporting an educational interest in racially integrated schools is well established and strong enough to permit a democratically elected school board reasonably to determine that this interest is a compelling one.

Third, there is a democratic element: an interest in producing an educational environment that reflects the "pluralistic society" in which our children will live. It is an interest in helping our children learn to work and play together with children of different racial backgrounds. It is an interest in teaching children to engage in the kind of cooperation among Americans of all races that is necessary to make a land of three hundred million people one Nation. [This] Court from *Swann* to *Grutter* has treated these civic effects as an important virtue of racially diverse education.

[In] light of this Courts conclusions in *Grutter*, the "compelling" nature of these interests in the context of primary and secondary public education follows here a fortiori. [If] an educational interest that combines these three elements is not "compelling," what is?

[Several] factors, taken together, [similarly lead] me to conclude that the boards' use of race-conscious criteria in these plans passes even the strictest "tailoring" test. First, the race-conscious criteria at issue only help set the outer bounds of *broad* ranges. They constitute but one part of plans that depend primarily upon other, nonracial elements. To use race in this way is not to set a forbidden "quota." [Indeed], the race-conscious ranges at issue in these cases often have no effect. * * *

Second, broad-range limits on voluntary school choice plans are less burdensome, and hence more narrowly tailored, than other race-conscious restrictions this Court has previously approved. Here, race becomes a factor only in a fraction of students' non-merit-based assignments—not in large numbers of students merit-based applications. Moreover, the effect of applying race-conscious criteria here affects potentially disadvantaged students *less severely*, not more severely, than the criteria at issue in *Grutter*. Disappointed students are not rejected from a State's flagship graduate program; they simply attend a different one of the district's many public schools, which in aspiration and in fact are substantially equal. * * *

Third, the manner in which the school boards developed these plans itself reflects "narrow tailoring." [Each] plan embodies the results of local experience and community consultation. Each plan is the product of a process that has sought to enhance student choice, while diminishing the need for mandatory busing. And each plan's use of race-conscious elements *is diminished* compared to the use of race in preceding integration plans. * * *

Justice Kennedy suggests that school boards "may pursue the goal of bringing together students of diverse backgrounds and races through other means, including strategic site selection of new schools; drawing attendance zones with general recognition of the demographics of neighborhoods; allocating resources for special programs; recruiting students and faculty in a targeted fashion; and tracking enrollments, performance, and other statistics by race." But, as to "strategic site selection," Seattle has built one new high school in the last 44 years (and that specialized school serves only 300 students). [As] to "drawing" neighborhood "attendance zones" on a racial basis, Louisville tried it, and it worked only when forced busing was also part of the plan. As to "allocating resources for special programs," Seattle and Louisville have both experimented with this; indeed, these programs are often referred to as "magnet schools," but the limited desegregation effect of these efforts extends at most to those few schools to which additional resources are granted. In addition, there is no evidence from the experience of these school districts that it will make any meaningful impact. * * *

V.   The Founders meant the Constitution as a practical document that would transmit its basic values to future generations through principles that remained workable over time. [As] I have pointed out, de facto resegregation is on the rise. It is reasonable to conclude that such resegregation can create serious educational, social, and civic problems. Given the conditions in which school boards work to set policy, they may need all of the means presently at their disposal to combat those problems.* * * I use the words "may need" here deliberately. The plurality, or at least those who follow Justice Thomas' "color-blind" approach, may feel confident that, to end invidious discrimination, one must end *all* governmental use of race-conscious criteria including those with inclusive objectives. By way of contrast, I do not claim to know how best to stop harmful discrimination; how best to create a society that includes all Americans; how best to overcome our serious problems of increasing de facto segregation, troubled inner city schooling, and poverty correlated with race. [But] I do know that the Constitution does not authorize judges to dictate solutions to these problems.

VI.   [To] invalidate the plans under review is to threaten the promise of *Brown*. The plurality's position, I fear, would break that promise. This is a decision that the Court and the Nation will come to regret.

B. AFFIRMATIVE ACTION IN GOVERNMENT CONTRACTS AND EMPLOYMENT

In CITY OF RICHMOND v. J.A. CROSON a majority of the Justices applied strict judicial scrutiny and invalidated a requirement by the City of Richmond that prime contractors on city projects award at least 30% of their subcontracts to minority firms, defined as those owned by " '[c]itizens of the United States who are Blacks, Spanish-speaking, Orientals, Indians, Eskimos, or Aleuts.' [The] Plan declared that it was 'remedial.' [It] 'allowed[ed] waivers in those individual situations where a contractor can prove to the satisfaction of the director that the requirements herein cannot be achieved.' " Writing in parts of the opinion for a plurality and in parts for a majority, O'CONNOR, J., distinguished a prior decision that had upheld affirmative action preferences in the award of *federal* construction contracts (without applying strict scrutiny) and found the Richmond scheme unconstitutional: "[We reaffirm] the view expressed by the plurality in *Wygant* [*v. Jackson Bd. of Educ.*, 476 U.S. 267 (1986),]a that the standard of review under the Equal Protection Clause is not dependent on the race of those burdened or benefitted by a particular classification. [But e]ven were we to accept a reading of the guarantee of equal protection under which the level of scrutiny varies according to the ability of different groups to defend their interests in the representative process, heightened scrutiny would still be appropriate in the circumstances of this case. [B]lacks comprise approximately 50% of the population of the city of Richmond. Five of the nine seats on the City Council are held by blacks.

"[The] District Court found the City Council's 'findings sufficient to ensure that, in adopting the Plan, it was remedying the present effects of past discrimination in the *construction industry*.' [A] generalized assertion that there has been past discrimination in an entire industry provides no guidance for a legislative body to determine the precise scope of the injury it seeks to remedy. It 'has no logical stopping point.' *Wygant*. 'Relief' for such an ill-defined wrong could extend until the percentage of public contracts awarded to MBEs in Richmond mirrored the percentage of minorities in the population as a whole.[There] is nothing approaching a prima facie case of a constitutional or statutory violation by *anyone* in the Richmond construction industry. [And the] foregoing analysis applies only to the inclusion of blacks within the Richmond set-aside program. There is *absolutely no evidence* of past discrimination against Spanish-speaking, Oriental,

---

a. Without majority opinion, *Wygant* held that a school board violated the Equal Protection Clause when, in effecting teacher lay-offs in response to a budget crisis, it laid off more senior white teachers in order to retain less senior minority teachers.

Indian, Eskimo, or Aleut persons in any aspect of the Richmond construction industry. * * *

"[I]t is almost impossible to assess whether the Richmond Plan is narrowly tailored to remedy prior discrimination since it is not linked to identified discrimination in any way. We limit ourselves to two observations in this regard.

"First, there does not appear to have been any consideration of the use of race-neutral means to increase minority business participation in city contracting. [Second,] the 30% quota cannot be said to be narrowly tailored to any goal, except perhaps outright racial balancing. It rests upon the 'completely unrealistic' assumption that minorities will choose a particular trade in lockstep proportion to their representation in the local population.

"[N]othing we say today precludes a state or local entity from taking action to rectify the effects of identified discrimination within its jurisdiction. If the city of Richmond had evidence before it that nonminority contractors were systematically excluding minority businesses from subcontracting opportunities it could take action to end the discriminatory exclusion. Where there is a significant statistical disparity between the number of qualified minority contractors willing and able to perform a particular service and the number of such contractors actually engaged by the locality or the locality's prime contractors, an inference of discriminatory exclusion could arise. Under such circumstances, the city could act to dismantle the closed business system by taking appropriate measures against those who discriminate on the basis of race or other illegitimate criteria. In the extreme case, some form of narrowly tailored racial preference might be necessary to break down patterns of deliberate exclusion. * * *

"Proper findings in this regard are necessary to define both the scope of the injury and the extent of the remedy necessary to cure its effects. Such findings also serve to assure all citizens that the deviation from the norm of equal treatment of all racial and ethnic groups is a temporary matter, a measure taken in the service of the goal of equality itself. Absent such findings, there is a danger that a racial classification is merely the product of unthinking stereotypes or a form of racial politics."

STEVENS, J. concurred in part and concurred in the judgment: "[I] believe the Constitution requires us to evaluate our policy decisions—including those that govern the relationships among different racial and ethnic groups—primarily by studying their probable impact on the future. I therefore do not agree with the premise that seems to underlie today's decision, as well as the decision in *Wygant,* that a governmental decision that rests on a racial classification is never permissible except as a remedy for a past wrong.[1] I do, however, agree with the Court's

---

1. In my view the Court's approach to this case gives unwarranted deference to race-based legislative action that purports to serve a purely remedial goal, and overlooks the potential value of race-based determinations that may serve other valid purposes. With regard to the former point [I] am not prepared to assume that even a more narrowly tailored set-aside program supported by stronger findings would be constitutionally justified. Unless the legislature can identify both the particular victims and the particular perpetrators of past discrimination, which is precisely what a court does when it makes findings of fact and conclusions of law, a *remedial* justification for race-based legislation will almost certainly sweep too broadly. With regard to the latter point: I think it unfortunate that the Court in neither *Wygant* nor this case seems prepared to acknowledge that some race-based policy decisions may serve a legitimate public purpose. I agree, of course, that race is so seldom relevant to legislative decisions on how best to foster the public good that legitimate justifications for race-based legislation will usually not be available. But unlike the Court, I would not totally discount the legitimacy of race-based decisions that may produce tangible and fully justified future benefits.

explanation of why the Richmond ordinance cannot be justified as a remedy for past discrimination.

"[T]he city makes no claim that the public interest in the efficient performance of its construction contracts will be served by granting a preference to minority-business enterprises. This case is therefore completely unlike *Wygant,* in which I thought it quite obvious that the School Board had reasonably concluded that an integrated faculty could provide educational benefits to the entire student body that could not be provided by an all-white, or nearly all-white faculty. * * * "

KENNEDY, J. concurred in part and concurred in the judgment: "[The] moral imperative of racial neutrality is the driving force of the Equal Protection Clause. [Nevertheless], given that a rule of automatic invalidity for racial preferences in almost every case would be a significant break with our precedents that require a case-by-case test, I am not convinced we need adopt it at this point."

SCALIA, J., concurred in the judgment: "I agree with much of the Court's opinion, and, in particular, with its conclusion that strict scrutiny must be applied to all governmental classification by race, whether or not its asserted purpose is 'remedial' or 'benign.' I do not agree, however, with the Court's dicta suggesting that, despite the Fourteenth Amendment, state and local governments may in some circumstances discriminate on the basis of race in order (in a broad sense) 'to ameliorate the effects of past discrimination.' The benign purpose of compensating for social disadvantages, whether they have been acquired by reason of prior discrimination or otherwise, can no more be pursued by the illegitimate means of racial discrimination than can other assertedly benign purposes we have repeatedly rejected. See, e.g., [*Wygant*]. At least where state or local action is at issue, only a social emergency rising to the level of imminent danger to life and limb—for example, a prison race riot, requiring temporary segregation of inmates, cf. *Lee v. Washington,* 390 U.S. 333 (1968)—can justify an exception to the principle embodied in the Fourteenth Amendment that '[o]ur Constitution is color-blind, and neither knows nor tolerates classes among citizens,' *Plessy* (Harlan, J., dissenting)."

MARSHALL, J., joined by BRENNAN and BLACKMUN, JJ., dissented: "My view has long been that race-conscious classifications designed to further remedial goals 'must serve important governmental objectives and must be substantially related to achievement of those objectives' in order to withstand constitutional scrutiny. Analyzed in terms of this two-prong standard, Richmond's set-aside, like the federal program on which it was modeled, is 'plainly constitutional.' *Fullilove v. Klutznick,* 448 U.S. 448 (1980) (Marshall, J., concurring in judgment).

"Turning first to the governmental interest inquiry, Richmond has two powerful interests in setting aside a portion of public contracting funds for minority-owned enterprises. The first is the city's interest in eradicating the effects of past racial discrimination. * * *

"Richmond has a second compelling interest in setting aside, where possible, a portion of its contracting dollars. [When] government channels all its contracting funds to a white-dominated community of established contractors whose racial homogeneity is the product of private discrimination, it does more than place its imprimatur on the practices which forged and which continue to define that community. It also provides a measurable boost to those economic entities that have thrived within it, while denying important economic benefits to those entities which, but for prior discrimination, might well be better qualified to receive valuable government contracts. In my view, the interest in ensuring that the government does not reflect and reinforce prior private discrimination in dispensing public contracts is every bit as strong as the interest in eliminating private discrimination—an interest which this Court has repeatedly deemed compelling. See, e.g., *Roberts v. United States Jaycees,* [Ch. 7, Sec. 9, III].

"In my judgment, Richmond's set-aside plan also comports with the second prong of the equal protection inquiry, for it is substantially related to the interests it seeks to serve in remedying past discrimination and in ensuring that municipal contract procurement does not perpetuate that discrimination."

———

Title VII of the 1964 Civil Rights Act. RICCI v. DeSTEFANO, 129 S.Ct. 2658 (2009), per KENNEDY, J., avoided questions involving the constitutionality of New Haven, Connecticut's decision to discard an employment test after minority candidates scored less well than whites—and, equally importantly, avoided constitutional questions about some applications of Title VII of the 1964 Civil Rights Act. City officials decided not to certify the test results, which would have determined promotions of firefighters to lieutenant and captain, in order to avoid a suit by minority applicants under the "disparate impact" provision of Title VII, which bars employment tests that disproportionately exclude minority applicants and are not justified by "business necessity." But the City's action to avoid one lawsuit triggered another, brought primarily by white firefighters, who claimed that the defendants violated another Title VII provision, which bars racially "disparate treatment" or intentional discrimination, as well as the Equal Protection Clause.

The Court avoided the constitutional issue by holding that the City's action in discarding the challenged test violated Title VIIs prohibition against racially "disparate treatment": "The City rejected the test results solely because the higher scoring candidates were white. [Fear] of litigation alone cannot justify an employer's reliance on race to the detriment of individuals who passed the examinations and qualified for promotions." Although the City acted with good intentions to avoid a disparate impact lawsuit by disappointed minority applicants, "race-based action like the City's [is] impermissible under Title VII unless the employer can demonstrate a strong basis in evidence that, had it not taken the action, it would have been liable under the disparate impact statute. [There was no such basis in this case. The City had sufficient reason to think its test was justified by 'business necessity' and the absence of a suitable identified alternative test. Because the City's action violated Title VII,] we need not decide whether a legitimate fear of disparate impact is ever sufficient to justify discriminatory treatment under the Constitution."

SCALIA, J., concurred: The Courts "resolution of this dispute merely postpones the evil day on which the Court will have to [decide whether] the disparate impact provisions of Title VII [are] consistent with the Constitution's guarantee of equal protection."

Ginsburg, J., joined by Stevens, Souter, and Breyer, JJ., dissented on statutory grounds.

———

In ADARAND CONSTRUCTORS, INC. v. PENA, 515 U.S. 200 (1995), the Court, per O'CONNOR, J. overruled an earlier decision in *Metro Broadcasting, Inc. v. FCC,* 497 U.S. 547 (1990), which had held that *federal* affirmative action programs would trigger only intermediate scrutiny, and subjected a preference for minority contractors and subcontractors on highway projects financed with federal money to strict judicial scrutiny. But the Court also said that "we wish to dispel the notion that strict scrutiny is 'strict in theory, but fatal in fact.' The unhappy persistence of both the practice and the lingering effects of racial discrimination against minority groups in this country is an unfortunate reality, and government is not disqualified from acting in response to it. As recently as 1987, for example, every Justice of this Court agreed that the Alabama Department of Public Safety's 'pervasive, systematic, and obstinate discriminatory conduct' justified a narrowly tailored race-based remedy. See *United States v. Paradise*, 480 U.S. 149 (1987).a When race-based action is necessary to further a compelling interest, such action is within constitutional constraints if it satisfies the 'narrow tailoring' test this Court has set out in previous cases."

STEVENS, J., joined by Ginsburg, J., dissented: "[The] majority in *Metro Broadcasting* [was] not alone in relying upon a critical distinction between federal and state programs. In his separate opinion in [*Croson*], Justice Scalia discussed the basis for this distinction. He observed that 'it is one thing to permit racially based conduct by the Federal Government—whose legislative powers concerning matters of race were explicitly enhanced by the Fourteenth Amendment—and quite another to permit it by the precise entities against whose conduct in matters of race that Amendment was specifically directed.' [In] her plurality opinion in *Croson*, Justice O'Connor also emphasized the importance of this distinction when she responded to the City's argument that *Fullilove* was controlling." Souter, J., joined by Ginsburg and Breyer, JJ., also dissented.

SECTION 3.   DISCRIMINATIONS
BASED ON GENDER

I. DEFINING THE LEVEL OF SCRUTINY

Prior to 1971, the Court used the deferential "traditional approach" (see Sec. 1 supra) to test the constitutionality of classifications based on gender. *Muller v. Oregon*, 208 U.S. 412 (1908), per Brewer, J., upheld a law barring factory work by women for more than ten hours a day, reasoning that "as healthy mothers are essential to vigorous offspring, the physical well-being of a woman becomes an object of public interest and care."a *Goesaert v. Cleary*, 335 U.S. 464 (1948), per Frankfurter, J., upheld a law denying bartender's licenses to most women, reasoning that "the fact that women may now have achieved the virtues that men have long claimed as their prerogatives and now indulge in vices that men have long practiced, does not preclude the States from drawing a sharp line between the sexes, certainly in such matters as the regulation of the liquor traffic."b Finally, *Hoyt v. Florida*, 368 U.S. 57 (1961), per Harlan, J., sustained a law

---

a. *Paradise* upheld a *judicially* ordered race-conscious remedy. The Court was unanimous that the federal government has a compelling interest in remedying proven race discrimination. Per Brennan, J., it found the particular order at issue to be "narrowly tailored," and thus upheld it, by a closely divided vote of 5–4.

a. But see *Adkins v. Children's Hospital*, 261 U.S. 525 (1923) (minimum wage for women violates due process), overruled, *West Coast Hotel Co. v. Parrish*, Ch. 5, Sec. 3.

b. See also the concurring opinion of Bradley, J., joined by Swayne and Field, JJ., in *Bradwell v. Illinois*, 83 U.S. (16 Wall.) 130 (1873), which upheld a statute denying women the right to practice law against challenge based on the privileges or immunities clause: "[T]he natural and proper timidity and delicacy which belongs to the female sex evidently unfits it for many of the occupations of civil life. [The] paramount destiny and mission of woman are to fulfill the noble and benign offices of wife and mother. This is the law of the Creator."

placing women on the jury list only if they made special request, stating that a "woman is still regarded as the center of home and family life."c

––––––

The first decision holding sex discrimination violative of equal protection, REED v. REED, 404 U.S. 71 (1971), per Burger, C.J., involved a law preferring males to females when two persons were otherwise equally entitled to be the administrator of an estate: "A classification 'must be reasonable, not arbitrary, and must rest upon some ground of difference having a fair and substantial relation to the object of the [law].' The question" is whether the classification "bears a rational relationship to a state objective that is sought to be advanced by the [law]." It was contended that the law had the reasonable "objective of reducing the workload on probate courts by eliminating one class of contests" and that the legislature might reasonably have "concluded that in general men are better qualified to act as an administrator than are women." But "to give a mandatory preference to members of either sex over members of the other, merely to accomplish the elimination of hearings on the merits, is to make the very kind of arbitrary legislative choice forbidden by [equal protection]."

––––––

Reed was followed by FRONTIERO v. RICHARDSON, 411 U.S. 677 (1973), which invalidated a federal statute permitting males in the armed services an automatic dependency allowance for their wives but requiring servicewomen to prove that their husbands were dependent. Brennan, J., joined by Douglas, White, and Marshall, JJ., argued that "classifications based upon sex [are] inherently suspect and must therefore be subjected to close judicial scrutiny." The plurality found "at least implicit support for such an approach in [*Reed's*] departure from 'traditional' rational basis analysis": "[O]ur Nation has had a long and unfortunate history of sex discrimination. Traditionally, such discrimination was rationalized by an attitude of 'romantic paternalism' which, in practical effect, put women not on a pedestal, but in a cage. * * *

"As a result of notions such as these, [statutes] became laden with gross, stereotypical distinctions between the sexes and, indeed, throughout much of the 19th century the position of women in our society was, in many respects, comparable to that of blacks under the pre-Civil War slave codes. Neither slaves nor women could hold office, serve on juries, or bring suit in their own names, and married women traditionally were denied the legal capacity to hold or convey property or to serve as legal guardians of their own children. And although blacks were guaranteed the right to vote in 1870, women were denied even [that] until adoption of the Nineteenth Amendment half a century later.

"It is true, of course, that the position of women in America has improved markedly in recent decades. [But] in part because of the high visibility of the sex characteristic, women still face pervasive, although at times more subtle, discrimination in our educational institutions, on the job market and, perhaps most conspicuously, in the political arena.17

c. *Hoyt* was effectively overruled in *Taylor v. Louisiana,* 419 U.S. 522 (1975), holding that a similar statute, operating largely to exclude women from jury service, deprived a criminal defendant of the Sixth and Fourteenth Amend- ment right to an impartial jury drawn from a fair cross section of the community.

17. It is true [that] when viewed in the abstract, women do not constitute a small and powerless minority. Nevertheless, in part be-

"Moreover, since sex, like race and national origin, is an immutable charac-teristic [the] imposition of special disabilities [would] seem to violate 'the basic concept of our system that legal burdens should bear some relationship to individual responsibility.' And what differentiates sex from such non-suspect statuses as intelligence or physical disability [is] that the sex characteristic frequently bears no relation to ability to perform or contribute to society.

"[The] Government [maintains] that, as an empirical matter, wives in our society frequently are dependent upon their husbands, while husbands rarely are dependent upon their wives. Thus, the Government argues that Congress might reasonably have concluded that it would be both cheaper and easier simply conclusively to presume that wives of male members are financially dependent upon their husbands, while burdening female members with the task of establish-ing dependency in fact.

"The Government offers no concrete evidence, however, tending to support its view that such differential treatment in fact saves the Government any money. [And any] statutory scheme which draws a sharp line between the sexes, *solely* [for] administrative convenience [violates equal protection]."

POWELL, J., joined by Burger, C.J., and Blackmun, J., concurring, would rely "on the authority of *Reed* and reserve for the future any expansion of its rationale" because of the "Equal Rights Amendment, which if adopted will resolve [the] question." Stewart, J., concurred, "agreeing that the [statutes] work an invidious discrimination." Rehnquist, J., dissented.

CRAIG v. BOREN

429 U.S. 190, 97 S.Ct. 451, 50 L.Ed.2d 397 (1976).

JUSTICE BRENNAN delivered the opinion of the Court.

The interaction of two sections of an Oklahoma statute prohibits the sale of "nonintoxicating" 3.2% beer to males under the age of 21 and to females under the age of 18. The question to be decided is whether such a gender-based differential constitutes a denial to males 18–20 years of age of the equal protection of the laws in violation of the Fourteenth Amendment.

[To] withstand constitutional challenge, previous cases establish that classifi-cations by gender must serve important governmental objectives and must be substantially related to achievement of those objectives. * * * Decisions following *Reed* [have] rejected administrative ease and convenience as sufficiently important objectives to justify gender-based classifications. * * *6

Reed has also provided the underpinning for decisions that have invalidated statutes employing gender as an inaccurate proxy for other, more germane bases of classification. Hence, "archaic and overbroad" generalizations concerning the financial position of servicewomen, *Frontiero,* and working women, *Wiesenfeld* [Part III infra], could not justify use of a gender line in determining eligibility for certain governmental entitlements. Similarly, increasingly outdated misconcep-tions concerning the role of females in the home rather than in the 'marketplace

---

cause of past discrimination, women are vastly underrepresented in this Nation's decision-making councils. * * *

6. *Kahn v. Shevin,* [Part III infra], and *Schlesinger v. Ballard,* [Part III infra], uphold-ing the use of gender-based classifications, rested upon the Court's perception of the lau-datory purposes of those laws as remedying disadvantageous conditions suffered by women in economic and military life. Needless to say, Oklahoma does not suggest that the age-sex differential was enacted to ensure the availabil-ity of 3.2% beer for women as compensation for previous deprivations.

and world of ideas' were rejected as loose-fitting characterizations incapable of supporting state statutory schemes that were premised upon their accuracy. In light of the weak congruence between gender and the characteristic or trait that gender purported to represent, it was necessary that the legislatures choose either to realign their substantive laws in a gender-neutral fashion, or to adopt procedures for identifying those instances where the sex-centered generalization actually comported with fact.

[We] turn then to the question whether, under *Reed*, the difference between males and females with respect to the purchase of 3.2% beer warrants the differential in age drawn by the Oklahoma statute. We conclude it does not.

[We] accept for purposes of discussion the District Court's identification of the objective underlying [the challenged statute] as the enhancement of traffic safety. Clearly, the protection of public health and safety represents an important function of state and local governments. However, appellees' statistics in our view cannot support the conclusion that the gender-based distinction closely serves to achieve that objective and therefore the distinction cannot under *Reed* withstand equal protection. The appellees introduced a variety of statistical surveys [to support the statute, but the] most focused and relevant of the statistical surveys, arrests of 18–20–year-olds for alcohol-related driving offenses, exemplifies the ultimate unpersuasiveness of this evidentiary record. Viewed in terms of the correlation between sex and the actual activity that Oklahoma seeks to regulate—driving while under the influence of alcohol—the statistics broadly establish that 18% of females and 2% of males in that age group were arrested for that offense. While such a disparity is not trivial in a statistical sense, it hardly can form the basis for employment of a gender line as a classifying device. Certainly if maleness is to serve as a proxy for drinking and driving, a correlation of 2% must be considered an unduly tenuous "fit." [Indeed,] prior cases have consistently rejected the use of sex as a decisionmaking factor even though the statutes in question certainly rested on far more predictive empirical relationships than this.

Moreover, the statistics exhibit a variety of other shortcomings that seriously impugn their value to equal protection analysis. Setting aside the obvious methodological problems,14 the surveys do not adequately justify the salient features of Oklahoma's gender-based traffic-safety law. None purports to measure the use and dangerousness of 3.2% beer as opposed to alcohol generally, a detail that is of particular importance since, in light of its low alcohol level, Oklahoma apparently considers the 3.2% beverage to be "nonintoxicating."

[W]hen it is further recognized that Oklahoma's statute prohibits only the selling of 3.2% beer to young males and not their drinking the beverage once acquired (even after purchase by their 18–20–year-old female companions), the relationship between gender and traffic safety becomes far too tenuous to satisfy *Reed's* requirement that the gender-based difference be substantially related to achievement of the statutory objective. We hold, therefore, that [Oklahoma's] 3.2% beer statute invidiously discriminates against males 18–20 years of age. * * *

JUSTICE POWELL concurring.

I join the opinion of the Court as I am in general agreement with it. I do have reservations as to some of the discussion concerning the appropriate standard for equal protection analysis and the relevance of the statistical evidence. * * *

---

14. The very social stereotypes that find reflection in age-differential laws are likely substantially to distort the accuracy of these comparative statistics. Hence, "reckless" young men who drink and drive are transformed into arrest statistics, whereas their female counterparts are chivalrously escorted home. * * *

With respect to the equal protection standard, I agree that *Reed* is the most relevant precedent. But I find it unnecessary, in deciding this case, to read that decision as broadly as some of the Court's language may imply. *Reed* and subsequent cases involving gender-based classifications make clear that the Court subjects such classifications to a more critical examination than is normally applied when "fundamental" constitutional rights and "suspect classes" are not present.

I view this as a relatively easy case. [T]his gender-based classification does not bear a fair and substantial relation to the object of the legislation. * * *

JUSTICE STEVENS concurring.

I am inclined to believe that what has become known as the two-tiered analysis of equal protection claims does not describe a completely logical method of deciding cases, but rather is a method the Court has employed to explain decisions that actually apply a single standard in a reasonably consistent fashion. * * *

In this case, the classification is not as obnoxious as some the Court has condemned, nor as inoffensive as some the Court has accepted. It is objectionable because it is based on an accident of birth, because it is a mere remnant of the now almost universally rejected tradition of discriminating against males in this age bracket, and because, to the extent it reflects any physical difference between males and females, it is actually perverse.4 * * *

The classification is not totally irrational. For the evidence does indicate that there are more males than females in this age bracket who drive and also more who drink. Nevertheless, [i]t is difficult to believe that the statute was actually intended to cope with the problem of traffic safety, since it has only a minimal effect on access to a not very intoxicating beverage and does not prohibit its consumption. [But] even assuming some such slight benefit, it does not seem to me that an insult to all of the young men of the State can be justified by visiting the sins of the 2% on the 98%.

JUSTICE REHNQUIST, [with whom CHIEF JUSTICE BURGER was "in general agreement"] dissenting.

The Court's disposition of this case is objectionable on two grounds. First is its conclusion that *men* challenging a gender-based statute which treats them less favorably than women may invoke a more stringent standard of judicial review than pertains to most other types of classifications. Second is the Court's enunciation of this standard, without citation to any source, as being that "classifications by gender must serve *important* governmental objectives and must be *substantially* related to achievement of those objectives." The only redeeming feature of the Court's opinion, to my mind, is that it apparently signals a retreat by those who joined the plurality opinion in *Frontiero* from their view that sex is a "suspect" classification for purposes of equal protection analysis. I think the Oklahoma statute challenged here need pass only the "rational basis" equal protection analysis expounded in [prior cases].

[T]here being no plausible argument that this is a discrimination against females,2 the Court's reliance on our previous sex-discrimination cases is ill-

---

4. Because males are generally heavier than females, they have a greater capacity to consume alcohol without impairing their driving ability than do females.

2. I am not unaware of the argument from time to time advanced, that all discriminations

between the sexes ultimately redound to the detriment of females, because they tend to reinforce "old notions" restricting the roles and opportunities of women. As a general proposition applying equally to all sex categorizations, I believe that this argument was implic-

founded. It treats gender classification as a talisman which—without regard to the rights involved or the persons affected—calls into effect a heavier burden of judicial review.

The Court's [standard of review] apparently comes out of thin air. The Equal Protection Clause contains no such language, and none of our previous cases adopt that standard. I would think we have had enough difficulty with the two standards of review which our cases have recognized—the norm of "rational basis," and the "compelling state interest" required where a "suspect classification" is involved—so as to counsel weightily against the insertion of still another "standard" between those two. How is this Court to divine what objectives are important? How is it to determine whether a particular law is "substantially" related to the achievement of such objective, rather than related in some other way to its achievement?

[Under the] applicable rational-basis test [the] evidence suggests clear differences between the drinking and driving habits of young men and women. Those differences are grounds enough for the State reasonably to conclude that young males pose by far the greater drunk-driving hazard, both in terms of sheer numbers and in terms of hazard on a per-driver basis. The gender-based difference in treatment in this case is therefore not irrational.

UNITED STATES v. VIRGINIA

518 U.S. 515, 116 S.Ct. 2264, 135 L.Ed.2d 735 (1996).

JUSTICE GINSBURG delivered the opinion of the Court.

Virginia's public institutions of higher learning include an incomparable military college, Virginia Military Institute (VMI). The United States maintains that the Constitution's equal protection guarantee precludes Virginia from reserving exclusively to men the unique educational opportunities VMI affords. We agree.

Founded in 1839, VMI is today the sole single-sex school among Virginia's 15 public institutions of higher learning. VMI's distinctive mission is to produce "citizen-soldiers." [Assigning] prime place to character development, VMI uses an "adversative method" modeled on English public schools and once characteristic of military instruction. [This model] features "physical rigor, mental stress, absolute equality of treatment, absence of privacy, minute regulation of behavior, and indoctrination in desirable values." [VMI] cadets live in spartan barracks where surveillance is constant and privacy nonexistent. [Entering] students are incessantly exposed to the rat line, "an extreme form of the adversative model," [which] bonds new cadets to their fellow sufferers and, when they have completed the 7–month experience, to their former tormentors.

In 1990, prompted by a complaint filed with the Attorney General by a female high-school student seeking admission to VMI, the United States sued the Commonwealth of Virginia and VMI, alleging that VMI's exclusively male admission policy violated the Equal Protection Clause of the Fourteenth Amendment. [The district court upheld the policy, but the court of appeals reversed, finding an equal protection violation. Following the remand, the state of Virginia proposed a remedial plan, under which the state would adopt] a parallel program for women: Virginia Women's Institute for Leadership (VWIL). The 4–year, state-sponsored

itly found to carry little weight in [several decisions upholding classifications designed to compensate women for actual or presumed employment and economic disadvantages]. Seeing

no assertion that it has special applicability to the situation at hand, I believe it can be dismissed as an insubstantial consideration.

undergraduate program would be located at Mary Baldwin College, a private liberal arts school for women, and would be open, initially, to about 25 to 30 students. Although VWIL would share VMI's mission—to produce "citizen-soldiers"—the VWIL program would differ, as does Mary Baldwin College, from VMI in academic offerings, methods of education, and financial resources.

The average combined SAT score of entrants at Mary Baldwin is about 100 points lower than the score for VMI freshmen. [While] VMI offers degrees in liberal arts, the sciences, and engineering, Mary Baldwin, at the time of trial, offered only bachelor of arts degrees. [Under the proposed remedial plan,] VWIL students would participate in ROTC programs [but in] lieu of VMI's adversative method, [VWIL would offer] "a cooperative method which reinforces self-esteem."

Virginia represented that it will provide equal financial support for in-state VWIL students and VMI cadets, and the VMI Foundation agreed to supply a $5.4625 million endowment for the VWIL program. Mary Baldwin's own endowment is about $19 million; VMI's is $131 million. Mary Baldwin will add $35 million to its endowment based on future commitments; VMI will add $220 million. [Both the district court and the court of appeals held that the proposed remedial plan satisfied the Equal Protection Clause.]

The cross-petitions in this case present two ultimate issues. First, does Virginia's exclusion of women from the educational opportunities provided by VMI—extraordinary opportunities for military training and civilian leadership development—deny to women "capable of all of the individual activities required of VMI cadets," the equal protection of the laws guaranteed by the Fourteenth Amendment? Second, if VMI's "unique" situation—as Virginia's sole single-sex public institution of higher education—offends the Constitution's equal protection principle, what is the remedial requirement?

We note, once again, the core instruction of this Court's pathmarking decisions in *J.E.B. v. Alabama ex rel. T.B.*, 511 U.S. 127 (1994), and *Mississippi Univ. for Women*, [Part III infra]: Parties who seek to defend gender-based government action must demonstrate an "exceedingly persuasive justification" for that action. [The] burden of justification is demanding and it rests entirely on the State. The State must show "at least that the [challenged] classification serves 'important governmental objectives and that the discriminatory means employed' are 'substantially related to the achievement of those objectives.' " The justification must be genuine, not hypothesized or invented post hoc in response to litigation. And it must not rely on overbroad generalizations about the different talents, capacities, or preferences of males and females.

The heightened review standard our precedent establishes does not make sex a proscribed classification. Supposed "inherent differences" are no longer accepted as a ground for race or national origin classifications. See *Loving v. Virginia*. Physical differences between men and women, however, are enduring. Inherent differences between men and women, we have come to appreciate, remain cause for celebration, but not for denigration of the members of either sex or for artificial constraints on an individual's opportunity. Sex classifications may be used to compensate women "for particular economic disabilities [they have] suffered," *Califano v. Webster,* [Part III infra], to "promote equal employment opportunity," see *California Federal Sav. & Loan Assn. v. Guerra,* 479 U.S. 272 (1987), [and] to advance full development of the talent and capacities of our Nation's people.[7] But such classifications may not be used, as they once were, to

---

7. Several amici have urged that diversity in educational opportunities is an altogether appropriate governmental pursuit and that single-sex schools can contribute importantly to

create or perpetuate the legal, social, and economic inferiority of women. [Measuring] the record in this case against the review standard just described, we conclude that Virginia has shown no "exceedingly persuasive justification" for excluding all women from the citizen-soldier training afforded by VMI.

[Single-sex] education affords pedagogical benefits to at least some students, Virginia emphasizes, and that reality is uncontested in this litigation. Similarly, it is not disputed that diversity among public educational institutions can serve the public good. But Virginia has not shown that VMI was established, or has been maintained, with a view to diversifying, by its categorical exclusion of women, educational opportunities within the State. In cases of this genre, our precedent instructs that "benign" justifications proffered in defense of categorical exclusions will not be accepted automatically; a tenable justification must describe actual state purposes, not rationalizations for actions in fact differently grounded.

[Neither] recent nor distant history bears out Virginia's alleged pursuit of diversity through single-sex educational options. In 1839, when the State established VMI, a range of educational opportunities for men and women was scarcely contemplated. [In] admitting no women, VMI followed the lead of [the] University of Virginia, founded in 1819. [Beginning in 1884,] Virginia eventually provided for several women's seminaries and colleges. [By] the mid–1970's, [however,] all [had] become coeducational. [The] University of Virginia introduced coeducation [in 1970] and, in 1972, began to admit women on an equal basis with men.

[Virginia] describes the current absence of public single-sex higher education for women as "an historical anomaly." But the historical record indicates action more deliberate than anomalous: First, protection of women against higher education; next, schools for women far from equal in resources and stature to schools for men; finally, conversion of the separate schools to coeducation. [In] sum, we find no persuasive evidence in this record that VMI's male-only admission policy "is in furtherance of a state policy of 'diversity.'"

[Virginia] next argues that VMI's adversative method of training provides educational benefits that cannot be made available, unmodified, to women. Alterations to accommodate women would necessarily be "radical," so "drastic," Virginia asserts, as to transform, indeed "destroy," VMI's program. [The] District Court [found] that coeducation would materially affect "at least these three aspects of VMI's program—physical training, the absence of privacy, and the adversative approach." And it is uncontested that women's admission would require accommodations, primarily in arranging housing assignments and physical training programs for female cadets. It is also undisputed, however, that "the VMI methodology could be used to educate women."

[The] notion that admission of women would downgrade VMI's stature, destroy the adversative system and, with it, even the school, is a judgment hardly proved, a prediction hardly different from other "self-fulfilling prophecies" once routinely used to deny rights or opportunities. [Women's] successful entry into the federal military academies, and their participation in the Nation's military forces, indicate that Virginia's fears for the future of VMI may not be solidly grounded. [Virginia], in sum, "has fallen far short of establishing the 'exceedingly persuasive justification'" that must be the solid base for any gender-defined classification.

such diversity. Indeed, it is the mission of some single-sex schools "to dissipate, rather than perpetuate, traditional gender classifications." We do not question the State's prerogative evenhandedly to support diverse educational opportunities. We address specifically and only an educational opportunity recognized by the District Court and the Court of Appeals as "unique," an opportunity available only at Virginia's premier military institute, the State's sole single-sex public university or college.

In the second phase of the litigation, Virginia presented its remedial plan—maintain VMI as a male-only college and create VWIL as a separate program for women. [Having] violated the Constitution's equal protection requirement, Virginia was obliged to show that its remedial proposal "directly addressed and related to" the violation, i.e., the equal protection denied to women ready, willing, and able to benefit from educational opportunities of the kind VMI offers. Virginia described VWIL as a "parallel program," and asserted that VWIL shares VMI's mission of producing "citizen-soldiers" and VMI's goals of providing "education, military training, mental and physical discipline, character [and] leadership development." [But] VWIL affords women no opportunity to experience the rigorous military training for which VMI is famed. Instead, the VWIL program "deemphasizes" military education, and uses a "cooperative method" of education "which reinforces self-esteem."

[Virginia] maintains that these methodological differences are "justified pedagogically," based on "important differences between men and women in learning and developmental needs," "psychological and sociological differences" Virginia describes as "real" and "not stereotypes." [As] earlier stated, [however], generalizations about "the way women are," estimates of what is appropriate for most women, no longer justify denying opportunity to women whose talent and capacity place them outside the average description. "[S]ome women, at least, would want to attend [VMI] if they had the opportunity"; "some women are capable of all of the individual activities required of VMI cadets" and "can meet the physical standards [VMI] now imposes on men". It is on behalf of these women that the United States has instituted this suit, and it is for them that a remedy must be crafted.19

[In] myriad respects other than military training, VWIL does not qualify as VMI's equal. VWIL's student body, faculty, course offerings, and facilities hardly match VMI's. Nor can the VWIL graduate anticipate the benefits associated with VMI's 157–year history, the school's prestige, and its influential alumni network.

[Virginia's] VWIL solution is reminiscent of the remedy Texas proposed 50 years ago, in response to a state trial court's 1946 ruling that, given the equal protection guarantee, African–Americans could not be denied a legal education at a state facility. See *Sweatt v. Painter,* [Sec. 2, II supra]. Reluctant to admit African–Americans to its flagship University of Texas Law School, the State set up a separate school for Heman Sweatt and other black law students. [This] Court contrasted resources at the new school with those at the school from which Sweatt had been excluded. Accordingly, the Court held, the Equal Protection Clause required Texas to admit African–Americans to the University of Texas Law School. In line with *Sweatt,* we rule here that Virginia has not shown substantial equality in the separate educational opportunities the State supports at VWIL and VMI. * * *

JUSTICE THOMAS took no part in the consideration or decision of this case.

CHIEF JUSTICE REHNQUIST, concurring in the judgement.

Two decades ago in *Craig v. Boren,* we announced that "to withstand constitutional challenge, * * * classifications by gender must serve important governmental objectives and must be substantially related to achievement of those objectives." [While] the majority adheres to this test today, it also says that the State must demonstrate an " 'exceedingly persuasive justification' " to support a

---

19. Admitting women to VMI would undoubtedly require alterations necessary to afford members of each sex privacy from the other sex in living arrangements, and to adjust aspects of the physical training programs. Experience [at the United States military academies] shows such adjustments are manageable.

gender-based classification. [To] avoid introducing potential confusion, I would have adhered more closely to our traditional [standard].

[I] agree with the Court that there is scant evidence in the record that [diversity] was the real reason that Virginia decided to maintain VMI as men only. [Even] if diversity in educational opportunity were the Commonwealth's actual objective, the Commonwealth's position would still be problematic. The difficulty is that the diversity benefited only one sex.

[Virginia] offers a second justification for the single-sex admissions policy: maintenance of the adversative method. [But a] State does not have substantial interest in the adversative methodology unless it is pedagogically beneficial. While considerable evidence shows that a single-sex education is pedagogically beneficial for some students, and hence a State may have a valid interest in promoting that methodology, there is no similar evidence in the record that an adversative method is pedagogically beneficial or is any more likely to produce character traits than other methodologies.

The Court defines the constitutional violation in this case as "the categorical exclusion of women from an extraordinary educational opportunity afforded to men." By defining the violation in this way, [the] Court necessarily implies that the only adequate remedy would be the admission of women to the all-male institution. [I] would not define the violation in this way; it is not the "exclusion of women" that violates the Equal Protection Clause, but the maintenance of an all-men school without providing any—much less a comparable—institution for women. * * *

JUSTICE SCALIA, dissenting.

* * * Much of the Court's opinion is devoted to deprecating the closed-mindedness of our forebears with regard to women's education, and even with regard to the treatment of women in areas that have nothing to do with education. Closed-minded they were—as every age is, including our own, with regard to matters it cannot guess, because it simply does not consider them debatable. The virtue of a democratic system with a First Amendment is that it readily enables the people, over time, to be persuaded that what they took for granted is not so, and to change their laws accordingly. That system is destroyed if the smug assurances of each age are removed from the democratic process and written into the Constitution. So to counterbalance the Court's criticism of our ancestors, let me say a word in their praise: they left us free to change. The same cannot be said of this most illiberal Court, which has embarked on a course of inscribing one after another of the current preferences of the society (and in some cases only the counter-majoritarian preferences of the society's law-trained elite) into our Basic Law. Today it enshrines the notion that no substantial educational value is to be served by an all-men's military academy—so that the decision by the people of Virginia to maintain such an institution denies equal protection to women who cannot attend that institution but can attend others.

[In] my view the function of this Court is to preserve our society's values regarding (among other things) equal protection, not to revise them. [Whatever] abstract tests we may choose to devise, they cannot supersede—and indeed ought to be crafted so as to reflect—those constant and unbroken national traditions that embody the people's understanding of ambiguous constitutional texts. More specifically, it is my view that "when a practice not expressly prohibited by the text of the Bill of Rights bears the endorsement of a long tradition of open, widespread, and unchallenged use that dates back to the beginning of the Republic, we have no proper basis for striking it down."

The all-male constitution of VMI comes squarely within such a governing tradition. For almost all of VMI's more than a century and a half of existence, its single-sex status reflected the uniform practice for government-supported military colleges.

[To] reject the Court's disposition today, however, it is [only] necessary to apply honestly the test the Court has been applying to sex-based classifications for the past two decades. [Only] the amorphous "exceedingly persuasive justification" phrase, and not the standard elaboration of intermediate scrutiny, can be made to yield [the] conclusion that VMI's single-sex composition is unconstitutional because there exist several women (or, one would have to conclude under the Court's reasoning, a single woman) willing and able to undertake VMI's program. Intermediate scrutiny has never required a least-restrictive-means analysis, but only a "substantial relation" between the classification and the state interests that it serves.

[It] is beyond question that Virginia has an important state interest in providing effective college education for its citizens. That single-sex instruction is an approach substantially related to that interest should be evident enough from the long and continuing history in this country of men's and women's colleges. But beyond that, [there was] "virtually uncontradicted" [expert evidence introduced in this case tending to show the benefits of single-sex education].

[Besides] its single-sex constitution, VMI [employs] a "distinctive educational method," sometimes referred to as the "adversative, or doubting, model of education." [It] was uncontested that "if the state were to establish a women's VMI-type [i.e., adversative] program, the program would attract an insufficient number of participants to make the program work"; and it was found by the District Court that if Virginia were to include women in VMI, the school "would eventually find it necessary to drop the adversative system altogether." Thus, Virginia's options were an adversative method that excludes women or no adversative method at all.

There can be no serious dispute that single-sex education and a distinctive educational method "represent legitimate contributions to diversity in the Virginia higher education system." As a theoretical matter, Virginia's educational interest would have been best served (insofar as the two factors we have mentioned are concerned) by six different types of public colleges—an all-men's, an all-women's, and a coeducational college run in the "adversative method," and an all-men's, an all-women's, and a coeducational college run in the "traditional method." But as a practical matter, of course, Virginia's financial resources, like any State's, are not limitless, and the Commonwealth must select among the available options. [In] these circumstances, Virginia's election to fund one public all-male institution and one on the adversative model—and to concentrate its resources in a single entity that serves both these interests in diversity—is substantially related to the State's important educational interests.

[The] Court argues that VMI would not have to change very much if it were to admit women. The principal response to that argument is that it is irrelevant: If VMI's single-sex status is substantially related to the government's important educational objectives, as I have demonstrated above and as the Court refuses to discuss, that concludes the inquiry. [But] if such a debate were relevant, the Court would certainly be on the losing side.

[Finally], the absence of a precise "all-women's analogue" to VMI is irrelevant. [VWIL] was carefully designed by professional educators who have long experience in educating young women. [None] of the United States' own experts in the remedial phase of this case was willing to testify that VMI's adversative method was an appropriate methodology for educating women.

[The] Court's decision today will have consequences that extend far beyond the parties to the case. [Under] the constitutional principles announced and applied today, single-sex public education is unconstitutional. [Although] the Court [purports] to have said nothing of relevance to other public schools [and to have considered] only an educational opportunity recognized [as] "unique," [footnote 7, supra], I suggest that the single-sex program that will not be capable of being characterized as "unique" is not only unique but nonexistent.

[A broader] potential of today's decision for widespread disruption of existing institutions lies in its application to private single-sex education. Government support is immensely important to private educational institutions. [When government funding is challenged, the] issue will be not whether government assistance turns private colleges into state actors, but whether the government itself would be violating the Constitution by providing state support to single-sex colleges. For example, in *Norwood v. Harrison*, [Ch. 10, Sec. 3 infra], we saw no room to distinguish between state operation of racially segregated schools and state support of privately run segregated schools. [The] only hope for state-assisted single-sex private schools is that the Court will not apply in the future the principles of law it has applied today. * * *

II. DIFFERENCES—REAL AND IMAGINED

Whatever standard of scrutiny applies, the Court has consistently assumed that differences between men and women sometimes justify different treatment. But a recurrent problem has been to distinguish "real" differences and permissible distinctions based upon them from impermissible reliance on and reinforcement of gender-based stereotypes. As you read the cases in this section, consider how consistent and successful the Court's efforts have been, and how much the Court has been aided—if at all—by the doctrinal tests that it has purported to apply.

———

GEDULDIG v. AIELLO, 417 U.S. 484 (1974), per STEWART, J., held that exclusion of "disability that accompanies normal pregnancy and childbirth" from California's disability insurance system "does not exclude [anyone] because of gender * * *. While it is true that only women can become pregnant, it does not follow that every legislative classification concerning pregnancy is [sex-based]. Absent a showing that distinctions involving pregnancy are mere pretexts designed to effect an invidious discrimination against the members of one sex or the other, lawmakers are constitutionally free to include or exclude pregnancy from the coverage of legislation such as this on any reasonable basis, just as with respect to any other physical condition. [The] program divides potential recipients into two groups—pregnant women and nonpregnant persons. While the first group is exclusively female, the second includes members of both sexes. The fiscal and actuarial benefits of the program thus accrue to members of both sexes. [There] is no risk from which men are protected and women are not. Likewise, there is no risk from which women are protected and men are not.[1]"

1. Indeed, the [data indicated] that both the annual claim rate and the annual claim cost are greater for women than for [men.]

BRENNAN, J., joined by Douglas and Marshall, JJ., dissented, finding "sex discrimination" in the state's "singling out for less favorable treatment a gender-linked disability peculiar to women [while] men receive full compensation for all disabilities suffered, including those that affect only or primarily their sex, such as prostatectomies, circumcision, hemophilia and gout."a

———

DOTHARD v. RAWLINSON, 433 U.S. 321 (1977), per STEWART, J., upheld the exclusion of women prison guards from duty in "contact positions" in all-male prisons: "In this environment of violence and disorganization, it would be an oversimplification to characterize [the exclusion of women] as an exercise in 'romantic paternalism.' [A] woman's relative ability to maintain order in a male, maximum-security, unclassified penitentiary could [be] directly reduced by her womanhood. There is a basis in fact for expecting that sex offenders who have criminally assaulted women in the past would be moved to do so again if access to women were established within the prison. There would also be a real risk that other inmates, deprived of a normal heterosexual environment, would assault women guards because they were women."

———

MICHAEL M. v. SUPERIOR COURT, 450 U.S. 464 (1981), upheld a "statutory rape" law that punished the male, but not the female, party to intercourse when the female was under 18 and not the male's wife. REHNQUIST, J., joined by Burger, C.J., and Stewart and Powell, JJ., observed that "the traditional minimum rationality test takes on a somewhat 'sharper focus' when gender-based classifications are challenged. See *Craig* (Powell, J., concurring). [But] this Court has consistently upheld statutes where the gender classification is not invidious, but rather realistically reflects the fact that the sexes are not similarly situated in certain circumstances. * * *

"We are satisfied not only that the prevention of illegitimate [teenage] pregnancy is at least one of the 'purposes' of the statute, but that the State has a strong interest in preventing such pregnancy.7

"Because virtually all of the significant harmful and inescapably identifiable consequences of teenage pregnancy fall on the young female, a legislature acts well within its authority when it elects to punish only the participant who, by nature, suffers few of the consequences of his conduct. It is hardly unreasonable for a legislature acting to protect minor females to exclude them from punishment. Moreover, the risk of pregnancy itself constitutes a substantial deterrence to young females. [A] criminal sanction imposed solely on males thus serves to roughly 'equalize' the deterrents on the sexes.

---

a. Cf. *Cleveland Bd. of Educ. v. LaFleur,* 414 U.S. 632 (1974) (invalidating a requirement that pregnant teachers go on leave on the ground that an "irrebuttable presumption" of inability to teach during pregnancy violated due process).

7. Although petitioner concedes that the State has a "compelling" interest in preventing teenage pregnancy, he contends that the "true" purpose [is] to protect the virtue and chastity of young women. As such, the statute is unjustifiable because it rests on archaic stereotypes. [Even] if the preservation of female chastity were one of the motives of the statute, and even if that motive be impermissible, petitioner's argument must fail because "[this] court will not strike down an otherwise constitutional statute on the basis of an alleged illicit legislative motive." *United States v. O'Brien,* [Ch. 7, Sec. 2].

"[The] State persuasively contends that a gender-neutral statute would frustrate its interest in effective enforcement. Its view is that a female is surely less likely to report violations of the statute if she herself would be subject to criminal prosecution. In an area already fraught with prosecutorial difficulties, we decline to hold that the Equal Protection Clause requires a legislature to enact a statute so broad that it may well be incapable of enforcement."

BLACKMUN, J., concurred: "I [cannot] vote to strike down the California statutory rape law, for I think it is a sufficiently reasoned and constitutional effort to control the problem at its inception. [I] am persuaded that, although a minor has substantial privacy rights in intimate affairs connected with procreation, California's [efforts] to prevent teenage pregnancy are to be viewed differently from efforts to inhibit a woman from dealing with pregnancy once it has become an inevitability. * * *

"I think [it] is only fair, with respect to this particular petitioner, to point out that his partner, Sharon, appears not to have been an unwilling participant in at least the initial stages of the intimacies that took place the night of June 3, 1978.[*] Petitioner's and Sharon's nonacquaintance with each other before the incident; their drinking; their withdrawal from the others of the group; their foreplay, in which she willingly participated and seems to have encouraged; and the closeness of their ages (a difference of only one year and 18 days) are factors that should make this case an unattractive one to prosecute at all, and especially to prosecute as a felony, rather than as a misdemeanor. But the State has chosen to prosecute in that manner, and the facts, I reluctantly conclude, may fit the crime."[a]

BRENNAN, J., joined by White and Marshall, JJ., dissented: "None of the three opinions upholding the California statute fairly applies the equal protection analysis this Court has so carefully developed since *Craig*. [The] plurality assumes that a gender-neutral statute would be less effective [in] deterring sexual activity because a gender-neutral statute would create significant enforcement problems. [But] a State's bare assertion [is] not enough to meet its burden of proof under *Craig*. Rather, the State must produce evidence that will persuade the Court that its assertion is true [and the] State has [not].

[*] Sharon at the preliminary hearing testified as follows: * * *

"We were drinking at the railroad tracks and we walked over to this bush and he started kissing me and stuff, and I was kissing him back, too, at first. Then, I was telling him to stop * * *.

"[T]hen he asked me if I wanted to walk him over to the park; so we walked over to the park and we sat down on a bench and then he started kissing me again and we were laying on the bench. And he told me to take my pants off.

"I said, 'No,' and I was trying to get up and he hit me back down on the bench and then I just said to myself, 'Forget it,' and I let him do what he wanted to do. * * *

"Q. Did you have sexual intercourse with the defendant?

"A. Yeah. * * *

"Q. You said that he hit you?

"A. Yeah.

"Q. How did he hit you?

"A. He slugged me in the face.

"[The Court]: Did he hit you one time or did he hit you more than once?

"The Witness: He hit me about two or three times. * * * "

[a]. Stewart, J., also concurred, noting "that the statutory discrimination, when viewed as part of the wider scheme of California law, is not as clearcut as might at first appear. Females are not freed from criminal liability in California for engaging in sexual activity that may be harmful. It is unlawful, for example, for any person, of either sex, [to] contribute to the delinquency of anyone under 18 years of age. All persons are prohibited [from] consensual intercourse with a child under 14. [Finally,] females may be brought within the proscription of § 261.5 itself, since a female may be charged with aiding and abetting its violation. [A]pproximately 14% of the juveniles arrested for participation in acts made unlawful by § 261.5 between 1975 and 1979 were females. Moreover, an underage female who is as culpable as her male partner, or more culpable, may be prosecuted as a juvenile delinquent."

"The second flaw in the State's assertion is that even assuming that a gender-neutral statute would be more difficult to enforce, the State has still not shown that those enforcement problems would make such a statute less effective than a gender-based statute in deterring minor females from engaging in sexual intercourse. Common sense, however, suggests that a gender-neutral statutory rape law is potentially a *greater* deterrent of sexual activity than a gender-based law, for the simple reason that a gender-neutral law subjects both men and women to criminal sanctions and thus arguably has a deterrent effect on twice as many potential violators. Even if fewer persons were prosecuted under the gender-neutral law, as the State suggests, it would still be true that twice as many persons would be *subject* to arrest."

STEVENS, J., also dissented: "[T]hat a female confronts a greater risk of harm than a male is a reason for applying the prohibition to her—not a reason for granting her a license to use her own judgment on whether or not to assume the risk. Surely, if we examine the problem from the point of view of society's interest in preventing the risk-creating conduct from occurring at all, it is irrational to exempt 50% of the potential violators. * * *

"Finally, even if my logic is faulty and there actually is some speculative basis for treating equally guilty males and females differently, I still believe that any such speculative justification would be outweighed by the paramount interest in even-handed enforcement of the law. A rule that authorizes punishment of only one of two equally guilty wrongdoers violates the essence of the constitutional requirement that the sovereign must govern impartially."

———

NGUYEN v. INS, 533 U.S. 53 (2001), upheld a provision of the Immigration and Naturalization Act that distinguishes between American citizen mothers and American citizen fathers who are the parents of illegitimate children born abroad: Whereas the mothers pass their American citizenship automatically to their illegitimate offspring, the statute establishes various procedural barriers before the illegitimate child of a citizen father can become a citizen. Writing for the Court, KENNEDY, J., recognized that heightened scrutiny applied, but he found the different treatment of illegitimate mothers and illegitimate fathers substantially related to two important governmental interests: "assuring that a biological parent-child relationship exists" and "ensur[ing] that the child and the citizen parent have some demonstrated opportunity or potential to develop [a] relationship [that] consists of the real, everyday ties that provide a connection between child and citizen parent and, in turn, the United States."

O'CONNOR, J., joined by Souter, Ginsburg, and Breyer, JJ., dissented: "While the Court invokes heightened scrutiny, the manner in which it [applies] this standard is a stranger to our precedents." According to O'Connor, J., no real differences justified the differential treatment. As a result of "[m]odern DNA testing," it was not substantially more difficult to determine biological fatherhood than motherhood in most cases. And if Congress cared about parent-child relationships, it "could require some degree of regular contact between the child and the citizen parent over a period of time" in order for either a mother or a father to be able to pass on American citizenship to an illegitimate child born abroad: "[The statute] finds support not in biological differences but instead in a stereotype—i.e., 'the generalization that mothers are significantly more likely than fathers [to] develop caring relationships with their children.' [No] one should mistake the majority's analysis for a careful application of this Court's equal protection jurisprudence concerning sex-based classifications. Today's decision instead represents a deviation from a line of cases in which we have vigilantly applied heightened scrutiny."b

III. "BENIGN"—"COMPENSATORY"— "REMEDIAL" DISCRIMINATION

CALIFANO v. WEBSTER

430 U.S. 313, 97 S.Ct. 1192, 51 L.Ed.2d 360 (1977).

PER CURIAM.

[Social Security Act § 215(b)(3)'s formula—which has since been amended— afforded the chance of higher old-age benefits to female wage earners than to similarly situated males.]

To withstand scrutiny under [equal protection], "classifications by gender must serve important governmental objectives and must be substantially related to achievement of those objectives." *Craig*. Reduction of the disparity in economic condition between men and women caused by the long history of discrimination against women has been recognized as such an important governmental objective. *Schlesinger v. Ballard*, 419 U.S. 498 (1975);a *Kahn v. Shevin*, 416 U.S. 351 (1974).b But "the mere recitation of a benign, compensatory purpose is not an automatic shield which protects against any inquiry into the actual purposes underlying a statutory scheme." *Weinberger v. Wiesenfeld*, 420 U.S. 636 (1975).c Accordingly, we have rejected attempts to justify gender classifications as compensation for past discrimination against women when the classifications in fact penalized women wage earners, *Califano v. Goldfarb*, 430 U.S. 199 (1977);d *Wiesenfeld*, or when the statutory structure and its legislative history revealed

b. The Court's previous cases involving discrimination against unmarried fathers in comparison with unmarried mothers, both decided by 5–4, are hard to reconcile. Compare *Caban v. Mohammed*, 441 U.S. 380 (1979) (holding violative of equal protection a New York statute granting the mother—but not the father— of an illegitimate child the right to veto the child's adoption) with *Parham v. Hughes*, 441 U.S. 347 (1979) (upholding a law denying the father—but not the mother—of an illegitimate child the right to sue for the child's wrongful death unless he had legitimated the child). In *Miller v. Albright*, 523 U.S. 420 (1998), a sharply divided Court had upheld the same provision involved in *Nguyen v. INS*, but had done so without majority opinion, with two Justices concurring in the result only because they thought that the illegitimate child seeking to establish citizenship in that case lacked standing to assert the rights of the biological father to be free from gender-based discrimination.

a. *Schlesinger*, per Stewart, J., upheld a federal statute providing for the discharge of naval "line" officers who had not been promoted for nine years (males) or thirteen years (females): Because of Navy restrictions on combat and sea duty for women, "Congress [may] quite rationally have believed that women line officers had less opportunity for promotion than did their male counterparts, and that a longer period of tenure for women officers

would, therefore, be consistent with the goal to provide women officers with 'fair and equitable career advancement programs.'"

b. *Kahn*, per Douglas, J., upheld a property tax exemption for widows (but not widowers) on the ground that the law was "reasonably designed to further the state policy of cushioning the financial impact of spousal loss upon the sex for whom that loss imposes a disproportionately heavy burden."

c. *Weinberger*, per Brennan, J., held that Social Security Act § 402(g)'s payment of benefits to the wife—but not the husband—of a deceased wage earner with minor children violated equal protection because it "unjustifiably discriminated against women wage-earners": as in *Frontiero*, an " 'archaic and overbroad' generalization [underlies] the distinction drawn by § 402(g), namely, that male [but not female] workers' earnings are vital to the support of their families." Unlike in *Kahn*, "[i]t is apparent both from the statutory scheme itself and from the legislative history of § 402(g) that Congress' purpose [was] not to provide an income to women who were, because of economic discrimination, unable to provide for themselves."

d. *Goldfarb* held that Social Security Act § 402(f)'s payment of benefits to a widow of a covered employee, but not to a widower unless he proves dependency on his deceased wife-employee, violated equal protection.

that the classification was not enacted as compensation for past discrimination. *Goldfarb; Wiesenfeld.*

[The] more favorable treatment of the female wage earner enacted here was not a result of "archaic and overbroad generalizations" about women, or of "the role-typing society has long imposed" upon women such as casual assumptions that women are "the weaker sex" or are more likely to be child-rearers or dependents. Rather, "the only discernible purpose of [§ 215's more favorable treatment is] the permissible one of redressing our society's longstanding disparate treatment of women." *Goldfarb.*

The challenged statute operated directly to compensate women for past economic discrimination. Retirement benefits [are] based on past earnings. But as we have recognized: "Whether from overt discrimination or from the socialization process of a male-dominated culture, the job market is inhospitable to the woman seeking any but the lowest paid jobs." *Kahn.* Thus, allowing women, who as such have been unfairly hindered from earning as much as men, to eliminate additional low-earning years from the calculation of their retirement benefits works directly to remedy some part of the effect of past discrimination.5

[T]he legislative history is clear that the differing treatment of men and women in former § 215(b)(3) was not "the accidental byproduct of a traditional way of thinking about females," *Goldfarb* (Stevens, J., concurring in the result), but rather was deliberately enacted to compensate for particular economic disabilities suffered by women. * * *

Reversed.

CHIEF JUSTICE BURGER, with whom JUSTICE STEWART, JUSTICE BLACKMUN, and JUSTICE REHNQUIST join, concurring in the judgment.

* * * I question whether certainty in the law is promoted by hinging the validity of important statutory schemes on whether five Justices view them to be more akin to the "offensive" provisions struck down in *Wiesenfeld* and *Frontiero,* or more like the "benign" provisions upheld in *Ballard* and *Kahn.* I therefore concur in the judgment [for] reasons stated by Mr. Justice Rehnquist in his dissenting opinion in *Goldfarb*: ["Favoring aged widows is scarcely an invidious discrimination. [It] in no way perpetuates the economic discrimination which has been the basis for heightened scrutiny of gender-based classifications, and is, in fact, explainable as a measure to ameliorate the characteristically depressed condition of aged widows."]

MISSISSIPPI UNIV. FOR WOMEN v. HOGAN

458 U.S. 718, 102 S.Ct. 3331, 73 L.Ed.2d 1090 (1982).

JUSTICE O'CONNOR delivered the opinion of the Court.

[Mississippi University for Women ("MUW"), "the oldest state-supported all-female college in the United States," denied Hogan admission to its School of Nursing solely because of his sex.a] Our decisions [establish] that the party seeking to uphold a statute that classifies individuals on the basis of their gender must carry the burden of showing an "exceedingly persuasive justification" for

---

5. Even with the advantage[,] women on the average received lower retirement benefits than men. "As of December 1972, the average monthly retirement insurance benefit for males was $179.60 and for females, $140.50."

a. The Court declined "to address the question of whether MUW's admissions policy, as applied to males seeking admission to schools other than the School of Nursing, violates the Fourteenth Amendment."

the classification. The burden is met only by showing at least that the classification serves "important governmental objectives and that the discriminatory means employed" are "substantially related to the achievement of those objectives."9

Although the test [is] straightforward, it must be applied free of fixed notions concerning the roles and abilities of males and females. [Thus,] if the statutory objective is to exclude or "protect" members of one gender because they are presumed to suffer from an inherent handicap or to be innately inferior, the objective itself is illegitimate. See *Frontiero*.

If the State's objective is legitimate and important, we next determine whether the requisite direct, substantial relationship between objective and means is present. The purpose of requiring that close relationship is to assure that the validity of a classification is determined through reasoned analysis rather than through the mechanical application of traditional, often inaccurate, assumptions about the proper roles of men and women. The need for the requirement is amply revealed by reference to the broad range of statutes already invalidated by this Court, statutes that relied upon the simplistic, outdated assumption that gender could be used as a "proxy for other, more germane bases of classification," *Craig*, to establish a link between objective and classification. * * *

The State's primary justification for maintaining the single-sex admissions policy of MUW's School of Nursing is that it compensates for discrimination against women and, therefore, constitutes educational affirmative action. [A] state can evoke a compensatory purpose to justify an otherwise discriminatory classification only if members of the gender benefited by the classification actually suffer a disadvantage related to the classification. We considered such a situation in *Webster* [and *Ballard*].

In sharp contrast, Mississippi has made no showing that women lacked opportunities to obtain training in the field of nursing or to attain positions of leadership in that field when the MUW School of Nursing opened its door or that women currently are deprived of such opportunities. In fact, in 1970, the year before the School of Nursing's first class enrolled, women earned 94 percent of the nursing baccalaureate degrees conferred in Mississippi and 98.6 percent of the degrees earned nationwide.

Rather than compensate for discriminatory barriers faced by women, MUW's [policy] tends to perpetuate the stereotyped view of nursing as an exclusively woman's job.15 By assuring that Mississippi allots more openings in its state-supported nursing schools to women than it does to men, MUW's admissions policy lends credibility to the old view that women, not men, should become nurses, and makes the assumption that nursing is a field for women a self-fulfilling prophecy. Thus, we conclude that, although the State recited a "benign, compensatory purpose," it failed to establish that the alleged objective is the actual purpose underlying the discriminatory classification.

The policy is invalid also because [the] State has made no showing that the gender-based classification is substantially and directly related to its proposed compensatory objective. To the contrary, MUW's policy of permitting men to

9. [Because] we conclude that the challenged statutory classification is not substantially related to an important objective, we need not decide whether classifications based upon gender are inherently suspect.

15. Officials of the American Nurses Association have suggested that excluding men

from the field has depressed nurses' wages. To the extent the exclusion of men has that effect, MUW's admissions policy actually penalizes the very class the State purports to benefit. Cf. *Wiesenfeld*.

attend classes as auditors fatally undermines its claim that women, at least those in the School of Nursing, are adversely affected by the presence of men.17

Affirmed.

CHIEF JUSTICE BURGER, dissenting.

I agree generally with Justice Powell's dissenting opinion. I write separately, however, to emphasize that [s]ince the Court's opinion relies heavily on its finding that women have traditionally dominated the nursing profession, it suggests that a State might well be justified in maintaining, for example, the option of an all-women's business school or liberal arts program.

JUSTICE POWELL, with whom JUSTICE REHNQUIST joins, dissenting.b

[T]he Court errs seriously by assuming [that] the equal protection standard generally applicable to sex discrimination is appropriate here. That standard was designed to free women from "archaic and overbroad generalizations." *Ballard.* In no previous case have we applied it to invalidate state efforts to *expand* women's choices. * * *

By applying heightened equal protection analysis to this case, the Court frustrates the liberating spirit of the Equal Protection Clause. It forbids the States from providing women with an opportunity to choose the type of university they prefer. And yet it is these women whom the Court regards as the *victims* of an illegal, stereotyped perception of the role of women in our society. The Court reasons this way in a case in which no woman has complained, and the only complainant is a man who advances no claims on behalf of anyone else. His claim [is] not that he is being denied a substantive educational opportunity, or even the right to attend an all-male or a coeducational college. It is *only* that the colleges open to him are located at inconvenient distances.

* * * I would sustain Mississippi's right to continue MUW on a rational basis analysis. But I need not apply this "lowest tier" of scrutiny. [More] than 2,000 women presently evidence their preference for MUW by having enrolled [there.] Generations of our finest minds, both among educators and students, have believed that single-sex, college-level institutions afford distinctive benefits. There are many persons, of course, who have different views. But simply because there are these differences is no reason—certainly none of constitutional dimension—to conclude that no substantial state interest is served when such a choice is made available.17

---

17. Justice Powell's dissent suggests that a second objective is served by the gender-based classification in that Mississippi has elected to provide women a choice of educational environments. Since any gender-based classification provides one class a benefit or choice not available to the other class, however, that argument begs the question. The issue is not whether the benefitted class profits from the classification, but whether the State's decision to confer a benefit only upon one class by means of a discriminatory classification is substantially related to achieving a legitimate and substantial goal.

b. Blackmun, J.'s brief dissent—agreeing essentially with Powell, J.—is omitted.

17. [It] is understandable that MUW might believe that it could allow men to audit courses without materially affecting its environment. MUW charges tuition but gives no academic credit for auditing. The University evidently is correct in believing that few men will choose to audit under such circumstances. This deviation from a perfect relationship between means and ends is insubstantial.

SECTION 4. SPECIAL SCRUTINY FOR OTHER CLASSIFICATIONS: DOCTRINE AND DEBATES

Are there are other classifications besides those based on race and gender that should be subject to special scrutiny? If so, by what criteria should those classifications be identified?

I. ALIENAGE

Up to the late 1940s, the Supreme Court found a "special public interest"a in rejecting almost all challenges to state discriminations against aliens involving such activities as land ownership, *Terrace v. Thompson,* 263 U.S. 197 (1923); killing wild game, *Patsone v. Pennsylvania,* 232 U.S. 138 (1914); operating poolhalls, *State of Ohio ex rel. Clarke v. Deckebach,* 274 U.S. 392 (1927); and working on public construction projects, *Crane v. New York,* 239 U.S. 195 (1915).b But *Takahashi v. Fish & Game Com'n,* 334 U.S. 410 (1948), relying on both Congress' "broad constitutional powers in determining what aliens shall be admitted to the United States" and the Fourteenth Amendment's "general policy" of "equality," invalidated California's denial of licenses for commercial fishing in coastal waters to aliens lawfully residing in the state.

GRAHAM v. RICHARDSON, 403 U.S. 365 (1971), took a much further step. Reasoning that "aliens as a class are a prime example of a 'discrete and insular minority,'" the Court ruled that "classifications based on alienage [are] inherently suspect and subject to close judicial scrutiny" and held that state laws denying welfare benefits to aliens violate equal protection.

Two years later, SUGARMAN v. DOUGALL, 413 U.S. 634 (1973), applied the close scrutiny prescribed by *Graham* to invalidate Section 53 of New York's Civil Service Law, which required citizenship as a condition of public employment in positions subject to competitive examination. The Court, per BLACKMUN, J., held that Section 53 unconstitutionally discriminated against aliens: "It is established, of course, that an alien is entitled to the shelter of the Equal Protection Clause[,] that aliens as a class 'are a prime example of a 'discrete and insular' minority (see *United States v. Carolene Products Co.* [Ch. 5, Sec. 3]),' and that classifications based on alienage are 'subject to close judicial scrutiny.'"

REHNQUIST, J., dissented in *Sugarman* and a companion case: "The Court, by holding in these cases and in *Graham,* that a citizen-alien classification is 'suspect' in the eyes of our Constitution, fails to mention, let alone rationalize, the fact that the Constitution itself recognizes a basic difference between citizens and aliens. That distinction is constitutionally important in no less than 11 instances in a political document noted for its brevity. [Indeed,] the very Amendment which the Court reads to prohibit classifications based on citizenship establishes the very distinction which the Court now condemns as 'suspect.' [The] language of that Amendment carefully distinguishes between 'persons' who, whether by birth or naturalization, had achieved a certain status, and 'persons' in general. That a 'citizen' was considered by Congress to be a rationally distinct subclass of all 'persons' is obvious from the language of the Amendment. * * *

"The mere recitation of the words 'insular and discrete minority' is hardly a *constitutional* reason for prohibiting state legislative classifications such as are involved here. [Our] society, consisting of over 200 million individuals of multitudinous origins, customs, tongues, beliefs, and cultures is, to say the least, diverse. It would hardly take extraordinary ingenuity for a lawyer to find 'insular and

---

a. *Truax v. Raich,* 239 U.S. 33 (1915).

b. *Truax,* however, invalidated Arizona's forbidding employers of five or more persons from hiring over 20% aliens.

discrete' minorities at every turn in the road. Yet, unless the Court can precisely define and constitutionally justify both the terms and analysis it uses, these decisions today stand for the proposition that the Court can choose a 'minority' it 'feels' deserves 'solicitude' and thereafter prohibit the States from classifying that 'minority' differently from the 'majority.' I cannot find, and the Court does not cite, any constitutional authority for such a 'ward of the Court' approach to equal protection."

AMBACH v. NORWICK

441 U.S. 68, 99 S.Ct. 1589, 60 L.Ed.2d 49 (1979).

JUSTICE POWELL delivered the opinion of the Court.

This case presents the question whether a State, consistently with the Equal Protection Clause, may refuse to employ as elementary and secondary school teachers aliens who are eligible for United States citizenship but who refuse to seek naturalization. * * *

[*Graham* for] the first time treated classifications based on alienage as "inherently suspect and subject to close judicial scrutiny." Applying *Graham*, this Court has held invalid statutes that prevented aliens from entering a State's classified civil service, *Sugarman*, practicing law, *In re Griffiths*, 413 U.S. 717 (1973),working as an engineer, *Examining Bd. v. Flores de Otero*, 426 U.S. 572 (1976), and receiving state educational benefits, *Nyquist v. Mauclet*, 432 U.S. 1 (1977). * * *

In *Sugarman*, we recognized that a State could, "in an appropriately defined class of positions, require citizenship as a qualification for office." [*Sugarman* thus contemplated that the] exclusion of aliens from [influential] governmental positions would not invite as demanding scrutiny from this Court.

Applying the rational basis standard, we held last Term that New York could exclude aliens from the ranks of its police force. *Foley v. Connelie*, 435 U.S. 291 (1978). Because the police function fulfilled "a most fundamental obligation of government to its constituency" and by necessity cloaked policemen with substantial discretionary powers, we viewed the police force as being one of those appropriately defined classes of positions for which a citizenship requirement could be imposed. Accordingly, the State was required to justify its classification "only by a showing of some rational relationship between the interest sought to be protected and the limiting classification."a

The rule for governmental functions, which is an exception to the general standard applicable to classifications based on alienage, rests on important principles inherent in the Constitution. The distinction between citizens and aliens, though ordinarily irrelevant to private activity, is fundamental to the definition and government of a State. [Citizenship] denotes an association with the polity which, in a democratic republic, exercises the powers of governance. The form of this association is important; an oath of allegiance or similar ceremony cannot substitute for the unequivocal legal bond citizenship represents. It is because of this special significance of citizenship that governmental entities, when exercising the functions of government, have wider latitude in limiting the participation of noncitizens.

a. *Cabell v. Chavez–Salido*, 454 U.S. 432 (1982), extended *Foley* to probation officers. Marshall, J., joined by Brennan, Blackmun, and Stevens, JJ., dissented in *Foley*. Blackmun, J., joined by Brennan, Marshall, and Stevens, JJ., dissented in *Cabell*.

In determining whether, for purposes of equal protection analysis, teaching in public schools constitutes a governmental function, we look to the role of public education and to the degree of responsibility and discretion teachers possess in fulfilling that role. Each of these considerations supports the conclusion that public school teachers may be regarded as performing a task "that go[es] to the heart of representative government." *Sugarman.*

Public education, like the police function, "fulfills a most fundamental obligation of government to its constituency." *Foley.* The importance of public schools in the preparation of individuals for participation as citizens, and in the preservation of the values on which our society rests, long has been recognized by our decisions [*Brown I*]. Within the public school system, teachers play a critical part in developing students' attitude toward government and understanding of the role of citizens in our society. [In] shaping the students' experience to achieve educational goals, teachers by necessity have wide discretion over the way the course material is communicated to students. [Further], a teacher serves as a role model for his students, exerting a subtle but important influence over their perceptions and values. Thus, [a] teacher has an opportunity to influence the attitudes of students toward government, the political process, and a citizen's social responsibilities. This influence is crucial to the continued good health of a democracy. * * *

As the legitimacy of the State's interest in furthering the educational goals outlined above is undoubted, it remains only to consider whether [the statute] bears a rational relationship to this interest. The restriction is carefully framed to serve its purpose, as it bars from teaching only those aliens who have demonstrated their unwillingness to obtain United States citizenship. Appellees [in] effect have chosen to classify themselves. They prefer to retain citizenship in a foreign country with the obligations it entails of primary duty and loyalty.14 [New York has] made a judgment that citizenship should be a qualification for teaching the young of the State in the public schools, and [the statute] furthers that judgment.

Reversed.

Justice Blackmun, with whom Justice Brennan, Justice Marshall, and Justice Stevens, join, dissenting.

[T]he New York classification is irrational. Is it better to employ a poor citizen-teacher than an excellent resident alien teacher? Is it preferable to have a citizen who has never seen Spain or a Latin American country teach Spanish to eighth graders and to deny that opportunity to a resident alien who may have lived for 20 years in the culture of Spain or Latin America? The State will know how to select its teachers responsibly, wholly apart from citizenship, and can do so selectively and intelligently. * * *

[Further], it is logically impossible to differentiate between this case [and *Griffiths*]. One may speak proudly of the role model of the teacher, of his ability to mold young minds, of his inculcating force as to national ideals, and of his profound influence in the impartation of our society's values. Are the attributes of an attorney any the less? [The attorney] is an influence in legislation, in the community, and in the role model figure that the professional person enjoys. * * *

---

14. As our cases have emphasized, resident aliens pay taxes, serve in the armed forces, and have made significant contributions to our country in private and public endeavors. No doubt [many] would make excellent public school teachers. But the legislature, having in mind the importance of education to state and local governments, may determine eligibility for the key position in discharging that function on the assumption that *generally* persons [who] have not declined the opportunity to seek United States citizenship, are better qualified than are those who have elected to remain aliens. * * *

Notes

1. *Discrimination against illegal aliens.* PLYLER v. DOE (1982), Sec. 5, III infra, "reject[ed] the claim that 'illegal aliens' are a 'suspect class.' [U]ndocumented status is not irrelevant to any proper legislative goal. Nor is [it] an absolutely immutable characteristic since it is the product of conscious, indeed unlawful, action." But the Court, per BRENNAN, J., invalidated a Texas statute denying free public education to illegal alien *children,* stressing both the special status of the children—who can " 'affect neither their parents' conduct nor their own status"—and "the importance of education," both to the children themselves and to the nation more generally, since so many undocumented residents were almost certain to remain in the United States.a

2. *Discrimination by the national government.* It has long been held that the *national* government has power "to exclude aliens altogether from the United States, or to prescribe the terms and conditions upon which they may come to this country." *Lem Moon Sing v. United States,* 158 U.S. 538 (1895). Relying on this traditionally recognized authority, MATHEWS v. DIAZ, 426 U.S. 67 (1976), per STEVENS, J., upheld a federal statute denying Medicare benefits to aliens unless they have (i) been admitted for permanent residence and (ii) resided for at least five years in the United States. Although "aliens and citizens alike, are protected by the Due Process Clause, [i]n the exercise of its broad power over naturalization and immigration, Congress regularly makes rules that would be unacceptable if applied to citizens.

"[T]he responsibility for regulating the relationship between the United States and [aliens] has been committed to the political branches of the Federal Government. Since decisions in these matters may implicate our relations with foreign powers, and since a wide variety of classifications must be defined in the light of changing political and economic circumstances, such decisions are frequently of a character more appropriate to either the Legislature or the Executive than to the Judiciary. [The] reasons that preclude judicial review of political questions also dictate a narrow standard of review of decisions made by the Congress or the President in the area of immigration and naturalization.

"Since it is obvious that Congress has no constitutional duty to provide *all aliens* with the welfare benefits provided to citizens, the party challenging the constitutionality of the particular line Congress has drawn" [—allowing benefits to some aliens but not to others—] "has the burden of advancing principled reasoning that will at once invalidate that line and yet tolerate a different line separating some aliens from others. [Since neither of the two requirements] is wholly irrational, this case essentially involves nothing more than a claim that it would have been more reasonable for Congress to select somewhat different requirements of the same kind. [But] it remains true that some line is essential, that any line must produce some harsh and apparently arbitrary consequences, and, of greatest importance, that those who qualify under the test Congress has chosen may reasonably be presumed to have a greater affinity with the United States than those who do not."a

---

a. Burger, C.J., joined by White, Rehnquist, and O'Connor, JJ., dissented.

a. Congress' power to exclude aliens or impose conditions on their admission to the United States does not, of course, imply a power to deny them all constitutional rights while they are here. E.g., *Almeida-Sanchez v. United States,* 413 U.S. 266, 273 (1973) (Fourth Amendment); *Wong Wing v. United States,* 163 U.S. 228, 237 (1896) (Fifth and Sixth Amendments).

II. SEXUAL ORIENTATION

ROMER v. EVANS

517 U.S. 620, 116 S.Ct. 1620, 134 L.Ed.2d 855 (1996).

JUSTICE KENNEDY delivered the opinion of the Court.

One century ago, the first Justice Harlan admonished this Court that the Constitution "neither knows nor tolerates classes among citizens." *Plessy v. Ferguson* (dissenting opinion). Unheeded then, those words are now understood to state a commitment to the law's neutrality where the rights of persons are at stake. The Equal Protection Clause enforces this principle and today requires us to hold invalid a provision of Colorado's Constitution.

[The] enactment challenged in this case is an amendment to the Constitution of the State of Colorado, adopted in a 1992 statewide referendum [and referred to] as "Amendment 2," its designation when submitted to the voters. [The] amendment reads: "No Protected Status Based on Homosexual, Lesbian, or Bisexual Orientation. Neither the State of Colorado, through any of its branches or departments, nor any of its agencies, political subdivisions, municipalities or school districts, shall enact, adopt or enforce any statute, regulation, ordinance or policy whereby homosexual, lesbian or bisexual orientation, conduct, practices or relationships shall constitute or otherwise be the basis of or entitle any person or class of persons to have or claim any minority status, quota preferences, protected status or claim of discrimination. This Section of the Constitution shall be in all respects self-executing."

[The] State's principal argument in defense of Amendment 2 is that it puts gays and lesbians in the same position as all other persons. So, the State says, the measure does no more than deny homosexuals special rights. This reading of the amendment's language is implausible. We rely not upon our own interpretation of the amendment but upon the authoritative construction of Colorado's Supreme Court, [which held that] "The immediate objective of Amendment 2 is, at a minimum, to repeal existing statutes, regulations, ordinances, and policies of state and local entities that barred discrimination based on sexual orientation." [Under Amendment 2 as thus construed, homosexuals], by state decree, are put in a solitary class with respect to transactions and relations in both the private and governmental spheres. The amendment withdraws from homosexuals, but no others, specific legal protection from the injuries caused by discrimination, and it forbids reinstatement of these laws and policies.

The change that Amendment 2 works in the legal status of gays and lesbians in the private sphere is far-reaching, both on its own terms and when considered in light of the structure and operation of modern antidiscrimination laws. That structure is well illustrated by contemporary statutes and ordinances prohibiting discrimination by providers of public accommodations. "At common law, innkeepers, smiths, and others who 'made profession of a public employment,' were prohibited from refusing, without good reason, to serve a customer." The duty was a general one and did not specify protection for particular groups. The common law rules, however, proved insufficient in many instances, and [most] States have chosen to counter discrimination by enacting detailed statutory schemes.

Colorado's state and municipal laws typify this emerging tradition of statutory protection and follow a consistent pattern. The laws first enumerate the persons or entities subject to a duty not to discriminate. The list goes well beyond the entities covered by the common law. The Boulder ordinance, for example, has a comprehensive definition of entities deemed places of "public accommodation." They include "any place of business engaged in any sales to the general public and any place that offers services, facilities, privileges, or advantages to the general public or that receives financial support through solicitation of the general public or through governmental subsidy of any kind."

[These] statutes and ordinances also depart from the common law by enumerating the groups or persons within their ambit of protection. [In] following this approach, Colorado's state and local governments have not limited anti-discrimination laws to groups that have so far been given the protection of heightened equal protection scrutiny under our cases. Rather, they set forth an extensive catalogue of traits which cannot be the basis for discrimination, including age, military status, marital status, pregnancy, parenthood, custody of a minor child, political affiliation, physical or mental disability of an individual or of his or her associates—and, in recent times, sexual orientation.

Amendment 2 bars homosexuals from securing protection against the injuries that these public-accommodations laws address. That in itself is a severe consequence, but there is more. Amendment 2, in addition, nullifies specific legal protections for this targeted class in all transactions in housing, sale of real estate, insurance, health and welfare services, private education, and employment.

[Not] confined to the private sphere, Amendment 2 also operates to repeal and forbid all laws or policies providing specific protection for gays or lesbians from discrimination by every level of Colorado government. The State Supreme Court cited two examples of protections in the governmental sphere that are now rescinded and may not be reintroduced. The first is [an] Executive Order which forbids employment discrimination against " 'all state employees, classified and exempt' on the basis of sexual orientation." Also repealed, and now forbidden, are "various provisions prohibiting discrimination based on sexual orientation at state colleges."

Amendment 2's reach may not be limited to specific laws passed for the benefit of gays and lesbians. It is a fair, if not necessary, inference from the broad language of the amendment that it deprives gays and lesbians even of the protection of general laws and policies that prohibit arbitrary discrimination [such as statutes subjecting agency action to judicial review under the arbitrary and capricious standard and making it a criminal offense for a public servant knowingly, arbitrarily, or capriciously to refrain from performing a duty imposed by law]. At some point in the systematic administration of these laws, an official must determine whether homosexuality is an arbitrary and thus forbidden basis for decision. Yet a decision to that effect would itself amount to a policy prohibiting discrimination on the basis of homosexuality, and so would appear to be no more valid under Amendment 2 than the specific prohibitions against discrimination the state court held invalid.

[The] state court did not decide whether the amendment has this effect, however, and neither need we. [Even] if, as we doubt, homosexuals could find some safe harbor in laws of general application, we cannot accept the view that Amendment 2's prohibition on specific legal protections does no more than deprive homosexuals of special rights. To the contrary, the amendment imposes a special disability upon those persons alone. Homosexuals are forbidden the safeguards that others enjoy or may seek without constraint. They can obtain specific protection against discrimination only by enlisting the citizenry of Colorado to amend the state constitution or perhaps, on the State's view, by trying to pass helpful laws of general applicability. This is so no matter how local or discrete the harm, no matter how public and widespread the injury. We find nothing special in the protections Amendment 2 withholds. These are protections taken for granted by most people either because they already have them or do not need them; these are protections against exclusion from an almost limitless number of transactions and endeavors that constitute ordinary civic life in a free society.

[If] a law neither burdens a fundamental right nor targets a suspect class, we will uphold the legislative classification so long as it bears a rational relation to some legitimate end. Amendment 2 fails, indeed defies, even this conventional inquiry. [Even] in the ordinary equal protection case calling for the most deferential of standards, we insist on knowing the relation between the classification adopted and the object to be attained. [By] requiring that the classification bear a rational relationship to an independent and legitimate legislative end, we ensure that classifications are not drawn for the purpose of disadvantaging the group burdened by the law.

Amendment 2 confounds this normal process of judicial review. It is at once too narrow and too broad. It identifies persons by a single trait and then denies them protection across the board. [It] is not within our constitutional tradition to enact laws of this sort. Central both to the idea of the rule of law and to our own Constitution's guarantee of equal protection is the principle that government and each of its parts remain open on impartial terms to all who seek its assistance. [Respect] for this principle explains why laws singling out a certain class of citizens for disfavored legal status or general hardships are rare. A law declaring that in general it shall be more difficult for one group of citizens than for all others to seek aid from the government is itself a denial of equal protection of the laws in the most literal sense. * * *

Davis v. Beason, 133 U.S. 333 (1890), not cited by the parties but relied upon by the dissent, is not evidence that Amendment 2 is within our constitutional tradition, and any reliance upon it as authority for sustaining the amendment is misplaced. In *Davis*, the Court approved an Idaho territorial statute denying Mormons, polygamists, and advocates of polygamy the right to vote and to hold office. [To] the extent *Davis* held that persons advocating a certain practice may be denied the right to vote, it is no longer good law. *Brandenburg v. Ohio*, [Ch. 7, Sec. 1, I]. To the extent it held that the groups designated in the statute may be deprived of the right to vote because of their status, its ruling could not stand without surviving strict scrutiny, a most doubtful outcome. *Dunn v. Blumstein*, [Sec. 5, II infra].

[A] second and related point is that laws of the kind now before us raise the inevitable inference that the disadvantage imposed is born of animosity toward the class of persons affected. "[I]f the constitutional conception of 'equal protection of the laws' means anything, it must at the very least mean that a bare * * * desire to harm a politically unpopular group cannot constitute a *legitimate* governmental interest." *Moreno*, [Sec. 1 supra]. Even laws enacted for broad and ambitious purposes often can be explained by reference to legitimate public policies which justify the incidental disadvantages they impose on certain persons. Amendment 2, however, in making a general announcement that gays and lesbians shall not have any particular protections from the law, inflicts on them immediate, continuing, and real injuries that outrun and belie any legitimate justifications that may be claimed for it.

[The] primary rationale the State offers for Amendment 2 is respect for other citizens' freedom of association, and in particular the liberties of landlords or employers who have personal or religious objections to homosexuality. Colorado also cites its interest in conserving resources to fight discrimination against other groups. The breadth of the Amendment is so far removed from these particular justifications that we find it impossible to credit them. [It] is a status-based enactment divorced from any factual context from which we could discern a relationship to legitimate state interests; it is a classification of persons undertaken for its own sake, something the Equal Protection Clause does not permit. * * *

JUSTICE SCALIA, with whom THE CHIEF JUSTICE and JUSTICE THOMAS join, dissenting.

[In] rejecting the State's arguments that Amendment 2 "puts gays and lesbians in the same position as all other persons," and "does no more than deny homosexuals special rights," [the] Court considers it unnecessary to decide the validity of the State's argument that Amendment 2 does not deprive homosexuals of the "protection [afforded by] general laws and policies that prohibit arbitrary discrimination in governmental and private settings." I agree that we need not resolve that dispute, because the Supreme Court of Colorado has resolved it for us. [The] Colorado court stated: "[I]t is significant to note that Colorado law currently proscribes discrimination against persons who are not suspect classes, including discrimination based on age, marital or family status, veterans' status, and for any legal, off-duty conduct such as smoking tobacco. *Of course Amendment 2 is not intended to have any effect on this legislation, but seeks only to prevent the adoption of antidiscrimination laws intended to protect gays, lesbians, and bisexuals.*" (emphasis added). [This] analysis, which is fully in accord with (indeed, follows inescapably from) the text of the constitutional provision, lays to rest such horribles [as] the prospect that assaults upon homosexuals could not be prosecuted. The amendment prohibits *special treatment* of homosexuals, and nothing more. It would not affect, for example, a requirement of state law that pensions be paid to all retiring state employees with a certain length of service; homosexual employees, as well as others, would be entitled to that benefit. But it would prevent the State or any municipality from making death-benefit payments to the "life partner" of a homosexual when it does not make such payments to the long-time roommate of a nonhomosexual employee.

[Despite] all of its hand-wringing about the potential effect of Amendment 2 on general antidiscrimination laws, the Court's opinion ultimately does not dispute all this, but assumes it to be true. The only denial of equal treatment it contends homosexuals have suffered is this: They may not obtain *preferential* treatment without amending the state constitution. That is to say, the principle underlying the Court's opinion is that one who is accorded equal treatment under the laws, but cannot as readily as others obtain *preferential* treatment under the laws, has been denied equal protection of the laws. If merely stating this alleged "equal protection" violation does not suffice to refute it, our constitutional jurisprudence has achieved terminal silliness.

The central thesis of the Court's reasoning is that any group is denied equal protection when, to obtain advantage (or, presumably, to avoid disadvantage), it must have recourse to a more general and hence more difficult level of political decisionmaking than others. The world has never heard of such a principle, which is why the Court's opinion is so long on emotive utterance and so short on relevant legal citation. And it seems to me most unlikely that any multilevel democracy can function under such a principle. For *whenever* a disadvantage is imposed, or conferral of a benefit is prohibited, at one of the higher levels of democratic decisionmaking (i.e., by the state legislature rather than local government, or by the people at large in the state constitution rather than the legislature), the affected group has (under this theory) been denied equal protection. To take the simplest of examples, consider a state law prohibiting the award of municipal contracts to relatives of mayors or city councilmen. Once such a law is passed, the group composed of such relatives must, in order to get the benefit of city contracts, persuade the state legislature—unlike all other citizens, who need only persuade the municipality. It is ridiculous to consider this a denial of equal protection, which is why the Court's theory is unheard of. * * *

I turn next to whether there was a legitimate rational basis for the substance of the constitutional amendment—for the prohibition of special protection for homosexuals.1 It is unsurprising that the Court avoids discussion of this question, since the answer is so obviously yes. The case most relevant to the issue before us today is not even mentioned in the Court's opinion: In *Bowers v. Hardwick*, [Ch. 6, Sec. 2], we held that the Constitution does not prohibit what virtually all States had done from the founding of the Republic until very recent years—making homosexual conduct a crime. [If] it is constitutionally permissible for a State to make homosexual conduct criminal, surely it is constitutionally permissible for a State to enact other laws merely *disfavoring* homosexual conduct. [And] a fortiori it is constitutionally permissible for a State to adopt a provision *not even* disfavoring homosexual conduct, but merely prohibiting all levels of state government from bestowing *special protections* upon homosexual conduct. Respondents (who, unlike the Court, cannot afford the luxury of ignoring inconvenient precedent) counter *Bowers* with the argument that a greater-includes-the-lesser rationale cannot justify Amendment 2's application to individuals who do not engage in homosexual acts, but are merely of homosexual "orientation."

[Assuming] that, in Amendment 2, a person of homosexual "orientation" is someone who does not engage in homosexual conduct but merely has a tendency or desire to do so, *Bowers* still suffices to establish a rational basis for the provision. If it is rational to criminalize the conduct, surely it is rational to deny special favor and protection to those with a self-avowed tendency or desire to engage in the conduct. Indeed, where criminal sanctions are not involved, homosexual "orientation" is an acceptable stand-in for homosexual conduct. A State "does not violate the Equal Protection Clause merely because the classifications made by its laws are imperfect." Just as a policy barring the hiring of methadone users as transit employees does not violate equal protection simply because *some* methadone users pose no threat to passenger safety, see *New York City Transit Authority v. Beazer*, [Sec. 1 supra], [Amendment] 2 is not constitutionally invalid simply because it could have been drawn more precisely so as to withdraw special antidiscrimination protections only from those of homosexual "orientation" who actually engage in homosexual conduct.

[The] Court's opinion contains grim, disapproving hints that Coloradans have been guilty of "animus" or "animosity" toward homosexuality, as though that has been established as UnAmerican. Of course it is our moral heritage that one should not hate any human being or class of human beings. But I had thought that one could consider certain conduct reprehensible—murder, for example, or polygamy, or cruelty to animals—and could exhibit even "animus" toward such conduct. Surely that is the only sort of "animus" at issue here: moral disapproval of homosexual conduct, the same sort of moral disapproval that produced the centuries-old criminal laws that we held constitutional in *Bowers*.

---

1. The Court evidently agrees that "rational basis"—the normal test for compliance with the Equal Protection Clause—is the governing standard. The trial court rejected respondents' argument that homosexuals constitute a "suspect" or "quasi-suspect" class, and respondents elected not to appeal that ruling to the Supreme Court of Colorado. And the Court implicitly rejects the Supreme Court of Colorado's holding that Amendment 2 infringes upon a "fundamental right" of "independently identifiable class[es]" to "participate equally in the political process."

[But] though Coloradans are, as I say, *entitled* to be hostile toward homosexual conduct, the fact is that the degree of hostility reflected by Amendment 2 is the smallest conceivable. The Court's portrayal of Coloradans as a society fallen victim to pointless, hate-filled "gay-bashing" is so false as to be comical. Colorado not only is one of the 25 States that have repealed their antisodomy laws, but was among the first to do so. But the society that eliminates criminal punishment for homosexual acts does not necessarily abandon the view that homosexuality is morally wrong and socially harmful; often, abolition simply reflects the view that enforcement of such criminal laws involves unseemly intrusion into the intimate lives of citizens.

There is a problem, however, which arises when criminal sanction of homosexuality is eliminated but moral and social disapprobation of homosexuality is meant to be retained. [Because] those who engage in homosexual conduct tend to reside in disproportionate numbers in certain communities, and of course care about homosexual-rights issues much more ardently than the public at large, they possess political power much greater than their numbers, both locally and statewide. Quite understandably, they devote this political power to achieving not merely a grudging social toleration, but full social acceptance, of homosexuality.

By the time Coloradans were asked to vote on Amendment 2, [three] Colorado cities—Aspen, Boulder, and Denver—had enacted ordinances that listed "sexual orientation" as an impermissible ground for discrimination, equating the moral disapproval of homosexual conduct with racial and religious bigotry[, and] the Governor of Colorado had signed an executive order [directing] state agency-heads to "ensure non-discrimination" in hiring and promotion based on, among other things, "sexual orientation." [I] do not mean to be critical of these legislative successes; homosexuals are as entitled to use the legal system for reinforcement of their moral sentiments as are the rest of society. But they are subject to being countered by lawful, democratic countermeasures as well.

That is where Amendment 2 came in. It sought to counter both the geographic concentration and the disproportionate political power of homosexuals by (1) resolving the controversy at the statewide level, and (2) making the election a single-issue contest for both sides. [The] Court today asserts that this most democratic of procedures is unconstitutional. Lacking any cases to establish that facially absurd proposition, it simply asserts that it *must* be unconstitutional, because it has never happened before. [But, as] I have noted above, this is proved false every time a state law prohibiting or disfavoring certain conduct is passed, because such a law prevents the adversely affected group—whether drug addicts, or smokers, or gun owners, or motorcyclists—from changing the policy thus established in "each of [the] parts" of the State.

[But] there is a much closer analogy, one that involves precisely the effort by the majority of citizens to preserve its view of sexual morality statewide, against the efforts of a geographically concentrated and politically powerful minority to undermine it. The constitutions of the States of Arizona, Idaho, New Mexico, Oklahoma, and Utah *to this day* contain provisions stating that polygamy is "forever prohibited." Polygamists, and those who have a polygamous "orientation," have been "singled out" by these provisions for much more severe treatment than merely denial of favored status; and that treatment can only be changed by achieving amendment of the state constitutions. The Court's disposition today suggests that these provisions are unconstitutional, and that polygamy must be permitted in these States on a state-legislated, or perhaps even local-option, basis—unless, of course, polygamists for some reason have fewer constitutional rights than homosexuals.

[Has] the Court concluded that the perceived social harm of polygamy is a "legitimate concern of government," and the perceived social harm of homosexuality is not? [I] strongly suspect that the answer [to the last question is] yes, which leads me to the last point I wish to make: [To] suggest [that] this constitutional amendment springs from nothing more than " 'a bare * * * desire to harm a politically unpopular group,' " is nothing short of insulting. (It is also nothing short of preposterous to call "politically unpopular" a group which enjoys enormous influence in American media and politics, and which, as the trial court here noted, though composing no more than 4% of the population had the support of 46% of the voters on Amendment 2.) [When] the Court takes sides in the culture wars, it tends to be with the knights rather than the villeins—and more specifically with the Templars, reflecting the views and values of the lawyer class from which the Court's Members are drawn. How that class feels about homosexuality will be evident to anyone who wishes to interview job applicants at virtually any of the Nation's law schools. The interviewer may refuse to offer a job because the applicant is a Republican; because he is an adulterer; [or] because he went to the wrong prep school or belongs to the wrong country club. But if the interviewer should wish not to be an associate or partner of an applicant because he disapproves of the applicant's homosexuality, *then* he will have violated the pledge which the Association of American Law Schools requires all its member-schools to exact from job interviewers: "assurance of the employer's willingness" to hire homosexuals. This law-school view of what "prejudices" must be stamped out may be contrasted with the more plebeian attitudes that apparently still prevail in the United States Congress, which has been unresponsive to repeated attempts to extend to homosexuals the protections of federal civil rights laws.

[Today's] opinion has no foundations in American constitutional law, and barely pretends to. The people of Colorado have adopted an entirely reasonable provision which does not even disfavor homosexuals in any substantive sense, but merely denies them preferential treatment. Amendment 2 is designed to prevent piecemeal deterioration of the sexual morality favored by a majority of Coloradans, and is not only an appropriate means to that legitimate end, but a means that Americans have employed before. Striking it down is an act, not of judicial judgment, but of political will. * * *

LAWRENCE v. TEXAS, Ch. 6, Sec. 2, per KENNEDY, J., overruled *Bowers* and held that a Texas statute prohibiting homosexual but not heterosexual sodomy lacked a legitimate purpose and violated a liberty right protected under the Due Process Clause. The Court passed quickly by an equal protection argument: "[P]etitioners [contend] that *Romer* provides the basis for declaring the Texas statute invalid under the Equal Protection Clause. That is a tenable argument, but we conclude the instant case requires us to address whether *Bowers* [has] continuing validity."

O'CONNOR, J., concurring, would have put the decision wholly on equal protection grounds: "When a law exhibits [a bare] desire to harm a politically unpopular group, we have applied a more searching form of rational basis review to strike down such laws under the Equal Protection Clause. [And we] have been most likely to apply rational basis review to hold a law unconstitutional under the Equal Protection Clause where, as here, the challenged legislation inhibits personal relationships. [O'Connor, J., here cited, inter alia, *Moreno, Eisenstadt v. Baird*, and *Romer*.] The statute at issue here [treats] the same conduct differently based solely on the participants. Those harmed by this law are people who have a same-sex sexual orientation. [The] Texas statute makes homosexuals unequal in the eyes of the law by making particular conduct—and only that conduct—subject to criminal sanction. [Texas] attempts to justify its law [by] arguing that the statute satisfies rational basis review because it furthers the legitimate governmental interest of the promotion of morality. In *Bowers*, we [rejected] the argument that no rational basis existed to justify [a prohibition against sodomy], pointing to the government's interest in promoting morality. [But] *Bowers* did not hold that moral disapproval of a group is a rational basis under the Equal Protection Clause to criminalize homosexual sodomy when heterosexual sodomy is not punished. [Moral] disapproval of a group cannot be a legitimate governmental interest under the Equal Protection Clause because legal classifications must not be 'drawn for the purpose of disadvantaging the group burdened by the law.' Texas' invocation of moral disapproval as a legitimate state interest proves nothing more than Texas' desire to criminalize homosexual sodomy. But the Equal Protection Clause prevents a State from creating 'a classification of persons undertaken for its own sake.'

"Texas argues [that] the law discriminates only against homosexual conduct. While it is true that the law applies only to conduct, the conduct targeted by this law is conduct that is closely correlated with being homosexual. Under such circumstances, Texas' sodomy law is targeted at more than conduct. It is instead directed toward gay persons as a class."

SCALIA, J., joined by Rehnquist, C.J., and Thomas, J., dissenting, rejected the equal protection as well as the due process argument: "On its face [the challenged statute] applies equally to all persons. [To] be sure, § 21.06 does distinguish between the sexes insofar as concerns the partner with whom the sexual acts are performed: men can violate the law only with other men, and women only with other women. But this cannot itself be a denial of equal protection, since it is precisely the same distinction regarding partner that is drawn in state laws prohibiting marriage with someone of the same sex while permitting marriage with someone of the opposite sex. The objection is made, however, that the antimiscegenation laws invalidated in *Loving* similarly were applicable to whites and blacks alike, and only distinguished between the races insofar as the partner was concerned. In *Loving*, however, we correctly applied heightened scrutiny, rather than the usual rational-basis review, because the Virginia statute was 'designed to maintain White Supremacy.' [By contrast, no] purpose to discriminate against men or women as a class can be gleaned from the Texas law, so rational-basis review applies. That review is readily satisfied here by the same rational basis that satisfied it in *Bowers*—society's belief that certain forms of sexual behavior are 'immoral and unacceptable.' This is the same justification that supports many other laws regulating sexual behavior that make a distinction based upon the identity of the partner—for example, laws against adultery, fornication, and adult incest, and laws refusing to recognize homosexual marriage.

"Justice O'Connor argues that [this law discriminates] with regard to the sexual proclivity of the principal actor. [But a similar claim could be made about] any law. A law against public nudity targets 'the conduct that is closely correlated with being a nudist,' and hence 'is targeted at more than conduct'; it is 'directed toward nudists as a class.' But be that as it may. Even if the Texas law does deny equal protection to 'homosexuals as a class,' that denial still does not need to be justified by anything more than a rational basis, which our cases show is satisfied by the enforcement of traditional notions of sexual morality. Justice O'Connor simply decrees application of 'a more searching form of rational basis review' to the Texas statute. [She does not] explain precisely what her 'more searching form' of rational-basis review consists of. It must at least mean, however, that laws exhibiting 'a ... desire to harm a politically unpopular group,' are invalid even though there may be a conceivable rational basis to support them. This reasoning leaves on pretty shaky grounds state laws limiting marriage to opposite-sex couples. Justice O'Connor seeks to preserve them by the conclusory statement that 'preserving the traditional institution of marriage' is a legitimate state interest. But 'preserving the traditional institution of marriage' is just a kinder way of describing the State's moral disapproval of same-sex couples. Texas's interest in § 21.06 could be recast in similarly euphemistic terms: 'preserving the traditional sexual mores of our society.' "

III. OTHER CHALLENGED BASES FOR DISCRIMINATION

1. *Illegitimacy.* MATHEWS v. LUCAS, 427 U.S. 495 (1976), per BLACKMUN, J., rejected arguments that statutes that disadvantage children born out of wedlock should be subjected to strict judicial scrutiny and upheld a provision of the Social Security Act that automatically provided survivors' benefits to the legitimate children of deceased wage-earners, based on a presumption of financial dependency, but required illegitimate children to prove their financial dependency in order to receive benefits: "It is true, of course, that the legal status of illegitimacy, however defined, is, like race or national origin, a characteristic determined by causes not within the control of the illegitimate individual, and it bears no relation to the individual's ability to participate in and contribute to society. The Court recognized in *Weber v. Aetna Casualty & Surety Co.,* 406 U.S. 164 (1972), that visiting condemnation upon that child in order to express society's disapproval of the parents' liaisons 'is illogical and unjust.' [But] where the law is arbitrary in such a way, we have had no difficulty in finding the discrimination impermissible on less demanding standards than those advocated here. *Levy v. Louisiana,* 391 U.S. 68 (1968).a And such irrationality in some classifications does not in itself demonstrate that other, possibly rational, distinctions made in part on the basis of legitimacy are inherently untenable. Moreover, discrimination against illegitimates has never approached the severity or pervasiveness of the historic legal and political discrimination against women and Negroes. [We] therefore adhere to [the] view [that] the Act's discrimination between individuals on the basis of their legitimacy does not 'command extraordinary protection from the majoritarian political process,' which our most exacting scrutiny would entail.

"[The] Court, in *Gomez v. Perez,* 409 U.S. 535, 538 (1973), held that 'once a State posits a judicially enforceable right on behalf of children to needed support from their natural fathers there is no constitutionally sufficient justification for denying such an essential right to a child simply because its natural father has not married its mother.' The same principle, which we adhere to now, applies when the judicially enforceable right to needed support lies against the Government rather than a natural father.

"[But] Congress' purpose in adopting [the] presumptions of dependency was obviously to serve administrative convenience. Although this rationale would not have survived strict scrutiny, under rational basis review Congress was entitled to rely on proxies rather than individual fact-finding to determine which survivors were financially dependent on their deceased parents and which were not. [W]hile

---

a. *Levy,* per Douglas, J., invalidated a statute denying illegitimate children the right to recover for the wrongful death of their mother: "[The test] is whether the line drawn is a rational one [but] we have been extremely sensitive when it comes to basic civil rights and have not hesitated to strike down an invidious classification even though it had history and tradition on its side."

the scrutiny by which their showing is to be judged is not a toothless one, the burden remains upon the appellees to demonstrate the insubstantiality of that relation. Under that test, the challengers could not carry the burden of proving irrationality."

STEVENS, J., joined by BRENNAN and MARSHALL, JJ.,dissented: "I am persuaded that the classification [is] more probably the product of a tradition of thinking of illegitimates as less deserving persons than legitimates. The sovereign should firmly reject that tradition. The fact that illegitimacy is not as apparent to the observer as sex or race does not make this governmental classification any less odious. It cannot be denied that it is a source of social opprobrium, even if wholly unmerited, or that it is a circumstance for which the individual has no responsibility whatsoever."

Following *Mathews*, the Court appeared to elevate the applicable standard of scrutiny for statutes that disadvantage illegitimates, while still withholding strict scrutiny, in CLARK v. JETER, 486 U.S. 456 (1988), which unanimously concluded that between the "extremes of rational basis review and strict scrutiny lies a level of intermediate scrutiny, which generally has been applied to discriminatory classifications based on sex or illegitimacy. To withstand intermediate scrutiny, a statutory classification must be substantially related to an important governmental objective." Applying that standard, *Clark* invalidated a statute providing that child-support actions for out-of-wedlock children must be brought before the child turns six. Although acknowledging an important state interest in avoiding litigation of stale or fraudulent claims, the Court found the six-year statute of limitations not substantially related to that interest. The six-year period was not necessarily a reasonable one, given the social pressures that might stop an unmarried mother from filing a claim, and "increasingly sophisticated tests for genetic markers permit the exclusion of over 99% of those who might be accused of paternity" regardless of when a claim is filed.

2. *Mental retardation.* CLEBURNE v. CLEBURNE LIVING CENTER, INC., 473 U.S. 432 (1985), per WHITE, J., declined to apply strict scrutiny to a challenge to a zoning ordinance that required a special permit for a group home for the retarded but held nonetheless that the city's refusal to grant a permit failed rational basis review: "[We] conclude [that] the Court of Appeals erred in holding mental retardation a quasi-suspect classification. [First, those] who are mentally retarded have a reduced ability to cope with and function in the everyday world. [They] are thus different, immutably so, in relevant respects, and the states' interest in dealing with and providing for them is plainly a legitimate one. How this large and diversified group is to be treated under the law is a difficult and often a technical matter, very much a task for legislators guided by qualified professionals and not by the perhaps ill-informed opinions of the judiciary. Heightened scrutiny inevitably involves substantive judgments about legislative decisions, and we doubt that the predicate for such judicial oversight is present where the classification deals with mental retardation.

"Second, [both national and state] lawmakers have been addressing [the difficulties of the retarded] in a manner that belies a continuing antipathy or prejudice and a corresponding need for more intrusive oversight by the judiciary. [Third,] the legislative response, which could hardly have occurred and survived without public support, negates any claim that the mentally retarded are politically powerless in the sense that they have no ability to attract the attention of the lawmakers. [Fourth,] if the large and amorphous class of the mentally retarded were deemed quasi-suspect, [it] would be difficult to find a principled way to distinguish a variety of other groups who have perhaps immutable disabilities setting them off from others, who cannot themselves mandate the desired legislative responses, and who can claim some degree of prejudice from at least part of the public at large. One need mention in this respect only the aging, the disabled, the mentally ill, and the infirm. We are reluctant to set out on that course, and we decline to do so.

"[Our] refusal to recognize the retarded as a quasi-suspect class does not leave them entirely unprotected from invidious discrimination. [The] State may not rely on a classification whose relationship to an asserted goal is so attenuated as to render the distinction arbitrary or irrational. Furthermore, some objectives—such as 'a bare * * * desire to harm a politically unpopular group,' *U.S. Dep't of Agriculture v. Moreno*—are not legitimate state interests. * * *

"The City does not require a special use permit in an R–3 zone for apartment houses, multiple dwellings, boarding and lodging houses, fraternity or sorority houses, dormitories, apartment hotels, hospitals, sanitariums, nursing homes for convalescents or the aged (other than for the insane or feebleminded or alcoholics or drug addicts), private clubs or fraternal orders, and other specified uses. [I]n our view the record does not reveal any rational basis for believing that the Featherston home would pose any special threat to the city's legitimate interests. [The City's action] appears to us to rest on an irrational prejudice against the mentally retarded."

STEVENS, J.,joined by Burger, C.J., concurred: "[O]ur cases reflect a continuum of judgmental responses to differing classifications which have been explained in opinions by terms ranging from 'strict scrutiny' at one extreme to 'rational basis' at the other. I have never been persuaded that these so called 'standards' adequately explain the decisional process. Cases involving classifications based on alienage, illegal residency, illegitimacy, gender, age, or—as in this case—mental retardation, do not fit well into sharply defined classifications.

"[I] have always asked myself whether I could find a 'rational basis' for the classification at issue. The term 'rational,' of course, includes a requirement that an impartial lawmaker could logically believe that the classification would serve a legitimate public purpose that transcends the harm to the members of the disadvantaged class. Thus, the word 'rational' * * * includes elements of legitimacy and neutrality that must always characterize the performance of the sovereign's duty to govern impartially. The rational basis test, properly understood, adequately explains why a law that deprives a person of the right to vote because his skin has a different pigmentation than that of other voters violates [equal protection]. We do not need to apply a special standard, or to apply 'strict scrutiny,' or even 'heightened scrutiny,' to decide such cases.

"In every equal protection case, we have to ask certain basic questions. What class is harmed by the legislation, and has it been subjected to a 'tradition of disfavor' by our laws? What is the public purpose that is being served by the law? What is the characteristic of the disadvantaged class that justifies the disparate treatment? In most cases the answer to these questions will tell us whether the statute has a 'rational basis.' [Every] law that places the mentally retarded in a special class is not presumptively irrational. The differences between mentally retarded persons and those with greater mental capacity are obviously relevant to certain legislative decisions. [But the record in this case] convinces me that this permit was required because of the irrational fears of neighboring property owners, rather than for the protection of the mentally retarded persons who would reside in respondent's home."

MARSHALL, J., joined by Brennan and Blackmun, JJ., concurred in the judgment in part and dissented in part: "The Court holds [the] ordinance invalid on rational basis grounds and disclaims that anything special, in the form of heightened scrutiny, is taking place. Yet Cleburne's ordinance surely would be valid under the traditional rational basis test applicable to economic and commercial regulation. [The] Court, for example, concludes that legitimate concerns for fire hazards or the serenity of the neighborhood do not justify singling out respondents to bear the burdens of these concerns, for analogous permitted uses appear to pose similar threats. Yet under the traditional and most minimal version of the rational basis test, 'reform may take one step at a time, addressing itself to the phase of the problem which seems most acute to the legislative mind.'

"[The] refusal to acknowledge that something more than minimum rationality review is at work here is, in my view, unfortunate [because it could encourage lower courts] to subject economic and commercial classifications to similar and searching 'ordinary' rational basis review—a small and regrettable step back toward the days of *Lochner v. New York*. Moreover, by failing to articulate the factors that justify today's 'second order' rational basis review,

"[I] have long believed the level of scrutiny employed in an equal protection case should vary with 'the constitutional and societal importance of the interest adversely affected and the recognized invidiousness of the basis upon which the particular classification is drawn.' *San Antonio Ind. Sch. Dist. v. Rodriguez* [Sec. 5, III infra] (Marshall, J., dissenting). [Here] the interest [in] establishing group homes is substantial, [for] as deinstitutionalization has progressed, group homes have become the primary means by which retarded adults can enter life in the community. [Second,] the mentally retarded have been subject to a 'lengthy and tragic history' of segregation and discrimination that can only be called grotesque. [For] the retarded, just as for Negroes and women, much has changed in recent years, but much remains the same; outdated statutes are still on the books, and irrational fears or ignorance, traceable to the prolonged social and cultural isolation of the retarded, continue to stymie recognition of the dignity and individuality of retarded people.

"[The] Court's [assumption] that the standard of review must be fixed with reference to the number of classifications to which a characteristic would validly be relevant [is] flawed. [An] inquiry into constitutional principle, not mathematics, determines whether heightened scrutiny is appropriate. Whenever evolving principles of equality, rooted in the Equal Protection Clause, require that certain classifications be viewed as *potentially* discriminatory, and when history reveals systemic unequal treatment, more searching judicial inquiry than minimum rationality becomes relevant. * * *3"

3. No single talisman can define those groups likely to be the target of classifications offensive to the Fourteenth Amendment and therefore warranting heightened or strict scrutiny; experience, not abstract logic, must be the primary guide. The "political powerlessness" of a group may be relevant, but that factor is neither necessary, as the gender cases demonstrate, nor sufficient, as the example of minors illustrates. [W]e see few statutes reflecting prejudice or indifference to minors, and I am not aware of any suggestion that legislation affecting them be viewed with the suspicion of heightened scrutiny. Similarly, immutability of the trait at issue may be relevant, but many immutable characteristics, such as height or blindness, are valid bases of governmental action and classifications under a variety of circumstances.

The political powerlessness of a group and the immutability of its defining trait are relevant insofar as they point to a social and cultural isolation that gives the majority little reason to respect or be concerned with that group's interests and needs. Statutes discriminating against the young have not been common nor need be feared because those who do vote and legislate were once themselves young, typically have children of their own, and certainly interact regularly with minors. Their social integration means that minors, unlike discrete and insular minorities, tend to be treated in legislative arenas with full concern and respect, despite their formal and complete exclusion from the electoral process.

The discreteness and insularity warranting a "more searching judicial inquiry" must therefore be viewed from a social and cultural per-

Although the Court invalidated a discrimination against the retarded pursuant to rational basis review in *Celburne*, it appears to have applied a much less stringent form of "rational basis" review in HELLER v. DOE, 509 U.S. 312 (1993). *Heller* per KENNEDY, J., upheld a Kentucky scheme that allowed the involuntary commitment of the mentally retarded under less stringent standards than those employed for the involuntary commitment of the mentally ill. Treating as canonical the formulation that "a classification 'must be upheld against equal protection challenge if there is any reasonably conceivable state of facts that could provide a rational basis for the classification,'" the Court concluded that the lesser standard of proof was justified because it was "reasonably conceivable" that violent behavior by the mentally retarded was easier to predict than such behavior by the mentally ill, and because the treatment afforded to the mentally retarded is less invasive than that provided to the mentally ill. Souter, J., joined by Blackmun and Stevens, JJ., dissented.

3. *Age.* MASSACHUSETTS BD. OF RETIREMENT v. MURGIA, 427 U.S. 307 (1976), per curiam, upheld—"under the rational basis standard"—a law requiring uniformed state police officers to retire at age 50. After first rejecting the contention "that a right of governmental employment per se is fundamental" and thus makes the legislative classification subject to "strict scrutiny" (see Sec. 5 infra), the Court continued: "While the treatment of the aged in this Nation has not been wholly free of discrimination, such persons, unlike, say, those who have been discriminated against on the basis of race or national origin, have not experienced a 'history of purposeful unequal treatment' or been subjected to unique disabilities on the basis of stereotyped characteristics not truly indicative of their abilities. The [Massachusetts statute] cannot be said to discriminate only against the elderly. Rather, it draws the line at a certain age in middle life. But even old age does not define a 'discrete and insular' group, *Carolene Products,* n. 4, in need of 'extraordinary protection from the majoritarian political process.' Instead, it marks a stage that each of us will reach if we live out our normal span. Even if the statute could be said to impose a penalty upon a class defined as the aged, it would not impose a distinction sufficiently akin to those classifications that we have found suspect to call for strict judicial scrutiny."

MARSHALL, J., dissented from "the rigid two-tier model [that] still holds sway as the Court's articulated description of the equal protection test," urging a "flexible equal protection standard" of the kind discussed in his concurring opinion in *Cleburne*, supra: "[T]he Court is quite right in suggesting that distinctions exist between the elderly and traditional suspect classes such as [blacks]. The elderly are protected not only by certain antidiscrimination legislation, but by legislation that provides them with positive benefits not enjoyed by the public at large. Moreover, the elderly are not isolated in society, and discrimination against them is not pervasive but is centered primarily in employment. The advantage of a flexible equal protection standard, however, is that it can readily accommodate such variables. The elderly are undoubtedly discriminated against, and when legislation denies them an important benefit—employment—I conclude that to sustain the legislation the Commonwealth must show a reasonably

spective as well as a political one. To this task judges are well suited, for the lessons of history and experience are surely the best guide as to when, and with respect to what interests, society is likely to stigmatize individuals as members of an inferior caste or view them as not belonging to the community. Because prejudice spawns prejudice, and stereotypes produce limitations that confirm the stereotype on which they are based, a history of unequal treatment requires sensitivity to the prospect that its vestiges endure. In separating those groups that are discrete and insular from those that are not, as in many important legal distinctions, "a page of history is worth a volume of logic."

substantial interest and a scheme reasonably closely tailored to achieving that interest.''

4. ***Wealth***. Laws that explicitly distinguish on the basis of wealth or poverty, and work directly to the disadvantage of the poor, are rare.a Today, laws seldom if ever prescribe that the poor cannot vote, attend public universities, utilize legal processes, or receive medical care in public hospitals. The disadvantage experienced by the poor more typically arises from the discriminatory impact of statutes that condition opportunities on the payment of money, or that draw lines—such as those separating relatively poor from relatively wealthy school districts—that strongly correlate with wealth. Equal protection issues involving discriminatory impact on the poor are discussed in Sec. 5, Parts II–III infra.

Although the Warren Court *stated* on several occasions that ''lines drawn on the basis of wealth or property'' ''render a classification highly suspect,''b the Burger Court observed in 1973 that the Court had ''never held that wealth discrimination alone provides an adequate basis for invoking strict scrutiny,''c and, in 1980, *Harris v. McRae,* Ch. 6, Sec. 2, said that ''this Court has held repeatedly that poverty, standing alone, is not a suspect classification. See, e.g. *James v. Valtierra.*''

JAMES v. VALTIERRA, 402 U.S. 137 (1971), per BLACK, J., upheld Art. 34 of the California Constitution, which provided that no ''low-rent housing project''— defined as any development ''for persons of low income''—could be constructed unless approved by local referendum: ''Provisions for referendums demonstrate devotion to democracy, not to bias, discrimination, or prejudice.'' A ''law making procedure that 'disadvantages' a particular group does not always deny equal protection.'' Nor were ''persons advocating low-income [housing] singled out'': Mandatory referendums were ''required for approval of state constitutional amendments, for the issuance of general obligation long-term bonds by local governments, and for certain municipal territorial annexations.''

MARSHALL, J., joined by Brennan and Blackmun, JJ., dissented. Under California law, ''publicly assisted housing developments designed to accommodate the aged, veterans, state employees, persons of moderate income, or any class of citizens other than the poor, need not be approved by prior referenda. [Art. 34 is] an explicit classification on the basis of poverty—a suspect classification which demands exacting judicial scrutiny.''d

SECTION 5.   FUNDAMENTAL RIGHTS

In the equal protection cases studied thus far, the crucial variable has been the basis on which the government draws classificatory lines. Beginning in the late 1950s, however, and especially in the 1960s and 1970s, the Court began to develop the notion that discriminatory classifications burdening ''fundamental'' rights will trigger strict judicial scrutiny even if they do not employ an otherwise suspect classification. In other words, the Court adopted a methodology pursuant to which there are two distinct ways to trigger strict scrutiny under the Equal Protection Clause (and the equal protection component of the Fifth Amendment), one involving suspect classifications and the other involving fundamental rights.

---

a. But cf. *Edwards v. California,* 314 U.S. 160 (1941), invalidating, under the Commerce Clause, a California statute making it a misdemeanor knowingly to transport a non-resident indigent into the state.

b. *Harper v. Virginia Bd. of Elections,* Sec. 5, I infra, and *McDonald v. Board of Elec. Comm'rs,* 394 U.S. 802 (1969).

c. *San Antonio Ind. School Dist. v. Rodriguez,* Sec. 5, III infra.

d. Douglas, J., did not participate.

This Part begins by examining two rights that the Court has recognized as fundamental under the Equal Protection Clause: the right to vote and the right to travel. It then examines cases in which the Court has refused to classify the rights to welfare and to education as fundamental for purposes of equal protection analysis.

I. VOTING

A. DENIAL OR QUALIFICATION OF THE RIGHT

HARPER v. VIRGINIA STATE BD. OF ELEC., 383 U.S. 663 (1966), per DOUGLAS, J., built upon earlier cases to overrule *Breedlove v. Suttles,* 302 U.S. 277 (1937), and hold that Virginia's $1.50 poll tax as "a prerequisite of voting" violated the Equal Protection Clause because the right to vote was a fundamental right: "[T]he right to vote in state elections is nowhere expressly mentioned" in the Constitution, but "once the franchise is [granted] lines may not be drawn which [violate equal protection]."3

"Long ago in *Yick Wo,* [Sec. 2, II supra], the Court referred to 'the political franchise of voting' as a 'fundamental political right, because preservative of all rights.' * * * Wealth, like race, creed, or color, is not germane to one's ability to participate intelligently in the electoral process. Lines drawn on the basis of wealth or property, like those of race, are traditionally disfavored. To introduce wealth or payment of a fee as a measure of a voter's qualifications is to introduce a capricious or irrelevant factor. * * *

"In determining what lines are unconstitutionally discriminatory, we have never been confined to historic notions of equality" and "notions of what constitutes equal treatment for purposes of the Equal Protection Clause *do* change [citing *Plessy* and *Brown*]. * * * Our conclusion, like that in *Reynolds v. Sims,*a is founded not on what we think governmental policy should be, but on what the Equal Protection Clause requires.

"We have long been mindful that where fundamental rights and liberties are asserted under the Equal Protection Clause, classifications which might invade or restrain them must be closely scrutinized and carefully confined. See, e.g., *Reynolds*; *Carrington v. Rash.*"b

BLACK, J., dissented: "[U]nder a proper interpretation of the Equal Protection Clause States are to have the broadest kind of leeway in areas where they have a general constitutional competence to act. [P]oll tax legislation can 'reasonably,' 'rationally' and without an 'invidious' or evil purpose to injure anyone be found to rest on a number of state policies including (1) the State's desire to collect its revenue, and (2) its belief that voters who pay a poll tax will be interested in furthering the State's welfare when they vote. [H]istory is on the side of 'rationality' of the State's poll tax policy. Property qualifications existed in the Colonies

---

3. [While] the "Virginia poll tax was born of a desire to disenfranchise the Negro," we do not stop to determine whether [the] Virginia tax in its modern setting serves the same end.

a. *Reynolds,* Part B infra, was among the first of the Court's so-called "one-person, one-vote" decisions requiring that voting districts have roughly equal populations.

b. *Carrington,* 380 U.S. 89 (1965), held a Texas provision, barring members of the military who moved to Texas from voting in state elections so long as they remained in the mili-

tary, "an invidious discrimination": "We deal here with matters close to the core of our constitutional system." Only "where military personnel are involved has Texas been unwilling to develop more precise tests to determine the bona fides on an individual claiming to have actually made his home in the state long enough to vote. * * * 'Fencing out' from the franchise a sector of the population because of the way they may vote is constitutionally impermissible."

and were continued by many States after the Constitution was adopted. [The Court] seems to be using the old 'natural-law-due-process formula' to justify striking down state laws as violations of [equal protection]."

HARLAN, J., joined by Stewart, J., dissented: "The [equal protection] test evolved by this Court [is whether] a classification can be deemed to be founded on some rational and otherwise constitutionally permissible state [policy].3 *Reynolds* [also] marked a departure from these traditional and wise principles. [I]t was probably accepted as sound political theory by a large percentage of Americans through most of our history, that people with some property have a deeper stake in community affairs, and are consequently more responsible, more educated, more knowledgeable, more worthy of [confidence. It] is all wrong, in my view, for the Court to adopt the political doctrines popularly accepted at a particular moment of our history and to declare all others to be irrational and invidious."

KRAMER v. UNION FREE SCHOOL DISTRICT

395 U.S. 621, 89 S.Ct. 1886, 23 L.Ed.2d 583 (1969).

CHIEF JUSTICE WARREN delivered the opinion of the Court.

[§ 2012 of the New York Education Law] provides that in certain New York school districts residents [may] vote in the school district election only if they [or their spouse] (1) own (or lease) taxable real property within the district, or (2) are parents (or have custody of) children enrolled in the local public schools. Appellant, a bachelor who neither owns nor leases taxable real property, [claimed] § 2012 denied him equal protection * * *.

[I]t is important to note what is *not* at issue in this case. The requirements of § 2012 that school district voters must (1) be citizens of the United States, (2) be bona fide residents of the school district, and (3) be at least 21 years of age are not challenged. * * *

In determining whether or not [this statute] violates the Equal Protection Clause, [we] must give the statute a close and exacting examination. [This] careful examination is necessary because statutes distributing the franchise constitute the foundation of our representative society. Any unjustified discrimination in determining who may participate in political affairs or in the selection of public officials undermines the legitimacy of representative government. [Therefore,] if a [statute] grants the right to vote to some bona fide residents of requisite age and citizenship and denies the franchise to others, the Court must determine whether the exclusions are necessary to promote a compelling state interest. See *Carrington.*

[The] presumption of constitutionality and the approval given "rational" classifications in other types of enactments are based on an assumption that the institutions of state government are structured so as to represent fairly all the people. However, when the challenge to the statute is in effect a challenge of this basic assumption, the assumption can no longer serve as the basis for presuming constitutionality. And, the assumption is no less under attack because the legislature which decides who may participate at the various levels of political choice is fairly elected. * * *

3. I think the somewhat different application of the Equal Protection Clause to racial discrimination cases finds justification in the fact that insofar as that clause may embody a particular value in addition to rationality, the historical origins of the Civil War Amendments might attribute to racial equality this special status. * * *

The need for exacting judicial scrutiny of statutes distributing the franchise is undiminished simply because, under a different statutory scheme, the offices subject to election might have been filled through appointment10 [since] "once the franchise is granted to the electorate, lines may not be drawn which are inconsistent with [equal protection]." *Harper.* Nor is the need for close judicial examination affected because the district [and] the school board do not have "general" legislative powers. Our exacting examination is not necessitated by the subject of the election [but] because some resident citizens are permitted to participate and some are not. * * *

Besides appellant and others who similarly live in their parents' homes, the statute also disenfranchises the following persons (unless they are parents or guardians of children enrolled in the district public school): senior citizens and others living with children or relatives; clergy, military personnel and others who live on tax-exempt property; boarders and lodgers; parents who neither own nor lease qualifying property and whose children are too young to attend school [or] attend private schools.

[A]ppellees argue that the State has a legitimate interest in limiting the franchise in school district elections [to] those "primarily interested in such elections" [and] that the State may reasonably and permissibly conclude that "property taxpayers" (including lessees of taxable property who share the tax burden through rent payments) and parents of the children enrolled in the district's schools are those "primarily interested" in school affairs. * * *

[A]ssuming, arguendo, that New York legitimately might limit the franchise in these school district elections to those "primarily interested in school affairs," close scrutiny of the § 2012 classifications demonstrates that they do not accomplish this purpose with sufficient precision to justify denying appellant the franchise.

[T]he classifications must be tailored so that the exclusion of appellant and members of his class is necessary to achieve the articulated state goal.14 Section 2012 does not meet the exacting standard of precision [because it permits] inclusion of many persons who have, at best, a remote and indirect interest in school affairs and on the other hand, exclude[s] others who have a distinct and direct interest in the school meeting decisions.15 * * *

JUSTICE STEWART, with whom JUSTICE BLACK and JUSTICE HARLAN join, dissenting. * * *

Clearly a State may reasonably assume that its residents have a greater stake in the outcome of elections held within its boundaries than do other persons [and] that residents, being generally better informed regarding state affairs than are nonresidents, will be more likely [to] vote responsibly. And the same may be said of legislative assumptions regarding the electoral competence of adults and literate persons on the one hand, and of minors and illiterates on the other. It is clear, of course, that lines thus drawn cannot infallibly perform their intended legislative

10. Similarly, no less a showing of a compelling justification for disenfranchising residents is required merely because the questions scheduled for the election need not have been submitted to the voters.

14. Of course, if the exclusions are necessary to promote the articulated state interest, we must then determine whether the interest promoted by limiting the franchise constitutes a compelling state interest. We do not reach that issue in this case.

15. For example, appellant resides with his parents in the school district, pays state and federal taxes and is interested in and affected by school board decisions [but cannot vote, whereas] an uninterested unemployed young man who pays no state or federal taxes, but who rents an apartment in the district, can [vote].

function. Just as "[i]lliterate people may be intelligent voters," nonresidents or minors might also in some instances be interested, informed, and intelligent participants in the electoral process. Persons who commute across a state line to work may well have a great stake in the affairs of the State in which they are employed; some college students under 21 may be both better informed and more passionately interested in political affairs than many adults. But such discrepancies are the inevitable concomitant of the line-drawing that is essential to lawmaking. So long as the classification is rationally related to a permissible legislative end, therefore—as are residence, literacy, and age requirements imposed with respect to voting—there is no denial of equal protection.

Thus judged, the statutory classification involved here seems to me clearly to be valid [and] the Court does not really argue the contrary. Instead, it [asserts] that the traditional equal protection standard is [inapt]. But the asserted justification for applying [a stricter] standard cannot withstand analysis. [The] voting qualifications at issue have been promulgated not by Union Free School District, but by the New York State Legislature, and the appellant is of course fully able to participate in the election of representatives in that body. There is simply no claim whatever here that the state government is not "structured so as to represent fairly all the people," including the appellant.

[§ 2012] does not involve racial classifications [and] is not one that impinges upon a constitutionally protected right, and that consequently can be justified only by a "compelling" state interest. For "the Constitution of the United States does not confer the right of suffrage upon any one."

In any event, it seems to me that under *any* equal protection standard, short of a doctrinaire insistence that universal suffrage is somehow mandated by the Constitution, the appellant's claim must be rejected. * * *

CRAWFORD v. MARION COUNTY ELEC. BD., 553 U.S. 181 (2008), rejected a facial challenge to an Indiana law requiring each voter to present government-issued photo identification as a condition of voting. STEVENS, J., announced the judgment in a plurality opinion joined by Roberts, C.J., and Kennedy, J.: "Under the standard applied in *Harper* [*v. Virginia Bd. of Elections*,] even rational restrictions on the right to vote are invidious [and unconstitutional] if they are unrelated to voter qualifications [but] 'evenhanded restrictions that protect the integrity and reliability of the electoral process itself' are not invidious" and may be upheld based on "relevant and legitimate state interests 'sufficiently weighty to justify the limitation.' [T]he state interests [asserted by Indiana, including deterring voter fraud and safeguarding voter confidence,] are both neutral and sufficiently strong to require us to reject petitioners' facial attack." Stevens, J., left open the possibility, however, that some otherwise qualified voters might be able to establish on an individual basis that they faced such severe difficulties in obtaining government-issued photo identification that the statute would be unconstitutional as applied to them.

SCALIA, J., joined by Thomas and Alito, JJ., concurred in the judgment: "*Burdick v. Takushi*, 504 U.S. 428 (1992), [calls] for application of a deferential [standard] for nonsevere, nondiscriminatory restrictions, reserving strict scrutiny for laws that severely restrict the right to vote. [T]he Indiana photo-identification law is a generally applicable, nondiscriminatory voting regulation" that easily survives deferential review, and does not trigger the "balancing" approach apparently contemplated by Stevens, J. The law's effects on individual voters should not matter: "A voter complaining about [the] law's effect on him has no valid equal protection claim because, without proof of discriminatory intent, a generally applicable law with disparate impact is not unconstitutional."

SOUTER, J., joined by Ginsburg, J., dissented: "Indiana's 'Voter ID Law' threatens to impose nontrivial burdens on the voting rights of [an estimated 43,000 citizens, or roughly 1% of all eligible voters,] and a significant number of those individuals are likely to be deterred from voting [by the costs of time and money involved in traveling to the offices of the Bureau of Motor Vehicles where photo identification must be obtained. A] state may not burden the right to vote merely by invoking abstract interests, [but] must make a particular, factual showing. [T]he State has made no such justification here. [Without] a shred of evidence that in-person voter impersonation is a problem in the State, [Indiana] has adopted one of the most restrictive photo identification requirements in the country."

B. "DILUTION" OF THE RIGHT: APPORTIONMENT

Distinct from the question of who gets to cast a vote in elections are questions involving how the lines dividing electoral districts are drawn and, relatedly, whether it is constitutionally permissible for voters in some districts to have proportionally more voting power than voters in others. (If there are more voters in one district then in another, then individual voters in the larger districts will have proportionally less voting power than voters in the smaller districts.) In *Colegrove v. Green*, 328 U.S. 549 (1946), which presented a challenge to malapportioned congressional districts, the principal opinion, by Frankfurter, J., characterized apportionment issues as being "of a peculiarly political nature" and beyond the capacity of courts to resolve under the political question doctrine. A bitterly divided Court subsequently distinguished *Colegrove* (on the ground that it arose under the Guarantee Clause) and held equal protection challenges to legislative apportionments justiciable in a 1962 decision in *Baker v. Carr*, Chap. 1, Sec. 2. But *Baker* left unresolved the substantive question of what rights, if any, voters have under the Equal Protection Clause to be free from what is sometimes called vote dilution.

REYNOLDS v. SIMS

377 U.S. 533, 84 S.Ct. 1362, 12 L.Ed.2d 506 (1964).

CHIEF JUSTICE WARREN delivered the opinion of the Court.

[Although the Alabama constitution required the legislature to reapportion decennially on the basis of population, none had taken place since 1901. The federal district court held the existing malapportionment violative of equal protection. Under] 1960 census figures, only 25.1% of the State's total population resided in districts represented by a majority of the members of the Senate, and only 25.7% lived in counties which could elect a majority of the members of the House of Representatives. Population-variance ratios of up to about 41–to–1 existed in the Senate, and up to about 16–to–1 in the House. * * *

We indicated in *Baker* that the Equal Protection Clause provides discoverable and manageable standards for [determining] the constitutionality of a state legislative apportionment scheme. [In this case] we are faced with the problem [of] determining the basic standards and stating the applicable guidelines for implementing our decision in *Baker*.

Gray v. Sanders, 372 U.S. 368 (1963),a and *Wesberry v. Sanders*, 376 U.S. 1 (1964),b are of course [relevant to but] not dispositive [of] these cases involving state legislative [apportionment]. But neither are they wholly inapposite. [*Gray*] established the basic principle of equality among voters within a State, [and] *Wesberry* clearly established that the fundamental principle of representative government in this country is one of equal representation for equal numbers of people, without regard to race, sex, economic status, or place of residence within a State. Our problem, then, is to ascertain [whether] there are any constitutionally cognizable principles which would justify departures from the basic standard of equality among voters in the apportionment of seats in state legislatures.

A predominant consideration in determining whether a State's legislative apportionment scheme constitutes an invidious discrimination [is] that the rights allegedly impaired are individual and personal in nature. [Since] the right of suffrage is a fundamental matter in a free and democratic society [and] is preservative of other basic civil and political rights, any alleged infringement [must] be carefully and meticulously scrutinized. * * *

Legislators represent people, not trees or acres. Legislators are elected by voters, not farms or cities or economic interests. As long as ours is a representative form of government, [the] right to elect legislators in a free and unimpaired fashion is a bedrock of our political system. [It] is inconceivable that a state law to the effect that, in counting votes for legislators, the votes of citizens in one part of the State would be multiplied by two, five, or 10, while the votes of persons in another area would be counted only at face value, could be [constitutional]. Of course, the effect of state legislative districting schemes which give the same number of representatives to unequal numbers of constituents is identical. * * *

Logically, in a society ostensibly grounded on representative government, it would seem reasonable that a majority of the people of a State could elect a majority of that State's legislators. [T]o sanction minority control of state legislative bodies would appear to deny majority rights in a way that far surpasses any possible denial of minority rights that might otherwise be thought to result. [T]he concept of equal protection has been traditionally viewed as requiring the uniform treatment of persons standing in the same relation to the governmental action questioned or challenged. With respect to the allocation of legislative representation, all voters, as citizens of a State, stand in the same relation regardless of where they live. Any suggested criteria for the differentiation of citizens are insufficient to justify any discrimination, as to the weight of their votes, unless relevant to the permissible purposes of legislative apportionment. Since the achieving of fair and effective representation for all citizens is concededly the basic aim of legislative apportionment, we conclude that the Equal Protection Clause guarantees the opportunity for equal participation by all voters in the election of state legislators. Diluting the weight of votes because of place of residence impairs basic constitutional rights under the Fourteenth Amendment just as much as

a. *Gray* invalidated the "county unit system" employed in Georgia primaries for statewide offices, under which the candidate receiving the highest number of votes in each county obtained "two votes for each representative to which the county is entitled in the lower House of the General Assembly," and the winner was determined on the basis of the county unit vote. Because counties were not represented in the state legislature in accordance with their population, counties comprising only a third of the state's population had "a clear majority of

county units." *Gray* was not dispositive in *Reynolds* since it involved "the weighing of votes in statewide elections."

b. *Wesberry* struck down Georgia's congressional districting statute, under which some districts had more than twice the population of others: "[T]he command of Art. I, § 2, that representatives be chosen 'by the people of the several states' means that as nearly as is practicable one man's vote in a congressional election is to be worth as much as another's."

invidious discriminations based upon factors such as race, or economic status. Our constitutional system amply provides for the protection of minorities by means other than giving them majority control of state legislatures. * * *

We are told that the matter of apportioning representation in a state legislature is a complex and many-faceted one. We are advised that States can rationally consider factors other than [population]. We are admonished not to restrict the power of the States to impose differing views as to political philosophy on their citizens. We are cautioned about the dangers of entering into political thickets and mathematical quagmires. Our answer is this: a denial of constitutionally protected rights demands judicial protection; our oath and our office require no less of us. [To] the extent that a citizen's right to vote is debased, he is that much less a citizen. [A] nation once primarily rural in character becomes predominantly urban. Representation schemes once fair and equitable become archaic and outdated. But the basic principle of representative government remains, and must remain, unchanged—the weight of a citizen's vote cannot be made to depend on where he lives. Population is, of necessity, [the] controlling criterion for judgment in legislative [apportionment]. This is the clear and strong command of our Constitution's Equal Protection Clause. This is an essential part of the concept of a government of laws and not men. This is at the heart of Lincoln's vision of "government of the people, by the people, [and] for the people." * * *

We hold that, as a basic constitutional standard, the Equal Protection Clause requires that the seats in both houses of a bicameral state legislature must be apportioned on a population basis. [We] find the federal analogy inapposite and irrelevant to state legislative districting schemes. [T]he Founding Fathers clearly had no intention of establishing a pattern or model for the apportionment of seats in state legislatures when the system of representation in the Federal Congress was adopted. Demonstrative of this is the fact that the Northwest Ordinance, adopted in the same year, 1787, as the Federal Constitution, provided for the apportionment of seats in territorial legislatures solely on the basis of population.

The system of representation in the two Houses of the Federal Congress [is] based on the consideration that in establishing our type of federalism a group of formerly independent States bound themselves together under one national government. [A] compromise between the larger and smaller States on this matter averted a deadlock in the Constitutional Convention * * *.

Political subdivisions of States [never] have been considered as sovereign entities. Rather, they have been traditionally regarded as subordinate governmental instrumentalities created by the State. * * *

We do not believe that the concept of bicameralism is rendered anachronistic and meaningless when the predominant basis of representation in the two state legislative bodies is required to be the same—population. A prime reason for bicameralism, modernly considered, is to insure mature and deliberate consideration of, and to prevent precipitate action on, proposed legislative measures. Simply because the controlling criterion for apportioning representation is required to be the same in both houses does not mean that there will be no differences in the composition and complexion of the two bodies. [The] numerical size of the two bodies could be made to differ, even significantly, and the geographical size of districts from which legislators are elected could also be made to differ. [T]he Equal Protection Clause requires that a State make an honest and good faith effort to construct districts, in both houses of its legislature, as nearly of equal population as is practicable. We realize that it is a practical impossibility to arrange legislative districts so that each one has an identical number of residents, or citizens, or voters. Mathematical exactness or precision is hardly a workable constitutional requirement.

[So] long as the divergences from a strict population standard are based on legitimate considerations incident to the effectuation of a rational state policy, some deviations from the equal-population principle are constitutionally permissible, [b]ut neither history alone, nor economic or other sorts of group interests, are permissible factors in attempting to justify disparities from population-based representation. Citizens, not history or economic interests, cast votes.

* * * Decennial reapportionment appears to be a rational approach to readjustment of legislative representation in order to take into account population shifts and growth [and] if reapportionment were accomplished with less frequency, it would assuredly be constitutionally suspect. * * *c

[Clark and Stewart, JJ., concurred in the result in *Reynolds,* but STEWART, J., joined by Clark, J., dissented in two of the companion cases in an opinion sharply at odds with the *Reynolds* rationale:]

First, says the Court, it is "established that the fundamental principle of representative government in this country is one of equal representation for equal numbers of [people]." [But] this "was not the colonial system, it was not the system chosen for the national government by the Constitution, it was not the system exclusively or even predominantly practiced by the States at the time of adoption of the Fourteenth Amendment, it is not predominantly practiced by the States today." Secondly, says the Court, unless legislative districts are equal in population, voters in the more populous districts will suffer a 'debasement' amounting to a constitutional injury. [I] find it impossible to understand how or why a voter in California, for instance, either feels or is less a citizen than a voter in Nevada, simply because, despite their population disparities, each of those States is represented by two United States Senators.

[My] own understanding of the various theories of representative government is that no one theory has ever commanded unanimous [assent]. But even if it were thought that the rule announced today by the Court is, as a matter of political theory, the most desirable, [I] could not join in the fabrication of a constitutional mandate which imports and forever freezes one theory of political thought into our Constitution, and forever denies to every State any opportunity for enlightened and progressive innovation * * *.

[The] fact of geographic districting, the constitutional validity of which the Court does not question, carries with it an acceptance of the idea of legislative representation of regional needs and interests. Yet if geographical residence is irrelevant, as the Court suggests, and the goal is solely that of equally "weighted" votes, I do not understand why the Court's constitutional rule does not require the abolition of districts and the holding of all elections at large. * * *

JUSTICE HARLAN, dissenting [in all the cases decided that day.]

The Court's constitutional discussion [is] remarkable [for] its failure to address itself at all to the Fourteenth Amendment as a whole or to the legislative history of the Amendment pertinent to the matter at hand. [I] am unable to

c. In addition to *Reynolds,* the Court invalidated apportionments in Colorado, *Lucas v. Forty–Fourth Gen. Assembly,* 377 U.S. 713; Delaware, *Roman v. Sincock,* 377 U.S. 695; Maryland, *Maryland Comm. for Fair Rep. v. Tawes,* 377 U.S. 656; New York, *WMCA, Inc. v. Lomenzo,* 377 U.S. 633; and Virginia, *Davis v. Mann,* 377 U.S. 678.

understand the Court's utter disregard of [§ 2 of the Fourteenth Amendment], which expressly recognizes the States' power to deny "or in any way" abridge the right of their inhabitants to vote for "the members of the [State] Legislature," and its express provision of a remedy for such denial or abridgement. The comprehensive scope of the second section and its particular reference to the state legislatures precludes the suggestion that the first section was intended to have the result reached by the [Court].

The history of the adoption of the Fourteenth Amendment provides conclusive evidence that neither those who proposed nor those who ratified the Amendment believed that the Equal Protection Clause limited the power of the States to apportion their legislatures as they saw fit. Moreover, the history demonstrates that the intention to leave this power undisturbed was deliberate and was widely believed to be essential to the adoption of the Amendment. [N]ote should [also] be taken of the Fifteenth and Nineteenth Amendments. [If] constitutional amendment was the only means by which all men and, later, women, could be guaranteed the right to vote at all, even for *federal* officers, how can it be that the far less obvious right to a particular kind of apportionment of *state* legislatures—a right to which is opposed a far more plausible conflicting interest of the State than the interest which opposes the general right to vote—can be conferred by judicial construction of the Fourteenth Amendment?

[The] consequence of today's decision is that in all but the handful of States which may already satisfy the new requirements the [courts] are given blanket authority and the constitutional duty to supervise apportionment of the State Legislatures. It is difficult to imagine a more intolerable and inappropriate interference by the judiciary with the independent legislatures of the States. * * *

Although the Court—necessarily, as I believe—provides only generalities in elaboration of its main thesis, its opinion nevertheless fully demonstrates how far removed these problems are from fields of judicial competence. Recognizing that "indiscriminate districting" is an invitation to "partisan gerrymandering," the Court nevertheless excludes virtually every basis for the formation of electoral districts other than "indiscriminate districting." In one or another of today's opinions, the Court declares it unconstitutional for a State to give effective consideration to any of the following in establishing legislative districts: (1) history; (2) "economic or other sorts of group interests"; (3) area; (4) geographical considerations; (5) a desire "to insure effective representation for sparsely settled areas"; (6) "availability of access of citizens to their representatives"; (7) theories of bicameralism (except those approved by the Court); (8) occupation; (9) "an attempt to balance urban and rural power"; (10) the preference of a majority of voters in the State. So far as presently appears, the *only* factor which a State may consider, apart from numbers, is political subdivisions. But even "a clearly rational state policy" recognizing this factor is unconstitutional if "population is submerged as the controlling consideration * * *."

I know of no principle of logic or practical or theoretical politics, still less any constitutional principle, which establishes all or any of these exclusions. [The] Constitution is not a panacea for every blot upon the public welfare, nor [does] this Court [serve] its high purpose when it exceeds its authority, even to satisfy justified impatience with the slow workings of the political [process.]

C. "DILUTION" OF THE RIGHT: PARTISAN GERRYMANDERS

DAVIS v. BANDEMER

478 U.S. 109, 106 S.Ct. 2797, 92 L.Ed.2d 85 (1986).

[Democrats challenged Indiana's 1981 state apportionment—enacted by Republican majorities in both houses of the legislature and signed by a Republican governor—on the ground that it "constituted a political gerrymander intended to disadvantage Democrats on a statewide basis." A majority of the Court, per White, J.—relying on cases such as *Baker* and *Reynolds* (indicating "the justiciability of claims going to the adequacy of state representation in state legislatures") and, particularly, *Gaffney v. Cummings,* 412 U.S. 735 (1973)a—held that a "political gerrymandering claim [is] justiciable."]

JUSTICE WHITE announced the judgment of the Court and delivered [an] opinion in which JUSTICE BRENNAN, JUSTICE MARSHALL, and JUSTICE BLACKMUN joined * * *.

We [agree] with the District Court that in order to succeed the Bandemer plaintiffs were required to prove both intentional discrimination against an identifiable political group and an actual discriminatory effect on that group. [As] long as redistricting is done by a legislature, it should not be very difficult to prove that the likely political consequences of the reapportionment were intended.11

[With respect to effects, our prior holdings] foreclose any claim that the Constitution requires proportional representation or that legislatures in reapportioning must draw district lines to come as near as possible to allocating seats to the contending parties in proportion to what their anticipated statewide vote will be.

[These] holdings rest on a conviction that the mere fact that a particular apportionment scheme makes it more difficult for a particular group in a particular district to elect the representatives of its choice does not render that scheme constitutionally infirm. This conviction, in turn, stems from a perception that the power to influence the political process is not limited to winning elections. An individual or a group of individuals who votes for a losing candidate is usually deemed to be adequately represented by the winning candidate and to have as much opportunity to influence that candidate as other voters in the district. * * *

As with individual districts, where unconstitutional vote dilution is alleged in the form of statewide political gerrymandering, the mere lack of proportional representation will not be sufficient to prove unconstitutional discrimination. [Rather], unconstitutional discrimination occurs only when the electoral system is arranged in a manner that will consistently degrade a voter's or a group of voters' influence on the political process as a [whole. S]uch a finding of unconstitutionality must be supported by evidence of continued frustration of the will of a majority of the voters or effective denial to a minority of voters of a fair chance to influence the political process.

---

a. *Gaffney* ruled that the fact "that virtually every Senate and House district line [in Connecticut] was drawn with the conscious intent to create a districting plan that would achieve a rough approximation of the statewide political strengths of the Democratic and Republican Parties, the only two parties in the state large enough to elect legislators from discernible geographic areas" did not invalidate the plan.

11. That discriminatory intent may not be difficult to prove in this context does not, of course, mean that it need not be proved at all to succeed on such a claim.

Based on these views, we would reject the District Court's apparent holding that *any* interference with an opportunity to elect a representative of one's choice would be sufficient to allege or make out an equal protection violation, unless justified by some acceptable state interest that the State would be required to demonstrate. [S]uch a low threshold for legal action would invite attack on all or almost all reapportionment statutes. [Inviting] attack on minor departures from some supposed norm would too much embroil the judiciary in second-guessing what has consistently been referred to as a political task for the legislature * * *.

[The] District Court's findings do not satisfy this threshold condition to stating and proving a cause of action. In reaching its conclusion, the District Court relied primarily on the results of the 1982 elections: Democratic candidates for the State House of Representatives had received 51.9% of the votes cast statewide and Republican candidates 48.1%; yet, out of the 100 seats to be filled, Republican candidates won 57 and Democrats 43. In the Senate, 53.1% of the votes were cast for Democratic candidates and 46.9% for Republicans; of the 25 Senate seats to be filled, Republicans won 12 and Democrats 13. The court also relied upon the use of multi-member districts in Marion and Allen counties, where Democrats or those inclined to vote Democratic in 1982 amounted to 46.6% of the population of those counties but Republicans won 86 percent—18 of 21—seats allocated to the districts in those counties. These disparities were enough to require a neutral justification by the State, which in the eyes of the District Court was not forthcoming.

Relying on a single election to prove unconstitutional discrimination is unsatisfactory. [The] appellants argue here, without a persuasive response from appellees, that had the Democratic candidates received an additional few percentage points of the votes cast statewide, they would have obtained a majority of the seats in both houses. Nor was there any finding that the 1981 reapportionment would consign the Democrats to a minority status in the Assembly throughout the 1980's or that the Democrats would have no hope of doing any better in the reapportionment that would occur after the 1990 census.

[We] recognize that our [test] may be difficult of application. Determining when an electoral system has been "arranged in a manner that will consistently degrade a voter's or a group of voters' influence on the political process as a whole" is of necessity a difficult inquiry. Nevertheless, we believe that it recognizes the delicacy of intruding on this most political of legislative functions and is at the same time consistent with our prior cases regarding individual multi-member districts, which have formulated a parallel standard. * * *

JUSTICE POWELL, with whom JUSTICE STEVENS joins, concurring [on the issue of justiciability], and dissenting.

[T]he plurality expresses the view, with which I agree, that a partisan political gerrymander violates the Equal Protection Clause only on proof of "both intentional discrimination against an identifiable political group and an actual discriminatory effect on that group." The plurality acknowledges that the record in this case supports a finding that the challenged redistricting plan was adopted for the purpose of discriminating against Democratic voters. The plurality argues, however, that appellees failed to establish that their voting strength was diluted statewide despite uncontradicted proof that certain key districts were grotesquely gerrymandered to enhance the election prospects of Republican candidates. * * *

[The] Equal Protection Clause guarantees citizens that their State will govern them impartially [and accordingly requires that] district lines should be determined in accordance with neutral and legitimate criteria.

[The] most basic flaw in the plurality's opinion is its failure to enunciate any standard that affords guidance to legislatures and courts. [This] places the plurality in the curious position of inviting further litigation even as it appears to signal the "constitutional green light" to would-be gerrymanderers. * * *

[To determine whether the state has met its obligation to govern impartially, courts must attend to several factors, the most important of which] are the shapes of voting districts and adherence to established political subdivision boundaries. Other relevant considerations include the nature of the legislative procedures [and] legislative history reflecting contemporaneous legislative goals. To make out a case of unconstitutional partisan gerrymandering, the plaintiff should be required to offer proof concerning these factors, as well as evidence concerning population disparities and statistics tending to show vote dilution. No one factor should be dispositive.

[Here], the District Court found that the procedures used in redistricting Indiana were carefully designed to exclude Democrats from participating in the legislative process [and] consisted of nothing more than the majority party's private application of computer technology to mapmaking. [T]he only data used in the computer program were precinct population, race of precinct citizens, precinct political complexion, and statewide party voting trends. [Next], the District Court found [how] the mapmakers carved up counties, cities, and even townships in their effort to draw lines beneficial to the majority party.

[Confronted with these findings,] appellants failed to justify the discriminatory impact of the plan by showing that the plan had a rational basis in permissible neutral criteria. * * *

JUSTICE O'CONNOR, with whom THE CHIEF JUSTICE and JUSTICE REHNQUIST join, concurring in the judgment.

[T]he legislative business of apportionment is fundamentally a political affair, and challenges to the manner in which an apportionment has been carried out— by the very parties that are responsible for this process—present a political question in the truest sense of the term. To turn these matters over to the federal judiciary is to inject the courts into the most heated partisan issues. It is predictable that the courts will respond by moving away from the nebulous standard a plurality of the Court fashions today and toward some form of rough proportional representation for all political groups.

[The] Equal Protection Clause does not supply judicially manageable standards for resolving purely political gerrymandering claims, and no group right to an equal share of political power was ever intended by the Framers. [Unlike racial minorities], members of the Democratic and Republican parties cannot claim that they are a discrete and insular group vulnerable to exclusion from the political process by some dominant group: these political parties *are* the dominant groups, and the Court has offered no reason to believe that they are incapable of fending for themselves through the political process. * * *

Furthermore, the Court fails to explain why a bipartisan gerrymander—which is what was approved in *Gaffney*—affects individuals any differently than a partisan gerrymander. [As] the plurality acknowledges, the scheme upheld in *Gaffney* tended to "deny safe district minorities any realistic chance to elect their own representatives." If this bipartisan arrangement between two groups of self-interested legislators is constitutionally permissible, as I believe and as the Court held in *Gaffney,* then—in terms of the rights of individuals—it should be equally permissible for a legislative majority to employ the same means to pursue its own interests over the opposition of the other party.

VIETH v. JUBELIRER

541 U.S. 267, 124 S.Ct. 1769, 158 L.Ed.2d 546 (2004).

JUSTICE SCALIA announced the judgment of the Court and delivered an opinion, in which THE CHIEF JUSTICE, JUSTICE O'CONNOR, and JUSTICE THOMAS join.

[After the 2000 census showed that Pennsylvania was entitled to only 19 Representatives in the U.S. House of Representatives, a decrease of two from its previous delegation, the Republican-controlled Pennsylvania legislature adopted and the Republican governor signed into law a redistricting plan designed to advantage Republicans. The plaintiff Democratic voters brought suit alleging that the "meandering and irregular" districts created by the plan "ignored all traditional redistricting criteria, including the preservation of local government boundaries, solely for the sake of partisan advantage," and thereby violated the Equal Protection Clause.]

Political gerrymanders are not new to the American scene. [It] is significant that the Framers provided a remedy for such practices in the Constitution, Article 1, § 4, while leaving in state legislatures the initial power to draw districts for federal elections, permitted Congress to "make or alter" those districts if it wished.

[Eighteen] years ago, [over] the dissent of three Justices, the Court held in *Bandemer* that, since it was "not persuaded that there are no judicially discernible and manageable standards by which political gerrymander cases are to be decided," such cases *were* justiciable. [But there was no majority on what the appropriate standards were. Nor] can it be said that the lower courts have, over 18 years, succeeded in shaping the standard that this Court was initially unable to enunciate. As one commentary has put it, "throughout its subsequent history, *Bandemer* has served almost exclusively as an invitation to litigation without much prospect of redress." S. Issacharoff, P. Karlan, & R. Pildes, *The Law of Democracy* 886 (rev. 2d ed. 2002). The [only lower court] case in which relief was provided (and merely preliminary relief, at that) did *not* involve the drawing of district lines [but instead involved a North Carolina system of electing all superior court judges statewide— a system that had resulted in the election of only a single Republican since 1900]; in *all* of the cases we are aware of involving that most common form of political gerrymandering, relief was denied. [Eighteen] years of judicial effort with virtually nothing to show for it [demonstrate that] no judicially discernible and manageable standards for adjudicating political gerrymandering claims have emerged. Lacking them, we must conclude that political gerrymandering claims are nonjusticiable and that *Bandemer* was wrongly decided.

We begin our review of possible standards with that proposed by Justice White's plurality opinion in *Bandemer* because, as the narrowest ground for our decision in that case, it has been the standard employed by the lower courts. The plurality concluded that a political gerrymandering claim could succeed only where plaintiffs showed "both intentional discrimination against an identifiable political group and an actual discriminatory effect on that group" [so severe that it was] "denied its chance to effectively influence the political process" as a whole, which could be achieved even without electing a candidate. [In] the lower courts, the legacy of the plurality's test is one long record of puzzlement and consternation. [We] decline to affirm it as a constitutional requirement.

Appellants take a run at enunciating their own workable standard. [Their proposal] retains the two-pronged framework of the *Bandemer* plurality—intent plus effect—but modifies the type of showing sufficient to satisfy each. [But it too is unworkable.]

For many of the same reasons, we also reject the standard suggested by Justice Powell in *Bandemer*. He agreed with the plurality that a plaintiff should show intent and effect, but believed that the ultimate inquiry ought to focus on whether district boundaries had been drawn solely for partisan ends to the exclusion of "all other neutral factors relevant to the fairness of redistricting." [This] is essentially a totality-of-the-circumstances analysis, where all conceivable factors, none of which is dispositive, are weighed with an eye to ascertaining whether the particular gerrymander has gone too far—or, in Justice Powell's terminology, whether it is not "fair." "Fairness" does not seem to us a judicially manageable standard. Fairness is compatible with noncontiguous districts, it is compatible with districts that straddle political subdivisions, and it is compatible with a party's not winning the number of seats that mirrors the proportion of its vote.

IV. We turn next to consideration of the standards proposed by today's dissenters. [The] mere fact that these four dissenters come up with three different standards—all of them different from the two proposed in *Bandemer* and the one proposed here by appellants—goes a long way to establishing that there is no constitutionally discernible standard. [Careful assessment of the proposed standards confirms that they are either not judicially manageable or not discernible in the Constitution.]

V. Justice Kennedy [who concurs in the Court's judgment dismissing the case before it but does not join this opinion holding all allegations of political gerrymanders to present nonjusticiable political questions] recognizes that we have "demonstrated the shortcomings of the other standards that have been considered to date." [Yet] he concludes that courts should continue to adjudicate such claims because a standard *may* one day be discovered.

[Reduced] to its essence, Justice Kennedy's opinion boils down to this: "As presently advised, I know of no discernible and manageable standard that can render this claim justiciable. I am unhappy about that, and hope that I will be able to change my opinion in the future." What are the lower courts to make of this pronouncement? We suggest that they must treat it as a reluctant fifth vote against justiciability at district and statewide levels—a vote that may change in some future case but that holds, for the time being, that this matter is nonjusticiable.

Justice Kennedy, concurring in the judgment.

[The] plurality demonstrates the shortcomings of the [standards] that have been considered to date. [But the fact that] no [adequate] standard has emerged in this case should not be taken to prove that none will emerge in the future. Where important rights are involved, the impossibility of full analytical satisfaction is reason to err on the side of caution.

[Because], in the case before us, we have no standard by which to measure the burden appellants claim has been imposed on their representational rights, appellants cannot establish that the alleged political classifications burden those same rights.

Justice Stevens, dissenting.

The central question presented by this case is whether political gerrymandering claims are justiciable. Although our reasons for coming to this conclusion differ, five Members of the Court are convinced that the plurality's answer to that question is erroneous.

[In] evaluating a challenge to a specific district, I would apply the standard set forth in [cases involving the deliberate creation of majority-minority districts] and ask whether the legislature allowed partisan considerations to dominate and control the lines drawn, forsaking all neutral principles. Under my analysis, if no neutral criterion can be identified to justify the lines drawn, and if the only possible explanation for a district's bizarre shape is a naked desire to increase partisan strength, then no rational basis exists to save the district from an equal protection challenge. * * *

Justice Souter, with whom Justice Ginsburg joins, dissenting.

For a claim based on a specific single-member district, I would require the plaintiff to make out a prima facie case with five elements. First, the resident plaintiff would identify a cohesive political group to which he belonged, which would normally be a major party, as in this case and in *Davis*. [Second], a plaintiff would need to show that the district of his residence paid little or no heed to those traditional districting principles whose disregard can be shown straightforwardly: contiguity, compactness, respect for political subdivisions, and conformity with geographic features like rivers and mountains. [Third], the plaintiff would need to establish specific correlations between the district's deviations from traditional districting principles and the distribution of the population of his group. [Fourth], a plaintiff would need to present the court with a hypothetical district including his residence, one in which the proportion of the plaintiff's group was lower (in a packing claim) or higher (in a cracking one) and which at the same time deviated less from traditional districting principles than the actual district. [Fifth], and finally, the plaintiff would have to show that the defendants acted intentionally to manipulate the shape of the district in order to pack or crack his group. [A] plaintiff who got this far would [then] shift the burden to the defendants to justify their decision by reference to objectives other than naked partisan advantage.

[As] for a statewide claim, I would not attempt an ambitious definition without the benefit of experience with individual district claims, and for now I would limit consideration of a statewide claim to one built upon a number of district-specific ones.

Justice Breyer, dissenting.

[T]he legislature's use of political boundary drawing considerations ordinarily does *not* violate the Constitution's Equal Protection Clause. [But there is] at least one circumstance where use of purely political boundary-drawing factors can amount to a serious, and remediable, abuse, namely the *unjustified* use of political factors to entrench a minority in power. By entrenchment I mean a situation in which a party that enjoys only minority support among the populace has nonetheless contrived to take, and hold, legislative power. * * *

D. "DILUTION" OF THE RIGHT: ISSUES INVOLVING RACE

MOBILE v. BOLDEN
446 U.S. 55, 100 S.Ct. 1490, 64 L.Ed.2d 47 (1980).

Justice Stewart announced the judgment of the Court and delivered an opinion in which The Chief Justice, Justice Powell, and Justice Rehnquist join.

The City of Mobile, Ala., has since 1911 been governed by a City Commission consisting of three members elected by the voters of the city at-large. [This] is the same basic electoral system that is followed by literally thousands of municipalities and other local governmental units throughout the Nation.

[The] constitutional objection to multimember districts is not and cannot be that, as such, they depart from apportionment on a population basis in violation of *Reynolds* and its progeny. Rather the focus in such cases has been on the lack of representation multimember districts afford various elements of the voting population in a system of representative legislative democracy. "Criticism [of multimember districts] is rooted in their winner-take-all aspects, their tendency to submerge minorities, [a] general preference for legislatures reflecting community interests as closely as possible and disenchantment with political parties and elections as devices to settle policy differences between contending interests." *Whitcomb v. Chavis,* 403 U.S. 124 (1971).

Despite repeated constitutional attacks upon multimember legislative districts, the Court has consistently held that they are not unconstitutional per se, e.g., *White v. Regester,* 412 U.S. 755 (1973); *Burns v. Richardson.* We have recognized, however, that such legislative apportionments could violate the Fourteenth Amendment if their purpose were invidiously to minimize or cancel out the voting potential of racial or ethnic minorities. To prove such a purpose it is not enough to show that the group allegedly discriminated against has not elected representatives in proportion to its numbers. A plaintiff must prove that the disputed plan was "conceived or operated as [a] purposeful devic[e] to further racial discrimination."

This burden of proof is simply one aspect of the basic principle that only if there is purposeful discrimination can there be a violation of [equal protection]. See *Washington v. Davis*; *Arlington Heights*; *Personnel Adm'r v. Feeney,* [Sec. 2, II supra]. Although dicta may be drawn from a few of the Court's earlier opinions suggesting that disproportionate effects alone may establish a claim of unconstitutional racial vote dilution, the fact is that such a view is not supported by any decision of this Court. More importantly, such a view is not consistent with the meaning of the Equal Protection Clause as it has been understood in a variety of other contexts involving alleged racial discrimination. *Davis* (employment); *Akins v. Texas,* 325 U.S. 398 (1945) (jury selection).

[It] is clear that the evidence in the present case fell far short of showing [purposeful] discrimination. [T]he District Court [affirmed by the Court of Appeals] based its conclusion of unconstitutionality primarily on the fact that no Negro had ever been elected to the City Commission, apparently because of the pervasiveness of racially polarized voting in Mobile. The trial court also found that city officials had not been as responsive to the interests of Negroes as to those of white persons. On the basis of these findings, the court concluded that the political processes in Mobile were not equally open to Negroes, despite its seemingly inconsistent findings that there were no inhibitions against Negroes becoming candidates, and that in fact Negroes had registered and voted without hindrance. [But] past discrimination cannot, in the manner of original sin, condemn governmental action that is not itself unlawful. The ultimate question remains whether a discriminatory intent has been proved in a given [case].

[We] turn finally [to] Justice Marshall's dissenting opinion. The theory [appears] to be that every "political group," or at least every such group that is in the minority, has a federal constitutional right to elect candidates in proportion to its numbers. Moreover, a political group's "right" to have its candidates elected is said to be a "fundamental interest," the infringement of which may be established without proof that a State has acted with the purpose of impairing anybody's access to the political process. This dissenting opinion finds the "right" infringed [because] no Negro has been elected to the Mobile City Commission.

Whatever appeal the dissenting opinion's view may have as a matter of political theory, it is not the law. The Equal Protection Clause [does] not require proportional representation as an imperative of political organization. * * *

It is of course true that a law that impinges upon a fundamental right explicitly or implicitly secured by the Constitution is presumptively unconstitutional. See *Shapiro v. Thompson,* [Part II infra]. See also *San Antonio Ind. School Dist. v. Rodriguez,* [Part III infra]. But plainly "[i]t is not the province of this Court to create substantive constitutional rights in the name of guaranteeing equal protection of the laws," id. [In] *Whitcomb,* the trial court had found that a multimember state legislative district had invidiously deprived Negroes and poor persons of rights guaranteed them by the Constitution, notwithstanding the absence of any evidence whatever of discrimination against them. Reversing the trial court, this Court said: "The District Court's holding, although on the facts of this case limited to guaranteeing one racial group representation, is not easily contained. It is expressive of the more general proposition that any group with distinctive interests must be represented in legislative halls if it is numerous enough to command at least one seat and represents a majority living in an area sufficiently compact to constitute a single-member district. This approach would make it difficult to reject claims of Democrats, Republicans, or members of any political [organization]. There are also union oriented workers, the university community, religious or ethnic groups occupying identifiable areas of our heterogeneous cities and urban areas. Indeed, it would be difficult for a great many, if not most, multi-member districts to survive analysis under the District Court's view unless combined with some voting arrangement such as proportional representation or cumulative voting aimed at providing representation for minority parties or interests. At the very least, affirmance [would] spawn endless litigation concerning the multi-member district systems now widely employed in this country." * * *

JUSTICE BLACKMUN, concurring in the result.

Assuming that proof of intent is a prerequisite to appellees' prevailing on their constitutional claim of vote dilution, I am inclined to agree with Justice White that, in this case, "the findings of the District Court amply support an inference of purposeful discrimination." I concur in the Court's judgment of reversal, however, because I believe that the relief afforded appellees by the District Court [ordering a new form of government "of a Mayor and a City Council with members elected from single-member districts"] was not commensurate with the sound exercise of judicial discretion. * * *

JUSTICE STEVENS, concurring in the judgment.

[The antidiscrimination command] is applicable, not merely to gerrymanders directed against racial minorities, but to those aimed at religious, ethnic, economic and political groups as well. My conclusion that the same standard should be applied to racial groups as is applied to other groups leads me also to conclude that the standard cannot condemn every adverse impact on one or more political groups without spawning more dilution litigation than the judiciary can manage. [N]othing comparable to the mathematical yardstick used in apportionment cases is available to identify the difference between permissible and impermissible adverse impacts on the voting strength of political groups. * * *

In my view, the proper standard is suggested by three characteristics of the gerrymander condemned in *Gomillion:* (1) the 28–sided configuration [was] manifestly not the product of a routine or a traditional political decision; (2) it had a significant adverse impact on a minority group; and (3) it was unsupported by any neutral justification and thus was either totally irrational or entirely motivated by a desire to curtail the political strength of the minority. These characteristics suggest that a proper test should focus on the objective effects of the political decision rather than the subjective motivation of the decisionmaker. [A] political decision that is supported by valid and articulable justifications cannot be invalid simply because some participants in the decisionmaking process were motivated by a purpose to disadvantage a minority group. [A] contrary view "would spawn endless litigation concerning the multimember districts now widely employed in this Country," and would entangle the judiciary in a voracious political thicket.

JUSTICE BRENNAN, dissenting.

I dissent because I agree with Justice Marshall that proof of discriminatory impact is sufficient in these cases. I also dissent because, even accepting the plurality's premise that discriminatory purpose must be shown, I agree with [Marshall and White, JJ.,] that the appellees have clearly met that burden.

JUSTICE WHITE, dissenting.

[The] District Court and the Court of Appeals properly found that an invidious discriminatory purpose could be inferred from the totality of facts in this case. * * *

JUSTICE MARSHALL, dissenting. * * *

The Court does not dispute the proposition that multimember districting can have the effect of submerging electoral minorities. [Further], we decided a series of vote-dilution cases under the Fourteenth Amendment that were designed to protect electoral minorities from precisely the combination of electoral laws and historical and social factors found in the present cases. [Although] we have held that multimember districts are not unconstitutional per se, there is simply no basis for the plurality's conclusion that under our prior cases proof of discriminatory intent is a necessary condition for the invalidation of multimember districting.

[Under] this line of cases, an electoral districting plan is invalid if it has the effect of affording an electoral minority "less opportunity [than] other residents in the district to participate in the political processes and to elect legislators of their choice," *Regester*. It is also apparent that the Court in *Regester* considered equal access to the political process as meaning more than merely allowing the minority the opportunity to vote. *Regester* stands for the proposition that an electoral system may not relegate an electoral minority to political impotence by diminishing the importance of its [vote].

The plurality fails to apply the discriminatory effect standard of *Regester* because that approach conflicts with what the plurality takes to be an elementary principle of law. "[O]nly if there is purposeful discrimination," announces the plurality, "can there be a violation of [equal protection]." That proposition [fails] to distinguish between two distinct lines of equal protection decisions: those involving suspect classifications, and those involving fundamental rights. * * *

Under the Equal Protection Clause, if a classification "impinges upon a fundamental right explicitly or implicitly protected by the [Constitution], strict judicial scrutiny" is required, *Rodriguez,* regardless of whether the infringement was intentional. As I will explain, our cases recognize a fundamental right to equal electoral participation that encompasses protection against vote dilution. Proof of discriminatory purpose is, therefore, not required to support a claim of vote dilution.[10] The plurality's erroneous conclusion to the contrary is the result of a

10. [Although] the right to vote is distinguishable for present purposes from the other fundamental rights our cases have recognized, surely the plurality would not require proof of

failure to recognize the central distinction between *Regester* and *Davis:* the former involved an infringement of a constitutionally protected right, while the latter dealt with a claim of racially discriminatory distribution of an interest to which no citizen has a constitutional entitlement. * * *

Reynolds and its progeny focused solely on the discriminatory *effects* of malapportionment. [In] the present cases, the alleged vote dilution, though caused by the combined effects of the electoral structure and social and historical factors rather than by unequal population distribution, is analytically the same concept: the unjustified abridgement of a fundamental right. It follows, then, that a showing of discriminatory intent is just as unnecessary under the vote-dilution approach [applied] in *Regester,* as it is under our reapportionment cases. * * *

The plurality's response is that my approach amounts to nothing less than a constitutional requirement of proportional representation for groups. That assertion amounts to nothing more than a red herring. [Appellees] proved that no Negro had ever been elected to the Mobile City Commission, despite the fact that Negroes constitute about one-third of the electorate, and that the persistence of severe racial bloc voting made it highly unlikely that any Negro could be elected at-large in the foreseeable future. Contrary to the plurality's contention, however, I do not find unconstitutional vote dilution in this case simply because of that showing. The plaintiffs convinced the District Court that Mobile Negroes were unable to use alternative avenues of political influence. They showed that Mobile Negroes still suffered pervasive present effects of massive historical official and private discrimination, and that the city commission had been quite unresponsive to the needs of the minority community. Mobile has been guilty of such pervasive racial discrimination in hiring employees that extensive intervention by the Federal District Court has been required. Negroes are grossly underrepresented on city boards and committees. The city's distribution of public services is racially discriminatory. City officials and police were largely unmoved by Negro complaints about police brutality and "mock lynchings." The District Court concluded that "[t]his sluggish and timid response is another manifestation of the low priority given to the needs of the black citizens and of the [commissioners'] political fear of a white backlash vote when black citizens' needs are at stake."

[The] plurality's requirement of proof of *intentional discrimination* [may] represent an attempt to bury the legitimate concerns of the minority beneath the soil of a doctrine almost as impermeable as it is specious. If so, the superficial tranquility created by such measures can be but short-lived. If this Court refuses to honor our long-recognized principle that the Constitution "nullifies sophisticated as well as simple-minded modes of discrimination," it cannot expect the victims of discrimination to respect political channels of seeking redress. I dissent.

ROGERS v. LODGE, 458 U.S. 613 (1982), per WHITE, J., affirmed a decision that the at-large election system for a Georgia County Board of Commissioners violated equal protection: "The district court [demonstrated] its understanding of the controlling standard by observing that a determination of discriminatory intent is 'a requisite to a finding of unconstitutional vote dilution' [and] concluded that the [system] 'although racially neutral when adopted, is being *maintained* for invidious purposes.' [This Court has] noted that issues of intent are commonly

discriminatory purpose in those cases. [For] example, it would make no sense to require such a showing when the question is whether a state statute regulating abortion violates the right of personal choice recognized in *Roe v. Wade.* The only logical inquiry is whether, regardless of the legislature's motive, the statute has the effect of infringing that right.

treated as factual matters [and] has frequently noted its reluctance to disturb findings of fact concurred in by two lower courts."

POWELL, J., joined by Rehnquist, J., dissented: "[T]he Court's opinion cannot be reconciled persuasively with [*Mobile*]. There are some variances in the largely sociological evidence presented in the two cases. But *Mobile* held that this *kind* of evidence was not enough. * * * I would hold that the factors cited by the Court of Appeals are too attenuated as a matter of law to support an inference of discriminatory intent."

———

Whereas *Mobile v. Bolden* involved issues of minority vote dilution, partly symmetrical issues may arise in cases in which legislatures act with the goal of *increasing* the voting power of racial minorities through the deliberate design of so-called majority-minority districts. There are a variety of reasons that legislatures might seek to create majority-minority districts, including the need to comply with the Voting Rights Act of 1965 ("VRA"), 42 U.S.C. § 1973c. As amended by Congress following *Mobile v. Bolden*, § 2 of the VRA permits plaintiffs to prove a *statutory* claim of minority vote dilution, without needing to prove discriminatory intent, by establishing that (i) a minority community is large and compact enough to constitute the majority in a voting district, (ii) the minority community is politically cohesive, and (iii) the majority has engaged in racially polarized voting practices. *See Thornburg v. Gingles*, 478 U.S. 30 (1986). In addition, § 5 of the VRA mandates that any proposed districting changes in covered jurisdictions should not be "retrogressive" with respect to the representation of racial minorities. To enforce this requirement, § 5 provides that covered jurisdictions must "pre-clear" proposed districting changes with either a federal court or the Department of Justice. The VRA thus not only permits, but sometimes actually requires, policy-makers to be race-conscious in drawing electoral districts.

SHAW v. RENO

509 U.S. 630, 113 S.Ct. 2816, 125 L.Ed.2d 511 (1993).

JUSTICE O'CONNOR delivered the opinion of the Court.

[As] a result of the 1990 census, North Carolina became entitled to a twelfth seat in the United States House of Representatives. The General Assembly enacted a reapportionment plan that included one majority-black congressional district. After the Attorney General of the United States objected to the plan pursuant to § 5 of the Voting Rights Act of 1965, the General Assembly passed new legislation creating a second majority-black district. Appellants allege that the revised plan, which contains district boundary lines of dramatically irregular shape, constitutes an unconstitutional racial gerrymander. * * *

The voting age population of North Carolina is approximately 78% white, 20% black, and 1% Native American; the remaining 1% is predominantly Asian. The black population is relatively dispersed; blacks constitute a majority of the general population in only 5 of the State's 100 counties. [The] largest concentrations of black citizens live in the Coastal Plain, primarily in the northern part. The General Assembly's first redistricting plan contained one majority-black district centered in that area of the State. [I]t moves southward until it tapers to a narrow band; then, with finger-like extensions, it reaches far into the southern-most part of the State near the South Carolina border. District 1 has been compared to a "Rorschach ink-blot test," and a "bug splattered on a windshield."

The second majority-black district, District 12, is even more unusually shaped. It is approximately 160 miles long and, for much of its length, no wider than the I–85 corridor. It winds in snake-like fashion through tobacco country, financial centers, and manufacturing areas "until it gobbles in enough enclaves of black neighborhoods." Northbound and southbound drivers on I–85 sometimes find themselves in separate districts in one county, only to "trade" districts when they enter the next county. Of the 10 counties through which District 12 passes, five are cut into three different districts; even towns are divided. At one point the district remains contiguous only because it intersects at a single point with two other districts before crossing over them. One state legislator has remarked that "[i]f you drove down the interstate with both car doors open, you'd kill most of the people in the district." * * *

An understanding of the nature of appellants' claim is critical to our resolution of the case. In their complaint, appellants did not claim that the General Assembly's reapportionment plan unconstitutionally "diluted" white voting strength. They did not even claim to be white. Rather, appellants' complaint alleged that the deliberate segregation of voters into separate districts on the basis of race violated their constitutional right to participate in a "color-blind" electoral process. [This] Court never has held that race-conscious state decisionmaking is impermissible in all circumstances. What appellants object to is redistricting legislation that is so extremely irregular on its face that it rationally can be viewed only as an effort to segregate the races for purposes of voting, without regard for traditional districting principles and without sufficiently compelling justification. For the reasons that follow, we conclude that appellants have stated a claim upon which relief can be granted under the Equal Protection Clause.

[R]edistricting differs from other kinds of state decisionmaking in that the legislature always is aware of race when it draws district lines, just as it is aware of age, economic status, religious and political persuasion, and a variety of other demographic factors. That sort of race consciousness does not lead inevitably to impermissible race discrimination. [W]hen members of a racial group live together in one community, a reapportionment plan that concentrates members of the group in one district and excludes them from others may reflect wholly legitimate purposes. The district lines may be drawn, for example, to provide for compact districts of contiguous territory, or to maintain the integrity of political subdivisions.

The difficulty of proof, of course, does not mean that a racial gerrymander, once established, should receive less scrutiny under the Equal Protection Clause than other state legislation classifying citizens by race. Moreover, it seems clear to us that proof sometimes will not be difficult at all. In some exceptional cases, a reapportionment plan may be so highly irregular that, on its face, it rationally cannot be understood as anything other than an effort to "segregat[e] voters" on the basis of race. *Gomillion,* in which a tortured municipal boundary line was drawn to exclude black voters, was such a case. So, too, would be a case in which a State concentrated a dispersed minority population in a single district by disregarding traditional districting principles such as compactness, contiguity, and respect for political subdivisions. We emphasize that these criteria are important not because they are constitutionally required—they are not—but because they are objective factors that may serve to defeat a claim that a district has been gerrymandered on racial lines.

[A] reapportionment plan that includes in one district individuals who belong to the same race, but who are otherwise widely separated by geographical and political boundaries, and who may have little in common with one another but the color of their skin, bears an uncomfortable resemblance to political apartheid. It reinforces the perception that members of the same racial group—regardless of their age, education, economic status, or the community in which they live—think alike, share the same political interests, and will prefer the same candidates at the polls. We have rejected such perceptions elsewhere as impermissible racial stereotypes. By perpetuating such notions, a racial gerrymander may exacerbate the very patterns of racial bloc voting that majority-minority districting is sometimes said to counteract.

The message that such districting sends to elected representatives is equally pernicious. When a district obviously is created solely to effectuate the perceived common interests of one racial group, elected officials are more likely to believe that their primary obligation is to represent only the members of that group, rather than their constituency as a whole. This is altogether antithetical to our system of representative democracy. * * *

For these reasons, we conclude that a plaintiff challenging a reapportionment statute under the Equal Protection Clause may state a claim by alleging that the legislation, though race-neutral on its face, rationally cannot be understood as anything other than an effort to separate voters into different districts on the basis of race, and that the separation lacks sufficient justification. * * *

The dissenters suggest that a racial gerrymander of the sort alleged here is functionally equivalent to gerrymanders for nonracial purposes, such as political gerrymanders. This Court has held political gerrymanders to be justiciable under the Equal Protection Clause. See *Bandemer.* But nothing in our case law compels the conclusion that racial and political gerrymanders are subject to precisely the same constitutional scrutiny. In fact, our country's long and persistent history of racial discrimination in voting—as well as our Fourteenth Amendment jurisprudence, which always has reserved the strictest scrutiny for discrimination on the basis of race—would seem to compel the opposite conclusion. * * *

Justice Souter contends that exacting scrutiny of racial gerrymanders under the Fourteenth Amendment is inappropriate because reapportionment "nearly always require[s] some consideration of race for legitimate reasons." "As long as members of racial groups have [a] commonality of interest" and "racial block voting takes place," he argues, "legislators will have to take race into account" in order to comply with the Voting Rights Act. Justice Souter's reasoning is flawed.

[That] racial bloc voting or minority political cohesion may be found to exist in some cases, of course, is no reason to treat all racial gerrymanders differently from other kinds of racial classification. Justice Souter apparently views racial gerrymandering of the type presented here as a special category of "benign" racial discrimination that should be subject to relaxed judicial review. As we have said, however, the very reason that the Equal Protection Clause demands strict scrutiny of all racial classifications is because without it, a court cannot determine whether or not the discrimination truly is "benign." * * *

Racial classifications of any sort pose the risk of lasting harm to our society. They reinforce the belief, held by too many for too much of our history, that individuals should be judged by the color of their skin. Racial classifications with respect to voting carry particular dangers. Racial gerrymandering, even for remedial purposes, may balkanize us into competing racial factions; it threatens to carry us further from the goal of a political system in which race no longer matters—a goal that the Fourteenth and Fifteenth Amendments embody, and to which the Nation continues to aspire. It is for these reasons that race-based districting by our state legislatures demands close judicial scrutiny. * * *

JUSTICE WHITE, with whom JUSTICE BLACKMUN and JUSTICE STEVENS join, dissenting.

[Because] districting inevitably is the expression of interest group politics, and because "the power to influence the political process is not limited to winning elections," the question in gerrymandering cases is "whether a particular group has been unconstitutionally denied its chance to effectively influence the political process." [By] this, I meant that the group must exhibit "strong indicia of lack of political power and the denial of fair representation," so that it could be said that it has "essentially been shut out of the political process." In short, even assuming that racial (or political) factors were considered in the drawing of district boundaries, a showing of discriminatory effects is a "threshold requirement" in the absence of which there is no equal protection violation, and no need to "reach the question of the state interests [served] by the particular districts."

To distinguish a claim that alleges that the redistricting scheme has discriminatory intent and effect from one that does not has nothing to do with dividing racial classifications between the "benign" and the malicious—an enterprise which, as the majority notes, the Court has treated with skepticism. Rather, the issue is whether the classification based on race discriminates against anyone by denying equal access to the political process.

[I]t strains credulity to suggest that North Carolina's purpose in creating a second majority-minority district was to discriminate against members of the majority group by "impair[ing] or burden[ing their] opportunity [to] participate in the political process." The State has made no mystery of its intent, which was to respond to the Attorney General's objections by improving the minority group's prospects of electing a candidate of its choice. I doubt that this constitutes a discriminatory purpose as defined in the Court's equal protection cases—i.e., an intent to aggravate "the unequal distribution of electoral power." But even assuming that it does, there is no question that appellants have not alleged the requisite discriminatory effects. Whites constitute roughly 76 percent of the total population and 79 percent of the voting age population in North Carolina. Yet, under the State's plan, they still constitute a voting majority in 10 (or 83 percent) of the 12 congressional districts. * * *

[In other cases] we have put the plaintiff challenging district lines to the burden of demonstrating that the plan was meant to, and did in fact, exclude an identifiable racial group from participation in the political process. Not so, apparently, when the districting "segregates" by drawing odd-shaped lines. In that case, we are told, such proof no longer is needed. Instead, it is the State that must rebut the allegation that race was taken into account, a fact that, together with the legislators' consideration of ethnic, religious, and other group characteristics, I had thought we practically took for granted.

[Although] I disagree with the holding that appellants' claim is cognizable, the Court's discussion of the level of scrutiny it requires warrants a few comments. I have no doubt that a State's compliance with the Voting Rights Act clearly constitutes a compelling interest. [The] Court, while seemingly agreeing with this position, warns that the State's redistricting effort must be "narrowly tailored" to further its interest in complying with the law. It is evident to me, however, that what North Carolina did was precisely tailored to meet the objection of the Attorney General to its prior plan. * * *

State efforts to remedy minority vote dilution are wholly unlike what typically has been labeled "affirmative action." To the extent that no other racial group is injured, remedying a Voting Rights Act violation does not involve preferential treatment. It involves, instead, an attempt to equalize treatment, and to provide minority voters with an effective voice in the political process. The Equal Protection Clause of the Constitution, surely, does not stand in the way. * * *

JUSTICE STEVENS, dissenting.

[If] it is permissible to draw boundaries to provide adequate representation for rural voters, for union members, for Hasidic Jews, for Polish Americans, or for Republicans, it necessarily follows that it is permissible to do the same thing for members of the very minority group whose history in the United States gave birth to the Equal Protection Clause. A contrary conclusion could only be described as perverse.

JUSTICE SOUTER, dissenting.

[Unlike] other contexts in which we have addressed the State's conscious use of race, see, e.g., *Croson,* electoral districting calls for decisions that nearly always require some consideration of race for legitimate reasons where there is a racially mixed population. As long as members of racial groups have the commonality of interest implicit in our ability to talk about concepts like "minority voting strength," and "dilution of minority votes," and as long as racial bloc voting takes place, legislators will have to take race into account in order to avoid dilution of minority voting strength in the districting plans they adopt. [A] second distinction between districting and most other governmental decisions in which race has figured is that those other decisions using racial criteria characteristically occur in circumstances in which the use of race to the advantage of one person is necessarily at the obvious expense of a member of a different race. * * *

In districting, by contrast, the mere placement of an individual in one district instead of another denies no one a right or benefit provided to others. [Under] our cases there is in general a requirement that in order to obtain relief under the Fourteenth Amendment, the purpose and effect of the districting must be to devalue the effectiveness of a voter compared to what, as a group member, he would otherwise be able to enjoy. * * *

There is thus no theoretical inconsistency in having two distinct approaches to equal protection analysis, one for cases of electoral districting and one for most other types of state governmental decisions. Nor, because of the distinctions between the two categories, is there any risk that Fourteenth Amendment districting law as such will be taken to imply anything for purposes of general Fourteenth Amendment scrutiny about "benign" racial discrimination, or about group entitlement as distinct from individual protection, or about the appropriateness of strict or other heightened scrutiny. * * *

———

MILLER v. JOHNSON, 515 U.S. 900 (1995), involved Georgia's creation of three majority-minority congressional districts (out of a total of eleven) in response to the Justice Department's earlier refusals to grant preclearance under the Voting Rights Act to plans that created only two such districts. Georgia's population was about 27% black. One of the majority-minority districts created by the state—the Eleventh—cut through eight counties and five municipalities. The Court, per KENNEDY, J., held that this plan violated equal protection because "race was the predominant factor motivating the drawing of the eleventh district.":

"Our observation in *Shaw* of the consequences of racial stereotyping was not meant to suggest that a district must be bizarre on its face before there is a constitutional violation. * * * Shape is relevant not because bizarreness is a necessary element of the constitutional wrong or a threshold requirement of proof, but because it may be persuasive circumstantial evidence that race for its own sake, and not other districting principles, was the legislature's dominant and controlling rationale in drawing its district lines. The logical implication, as courts applying *Shaw* have recognized, is that parties may rely on evidence other than bizarreness to establish race-based districting.

"[Whether] or not in some cases compliance with the Voting Rights Act, standing alone, can provide a compelling interest independent of any interest in remedying past discrimination, it cannot do so here. [Georgia's] drawing of the Eleventh District was not required under the Act because there was no reasonable basis to believe that Georgia's earlier enacted plans violated [§ 5]. Georgia's first and second proposed plans increased the number of majority-black districts from 1 out of 10 (10%) to 2 out of 11 (18.18%). These plans were 'ameliorative' and could not have violated § 5's non-retrogression principle. [There] is no indication Congress intended such a far-reaching application of § 5, so we reject the Justice Department's interpretation of the statute and avoid the constitutional problems that interpretation raises."

GINSBURG, J., joined by Stevens, Souter and Breyer, JJ., dissented: "Although the Georgia General Assembly prominently considered race in shaping the Eleventh District, race did not crowd out all other factors, [Tellingly,] the District that the Court's decision today unsettles is not among those on a statistically calculated list of the 28 most bizarre districts in the United States, a study prepared in the wake of our decision in *Shaw*. * * *

"To accommodate the reality of ethnic bonds, legislatures have long drawn voting districts along ethnic lines. Our Nation's cities are full of districts identified by their ethnic character—Chinese, Irish, Italian, Jewish, Polish, Russian, for example. The creation of ethnic districts reflecting felt identity is not ordinarily viewed as offensive or demeaning to those included in the delineation. [If] Chinese–Americans and Russian–Americans may seek and secure group recognition in the delineation of voting districts, then African–Americans should not be dissimilarly treated. Otherwise, in the name of equal protection, we would shut out 'the very minority group whose history in the United States gave birth to the Equal Protection Clause.' "

———

BUSH v. VERA, 517 U.S. 952 (1996), struck down congressional districts crafted to meet what Texas argued were the requirements of the Voting Rights Act. Although race was a factor in drawing the lines, Texas argued that the predominant factor was the protection of incumbents. O'CONNOR, J., joined by Rehnquist, C.J., and Kennedy, J., agreed that avoiding contests between incumbents was a legitimate districting consideration, and she emphasized that the "decision to create majority-minority districts was not objectionable in and of itself." O'Connor, J., noted that "[o]ur precedents have used a variety of formulations to describe the threshold for the application of strict scrutiny" and cited as possible triggering standards for strict scrutiny language from both *Shaw* ("so extremely irregular on its face that it rationally can be viewed only as an effort to segregate the races for purposes of voting, without regard for traditional districting principles") and *Miller* ("race for its own sake, and not other districting principles, was the legislature's dominant and controlling rationale"). Noting that strict scrutiny does not "apply to all cases of intentional creation of majority-minority districts," she nonetheless concluded on the facts that strict scrutiny was appropriate because race had predominated over legitimate districting considerations. Among the findings weighing in favor of the application of strict scrutiny were "that the State substantially neglected traditional districting criteria such as compactness, that it was committed from the outset to creating majority-minority districts, and that it manipulated district lines to exploit unprecedentedly detailed racial data."

"As we have done in each of our previous cases, in which [compliance with Section 2 of the Voting Rights Act] has been raised as a defense to charges of racial gerrymandering, we assume without deciding that compliance with [Section 2's] results test [can be] a compelling state interest." O'Connor, J., concluded, however, that the Texas districts were not narrowly tailored to meet the requirements of the Voting Rights Act because the act does not require a state to create districts that are not reasonably compact:**a** "If, because of the dispersion of the minority population, a reasonably compact majority-minority district cannot be created, the [Voting Rights Act] does not require a majority-minority district; if a reasonably compact district can be created, nothing in [the Voting Rights Act] requires the race-based creation of a district that is far from compact."

THOMAS, J., joined by Scalia, J., concurring, maintained that the intentional creation of majority-minority districts should be enough to invoke strict scrutiny: "In my view, application of strict scrutiny in this suit was never a close question," because "a majority-minority district is created 'because of,' and not merely 'in spite of,' racial demographics." Kennedy, J., concurring separately, strongly suggested he would join Thomas and Scalia, JJ., on that point if the issue were presented.

STEVENS, J., joined by Ginsburg and Breyer, JJ., dissenting, denied that race was a predominant consideration in the formation of the Texas districts and maintained that the creation of districts that were not reasonably compact was consistent with the Voting Rights Act. (He conceded, however, that a state was not *compelled* by the VRA to a create majority-minority district unless it could create a majority-minority district that was reasonably compact).

SOUTER, J., joined by Ginsburg and Breyer, JJ., dissenting, raised administrability, separation of powers, and federalism objections to the Court's *Shaw* jurisprudence: "The result of [the Court's] failure to provide a practical standard for distinguishing between lawful and unlawful use of race has not only been inevitable confusion in statehouses and courtrooms, but a consequent shift in responsibility for setting district boundaries from state legislatures, which are invested with front-line authority by Article I of the Constitution, to the courts, and truly to this Court, which is left to superintend the drawing of every legislative district in the land."

O'CONNOR, J., who wrote the plurality opinion in *Bush v. Vera*, also wrote a separate concurring opinion in which she attempted to summarize "the rules governing the States' consideration of race in the districting process[:] First, so long as they do not subordinate traditional districting criteria to the use of race for its own sake or as a proxy, States may intentionally create majority-minority districts, and may otherwise take race into consideration, without coming under strict scrutiny. See [the plurality opinion and the dissenting opinions of Stevens

---

a. The Court reached the same conclusion, again over the vigorous dissents of Stevens, J., and Souter, J., both joined by Breyer and Gins- burg, J.J., in the companion case of *Shaw v. Hunt* ("*Shaw II*"), 517 U.S. 899 (1996).

and Souter, JJ.]. Only if traditional districting criteria are neglected and that neglect is predominantly due to the misuse of race does strict scrutiny apply.

"Second, where voting is racially polarized, § 2 [of the Voting Rights Act] prohibits States from adopting districting schemes that would have the effect that minority voters 'have less opportunity than other members of the electorate [to] elect representatives of their choice.' § 2(b). That principle may require a State to create a majority-minority district where the three *Gingles* factors are present— viz., (i) the minority group 'is sufficiently large and geographically compact to constitute a majority in a single-member district,' (ii) 'it is politically cohesive,' and (iii) 'the white majority votes sufficiently as a bloc to enable it * * * usually to defeat the minority's preferred candidate.'

"Third, the state interest in avoiding liability under [§ 2] is compelling.b If a State has a strong basis in evidence for concluding that the *Thornburg v. Gingles* factors are present, it may create a majority-minority district without awaiting judicial findings. Its 'strong basis in evidence' need not take any particular form, although it cannot simply rely on generalized assumptions about the prevalence of racial bloc voting.

"Fourth, if a State pursues that compelling interest by creating a district that 'substantially addresses' the potential liability, and does not deviate substantially from a hypothetical court-drawn § 2 district for predominantly racial reasons, its districting plan will be deemed narrowly tailored. Cf. (plurality opinion)(acknowledging this possibility); (Souter, J., dissenting)(same); (Stevens, J., dissenting)(contending that it is applicable here).

"Finally, however, districts that are bizarrely shaped and non-compact, and that otherwise neglect traditional districting principles and deviate substantially from the hypothetical court-drawn district, for predominantly racial reasons, are unconstitutional. (plurality opinion)."

E. EQUALITY IN THE COUNTING
AND RECOUNTING OF VOTES

BUSH v. GORE

531 U.S. 98, 121 S.Ct. 525, 148 L.Ed.2d 388 (2000).

PER CURIAM.

[After a machine count and recount of ballots in the 2000 Florida presidential election, Democrat Albert Gore trailed Republican George W. Bush by fewer than 1,000 votes. Returns from other states made it clear that the winner of Florida's electoral votes would have an electoral college majority. With the election thus in the balance, Gore sought further manual recounts in selected, heavily Democratic Florida counties, and a complex series of legal battles unfolded. Among the signal events was a United States Supreme Court decision, entered on December 4, vacating a decision of the Florida Supreme Court that effectively extended the deadline established by Florida's Secretary of State for the completion of recounts. When the deadline for "recounts" passed with a full manual recount having been completed in only one county, the legal battles entered a second phase in which Florida law permits legal "contests" of disputed elections. In an appeal from a lower court ruling, the Florida Supreme Court, by 4–3, ordered a manual recount

---

b. The four dissenters in *Vera* (who also dissented in *Hunt*), together with O'Connor, J.,   supported this proposition.

of all so-called "undervotes"—ballots on which the earlier machine counts had failed to record any presidential choice—in one of the counties in which Gore had sought a recount and further directed a manual recount of "undervotes" in all counties. Many of the "undervote" ballots were punchcards on which voters using a stylus had apparently left hanging "chads" or produced "dimples" but made no full perforation. In determining when votes should be recorded, the Florida Supreme Court said only that election officials and lower court judges should follow the legislatively prescribed standard of attempting to discern "the will of the voter."]

[Bush immediately sought a Supreme Court stay of the Florida Supreme Court's ruling, alleging that the state court's decision lacked any foundation in pre-existing Florida law and thus violated both a federal statute and the command of Art. II of the federal constitution that the choice of presidential electors should occur "in such Manner as the [state] Legislature"—as distinguished, Bush argued, from the state constitution or state courts—"may direct." Bush also contended that the unelaborated "will of the voter" standard for counting or not counting ballots with hanging chads and dimples would produce unjustified disparities and violate the Due Process and Equal Protection Clauses. The Supreme Court stayed the Florida Supreme Court's order on Saturday, December 9—just three days before what a majority of the Justices understood to be a Florida statutory deadline of December 12 for the completion of proceedings bearing on the final certification of the state's electors. The Court held oral argument in the case on Monday December 11 and handed down its decision shortly after 10 p.m. on December 12.]

[When] the state legislature vests the right to vote for President in its people, the right to vote as the legislature has prescribed is fundamental; and one source of its fundamental nature lies in the equal weight accorded to each vote and the equal dignity owed to each voter. See [*McPherson v. Blacker*, 146 U.S. 1, 35 (1892)].

The right to vote is protected in more than the initial allocation of the franchise. Equal protection applies as well to the manner of its exercise. Having once granted the right to vote on equal terms, the State may not, by later arbitrary and disparate treatment, value one person's vote over that of another. See, e.g., *Harper v. Virginia Bd. of Elections,* [supra]. * * *

The question before us [is] whether the recount procedures the Florida Supreme Court has adopted are consistent with its obligation to avoid arbitrary and disparate treatment of the members of its electorate. * * *

For purposes of resolving the equal protection challenge, it is not necessary to decide whether the Florida Supreme Court had the authority under the legislative scheme for resolving election disputes to define what a legal vote is and to mandate a manual recount implementing that definition. The recount mechanisms implemented in response to the decisions of the Florida Supreme Court do not satisfy the minimum requirement for non-arbitrary treatment of voters necessary to secure the fundamental right. Florida's basic command for the count of legally cast votes is to consider the "intent of the voter." This is unobjectionable as an abstract proposition and a starting principle. The problem inheres in the absence of specific standards to ensure its equal application.

[T]he standards for accepting or rejecting contested ballots might vary not only from county to county but indeed within a single county from one recount team to another. The record provides some examples. A monitor in Miami–Dade County testified at trial that he observed that three members of the county canvassing board applied different standards in defining a legal vote. * * *

[The Court also expressed concern about the disparate treatment of so-called "overvotes," involving ballots on which a voter made a mark next to the name of more than one candidate. Under the recount scheme mandated by the Florida Supreme Court,] the citizen whose ballot was not read by a machine because he failed to vote for a candidate in a way readable by machine may still have his vote counted in a manual recount; on the other hand, the citizen who marks two candidates in a way discernable by the machine will not have the same opportunity to have his vote count, even if a manual examination of the ballot would reveal the requisite indicia of intent. * * *

In addition [the] Florida Supreme Court's [order] did not specify who would recount the ballots. The county canvassing boards were forced to pull together ad hoc teams comprised of judges from various Circuits who had no previous training in handling and interpreting ballots. Furthermore, while others were permitted to observe, they were prohibited from objecting during the recount.

The recount process, in its features here described, is inconsistent with the minimum procedures necessary to protect the fundamental right of each voter in the special instance of a statewide recount under the authority of a single state judicial officer. Our consideration is limited to the present circumstances, for the problem of equal protection in election processes generally presents many complexities.

The question before the Court is not whether local entities, in the exercise of their expertise, may develop different systems for implementing elections. Instead, we are presented with a situation where a state court with the power to assure uniformity has ordered a statewide recount with minimal procedural safeguards. When a court orders a statewide remedy, there must be at least some assurance that the rudimentary requirements of equal treatment and fundamental fairness are satisfied. * * *

Upon due consideration of the difficulties identified to this point, it is obvious that the recount cannot be conducted in compliance with the requirements of equal protection and due process without substantial additional work. * * *

The Supreme Court of Florida has said that the legislature intended the State's electors to [be chosen] by December 12. That date is upon us, and there is no recount procedure in place under the State Supreme Court's order that comports with minimal constitutional standards. Because it is evident that any recount seeking to meet the December 12 date will be unconstitutional for the reasons we have discussed, we reverse the judgment of the Supreme Court of Florida ordering a recount to proceed. * * *

[Rehnquist, C.J., joined by Scalia and Thomas, J.J., joined the per curiam opinion, but wrote separately, concluding that the Florida Supreme Court violated Art. II by applying rules of decision at odds with those mandated by the Florida legislature.]

Justice STEVENS, with whom Justices GINSBURG and BREYER, join, dissenting.

* * * [Although we have previously found equal protection violations] when individual votes within the same State were weighted unequally, [we] have never before called into question the substantive standard by which a State determines that a vote has been legally cast. And there is no reason to think that the guidance provided to the factfinders, specifically the various canvassing boards, by the "intent of the voter" standard is any less sufficient—or will lead to results any less uniform—than, for example, the "beyond a reasonable doubt" standard employed everyday by ordinary citizens in courtrooms across this country.

Admittedly, the use of differing substandards for determining voter intent in different counties employing similar voting systems may raise serious concerns. Those concerns are alleviated—if not eliminated—by the fact that a single impartial magistrate will ultimately adjudicate all objections arising from the recount process. Of course, as a general matter, "[t]he interpretation of constitutional principles must not be too literal. We must remember that the machinery of government would not work if it were not allowed a little play in its joints." *Bain Peanut Co. of Tex. v. Pinson*, 282 U.S. 499, 501 (1931) (Holmes, J.). If it were otherwise, Florida's decision to leave to each county the determination of what balloting system to employ—despite enormous differences in accuracy—might run afoul of equal protection. So, too, might the similar decisions of the vast majority of state legislatures to delegate to local authorities certain decisions with respect to voting systems and ballot design. * * *

If we assume—as I do—that the [Florida Supreme Court] and the judges who would have carried out its mandate are impartial, its decision does not even raise a colorable federal question. What must underlie petitioners' entire [case] is an unstated lack of confidence in the impartiality and capacity of the state judges who would make the critical decisions if the vote count were to proceed. [The] endorsement of that position by a majority of this Court can only lend credence to the most cynical appraisal of the work of judges throughout the land. [Although] we may never know with complete certainty the winner of this year's Presidential election, the identity of the loser is perfectly clear. It is the Nation's confidence in the judge as an impartial guardian of the rule of law.

Justice SOUTER, with whom Justice BREYER, joins, dissenting.

* * * I would [remand] the case to the courts of Florida with instructions to establish uniform standards for evaluating the several types of ballots that have prompted differing treatments, to be applied within and among counties when passing on such identical ballots in any further recounting (or successive recounting) that the courts might order. * * *

Justice GINSBURG, with whom Justice STEVENS, joins, dissenting:

* * * Ideally, perfection would be the appropriate standard for judging the recount. But we live in an imperfect world, one in which thousands of votes have not been counted. I cannot agree that the recount adopted by the Florida court, flawed as it may be, would yield a result any less fair or precise than the certification that preceded that recount. See, e.g., *McDonald v. Board of Election Comm'rs of Chicago*, 394 U.S. 802, 807 (1969) (even in the context of the right to vote, the state is permitted to reform " 'one step at a time' "). * * *

Justice BREYER, with whom Justice STEVENS, Justice SOUTER, and Justice GINSBURG, join, dissenting.

* * * By halting the manual recount, and thus ensuring that the uncounted legal votes will not be counted under any standard, this Court crafts a remedy out of proportion to the asserted harm. [I]n a system that allows counties to use different types of voting systems, voters already arrive at the polls with an unequal chance that their votes will be counted. I do not see how the fact that this results from counties' selection of different voting machines rather than a court order makes the outcome any more fair. Nor do I understand why the Florida Supreme Court's recount order, which helps to redress this inequity, must be entirely prohibited based on a deficiency that could easily be remedied. * * *

II. TRAVEL

CRANDALL v. NEVADA, 73 U.S. (6 Wall.) 35 (1867), Struck down a state tax of $1 on rail and stage tickets for out-of-state destinations on the ground that the tax violated a constitutionally protected right to travel. In ruling as it did, however, the Court pointedly declined to identify any particular provision of the Constitution as the source of the right. "The people of these United States constitute one nation," the Court emphasized, and it suggested that implicit in the idea of nationhood was a prohibition against state interferences with the right to travel from one state to another. Since *Crandall*, the Court has consistently recognized a right to travel, but it has had far more difficulty identifying the specific bounds of that right.

SAENZ v. ROE

526 U.S. 489, 119 S.Ct. 1518, 143 L.Ed.2d 689 (1999).

JUSTICE STEVENS delivered the opinion of the Court.

In 1992, California enacted a statute limiting the maximum welfare benefits available to newly arrived residents. The scheme limits the amount payable to a family that has resided in the State for less than 12 months to the amount payable by the State of the family's prior residence. The questions presented by this case are whether the 1992 statute was constitutional when it was enacted and, if not, whether an amendment to the Social Security Act enacted by Congress in 1996 affects that determination. * * *

The word "travel" is not found in the text of the Constitution. Yet the "constitutional right to travel from one State to another" is firmly embedded in our jurisprudence. [In] *Shapiro* [*v. Thompson*, 394 U.S. 618 (1969)], we reviewed the constitutionality of three statutory provisions that denied welfare to residents of [states] who had resided within those respective jurisdictions less than one year immediately preceding their applications for assistance. Without pausing to identify the specific source of the right, [we] squarely held that it was "constitutionally impermissible" for a State to enact durational residency requirements for the purpose of inhibiting the migration by needy persons into the State. We further held that a classification that had the effect of imposing a penalty on the exercise of the right to travel violated the Equal Protection Clause "unless shown to be necessary to promote a *compelling* governmental interest" and that no such showing had been made. In this case, California argues that [its statute], unlike the legislation reviewed in *Shapiro*, [does] not penalize the right to travel because new arrivals are not ineligible for benefits during their first year of residence. California submits that, instead of being subjected to the strictest scrutiny, the statute should be upheld if it is supported by a rational basis and that the State's legitimate interest in saving over $10 million a year satisfies that test.

[The] "right to travel" discussed in our cases embraces at least three different components. It protects the right of a citizen of one State to enter and to leave another State, the right to be treated as a welcome visitor rather than an unfriendly alien when temporarily present in the second State, and, for those travelers who elect to become permanent residents, the right to be treated like other citizens of that State.* * *

What is at issue in this case [is the] third aspect of the right to travel—the right of the newly arrived citizen to the same privileges and immunities enjoyed by other citizens of the same State. That right is protected not only by the new arrival's status as a state citizen, but also by her status as a citizen of the United States. That additional source of protection is plainly identified in the opening words of the Fourteenth Amendment: "All persons born or naturalized in the United States, and subject to the jurisdiction thereof, are citizens of the United States and of the State wherein they reside. No state shall make or enforce any law which shall abridge the privileges or immunities of citizens of the United States."

Despite fundamentally differing views concerning the coverage of the Privileges or Immunities Clause of the Fourteenth Amendment, most notably expressed in the majority and dissenting opinions in the *Slaughter–House Cases*, [Chap. 5. Sec. 1, III] it has always been common ground that this Clause protects the third component of the right to travel. Writing for the majority in the *Slaughter–House Cases*, Justice Miller explained that one of the privileges conferred by this Clause "is that a citizen of the United States can, of his own volition, become a citizen of any State of the Union by a *bona fide* residence therein, with the same rights as other citizens of that State." * * *

Neither mere rationality nor some intermediate standard of review should be used to judge the constitutionality of a state rule that discriminates against some of its citizens because they have been domiciled in the State for less than a year. The appropriate standard may be more categorical than that articulated in *Shapiro*, but it is surely no less strict. * * *

Because this case involves discrimination against citizens who have completed their interstate travel, the State's argument that its welfare scheme affects the right to travel only "incidentally" is beside the point. Were we concerned solely with actual deterrence of migration, we might be persuaded that a partial withholding of benefits constitutes a lesser incursion on the right to travel than an outright denial of all benefits. But since the right to travel embraces the citizen's right to be treated equally in her new State of residence, the discriminatory classification is itself a penalty.

It is undisputed that respondents and the members of the class that they represent are citizens of California and that their need for welfare benefits is unrelated to the length of time that they have resided in California. We thus have no occasion to consider what weight might be given to a citizen's length of residence if the bona fides of her claim to state citizenship were questioned. Moreover, because whatever benefits they receive will be consumed while they remain in California, there is no danger that recognition of their claim will encourage citizens of other States to establish residency for just long enough to acquire some readily portable benefit, such as a divorce or a college education, that will be enjoyed after they return to their original domicile. See, e.g., *Sosna* [*v. Iowa*, 419 U.S. 393 (1975) (upholding a one-year residency requirement to file for divorce)]; *Vlandis v. Kline*, 412 U.S. 441 (1973) [invalidating a conclusive presumption that a student who filed an out-of-state application to a state university was not thereafter a state resident but appearing to contemplate the permissibility of other tests for the bona fides residency claims]. * * *

Disavowing any desire to fence out the indigent, California has instead advanced an entirely fiscal justification for its [scheme]. The enforcement of [the statute] will save the State approximately $10.9 million a year. The question is not whether such saving is a legitimate purpose but whether the State may accomplish that end by the discriminatory means it has chosen. An evenhanded, across-the-board reduction of about 72 cents per month for every beneficiary would produce the same result. But our negative answer to the question does not rest on the weakness of the State's purported fiscal justification. It rests on the fact that the Citizenship Clause of the Fourteenth Amendment expressly equates citizenship with residence: "That Clause does not provide for, and does not allow for, degrees of citizenship based on length of residence." *Zobel* [*v. Williams*, 457 U.S. 55 (1982) (invalidating an Alaska scheme for distributing state oil revenue to Alaska residents based on the length of citizens' residency in the state)]. [Neither] the duration of respondents' California residence, nor the identity of their prior States of residence, has any relevance to their need for benefits. Nor do those factors bear any relationship to the State's interest in making an equitable allocation of the funds to be distributed among its needy citizens. As in *Shapiro*, we reject any contributory rationale for the denial of benefits to new residents. [S]ee also *Zobel*. In short, the State's legitimate interest in saving money provides no justification for its decision to discriminate among equally eligible citizens.

The question that remains is whether congressional approval of durational residency requirements in the 1996 amendment to the Social Security Act somehow resuscitates the constitutionality of [the statute]. That question is readily answered, for we have consistently held that Congress may not authorize the States to violate the Fourteenth Amendment.

CHIEF JUSTICE REHNQUIST, with whom JUSTICE THOMAS joins, dissenting:

The Court today breathes new life into the previously dormant Privileges or Immunities Clause of the Fourteenth Amendment—a Clause relied upon by this Court in only one other decision, *Colgate v. Harvey*, 296 U.S. 404 (1935), overruled five years later by *Madden v. Kentucky*, 309 U.S. 83 (1940). It uses this Clause to strike down what I believe is a reasonable measure falling under the head of a "good-faith residency requirement." Because I do not think any provision of the Constitution—and surely not a provision relied upon for only the second time since its enactment 130 years ago—requires this result, I dissent. * * *

I agree with the proposition that a "citizen of the United States can, of his own volition, become a citizen of any State of the Union by a *bona fide* residence therein, with the same rights as other citizens of that State." *Slaughter–House Cases*. But I cannot see how the right to become a citizen of another State is a necessary "component" of the right to travel, or why the Court tries to marry these separate and distinct rights. A person is no longer "traveling" in any sense of the word when he finishes his journey to a State which he plans to make his home. Indeed, under the Court's logic, the protections of the Privileges or Immunities Clause recognized in this case come into play only when an individual *stops* traveling with the intent to remain and become a citizen of a new State. [At] most, restrictions on an individual's right to become a citizen indirectly affect his calculus in deciding whether to exercise his right to travel in the first place, but such an attenuated and uncertain relationship is no ground for folding one right into the other.

No doubt the Court has, in the past 30 years, essentially conflated the right to travel with the right to equal state citizenship in striking down durational residence requirements similar to the one challenged here. See, e.g., *Shapiro*; *Memorial Hospital v. Maricopa County*, 415 U.S. 250, 280–83 (1974) (striking down 1–year county residency requirement before receiving entitlement to nonemergency hospitalization or emergency care). These cases marked a sharp departure from the Court's prior precedents because in none of them was travel itself prohibited. * * *

The Court today tries to clear much of the underbrush created by these prior right-to-travel cases, abandoning its effort to define what residence requirements deprive individuals of "important rights and benefits" or "penalize" the right to travel. Under its new analytical framework, a State, outside certain ill-defined circumstances, cannot classify its citizens by the length of their residence in the State without offending the Privileges or Immunities Clause of the Fourteenth Amendment. The Court thus departs from *Shapiro* and its progeny, and, while paying lip service to the right to travel, the Court does little to explain how the right to travel is involved at all. Instead, as the Court's analysis clearly demonstrates, this case is only about respondents' right to immediately enjoy all the privileges of being a California citizen in relation to that State's ability to test the good-faith assertion of this right. * * *

In unearthing from its tomb the right to become a state citizen and to be treated equally in the new State of residence, however, the Court ignores a State's need to assure that only persons who establish a bona fide residence receive the benefits provided to current residents of the State. [T]he Court has consistently recognized that while new citizens must have the same opportunity to enjoy the privileges of being a citizen of a State, the States retain the ability to use bona fide residence requirements to ferret out those who intend to take the privileges and run.* * *

If States can require individuals to reside in-state for a year before exercising the right to educational benefits [as contemplated in cases such as *Vlandis*], the right to terminate a marriage [as upheld in *Sosna*],or the right to vote in primary elections that all other state citizens enjoy, then States may surely do the same for welfare benefits. Indeed, there is no material difference between a 1–year residence requirement applied to the level of welfare benefits given out by a State, and the same requirement applied to the level of tuition subsidies at a state university. The welfare payment here and in-state tuition rates are cash subsidies provided to a limited class of people, and California's standard of living and higher education system make both subsidies quite attractive. Durational residence requirements were upheld when used to regulate the provision of higher education subsidies, and the same deference should be given in the case of welfare payments.

The Court today recognizes that States retain the ability to determine the bona fides of an individual's claim to residence, but then tries to avoid the issue. It asserts that because respondents' need for welfare benefits is unrelated to the length of time they have resided in California, it has "no occasion to consider what weight might be given to a citizen's length of residence if the bona fides of her claim to state citizenship were questioned." But I do not understand how the absence of a link between need and length of residency bears on the State's ability to objectively test respondents' resolve to stay in California. There is no link between the need for an education or for a divorce and the length of residence, and yet States may use length of residence as an objective yardstick to channel their benefits to those whose intent to stay is legitimate. * * *

The Court tries to distinguish education and divorce benefits by contending that the welfare payment here will be consumed in California, while a college education or a divorce produces benefits that are "portable" and can be enjoyed after individuals return to their original domicile. But this "you can't take it with you" distinction is more apparent than real, and offers little guidance to lower courts who must apply this rationale in the future. Welfare payments are a form of insurance, giving impoverished individuals and their families the means to meet the demands of daily life while they receive the necessary training, education, and time to look for a job. The cash itself will no doubt be spent in California, but the benefits from receiving this income and having the opportunity to become employed or employable will stick with the welfare recipient if they stay in California or go back to their true domicile. Similarly, tuition subsidies are "consumed" in-state but the recipient takes the benefits of a college education with him wherever he goes. A welfare subsidy is thus as much an investment in human capital as is a tuition subsidy, and their attendant benefits are just as "portable." More importantly, this foray into social economics demonstrates that the line drawn by the Court borders on the metaphysical, and requires lower courts to plumb the policies animating certain benefits like welfare to define their "essence" and hence their "portability." * * *

I therefore believe that the durational residence requirement challenged here is a permissible exercise of the State's power to "assur[e] that services provided for its residents are enjoyed only by residents."

JUSTICE THOMAS, with whom THE CHIEF JUSTICE joins, dissenting.

* * * Unlike the Equal Protection and Due Process Clauses, which have assumed near-talismanic status in modern constitutional law, the Court all but read the Privileges or Immunities Clause out of the Constitution in the *Slaughter–House Cases*. * * *

As The Chief Justice points out, it comes as quite a surprise that the majority relies on the Privileges or Immunities Clause at all in this case. [Although] the majority appears to breathe new life into the Clause today, it fails to address its historical underpinnings or its place in our constitutional jurisprudence. Because I believe that the demise of the Privileges or Immunities Clause has contributed in no small part to the current disarray of our Fourteenth Amendment jurisprudence, I would be open to reevaluating its meaning in an appropriate case. Before invoking the Clause, however, we should endeavor to understand what the framers of the Fourteenth Amendment thought that it meant. We should also consider whether the Clause should displace, rather than augment, portions of our equal protection and substantive due process jurisprudence. The majority's failure to consider these important questions raises the specter that the Privileges or Immunities Clause will become yet another convenient tool for inventing new rights, limited solely by the "predilections of those who happen at the time to be Members of this Court." * * *

III. WELFARE AND EDUCATION

Based on a number of Warren Court decisions that seemed to have as their practical aim ensuring that the poor would have access to opportunities that are routinely enjoyed by the economically better off, by the late 1960s a number of commentators thought that the Justices might be poised either to recognize fundamental rights to education and possibly welfare or to identify the poor as a suspect class. The Court, however, never formally confronted whether to do so during the Warren years. Subsequent decisions have rejected claims that welfare and education are fundamental rights for purposes of equal protection analysis.

DANDRIDGE v. WILLIAMS, 397 U.S. 471 (1970): Maryland's Aid to Families With Dependent Children Program gave most eligible families their computed "standard of need," but imposed a "maximum limitation" on the total amount any family could receive. The Court, per STEWART, J., held that the statutory ceiling did not violate equal protection: "[H]ere we deal with state regulation in the social and economic field, not affecting freedoms guaranteed by the Bill of Rights, and claimed to violate the Fourteenth Amendment only because the regulation results in some disparity in grants of welfare payments to the largest AFDC families.16 In [this area] a state does not violate [equal protection] merely because the classifica-

---

16. Cf. *Shapiro*, where, by contrast, the Court found state interference with the consti- tutionally protected freedom of interstate travel.

tions made by its laws are imperfect." "It is enough that the state's action be rationally based and free from invidious discrimination."

"To be sure, [many cases] enunciating this [standard] have in the main involved state regulation of business or industry. The administration of public welfare assistance, by contrast, involves the most basic economic needs of impoverished human beings, [but] we can find no basis for applying a different constitutional standard. [By] combining a limit on the recipient's grant with permission to retain money earned, without reduction in the amount of the grant, Maryland provides an incentive to seek gainful employment. And by keeping the maximum family AFDC grants to the minimum wage a steadily employed head of a household receives, the State maintains some semblance of an equitable balance between families on welfare and those supported by an employed breadwinner."

MARSHALL, J., joined by Brennan, J., dissented:a "[T]he only distinction between those children with respect to whom assistance is granted and those [denied] is the size of the family into which the child permits himself to be born. [This] is grossly underinclusive in terms of the class which the AFDC program was designed to assist, namely *all* needy dependent children, [and requires] a persuasive justification * * *.

"The Court never undertakes to inquire for such a justification; rather it avoids the task by focusing upon the abstract dichotomy between two different approaches to equal protection problems which have been utilized by this Court.

"[The] cases relied on by the Court, in which a 'mere rationality' test was actually used, [involve] regulation of business interests. The extremes to which the Court has gone in dreaming up rational bases for state regulation in that area may in many instances be ascribed to a healthy revulsion from the Court's earlier excesses in using the Constitution to protect interests which have more than enough power to protect themselves in the legislative halls. This case, involving the literally vital interests of a powerless minority—poor families without breadwinners—is far removed from the area of business regulation, as the Court concedes. * * *

"In my view, equal protection analysis of this case is not appreciably advanced by the a priori definition of a 'right,' fundamental [and thus invoking the 'compelling' interest test] or otherwise.14 Rather, concentration must be placed upon the character of the classification in question, the relative importance to individuals in the class discriminated against of the governmental benefits which they do not receive, and the asserted state interests in support of the classification. * * *

"It is the individual interests here [that] most clearly distinguish this case from the 'business regulation' [cases]. AFDC support to needy dependent children provides the stuff which sustains those children's lives: food, clothing, shelter. And this Court has already recognized [that] when a benefit, even a 'gratuitous' benefit, is necessary to sustain life, stricter constitutional standards, both procedural17 and substantive,18 are applied to the deprivation of that benefit.

---

a. Douglas, J., dissented on the ground (agreed to also by Marshall and Brennan, JJ.) that the Maryland law was inconsistent with the Social Security Act.

14. [T]he Court's insistence that equal protection analysis turns on the basis of a closed category of "fundamental rights" involves a curious value judgment. It is certainly difficult to believe that a person whose very survival is at stake would be comforted by the knowledge that his "fundamental" rights are preserved intact. * * *

17. See *Goldberg v. Kelly*, 397 U.S. 254 (1970).

18. [See] *Kirk v. Board of Regents*, 273 Cal.App.2d 430, 440–441, 78 Cal.Rptr. 260, 266–267 (1969), appeal dismissed, 396 U.S. 554 (1970), upholding a one-year residency requirement for tuition-free graduate education at

"Nor is the distinction upon which the deprivation is here based—the distinction between large and small families—one which readily commends [itself]. Indeed, governmental discrimination between children on the basis of a factor over which they have no control [bears] some resemblance to the classification between legitimate and illegitimate children which we condemned [in cases discussed in Sec. 4, II supra]."

On examination, the asserted state interests were either "arbitrary," impermissible, of "minimum rationality," "drastically overinclusive," or "grossly underinclusive." "The existence of [other] alternatives [to satisfy asserted state interests] does not, of course, conclusively establish the invalidity of the maximum grant regulation. It is certainly relevant, however, in appraising the overall interest of the State in the maintenance of the regulation [against] a fundamental constitutional challenge."

SAN ANTONIO IND. SCHOOL DIST. v. RODRIGUEZ

411 U.S. 1, 93 S.Ct. 1278, 36 L.Ed.2d 16 (1973).

JUSTICE POWELL delivered the opinion of the Court.

This suit attacking the Texas system of financing public education was initiated by Mexican–American parents [as] a class action on behalf of schoolchildren throughout the State who are members of minority groups or who are poor and reside in school districts having a low property tax base. * * *

Recognizing the need for increased state funding to help offset disparities in local spending [because of sizable differences in the value of assessable property between local school districts,] the state legislature [established the] Minimum Foundation School Program [which] accounts for approximately half of the total educational expenditures in Texas. [It] calls for state and local contributions to a fund earmarked specifically for teacher salaries, operating expenses, and transportation costs. The State [finances] approximately [80%]. The districts' share, known as the Local Fund Assignment, is apportioned among the school districts under a formula designed to reflect each district's relative taxpaying ability. * * *

The school district in which appellees reside, [Edgewood,] has been compared throughout this litigation with the Alamo Heights [District. Edgewood] is situated in the core-city sector of San Antonio in a residential neighborhood that has little commercial or industrial property. [A]pproximately 90% of the student population is Mexican–American and over 6% is Negro. The average assessed property value per pupil is $5,960—the lowest in the metropolitan area—and the median family income ($4,686) is also the lowest. At an equalized tax rate of $1.05 per $100 of assessed property—the highest in the metropolitan area—the district contributed $26 to the education of each child for the 1967–1968 school year above its Local Fund Assignment for the Minimum Foundation Program. The Foundation Program contributed $222 per pupil for a state-local total of $248. Federal funds added another $108 for a total of $356 per pupil.

Alamo Heights is the most affluent school district in San Antonio. [Its] school population [has] only 18% Mexican–Americans and less than 1% Negroes. The assessed property value per pupil exceeds $49,000 and the median family income is $8,001. In 1967–1968 the local tax rate of $.85 per $100 of valuation yielded $333 per pupil over and above its contribution to the Foundation Program.

state university, and distinguishing *Shapiro* on the ground that it "involved the immediate and pressing need for preservation of life and health of persons unable to live without public assistance, and their dependent children."

Coupled with the $225 provided from that Program, the district was able to supply $558 per student. Supplemented by a $36 per pupil grant from federal sources, Alamo Heights spent $594 per pupil.

[Finding] that wealth is a "suspect" classification and that education is a "fundamental" interest, the District Court held that the Texas system could be sustained only if the State could show that it was premised upon some compelling state interest. * * *

II.   [The] wealth discrimination discovered [is] quite unlike any of the forms of wealth discrimination heretofore reviewed by this Court. [The] individuals [who] constituted the class discriminated against in our prior cases shared two distinguishing characteristics: because of their impecunity they were completely unable to pay for some desired benefit, and as a consequence, they sustained an absolute deprivation of a meaningful opportunity to enjoy that benefit. [For example,] *Douglas v. California,* 372 U.S. 353 (1963), [which held that a state must appoint counsel for an indigent criminal defendant for a first appeal granted as a matter of statutory right, provides] no relief for those on whom the burdens of paying for a criminal defense are, relatively speaking, great but not insurmountable. Nor does it deal with relative differences in the quality of counsel acquired by the less wealthy.

[Neither] of the two distinguishing characteristics of wealth classifications can be found here. First, [there] is reason to believe that the poorest families are not necessarily clustered in the poorest property districts. * * *

Second, [lack] of personal resources has not occasioned an absolute deprivation of the desired benefit. The argument here is not that the children [are] receiving no public education; rather, it is that they are receiving a poorer quality education [than] children in districts having more assessable wealth. [A] sufficient answer to appellees' argument is that at least where wealth is involved the Equal Protection Clause does not require absolute equality or precisely equal advantages. [Texas] asserts that the Minimum Foundation Program provides an "adequate" education for all children in the State. [No] proof was offered at trial persuasively discrediting or refuting the State's assertion. * * *60

This brings us [to] the third way in which the classification scheme might be defined—*district* wealth discrimination. Since the only correlation indicated by the evidence is between district property wealth and expenditures, it may be argued that discrimination might be found without regard to the individual income characteristics of district residents. * * *

However described, it is clear that appellees' suit asks this Court to extend its most exacting scrutiny to review a system that allegedly discriminates against a large, diverse, and amorphous class, unified only by the common factor of residence in districts that happen to have less taxable wealth than other districts. The system of alleged discrimination and the class it defines have none of the traditional indicia of suspectness: the class is not saddled with such disabilities, or subjected to such a history of purposeful unequal treatment, or relegated to such a position of political powerlessness as to command extraordinary protection from the majoritarian political process.

We thus conclude that the Texas system does not operate to the peculiar disadvantage of any suspect class.

---

60. [If] elementary and secondary education were made available by the State only to those able to pay a tuition assessed against each pupil, there would be a clearly defined class of "poor" people—definable in terms of their inability to pay the prescribed sum—who would be absolutely precluded from receiving an education. That case would present a far more compelling set of circumstances for judicial assistance than [this one].

[Recognizing] that this Court has never heretofore held that wealth discrimination alone provides an adequate basis for invoking strict scrutiny, appellees [also] assert that the State's system impermissibly interferes with the exercise of a "fundamental" right [requiring] the strict standard of judicial review. * * *

Nothing this Court holds today in any way detracts from our historic dedication to public education. [But] the importance of a service performed by the State does not determine whether it must be regarded as fundamental for purposes of examination under the Equal Protection Clause. [In *Shapiro,* the] right to interstate travel had long been recognized as a right of constitutional significance, and the Court's decision, therefore, did not require an ad hoc determination as to the social or economic importance of that right. [In *Dandridge*], the central importance of welfare benefits to the poor was not an adequate foundation for requiring the State to justify its law by showing some compelling state interest. * * *

The lesson of these cases [is that it] is not the province of this Court to create substantive constitutional rights in the name of guaranteeing equal protection of the laws. Thus the key to discovering whether education is "fundamental" is not to be found in comparisons of the relative societal significance of education as opposed to subsistence or housing [or] by weighing whether education is as important as the right to travel. Rather, the answer lies in assessing whether there is a right to education explicitly or implicitly guaranteed by the Constitution. *Dunn v. Blumstein,* 405 U.S. 330 (1972);[74] *Skinner.*[76]

Education, of course, is not among the rights afforded explicit protection under [the] Constitution. Nor do we find any basis for saying it is implicitly so protected. [But] appellees [contend] that education is distinguishable from other services and benefits provided by the State because it bears a peculiarly close relationship to other rights and liberties accorded protection under the Constitution [in that] it is essential to the effective exercise of First Amendment freedoms and to intelligent utilization of the right to vote. In asserting a nexus between speech and education, appellees urge that the right to speak is meaningless unless the speaker is capable of articulating his thoughts intelligently and persuasively. [A] similar line of reasoning is pursued with respect to the right to [vote]: a voter cannot cast his ballot intelligently unless his reading skills and thought processes have been adequately developed.

We need not dispute any of these propositions. [Yet] we have never presumed to possess either the ability or the authority to guarantee to the citizenry the most *effective* speech or the most *informed* electoral choice. That these may be desirable goals [is] not to be doubted. [But] they are not values to be implemented by judicial intrusion into otherwise legitimate state activities.

[The] logical limitations on appellees' nexus theory are difficult to perceive. [Empirical] examination might well buttress an assumption that the ill-fed, ill-clothed, and ill-housed are among the most ineffective participants in the political

---

74. *Dunn* fully canvasses this Court's voting rights cases and explains that "this Court has made clear that a citizen has a *constitutionally protected right* to participate in elections on an equal basis with other citizens in the jurisdiction." (emphasis supplied). The constitutional underpinnings of [this right] can no longer be doubted even though, as the Court noted in *Harper,* "the right to vote in state elections is nowhere expressly mentioned."

76. *Skinner* applied the standard of close scrutiny to a state law permitting forced sterilization of "habitual criminals." Implicit in the Court's opinion is the recognition that the right of procreation is among the rights of personal privacy protected under the Constitution. See *Roe v. Wade.*

process and that they derive the least enjoyment from the benefits of the First Amendment. * * *

[The] present case, in another basic sense, is significantly different from any of the cases in which the Court has applied strict scrutiny [to] legislation touching upon constitutionally protected rights. [These] involved legislation which "deprived," "infringed," or "interfered" with the free exercise of some such fundamental personal right or liberty. [We] think it plain that, in substance, the thrust of the Texas system is affirmative and reformatory and, therefore, should be scrutinized under judicial principles sensitive to the nature of the State's efforts and to the rights reserved to the States under the Constitution.

[This] case represents [a] direct attack on the way in which Texas has chosen to raise and disburse state and local tax revenues. [This] Court has often admonished against such interferences with the State's fiscal policies under the Equal Protection Clause [and] we continue to acknowledge that the Justices of this Court lack both the expertise and the familiarity with local problems so necessary to the making of wise decisions with respect to the raising and disposition of public revenues. [No] scheme of taxation [has] yet been devised which is free of all discriminatory impact. [I]t would be difficult to imagine a case having a greater potential impact on our federal system than the one now before us, in which we are urged to abrogate systems of financing public education presently in existence in virtually every State. * * * The need is apparent for reform in tax systems which may well have relied too long and too heavily on the local property tax. [But] the ultimate solutions must come from the lawmakers and from the democratic pressures of those who elect them.

Reversed.

JUSTICE BRENNAN, dissenting.

Although I agree with my Brother White that the Texas statutory scheme is devoid of any rational basis, [I] also record my disagreement with the Court's rather distressing assertion that a right may be deemed "fundamental" for the purposes of equal protection analysis only if it is "explicitly or implicitly guaranteed by the Constitution." As my Brother Marshall convincingly demonstrates our prior cases stand for the proposition that "fundamentality" is, in large measure, a function of the right's importance in terms of the effectuation of those rights which are in fact constitutionally guaranteed. * * *

JUSTICE WHITE, with whom JUSTICE DOUGLAS and JUSTICE BRENNAN join, dissenting.

[T]his case would be quite different if it were true that the Texas system, while insuring minimum educational expenditures in every district through state funding, extended a meaningful option to all local districts to increase their per-pupil [expenditures. But for] districts with a low per-pupil real estate tax base [the] Texas system utterly fails to extend a realistic choice to parents because the property tax, which is the only revenue-raising mechanism extended to school districts, is practically and legally unavailable. * * *

In order to equal the highest yield in any other Bexar County district, Alamo Heights would be required to tax at the rate of 68 cents per $100 of assessed valuation. Edgewood would be required to tax at the prohibitive rate of $5.76 per $100. But state law places a $1.50 per $100 ceiling on the maintenance tax [rate]. Requiring the State to establish only that unequal treatment is in furtherance of a permissible goal, without also requiring the State to show that the means chosen to effectuate that goal are rationally related to its achievement, makes equal protection analysis no more than an empty gesture. * * *

Justice Marshall, with whom Justice Douglas, concurs, dissenting.

[T]he majority's holding can only be seen as a retreat from our historic commitment to equality of educational opportunity. [At] the very least, in view of the substantial interdistrict disparities in funding, [the] burden of proving that these disparities do not in fact affect the quality of children's education must fall upon the appellants. Yet [they] have argued no more than that the relationship is ambiguous. * * *

[The] Court apparently seeks to establish [that] equal protection cases fall into one of two neat categories which dictate the appropriate standard of review—strict scrutiny or mere rationality. But [a] principled reading of what this Court has done reveals that it has applied a spectrum of standards [which] clearly comprehends variations in the degree of care with which the Court will scrutinize particular classifications, depending [on] the constitutional and societal importance of the interest adversely affected and the recognized invidiousness of the basis upon which the particular classification is drawn. * * *

I therefore cannot accept the majority's labored efforts to demonstrate that fundamental interests, which call for strict scrutiny of the challenged classification, encompass only established rights which we are somehow bound to recognize from the text of the Constitution itself. * * *59

I would like to know where the Constitution guarantees the right to procreate, *Skinner,* or the right to vote in state elections, e.g., *Reynolds v. Sims,*[60] or the right to an appeal from a criminal conviction, e.g., *Griffin v. Illinois,* 351 U.S. 12 (1956)[61] These are instances in which, due to the importance of the interests at stake, the Court has displayed a strong concern with the existence of discriminatory state treatment. But the Court has [never] indicated that these are interests which independently enjoy full-blown constitutional protection. * * *

The majority is, of course, correct when it suggests that the process of determining which interests are fundamental is a difficult one. But I do not think the problem is insurmountable. [The task] should be to determine the extent to which constitutionally guaranteed rights are dependent on interests not mentioned in the Constitution. As the nexus between the specific constitutional guarantee and the nonconstitutional interest draws closer, the nonconstitutional interest becomes more fundamental and the degree of judicial scrutiny applied when the interest is infringed on a discriminatory basis must be adjusted accordingly. * * * Procreation is now understood to be important because of its interaction with the established constitutional right of privacy. The exercise of the state franchise is closely tied to basic civil and political rights inherent in the First Amendment. And access to criminal appellate processes enhances the integrity of

59. Indeed, the Court's theory would render the established concept of fundamental interests in the context of equal protection analysis superfluous, for the substantive constitutional right itself requires that this Court strictly scrutinize any asserted state interest for restricting or denying access to any particular guaranteed right.

60. It is interesting that in its effort to reconcile the state voting rights cases with its theory of fundamentality the majority can muster nothing more than the contention that "[t]he constitutional underpinnings of the *right to equal treatment in the voting process* can no longer be doubted." If, by this, the Court intends to recognize a substantive con-

stitutional "right to equal treatment in the voting process" independent of the Equal Protection Clause, the source of such a right is certainly a mystery to me.

61. It is true that *Griffin* [also] involved discrimination against [indigents]. But, as the majority points out, the Court has never deemed wealth discrimination alone to be sufficient to require strict judicial scrutiny; rather, such review of wealth classifications has been applied only where the discrimination affects an important individual interest, see, e.g., *Harper.* Thus, I believe *Griffin* [can] only be understood as premised on a recognition of the fundamental importance of the criminal appellate process.

the range of rights implicit in the Fourteenth Amendment guarantee of due process of law. Only if we closely protect the related interests from state discrimination do we ultimately ensure the integrity of the constitutional guarantee itself. This is the real lesson that must be taken from our previous decisions involving interests deemed to be fundamental.

[It] is true that this Court has never deemed the provision of free public education to be required by the Constitution. [But] the fundamental importance of education is amply indicated by the prior decisions of this Court, by the unique status accorded public education by our society, and by the close relationship between education and some of our most basic constitutional [values].

[I] do not question that local control of public education, as an abstract matter, constitutes a very substantial state interest. [But] on this record, it is apparent that the State's purported concern with local control is offered primarily as an excuse rather than as a justification for interdistrict inequality.

In Texas statewide laws regulate [the] most minute details of local public education. For example, the State prescribes required courses. All textbooks must be submitted for state [approval]. The State has established the qualifications necessary for teaching in Texas public schools and the procedures for obtaining certification. The State has even legislated on the length of the school [day.]

[In] my judgment, any substantial degree of scrutiny of the operation of the Texas financing scheme reveals that the State has selected means wholly inappropriate to secure its purported interest in assuring its school districts local fiscal control.96 At the same time, appellees have pointed out a variety of alternative financing schemes which may serve the State's purported interest in local control as well as, if not better than, the present scheme without the current impairment of the educational opportunity of vast numbers of Texas schoolchildren.[98] * * *

PLYLER v. DOE, 457 U.S. 202 (1982), per BRENNAN, J., held that a Texas statute (§ 21.031) denying free public education to illegal alien children violated equal protection: "Persuasive arguments support the view that a State may withhold its beneficence from those whose very presence within the United States is the product of their own unlawful conduct. [But the children] in these cases 'can affect neither their parents' conduct nor their own status.' Even if the State found it expedient to control the conduct of adults by acting against their children, legislation directing the onus of a parent's misconduct against his children does not comport with fundamental conceptions of justice. [Citing cases involving discrimination against illegitimates, Sec. 4, II supra].

96. [Although] my Brother White purports to reach this result by application of that lenient standard of mere rationality, [it] seems to be that the care with which he scrutinizes the practical effectiveness of the present local property tax as a device for affording local fiscal control reflects the application of a more stringent standard of [review].

98. * * * Central financing would leave in local hands the entire gamut of local educational policy-making—teachers, curriculum, school sites, the whole process of allocating resources among alternative educational objectives.

A second possibility is the much discussed theory of district power equalization put forth by Professors Coons, Clune, and Sugarman in their seminal work, *Private Wealth and Public Education* 201–242 (1970). Such a scheme would truly reflect a dedication to local fiscal control. Under their system, each school district would receive a fixed amount of revenue per pupil for any particular level of tax effort regardless of the level of local property tax base. * * *

"We reject the claim that 'illegal aliens' are a 'suspect class.' [U]ndocumented status is not irrelevant to any proper legislative goal. Nor is [it] an absolutely immutable characteristic since it is the product of conscious, indeed unlawful, action. But § 21.031 [imposes] its discriminatory burden on the basis of a legal characteristic over which children can have little control. It is thus difficult to conceive of a rational justification for penalizing these children for their presence within the United States. * * *

"Public education is not a 'right' granted to individuals by the Constitution. *Rodriguez.* But neither is it merely some governmental 'benefit' indistinguishable from other forms of social welfare legislation. Both the importance of education in maintaining our basic institutions, and the lasting impact of its deprivation on the life of the child, mark the distinction. [We] cannot ignore the significant social costs borne by our Nation when select groups are denied the means to absorb the values and skills upon which our social order rests.20 [Thus], the discrimination contained in § 21.031 can hardly be considered rational unless it furthers some substantial goal of the State.

"[First,] appellants appear to suggest that the State may seek to protect the State from an influx of illegal immigrants. While a State might have an interest in mitigating the potentially harsh economic effects of sudden shifts in population, [t]here is no evidence in the record suggesting that illegal entrants impose any significant burden on the State's economy. To the contrary, the available evidence suggests that illegal aliens underutilize public services, while contributing their labor to the local economy and tax money to the State fisc. The dominant incentive for illegal entry [into] Texas is the availability of employment; few if any illegal immigrants come to this country [to] avail themselves of a free education. * * *

"Second, [appellants] suggest that undocumented children are appropriately singled out for exclusion because of the special burdens they impose on the State's ability to provide high quality public education. [In] terms of educational cost and need, however, undocumented children are 'basically indistinguishable' from legally resident alien children.

"Finally, appellants suggest that undocumented children are appropriately singled out because their unlawful presence within the United States renders them less likely than other children to remain within the boundaries of the State, and to put their education to productive social or political use within the State. Even assuming that such an interest is legitimate, it is an interest that is most difficult to quantify. The State has no assurance that any child, citizen or not, will employ the education provided by the State within the confines of the State's borders. In any event, the record is clear that many of the undocumented children disabled by this classification will remain in this country indefinitely, and that some will become lawful residents or citizens of the United States. It is difficult to understand precisely what the State hopes to achieve by promoting the creation and perpetuation of a subclass of illiterates within our boundaries, surely adding to the problems and costs of unemployment, welfare, and crime. It is thus clear that whatever savings might be achieved [are] wholly insubstantial in light of the costs involved to these children, the State, and the Nation."

BLACKMUN, J., who joined the Court's opinion, concurred: "I joined [the] Court in *Rodriguez,* and I continue to believe that it provides the appropriate model for resolving most equal protection disputes. [Classifications] involving the complete

---

20. [Whatever] the current status of these children, the courts below concluded that many will remain here permanently and that some indeterminate number will eventually become citizens. * * *

denial of education are in a sense unique, for they strike at the heart of equal protection values by involving the State in the creation of permanent class distinctions."

POWELL, J., who joined the Court's opinion, concurred "to emphasize the unique character of the case": "Although the analogy is not perfect, our holding today does find support in decisions of this Court with respect to the status of illegitimates. [Thus,] review in a case such as this is properly heightened. [These children] have been singled out for a lifelong penalty and stigma. A legislative classification that threatens the creation of an underclass of future citizens and residents cannot be reconciled with one of the fundamental purposes of the Fourteenth Amendment. In these unique circumstances, the Court properly may require that the State's interests be substantial and that the means bear a 'fair and substantial relation' to these interests.3"

BURGER, C.J., joined by White, Rehnquist and O'Connor, JJ., dissented: "[B]y patching together bits and pieces of what might be termed quasi-suspect-class and quasi-fundamental-rights analysis, the Court spins out a theory custom-tailored to the facts [and its] opinion rests on such a unique confluence of theories and rationales that it will likely stand for little beyond the results in these particular [cases].

"[Once] it is conceded—as the Court does—that illegal aliens are not a suspect class, and that education is not a fundamental right, our inquiry should focus on and be limited to whether the legislative classification at issue bears a rational relationship to a legitimate state purpose. [I]t simply is not 'irrational' for a State to conclude that it does not have the same responsibility to provide benefits for persons whose very presence in the State and this country is illegal as it does to provide for persons lawfully present."

---

3. [I]n *Rodriguez* no group of children was singled out by the State and then penalized because of their parents' status. [Nor] was any group of children totally deprived of all education as in this case. If the resident children of illegal aliens were denied welfare assistance, made available by government to all other children who qualify, this also—in my opinion—would be an impermissible penalizing of children because of their parents' status.

Chapter 10

THE CONCEPT OF STATE ACTION

SECTION 1. INTRODUCTION

The "state action" doctrine has long established that, because of their language or history, most provisions of the Constitution that protect individual liberty—including those set forth in Art. 1, §§ 9 and 10, the Bill of Rights, and the Fourteenth and Fifteenth Amendments—impose restrictions or obligations only on government. The subject received its first extensive treatment in the CIVIL RIGHTS CASES, 109 U.S. 3 (1883), per BRADLEY, J., which held that neither the Thirteenth nor Fourteenth Amendments empowered Congress to pass the Civil Rights Act of 1875, making racial discrimination unlawful in public accommodations (inns, public conveyances, places of public amusement, etc.)—"and no other ground of authority for its passage being suggested, it must necessarily be declared void." Although the issue presented did not simply concern the authority granted the *Court* under § 1 of the Thirteenth and Fourteenth Amendments, but rather involved the scope of *Congress'* power under the final sections of these amendments to enforce their substantive provisions "by appropriate legislation" (a topic to be considered in detail in Ch. 11), the Court's discussion of "state action" remains the classic exposition.

The Court held that, under the Fourteenth Amendment, "individual invasion of individual rights is not the subject-matter of the amendment. [It] nullifies and makes void all state legislation, and state action of every kind, which impairs the privileges and immunities of citizens of the United States, or which injures them in life, liberty, or property without due process of law, or which denies to any of them the equal protection of the laws. [T]he last section of the amendment [does] not authorize Congress to create a code of municipal law for the regulation of private rights; but to provide modes of redress against the operation of state laws, and the action of state officers, executive or judicial, when these are subversive of the fundamental rights specified in the amendment. * * *

"An inspection of the [Civil Rights Act of 1875] shows that [it] proceeds ex directo to declare that certain acts committed by individuals shall be deemed offenses. [It] does not profess to be corrective of any constitutional wrong committed by the states; [it] applies equally to cases arising in states which have the justest laws respecting the personal rights of citizens, and whose authorities are ever ready to enforce such laws as to those which arise in states that may have violated the prohibition of the amendment. In other words, it steps into the domain of local jurisprudence, and lays down rules for the conduct of individuals in society towards each other. [C]ivil rights, such as are guaranteed by the Constitution against state aggression, cannot be impaired by the wrongful acts of individuals, unsupported by state authority in the shape of laws, customs, or judicial or executive proceedings. [An] individual cannot deprive a man of his right to vote, to hold property, to buy and to sell, to sue in the courts, or to be a witness or a juror; he may, by force or fraud, interfere with the enjoyment of the right in a particular case; [but] unless protected in these wrongful acts by some shield of state law or state authority, he cannot destroy or injure the right; he will only render himself amenable [to] the laws of the state where the wrongful acts are committed. [The] abrogation and denial of rights, for which the states alone were or could be responsible, was the great seminal and fundamental wrong which was intended to be remedied."

The Court recognized that the Thirteenth Amendment "is not a mere prohibition of state laws establishing or upholding slavery, but an absolute declaration that slavery or involuntary servitude shall not exist in any part of the United States [and] that the power vested in Congress to enforce the article by appropriate legislation, clothes Congress with power to pass all laws necessary and proper for abolishing all badges and incidents of slavery, in the United States. [T]he civil rights bill of 1866, passed in view of the Thirteenth Amendment, before the fourteenth was adopted, undertook to wipe out these burdens and disabilities, [namely,] the same right to make and enforce contracts, to sue, be parties, give evidence, and to inherit, purchase, lease, sell, and convey property, as is enjoyed by white citizens. [At] that time (in 1866) Congress did not assume, under the authority given by the Thirteenth Amendment, to adjust what may be called the social rights of men and races in the community; but only to declare and vindicate those fundamental rights which appertain to the essence of citizenship, and the enjoyment or deprivation of which constitutes the essential distinction between freedom and slavery.

"[It] would be running the slavery argument into the ground to make it apply to every act of discrimination which a person may see fit to make as to the guests he will entertain, or as to the people he will take into his coach or cab or car, or admit to his concert or theater, or deal with in other matters of intercourse or business. Innkeepers and public carriers, by the laws of all the states, so far as we are aware, are bound, to the extent of their facilities, to furnish proper accommodation to all unobjectionable persons who in good faith apply for them. If the laws themselves make any unjust discrimination, amenable to the prohibitions of the Fourteenth Amendment, Congress has full power to afford a remedy under that amendment and in accordance with it."a

HARLAN, J., dissented: "Was it the purpose of the nation [by the Thirteenth Amendment] simply to destroy the institution [of slavery], and remit the race, theretofore held in bondage, to the several states for such protection, in their civil rights, necessarily growing out of freedom, as those states [choose] to provide? [S]ince slavery [rested] wholly upon the inferiority, as a race, of those held in bondage, their freedom necessarily involved immunity from, and protection against, all discrimination against them, because of their race, in respect of such civil rights as belong to freemen of other races. Congress, therefore, [may] enact laws of a direct and primary character, operating upon states, their officers and

a. In *Bell v. Maryland,* 378 U.S. 226 (1964), Goldberg, J., joined by Warren, C.J., and Douglas, J., examining the "historical evidence" in detail, concluded that the *Civil Rights Cases* were based on the assumption of the framers of the Fourteenth Amendment that "under state law, when the Negro's disability as a citizen was removed, he would be assured the same public civil rights that the law had guaranteed white persons," and that "the duties of the proprietors of places of public accommodation would remain as they had long been and that the States would now be affirmatively obligated to insure that these rights ran to Negro as well as white citizens." Black, J., joined by Harlan and White, JJ., disagreed.

agents, and also upon, at least, such individuals and corporations as exercise public functions and wield power and authority under the state. * * *

"It remains now to inquire what are the legal rights of colored persons in respect of the accommodations * * *.

"1. As to public conveyances on land and water. [R]ailroads [are] none the less public highways because controlled and owned by private corporations; that it is a part of the function of government to make and maintain highways for the conveyance of the public; that no matter who is the agent, and what is the agency, the function performed is *that of the state* * * *.

"Such being the relations these corporations hold to the public, it would seem that the right of a colored person to use an improved public highway, upon the terms accorded to freemen of other races, is as fundamental in the state of freedom, established in this country, as are any of the rights which my brethren concede to be so far fundamental as to be deemed the essence of civil freedom.

"2. As to inns. [A] keeper of an inn is in the exercise of a quasi public employment. The law gives him special privileges, and he is charged with certain duties and responsibilities to the public [which] forbids him from discriminating against any person asking admission as a guest on account of [race].

"3. As to places of public amusement. [W]ithin the meaning of the act of 1875, [they] are such as are established and maintained under direct license of the law. [The] local government granting the license represents [the colored race] as well as all other races within its jurisdiction. A license from the public to establish a place of public amusement, imports, in law, equality of right, at such [places]."

Turning to the Fourteenth Amendment, "the first clause of the first section— 'all persons born or naturalized in the United States, and subject to the jurisdiction thereof, are citizens of the United States, and of the state wherein they reside'—is of a distinctly affirmative character. In its application to the colored race, previously liberated, it [granted] citizenship of the state in which they respectively resided. [Further], they were brought, by this supreme act of the nation, within the direct operation of that provision of the Constitution which declares that 'the citizens of each state shall be entitled to all privileges and immunities of citizens in the several states.' Article IV, § 2.

"The citizenship thus acquired [may be protected] by congressional legislation of a primary direct character; this, because the power of Congress is not restricted to the enforcement of prohibitions upon state laws or state action. It is, in terms distinct and positive, to enforce 'the *provisions of this article*' of amendment * * * *all* of the provisions,—affirmative and prohibitive * * *.

"But what was secured to colored citizens of the United States—as between them and their respective states—by the grant to them of state citizenship? With what rights, privileges, or immunities did this grant from the nation invest them? There is one, if there be no others—exemption from race discrimination in respect of any civil right belonging to citizens of the white race in the same state [by] the state, or its officers, or by individuals, or corporations exercising public functions or authority. [It] was perfectly well known that the great danger to the equal enjoyment by citizens of their rights, as citizens, was to be apprehended, not altogether from unfriendly state legislation, but from the hostile action of corporations and individuals in the states. * * *

"But if it were conceded that the power of Congress could not be brought into activity until the rights specified in the act of 1875 had been abridged or denied by some state law or state action, I maintain that the decision of the court is erroneous. [In] every material sense applicable to the practical enforcement of the

Fourteenth Amendment, railroad corporations, keepers of inns, and managers of places of public amusement are agents of the state, because amenable, in respect of their public duties and functions, to public regulation. * * * I agree that if one citizen chooses not to hold social intercourse with another, he is not and cannot be made amenable to the law for his conduct in that regard. [The] rights which Congress, by the act of 1875, endeavored to secure and protect are legal, not social, rights. The right, for instance, of a colored citizen to use the accommodations of a public highway upon the same terms as are permitted to white citizens is no more a social right than his right, under the law, to use the public streets of a city, or a town, or a turnpike road, or a public market, or a post-office, or his right to sit in a public building with others, of whatever race, for the purpose of hearing the political questions of the day discussed."

———

The basic doctrine of the *Civil Rights Cases*—that it is "state action" that is prohibited by the Fourteenth Amendment—has remained undisturbed. But the question of what constitutes "state action" has generated significant controversy. It is settled that the term comprehends statutes enacted by national, state and local legislative bodies and the official actions of all government officers.b The more difficult problems arise when the conduct of private individuals or groups is challenged as being unconstitutional. Although—as will be pointed out in the materials that follow (see, e.g., note 7 after *Shelley v. Kraemer,* Sec. 3 infra)—it has often been argued that the inquiries are misperceived, the questions that the Court has asked are whether the private actor (a) is performing a "government function," or (b) is sufficiently "involved with" or "encouraged by" the state so as to be held to the state's constitutional obligations. These subjects will be developed in the next two sections of this chapter.

Until recent decades, most cases involved racial discrimination (or, occasionally, denial of free speech). But, as will be detailed in Ch. 11, the enactment and strengthening of federal (and state) civil rights statutes since the 1960s has largely mooted the problem of private racial discrimination. Further, with the growth under the Equal Protection Clause of the number of "suspect" and "quasi-suspect" classifications (see Ch. 9, Secs. 3 and 4) and the expansion under the Due Process Clause of the procedural rights that the state must afford persons before depriving them of liberty or property (see Ch. 6, Sec. 5), an increasing number of cases (as will be seen in the final section of this chapter) have involved attempts to require "private" adherence to these constitutional responsibilities.

SECTION 2.   "GOVERNMENT FUNCTION"

SMITH v. ALLWRIGHT, 321 U.S. 649 (1944), held that the Fifteenth Amendment forebade exclusion of African–Americans from primary elections conducted by the Democratic Party of Texas, pursuant to party resolution. The Court, per REED, J., relied heavily on a case from Louisiana, *United States v. Classic,* 313 U.S. 299 (1941), which "makes clear that state delegation to a party of the power to fix the qualifications of primary elections is delegation of a state function that may make

b. On the question of what constitutes a "government" agency, *Lebron v. National R.R. Passenger Corp.,* 513 U.S. 374 (1995), per Scalia, J., held that Amtrak—created by a special federal statute as a corporation "for the furtherance of governmental objectives," with the President having "permanent authority to appoint a majority of the directors"—"is part of the government for purposes of the First Amendment," even though the authorizing statute disclaims this fact. O'Connor, J., dissented.

the party's action the action of the state. [The] right to participate in the choice of elected officials without restriction by any state because of race [is] not to be nullified by a state through casting its electoral process in a form which permits a private organization to practice racial discrimination in the election." Frankfurter, J., concurred in the result. Roberts, J., dissented.

TERRY v. ADAMS, 345 U.S. 461 (1953), involved the exclusion of African–Americans from the "pre-primary" elections of the Jaybird Democratic Association, an organization of all the white voters in a Texas county that was run like a regular political party and whose candidates since 1889 had nearly always run unopposed and won in the regular Democratic primary and the general election. The record showed "complete absence of any compliance with the state law or practice, or cooperation by or with the State." The Court held the election subject to the Fifteenth Amendment.

BLACK, J., joined by Douglas and Burton, JJ., found that "the admitted party purpose" was "to escape the Fifteenth Amendment's command." The "Amendment excludes social or business clubs" but "no election machinery could be sustained if its purpose or effect was to deny Negroes on account of their race an effective voice in the governmental affairs. [The] only election that has counted in this Texas county for more than fifty years has been that held by the Jaybirds. [For] a state to permit such a duplication of its election processes is to permit a flagrant abuse [of] the Fifteenth Amendment."

CLARK, J., joined by Vinson, C.J., and Reed and Jackson, JJ., described the Jaybirds as not merely a "private club" "organized to influence public candidacies or political action," but rather a "part and parcel of the Democratic Party, an organization existing under the auspices of Texas law. [W]hen a state structures its electoral apparatus in a form which devolves upon a political organization the uncontested choice of public officials, that organization itself, in whatever disguise, takes on those attributes of government which draw the Constitution's safeguards into play." Frankfurter, J., also concurred.

MINTON, J., dissented: The Jaybird's activity "seems to differ very little from situations common in many other places [where] a candidate must obtain the approval of a religious group. [E]lections and other public business are influenced by all sorts of pressures from carefully organized groups. [Far] from the activities of these groups being properly labeled as state action, [they] are to be considered as attempts to influence or obtain state action."

MARSH v. ALABAMA, 326 U.S. 501 (1946): A Jehovah's Witness sought "to distribute religious literature on the premises of a company-owned town contrary to the wishes of the town's management." The town, owned by a shipbuilding company, had "all the characteristics of any other American town." Appellant was warned that she could not distribute the literature and when she refused to leave the sidewalk of the town's "business block," a deputy sheriff, who was paid by the company to serve as the town's policeman, arrested her and she was convicted of trespass.

The Court, per BLACK, J., reversed: Under *Lovell v. Griffin,* Ch.7, Sec. 4, I, A, an ordinary municipality could not have barred appellant's activities, and the fact that "a single company had legal title to all the town" may not result in impairing "channels of communication" of its inhabitants or those persons passing through. "Ownership does not always mean absolute dominion. The more an owner, for his advantage, opens up his property for use by the public in general, the more do his rights become circumscribed by the statutory and constitutional rights of those who use it. Thus, the owners of privately held bridges, ferries, turnpikes and railroads may not operate them as freely as a farmer does his farm. Since these facilities are built and operated primarily to benefit the public and since their operation is essentially a public function, it is subject to state regulation." In balancing property rights against freedom of press and religion, "the latter occupy a preferred position" and the former do not "justify the State's permitting a corporation to govern a community of citizens so as to restrict their fundamental liberties and the enforcement of such restraint by the application of a State statute." Frankfurter, J., concurred. Jackson, J., did not participate.a

———

AMALGAMATED FOOD EMPLOYEES UNION v. LOGAN VALLEY PLAZA, 391 U.S. 308 (1968), per MARSHALL, J.—reasoning that a large privately owned shopping center was the "functional equivalent of the business district [in] *Marsh*"— held that it could not enjoin peaceful union picketing on its property against a store located in the shopping center. Black and White, JJ., dissented. Harlan, J., did not reach the merits.

Four years later, LLOYD CORP. v. TANNER, 407 U.S. 551 (1972), per POWELL, J., held that a shopping center's refusal to permit antiwar handbilling on its premises was not state action. *Logan Valley* was distinguished because the picketing there had been specifically directed to a store in the shopping center and the pickets had no other reasonable opportunity to reach their audience. In *Marsh*, "the company town was performing the full spectrum of municipal powers and stood in the shoes of the State. In the instant case there is no comparable assumption or exercise of municipal functions or power." Marshall, J., joined by Douglas, Brennan and Stewart, JJ., dissented, finding "no valid distinction" from *Logan Valley*.

Finally, HUDGENS v. NLRB, 424 U.S. 507 (1976), per STEWART, J.—involving picketing of a store in a shopping center by a union with a grievance against the store's warehouse (located elsewhere)—overruled *Logan Valley* on the ground that "*Lloyd* amounted to [its] total rejection."b MARSHALL, J., joined by Brennan, J., dissented: "*Logan Valley* [recognized] that the owner of the modern shopping center complex, by dedicating his property to public use as a business district, to some extent displaces the 'State' from control of historical First Amendment forums, and may acquire a virtual monopoly of places suitable for effective communication. The roadways, parking lots, and walkways of the modern shopping center may be as essential for effective speech as the streets and sidewalks in the municipal or company-owned town."

———

a. Reed, J., joined by Vinson, C.J., and Burton, J., dissented, noting that "there was [no] objection to appellant's use of the nearby public highway and under our decisions she could rightfully have continued her activities [thirty feet parallel] from the spot she insisted upon using."

b. White, J., concurred in the result, finding that *Logan Valley* "does not cover the facts of this case [which concern] a warehouse not located on the center's premises. The picketing was thus not 'directly related in its purpose to the use to which the shopping center property was being put.'" Stevens, J., did not participate.

EVANS v. NEWTON, 382 U.S. 296 (1966): In 1911, Senator A.O. Bacon devised land to Macon, Ga., to be used as a park for whites only. After *Pennsylvania v. Board of City Trusts,* 353 U.S. 230 (1957)—finding "state action" when public officials act as trustees under a private will requiring racial discrimination—the city permitted African–Americans to use the park. When Bacon's heirs sued to remove the city as trustee, the Georgia courts accepted the city's resignation and appointed private individuals as trustees so that the trust's purpose would not fail.

The Court, per DOUGLAS, J., reversed, reasoning, inter alia, that "the service rendered even by a private park of this character is municipal in nature, [more] like a fire department or police department [than like] golf clubs, social centers, luncheon clubs, schools such as Tuskegee was at least in origin, and other like organizations in the private sector. * * * Mass recreation through the use of parks is plainly in the public domain and state courts that aid private parties to perform that public function on a segregated basis implicate the State in conduct proscribed by the Fourteenth Amendment. Like the streets of the company town in *Marsh,* the elective process of *Terry,* and the transit system of *Pollak,*c the predominant character and purpose of this park are municipal." White, J., concurred on a separate ground.

HARLAN, J., joined by Stewart, J., dissented: The failing of the majority's theory "can be shown by comparing [the] 'public function' of privately established schools with that of privately owned parks.d Like parks, the purpose schools serve is important to the public. Like parks, private control exists, but there is also a very strong tradition of public control in this field. Like parks, schools may be available to almost anyone of one race or religion but to no others. Like parks, there are normally alternatives for those shut out but there may also be inconveniences and disadvantages caused by the restriction. Like parks, the extent of school intimacy varies greatly depending on the size and character of the institution."e

––––––

JACKSON v. METROPOLITAN EDISON CO., 419 U.S. 345 (1974): Respondent, "a heavily regulated private utility" with a state certificate of public convenience to sell electricity, terminated service to petitioner for nonpayment pursuant to a provision of its general tariff that had been filed with the Pennsylvania public Utilities Commission. Petitioner claimed that termination "without adequate notice and a hearing before an impartial body" deprived her of property without due process of law. The Court, per REHNQUIST, J., held "that the termination did not constitute state action": "It may well be that acts of a heavily regulated utility with at least something of a governmentally protected monopoly will more readily be found to be 'state' [acts]. But the inquiry must be whether there is a sufficiently close nexus between the state and the challenged action of

c. In *Public Utilities Com'n v. Pollak,* 343 U.S. 451 (1952), a city transit company subject to public regulation was considered in "sufficiently close relation" with the government as to cause the Court to determine whether the company's playing of radio programs on buses violated the Due Process Clause.

d. For further consideration of "private schools," see note 3 after *Moose Lodge v. Irvis,* Sec. 3 infra.

e. Black, J., "agreed with the position also stated in Harlan, J.'s opinion that 'the writ of certiorari should have been dismissed as improvidently granted.'"

For subsequent litigation in respect to this park, see *Evans v. Abney,* Sec. 3 infra.

the regulated entity so that the action of the latter may be fairly treated as that of the state itself."

Even assuming that the state had granted Metropolitan a monopoly, "this fact is not determinative." As to the contention that respondent performs a "public function," "if we were dealing with the exercise by Metropolitan of some power delegated to it by the State which is traditionally associated with sovereignty, such as eminent domain, our case would be [different]. But while the Pennsylvania statute imposes an obligation to furnish service on regulated utilities," unlike the situation in *Terry, Marsh* and *Evans v. Newton*, "the supplying of utility service is not traditionally the exclusive prerogative of the State." Further, although Metropolitan may have been a regulated business "providing arguably essential goods and services, 'affected with a public interest,' " so too are "doctors, optometrists, lawyers" and many others. "We do not believe that such a status converts their every action, absent more, into that of the State." Finally, *Pollak* was distinguishable because there the government agency had its "imprimatur placed on the practice" complained of. Here, the termination provision "has appeared in Metropolitan's previously filed tariffs for many years and has never been the subject of a hearing or other scrutiny by the commission."

Douglas, J., dissented: Metropolitan "is the only public utility furnishing electric power to the town. When power is denied a householder, the home, under modern conditions, is likely to become unlivable." Further, "Pennsylvania has undertaken to regulate numerous aspects of respondent's operations [and] the State would presumably lend its weight and authority to facilitate the enforcement of respondent's published procedures. Cf. *Reitman*; *Shelley* [infra]. Finally, under Burton, 'it is not enough to examine seriatim each of the factors upon which a claimant relies and to dismiss each individually as being insufficient to support a finding of state action. It is the aggregate that is controlling.' "

Marshall, J., also dissented: "[W]here the State has so thoroughly insinuated itself into the operations of the enterprise, it should not be fatal if the State has not affirmatively sanctioned the particular practice in question." That the termination provision "was not seriously questioned before approval [suggests], that the commission was satisfied to permit the company to proceed in the termination area as it had done in the past." Under the majority's rationale, "authorization and approval would require the kind of hearing that was held in *Pollak*, where the Public Utilities Commission expressly stated that the bus company's installation of radios in buses and streetcars was not inconsistent with the public convenience, safety and necessity. I am afraid that the majority has in effect restricted *Pollak* to its [facts]."

The Court "reads the 'public function' argument too narrowly. [W]hen the activity in question is of such public importance that the State invariably either provides the service itself or permits private companies to act as state surrogates in providing it, much more is involved than just a matter of public interest. In those cases, the State has determined that if private companies wish to enter the field, they will have to surrender many of the prerogatives normally associated with private enterprise and behave in may ways like a governmental body. And when the State's regulatory scheme has gone that far, it seems entirely consistent to impose on the public utility the constitutional burdens normally reserved for the State.

"Private parties performing functions affecting the public interest can often make a persuasive claim to be free of the constitutional requirements applicable to governmental institutions because of the value of preserving a private sector in which the opportunity for individual choice is maximized. Maintaining the private status of parochial schools [advances] just this value. In the due process area, a similar value of diversity' may often be furthered by allowing various private institutions the flexibility to select procedures that fit their particular needs. But [t]he values of pluralism and diversity are simply not relevant when the private company is the only electric company in town.

"[The] Court has not adopted the notion, accepted elsewhere, that different standards should apply to state action analysis when different constitutional claims are presented. Thus, the majority's analysis would seemingly apply as well to a company that refused to extend service to Negroes, welfare recipients, or any other group that the company preferred, for its own reasons, not to serve. I cannot believe that this Court would hold that the State's involvement with the utility company was not sufficient to impose upon the company an obligation to meet the constitutional mandate of nondiscrimination." BRENNAN, J., dissented on procedural grounds.

———

In CBS v. DEMOCRATIC NAT'L COMM., Ch. 7, Sec. 8, I—in which the FCC had ruled that a broadcaster is not required to accept editorial advertisements—some Justices addressed the question of whether the action of the broadcast licensee was "governmental action" for purposes of the First Amendment. BURGER, C.J., joined by Stewart and Rehnquist, JJ., concluded that it was not: "[T]he Commission has not fostered the licensee policy challenged here; it has simply declined to command particular action because it fell within the area of journalistic discretion. [Were] we to read the First Amendment to spell out governmental action in the circumstances presented here, few licensee decisions on the content of broadcasts or the processes of editorial evaluation would escape constitutional scrutiny. In this sensitive area so sweeping a concept of governmental action would go far in practical effect to undermine nearly a half century of unmistakable congressional purpose to maintain—no matter how difficult the task—essentially private broadcast journalism held only broadly accountable to public interest standards."

BRENNAN, J., joined by Marshall, J., disagreed: "[T]he public nature of the airwaves, the governmentally created preferred status of broadcast licensees, the pervasive federal regulation of broadcast programming, and the Commission's specific approval of the challenged broadcaster policy combine in this case to bring the promulgation and enforcement of that policy within the orbit of constitutional imperatives. [Compared to *Pollak*], this case concerns not an incidental activity of a bus company but, rather, the primary activity of the regulated entities—communication.* * *12"a

12. [W]here, as here, the Government has implicated itself in the actions of an otherwise private individual, that individual must exercise his own rights with due regard for the First Amendment rights of others. In other words, an accommodation of competing rights is required, and "balancing" [is] the result. * * * I might also note that [a] finding of governmental involvement in this case does not in any sense command a similar conclusion with respect to newspapers. [The] decision as to who shall operate newspapers is made in the free market, not by Government fiat. The newspaper industry is not extensively regulated * * *.

a. The "government function" issue is considered further in Sec. 4 infra.

SECTION 3.   STATE "INVOLVEMENT" OR "ENCOURAGEMENT"

SHELLEY v. KRAEMER
334 U.S. 1, 68 S.Ct. 836, 92 L.Ed. 1161 (1948).

CHIEF JUSTICE VINSON delivered the opinion of the Court.

[In two cases from Missouri and Michigan, petitioners were African–Americans who had purchased houses from whites despite the fact that the properties were subject to restrictive covenants, signed by most property owners in the block, providing that for a specified time (in one case fifty years from 1911) the property would be sold only to Caucasians. Respondents, owners of other property subject to the covenants, sued to enjoin the buyers from taking possession and to divest them of title. The state courts granted the relief.]

Equality in the enjoyment of property rights was regarded by the framers of [the Fourteenth] Amendment as an essential pre-condition to the realization of other basic civil rights and liberties which the Amendment was intended to guarantee.7 Thus, [42 U.S.C. § 1982] derived from § 1 of the Civil Rights Act of 1866 which was enacted by Congress while the Fourteenth Amendment was also under consideration, provides: "All citizens of the United States shall have the same right, in every State and Territory, as is enjoyed by white citizens thereof to inherit, purchase, lease, sell, hold, and convey real and personal property." * * *

It is likewise clear that restrictions on the right of occupancy of the sort sought to be created by the private agreements in these cases could not be squared with the requirements of the Fourteenth Amendment if imposed by state statute or local ordinance. [But here] the particular patterns of discrimination and the areas in which the restrictions are to operate, are determined, in the first instance, by the terms of agreements among private individuals. Participation of the State consists in the enforcement of the restrictions so defined. * * *

Since [the] *Civil Rights Cases,* the principle has become firmly embedded in our constitutional law that the action inhibited by the first section of the Fourteenth Amendment is only such action as may fairly be said to be that of the States. That Amendment erects no shield against merely private conduct, however discriminatory or wrongful. We conclude, therefore, that the restrictive agreements standing alone cannot be regarded as a violation of any rights guaranteed to petitioners by the Fourteenth Amendment. So long as the purposes of those agreements are effectuated by voluntary adherence to their terms, it would appear clear that there has been no action by the State and the provisions of the Amendment have not been violated.

But here [the] purposes of the agreements were secured only by judicial enforcement by state courts of the restrictive terms of the agreements. [That] the action of state courts and of judicial officers in their official capacities is to be regarded as action of the State within the meaning of the Fourteenth Amendment, is a proposition which has long been established. [In] the *Civil Rights Cases,* this Court pointed out that the Amendment makes void "state action of every kind" which is inconsistent with the guaranties therein contained, and extends to manifestations of "state authority in the shape of laws, customs, or judicial or executive proceedings." * * *

One of the earliest applications of the prohibitions contained in the Fourteenth Amendment to action of state judicial officials occurred in cases in which Negroes had been excluded from jury service. [These] cases demonstrate, also, the early recognition by this Court that state action in violation of the Amendment's

7. *Slaughter–House Cases* [Ch. 5, Sec. 1, III].

provisions is equally repugnant to the constitutional commands whether directed by state statute or taken by a judicial official in the absence of statute. * * *

The action of state courts in imposing penalties or depriving parties of other substantive rights without providing adequate notice and opportunity to defend, has, of course, long been regarded as a denial of the due process of law guaranteed by the Fourteenth Amendment. In numerous cases, this Court has reversed criminal convictions in state courts for failure of those courts to provide the essential ingredients of a fair hearing. Thus it has been held that convictions obtained in state courts under the domination of a mob are void. Convictions obtained by coerced confessions, by the use of perjured testimony known by the prosecution to be such, or without the effective assistance of counsel, have also been held to be exertions of state authority in conflict with the fundamental rights protected by the Fourteenth Amendment.

But the examples of state judicial action which have been held by this Court to violate the Amendment's commands are not restricted to situations in which the judicial proceedings were found in some manner to be procedurally unfair. It has been recognized that the action of state courts in enforcing a substantive common-law rule formulated by those courts, may result in the denial of rights guaranteed by the Fourteenth Amendment. [Thus,] in *AFL v. Swing,* 1941, 312 U.S. 321, enforcement by state courts of the common-law policy of the State, which resulted in the restraining of peaceful picketing, was held to be state action of the sort prohibited by the Amendment's guaranties of freedom of discussion. In *Cantwell v. Connecticut,* 1940, [Ch. 8, Sec. 2, I], a conviction in a state court of the common-law crime of breach of the peace was, under the circumstances of the case, found to be a violation of the Amendment's commands relating to freedom of religion. In *Bridges v. California,* 1941, 314 U.S. 252, enforcement of the state's common-law rule relating to contempts by publication was held to be state action inconsistent with the prohibitions of the Fourteenth Amendment. * * *

We have no doubt that there has been state action in these cases in the full and complete sense of the phrase. The undisputed facts disclose that petitioners were willing purchasers of properties upon which they desired to establish homes. The owners of the properties were willing sellers; and contracts of sale were accordingly consummated. It is clear that but for the active intervention of the state courts, supported by the full panoply of state power, petitioners would have been free to occupy the properties in question without restraint.

These are not cases, as has been suggested, in which the States have merely abstained from action, leaving private individuals free to impose such discriminations as they see fit. Rather, these are cases in which the States have made available to such individuals the full coercive power of government to deny to petitioners, on the grounds of race or color, the enjoyment of property rights in premises which petitioners are willing and financially able to acquire and which the grantors are willing to sell. * * *

The enforcement of the restrictive agreements by the state courts in these cases was directed pursuant to the common-law policy of the States as formulated by those courts in earlier decisions. [The] judicial action in each case bears the clear and unmistakable imprimatur of the State. We have noted that previous decisions of this Court have established the proposition that judicial action is not immunized from the operation of the Fourteenth Amendment simply because it is taken pursuant to the state's common-law policy. Nor is the Amendment ineffective simply because the particular pattern of discrimination, which the State has enforced, was defined initially by the terms of a private agreement. * * * We have noted that freedom from discrimination by the States in the enjoyment of property rights was among the basic objectives sought to be effectuated by the framers of the Fourteenth Amendment. That such discrimination has occurred in these cases is clear. * * *

Respondents urge, however, that since the state courts stand ready to enforce restrictive covenants excluding white persons[,] enforcement of covenants excluding colored persons may not be deemed a denial of equal protection of the laws to the colored persons who are thereby affected. [But the] rights created by the first section of the Fourteenth Amendment are, by its terms, guaranteed to the individual. The rights established are personal rights. It is, therefore, no answer to these petitioners to say that the courts may also be induced to deny white persons rights of ownership and occupancy on grounds of race or color. Equal protection of the laws is not achieved through indiscriminate imposition of inequalities. * * *

Reversed.a

JUSTICE REED, JUSTICE JACKSON, and JUSTICE RUTLEDGE took no part in the consideration or decision of these cases.

On remand, after *Evans v. Newton,* the Georgia courts interpreted Senator Bacon's will and held that "because the park's segregated, whites-only character was an essential and inseparable part of the testator's plan," the "cy pres doctrine to amend the terms of the will by striking the racial restrictions" was inapplicable; that, therefore, the trust failed and the trust property "by operation of law reverted to the heirs of Senator Bacon." EVANS v. ABNEY, 396 U.S. 435 (1970), per BLACK, J., affirmed, finding that "the Georgia court had no alternative under its relevant trust laws, which are long standing and neutral with regard to race, but to end the Baconsfield trust": "[T]he Constitution imposes no requirement upon the Georgia court to approach Bacon's will any differently than it would approach any will creating any charitable trust of any kind. [T]here is not the slightest indication that any of the Georgia judges involved were motivated by racial animus or discriminatory intent of any sort in construing and enforcing Senator Bacon's will. Nor is there any indication that Senator Bacon in drawing up his will was persuaded or induced to include racial restrictions by the fact that such restrictions were permitted by the Georgia trust statutes." *Shelley* was "easily distinguishable" because here "the termination of the park was a loss shared equally by the white and Negro citizens of Macon."

BRENNAN, J., dissented: "For almost half a century Baconsfield has been a public park. [When] a public facility would remain open but for the constitutional command that it be operated on a nonsegregated basis, the closing of that facility conveys an unambiguous message of community involvement in racial discrimination": "First, there is state action whenever a State enters into an arrangement which creates a private right to compel or enforce the reversion of a public facility" and, here, "in accepting title to the park," city officials agreed to that "if the city should ever incur a constitutional obligation to desegregate the park." Second, "nothing in the record suggests that after our decision in *Evans v. Newton* the City of Macon retracted its previous willingness to manage Baconsfield on a nonsegregated basis, or that the white beneficiaries of Senator Bacon's generosity were unwilling to share it with Negroes, rather than have the park revert to his heirs." Thus, contrary to *Shelley,* "this is a case of a state court's

---

a. See also *Barrows v. Jackson*, 346 U.S. 249 (1953) (action by a co-covenantor to recover damages from a property owner who sold to an African–American barred by equal protection).

enforcement of a racial restriction to prevent willing parties from dealing with one another." Douglas, J., also dissented. Marshall, J., did not participate.

REITMAN v. MULKEY, 387 U.S. 369 (1967), per WHITE, J., held violative of equal protection an amendment to the California constitution [§ 26] that prohibited any state law restricting the right of homeowners to sell (or not to sell) their residential property to any persons they wish: "[§ 26's] immediate design and intent, the California court said, was 'to overturn state laws that bore on the right of private sellers and lessors to discriminate,' [and] 'to forestall future state action that might circumscribe this right.' [T]he state court [reasoned] that a prohibited state involvement could be found 'even where the state can be charged with only encouraging,' rather than commanding discrimination. [To] the California court '[t]he instant case [was one]' wherein the State had taken affirmative action designed to make private discriminations legally possible. Section 26 was said to have changed the situation from one in which discriminatory practices were restricted 'to one wherein it is encouraged, within the meaning of the cited decisions'; § 26 was legislative action 'which authorized private discrimination' and made the State 'at least a partner in the instant act of discrimination * * *.' The court could 'conceive of no other purpose for an application of section 26 aside from authorizing the perpetration of a purported private discrimination * * *.' * * *

"The California court could very reasonably conclude that § 26 would and did have wider impact than a mere repeal of existing statutes. [The] right to discriminate, including the right to discriminate on racial grounds, was now embodied in the State's basic charter, immune from legislative, executive, or judicial regulation at any level of the state government."

HARLAN, J., joined by Black, Clark and Stewart, JJ., dissented: "[A]ll that has happened is that California has effected a pro tanto repeal of its prior statutes forbidding private discrimination. This runs no more afoul of the Fourteenth Amendment than would have California's failure to pass any such antidiscrimination statutes in the first instance. [A] state enactment, particularly one that is simply permissive of private decision-making rather than coercive[,] should not be struck down [without] persuasive evidence of an invidious purpose or effect. [§ 26 is] a neutral provision restoring to the sphere of free choice, left untouched by the Fourteenth Amendment, private behavior within a limited area of the racial problem."[a]

MOOSE LODGE v. IRVIS
407 U.S. 163, 92 S.Ct. 1965, 32 L.Ed.2d 627 (1972).

JUSTICE REHNQUIST delivered the opinion of the Court.

Appellee Irvis, a Negro, [who] was refused service [as the guest of a member] by appellant Moose Lodge, [claimed] that because the Pennsylvania liquor board had issued appellant Moose Lodge a private club license that authorized the sale of alcoholic beverages on its premises, the refusal of service to him was "state action." * * *

a. In the early 1960s, the Court—employing a variety of doctrines, but never relying on *Shelley*—reversed a long series of trespass convictions of "sit-in" demonstrators who were protesting racial discrimination by restaurants and other businesses. The Civil Rights Act of 1964 (Ch. 2, Sec. 2, III) largely mooted the constitutional problem of equal rights in public accommodations.

While the principle is easily stated, the question of whether particular discriminatory conduct is private, on the one hand, or amounts to "state action," on the other hand, frequently admits of no easy answer. "Only by sifting facts and weighing circumstances can the non-obvious involvement of the State in private conduct be attributed its true significance." *Burton v. Wilmington Parking Authority*, 365 U.S. 715 (1961).

[*Burton* held] that a private restaurant owner who refused service because of a customer's race violated the Fourteenth Amendment, where the restaurant was located in a building owned by a state-created parking authority and leased from the authority. The Court, after a comprehensive review of the relationship between the lessee and the parking authority concluded that the latter had "so far insinuated itself into a position of interdependence with Eagle [the restaurant owner] that it must be recognized as a joint participant in the challenged activity, which, on that account, cannot be considered to have been so 'purely private' as to fall without the scope of the Fourteenth Amendment." * * *

In *Burton*, the Court's full discussion of the facts in its opinion indicates the significant differences between that case and this: "The land and building were publicly owned. As an entity, the building was dedicated to 'public uses' in performance of the Authority's 'essential governmental functions.' The costs of land acquisition, construction, and maintenance are defrayed entirely from donations by the City of Wilmington, from loans and revenue bonds and from the proceeds of rentals and parking services out of which the loans and bonds were payable. Assuming that the distinction would be significant, the commercially leased areas were not surplus state property, but constituted a physically and financially integral and, indeed, indispensable part of the State's plan to operate its project as a self-sustaining unit.a Upkeep and maintenance of the building, including necessary repairs, were responsibilities of the Authority and were payable out of public funds. It cannot be doubted that the peculiar relationship of the restaurant to the parking facility in which it is located confers on each an incidental variety of mutual benefits. Guests of the restaurant are afforded a convenient place to park their automobiles, even if they cannot enter the restaurant directly from the parking area. Similarly, its convenience for diners may well provide additional demand for the Authority's parking facilities. Should any improvements effected in the leasehold by Eagle become part of the realty, there is no possibility of increased taxes being passed on to it since the fee is held by a tax-exempt government agency. Neither can it be ignored, especially in view of Eagle's affirmative allegation that for it to serve Negroes would injure its business, that profits earned by discrimination not only contribute to, but also are indispensable elements in, the financial success of a governmental agency."b

a. "Other portions of the structure were leased to other tenants, including a bookstore, a retail jeweler, and a food store. Upon completion of the building, the Authority located at appropriate places thereon official signs indicating the public character of the building, and flew from mastheads on the roof both the state and national flags." *Burton*.

b. *Burton* added: "It is irony amounting to grave injustice that in one part of a single building, erected and maintained with public funds by an agency of the State to serve a public purpose, all persons have equal rights, while in another portion, also serving the public, a Negro is a second-class citizen [but] at the same time fully enjoys equal access to nearby restaurants in wholly privately owned

buildings. [I]n its lease with Eagle the Authority could have affirmatively required Eagle to discharge the responsibilities under the Fourteenth Amendment imposed upon the private enterprise as a consequence of state participation. But no State may effectively abdicate its responsibilities by either ignoring them or by merely failing to discharge them whatever the motive may be."

Harlan, J., joined by Whittaker, J., dissented: "The Court's opinion, by a process of first undiscriminatingly throwing together various factual bits and pieces and then undermining the resulting structure by an equally vague disclaimer, seems to me to leave completely at sea just what it is in this record that satisfies the requirement of 'state action.'"

Here there is nothing approaching the symbiotic relationship between lessor and lessee that was present in [*Burton*]. Moose Lodge quite ostentatiously proclaims the fact that it is not open to the public at large. Nor is it located and operated in such surroundings that although private in name, it discharges a function or performs a service that would otherwise in all likelihood be performed by the State. In short, while Eagle was a public restaurant in a public building, Moose Lodge is a private social club in a private building. * * *

JUSTICE DOUGLAS, with whom JUSTICE MARSHALL joins, dissenting.

My view of the First Amendment and the related guarantees of the Bill of Rights is that they create a zone of privacy which precludes government from interfering with private clubs or groups. [And] the fact that a private club gets some kind of permit from the State or municipality does not make it ipso facto a public enterprise or undertaking, any more than the grant to a householder of a permit to operate an incinerator puts the householder in the public domain. [But in this case, there] is a complex quota system, [for liquor licenses which makes it difficult for a] group desiring to form a nondiscriminatory club. [Thus,] the State of Pennsylvania is putting the weight of its liquor license, concededly a valued and important adjunct to a private club, behind racial discrimination. * * *

JUSTICE BRENNAN, with whom JUSTICE MARSHALL joins, dissenting.

When Moose Lodge obtained its liquor license, the State of Pennsylvania became an active participant in the operation of the Lodge bar. Liquor licensing laws [are] primarily pervasive regulatory schemes under which the State dictates and continually supervises virtually every detail of the operation of the licensee's business. * * *

NORWOOD v. HARRISON, 413 U.S. 455 (1973), per BURGER, C.J., enjoined Mississippi's lending of textbooks to all students in public and private schools as applied to racially segregated private schools: "[T]hat the Constitution may compel toleration of private discrimination in some circumstances does not mean that it requires state support for such discrimination." * * * Textbooks are a basic educational tool and, like tuition grants, they are provided only in connection with schools; they are to be distinguished from generalized services government might provide to schools in common with others. Moreover, the textbooks provided to private school students by the State in this case are a form of assistance readily available from sources entirely independent of the State— unlike, for example, "such necessities of life as electricity, water, and police and fire protection." "Douglas and Brennan, JJ., concurred in the result."

In GILMORE v. MONTGOMERY, 417 U.S. 556 (1974), a federal court enjoined the city's "permitting the use of public park recreational facilities by private segregated school groups and by other non-school groups that racially discriminate in their membership." The Court, per BLACKMUN, J., modified the decree in part: It "was wholly proper for the city to be enjoined from permitting *exclusive* access to public recreational facilities by segregated private schools" (emphasis added), which had been "formed in reaction against" the federal court's school desegregation order. "[T]his assistance significantly tended to undermine the federal court order mandating [a] unitary school system in Montgomery." But, "upon this record, we are unable to draw a conclusion as to whether the use of zoos, museums, parks, and other recreational facilities by private school groups *in common with others,* and by private nonschool organizations, involves government so directly in the actions of those users as to warrant" intervention (emphasis added).

"It is possible that certain uses of city facilities will be judged to be in contravention of the parks [or school] desegregation order, [or] in some way to constitute impermissible 'state action' ascribing to the city the discriminatory actions of the groups." This concerns "whether there is significant state involvement in the private discrimination alleged. * * * Traditional state monopolies, such as electricity, water, and police and fire protection—all generalized governmental services—do not by their mere provision constitute a showing of state involvement in invidious discrimination. *Norwood.* The same is true of a broad spectrum of municipal recreational [facilities].

"If, however, the city or other governmental entity rations otherwise freely accessible recreational facilities, the case for state action will naturally be stronger than if the facilities are simply available to all comers without condition or reservation. Here, for example, petitioners allege that the city engages in scheduling softball games for an all-white church league and provides balls, equipment, fields, and lighting. The city's role in that situation would be dangerously close to what was found to exist in *Burton* * * *."a

WHITE, J., joined by Douglas, J., concurred: "[T]he question is not whether there is state action, but whether the conceded action by the city [must] be deemed to have denied the equal protection of the laws. In other words, by permitting a segregated school or group to use city-owned facilities, has the State furnished such aid to the group's segregated policies or become so involved in them that the State itself may fairly be said to have denied equal protection? Under *Burton,* it is perfectly clear that to violate the Equal Protection Clause the State itself need not make, advise, or authorize the private decision to discriminate that involves the State in the practice of segregation or would appear to do so in the minds of ordinary citizens." Marshall, J. generally agreed with White, J.

SECTION 4.   DEVELOPMENTS IN THE LAST THREE DECADES

RENDELL–BAKER v. KOHN

457 U.S. 830, 102 S.Ct. 2764, 73 L.Ed.2d 418 (1982).

CHIEF JUSTICE BURGER delivered the opinion of the Court.

[New Perspectives is a private school that] specializes in dealing with students who have experienced difficulty completing public high [schools]. In recent years, nearly all of the students at the school have been referred to it by the Brookline or Boston school committees, or by the Drug Rehabilitation Division of the Massachusetts Department of Mental Health. [In] recent years, public funds have accounted for at least 90%, and in one year 99%, of respondent's operating budget. [T]he school must comply with a variety [of] detailed regulations concerning matters ranging from recordkeeping to student-teacher ratios. [T]he regulations require the school to [maintain] personnel standards and procedures, but they impose few specific requirements.

---

a. Brennan, J., concurred in part but would enjoin *any* "school-sponsored or directed uses of the city recreational facilities that enable private segregated schools to duplicate public school operations at public expense."

[Petitioners were teachers and a vocational counselor discharged by the school for, inter alia, supporting student criticisms against various school policies. They sued under 42 U.S.C. § 1983. The] core issue presented [is] not whether petitioners were discharged because of their speech or without adequate procedural protections, but whether the school's action in discharging them can fairly be seen as state action. * * *

In *Blum v. Yaretsky,* 457 U.S. 991 (1982), [t]he Court considered whether certain nursing homes were state actors for the purpose of determining whether decisions regarding transfers of patients could [be] subjected to Fourteenth Amendment due process requirements. [Like] the New Perspectives School, the nursing homes were privately owned and operated. [T]he Court held that, "[A] State normally can be held responsible for a private decision only when it has exercised coercive power or has provided such significant encouragement, either overt or covert, that the choice must in law be deemed to be that of the State." In determining that the transfer decisions were not actions of the state, the Court considered each of the factors alleged by petitioners [here].

First, [the] State subsidized the operating and capital costs of the nursing homes, and paid the medical expenses of more than 90% of the patients. * * *

The school, like the nursing homes, is not fundamentally different from many private corporations whose business depends primarily on contracts to build roads, bridges, dams, ships, or submarines for the government. Acts of such private contractors do not become acts of the government by reason of their significant or even total engagement in performing public contracts. * * *

A second factor considered in *Blum* was the extensive regulation of the nursing homes by the State. There the State was indirectly involved in the transfer decisions challenged in that case because a primary goal of the State in regulating nursing homes was to keep costs down by transferring patients from intensive treatment centers to less expensive facilities when possible.a [The] nursing homes were extensively regulated in many other ways as well. The Court relied on *Jackson,* where we held that state regulation, even if "extensive and detailed," did not make a utility's actions state action. Here the decisions to discharge the petitioners were not compelled or even influenced by any state regulation. * * *

The third factor asserted to show that the school is a state actor is that it performs a "public function." However, our holdings have made clear that the relevant question [is] whether the function performed has been "traditionally the *exclusive* prerogative of the State." [U]ntil recently the State had not undertaken to provide education for students who could not be served by traditional public schools. That a private entity performs a function which serves the public does not make its acts state action.7

a. Brennan, J., joined by Marshall, J., dissented in *Blum:* "[Not] only has the State established the system of treatment levels and utilization review in order to further its own fiscal goals, [but] the State prescribes with as much precision as is possible the standards by which individual determinations are to be made. [The] Court thus fails to perceive the decisive involvement of the State in the private conduct challenged by the respondents."

7. There is no evidence that the State has attempted to avoid its constitutional duties by a sham arrangement which attempts to disguise provision of public services as acts of private parties. Cf. *Evans v. Newton.*

[Compare Brennan, J., joined by Marshall, J., dissenting in *Blum:* "For many, the totality of their social network is the nursing home community. Within that environment, the nursing home operator is the immediate authority, the provider of food, clothing, shelter, and health care, and, in every significant respect, the functional equivalent of a State. Cf. *Marsh.*"]

Fourth, petitioners argue that there is a "symbiotic relationship" [as] in *Burton.* Such a claim was rejected in *Blum,* and we reject it here. In *Burton,* [i]n response to the argument that the restaurant's profits, and hence the State's financial position, would suffer if it did not discriminate, the Court concluded that this showed that the State profited from the restaurant's discriminatory conduct. [Here] the school's fiscal relationship with the State is not different from that of many contractors performing services for the government. * * *

Affirmed.**b**

JUSTICE MARSHALL, with whom JUSTICE BRENNAN joins, dissenting.

[I]t is difficult to imagine a closer relationship between a government and a private enterprise. [The] school's very survival depends on the State. If the State chooses, it may exercise complete control over the school's operations simply by threatening to withdraw financial support if the school takes action that it considers objectionable. [Almost] every decision the school makes is substantially affected in some way by the State's regulations.**1**

[Under state law], the State is *required* to provide a free education to all children, including those with special needs. [The] State should not be permitted to avoid constitutional requirements simply by delegating its statutory duty to a private entity. * * *

The majority repeatedly compares the school to a private contractor. [Although] shipbuilders and dambuilders, like the school, may be dependent on government funds, they are not so closely supervised by the government. And unlike most private contractors, the school is performing a statutory duty of the State. * * *

In SAN FRANCISCO ARTS & ATHLETICS, INC. v. UNITED STATES OLYMPIC COMM., 483 U.S. 522 (1987), USOC, to which Congress granted the right to prohibit certain uses of the word "Olympic," enjoined petitioner from calling its athletic competitions the "Gay Olympic Games." Petitioner claimed that USOC's enforcement violated equal protection. The Court, per POWELL, J.— relying mainly on *Rendell–Baker, Blum* and *Jackson*—held that USOC is not a "governmental actor."

BRENNAN, J., joined by Marshall, J.—and "largely" by O'Connor and Blackmun, JJ.—dissented on the basis of "a symbiotic relationship sufficient to provide a nexus between the USOC's challenged action and the Government": "The Act gave the USOC authority and responsibilities that no private organization in this country had ever held. The Act also [authorized USOC] to seek up to $16 million annually in grants from the Secretary of Commerce, and afford[ed] it unprecedented power to control the use of the word 'Olympic' and related emblems to raise additional funds. As a result of the Act, the United States obtained, for the first time in its history, an exclusive and effective organization to coordinate and administer all amateur athletics related to international competition* * *.

"Second, in the eye of the public, both national and international, the connection between the decisions of the United States Government and those of

---

b. White, J., concurred in the judgment (and in *Blum*): "For me, the critical factor is the absence of any allegation that the employment decision was itself based upon some rule of conduct or policy put forth by the State."

1. [By] analyzing the various indicia of state action separately, without considering their cumulative impact, the majority commits a fundamental error.

the United States Olympic Committee is profound. The President of the United States has served as the Honorary President of the USOC. The national flag flies both literally and figuratively over the central product of the USOC, the United States Olympic Team.a [While] in *Burton* the restaurant was able to pursue a policy of discrimination because the State had failed to impose upon it a policy of non-discrimination, the USOC could pursue its alleged policy of selective enforcement only because Congress *affirmatively* granted it power that it would not otherwise have to control the use of the word 'Olympic.' "b

FLAGG BROS., INC. v. BROOKS

436 U.S. 149, 98 S.Ct. 1729, 56 L.Ed.2d 185 (1978).

JUSTICE REHNQUIST delivered the opinion of the Court.

The question presented [is] whether a warehouseman's proposed sale of goods entrusted to him for storage, as permitted by New York Uniform Commercial Code § 7–210, is an action properly attributable to the State * * *.

[R]espondent Shirley Brooks and her family were evicted from their apartment in Mount Vernon, N.Y., on June 13, 1973. The city marshal arranged for Brooks' possessions to be stored by petitioner Flagg Brothers, Inc., in its warehouse. Brooks was informed of the cost of moving and storage, and she instructed the workmen to proceed, although she found the price too high. On August 25, 1973, after a series of disputes over the validity of the charges being claimed by petitioner Flagg Brothers, Brooks received a letter demanding that her account be brought up to date within 10 days "or your furniture will be sold." A series of subsequent letters from respondent and her attorneys produced no satisfaction.

Brooks thereupon initiated this class action in the District Court under 42 U.S.C. § 1983, seeking damages, an injunction against the threatened sale [and] the declaration that such a sale pursuant to § 7–210 would violate [due process].

It must be noted that respondents have named no public officials as defendants in this action. The city marshal, who supervised their evictions, was dismissed from the case by the consent of all the parties. This total absence of overt official involvement plainly distinguishes this case from earlier decisions imposing procedural restrictions on creditors' remedies such as *North Georgia Finishing, Inc. v. Di–Chem, Inc.*, 419 U.S. 601 (1975); *Fuentes v. Shevin*, 407 U.S. 67 (1972); *Sniadach v. Family Finance Corp.*, 395 U.S. 337 (1969).c [While] any

a. The Court responded that "all sorts of private organizations send 'national representatives' to participate in world competitions. Although many are of interest only to a select group, others, like the Davis Cup Competition, the America's Cup, and the Miss Universe Pageant, are widely viewed as involving representation of our country. The organizations that sponsor United States participation in these events all perform 'national representational,' as well as 'administrative [and] adjudicative role[s],' in selecting and presenting the national representatives."

b. The Court responded that petitioner "has failed to demonstrate that the Federal Government can or does exert any influence over the exercise of the USOC's enforcement decisions. Absent proof of this type of 'close nexus between the [Government] and the challenged action of the [USOC],' the challenged

action may not be 'fairly treated as that of the [Government] itself.' *Jackson*."

c. *Sniadach* held that a statute—authorizing a creditor to get a summons from a court clerk and thereby obtain prejudgment garnishment of a debtor's wages—violated due process because the statute did not provide debtor with prior notice and opportunity for a hearing.

Fuentes held that a statute—authorizing a seller of goods under a conditional sales contract to get a writ from a court clerk and thereby obtain prejudgment repossession with the sheriff's help—violated due process because the statute did not provide the buyer with prior notice and opportunity for a hearing.

North Georgia Finishing held violative of due process a statute authorizing a creditor to obtain prejudgment garnishment of a debtor's assets by filing an affidavit with a court clerk

person with sufficient physical power may deprive a person of his property, only a State or a private person whose action "may be fairly treated as that of the State itself," *Jackson,* may deprive him of "an interest encompassed within the Fourteenth Amendment's protection," *Fuentes* * * *.

Respondents' primary contention is that New York has delegated to Flagg Brothers a power "traditionally exclusively reserved to the State." *Jackson.* They argue that the resolution of private disputes is a traditional function of civil government, and that the State in § 7–210 has delegated this function to Flagg Brothers. Respondents, however, have read too much into the language of our previous cases. While many functions have been traditionally performed by governments, very few have been "exclusively reserved to the State."

One such area has been elections. [*Terry v. Adams; Smith v. Allwright.* A second] originated with *Marsh.* Just as the Texas Democratic Party in *Smith* and the Jaybird Democratic Association in *Terry* effectively performed the entire public function of selecting public officials, so too the Gulf Shipbuilding Corp. performed all the necessary municipal functions in the town of Chickasaw * * *.

These two branches of the public-function doctrine have in common the feature of exclusivity.[8] Although the elections held by the Democratic Party and its affiliates were the only meaningful elections in Texas, and the streets owned by the Gulf Shipbuilding Corp. were the only streets in Chickasaw, the proposed sale by Flagg Brothers under § 7–210 is not the only means of resolving this purely private dispute. Respondent Brooks has never alleged that state law barred her from seeking a waiver of Flagg Brothers' right to sell her goods at the time she authorized their storage. Presumably, [a person] who alleges that she never authorized the storage of her goods, could have sought to replevy her goods at any time under state law. The challenged statute itself provides a damages remedy against the warehouseman for violations of its provisions. This system of rights and remedies, recognizing the traditional place of private arrangements in ordering relationships in the commercial world,[9] can hardly be said to have delegated to

stating reasons to fear that the property would otherwise be lost. The Court distinguished *Mitchell v. W.T. Grant Co.,* 416 U.S. 600, which had upheld a statute that, without requiring prior notice to a buyer-debtor, permitted a seller-creditor holding a vendor's lien to secure a writ of sequestration and, having filed a bond, to cause the sheriff to take possession of the property at issue. *North Georgia Finishing* emphasized that under the sequestration statute in *Mitchell,* unlike the garnishment statute at bar, the writ "was issuable only by a judge upon the filing of an affidavit going beyond mere conclusory allegations and clearly setting out the facts entitling the creditor to sequestration" and that the *Mitchell* statute "expressly entitled the debtor to an immediate hearing after seizure and to dissolution of the writ absent proof by the creditor of the grounds on which the writ was issued."

Subsequently, *Connecticut v. Doehr,* 501 U.S. 1 (1991), held that a state statute authorizing prejudgment attachment of real estate upon plaintiff's ex parte showing that there is probable cause to sustain the validity of his or her claim—without a showing of extraordinary circumstances, and without a requirement that the person seeking the attachment post a bond—violated due process. Petitioner sought

an attachment on respondent's home in conjunction with a civil action for assault and battery that he was seeking to institute against respondent in the same court. On the strength of statements in petitioner's affidavit, the court ordered the attachment. Only after the sheriff attached his property did respondent receive notice, which informed him of his right to a postattachment hearing. Instead, respondent filed a federal action, successfully arguing that the state statute violated due process.

8. Respondents also contend that *Evans v. Newton* establishes that the operation of a park for recreational purposes is an exclusively public function. We doubt that *Newton* intended to establish any such broad doctrine in the teeth of the experience of several American entrepreneurs who amassed great fortunes by operating parks for recreational purposes. We think *Newton* rests on a finding of ordinary state action under extraordinary circumstances. The Court's opinion emphasizes that the record showed "no change in the municipal maintenance and concern over this facility" after the transfer of title to private trustees. * * *

9. Unlike the parade of horribles suggested by our Brother Stevens in dissent, this case does not involve state authorization of private breach of the peace.

Flagg Brothers an exclusive prerogative of the sovereign.10

Whatever the particular remedies available under New York law, we do not consider a more detailed description of them necessary to our conclusion that the settlement of disputes between debtors and creditors is not traditionally an exclusive public function.11 Creditors and debtors have had available to them historically a far wider number of choices than has one who would be an elected public official, or a member of Jehovah's Witnesses who wished to distribute literature in Chickasaw, Ala. * * * This is true whether these commercial rights and remedies are created by statute or decisional law. To rely upon the historical antecedents of a particular practice would result in the constitutional condemnation in one State of a remedy found perfectly permissible in another.

[T]here are a number of state and municipal functions not covered by our election cases or governed by the reasoning of *Marsh* which have been administered with a greater degree of exclusivity by States and municipalities than has the function of so-called "dispute resolution." Among these are such functions as education, fire and police protection, and tax collection. We express no view as to the extent, if any, to which a city or State might be free to delegate to private parties the performance of such functions and thereby avoid the strictures of the Fourteenth Amendment. * * *

Respondents further urge that Flagg Brothers' proposed action is properly attributable to the State because the State has authorized and encouraged it in enacting § 7–210. Our cases state "that a State is responsible for [the] act of a private party when the State, by its law, has compelled the act." This Court, however, has never held that a State's mere acquiescence in a private action converts that action into that of the State. * * *

10. [It] would intolerably broaden [the] notion of state action [to] hold that the mere existence of a body of property law in a State, whether decisional or statutory, itself amounted to "state action" even though no state process or state officials were ever involved in enforcing that body of law.

This situation is clearly distinguishable from cases such as *North Georgia Finishing; Fuentes;* and *Sniadach.* In each of those cases a government official participated in the physical deprivation of what had concededly been the constitutional plaintiff's property under state law before the deprivation occurred. The constitutional protection attaches not because, as in *North Georgia Finishing,* a clerk issued a ministerial writ out of the court, but because as a result of that writ the property of the debtor was seized and impounded by the affirmative command of the law of Georgia. The creditor in *North Georgia Finishing* had not simply sought to pursue the collection of his debt by private means permissible under Georgia law; he had invoked the authority of the Georgia court, which in turn had ordered the garnishee not to pay over money which previously had been the property of the debtor. See *Shelley v. Kraemer.* * * *

11. It may well be, as my Brother Stevens' dissent contends, that "[t]he power to order legally binding surrenders of property and the constitutional restrictions on that power are

necessary correlatives in our system." But here New York, unlike Florida in *Fuentes,* Georgia in *North Georgia Finishing,* and Wisconsin in *Sniadach,* has not ordered respondents to surrender any property whatever. It has merely enacted a statute which provides that a warehouseman conforming to the provisions of the statute may convert his traditional lien into good title. There is no reason whatever to believe that either Flagg Brothers or respondents could not, if they wished, seek resort to the New York courts in order to either compel or prevent the "surrenders of property" to which that dissent refers, and that the compliance of Flagg Brothers with applicable New York property law would be reviewed after customary notice and hearing in such a proceeding.

The fact that such a judicial review of a self-help remedy is seldom encountered bears witness to the important part that such remedies have played in our system of property rights. This is particularly true of the warehouseman's lien, which [is] burdened by procedural constraints and provides for a compensatory remedy and judicial relief against abuse, [and] is not atypical of creditors' liens historically, whether created by statute or legislatively enacted. The conduct of private actors in relying on the rights established under these liens to resort to self-help remedies does not permit their conduct to be ascribed to the State.

It is quite immaterial that the State has embodied its decision not to act in statutory form. If New York had no commercial statutes at all, its courts would still be faced with the decision whether to prohibit or to permit the sort of sale threatened here the first time an aggrieved bailor came before them for relief. [If] the mere denial of judicial relief is considered sufficient encouragement to make the State responsible for those private acts, all private deprivations of property would be converted into public acts whenever the State, for whatever reason, denies relief sought by the putative property owner. * * *

Here, the State of New York has not compelled the sale of a bailor's goods, but has merely announced the circumstances under which its courts will not interfere with a private sale. Indeed, the crux of respondents' complaint is not that the State *has* acted, but that it has *refused* to act. This statutory refusal to act is no different in principle from an ordinary statute of limitations whereby the State declines to provide a remedy for private deprivations of property after the passage of a given period of time. * * *

Reversed.

JUSTICE STEVENS, with whom JUSTICE WHITE and JUSTICE MARSHALL join, dissenting.

[Under the Court's] approach a State could enact laws authorizing private citizens to use self-help in countless situations without any possibility of federal challenge. [It] could authorize the warehouseman to retain all proceeds of the lien sale, even if they far exceeded the amount of the alleged debt; it could authorize finance companies to enter private homes to repossess merchandise; or indeed, it could authorize "any person with sufficient physical power" to acquire and sell the property of his weaker neighbor. [The] Court's rationale would characterize action pursuant to such a statute as purely private action, which the State permits but does not compel, in an area not exclusively reserved to the State.

As these examples suggest, [t]here is no great chasm between "permission" and "compulsion" requiring particular state action to fall within one or the other definitional camp. [In] this case, the State of New York, by enacting § 7–210 of the Uniform Commercial Code, has acted in the most effective and unambiguous way a State can act. This section specifically authorizes petitioner Flagg Brothers to sell respondents' possessions; it details the procedures that petitioner must follow; and it grants petitioner the power to convey good title to goods that are now owned by respondents to a third party.

[Petitioners] argue that the nonconsensual transfer of property rights is not a traditional function of the sovereign. The overwhelming historical evidence is to the contrary, however, and the Court wisely does not adopt this position. Instead, the Court reasons that state action cannot be found because the State has not delegated to the warehouseman an *exclusive* sovereign function.[8] This distinction [is] inconsistent with the line of cases beginning with *Sniadach* [which have] scrutinized various state statutes regulating the debtor-creditor relationship for

---

8. [Even] if I were to accept the notion that sovereign functions must be "exclusive," the Court's description of exclusivity is incomprehensible. The question is whether a particular action is a uniquely sovereign function, not whether state law forecloses any possibility of recovering for damages for such activity. For instance, it is clear that the maintenance of a police force is a unique sovereign function, and the delegation of police power to a private party will entail state action. Under the Court's analysis, however, there would be no state action if the State provided a remedy, such as an action for wrongful imprisonment, for the individual injured by the "private" policeman. [Of] course, the availability of other state remedies may be relevant in determining whether the statute provides sufficient procedural protections under the Due Process Clause, but it is not relevant to the state-action issue.

compliance with the Due Process Clause. [The] Court today seeks to explain these [on] the ground that in each case there was some element of "overt official involvement." [But] until today, this Court had never held that purely ministerial acts of "minor governmental functionaries" were sufficient to establish state action. [The] number of private actions in which a governmental functionary plays some ministerial role is legion;[12] to base due process review on the fortuity of such governmental intervention would demean the majestic purposes of the Due Process Clause.

Instead, cases such as *North Georgia Finishing* must be viewed as reflecting this Court's recognition of the significance of the State's role in defining *and controlling* the debtor-creditor relationship. [In *Fuentes*, the] statutes placed the state power to repossess property in the hands of an interested private party, just as the state statute in this case places the state power to conduct judicially binding sales in satisfaction of a lien in the hands of the warehouseman. "Private parties, serving their own private advantage, may unilaterally invoke state power to replevy goods from another. No state official participates in the decision to seek a writ; no state official reviews the basis for the claim to repossession; and no state official evaluates the need for immediate seizure. There is not even a requirement that the plaintiff provide any information to the court on these matters." Ibid. [Yet] the very defect that made the statutes in *Fuentes* and *North Georgia Finishing* unconstitutional—lack of state control—is, under today's decision, the factor that precludes constitutional review of the state statute. The Due Process Clause cannot command such incongruous results. If it is unconstitutional for a State to allow a private party to exercise a traditional state power because the state supervision of that power is purely mechanical, the State surely cannot immunize its actions from constitutional *scrutiny* by removing even the mechanical supervision. * * *

It is important to emphasize that, contrary to the Court's apparent fears, this conclusion does not even remotely suggest that "all private deprivations of property [will] be converted into public acts whenever the State, for whatever reason, denies relief sought by the putative property owner." The focus is not on the private deprivation but on the state authorization. [The] State's conduct in this case takes the concrete form of a statutory enactment, and it is that statute that may be challenged. * * *

Finally, it is obviously true that the overwhelming majority of disputes in our society are resolved in the private sphere. But it is no longer possible, if it ever was, to believe that a sharp line can be drawn between private and public actions. [In] the broadest sense, we expect government "to provide a reasonable and fair framework of rules which facilitate commercial transactions." This "framework of rules" is premised on the assumption that the State will control nonconsensual deprivations of property and that the State's control will, in turn, be subject to the restrictions of the Due Process Clause. * * *d

---

LUGAR v. EDMONDSON OIL CO., 457 U.S. 922 (1982), per WHITE, J.,— involving a statute that authorized a creditor to file a petition with a court clerk and thus obtain a prejudgment attachment of a debtor's property which was

---

12. For instance, state officials often perform ministerial acts in the transferring of ownership in motor vehicles or real estate. It is difficult to believe that the Court would hold that all car sales are invested with state action.

d. The separate dissent of Marshall, J., is omitted. Brennan, J., did not participate.

executed by the sheriff—relied on all the debtor-creditor decisions as establishing the doctrine "that a private party's joint participation with state officials in the seizure of disputed property is sufficient to characterize that party as a 'state actor' for purposes of the Fourteenth Amendment." POWELL, J., joined by Rehnquist and O'Connor, JJ., dissented: "It is unclear why a private party engages in state action when filing papers seeking an attachment of property, but not [when] summoning police to investigate a suspected crime." Burger, C.J., also dissented.

NATIONAL COLLEGIATE ATHLETIC ASS'N v. TARKANIAN, 488 U.S. 179 (1988): The NCAA is an association of virtually all colleges with major athletic programs, and its rules governing these programs are binding on its members. After its investigation that found 38 recruitment violations by the staff of the University of Nevada, Las Vegas (including 10 by Tarkanian, who was UNLV's basketball coach), NCAA imposed sanctions on UNLV and requested it to show cause why additional penalties should not be imposed if it failed to suspend Tarkanian. The Court, per STEVENS, J., conceded that UNLV's suspension of Tarkanian, which was clearly state action, "was influenced by the rules and recommendations of the NCAA," but held that this did not turn the NCAA's conduct into "state action," and thus the NCAA did not violate Tarkanian's right to procedural due process: Although, as a member of the NCAA, UNLV played a role in formulating its rules, "UNLV delegated no power to the NCAA to take specific action against any University employee. The commitment by UNLV to adhere to NCAA enforcement procedures was enforceable only by sanctions that the NCAA might impose on UNLV," and which UNLV could choose to ignore by withdrawing from the NCAA. And even if "the power of the NCAA is so great that the UNLV had no practical alternative to compliance with its demands, [it] does not follow that such a private party [is] acting under color of state law." Finally, "in the case before us the state and private parties' relevant interests do not coincide, as they did in *Burton;* rather, they have clashed throughout the investigation, the attempt to discipline Tarkanian, and this litigation. UNLV and the NCAA were antagonists, not joint participants, and the NCAA may not be deemed a state actor on this ground."

WHITE, J., joined by Brennan, Marshall and O'Connor, JJ., dissented: "[I]t was the NCAA's findings that Tarkanian had violated NCAA rules, made at NCAA-conducted hearings, all of which were agreed to by UNLV in its membership agreement with the NCAA, that resulted in Tarkanian's suspension by UNLV. On these facts, the NCAA was 'jointly engaged with [UNLV] officials in the challenged action,' and therefore was a state actor."

BRENTWOOD ACADEMY v. TENNESSEE SECONDARY SCHOOL ATHLETIC ASS'N, 531 U.S. 288 (2001): TSSAA was a membership corporation organized (and so designated by the state board of education in 1972) to regulate interscholastic sports among the public and private high schools in Tennessee. Almost all of the state's public high schools (290) and 55 private schools belonged. Its rules (specifically approved by the state board in 1972, and subject to subsequent review) governed such matters as student eligibility and academic standards and financial aid. Its operating committees were limited to principals elected by member schools, all of whom at the time of the action challenged in this case were from public schools, and ex-officio appointees of the state board. In

1997, TSSAA penalized Brentwood Academy, a parochial school, for violating a rule against "undue influence" in recruiting. The Court, per SOUTER, J., held that this was "state action": "The nominally private character of the Association is overborne by the pervasive entwinement of public institutions and public officials in its composition and workings.

"[Although] the terms of the State Board's Rule expressly designating the Association as regulator of interscholastic athletics in public schools was deleted in 1996, the year after a Federal District Court held that the Association was a state actor because its rules were 'caused, directed and controlled by the Tennessee Board of Education' [this] affected nothing but words." Nor is it dispositive "that the State neither coerced nor encouraged the actions complained of. 'Coercion' and 'encouragement' are like 'entwinement' in referring to kinds of facts that can justify characterizing an ostensibly private action as public instead. [When] the relevant facts show pervasive entwinement to the point of largely overlapping identity, the implication of state action is not affected by pointing out that the facts might not loom large under a different test.

"[Even] facts that suffice to show public action [may] be outweighed in the name of some value at odds with finding public accountability in the circumstances. [For example], full-time public employment would be conclusive of state action for some purposes, but not when the employee is doing a defense lawyer's primary job; then, the public defender does 'not ac[t] on behalf of the State; he is the State's adversary.' *Polk County v. Dodson.*"

THOMAS, J., joined by Rehnquist, C.J. and Scalia and Kennedy, JJ., dissented: "We have never found state action based upon mere 'entwinement.' Until today, we have found a private organization's acts to constitute state action only when the organization performed a public function; was created, coerced, or encouraged by the government; or acted in a symbiotic relationship with the government. [Although *Evans v. Newton*] uses the word 'entwined,' [our] analysis rested on the recognition that the subject of the dispute, a park, served a 'public function,' much like a fire department or a police department. [Even] if the city severed all ties to the park and placed its operation in private hands, the park still would be 'municipal in nature,' analogous to other public facilities that have given rise to a finding of state action: the streets of a company town in *Marsh*; the elective process in *Terry*; and the transit system in *Pollak.*"

———

EDMONSON v. LEESVILLE CONCRETE CO., 500 U.S. 614 (1991), per KENNEDY, J., held that use by a private litigant in a civil trial of a peremptory challenge to exclude jurors on the basis of race violated "the excluded jurors' equal protection rights": "Although private use of state-sanctioned private remedies or procedures does not rise, by itself, to the level of state action, our cases have found state action when private parties make extensive use of state procedures with 'the overt, significant assistance of state officials.' See *Lugar*. [The] government summons jurors, constrains their freedom of movement, and subjects them to public scrutiny and examination. The party who exercises a challenge invokes the formal authority of the court, which must discharge the prospective juror, thus effecting the 'final and practical denial' of the excluded individual's opportunity to serve on the petit jury. [By] enforcing a discriminatory peremptory challenge, the court 'has not only made itself a party to the [biased act], but has elected to place its power, property and prestige behind the [alleged] discrimination.' *Burton.*

"[Further, a] traditional function of government is evident here. The peremptory challenge is used in selecting an entity that is a quintessential governmental body, having no attributes of a private actor. [If] a government confers on a private body the power to choose the government's employees or officials, the private body will be bound by the constitutional mandate of race neutrality [*Terry*]. If peremptory challenges based on race were permitted, persons could be required by summons to be put at risk of open and public discrimination as a condition of their participation in the justice system. The injury to excluded jurors would be the direct result of governmental delegation and participation."

O'CONNOR, J., joined by Rehnquist, C.J., and Scalia, J., dissented: "It is the nature of a peremptory that its exercise is left wholly within the discretion of the litigant. [The] peremptory is, by design, an enclave of private action in a government-managed proceeding.

"[The] government 'normally can be held responsible for a private decision only when it has exercised coercive power or has provided such significant encouragement, either overt or covert, that the choice must in law be deemed to be that of the State.' *Blum*. [A] judge does not 'significantly encourage' discrimination by the mere act of excusing a juror in response to an unexplained request. [In] order to constitute state action under [the government function] doctrine, private conduct must not only comprise something that the government traditionally does, but something that *only* the government traditionally does. Even if one could fairly characterize the use of a peremptory strike as the performance of the traditional government function of jury selection, it has never been exclusively the function of the government to select juries; peremptory strikes are older than the Republic."

DeSHANEY v. WINNEBAGO COUNTY DEP'T OF SOCIAL SERV.

489 U.S. 189, 109 S.Ct. 998, 103 L.Ed.2d 249 (1989).

CHIEF JUSTICE REHNQUIST delivered the opinion of the Court.

[I]n January 1982, [the] Department of Social Services (DSS) interviewed [Joshua DeShaney's father about alleged child abuse], but he denied the accusations, and DSS did not pursue them. [In] January 1983, Joshua was admitted to a local hospital with multiple bruises and abrasions. The examining physician suspected child abuse and notified DSS. [T]he county convened an ad hoc "Child Protection Team" [which] decided that there was insufficient evidence of child abuse to retain Joshua in the custody of the court. The Team did, however, decide to recommend several measures to protect Joshua, including enrolling him in a preschool program, providing his father with certain counselling services, and encouraging his father's girlfriend to move out of the home. [A month later] emergency room personnel called the DSS caseworker handling Joshua's case to report that he had once again been treated for suspicious injuries. The caseworker concluded that there was no basis for action. [For] six months, the caseworker made monthly visits to the DeShaney home, during which she observed a number of suspicious injuries on Joshua's head; [and] that he had not been enrolled in school and that the girlfriend had not moved out. The caseworker dutifully recorded these incidents in her files, along with her continuing suspicions that someone in the DeShaney household was physically abusing Joshua, but she did nothing more. In November 1983, the emergency room notified DSS that Joshua had been treated once again for injuries that they believed to be caused by child abuse. On the caseworker's next two visits to the DeShaney home, she was told that Joshua was too ill to see her. Still DSS took no action.

In March 1984, Randy DeShaney beat 4–year-old Joshua so severely that he fell into a life-threatening coma [and] is expected to spend the rest of his life confined to an institution for the profoundly retarded. Randy DeShaney was subsequently tried and convicted of child abuse.

"[N]othing in the language of the Due Process Clause itself requires the State to protect the life, liberty, and property of its citizens against invasion by private actors. [Nor] does history support such an expansive reading of the constitutional text. [The Clause's] purpose was to protect the people from the State, not to ensure that the State protected them from each other. The Framers were content to leave the extent of governmental obligation in the latter area to the democratic political processes. * * *

Petitioners contend, however, that even if the Due Process Clause imposes no affirmative obligation on the State to provide the general public with adequate protective services, such a duty may arise out of certain "special relationships" created or assumed by the State with respect to particular individuals [and] that such a "special relationship" existed here because the State knew that Joshua faced a special danger of abuse at his father's hands, and specifically proclaimed, by word and by deed, its intention to protect him against that danger. * * *

We reject this argument. [I]ncarceration, institutionalization, or other similar restraint of personal liberty [is] the "deprivation of liberty" triggering the protections of the Due Process Clause. [While] the State may have been aware of the dangers that Joshua faced in the free world, it played no part in their creation, nor did it do anything to render him any more vulnerable to them. That the State once took temporary custody of Joshua does not alter the analysis, for when it returned him to his father's custody, it placed him in no worse position than that in which he would have been had it not acted at all; the State does not become the permanent guarantor of an individual's safety by having once offered him shelter. * * *

JUSTICE BRENNAN, with whom JUSTICE MARSHALL and JUSTICE BLACKMUN join, dissenting.

* * * I [would] recognize, as the Court apparently cannot, that "the State's knowledge of [an] individual's predicament [and] its expressions of intent to help him" can amount to a "limitation of his freedom to act on his own behalf" or to obtain help from others. Thus, [if] a State cuts off private sources of aid and then refuses aid itself, it cannot wash its hands of the harm that results from its inaction. * * *

The specific facts before us bear out this view of Wisconsin's system of protecting children. Each time someone voiced a suspicion that Joshua was being abused, that information was relayed to the Department for investigation and possible action. [If] DSS ignores or dismisses these suspicions, no one will step in to fill the gap. * * * My disagreement with the Court arises from its failure to see that inaction can be every bit as abusive of power as action, that oppression can result when a State undertakes a vital duty and then ignores it. * * *

JUSTICE BLACKMUN, dissenting. * * *

Like the antebellum judges who denied relief to fugitive slaves, the Court today claims that its decision, however harsh, is compelled by existing legal doctrine. On the contrary, the question presented by this case is an open one, and our Fourteenth Amendment precedents may be read more broadly or narrowly depending upon how one [chooses]. I would adopt a "sympathetic" reading, one which comports with dictates of fundamental justice and recognizes that compassion need not be exiled from the province of judging. * * *

Chapter 11

CONGRESSIONAL ENFORCEMENT
OF CIVIL RIGHTS

The exercise of congressional authority under the commerce power to protect civil rights was examined in detail in Ch. 2, Sec. 2, III. But the potentially most pervasive sources of federal legislative power to enforce personal liberty are found in the final sections of the Thirteenth, Fourteenth, and Fifteenth Amendments which grant Congress power to enforce the substantive provisions of these amendments "by appropriate legislation."

SECTION 1. REGULATION
OF PRIVATE PERSONS

I. THIRTEENTH AMENDMENT

JONES v. ALFRED H. MAYER CO.

392 U.S. 409, 88 S.Ct. 2186, 20 L.Ed.2d 1189 (1968).

JUSTICE STEWART delivered the opinion of the Court.

[P]etitioners filed a complaint [that] respondents had refused to sell them a home [for] the sole reason that petitioner [is] a Negro. Relying in part upon 42 U.S.C. § 1982, the petitioners sought injunctive and other relief. The [courts below] sustained the respondents' motion to dismiss [concluding] that § 1982 applies only to state action * * *.

On its [face] § 1982 appears to prohibit *all* discrimination against Negroes in the sale or rental of property—discrimination by private owners as well as discrimination by public [authorities.] Stressing what they consider to be the revolutionary implications of so literal a reading of § 1982, the respondents argue that Congress cannot possibly have intended any such result. Our examination of the relevant history, however, persuades us that Congress meant exactly what it said. * * *

The remaining question is whether Congress has power under the Constitution to do what § 1982 purports to [do]. Our starting point is the Thirteenth Amendment, for it was pursuant to that constitutional provision that Congress originally enacted what is now § 1982. [It] has never been [doubted] "that the power vested in Congress to enforce the article by appropriate legislation," [*Civil Rights Cases,*] includes the power to enact laws "direct and primary, operating upon the acts of individuals, whether sanctioned by State legislation or not." [Id.]

"By its own unaided force and effect," the Thirteenth Amendment "abolished slavery, and established universal freedom." *Civil Rights Cases*. Whether or not the Amendment *itself* did any more than that—a question not involved in this case—it is at least clear that the Enabling Clause of that Amendment empowered Congress to do much more. For that clause clothed "Congress with power to pass *all laws necessary and proper for abolishing all badges and incidents of slavery in the United States.*" Ibid. (Emphasis added.)

Those who opposed passage of the Civil Rights Act of 1866 argued in effect that the Thirteenth Amendment merely authorized Congress to dissolve the legal bond by which the Negro slave was held to his master. Yet [the] majority leaders in Congress—who were, after all, the authors of the Thirteenth Amendment—had no doubt that its Enabling Clause contemplated the sort of positive legislation that was embodied in the 1866 Civil Rights Act. [Surely] Congress has the power under the Thirteenth Amendment rationally to determine what are the badges and the incidents of slavery, and the authority to translate that determination into effective legislation. Nor can we say that the determination Congress has made is an irrational one. For this Court recognized long ago that, whatever else they may have encompassed, the badges and incidents of slavery—its "burdens and disabilities"—included restraints upon "those fundamental rights which are the essence of civil freedom, namely the same right [to] inherit, purchase, lease, sell and convey property, as is enjoyed by white citizens." *Civil Rights Cases*. Just as the Black Codes, enacted after the Civil War to restrict the free exercise of those rights, were substitutes for the slave system, so the exclusion of Negroes from white communities became a substitute for the Black Codes. And when racial discrimination herds men into ghettos and makes their ability to buy property turn on the color of their skin, then it too is a relic of slavery.

[At] the very least, the freedom that Congress is empowered to secure under the Thirteenth Amendment includes the freedom to buy whatever a white man can buy, the right to live wherever a white man can live. If Congress cannot say that being a free man means at least this much, then the Thirteenth Amendment made a promise the Nation cannot keep. * * *

Reversed.a

———

RUNYON v. McCRARY, 427 U.S. 160 (1976), per STEWART, J., relying on *Mayer's* interpretation of § 1982, held that § 1981 (Sec. 1, I supra), prohibits private schools—that were operated commercially and open to the public in that they engaged in general advertising to attract students—from refusing to accept black students. POWELL, J., joined the opinion, but added that "choices, including those involved in entering into a contract, that are 'private' in the sense that they are not part of a commercial relationship offered generally or widely, and that reflect the selectivity exercised by an individual entering into a personal relationship, certainly were never intended to be restricted by" § 1981. Stevens, J., joined the court's opinion, feeling bound by, but disagreeing with, the statutory interpretation in *Mayer*. White, J., joined by Rehnquist, J., dissented on grounds of statutory interpretation.

a. The concurring opinion of Douglas, J., is omitted, as is a lengthy opinion, Harlan, J., joined by White, J., dissenting. He relied on statements in prior Supreme Court opinions, the use of the word "right" in § 1982, the legislative history and debates of the Civil Rights Act of 1866 and of companion legislation, and on the ethics of the times to demonstrate that the Court's construction of § 1982 was "open to the most serious doubt" if not "wholly untenable."

II. STATE "INVOLVEMENT"

UNITED STATES v. PRICE, 383 U.S. 787 (1966), involved indictments for conspiracy and substantive violations under 18 U.S.C. §§ 241 and 242, against three Mississippi police officials and fifteen "nonofficial persons," for having willfully killed three civil rights workers—the police officials first jailing the victims, then releasing them and intercepting them and, then, all 18 defendants "punishing" the victims by shooting them—thus depriving "the victims due process of law."

A unanimous Court, per FORTAS, J., treating the case as raising issues "of construction, not of constitutional power," held that, as to the conspiracy count against the "private persons" under § 242, " '[I]t is immaterial to the conspiracy that these private individuals were not acting under color of law' because the count charges that they were conspiring with persons who were so acting." As to the substantive counts against the "private persons" under § 242, the Court, stating that the statutory language "under color of law" has "consistently been treated as the same thing as the 'state action' required by the Fourteenth Amendment," held that "private persons, jointly engaged with state officials in the prohibited action, are acting 'under color' of law for purposes of the statute. To act 'under color' of law does not require that the accused be an officer of the State. It is enough that he is a wilful participant in joint activity with the State or its agents," citing *Burton v. Wilmington Parking Auth.*, Ch. 10, Sec. 3. "[A]ccording to the indictment, the brutal joint adventure was made possible by state detention and calculated release of the prisoners by an officer of the State."a "Those who took advantage of participation by state officers in accomplishment of the foul purpose alleged must suffer the consequences of that participation."b

SECTION 2. REGULATION OF STATE ACTORS

SOUTH CAROLINA v. KATZENBACH, 383 U.S. 301 (1966): South Carolina challenged the Voting Rights Act of 1965—"the heart of [which] is a complex scheme of stringent remedies aimed at areas where voting discrimination has been most flagrant." The Court, per WARREN, C.J., referred to "the voluminous legislative history" that showed, inter alia, "unremitting and ingenious defiance of the Constitution," the enactment of literacy tests in Alabama, Georgia, Louisiana, Mississippi, North Carolina, South Carolina, and Virginia, still in use, which, because of their various qualifications, "were specifically designed to prevent Negroes from voting." It pointed out that "discriminatory application of voting tests" "pursuant to a widespread 'pattern or practice' ""is now the principal method used to bar Negroes from the polls," and that "case-by-case litigation against voting discrimination" under federal statutes of 1957, 1960 and 1964 has "done little to cure the problem."

"As against the reserved powers of the States, Congress may use any rational means to effectuate the constitutional prohibition of racial discrimination in voting. [The] basic test to be applied in a case involving § 2 of the Fifteenth

---

a. See also *United States v. Guest*, 383 U.S. 745 (1966).

b. See also *Screws v. United States*, 325 U.S. 91 (1945) holding that it was no defense under § 242 that defendant's actions were in violation of state law: "Misuse of power, possessed by virtue of state law and made possible only because the wrongdoer is clothed with the authority of state law, is action taken 'under color of' state law. [It] is clear that under 'color' of law means under 'pretense' of law. Thus acts of officers in the ambit of their personal pursuits are plainly excluded. Acts of officers who undertake to perform their official duties are included whether they hew to the line of their authority or overstep it."

Amendment is the same as in all cases concerning the express powers of Congress with relation to the reserved powers of the [states.] 'Let the end be legitimate, let it be within the scope of the constitution, and all means which are appropriate, which are plainly adapted to that end, which are not prohibited, but consist with the letter and spirit of the constitution, are constitutional.' *McCulloch v. Maryland* [Ch. 2, Sec. 1]."

The "coverage formula" of the Act applied "to any State, or to any separate political subdivision [for] which two findings have been made: (1) [on] November 1, 1964, it maintained a 'test or device,' and (2) [that] less than 50% of its voting-age residents were registered on November 1, 1964, or voted in the presidential election of November 1964. * * * § 4(b). [T]he phrase 'test or device' means any requirement that a registrant or voter must '(1) demonstrate the ability to read, write, understand, or interpret any matter, (2) demonstrate any educational achievement or his knowledge of any particular subject, (3) possess good moral character, or (4) prove his qualifications by the voucher of registered voters or members of any other class.' § 4(c)." Statutory coverage was terminated by a so-called "bail out" provision—if the area obtained a judgment from a three-judge federal court in the District of Columbia "that tests and devices have not been used during the preceding five years to abridge the franchise on racial grounds." "In acceptable legislative fashion, Congress chose to limit its attention to the geographic areas where immediate action seemed necessary."

The areas covered, "for which there was evidence of actual voting discrimination,"—Alabama, Georgia, Louisiana, Mississippi, South Carolina and much of North Carolina—shared the "two characteristics incorporated by Congress into the coverage formula." "It was therefore permissible to impose the new remedies on the few remaining States and political subdivisions covered by the formula, at least in the absence of proof that they have been free of substantial voting discrimination in recent years." That there are excluded areas "for which there is evidence of voting discrimination by other means" is irrelevant: "Legislation need not deal with all phases of a problem in the same way, so long as the distinctions drawn have some basis in political experience." "There are no States or political subdivisions exempted from coverage under § 4(b) in which the record reveals recent racial discrimination involving tests and devices. This fact confirms the rationality of the formula."

In areas covered, § 4(a) suspended "literacy tests and similar voting qualifications for a period of five years from the last occurrence of substantial voting discrimination," and § 5 suspended "all new voting regulations pending review by [the Attorney General or a three-judge court in the District of Columbia] to determine whether their use would perpetuate voting discrimination."[a] Both were upheld as a "legitimate response to the problem," the Court recounting the evidence Congress had before it of prior discriminatory administration of old tests and use of new tests to evade court decrees.[b]

---

a. For examples of the Court's subsequent broad interpretation of "voting regulations" that are subject to the suspension provision of section 5, see *United Jewish Orgs. v. Carey,* Ch. 9, Sec. 5, I, D (new or revised reapportionment plan); *Rome v. United States,* infra (election of officials "at large" rather than by district; annexation of adjacent area thus increasing number of eligible voters).

b. Black, J., agreed "with substantially all of the Court's opinion" but dissented in respect to § 5 of the Act: "[I]f all the provisions of our Constitution which limit the power of the Federal Government and reserve other power to the States are to mean anything, they mean at least that the States have power to pass laws [without] first sending their officials hundreds of miles away to beg federal authorities to approve them."

KATZENBACH v. MORGAN

384 U.S. 641, 86 S.Ct. 1717, 16 L.Ed.2d 828 (1966).

JUSTICE BRENNAN delivered the opinion of the Court.

[Section] 4(e) of the Voting Rights Act of 1965 [provides] that no person who has successfully completed the sixth primary grade in a [school] accredited by the Commonwealth of Puerto Rico in which the language of instruction was other than English shall be denied the right to vote in any election because of his inability to read or write English. [Thus, it] prohibits the enforcement of the election laws of New York requiring an ability to read and write English * * *.

The Attorney General of New York argues that an exercise of congressional power under § 5 of the Fourteenth Amendment that prohibits the enforcement of a state [law] cannot be sustained as appropriate legislation to enforce the Equal Protection Clause unless the judiciary decides—even with the guidance of a congressional judgment—that the application of the English literacy requirement prohibited by § 4(e) is forbidden by the Equal Protection Clause itself. We disagree. Neither the language nor history of § 5 supports such a construction.[7] [A] construction of § 5 that would require a judicial determination that the enforcement of the state law precluded by Congress violated the Amendment, as a condition of sustaining the congressional enactment [would] confine the legislative power in this context to the insignificant role of abrogating only those state laws that the judicial branch was prepared to adjudge unconstitutional, or of merely informing the judgment of the judiciary by particularizing the "majestic generalities" of [§ 1]. Accordingly, our decision in *Lassiter v. Northampton Cty. Bd. of Elec.*, 360 U.S. 45 (1959), sustaining the North Carolina English literacy requirement as not in all circumstances prohibited by the first sections of the Fourteenth and Fifteenth Amendments, [did] not present the question before us here: Without regard to whether the judiciary would find that the Equal Protection Clause itself nullifies New York's English literacy requirement as so applied, could Congress prohibit the enforcement of the state law by legislating under § 5? In answering this question, our task is limited to determining whether such legislation is, as required by § 5, appropriate legislation to enforce the Equal Protection Clause.

By including § 5 the draftsmen sought to grant to Congress [the] same broad powers expressed in the Necessary and Proper Clause.[9] The classic formulation of the reach of those powers was established by Chief Justice Marshall in *McCulloch v. Maryland*, [Ch. 2, Sec. 1]. *Ex parte Virginia*, 100 U.S. 339, 25 L.Ed. 676 (1879), decided 12 years after the adoption of the Fourteenth Amendment, held that congressional power under § 5 had this same broad [scope]. Section 2 of the Fifteenth Amendment grants Congress a similar power [and] we recently held in *South Carolina* that [the test was] the one formulated in *McCulloch*. * * * Correctly viewed, § 5 is a positive grant of legislative power authorizing Congress

---

7. For the historical evidence suggesting that the sponsors and supporters of the Amendment were primarily interested in augmenting the power of Congress, rather than the judiciary, see generally Laurent B. Frantz, *Congressional Power to Enforce the Fourteenth Amendment Against Private Acts*, 73 Yale L.J. 1353, 1356–1357 (1964); Robert J. Harris, *The Quest for Equality*, 33–56 (1960); Jacobus tenBroek, *The Antislavery Origins of the Fourteenth Amendment* 187–217 (1951). [But see

Robert A. Burt, *Miranda and Title II: A Morganatic Marriage*, 1969 Sup.Ct.Rev. 81–100.]

9. In fact, earlier drafts of the proposed Amendment employed the "necessary and proper" terminology to describe the scope of congressional power under the Amendment. The substitution of the "appropriate legislation" formula was never thought to have the effect of diminishing the scope of this congressional power. See, e.g., Cong. Globe, 42d Cong., 1st Sess., App. 83. * * *

to exercise its discretion in determining whether and what legislation is needed to secure the guarantees of the Fourteenth Amendment. * * *10

There can be no doubt that § 4(e) may be regarded as an enactment to enforce the Equal Protection Clause. [S]pecifically, § 4(e) may be viewed as a measure to secure for the Puerto Rican community residing in New York nondiscriminatory treatment by government—both in the imposition of voting qualifications and the provision or administration of governmental services, such as public schools, public housing and law enforcement.

Section 4(e) may be readily seen as "plainly adapted" to furthering these aims of the Equal Protection Clause. The practical effect of § 4(e) is to prohibit New York from denying the right to vote to large segments of its Puerto Rican community [—the] right that is "preservative of all rights." This enhanced political power will be helpful in gaining nondiscriminatory treatment in public services for the entire Puerto Rican community.11 [It] was for Congress, as the branch that made this judgment, to assess and weigh the various conflicting considerations—the risk or pervasiveness of the discrimination in governmental services, the effectiveness of eliminating the state restriction on the right to vote as a means of dealing with the evil, the adequacy or availability of alternative remedies, and the nature and significance of the state interests that would be affected by the nullification of the English literacy requirement. [It] is enough that we be able to perceive a basis upon which the Congress might resolve the conflict as it did. There plainly was such a [basis]. Any contrary conclusion would require us to be blind to the realities familiar to the legislators.

The result is no different if we confine our inquiry to the question whether § 4(e) was merely legislation aimed at the elimination of an invidious discrimination in establishing voter qualifications. We are told that New York's English literacy requirement originated in the desire to provide an incentive for non-English speaking immigrants to learn the English language and in order to assure the intelligent exercise of the franchise. Yet Congress might well have questioned, in light of the many exemptions provided,13 and some evidence suggesting that prejudice played a prominent role in the enactment of the requirement,14 whether these were actually the interests being served. Congress might have also questioned whether denial of a right deemed so precious and fundamental in our society was a necessary or appropriate means of encouraging persons to learn English, or of furthering the goal of an intelligent exercise of the franchise. Finally, Congress might well have concluded that as a means of furthering the intelligent exercise of the franchise, an ability to read or understand Spanish is as effective as ability to read English for those to whom Spanish-language newspapers and Spanish-language radio and television programs are available to inform

10. Contrary to the suggestion of the [dissent,] § 5 is limited to adopting measures to enforce the guarantees of the Amendment; § 5 grants Congress no power to restrict, abrogate, or dilute these guarantees. Thus, for example, an enactment authorizing the States to establish racially segregated systems of education would not be—as required by § 5—a measure "to enforce" the Equal Protection Clause since that clause of its own force prohibits such state laws.

11. Cf. * * * United States v. Darby [Ch. 2, Sec. 2, II, B], that the power of Congress to regulate interstate commerce "extends to those activities intrastate which so affect interstate commerce or the exercise of the power of Con-

gress over it as to make regulation of them appropriate means to the attainment of a legitimate end * * *."

13. The principal exemption complained of is that for persons who had been eligible to vote before January 1, 1922.

14. This evidence consists in part of statements made in the Constitutional Convention first considering the English literacy requirement * * *. Congress was aware of this evidence. See, e.g., Literacy Tests and Voter Requirements in Federal and State Elections, Senate Hearings 507–513; Voting Rights, House Hearings 508–513.

them of election issues and governmental affairs.16 Since Congress undertook to legislate so as to preclude the enforcement of the state law, and did so in the context of a general appraisal of literacy requirements for voting, see *South Carolina,* to which it brought a specially informed legislative competence,17 it was Congress' prerogative to weigh these competing considerations. Here again, it is enough that we perceive a basis upon which Congress might predicate a judgment that the application of New York's English literacy [requirement] constituted an invidious discrimination in violation of the Equal Protection Clause.

[The Court rejected the contention that the "American-flag schools" limitation itself violates "the letter and spirit of the Constitution"].

Reversed.

JUSTICE HARLAN, whom JUSTICE STEWART joins, dissenting.

[The dissent first argued that the New York law was not forbidden by the Equal Protection Clause itself.] I believe the Court has confused the issue of how much enforcement power Congress possesses under § 5 with the distinct issue of what questions are appropriate for congressional determination and what questions are essentially judicial in nature.

When recognized state violations of federal constitutional standards have occurred, Congress is of course empowered by § 5 to take appropriate remedial measures. [But the] question here is not whether the statute is appropriate remedial legislation to cure an established violation of a constitutional command, but whether [a] particular state practice or, as here, a statute is so arbitrary or irrational as to offend the command of [equal protection]. That question is one for the judicial branch ultimately to determine. [In] view of [*Lassiter*], I do not think it is open to Congress to limit the effect of that decision as it has undertaken to do by § 4(e). In effect the Court reads § 5 of the Fourteenth Amendment as giving Congress the power to define the *substantive* scope of the Amendment. If that indeed be the true reach of § 5, then I do not see why Congress should not be able as well to exercise its § 5 "discretion" by enacting statutes so as in effect to dilute equal protection and due process decisions of this Court. In all such cases there is room for reasonable men to differ as to whether or not a denial of equal protection or due process has occurred, and the final decision is one of judgment. Until today this judgment has always been one for the judiciary to resolve.

I do not mean to suggest in what has been said that a legislative judgment of the type incorporated in § 4(e) is without any force whatsoever. Decisions on questions of equal protection and due process are based not on abstract logic, but on empirical foundations. To the extent "legislative facts" are relevant to a judicial determination, Congress is well equipped to investigate them, and such determinations are of course entitled to due respect. In *South Carolina,* such legislative findings were made to show that racial discrimination in voting was actually occurring. Similarly, in *Heart of Atlanta* and *Katzenbach v. McClung,* [Ch. 2, Sec. 2, III], the congressional determination that racial discrimination in a clearly defined group of public accommodations did effectively impede interstate commerce was based on "voluminous testimony" which had been put before the Congress and in the context of which it passed remedial legislation.

16. See, e.g., 111 Cong.Rec. 10675 (May 20, 1965), 15102 (July 6, 1965), 15666 (July 9, 1965). The record in this case includes affidavits describing the nature of New York's two major Spanish-language newspapers [and] its three full-time Spanish-language radio stations and affidavits from those who have campaigned in Spanish speaking areas.

17. See, e.g., 111 Cong.Rec. 10676 (Senator Long of Louisiana and Senator Young), 10678 (Senator Holland) (May 20, 1965), drawing on their experience with voters literate in a language other than English. * * *

But no such factual data provide a legislative record supporting § 4(e)9 by way of showing that Spanish-speaking citizens are fully as capable of making informed decisions in a New York election as are English-speaking citizens. Nor was there any showing whatever to support the Court's alternative argument that § 4(e) should be viewed as but a remedial measure designed to cure or assure against unconstitutional discrimination of other varieties, e.g., in "public schools, public housing and law enforcement" * * *.

Thus, we have [here] what can at most be called a legislative announcement that Congress believes a state law to entail an unconstitutional deprivation of equal protection. Although this kind of declaration is of course entitled to the most respectful consideration, coming as it does from a concurrent branch and one that is knowledgeable in matters of popular political participation, I do not believe it lessens our responsibility to decide the fundamental issue of whether in fact the state enactment violates federal constitutional rights.

In assessing the deference we should give to this kind of congressional expression of policy, it is relevant that the judiciary has always given to congressional enactments a presumption of validity. However, it is also a canon of judicial review that state statutes are given a similar presumption, [and] although it has been suggested that this Court should give somewhat more deference to Congress than to a State Legislature, such a simple weighing of presumptions is hardly a satisfying way of resolving a matter that touches the distribution of state and federal power in an area so sensitive as that of the regulation of the franchise. Rather it should be recognized that while the Fourteenth Amendment is a "brooding omnipresence" over all state legislation, the substantive matters which it touches are all within the primary legislative competence of the States. Federal authority, legislative no less than judicial, does not intrude unless there has been a denial by state action of Fourteenth Amendment [limitations]. At least in the area of primary state concern a state statute that passes constitutional muster under the judicial standard of rationality should not be permitted to be set at naught by a mere contrary congressional pronouncement unsupported by a legislative record justifying that conclusion. * * *

BOERNE v. FLORES

521 U.S. 507, 117 S.Ct. 2157, 138 L.Ed.2d 624 (1997).

JUSTICE KENNEDY delivered the opinion of the Court.

A decision by local zoning authorities to deny a church a building permit was challenged under the Religious Freedom Restoration Act of 1993 (RFRA). * * *

Congress enacted RFRA in direct response to the Court's decision in *Employment Div. v. Smith*, [Ch. 8, Sec. 2, I]. *Smith* held that neutral, generally applicable laws may be applied to religious practices even when not supported by a compelling governmental interest. [Many] criticized the Court's reasoning, and this disagreement resulted in the passage of RFRA. * * *

RFRA prohibits "[g]overnment" from "substantially burden[ing]" a person's exercise of religion even if the burden results from a rule of general applicability unless the government can demonstrate the burden "(1) is in furtherance of a compelling governmental interest; and (2) is the least restrictive means of furthering that compelling governmental interest." * * *

Congress relied on its Fourteenth Amendment enforcement power in enacting the most far reaching and substantial of RFRA's provisions, those which impose

9. There were no committee hearings or reports referring to this section, which was introduced from the floor during debate on the full Voting Rights Act.

its requirements on the [States.] Legislation which deters or remedies constitutional violations can fall within the sweep of Congress' enforcement power even if in the process it prohibits conduct which is not itself unconstitutional and intrudes into "legislative spheres of autonomy previously reserved to the States." *Fitzpatrick v. Bitzer*, 427 U.S. 445, 455 (1976). [As examples, the Court discussed the practices that Congress had made unlawful in *South Carolina, Morgan* and *Rome*, note 3(c) infra.] We agree with respondent, of course, that Congress can enact legislation under § 5 enforcing the constitutional right to the free exercise of religion. * * *

Congress' power under § 5, however, extends only to "enforc[ing]" the provisions of the Fourteenth Amendment. The Court has described this power as "remedial," *South Carolina*. The design of the Amendment and the text of § 5 are inconsistent with the suggestion that Congress has the power to decree the substance of the Fourteenth Amendment's restrictions on the States. Legislation which alters the meaning of the Free Exercise Clause cannot be said to be enforcing the Clause. * * *

While the line between measures that remedy or prevent unconstitutional actions and measures that make a substantive change in the governing law is not easy to discern, and Congress must have wide latitude in determining where it lies, the distinction exists and must be observed. There must be a congruence and proportionality between the injury to be prevented or remedied and the means adopted to that end. Lacking such a connection, legislation may become substantive in operation and effect. * * *

The Fourteenth Amendment's history confirms the remedial, rather than substantive, nature of the Enforcement Clause. [The] objections to the [Joint] Committee's first draft of the Amendment [had] a common theme: The proposed Amendment gave Congress [a] power to intrude into traditional areas of state responsibility, a power inconsistent with the federal design central to the Constitution. [Under] the revised Amendment, Congress' power was no longer plenary but remedial [and] did not raise the concerns expressed earlier regarding broad congressional power to prescribe uniform national laws with respect to life, liberty, and property. * * *

The design of the Fourteenth Amendment has proved significant also in maintaining the traditional separation of powers between Congress and the Judiciary. The first eight Amendments to the Constitution set forth self-executing prohibitions on governmental action, and this Court has had primary authority to interpret those prohibitions. The [Joint Committee's first] draft, some thought, departed from that tradition by vesting in Congress primary power to interpret and elaborate on the meaning of the new Amendment through legislation. [As] enacted, the Fourteenth Amendment confers substantive rights against the States which, like the provisions of the Bill of Rights, are self-executing. The power to interpret the Constitution in a case or controversy remains in the Judiciary. * * *

Any suggestion that Congress has a substantive, non-remedial power under the Fourteenth Amendment is not supported by our case law. In *Oregon v. Mitchell*, [400 U.S. 112 (1970)], a majority of the Court concluded Congress had exceeded its enforcement powers by enacting legislation lowering the minimum age of voters from 21 to 18 in state and local elections.[a] The five Members of the Court who reached this conclusion explained that [the] legislation was unconstitu-

---

a. A different majority—Black, Douglas, Brennan, White and Marshall, JJ.—voted to uphold this provision as to federal elections. Black, J., who was in both majorities, distinguished the situations on the ground (which no other justice joined) that Congress had power under Art. I, § 4 to set qualifications for voters in federal elections.

tional because the Constitution "reserves to the States the power to set voter qualifications in state and local elections." Four of these five were explicit in rejecting the position that § 5 endowed Congress with the power to establish the meaning of constitutional provisions. See (opinion of Harlan, J.); (opinion of Stewart, J., joined by Burger, C. J., and Blackmun, J.). Justice Black's rejection of this position might be inferred from his disagreement with Congress' interpretation of the Equal Protection Clause.b

There is language in our opinion in *Morgan* which could be interpreted as acknowledging a power in Congress to enact legislation that expands the rights contained in § 1 of the Fourteenth Amendment. This is not a necessary interpretation, however, or even the best one. [As] Justice Stewart explained in *Mitchell*, interpreting *Morgan* to give Congress the power to interpret the Constitution "would require an enormous extension of that decision's rationale."

If Congress could define its own powers by altering the Fourteenth Amendment's meaning, no longer would the Constitution be "superior paramount law, unchangeable by ordinary means." It would be "on a level with ordinary legislative acts, and, like other [acts,] alterable when the legislature shall please to alter it." *Marbury v. Madison.* Under this approach, it is difficult to conceive of a principle that would limit congressional power. Shifting legislative majorities could change the Constitution and effectively circumvent the difficult and detailed amendment process contained in Article V. * * *

Respondent contends that RFRA is a proper exercise of Congress' remedial or preventive power. The Act, it is [said,] prevents and remedies laws which are enacted with the unconstitutional object of targeting religious beliefs and practices. See *Church of the Lukumi Babalu Aye, Inc. v. Hialeah,* [Ch. 8, Sec. 2, I]. To avoid the difficulty of proving such violations, it is said, Congress can simply invalidate any law which imposes a substantial burden on a religious practice unless it is justified by a compelling interest and is the least restrictive means of accomplishing that interest. If Congress can prohibit laws with discriminatory effects in order to prevent racial discrimination in violation of the Equal Protection Clause, then it can do the same, respondent argues, to promote religious liberty.

While preventive rules are sometimes appropriate remedial measures, there must be a congruence between the means used and the ends to be achieved. * * * Strong measures appropriate to address one harm may be an unwarranted response to another, lesser one.

A comparison between RFRA and the Voting Rights Act is instructive. In contrast to the record which confronted Congress and the judiciary in the voting rights cases, RFRA's legislative record lacks examples of modern instances of generally applicable laws passed because of religious bigotry. [Rather,] the emphasis of the hearings was on laws of general applicability which place incidental burdens on religion. * * *

Regardless of the state of the legislative record, RFRA [is] so out of proportion to a supposed remedial or preventive object that it cannot be understood as responsive to, or designed to prevent, unconstitutional behavior. It appears,

b. Black, J., stated: "Congress made no legislative findings that 21–year-old vote requirements were used by the States to disenfranchise voters on account of race. I seriously doubt that such a finding, if made, could be supported by substantial evidence. Since Congress has attempted to invade an area preserved to the States by the Constitution without a foundation for enforcing the Civil War Amendments' ban on racial discrimination, I would hold that Congress has exceeded its powers in attempting to lower the voting age in state and local elections."

instead, to attempt a substantive change in constitutional protections. Preventive measures prohibiting certain types of laws may be appropriate when there is reason to believe that many of the laws affected by the congressional enactment have a significant likelihood of being unconstitutional. See *Rome* [note 1 infra].

RFRA is not so confined. Sweeping coverage ensures its intrusion at every level of government, displacing laws and prohibiting official actions of almost every description and regardless of subject matter. * * *

The reach and scope of RFRA distinguish it from other measures passed under Congress' enforcement power, even in the area of voting rights. In *South Carolina,* the challenged provisions were confined to those regions of the country where voting discrimination had been most flagrant, and affected a discrete class of state laws, i.e., state voting laws. Furthermore, to ensure that the reach of the Voting Rights Act was limited to those cases in which constitutional violations were most likely (in order to reduce the possibility of overbreadth), the coverage under the Act would terminate "at the behest of States and political subdivisions in which the danger of substantial voting discrimination has not materialized during the preceding five years." The provisions restricting and banning literacy tests, upheld in *Morgan,* attacked a particular type of voting qualification, one with a long history as a "notorious means to deny and abridge voting rights on racial grounds." [This] is not to say, of course, that § 5 legislation requires termination dates, geographic restrictions or egregious predicates. Where, however, a congressional enactment pervasively prohibits constitutional state action in an effort to remedy or to prevent unconstitutional state action, limitations of this kind tend to ensure Congress' means are proportionate to ends legitimate under § 5. * * *

When [the] Court has interpreted the Constitution, it has acted within the province of the Judicial Branch, which embraces the duty to say what the law is. When the political branches of the Government act against the background of a judicial interpretation of the Constitution already issued, it must be understood that in later cases and controversies the Court will treat its precedents with the respect due them under settled principles, including stare decisis, and contrary expectations must be disappointed. RFRA was designed to control cases and controversies, such as the one before us; but as the provisions of the federal statute here invoked are beyond congressional authority, it is this Court's precedent, not RFRA, which must control. * * *

JUSTICE STEVENS, concurring.

In my opinion, RFRA is a "law respecting an establishment of religion" that violates the First Amendment * * *.c

JUSTICE O'CONNOR, with whom JUSTICE BREYER joins except as to [the first two sentences below].

* * * I agree with much of the reasoning set forth in [the] Court's opinion. Indeed, if I agreed with the Court's standard in *Smith,* I would join the opinion. [But] I remain of the view that *Smith* was wrongly decided, and I would use this case to reexamine the Court's holding there. Therefore, I would direct the parties to brief the question whether *Smith* represents the correct understanding of the Free Exercise Clause and set the case for reargument. * * *

JUSTICE SOUTER, dissenting.

c. The concurring opinion of Scalia, J.,   Court's opinion, is omitted.
joined by Stevens, J., both of whom joined the

* * * Justice O'Connor's opinion [raises] very substantial issues about the soundness of the *Smith* rule. [In] order to provide full adversarial consideration, this case should be set down for reargument. * * * I would therefore dismiss the writ of certiorari as improvidently granted * * *.

Notes

1. ***Changed circumstances over time.*** NORTHWEST AUSTIN MUNICI-PAL UTILITY DIST. v. HOLDER, 129 S.Ct. 2504 (2009), per ROBERTS, C.J., interpreted the Voting Rights Act of 1965 (as reauthorized most recently in 2006) to permit *all* political subdivisions, including a small utility district with an elected board, to "bailout [from the § 5] preclearance requirements if certain rigorous conditions are met," and thus followed "our usual practice [to] avoid the unnecessary resolution of constitutional questions." The Court nonetheless opined:

"Some of the conditions that we relied upon in upholding this statutory scheme in *South Carolina v. Katzenbach* and *Rome* [infra] have unquestionably improved. Things have changed in the South. Voter turnout and registration rates now approach parity. Blatantly discriminatory evasions of federal decrees are rare. And minority candidates hold office at unprecedented levels.

"These improvements are no doubt due in significant part to the Voting Rights Act itself, and stand as a monument to its success. Past success alone, however, is not adequate justification to retain the preclearance requirements. It may be that these improvements are insufficient and that conditions continue to warrant preclearance under the Act. But the Act imposes current burdens and must be justified by current needs.

The Act also differentiates between the States, [and] a departure from the fundamental principle of equal sovereignty requires a showing that a statute's disparate geographic coverage is sufficiently related to the problem that it targets. [The] statute's coverage formula is based on data that is now more than 35 years old, and there is considerable evidence that it fails to account for current political conditions. * * *

"The parties do not agree on the standard to apply in deciding whether, in light of the foregoing concerns, Congress exceeded its Fifteenth Amendment enforcement power in extending the preclearance requirements. The district argues that '[t]here must be a congruence and proportionality between the injury to be prevented or remedied and the means adopted to that end,' [*Boerne*]; the Federal Government asserts that it is enough that the legislation be a 'rational means to effectuate the constitutional prohibition,' [*South Carolina*]. That question has been extensively briefed in this case, but we need not resolve it. The Act's preclearance requirements and its coverage formula raise serious constitutional questions under either test."

THOMAS, J., concurred and dissented in part: Although "by 1965, Congress had every reason to conclude that States with a history of disenfranchising voters based on race would continue to do all they could to evade the constitutional ban on voting discrimination, * * * I conclude that the lack of current evidence of intentional discrimination with respect to voting renders § 5 unconstitutional. [The] burden remains with Congress to prove that the extreme circumstances warranting § 5's enactment persist today. A record of scattered infringement of the right to vote is not a constitutionally acceptable substitute."

2. ***De facto discrimination.*** ROME v. UNITED STATES, 446 U.S. 156 (1980), involved the Attorney General's refusal to approve, under § 5 of the Voting Rights Act, various changes in the Rome, Ga.'s electoral system and a

number of city annexations. A federal court found that the city had not employed any discriminatory barriers to black voting or black candidacy in the past 17 years and that the city had proved that the electoral changes and annexations were not discriminatorily motivated, but that they were prohibited by the Act because they had a discriminatory effect. The Court, per MARSHALL, J., affirmed: "[T]he Act's ban on electoral changes that are discriminatory in effect is an appropriate method of promoting the purposes of the Fifteenth Amendment, even if it is assumed that § 1 of the Amendment prohibits only intentional discrimination in voting. [See *Mobile v. Bolden,* Ch. 9, Sec. 5, I, B.] Congress could rationally have concluded that, because electoral changes by jurisdictions with a demonstrable history of intentional racial discrimination in voting create the risk of purposeful discrimination, it was proper to prohibit changes that have a discriminatory impact. See *South Carolina v. Katzenbach.*"

REHNQUIST, J., joined by Stewart, J., dissented: "Congress had before it evidence that various governments were enacting electoral changes and annexing territory to prevent the participation of blacks in local government by measures other than outright denial of the franchise. [G]iven the difficulties of proving that an electoral change or annexation has been undertaken for the purpose of discriminating against blacks, Congress could properly conclude that as a remedial matter it was necessary to place the burden of proving lack of discriminatory purpose on the localities. But all of this does not support the conclusion that Congress is acting remedially when it continues the presumption of purposeful discrimination even after the locality has disproved that presumption. Absent other circumstances, it would be a topsy-turvy judicial system which held that electoral changes which have been affirmatively proven to be permissible under the Constitution nonetheless violate the Constitution. [Thus,] the result of the Court's holding is that Congress effectively has the power to determine for itself that this conduct violates the Constitution. This result violates previously well-established distinctions between the Judicial Branch and the Legislative or Executive Branches of the Federal Government." Powell, J., dissented on narrower grounds.

3. ***Further restrictions on § 5.*** (a) ***Equal protection.*** (i) KIMEL v. FLORIDA BD. OF REGENTS, 528 U.S. 62 (2000), per O'CONNOR, J., explored *Boerne's* scope in the context of Congress' exercising its § 5 power—which may be used to abrogate the states' immunity from suits in federal court guaranteed by the Eleventh Amendment—to make states subject to federal court actions for violating the Age Discrimination in Employment Act: "We have considered claims of unconstitutional age discrimination under the Equal Protection Clause three times [and held that] age is not a suspect classification [Ch. 9, Sec. 4, V]. Our Constitution permits States to draw lines on the basis of age when they have a rational basis for doing so at a class-based level, even if it 'is probably not true' that those reasons are valid in the majority of cases.

"Judged against the backdrop of our equal protection jurisprudence, it is clear that the ADEA is 'so out of proportion to a supposed remedial or preventive object that it cannot be understood as responsive to, or designed to prevent, unconstitutional behavior.' *Boerne.* The Act, through its broad restriction on the use of age as a discriminating factor, prohibits substantially more state employment decisions and practices than would likely be held unconstitutional under the applicable equal protection, rational basis standard. * * *

"That the ADEA prohibits very little conduct likely to be held unconstitutional, while significant, does not alone provide the answer to our § 5 inquiry. Difficult and intractable problems often require powerful remedies, and we have never held that § 5 precludes Congress from enacting reasonably prophylactic legislation. Our task is to determine whether the ADEA is in fact just such an appropriate remedy or, instead, merely an attempt to substantively redefine the States' legal obligations with respect to age discrimination. Our examination of the ADEA's legislative record confirms [that] Congress never identified any pattern of age discrimination by the States, much less any discrimination whatsoever that rose to the level of constitutional violation."a

STEVENS, J., joined by Souter, Ginsburg and Breyer, JJ., dissented, relying on their dissenting view in *Seminole Tribe*, fn. a: "Congress' power to authorize federal remedies against state agencies that violate federal statutory obligations is coextensive with its power to impose those obligations on the States in the first place. Neither the Eleventh Amendment nor the doctrine of sovereign immunity places any limit on that power."b

(ii) *Required congressional record.* BOARD OF TRUSTEES OF UNIV. OF ALA. v. GARRETT, 531 U.S. 356 (2001), per REHNQUIST, C.J. held that Congress had no §§ 5 power to abrogate state immunity and provide its employees a damages remedy under Title I of the Americans with Disabilities Act, which forbids employment discrimination against "a qualified individual" because of "disability" and requires "reasonable accommodations" to achieve this end: "[*Cleburne*, Ch. 9, Sec. 4, III, held that a legislative classification based on disability] incurs only the minimum 'rational-basis' review applicable to general social and economic legislation. [Breyer, J.'s dissent suggests] that state decision-making reflecting 'negative attitudes' or 'fear' necessarily runs afoul of the Fourteenth Amendment. Although such biases may often accompany irrational (and therefore unconstitutional) discrimination, their presence alone does not a constitutional violation make. [Thus,] States are not required by the Fourteenth Amendment to make special accommodations for the disabled, so long as their actions towards such individuals are rational. They could quite hard headedly—

a. The scope of the Eleventh Amendment is considered in detail in Federal Courts courses. But several recent decisions—by the same 5–4 split as in *Lopez, Morrison, Printz* [Ch. 2, Secs. 2, IV and 5, IV], and *Kimel*—have interpreted it to similarly enforce principles of federalism and state sovereignty. *Seminole Tribe v. Florida*, 517 U.S. 44 (1996)—overruling *Pennsylvania v. Union Gas Co.*, 491 U.S. 1 (1989)—per Rehnquist C.J., held that, unlike under its § 5 power, Congress has *no* authority under the Commerce Clause to abrogate state immunity under the Eleventh Amendment, and *Florida Prepaid Postsecondary Educ. Expense Bd. v. College Savings Bank*, below, extended this limitation to other Art. I powers (Patent Clause). *Alden v. Maine*, 527 U.S. 706 (1999), per Kennedy, J., while agreeing that the Fair Labor Standards Act could constitutionally be applied to states (see *Garcia*, Ch. 2, Sec. 5, IV), held that, just as under *Seminole Tribe* private parties could not sue states under such federal statutes in federal court without their consent, so, too, states could not be sued in their own courts under such circumstances:

"[T]he sovereign immunity of the States neither derives from nor is limited by the terms of the Eleventh Amendment. Rather, as the Constitution's structure, and its history, and the authoritative interpretations by this Court

make clear, the States' immunity from suit is a fundamental aspect of the sovereignty which the States enjoyed before the ratification of the Constitution, and which they [retain] except as altered by the plan of the Convention or certain constitutional Amendments."

Souter J., spoke for the dissenters: "[T]oday the Court has no qualms about saying frankly that the federal right to damages afforded by Congress under the FLSA cannot create a concomitant private remedy. [The] Court calls 'immunity from private suits central to sovereign dignity,' [but] this dignity is [not] a quality easily translated from the person of the King to the participatory abstraction of a republican State. [It] would be hard to imagine anything more inimical to the republican conception, which rests on the understanding of its citizens precisely that the government is not above them, but of them, its actions being governed by law just like their own."

b. *Central Va. Comm. College v. Katz,* 546 U.S. 356 (2006), per Stevens, J., held that the Art. 1, § 8, cl. 4 bankruptcy power "was intended" to subordinate "state sovereign immunity in the bankruptcy arena" as "a uniform federal response" to the problems and injustice of the then existing "patchwork of insolvency and bankruptcy laws." Roberts, C.J., and Scalia, Kennedy and Thomas, JJ., dissented.

and perhaps hardheartedly—hold to job-qualification requirements which do not make allowance for the disabled. If special accommodations for the disabled are to be required, they have to come from positive law and not through the Equal Protection Clause.

"Once we have determined the metes and bounds of the constitutional right in question, we examine whether Congress identified a history and pattern of unconstitutional employment discrimination by the States against the disabled. * * *

"Respondents contend that the inquiry as to unconstitutional discrimination should extend not only to States themselves, but to units of local governments, such as cities and counties. [B]ut the Eleventh Amendment does not extend its immunity to units of local government. [It] would make no sense to consider constitutional violations on their part, as well as by the States themselves, when only the States are the beneficiaries of the Eleventh Amendment.

"Congress made a general finding in the ADA that 'historically, society has tended to isolate and segregate individuals with disabilities, and, despite some improvements, such forms of discrimination against individuals with disabilities continue to be a serious and pervasive social problem.' The record assembled by Congress includes many instances to support such a finding. But the great majority of these incidents do not deal with the activities of States.

"Respondents in their brief cite half a dozen examples from the record that did involve States. [But] these incidents taken together fall far short of even suggesting the pattern of unconstitutional discrimination on which §§ 5 legislation must be based. [Further, the] host of incidents [in Appendix C to Breyer, J.'s dissent] consists not of legislative findings, but of unexamined, anecdotal accounts of 'adverse, disparate treatment by state officials.' [Of course,] 'adverse, disparate treatment' often does not amount to a constitutional violation where rational-basis scrutiny applies. These accounts, moreover, were submitted not directly to Congress but to the Task Force on the Rights and Empowerment of Americans with Disabilities, which made no findings on the subject of state discrimination in employment.7 And, had Congress truly understood this information as reflecting a pattern of unconstitutional behavior by the States, one would expect some mention of that conclusion in the Act's legislative findings. There is none. Although Justice Breyer would infer from Congress' general conclusions regarding societal discrimination against the disabled that the States had likewise participated in such action, the House and Senate committee reports on the ADA flatly contradict this assertion. [The Senate] Committee's report reached, among others, the following conclusion: 'Discrimination still persists in such critical areas as *employment in the private sector,* public accommodations, public services, transportation, and telecommunications.' The House Committee [reached] the same conclusion * * *.

"Even were it possible to squeeze out of these examples a pattern of unconstitutional discrimination by the States, the rights and remedies created by the ADA against the States would raise the same sort of concerns as to congruence and proportionality as were found in *Boerne.* For example, whereas it would be entirely rational (and therefore constitutional) for a state employer to conserve

7. Only a small fraction of the anecdotes Justice Breyer identifies in his Appendix C relate to state discrimination against the disabled in employment. At most, somewhere around 50 of these allegations describe conduct that could conceivably amount to constitutional violations by the States, and most of them are so general and brief that no firm conclusion can be drawn. The overwhelming majority of these accounts pertain to alleged discrimination by the States in the provision of public services and public accommodations, which areas are addressed in Titles II and III of the ADA.

scarce financial resources by hiring employees who are able to use existing facilities, the ADA requires employers to 'make existing facilities used by employees readily accessible to and usable by individuals with disabilities.' The ADA does except employers from the 'reasonable accommodation' requirement where the employer 'can demonstrate that the accommodation would impose an undue hardship on the operation of the business of such covered entity.' However, even with this exception, the accommodation duty far exceeds what is constitutionally required. [The] Act also makes it the employer's duty to prove that it would suffer such a burden, instead of requiring (as the Constitution does) that the complaining party negate reasonable bases for the employer's decision.

"The ADA also forbids 'utilizing standards, criteria, or methods of administration' that disparately impact the disabled, without regard to whether such conduct has a rational basis. Although disparate impact may be relevant evidence of racial discrimination, see *Washington v. Davis,* [Ch. 9, Sec. 2, III] such evidence alone is insufficient even where the Fourteenth Amendment subjects state action to strict scrutiny.

"The ADA's constitutional shortcomings are apparent when the Act is compared to Congress' efforts in the Voting Rights Act of 1965 [in which] Congress documented a marked pattern of unconstitutional action by the States. State officials, Congress found, routinely applied voting tests in order to exclude African–American citizens from registering to vote. Congress also determined that litigation had proved ineffective and that there persisted an otherwise inexplicable 50–percentage-point gap in the registration of white and African–American voters in some States."

KENNEDY, J., joined by O'Connor, J., who joined the Court's opinion, concurred: "For the reasons explained by the Court, an equal protection violation has not been [shown]. If the States had been transgressing the Fourteenth Amendment by their mistreatment or lack of concern for those with impairments, one would have expected to find in decisions of the [courts] extensive litigation and discussion of the constitutional violations. This confirming judicial documentation does not exist. That there is a new awareness, a new consciousness, a new commitment to better treatment of those disadvantaged by mental or physical impairments does not establish that an absence of state statutory correctives was a constitutional violation."

BREYER, J. joined by Stevens, Souter and Ginsburg, JJ., dissented: "There are roughly 300 examples of discrimination by state governments themselves in the legislative record. I fail to see how this evidence 'fall[s] far short of even suggesting the pattern of unconstitutional discrimination on which §§ 5 legislation must be based.'

"The congressionally appointed task force collected numerous specific examples, provided by persons with disabilities themselves, of adverse, disparate treatment by state officials. They reveal, not what the Court describes as 'half a dozen' instances of discrimination, but hundreds of instances of adverse treatment at the hands of state officials—instances in which a person with a disability found it impossible to obtain a state job, to retain state employment, to use the public transportation that was readily available to others in order to get to work, or to obtain a public education, which is often a prerequisite to obtaining employment. State-imposed barriers also frequently made it difficult or impossible for people to vote, to enter a public building, to access important government services, such as calling for emergency assistance, and to find a place to live due to a pattern of irrational zoning decisions similar to the discrimination that we held unconstitutional in *Cleburne.*

"As the Court notes, those who presented instances of discrimination rarely provided additional, independent evidence sufficient to prove in court that, in each instance, the discrimination they suffered lacked justification from a judicial standpoint. [But] Congress, unlike courts, must, and does, routinely draw general conclusions—for example, of likely motive or of likely relationship to legitimate need—from anecdotal and opinion-based evidence of this kind, particularly when the evidence lacks strong refutation. In reviewing §§ 5 legislation, we have never required the sort of extensive investigation of each piece of evidence that the Court appears to contemplate. Nor has the Court traditionally required Congress to make findings as to state discrimination, or to break down the record evidence, category by category. * * * Congress could have reasonably believed that these examples represented signs of a widespread problem of unconstitutional discrimination. * * *

"The problem with the Court's approach is that neither the 'burden of proof' that favors States nor any other rule of restraint applicable to *judges* applies to *Congress* when it exercises its §§ 5 power. * * * Rational-basis review—with its presumptions favoring constitutionality—is 'a paradigm of *judicial* restraint.' *FCC v. Beach Communications,* [Ch. 9, Sec. 1]. And the Congress of the United States is not a lower court. Indeed, [*Cleburne*] made clear that the absence of a contrary congressional finding was critical to our decision to apply mere rational-basis review to disability discrimination claims—a 'congressional direction' to apply a more stringent standard would have been 'controlling.' * * *

"There is simply no reason to require Congress, seeking to determine facts relevant to the exercise of its §§ 5 authority, to adopt rules or presumptions that reflect a court's institutional limitations. Unlike courts, Congress can readily gather facts from across the Nation, assess the magnitude of a problem, and more easily find an appropriate remedy. Cf. *Cleburne* (addressing the problems of the 'large and diversified group' of persons with disabilities 'is a difficult and often a technical matter, very much a task for legislators guided by qualified professionals and not by the perhaps ill-informed opinions of the judiciary'). Unlike courts, Congress directly reflects public attitudes and beliefs, enabling Congress better to understand where, and to what extent, refusals to accommodate a disability amount to behavior that is callous or unreasonable to the point of lacking constitutional justification. Unlike judges, Members of Congress can directly obtain information from constituents who have first-hand experience with discrimination and related issues.

"Moreover, unlike judges, Members of Congress are elected. [To] apply a rule designed to restrict courts as if it restricted Congress' legislative power is to stand the underlying principle—a principle of judicial restraint—on its head. * * *

"The Court argues in alternative that the statute's damage remedy is not 'congruent' with and 'proportional' to the equal protection problem that Congress found. [But] it is just that power—the power to require more than the minimum that §§ 5 grants to Congress, as this Court has repeatedly confirmed. * * * Nothing in the words 'reasonable accommodation' suggests that the requirement has no 'tend[ency] to enforce' the Equal Protection Clause, *Ex parte Virginia,* that it is an irrational way to achieve the objective, *South Carolina,* that it would fall outside the scope of the Necessary and Proper Clause, *Morgan,* or that it somehow otherwise exceeds the bounds of the 'appropriate,' U.S. Const., Amdt. 14, §§ 5.* * *

"[The] legislation before us [does] not discriminate against anyone, nor does it pose any threat to basic liberty. And it is difficult to understand why the Court, which applies 'minimum "rational-basis" review' to statutes that *burden* persons with disabilities, subjects to far stricter scrutiny a statute that seeks to *help* those same individuals.

"I recognize nonetheless that this statute imposes a burden upon States in that it removes their Eleventh Amendment protection from suit, thereby subjecting them to potential monetary liability. Rules for interpreting §§ 5 that would provide States with special protection, however, run counter to the very object of the Fourteenth Amendment. By its terms, that Amendment prohibits *States* from denying their citizens equal protection of the laws."

(iii) ***Prophylactic legislation.*** NEVADA DEP'T OF HUMAN RESOURCES v. HIBBS, 538 U.S. 721 (2003), per REHNQUIST, C.J., upheld Congress' §§ 5 power to abrogate state sovereign immunity and provide state employees damages under the Family and Medical Leave Act which entitles eligible employees up to 12 work weeks of unpaid leave annually for several reasons, including onset of a "serious health condition" in an employee's spouse, child, or parent: "The FMLA aims to protect the right to be free from gender-based discrimination in the workplace. [According] to evidence that was before Congress when it enacted the FMLA, States continue to rely on invalid gender stereotypes in the employment context, specifically in the administration of leave benefits. Reliance on such stereotypes cannot justify the States' gender discrimination in this area. *United States v. Virginia*, [Ch. 9, Sec. 3, I]. The long and extensive history of sex discrimination prompted us to hold that measures that differentiate on the basis of gender warrant heightened scrutiny; [the] persistence of such unconstitutional discrimination by the States justifies Congress' passage of prophylactic §§ 5 legislation.

"As the FMLA's legislative record reflects, a 1990 Bureau of Labor Statistics (BLS) survey stated that 37 percent of surveyed private-sector employees were covered by maternity leave policies, while only 18 percent were covered by paternity leave policies. [The] data show an increase in the percentage of employees eligible for such leave, [but] they also show a widening of the gender gap [from 1989]. Thus, stereotype-based beliefs about the allocation of family duties remained firmly rooted, and employers' reliance on them in establishing discriminatory leave policies remained widespread.3

"Congress also heard testimony that '[p]arental leave for fathers [is] rare. Even [w]here child-care leave policies do exist, men, *both in the public and private sectors,* receive notoriously, discriminatory treatment in their requests for such leave.' " [This] and other differential leave policies [e.g., state employers' collective bargaining agreements] were not attributable to any differential physical needs of men and women, but rather to the pervasive sex-role stereotype that caring for family members is women's work.5

"Finally, Congress had evidence that, even where state laws and policies were not facially discriminatory, they were applied in discriminatory ways. It was aware of the 'serious problems with the discretionary nature of family leave,' because when 'the authority to grant leave and to arrange the length of that leave rests

3. While this and other material described leave policies in the private sector, a 50–state survey also before Congress demonstrated that "[t]he proportion and construction of leave policies available to public sector employees differs little from those offered private sector employees."

5. * * *Justice Kennedy's dissent ignores this common foundation that, as Congress found, has historically produced discrimination in the hiring and promotion of women. Consideration of such evidence does not, as the dissent contends, expand our §§ 5 inquiry to include "*general* gender-based stereotypes in employment." To the contrary, because parenting and family leave address very similar situations in which work and family responsibilities conflict, they implicate the same stereotypes.

with individual supervisors,' it leaves 'employees open to discretionary and possibly unequal treatment.' * * *

"In spite of all of the above evidence, Justice Kennedy argues in dissent that Congress' passage of the FMLA was unnecessary because 'the States appear to have been ahead of Congress in providing gender-neutral family leave benefits,' and points to Nevada's leave policies in particular. However, it was only '[s]ince Federal family leave legislation was first introduced' that the States had even 'begun to consider similar family leave initiatives.'

"Furthermore, the dissent's statement that some States 'had adopted some form of family-care leave' before the FMLA's enactment, glosses over important shortcomings of some state policies. First, seven States had childcare leave provisions that applied to women only. [Second,] 12 States provided their employees no family leave, beyond an initial childbirth or adoption, to care for a seriously ill child or family member. Third, many States provided [only] voluntary or discretionary leave programs.a Three States left the amount of leave time primarily in employers' hands. Congress could reasonably conclude that such discretionary family-leave programs would do little to combat the stereotypes about the roles of male and female employees that Congress sought to eliminate. [N]o matter how generous petitioner's own may have been, Congress was justified in enacting the FMLA as remedial legislation.

"In sum, the States' record of unconstitutional participation in, and fostering of, gender-based discrimination in the administration of leave benefits is weighty enough to justify the enactment of prophylactic §§ 5 legislation.

"[Here, unlike *Kimel* and *Garrett*,] Congress directed its attention to state gender discrimination, which triggers a heightened level of scrutiny [that makes it] easier for Congress to show a pattern of state constitutional violations. Congress was similarly successful in *South Carolina.* * * *

"We believe that Congress' chosen remedy [is] 'congruent and proportional to the targeted violation.' [By] setting a minimum standard of family leave for *all* eligible employees, irrespective of gender, the FMLA attacks the formerly state-sanctioned stereotype that only women are responsible for family caregiving, thereby reducing employers' incentives to engage in discrimination by basing hiring and promotion decisions on stereotypes.

"[In] the dissent's view, in the face of evidence of gender-based discrimination by the States in the provision of leave benefits, Congress could do no more in exercising its §§ 5 power than simply proscribe such discrimination. But this position cannot be squared with our recognition that Congress 'is not confined to the enactment of legislation that merely parrots the precise wording of the Fourteenth Amendment,' but may prohibit 'a somewhat broader swath of conduct, including that which is not itself forbidden by the Amendment's text.' [*Kimel.*]

"Indeed, in light of the evidence before Congress, a statute mirroring Title VII, that simply mandated gender equality in the administration of leave benefits, would not have achieved Congress' remedial object. Such a law would allow States to provide for no family leave at all. Where '[t]wo-thirds of the nonprofessional caregivers for older, chronically ill, or disabled persons are working women,' and state practices continue to reinforce the stereotype of women as caregivers, such a policy would exclude far more women than men from the workplace.

a. Kennedy, J., responded: "The Court does not argue the States intended to enable employers to discriminate in the provision of family leave; nor [is] there evidence state employers discriminated in the administration of leave benefits."

"Unlike the statutes at issue in *Boerne, Kimel,* and *Garrett,* which applied broadly to every aspect of state employers' operations, the FMLA is narrowly targeted at the fault line between work and family—precisely where sex-based overgeneralization has been and remains strongest—and affects only one aspect of the employment relationship."

"We also find significant the many other limitations that Congress placed on the scope of this measure. The FMLA requires only unpaid leave, and applies only to employees who have worked for the employer for at least one year and provided 1,250 hours of service within the last 12 months. Employees in high-ranking or sensitive positions are simply ineligible for FMLA leave; of particular importance to the States, the FMLA expressly excludes from coverage state elected officials, their staffs, and appointed policymakers. [In] choosing 12 weeks as the appropriate leave floor, Congress chose a middle ground, a period long enough to serve 'the needs of families' but not so long that it would upset 'the legitimate interests of employers.' [The] damages recoverable are strictly defined and measured by actual monetary losses, and the accrual period for backpay is limited by the Act's 2–year statute of limitations (extended to three years only for willful violations)."

KENNEDY, J., joined by Scalia and Thomas, JJ., dissented on the ground that Congress had failed "to make the requisite showing. [The] Act's findings of purpose are devoid of any discussion of the relevant evidence." See *Chittister v. Department of Community and Econ. Dev.,* 226 F.3d 223, 228–229 (C.A.3 2000) ("Notably absent is any finding concerning the existence, much less the prevalence, in public employment of personal sick leave practices that amounted to intentional gender discrimination in violation of the Equal Protection Clause"). * * *

"The Court seeks to connect the evidence of private discrimination to an alleged pattern of unconstitutional behavior by States through inferences drawn from two sources. [Both] statements were made during the hearings on the proposed 1986 national leave legislation, and so preceded the Act by seven years. The 1986 bill, which was not enacted, differed in an important respect from the legislation Congress eventually passed. That proposal sought to provide parenting leave, not leave to care for another ill family member. [Thus, this] evidence concerns the Act's grant of parenting leave, and is too attenuated to justify the family leave provision.* * *

"The Court next argues [that] many States did not guarantee the right to family leave by statute, instead leaving the decision up to individual employers, who could subject employees to 'discretionary and possibly unequal treatment.' The study from which the Court derives this conclusion examined 'the parental leave policies of Federal executive branch agencies.' [A] history of discrimination on the part of the Federal Government may, in some situations, support an inference of similar conduct by the States, but the Court does not explain why the inference is justified here.* * *

"The Court acknowledges that States have adopted family leave programs prior to federal intervention, but argues these policies suffered from serious imperfections. [Given] that the States assumed a pioneering role in the creation of family leave schemes, it is not surprising these early efforts may have been imperfect. This is altogether different, however, from purposeful discrimination. * * *

"Stripped of the conduct which exhibits no constitutional infirmity, the Court's 'exten[sive] and specifi[c] record of unconstitutional state conduct,' boils down to the fact that three States, Massachusetts, Kansas, and Tennessee, provided parenting leave only to their female employees, and had no program for granting their employees (male or female) family leave. [The] few incidents identified by the Court 'fall far short of even suggesting the pattern of unconstitutional discrimination on which §§ 5 legislation must be based.' *Garrett.* [Given] the insufficiency of the evidence that States discriminated in the provision of family leave, the unfortunate fact that stereotypes about women continue to be a serious and pervasive social problem would not alone support the charge that a State has engaged in a practice designed to deny its citizens the equal protection of the laws. *Garrett.*

"[If] Congress had been concerned about different treatment of men and women with respect to family leave, a congruent remedy would have sought to ensure the benefits of any leave program enacted by a State are available to men and women on an equal basis. Instead, the Act imposes, across the board, a requirement that States grant a minimum of 12 weeks of leave per year. This requirement may represent Congress' considered judgment as to the optimal balance. [It] does not follow, however, that if the States choose to enact a different benefit scheme, they should be deemed to engage in unconstitutional conduct and forced to open their treasuries to private suits for damages."

SCALIA, J., dissenting, added: "The constitutional violation that is a prerequisite to 'prophylactic' congressional action to 'enforce' the Fourteenth Amendment is a violation *by the State against which the enforcement action is taken*. There is no guilt by association, enabling the sovereignty of one State to be abridged under §§ 5 of the Fourteenth Amendment because of violations by another State, or by most other States, or even by 49 other States. [T]he Court does not even attempt to demonstrate that each one of the 50 States covered by [the Act] was in violation of the Fourteenth Amendment. [This] will not do. Prophylaxis in the sense of extending the remedy beyond the violation is one thing; prophylaxis in the sense of extending the remedy beyond the violator is something else. See *Rome.*"

(b) ***Due process.*** (i) FLORIDA PREPAID POSTSECONDARY EDUCATION EXPENSE BOARD v. COLLEGE SAVINGS BANK, 527 U.S. 627 (1999), per REHNQUIST, C.J., concerned Congress' § 5 power to expressly make states subject to federal court actions for patent infringement: Although patents "have long been considered a species [of] 'property' of which no person may be deprived by a State without due process [,] Congress identified no pattern of patent infringement by the States, let alone a pattern of constitutional violations. [At] most, Congress heard testimony that patent infringement by States might increase in the future. [Further,] only where the State provides no remedy, or only inadequate remedies, to injured patent owners [could] a deprivation of property without due process result. [The] legislative record thus suggests that the Patent Remedy Act does not respond to a history of 'widespread and persisting deprivation of constitutional rights' of the sort Congress has faced in enacting proper prophylactic § 5 legislation. * * * [*Boerne.*]"

STEVENS, J., joined by Souter, Ginsburg and Breyer, JJ., dissented: "[I]t is well known that not all States have waived their sovereign immunity from suit, and among those States that have, the contours of this waiver vary widely. Even if such remedies might be available in theory, it would have been 'appropriate' for Congress to conclude that they would not guarantee patentees due process in infringement actions against state defendants. State judges have never had the exposure to patent litigation that federal judges have experienced for decades, [and] the entire category of such cases would raise questions of impartiality."

(ii) ***Fundamental rights.*** TENNESSEE v. LANE, 541 U.S. 509 (2004), per STEVENS, J., upheld Congress' § 5 power to authorize private citizens to sue states for damages under Title II of the ADA, which "seeks to enforce a variety [of] basic constitutional guarantees [like] the right of access to the courts at issue in this case, that are protected by the Due Process Clause": "Congress identified important shortcomings in existing laws that [disclosed] hundreds of examples of unequal treatment of persons with disabilities by States and their political subdivisions. [As] *Garrett* observed, the 'overwhelming majority' of these examples concerned discrimination in the administration of public programs and services.

"With respect to the particular services at issue in this case, Congress learned that many individuals, in many States across the country, were being excluded from courthouses and court proceedings by reason of their disabilities. [And various judicial decisions] also demonstrate a pattern of unconstitutional treatment in the administration of justice.

"[T]he dissent's contention that the record is insufficient to justify Congress' exercise of its prophylactic power is puzzling, to say the least. Just last Term in *Hibbs*, we approved the [FMLA] based primarily on evidence of disparate provision of parenting leave, little of which concerned unconstitutional state conduct. We explained that because the FMLA was targeted at sex-based classifications, which are subject to a heightened standard of judicial scrutiny, 'it was easier for Congress to show a pattern of state constitutional violations' than in *Garrett* or *Kimel*, both of which concerned legislation that targeted classifications subject to rational-basis review. Title II is aimed at the enforcement of a variety of basic rights, including the right of access to the courts at issue in this case, that call for a standard of judicial review at least as searching, and in some cases more searching, than the standard that applies to sex-based classifications.

" * * * Title II reaches a wide array of official conduct in an effort to enforce an equally wide array of constitutional guarantees. Petitioner urges [that] the fact that Title II applies not only to public education and voting-booth access but also to seating at state-owned hockey rinks indicates that Title II is not appropriately tailored to serve its objectives. But [the] question presented in this case is not whether Congress can validly subject the States to private suits for money damages for failing to provide reasonable access to hockey rinks, or even to voting booths, but whether Congress had the power under §§ 5 to enforce the constitutional right of access to the courts. [See] *United States v. Raines*, 362 U.S. 17 (1960).19

" * * * Title II's requirement of program accessibility, is congruent and proportional to its object of enforcing the right of access to [courts.] Congress required the States to take reasonable measures to remove architectural and other barriers to accessibility. [It] requires only 'reasonable modifications.' [In] the case of facilities built or altered [before] 1992, [for] which structural change is likely to be more difficult, a public entity may comply with Title II by adopting a variety of less costly measures, including relocating services to alternative, accessible sites and assigning aides to assist persons with disabilities in accessing services. Only if these measures are ineffective in achieving accessibility is the public entity required to make reasonable structural changes. And in no event is the entity required to undertake measures that would impose an undue financial or administrative burden, threaten historic preservation interests, or effect a fundamental alteration in the nature of the service.

---

19. In *Raines*, a State subject to suit under the Civil Rights Act of 1957 contended that the law exceeded Congress' power to enforce the Fifteenth Amendment because it prohibited "any person," and not just state actors, from interfering with voting rights. We rejected that argument, concluding that "if the complaint here called for an application of the statute clearly constitutional under the Fifteenth Amendment, that should have been an end to the question of constitutionality."

"[Under due process,] a State must afford to all individuals '[a] meaningful opportunity to be heard' in its courts. *Boddie v. Connecticut*, 401 U.S. 371 (1971).20 Our cases have recognized a number of affirmative obligations that flow from this principle: the duty to waive filing fees in certain family-law and criminal cases, the duty to provide transcripts to criminal defendants seeking review of their convictions, and the duty to provide counsel to certain criminal defendants. Each of these cases makes clear that ordinary considerations of cost and convenience alone cannot justify a State's failure to provide individuals with a meaningful right of access to the courts.[24]"a

REHNQUIST, J., joined by Kennedy and Thomas, JJ., dissented: "[T]he majority identifies nothing in the legislative record that shows Congress was responding to widespread violations of the due process rights of disabled persons. Rather, [the] majority sets out on a wide-ranging account of societal discrimination against the disabled [through] institutionalization laws, restrictions on marriage, voting, and public education, conditions in mental hospitals, and various other forms of unequal treatment in the administration of public programs and services. Some of this evidence would be relevant if the Court were considering the constitutionality of the statute as a whole; but the Court rejects that approach in favor of a narrower 'as-applied' inquiry. We discounted much the same type of outdated, generalized evidence in [*Garrett*].

"With respect to the due process 'access to the courts' rights on which the Court ultimately relies, [there] is nothing in the legislative record or statutory findings to indicate that disabled persons were systematically denied the right to be present at criminal trials, denied the meaningful opportunity to be heard in civil cases, unconstitutionally excluded from jury service, or denied the right to attend criminal trials.4 [8,9]

20. Because this case implicates the right of access to the courts, we need not consider whether Title II's duty to accommodate exceeds what the Constitution requires in the class of cases that implicate only *Cleburne's* prohibition on irrational discrimination.

24. The Chief Justice contends that Title II cannot be understood as remedial legislation because it "subjects a State to liability for failing to make a vast array of special accommodations, *without regard for whether the failure to accommodate results in a constitutional wrong*." (emphasis in original). But as we have often acknowledged, Congress "is not confined to the enactment of legislation that merely parrots the precise wording of the Fourteenth Amendment," and may prohibit "a somewhat broader swath of conduct, including that which is not itself forbidden by the Amendment's text." *Kimel.*

a. The Court upheld the Sixth Circuit's affirmance of the federal district judge's denial of the state's motion to dismiss on Eleventh Amendment grounds. The Sixth Circuit "noted that the case presented difficult questions that 'cannot be clarified absent a a factual record,' and remanded for further proceedings."

Similarly, see *United States v. Georgia*, 546 U.S. 151 (2006), per Scalia, J., unanimously upholding Congress' § 5 power to authorize damages against states under Title II of the ADA for conditions of confinement for disabled prisoners that violate the Eighth Amendment's

prohibition of cruel and unusual punishment, made applicable to the states through the Due Process Clause.

4. Certainly, respondents Lane and Jones were not denied these constitutional rights. The majority admits that Lane was able to attend the initial hearing of his criminal trial [by crawling up two flights of stairs]. Lane was arrested for failing to appear at his second hearing only after he refused assistance from officers dispatched by the court to help him to the courtroom. The court conducted a preliminary hearing in the first-floor library to accommodate Lane's disability, and later offered to move all further proceedings in the case to a handicapped-accessible courthouse in a nearby town. Respondent Jones, a disabled court reporter, does not seriously contend that she suffered a constitutional injury.

8. The majority rather peculiarly points to Congress' finding that "discrimination against individuals with disabilities persists in such critical areas as *access to public services*" as evidence that Congress sought to vindicate the Due Process rights of disabled persons. However, one does not usually refer to the right to attend a judicial proceeding as "access to [a] public servic[e]." Given the lack of any concern over courthouse accessibility issues in the legislative history, it is highly unlikely that this legislative finding obliquely refers to state violations of the due process rights of disabled persons to attend judicial proceedings.

"Even if the anecdotal evidence and conclusory statements relied on by the majority could be properly considered, the mere existence of an architecturally 'inaccessible' courthouse—i.e., one a disabled person cannot utilize without assistance—does not state a constitutional violation. A violation of due process occurs only when a person is actually denied the constitutional right to access a given judicial proceeding. We have never held that a person has a *constitutional* right to make his way into a courtroom without any external assistance. * * *

"The majority concludes that Title II's massive overbreadth can be cured by considering the statute only 'as it applies to the class of cases implicating the accessibility of judicial services.' [In] conducting its as-applied analysis, however, the majority posits a hypothetical statute, never enacted by Congress, that applies only to courthouses. [If] we had arbitrarily constricted the scope of the statutes to match the scope of a core constitutional right, [our § 5 precedents] might have come out differently. In *Garrett*, for example, Title I might have been upheld 'as applied' to irrational employment discrimination; or in *Florida Prepaid*, the Patent Remedy Act might have been upheld 'as applied' to intentional, uncompensated patent infringements.b It is thus not surprising that the only authority cited by the majority is *Raines*, a case decided long before we enunciated the congruence-and-proportionality test.

"I fear that the Court's adoption of an as-applied approach eliminates any incentive for Congress to craft § 5 legislation for the purpose of remedying or deterring actual constitutional violations. Congress can now simply rely on the courts to sort out which hypothetical applications of an undifferentiated statute, such as Title II, may be enforced against the States. All the while, States will be subjected to substantial litigation in a piecemeal attempt to vindicate their Eleventh Amendment rights. * * *

"The majority's reliance on *Boddie*, and other cases in which we held that due process requires the State to waive filing fees for indigent litigants, is unavailing. While these cases support the principle that the State must remove financial requirements that in fact prevent an individual from exercising his constitutional rights, they certainly do not support a statute that subjects a State to liability for failing to make a vast array of special accommodations, *without regard for whether the failure to accommodate results in a constitutional wrong.*"

Scalia, J., also dissented because "the 'congruence and proportionality' standard, like all such flabby tests, is a standing invitation to judicial arbitrariness and policy-driven decisionmaking. Worse still, it casts this Court in the role of Congress's taskmaster. Under it, the courts (and ultimately this Court) must regularly check Congress's homework to make sure that it has identified sufficient constitutional violations to make its remedy congruent and proportional. As a general matter, we are ill advised to adopt or adhere to constitutional rules that bring us into constant conflict with a coequal branch of Government. * * *

"I would replace 'congruence and proportionality' with another test—one that provides a clear, enforceable limitation supported by the text of § 5. * * * Section

9. The Court correctly explains that "it [i]s easier for Congress to show a pattern of state constitutional violations" when it targets state action that triggers a higher level of constitutional scrutiny. [But] Congress may not dispense with the required showing altogether simply because it purports to enforce due process rights. See *Florida Prepaid*; *Boerne*. * * *

b. Stevens, J., replied: "[N]either *Garrett* nor *Florida Prepaid* lends support to the proposition that the ["congruence-and-proportionality"] test requires courts in all cases to 'measur[e] the full breadth of the statute or relevant provision that Congress enacted against the scope of the constitutional right it purported to enforce.' In fact, the decision in *Garrett*, which severed Title I of the ADA from Title II for purposes of the § 5 inquiry, demonstrates that courts need not examine 'the full breadth of the statute' all at once."

5 authorizes Congress to create a cause of action through which the citizen may vindicate his Fourteenth Amendment rights. One of the first pieces of legislation passed under Congress's § 5 power [is now codified in § 1983]. Section 5 would also authorize measures that do not restrict the States' substantive scope of action but impose requirements directly related to the facilitation of 'enforcement'—for example, reporting requirements that would enable violations of the Fourteenth Amendment to be identified. But what § 5 does not authorize is so-called 'prophylacti; measures, prohibiting primary conduct that is itself not forbidden by the Fourteenth Amendment.

"[P]rincipally for reasons of stare decisis, I shall henceforth apply the permissive *McCulloch* standard [used in *South Carolina* and *Morgan*] to congressional measures designed to remedy racial discrimination by the States. I would not, however, abandon the requirement that Congress may impose prophylactic § 5 legislation only upon those particular States in which there has been an identified history of relevant constitutional violations."c

(c) *State action.* UNITED STATES v. MORRISON, Ch. 2, Sec. 2, IV, per REHNQUIST, C.J., held that Congress had no § 5 power to grant a civil remedy to victims of gender-motivated violence despite Congress' (1) receiving "evidence that many participants in state justice systems are perpetuating an array of erroneous stereotypes and assumptions," and (2) concluding "that these discriminatory stereotypes often result in insufficient investigation and prosecution of gender-motivated crime, inappropriate focus on the behavior and credibility of the victims of that crime, and unacceptably lenient punishments for those who are actually convicted of gender-motivated violence":

"[S]tate-sponsored gender discrimination violates equal protection unless it 'serves "important governmental objectives and [the] discriminatory means employed" are "substantially related to the achievement of those objectives." ' *United States v. Virginia.* However, the language and purpose of the Fourteenth Amendment place certain limitations on the manner in which Congress may attack discriminatory conduct. [Foremost] is the time-honored principle that the Fourteenth Amendment, by its very terms, prohibits only state action. * * *

"Shortly after the Fourteenth Amendment was adopted, we decided two cases interpreting the Amendment's provisions, *United States v. Harris*, 106 U.S. 629 (1883), and the *Civil Rights Cases*. [*Harris*] considered a challenge to § 2 of the Civil Rights Act of 1871. That section sought to punish 'private persons' for 'conspiring to deprive any one of the equal protection of the laws enacted by the State.' We concluded that this law exceeded Congress' § 5 power because the law was 'directed exclusively against the action of private persons, without reference to the laws of the State, or their administration by her officers.' [We] reached a similar conclusion in the *Civil Rights Cases.* * * *

"Petitioners rely on *Guest* for the proposition that the rule laid down in the *Civil Rights Cases* is no longer good law. In *Guest*, [t]hree Members of the Court, in a separate opinion by Justice Brennan, expressed the view that the *Civil Rights Cases* were wrongly decided, and that Congress could under § 5 prohibit actions by private individuals. Three other Members of the Court, who joined the opinion of the Court, joined a separate opinion by Justice Clark which in two or three sentences stated the conclusion that Congress could 'punis[h] all conspiracies—

c. In a separate concurring opinion, Ginsburg, J., joined by Souter and Breyer, JJ., responded: "Members of Congress are understandably reluctant to condemn their own States as constitutional violators, complicit in maintaining the isolated and unequal status of persons with disabilities. I would not disarm a National Legislature for resisting an adversarial approach to lawmaking better suited to the courtroom."

with or without state action—that interfere with Fourteenth Amendment rights.' [We] have no hesitation in saying that it would take more than the naked dicta contained in Justice Clark's opinion, when added to Justice Brennan's opinion, to cast any doubt upon the enduring vitality of the *Civil Rights Cases* and *Harris*."

Sec. 13981 "is directed not at any State or state actor, but at individuals who have committed criminal acts motivated by gender bias. [It] visits no consequence whatever on any Virginia public official involved in investigating or prosecuting Brzonkala's assault. The section is, therefore, unlike any of the § 5 remedies that we have previously upheld"—as in *Morgan, South Carolina*, and *Ex parte Virginia*, which were directed at states or state officials. The "remedy is not 'corrective in its character, adapted to counteract and redress the operation of such prohibited state laws or proceedings of state officers.' *Civil Rights Cases*.a Or, as we have phrased it in more recent cases, prophylactic legislation under § 5 must have a 'congruence and proportionality between the injury to be prevented or remedied and the means adopted to that end.'

"Section 13981 is also different from these previously upheld remedies in that it applies uniformly throughout the Nation. Congress' findings indicate that the problem of discrimination against the victims of gender-motivated crimes does not exist in all States, or even most States. By contrast, the § 5 remedy upheld in *Morgan* was directed only to the State where the evil found by Congress existed, and in *South Carolina,* the remedy was directed only to those States in which Congress found that there had been discrimination."

BREYER, J., joined by Stevens, J., "doubt[ed] the Court's reasoning," but did not "answer the § 5 question"b: "The Federal Government's argument [is] that Congress used § 5 to remedy the actions of *state actors*, namely, those States which, through discriminatory design or the discriminatory conduct of their officials, failed to provide adequate (or any) state remedies for women injured by gender-motivated violence—a failure that the States, and Congress, documented in depth." Breyer J., argued that the *Civil Rights Cases* did not consider "this kind of claim," because the statute "did 'not profess to be corrective of any constitutional wrong committed by the States' [but] established 'rules for the conduct of individuals in society towards each other, [without] referring in any manner to any supposed action of the State or its authorities.'

"[W]hy can Congress not provide a remedy against private actors? Those private actors, of course, did not themselves violate the Constitution. But this Court has held that Congress at least sometimes can enact remedial 'legislation [that] prohibits conduct which is not itself unconstitutional.' The statutory remedy [may] lead state actors to improve their own remedial systems, primarily through example. It restricts private actors only by imposing liability for private conduct that is, in the main, already forbidden by state law. Why is the remedy 'disproportionate'? And given the relation between remedy and violation—the creation of a federal remedy to substitute for constitutionally inadequate state remedies—where is the lack of 'congruence'?

" * * * Congress had before it the task force reports of at least 21 States documenting constitutional violations. And it made its own findings about pervasive gender-based stereotypes hampering many state legal systems, sometimes

a. The Court noted: "There is abundant evidence [t]o show that the Congresses that enacted the [laws in the *Civil Rights Cases*] had a purpose similar to that of Congress in enacting § 13981: There were state laws on the books bespeaking equality of treatment, but in the administration of these laws there was discrimination against newly freed slaves."

b. Souter and Ginsburg, JJ., having found the law valid under the Commerce Clause, felt no occasion to reach the § 5 issue.

unconstitutionally so. The record nowhere reveals a congressional finding that the problem 'does not exist' elsewhere. [This] Court has not previously held that Congress must document the existence of a problem in every State prior to proposing a national solution."c

c. *Mitchell* unanimously upheld the extension *nationwide* of Voting Rights Act of 1965 § 4a's prohibition of "any test or device" (including literacy tests) "as a prerequisite for voting or registration." Black, J., reasoned that "Congress had before it a long history of the discriminatory use of literacy tests to disfranchise voters on account of their race. [A]s to the Nation as a whole, Congress had before it statistics which demonstrate that voter registration and voter participation are consistently greater in States without literacy tests." Harlan, J., added: "Despite the lack of evidence of specific instances of discriminatory application or effect, Congress could have determined that racial prejudice is prevalent throughout the Nation, and that literacy tests unduly lend themselves to discriminatory application, either conscious or unconscious. This danger of violation of § 1 of the Fifteenth Amendment was sufficient to authorize the exercise of congressional power under § 2. [While] a less sweeping approach in this delicate area might well have been appropriate, the choice which Congress made was within the range of the reasonable." Stewart, J., joined by Burger, C.J., and Blackmun, J., held: "Because the justification for extending the ban on literacy tests to the entire Nation need not turn on whether literacy tests unfairly discriminate against Negroes in every State in the Union, Congress was not required to make state-by-state [findings]. In the interests of uniformity, Congress may paint with a much broader brush than may this Court, which must confine itself to the judicial function of deciding individual cases and controversies upon individual records. * * * Experience gained under the 1965 Act has now led Congress to conclude that it should go the whole distance. This approach to the problem is a rational one; consequently it is within [the] power of Congress under § 2 of the Fifteenth Amendment."

Chapter 12

LIMITATIONS ON JUDICIAL POWER AND REVIEW

SECTION 2. STANDING

I. THE STRUCTURE OF STANDING DOCTRINE

ALLEN v. WRIGHT

468 U.S. 737, 104 S.Ct. 3315, 82 L.Ed.2d 556 (1984).

Justice O'Connor delivered the opinion of the Court.

Parents of black public school children allege in this nation-wide class action that the Internal Revenue Service (IRS) has not adopted sufficient standards and procedures to fulfill its obligation to deny tax-exempt status to racially discriminatory private schools. They assert that the IRS thereby harms them directly and interferes with the ability of their children to receive an education in desegregated public schools. The issue before us is whether plaintiffs have standing to bring this suit. We hold that they do not.

[Respondents] allege in their complaint that many racially segregated private schools were created or expanded in their communities at the time the public schools were undergoing desegregation. According to the complaint, many such private schools, including 17 schools or school systems identified by name in the complaint (perhaps some 30 schools in all), receive tax exemptions either directly or through the tax-exempt status of "umbrella" organizations that operate or support the [schools.]11 Respondents allege that the IRS grant of tax exemptions to such racially discriminatory schools is unlawful [under federal statutes and the Constitution, and they seek declaratory and injunctive relief].

[R]espondents do not allege that their children have been the victims of discriminatory exclusion from the schools whose tax exemptions they challenge as unlawful. [Rather,] respondents claim a direct injury from the mere fact of the challenged Government conduct and, as indicated by the restriction of the plaintiff class to parents of children in desegregating school districts, injury to their children's opportunity to receive a desegregated education. * * *

II.   Article III of the Constitution confines the federal courts to adjudicating actual "cases" and "controversies." As the Court explained in *Valley Forge Christian College v. Americans United for Separation of Church and State, Inc.*,

---

11. * * * Contrary to Justice Brennan's statement, the complaint does not allege that each desegregating district in which they re-side contains one or more racially discriminatory private schools unlawfully receiving a tax exemption.

454 U.S. 464 (1982), the "case or controversy" requirement defines with respect to the Judicial Branch the idea of separation of powers on which the Federal Government is founded. The several doctrines that have grown up to elaborate that requirement are "founded in concern about the proper—and properly limited—role of the courts in a democratic society." * * *

The Art. III doctrine that requires a litigant to have "standing" to invoke the power of a federal court is perhaps the most important of these doctrines. "In essence the question of standing is whether the litigant is entitled to have the court decide the merits of the dispute or of particular issues." Standing doctrine embraces several judicially self-imposed limits on the exercise of federal jurisdiction, such as the general prohibition on a litigant's raising another person's legal rights, the rule barring adjudication of generalized grievances more appropriately addressed in the representative branches, and the requirement that a plaintiff's complaint fall within the zone of interests protected by the law invoked. The requirement of standing, however, has a core component derived directly from the Constitution. A plaintiff must allege personal injury fairly traceable to the defendant's allegedly unlawful conduct and likely to be redressed by the requested relief.

Like the prudential component, the constitutional component of standing doctrine incorporates concepts concededly not susceptible of precise definition. The injury alleged must be, for example, "distinct and palpable," and not "abstract" or "conjectural" or "hypothetical," *Los Angeles v. Lyons*, [infra]. The injury must be "fairly" traceable to the challenged action, and relief from the injury must be "likely" to follow from a favorable decision. See *Simon v. Eastern Kentucky Welfare Rights Org.*, 426 U.S. 26 (1976). (These terms cannot be defined so as to make application of the constitutional standing requirement a mechanical exercise.)

The absence of precise definitions, however, [hardly] leaves courts at sea in applying the law of standing. Like most legal notions, the standing concepts have gained considerable definition from developing case law. [More] important, the law of Art. III standing is built on a single basic idea—the idea of separation of powers. It is this fact which makes possible the gradual clarification of the law through judicial application. * * *

Respondents allege two injuries in their complaint to support their standing to bring this lawsuit. First, they say that they are harmed directly by the mere fact of Government financial aid to discriminatory private schools. Second, they say that the federal tax exemptions to racially discriminatory private schools in their communities impair their ability to have their public schools desegregated. [N]either suffices to support respondents' standing.

Respondents' first claim of injury [might] be a claim simply to have the Government avoid the violation of law alleged in respondents' complaint. Alternatively, it might be a claim of stigmatic injury, or denigration, suffered by all members of a racial group when the Government discriminates on the basis of race. Under neither interpretation is this claim of injury judicially cognizable.

This Court has repeatedly held that an asserted right to have the Government act in accordance with law is not sufficient, standing alone, to confer jurisdiction on a federal court. In *Schlesinger v. Reservists Committee to Stop the War*, 418 U.S. 208 (1974), for example, the Court rejected a claim of citizen standing to challenge Armed Forces Reserve commissions held by Members of Congress as violating the Incompatibility Clause of Art. I, § 6, of the Constitution. As citizens, the Court held, plaintiffs alleged nothing but "the abstract injury in nonobservance of the Constitution...." More recently, in *Valley Forge*, we rejected a claim of standing to challenge a Government conveyance of property to a religious institution. Insofar as the plaintiffs relied simply on "their shared individuated right" to a Government that made no law respecting an establishment of religion, we held that plaintiffs had not alleged a judicially cognizable injury. * * *

Neither do they have standing to litigate their claims based on the stigmatizing injury often caused by racial discrimination. There can be no doubt that this sort of noneconomic injury is one of the most serious consequences of discriminatory government action and is sufficient in some circumstances to support standing. Our cases make clear, however, that such injury accords a basis for standing only to "those persons who are personally denied equal treatment" by the challenged discriminatory conduct. [If an] abstract stigmatic injury were cognizable, standing would extend nationwide to all members of the particular racial groups against which the Government was alleged to be discriminating by its grant of a tax exemption to a racially discriminatory school, regardless of the location of that school. [A] black person in Hawaii could challenge the grant of a tax exemption to a racially discriminatory school in Maine. Recognition of standing in such circumstances would transform the federal courts into "no more than a vehicle for the vindication of the value interests of concerned bystanders." Constitutional limits on the role of the federal courts preclude such a transformation.

It is in their complaint's second claim of injury that respondents allege harm to a concrete, personal interest that can support standing in some circumstances. The injury they identify—their children's diminished ability to receive an education in a racially integrated school—is, beyond any doubt, not only judicially cognizable but, as shown by cases [since] *Brown v. Board of Education*, [Ch. 9, Sec. 2, supra] one of the most serious injuries recognized in our legal system. Despite the constitutional importance of curing the injury alleged by respondents, however, the federal judiciary may not redress it unless standing requirements are met. In this case, respondents' second claim of injury cannot support standing because the injury alleged is not fairly traceable to the Government conduct respondents challenge as unlawful.[22]

The illegal conduct challenged by respondents is the IRS's grant of tax exemptions to some racially discriminatory schools. The line of causation between that conduct and desegregation of respondents' schools is attenuated at best. From the perspective of the IRS, the injury to respondents is highly indirect and "results from the independent action of some third party not before the court." *Simon.* * * *

The diminished ability of respondents' children to receive a desegregated education would be fairly traceable to unlawful IRS grants of tax exemptions only if there were enough racially discriminatory private schools receiving tax exemptions in respondents' communities for withdrawal of those exemptions to make an

---

22. Respondents' stigmatic injury, though not sufficient for standing in the abstract form in which their complaint asserts it, is judicially cognizable to the extent that respondents are personally subject to discriminatory treatment. See *Heckler v. Mathews*, 465 U.S. 728 (1984) [upholding standing to challenge the denial of monetary benefits on an allegedly discriminatory basis even though the plaintiffs could not gain enhanced benefits by prevailing because the result instead would be lower benefits for others]. The stigmatic injury thus requires identification of some concrete interest with respect to which respondents are personally subject to discriminatory treatment. That interest must independently satisfy the causation requirement of standing doctrine.

[Here,] respondents identify only one interest that they allege is being discriminatorily impaired—their interest in desegregated public school education. Respondents' asserted stigmatic injury, therefore, is sufficient to support their standing in this litigation only if their school-desegregation injury independently meets the causation requirement of standing doctrine.

appreciable difference in public school integration. Respondents have made no such allegation. It [is] entirely speculative, as respondents themselves conceded in the Court of Appeals, whether withdrawal of a tax exemption from any particular school would lead the school to change its policies. It is just as speculative whether any given parent of a child attending such a private school would decide to transfer the child to public school as a result of any changes in educational or financial policy made by the private school once it was threatened with loss of tax-exempt status. It is also pure speculation whether, in a particular community, a large enough number of the numerous relevant school officials and parents would reach decisions that collectively would have a significant impact on the racial composition of the public schools. * * *

The Court of Appeals relied for its contrary conclusion on *Gilmore v. City of Montgomery* [and] *Norwood v. Harrison*, [both discussed in Ch. 10, Sec. 3 supra. Neither], however, requires that we find standing in this lawsuit.

In *Gilmore*, the plaintiffs [alleged] that the city was violating [their] equal protection right by permitting racially discriminatory private schools and other groups to use the public parks. The Court recognized plaintiffs' standing to challenge this city policy insofar as the policy permitted the exclusive use of the parks by racially discriminatory private [schools]. Standing in *Gilmore* thus rested on an allegation of direct deprivation of a right to equal use of the parks. * * *

In *Norwood v. Harrison*, parents of public school children in Tunica County, Miss., filed a statewide class action challenging the State's provision of textbooks to students attending racially discriminatory private schools in the State. The Court held the State's practice unconstitutional because it breached "the State's acknowledged duty to establish a unitary school system." The Court did not expressly address the basis for the plaintiffs' standing.

In *Gilmore*, however, the Court identified the basis for standing in *Norwood*: "The plaintiffs in Norwood were parties to a school desegregation order and the relief they sought was directly related to the concrete injury they suffered." Through the school-desegregation decree, the plaintiffs had acquired a right to have the State "steer clear" of any perpetuation of the racially dual school system that it had once sponsored. The interest acquired was judicially cognizable because it was a personal interest, created by law, in having the State refrain from taking specific actions. * * *

III. "The necessity that the plaintiff who seeks to invoke judicial power stand to profit in some personal interest remains an Art. III requirement." *Simon*. Respondents have not met this fundamental requirement. The judgment of the Court of Appeals is accordingly reversed, and the injunction issued by that court is vacated.

JUSTICE BRENNAN, dissenting.

[In] these cases, the respondents have alleged at least one type of injury that satisfies the constitutional requirement of "distinct and palpable injury."[3] In particular, they claim that the IRS's grant of tax-exempt status to racially discriminatory private schools directly injures their children's opportunity and ability to receive a desegregated education. * * *

The Court acknowledges that this alleged injury is sufficient to satisfy constitutional standards. [Moreover,] in light of the injuries they claim, the respondents have alleged a direct causal relationship between the Government

---

3. Because I conclude that the second injury alleged by the respondents is sufficient to satisfy constitutional requirements, I do not need to reach what the Court labels the "stigmatic injury." * * *

action they challenge and the injury they suffer: [Common] sense alone would recognize that the elimination of tax-exempt status for racially discriminatory private schools would serve to lessen the impact that those institutions have in defeating efforts to desegregate the public schools.

The Court admits that "[t]he diminished ability of respondents' children to receive a desegregated education would be fairly traceable to unlawful IRS grants of tax exemptions [if] there were enough racially discriminatory private schools receiving tax exemptions in respondents' communities for withdrawal of those exemptions to make an appreciable difference in public school integration," but concludes that "[r]espondents have made no such allegation." With all due respect, the Court has either misread the complaint or is improperly requiring the respondents to prove their case on the merits in order to defeat a motion to dismiss. For example, the respondents specifically refer by name to at least 32 private schools that discriminate on the basis of race and yet continue to benefit illegally from tax-exempt status. Eighteen of those schools [are] located in the city of Memphis, Tenn., which has been the subject of several court orders to desegregate. * * *

More than one commentator has noted that the causation component of the Court's standing inquiry is no more than a poor disguise for the Court's view of the merits of the underlying claims. The Court today does nothing to avoid that criticism. * * *

JUSTICE STEVENS, with whom JUSTICE BLACKMUN joins, dissenting.

[In the] final analysis, the wrong respondents allege that the Government has committed is to subsidize the exodus of white children from schools that would otherwise be racially integrated. The critical question in these cases, therefore, is whether respondents have alleged that the Government has created that kind of subsidy.

[If] the granting of preferential tax treatment would "encourage" private segregated schools to conduct their "charitable" activities, it must follow that the withdrawal of the treatment would "discourage" them, and hence promote the process of desegregation. [This] causation analysis is nothing more than a restatement of elementary economics: when something becomes more expensive, less of it will be purchased. [W]ithout tax-exempt status, private schools will either not be competitive in terms of cost, or have to change their admissions policies, hence reducing their competitiveness for parents seeking "a racially segregated alternative" to public schools, which is what respondents have alleged many white parents in desegregating school districts seek.

[Because] [c]onsiderations of tax policy, economics, and pure logic all confirm the conclusion that respondents' injury in fact is fairly traceable to the Government's allegedly wrongful conduct[,] [t]he Court [is] forced to introduce the concept of "separation of powers" into its analysis. [In doing so,] the Court could be saying that it will require a more direct causal connection when it is troubled by the separation of powers implications of the case before it. That approach confuses the standing doctrine with the justiciability of the issues that respondents seek to raise. The purpose of the standing inquiry is to measure the plaintiff's stake in the outcome, not whether a court has the authority to provide it with the outcome it seeks.

[As the Court has previously recognized,] the " 'fundamental aspect of standing' is that it focuses primarily on the *party* seeking to get his complaint before the federal court rather than 'on the issues he wishes to have adjudicated,' " *United States v. Richardson*, 418 U.S. 166, 174 (1974). [If] a plaintiff presents a nonjusticiable issue, or seeks relief that a court may not award, then its complaint should be dismissed for those reasons, and not because the plaintiff lacks a stake in obtaining that relief and hence has no standing. Imposing an undefined but clearly more rigorous standard for redressability for reasons unrelated to the causal nexus between the injury and the challenged conduct can only encourage undisciplined, ad hoc litigation.

[Alternatively], the Court could be saying that it will not treat as legally cognizable injuries that stem from an administrative decision concerning how enforcement resources will be allocated. This surely is an important point. Respondents do seek to restructure the IRS's mechanisms for enforcing the legal requirement that discriminatory institutions not receive tax-exempt status. Such restructuring would dramatically affect the way in which the IRS exercises its prosecutorial discretion. The Executive requires latitude to decide how best to enforce the law, and in general the Court may well be correct that the exercise of that discretion, especially in the tax context, is unchallengeable.

However, as the Court also recognizes, this principle does not apply when suit is brought "to enforce specific legal obligations whose violation works a direct harm." [Here,] respondents contend that the IRS is violating a specific constitutional limitation on its enforcement discretion. There is a solid basis for that contention. In *Norwood*, we wrote: "A State's constitutional obligation requires it to steer clear, not only of operating the old dual system of racially segregated schools, but also of giving significant aid to institutions that practice racial or other invidious discrimination."

Deciding whether the Treasury has violated a specific legal limitation on its enforcement discretion does not intrude upon the prerogatives of the Executive, for in so deciding we are merely saying "what the law is." * * *

In short, I would deal with the question of the legal limitations on the IRS's enforcement discretion on its merits, rather than by making the untenable assumption that the granting of preferential tax treatment to segregated schools does not make those schools more attractive to white students and hence does not inhibit the process of desegregation.a

Note

Standing and non-economic injuries. Although unwilling to find an actionable stigmatic injury in *Allen*, the Court has regularly accepted the proposition that non-economic injuries can satisfy the constitutional requirement, provided that they are pleaded with sufficient specificity. For example, FRIENDS OF THE EARTH, INC. v. LAIDLAW ENVIRONMENTAL SERVICES (TOC), INC., 528 U.S. 167 (2000), upheld standing under the citizen suit provisions of the Clean Water Act. The defendant argued that standing was defeated because the District Court, in imposing a penalty, ruled that the defendant's illegal actions had not been proved to "result in any health risk or environmental harm." But the Court, per GINSBURG, J., held that the relevant injury "is not injury to the environment but injury to the plaintiff" and that the plaintiffs suffered injury from their "reasonable concerns" that pollution had damaged land that they otherwise would have used. Scalia, J., joined by Thomas, J., dissented.

The causation requirement. With the application of the causation requirement in *Allen*, compare the analysis in REGENTS OF THE UNIVERSITY OF CALIFORNIA v. BAKKE, Ch. 9, Sec. 2, III, in which the Court upheld the

a. Marshall, J., did not participate in the decision.

standing of a white plaintiff to challenge a special admissions program for minority applicants to medical school. A standing question arose because it was not clear that the existence of an affirmative action program caused Bakke's rejection (he might have been turned down anyway). Rebuffing a standing challenge, Powell, J., wrote for a majority of five that Bakke suffered injury through his deprivation, on grounds of race, of the chance to compete for every place in the entering class regardless of whether the affirmative action program caused his being ultimately rejected.

Redressability. In perhaps the majority of cases, the requirement that an injury be redressable can be viewed as an aspect of the causation requirement: if a defendant has caused injury, relief against the defendant will ordinarily remedy the injury. Occasionally, however, the redressability requirement exercises independent bite. In LOS ANGELES v. LYONS, 461 U.S. 95 (1983), for example, the plaintiff had been choked to unconsciousness by the Los Angeles police after being stopped for a traffic violation. Alleging that the department had a policy of applying life-threatening chokeholds unnecessarily, Lyons sued for injunctive relief. Standing could not be grounded on the threat of future injury, the Court held, because it was too speculative that Lyons himself would be subjected to a choke-hold again. And, although Lyons undoubtedly had suffered an injury in the past, that injury could not be redressed by an injunction against future police conduct.[b]

Compare SPRINT COMMUNICATIONS CO. v. APCC SERVICES, INC., 554 U.S. 269 (2008), per BREYER, J., which held that the assignee of a legal claim for money has standing to sue in federal court, even when the assignee is a "collection firm" that has promised to remit the proceeds to the assignor: For purposes of Art. III's injury requirement, the assignee stands in the shoes of the assignor, and an award of damages would redress the assigned injury, regardless of whether the plaintiff kept the proceeds. ROBERTS, C.J., joined by Scalia, Thomas, and Alito, JJ., dissented: "The Court goes awry when it asserts that the standing inquiry focuses on whether the *injury* is likely to be redressed, not whether the *complaining party's* injury is likely to be redressed."

II. CONGRESSIONAL POWER TO CREATE STANDING

LUJAN v. DEFENDERS OF WILDLIFE

504 U.S. 555, 112 S.Ct. 2130, 119 L.Ed.2d 351 (1992).

JUSTICE SCALIA delivered the opinion of the Court with respect to Parts I, II, III–A, and IV, and an opinion with respect to Part III–B in which the CHIEF JUSTICE, JUSTICE WHITE, and JUSTICE THOMAS join.

[The Endangered Species Act of 1973 (ESA) § 7(a)(2) requires federal agencies to consult with the Secretary of the Interior to "insure" that projects that they fund do not threaten endangered species. Regulations promulgated in 1978 construed the consultation requirement as extending to actions taken in foreign nations. In 1986, however, the Department of the Interior reinterpreted the ESA to require consultation only for actions taken in the United States or on the high seas. Several organizations filed suits challenging the new regulation as contrary to law.]

IIIA. [The Court first held that the groups and their members had failed to present sufficient evidence of injury in fact. Although affidavits testified that at least two members had previously traveled abroad to observe endangered species

---

b. Marshall, J., joined by Brennan, Blackmun, and Stevens, JJ., dissented.

and intended to do so again,] [t]hat the women "had visited" the areas of [identified] projects before the projects commenced proves nothing. [And] the affiants' profession of an "inten[t]" to return to the places they had visited [before]—without any description of concrete plans, or indeed even any specification of *when* the some day will be—do not support a finding of the "actual or imminent" injury that our cases require.

[No more persuasive are] a series of novel standing theories, [including] the "animal nexus" approach, whereby anyone who has an interest in studying or seeing the endangered animals anywhere on the globe has standing; and the "vocational nexus" approach, under which anyone with a professional interest in such animals can sue. Under these theories, anyone who goes to see Asian elephants in the Bronx Zoo, and anyone who is a keeper of Asian elephants in the Bronx Zoo, has standing to sue because the Director of AID did not consult with the Secretary regarding the AID-funded project in Sri Lanka. This is beyond all reason. [It is] pure speculation and fantasy, to say that anyone who observes or works with an endangered species, anywhere in the world, is appreciably harmed by a single project affecting some portion of that species with which he has no more specific connection.

B. Besides failing to show injury, respondents failed to demonstrate redressability. [Since] the agencies funding the projects were not parties to the case, the District Court could accord relief only against the Secretary. [There was no assurance that other agencies would feel bound by the Secretary's regulation, or that the withdrawal of American funding would cause projects to be terminated and the threat to endangered species thereby eliminated.]

IV. The Court of Appeals found that respondents had standing for an additional reason: because they had suffered a "procedural injury." The so-called "citizen-suit" provision of the ESA provides, in pertinent part, that "any person may commence a civil suit on his own behalf (A) to enjoin any person, including the United States and any other governmental instrumentality or agency [who] is alleged to be in violation of any provision of this chapter." The court held that, because § 7(a)(2) requires inter-agency consultation, the citizen-suit provision creates a "procedural righ[t]" to consultation in all "persons"—so that *anyone* can file suit in federal court to challenge the Secretary's (or presumably any other official's) failure to follow the assertedly correct consultative procedure, notwithstanding their inability to allege any discrete injury flowing from that failure. To understand the remarkable nature of this holding one must be clear about what it does *not* rest upon: This is not a case where plaintiffs are seeking to enforce a procedural requirement the disregard of which could impair a separate concrete interest of theirs (e.g., the procedural requirement for a hearing prior to denial of their license application, or the procedural requirement for an environmental impact statement before a federal facility is constructed next door to them).6 Nor is it simply a case where concrete injury has been suffered by many persons, as in

6. There is this much truth to the assertion that "procedural rights" are special: The person who has been accorded a procedural right to protect his concrete interests can assert that right without meeting all the normal standards for redressability and immediacy. Thus, under our case-law, one living adjacent to the site for proposed construction of a federally licensed dam has standing to challenge the licensing agency's failure to prepare an Environmental Impact Statement, even though he cannot establish with any certainty that the Statement will cause the license to be withheld or altered, and even though the dam will not be completed for many years. (That is why we do not rely, in the present case, upon the Government's argument that, *even if* the other agencies were obliged to consult with the Secretary, they might not have followed his advice.) What respondents' "procedural rights" argument seeks, however, is quite different from this: standing for persons who have no concrete interests affected—persons who live (and propose to live) at the other end of the country from the dam.

mass fraud or mass tort situations. Nor, finally, is it the unusual case in which Congress has created a concrete private interest in the outcome of a suit against a private party for the government's benefit, by providing a cash bounty for the victorious plaintiff. Rather, the court held that the injury-in-fact requirement had been satisfied by congressional conferral upon *all* persons of an abstract, self-contained, non-instrumental "right" to have the Executive observe the procedures required by law.

[The] question presented here is whether the public interest in proper administration of the laws (specifically, in agencies' observance of a particular, statutorily prescribed procedure) can be converted into an individual right by a statute that denominates it as such, and that permits all citizens (or, for that matter, a subclass of citizens who suffer no distinctive concrete harm) to sue. If the concrete injury requirement has the separation-of-powers significance we have always said, the answer must be obvious: To permit Congress to convert the undifferentiated public interest in executive officers' compliance with the law into an "individual right" vindicable in the courts is to permit Congress to transfer from the President to the courts the Chief Executive's most important constitutional duty, to "take Care that the Laws be faithfully executed," Art. II, § 3. It would enable the courts, with the permission of Congress, "to assume a position of authority over the governmental acts of another and co-equal department," *Frothingham*, and to become "virtually continuing monitors of the wisdom and soundness of Executive action." *Allen*. We have always rejected that vision of our role * * *.

Nothing in this contradicts the principle that "[the] injury required by Art. III may exist solely by virtue of 'statutes creating legal rights, the invasion of which creates standing.'" *Warth v. Seldin*, 422 U.S. 490 (1975). [T]he cases [previously cited by the Court] as an illustration of that principle involved Congress's elevating to the status of legally cognizable injuries concrete, de facto injuries that were previously inadequate in law (namely, injury to an individual's personal interest in living in a racially integrated community, see *Trafficante v. Metropolitan Life Ins. Co.*, 409 U.S. 205, 208–12 (1972), and injury to a company's interest in marketing its product free from competition, see *Hardin v. Kentucky Utilities Co.*, 390 U.S. 1, 6 (1968)). As we said in *Sierra Club v. Morton*, 405 U.S. 727 (1972), "[Statutory] broadening [of] the categories of injury that may be alleged in support of standing is a different matter from abandoning the requirement that the party seeking review must himself have suffered an injury." Whether or not the principle set forth in *Warth* can be extended beyond that distinction, it is clear that in suits against the government, at least, the concrete injury requirement must remain.

Justice Kennedy, with whom Justice Souter joins, concurring in part and concurring in the judgment.

[I] join Part IV of the Court's opinion with the following observations. As government programs and policies become more complex and far-reaching, we must be sensitive to the articulation of new rights of action that do not have clear analogs in our common-law tradition. Modern litigation has progressed far from the paradigm of Marbury suing Madison to get his commission. [In] my view, Congress has the power to define injuries and articulate chains of causation that will give rise to a case or controversy where none existed before, and I do not read the Court's opinion to suggest a contrary view. [In] exercising this power, however, Congress must at the very least identify the injury it seeks to vindicate and relate the injury to the class of persons entitled to bring suit. The citizen-suit provision of the Endangered Species Act does not meet these minimal requirements, because [it] does not of its own force establish that there is an injury in "any person" by virtue of any "violation."

The Court's holding that there is an outer limit to the power of Congress to confer rights of action is a direct and necessary consequence of the case and controversy limitations found in Article III. I agree that it would exceed those limitations if, at the behest of Congress and in the absence of any showing of concrete injury, we were to entertain citizen-suits to vindicate the public's nonconcrete interest in the proper administration of the laws. While it does not matter how many persons have been injured by the challenged action, the party bringing suit must show that the action injures him in a concrete and personal way. This requirement is not just an empty formality. It preserves the vitality of the adversarial process by assuring both that the parties before the court have an actual, as opposed to professed, stake in the outcome, and that "the legal questions presented [will] be resolved, not in the rarefied atmosphere of a debating society, but in a concrete factual context conducive to a realistic appreciation of the consequences of judicial action." *Valley Forge*. In addition, the requirement of concrete injury confines the Judicial Branch to its proper, limited role in the constitutional framework of government. * * *

JUSTICE STEVENS, concurring in the judgment.

Because I am not persuaded that Congress intended the consultation requirement in § 7(a)(2) [to] apply to activities in foreign countries, I concur in the judgment of reversal. I do not, however, agree with the Court's conclusion that respondents lack standing because the threatened injury to their interest in protecting the environment and studying endangered species is not "imminent." Nor do I agree with the plurality's additional conclusion that respondents' injury is not "redressable" in this litigation. * * *

JUSTICE BLACKMUN, with whom JUSTICE O'CONNOR joins, dissenting.

I part company with the Court in this case in two respects. First, I believe that respondents have raised genuine issues of fact—sufficient to survive summary judgment—both as to injury and as to redressability. Second, I question the Court's breadth of language in rejecting standing for "procedural" injuries. * * *

The Court concludes that any "procedural injury" suffered by respondents is insufficient to confer standing. It rejects the view that the "injury-in-fact requirement [is] satisfied by congressional conferral upon *all* persons of an abstract, self-contained, noninstrumental 'right' to have the Executive observe the procedures required by law." Whatever the Court might mean with that very broad language, it cannot be saying that "procedural injuries" *as a class* are necessarily insufficient for purposes of Article III standing.

Most governmental conduct can be classified as "procedural." [When] the Government, for example, "procedurally" issues a pollution permit, those affected by the permittee's pollutants are not without standing to sue. Only later cases will tell just what the Court means by its intimation that "procedural" injuries are not constitutionally cognizable injuries. In the meantime, I have the greatest of sympathy for the courts across the country that will struggle to understand the Court's standardless exposition of this concept today.

The Court expresses concern that allowing judicial enforcement of "agencies' observance of a particular, statutorily prescribed procedure" would "transfer from the President to the courts the Chief Executive's most important constitutional duty, to 'take Care that the Laws be faithfully executed,' Art. II, sec. 3." In fact, the principal effect of foreclosing judicial enforcement of such procedures is to transfer power into the hands of the Executive at the expense—not of the courts—but of Congress, from which that power originates and emanates.

Under the Court's anachronistically formal view of the separation of powers, Congress legislates pure, substantive mandates and has no business structuring the procedural manner in which the Executive implements these mandates. To be sure, in the ordinary course, Congress does legislate in black-and-white terms of affirmative commands or negative prohibitions on the conduct of officers of the Executive Branch. In complex regulatory areas, however, Congress often legislates, as it were, in procedural shades of gray. That is, it sets forth substantive policy goals and provides for their attainment by requiring Executive Branch officials to follow certain procedures, for example, in the form of reporting, consultation, and certification requirements.

[There] may be factual circumstances in which a congressionally imposed procedural requirement is so insubstantially connected to the prevention of a substantive harm that it cannot be said to work any conceivable injury to an individual litigant. But, as a general matter, the courts owe substantial deference to Congress' substantive purpose in imposing a certain procedural requirement. In all events, [t]here is no room for a per se rule or presumption excluding injuries labeled "procedural" in nature. * * *

———

FEC v. AKINS, 524 U.S. 11 (1998), per Breyer, J., upheld the power of Congress to confer standing on any "aggrieved" person who suffers the harm of "inability to obtain information" as a result of a decision by the FEC that reporting and disclosure requirements are not applicable to a private party. Although the interest in acquiring information was not protected at common law, and although "prudential" considerations might have precluded recognition of standing to sue based on so widespread an injury in the absence of a statute, Congress had specifically authorized suit under the Federal Election Campaign Act. Judicially imposed "prudential" limitations on standing therefore had to give way; the "failure to obtain relevant information" is a "concrete" enough injury to satisfy the requirements of Art. III.

Scalia, J., joined by O'Connor and Thomas, JJ., dissented on the ground that the asserted injury was too generalized and undifferentiated to support standing, and a statute could not cure the constitutional defect. "If today's decision is correct, it is within the power of Congress to authorize any interested person to manage (through the courts) the Executive's enforcement of any law that includes a requirement for the filing and public availability of a piece of paper. This is not the system we have had, and it is not the system we should desire."

———

MASSACHUSETTS v. EPA, 549 U.S. 497 (2007), per Stevens, J., upheld the standing of a state to challenge a refusal by the EPA to issue regulations governing greenhouse gas emissions by motor vehicles: Congress had authorized "this type of challenge to EPA action," albeit in a statutory provision that otherwise made no specific reference to standing, and said that "a litigant to whom Congress has 'accorded a procedural right to protect his interests' * * * 'can assert that right without meeting all the normal standards for redressability and immediacy.' When a litigant is vested with a procedural right, that litigant has standing if there is some possibility that the requested relief will prompt the injury-causing party to reconsider the decision that allegedly harmed the litigant. [Moreover,] Massachusetts' stake in protecting its quasi-sovereign interests," which set it apart from ordinary litigants, entitled it to "special solicitude in our standing analysis." With the framework for standing analysis thus apparently loosened, Stevens, J., concluded that Massachusetts had alleged an injury, involving the threatened loss of state-owned coastal property as a result of global warning that was traceable to greenhouse gas emissions and a consequent rise in sea levels. Domestic greenhouse gas traceable to automobile emissions contributed causally to the threat of loss even if "predicted increases in greenhouse gas emissions from developing nations, especially China and India, are likely to offset any marginal domestic decrease." And the redressability requirement was met because the risk of catastrophic environmental damages "would be reduced to some extent if the petitioners received the relief they seek."

ROBERTS, C.J., joined by Scalia, Thomas and Alito, JJ., dissenting, argued that the state had alleged no threat of imminent or particularized injury: "Global warming is a phenomenon 'harmful to humanity at large,' and the redress petitioners seek is focused no more on them than on the public generally—it is literally to change the atmosphere of the world. [Petitioners] are never able to trace their alleged injuries [to] the fractional amount of global emissions that might have been limited with EPA standards [and] given events elsewhere in the world [the] Court never explains" why the injury resulting from its alleged, impending loss of land would be redressed. "The good news is that the Court's 'special solicitude' for Massachusetts limits the future applicability of the diluted standing requirements applied in this case. The bad news is that the Court's self-professed relaxation of [Article] III requirements has caused us to transgress 'the proper—and properly limited—role of the courts in a democratic society.' "

SECTION 3. TIMING OF ADJUDICATION

I. MOOTNESS

DeFUNIS v. ODEGAARD

416 U.S. 312, 94 S.Ct. 1704, 40 L.Ed.2d 164 (1974).

PER CURIAM.

[Petitioner was admitted to the University of Washington Law School after a state trial court had sustained his claim that the school's special admissions policy violated equal protection. The Washington Supreme Court reversed, but its judgment was stayed. By the time the case was argued in the Supreme Court, petitioner had registered for the final term of his third year. Although the school stated that if its admissions policy were upheld, petitioner would be subject to it if he had to register for any additional terms, his present registration "would not be canceled [regardless] of the outcome of this litigation."]

The starting point for analysis is the familiar proposition that "federal courts are without power to decide questions that cannot affect the rights of litigants in the case before them." *North Carolina v. Rice*, 404 U.S. 244, 246 (1971). The inability of the federal judiciary "to review moot cases derives from the requirement of Art. III of the Constitution under which the exercise of judicial power depends upon the existence of a case or controversy." *Liner v. Jafco, Inc.*, 375 U.S. 301, 306 n. 3 (1964).

[A]ll parties agree that DeFunis is now entitled to complete his legal studies at the University of Washington and to receive his degree from that institution. A determination by this Court of the legal issues tendered by the parties is no longer necessary to compel that result, and could not serve to prevent it. DeFunis did not cast his suit as a class action, and the only remedy he requested was an injunction commanding his admission to the Law School. He was not only accorded that remedy, but he now has also been irrevocably admitted to the final term of the final year of the Law School course. The controversy between the parties has thus clearly ceased to be "definite and concrete" and no longer "touch[es] the legal relations of parties having adverse legal interests." *Aetna Life Ins. Co. v. Haworth*, 300 U.S. 227, 240–241 (1937).

[There] is a line of decisions in this Court standing for the proposition that the "voluntary cessation of allegedly illegal conduct does not deprive the tribunal of power to hear and determine the case, i.e., does not make the case moot." [E.g.,] *United States v. W.T. Grant Co.*, 345 U.S. 629, 632 (1953). These decisions and the doctrine they reflect would be quite relevant if the question of mootness here had arisen by reason of a unilateral change in the *admissions procedures* of the Law School. For it was the admissions procedures that were the target of this litigation, and a voluntary cessation of the admissions practices complained of could make this case moot only if it could be said with assurance "that 'there is no reasonable expectation that the wrong will be repeated.'" *W.T. Grant Co.* Otherwise, "[t]he defendant is free to return to his old ways," id., and this fact would be enough to prevent mootness because of the "public interest in having the legality of the practices settled." Ibid. But mootness in the present case depends not at all upon a "voluntary cessation" of the admissions practices that were the subject of this litigation. It depends, instead, upon the simple fact that DeFunis is now in the final quarter of the final year of his course of study, and the settled and unchallenged policy of the Law School to permit him to complete the term for which he is now enrolled.

It might also be suggested that this case presents a question that is "capable of repetition, yet evading review," *Southern Pacific Terminal Co. v. ICC*, 219 U.S. 498, 515 (1911); *Roe v. Wade*, [Ch. 6, Sec. 2], and is thus amenable to federal adjudication even though it might otherwise be considered moot.a But DeFunis will never again be required to run the gauntlet of the Law School's admission process, and so the question is certainly not "capable of repetition" so far as he is concerned. Moreover, just because this particular case did not reach the Court until the eve of the petitioner's graduation from law school, it hardly follows that the issue he raises will in the future evade review. If the admissions procedures of the Law School remain unchanged, there is no reason to suppose that a subsequent case attacking those procedures will not come with relative speed to this Court, now that the Supreme Court of Washington has spoken. This case, therefore, in no way presents the exceptional situation in which the *Southern Pacific Terminal* doctrine might permit a departure from "[t]he usual rule in federal cases [that] an actual controversy must exist at stages of appellate or certiorari review, and not simply at the date the action is initiated." *Roe v. Wade*.

a. When a statute directly applies to particular plaintiffs only for a short period, it may sometimes be difficult for plaintiffs to prosecute a legal challenge to its conclusion before the statute has ceased to apply to them. For example, by the time a court is ready to rule on the constitutionality of a statute conditioning the right to vote on residency in a district for three or six months, the election may have passed. Or a pregnancy may have run its course before an affected woman could secure a court ruling on a statute regulating abortion. In response to cases such as these, the Court has established an exception to otherwise applicable mootness doctrine for cases in which the issue presented is "capable of repetition, yet evading review." See, e.g., *Moore v. Ogilvie*, 394 U.S. 814 (1969). In applying this exception, however, the Court sometimes demands assurances that the plaintiff may again be *personally* affected by the challenged statute. E.g., *Weinstein v. Bradford*, 423 U.S. 147 (1975).

[W]e conclude that the Court cannot, consistently with the limitations of Art. III of the Constitution, consider the substantive constitutional issues tendered by the parties.5

JUSTICE BRENNAN, with whom JUSTICE DOUGLAS, JUSTICE WHITE, and JUSTICE MARSHALL concur, dissenting.

[Many] weeks of the school term remain, and [a]ny number of unexpected events—illness, economic necessity, even academic failure—might prevent [petitioner's] graduation at the end of the term. Were that misfortune to befall, and were petitioner required to register for yet another term, the prospect that he would again face the hurdle of the admissions policy is real, not fanciful * * *.

In these circumstances, and because the University's position implies no concession that its admissions policy is unlawful, this controversy falls squarely within the Court's long line of decisions holding that the "[m]ere voluntary cessation of allegedly illegal conduct does not moot a case." *United States v. Concentrated Phosphate Export Assn.*, 393 U.S. 199, 203 (1968).

[T]he Court concedes that, if petitioner has lost his stake in this controversy, he did so only when he registered for the spring term. But petitioner took that action only after the case had been fully litigated in the state courts, briefs had been filed in this Court, and oral argument had been heard. The case is thus ripe for decision on a fully developed factual record with sharply defined and fully canvassed legal issues.

Moreover, in endeavoring to dispose of this case as moot, the Court clearly disserves the public interest. The constitutional issues which are avoided today concern vast numbers of people, organizations, and colleges and universities, as evidenced by the filing of twenty-six amicus curiae briefs. Few constitutional questions in recent history have stirred as much debate, and they will not disappear. [Because] avoidance of repetitious litigation serves the public interest, that inevitability counsels against mootness determinations, as here, not compelled by the record.

Note

Mootness and standing. Although the Court on several occasions had characterized mootness as "the doctrine of standing set in a time frame,"a the Court reconsidered that description in FRIENDS OF THE EARTH v. LAIDLAW ENV. SERVS. (TOC), INC., 528 U.S. 167 (2000). After Friends of the Earth sued to enjoin a violation of the environmental laws, the defendants ceased their illegal conduct, and the court of appeals ordered the case dismissed as moot. Reasoning that all elements of Article III standing must persist throughout federal litigation, the lower court found it too unlikely that a judicial remedy would effectively redress any current injury to the plaintiffs.b The Court, per GINSBURG, J., reversed, holding that "the Court of Appeals confused mootness with standing": "[T]here

---

5. It is suggested in dissent that "[a]ny number of unexpected events—illness, economic necessity, even academic failure—might prevent his graduation at the end of the term." "But such speculative contingencies afford no basis for our passing on the substantive issues [the petitioner] would have us decide," *Hall v. Beals*, 396 U.S. 45, 49 (1969), in the absence of "evidence that this is a prospect of 'immediacy and reality.'" *Golden v. Zwickler*, 394 U.S. 103, 109 (1969).

a. See *Arizonans for Official English v. Arizona*, 520 U.S. 43, 68 n.22 (1997), quoting *United States Parole Comm'n v. Geraghty*, 445 U.S. 388, 397 (1980), in turn quoting Henry P. Monaghan, *Constitutional Adjudication: The Who and When*, 82 Yale L.J. 1363, 1384 (1973).

b. The clearly available remedy under the Clean Water Act on which the "redressability" debate focused was a civil money penalty payable to the government, not to the plaintiffs.

are circumstances in which the prospect that a defendant will engage in (or resume) harmful conduct may be too speculative to support standing, but not too speculative to overcome mootness. [Standing] doctrine functions to ensure, among other things, that the scarce resources of the federal courts are devoted to those disputes in which the parties have a concrete stake. In contrast, by the time mootness is an issue, the case has been brought and litigated, often (as here) for years. To abandon the case at an advanced stage may prove more wasteful than frugal. This argument from sunk costs does not license courts to retain jurisdiction over cases in which one or both of the parties plainly lacks a continuing interest [but it] surely highlights an important difference between the two doctrines."

Scalia, J., joined by Thomas, J., dissented on the ground that the plaintiffs never possessed standing.

Mootness in class actions. If the *DeFunis* case had been filed as a class action, would the result have been the same? The Court apparently gave a negative answer in UNITED STATES PAROLE COMM'N v. GERAGHTY, 445 U.S. 388 (1980), in which a federal prisoner filed a class action challenging the guidelines governing release on parole. The district court denied class certification and rejected the claim on the merits, and Geraghty himself had been released from prison before the case reached the Court, but the Court, per BLACKMUN, J., held the case not moot. "[A]n action brought on behalf of a class does not become moot upon expiration of the named plaintiff's substantive claim," and it made no difference that the plaintiff's substantive claim had been mooted before the class had been certified: "The proposed [class] representative retains a 'personal stake' in obtaining class certification sufficient to assure that Art. III values are not undermined. If the appeal results in a reversal of the class certification denial, and a class subsequently is properly certified, the merits of the class claim then may be adjudicated."

POWELL, J., joined by Burger, C.J., and Stewart and Rehnquist, JJ., dissented: "The Court makes no effort to identify any injury to respondent that may be redressed by, or any benefit to respondent that may accrue from, a favorable ruling on the certification question. Instead, respondent's 'personal stake' is said to derive from two factors having nothing to do with concrete injury or stake in the outcome. First, the Court finds that the Federal Rules of Civil Procedure create a 'right,' 'analogous to the private attorney general concept,' to have a class certified. Second, the Court thinks that the case retains the 'imperatives of a dispute capable of judicial resolution,' which are identified as (i) a sharply presented issue, (ii) a concrete factual setting, and (iii) a self-interested party actually contesting the case.

"The Court's reliance on some new 'right' inherent in Rule 23 is misplaced. We have held that even Congress may not confer federal court jurisdiction when Art. III does not. Far less so may a rule of procedure which 'shall not be construed to extend [the] jurisdiction of the United States district courts.' Fed.Rule Civ.Proc. 82. [Although] we have refused steadfastly to countenance the 'public action,' the Court's redefinition of the personal stake requirement leaves no principled basis for that practice."

II. RIPENESS

Although the Court regularly enforces a "ripeness" doctrine, that doctrine's exact purposes and contours, and in particular its relation to standing doctrine, are not always clear. Writes Erwin Chemerinsky, *Federal Jurisdiction* § 2.4.1 at

113–15 (4th ed. 2003): "Ripeness [is] a justiciability doctrine determining *when* review is appropriate. [Specifically], the ripeness doctrine seeks to separate matters that are premature for review because the injury is speculative and never may occur, from those cases that are appropriate for federal court action. Although the phrasing makes the questions of who may sue and when may they sue seem distinct, in practice there is an obvious overlap between the doctrines of standing and ripeness. If no injury has occurred, the plaintiff might be denied standing or the case might be dismissed as not ripe. * * * However, for the sake of clarity, especially in those cases where the law of standing and ripeness is not identical, ripeness can be given a narrower definition that distinguishes it from standing and explains the existing case law. Ripeness properly should be understood as involving the question of *when may a party seek preenforcement review of a statute or regulation.* Customarily, a person can challenge the legality of a statute or regulation only when he or she is prosecuted for violating it. At that time, a defense can be that the law is invalid, for example, as being unconstitutional."

See also *Abbott Laboratories v. Gardner*, 387 U.S. 136, 148 (1967) (asserting that the "basic rationale" of ripeness doctrine is "to prevent the courts, through avoidance of premature adjudication, from entangling themselves in abstract disagreements"). In *Abbott Laboratories*, the Court characterized the ripeness inquiry as having two aspects: (i) "the hardship to the parties of withholding court consideration" and (ii) "the fitness of the issues for judicial decision." Consider whether the ripeness analysis in the following cases matches these descriptions.

UNITED PUBLIC WORKERS v. MITCHELL

330 U.S. 75, 67 S.Ct. 556, 91 L.Ed. 754 (1947).

JUSTICE REED delivered the opinion of the Court.

[Appellants, federal civil service employees, sought a federal declaratory judgment that the Hatch Act's prohibition against taking "any active part in political management or in political campaigns" violated their first amendment rights. They also requested injunctive relief. Only one appellant (Poole) had actually violated the Act. The others alleged that they desired to do so by, inter alia, serving as party officials, writing articles and circulating petitions to support candidates, acting as poll watchers, and transporting voters to the polls.a]

At the threshold of consideration, we are called upon to decide whether the complaint states a controversy cognizable in this Court. [Except with respect to Poole, the affidavits submitted by the plaintiffs] follow the generality of purpose expressed by the complaint. They declare a desire to act contrary to the rule against political activity but not that the rule has been violated. * * *

As is well known, the federal courts established pursuant to Article III of the Constitution do not render advisory opinions. For adjudication of constitutional issues, "concrete legal issues, presented in actual cases, not abstractions," are requisite. This is as true of declaratory judgments as any other field. These appellants seem clearly to seek advisory opinions upon broad claims of [constitutional rights]. As these appellants are classified employees, they have a right superior to the generality of citizens, [but] the facts of their personal interest in their civil rights, of the general threat of possible interference with those rights by

a. One did allege that, at the last congressional election, he wanted to be a poll watcher but was informed by a Civil Service Commission official "that if I used my watcher's certif- icate, the Civil Service Commission would see that I was dismissed from my job." This matter, the Court found, "had long been moot when this complaint was filed."

the Civil Service Commission under its rules, if specified things are done by appellants, does not make a justiciable case or controversy. Appellants want to engage in "political management and political campaigns," to persuade others to follow appellants' views by discussion, speeches, articles and other acts reasonably designed to secure the selection of appellants' political choices. Such generality of objection is really an attack on the political expediency of the Hatch Act, not the presentation of legal issues. It is beyond the competence of courts to render such a decision.

The power of courts, and ultimately of this Court, to pass upon the constitutionality of acts of Congress arises only when the interests of litigants require the use of this judicial authority for their protection against actual interference. A hypothetical threat is not enough. We can only speculate as to the kinds of political activity the appellants desire to engage in or as to the contents of their proposed public statements or the circumstances of their publication. It would not accord with judicial responsibility to adjudge, in a matter involving constitutionality, between the freedom of the individual and the requirements of public order except when definite rights appear upon the one side and definite prejudicial interferences upon the other.

The Constitution allots the nation's judicial power to the federal courts. Unless these courts respect the limits of that unique authority, they intrude upon powers vested in the legislative or executive branches. [Should] the courts seek to expand their power so as to bring under their jurisdiction ill-defined controversies over constitutional issues, they would become the organ of political theories. Such abuse of judicial power would properly meet rebuke and restriction from other branches. [No] threat of interference by the Commission with rights of these appellants appears beyond that implied by the existence of the law and the regulations.

[Poole, however] has been charged by the Commission with political activity and a proposed order for his removal from his position adopted subject to his right under Commission procedure to [reply]. Since Poole admits that he violated the rule against political activity and that removal from office is therefore mandatory under the [act,] we see no reason why a declaratory judgment action, even though constitutional issues are involved, does not lie. [The Court then rejected Poole's challenge on the merits.]

JUSTICE DOUGLAS, dissenting in part:

[What] these appellants propose to do is plain enough. If they do what they propose to do, it is clear that they will be discharged * * *.2 The threat against them is real not fanciful, immediate not remote. The case is therefore an actual not a hypothetical one. [T]o require these employees first to suffer the hardship of a discharge is not only to make them incur a penalty; it makes inadequate, if not wholly illusory, any legal remedy which they may have. [At] least to the average person in the lower income groups the burden of taking that course is irreparable injury* * *.b

2. The case is, therefore, unlike those situations where the Court refused to entertain actions for declaratory judgments, the state of facts being hypothetical in the sense that the challenge was to statutes which had not as yet been construed or their specific application known.

b. Black, J., agreed with Douglas, J., "that all the petitioners' complaints state a case or controversy" and further that "the challenged provision is unconstitutional on its face." Rutledge, J., agreed with Black, J., as to Poole; as to the others, however, the controversy "is not yet appropriate for the discretionary exercise of declaratory judgment jurisdiction." Frankfurter, J., concurred in the Court's opinion. Murphy and Jackson, JJ., took no part.

Note

Case-by-case variations. Not all decisions have applied the ripeness analysis as stringently as *UPW v. Mitchell*. For example, *Epperson v. Arkansas*, Ch. 8, Sec. 1, III, found no ripeness difficulty with a challenge to a forty-year-old statute making the teaching of evolution unlawful, despite the absence of any record of enforcement: Although the law might be "more of a curiosity than a vital fact of life," the case was "properly here [on appeal from a state court], and it is our duty to decide the issues presented."

Challenges to conduct rather than statutes. In contrast with *UPW v. Mitchell* and *Epperson v. Arkansas*, which involved attacks on the constitutionality of statutes, the plaintiffs in O'SHEA v. LITTLETON, 414 U.S. 488 (1974), mounted a constitutional challenge to official conduct not mandated by any law. In the lower courts, black and white residents who had protested racial discrimination in Cairo, Illinois, had obtained a federal injunction against state judicial officers based on an alleged pattern of illegal bail, sentencing, and law enforcement practices against them due to their race and their exercise of first amendment rights. Although some respondents "had actually been defendants in proceedings before petitioners and had suffered from the alleged unconstitutional practices," the Court, per WHITE, J., reversed: "Of course, past wrongs are evidence bearing on whether there is a real and immediate threat of repeated injury. [But] respondents here have not pointed to any imminent prosecutions contemplated against any of their number and they naturally do not suggest that any one of them expects to violate valid criminal laws. [Thus], the threat of injury from the alleged course of conduct they attack is simply too remote to satisfy the case-or-controversy requirement and permit adjudication by a federal court."c

Even if there were "an existing case or controversy," however, "a proper balance in the concurrent operation of federal and state courts" precludes federal equitable relief. The decision below "would contemplate interruption of state proceedings to adjudicate assertions of noncompliance by petitioners. This seems to us nothing less than an ongoing federal audit of state criminal proceedings [that] is antipathetic to established principles of comity.d * * * Respondents have failed, moreover, to establish the basic requisites of the issuance of equitable relief in these circumstances—the likelihood of substantial and immediate irreparable injury, and the inadequacy of remedies at law. [I]f any of the respondents are ever prosecuted and face trial, or if they are illegally sentenced, there are available state and federal procedures which could provide relief from the wrongful conduct alleged."e

c. For similar analysis, see *Rizzo v. Goode*, 423 U.S. 362 (1976).

d. Compare *Allee v. Medrano*, 416 U.S. 802 (1974)(upholding a federal injunction against state police disruption of unionization efforts).

e. Blackmun, J., concurred in the first part of the Court's opinion. Douglas, J., joined by Brennan and Marshall, JJ., dissented.

Appendix A

THE JUSTICES OF THE SUPREME COURT

Originally prepared by JOHN J. COUND

Professor of Law, University of Minnesota

The following data summarize the prior public careers of the justices of the Supreme Court. The first dates in parentheses are those of birth and death; these are followed by the name of the appointing President and the dates of service on the Court. The states in which the justices were residing when appointed and their political affiliations at that time are then given. In detailing prior careers, I have followed chronological order, with two exceptions: I have listed first that a justice was a signer of the Declaration of Independence or the Federal Constitution, and I have indicated state legislative experience only once for each justice. I have not distinguished between different bodies in the state legislature, and I have omitted service in the Continental Congresses. Private practice, except where deemed especially significant, and law teaching have been omitted, except where a justice was primarily engaged therein upon appointment. (Blackmun, Breyer, Burger, Douglas, Fortas, Ginsburg, Holmes, Hughes, Kennedy, L.Q.C. Lamar, Lurton, McReynolds, Murphy, Roberts, W. Rutledge, Scalia, Stevens, Stone and Van Devanter, in addition to Taft and Frankfurter, had all taught before going on the Court; Story, Strong and Wilson taught while on the court or after leaving it). The activity in which a justice was engaged upon appointment has been italicized. Figures in parentheses indicate years of service in the position. In only a few cases, a justice's extra-Court or post-Court activity has been indicated or some other note made. An asterisk designates the Chief Justices.

The accompanying Table of Justices on pages [___] and [___] has been planned so that the composition of the Court at any time can be readily ascertained.

(This material has been compiled from a great number of sources, but special acknowledgment must be made to the *Dictionary of American Biography* (Charles Scribner's Sons), the A.N. Marquis Company works, and Ewing, *The Judges of the Supreme Court, 1789–1937* (University of Minnesota Press, 1938).)

ALITO, JR., SAMUEL A. (1950–____; G.W. Bush, 2006–____). N.J. Rep.—U.S., Assistant U.S. Attorney (4); Assistant to Solicitor General (4); Deputy Assistant Attorney General (3); U.S. Attorney (4); *Judge, Court of Appeals (16).*

BALDWIN, HENRY (1780–1844; Jackson, 1830–1844). Pa.Dem.—U.S., House of Representatives (5). *Private practice.*

BARBOUR, PHILIP P. (1783–1841; Jackson, 1836–1841). Va.Dem.—Va., Legislature (2). U.S., House of Representatives (14). Va., Judge, General Court (2); President, State Constitutional Convention, 1829–30. *U.S., Judge, District Court (5).*

BLACK, HUGO L. (1886–1971; F.D. Roosevelt, 1937–1971). Ala.Dem.—Captain, Field Artillery, World War I. Ala., Judge, Police Court (1); County Solicitor (2). *U.S., Senate (10).*

BLACKMUN, HARRY A. (1908–1999; Nixon, 1970–1994). Minn.Rep.—Resident Counsel, Mayo Clinic, (10). *U.S., Judge, Court of Appeals (11).*

BLAIR, JOHN (1732–1800; Washington, 1789–1796). Va.Fed.—Signer, U.S. Constitution, 1787. Va., Legislature (9); Judge and Chief Justice, General Court (2), *Court of Appeals (9).* His opinion in *Commonwealth v. Caton,* 4 Call 5, 20 (Va.1782), is one of the earliest expressions of the doctrine of judicial review.

BLATCHFORD, SAMUEL (1820–1893; Arthur, 1882–1893). N.Y.Rep.—U.S., Judge, District Court (5); *Circuit Court (10).*

BRADLEY, JOSEPH P. (1803–1892; Grant, 1870–1892). N.J.Rep.—Actuary. *Private practice.*

BRANDEIS, LOUIS D. (1856–1941; Wilson, 1916–1939). Mass.Dem.—*Private practice.* Counsel, variously for the government, for industry, and "for the people," in numerous administrative and judicial proceedings, both state and federal.

BRENNAN, WILLIAM J. (1906–1997; Eisenhower, 1956–1990). N.J.Dem.—U.S. Army, World War II. N.J., Judge, Superior Court (1); Appellate Division (2); *Supreme Court (4).*

BREWER, DAVID J. (1837–1910; B. Harrison, 1889–1910). Kans.Rep.—Kans., Judge, County Criminal and Probate Court (1), District Court (4); County Attorney (1); Judge, Supreme Court (14), *U.S., Judge, Circuit Court (5).*

BREYER, STEPHEN GERALD (1937–____; Clinton, 1994–____). Mass. Dem.—U.S., Special Assistant to Assistant Attorney General for Antitrust (2); Assistant Special Prosecutor (during Watergate) (1); Special Counsel of the Senate Judiciary Committee (1); Chief Counsel, same (2); Judge, Court of Appeals (10); Member (while a judge) of the United States Sentencing Commission (4), and of the Judicial Conference of the United States (4); *Chief Judge, Court of Appeals (4).*

BROWN, HENRY, B. (1836–1913; B. Harrison, 1890–1906). Mich.Rep.—U.S., Assistant U.S. Attorney (5). Mich., Judge, Circuit Court (1). *U.S., Judge, District Court (15).*

Year	Seat 1	Seat 2	Seat 3	Seat 4	Seat 5	Seat 6	Seat 7	Seat 8	Seat 9	Seat 10
1789	Jay	Rutledge, J.	Cushing	Wilson	Blair					
1790						Iredell				
1791		Johnson, T.								
1793		Paterson								
1795	Rutledge, J.									
1796	Ellsworth				Chase, Samuel					
1798				Washington						
1799						Moore				
1801	Marshall, J.									
1804						Johnson, W.				
1806		Livingston								
1807							Todd			
1811			Story		Duval					
1823		Thompson								
1826							Trimble			
1829							McLean			
1830				Baldwin						
1835						Wayne				
1836	Taney				Barbour					
1837								Catron	McKinley	
1841					Daniel					
1845		Nelson	Woodbury							
1846				Grier						
1851			Curtis							
1853									Campbell	
1858			Clifford							
1862					Miller		Swayne		Davis	
1863										Field
1864	Chase, Salmon									
1865										
1867										
1870				Strong		Bradley				
1872		Hunt								
1874	Waite									
1877								Harlan		
1880				Woods						
1881			Gray				Matthews			
1882		Blatchford								
1888	Fuller			Lamar, L.						
1889							Brewer			
1890					Brown					
1892						Shiras				
1893				Jackson, H.						
1894		White, E.								
1895				Peckham						
1898									McKenna	
1902			Holmes							
1903					Day					
1906				Moody						

Catron died in 1865, Wayne in 1867; their positions were abolished by Congress to prevent their being filled by President Johnson; a new position was created in 1869, which traditionally has been regarded as a re-creation of Wayne's seat.

Years: 1909, 1910, 1912, 1914, 1916, 1921, 1922, 1923, 1925, 1930, 1932, 1937, 1938, 1939, 1940, 1941, 1943, 1945, 1946, 1949, 1953, 1955, 1956, 1957, 1958, 1962, 1965, 1966, 1967, 1968, 1969, 1970, 1972, 1975, 1981, 1982

Chief Justices: White, E.; Taft; Hughes; Stone; Vinson; Warren; Burger

Seat: ** Van Devanter; Black; Powell

Seat: Cardozo; Frankfurter; Goldberg; Fortas; Blackmun

Seat: Lurton; McReynolds; Byrnes; Rutledge; Minton; Brennan

Seat: Lamar, J; Brandeis; Douglas; Stevens

Seat: Butler; Murphy; Clark; Marshall, T.

Seat: Hughes; Clarke; Sutherland; Reed; Whittaker; White, B.

Seat: Pitney; Sanford; Roberts; Burton; Stewart; O'Connor

Seat: Stone; ** Jackson, R.; Harlan; Rehnquist

** Fuller died in 1910 and White was named Chief Justice. Hughes resigned in 1941, and Stone was named Chief Justice.
Burger resigned in 1986 and Rehnquist was named Chief Justice.

1983	1986	1987	1988	1989	1990	1991	1993	1994	1995	1996	1997	1998	1999	2000	2001	2002	2003	2004	2005	2006

Scalia

Alito

Ginsburg

Thomas, C.

Souter

Breyer

Kennedy

Rehnquist

Roberts

** Fuller died in 1910 and White was named Chief Justice. Hughes resigned in 1941, and Stone was named Chief Justice. Burger resigned in 1986 and Rehnquist was named Chief Justice.

1983	1986	1987	1988	1989	1990	1991	1993	1994	1995	1996	1997	1998	1999	2000	2001	2002	2003	2004	2005	2006

*BURGER, WARREN E. (1907–1995; Nixon, 1969–1986). Va.Rep.—U.S., Assistant Attorney General, Civil Division (3), *Judge, Court of Appeals (13)*.

BURTON, HAROLD H. (1888–1964; Truman, 1945–1958). Ohio Rep.—Capt., U.S.A., World War I. Ohio, Legislature (2). Mayor, Cleveland, OH. (5). *U.S., Senate (4).*

BUTLER, PIERCE (1866–1939; Harding, 1922–1939). Minn.Dem.—Minn., County Attorney (4). *Private practice.*

BYRNES, JAMES F. (1879–1972; F.D. Roosevelt, 1941–1942). S.C.Dem.— S.C., Solicitor, Circuit Court (2). U.S., House of Representatives (14); *Senate (12).* Resigned from the Court to become U.S. Director of Economic Stabilization.

CAMPBELL, JOHN A. (1811–1889; Pierce, 1853–1861). Ala.Dem.—*Private practice.* After his resignation, he became Assistant Secretary of War, C.S.A.

CARDOZO, BENJAMIN N. (1870–1938; Hoover, 1932–1938). N.Y.Dem.— N.Y., Judge, Supreme Court (6 weeks); Associate Judge and *Chief Judge, Court of Appeals (18).*

CATRON, JOHN (1778–1865; Van Buren, 1837–1865). Tenn.Dem.—Tenn., Judge and Chief Justice, Supreme Court of Errors and Appeals (10). *Private practice.*

*CHASE, SALMON P. (1808–1873; Lincoln, 1864–1873). Ohio Rep.—U.S., Senate (6). Ohio, Governor (4). *U.S., Secretary of the Treasury (3).*

CHASE, SAMUEL (1741–1811; Washington, 1796–1811). Md.Fed.—Signer, U.S. Declaration of Independence, 1776. Md., Legislature (20); Chief Judge, Court of Oyer and Terminer (2), *General Court (5).* Impeached and acquitted, 1804–05.

CLARK, TOM C. (1899–1977; Truman, 1949–1967). Tex.Dem.—U.S. Army, World War I. Tex., Civil District Attorney (5). U.S., Assistant Attorney General (2), *Attorney General (4).*

CLARKE, JOHN H. (1857–1945; Wilson, 1916–1922). Ohio Dem.—*U.S. Judge, District Court (2).*

CLIFFORD, NATHAN (1803–1881; Buchanan, 1858–1881). Me.Dem.—Me., Legislature (4); Attorney General (4). U.S., House of Representatives (4); Attorney General (2); Minister Plenipotentiary to Mexico, 1848. *Private practice.*

CURTIS, BENJAMIN R. (1809–1874; Fillmore, 1851–1857). Mass.Whig.— Mass., Legislature (1). *Private practice.*

CUSHING, WILLIAM (1732–1810; Washington, 1789–1810). Mass.Fed.— Mass., Judge, Superior Court (3); Justice and *Chief Justice, Supreme Judicial Court (14).*

DANIEL, PETER V. (1784–1860; Van Buren, 1841–1860). Va.Dem.—Va., Legislature (3); Member, Privy Council (23). *U.S., Judge, District Court (5).*

DAVIS, DAVID (1815–1886; Lincoln, 1862–1877). Ill.Rep.—Ill., Legislature (2); *Judge, Circuit Court (14).* His resignation to become U.S. Senator upset the agreed-upon composition of the Hayes–Tilden Electoral Commission.

DAY, WILLIAM R. (1849–1923; T. Roosevelt, 1903–1922). Ohio Rep.—Ohio, Judge, Court of Common Pleas (4). U.S., Assistant Secretary of State (1), Secretary of State (½); Chairman, U.S. Peace Commissioners, 1898; *Judge, Circuit Court of Appeals (4).*

DOUGLAS, WILLIAM O. (1898–1980; F.D. Roosevelt, 1939–1975). Conn. Dem.—Pvt., U.S. Army, World War I. *U.S., Chairman, Securities and Exchange Commission (3).* His was the longest tenure in the history of the Court.

[6]

DUVAL(L), GABRIEL (1752–1844; Madison, 1811–1835). Md.Rep.—Declined to serve as delegate, U.S. Constitutional Convention, 1787. Md., State Council (3). U.S., House of Representatives (2). Md., Judge, General Court (6). *U.S., Comptroller of the Treasury (9).*

*ELLSWORTH, OLIVER (1745–1807; Washington, 1796–1800). Conn.Fed.— Delegate, U.S. Constitutional Convention, 1787. Conn., Legislature (2); Member, Governor's Council (4); Judge, Superior Court (5). *U.S., Senate (7).*

FIELD, STEPHEN J. (1816–1899; Lincoln, 1863–1897). Calif.Dem.—*Calif., Justice, and Chief Justice, Supreme Court (6).*

FORTAS, ABE (1910–1982; L.B. Johnson, 1965–1969). Tenn.Dem.—U.S. Government attorney and consultant (A.A.A., S.E.C., P.W.A., Dep't of Interior) (9); Undersecretary of Interior (4). *Private practice in Washington, D.C.* Nominated as Chief Justice; nomination withdrawn, 1968. Resigned.

FRANKFURTER, FELIX (1882–1965; F.D. Roosevelt, 1939–1962). Mass. Independent.—U.S., Assistant U.S. Attorney (4); Law Officer, War Department, Bureau of Insular Affairs (3); Assistant to Secretary of War (1). *Professor of Law (25).*

*FULLER, MELVILLE W. (1833–1910; Cleveland, 1888–1910). Ill.Dem.—Ill., Legislature (2). *Private practice.*

GINSBURG, RUTH BADER (1933–___; Clinton, 1993–___); N.Y.Dem.—*U.S., Judge, Court of Appeals (13).*

GOLDBERG, ARTHUR J. (1908–1990; Kennedy, 1962–1965). Ill.Dem.—Major, U.S.A., World War II. General Counsel, USW–AFL–CIO (13). *U.S., Secretary of Labor (1).* Resigned to become Ambassador to U.N.

GRAY, HORACE (1828–1902; Arthur, 1881–1902). Mass.Rep.—*Mass., Associate Justice and Chief Justice, Supreme Judicial Court (18).*

GRIER, ROBERT O. (1794–1870; Polk, 1846–1870). Pa.Dem.—*Pa., Presiding Judge, District Court (13).*

HARLAN, JOHN M. (1833–1911; Hayes, 1877–1911). Ky.Rep.—Ky., Judge, County Court (1). Col., Union Army, 1861–63. Ky., Attorney General (4). U.S., Member, President's Louisiana Commission, 1877. *Private practice.* Grandfather of:

HARLAN, JOHN M. (1899–1971; Eisenhower, 1955–1971). N.Y.Rep.—Col., U.S.A.A.F., World War II. N.Y. Chief Counsel, State Crime Commission (2). *U.S., Judge, Court of Appeals (1).*

HOLMES, OLIVER W., JR. (1841–1935; T. Roosevelt, 1902–1932). Mass. Rep.—Lt. Col., Mass. Volunteers, Civil War. *Mass., Associate Justice, and Chief Justice, Supreme Judicial Court (20).*

*HUGHES, CHARLES E. (1862–1948; Taft, 1910–1916, and Hoover, 1930–1941). N.Y.Rep.—N.Y., Counsel, legislative committees investigating gas and insurance industries (2); U.S., Special Assistant to Attorney General for Coal Investigation (1). *N.Y., Governor (3).* [Between appointments to the Supreme Court: Presidential Nominee, Republican Party, 1916. U.S., Secretary of State (4). *Member, Permanent Court of Arbitration, The Hague (4). Judge, Permanent Court of International Justice (2).*] Chief Justice on second appointment.

HUNT, WARD (1810–1886; Grant, 1872–1882). N.Y.Rep.—N.Y., Legislature (2). Mayor of Utica, N.Y. (1). N.Y., Associate Judge, and Chief Judge, Court of

Appeals (4); *Commissioner of Appeals (4).* He did not sit from 1879 to his retirement in 1882.

IREDELL, JAMES (1750–1799; Washington, 1790–1799). N.C.Fed.—Comptroller of Customs (6), Collector of Port (2), Edenton, N.C. N.C., Judge, Superior Court (½); Attorney General (2); Member, Council of State, 1787; *Reviser of Statutes (3).*

JACKSON, HOWELL E. (1832–1895; B. Harrison, 1893–1895). Tenn.Dem.—Tenn., Judge, Court of Arbitration (4); Legislature (1). U.S. Senate (5); *Judge, Circuit Court of Appeals (7).*

JACKSON, ROBERT H. (1892–1954; F.D. Roosevelt, 1941–1954). N.Y.Dem.—U.S., General Counsel, Bureau of Internal Revenue (2); Assistant Attorney General (2); Solicitor General (2); *Attorney General (1).*

*JAY, JOHN (1745–1829; Washington, 1789–1795). N.Y.Fed.—N.Y., Chief Justice, Supreme Court (2). U.S., Envoy to Spain (2); Commissioner, Treaty of Paris, 1782–83; Secretary for Foreign Affairs (6). Co-author, The Federalist.

JOHNSON, THOMAS (1732–1819; Washington, 1791–1793). Md.Fed.—Md., Brigadier–General, Militia (1); Legislature (5); Governor (2); *Chief Judge, General Court (1).*

JOHNSON, WILLIAM (1771–1834; Jefferson, 1804–1834). S.C.Rep.—S.C., Legislature (4); *Judge, Court of Common Pleas (6).*

KENNEDY, ANTHONY M. (1936–___; Reagan, 1988–___). Calif.Rep.—Calif. Army National Guard (1). *U.S., Judge, Court of Appeals (11).*

LAMAR, JOSEPH R. (1857–1916; Taft, 1910–1916). Ga.Dem.—Ga., Legislature (3); Commissioner to Codify Laws (3); Associate Justice, Supreme Court (4). *Private practice.*

LAMAR, LUCIUS Q.C. (1825–1893; Cleveland, 1888–1893). Miss.Dem.—Ga., Legislature (2). U.S., House of Representatives (4). Draftsman, Mississippi Ordinance of Secession, 1861. C.S.A., Lt. Col. (1); Commissioner to Russia (1); Judge–Advocate, III Corps. Army of No. Va. (1). U.S., House of Representatives (4); Senate (8); *Secretary of the Interior (3).*

LIVINGSTON, (HENRY) BROCKHOLST (1757–1823; Jefferson, 1806–1823). N.Y.Rep.—Lt. Col., Continental Army. *N.Y., Judge, Supreme Court (4).*

LURTON, HORACE H. (1844–1914; Taft, 1909–1914). Tenn.Dem.—Sgt. Major, C.S.A. Tenn., Chancellor (3); Associate Justice and Chief Justice, Supreme Court (7). *U.S., Judge, Circuit Court of Appeals (16).*

McKENNA, JOSEPH (1843–1926; McKinley, 1898–1925). Calif.Rep.—Calif., District Attorney (2); Legislature (2). U.S., House of Representatives (7); Judge, Circuit Court of Appeals (5); Attorney General (1).

McKINLEY, JOHN (1780–1852; Van Buren, 1837–1852). Ala.Dem.—Legislature (4). U.S., Senate (5); House of Representatives (2); *re-elected to Senate,* but appointed to Court before taking seat.

McLEAN, JOHN (1785–1861; Jackson, 1829–1861). Ohio Dem.—U.S., House of Representatives (4). Ohio, Judge, Supreme Court (6). U.S., Commissioner, General Land Office (1); *Postmaster-General (6).*

McREYNOLDS, JAMES C. (1862–1946; Wilson, 1914–1941). Tenn.Dem.—U.S., Assistant Attorney General (4); *Attorney General (1).*

*MARSHALL, JOHN (1755–1835; J. Adams, 1801–1835). Va.Fed.—Va., Legislature (7); U.S., Envoy to France (1); House of Representatives (1); *Secretary of State (1).*

MARSHALL, THURGOOD (1908–1993; L.B. Johnson, 1967–1991). N.Y.Dem.—Counsel, Legal Defense and Educational Fund, NAACP (21). U.S., Judge, Court of Appeals (4); *Solicitor General (2).*

MATTHEWS, STANLEY (1824–1889; Garfield, 1881–1889). Ohio Rep.—Ohio, Judge, Court of Common Pleas (2); Legislature (3). U.S., District Attorney (3). Col., Ohio Volunteers. Ohio, Judge, Superior Court (2). Counsel before Hayes–Tilden Electoral Commission, 1877. U.S., Senate (2). *Private practice.* His first appointment to the Court by Hayes in 1881 was not acted upon by the Senate.

MILLER, SAMUEL F. (1816–1890; Lincoln, 1862–1890). Iowa Rep.—Physician. *Private practice.*

MINTON, SHERMAN (1890–1965; Truman, 1949–1956). Ind.Dem.—Capt., Inf., World War I. U.S., Senate (6); *Judge, Court of Appeals (8).*

MOODY, WILLIAM H. (1853–1917; T. Roosevelt, 1906–1910). Mass.Rep.—U.S., District Attorney (5), House of Representatives (7); Secretary of the Navy (2); *Attorney General (2).*

MOORE, ALFRED (1755–1810; J. Adams, 1799–1804). N.C.Fed.—N.C., Col. of Militia; Legislature (2); Attorney General (9). U.S. Commissioner, Treaty with Cherokee Nation (1); *N.C., Judge, Superior Court (1).*

MURPHY, FRANK (1893–1949; F.D. Roosevelt, 1940–1949). Mich.Dem.—Capt., Inf., World War I. U.S., Assistant U.S. Attorney (1). Mich., Judge, Recorder's Court (7). Mayor, Detroit, Mich. (3). U.S., Governor–General, and High Commissioner, P.I. (3). Mich., Governor (2). *U.S., Attorney General (1).*

NELSON, SAMUEL (1792–1873; Tyler, 1845–1872). N.Y.Dem.—N.Y., Judge, Circuit Court (8); Associate Justice, and *Chief Justice, Supreme Court (14).*

O'CONNOR, SANDRA DAY (1930–____; Reagan, 1981–2006). Ariz.Rep.—Calif., Deputy County Attorney (2); Ariz., Assistant Attorney General (4); Legislature (6); Judge, Superior Court (4); *Court of Appeals (2).*

PATERSON, WILLIAM (1745–1806; Washington, 1793–1806). N.J.Fed.—Signer, U.S. Constitution, 1787. N.J., Legislature (2); Attorney General (7). U.S., Senate (1). *N.J., Governor (3).* Reviser of English Pre–Revolutionary Statutes in Force in N.J.

PECKHAM, RUFUS W. (1838–1909; Cleveland, 1895–1909). N.Y.Dem.—N.Y., District Attorney (1); Justice, Supreme Court (3); *Associate Judge, Court of Appeals (9).*

PITNEY, MAHLON (1858–1924; Taft, 1912–1922). N.J.Rep.—U.S., House of Representatives (4). N.J., Legislature (2); Associate Justice, Supreme Court (7); Chancellor (4).

POWELL, LEWIS F. (1907–1998; Nixon, 1972–1987). Va.Dem.—Col., U.S.A.A.F., World War II. U.S., Special Assistant to the Attorney General on Selective Service (4). Va., Member, State Board of Education (8). *Private practice.*

REED, STANLEY F. (1884–1980; F.D. Roosevelt, 1938–1957). Ky.Dem.—Ky., Legislature (4). 1st Lt., U.S.A., World War I. U.S., General Counsel, Federal Farm Board (3); General Counsel, Reconstruction Finance Corporation (3); *Solicitor General (3).*

*REHNQUIST, WILLIAM H. (1924–2005; Nixon, later Reagan, 1972–2005). Ariz.Rep.—U.S.A.F., World War II. *U.S., Assistant Attorney General, Office of Legal Counsel (3).*

*ROBERTS, JOHN G. (1955–____); G.W. Bush, 2005—____). D.C. Rep.—U.S., Special Assistant to Attorney General (1); Associate Counsel to the President (4); Principal Deputy Solicitor General (4). Private practice (14). *U.S., Judge, Court of Appeals (2).*

ROBERTS, OWEN J. (1875–1955; Hoover, 1930–1945). Pa.Rep.—Pa., Assistant District Attorney (3). U.S., Special Deputy Attorney General in Espionage Act Cases, World War I; Special Prosecutor, Oil Cases, 1924. *Private practice.*

*RUTLEDGE, JOHN (1739–1800; Washington, 1789–1791, and Washington, 1795). S.C.Fed.—Signer, U.S. Constitution, 1787. S.C., Legislature (18); Attorney General (1); President and Governor (6); *Chancellor (7).* [Between appointments to the Supreme Court: *S.C., Chief Justice, Court of Common Pleas and Sessions (4).*] He did not sit under his first appointment; he sat with a recess appointment as Chief Justice, but his regular appointment was rejected by the Senate.

RUTLEDGE, WILEY B. (1894–1949; F.D. Roosevelt, 1943–1949). Iowa Dem.—Mo., then Iowa, Member, National Conference of Commissioners on Uniform State Laws (10). *U.S., Judge, Court of Appeals (4).*

SANFORD, EDWARD T. (1865–1930; Harding, 1923–1930). Tenn.Rep.—U.S., Assistant Attorney General (1); *Judge, District Court (15).*

SCALIA, ANTONIN (1936–____; Reagan, 1986–____). Va.Rep.—U.S., General Counsel, Office of Telecommunications Policy (1); Chairman, Administrative Conference of the United States (2); Assistant Attorney General, Office of Legal Counsel (3); *Judge, Court of Appeals (4).*

SHIRAS, GEORGE (1832–1924; B. Harrison, 1892–1903). Pa.Rep.—*Private practice.*

SOUTER, DAVID H. (1939–____; G.H.W. Bush, 1990–____). N.H.Rep.—N.H., Assistant Attorney General (3); Deputy Attorney General (5); Attorney General (2); Associate Justice, Superior Court (5); Associate Justice, Supreme Court (7). *U.S., Judge, Court of Appeals ($^1\!/\!_2$) .*

STEVENS, JOHN PAUL (1920–____; Ford, 1975–____). Ill.Independent.— U.S.N.R., World War II. U.S., Associate Counsel, Subcommittee on the Study of Monopoly Power, Committee on the Judiciary, House of Representatives (1); Member, Attorney General's National Committee to Study the Antitrust Laws (2). Ill., Chief Counsel, Special Commission of the Supreme Court. *U.S., Judge, Court of Appeals (5).*

STEWART, POTTER (1915–1985; Eisenhower, 1958–1981). Ohio Rep.—Lt., U.S.N.R., World War II. *U.S., Judge, Court of Appeals (4).*

*STONE, HARLAN F. (1872–1946; Coolidge, later F.D. Roosevelt, 1925–1946). N.Y.Rep.—*U.S., Attorney General (1).* Chief Justice, 1941–1946.

STORY, JOSEPH (1779–1845; Madison, 1811–1845). Mass.Rep.—Mass., Legislature (5). U.S., House of Representatives (2). *Private practice.*

STRONG, WILLIAM (1808–1895; Grant, 1870–1880). Pa.Rep.—U.S., House of Representatives (4). Pa., Justice, Supreme Court (11). *Private practice.*

SUTHERLAND, GEORGE (1862–1942; Harding, 1922–1938). Utah Rep.— Utah, Legislature (4). U.S., House of Representatives (2); Senate (12). *Private practice.*

SWAYNE, NOAH H. (1804–1884; Lincoln, 1862–1881). Ohio Rep.—Ohio, County Attorney (4); Legislature (2). U.S., District Attorney (9). *Private practice.*

*TAFT, WILLIAM H. (1857–1930; Harding, 1921–1930). Conn.Rep.—U.S., Collector of Internal Revenue (1). Ohio, Judge, Superior Court (3). U.S., Solicitor General (2); Judge, Circuit Court of Appeals (8); Governor–General, P.I. (3); Secretary of War (4); President (4). *Professor of Law.*

*TANEY, ROGER B. (1777–1864; Jackson, 1836–1864). Md.Dem.—Md., Legislature (7); Attorney General (2). U.S., Attorney General (2), Secretary of the Treasury (¾; rejected by the Senate). *Private practice.*

THOMAS, CLARENCE (1948–___; G.H.W. Bush, 1991–___). Ga.Rep.—Mo., Assistant Attorney General (3). U.S., Legislative Assistant (2); Assistant Secretary for Civil Rights, Department of Education (1); Chairman, Equal Employment Opportunity Commission (8); *Judge, Court of Appeals (1).*

THOMPSON, SMITH (1768–1843; Monroe, 1823–1843). N.Y.Rep.—N.Y., Legislature (2); Associate Justice, and Chief Justice, Supreme Court (16). *U.S., Secretary of the Navy (4).*

TODD, THOMAS (1765–1826; Jefferson, 1807–1826). Ky.Rep.—*Ky., Judge, and Chief Justice, Court of Appeals (6).*

TRIMBLE, ROBERT (1777–1828; J.Q. Adams, 1826–1828). Ky.Rep.—Ky., Legislature (2). Judge, Court of Appeals (2). U.S., District Attorney (4); *Judge, District Court (9).*

VAN DEVANTER, WILLIS (1859–1941; Taft, 1910–1937). Wyo.Rep.—Wyo., Legislature (2); Chief Justice, Supreme Court (1). U.S., Assistant Attorney General (Interior Department) (6); *Judge, Circuit Court of Appeals (7).*

*VINSON, FRED M. (1890–1953; Truman, 1946–1953). Ky.Dem.—Ky., Commonwealth Attorney (3). U.S., House of Representatives (14); Judge, Court of Appeals (5); Director, Office of Economic Stabilization (2); Federal Loan Administrator (1 mo.); Director, Office of War Mobilization and Reconversion (3 mo.); *Secretary of the Treasury (1).*

*WAITE, MORRISON R. (1816–1888; Grant, 1874–1888). Ohio Rep.—Ohio, Legislature (2). Counsel for United States, U.S.—Gr. Brit. Arbitration ("Alabama" Claims), 1871–72. *Private practice.*

*WARREN, EARL (1891–1974; Eisenhower, 1953–1969). Calif.Rep.—1st Lt., Inf., World War I. Deputy City Attorney (1); Deputy District Attorney (5); District Attorney (14); Attorney General (4); *Governor (10).*

WASHINGTON, BUSHROD (1762–1829; J. Adams, 1798–1829). Pa.Fed.—Va., Legislature (1). *Private practice.*

WAYNE, JAMES M. (1790–1867; Jackson, 1835–1867). Ga.Dem.—Ga., Officer, Hussars, War of 1812; Legislature (2). Mayor of Savannah, Ga. (2). Ga., Judge, Superior Court (5). *U.S., House of Representatives (6).*

WHITE, BYRON R. (1917–2002; Kennedy, 1962–1993). Colo.Dem.—U.S.N.R., World War II. *U.S., Deputy Attorney General (1).*

*WHITE, EDWARD D. (1845–1921; Cleveland, later Taft, 1894–1921). La. Dem.—La., Legislature (4); Justice, Supreme Court (2). *U.S., Senate (3).* Chief Justice, 1910–1921.

WHITTAKER, CHARLES E. (1901–1973; Eisenhower, 1957–1962). Mo.Rep.—U.S., Judge, District Court (2); *Court of Appeals (1).*

WILSON, JAMES (1724–1798; Washington, 1789–1798). Pa.Fed.—Signer, U.S. Declaration of Independence, 1776, and U.S. Constitution, 1787. Although he was strongly interested in western-land development companies for several years prior to his appointment, his primary activity in the period immediately preceding his appointment was in obtaining ratification of the Federal and Pennsylvania Constitutions.

WOODBURY, LEVI (1789–1851; Polk, 1845–1851). N.H. Dem.—N.H., Associate Justice, Superior Court (6); Governor (2); Legislature (1). U.S., Senate (6); Secretary of the Navy (3); Secretary of the Treasury (7); *Senate (4)*.

WOODS, WILLIAM B. (1824–1887; Hayes, 1880–1887). Ga.Rep.—Mayor, Newark, Oh. (1). Ohio, Legislature (4). Brevet Major General, U.S. Vol., Civil War. Ala., Chancellor (1). *U.S., Judge, Circuit Court (11)*.

Appendix B

THE CONSTITUTION OF THE UNITED STATES

PREAMBLE

We the People of the United States, in Order to form a more perfect Union, establish Justice, insure domestic Tranquility, provide for the common defence, promote the general Welfare, and secure the Blessings of Liberty to ourselves and our Posterity, do ordain and establish this Constitution for the United States of America.

ARTICLE I

Section 1. All legislative Powers herein granted shall be vested in a Congress of the United States, which shall consist of a Senate and House of Representatives.

Section 2. [1] The House of Representatives shall be composed of Members chosen every second Year by the People of the several States, and the Electors in each State shall have the Qualifications requisite for Electors of the most numerous Branch of the State Legislature.

[2] No Person shall be a Representative who shall not have attained to the Age of twenty five Years, and been seven Years a Citizen of the United States, and who shall not, when elected, be an Inhabitant of that State in which he shall be chosen.

[3] Representatives and direct Taxes shall be apportioned among the several States which may be included within this Union, according to their respective Numbers, which shall be determined by adding to the whole Number of free Persons, including those bound to Service for a Term of Years, and excluding Indians not taxed, three fifths of all other Persons. The actual Enumeration shall be made within three Years after the first Meeting of the Congress of the United States, and within every subsequent Term of ten Years, in such Manner as they shall by Law direct. The Number of Representatives shall not exceed one for every thirty Thousand, but each State shall have at Least one Representative; and until such enumeration shall be made, the State of New Hampshire shall be entitled to chuse three, Massachusetts eight, Rhode Island and Providence Plantations one, Connecticut five, New York six, New Jersey four, Pennsylvania eight, Delaware one, Maryland six, Virginia ten, North Carolina five, South Carolina five, and Georgia three.

[4] When vacancies happen in the Representation from any State, the Executive Authority thereof shall issue Writs of Election to fill such Vacancies.

[5] The House of Representatives shall chuse their Speaker and other Officers; and shall have the sole Power of Impeachment.

Section 3. [1] The Senate of the United States shall be composed of two Senators from each State, chosen by the Legislature thereof, for six Years; and each Senator shall have one Vote.

[2] Immediately after they shall be assembled in Consequence of the first Election, they shall be divided as equally as may be into three Classes. The Seats of the Senators of the first Class shall be vacated at the Expiration of the Second Year, of the second Class at the Expiration of the fourth Year, and of the third Class at the Expiration of the sixth Year, so that one third may be chosen every second Year; and if Vacancies happen by Resignation, or otherwise, during the Recess of the Legislature of any State, the Executive thereof may make temporary Appointments until the next Meeting of the Legislature, which shall then fill such Vacancies.

[3] No Person shall be a Senator who shall not have attained to the Age of thirty Years, and been nine Years a Citizen of the United States, and who shall not, when elected, by an Inhabitant of that State for which he shall be chosen.

[4] The Vice President of the United States shall be President of the Senate, but shall have no Vote, unless they be equally divided.

[5] The Senate shall chuse their other Officers, and also a President pro tempore, in the Absence of the Vice President, or when he shall exercise the Office of President of the United States.

[6] The Senate shall have the sole Power to try all Impeachments. When sitting for that Purpose, they shall be on Oath or Affirmation. When the President of the United States is tried, the Chief Justice shall preside: And no Person shall be convicted without the Concurrence of two thirds of the Members present.

[7] Judgment in Cases of Impeachment shall not extend further than to removal from Office, and disqualification to hold and enjoy any Office of honor, Trust, or Profit under the United States: but the Party convicted shall nevertheless be liable and subject to Indictment, Trial, Judgment, and Punishment, according to Law.

Section 4. [1] The Times, Places and Manner of holding Elections for Senators and Representatives, shall be prescribed in each State by the Legislature thereof; but the Congress may at any time by Law make or alter such Regulations, except as to the Places of chusing Senators.

[2] The Congress shall assemble at least once in every Year, and such Meeting shall be on the first Monday in December, unless they shall by Law appoint a different Day.

Section 5. [1] Each House shall be the Judge of the Elections, Returns, and Qualifications of its own Members, and a Majority of each shall constitute a Quorum to do Business; but a smaller Number may adjourn from day to day, and may be authorized to compel the Attendance of absent Members, in such Manner, and under such Penalties as each House may provide.

[2] Each House may determine the Rules of its Proceedings, punish its Members for disorderly Behavior, and, with the Concurrence of two thirds, expel a Member.

[3]   Each House shall keep a Journal of its Proceedings, and from time to time publish the same, excepting such Parts as may in their Judgment require Secrecy; and the Yeas and Nays of the Members of either House on any question shall, at the Desire of one fifth of those Present, be entered on the Journal.

[4]   Neither House, during the Session of Congress, shall without the Consent of the other, adjourn for more than three days, nor to any other Place than that in which the two Houses shall be sitting.

Section 6. [1] The Senators and Representatives shall receive a Compensation for their Services, to be ascertained by Law, and paid out of the Treasury of the United States. They shall in all Cases, except Treason, Felony and Breach of the Peace, be privileged from Arrest during their Attendance at the Session of their respective Houses, and in going to and returning from the same; and for any Speech or Debate in either House, they shall not be questioned in any other Place.

[2]   No Senator or Representative shall, during the Time for which he was elected, be appointed to any civil Office under the Authority of the United States, which shall have been created, or the Emoluments whereof shall have been increased during such time; and no Person holding any Office under the United States, shall be a Member of either House during his Continuance in Office.

Section 7. [1] All Bills for raising Revenue shall originate in the House of Representatives; but the Senate may propose or concur with Amendments as on other Bills.

[2]   Every Bill which shall have passed the House of Representatives and the Senate, shall, before it become a Law, be presented to the President of the United States; If he approve he shall sign it, but if not he shall return it, with his Objections to the House in which it shall have originated, who shall enter the Objections at large on their Journal, and proceed to reconsider it. If after such Reconsideration two thirds of that House shall agree to pass the Bill, it shall be sent together with the Objections, to the other House, by which it shall likewise be reconsidered, and if approved by two thirds of that House, it shall become a Law. But in all such Cases the Votes of both Houses shall be determined by yeas and Nays, and the Names of the Persons voting for and against the Bill shall be entered on the Journal of each House respectively. If any Bill shall not be returned by the President within ten Days (Sundays excepted) after it shall have been presented to him, the Same shall be a Law, in like Manner as if he had signed it, unless the Congress by their Adjournment prevent its Return in which Case it shall not be a Law.

[3]   Every Order, Resolution, or Vote, to Which the Concurrence of the Senate and House of Representatives may be necessary (except on a question of Adjournment) shall be presented to the President of the United States; and before the Same shall take Effect, shall be approved by him, or being disapproved by him, shall be repassed by two thirds of the Senate and House of Representatives, according to the Rules and Limitations prescribed in the Case of a Bill.

Section 8. [1] The Congress shall have Power To lay and collect Taxes, Duties, Imposts and Excises, to pay the Debts and provide for the common Defence and general Welfare of the United States; but all Duties, Imposts and Excises shall be uniform throughout the United States;

[2]   To borrow money on the credit of the United States;

[3]   To regulate Commerce with foreign Nations, and among the several States, and with the Indian Tribes;

[4]   To establish an uniform Rule of Naturalization, and uniform Laws on the subject of Bankruptcies throughout the United States;

[5]   To coin Money, regulate the Value thereof, and of foreign Coin, and fix the Standard of Weights and Measures;

[6]   To provide for the Punishment of counterfeiting the Securities and current Coin of the United States;

[7]   To Establish Post Offices and Post Roads;

[8]   To promote the Progress of Science and useful Arts, by securing for limited Times to Authors and Inventors the exclusive Right to their respective Writings and Discoveries;

[9]   To constitute Tribunals inferior to the supreme Court;

[10]   To define and punish Piracies and Felonies committed on the high Seas, and Offenses against the Law of Nations;

[11]   To declare War, grant Letters of Marque and Reprisal, and make Rules concerning Captures on Land and Water;

[12]   To raise and support Armies, but no Appropriation of Money to that Use shall be for a longer Term than two Years;

[13]   To provide and maintain a Navy;

[14]   To make Rules for the Government and Regulation of the land and naval Forces;

[15]   To provide for calling forth the Militia to execute the Laws of the Union, suppress Insurrections and repel Invasions;

[16]   To provide for organizing, arming, and disciplining, the Militia, and for governing such Part of them as may be employed in the Service of the United States, reserving to the States respectively, the Appointment of the Officers, and the Authority of training the Militia according to the discipline prescribed by Congress;

[17]   To exercise exclusive Legislation in all Cases whatsoever, over such District (not exceeding ten Miles square) as may, by Cession of particular States, and the Acceptance of Congress, become the Seat of the Government of the United States, and to exercise like Authority over all Places purchased by the Consent of the Legislature of the State in which the Same shall be, for the Erection of Forts, Magazines, Arsenals, dock-Yards, and other needful Buildings;—And

[18]   To make all Laws which shall be necessary and proper for carrying into Execution the foregoing Powers, and all other Powers vested by this Constitution in the Government of the United States, or in any Department or Officer thereof.

Section 9. [1] The Migration or Importation of Such Persons as any of the States now existing shall think proper to admit, shall not be prohibited by the Congress prior to the Year one thousand eight hundred and eight, but a Tax or duty may be imposed on such Importation, not exceeding ten dollars for each Person.

[2]   The privilege of the Writ of Habeas Corpus shall not be suspended, unless when in Cases of Rebellion or Invasion the public Safety may require it.

[3]   No Bill of Attainder or ex post facto Law shall be passed.

[4]   No Capitation, or other direct, Tax shall be laid, unless in Proportion to the Census or Enumeration herein before directed to be taken.

[5]   No Tax or Duty shall be laid on Articles exported from any State.

[6]   No Preference shall be given by any Regulation of Commerce or Revenue to the Ports of one State over those of another: nor shall Vessels bound to, or from, one State be obliged to enter, clear, or pay Duties in another.

[7]   No money shall be drawn from the Treasury, but in Consequence of Appropriations made by Law; and a regular Statement and Account of the Receipts and Expenditures of all public Money shall be published from time to time.

[8]   No Title of Nobility shall be granted by the United States: And no Person holding any Office of Profit or Trust under them, shall, without the Consent of the Congress, accept of any present, Emolument, Office, or Title, of any kind whatever, from any King, Prince, or foreign State.

Section 10. [1] No State shall enter into any Treaty, Alliance, or Confederation; grant Letters of Marque and Reprisal; coin Money; emit Bills of Credit; make any Thing but gold and silver Coin a Tender in Payment of Debts; pass any Bill of Attainder, ex post facto Law, or Law impairing the Obligation of Contracts, or grant any Title of Nobility.

[2]   No State shall, without the Consent of the Congress, lay any Imposts or Duties on Imports or Exports, except what may be absolutely necessary for executing it's inspection Laws: and the net Produce of all Duties and Imposts, laid by any State on Imports or Exports, shall be for the Use of the Treasury of the United States; and all such Laws shall be subject to the Revision and Controul of the Congress.

[3]   No State shall, without the Consent of Congress, lay any Duty of Tonnage, keep Troops, or Ships of War in time of Peace, enter into any Agreement or Compact with another State, or with a foreign Power, or engage in War, unless actually invaded, or in such imminent Danger as will not admit of delay.

ARTICLE II

Section 1. [1] The executive Power shall be vested in a President of the United States of America. He shall hold his Office during the Term of four Years, and, together with the Vice President, chosen for the same Term, be elected, as follows:

[2]   Each State shall appoint, in such Manner as the Legislature thereof may direct, a Number of Electors, equal to the whole Number of Senators and Representatives to which the State may be entitled in the Congress; but no Senator or Representative, or Person holding an Office of Trust or Profit under the United States, shall be appointed an Elector.

[3]   The Electors shall meet in their respective States, and vote by Ballot for two Persons, of whom one at least shall not be an Inhabitant of the same State with themselves. And they shall make a List of all the Persons voted for, and of the Number of Votes for each; which List they shall sign and certify, and transmit sealed to the Seat of the Government of the United States, directed to the President of the Senate. The President of the Senate shall, in the Presence of the Senate and House of Representatives, open all the Certificates, and the Votes shall then be counted. The Person having the greatest Number of Votes shall be the President, if such Number be a Majority of the whole Number of Electors appointed; and if there be more than one who have such Majority, and have an equal Number of Votes, then the House of Representatives shall immediately chuse by Ballot one of them for President; and if no Person have a Majority, then

from the five highest on the List the said House shall in like Manner chuse the President. But in chusing the President, the Votes shall be taken by States the Representation from each State having one Vote; A quorum for this Purpose shall consist of a Member or Members from two thirds of the States, and a Majority of all the States shall be necessary to a Choice. In every Case, after the Choice of the President, the Person having the greater Number of Votes of the Electors shall be the Vice President. But if there should remain two or more who have equal Votes, the Senate shall chuse from them by Ballot the Vice President.

[4]   The Congress may determine the Time of chusing the Electors, and the Day on which they shall give their Votes; which Day shall be the same throughout the United States.

[5]   No person except a natural born Citizen, or a Citizen of the United States, at the time of the Adoption of this Constitution, shall be eligible to the Office of President; neither shall any Person be eligible to that Office who shall not have attained to the Age of thirty five Years, and been fourteen Years a Resident within the United States.

[6]   In case of the removal of the President from Office, or of his Death, Resignation or Inability to discharge the Powers and Duties of the said Office, the Same shall devolve on the Vice President, and the Congress may by Law provide for the Case of Removal, Death, Resignation or Inability, both of the President and Vice President, declaring what Officer shall then act as President, and such Officer shall act accordingly, until the Disability be removed, or a President shall be elected.

[7]   The President shall, at stated Times, receive for his Services, a Compensation, which shall neither be increased nor diminished during the Period for which he shall have been elected, and he shall not receive within that Period any other Emolument from the United States, or any of them.

[8]   Before he enter on the Execution of his Office, he shall take the following Oath or Affirmation: "I do solemnly swear (or affirm) that I will faithfully execute the Office of President of the United States, and will to the best of my Ability, preserve, protect and defend the Constitution of the United States."

Section 2. [1] The President shall be Commander in Chief of the Army and Navy of the United States, and of the militia of the several States, when called into the actual Service of the United States; he may require the Opinion, in writing, of the principal Officer in each of the Executive Departments, upon any Subject relating to the Duties of their respective Offices, and he shall have Power to grant Reprieves and Pardons for Offenses against the United States, except in Cases of Impeachment.

[2]   He shall have Power, by and with the Advice and Consent of the Senate to make Treaties, provided two thirds of the Senators present concur; and he shall nominate, and by and with the Advice and Consent of the Senate, shall appoint Ambassadors, other public Ministers and Consuls, Judges of the supreme Court, and all other Officers of the United States, whose Appointments are not herein otherwise provided for, and which shall be established by Law; but the Congress may by Law vest the Appointment of such inferior Officers, as they think proper, in the President alone, in the Courts of Law, or in the Heads of Departments.

[3]   The President shall have Power to fill up all Vacancies that may happen during the Recess of the Senate, by granting Commissions which shall expire at the End of their next Session.

Section 3. He shall from time to time give to the Congress Information of the State of the Union, and recommend to their Consideration such Measures as he shall judge necessary and expedient; he may, on extraordinary Occasions, convene both Houses, or either of them, and in Case of Disagreement between them, with Respect to the Time of Adjournment, he may adjourn them to such Time as he shall think proper; he shall receive Ambassadors and other public Ministers; he shall take Care that the Laws be faithfully executed, and shall Commission all the Officers of the United States.

Section 4. The President, Vice President and all civil Officers of the United States, shall be removed from Office on Impeachment for, and Conviction of, Treason, Bribery, or other high Crimes and Misdemeanors.

Article III

Section 1. The judicial Power of the United States, shall be vested in one supreme Court, and in such inferior Courts as the Congress may from time to time ordain and establish. The Judges, both of the supreme and inferior Courts, shall hold their Offices during good Behaviour, and shall, at stated Times, receive for their Services a Compensation, which shall not be diminished during their Continuance in Office.

Section 2. [1] The judicial Power shall extend to all Cases, in Law and Equity, arising under this Constitution, the Laws of the United States, and Treaties made, or which shall be made, under their Authority;—to all Cases affecting Ambassadors, other public Ministers and Consuls;—to all Cases of admiralty and maritime Jurisdiction;—to Controversies to which the United States shall be a Party;—to Controversies between two or more States;—between a State and Citizens of another State;—between Citizens of different States;—between Citizens of the same State claiming Lands under the Grants of different States, and between a State, or the Citizens thereof, and foreign States, Citizens or Subjects.

[2] In all Cases affecting Ambassadors, other public Ministers and Consuls, and those in which a State shall be a Party, the supreme Court shall have original Jurisdiction. In all the other Cases before mentioned, the supreme Court shall have appellate Jurisdiction, both as to Law and Fact, with such Exceptions, and under such Regulations as the Congress shall make.

[3] The trial of all Crimes, except in Cases of Impeachment, shall be by Jury; and such Trial shall be held in the State where the said Crimes shall have been committed; but when not committed within any State, the Trial shall be at such Place or Places as the Congress may by Law have directed.

Section 3. [1] Treason against the United States, shall consist only in levying War against them, or, in adhering to their Enemies, giving them Aid and Comfort. No Person shall be convicted of Treason unless on the Testimony of two Witnesses to the same overt Act, or on Confession in open Court.

[2] The Congress shall have Power to declare the Punishment of Treason, but no Attainder of Treason shall work Corruption of Blood, or Forfeiture except during the Life of the Person attainted.

Article IV

Section 1. Full Faith and Credit shall be given in each State to the public Acts, Records, and judicial Proceedings of every other State. And the Congress may by general Laws prescribe the Manner in which such Acts, Records and Proceedings shall be proved, and the Effect thereof.

Section 2. [1] The Citizens of each State shall be entitled to all Privileges and Immunities of Citizens in the several States.

[2] A Person charged in any State with Treason, Felony, or other Crime, who shall flee from Justice, and be found in another State, shall on demand of the executive Authority of the State from which he fled, be delivered up, to be removed to the State having Jurisdiction of the Crime.

[3] No Person held to Service or Labour in one State, under the Laws thereof, escaping into another, shall, in Consequence of any Law or Regulation therein, be discharged from such Service or Labour, but shall be delivered up on Claim of the Party to whom such Service or Labour may be due.

Section 3. [1] New States may be admitted by the Congress into this Union; but no new State shall be formed or erected within the Jurisdiction of any other State; nor any State be formed by the Junction of two or more States, or Parts of States, without the Consent of the Legislatures of the States concerned as well as of the Congress.

[2] The Congress shall have Power to dispose of and make all needful Rules and Regulations respecting the Territory or other Property belonging to the United States; and nothing in this Constitution shall be so construed as to Prejudice any Claims of the United States, or of any particular State.

Section 4. The United States shall guarantee to every State in this Union a Republican Form of Government, and shall protect each of them against Invasion; and on Application of the Legislature, or of the Executive (when the Legislature cannot be convened) against domestic Violence.

ARTICLE V

The Congress, whenever two thirds of both Houses shall deem it necessary, shall propose Amendments to this Constitution, or, on the Application of the Legislatures of two thirds of the several States, shall call a Convention for proposing Amendments, which, in either Case, shall be valid to all Intents and Purposes, as part of this Constitution, when ratified by the Legislatures of three fourths of the several States, or by Conventions in three fourths thereof, as the one or the other Mode of Ratification may be proposed by the Congress; Provided that no Amendment which may be made prior to the Year One thousand eight hundred and eight shall in any Manner affect the first and fourth Clauses in the Ninth Section of the first Article; and that no State, without its Consent, shall be deprived of its equal Suffrage in the Senate.

ARTICLE VI

[1] All Debts contracted and Engagements entered into, before the Adoption of this Constitution shall be as valid against the United States under this Constitution, as under the Confederation.

[2] This Constitution, and the Laws of the United States which shall be made in Pursuance thereof; and all Treaties made, or which shall be made, under the Authority of the United States, shall be the supreme Law of the Land; and the Judges in every State shall be bound thereby, any Thing in the Constitution or Laws of any State to the Contrary notwithstanding.

[3] The Senators and Representatives before mentioned, and the Members of the several State Legislatures, and all executive and judicial Officers, both of the United States and of the several States, shall be bound by Oath or Affirma-

tion, to support this Constitution; but no religious Test shall ever be required as a Qualification to any Office or public Trust under the United States.

ARTICLE VII

The Ratification of the Conventions of nine States shall be sufficient for the Establishment of this Constitution between the States so ratifying the Same.

AMENDMENTS OF THE CONSTITUTION OF THE UNITED STATES OF AMERICA, PROPOSED BY CONGRESS AND RATIFIED BY THE LEGISLATURES OF THE SEVERAL STATES PURSUANT TO THE FIFTH ARTICLE OF THE ORIGINAL CONSTITUTION.

AMENDMENT I [1791]

Congress shall make no law respecting an establishment of religion, or prohibiting the free exercise thereof; or abridging the freedom of speech, or of the press; or the right of the people peaceably to assemble, and to petition the Government for a redress of grievances.

AMENDMENT II [1791]

A well regulated Militia, being necessary to the security of a free State, the right of the people to keep and bear Arms, shall not be infringed.

AMENDMENT III [1791]

No Soldier shall, in time of peace be quartered in any house, without the consent of the Owner, nor in time of war, but in a manner to be prescribed by law.

AMENDMENT IV [1791]

The right of the people to be secure in their persons, houses, papers, and effects, against unreasonable searches and seizures, shall not be violated, and no Warrants shall issue, but upon probable cause, supported by Oath or affirmation and particularly describing the place to be searched, and the persons or things to be seized.

AMENDMENT V [1791]

No person shall be held to answer for a capital, or otherwise infamous crime, unless on a presentment or indictment of a Grand Jury, except in cases arising in the land or naval forces, or in the Militia, when in actual service in time of War or public danger; nor shall any person be subject for the same offence to be twice put in jeopardy of life or limb; nor shall be compelled in any criminal case to be a witness against himself, nor be deprived of life, liberty, or property, without due process of law; nor shall private property be taken for public use, without just compensation.

AMENDMENT VI [1791]

In all criminal prosecutions, the accused shall enjoy the right to a speedy and public trial, by an impartial jury of the State and district wherein the crime shall have been committed, which district shall have been previously ascertained by law, and to be informed of the nature and cause of the accusation; to be confronted with the witnesses against him; to have compulsory process for obtaining witnesses in his favor, and to have the Assistance of Counsel for his defence.

AMENDMENT VII [1791]

In Suits at common law, where the value in controversy shall exceed twenty dollars, the right of trial by jury shall be preserved, and no fact tried by jury, shall be otherwise re-examined in any Court of the United States, than according to the rules of the common law.

AMENDMENT VIII [1791]

Excessive bail shall not be required, nor excessive fines imposed, nor cruel and unusual punishments inflicted.

AMENDMENT IX [1791]

The enumeration in the Constitution, of certain rights, shall not be construed to deny or disparage others retained by the people.

AMENDMENT X [1791]

The powers not delegated to the United States by the Constitution, nor prohibited by it to the States, are reserved to the States respectively, or to the people.

AMENDMENT XI [1798]

The Judicial power of the United States shall not be construed to extend to any suit in law or equity, commenced or prosecuted against one of the United States by Citizens of another State, or by Citizens or Subjects of any Foreign State.

AMENDMENT XII [1804]

The Electors shall meet in their respective states and vote by ballot for President and Vice-President, one of whom, at least, shall not be an inhabitant of the same state with themselves; they shall name in their ballots the person voted for as President, and in distinct ballots the person voted for as Vice-President, and they shall make distinct lists of all persons voted for as President, and of all persons voted for as Vice-President, and of the number of votes for each, which lists they shall sign and certify, and transmit sealed to the seat of the government of the United States, directed to the President of the Senate;—The President of the Senate shall, in the presence of the Senate and House of Representatives, open all the certificates and the votes shall then be counted;—The person having the greatest number of votes for President, shall be the President, if such number be a majority of the whole number of Electors appointed; and if no person have such majority, then from the persons having the highest numbers not exceeding three on the list of those voted for as President, the House of Representatives shall choose immediately, by ballot, the President. But in choosing the President, the votes shall be taken by states, the representation from each state having one vote; a quorum for this purpose shall consist of a member or members from two-thirds of the states, and a majority of all the states shall be necessary to a choice. And if the House of Representatives shall not choose a President whenever the right of choice shall devolve upon them before the fourth day of March next following, then the Vice-President shall act as President, as in the case of the death or other constitutional disability of the President.—The person having the greatest number of votes as Vice-President, shall be the Vice-President, if such number be a majority of the whole number of Electors appointed, and if no person have a majority, then from the two highest numbers on the list, the Senate shall choose the Vice-President; a quorum for the purpose shall consist of two-thirds of the whole number of Senators, and a majority of the whole number shall be necessary to a choice. But no person constitutionally ineligible to the office of President shall be eligible to that of Vice-President of the United States.

AMENDMENT XIII [1865]

Section 1. Neither slavery nor involuntary servitude, except as a punishment for crime whereof the party shall have been duly convicted, shall exist within the United States, or any place subject to their jurisdiction.

Section 2. Congress shall have power to enforce this article by appropriate legislation.

AMENDMENT XIV [1868]

Section 1. All persons born or naturalized in the United States, and subject to the jurisdiction thereof, are citizens of the United States and of the State wherein they reside. No State shall make or enforce any law which shall abridge the privileges or immunities of citizens of the United States; nor shall any State deprive any person of life, liberty, or property, without due process of law; nor deny to any person within its jurisdiction the equal protection of the laws.

Section 2. Representatives shall be apportioned among the several States according to their respective numbers, counting the whole number of persons in each State, excluding Indians not taxed. But when the right to vote at any election for the choice of electors for President and Vice President of the United States, Representatives in Congress, the Executive and Judicial officers of a State, or the members of the Legislature thereof, is denied to any of the male inhabitants of such State, being twenty-one years of age, and citizens of the United States, or in any way abridged, except for participation in rebellion, or other crime, the basis of representation therein shall be reduced in the proportion which the number of such male citizens shall bear to the whole number of male citizens twenty-one years of age in such State.

Section 3. No person shall be a Senator or Representative in Congress, or elector of President and Vice President, or hold any office, civil or military, under the United States, or under any State, who having previously taken an oath, as a member of Congress, or as an officer of the United States, or as a member of any State legislature, or as an executive or judicial officer of any State, to support the Constitution of the United States, shall have engaged in insurrection or rebellion against the same, or given aid or comfort to the enemies thereof. But Congress may by a vote of two-thirds of each House, remove such disability.

Section 4. The validity of the public debt of the United States, authorized by law, including debts incurred for payment of pensions and bounties for services in suppressing insurrection or rebellion, shall not be questioned. But neither the United States nor any State shall assume or pay any debt or obligation incurred in aid of insurrection or rebellion against the United States, or any claim for the loss or emancipation of any slave; but all such debts, obligations and claims shall be held illegal and void.

Section 5. The Congress shall have power to enforce, by appropriate legislation, the provisions of this article.

AMENDMENT XV [1870]

Section 1. The right of citizens of the United States to vote shall not be denied or abridged by the United States or by any State on account of race, color, or previous condition of servitude.

Section 2. The Congress shall have power to enforce this article by appropriate legislation.

AMENDMENT XVI [1913]

The Congress shall have power to lay and collect taxes on incomes, from whatever source derived, without apportionment among the several States, and without regard to any census or enumeration.

AMENDMENT XVII [1913]

[1] The Senate of the United States shall be composed of two Senators from each State, elected by the people thereof, for six years; and each Senator shall have one vote. The electors in each State shall have the qualifications requisite for electors of the most numerous branch of the State legislatures.

[2] When vacancies happen in the representation of any State in the Senate, the executive authority of such State shall issue writs of election to fill such vacancies: *Provided,* That the legislature of any State may empower the executive thereof to make temporary appointments until the people fill the vacancies by election as the legislature may direct.

[3] This amendment shall not be so construed as to affect the election or term of any Senator chosen before it becomes valid as part of the Constitution.

AMENDMENT XVIII [1919]

Section 1. After one year from the ratification of this article the manufacture, sale, or transportation of intoxicating liquors within, the importation thereof into, or the exportation thereof from the United States and all territory subject to the jurisdiction thereof for beverage purposes is hereby prohibited.

Section 2. The Congress and the several States shall have concurrent power to enforce this article by appropriate legislation.

Section 3. This article shall be inoperative unless it shall have been ratified as an amendment to the Constitution by the legislatures of the several States, as provided in the Constitution, within seven years from the date of the submission hereof to the States by the Congress.

AMENDMENT XIX [1920]

[1] The right of citizens of the United States to vote shall not be denied or abridged by the United States or by any State on account of sex.

[2] Congress shall have power to enforce this article by appropriate legislation.

AMENDMENT XX [1933]

Section 1. The terms of the President and Vice President shall end at noon on the 20th day of January, and the terms of Senators and Representatives at noon on the 3d day of January, of the years in which such terms would have ended if this article had not been ratified; and the terms of their successors shall then begin.

Section 2. The Congress shall assemble at least once in every year, and such meeting shall begin at noon on the 3d day of January, unless they shall by law appoint a different day.

Section 3. If, at the time fixed for the beginning of the term of the President, the President elect shall have died, the Vice President elect shall become President. If the President shall not have been chosen before the time fixed for the beginning of his term, or if the President elect shall have failed to qualify, then the Vice President elect shall act as President until a President shall have qualified; and the Congress may by law provide for the case wherein neither a President elect nor a Vice President elect shall have qualified, declaring who shall then act as President, or the manner in which one who is to act shall be selected, and such person shall act accordingly until a President or Vice President shall have qualified.

Section 4. The Congress may by law provide for the case of the death of any of the persons from whom the House of Representatives may choose a President whenever the right of choice shall have devolved upon them, and for the case of the death of any of the persons from whom the Senate may choose a Vice President whenever the right of choice shall have devolved upon them.

Section 5. Sections 1 and 2 shall take effect on the 15th day of October following the ratification of this article.

Section 6. This article shall be inoperative unless it shall have been ratified as an amendment to the Constitution by the legislatures of three-fourths of the several States within seven years from the date of its submission.

Amendment XXI [1933]

Section 1. The eighteenth article of amendment to the Constitution of the United States is hereby repealed.

Section 2. The transportation or importation into any State, Territory, or possession of the United States for delivery or use therein of intoxicating liquors, in violation of the laws thereof, is hereby prohibited.

Section 3. This article shall be inoperative unless it shall have been ratified as an amendment to the Constitution by conventions in the several States, as provided in the Constitution, within seven years from the date of the submission hereof to the States by the Congress.

Amendment XXII [1951]

Section 1. No person shall be elected to the office of the President more than twice, and no person who has held the office of President, or acted as President, for more than two years of a term to which some other person was elected President shall be elected to the office of President more than once. But this Article shall not apply to any person holding the office of President when this Article was proposed by the Congress, and shall not prevent any person who may be holding the office of President, or acting as President, during the term within which this Article becomes operative from holding the office of President or acting as President during the remainder of such term.

Section 2. This article shall be inoperative unless it shall have been ratified as an amendment to the Constitution by the legislatures of three-fourths of the several States within seven years from the date of its submission to the States by the Congress.

Amendment XXIII [1961]

Section 1. The District constituting the seat of Government of the United States shall appoint in such manner as the Congress may direct:

A number of electors of President and Vice President equal to the whole number of Senators and Representatives in Congress to which the District would be entitled if it were a State, but in no event more than the least populous state; they shall be in addition to those appointed by the states, but they shall be considered, for the purposes of the election of President and Vice President, to be electors appointed by a state; and they shall meet in the District and perform such duties as provided by the twelfth article of amendment.

Section 2. The Congress shall have power to enforce this article by appropriate legislation.

AMENDMENT XXIV [1964]

Section 1. The right of citizens of the United States to vote in any primary or other election for President or Vice President, for electors for President or Vice President, or for Senator or Representative in Congress, shall not be denied or abridged by the United States or any State by reason of failure to pay any poll tax or other tax.

Section 2. The Congress shall have power to enforce this article by appropriate legislation.

AMENDMENT XXV [1967]

Section 1. In case of the removal of the President from office or of his death or resignation, the Vice President shall become President.

Section 2. Whenever there is a vacancy in the office of the Vice President, the President shall nominate a Vice President who shall take office upon confirmation by a majority vote of both Houses of Congress.

Section 3. Whenever the President transmits to the President pro tempore of the Senate and the Speaker of the House of Representatives his written declaration that he is unable to discharge the powers and duties of his office, and until he transmits to them a written declaration to the contrary, such powers and duties shall be discharged by the Vice President as Acting President.

Section 4. Whenever the Vice President and a majority of either the principal officers of the executive departments or of such other body as Congress may by law provide, transmit to the President pro tempore of the Senate and the Speaker of the House of Representatives their written declaration that the President is unable to discharge the powers and duties of his office, the Vice President shall immediately assume the powers and duties of the office as Acting President.

Thereafter, when the President transmits to the President pro tempore of the Senate and the Speaker of the House of Representatives his written declaration that no inability exists, he shall resume the powers and duties of his office unless the Vice President and a majority of either the principal officers of the executive department or of such other body as Congress may by law provide, transmit within four days to the President pro tempore of the Senate and the Speaker of the House of Representatives their written declaration that the President is unable to discharge the powers and duties of his office. Thereupon Congress shall decide the issue, assembling within forty-eight hours for that purpose if not in session. If the Congress, within twenty-one days after receipt of the latter written declaration, or, if Congress is not in session, within twenty-one days after Congress is required to assemble, determines by two-thirds vote of both Houses that the President is unable to discharge the powers and duties of his office, the

Vice President shall continue to discharge the same as Acting President; otherwise, the President shall resume the powers and duties of his office.

Amendment XXVI [1971]

Section 1. The right of citizens of the United States, who are eighteen years of age or older, to vote shall not be denied or abridged by the United States or by any State on account of age.

Section 2. The Congress shall have power to enforce this article by appropriate legislation.

Amendment XXVII [1992]*

No law, varying compensation for the services of Senators and Representatives, shall take effect, until an election of Representatives shall have intervened.

* On May 7, 1992, more than 200 years after it was first proposed by James Madison, the Twenty-Seventh Amendment was ratified by a 38th State (Michigan). Although Congress set no time limit for ratification of this amendment, ten of the *other* amendments proposed at the same time (1789)—now known as the Bill of Rights—were ratified in a little more than two years. After all this time, is the ratification of the Twenty–Seventh Amendment valid? Does it matter that many of the states that ratified the amendment did not exist at the time it was first proposed?

†